Blackstone's

Handbook for Policing Students

Blackstone's

Handbook for Policing Students

Fifteenth Edition

Edited by

Professor Robin Bryant and Sarah Bryant

Additional editorial support provided by
Dr Dominic Wood, Dr Sarah Bradshaw, Alex Leek,
and Graham Weaver.

Contributors:

Barry Blackburn, Candice Francis, Dr Paul Gilbert,
Dr Sofia Graça, Rich Honess, Graham Hooper,
Anjali Howard, Kevin Lawton-Barrett, Dr Vincent Leonard,
Susanna Mitchell, Paul Norman, James Nunn,
Dr Martin O'Neill, Jane Owens, Mark Robinson,
Vince Straine-Francis, Robert Underwood,
and Dr Dominic Wood

OXFORD
UNIVERSITY PRESS

OXFORD
UNIVERSITY PRESS

Great Clarendon Street, Oxford, OX2 6DP,
United Kingdom

Oxford University Press is a department of the University of Oxford.
It furthers the University's objective of excellence in research, scholarship,
and education by publishing worldwide. Oxford is a registered trade mark of
Oxford University Press in the UK and in certain other countries

First Edition published in 2006
Fifteenth Edition published in 2020

Impression: 1

Published in the United States of America by Oxford University Press
198 Madison Avenue, New York, NY 10016, United States of America

British Library Cataloguing in Publication Data

Data available

ISBN 978-0-19-887035-7

Printed in Italy by
L.E.G.O. S.p.A.

Contents

About the Authors

Barry Blackburn

Barry is a Lecturer in Criminal Justice at Canterbury Christ Church University following a career within various sectors of the criminal justice system. He specializes in the interpretation of forensic evidence and the use of research methods within the criminal justice system. Barry has recently completed research on predictive policing and firearms licensing in the UK for the Metropolitan Police.

Sarah Bradshaw

Sarah is a Professor and Head of the School of Law at Middlesex University. Her research is focused on gender equality and human rights. She also works on post-disaster response and recovery. She has advised many organizations on gender issues including the United Nations, and briefed the armed forces and first responders on gendered response to disaster including a high-level military conference at the invitation of the Supreme Commander of the Swedish Armed Forces.

Candice Francis

Candice is currently a serving Police Officer in London, with around five years' experience. Prior to this, she completed a degree in Crime and Policing at Canterbury Christ Church University, and spent time working in a police custody unit. Her professional interests include improving the use of stop and search in relation to controlled drugs.

Dr Paul Gilbert

Paul is a civil servant in the Police Service of Northern Ireland and has more than 30 years' experience of policing in Northern Ireland as a frontline officer, police trainer, and civil servant. He is also a sessional lecturer at Canterbury Christ Church University and a Teaching Assistant at Queen's University, Belfast. Paul's PhD research was on the reform of policing in Northern Ireland.

Dr Sofia Graça

Sofia is a Principal Lecturer at the School of Law, Criminal Justice and Computing at Canterbury Christ Church University. Her research interests include domestic violence and individuals' relationship with the justice system. Sofia is also interested in law enforcement and transnational cooperation, having been invited to develop research for and present at conferences organized by Europol and CEPOL.

Rich Honess

Richard is a Senior Lecturer in Policing at Canterbury Christ Church University. He is a former police officer from the Metropolitan Police having served in the City of Westminster, Lambeth, and Bromley boroughs on frontline teams including emergency response, Safer Neighbourhoods, and Safer Transport Teams. His research interests are police education and training, police self-legitimacy, and organizational improvement. He is also the Learning and Development Co-Ordinator for the Society of Evidence-Based Policing.

Graham Hooper

Graham holds a senior police staff position with Kent Police. His has also held policing lectureship posts in London and at Canterbury Christ Church University. He served for over 30 years as a police officer rising to the rank of Assistant Chief Constable. During his police career he worked in two forces—Thames Valley Police and (on secondment) to the Metropolitan Police, where he led an initiative to tackle knife crime. Graham also has extensive experience of national policing having performed a variety of senior appointments in organizations such as Her Majesty's Inspectorate of Constabulary, the Home Office, and the National Policing Improvement Agency.

Anjali Howard

Anjali is a serving Kent Police detective with 11 years' experience. She is responsible for ensuring the quality of investigator developmental portfolios in Kent Police and also trains detective assessors and tutors. Anjali is currently studying for an MSc in Applied Policing Practice with Canterbury Christ Church University.

Jo Lawry

Jo is a Detective Constable with Kent Police and a Family Liaison Officer. She has served with the force for over 30 years, including 20 years as a Detective working across volume crime, in addition to serious and complex investigations. She is also an accredited trainer in crime investigation, foundation training, witness interviewing and specialist child abuse investigations.

Kevin Lawton-Barrett

Kevin is a Senior Lecturer for the BSc (Hons) degree in Forensic Investigation at Canterbury Christ Church University. Prior to this he was an operational Senior CSI at Kent Police and a trainer attached to Kent Police College, involved in the training and development of CSIs, police recruits, and detectives. His current interests, apart from CSI, include the prevention and investigation of heritage crimes such as thefts of maritime artefacts and heritage metals.

Alex Leek

Alex is a Senior Lecturer in Policing at the University of Cumbria, having enjoyed a career that encompassed the criminal justice sector, local government, multi-agency partnerships and in an international setting at a post graduate university of science and technology in the Middle East. Alex has been a member of the PEQF Initial Policing Education Board, College of Policing since its inception and is a Fellow of the Higher Education Academy.

Dr Vincent Leonard

Vince is the Chief Firearms Instructor for Kent Police, a position he has held as a police officer since 2004 and as a member of police staff since 2009. He has over 40 years' professional experience in the field of firearms, the majority of which has been in the area of armed policing, as a practitioner, commander, trainer, and manager. Vince's research interests are in the area of judgement and decision-making.

Susanna Mitchell

Susanna joined Canterbury Christ Church University in 2015 and currently lectures in evidence in relation to criminal investigation, and about the investigation of rape and domestic abuse. Prior to this she was a senior crown prosecutor for the CPS specializing in the prosecution of rape and serious sexual offences. Susanna is still a practising lawyer and is regularly instructed by the CPS.

Paul Norman

Paul is a serving Kent Police detective with over 23 years' experience. He is a registered digital media investigator and a cybercrime specialist. As well as being the lead trainer for Kent Police in open source intelligence research and digital investigations, he is also a sessional lecturer at Canterbury Christ Church University. In addition to this, Paul has worked with other UK agencies to help them develop their cybercrime investigation capabilities.

James Nunn

James was formerly a roads policing inspector with the Metropolitan Police serving nearly 29 years, more than half of this within his specialism. He was lead for the implementation of drug-drive over-the-prescribed-limit enforcement in London, and has advised the Canadian Ministry of Justice on this subject. James has an MA in Policing and Criminal Justice from Canterbury Christ Church University and is currently a PhD candidate researching traffic injury prevention at Loughborough University.

Dr Martin O'Neill

Martin is a Senior Lecturer in Criminal Investigation, and the programme director for the newly formed BSc in Criminal Investigation at Canterbury Christ Church University. He specializes in all aspects of criminal investigation and aspires to research areas such as sexual offences, domestic abuse investigations, investigative decision-making, and death investigation.

Jane Owens

Jane is a Senior Lecturer in Policing at Canterbury Christ Church University. She has served as a police officer in both Surrey and Bedfordshire Police Forces, ending her career seconded to the National Policing Improvement Agency, where she was an Implementation Officer for the development and delivery of national leadership and management training for sergeants and inspectors. Jane's research interests include neighbourhood policing, police governance (in particular the role of the Police and Crime Commissioner), and 'private' policing.

Vincent Straine-Francis

Vince was a Module Leader for the BSc (Hons) in Policing Cyber Security and an Instructor on the Certificate in Knowledge of Policing for Canterbury Christ Church University. He is a retired Metropolitan and Kent Police Detective. Vince spent the last seven years of his career devising Kent Police Detective training programmes, and training new recruits and specials. In 2018, he went back to Kent Police detective training.

Robert Underwood

Bob is a Senior Lecturer in Policing at Canterbury Christ Church University. He was a Kent Police Officer and helped devise the Kent Student Officer Programme. Together with colleagues, Bob was jointly responsible for the design of the Foundation Degree in Policing, which formed the basis of initial police learning in Kent.

Graham Weaver

Graham is an Inspector in Surrey Police. He is the PEQF Implementation Lead for Surrey Police and Sussex Police and a member of the Partnership Strategic Group overseeing the PCDA and DHEP programmes run in collaboration with the Policing Education Consortium. He also sits on the College of Policing Initial Police Education Board.

Dr Dominic Wood

Dominic is Head of the School of Law, Criminal Justice and Policing at Canterbury Christ Church University. After organizing and chairing an international policing conference at CCCU on Knowledge Led Policing, Dominic helped to establish the Higher Education Forum for Learning and Development in Policing.

Table of Cases

Table of Legislation

EU Legislation

Directives

Regulations

Table of International Instruments

Table of Secondary Legislation

Table of Codes of Practice

Table of Circulars

Introduction

This fifteenth edition of *Blackstone's Handbook for Policing Students* is designed and written to support trainee and apprentice police officers, and students on policing pre-join programmes at colleges, universities, or private sector training providers. The Handbook has six main parts (Overview, Policing in Context, Qualifications and Training, General Procedures, Specific Incidents, and Investigation and Prosecution). Each part is divided into a number of chapters and addresses a different aspect of policing and initial police training. The chapters focus in more detail on specific topics—such as Chapter 4 on the Criminal Justice System in England and Wales (in 'Policing in Context'), Chapter 15 on Unlawful Violence (in 'Specific Incidents'), and Chapter 25 on Investigative Interviewing (in 'Investigation and Prosecution').

The authors of the Handbook have taken care to ensure the accuracy of the information contained within. However, neither the authors nor the publisher can accept any responsibility for any actions taken, or not taken, as a consequence of the information it contains. We would be grateful for feedback on the new Handbook, and for the identification of errors. Please email police.uk@OUP.com with your comments or queries.

Please note that references in the Handbook to College of Policing materials (including Authorised Professional Practice and other forms of guidance) have not been reviewed or endorsed by the College of Policing.

For this edition, the editorial process was supported by colleagues from the Police Education Consortium, Dr Dominic Wood, Canterbury Christ Church University, Dr Sarah Bradshaw, Middlesex University, Alex Leek, University of Cumbria, and Graham Weaver, Sussex Police.

1 | Introducing the Handbook

1.1 Introduction

In this chapter we provide you with guidance about how to use the Handbook, and some background information and advice on studying policing. We are familiar with the wide range of experiences that learners (either on pre-join programmes at a college, university, or private training provider, or as trainee police officers) bring to their education and training, and the Handbook has been written and set out to be both accessible and of value to all our readers.

We also provide a glossary in 1.4 which is likely to be of value to learners on 'pre-join' policing programmes and during initial training as a student police officer. For example, you might hear more experienced police colleagues, or fellow students, using an acronym or a form of jargon that you have not encountered, and the glossary might well provide an answer.

1.2 The Handbook as a Survival Guide

The Handbook is designed to support both trainee police officers (eg undertaking the Police Constable Degree Apprenticeship (PCDA) or the Degree Holders Entry Programme (DHEP), see 6.4) and those learners who are preparing to join the police on a College of Policing approved pre-join undergraduate degree. For example, to help you learn more effectively, we have omitted some of the more detailed aspects of the law and police procedure, and instead provide a simplified version that shows the key points. Of course, this does not mean that the detail is not important; it is just that learning is usually easier when moving from the simple to the complex, so we start you off with the simple. In the case of the law, the full complexity will normally be introduced and explained to you by your tutors and trainers using a variety of teaching and learning methods. However, you may be expected to learn new material for yourself, and if this is so then you are likely to find Chapter 7 of the Handbook particularly useful.

The style of the Handbook represents a judgement concerning the best ways of introducing and describing a subject area. For many aspects of the law (eg as covered in Chapters 9 to 22 inclusive) we have adopted a bite-size approach for legislation and police practice. We have simplified and condensed the topics into relatively short sections of text and diagrams, each dealing with a particular topic. This would seem to suit the subject matter and the need for you, on many occasions, to assimilate and be able to reproduce the facts. In other parts of the book we have adopted a more holistic approach—for example to investigation and interviewing, covered in Chapters 24 and 25. This reflects the reality that learning the skills of investigation and interviewing involves much more than simply following the codes and legislation. You will also need, for example, to appreciate the structure an interview can take, the forms of communication used (particularly for questioning), and the role of the interview within a wider criminal investigation.

1.3 Using the Handbook

You will sometimes look up a particular topic, but at other times you might read several sections to gain an overview. If you are an activist learner (see 7.3.2) you might find completing some of the tasks provides a welcome relief from simple reading! This Handbook, although large enough, does not contain the full level of detail you will need either to complete your pre-join programme or to qualify as a police officer with the PCDA or DHEP, so we frequently refer you to further sources of information after hopefully providing you with a good general understanding of the topic in question.

1.3.1 Tasks, references, and further reading

Many of the chapters include tasks to check your understanding, with the answers provided at the end of each chapter. In many cases the tasks provide further ideas for you to explore, or point you in the direction of additional reading and study. For this reason it is helpful to read the answers to the tasks even though you may already be confident that you know the answer to a question.

Referencing is a standard academic system for producing evidence for your arguments, or for directing the reader towards further information. We have deliberately kept the volume of referencing in this Handbook to a minimum, generally restricting it to where the source of the ideas and information might be useful. Referencing sources is a common courtesy to those authors whose work we have utilized, and respects the intellectual property rights of others, but we have minimized it to make the Handbook more accessible to a wider range of readers: in this way the flow is not disturbed by frequent references to other material.

We also indicate where further reading might be useful, as the Handbook is very much a survival guide (see 1.2). You will find more detail and further explanation in your university library (including electronic resources) and in your College of Policing notes (if you are on an approved pre-join programme, the PCDA or DHEP). If you are a special constable or undertaking the PCDA or DHEP, you will also have access to your force notes, and information from organizations such as NCALT (the National Centre for Applied Learning Technology, a password-protected, online police learning portal for the police service) and the PNLD (Police National Legal Database, again password-protected), through their websites in particular. We frequently state that further information, or the source of the underpinning material we have utilized, is available 'online'. The usual search techniques (using web-based search engines such as Google) should provide the relevant hypertext links.

1.3.2 Extracts from legislation, circulars, and codes

Throughout the Handbook there are numerous extracts from primary legislation or codes—often from Acts of Parliament. These are quoted in their original form, but sometimes with minor changes to make the meaning clearer. Often an explanation in everyday language is also given, normally in a text box to the right of the original legislation. Quotations are signified by the use of a different font (or quotation marks), while explanations and comments are in ordinary text, like this:

| if when not at [his/her] place of abode. | The term 'place of abode' means the place or site where someone lives. It normally includes the garage and garden of a house and should be given its normal meaning, but it will be a question of fact for the court to decide. If a homeless person sleeps in his/her car, the car counts as an abode while he/she is asleep. However, when the same car is being driven by the same person, it is not considered as a place of abode for the purposes of the offence of going equipped (see *R v Bundy* 1977). |

When changes have been made to the original, this is usually because legislation tends to use the word 'he' to cover 'he or she'. (However, in some legislation (eg for some sexual offences), 'he' really does mean just 'he'.) We have changed 'he' to 'he/she' and 'him' to 'him/her', and so on, where appropriate. We have also occasionally changed a particular word if it helps the sentence make more sense when quoted alone. Minor changes to the wording of legislation or codes in the Handbook are shown in square brackets, as in the following example.

The original, from s 74 of the Sexual Offences Act 2003, states:

For the purposes of this Part, a person consents if he agrees by choice, and has the freedom and capacity to make that choice.

Our revised version reads:

For the purposes of this [offence], a person consents if [he/she] agrees by choice, and has the freedom and capacity to make that choice.

As you can see we have changed 'Part' to '[offence]' and 'he' to '[he/she]'. You will also find the detail of legislation covered in other publications. Most recent legislation is available from the government website <http://www.legislation.gov.uk>. Legislation can be confusing as it may have been subject to amendment and changed by subsequent legislation, for example the definition of a religiously aggravated offence in the Crime and Disorder Act 1998 (see 14.10) was subsequently added to by the Anti-terrorism, Crime and Security Act 2001. This added a new subsection 28(5) to the four subsections of the 1998 legislation. The government website at <http://www.legislation.gov.uk> provides 'updated' versions of much (but not all) original legislation.

It is also often the case that the words and phrases used in legislation have specific meanings that do not always correspond exactly to the same words or phrases used in everyday life, for example, you might think that 'assault' always means physically hurting somebody, but see Chapter 15.

Further explanation of legislation can be found in sources such as:

- Oxford University Press publications such as *Blackstone's Police Operational Handbook 2019: Law* and the Blackstone's Police Manuals;
- the PNLD website at <https://www.pnld.co.uk/> (note that this is a subscription service unless you have a police.uk email address);
- prosecution guidance from the CPS at <https://www.cps.gov.uk/prosecution-guidance>;
- the 'official' home of UK legislation at <http://www.legislation.gov.uk> (turning on the 'explanatory notes' can be helpful);
- the monthly College of Policing digests (if you are a trainee police constable you can sub-scribe to these by sending an email including your full name, force name, and email address to <digestregistration@college.pnn.police.uk>, otherwise monitor the website <http://www.college.police.uk/What-we-do/Standards/Pages/College-Digest.aspx> on a regular basis);
- the online legal databases Westlaw (<https://legalresearch.westlaw.co.uk>) and Lawtel (<https://www.lawtel.com>) if you are studying at university or college; and
- subscription policing publications such as *Police Professional*.

PCDA apprentices, DHEP trainees, and special constables can also use police force resources (eg the force intranet) and the NCALT learning portal for the police service at <http://www.ncalt.com>. There is also the Police OnLine Knowledge Area (POLKA); registering and access details may be found at the College of Policing website <http://www.college.police.uk/What-we-do/Research/polka/Pages/POLKA.aspx>.

> **TASK 1** Use the internet to find out about the two conditions that constitute the test for making a Criminal Behaviour Order (CBO) against a person.

1.3.3 Structure of the Handbook

As you might have already discovered through reading the Contents, the Handbook is divided into five parts after the introductory material provided in Chapters 1 and 2, as follows:

- **Policing in Context**—this provides the background and context to policing and law enforcement in England and Wales, including an overview of policing professional issues, the nature of crime and disorder, and the Criminal Justice System. This part of the Handbook provides you with a starting point for the required reading and research.
- **Qualifications and Training**—this is a description and discussion of what it means to work within the profession of policing, from standards of behaviour, to qualifications, to the detail of training itself.
- **General Procedures**—this examines general policing powers and procedures in detail, to the level required for initial training as a police officer.
- **Specific Incidents**—this covers the knowledge of criminal law required to undertake policing of a wide variety of incidents up to the stage of initial qualification, and hence is a particularly long and demanding part of the Handbook.
- **Investigation and Prosecution**—this looks at the processes and procedures for police investigations (including interviewing and forensic investigation), and concludes with a chapter on prosecution.

1.3.4 Local force policies

If you are a special constable or undertaking initial police training with a police force then this Handbook should always be read in conjunction with local force policies. This applies particularly for procedures such as writing a statement or making a pocket notebook entry, and where new technology is being introduced. You are likely to find your local policies referred to as 'Force Orders', 'Standard Operating Procedures (SOP)', or 'Policies' on your organization's intranet.

Apprentice police constables may also be required to learn verbatim definitions. These are often concerned with the law, for example the definition of what constitutes theft. In this case we advise you to use the definitions given to you by your force rather than those reproduced in this Handbook or, indeed, in other textbooks. This is because there is sometimes a slight variation between forces—for example, whether the wording uses 'he' as in the original Act, or 'he/she'.

1.4 Glossary of Terms Used in Policing

You will encounter many acronyms and forms of jargon during your training and thereafter in your police career. The following glossary of terms covers a wide range of the often bewildering words and phrases used within policing. Note that many police forces also publish their own glossary of terms.

3 × 5 × 2 A 'three by five by two' intelligence form. The numbers refer to 'qualities' of the intelligence, measured in three categories, using the scales 1 to 5 and A to E, and the letters P or C.

5 × 5 × 5 A 'five by five by five' intelligence report. The numbers refer to a scale that is used to attempt to measure the reliability of, access to, and other factors about the source providing the intelligence.

16 + 1 Reference to the system used to record self-defined (as distinct from officer-defined (see IC1)) ethnicity: eg A1 is used for Indian.

ABC (1) Acceptable Behaviour Contract; (2) Activity-Based Costing, a finance/budgeting methodology that enables costs of an activity to be calculated (as opposed to a value which can only be assessed).

ABE ('A-B-E') Achieving Best Evidence, guidance on interviewing victims and witnesses, and using 'special measures' (qv), usually employed in more serious crimes such as rape.

ABH Assault resulting in actual bodily harm.

ACC Assistant chief constable; a senior police officer command rank (see 2.3.1).

ACPO ('Ack-poh') Association of Chief Police Officers (replaced in 2015 by the National Police Chiefs' Council (NPCC, qv)).

Active Defence A proactive approach to defence which involves a rigorous examination of police investigation procedures and the prosecution case; the title of an influential book by Roger Ede and Eric Shepherd.

Ad hoc A Latin phrase meaning 'for this special purpose', which has come to mean 'off the cuff' or 'unrehearsed'.

ADVOKATE ('advokate') Mnemonic used in police training to assist the recollection of the so-called 'Turnbull' rules for witness recall (see 10.5).

AFO ('A-F-O') Authorized Firearms Officer.

Airwave The digital national police radio communication system.

AirwaveSpeak A standardized form of communication when using Airwave (qv).

Alpha/Bravo, etc The phonetic alphabet used in police communication (see 5.9.4.1).

AMHP Approved mental health professional.

Analyst A professional police staff member whose role (usually) is to analyse and assess crime data and intelligence, and present research findings.

ANPR Automatic Number Plate Recognition system: see 'Nexus'.

APA ('A-P-A') Association of Police Authorities (now replaced in part by APACE, qv).

APACE Association of Policing & Crime Chief Executives.

APACS ('aippax') Association of Payments and Clearing Services.

APEL ('A-P-E-L' or sometimes 'aipell') Accreditation of Prior Experiential Learning.

APL ('A-P-L' or sometimes 'aipull') Accreditation of Prior Learning.

APP ('A-P-P') Authorised Professional Practice.

ARU ('A-R-U') Armed Response Unit.

ARV ('A-R-V') Armed Response Vehicle.

ASB ('A-S-B') Anti-social Behaviour.

ASBO ('azboh') Anti-social Behaviour Order, discontinued in 2015. The Injunction to Prevent Nuisance and Annoyance (IPNA) is seen by some as a replacement.

ASP ('asp') An informal term for an extendable metal baton (a reference to the US company Armament Systems and Procedures Inc).

Assistant commissioner Senior police rank in the Metropolitan Police, generally considered to be equivalent to a chief constable.

ASU ('A-S-U') Air Support Unit, usually in the form of police helicopters.

Attestation The formal point at which the powers and responsibilities of the office of constable are assumed, accompanied by the swearing of an oath.

AVLS Automatic (or Automated) Vehicle Location System.

Awarding Bodies Organizations permitted to issue awards and qualifications.

Baton A side-handled self-protection weapon carried by uniformed police officers.

Baton round The formal term for a rubber or plastic bullet.

BAWP ('B-A-W-P') British Association for Women in Policing.

BCE Bad-character evidence.

BCS British Crime Survey (now replaced by the Crime Survey for England and Wales).

BCU Basic Command Unit (Area, Division) or sometimes Borough Command Unit (particularly amongst MPS officers).

Biometrics The use of unique human physical characteristics (such as the iris of the eye) as identifiers.

BLS Basic Life Support (part of First Aid training).

BME Black and Minority Ethnic (groups).

Border Force The UK's law enforcement body responsible for immigration and customs control.

BPA Black Police Association.

BTP British Transport Police.

BWC Body-Worn Camera qv BWV.

BWV Body-Worn Video.

Byford Report A review by Sir Lawrence Byford on the police investigation into the 'Yorkshire Ripper' (Peter Sutcliffe) murders between 1975 and 1981; the report was instrumental in the establishment of HOLMES (qv).

CAP ('C-A-P' or 'cap') Common Approach Path.

CAR (often 'car') Cumulative Assessment Record.

Cat A/B/C murders ('cat A', etc) Categories of homicide (see 11.3.4).

CBO Criminal Behaviour Order.

CBRN Chemical, Biological, Radiological, or Nuclear (hazard, etc).

CCR Contact and Control Room.

CCTV Closed-Circuit Television.

CCU Computer Crime Unit.

CDI Crime data integrity, a general term referring to the accuracy of a force's crime recording, according to national (crime) counting rules set by the Home Office.

CDRP Crime and Disorder Reduction Partnership.

CEOP ('see-op') Child Exploitation and Online Protection Centre.

CEPOL ('seepol') European Police College.

Certificate in Knowledge of Policing The knowledge requirement for the assessed units of the Diploma in Policing (qv), usually undertaken as part of a pre-join programme (qv). It ceased to be accepted at the end of 2019.

cf Latin for 'compare'.

Chief Officer A police officer with the rank of assistant chief constable and above: command rank.

CHIS ('chiss') Covert Human Intelligence Source (informant).

Child Sexual Abuse The collective term used to describe any form of sexual abuse of children and young persons both historically and in the present day. CSA is now a major priority for police forces.

CI ('C-I') (1) Cognitive Interview; (2) Cell Intervention.

CIAPOAR ('see-a-poor') Mnemonic for factors to remember when making decisions within the NDM (qv); Code of ethics, Information, Assessment, Powers and policy, Options, Actions, and Review.

CID ('C-I-D') Criminal Investigation(s) Department, now replaced in many police forces by Specialist Crime Investigations, SCI, or similar.

Civil Nuclear Constabulary A non-Home Office police force that provides security and protection to civil (non-military) nuclear sites in the UK.

CJPOA Criminal Justice and Public Order Act 1994.

CJ(S) A process or unit concerned with Criminal Justice (Systems).

CKP Certificate in Knowledge of Policing (qv).

CLDP Core Leadership Development Programme.

CLO ('C-L-O') Community Liaison Officer.

CLUE2 ('klue-too') A case-tracking data system.

CNC Civil Nuclear Constabulary.

CnC Command and Control system used by a number of police forces and other agencies.

Collar To make an arrest (vernacular).

College of Policing The professional body for policing (successor to the NPIA, qv).

Commander Metropolitan and City of London chief police officer rank, equivalent to assistant chief constable in all other forces.

Commissioner Top rank (head of force) in the MPS and the City of London police. The commissioner of the Metropolitan Police is considered to be the most senior police officer in the UK.

Compromise When a criminal target (a suspect) detects covert surveillance.

Confirmation The final stage of successful initial training, when a student police officer/trainee is confirmed as a police constable.

Continuity (of evidence); an audited and continuous trail for evidential items from crime scene or suspect to court, to prevent interference or contamination.

CoP see College of Policing.

CPA (1) Crime Pattern Analysis; (2) Child Protection Agency.

CPIA Criminal Procedure and Investigations Act 1996.

CPN Community Protection Notice.

CPO Crime Prevention Officer.

CPOSA Chief Police Officers' Staff Association.

CPP Crime Prevention Panels.

CPR Cardio-pulmonary resuscitation.

CPS Crown Prosecution Service, the governmental body of qualified lawyers who prosecute criminal cases before the courts.

CRaSH/CRASH Collision recording and data sharing digital system.

CRE Commission for Racial Equality, disbanded in 2007; now the EHRC (qv).

Crimelink Crime analysis software used by some force analysts, developed by the company 'Precision' Computing Intelligence.

Crimewatch discontinued BBC TV programme that highlighted unsolved crimes, usually of a serious nature.

CRO ('C-R-O') (1) Criminal Records Office; (2) Criminal (vernacular).

CROPS ('crops') Covert Rural Observation Posts (or Points).

CSAI Child Sex Abuse Images.

CSI Crime Scene Investigator.

CSM Crime Scene Manager.

CSO Community Support Officer.

CSODS Child Sex Offender Disclosure Scheme.

CSP (1) Communications Service Provider; (2) Community Safety Partnership.

CSU Community Safety Unit.

CT Counter Terrorism.

CT Units Regional (outside London) counter-terrorism units where forces collaborate to create additional capability and capacity to tackle terrorism and extremism.

CTM Contact Trace Material.

Cuff (1) Police vernacular for not doing something which one is supposed to do as a matter of duty or obligation; (2) To handcuff (vernacular).

Custody or custody suite A designated area in a police station (usually close to the cells), where arrested persons are logged and processed.

CW Cannabis Warning.

Cybercrime An all-embracing and somewhat ambiguous term for crimes committed using computers and/or digital networks, or against computer systems.

Dabs Colloquial term for fingerprints.

DC Detective Constable.

DCC Deputy Chief Constable.

DCI Detective Chief Inspector.

DCS Detective Chief Superintendent; command rank.

DDA Disability Discrimination Act 1995.

Deputy assistant commissioner Senior police officer rank in the Metropolitan and City of London police forces. Equivalent to deputy chief constable in other police forces.

DFU Digital Forensics Unit.

DHEP Degree-Holder Entry Programme: a short programme for graduates (in any subject) to fully qualify as a police constable.

DHRs Domestic Homicide Reviews.

DI ('D-I') Detective Inspector.

DIC ('D-I-C') Drunk in charge (of a person or object).

Diploma in Policing The minimum national qualification for trainee police officers, soon to be replaced.

Disclosure The police and the prosecution provide the defence with certain information and documents which might be pertinent evidence in a criminal case.

DNA Deoxyribonucleic Acid, the genetic material from cells (can be used to obtain a 'genetic fingerprint').

DNA-17 A DNA profiling technique (uses all the DNA areas for SGM+ and six additional areas).

Doctrine A body of knowledge and procedure concerned with police practice, notably criminal investigation—eg as expressed in the MIM (qv) and the NCPE Volume Crime Investigation Manuals.

DPP Director of Public Prosecutions (also head of the Crown Prosecution Service).

DS Detective Sergeant.

DVCVA Domestic Violence, Crime and Victims Act 2004.

DVLA Driver and Vehicle Licensing Agency.

DVPN Domestic Violence Protection Notice.

DVPO Domestic Violence Protection Order.

EAW European Arrest Warrant.

EBP Evidence-based policing.

ECHR European Convention on Human Rights.

EEK Early Evidence Kit for use after a sexual assault.

EHRC Equality and Human Rights Commission.

Element (within a unit of an NOS (qv)). NOS units are usually divided into two or more elements which describe more precisely a skill or competence.

EPO Emergency Protection Order, used for protecting children from imminent harm.

ERO ('E-R-O') Evidence Review Officer.

ESDA ('ezzder') Electrostatic Detection Apparatus.

ETA ('E-T-A') Estimated time of arrival.

et al Latin for 'and others'.

Europol The European Union law enforcement organization.

Extended police family A reference to the wider group of law enforcement and pubic order staff, beyond the traditional full-time police—eg special constables and PCSOs (qv).

FA ('F-A') Forensic Alliance (an independent forensic science laboratory and service).

Family of forces Older term for police forces that are similar in terms of their structure, size, budget, etc. Now largely replaced by the Home Office designation 'Most Similar Forces' (MSF (qv)).

FAO or FOAS ('F-A-O' or 'F-O-A-S') First Attending Officer/First Officer Attending the Scene/first responder.

FBO Football Banning Order.

FCA Forensic Computer Analyst.

FCC Force Communications (or Control) Centre.

FCP Forward Control Point.

FDR Firearm Discharge Residue.

'Federation' The Police Federation of England and Wales (qv).

Fence Vernacular for a person who buys or exchanges stolen goods.

FERRT ('fert') Fingerprint Evidence Recovery and Recording Techniques.

FGM Female Genital Mutilation.

FIO ('F-I-O') Field Intelligence Officer or Financial Intelligence Officer.

Fishing Police vernacular for any speculative attempt, particularly where the intention is to try to recover evidence of potential value in a criminal case but the grounds for doing so (and the form of evidence) are uncertain.

FLA ('F-L-A') Family Law Act 1996.

FLINTS Forensic Linked Intelligence System: a database and comparative analysis system developed by West Midlands Police.

FLO ('F-L-O') (1) Family Liaison Officer; (2) Forensic Laboratory Officer.

FME Forensic medical examiner.

FMPO Forced Marriage Protection Order.

FMS Force Management Statement. An annual document required of each force by HMICFRS (qv) detailing likely demand over the next four years.

FOD ('fod') Fact of Death, a statement from a medical professional confirming a person is dead.

FOI ('F-O-I') Freedom of Information, as in a request under the Freedom of Information Act 2000.

Forensics21 A discontinued initiative to improve police forensic services (ended in 2012).

Foundation degree/FD A qualification at higher education level. Foundation degrees in policing often incorporate the NOS (qv) and the Diploma in Policing (qv) units for initial policing.

FPN Fixed Penalty Notice.

FSS (1) Forensic Science Society; (2) Forensic Science Service (closed in 2012).

FSU (1) Family Support Unit; (2) Firearms Support Unit.

FTS Forensic Telecommunications Services.

Garda Síochána The police force of the Republic of Ireland.

GBH Grievous Bodily Harm; a category of assault.

GMP Greater Manchester Police.

Gong A police medal.

GPA Gay Police Association.

H2H House-to-house (as in conducting enquiries).

Handler Vernacular term for police officer responsible for liaising with and tasking a CHIS (qv).

Handling Taking illegal ownership of stolen or otherwise illegally obtained goods.

Hate crime ACPO (qv) defined a hate crime as any hate incident (qv), which constitutes a criminal offence and is perceived by the victim, or any other person, as being motivated by prejudice or hate.

Hate incident ACPO (qv) defined a hate incident as any incident, which may or may not constitute a criminal offence, that is perceived by the victim, or any other person, as being motivated by prejudice or hate.

HATOS ('hay-toes') Informal term for highways authority traffic officers.

Hearsay A reference to information that is not given directly (orally) to the court, but is somehow second-hand. It is generally not accepted as evidence in a court.

HEI Higher Education Institution

Hermes A database of missing persons maintained by the MPB (qv).

Highways Agency The highways authority that preceded Highways England.

Hillsborough The grounds of Sheffield Wednesday football club, where 96 Liverpool fans were unlawfully killed in 1989. The events have come to symbolize failures in police leadership.

Hit A DNA sample which can be matched with an identified person (not always criminal).

HMCPSI Her Majesty's Crown Prosecution Service Inspectorate

HMIC Now replaced by HMICFRS (qv).

HMICFRS Her Majesty's Inspectorate of Constabulary Fire & Rescue Services (replaces HMIC). It inspects at BCU (qv) and force levels, and carries out thematic inspections (eg into police training). It also inspects fire and rescue services throughout England & Wales.

HMPS Her Majesty's Prison Service.

HMRC Her Majesty's Revenue and Customs (previously 'Customs and Excise' and the 'Inland Revenue').

HOLMES, HOLMES2 Home Office Large Major Enquiry System: an information system designed to support large-scale police investigations (eg homicide).

Home Office A government department responsible for policy relating to policing and crime.

Home Secretary The senior government minister responsible for policing and security in England and Wales, including police reform (the Welsh Assembly has some devolved powers for policing in Wales).

HORTies ('hortiz') Police vernacular for the HORT/1 and HORT/2 forms for requiring the production of driving documents.

HOSDB Home Office Scientific Development Branch, was part of NPIA (qv).

Hot spot A geographical location with a high incidence of crime and criminality.

HPDS High Potential Development Scheme for police promotions.

HQ Headquarters.

HRA Human Rights Act 1998.

HSE Health and Safety Executive.

Ibid Latin for 'in the same place'.

IC1, IC2 to IC9 (eg 'I-C-2') A reference to Identity Codes used by police officers to record ethnicity (eg IC1 is White European).

ICF Integrated Competency Framework (replaced in 2011 by the Policing Professional Framework (qv)). It combined descriptions of behavioural requirements with the NOS (qv) and profiles for certain policing roles.

ICIDP Initial Crime Investigators' Development Programme.

ICO Information Commissioner's Office, the regulatory office for data protection and electronic privacy.

ICV Incident Command Vehicle used in situations where public order might be a problem.

IDENT1 ('ident-wun') The national database of fingerprints.

Idents Identifications (vernacular).

IDIOM Information Database for IOM (qv); for tracking and monitoring prolific offenders.

IED ('I-E-D') Improvised Explosive Device (a 'bomb').

IIMARCH ('eye-eye-march') Mnemonic for content of briefings: Information, Intention, Method, Administration, Risk assessment, Communications, Human rights compliance.

IL4SP Initial Learning for the Special Constabulary.

ILP/ILPM ('I-L-P') Intelligence-Led Policing and hence Intelligence-Led Policing Model; sometimes referred to as Intelligence-Based Policing. Also related to Information-Based Policing or Information-Led Policing.

IMPACT A College of Policing (qv) programme to improve police information access and sharing.

IMSC Initial Management of Serious Crime course.

IND Immigration and Nationality Directorate.

Independent Inquiry into Child Sexual Abuse A public inquiry (likely to last several years) to examine the extent to which institutions and organizations in England and Wales have made a serious attempt to fulfil their responsibility to protect children.

Independent Patrol The ability of a trainee police officer to conduct a police patrol without the constant supervision of a qualified police officer.

Informant A person (often a criminal) who passes intelligence to a source handler: a CHIS (qv). Known by other criminals as a snout, grass, or nark.

INI The IMPACT (qv) Nominal Index—a 'mega' database for searching many smaller databases for information about named individuals.

Insp. or Ins. Abbreviation for 'Inspector', a policing rank.

Institutional racism The idea that institutions can unintentionally behave in a manner prejudicial to ethnic minorities, through their written and unwritten policies and procedures.

Inter-agency Approaches that involve partnership between several agencies: for example, collaboration with the Probation Service and Social Services. See also CDRP (qv).

inter alia Latin for 'among other things'.

Interpol International policing organization.

Intranet Often refers in police circles to a police internal electronic information system, with restricted access rights.

IO Investigating (police) Officer, usually a detective officer (for a crime), but can be a uniformed officer (eg for traffic collisions).

IOM Integrated offender management

IOPC The 'Independent Office for Police Conduct'; deals with serious complaints against the police, and investigates all instances where police officers have used firearms in the course of their duties.

IP ('I-P') Injured Person or Party (often literally the person injured in a crime involving personal violence).

IPCC Independent Police Complaints Commission: now replaced by the IOPC (qv).

IPLDP (I-P-L-D-P or 'ipple-dip') (1) Initial Police Learning and Development Programme: the programme for initial police training since 2006; (2) Central Authority Responsible for the implementation and policy direction of IPLDP training programme.

ISA Information Sharing Agreement (between the police and other agencies).

ISO ('I-S-O') Individual Support Order, for a young person aged 10–17 years.

ISVAs Independent Sexual Violence Advisors.

JAPAN *J*ustification, *A*uthorization, *P*roportionality, *A*uditable, and *N*ecessary; a checklist for policing actions.

JBB Joint Branch Board of the Police Federation of England and Wales (qv).

Job Informal term for having a commitment or assignment such as attending the scene of a burglary, eg 'I've got a job to go to'.

JRFT Job-Related Fitness Test.

Justice Ministry Responsible for the courts, prisons, probation, criminal law, and sentencing.

KSB *K*nowledge, *S*kills and *B*ehaviours, for trainee police officers.

Latent prints/marks These are invisible until revealed by dusting or other techniques.

Lawrence, Stephen/the Lawrence Inquiry/the Macpherson Inquiry References to the death of the black teenager Stephen Lawrence in 1993, the subsequent investigation conducted by the MPS (qv), and the reports that followed (eg as conducted by Lord Macpherson, 1999).

LCN Low Copy Number; a tiny amount of DNA recovered through advanced scientific processes.

LEA Law Enforcement Agency.

Learning Diary Sometimes kept by trainee police officers as part of the process of reflective learning.

Learning Requirement A set of learning requirements that underpin the IPLDP (qv) curriculum.

Level 1 Local crime signifier (used within NIM (qv)). Illegal possession of a controlled drug is a Level 1 crime.

Level 2 Cross-BCU or cross-force crime signifier (used within NIM (qv)). Dealing in illegal drugs is a Level 2 crime.

Level 3 National or international crime signifier (used within NIM (qv)). Organizing the importing or distribution of illegal drugs is a Level 3 crime.

LGC Laboratory of Government Chemists (service provider for scientific analysis).

LIVESCAN Commercial computerized database and digital system for taking fingerprints.

LOCARD Forensic database system.

loc cit Latin for 'at the place quoted'.

LPG Legislation, Policy, and Guidelines modules, part of the IPLDP curriculum (qv).

MAPPA ('mapper') Multi-Agency Public Protection Arrangements (part of the joint agency approach to managing violent and sex offenders).

MARAC Multi-agency Risk Assessment Conference.

MASH Multi-agency sharing hub.

Match An identified DNA (qv) sample.

MG forms The forms for recording information from investigations; sent to the CPS (qv) for an initial charging decision.

MG11 Witness statement form.

MIM ('mim') Murder Investigation Manual (sometimes called the 'Murder Manual'). It was the first example of a comprehensive doctrine (qv) to assist in the investigation of serious crime, and sets out possible investigative strategies (eg forensic and the interview strategy). It was written partly as a result of the enquiry into the death of Stephen Lawrence.

minutiae Latin for 'of small parts'; the individuality of a fingerprint or mark through examination of its ridge (qv) characteristics (up to 150 characteristics in a single finger print).

Misper Missing person, or the forms used during an investigation about a missing person.

MO ('M-O') Modus operandi is Latin for a characteristic way of doing something. Often used to refer to a particular way of committing a crime.

MoDP Ministry of Defence Police.

MOPAC Mayor's Office for Policing and Crime (London's equivalent of a police and crime commissioner).

MoPI ('moppy') Management of Police Information.

Morris Inquiry A 2004 inquiry into professional standards and employment issues in the MPS (qv).

MOU ('M-O-U') Memorandum of Understanding.

MPS Metropolitan Police Service: London's police force.

MSF Most Similar Force (for comparing police forces).

Multi-agency Approaches to crime investigation and reduction that involve partnership between the police and non-police agencies.

NABIS ('nay-biss') National Ballistics Intelligence Service.

NACRO ('nak-roh') National Association for the Care and Resettlement of Offenders.

NAFIS ('naffiss') National Automated Fingerprint Identification System, now replaced by IDENT1 (qv).

National Crime Agency The National Crime Agency, the national law enforcement agency (takes responsibility for some of the work previously undertaken by the NPIA (qv), SOCA (qv), and the CEOP (qv)).

National Injuries Database A searchable national database of wounds (mainly victims'), enabling comparisons.

National Occupational Standards The National Occupational Standards (NOS) for policing, developed by Skills for Justice (qv).

NB Latin for 'take especial note of'.

NBPA National Black Police Association.

NCA National Crime Agency (qv).

NCALT ('enn-kalt') National Centre for Applied Learning Technology, a password-protected, online police learning portal for the police service.

NCDV National Centre for Domestic Violence.

NCLCC National County Lines Coordination Centre

NCSP National Community Safety Plan.

NDM National Decision Model.

NDNAD National DNA (qv) Database.

NDORS National Driver Offender Re-training Scheme.

NEFPN Non-endorsable Fixed Penalty Notice.

NFA (1) No Further (police or CPS) Action; (2) No Fixed Abode; (3) National Fraud Authority (disbanded in 2014).

NFD National Footwear Database (replaces the NFRC).

NFFID National Firearms Forensic Intelligence Database.

NFIB National Fraud Intelligence Bureau, a central access point for individuals and organizations for suspected cybercrime, overseen by the City of London police.

NFIU National Football Intelligence Unit.

NFLMS National Firearms Licensing Management System: a database containing details of all firearm or shotgun certificate holders (and those in the process of applying for certificates).

NFRC National Footwear Reference Collection (previous name for the National Footwear Database).

Nick Vernacular for: (1) a police station; (2) to arrest a person.

NID ('N-I-D' or 'nid') National Injuries Database (qv).

NIE ('N-I-E') National Investigators' Examination.

NIM ('nim' or 'N-I-M') National Intelligence Model, sometimes described as a business model for policing. All police forces are required to follow the NIM,

NMAT ('en-mat') National Mutual Aid Telephony, a national call-handling system for use in emergencies.

NMPR National Mobile Phone Register/National Mobile Property Register.

Nominals Vernacular police term for those perceived to be active and often recidivist, high-volume criminals.

Non-Home Office forces Police forces that are not one of the 43 county or city-based 'territorial' forces, eg BTP (qv).

NOS ('N-O-S' or rarely 'noz') National Occupational Standards (qv).

NPAS National Police Air Service.

NPB National Policing Board.

NPC National Policing Curriculum.

NPCC National Police Chiefs' Council, established in 2015 with the objective of coordinating operational policing at national levels, replaces ACPO (qv).

NPIA National Police Improvement Agency, phased out in 2013. Much of its previous work is now managed by the College of Policing (qv), the National Crime Agency (qv), and the Home Office (qv).

NPPF The National Police Promotion Framework, for promotions to sergeant and inspector ranks.

NPT Neighbourhood Policing Team.

NSPIS National Strategy for Police Information Systems: a suite of databases and software to support case preparation, command and control, and custody processes.

NSY New Scotland Yard.

NTSU National Technical Services Unit.

NVQ National Vocational Qualification. There are NVQs at Levels 3 and 4 in policing and other law enforcement roles, incorporating the relevant NOS (qv).

OCC Operations and Communications Centre.

OCD Out-of court-disposal (OOCD is also used).

OIC ('O-I-C') Officer in Charge.

OOCD Out of court disposal (OCD is also used).

OP ('O-P') Observation point for carrying out surveillance.

Op Operation, usually refers to a targeted police operation against a criminal problem, eg 'Op Damocles'. The name does not reflect the nature of the operation.

op cit Latin for 'see the work cited'.

ORC ('O-R-C' or 'ork') Operational Response Commander.

OSPRE® ('osspray') Objective Structured Performance-Related Examination, written tests for potential police sergeants or inspectors, now subsumed within the NPPF (qv).

OST Officer Safety Training.

PAC ('P-A-C' or 'pack') Police Action Checklist. In many forces the satisfactory completion of the PAC is one of the criteria for Independent Patrol Status (qv).

PACE ('pace') Police and Criminal Evidence Act 1984.

PAS ('P-A-S') Police Advisers' (or Advisory) Service.

passim Latin for 'everywhere', but used in the sense of 'throughout'.

PBE Pocket book entry.

PC or Pc Police constable.

PCC Police and Crime Commissioner.

PCDA Police Constable Degree Apprenticeship.

PCeU Police Central e-Crime Unit, a national resource based at the MPS (qv). It is partly funded by the Home Office (qv).

PCP (1) Police and Crime Panel; (2) Police and Crime Plan.

PCR Postal Charge and Requisition, a formal charge and direction to attend court is issued by post.

PCSO Police Community Support Officer.

PDP The Professional Development Portfolio is a tool for recording an individual police officer's professional development.

PDPP Pre-join Degree in Professional Policing, see PJDPP.

PDU Professional Development Unit for police employees, including trainee officers.

PEACE ('peace') Mnemonic for an interviewing model used by all UK forces, *P*lanning and preparation; *E*ngage and explain; *A*ccount, clarification and challenge; *C*losure; and *E*valuation.

PEEL The acronym for describing the three areas ('pillars') used when inspecting forces: P (police), E (effectiveness), E (efficiency), and L (legitimacy).

PentiP The Penalty Notice Processing system.

PEQF Police Education Qualifications Framework, encompasses all professional qualifications in policing from 2020 onwards.

Phonetic Alphabet The system commonly used by the police to communicate letters of the alphabet.

PI ('P-I') Performance Indicator; a type of quantitative measure, used by the Home Office to assess the police service.

PIMS ('pimz') Performance Indicator Management System.

PIP ('pip') 'Professionalising Investigation Programme' at levels 1–4. Level 1 is embedded in the initial police officer training (mapped to the NOS (qv) 2G2, 2H1, and 2H2).

PIRA ('peer-rah') Provisional Irish Republican Army, a proscribed terrorist group.

PJDPP Pre-join Degree in Professional Policing: a policing degree after which the student is eligible to apply to a force for a police officer post (also known as PDPP).

PLO ('P-L-O') Prison Liaison Officer (a police officer).

PM Post mortem examination.

PNAC (sometimes 'p-nack') Police National Assessment Centre for superintendents and chief superintendents who aspire to chief officer (qv) ranks (also called 'Senior PNAC').

PNB (1) Pocket notebook; (2) Police Negotiation Board.

PNC Police National Computer.

PND (1) Penalty Notice for Disorder; (2) Police National Database.

PNLD Police National Legal Database.

POCA ('pocker') Proceeds of Crime Act 2002.

Police and Crime Panels Set up by the Police Reform & Social Responsibility Act 2011 to act as a 'check and a balance' on a PCC's performance.

Police Degree Apprenticeships A new entry route into policing via an apprenticeship programme (from 2020). Officers will have to undergo police training and complete a degree in policing to be confirmed in the rank.

Police Federation of England and Wales The national staff association for the federated ranks of constable, sergeant, inspector, and chief inspector, resembling a trade union.

Police Memorial Trust Charitable organization for police officers killed in the line of duty (has a national memorial in London).

Police Now An initiative where graduates are trained as police officers for a two-year period, with particular emphasis on developing 'leadership skills'.

Police Scotland The single police force in Scotland, created in 2013 (eight regional forces were merged).

Police Staff Official designation of support (civilian) staff, some of whom are operational but do not have the police officer warranted powers. Includes PCSOs (qv).

Policing Protocol Order 2011 A statute-based description of the legal responsibilities of chief constables, police and crime commissioners, the Home Secretary, and police and crime panels.

POLKA ('polka') Police OnLine Knowledge Area, a restricted-access online collaborative site for sharing policing knowledge and information.

PolSA/POLSA ('polsah') Police Search Adviser.

POP/BritPOP ('pop') Problem-Oriented Policing and its UK derivative.

PPF Policing Professional Framework, soon to be discontinued and replaced by the PPP (qv).

PPP Policing Professional Profiles.

Predictive Policing Uses software based on mathematical algorithms to predict crime patterns, to decide how to deploy police resources.

Pre-entry course/programme See pre-join programme.

Pre-join programme A course of study leading to entry to the police service as a trainee officer.

Probationer An older informal term for a police officer in initial training. The terms apprentice police constable, student police officer, or trainee police officer are now more commonly used.

Profiler An informal term for a behavioural analyst or behavioural adviser, who carries out 'profiling' (qv).

Profiling An informal and imprecise term, as in 'offender profiling' and 'geographical profiling'. Often predicts the psychological traits of an unknown offender.

PRRB Police Remuneration Review Body.

PS or Ps Police sergeant.

PSAEW Police Superintendents' Association of England and Wales, the national staff association for the ranks of superintendent and chief superintendent.

PSB or PSBM The basic personal safety course often included by forces as part of IPLDP (qv).

PSD Professional Standards Department.

PSNI Police Service of Northern Ireland (previously called the RUC, Royal Ulster Constabulary).

PSO Prohibited Steps Order (for protecting children).

PSPO Public Spaces Protection Order.

PWITS ('pee-wits') Possession (of drugs) with intent to supply.

QPM Queen's Police Medal.

qv Latin for 'for which, see …'. It refers the reader to another item or word.

R&D Research and Development Unit (usually for intelligence analysis and tasking at BCU (qv) level).

RCT Randomised Control Trial, a research method often employed to support Evidence Based Policing (qv).

Re-coursing/Back-coursing An informal term for trainee police officers having to repeat elements of initial training, normally as a result of failure or for personal reasons.

Redcap Vernacular term for an officer of the RMP (qv).

Reflex Nationally funded project to deal with organized immigration crime.

Refs A vernacular reference to a refreshment break during a tour of duty.

Ridge and furrow Identifying features in fingerprints.

RIPA ('ripper') Regulation of Investigatory Powers Act 2000. It regulates undercover police work and the use of informants, but is now partly subsumed by the Investigatory Powers Act 2016.

RIRA ('real I-R-A') Real Irish Republican Army, a proscribed terrorist organization.

RMP Royal Military Police.

ROLE ('role') Recognition of Life Extinct. A statement from a medical professional confirming a person is dead.

ROTI ('roh-tee') A written summary of an audio recorded interview (previously taped).

ROVI ('roh-vee') A written summary of an audio-visually recorded interview.

RSHO Risk of Sexual Harm Order, superseded by SROs in 2015.

RTA (1) Road Traffic Act; (2) Road Traffic Accident—now largely replaced by RTI (qv) or RTC (qv).

RTC Road Traffic Collision. The term 'collision' is preferred to 'accident' as most collisions on roads are due to human error, negligence, or a criminal act, rather than a chance event. However, the term 'accident' is still present in legislation.

RTI Road Traffic Incident.

RUC Royal Ulster Constabulary—the former police force for Northern Ireland, replaced by the Police Service of Northern Ireland (PSNI) in 2001.

RV(P) Rendezvous (point) at a crime scene or major incident.

SAB Safeguarding Adult Board.

Safeguarding A term used increasingly in policing to describe policies to address vulnerable adults and children/young persons, who may be at risk of harm through exploitation by criminals.

Sanitized The term for describing intelligence from which the identifying features and origins have been omitted.

SARA ('sarr-rer' or 'S-A-R-A') *S*can, *A*nalyse, *R*espond, and *A*ssess.

SARC ('sark') Sexual Assault Referral Centre.

SB Special Branch: the part of every police force that specializes in matters of national security. SB officers do not wear uniforms.

SCAIDP Specialist Child Abuse Investigation Development Programme.

Scarman Inquiry (Scarman Report) An official inquiry into the rioting in the Brixton area of London in 1981. It recommended reforming the law, changing police training and practice, and improving community relations.

SCAS ('Scaz') Serious Crime Analysis Section. A database of homicides and stranger rapes maintained by the NCA (qv).

SDE Self-defined Ethnicity.

SDN Short Descriptive Note (part of a case file, such as a reference to a transcription of an interview with a suspect).

Secret Policeman A 2003 documentary made by an undercover reporter and subsequently aired by BBC television. It produced evidence of racist behaviour by police recruits at a police regional training centre.

SFO Serious Fraud Office.

SGM Second Generation Multiplex: a DNA-profiling system using seven areas for discriminating between people.

SGM+ A DNA-profiling system similar to SGM, but more accurate as it uses 11 areas for discrimination.

Sgt Abbreviation for 'sergeant', a policing rank sometimes also referred to as 'skipper'.

Shoe marks Informal term for footwear prints which can match a suspect to a crime scene.

SHPO Sexual Harm Prevention Order.

Show out An informal term for a security problem on a surveillance operation when the suspect realizes that he/she is being observed.

SIA ('S-I-A') Security Industry Association.

sic Latin for 'just as it is written'.

SIO ('S-I-O') Senior Investigating Officer (usually a detective officer) investigating a serious or major crime, such as a Category A or B murder (qv), or a rape.

SIODP Senior Investigating Officers' Development Programme.

SIU ('S-I-U') Special Investigation Unit (for child abuse and child protection investigations).

Skills for Justice/SfJ/S4J The Sector Skills Council (SSC) for Criminal Justice, including Policing. Skills for Justice is responsible for the National Occupational Standards (qv) for Policing, and other justice-related bodies and organizations (such as the Probation Service).

Skillsmark Quality assurance scheme introduced by Skills for Justice (qv).

SLA Service Level Agreement.

SLDP Senior Leadership Development Programmes (SLDP1 and SLDP2) for chief inspector roles or above.

SLP Senior Leadership Programme.

SMART(ER) Used in reference to objectives: *S*pecific, *M*easurable, *A*chievable, *R*ealistic, *T*imely (and *E*valuated and *R*eviewed).

SMT Senior Management Team (on a BCU (qv), usually the commander, a superintendent (or a chief superintendent on large BCUs), together with one or more chief inspectors (Crime and Operations) and a business manager).

SNT Safer Neighbourhood Teams (an alternative name for Neighbourhood Policing Teams).

SO 19 Firearms unit in the MPS (qv).

SOCA ('socker') Serious Organised Crime Agency: phased out in 2013, its work is now carried out by the NCA (qv).

SOCO ('sockoh') Scenes of Crime Officer; older term replaced in many police forces by CSI (qv).

SOCPA ('sockper') The Serious Organised Crime and Police Act 2005.

SOIT ('S-O-I-T') Sexual Offences Investigative Trained (officer), an MPS role.

SOLAP ('soh-lap') Student Officer Learning Assessment Portfolio, now replaced by an electronic assessment portfolio in many forces.

SOLO ('solo') Sex Offender Liaison Officer.

SOP ('S-O-P') Standard Operating Procedure.

SOPO ('sop-oh') Sexual Offences Protection Order, superseded by SHPOs in 2015.

Special measures Used in investigations and courts to provide support and protection for witnesses of more serious crimes.

Spit hood A shroud to cover a detained person's face and head, to protect police officers and others from spitting or biting.

SPoC/SPOC/spoc ('spock') Single Point of Contact.

SPP Strategic Policing Priorities.

SPR Strategic Policing Requirement (qv).

SRO Sexual Risk Order, supersedes RSHOs.

Stinger Pronged device for stopping cars by puncturing their tyres.

STO ('S-T-O') Specially trained officer.

STR Short Tandem Repeat: a section of DNA that can be used in profiling methodologies such as SGM+ and DNA-17 (qv).

Strategic Policing Requirement A statement by the Home Secretary outlining national risks and threats to England and Wales. It also states the government's expectations of police forces in terms of capacity and capability to collectively address such threats. The SPR is regularly updated.

Superintendents' Association The Police Superintendents' Association of England and Wales.

Supervised Patrol Undertaken by trainee police officers under the supervision of a qualified police officer or officers.

T&CG Tasking and Coordinating Group.

Tac/TAC team (1) Tactical Support Team—eg used to serve a warrant; (2) Terrorism and Crime Team (MPS (qv)).

TDA or TADA Taking and Driving Away: a reference to a form of vehicle crime. Also known as TWOC (qv).

Tenprint A fingerprinting process whereby prints of all ten fingers are recorded.

Test Purchase The authorized purchase of drugs, alcohol, or other items by an undercover police officer or another person, to provide evidence of illegal activity.

TFU Tactical Firearms Unit.

TIC ('T-I-C') Acronym for offences 'taken into consideration' by a court.

TIE (sometimes 'ty') *T*race, *I*mplicate, and/or *E*liminate (in investigations).

TNA Training Needs Analysis.

TOS ('T-O-S') Traffic Officers Service (part of Highways England Traffic Officers Service). Such officers are often still known as HATOs (qv).

TWOC ('twok') Taken Without (Owner's) Consent—normally used in reference to a motor vehicle: see also TDA or TADA.

UC (or UC officer) Abbreviation for an undercover officer.

Undercover Policing Inquiry Judge-led public inquiry into all undercover policing since 1968.

UKBA UK Border Agency, now dissolved and replaced by Border Force (qv) and Immigration Enforcement.

UVP Ultra-Violet (Light) Photography.

VCMM Volume Crime Management Model (Practice Advice on the Management of Priority and Volume Crime).

VCSE Volume Crime Scene Examiner (forensic).

VDRS Vehicle Defect Rectification Scheme.

VEM ('V-E-M') Visible Ethnic Minority: refers to both individuals and communities.

VIAPOAR ('via-por') Mnemonic that was used for the factors to take into account when making decisions, now replaced by CIAPOAR (qv).

ViCLAS ('vy-class') Violent Crime Linkage Analysis System—a database used by SCAS (qv) in the UK, originally devised by the Royal Canadian Mounted Police (RCMP).

VIPER ('viper') Video Identification Parade Electronic Recording.

ViSOR ('vy-zor') Violent and Sex Offender Register: a database of individuals considered a potential danger to the public because of their history of violence and/or sex offending.

VOO Violent Offender Order.

VPS Victim Personal Statement.

Vulnerability A now common overarching term used in policing to describe people who are especially vulnerable by reasons of age (a child or young person), their relationship to the suspect or offender, or the mental health of the victim.

WBA Work-based Assessment.

Whorl Characteristic pattern seen in fingerprints.

Winsor Review(s) Two reports (2011 and 2012) by Tom Winsor on pay, conditions, entry routes, and career pathways for police staff.

WPLDP Wider Police Learning and Development Programme.

YOT ('yot') Youth Offending Team.

YPVA Young People's Violence Advisor.

TASK 2 There might be terms, acronyms, and jargon particular to your local police organizations not included here. Your local force might have a list on its intranet, or on a publicly available website, or (more rarely) in a published form. Use the internet to track down a list.

1.5   Answers to Tasks

TASK 1 You should have found that the two conditions of making a CBO are given in s 22(3) (4) of Part 2 of the Anti-social Behaviour, Crime and Policing Act 2014. The legislation itself can be found at <http://www.legislation.gov.uk/ukpga/2014/12/contents/enacted>.

The first condition is that 'the court is satisfied, beyond reasonable doubt, that the offender has engaged in behaviour that caused or was likely to cause harassment, alarm or distress to any person'.

The second condition is that the CBO may be ordered if 'the court considers that making the order will help in preventing the offender from engaging in such behaviour'. In this case the explanatory notes provided on the official legislation site are very general in nature, and it is best also to consult the CPS guidance at <https://www.cps.gov.uk/legal-guidance/criminal-behaviour-orders>. This explains the test in more detail.

TASK 2 Police forces often publish a glossary of terms used in their documentation, available under the Freedom of Information Act 2000. An example of a glossary may be found at: <http://www.northants.police.uk/simple/page/glossary-terms>.

2 | Policing

2.1 Introduction

The title of this chapter is 'Policing' rather than 'The Police'. This reflects Reiner's distinction that the term ' "Police" refers to a particular kind of social institution, while "policing" implies a set of processes with specific social functions' (Reiner, 2000, p 1). Policing is undertaken by a range of organizations and not just the police, so we also consider the 'extended policing family' (see 2.2.2). In addition, we examine the claim that policing is a profession, taking into account the learning and development requirements for trainee police officers and students on pre-join programmes; the demonstration of certain professional qualities is likely to be required. These qualities are sometimes less easy to pinpoint and identify than other aspects of learning and development (such as the acquisition of knowledge and demonstration of competencies and skills as outlined in Part III of this book), but they are just as important for twenty-first-century police officers. We also include in this chapter a list of dates and key events in the history of law enforcement and policing, which provides some perspective for current practices (and may help you understand some of the reactions to proposed changes). Additionally, we explain the basic configuration of the rank structure in policing and give an overview of a typical police force organizational structure.

Policing is always changing and evolving, but this is particularly true at the time of writing. The College of Policing, the professional body for policing established in 2012, continues to develop, and the introduction of directly elected Police and Crime Commissioners was a further significant change (see 2.3.2).

The relatively recent recognition that vulnerability (particularly surrounding victims and witnesses) should be very much taken into account in today's policing, and the need to respond to global movements such as #MeToo demonstrate the very fast-moving nature of the policing domain at this time.

2.2 Perspectives in Policing

It is perhaps surprising to note that the public police (in the UK and elsewhere) are a relatively modern phenomenon, and that there have been a number of notable occasions when their very existence has been challenged. If there is one key date in modern-day policing it is probably 1829, when Sir Robert Peel, then Home Secretary, introduced a Bill in Parliament for the establishment of a 'Metropolitan Police Force' for London. Perhaps this is the primary observation here: the police service as we would recognize it today is not even 200 years old, and fundamental challenges to its purpose and structure still abound. However, the formation of the 'Met' is often referred to by police historians as the beginning of the 'new police', as it clearly delineates the police we know today from the previous ad hoc local policing bodies and watch systems.

2.2.1 Law enforcement

Law enforcement in England and Wales has rarely been simply the province of the police alone. Many responsibilities for law enforcement and public order continue to be shared amongst a large number of agencies, as shown in the table.

Type	Description	Examples	Comments
The 'territorial' or 'Home Office' police forces	The 43 county or metropolitan police forces in England and Wales, and the single Police Services of Scotland and of Northern Ireland	Essex Police, MPS, Derbyshire Constabulary, PSNI	What most people mean when they refer to the 'police'
Sector-specific police forces	Police forces for specific sectors or industries (eg transport, nuclear power)	BTP, CNC	Powers are at least equal to those of the territorial police forces
'Heritage' constabularies and police forces	Individual constabularies established previously under Acts of Parliament, restricted to small geographical areas	Port of Dover Police, Royal Parks Constabulary, Cambridge University Constabulary	Powers are the same as those for territorial police but the forces are smaller
Armed services police	Organizations responsible for policing the armed forces (eg the navy)	MoD Police, Royal Military Police	Some armed services police are civilians (ie not members of the armed forces)
Agencies	Home Office or non-statutory bodies with extensive powers of search, detention, arrest, and investigation	NCA for England and Wales	The NCA has now subsumed many former agencies such as SOCA
National police 'units' or 'sections'	Normally NPCC or College of Policing supported units offering specialist support to police forces	National Wildlife Crime Unit (NWCU), SCAS	Normally made up of seconded police officers, but not exclusively
Other organizations with investigatory powers	Non-police organizations with limited powers of investigation (but might have surveillance powers)	Local authorities, HM Revenue and Customs, IOPC	Some powers are governed by RIPA 2000 and IPA 2016
Other organizations with enforcement and/or regulatory powers	Regulatory bodies with responsibility for enforcing regulations	Trading Standards, HSE	Powers normally fall short of arrest, although they can usually prosecute
Other 'emergency services'	Services (other than the police) usually involved in the case of fire, vehicle collisions, and apparent accidents etc.	Fire and Rescue Services	Some emergency services have powers for stopping people and vehicles, entry, investigation, and prosecution
'Private' security or investigatory services	Companies and individuals from the private security industry	Security guards, 'private detectives', debt collectors	In some cases licensing is required or forms of self-regulation
Informal policing	Social control and enforcement as a secondary occupational responsibility	Teachers, park rangers, bus drivers	Normally no powers beyond those of any civilian

Informal policing activities are also undertaken at the so-called 'secondary' and 'tertiary' levels of social control, for example by teachers and security staff, and even through institutions such as the church and trade union organizations. These informal policing mechanisms are not underpinned by particular powers (beyond those of every citizen) and such activities are better understood as secondary occupational responsibilities, or even as less tangible societal responsibilities.

Despite the increased sharing of policing powers the 'public police' still retain unique and profound powers, including those surrounding discretion (see 5.5.3). We still often refer to our police organizations as 'forces' although some prefer the term 'police service'.

2.2.2   The extended policing family

Policing involves an array of providers which together form an extended policing family which includes special constables, police support staff and police community support officers, police volunteers, and private security firms. This is not an exhaustive list, but it does provide an indication of the various different kinds of policing arrangements, including voluntary, regulatory, and private policing providers. Many members of the extended policing family are important in policing communities (see Chapter 8).

At 31 March 2019 there were 202,023 staff working for the police forces of England and Wales of which about 61 per cent were police officers, 34 per cent police support staff, and 5 per cent PCSOs (author's rounded calculations, based on data available at Home Office, 2019h). In addition, there were 10,640 special constables serving with police forces in the UK in 2019, a reduction of just over 1,000 compared with 2018.

2.2.2.1 Special constables

Special constables ('specials') are volunteers, who are sworn officers with full powers. They undertake police duties on a part-time basis (a minimum of 96 hours per year). Most specials are not paid employees of a police force but they are reimbursed expenses. However, a number of measures have been introduced by some forces or local authorities to 'reward' specials for their service such as an 'allowance' or a council tax discount. They must be over the age of 18 and be a national of a country within the European Economic Area (EEA), or a national of a country outside the EEA with the right to reside in this country without restrictions.

Most special constables undertake paid employment elsewhere; the system functions very much in the same way as the Territorial Army, or RAF, or Naval volunteer reserve forces. In most forces they work alongside regular officers, go out on patrol, and deal with the range of activities which a patrol constable would encounter during an ordinary shift. Specials are subject to the same Code of Ethics as other police officers, which means, for example, that they must not take any active part in politics.

Some police services now require future applicants to the police service to serve as special constables before applying for full-time employment, so there are a growing number of specials who are in full- or part-time education. The training for specials in most forces is the College of Policing IL4SC (Initial Learning for the Special Constabulary) programme, and utilizes both workplace assessments (against the National Occupational Standards (NOS)) and the assessment of knowledge and understanding.

Whilst such initiatives are currently welcomed (primarily on economic grounds) there might be issues further down the line with respect to the status of specials as more focus is placed on what a police officer needs to know before being issued with a warrant card. For example, consider the implications if a special constable applies to his/her force to become a paid full-time police officer through the national SEARCH© assessment process (see Chapter 6), but is rejected (perhaps on the grounds of respect for diversity). This could raise concerns over whether he/she should retain the status of a warranted officer.

2.2.2.2 Police support staff

There were 69,365 police support staff in England and Wales in 2019 (Home Office, 2019h). In many forces, support staff can make up to a third of total numbers, and they undertake a wide range of tasks. For some areas in policing it may be more appropriate to employ specialist support staff (cybercrime and fraud being two obvious examples) than to rely on 'omnicompetent' officers. This issue touches on a wider debate about the purpose of sworn officers, and the responsibilities and tasks assigned to this role.

> **TASK 1** Suggest some examples of the types of work police support staff might carry out.

2.2.2.3 Non-territorial police forces

As noted in 2.2.1, in addition to the Home Office 'territorial' forces of England and Wales there are other police forces such as:

- The British Transport Police (BTP), mainly responsible for policing the UK railway network (over- and underground). Uniformed and plain clothes BTP officers travel on the railways performing police functions. BTP worked very closely with the MPS after the London tube train bombings in 2005.

Policing in Context

- The Ministry of Defence (MoD) Police, who guard MoD establishments across the UK (including Scotland). Other police forces within the armed forces are the Royal Military Police (RMP) and the RAF's Provost and Security Services (P&SS). These only have jurisdiction within their force establishments, and only for less serious crimes.
- The Civil Nuclear Constabulary (CNC), who protect civil nuclear installations and fuels in shipment and storage. All CNC officers are firearms-trained.

2.2.2.4 Police Community Support Officers

The Police Community Support Officer (PCSO) role was specifically designed to provide presence and to be accessible to the community, and also to enable local people to contribute to Neighbourhood Policing Teams. PCSOs work alongside police constables, to help reduce crime and anti-social behaviour in local neighbourhoods, and to provide reassurance to the public. In some forces, PCSOs now undertake specialist roles such as victim liaison.

PCSOs engage with the public, identifying their concerns and supporting people who are affected by anti-social behaviour, crime, or the fear of crime. They patrol a limited beat where they can be seen and spoken to, and there is an emphasis on meeting and talking to young people. PCSO uniforms are similar to those of warranted police officers but they have blue ties, and their epaulettes clearly identify them as PCSOs.

PCSOs do not have a power of arrest but do have many other powers (see CoP, 2015f). Each PCSO officer carries documentation detailing the powers he/she has been granted.

There are 20 potentially available 'standard' PCSO powers, which include the power to:

- enter and search any premises for the purposes of saving life and limb or preventing serious damage to property;
- require the name and address of a person in specified circumstances (eg for anti-social behaviour, for road traffic offences or if the suspect is believed to have committed certain offences such as causing injury, alarm, or distress to another);
- control traffic (under certain circumstances);
- issue certain fixed penalty notices (eg for cycling on a footpath, or littering);
- require surrender of certain items (eg alcohol from people under 18, or from people drinking in a designated place);
- seize certain items (eg tobacco from a person aged under 16) and vehicles which have been used to cause alarm; and
- remove abandoned vehicles.

Another 43 'discretionary additional powers' can be granted by chief officers, such as the power to:

- issue fixed penalty notices (eg for disorder, truancy, dog fouling, graffiti, fly posting, driving the wrong way along a one-way street, and unlicensed street vending);
- 'deal with' begging;
- detain a person for up to 30 minutes, using reasonable force to prevent him/her from escaping;
- search detained persons for dangerous items, and use reasonable force to prevent escape;
- require a person claiming to be a charity collector to provide his/her certificate, name, address, and signature.

In many police forces PCSO training follows the National Policing Curriculum. It involves learning across ten categories: Ethics and values; Personal and public safety; Information management; Community engagement and crime prevention; Forensics and evidence gathering; Public protection; Intelligence and counter-terrorism; Crime and investigation; Planned operations and emergency procedures; and finally, Leadership and strategic command. The *National Policing PCSO Operational Handbook* (2015) provides full details on all aspects of the role and function of the PCSO, and is available online. Note, however, that a PCSO version of the new Police Constable Degree Apprenticeship is currently under development by the College of Policing, and this is likely to lead to significant changes.

TASK 2

1. What discretionary powers are given to PCSOs by your local police force?
2. Think about what you know about PCSOs and the work they do. What form do you imagine PCSO training takes, and how long might it last?

2.2.2.5 Other policing and law enforcement agencies

Many aspects of our lives are predominantly policed by individuals other than sworn police officers, for example at most football grounds the policing is provided by stewards. Likewise, the policing of the night-time economy in our town and city centres (with regard to reducing the likelihood of serious disorder) involves a range of privately employed individuals, who will be present in far greater numbers than sworn police officers. There are also non-police agencies which have investigative powers and can also prosecute their own cases, while others will investigate certain matters, and then turn their findings over to the police to take to court. HM Revenue and Customs, for example, has powers to investigate crimes such as evasion of VAT or other taxes, and improper importing. Likewise, the UK's Border Force employees have specific powers in relation to immigration and customs matters. There have been moves to centralize and coordinate investigative capacities across different agencies, for example through the establishment of the National Crime Agency (NCA) in 2013. The NCA 'command' units include Border Policing Command, Economic Crime Command, Organised Crime Command, and Child Exploitation and Online Protection Command.

2.2.2.6 Regulatory bodies

These are bodies which have a particular interest in specialized matters such as public health or environmental crime, and can prosecute offenders. This category includes:

- the Health and Safety Executive (HSE);
- Trading Standards Authorities;
- the National Society for the Prevention of Cruelty to Children (NSPCC);
- the Royal Society for the Prevention of Cruelty to Animals (RSPCA); and
- the Royal Society for the Protection of Birds (RSPB).

In a sense, most of these bodies focus on niche crime, such as maltreatment of animals and stealing birds' eggs. Only the work of the HSE and the NSPCC impact substantially on police work, although it seems likely that environmental crime will have a higher profile in the future.

2.2.2.7 The private sector

Successive governments have demonstrated the belief that private companies have an important role to play within the extended policing family. The private security industry is expanding rapidly and includes staff such as door stewards at clubs, shopping centre security personnel, train guards, security guards who patrol areas frequented by the public, and detention officers in privatized prisons. The last few years have seen an increase in the number of 'gated communities' (following a US model), where access to a group of private and exclusive dwellings is controlled by uniformed guards 24 hours a day. This reassures the householders that privacy is guaranteed and increases physical security, and makes burglaries, robberies, and assaults more difficult to commit or attempt.

Compulsory licensing for staff applies for many security occupations, such as security guards, door stewards, and for vehicle immobilizer personnel (clampers). There is a voluntary (non-statutory) scheme in place for 'approved contractors'—the companies supplying private security services. More information is available on the Security Industry Authority (SIA) website.

Security extends across the community, for example through bailiffs and the use of CCTV. Bailiffs recover property that has not been fully paid for, or seize goods in lieu of debt. Their work may involve the police, particularly for evictions or where there is concern about public order. The extension of the policing family also includes the large surveillance system (eg monitored CCTV) across the UK, and automated number plate readers (ANPR) linked to cameras mounted on bridges and gantries to monitor vehicle movements. The use of CCTV in police surveillance work is discussed in 23.4.1.

When considering the steady growth of private security, we should not ignore the large established security companies, such as G4S and the Securitas Group. They are involved in all aspects of private security, such as cash collection from businesses, the provision of physical security, and the transportation of prisoners. When private companies provide security for organizations there can be a blurring of roles between public policing and private policing. For example, at some animal research facilities external security is run by the police whilst internal security is managed by a private company. However, the degree of cooperation that exists between the two is not always clear, which has implications for formal police accountability mechanisms.

An important question raised in relation to private policing concerns the very purpose of the police. The police carry out a variety of activities with a common purpose; to serve the public interest. It is this public service, perhaps more than how the police are funded, that means the police are deemed to be a public, as opposed to private, service. Many police organizations receive private funding; for example, BTP are partially funded by the rail companies. Indeed, all public police services are increasingly generating income beyond that provided by government through the Home Office, and it seems likely that an increased reliance on such funding will be required to sustain an effective and efficient police service.

Finally (though we have by no means exhausted the examples of the private security industry), there are private investigators. These are generally small-scale enquiry companies (seldom exceeding half a dozen employees) which are usually staffed by ex-police officers. They are principally engaged in matters such as gathering evidence for presentation in divorce cases, or tracking down missing persons. They present little in the way of conflict with the regular police, except when attempts are made to access official records or data such as vehicle registration numbers.

2.2.2.8 Volunteer roles in police work

There are two key volunteering roles in the police namely 'special constables' (see 2.2.2.1) and 'police support volunteers' (or simply 'police volunteers'). Police volunteers are individuals who work for the police in a variety of non-enforcement roles—these include helping with front desk responsibilities, neighbourhood watch support (see 2.2.2.9), and assisting neighbourhood policing teams with community initiatives. Typically a non-metropolitan police force will have between 100 and 200 volunteers. Police volunteers are security checked but do not hold any police powers. The police are now exploring the recruitment of volunteers to specialist roles such as computing and cybersecurity.

2.2.2.9 Neighbourhood Watch

The Neighbourhood Watch (NhW) scheme involves bringing groups of residents together to 'create ... communities where crime and anti-social behaviour are less likely to happen' (Neighbourhood Watch, 2014). It was established in 1982 and there are now approximately 150,000 schemes in the UK covering some 5 million households. NhW is usually organized by volunteers and led by a coordinator who is supported by a liaison officer linked to the local police station. These local networks are part of a larger national structure supported by the National Police Chiefs' Council and the Home Office, and need to be registered with the police. NhW groups collect information about local concerns (eg criminal damage, anti-social behaviour, bogus callers, etc), and provide the police with any information regarding crimes or suspects. The police can also share information about crimes committed in the NhW area, and offer advice on how community members can protect themselves. Police officers can encourage communities or individuals to start new schemes or join established schemes by directing people to liaison officers or established coordinators. Police forces throughout the country are now engaged in a whole range of 'watch' schemes, including Hospital Watch, Boat Watch, Business Watch, National Pubwatch, Shed Watch, Church Watch, Forecourt Watch, Bicycle Watch, Country Eye, Horse Watch, Farm Watch, School Watch, and Shop Watch. These schemes are very important in the policing of our local communities (see Chapter 8).

2.2.3 Policing as a profession

Trainee officers will often hear references during training to 'adopting a professional attitude' or 'behaving in a professional manner', but what does this actually mean? Here we consider what it means to professionalize policing and what this means for the trainee officer. But before we examine what 'professional policing' might mean, we need to consider what we might mean generally by a 'profession'.

> **TASK 3** Make a list of professions. What features do you look for in an occupation that makes it a profession? Are there any common features that are found in all the professions you have listed?

We encounter the word 'profession' in many different contexts and applied to numerous occupational groups. There is no universally accepted definition of profession, although there is a general agreement that only some occupations qualify as professions. It is also potentially confusing that the word 'professional' is often appended to an activity simply to acknowledge that its practitioners receive some form of payment for it, or that it is undertaken more seriously. For example, we know that a reference to a 'professional gambler' means that he/she probably earns a living from gambling. However, there is likely to be more to a profession than this. Traditionally, there were just four professions: law, medicine, the church, and the military. Later, accountancy became a profession, and now there are many more occupations commonly regarded as professions, for example teaching. There is a broad consensus in the academic world that at least some of the following are required for an occupation to also be a profession:

- an accepted corpus of knowledge and theory underpinning the practice of the profession;
- controls on entry to the profession, normally through qualification, coupled with a need to maintain the currency of qualification;
- autonomy, discretion, and a degree of self-regulation;
- its practitioners have a form of vocational calling; and
- a code of ethics.

In addition, for most professions, many of the control and regulatory functions are carried out by a professional body.

To illustrate these ideas and to explore them further, we now consider medical practice as an example of a profession and measure it against our list of features for a profession.

Requirements of a profession	The medical profession
Corpus of knowledge and theory	The scientific basis to medical practice (eg physiology and biochemistry), knowledge of clinical practice (eg conducting physical examinations), aspects of the behavioural and social sciences
Controls on entry to the profession and continuing professional development	Completing a recognized medical degree, followed by a period of supervised practice (eg foundation training followed by postgraduate training). There is a need to demonstrate regular Continuous Professional Development (CPD) under seven headings in order to maintain a place on the professional register
Autonomy, discretion, and self-regulation	Medical doctors have significant autonomy and discretion. Their conduct is regulated by the General Medical Council (GMC). Their representative body is the British Medical Association (BMA). Their authority is largely epistemic in nature (see 5.11.5.1)
Vocational calling	Difficult to prove, as no clear definitions of a vocation exist. However, interviews for entry to medical degrees often attempt to test applicants for this
Code of ethics	A code is published by the GMC. Doctors are informed to 'make the care of your patient your first concern', to 'respect patients' dignity and privacy', and 'to give patients information in a way they can understand'

We can see that medicine matches our working definition of a profession very closely. We can now compare the features of policing work with our definition of what makes an occupation a profession.

TASK 4 Complete the following table for the occupation of policing:

Requirements of a profession	The policing profession
Corpus of knowledge and theory	
Controls on entry to the profession and maintenance of position	
Autonomy, discretion, and self-regulation	
Vocational calling	
Code of ethics	

You probably established that policing in the UK meets many, but not all, of our criteria for being a profession. Some of the necessary elements (such as the need to maintain skills and knowledge) were originally developed by the NPIA and others, and more recently the College of Policing has taken on this responsibility. There is now also a 'National SIO Register' for senior investigating officers (SIOs), and it is envisaged that it will eventually contain the details of all investigators accredited through the Senior Investigating Officer Development Programme (SIODP), or through other means of demonstrating competence, although progress on this appears slow. As Bryant (2009, p 29) notes, 'to remain "live" on the register an SIO will be required to provide details of' his/her relevant 'CPD activity'. A similar system applies for doctors—to retain their place on a professional register they have to provide evidence to show they have kept up to date and are fit to practise (GMC, 2008).

Some would argue that establishing and maintaining policing as a full profession is important for the following reasons:

- to develop the body of knowledge, doctrines, and skills required for modern-day policing;
- to protect the right of the police, in certain key respects, to regulate themselves;
- to improve public confidence in the work of the police by providing a full professional register implying the need for its members to regularly demonstrate that they have met the requirement to maintain their skills and knowledge; and
- to distinguish the work and the professional standing of the police officer from others, including members of the extended policing family (see 2.2) and other law enforcers.

While professionalization is largely seen as a positive, this final bullet point shows that there are other not so positive considerations with regard to professionalizing policing. For example, many of the traditional professions such as law are not noted for their inclusivity, and striving for a professional status may reduce the representative nature of the policing family.

2.2.3.1 The College of Policing

The College of Policing was established in 2012 as the official professional body for policing. It has assumed many of the standards and training responsibilities of its predecessor, the NPIA. Its focus is on:

- Knowledge (the development of research and evidence of *What Works*);
- Education (the development of individual members of the profession); and
- Standards for police forces and individuals.

The College has developed a National Policing Curriculum, for which it has secured accredited providers. In the long term, the College of Policing aspires to achieve charter status ('The Royal College of Policing') and be independent of government, for example in terms of its funding. Membership of the College of Policing is open to all police staff, but police staff awareness of the College appears to be low, a problem exacerbated by the inability of the College to communicate directly with members and potential members (Home Affairs Select Committee, 2015).

A key requirement for professionalization appears to be specialist knowledge and expertise. The 2011 Neyroud Review into police leadership and training made proposals on how to align policing more fully with other professions, including the establishment of a new professional body. This is an ongoing remit of the College of Policing as indicated, for example, by the development of the new Code of Ethics for policing, the extensive ongoing development of

Authorised Professional Practice, and the new qualifications framework for policing (pitched at HE (higher education) level).

2.2.4 Approaches to policing

There are a number of different models or approaches to policing. It is perhaps misleading to suggest they are somehow in competition or are mutually exclusive, although there are significant points of departure between them, and each has a separate focus. For example, the intelligence-led policing model tends to be seen as a response to the inevitable and unavoidable existence of criminals in society, and the existence of high-volume repeat criminals. In contrast, problem-oriented policing (see 8.3.2.2) attempts to model crime or disorder in terms of problems that we can then analyse and attempt to solve. Zero-tolerance policing (see 8.3.3.2) is based on the idea that an absence of effective police responses is likely to lead to an escalation of problems.

> **TASK 5** What do you think characterizes the British approach to policing? What can you point to that is essentially British about it?

The different approaches to policing are to some extent due to conflicting views regarding the most pressing policing problems in society, and what are the most appropriate and effective means of addressing them.

2.2.4.1 Intelligence-led policing

Intelligence-led policing (ILP) was introduced in the UK in the 1990s as a new model of policing (it is also known as intelligence-based policing). Within this model, intelligence from a number of agencies is pooled with the explicit intention to 'disrupt, disable or undermine criminal behaviour' (Stelfox, 2008, in Newburn and Neyroud, 2008, p 146). Ratcliffe (2008) defined intelligence-led policing as:

> a business model and managerial philosophy where data analysis and crime intelligence are pivotal to an objective, decision-making framework that facilitates crime and problem reduction, disruption and prevention through both strategic management and effective enforcement strategies that target prolific and serious offenders.

ILP was progressively adopted (with varying degrees of enthusiasm) by police forces in England and Wales during the late 1990s, and retains a significant influence on strategic and tactical policing methods in the UK. Thornton claimed that 'the concept of intelligence-led policing underpins all aspects of policing, from neighbourhood policing and partnership work to the investigation of serious and organised crime and terrorism' (Thornton, 2007, p 3).

ILP, at its outset at least, was a crime-focused model of policing which emphasized the countering of crime through detection, disruption, or dissuasion. In practical terms, ILP derives its philosophy and principles from the recognition that crime and criminality can be understood at some level in terms of its perpetrators, its temporal and spatial patterns, and the linkages between crimes (eg common case analysis). In terms of the perpetrators of crime, the 1993 Audit Commission report (Audit Commission, 1993) and the unpublished research of Kent Police and others appeared to demonstrate clearly that a minority of criminals are responsible for the majority of most types of volume crime. The logic ran that this minority could be identified (eg through the use of paid informants) and then targeted and 'removed' through successful detection and prosecution. This, it was hoped, could be a more effective use of police resources, compared with more reactive models. Indeed, as Heaton (2008) and others have observed, this 'targeting' of high-volume and often recidivist offenders became a cornerstone of ILP. Thus, the mantra of ILP became to 'target the criminal and not just the crime' (adapted from an observation made by the Audit Commission, 1993), and this led to a much greater emphasis on intelligence gathering and analysis (and the associated employment of increasing numbers of analysts), and a reduction in reactive policing.

Opinion and research continue to differ concerning just how small a minority of criminals are responsible for just how large a majority of crime. For example, the Audit Commission cited Home Office research, which claimed that '7% of males who had been convicted of 6 or more offences accounted for 65% of all convictions' (Home Office, 1989, p 2). While there was probably some exaggeration in this oft-repeated '7% responsible for 65%' claim, which was derived in a very particular context, there is nonetheless clear evidence for a skew in offending. Heaton (2000) argued that a more 'realistic' ratio would be 3 per cent of offenders being responsible for 24 per cent of offences. A 2004 study in Brighton and Hove supports this more conservative estimate with the 'top' 40 of the 400 identified high-volume offenders (10 per cent) being responsible for 691 convictions out of the 3,453 total (20 per cent) (Center for Problem-Oriented Policing, 2009). Further, research on repeat victimization (Everson and Pease, 2001) suggests that prolific offenders may be responsible for the bulk of these repeated crimes against the same person or target.

The identification of 'patterns of crime' and linking crimes together is also an important (although not a unique) feature of ILP, giving rise to the ability to deploy policing resources more effectively. This is often combined with an increased multi-agency approach to the sharing of intelligence. The analysis of crime data and intelligence (see 23.5) by both the police and partner agencies (often through CSPs) is a key factor in identifying temporal and spatial aspects of crime. This can help ensure that resources are deployed appropriately and proactively where possible.

2.2.4.2 Predictive policing

Predictive policing is concerned with the use of mathematical, analytical, and predictive techniques which are designed to identify potential criminal activity in a policing area. Perry *et al* (2013) have highlighted the potential strengths and outcomes of such an approach, in that it provides the ability to identify and prevent crime or to solve past crimes by making statistical predictions. However, they go on to identify certain weaknesses, for example issues around data-collection techniques, failures to address the underlying causes of crime, and the fact that stop and search cannot be used with a predictive model of crime detection. They also observe that predictive policing is very resource-intensive.

We could also add that predictive policing thus far has been predominantly concerned with forecasting locations of crimes which follow spatial and temporal (time-dependent) patterns. This raises concerns about societal justice: predictive policing algorithms have been deployed for crimes such as street robbery but not for 'insider trading' in the City of London. Concerns have also been expressed about the possibly inadvertent discriminatory effects of employing predictive policing algorithms based on past events (Smith, 2016).

Despite these concerns, a principal theme of the 2017 annual report by the Chief HMI, Sir Thomas Winsor, was that the police should be able to 'understand, predict and meet demand' (HMIC, 2017b, p 16) so that increasingly scarce resources can be deployed more effectively, and HMICFRS (previously HMIC) has been working with the London School of Economics 'to develop a statistical model that can with accuracy predict demand for police services' (HMIC, 2017b, p 17).

2.2.5 Legitimacy

The issue of legitimacy is central to debates about the police role in democratic societies. The existence of police authority requires individuals to willingly sacrifice a degree of personal freedom and liberty in order to secure a greater degree of collective freedom and liberty. The logic behind this way of thinking is made explicit in the writings of the seventeenth-century English philosopher Thomas Hobbes: without authority in society there would exist 'a war of all against all'. For Hobbes, therefore, the existence of any authority is preferable to none at all. This is an important point to note because, as Nozick (1974) and Simmons (2001) have argued, the necessity for authority must be considered before questioning the legitimacy of authority. The difficulty in justifying police authority is illustrated by the fact that it took six attempts (from 1785 onwards) to pass a Police Bill through the Houses of Parliament, to create the 'new' police in 1829. Clearly there was opposition at the time to the very existence of a professional standing body of police in England and Wales. Today, we largely take the existence of the police for granted, and very few people seriously question whether we would be better off without any police. The benefits of having a police presence need to be balanced against both the financial cost and the loss of civil liberties arising from policing activities.

The continuing importance of legitimacy in policing is clear; it is one of the areas assessed in HMICFRS in its annual integrated PEEL inspection. There are two distinct means through which legitimacy can be established: consensual and moral legitimacy.

2.2.5.1   Consensual and moral legitimacy of the police

The police are quite rightly governed by the law, but the issue of legitimacy is central to debates about the police role in liberal democratic societies in other ways too. Consensual legitimacy is gained through the support of the people and communities who are being policed. It reflects the democratic aspect of policing within a liberal democracy, the notion of 'policing by consent' (Reiner, 2000). In the early years of the police the discussion about legitimacy was almost exclusively concerned with consent, and even today the Home Office focus on neighbourhood policing (see Chapter 8) places great emphasis on the importance of consent.

From the perspective of those advocating consensual legitimacy, the police are legitimate to the extent that the public consent to policing. Of course there are differing degrees to which we might say the public consents to the police. One view is to say that the public consents passively by not opposing what the police do. On the other hand, we might insist on the public having an ongoing engagement with the police, in order for consent to be given actively. In practice, the kind of consent gained will be dependent upon the type of police response and the particular problem addressed. For example, if the police are required to deal with a serious threat of terrorism, then the consent will have to be passive in order to allow the police to be effective. The more the public know about how the police intend to counter the terrorists, the more the terrorists would also know and the police intervention might fail as a consequence. Conversely, when the police are required to resolve low-level but persistent offending, there is a greater need for the police to communicate with the local community, to establish and agree the best way to address the problem. In this latter case, the consent must be active and ongoing. The police need to negotiate their response to the problem and ensure that the community supports, as much as is possible, any police interventions. In this respect, to ensure consensual legitimacy of the police there must be appropriate public involvement in negotiating police responses, and the response must deal effectively with the particular problem. An appeal for witnesses to an event is a common form of this nexus between police and public.

There are limits to consensual legitimacy, for example the police could theoretically be too responsive to the views of the communities being policed. As Waddington (1999) has noted, the police are required to deal with conflicts in society and in the exercise of this function they may have to police 'against' some sections of the community. A real concern exists that the police might be overly responsive to one section of the community against another. This could lead to the exclusion and/or targeting of groups of individuals who are seen to be on the periphery of a community. Put another way, the popularity of the police, which is effectively what consent measures, is no guarantee that the police are acting in a legitimate way. Equally, people's fears or concerns may not necessarily match the prevailing crime patterns, and may not help the police to focus effort appropriately.

There are various ways of establishing the legitimacy of police authority, and approval from citizens is just one. As Simmons (2001) observes, this particular way of establishing legitimacy focuses on how an authority is perceived, rather than what it does. It measures the attitudes of the recipients of the authority, rather than measuring the authority itself. In a similar vein, Bottoms and Tankebe (2012) draw attention to the limits of the procedural justice approach to ascertaining police legitimacy, on the grounds that it captures the perspective of the 'audience', but not the power-brokers themselves.

We might say that consent is a necessary, but not sufficient, aspect of police legitimacy. In liberal democratic terms, consent reflects democratic, but not liberal concerns. The liberal concerns within liberal democratic contexts are expressed more through the moral legitimacy of the police, rather than consensual legitimacy. It is becoming increasingly important for the police to 'do the right thing' from a moral perspective. The course of action that would be supported by a local community is not always the moral one, and the community might not support all morally correct policing actions. For example, the police will not always be able to gain consensual support for protecting a known paedophile living within a residential area, or allowing a racist organization to march through the town centre. However, the reason why the police do what they do is often a matter of moral legitimacy rather than consensual legitimacy.

Policing in Context

2.2.5.2 **Police legitimacy in practice**

As far as possible, the police will try to achieve both moral and consensual legitimacy, but this is not always possible. The former Chief Constable of Devon and Cornwall, John Alderson, advocated 'principled policing' (see Alderson, 1998), arguing that policing should be more firmly founded upon moral principles, rather than pragmatic concerns. The Human Rights Act 1998 gave legislative support to this point of view. Increasingly, police officers must take into account a number of (often different or contradictory) moral considerations in order to make professional judgements. Policing by consent remains an important part of police legitimacy, but the police must operate primarily within both legal and moral boundaries if they are to be truly legitimate.

> **TASK 6** What would you need to take into account if (as a police officer) you had to control a march by the Britain First organization through your town, knowing that a group of anti-racist protestors was planning to turn up in large numbers to oppose the march? (Note that our interest here is in judgements based on police legitimacy, rather than the detail of operational orders.)

2.2.6 Chronology of law enforcement and policing

An understanding of the past is an important precursor to understanding the present. Current practice and the reasons for it are sometimes easier to appreciate if we consider the historical context. We do not provide a comprehensive history of law enforcement and the police in the UK, nor do we offer much in the way of analysis, but we do provide you with some of the background and a number of key dates in the history of policing in England and Wales, dominated (at least in the nineteenth century) by the Metropolitan Police in London.

1829	Sir Robert Peel establishes the first civilian police force in London, with two Justices of the Peace in charge of the force—Richard Mayne and Charles Rowan.
1831	Period of considerable unrest and mob violence, especially in the north of England and in London.
1835	The Municipal Corporations Act 1835 establishes 'watch committees' to oversee policing of areas outside London.
1839–40	Provincial constabularies established across the country for the first time.
1842	Establishment of a detective force at the London Metropolitan Police HQ, Scotland Yard (still only ten staff in 1856).
1840s–50s	Considerable hostility towards the new police, with widespread resentment about the cost and the perceived lack of police officers when needed. Some believe that any police force is illiberal.
1856	Becomes mandatory for local government bodies to set up police forces. Financial support awarded by central government to forces proved to be efficient and reliable, paving the way for the modern inspection regime by Her Majesty's Inspectorate of Constabulary (HMIC).
1860	Over 200 borough and county police forces in England and Wales in existence. Unrest in Ireland leads to the formation of the Royal Irish Constabulary, which is paramilitary from the outset.
1872	Police officers go on strike for the first time.
1878	The Criminal Investigation Department (CID) formed, with Scotland Yard detectives being called in by county forces to lead criminal investigations well into the 1930s.
1883	The Special Irish Branch is set up as part of the Metropolitan Police to deal with attacks by Irish republicans in London. Later it becomes known simply as Special Branch.
1901	Scotland Yard's Fingerprint Bureau is formed.
1911	Police officers armed for the first time, after assisting the military to end a siege of armed anarchists in a London house.

1912	Establishment of special constables on a permanent basis.
1914	NUPPO, the first Police Union (unofficial) was formed. The 'Women Police' are founded.
1914–18	The First World War puts enormous pressure on the police due to enlistment in the armed forces, suspension of police recruitment, and new tasks such as the pursuit of deserters.
1916	The Commissioner of the Metropolitan Police rules that any officer joining a union was liable to dismissal.
	The regularizing of women police officers as equal members of the force is generally dated from 1916, although many would argue that women were not fully accepted in the police service until the Second World War, and even then, attitudes to female police officers were often negative. Moreover, those women officers who were appointed were largely confined to duties connected with children or women offenders. The Police Federation did not admit female officers as members until 1948.
1918–19	The police, particularly in Liverpool and London, embark on a series of strikes for better pay and conditions, and for recognition of police trades unions. New legislation bans police trades unions and denies the police the right to strike, but allows the formation of the Police Federation for negotiations over pay, etc.
1921	Police motorcycle patrols established.
1922	After the creation of Eire in 1922, the RIC become the Royal Ulster Constabulary (RUC).
1931	A two-tier entry system to the police operates briefly, based on the officer/non-commissioned ranks recruitment in the armed forces. Police officers are trained at Hendon, but this experiment with 'officer entry' is short-lived.
1935	The first police forensic laboratory is opened by the Metropolitan Police.
1937	The emergency telephone number 999 is introduced.
1946	The number of forces is reduced to 125.
1948	The Police Federation starts to admit female officers as members.
1950s	The so-called 'Golden Age' of policing, characterized by apparent widespread acceptance of the legitimacy of the police, and relatively low levels of crime and disorder begins. Popular belief in its existence probably derives at least in part from a television series of the time, *Dixon of Dock Green*.
1964	The number of separate and distinct forces is reduced to 49.
1965	Police officer personal radios are introduced.
1973	Women police officers are fully integrated directly into the police service, performing the same duties as male colleagues.
1981	The Scarman Report into the Brixton riots in April 1981 (involving mostly young black men) gives rise to a concerted effort to improve relations between the police and minority ethnic groups.
1984	The Police and Criminal Evidence Act 1984 (PACE Act) creates the Police Complaints Authority (PCA). This was in response to criticism of the police 'acting as judge and jury' in investigations into complaints from the public about the police.
1990	The Association of Chief Police Officers (ACPO) publishes its 'Statement of Common Purpose and Values', which emphasizes the police should be seen more as a service than as a force.
1990s	(onwards) The employment of civilian staff in police forces increases, as it is recognized that some traditional police officer roles can be performed just as effectively by non-warranted police staff (eg crime scene investigators).
1994	Creation of a centralized computer database for criminal records.
1997	NAFIS, the National Automated Fingerprint Identification System is created.

1999	The Macpherson Inquiry into the death of Stephen Lawrence (a black teenager murdered in London in 1993) criticizes the whole police service as 'institutionally racist'.
	The RUC becomes the Police Service of Northern Ireland (PSNI), following the Patten Inquiry.
2002	Introduction of Police Community Support Officers (PCSOs).
2003	TV airing by the BBC of *The Secret Policeman* uncovering racism at a regional police training centre.
	The Independent Police Complaints Commission (IPCC) is established to replace the Police Complaints Authority.
2005	Formation of the Serious Organised Crime Agency (SOCA), combining several existing agencies to counter level 3 crime and criminality.
2006	Following a 2005 HMIC report, an amalgamation of police forces is proposed but then rescinded in 2006.
2007	The National Police Improvement Agency (NPIA) is formed, incorporating Centrex (police training) and other national policing agencies such as the Police Information Technology Organisation (PITO). The Home Office is split into two parts: the 'justice' element is incorporated into a new Whitehall department—the Ministry of Justice—whilst the 'security' element (including the police) becomes part of a new Interior Ministry.
2008	Publication of the Flanagan Review of Policing, with recommendations on reducing unnecessary police bureaucracy and the implementation of Neighbourhood Policing.
2008–9	The 'Policing Pledge' was launched, setting out the public's right to a range of services from their local police force (eg that an emergency 999 call will be answered within ten seconds). It is subsequently withdrawn in 2010–11.
2010	A new government promises cuts in police bureaucracy, the return to the police of responsibility for charging suspects with 'low level' offences, and locally elected police and crime commissioners (PCCs).
2011	Against a backdrop of general austerity, the 2010 comprehensive spending review imposes significant budget reductions for police forces in England and Wales. By 2012 these cuts had led to tangible reductions in police staffing levels in all police forces in England and Wales. The first Winsor Review into police officer and staff remuneration and conditions is published, with detailed recommendations on police pay. The Neyroud Review into police training and leadership recommends the establishment of a chartered professional body for policing.
2012	The first Police and Crime Commissioners (PCCs) are elected to replace Police Authorities (which had been the main instrument of local police accountability since the 1960s). PCCs are responsible for 'hiring and firing' their chief constable and for setting out a five-year Police and Crime Plan. In London, the PCC role is assumed by the Mayor's Office.
	The second Winsor Review (into entry routes into policing, promotion, health and fitness requirements, and contribution-related pay) is published.
	The College of Policing is established as a professional body for policing, replacing the short-lived NPIA.
2013	The Home Office consults on measures intended to maintain and enhance the integrity of the police, including: a new code of ethics (covering all ranks); a single set of professional standards; a national register of chief officers' pay packages, gifts, hospitality, and second jobs; and a national register of officers who have been 'struck off'.
	Allegations that the Government chief whip Andrew Mitchell made particular derogatory remarks to police officers on duty in Downing Street leads to claims of collusion between some of the police officers involved (the repercussions were dubbed 'Plebgate' by some media).
	The Serious Crime Agency is formed, with a national remit to tackle serious and organized crime.

2014	An MPS police officer is jailed for a year for misconduct in public office after falsely claiming that he witnessed an altercation between the chief whip and other police officers in Downing Street in 2013.
	The Home Secretary sets out a package of reforms to the Police Federation, including plans to reduce its public funding and introducing an 'opt in' to the Federation rather than the existing 'opt out'.
	A new Police Code of Ethics is published by the College of Policing.
	The first 19 'direct entrants' to the police service (at superintendent level) are recruited (from a pool of almost 1,000 applicants).
2015	Further cuts (around £300 million) to the budgets of police forces begin to be implemented.
	The Independent Inquiry into Child Sexual Abuse begins. Its terms of reference include the role of the police (in England and Wales) in investigating child sexual abuse. The hearings begin for the judicial-led inquiry into undercover policing following revelations concerning undercover police officers using the identities of dead children, and fathering children with female suspects upon whom they were spying.
	The College of Policing commences consultation on the requirement for police officer applicants to have a degree.
	ACPO (Association of Chief Police Officers) is abolished and a new organization representing police chiefs is created—the National Police Chiefs' Council (NPCC).
2016	The new inquest into the 96 deaths at Hillsborough in 1989 finds that those who died in the disaster were unlawfully killed, and that a police commander was in breach of a duty of care and this amounted to gross negligence.
	The second election for police and crime commissioners in England and Wales takes place.
2017	The Metropolitan Police appoint the first ever female Commissioner— Cressida Dick. The three most senior positions in policing in England and Wales are all now headed by women—the 'Met' (MPS) (Cressida Dick), the National Crime Agency (Lynne Owens), and the chair of the National Police Chiefs' Council (Sara Thornton).
2018	The national police complaints structure is reorganized again, with the abolition of the IPCC and the creation, in its place, of the new Independent Office for Police Conduct (IOPC).
2018	Wiltshire Police respond to a chemical poisoning attack (Novichok) in the city of Salisbury. Later the same nerve agent kills a citizen.

> **TASK 7** What is the history of your local force? See if you can establish the dates of a few key events in the last 200 years or so.

2.3 **Police Organization and Ranks**

You may sometimes hear the police referred to as a 'disciplined organization'. This refers not only to the need for self-discipline and restraint but also to the fact that at least parts of the organization (those parts concerned with police officers) are organized into ranks in a hierarchical fashion, involving the issuing and receiving of orders. The diagram shows a typical structure for a police force with 6,000-plus staff. There are likely to be some variations between forces.

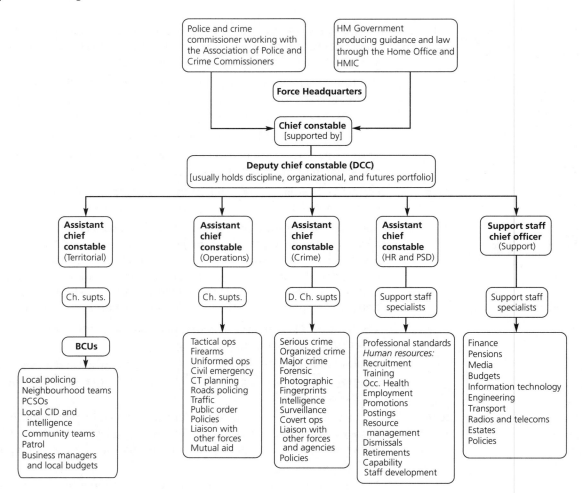

2.3.1 Police ranks

Apart from the MPS and one or two other forces (such as the City of London), the rank structure and the associated badges on the epaulettes of uniforms are as follows (in order of decreasing superiority):

- chief constable;
- deputy chief constable;
- assistant chief constable;
- chief superintendent;
- superintendent;
- chief inspector;
- inspector;
- sergeant; and
- constable.

In the non-uniformed equivalents 'detective' often precedes the rank, for example detective chief inspector. This does not signify a higher or more senior police rank—it simply defines the officer's *role*.

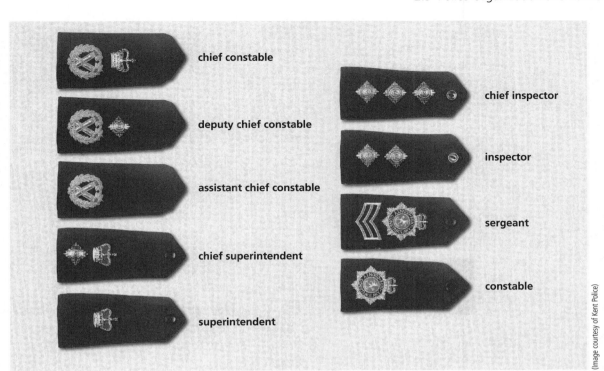

chief constable

deputy chief constable

assistant chief constable

chief superintendent

superintendent

chief inspector

inspector

sergeant

constable

(Image courtesy of Kent Police)

In the MPS the rank structure is different for the higher ranks; for example, there is a commissioner, a deputy commissioner, and a commander instead of a chief constable, deputy chief constable, and assistant chief constable. There are also two additional ranks (marked with asterisks) on the MPS rank list. The MPS ranks are as follows:

- commissioner;
- deputy commissioner;
- assistant commissioner;
- deputy assistant commissioner;*
- commander;*
- chief superintendent;
- superintendent;
- chief inspector;
- inspector;
- sergeant; and
- constable.

The rank structure for the City of London Police is similar to the MPS but without deputy assistant commissioners. Border Force also has a rank structure, and its officers also wear a uniform with epaulettes, but the names of the ranks differ slightly (ranging from 'administrative assistant' to 'director general').

The insignia of the ranks may vary from force to force. You should also take the time to familiarize yourself with the insignia of uniformed members of the extended police family (see 2.2.2), such as special constables and PCSOs.

TASK 8 Construct a set of memory cards to help you learn the police ranks and their associated insignia. On one side of the card put a photograph (or a simple drawing) of the associated insignia, and on the other the name of the rank, like so:

superintendent

(Image courtesy of Kent Police)

Now take cards at random from your collection. If the name of the rank turns up first then describe the insignia. Reverse the card and check your answer. If the insignia shows first, then you need to name the rank. As before, turn over to check your answer. Keep retesting (alone or in a group), until you have memorized all the ranks and insignia.

TASK 9 Find out the names and ranks of the individuals who lead your local police force. For example, who is responsible for training?

2.3.2 Police and crime commissioners and police and crime panels

Each police force now has a police and crime commissioner (PCC) who is responsible for holding chief officers to account, and managing the funding of the force from a precept (a type of local tax). PCCs are directly elected by the public every four years, and most are affiliated to a political party. The PCC is answerable to the local police and crime panel (PCP).

The police and crime panel members are appointed, with at least ten panel members being local authority councillors (elected). The other members are appointed, and they are usually individuals with specific skills or knowledge within their police locality. The panel has only limited powers, and functions mainly as a 'check and a balance' on the PCC and his/her actions. The PCC, however, needs only to 'have regard to' the panel's views. For example, the panel can 'review' a PCC's draft crime and police plan and make recommendations about it, but cannot reject it outright. Similarly, the panel can 'veto' the PCC's recommended precept the first time it is submitted, but cannot block a resubmitted precept.

There are three important differences between the PCC system and the previous local police authority in that:

- the PCC is a single person (as opposed to typically 17 individuals from different backgrounds, as was the case with the police authorities);
- the PCC is directly elected (rather than appointed, as was the case with local police authority members)—some have said this makes policing democratically accountable; and
- the panel and the PCC have a broader remit, as other local crime-related agencies can be held to account (compared with the much narrower scope of the local police authorities).

The introduction of PCCs has arguably made the political dimensions of police work more explicit and transparent, although there are still concerns that the new system could undermine police independence and lead to political interference.

The Policing and Crime Act 2017 places a duty on police, fire, and ambulance services to work together. PCCs can take on responsibility for fire and rescue services where a local case is made to support this.

2.3.2.1 Police and crime plans

Every PCC in England and Wales is required (by the Police Reform and Social Responsibility Act 2011) to produce a police and crime plan setting out a strategy for policing and crime reduction. The plan is devised in consultation with the chief constable and other community safety partners (eg health, local authorities, fire and rescue services). Other criminal justice agencies are also involved in setting priorities. Each plan covers a four-year period but can be revised annually.

The plans are likely to contain specific priorities, for example one priority in the PCP for the Thames Valley for April 2017–March 2021 is to 'target and manage harm and risk' (PCC Thames Valley, 2017). Undoubtedly, these police and crime plans have at least an indirect effect on the work of police service staff, and in many cases the effects will be relatively easy to see, in terms of changing priorities in operational policing.

2.3.2.2 Other force strategies, plans, and corporate statements

In addition to the formal, statutory plans they are required to hold, almost all police forces have their own statements of how they wish to operate and what they expect of their staff. These are sometimes referred to as the Mission, Vision, Values and Priorities (MVVP). Such pledges and aspirations will be very important to a force, and will guide actions and behaviours. MVVPs are often revised when a new chief constable takes charge of a force.

2.3.3 The Policing Protocol Order 2011

The Police Reform and Social Responsibility Act 2011 also sought to redefine and clarify the constitutional/governance positions of the key actors in policing in England and Wales—the Home Secretary, the chief constables, and the police authorities (now replaced by a PCC in each force). This was achieved in a document called the Policing Protocol Order 2011, and perhaps the most sensitive area the Protocol touches upon is police operational independence. The Order sought to reaffirm that operational control would remain solely in the hands of chief constables, and this has largely been achieved.

2.3.4 The Strategic Policing Requirement

The major police reforms around 2011 also included the creation of the Strategic Policing Requirement (SPR). This was a bold attempt by the Home Office to outline the commitments and priorities that would require a coordinated and joint response from the police service, and where a number of police forces could act in unison, to tackle a serious national threat or risk.

The first SPR was issued by the Home Secretary in 2012, and required both PCCs and chief constables to be ready to respond anywhere with trained, equipped, and deployable resources to address incidents of terrorism, serious public disorder, or civil disaster. In 2015 the SPR was reviewed and revised. Child sexual abuse was added to the list of national threats to which forces may have to respond in a collective and coordinated manner.

A number of regional collaborations have since been established between forces to deal with crime and policing issues that some found difficult to address alone, and the SPR remains one of the most important statements about how constabularies are expected to work together— in effect as a national police force.

2.4 Answers to Tasks

TASK 1 These vary from force to force, of course, but most forces have support staff engaged in some or all of the following:

- **Crime Scene Investigators**: an operational role which in the past was undertaken exclusively by police officers. CSIs are often now police staff with training and qualifications in forensic investigation (see 26.3).
- **Statement takers**: many of the statements taken from witnesses and victims of crime, particularly volume crime, are taken by support staff rather than police officers. Such statements do not have to be taken under caution (unlike statements by suspects), and therefore do not have to be taken by sworn officers. This can free up a great deal of time for police officers to pursue the investigation, and there can also be a marked increase in the professionalism

with which victims and witnesses are interviewed because the support staff are specialized in this task.

- **Volume Crime Scene Examiners (VCSEs)**: this role may not exist in all forces, but VCSEs are employed to undertake specialist forensic examination of extended areas of crime scenes. They are particularly used in vehicle crimes.
- **Detention officers ('jailers')**: these are support staff trained in custody and holding prisoners.
- **Human resources (HR)**: HR can include the whole range of specialists covering recruitment, promotions and postings, training, assessment and appraisal, retirement, secondment, dismissal, or capability issues. HR also deal with all matters relating to police support staff, including negotiations with staff associations.
- **Information technology**: these specialists are almost exclusively support staff, though some forces retain police officers where there is direct interface with police officers on patrol, for example in force communication centres or control rooms. The IT remit often includes telephony and wireless communications (including personal radios).
- **Lawyers**: legal advice (civil and/or criminal) to forces is now seen as an important resource, particularly for the chief officer team, and in dealing with complaints from the public, or litigation by employees (eg employment tribunals).
- **Estates**: police forces occupy many buildings and possess vast stocks of property which need specialist handling, particularly in negotiations with planning authorities.
- **Finance**: with annual police budgets often amounting to hundreds of millions of pounds, there is a need for specialist financial and budget management. In most forces, 80 per cent or more of the budget is spent on salaries or pensions, leaving a relatively small operational revenue budget to which is added the capital budget for aspects such as buildings and vehicles.
- **Administration**: from paper files to computerized records, from sickness certificates to awards ceremonies, from shotgun certificates to booking training courses, the administrative tasks in a police force are complex and numerous. The bureaucratic nature of policing inevitably creates a large administrative tail.

Force websites often provide descriptions of the roles undertaken by police staff. A good example is Essex Police and its website at <http://www.essex.police.uk/recruitment/police_staff_vacancies.aspx>.

TASK 2

1. In most cases you should be able to find this information through an internet search. Some forces publish this information only consequent to a freedom of information (FoI) request, but others provide the information as a matter of routine, for example the MPS lists the designated powers in its publicly available 'MPS Disclosure Log'.
2. All local PCSO training must follow the National Policing Curriculum. The College of Policing outlines a ten-week direct learning programme (CoP, 2015f) which is usually completed over a period of between six months and one year.

   PCSO initial training includes: corporate induction including professional standards, diversity, ethics and community awareness, inter-personal skills, first aid, self-defence ('empty hand skills'), communications and radio procedure, problem-solving approaches to crime and disorder, scene management, tasking and intelligence gathering, evidence gathering and witness skills, PCSO powers and procedures, citizens' powers and procedures, human rights, anti-social behaviour (including anti-social behaviour contracts and youth referral).

   After initial training there is a structured development process comparable to that of police probationer constables. PCSOs receive further training in areas such as RIPA, major incidents, mental health, and vulnerable persons.

TASK 3 It is highly likely that you included at least some of the following professions: medicine (eg a doctor); law (eg a barrister); church (eg a vicar); and teaching (eg a school teacher). You may also have thought of the military (eg a General), nursing, or accountancy. Did you include policing?

Professions are occupations that normally have the following qualities:

- They provide an income which is normally referred to as a salary. Interestingly, in many respects police officers are paid a wage rather than a salary—for example, below certain ranks they qualify for overtime payments calculated at an hourly rate.

- Entry to the profession is regulated and controlled. The title may be legally controlled, as in the case of the medical profession. Quite often a higher education degree in an approved area of study, or a licence, is required. Members of the profession are then licensed to practise, but there are procedures for removal of the licence (which in some professions is referred to as being struck off).
- There is a code of ethics and behaviour that members of the profession subscribe to.

TASK 4 Some possible answers are:

Requirements of a profession	The policing profession
Corpus of knowledge and theory	There is a growing body of underpinning knowledge and theory for many aspects of policing, for example in operational matters and application of the law. There was also doctrinal development, undertaken by the College of Policing (eg underpinning Authorised Professional Practice). However, there is as yet no universally accepted complete corpus of knowledge which is unique to policing
Controls on entry to the profession and maintenance of position	Entry is controlled through the national selection process. However, there are no formal academic requirements to enter the profession, beyond relatively simple tests of English and numeracy, although this might well change in the near future (see Chapter 6)
Autonomy, discretion, and self-regulation	Police officers enjoy relatively high levels of autonomy and discretion. The title of police constable is controlled so that only those that qualify are entitled to use it. Self-regulation of policing exists in a restricted form but is increasingly under challenge
Vocational calling	Policing is more than just a job and affects many aspects of an individual's life
Code of ethics	The Code of Ethics was created in 2014 (see 5.3)

TASK 5 You might have included:

- it is decentralized: public policing is still largely local, autonomous, and non-political (with shades of grey, for example the Miners' Strike in 1984/5);
- policing is consensual: it cannot operate without the active support of the public;
- approaches to policing are characterized by provisions in the Human Rights Act 1998 and the PACE Act 1984, which respect human dignity and ensure fairness of process;
- police officers, for the most part and on most occasions, are unarmed;
- police officers have independence in conducting investigations; they may still exercise initiative in whether to investigate or not;
- we have an adversarial criminal justice system, which requires the prosecution to disclose evidence;
- there is a presumption of innocence until proven guilty; the burden of proof lies with the prosecution.

TASK 6 You would have had to arbitrate between the right to freedom of expression (however extreme such views may be) and the need to sustain law and order. The legitimacy of your presence might not be consensual, but it may be both legitimized in law and necessary for preservation of the peace. The police would endeavour to control the marchers by determining the safest route for the parade to follow whilst also ensuring that direct clashes with the protesters were avoided. However, it is inevitable that someone, somewhere would have individual freedoms circumscribed (even if only the rights of Saturday shoppers to go about their lawful business), and thus the police are using moral as well as legal legitimacy in the policing of the march.

TASK 7 Some dedicated police history websites exist (eg the Friends of the Metropolitan Police Historical Collection at <https://www.metpolicehistory.co.uk/metpolicehistory.html>). Many forces also have museums (eg the Essex Police museum at Police HQ in Chelmsford) and some may also have a comprehensive and published written history (eg Ingleton, 2002).

TASK 8 Using memory cards (sometimes also called 'flashcards') in the era of modern information technology may seem somewhat old-fashioned but they are a tried-and-tested method that works.

TASK 9 Many police websites have a 'Who's Who', particularly for their Senior Management Team (SMT). Thames Valley Police SMT (for example) is described at <https://www.thamesvalley.police.uk/police-forces/thames-valley-police/areas/au/about-us/who-we-are/>.

3 | Crime and Criminality

3.1   Introduction

The subject matter covered in this chapter relates to the following parts of the National Policing Curriculum: 'Criminology and crime prevention', 'Evidence-based policing', and 'Research methods and skills'. If you are undertaking the PCDA or DHEP you will be expected to understand 'the causes, mitigations and prevention of crime and how this knowledge and understanding can influence and be applied to accountable decision-making in all operational policing environments'. Your lecturers, teachers, trainers, and tutors will no doubt refer you to more in-depth texts that cover theories on crime and criminality and their relevance to policing.

In this chapter we take a brief look at the nature of disorder, crime, and criminality in England and Wales. Every day, social media (particularly Twitter, Facebook, and WhatsApp), TV, radio, and newspapers contain reports of disorder and crime. Numerous articles and research papers are devoted to trying to understand why people commit crimes and why certain crimes are more prevalent than others. Some of the topics are very complex, drawing on psychological, philosophical, sociological, criminological, and political perspectives; in this chapter we have deliberately simplified these issues because this is not a handbook of crime or criminology. In a very real sense, you will be grappling with these ideas and questions throughout your police career, and most certainly during your time as a student or police trainee.

> **TASK 1**
>
> - What makes a particular crime sensational?
> - What sorts of crime are of little apparent interest?
> - Some sorts of crime have a serious impact on a community, while others cause little apparent concern. Why should this be the case?

Over the past 50 years, criminologists, social scientists, and ordinary members of the public have become increasingly interested in finding out more about policing and the police. Researchers and other academics have produced numerous publications concerning the organization, administration, governance, and general understanding of police work (eg Reiner, 2010; Newburn, 2011; Caless and Owens, 2016; Rowe, 2017; and O'Neill, 2018 to name but a few). Criminology has also provided the police with some important theories about the nature of crime and criminal behaviour, and these can help the police in various different ways. For example, the Neighbourhood Policing Model is supported by developments in criminological theories concerning crime prevention, the characteristics of victims, and the spatial movements of criminals, and also by evidence-based policing. Here, we provide a selection of important ways in which criminology informs contemporary policing, which may encourage you to delve deeper into the growing body of criminological research on many different policing matters. First we will consider some fundamental questions, such as the definition of crime, and possible causes of crime.

3.2   Definitions of Crime

What is crime? The answer may seem obvious until we begin to think through the details and test out our general ideas on some specific examples. Henry (2013, p 85) states 'Crime is not a self-evident and unitary concept. Its constitution is diverse, historically relative and continually contested.'

We might, for example, say that crime is what is forbidden, that crime is an activity which society would like to eradicate or prevent. On the other hand, technically, a particular activity is a crime because the law defines it as such. However, laws are created by people so, in the end, we are back to where we started: people (albeit only certain categories of people such as judges and MPs) determine which activities are criminal.

TASK 2

1. List three crimes that would appear to be universal.
2. List three offences that are considered criminal in the UK today but were not 100 years ago.
3. List three offences that are considered criminal in other parts of the world but not in the UK.

Without reference to existing concepts of crime and laws there is nothing about an activity in itself that marks it out as a crime. Consider, for example, how some forms of sexual activity between consenting adult men were officially viewed as crimes in the recent past but are no longer treated as such. There are in fact only a very few acts that have been consistently considered crimes throughout modern history (see Task 2). Other types and definitions of crime are mutable, and they change as society and our attitudes change. For example, collecting birds' eggs or hunting foxes with dogs are now seen by many as unacceptable, and the laws have followed suit. Currently there is debate around criminalizing so-called 'legal highs' and decriminalizing certain 'illegal' drugs such as cannabis; the law may be changed in response to these changing societal views on what should be 'legal' or not.

Hate crime is a particular case of subjectivity in law, as the opinion of a victim can determine whether a crime has occurred. This is because the hate element can be defined by the victim(s) or a witness, irrespective of whether hate was present and/or intended.

Once again, the close interrelationship between the law, society, and individuals is a key factor in understanding crime. The brief examples we have provided here demonstrate that crimes are social constructions, ie that no act or behaviour is in itself wrong, but rather that societies will identify different activities as crimes, according to the specific needs and views of a given society at a particular point in history.

3.2.1 Deviance and progress

It has been suggested that some types of deviant behaviour might have a role in promoting beneficial changes in society, and that we should therefore be wary of too hastily classifying deviant behaviour as criminal. John Stuart Mill (1806–73), an English philosopher, believed it was important for the development of a healthy society that individuals should have as much freedom as possible, primarily (he suggested) because individuals who deviate from the norm can help society to advance. There are numerous examples throughout history of individuals (some of whom we now celebrate as heroes) who were regarded as a threat to society at an earlier time. Consider, for example, the suppression of scientific thinkers such as Galileo, who were considered to be heretics, or (more recently) civil rights protesters such as Martin Luther King in the USA. In the UK today there are many examples of people and campaign groups willing to break the law, for example animal rights activists, Fathers 4 Justice, anti-abortionists, and environmentalists such as Extinction Rebellion (who espouse 'nonviolent civil disobedience'). These groups each believe they are promoting values or demanding changes that will become widely accepted in the future, in the same way that those fighting at previous times in history for equal rights for women or the abolition of the slave trade eventually came to be recognized as heroic figures. However, there is no possible way to foresee which views that are currently deviations from the norm might become the accepted view in the future. It is impossible to know for certain whether an individual who is taking action to promote a new or different view is innovative, or merely criminal.

Mill suggested that people should be permitted to make mistakes and act immorally, provided these acts do not harm others. This is Mill's famous 'harm to others' principle. It is largely from this perspective that we have established a separation between the law and morality; it is argued that the law pertains to public matters and morality to private individual concerns. This view was supported in 1957 in the Wolfenden Report into homosexuality and prostitution, in which it was argued that private acts between consenting adults should not be the concern of law enforcement (Wolfenden Report, 1957). Note, however, that some campaigners for LGBTQ rights have criticized this perspective as they feel it placed too much emphasis on the word 'private', which suggests that public expressions of some forms of sexuality should be regulated and controlled.

However, critics have challenged the view that law and morality can be so neatly separated. They argue that there is a significant grey area which we might characterize as social morality, and that it is simply not possible to insulate our private activities completely as there will always be 'leakage'. This would cause our actions to have consequences that we could not have predicted. This challenges Mill's 'harm to others' principle because it suggests that others can be unintentionally or unknowingly harmed by our actions. Perhaps a good example of this is smoking. For many years campaigns have encouraged smokers to stop for their own sake, but little was done to prohibit smoking in a public place as the dangers of passive smoking were not recognized. Smoking is now, however, increasingly regulated on the grounds of doing 'harm to others' by impacting on the health and safety of people in the vicinity (see 14.2.1.7).

3.3 The Causes of Crime

When examining the causes of crime, an important starting point is to acknowledge some fundamental differences in how we might understand the various reasons for criminal acts, and how these differences in turn can inform police work. Blackburn (1995) made a distinction between crimes and criminality. He stated that people commit crimes as a rational response to the environment in which they find themselves, and that criminality is a characteristic of an individual that emphasizes his/her propensity to commit crimes. This introduces us to an area of constant discussion and argument in criminological circles; namely the nature–nurture debate. Are criminals born as such, or do people become criminals due to the society they live in?

3.3.1 Criminal by nature?

It is difficult to understand the actions of a violent serial murderer as the consequence of injustices in society. No matter how bad society is, it is hard to view such brutality as a reasonable response. The concept of criminality developed from what is referred to as the positivist school of criminology associated with Cesare Lombroso's *L'Uomo Delinquente* (*The Criminal Man*), published in 1876. Positivists believe that social life can be studied objectively and scientifically by employing methods comparable to those used in the natural sciences (Tierney, 2009). They suggest criminals are pathological and distinct from non-criminal individuals, and as such criminality is determined by factors beyond the immediate control of an individual and is not a product of his/her free will (Jones and Newburn, 1998, pp 101–2).

There are three main types of positivist theories:

- 'biological positivism' which suggests that some forms of criminality are due to a biological abnormality in the individual, such as a chemical imbalance in the brain, or unusual levels of certain hormones;
- 'psychological positivism' which suggests that some forms of criminality are linked to a number of interrelated personality traits such as 'impulsivity'; and
- 'sociological positivism' which suggests that the social environment (such as the presence of anti-social subcultures) can increase some forms of crime.

3.3.2 Criminal through nurture?

Some crimes seem to be more easily explained as a product of the social situation in which they occur. Rational Choice Theory (Cornish and Clarke, 1986) argues that criminals make a rational decision before committing a crime, have thought through (at some level at least) their reasons for committing a criminal act, and rationalized the need to commit the act. For example, a single mother with no money who steals nappies for her baby is certainly committing a crime, but we can sympathize with some aspects of her motivation, and we might also think that she should not have been placed in such a difficult position in the first place. However, we also know that not all mothers in the same situation would resort to shoplifting, and would find another solution to the problem. Irrespective of which moral position is adopted, from a policing perspective this particular crime can be understood more readily as a social response rather than as an individual failing. This view is associated with what is referred to as classical criminology, which emerged in the late eighteenth century and informed the thinking of law reformers at the time (eg Bentham, Howard, Beccaria). This view of crime suggests that anyone could become a criminal given the right circumstances, and that punishment is required to act as a deterrent to crime.

3.3.3   Nature and nurture

The relative effects of nature (how we are 'pre-wired') and nurture (the effect of our environment, such as our upbringing) have been debated for centuries, but more recent research is beginning to clarify the relative contribution of each to our behaviour.

Nature refers to what we are born with or, in recent terms, our genetic make-up, and nurture relates to the environmental contexts in which we develop. Nurture includes everything from our schooling, how our parents raised us, our local community, and every arbitrary experience that has good, bad, or indifferent outcomes.

The debates have frequently been polemical and exclusionary; that is, those favouring nature explanations would dismiss nurture as an influence and those supporting nurture explanations would exclude completely the view that nature has any part to play. However, the nature/nurture dichotomy can often be over-simplified and therefore misleading. Increasingly today we recognize that both nature and nurture form part of the explanation and, indeed, that it is not always easy to distinguish one from the other, particularly as modern biology continues to uncover examples of genetic predispositions being either masked or revealed by various environmental factors.

3.3.4   Criminal careers and desistance

When we talk of a 'criminal career' (a concept that originated in the 1970s) we are usually referring to delinquent and criminal acts committed by an individual as he/she gets older and progresses from childhood through adolescence and into adulthood (a 'longitudinal' pattern of offending). The 'age-crime' curve for many offenders shows that the incidence of criminal behaviour, in terms of recorded crime at least, increases during adolescence but then decreases abruptly after the onset of adulthood. Many so-called 'criminals' in fact commit only one relatively serious offence (as a young person), and then desist from offending.

The academic study of criminal careers focuses on four key measures (Blumstein *et al*, 1986) as follows:

- the *participation rate* (or prevalence) is the proportion of the population that is actively committing offences;
- *frequency* (or incidence) is the rate of offending amongst the active 'offending population';
- *seriousness* refers to how serious the crimes are; and
- *career length* is how long each individual continues to offend.

We can apply these measures to 'career criminals' as an illustration. Career criminals form a small proportion of all offenders and frequently commit offences, the offences they commit are relatively serious, and their offending persists over time.

These measures can provide insight into the changes in patterns of criminal behaviour over the life course of an individual (Greenburg, 2019), and raise the prospect of identifying individuals who are on track to becoming career criminals, ie an individual's criminal activities are becoming more persistent, more frequent, and/or more serious over an increasingly longer timeframe. This may provide opportunities for intervention to help prevent future offending. It could also help with detecting crimes (see 2.2.4 on intelligence-led policing), and identifying high volume recidivist offenders.

3.3.4.1   **Desisting from crime**

Most people reduce or stop their offending after an initial period of committing frequent crimes (and sometimes never commit any further offences). The reasons for this desistance are not clear, and have only recently been subjected to rigorous academic enquiry; it is a developing area of study. It appears perhaps unsurprisingly that desistance is linked in part to the person's motivation and thinking, and that external threats (eg of punishment) will only have a limited effect. Personal relationships and the amount of social capital a person can access seem to be far more significant factors.

3.3.5   **Criminological theory and policing**

Criminology draws upon a wide range of disciplines, for example sociology, psychology, and history. Broadly, criminological theory can be conceptualized as falling under one of three main headings or 'schools':

- classical/neo-classical theory (rational choice theory, routine activity theory);
- positivist theory (biosocial and psychological theories, the Chicago school, social learning/ differential association theory); and
- sociological theory (strain/anomie theory, social control theory, labelling).

Dividing criminological theory into 'schools' can be somewhat misleading, as they are far from being mutually exclusive. For example, labelling theory is linked to sociological theory, but applying labelling theory at the level of the individual is also likely to invoke a psychological mechanism as part of the explanation.

The table provides a summary of the main theories, and includes examples to illustrate some of the ways in which each theory could apply within policing.

School	Example of theory	Brief description of theory	Possible application within policing
Classical or neo-classical	Rational Choice	Crime is a rational act that needs no special explanation; it results from a 'cost-benefits' analysis	Offering crime prevention advice after online fraud
	Routine Activity	Crime occurs when motivated offenders and attractive targets intersect in time and space, with no or ineffective capable guardianship	Policing of crime hotspots
	Control/General Theory of Crime	Crime is caused by a lack of effective control (external, or within the individual)	Conducting 'visible' police patrol
Sociological	Social Disorganization	The breakdown of informal social controls allows the progressive dominance of criminal cultures (see also 'Broken Windows' theory)	Police provide support for members of the public, and workers such as bus drivers and park keepers
	Social Learning/ Differential Association/ Subcultures	Crime is a form of behaviour that is learned through association with criminals or people who tolerate crime	Police referring suspected 'gang members' to other agencies
Positivist	Strain (anomie)	Some individuals lack legitimate opportunities to achieve their goals (for example wealth, status, authority) and therefore use illegal means instead	Use of police discretion in case of suspected shoplifting by a child
	Labelling	Some individuals are 'labelled' as criminal or anti-social, and they unwittingly adopt the label (a form of self-fulfilling prophecy)	Adopting a professional approach when conducting 'stop and search'

3.4   **Measuring Crime**

There are various means of measuring crime rates, for example police and criminal justice statistical records, large-scale surveys (mostly government-sponsored), and small-scale academic studies. The government and criminal justice agencies use recorded crime figures from the police and the Crime Survey for England & Wales (CSEW) and the Northern Ireland Crime Survey (NICS) as their key sources of information. In these crime surveys thousands of households are randomly selected, and interviews are conducted with the aim of measuring both recorded and unrecorded crime (see 3.4.1).

Various factors will tend to distort the accuracy of the measured levels of crime at any given time. These factors include the under-reporting of crime by the public, the under-recording of crime by the police, political interest, and intellectual bias. The distortion can also lead to difficulties in making meaningful comparisons between current crime levels and those in the past. Under-reporting and under-recording are particularly problematic for the police, and have received considerable attention, for example HMIC stated (2014b, p 49) that 'Victims of crime are being let down. The police are failing to record a large proportion of the crimes reported to them'. Research practices can also contribute to a distorted picture of the true extent of crime due to weaknesses in any research design that involves collecting data. For example, there may be distortions and inaccuracies due to small sample sizes, uneven access to research participants, ethical barriers, organizational limitations, and funding restrictions. The CSEW and its predecessor, the British Crime Survey, are considered by many to be the most comprehensive crime surveys in the world, but even here there are limitations. For example, it was only in January 2009 that the BCS began including 10 to 15-year-olds in the survey and recording their experiences of crime, and it was not until 2016 that the CSEW first included questions to assess the extent of fraud and computer misuse offences. It should also be noted that the wording of the questions in the survey has changed over the years, and because of this year-on-year comparisons may create a misleading picture. In addition, the wording of the questions has been shown to influence respondents' answers about 'fear of crime' (Farrall and Gadd, 2004). Recognizing the many limitations of existing measures, researchers constantly review their methods to ensure that the crime surveys are robust and as useful as possible. Establishing a more accurate picture of the extent of crime and ensuring that it is recorded properly are important aspects of modern policing.

3.4.1   Reported incidents and recorded crime

An important distinction needs to be made between *reported* crime-related incidents (eg reports made by a member of the public to the police) and *recorded* crime. Let us consider a particular incident where the police are contacted—it may or may not involve a crime. Imagine that I have witnessed a heated argument in the street, perhaps with some pushing, shoving, and screaming. I phone the police and report it; the police will take note of the contents of my call (it will be registered, or 'logged' in police jargon—see 24.4.1 for further discussion of police response to incoming calls). This registration of the incident is what most commentators mean when they refer to reported crime.

The police then have to decide whether the incident should be recorded as an actual crime (a so-called 'notifiable offence'). They will first need to decide whether the circumstances as reported by the caller amount to an offence, based on their knowledge and the counting rules from the National Crime Recording Standard (NCRS) and Home Office Counting Rules (HOCR) (see 3.4.1.1). The police will also consider whether there is any credible evidence to the contrary. If on 'the balance of probability' the circumstances described in the victim's report amount to an offence as defined by the law, then the incident should be recorded as a crime (Home Office, 2014c and 2016b).

As our incident illustrates, the decision is far from simple. In response to my call the police are required to make all reasonable enquiries to identify specific victims, and secure any supporting evidence. Although pushing and shoving could technically be an offence of assault or battery (see 15.2) or a public order offence (see 14.4), this would depend on the circumstances, and these would probably not be clear from my account over the phone. More importantly, a victim is unlikely to be identified, and the basic recording rule of 'no victim, no crime' would be applied (although there are exceptions to this rule). Hence it is highly unlikely that the pushing and shoving I saw would be recorded by the police as a crime.

It has been acknowledged that there is a 'degree of subjective interpretation in making decisions about how to record crimes' (HMIC, 2013a, p 3), and that in at least one police force there was serious under-recording of crime which led to victims not receiving the service they required. This particular situation has now improved, but there are still major issues regarding how the police deal with incidents reported by the public. For example, an HMIC report (2014b, p 63) found that when senior statisticians from the Home Office audited the police in England and Wales, the results showed that only 81 per cent of the total crimes reported to the police were in fact recorded correctly, meaning that approximately 800,000 crimes per year, despite being reported to police, were not being recorded as such.

The diagram shows some of the key decisions that are made after an incident is reported to the police.

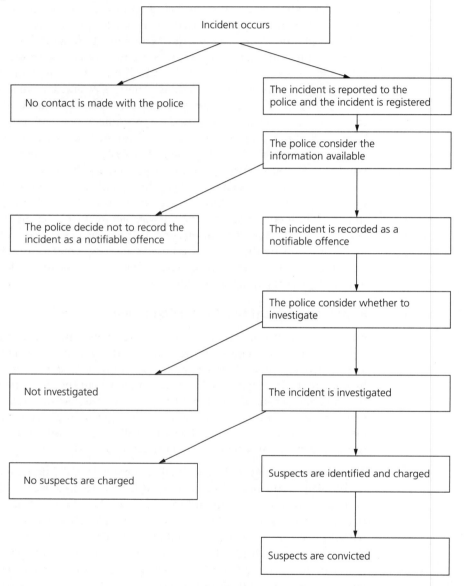

In terms of statistics, the Home Office (2019b), when commenting on how the police dealt with crimes recorded in the year ended March 2019, stated that police forces closed almost half (44 per cent) of offences with no suspect identified. Additionally, the proportion of crimes which resulted in a charge or summons fell from 9 per cent to 8 per cent and the numbers of offences which resulted in evidential difficulties rose from 29 per cent to 32 per cent compared with the previous year. Some of these changes are likely to be partly due to improved crime recording processes by the police. However, it has been estimated that recorded crime represents only a small proportion of all crime committed and so the Home Office data may be misleading. Data from 2002 (see the pie chart) suggested that for all crimes occurring, 53 per cent were not reported to the police at all. Of the total for all crimes, 47 per cent were reported, 27 per cent were reported and then recorded, 5 per cent were investigated to a conclusion, but only 2 per cent of the original total resulted in a conviction (Wright, 2002).

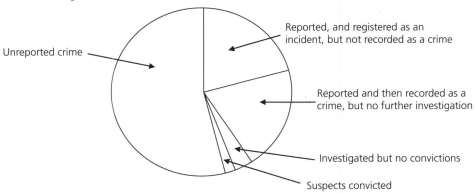

3.4.1.1   National Crime Recording Standard and Home Office Counting Rules

The National Crime Recording Standard (NCRS) considers victims' reports to the police and applies legal definitions of crime to identify which crimes have been committed. It is used to ensure crimes are recorded in accordance with the law. The Home Office Counting Rules for Recorded Crime (HOCR) help to ensure that crimes are recorded consistently and accurately. It could be said that the HOCR are 'what must be done', the NCRS are 'why it must be done' (HMIC, 2014a). The College of Policing 'Code of Ethics' emphasizes that complying with the National Crime Recording Standard is central to the Home Office Counting Rules for Recorded Crime.

Crime recording and counting methods were changed by the Home Office in 2013 and 2014, replacing the old system under which crimes were classed as either 'detected', 'undetected', or 'no crime'. There are now 21 possible outcomes for each recorded crime; for example, charge/summons, taken into consideration (TIC), community resolution, prosecution not in the public interest, and investigation complete—no suspect identified (for a full list see Heap, 2017, p 13).

The processes of reporting and recording crime are complex, and full details are provided by the Home Office (2019f). The Home Office (2014f) stated that the revised system would provide police forces in England and Wales with the best crime recording system in the world.

3.4.2   The perception of crime

There is a general acceptance that the fear of crime and disorder has increased in recent years. For example the CSEW ending March 2019 found that 81 per cent of adults believed that crime had risen nationally (ONS, 2019a). However, during this period most forms of recorded crime actually decreased, so it seems the year-on-year trends about perceptions in the survey might not be completely reliable (see 3.4 and Farrall and Gadd, 2004).

The survey also suggests that some sectors of the community are more likely to believe that crime has risen significantly, and to worry more about crime. For example, the CSEW ending March 2019 (ONS, 2019a) suggested that:

- women were more likely than men to believe that crime had risen in recent years, both nationally and locally;
- people aged 75 and over were most likely to believe that crime had risen nationally in recent years, while people in the 35–44 and the 45–54 age groups were more likely to believe that crime was increasing locally;
- individuals living in the most deprived areas perceived a larger rise in local and national crime in recent years (compared with people living in less deprived areas).

However, it is important to note that according to official statistics, those who feel most worried about crime or who perceive crime to be increasing are not necessarily the most likely to become victims of crime. Having said this, being fearful of crime is itself a form of harm to an individual, and the lifestyle implications can be profound. Therefore an elderly person's statistically 'irrational' fears about crime still need to be taken into account. Another factor to consider is that even if the risk of an incident (such as a physical attack) may be low, the negative consequences of such an incident could be very high in terms of recovery from an injury.

A key reason why many people overestimate the extent of crime and disorder is that people tend to base their judgements on the more obvious and visible local crimes or anti-social behaviour. Innes (2014) refers to these as 'signal crimes' or 'signal disorders', and believes they are perceived by residents as warning signals about the level of insecurity in their neighbourhood. Possible examples of signal crimes and disorder, particularly when a number of these examples coincide in a local community, include:

- public drinking, swearing, and rowdy and uncivil behaviour by groups of individuals;
- litter, graffiti, and other forms of damage and vandalism;
- evidence of drug taking and dealing, and prostitution;
- speeding;
- rubbish dumped in the street or outside houses; and
- abandoned or burnt-out vehicles.

As Innes (2005, p 192) notes:

> major crimes such as homicides can and do function as signals, but (for most people, most of the time) the signals that they attend to and that assume particular salience for them are what have tended to be treated by the criminal justice agencies as less serious.

Once spotted, these signals can give rise to a heightened sense of awareness, and individuals are more likely to notice other similar examples—a self-reinforcing and potentially harmful feedback loop.

3.5 Modelling Crime and Criminality

In 3.3 we provided an overview of some of the theories that attempt to explain crime and criminality. We now move on from these general theories (often concerned with human nature and society) to more detailed explanatory models and also suggest some possible responses for the police and others.

3.5.1 Opportunities for crime

There are many theories regarding how and why crimes are committed; here we will only briefly explore some of the key ideas. A good account of criminological theories can be found in Roger Hopkins Burke's *An Introduction to Criminological Theory*, 5th edn (2019).

Pease (2002) noted that crime has been understood in terms of structure, human psyche, and circumstance. By 'structure' he meant poverty and inequality, and other major social issues that are seen to be linked to crime. The 'human psyche' aspect concerns the attributes of the criminal as a person, in other words the reasons why he/she has a propensity to commit offences. However, Pease regarded 'circumstance' as the key factor for causing crime. In other words, it is the opportunity that is presented to the potential criminal that is the primary reason the crime will take place. For example, an unlocked parked car with the keys in the ignition presents an opportunity to a potential joy-rider or thief.

Related to this is rational-choice theory (Cornish and Clarke, 1986, see 3.3.2). This theory assumes that criminals who decide to commit offences employ the same kind of thought processes as non-criminals making everyday, non-criminal decisions:

> It is not the case (except for a tiny handful of pathological personalities) that criminals are so unlike the rest of us as to be indifferent to the costs and benefits of the opportunities open to them. (Wilson, 1996, p 312)

This suggests that crimes occur if they are easy to commit, and the results are sufficiently rewarding.

Routine-activity theory (Felson, 2002) is also predicated upon an understanding of the relationship between an individual's everyday experiences and his/her criminal behaviour. It defines criminal opportunities in terms of three interrelated and necessary components: a motivated offender; a suitable target; and the absence of a guardian. The idea is that criminal opportunities arise when these three components coincide. For example, in a certain situation the number of offences might increase if there are few guardians and plenty of suitable targets, even if there is no increase in the number of motivated offenders. Schools are a prime example of this kind of scenario: there are significant numbers of largely unsupervised vulnerable children with mobile phones, and there are other largely unsupervised children who are keen to acquire them.

3.5.2   The 'hot' model

Some of the constituent elements of crime can be considered as being 'hot': that is, both frequently occurring and worthy of attention. The following owes much to Clarke (1999), although some terms such as 'hot offender' are of our own devising. Therefore this section will discuss 'hot spots', 'hot offenders', and 'hot products'. It should be noted that the 'hot' model of crime might need to be adapted (or even abandoned) for cybercrime because it is difficult to determine the actual location for internet crimes, however, the notion of 'hot products' and repeat victimization is still relevant in cybercrime.

'Hot spots' are places that are particularly prone to crime, such as railway stations, shopping malls, town centres, particular shops and houses, post offices, or flats. This may be related to the easy pickings for people who are intent on theft, shoplifting, or mugging for example. In addition, it may also be related to opportunity, for example in the vicinity of cash machines or dog race courses, where people are more likely to be carrying large quantities of cash or other items of potential value (such as credit and debit cards). The hot spots create an uneven distribution of crime: in a city there will be some particular and relatively small geographical areas that always or nearly always have a high crime rate (of all types), while other areas will be virtually crime free. Until some preventative action is taken, these hot spots will persist, and even if action is taken they may still recur (see 3.6.2). However, Eck *et al* (2017, p 1) argue that the phenomenon of crime 'hot spots' is 'naturally occurring' and argue that 'the concentration of crime at places is unexceptional and should be treated as one manifestation of a general tendency of things to be concentrated'.

'Hot offenders' are defined as the relatively small number of people who are responsible for the majority of crime. A review by Marinez *et al* (2017, p 1) found that 'crime is highly concentrated in the population and across different types of offenders'. Furthermore, research, for example by Everson and Pease (2001), on repeat victimization (see 'hot victims' discussed later) suggests that prolific offenders may be responsible for the bulk of these repeated crimes against the same person or target. However, opinion and research continue to differ over just how small a minority of criminals is responsible for just how large a majority of crimes (see also 2.2.4.1).

'Hot products' are the items we know are more attractive to burglars or street robbers, and there is a logic to what they choose to steal. Clarke (1999) suggests a mnemonic for rating hot products: CRAVED.

C	Concealable
R	Removable
A	Available
V	Valuable
E	Enjoyable
D	Disposable

The CRAVED model can be used as a means of judging just how attractive an object will be for a thief. A score can be assigned for each factor, and a high total CRAVED score would indicate that the object is more likely to be stolen. While it is not as simple as this, the scoring system provides a relatively easy way of assessing what would be a 'hot product'.

In the original work by Clarke (1999), disposability was considered to be one of the most important factors. Thieves prefer items which they can get rid of quickly and without fuss to a trusted 'fence', although they will probably receive only a tenth or a fifth of the retail value of the item (handling stolen goods is covered in 16.5). The average, small-time, drug-abusing, volume criminal will go for small items of value which are easily transportable and not easily traced. This is why cash (pre-eminently) and jewellery are popular targets for thieves. Cash, of course, is easily disposed of and generally untraceable, and most rings and watches are easily converted into money. Smartphones and laptops are also popular targets. Interestingly, bicycles were the most commonly stolen home possession in 2015, according to insurance claim information.

TASK 3 Estimate how CRAVED the following articles might be:

- an iPad;
- an iPhone X or equivalent smartphone;
- a laptop;
- £642.89 in coins;
- a desktop computer with separate screen and keyboard;
- a CRT (non-flat-screen) television;
- a 2012 mobile phone;
- £350 in £50 notes;
- a manuscript copy of The Lindisfarne Gospels;
- 12 Japanese ivory netsuke dating from the late sixteenth century;
- a Rolex watch, engraved and dated; and
- an unframed oil painting by Rubens, measuring 23 × 19 cm.

Clearly, there are many possible interactions between hot spots, hot offenders, and hot products. Hot offenders are more likely to want hot products, and to target hot spots because, as we noted earlier, there are relatively easy opportunities for crime and relatively little chance of being caught. And of course the same offenders may return to burgle the same house again. It is hard to disentangle cause and effect, but the uneven distribution of crime cannot be ignored.

The concept of repeat victims, hotspots, and offenders forms part of the Problem-Orientated Policing (POP) approach (see 8.3.2.2). This was ultimately linked to Intelligence-led policing (see 2.2.4.1) and the National Intelligence Model (see 23.6), a core element of Neighbourhood Policing Strategy in England and Wales (see Chapter 8).

3.5.3 Repeat victimization

Research into repeat victimization was initiated in the 1970s. The Kirkholt Burglary Prevention Project which successfully targeted repeat burglaries for prevention (Seymore, 2001) was a major influence on the idea of repeat victimization from the late 1980s. This spurred other prevention efforts and a broader range of research into the extent and nature of repeat victimization, including methodological studies. The Home Office in particular supported a programme of research and development into repeat victimization with publications throughout the 1980s and 1990s.

It is important to note that 'victimization' in the academic literature (and to a lesser extent in policing circles) applies to more than people: it can include crime 'against' households, business premises and vehicles. While perhaps it would be better to use the word 'target' rather than 'victim', this is not common, and this despite the fact that the harm that can be done by labelling someone as a 'victim' has been critiqued in the wider social science literature.

One consequence of the increased interest in this phenomenon is the fact that it is now normal for most studies to incorporate a measure of repeat victimization. The previous practice of focusing on the number of crimes as 'the crime rate' was thought to be frequently misleading (Grove and Farrell, 2011).

The extent of repeat victimization in England and Wales is difficult to estimate for a number of reasons, including police recording systems. One study in 1998 found that approximately two per cent of the population experienced 44 per cent of property crime, and that 1 per cent of the population 'accounted for' 59 per cent of all personal crime (Pease, 1998).

An important distinction is between 'pure repeat' victims and 'near repeat' victims. Pure repeats are when the same person or household is victimized again (see 3.5.3.1), and 'near repeat victimization' is when the crime is repeated nearby, but with a different victim (see 3.5.3.2). This distinction is important as the two types of victimization are thought to occur for somewhat different reasons (see Chainey, 2012).

In terms of cybercrime, repeat victimization is less well understood; however, a similar phenomenon to non-virtual victimization appears to be emerging: a minority of victims (people, websites) account for the majority of the crimes (such as online fraud, DDos attacks).

3.5.3.1   Pure repeat victimization

Pure repeats are when the same 'target', for example the same person or household, is repeatedly victimized (eg repeated burglary at the same address). The repeat generally takes place quite soon after the original incident. Intuitively, it could be expected that old age, frailty, and naivety would make a person more vulnerable to 'pure repeat' victimization than the average person. There is, however, not much empirical evidence to support this, other than for distraction burglary (see the start of 16.4). The reasons for pure repeat victimization are not clearly understood, although research does suggest a number of possible factors (including combinations of factors). For example, the same household may be repeatedly burgled (sometimes by the same offender) and the reasons for this could be that:

- there is something inherently 'risky' about the location of the house or flat itself (it is close, but not too close, to the offender's 'anchor point'—see Routine Activities Theory);
- the perpetrator will be familiar with the layout of the dwelling;
- the perpetrator will be aware that stolen items may have been replaced with new items which can be taken on a subsequent burglary.

For interpersonal crimes (such as assault) there may be aspects of the victims' lifestyle that lead to an increased risk of pure repeat victimization, for example the kind of activities they undertake and their vulnerability in certain circumstances (see Chapter 4). A particularly important example of this kind of repeat victimization is domestic violence (see 13.6).

If you are undertaking initial police training (via the PCDA or DHEP) then you will probably receive inputs on the kind of crime prevention advice to provide for 'pure repeat' victims. Many police forces will also have repeat victimization policies and procedures which will outline 'victim management' and reduction measures available to both the force and individual officers. These are often available online.

3.5.3.2   Near repeat victimization

Near repeats are, for example, when one household in a street has been burgled, and then nearby households are burgled soon after. The phenomenon is probably one of the causes of geographically located crime hotspots (see 3.5.2). As Ken Pease claims, 'primarily high crime areas are high because of numbers of repeat victimisation' (Pease, 2018). The modelling of near repeat victimization is often built into the algorithms for so-called 'predictive policing', but the success of this approach has been queried. For example, Chainey *et al* conducted research on data from New Zealand, and pointed out that the 'use of repeats and near repeats as a prediction and prevention framework is unlikely to yield consistent positive results'(Chainey *et al* 2018, p 619).

> **TASK 4** Does your local police force use any 'predictive policing' algorithms? If so, how are they used to assist operational policing? How effective are they?

> **TASK 5** Consider the following quotation:
>
> > Becoming criminal can be explained in much the same way we explain becoming a midwife or buying a car. (Wilson, 1996, p 307)
>
> What practical policing implications could be derived from this, assuming that the argument being made is valid?

3.5.4 Social learning theory and differential association

One of the major criminological theories is 'social learning theory' (summarized in 3.3.6). It was developed from Edwin Sutherland's differential association theory, and subsequently revised by others. According to social learning theory, crime is a learned behaviour and in this sense is essentially no different from other more socially acceptable examples of learned behaviours such as waiting in queues and taking turns. Individuals, particularly young people, learn through communicating and participating in groups, and for young children this is mainly the family. The child assimilates a general sense of what is 'normal' from what he/she experiences and sees in day-to-day events. From adolescence onwards, other social groups become more influential, including peer groups. However, it is important to note that social learning theory is not the same as 'peer group pressure' but is instead a more subtle form of social learning. Social learning theory would predict that if a person associates mainly with groups that consider crime as normal and acceptable behaviour, and less frequently with those that consider criminal acts as unacceptable, the person is more likely to adopt the stance of the former than the latter. Hence 'differential association' underpins the rationale for the theory.

Social learning theory would therefore seem to provide a persuasive explanation for at least some forms of crime. However, there are some general limitations for such theories, for example differential association offers no explanation for why people in superficially similar circumstances behave so differently; why do some choose to 'learn' deviant behaviour whilst others do not (Newburn, 2007, p 152)? We would suggest that part of the explanation might be that a person is not merely a passive recipient of his/her environment; most people play an active role in creating and shaping their immediate environment, for instance when choosing friends and leisure activities.

3.5.5 Psychological perspectives on crime

Whereas the criminological theory discussed earlier is normally concerned with crime as a phenomenon, psychological perspectives are often based on the behaviour and motivation of the individual. Put simplistically, psychology is more concerned with 'criminals' than 'crimes'. General psychological perspectives on crime usually arise from four main traditions: psychodynamic theories, behaviourist theories, cognitive theories, and personality theories. Most of these traditions arose in the early to mid-twentieth century. It is clear that psychological theory needs to be applied in specific ways to specific contexts within crime and policing if it is to provide meaningful insights. We briefly describe the four main traditions here, and consider how they might apply to law enforcement and policing.

Psychodynamic theories are often associated with their founder, Sigmund Freud (1859–1939). Key features of this theory are that each person has a subconscious psyche that includes the id, ego, and superego. The theory would suggest that criminal behaviour is due to inadequate development of the superego. Freud himself had little to say about crime but one of his followers, John Bowlby (1907–90), developed an influential 'maternal deprivation' thesis, which was firmly rooted in the psychodynamic tradition. Psychodynamic theories could be used to try to understand the motivation of 'ego' criminals, for example in causing criminal damage such as obscene graffiti.

Behaviourist theories originated with the well-known classical conditioning experiments on dogs carried out by Ivan Pavlov (1848–1939). The key features include the concepts of stimulus and response, reinforcement (negative and positive), and punishment, and these can result in classical conditioning or operant conditioning. Such ideas were then extensively developed by John Watson (1878–1958) and B F Skinner (1904–90). Behaviourist theories might help us to understand some aspects of a stalker's behaviour; he/she might derive satisfaction observing the fear of a victim, and the behaviour could become a conditioned response.

Cognitive social psychology theories emphasize that humans are sentient beings with perception, memory, and reasoning. The theories are usually associated with Ulric Neisser (1928–2012) particularly in the USA. Other proponents include Lawrence Kohlberg (1927–87), whose notion of 'moral reasoning' has been particularly influential in the psychology of crime, and Albert Bandura (1929–), who has made many contributions in this field. Cognitive social psychology could be used to try to understand online child abuse groomers; they may repeat to themselves a consistent 'cognitive script', which is a form of memory structure, to rationalize and direct their behaviour.

Personality theories emphasize that individuals differ in terms of personality, and that each person has different levels of extraversion, neuroticism, and psychoticism. Eysenk (1916–90) suggested that high extraversion (a need for external stimulation) was associated with some forms of criminality, and more recently we might also consider that the desire of some offenders to promote their criminal activity via YouTube is another example of extraversion. Criminal psychology has long considered whether those who commit crime are in some way 'different' from those who do not; are there significant personality differences between the two groups? Obviously there can never be an unambiguous 'yes' or 'no' answer to such a question. For example, there is often no clear binary distinction *per se* between those that do and those that do not commit crime, given that crime itself is a social construct. Even if there were to be a clear distinction it would be impossible to separate cause and effect. A corollary to this, and perhaps an even more challenging question, is whether the personality traits of those who undertake specific types of crime (such as 'spree killing') differ from both the law abiding population as a whole, and/or from those who undertake more common, and less violent forms of crime.

3.6 Crime Reduction

We often hear the terms 'crime prevention', 'crime reduction', and 'community safety' used both within policing and more widely. Ekblom (2001) draws subtle distinctions between these concepts, whereas Pease (2002) suggests they are different expressions of the same thing. We will use the terms interchangeably.

Crime prevention is a long-standing but often neglected policing priority. Today we recognize that all police officers have a crime prevention responsibility, and that this is not simply the role of a designated 'Crime Prevention Officer' (as was the case in the recent past). The police now have a better understanding of how preventative measures can help to reduce crime, and that crime prevention is an integral aspect of a police officer's duties, alongside crime detection. Furthermore, crime prevention can be used in a targeted and directed manner to reduce crime and to thereby free more police resources for dedicated proactive police work. Given the apparent huge growth in online crime (see Chapter 21), and the current very low rates of detection for this form of criminal activity, crime prevention measures increasingly need to include public cyber-security awareness.

Crime can be reduced to some extent through detecting crimes and imprisoning the offenders, with the result that fewer prospective offenders have the opportunity to commit crime. However, preventing crimes from happening in the first place represents a far more rational and economical approach, and provides clear benefits to society. The targeted use of crime prevention forms part of a problem-oriented approach to reducing crime (see 8.3.2.2), and is informed by routine-activity theory (see the start of 3.5.1), and the idea that there are three components of crime: the offender, the victim, and the location of a crime. Police officers should consider why a crime has occurred, as this can help to identify the appropriate preventative measures. The police response then becomes more proactive (as opposed to reactive).

The crime reduction agenda has also been bolstered by the move towards partnership approaches in policing (see 8.4), and the increasing emphasis on crime prevention has altered the role of the police. Crime prevention requires good intelligence and it is therefore important that police officers make the most of information provided by local intelligence officers. In turn, investigators also need to share information with the local intelligence officers (see 23.5 and 25.7). This joined up approach was enshrined in the ten Principles of Neighbourhood Policing which were introduced by the National Centre for Policing Excellence in 2006 (NCPE/ACPO, 2006). The NCPE later merged with the National Police Improvement Agency and ultimately became part of the College of Policing.

It is important that any intervention is properly evaluated. Policing in general (and crime reduction in particular) is increasingly subject to research and evaluation, and the results of this research will help to ensure that any claims used to justify preventative strategies are based on firm evidence (see eg Smith and Tilley, 2005).

The new emphasis on integrating crime prevention into everyday police work means that police officers must continually anticipate, recognize, and assess the risk of criminal activity. Measures can then be taken to reduce the risk. These measures could be straightforward, for example simply providing the public with crime prevention advice, but in some situations a more concerted effort is required.

3.6.1   Reducing the opportunities for crime

As an example, consider an unlit pathway which provides criminals with an appropriate location for committing crime. A police officer needs to be able to evaluate what short-term measures can be taken to reduce the criminal opportunity (eg increase the guardianship of the unlit pathway by increasing police patrols), but the police must also ensure that a longer-term solution is provided, for example by contacting the local council to ensure the lighting problem is addressed.

Routine-activity theory (RAT) and rational-choice theory (RCT) are often used to explore the various causes of crime (see 3.3). Using these, it follows that preventative techniques could be organized under three headings: increasing the effort (eg target hardening); increasing the risks (eg CCTV); and reducing the rewards (eg marking property). Pease (2002) adds a fourth heading: 'reducing the excuses' or in other words making it harder for the offender to provide a valid or appropriate rationale for why they have carried out certain acts, and perhaps in the process causing him/her to feel guilty or ashamed. The relative significance of each of these strategies depends upon the particular crime in question: which strategy is most likely to have the greatest deterrent impact on the potential criminal? These ideas are illustrated in Task 6.

TASK 6 Consider the following scenarios and identify whether increasing the effort, increasing the risk, or reducing the reward would be the most effective preventative measure. We acknowledge that, to some extent, all three would be appropriate but try to identify the one that you think addresses the problem most directly.

1. There have been a number of thefts from vehicles in a supermarket car park. The cars targeted have had valuable items stolen from them.
2. A shop is being repeatedly targeted at night by a group of known drug addicts.
3. Small amounts of money are being stolen by a member of staff from within a bank.

Routine-activity theory (Felson, 2002) suggests some other approaches that may be used in crime reduction: for example, ensuring that motivated offenders are not left unobserved where there are easy criminal targets, for example goods that could be stolen. This theory suggests that the number of motivated offenders does not have to be reduced in order to reduce crime; they simply need to be monitored more closely. Goods could also be redesigned so that they are more difficult to sell on. To some extent routine-activity theory can also be applied to help to reduce the opportunities for online crime as well as the more 'well-established' crimes that involve physical locations. Online crime, however, does not have the relationship of proximity or distance between offenders and targets; the relevance of RAT is therefore more problematic (Leukfeldt and Var, 2016).

3.6.2   Environmental criminology

Environmental criminology (also known as socio-spatial criminology or sometimes the 'geography of crime') considers the spatial distribution of crime, criminality, and victimization. It is closely linked to 'situational crime prevention' (SCP), and also has links with routine activities theory. SCP involves designing products, services, environments, or systems to reduce the likelihood of crime. Examples include traffic enforcement cameras for motoring offences, increased use of CCTV, designing better laid out housing estates to restrict vehicular access, and using metal detectors at airports.

Environmental criminology focuses less on criminality (eg the motivation of the offender as an individual, ie the 'why?') and more on crime events (the 'where?' and the 'when?').

Two 'principles' (essentially assumptions based on empirical research) underpin environmental criminology:

- the behaviour of offenders is significantly affected by the environment; and
- crime is non-randomly distributed in space and time (see hotspots in 3.5.2).

In practical terms, environmental criminology considers 'crime patterns', 'crime trends', 'distance of travel to crime', and how these relate to the physical environment. Understanding these patterns could help to reduce crime or even to identify an unknown offender. For example, some offenders will only commit certain offences beyond a certain distance from where they live (the 'anchor point'), but not too far away. Thus, a series of such crimes will take place within a broad ring (known in the US as the 'doughnut theory' for obvious reasons). Beyond the crime-free zone around the offender's home location (the hole of the doughnut), the number of crimes committed by the offender decreases as the distance from the anchor point increases (a 'distance decay' effect) in a roughly mathematically predictable way. An application of environmental criminology would be to 'work backwards' from the crime location data, to try to establish where an unknown serial offender is likely to live; this is an example of 'geographical profiling'.

3.6.3   The prevention of hot spots

The persistent presence of police officers, PCSOs, or local authority wardens would undoubtedly have a deterrent effect on hot spots, but this cannot be sustained for long due to the cost. Researchers are looking at whether regular 10- to 15-minute patrols would provide a more cost-effective solution—the 'more but shorter' proposal. It has also been suggested that a more effective approach might be fewer visits of longer duration (Williams and Coupe, 2017). CCTV cameras are a possible short-term solution at a relatively lower cost, especially if coordinated with police action on the ground such as 'blitzes' on pickpockets, for example.

A longer-term and better solution is to 'design out' crime, for example by installing carefully designed walkways and better street lighting. Intelligence (see Chapter 24) is also likely to be an important part of any approach to dealing with hot spots. Analysts will consider the types of crime, the times when they occur, the sorts of people who commit those crimes, and the seasonal impact (if any) upon the nature of the crime. A detailed understanding and taking appropriate measures may lead to the cooling of a hot spot. Dealing with cybercrime hotspots on the internet normally involves a number of national agencies and private companies (such as ISPs).

3.6.4   Crime prevention advice

Crime prevention is the responsibility of all police officers, but a specialist Crime Prevention Officer (CPO) can provide further advice. The crime should be considered from the perspective of the victim, the offender, and the location. Pertinent questions can then be asked about why a crime has occurred, and this can help to provide the basis for practical solutions. The advice can be tailored to specific contexts, for example, regarding the most suitable locks, lighting, and other basic security measures in a home where a burglary has recently taken place. There is also a specific need to tailor crime prevention messages aimed at young people, children, and those at particular risk within online environments. The lessons learnt during the investigation of one particular crime incident should also be used to help to prevent future criminal activities.

Police officers can encourage communities as a whole to become involved in implementing effective crime prevention strategies, for example Neighbourhood Watch schemes (see 2.2.2.9), and Street Watch. In addition, Neighbourhood Policing Teams (sometimes known as Safer Neighbourhood Teams (SNTs)), Crime Prevention Panels (CPPs), and Community Safety Partnerships (CSPs), all provide a local focus for crime prevention measures, alongside the national Crimestoppers Trust which works in collaboration with the police (see Chapter 8 on community policing).

3.6.5   Displacement

Crime prevention can lead to crime displacement: crimes are not prevented, but merely displaced to other locations or to a later time (Johnson *et al*, 2014). Displaced crime may also occur through criminal innovation (see the following list). Displacement is often explained as a consequence of criminality: those with a disposition to commit crimes will adapt and find different ways in which to realize their criminal disposition. The following types of displacement have been identified.

- **Temporal displacement:** the crime takes place at a later time. As an example, consider the depot that introduces a security guard overnight to counter a string of night-time burglaries. However, there is a one-hour gap between the security guard finishing and the day staff arriving, so the criminals choose this time to commit the offence.
- **Spatial displacement:** the crime happens at another location. For example, a high police presence is introduced in Area 1 to address alleged incidents of anti-social behaviour from a group of young people. But some members of the group simply move to Area 2 and behave in the same way.
- **Displacement by type of crime:** the criminals turn to different crimes. Suppose that the local council introduces better street lighting on an estate prone to street robberies. The number of robberies falls but the number of burglaries increases in the area.
- **Displacement by innovation:** the criminals become better at what they do. An example is the fact that people no longer carry large amounts of cash, which reduces the cash reward for street robbers. But some criminals turn to using stolen credit cards, thereby gaining access to even larger sums of money.

Pease (1997) has suggested that the extent of displacement is often exaggerated, and that the issue is raised on ideological rather than empirical grounds, as an excuse for taking no action. He also argues that displacement is never likely to be 100 per cent, and illustrates ways in which displacement can be an advantage. For example, it might be beneficial to move a crime from one area to another to reduce its overall impact on society, or to change the type of crime committed. For instance, if sex-workers are operating on the street in a family residential area, it seems likely that a high police presence would move them on to another area. If they move to a non-residential area it would clearly reduce the concern that any children would be affected, but this might need to be balanced against a separate concern for the safety of the sex-workers. Some might innovate and use more discreet means of operating, while others might desist from sex-work. The effects of displacement can be predicted and then compared with the effect in practice. As Pease puts it, displacement is positive as long as 'the deflected crime causes less harm and misery than the original crime' (Pease, 1997, p 978).

3.6.6   Procedural justice

Procedural justice focuses on the way the police (and other legal authorities) interact with the public, particularly 'face to face', and how these interactions shape the public perception of the police. Claims have been made, particularly in the US, that 'if police treat citizens respectfully and make decisions in a fair way, then it can enhance public perceptions of police legitimacy' (Murphy, 2018, see also 2.2.5 on police legitimacy). This is thought to be true even if the outcome for a member of the public is a negative one, such as being arrested.

The concepts and research underpinning procedural justice are having a significant impact within both academic and professional policing spheres. For example, the College of Policing expects police officers to adopt a 'procedural justice approach' when conducting a stop and search (CoP, 2017b).

Procedural justice is based on some key principles; the police should treat people with dignity and respect, they must be neutral in their decision-making, and police actions must be seen to be fair and proportionate in the circumstances. It is important that policing is not seen as simply a rigid application of the law and associated police powers but also as acting fairly. A reasoned and principled use of professional discretion promotes police legitimacy, and procedural justice is likely to play a part in this. There is empirical evidence, for example, that the degree of procedural justice in a particular country is a good predictor of the level of state police legitimacy. It is also the case at the level of the individual, that the way a police officer behaves and reacts to others has a bearing on his/her personal authority.

However, simply applying procedural justice principles to everyday policing will not automatically lead to particular desirable outcomes, such as increasing the chances that people will comply with police instructions. As Waddington *et al* (2017) observe, different people will interpret the same action of the police in a particular situation ('vignette') in different ways. A person's judgement about police authority and legitimacy may be rooted in experiences (their own, and the experiences of others) that pre-date any direct contact with the police.

3.7 **Answers to Tasks**

TASK 1

What makes a crime sensational? There are many different explanations for what registers as a sensational crime in public imagination and the media. A sensational crime is often one which has something out of the ordinary, something different, even a little outrageous, to make it stand out. Some violent crimes involving children may feature highly in the media and thus public consciousness (possibly because many of us are expected to identify with the parents of the victim, or because the vulnerability of a child evokes sympathy and pity in us).

One category of crimes which tend not to make the headlines, unless very significant, are the so-called victimless crimes such as defrauding a large company or embezzling insurance money.

There are victims of course for any crime, but what frightens a community or spreads anxiety is the thought that some sort of terror or dread is stalking the streets. A series of rapes can have this effect, especially in a small community such as a town or a college, and the abduction of a child also causes widespread concern.

TASK 2 There are many possible answers, and we provide some suggestions here.

1. The answer is somewhat speculative, but they would seem likely to include theft, murder, and rape.
2. Activities that were not considered as crimes 100 years ago but are today include stalking and some types of outdoor night-time music and dancing events.
3. Activities that are not considered as crimes in the UK but are in some other countries include adultery (Nigeria), consuming alcohol (Saudi Arabia), and keeping African pygmy hedgehogs (some states of the USA).

TASK 3 There is a difference between intrinsic value and 'CRAVED'. The thieves would probably leave the coins behind because they are bulky and very heavy, but they would pocket the £350 in notes immediately. The PC would probably be left; again it is bulky and heavy. The iPad, iPhone X, and the Rolex would be easily pocketed for selling on. However, traffic in particular electronic goods is often short-lived as it is often the next-generation goods that the fences demand; the laptop may be old and heavy, and a 2012 mobile phone would yield no return. Apple Inc have introduced additional security measures in recent years to increase the difficulty of 'fencing' stolen iPads and iPhones. The Rolex might present problems because any engraving can help trace an item, but in a snatching or mugging the thieves would not stop to check. The engraving and date would reduce the price, so the fence might decide to file out the engraving.

The other items are small but would be very difficult to sell on. *The Gospels* and the Rubens' painting would be worth several million pounds, but they would be very difficult to fence on any art market. However, organized drugs importers and traffickers have used valuable art such as paintings or sculptures as 'cash' for their transactions—the more so since the Proceeds of Crime Act 2002 made depositing large amounts of cash in a bank account subject to scrutiny and investigation.

The *netsuke* (small carved figures) would be worth several thousand pounds each, but only through an expert dealer, and the average fence is unlikely to know what they are. That said, some thieves steal to order and might target such items specifically, but these are not likely to be volume criminals working on hot spots.

TASK 4

Kent Police started to use the commercial 'PredPol' predictive policing system in 2013, at a cost of around £100,000 per year (Chowdhury, 2018). However, in 2018 they cancelled their contract with the US firm concerned, explaining that it was 'challenging' to demonstrate whether the system had enabled police to reduce crime (BBC News, 2018b).

When predictive policing algorithms were first marketed it was usually on the basis of their supposed ability to accurately and precisely 'predict' crime using 'scientific' (mathematical) algorithms performed using computing technology. However, as Ratcliffe (2014, p 5) noted, predictive policing is better thought of as the 'use of historical data to create a spatiotemporal forecast of areas of criminality or crime hot spots that will be the basis for police resource allocation decisions'. It is this coupling of operational decision-making with crime forecasting that forms the basis of any claim of novelty for 'predictive policing'.

The crime forecasting aspects of predictive policing tend to be applied only to those crimes whose occurrence exhibits some mathematical relationship with physical space and particularly public places such as town centres (eg thefts). As far as we are aware, there are no predictive policing algorithms that forecast the types of crimes that have few correlations with public spaces (such as corporate fraud). Further, predictive policing, as a commercial product, is often based on the assumption that deploying police resources to a particular area will not simply lead to displacement of crime. For example, the model may suggest that visible patrols should be deployed to a certain shopping centre on Saturday afternoons to dissuade pickpockets, but the pickpockets might then simply move to another nearby shopping area.

Most of the algorithms are marginally better at predicting crime than 'average' (ie conventional crime forecasting techniques), but they tend to perform best for the more predictable offences such as theft in shopping centres during opening hours. A number of research studies are under way to test the predictive accuracy of the algorithms employed.

There has also been some controversy, particularly in the USA, around whether some of the algorithms involved lead to inadvertent and ongoing racial bias through a form of feedback loop.

TASK 5 The quotation assumes that criminal behaviour will follow a rational pattern, thus hot products will be targeted by certain people in hot spots, and markets will exist for the products of crime. The predictability of this should allow the police (in principle at least) to anticipate appropriate points at which to intervene.

TASK 6

1. Reducing the reward. The fact that the cars targeted have valuables on show suggests that the offenders are looking for easy rewards. Increasing the risk by introducing better lighting, CCTV cameras, or security guards would also be beneficial, but the most cost-effective measure is likely to be encouraging people not to leave valuables in the car.
2. Increasing the effort. We can assume that these particular offenders are desperate and therefore unlikely to be overly concerned at being caught (increasing the risk) and will be prepared to take risks for small rewards (reducing the reward). Therefore, making it physically difficult to break in by installing metal bars and stronger locks is likely to be the most effective measure.
3. Increasing the risk. The rewards are already limited and making it more difficult to take the money is impractical because of the need for employees to handle money. Therefore, increasing the risk, for example by installing CCTV, is likely to have a deterrent effect because the employees have a lot to lose if they are caught.

4 The Criminal Justice System in England and Wales

4.1   Introduction

This chapter covers some of the key features of the criminal justice system in England and Wales. The various types of legislation and the principles of criminal liability are explained, along with the hierarchy of the court system. We also provide a brief account of some of the legislation that protects the general rights of UK citizens, such as the Human Rights Act 1998 and the PACE Codes of Practice. The topics covered in this chapter are likely to contribute to the learning required for the National Policing Curriculum subject areas, 'Understanding the Police Constable Role', 'Criminal Justice', and 'Valuing Difference and Inclusion'.

In the UK the concept of the criminal justice system refers to the law, law enforcement, and dealing with transgressions of the law. The criminal justice system (CJS) in England and Wales includes the police, the courts of law, Her Majesty's Prison and Probation Service, the Youth Justice Board, and the Crown Prosecution Service (CPS).

Both students on pre-join programmes and trainee police officers undertaking the PCDA or the DHEP will need to understand the different types of law and court procedures.

A number of situations that involve specific types of legislation will be addressed in more detail in subsequent chapters (such as criminal and family law regarding domestic violence in 13.6), but here we will concentrate on the general aspects; how laws are made, some of the different branches of law, the principles behind criminal law, and the courts system.

The system used by the courts in England and Wales is adversarial, whereas elsewhere in Europe (eg in France) the system is inquisitorial. In an inquisitorial system the defendant is questioned by a judge during trial so the lawyers in court have a lower profile. The adversarial model in contrast requires that two advocates representing their parties (ie the prosecution and the defence) present their cases to an impartial person or persons (ie a judge and jury or magistrates) in order for the verdict to be determined.

A person who has been charged with an offence but has not yet appeared in court is known as the defendant. He/she is tried by a court (usually in open session), and the defendant's guilt must be proved beyond reasonable doubt. The prosecution is conducted on behalf of the Crown, often referred to in written case law as 'R' (this stands for Regina or Rex which is Latin for the Queen or the King, see 4.2.1 on the conventions for naming cases). The Crown Prosecutors (CP) and Senior Crown Prosecutors (SCP) are lawyers employed by the CPS to review and, when appropriate, prosecute cases investigated by the police. Associate Prosecutors (legally trained but not lawyers) may also perform some of these functions at the level of the magistrates' courts. The CPS also employs Crown Advocates who deal almost exclusively with cases at Crown Court and Court of Appeal. The CPS also instructs barristers from the independent bar to conduct some prosecutions at court, and to provide the CPS with advice on complex legal matters. The defendant is normally represented by a solicitor and in some circumstances by a barrister. They are known as 'defence counsel' or 'the defence' (see Chapter 27 for more details on these roles).

4.2 The Law in England and Wales

An understanding of the law in England and Wales is an important aspect of the police officer's epistemic authority (see 5.11.5.1). You may have heard law referred to as: common law, statute law, case law, Acts of Parliament, Statutory Instruments, and by-laws. These all interrelate in a number of ways.

Common law (also known as 'judge-made law') can be traced back to the Norman invasion of Britain in the eleventh century. Local courts made decisions that were then passed by word of mouth to other courts. Over time they were accepted by more courts throughout the country, creating a 'binding precedent'. Examples of common law offences include murder, manslaughter, perverting the course of justice, and escape from lawful custody. In the UK new common law offences are no longer created, but courts continue to interpret existing laws when setting precedents.

Statute law is the foundation of the current legal system in England and Wales. This primary source of law can be accessed electronically via the UK Statute Law Database at www.legislation.gov.uk. Bills or 'draft law' are needed to create new legislation; ministry officials write a proposal and submit it to the Houses of Parliament for a decision. If accepted it is given Royal Assent before becoming an Act of Parliament. For example, the Criminal Finances Bill was introduced in the House of Commons in October 2016 for discussion, and it received Royal Assent in April 2017, becoming the Criminal Finances Act 2017, and thereby becoming statute law. A regularly revised list of bills currently before parliament for consideration is available at <http://services.parliament.uk/bills/>.

Case law helps to establish the precise meaning of legislation, and sets precedents. Decisions made by higher courts about legislation are then accepted by lower courts throughout the country. This 'doctrine of precedent' sets out how the legislation should be used by a court in similar circumstances. Although the specific circumstances of the case might change (referred to as *obiter dicta*), the court should use the same reasoning (or *ratio decidendi*) that was used by previous courts to reach a decision. An example of this would be any decisions made about identification evidence; this would follow the precedents set in the case *R v Turnbull* [1976] 3 All ER 549. When case law has been used this is indicated as 'by way of case stated'.

Acts of Parliament are divided into sections containing, for example, definitions, offences, powers of arrest, exemptions, and interpretations of words and expressions used. An Act often includes technical details such as fines and penalties, which may need frequent revision and updating. The updates are provided as Statutory Instruments such as Orders, Regulations, and Rules, and are often left to government ministers, to reduce the pressure on parliamentary time.

Statutory Instruments (SIs) allow the details of an Act to be revised without using parliamentary procedures. They are as much part of the law of England and Wales as the main body of the Act of Parliament. SIs are given a number as well as a title, for example 'Criminal Justice (Electronic Monitoring) (Responsible Person) Order 2014' (SI 2014 No 163). The Home Secretary used this SI to enable private companies such as Capita and G4S to take responsibility for the electronic monitoring of people released on condition of bail or as part of a youth rehabilitation order, curfew, or community order.

By-laws are usually local laws which have been made by a local authority and approved by a Secretary of State of the government. They normally deal with local matters, for example dogs on leads in recreational areas. They can also refer to charters, which are documents created under a generic form of legislation to regulate certain activities within an organization. Examples of charters include Trades Union charters and the Department of Health Information Charter.

TASK 1 The Road Vehicle Lighting Regulations 1989 (SI 1989 No 1796) were introduced under s 41 of the Road Traffic Act 1988. Find out what regs 11–22 cover in relation to motor vehicles. (Use *Blackstone's Police Manual: Volume 3 Road Policing*, the internet, or other sources to look this up.)

4.2.1   The naming system for legal cases

Each legal case in court has an official title, for example *R v Turnbull* [1976] 3 All ER 549. There is an official system for naming cases, for example 'R' stands for 'Regina' or 'Rex' (the Queen or King respectively, depending whether a King or a Queen is on the throne when the case is heard). The letter 'v' stands for versus, and 'Turnbull' is the name of the defendant. The case was held in 1976, and can be found in Volume 3 of the 1976 All England Law Reports on p 549.

4.3   Principles of Criminal Liability

Most of the law relevant to a police officer's first few years of service is undoubtedly criminal, rather than civil law. We therefore begin with the notion of 'criminal liability'—how do we *know* and then prove that a person has broken the law? There are two elements of criminal liability:

1. The *actus reus*—the action the defendant carried out, which must be proved beyond reasonable doubt (see 4.3.1).
2. The *mens rea*—the guilty mind-set that the defendant had at the time the action was taken, which also must be proved; that is, that the defendant intended to commit the crime. However, there are some exceptions to this (see 4.3.2).

Although the use of Latin can seem off-putting and exclusionary, these terms are commonly used within the legal system and so are worth remembering (if you are unsure you will find a number of internet sites that will help you to pronounce these two Latin phrases). We will now look at these two building blocks of criminal liability in more detail.

4.3.1   *Actus reus*

This is about a person's actions (including a lack of action). If a person is to be found guilty of a criminal offence, then it must be proved that he/she either:

- acted criminally in some way, for example committed murder;
- omitted to do an act, and the omission brought about a criminal outcome, for example knowing that someone was going to commit a crime but doing nothing to stop it or report it;
- caused a state of affairs to happen, for example knowingly drinking a lot of alcohol and then driving a car; or
- failed to do an act which was required, and which brought about a criminal outcome, for example failing to ensure that a vehicle was roadworthy when offering it for hire, this leads to the criminal outcome of someone driving a car that is not in a safe condition to be driven.

4.3.2   *Mens rea*

This is about a person's thoughts or state of mind, and is about having guilty knowledge. The defendant's state of mind or *mens rea* is relevant to a number of offences, and to this end the legislation includes terms such as:

- 'dishonestly' such as for theft;
- 'wilfully' such as for neglect of children;
- 'recklessly' as in the offence of causing criminal damage; and
- 'with intent' as in burglary with intent to steal.

The degree of *mens rea* in criminal offences varies. For example, a person can deliberately commit an offence, but at the other end of the scale a person could simply fail to take appropriate care to avoid the criminal outcome of their action or inaction (usually called negligence).

The level of intent is assessed by comparing the actions of the defendant with those of a hypothetical 'reasonable' or average person under the circumstances of the alleged offence. For more serious situations (eg murder and 'wounding or inflicting grievous bodily harm with intent') the law requires that the suspect has a specific intent or *mens rea*. This would also include offences for which there is an ulterior purpose other than the main criminal act, for example when a defendant is charged with burglary with intent (see 16.4.1). Here, it would have to be proved that the defendant not only intended to enter a building as a trespasser, but also intended to inflict grievous bodily harm, cause damage, or steal. For other offences, such as common assault or battery, it is sufficient to prove basic intent. This requires that the defendant knew or at least closed his/her mind (ie was reckless) to the fact that his/her actions would result in harm being caused to the victim.

4.3.3 Strict liability offences

'Strict liability' offences are those for which only the guilty act (*actus reus*) needs to be proved. There is no need for a *mens rea* for a successful conviction (or a diminished *mens rea* may be sufficient). Two examples of strict liability offences are:

- paying for sexual services of a prostitute who is being subjected to force by another (s 14 of the Policing and Crime Act 2009, see 17.5.2)—it is irrelevant whether the suspect knows about the use of force by another; and
- the sale of faulty goods (s 14 of the Sale of Goods Act 1979)—it is irrelevant whether the suspect knows the goods are faulty.

Strict liability offences are usually less serious and often correspond to statutory violations, but they can also include offences where the action itself is considered so dangerous or socially unacceptable that there is no need to prove the offender's intention. However, it is not always clear whether a *mens rea* is required, and decisions concerning strict liability may be ultimately left to the courts.

4.3.4 Burden of proof

How do we prove that a person is guilty of a criminal offence? The law tells us that:

> throughout the web of the English criminal law one golden thread is always to be seen: that it is the duty of the prosecution to prove the prisoner's guilt. (*Woolmington v DPP* [1935] AC 462)

Therefore, in criminal proceedings the onus is on the prosecution to prove the guilt of the defendant, not on the defendant to prove his/her innocence. And furthermore, the degree of proof required for criminal cases is 'beyond reasonable doubt'. This was famously expressed by Geoffrey Lawrence (cited in Johnston and Hutton, 2005, p 133) in the following way:

> The possibility of guilt is not enough, suspicion is not enough, probability is not enough, likelihood is not enough. A criminal matter is not a question of balancing probabilities and deciding in favour of probability, a conviction must be formed beyond reasonable doubt that the accused is guilty, and this is done on the basis of the evidence provided in court.

The jury will therefore be directed by the judge that they should only return a guilty verdict if they are sure of the suspect's guilt, beyond any reasonable doubt. Magistrates will be aware of this responsibility from their training and may be reminded of it by their legal adviser.

4.4 Human Rights and Equality

The concept of human rights and the responsibilities of police officers in the preservation and maintenance of those rights runs throughout this Handbook. The police are expected to exercise their powers and procedures fairly and without bias, and in accordance with the Human Rights Act 1998, the Equality Act 2010, and PACE (the Police and Criminal Evidence Act 1984). Human rights legislation stresses the entitlement of individuals to expect certain fundamental rights as part of their social contract with the state and other forms of authority.

4.4.1 The Human Rights Act 1998

The Human Rights Act 1998 (HRA) lists a number of rights as shown in the table. Each right is considered as absolute (underlined), limited (L), or qualified (Q).

Article number	Article title
2	<u>Right to life</u>
3	<u>Prohibition of torture</u>
4	<u>Prohibition of slavery and forced labour</u>
5	Right to liberty and security (L)
6	Right to a fair trial (L)

Article number	Article title
7	No punishment without law
8	Right to respect for private and family life (Q)
9	Freedom of thought, conscience, and religion (Q)
10	Freedom of expression (Q)
11	Freedom of assembly and association (Q)
12	Right to marry (L)
14	Prohibition of discrimination (L)

The **absolute rights** of an individual cannot be restricted by the interests of the community as a whole.

Limited rights do not apply in all circumstances—for example the right to liberty (part of Article 5) does not apply if the detention is lawful, such as after arrest. However, although the right to liberty may be limited, a lawfully arrested person would still have the right to security under Article 5. A further example of a limited right occurs within Article 6, under which both the public and the press have the right to access to any court hearing, but this right is subject to certain restrictions in the interests of morality, public order, national security, or where the interests of young people under 18, or the privacy of the parties, require the exclusion of the press and public.

Qualified rights relate to matters where interference by the public authority is permissible if it is in the public interest and can be qualified, for example to prevent disorder or crime, for public safety, or for national security. However, a public authority (such as the police) may only interfere with a qualified right if the interference is:

- lawful and is part of existing common or statute law (see 4.2), such as the power to stop and search;
- made for one of the specifically listed permissible acts in the interests of the public, such as to prevent disorder for public safety; or
- necessary in a democratic society, where the wider interests of the community as a whole often have to be balanced against the rights of an individual (but it must still be proportionate).

There are certain aspects of the HRA 1998 which may seem strange (eg Article 1 does not contain any rights and Article 13 does not even exist), but this is partly because it is derived from the European Convention on the Protection of Human Rights and Fundamental Freedoms (ECHR).

All new statute law must be compatible with the HRA. An individual may take a public authority to a UK court (rather than directly to the European Court of Human Rights) if the authority has not acted in a manner compatible with the rights. UK courts are required to interpret all legislation in a way which is compatible with the Convention's rights, so far as is possible (s 3), and public authorities (eg government and the police) cannot act in a way which is incompatible with the Convention. Note, however, there is no retrospective effect on existing law (*R v Lambert* [2001] 2 WLR 211).

At the time of writing, the UK's position in relation to Brexit is unclear, but leaving the European Union (EU) will not impact UK citizens' rights under the European Court of Human Rights, as the Court comes under the auspices of the Council of Europe (and not the EU). The longer-term impact of Brexit on our equality and human rights will depend on the laws that are passed after leaving the EU. This chapter reflects the law at the time of writing, as the UK goes through the transition phase after leaving the EU.

4.4.1.1 Applying the Human Rights Act to everyday policing

A police officer should consider the following questions in relation to an individual or group before 'interfering' with another person's qualified rights:

1. Are my actions lawful? Is there common or statute law to support my interference with his/her rights?

2. Are my actions permissible? Am I permitted to interfere with his/her rights because it is in support of a duty, such as preventing crime?
3. Are my actions necessary? Do the needs of the many outweigh the needs of the few; in other words, must I take into account the interests of the community and balance one individual's rights against another's?
4. Are my actions proportionate? Having considered everything, will my actions be excessive or could I do something less intrusive and more in proportion to the outcome I need to achieve?

During initial police training mnemonics may be used with regard to these questions, for example *PLAN* (Proportionality, Legality, Accountability, and Necessity) and *JAPAN* (Justification, Authorization, Proportionality, Auditable, and Necessary).

4.4.2 The Equality Act 2010

The foundations of equality and diversity in the UK are enshrined in legislation. Under the Equality Act 2010 it is unlawful to discriminate on the grounds of certain 'protected characteristics'. These characteristics are: age, disability, race, religion or belief, sex, gender reassignment, sexual orientation, marriage and civil partnership, pregnancy or maternity.

The 2010 Equality Act brought together all of the previous anti-discrimination laws, for example the Sex Discrimination Act 1975 and the Race Relations Act 1976. This has simplified the legislative framework, and also provides better protection in some situations. The Equality Act has certain key aims including those that concern:

- personal characteristics—the Act restates the relevant enactments relating to discrimination and harassment;
- pay differences—certain employers will be required to publish information about the differences in pay between male and female employees;
- victimization—prohibition in law in certain circumstances;
- discrimination—action to be taken to eliminate discrimination and other prohibited conduct;
- equality of opportunity—to be increased; and
- family relationships—to amend the law relating to rights and responsibilities in family relationships.

Public authorities are now required to eliminate discrimination, harassment, victimization, and any other conduct prohibited by the Act in relation to the protected characteristics. They must also advance equality of opportunity and foster good relations between people who share a protected characteristic and people who do not share it.

4.4.2.1 Promoting equality

Given the powerful positions police officers hold in society it is important for all officers to ensure their own prejudices do not lead to discrimination. As the Institute for Apprenticeships explains, police constables:

> exercise wide-ranging powers to maintain the peace and uphold the law across complex and diverse communities. They must justify and personally account for their actions through differing legal frameworks including courts, while also under the close scrutiny of the public.

Our gender, life experiences, family, cultural, and social backgrounds can all influence our understanding and views of the world. They can be portrayed in a variety of verbal and non-verbal ways and each officer must manage all aspects of their communication during encounters with members of the public, in order to reduce potentially harmful impacts.

A number of important principles that support equality have been integrated into the standards of professional behaviour for the police (see 5.3.1). These standards are reflected in some of the specific requirements that apply for police responses to issues such as hate crime (see 14.10), harassment (see 14.5), confidentiality (see 5.8.1), human rights (see 4.4), and recording information in investigations (see 24.3).

The Institute of Apprenticeship's standard for those undertaking the PCDA is for trainees to exhibit professional integrity, which the Institute explains means to:

> maintain the highest standards of professionalism and trustworthiness, making sure that values, moral codes and ethical standards are always upheld, including challenging others where appropriate.

As a public service, police personnel should ideally reflect a representative cross-section of society. This would benefit policing in terms of gaining confidence and cooperation across the full range of groups within the community. Recruiting from the full range of society allows the police service to attract a wider range of skills and knowledge, as well as recruiting the best people to fill vacancies.

> **TASK 2** How would a trainee police officer seek to follow the principles of equality, diversity, and anti-discrimination practice?

4.5 The Criminal Justice System in Practice

Once an alleged crime has been reported, there will be an investigation at some level, usually by the police. The extent and nature of an investigation will inevitably vary with the circumstances (covered in more detail in Chapters 10 and 24). If the investigation leads to a prosecution it will usually be conducted by the CPS, on behalf of the Crown (the state). The prosecution will take place in a court, for example in a Crown Court for a more serious case (see 4.5.2 on the various types of court). The defendant will usually be represented by a solicitor or barrister, but can choose to represent him/herself. The courts may be assisted by Social Services and the National Probation Service. Chapters 23 to 27 provide more detailed information on investigation, prosecution, and court procedures.

4.5.1 The classification of criminal offences

Some offences are more serious than others, and can only be tried in particular courts. Offences are classified as summary-only offences, indictment-only offences, and either-way offences.

Summary-only offences are less serious and are normally dealt with in the magistrates' court where they are governed by Part 37 of the Criminal Procedure Rules 2010. Examples of summary-only offences are common assault and being drunk and disorderly. The Crown Court may, however, deal with a summary offence in certain circumstances. For example, there are a small number of summary-only offences that can be added to the indictment (the formal document that sets out the offences to be heard in the Crown Court) along with connected indictable or either-way offences. These summary-only offences are listed under s 40 of the Criminal Justice Act 1988, and include common assault, taking a vehicle without consent, and driving while disqualified. Summary-only offences must be charged within six months of the offence having taken place.

Indictment-only offences are the most serious cases and can only be dealt with in a Crown Court. Examples include murder, manslaughter, causing death by dangerous driving, rape, robbery, aggravated burglary, and wounding with intent.

Either-way offences can be tried in a magistrates' court or a Crown Court. Examples of either-way offences include theft, obtaining property by deception, and assault occasioning actual bodily harm. Certain either-way offences can only be tried at a magistrates' court, for example criminal damage or aggravated vehicle taking with a cost below £5,000, and low-level shoplifting of goods worth less than £200 (ss 22–22A of the Magistrates' Courts Act 1980). At the first hearing for an either-way offence (in the magistrates' court) the defendant will be asked whether he/she wishes to enter a plea. If the defendant enters a guilty plea the magistrates will consider whether their sentencing powers are sufficient to deal with the matter. If not, they will commit the case to the Crown Court for sentence. If the defendant pleads 'not guilty' or 'withholds' his/her plea at the first hearing in the magistrates' court, there will be a 'mode of trial' hearing to decide where the trial should be held. The crown prosecutor will make representations, and the defence may object to an either-way offence going to a Crown Court. The magistrates make the final decision, unless the defendant elects to be tried by judge and jury in a Crown Court, in which case the magistrates must comply.

The classification for each criminal offence and its mode of trial and penalty can be found either by reference to primary sources—that is, the legal texts themselves (eg through the Home Office website) or secondary sources, such as Blackstone's Police Manuals. For example, the relevant legislation for handling stolen goods is in s 22 of the Theft Act 1968. This, in conjunction with Sch 1 to and s 32 of the Magistrates' Courts Act 1980, states that handling stolen goods is triable either way, with a maximum penalty of 14 years' imprisonment on indictment, or if tried summarily six months' imprisonment and/or a fine.

TASK 3 Use an appropriate textbook or the internet to determine for the offence of robbery:

- the relevant Act, including section;
- the mode of trial; and
- the maximum penalty for a person found guilty.

4.5.2 The courts

The structure of the courts system in England and Wales relates to the nature of the matters in hand and the seriousness of the cases handled by each category of court. The diagram shows some key elements in the relationships between the various types of court in England and Wales.

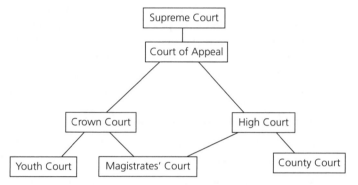

All of the courts shown here can deal with criminal cases, except for County Courts (which only deal with civil cases). The role of the courts that deal with criminal cases is our primary concern here, but police officers are occasionally required to give evidence in civil cases (eg an officer who attended a road traffic collision in which a pedestrian was seriously injured might be called as a witness in a civil court case in which claims for damages were in dispute).

The magistrates' courts are where all criminal cases start, regardless of classification. Around 95 per cent of all criminal cases are concluded in the magistrates' court. Summary matters stay in the magistrates' courts along with less serious either-way offences. The more serious either-way offences tend to be sent straight to the Crown Court following the first hearing. Indictable only offences will always be sent straight to the Crown Court from the magistrates' court. Magistrates deal with a variety of hearings, for example, applications for bail, pleas (guilty/not guilty), sentencing, trial management hearings, and trials. There are about 330 magistrates' courts across England and Wales. Hearings in magistrates' courts are presided over by a district judge (a qualified lawyer), or a bench of three magistrates (sometime referred to as the 'justices of the peace'). Magistrates are lay people drawn from the local community, and not professional judges or lawyers. They are advised on points of law by a legal adviser who is legally trained and is usually a solicitor or barrister. Magistrates' courts also hear non-criminal cases, such as family law disputes. The Specialist Domestic Violence Courts are held in magistrates' courts.

There are limits to the penalties that can be imposed at a magistrates' court, as follows:

- a custodial sentence must be no longer than six months per individual offence, with a maximum of two consecutive six-month sentences (s 154 of the Criminal Justice Act 2003); and
- fines at magistrates' courts cannot exceed £5,000.

For either-way offences (see 4.5.1), the offender can be sent to the Crown Court for sentence if the magistrates believe that a more severe sentence is appropriate. If a defendant is dissatisfied with a verdict from the magistrates' courts, he/she may appeal to the Crown Court for matters of fact and law, and to the High Court for matters of law only.

A youth court is normally used for defendants aged between 10 and 17 years (unless being charged jointly with an adult, or for murder or manslaughter). The procedures are very similar to those in a magistrates' court but are adapted to take account of the age of the defendant, and are not open to the public. A particular courtroom within a magistrates' court is often formally designated as a youth court. Appeals from a youth court generally go to the Crown Court.

The **Crown Court** is a first instance court (ie not an appeal court) for more serious criminal cases, including indictable offences such as murder, rape, or robbery. There are 77 Crown Courts across the UK. They also try appeals from magistrates' courts, and 'either-way' cases referred by magistrates' courts. The trial takes place before a judge and a jury, and members of the public (see Chapter 27). Police officers and other relevant experts may give evidence as witnesses. On matters of fact and law, it is possible to appeal from the Crown Court to the Criminal Division of the Court of Appeal.

The **High Court** is, alongside the Crown Court and the Appeal Courts, part of the higher courts of justice in England and Wales. It hears cases at first instance and on appeal. The High Court consists of three divisions, the Queen's Bench Division, the Chancery Division, and the Family Division, and each hears different types of cases. Judges from the Queen's Bench Division hear the most important criminal cases at Crown Court.

The **Court of Appeal** considers appeals from the Crown Court (criminal cases) and the High Court (civil cases) but it also takes a few appeals from magistrates' and youth courts. It normally sits in up to 12 courts in the Royal Courts of Justice in London. Some hearings may now be recorded and broadcast (Crime and Courts Act 2013), overturning a ban dating from 1925.

The **Supreme Court** is the highest court and the final instance of appeal on points of law and important legal disputes for criminal and civil cases in England and Wales. It is presided over by 12 appointed senior judges.

Summary of the courts

Courts	Type of cases	Features	Open to the public?	Appeals go to
Youth	Defendants aged 10 to 17 years	No jury	Not usually	Crown Court
Magistrates'	Offences triable summarily only, and either-way offences	No jury	Yes, usually	Crown Court or High Court
Crown	Offences triable only on indictment, and either-way offences referred from magistrates' courts. Appeals from magistrates' and youth courts	Judge and jury	Yes, usually	Court of Appeal (Criminal Division)
Appeal	Appeals from Crown Court	Judges only, no jury	Yes, usually	Supreme Court
Supreme	Appeals from Court of Appeal	Judges only, no jury	Yes, usually	Final point of appeal

The majority of courts are generally open to the public, but a small number of cases are heard in private, for example particularly sensitive cases or where intimidation is of concern (s 25 of the Youth Justice and Criminal Evidence Act 1999).

> **TASK 4** Find out the location of your nearest magistrates' court or Crown Court, and plan when to visit. You will be able to sit in the public gallery to observe proceedings.

4.5.3   Sentencing

Once a court has found a defendant guilty, it has three primary sentencing options: community orders, fines, and custodial sentences. These may be used together or separately, depending on the offence and the offender's circumstances. Community orders (such as removing graffiti from buildings) combine rehabilitation with punishment, and are supervised by the National Probation Service. For the most serious offences, courts may opt for custodial sentences. The length of the sentence imposed depends on the maximum penalty (as defined in the legislation for that offence), the circumstances in which the offence was committed, and on the offender (eg whether he/she was a repeat offender).

The court may also make a conditional or an absolute discharge. For the former, the offender is discharged but with the condition of not committing any other offence for a certain time period (three years maximum). An offender who does then commit an offence within the time period will be convicted for breaching the conditional discharge and re-sentenced. For an absolute discharge, the person has either admitted to an offence or been found guilty, but is not penalized as the process of investigation and prosecution is deemed to be a sufficient response to the offence committed.

Sentences must be appropriate and proportionate, taking into consideration all of the circumstances. The sentencing council sets out sentencing guidelines to help magistrates and judges decide on the appropriate sentence. For more information see <http://www.sentencingcouncil.org.uk/>.

4.6 The Police and Criminal Evidence Act 1984 (PACE)

The police have powers to arrest individuals, to search people and property, to enter buildings, and to seize objects. Many of these powers, and the restrictions on their use, are provided in the Police and Criminal Evidence Act 1984 (known as the PACE Act 1984, or simply as PACE), and some are considered in more detail later in this Handbook (in Chapters 9 and 10, for example).

The PACE Act 1984 contains key legislation in relation to:

- criminal investigation procedures in England and Wales;
- applying the principles of justice, honesty, and workability in the investigative process;
- protection of the rights of all individuals; and
- police powers for search and arrest.

The demonstration of knowledge of the PACE Act 1984 in practical policing contexts is an important element in both the knowledge and skills requirements of the PCDA and DHEP—for example in relation to conducting searches (see Chapter 9 on searches).

4.6.1 PACE Codes of Practice

The PACE Codes of Practice provide guidelines on how investigative processes should be conducted. The Codes are divided into eight main sections, and refer to contacts between the police and the public in the exercise of certain police powers.

Code	General areas covered
A	Stop and search
B	Search of premises
C	Detention, treatment, and questioning of suspects
D	Identification of suspects
E	Audio-only recording of interviews
F	Audio-visual recording of interviews
G	Power of arrest
H	Detention, treatment, and questioning of terrorist suspects

A brief summary of each code is provided here. The Codes are available as a smartphone app, and can also be downloaded in full from the Home Office website. The Codes were revised in 2019.

Code A covers the police statutory powers of stop and search, and the requirements for police officers and police staff to record public encounters. It provides guidelines on searching people who are not under arrest, and covers the key principles a police officer needs to apply when deciding whether to use a power of search. The considerations and recommendations for the protection of an individual's rights are also covered, leaving very little doubt about the proper extent of a search and where it can take place. In addition, the Code outlines what documentation must be completed at the end of such a search or encounter.

Code B covers searches of premises by police officers, and the seizure of any property found (including property found on people present on the premises). It provides guidelines on how to protect a person's rights in relation to the conduct of the search, and the record to be made after the search. The Code covers pre-planned searches (with warrants issued by magistrates), as well as searches for the purposes of making an arrest, or a search for stolen or unlawfully possessed property in premises (including items in the possession of people on the premises).

Code C covers the detention, treatment, and questioning of suspects not related to terrorism by police officers, and applies primarily to suspects under arrest. The Code outlines the procedure for protecting an arrested person's rights whilst in detention, and the care he/she must be given while in custody at a police station. However, any person who is not under arrest but who is assisting with an investigation should be treated with 'no less' consideration (Note 1A). The Code emphasizes that discrimination against a detained person with 'protected characteristics' (listed under the Equality Act 2010) is unlawful, and sets out how custody staff can exchange specified information with the detainee, using interpreters and written translations where necessary (see 10.8 for further details). Code C underlines the rights for detainees to communicate with other people, including legal representation, and describes how to protect those rights during questioning (a written notice of the rights is required, see 10.8). A detainee aged 10 to 17 years must have an appropriate adult present (see 25.5.1.1) and a person responsible for his/her welfare (usually a parent or guardian) must be informed. Particular requirements apply for 'vulnerable people' and the definition of 'vulnerable' has been recently updated (see para 1.13d). The Code also covers terrorism-related post-charge questioning and detention under code H.

Code D covers the identification of persons by police officers. It protects the rights of a suspect regarding identification before and after arrest and refers to identification parade procedures, identification by body samples and fingerprints, and showing witnesses photographs of suspects.

Code E covers the audio recording of interviews with suspects (arrested or not), and safeguards the rights of an individual. It sets out that the recordings must be handled securely and in confidence, and allows for breaks during interviews (see 25.5.7 for more details). Audio-recording of voluntary interviews with suspects who have not been arrested is not automatically required (see 25.5.7.1) for offences such as possession of cannabis or khat, shoplifting with a value up to £100, and criminal damage of up to a value of £300.

Code F covers audio-visually recorded interviews with suspects (arrested or not), and outlines the procedures to be followed. At the time of writing there is no statutory requirement to visually record interviews, but the practice is becoming more common.

Code G covers the statutory power of arrest by police officers. It outlines the correct procedures for arresting a person in order that his/her right to liberty is considered at all times (see 4.4), and that proper justification for the arrest is provided (see 10.6.2).

Code H covers suspects arrested on suspicion of being a terrorist under s 41 of the Terrorism Act 2000. Interpreters and written translations must be used where necessary and a written notice of rights and entitlements must be provided to each detainee (as for Code C). Code H ceases to apply once a terrorist suspect has been charged with an offence (Code C then applies), released without charge, or transferred to a prison.

A breach of any of the Codes could result in:

- disciplinary action for the police officer, depending on the circumstances (see 5.6);
- evidence being deemed inadmissible or unfair by a court (s 78(1) PACE Act 1984); and/or
- liability for civil or criminal proceedings.

TASK 5 For each Code, write a brief description of a situation when it might be applied. If you are a trainee officer you might have witnessed such incidents while on Supervised Patrol, and descriptions of these may provide you with material for completion of your assessment portfolio.

Policing in Context

4.7 Answers to Tasks

TASK 1 You should have found that these Regulations cover the fitting of lights, reflectors, and rear markings on vehicles.

TASK 2 You may have considered a number of possible scenarios that might take place on Supervised Patrol. Remember that these rights extend to suspects as well as victims and witnesses. For example, as a trainee officer you may be involved in the arrest and processing of an individual whose grasp of spoken English is poor or non-existent, and participate in the procedures to facilitate communication with him/her. Your assessor would be able to observe your actions directly in this case but you might also need to provide evidence of your knowledge and understanding—for example through evidence in your pocket notebook.

TASK 3 For the offence of robbery, you should have found:

- the Theft Act 1968, s 8(1);
- mode of trial: triable on indictment only;
- maximum penalty for a person found guilty: life imprisonment.

TASK 4 The website <https://courttribunalfinder.service.gov.uk> provides information on local courts.

TASK 5 Your answers might include the following:

Code A: You may have seen people being searched, for example under s 23 Misuse of Drugs Act 1971, s 47 Firearms Act 1968, and s 1 PACE Act 1984. Annex A of the PACE Act 1984 Code A lists the various powers of search (see 9.3 and 9.4).

Code B: you may have seen a premises being searched under s 17 of the PACE Act 1984, in order to find and arrest a suspect. You may also have seen searches of premises at the time of an arrest, under s 32 of the PACE Act 1984, and after arrest under s 18 of the PACE Act 1984. You may also have seen a warrant executed. All these searches would have been carried out with regard to Code B.

Code C: you may have observed people suspected of committing road traffic offences interviewed at the roadside, and the officer recording the interview contemporaneously in his/her pocket notebook.

Code D: you may have seen a witness or victim identify a suspect in the vicinity of an offence soon after the event. You may also have seen an identification parade, where a witness is asked to identify a suspect.

Codes E and F: you may have seen interviews with suspects at your local police station which were recorded, and the steps taken to respect the suspect's rights—for example, explaining how he/she can obtain a copy of the recording. Many forces routinely make AV recordings of interviews.

Code G: you are very likely to have seen suspects arrested (see 10.6), and cautioned at the time of arrest.

5 Roles, Responsibilities, and Support

5.1 Introduction

This chapter of the Handbook covers a wide range of topics that are relevant to the work of the individual police officer. We start with the process of induction into a police organization. Induction is the process of 'bringing in' or initiation, and in some senses, it also refers to a kind of transformation—in this case from being a member of the public to becoming both a member of the public and a police constable. This is likely to take a few months.

You will discover that there are certain symbolic aspects to induction, such as the ceremony that surrounds attestation. Induction is also the assimilation into an organizational culture or cultures. In policing, the process of 'buying into' the existing organizational culture has not been without controversy. For some observers, the prevailing cultures within the police have often been characterized as male-dominated and exclusionary. Allied to this view is the suggestion that initial police training moves you from being an individual to being part of a group, and into a group where it is 'dangerous to be different'. (This is the so-called police 'canteen culture' that you may hear or read about.) The police service is aware of these criticisms and one of the driving forces behind changes to initial police training during the last decade is to create a more inclusive learning environment.

We will examine the Code of Ethics produced by the College of Policing which sets out the necessary attitudes and behaviours, and Police Regulations which also address these matters. We also explain conduct, misconduct, discipline, and complaints, and introduce the various staff associations for police officers, and some of the specialist support groups such as the British Association for Women in Policing (BAWP). This is followed by a description of police IT systems (an increasingly important part of information management) and how information is stored, processed, and communicated, including confidentiality. The importance of effective communication is also considered as this is an essential part of discharging the responsibilities of the police officer. Understanding health and safety is an important part of a police officer's ability to make risk assessments, and this is often covered in conjunction with First Aid, a vital skill for patrol constables.

The topics covered in this chapter (particularly the first parts) are likely to contribute to the learning required for the National Policing Curriculum subject areas: 'Understanding the Police Constable Role', 'Valuing Difference and Inclusion', and 'Maintaining Professional Standards'. We also cover material relevant to 'Communication Skills', 'Decision-making and Discretion', 'Managing Conflict', 'Leadership and Team-working', and 'Well-being and Resilience'.

5.2 **Attestation and the Role of the Police Constable**

After attestation a trainee police officer holds the office of probationary constable, with the position being confirmed after about two calendar years. The origins of the office of constable within law enforcement in the UK can be traced back hundreds of years, although many commentators consider the most significant starting point for the modern-day police service as the year 1829 (see 2.2).

In recent years, constables have become just one of many members of the extended police family; they no longer have a monopoly on certain traditional policing powers. They nonetheless continue to hold a special position within a police organization, as you will discover when working through this chapter and those that follow. The role of police constable, however, is clearly defined in terms of its significant responsibilities, and the high standards required for attitudes, values, and professional knowledge.

There has been much discussion about the possible effects of an individual's personal beliefs and values, and the manner in which these are expressed in their day-to-day actions and decisions. Trainees may feel (somewhat defensively) that they are 'entitled to their opinions' with the implication that their attitudes would have no bearing on their actions. This is obviously an important issue for those engaged in police training and education, and is addressed in other parts of this Handbook. Here, however, we are concerned with how the professional development of a trainee (and the progression to confirmation as constable) links up with the wider common purpose and values of the police service.

We noted in 2.2.3 that having a code of professional conduct is a common feature of the professions. The Police Service Statement of Mission and Values (NPCC, 2016, p 4) is reflected today, almost word for word, in most police forces' own statements. It is a relatively consistent declaration of the guiding principles of the police service, and all police officers, including trainees, are required to work towards the achievement of this statement.

According to the statement, the mission of the police service is to:

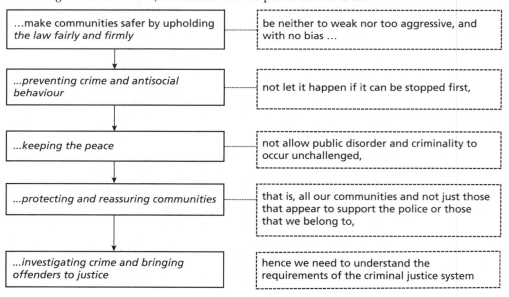

In 2017 a probationary constable was dismissed by Bedfordshire Police for 'discreditable conduct' after 'acting unprofessionally while off-duty' (Bedfordshire Police, 2017). Police officers had been called to the probationer's home in Cambridgeshire after reports that the individual concerned was drunk and behaving aggressively. The probationer was arrested for 'breach of the peace' (see 14.3) and then allegedly acted in an 'uncooperative and belligerent manner' (ibid) and continued being abusive whilst in police custody. Following a hearing for gross misconduct (see 5.6), he was dismissed from the force.

Qualifications and Training

5.2.1 Attestation of police constables

Attestation is the stage at which a trainee police officer is formally given the powers of a police constable—for example, he/she is then able to arrest someone according to the law and Codes of Practice. The legal detail is set out in s 29 of and Sch 4 to the Police Act 1996, as amended by s 83 of the Police Reform Act 2002. (Parallel legislation covers the 'non-Home Office' forces, eg in s 24 of the Railways and Transport Safety Act 2003, for BTP.)

In many forces, attestation occurs early on in a trainee officer's career—sometimes on initial appointment and certainly within the first few weeks. The warrant card can also be issued at attestation (although some forces instead issue a 'trainee police officer identity card').

There is often a formal attestation ceremony to which family and friends may be invited. The declaration is usually taken by a Justice of the Peace (magistrate). The trainee will make a formal declaration (sometimes referred to as an 'Oath') as follows:

> I . . . of . . . do solemnly and sincerely declare and affirm that I will well and truly serve the Queen in the office of constable, with fairness, integrity, diligence, and impartiality, upholding fundamental human rights and according equal respect to all people; and that I will, to the best of my power, cause the peace to be kept and preserved and prevent all offences against people and property; and that while I continue to hold the said office I will, to the best of my skill and knowledge, discharge all the duties thereof faithfully according to law.

An alternative Welsh-language version can be used in Wales and there are alternative versions for police officers in Scotland and Northern Ireland, and in the BTP.

The making of a declaration may seem somewhat old-fashioned. However, it is worth bearing in mind that the declaration police officers make has a statutory basis in law and its symbolic importance remains strong, both within police culture and in the wider political and social world.

> **TASK 1** Trainee police officers should learn the declaration for the attestation word for word! Note that you will probably be given a card to read from at actual attestation, or be asked to follow another's lead. However, you are likely to be required to memorize information on a number of occasions during training (eg definitions) and this task is good practice.

5.3 The Code of Ethics

The Code of Ethics was introduced by the College of Policing in July 2014 and is available from the College of Policing website. It was issued as a code of practice under s 39A(5) of the Police Act 1996, as amended by s 124 of the Anti-social Behaviour, Crime and Policing Act 2014 (CoP, 2014a). The Code of Ethics is central to the professionalization of the police service and police practices. All police officers and staff must observe the Code and ensure it is applied for all police officers, staff, and volunteers engaged in policing within the service.

The Code of Ethics is incorporated as a central feature of the National Decision Model (see 5.5.2). The Code comprises the standards of professional behaviour and the policing principles, and complements the Police Service Statement of Mission and Values (see 5.2). Initial police training will frequently involve direct contact with both the public and fellow members of the extended policing family (eg PCSOs), so it is important that all trainees read and understand the Code because it applies to all areas of police work.

Attested police officers are not employees in the conventional meaning of the term; they are instead holders of public office. One consequence of this is that all police officers' activities both on and off duty are covered by the Code of Ethics, and regulated by law through Statutory Instruments. Any breach of the Code can be dealt with in a variety of ways, from peer or group challenge through to using the police regulations. Professional judgement, proportionality, and the severity and impact of the breach will all need to be taken into account.

5.3.1 The Standards of Professional Behaviour and the Policing Principles

The ten standards of professional behaviour are the minimum standards that both trainee and confirmed police officers must maintain, and are listed c 2020. They are:

	Standard	Description
1	Honesty and Integrity	Police officers are honest, act with integrity, and do not compromise or abuse their position.
2	Authority, Respect, and Courtesy	Police officers act with self-control and tolerance, treating members of the public and colleagues with respect and courtesy. Police officers do not abuse their powers or authority and respect the rights of all individuals.
3	Equality and Diversity	Police officers act with fairness and impartiality. They do not discriminate unlawfully or unfairly.
4	Use of Force	Police officers only use force to the extent that it is necessary, proportionate, and reasonable in all the circumstances.
5	Orders and Instructions	Police officers only give and carry out lawful orders and instructions. Police officers abide by police regulations, force policies, and lawful orders.
6	Duties and Responsibilities	Police officers are diligent in the exercise of their duties and responsibilities. Police officers have a responsibility to give appropriate cooperation during investigations, inquiries and formal proceedings, participating openly and professionally in line with the expectations of a police officer when identified as a witness.
7	Confidentiality	Police officers treat information with respect and access or disclose it only in the proper course of police duties.
8	Fitness for Duty	Police officers when on duty or presenting themselves for duty are fit to carry out their responsibilities.
9	Discreditable Conduct	Police officers behave in a manner which does not discredit the police service or undermine public confidence in it, whether on or off duty. Police officers report any action taken against them for a criminal offence, any conditions imposed on them by a court or the receipt of any penalty notice.
10	Challenging and Reporting Improper Conduct	Police officers report, challenge, or take action against the conduct of colleagues which has fallen below the standards of professional behaviour.

Note that the Police Service of Northern Ireland (PSNI) has its own standards of professional behaviour, available on their website.

The general attitudes and approaches to police work are also underpinned by the Policing Principles which are 'Accountability, Fairness, Honesty, Integrity, Leadership, Objectivity, Openness, Respect and Selflessness' (CoP, 2014a). Further details are provided on the College of Policing website.

> **TASK 2** In December 2017 a sergeant from Sussex Police was dismissed from the service following a disciplinary hearing, after it had been discovered that he was spending parts of his night shifts visiting two women with whom he was having sexual relationships. Which of the standards of professional behaviour may have been breached by this officer's conduct?

5.4 The Police Regulations and Conditions of Service

Conditions of service for police constables are also regulated by law under various Police Regulations contained in Statutory Instruments. Because of their length and complexity these will not be dealt with in their entirety here, but they are presented here in a summarized and simplified form, with extra explanations in places. Full details may be found in other textbooks such as *Blackstone's Police Manual: Volume 4 General Police Duties 2020* and online. At the moment of attestation a trainee police officer becomes subject to police regulations, such as the 2003 Regulations as described in the following paragraphs. Note that the Police (Performance) Regulations 2012 do not apply for trainee officers.

5.4.1 Restrictions on private life and business interests

These are set out in Sch 1 to the Police Regulations 2003 which states that 'The restrictions on private life...shall apply to all members of a police force' (reg 6(1)) and that:

> A member of a police force shall at all times abstain from any activity which is likely to interfere with the impartial discharge of [his/her] duties or which is likely to give rise to the impression amongst members of the public that it may so interfere; and in particular a member of a police force shall not take any active part in politics. (Sch 1, para 1)

In other words, a police officer must not pursue a course of conduct which members of the public will perceive as favouritism, and especially must not be active in politics. In addition, a police officer 'shall not wilfully refuse or neglect to discharge any lawful debt' (Sch 1, para 4). This does not mean a police officer cannot have a mortgage or a car loan (as these are lawful), but any debt which could place the officer in danger of being coerced is unacceptable.

The Police (Amendment No 3) Regulations 2012 state in reg 8 that:

> [i]f a member of a police force has or proposes to have a business interest which has not previously been disclosed, or, is or becomes aware that a relative has or proposes to have a business interest which, in the opinion of the member, interferes or could be seen as interfering with the impartial discharge of the member's duties and has not previously been disclosed the member shall immediately give written notice of that business interest to the chief officer.

For the purposes of their integrity and credibility, police officers must disclose business interests in order that they may be checked for compatibility with the role of a constable.

> **TASK 3** Find out about the procedure in your police area for police officers to declare any business interests.

5.4.2 Personal records, fingerprints, and samples

In relation to personal records, reg 15 of the Police Regulations 2003 states that the chief officer of a police force 'shall cause a personal record of each member of the police force to be kept' throughout a police officer's service. It will contain details of the officer and his/her relatives, a history of courses attended, expertise gained, promotions achieved, and the outcomes of any disciplinary investigations.

Regulation 18 of the Police Regulations 2003 concerns taking and recording a police officer's fingerprints, for the purposes of eliminating him/her from any forensic investigation. Quite often this takes place early on in training, and sometimes as part of initial training on forensic awareness. Regulation 19 of the Police Regulations 2003 obliges an officer to supply a sample such as a mouth swab for DNA analysis, again for the purposes of elimination. In addition, any officer can be selected for random drug testing (Police Regulations 2003 and Police (Amendment No 2) Regulations 2012).

5.4.3 Duty to carry out lawful orders

Regulation 20 of the Police Regulations 2003 states that every member of a police force:

> shall carry out all lawful orders and shall at all times punctually and promptly perform all appointed duties and attend to all matters within the scope of [his/her] office as a constable.

The police service has a rank structure (see 2.3.1) in which supervisors and managers may require certain actions to be carried out. Police officers are expected to carry out these orders, if they are lawful.

> **TASK 4** If you are undertaking the Police Constable Degree Apprenticeship (PCDA) or the Degree Holders Entry Programme (DHEP), take the opportunity to reflect upon these regulations and the police Code of Ethics. Section 5.2 of the Code states that a police officer should:
>
> > follow lawful orders, recognizing that any decision not to follow an order needs to be objectively and fully justified.
>
> Which areas do you think are going to be easy for you to satisfy, and which areas do you need to consider at greater length? How, for example, would you know that an order was unlawful?

Qualifications and Training

5.4.4 Discharge of a trainee police officer

Under reg 13 of the Police Regulations 2003 a trainee officer can be dismissed. This is covered more fully in 6.6.4 along with extending the probationary period under reg 12. However, before being discharged, a trainee can give notice of 'retirement', ie resign, although he/she must first obtain the appropriate authority from the chief officer (or delegated authority), (Police (Conduct) (Amendment) Regulations 2014).

5.5 Decision-making in Policing

The legitimacy, authority, and even effectiveness of the police depend on the exercise of ethical decision-making. In essence this means that there is an expectation on the police, from the public and others, that they make decisions based on a set of ethical principles, and not in an arbitrary manner, or according to emotional response or prejudice. We will examine the ethical basis to policing, how ethics are reflected in decision-making, and finally the ways in which police officers might fall short of the ethical requirements expected of the police service.

5.5.1 Ethics and policing

Ethics are important for all police officers because if police methods and procedures do not meet high ethical standards then the authority of the police will be undermined, and the public may have less trust in the police and the law. The expected standards of behaviour are clearly defined in existing documents, but ethics is also about personal ideas, and if a police officer's actions are to ring true, his/her own rules of moral behaviour (or personal ethics) need to correspond with the force's formal requirements. Diversity training provides trainees with further opportunities for considering personal views and feelings about a range of possible attitudes and behaviours.

A number of official documents set out guidance (in varying degrees of detail and levels of official standing) concerning police ethics and behaviour. These documents include:

- the Policing Professional Profiles;
- the Police (Conduct) Regulations 2020;
- the Police (Complaints and Misconduct) Regulations 2020;
- the Police (Performance) Regulations 2020;
- the Police Regulations 2003; and
- the College of Policing Code of Ethics.

The Police (Conduct) Regulations 2020 contain the 'Standards of Professional Behaviour' (see 5.3.1), guidance on police officer behaviour when off duty (see also 5.4), and misconduct procedures (see 5.6). There are similar documents for police officers in Northern Ireland, Scotland, and non-Home Office Forces.

The police have always been affected by changes in customs, beliefs, and social morality. Policing norms are shaped by wider social norms, so any ethical questions about what police officers ought to do in particular circumstances are interpreted according to the moral values of the day. For example, there has been a shift in police practice from being responsive to being proactive, and more emphasis is placed on preventing crime.

> **TASK 5** What is policing by consent, and how might this differ from when police were introduced in 1829?

In recent years policing has been informed increasingly by the need to demonstrate value for money (sometimes through reductions in police staffing levels) and to meet targets set by government. This form of 'managerialism' has been criticized by some chief officers because it leads to police officers becoming over-concerned with meeting targets, and because it is not always easy to measure the wide variety of activities involved in professional policing.

The role of police in international peacekeeping (alongside a military presence and other supporting agencies from different parts of the world) demands an ethical consistency across different organizations with very different values and traditions. This might sometimes include British police officers working alongside officers from other countries where there may be widespread corruption and the status of police officers is very low.

TASK 6 Consider corruption, bribery, political use of the police, low pay, low status, and paramilitary policing, all of which can be found in some other countries. Draw a flow diagram showing how these factors might interact. Use arrows to show how one factor could be the cause of another. (An example of this particular use of arrows is shown in the diagram below: the arrow shows that poor pay leads to low status.)

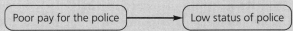

Note that there are no certain answers to this exercise; you might argue that it is the low status that is causing the low pay.

One of the key skills trainee police officers have to develop during training is the ability to apply discretion (see 5.5.3), and this is linked with ethics. For example, imagine a trainee on Supervised Patrol and her tutor are called to deal with a theft at a supermarket, with instructions to investigate the matter and decide upon a course of action. The offender is a confused 94-year-old man who has apparently picked up a bag of apples and wandered out of the store, pursued by store detectives. The old man had technically committed a crime, but there were mitigating circumstances: his age and frailty must be taken into account, and proving 'intention permanently to deprive' (the basis of the Theft Act 1968 (see 16.2)) would be somewhat difficult. Enforcing the law might not be the most appropriate response, but police officers have to be prepared to justify the reasons for any decision (see 5.5.2 on the NDM).

5.5.2 The National Decision Model

The police routinely make difficult decisions in fast moving situations, where the information may be incomplete, or some members of the public may be trying to deliberately mislead or undermine police responses. Ethical decision-making in policing is informed by the National Decision Model (NDM). The model consists of a number of elements, with the Code of Ethics being central. The wording of the NDM is mainly drawn from operational police culture, but the intention is that anyone making decisions in the police service (both operational and non-operational) should use it.

The NDM, introduced in 2012, appears to have been developed in part from the Conflict Management Model (CMM) which was employed for decision-making in the context of public order and firearms incidents. The models are similar, although the NDM is focused around the Code of Ethics, and includes 'review' as one of the essential elements. The NDM relates to ACPO's 2011 Statement of Mission and Values, and ACPO suggested it would support decision-making which had been undertaken by police officers who had followed the NDM; the IOPC will provide similar support. The topics covered in 5.5.2 are likely to contribute to the learning required for the National Policing Curriculum subject area: 'Decision-making and Discretion'.

When making decisions using the NDM the mnemonic CIAPOAR can be used as an aide-memoire:

- Code of Ethics—the policing principles and standards of professional behaviour;
- Information—gather information and intelligence;
- Assessment—assess threat and risk and develop a working strategy;
- Powers and policy—consider powers and policy;
- Options—identify the options and contingencies;
- Action—take action;
- Review.

In essence, the NDM seeks to provide the policy basis and ethical underpinning for taking action, or for deciding not to act. Police officers might sometimes need to work outside policy if the circumstances require, but justification and documentation is still required. Reservations concerning the applicability of the NDM have been expressed, particularly with respect to criminal investigations (see 24.2.1).

The College of Policing APP outlines a number of principles that are fundamental to the NDM (CoP, 2014c), to encourage and support professional judgement. As professionals, the police have to be able to make decisions in uncertain conditions, and the first consideration should be public safety and security. When judging possible risks from decisions the possible benefits and harm must be taken into account, and it must be accepted that harm can never be totally prevented. Therefore, a decision involving risk should be judged by how good the decision-making was, and not by the actual outcome, so any police officer who has followed these principles when making a decision should be supported. The principles clearly state that making decisions concerning risk is inherently difficult, that the extent to which an officer's decisions present risks should be judged in comparison with others in a similar professional position, and that deciding whether to record decisions about risk is a matter of professional judgement. It is emphasized that examples of good risk taking should be identified and shared, and that communication and cooperation with other agencies will help to improve decision-making (CoP, 2018m).

5.5.3 Police discretion

According to Jones, police discretion is the 'freedom of the individual officer to act according to his or her own judgement in particular situations' (as cited in Newburn and Neyroud, 2008, p 82). We could perhaps replace the word 'freedom' with 'duty' or 'obligation', and refer to 'professional judgement', to emphasize that the concept of police discretion is founded within the notion of the 'office of constable'. This establishes the legal status of a police officer as a holder of original authority. An example of this is that a police officer cannot be ordered to arrest a person, and must take responsibility for deciding whether arrest is appropriate or not, given the circumstances (see 10.6). In this sense, discretion should be seen more as a professional burden than a freedom, as freedom implies rather too much subjectivity. Police officers are not robots, programmed to respond to every crime they encounter by arrest and charge, and policing is about more than law enforcement; it is carried out in the public interest with a view to securing primarily a more peaceful society. In terms of good policing, law enforcement is just one means to an end, and would be inappropriate in some contexts. For example it would not be practical or legitimate to arrest and charge for every offence because it could undermine the relationship between police and public (see 2.2.5). Nor would it be likely to have any significant impact on levels of crime (although see zero-tolerance policing models (8.3.3.2) and also the association between offences and criminality discussed in Chapter 3).

Thus the exercise of discretion is an important, even fundamental policing skill. Indeed, Lord Scarman stated:

> [T]he exercise of discretion lies at the heart of the policing function. It is undeniable that there is only one law for all: and it is right that this should be so. But it is equally well recognised that successful policing depends on the exercise of discretion on how the law is enforced. . . . Discretion is the art of suiting action to particular circumstances. (Scarman, 1981, para 4.58)

Chan (2003) has noted that, in the early stages of initial police training, officers are hungry for basic technical knowledge; you might well agree! This is understandable because police officers require the basic know-how skills in order to feel confident enough to perform duties (under the supervision of a tutor) in operational settings such as Supervised Patrol (see 5.11.1.2 on epistemic authority). Police discretion is a subject that does not fit easily under the umbrella of basic technical knowledge, unlike most of the other learning for trainee officers. Nonetheless, it is important to understand what police discretion is (and what it is not), because it is relevant to much of the everyday work of a police officer. It is the vital ingredient which justifies police work as a profession, or in Neyroud and Beckley's words (2001, p 86), discretion is 'the essence of informed professionalism in policing'.

If police discretion is to be maintained, however, it is important that we make a positive case for it. We need to identify a number of ways in which police discretion is often misrepresented, for example the idea that police discretion is nothing more than applying common sense, or that it can amount to discrimination.

5.5.3.1   Defining and using discretion

Police discretion does not only apply to frontline officers. It also applies to the kinds of decisions that police managers and chief officers must make, described by Neyroud and Beckley (2001) as 'prioritizing decisions' and 'tactical decisions'. The former relates primarily to the allocation of limited resources and the latter relates to the balancing of liberty and order in a liberal democratic society. In a similar vein, Delattre (2002) discusses the need for senior investigative officers to make anticipatory and planning decisions about, for example, when to identify and release information about a serial killer. These are all good examples of police discretionary decisions and it is important for new police officers to be aware of why and how these kinds of decisions are made. However, here we will focus on discretion for frontline officers: in other words, the kind of decisions that patrol constables (and therefore trainee officers) are expected to make on a daily basis.

Discretion often involves choosing between different law enforcement options. For example, officers are regularly confronted with minor offences that present a choice of issuing fixed penalty tickets or making an arrest and taking the suspect to the police station. It has been argued that:

> Under-enforcement as opposed to choosing how to enforce the law, has led to concerns because it is seen by some to occur as a consequence of either an officer's 'misappropriation of judicial power' or an officer's 'discrimination'. (Neyroud and Beckley, 2001, pp 85–6)

Clearly anyone who is given a verbal warning or reprimand instead of being charged or arrested is unlikely to complain about it. But it could be argued that a person who has committed an offence merits the law's full weight of sanction, and that everyone (who has committed an identical offence) deserves to be punished in the same way. Some people think it is unfair that not all offenders have the law enforced against them, and critics of under-enforcement point to the inconsistency in applying the law. This calls into question the fundamental right of the police to employ discretionary powers.

One simple answer (proposed by the critics of police discretion) is to remove police discretion altogether, or at least reduce the extent to which officers can draw upon it. There would be practical problems with this. For instance, the criminal justice system already struggles to cope with the existing caseload; how would it cope if the police enforced the law without discretion? Another problem is that police work is extremely difficult to manage (see Chapter 2 in Reiner, 2000). Most officers operate alone or with a partner, and as Crawshaw *et al* note (1998, p 24), police supervision tends to occur after the event. These problems illustrate the extent and relevance of police discretion, but they are not really sufficient arguments for justifying its use; we will need to look more deeply!

Governments have periodically introduced legislation and guidelines to restrict the amount of discretion a police officer can use. This may be reflected in force policies as well, for example in relation to the policing of domestic violence, 'positive action' policies (including arrest at a domestic incident, see 13.6.1) have been applied across the UK, effectively reducing the use of discretion.

The police should make law-enforcement decisions based upon their interpretation of what is best for the public interest. It is this balancing act between law enforcement and the needs of society that gives rise to police discretion. The police are expected to use the law to maintain order, and therefore they need discretionary powers in order to use the law as effectively as possible, within legal boundaries. But they should not be required to enforce the law mechanically in every circumstance. In this respect the police are accountable not only to the law but also to the people they police.

5.5.3.2   Discretion and common sense

The view that police discretion is a matter of applying common sense to policing situations would initially appear to have some merit. It helps police officers understand how real operational experiences complement the necessarily theoretical and abstract learning which takes place during the initial period of police training. Officers learn to use the law as a means to an end rather than as an end in itself.

However, it is too simplistic to view police discretion as the mere application of common sense, as this suggests that discretionary decisions are straightforward and could be applied by anyone. It also fails to distinguish between the decisions that are just simple, common sense decisions and the decisions that genuinely require the use of discretion. As Davis (1996) notes, not all choices are discretionary. Police discretion cannot be simply reduced to being a matter of making choices or decisions.

5.5.3.3 Police discretion and subjectivity

Another way of considering discretion is that maybe every police officer has a unique subjectivity that produces different approaches to how the law is interpreted and enforced. However, although the individual subjectivities of officers clearly play an important role in day-to-day policing, this should not be confused with police discretion. Indeed, police discretion is necessary precisely because it provides a way of curbing the influence of individual subjectivity.

Should we expect all police officers to make the same decision in identical circumstances? We should note that the question is not entirely fair because in reality no two sets of circumstances are ever identical. Nonetheless, the existence of police discretion implies the answer cannot be a clear cut 'yes' or 'no'. But if every officer makes a different decision, in what sense are these decisions connected, and how do they relate to policing principles and practice? The answer is that we should expect officers' decisions to differ, but that there will be a finite number of decision categories, normally two or three. Ideally, each of these categories would represent good police decisions that could be justified and explained. (More realistically, we might expect a few officers to make decisions that fall into another separate category, one that represents bad police decisions.) There are only a limited number of valid options open for consideration because each option must adhere to professional standards, integrity, the law, and force policy. The legal philosopher Ronald Dworkin has explained this point by referring to discretion as the 'hole in the doughnut' (see Neyroud and Beckley, 2001, p 83). This analogy suggests that discretion is given meaning by the professionalism (the dough) surrounding it—the hole in a ring doughnut only exists because of the dough. If we eat the ring, the hole disappears too. Likewise, without professional standards, discretion becomes meaningless; police discretion cannot exist if there is no professional policing context.

Just as professional standards limit the number of options available to officers, the same standards also allow for different responses. Subjectivity is not an adequate answer because it would mean that law enforcement is too arbitrary. It is not acceptable that a man is arrested only because he encountered officer A, rather than officer B or C. All police responses are only valid to the extent that they can be explained and justified in terms of professional standards, and not just as a product of a subjective perspective. To reiterate and emphasize the point, discretion reduces the influence of subjectivity by providing an objective, professional guide to decision-making.

5.5.3.4 Discretion and judicial misappropriation

We have noted that some critics see police discretion as nothing more than an individual officer's misappropriation of judicial power. The reasoning behind this is that if an individual has clearly committed an offence an officer who decides not to enforce the law is effectively acting as judge and jury. This view is based upon a long-standing misconception of the police officer's role; that the police are merely law enforcers. Waddington (1999) observed (with reference to the surprise expressed by researchers into policing in the 1960s):

> the prevailing assumption had been that policing was little more than the application of the law ... Criminals committed crimes and the police captured the criminals who were tried and convicted by the courts. (Waddington, 1999, p 31)

Indeed, Waddington refers to the discretionary powers of the police as being 'discovered' in the 1960s. Of course police officers had been exercising discretion since the creation of the modern police in 1829, but it was not an aspect of police work that had received much attention. As more research has been conducted, it has been found that the police have consistently enforced the law more against certain sections of society and less against others, and to some extent the evidence suggests that this is still the case (see 5.5.3.5).

There can be no defence for the police discriminating against certain sections of society, but that does not mean that the police should have their power of discretion removed. Instead, maybe police officers should be seen more as 'peace officers' than law enforcers (Banton, 1964). Waddington (1999) has argued that the police use the law as and when appropriate in order to bring about a greater sense of peace and order in society. He refers also to Lord Scarman's warning following the Brixton riots in 1981 'that the maintenance of "public tranquillity" was a higher priority than "law enforcement"' (Waddington, 1999, p 42).

5.5.3.5 Discretion and discrimination

The view that discretion is the means by which certain sections of society are discriminated against has arisen from research conducted since the 1960s. Why are some sections of society more likely than others to have the law enforced against them? In their defence, police officers have argued that they do not discriminate against any sections of society but respond to each individual they encounter depending on how that individual responds to them. This is referred to in police circles as the attitude test. (You will no doubt hear more experienced police officers using this phrase, or more colloquial versions.) Quite simply, an individual who is polite and repentant is less likely to have the law enforced against him/her. The supposed rationale is that he/she appears to have learnt a lesson and seems unlikely to reoffend. An intervention by a police officer is in itself an effective form of remonstration and can help to prevent repeat offending. It may not be in the public interest to pursue certain cases further, as this would contribute nothing towards achieving a more ordered society (and apart from the wasted expense, it could have a negative effect on the individual stopped). On the other hand, it is argued that if the individual stopped by the police officer is rude, abusive, and unrepentant, then it is assumed that further action needs to be taken to make sure he/she feels sufficiently reprimanded.

But such practice may just perpetuate problems in society. People who regularly come into contact with the police are more likely to be immune to police warnings and will feel more confident in challenging authority. They are more likely to be abusive and to have an existing antagonistic relationship with the police. Historically, individuals from certain ethnic minority groupings have had a disproportionately high interaction with the police, and the attitude test helps to perpetuate this. Police officers must therefore take great care in such situations.

We discuss epistemic authority in 5.11.1.2, and note the need for police officers to have a sound knowledge of the law. Increasingly, however, in relation to police discretion, police officers also need to know what actually works in policing; what is effective and what is not effective, and why different individuals are likely to respond in different ways to similar police interventions. Clearly, a police officer with a better knowledge and understanding of the contexts in which he/she is operating will be able to apply discretionary reasoning more effectively.

Efforts have been made to promote this kind of information in police culture, and to rectify any resulting adverse or confrontational attitudes. There have undoubtedly been some low points; for example, see Macpherson (1999) and *The Secret Policeman* programme (2003). This programme was about an undercover journalist, Mark Daly, who joined Greater Manchester Police as a trainee officer and spent 15 weeks at the Bruche Centrex regional Police Training Centre, near Warrington. He secretly filmed some of his fellow trainees and the trainers delivering the programme, and recorded racist language and attitudes amongst some of his fellow trainees and inappropriate behaviour by some trainers. However, as Daly himself noted in 2003:

> The majority of the officers I met will undoubtedly turn out to be good, non-prejudiced ones intent on doing the job properly. But the next generation of officers from one of Britain's top police colleges contains a significant minority of people who are holding the progress of the police service back. (Daly, 2003)

Today's police officers are in a much better position to understand the negative way in which some people from ethnic minorities respond to the attitude test, and officers understand how to speak and act in a manner that can help break the cycle. This is due mostly to the programmes for equality and diversity training and development, which are compulsory for all officers.

The important difference between discriminatory and discretionary decisions is that discrimination is based upon prejudice, whereas discretion is premised upon professional judgement (which incorporates many different factors, including the prevalence of discrimination in previous times). This requires officers to go beyond simply providing a common standard

Qualifications and Training

by which every individual encounter is measured. Officers are required to respond to each encounter individually, taking into account the specifics of each situation. As Rowe (2002) has noted, since the Macpherson Report (1999) policing no longer treats everyone equally but rather pursues specific policies aimed at reducing discrimination, for example by actively promoting an anti-racist agenda. It is now part of the police officer's role to break the cycle of discrimination.

TASK 7 In the following task you are given two scenarios to consider. The first is taken from the 1995 National Police Training notes and the second is our own invention.

1. You see a woman, who appears to be slightly drunk, pick up a street sign that was on the ground, conceal it under her coat, and walk off. When stopped, she readily admits that she intends to keep it as a trophy. She is a medical student who is celebrating passing her final exam (NPT, 1995, p 4).
2. You are on duty outside a football ground when you observe a young man, clutching a can of super-strength lager, pick up an 'Away Supporters' sign from the ground, conceal it under his hoodie, and walk off. When stopped, he readily admits that he intends to keep it to start a collection. He is celebrating his club's victory in an important match.

In each case consider what discretion, if any, you would exercise.

5.5.4 Police corruption

In a culture where ethical decision-making in policing is not valued, corruption may flourish. Research has shown that corruption can occur in any part of the police service, and therefore we need to understand how widespread corruption is likely to be, and how we might prevent it. In December 2018, a former Cheshire police officer was sentenced to 25 years' imprisonment for a total of 37 sexual offences including rape (Halliday, 2018). In fact, 'corruption for the purposes of sexual gratification' amongst police officers seems to be on the increase (HMIC, 2015a, p 110). For example, in 2016 the BBC found there had been 436 reported allegations of abuse of authority by police officers for sexual gain in a period of two years (BBC, 2016).

TASK 8 What sort of opportunities do you think there might be for corruption in relation to drugs policing in particular?

TASK 9 Consider the following list of factors that might contribute to an officer's decision to act corruptly:

- lack of personal integrity;
- corrupt police officers providing a role model;
- the pressure for results;
- abuse or assault from members of the public;
- the difficulties in securing convictions;
- belief that sentencing was not adequate for the crime committed;
- the first arrival at the scene of a crime, when cash or goods may be lying about;
- personal financial pressures;
- handling and storing drugs from police investigations;
- the 'long hours, low reward' culture, leading to envy of others more fortunately placed;
- lack of effective supervision;
- the excessive exercise of discretion without challenge;
- feelings of bitterness or resentment at not receiving expected promotion; and
- managing informants without adequate supervision or scrutiny.

Most of them are about predisposition—motivations for an officer to act corruptly. But an opportunity is also required; list the five factors from the list which provide opportunities to act corruptly.

There are a number of more general theories about the causes of corruption. One such theory is that the metaphorical (in some cases, actual) free cup of coffee is enough to start a police officer on the slippery slope to corruption. The idea is that from a free cup of coffee it is but a short step to a free meal, then free entry to a club, then preferential treatment, then provision of goods and inducements, and finally the offer to engage in joint criminal exploits. By accepting the free cup of coffee, the officer could be indicating a willingness to be corrupted.

> **TASK 10** How convinced are you by the 'free cup of coffee' theory? Can you see any flaws in it? Can you think of examples that might challenge the theory?

The 'bad apple' theory argues that a corrupt police officer or staff member is an isolated instance, and that the solution is to simply remove the individual officer. The 'bent for the job' theory (also known as 'noble cause' corruption) is a third explanation for corruption. It was argued that the law was so inadequately structured that substantial numbers of the guilty went unpunished, and that officers felt obliged to be devious and underhand because it seemed the only way to achieve results (see Newburn, 2015, for a literature review of police integrity and corruption).

5.6   Misconduct and Complaints Procedures

Police misconduct and complaint procedures are primarily governed by three pieces of legislation namely: Police (Complaints and Misconduct) Regulations 2020, Police (Conduct) Regulations 2020, and Police (Performance) Regulations 2020. These regulations are outlined in *Home Office Guidance: Conduct, Efficiency and Effectiveness: Statutory Guidance on Professional Standards, Performance and Integrity in Policing* (Home Office, 2020b).

'Misconduct' under the Police (Conduct) Regulations 2020 is defined as 'a breach of the Standards of Professional Behaviour that is so serious as to justice disciplinary action'. 'Gross misconduct' is a more serious failure to meet the standards (so serious that it could lead to dismissal). Allegations concerning the conduct of a police officer fall into one of two categories:

- 'conduct matters', which concern allegations made against a police officer by a colleague; and
- 'complaints' which are allegations made by a member of the public about the conduct of a police officer.

The process of making such allegations, the investigation and subsequent methods of disposal, are together known as the Police Complaints System.

Complaints and conduct matters can be handled by a line manager or supervisor, or if more serious by the 'appropriate authority' or the Independent Office for Police Conduct (IOPC). The appropriate authority would be a chief officer (chief constable or commissioner), but he/she can delegate this function to a police officer of at least the rank of chief inspector, or another police staff member of at least a similar level of seniority. This will frequently be an officer within a Professional Standards Department.

5.6.1   Conduct matters

Police officers are required to abide by the standards of professional behaviour (see 5.3.1). This includes the tenth standard that requires a police officer to report, challenge, or take action against the conduct of any colleague whose behaviour has fallen below any of the other nine Standards. Failure to report such instances would render the officer liable for claims of misconduct. Normally, an officer should report any concerns to his/her supervisor or the Professional Standards Department, but concerns can also be raised confidentially with the IOPC (see 5.6.3) as it is designated as an official body for the purposes of public interest disclosure.

The flowchart summarizes the procedures for handling an allegation relating to 'conduct matters'. These decisions would be taken by the appropriate authority—usually local senior officers. The possible sanctions are described in 5.6.4.

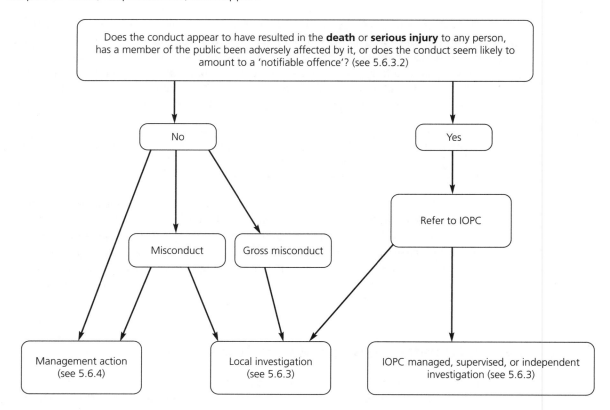

5.6.2   Complaints

Allegations made by members of the public concerning the conduct or behaviour of a police officer (trainee or confirmed) are called complaints. Examples might include complaints of rudeness, the use of excessive force, or unjustified arrest. Allegations can only be made by a member of the public who:

- claims to be the victim of the conduct;
- claims to have been adversely affected by the conduct (but is not the victim);
- claims to have witnessed the conduct; or
- is a person who is representing any of the above.

The appropriate course of action will be decided by the 'appropriate authority' (defined earlier).

Statutory guidance on the handling of complaints is available (IOPC, 2020) The flowchart summarizes the current process for managing complaints.

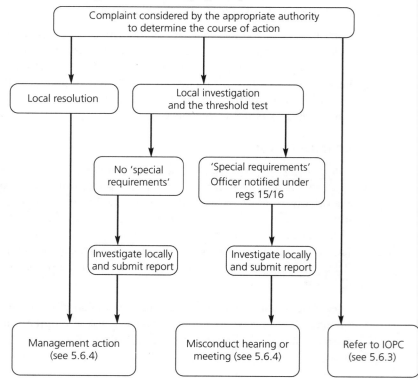

The threshold test establishes whether it appears likely that the officer who is the subject of the complaint has committed a criminal offence or behaved in such a way that disciplinary proceedings are likely to be required. If this applies, the investigation will be subject to 'special requirements', and the officer must be formally notified about the investigation (see 5.6.3.3).

5.6.3 Investigations and the Independent Office for Police Conduct

The Independent Office for Police Conduct (IOPC) can initiate investigations without the need for a force to record and refer a particular case for investigation. The Director General of the IOPC is Michael Lockwood, a former chief executive of Harrow Council. He is assisted by a board of directors (Home Office, 2017b). The IOPC will not only investigate allegations involving the police but they will also deal with serious complaints and conduct matters relating to staff at the NCA, GLAA, Home Office, HMRC, Mayor's Office for Policing and Crime (MOPAC), and Police and Crime Commissioners.

When the IOPC receives a referral from a police force the IOPC assessment unit reviews the information they have received. The IOPC then decide if the matter requires an investigation, and if so of what type. There are four different types of investigation: local, supervised, managed, and independent, as shown in the diagram.

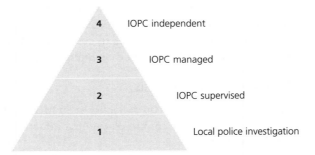

The diagram tapers towards the top as there are fewer high-level investigations, and as you might expect, the more serious the matter, the higher the level of the investigation, and the greater the level of direct IOPC involvement.

5.6.3.1 Local police investigations and local resolution

A local investigation is carried out for less serious matters and the IOPC will not be involved. It would usually be carried out by the force's Professional Standards Department, and be similar to any other police enquiry, including, for example, the collection of evidence through interviews from witnesses and suspects. The investigator is appointed by the appropriate authority, and the officer under investigation must be notified (under reg 15 of the Police (Conduct) Regulations 2012, or reg 16 of the Police (Complaints and Misconduct) Regulations 2012). Further information is provided in 5.6.3.3.

Local (or informal) resolution may be possible, in which case regulation 15/16 notices (see 5.6.3.3) are not required, no blame is attached, nor is there any need to involve disciplinary procedures. The process will not affect a trainee officer's personal development plan, staff appraisal, or any subsequent misconduct hearing. Note that a police force cannot make an apology to the complainant unless this is authorized by the officer against whom the complaint was made.

5.6.3.2 Investigations involving the IOPC

Investigations into more serious matters will involve the IOPC. An IOPC-**supervised** investigation is used for complaints or allegations of misconduct which are of considerable significance and probable public concern. It will be supervised by the IOPC but conducted, directed, and controlled by the police. The complainant has the right of appeal to the IOPC. An IOPC-**managed** investigation takes place when the alleged incident is more serious and likely to cause higher levels of public concern, and therefore the subsequent investigation must have an independent element. The IOPC direct and control the process, whilst the police conduct the investigation. An **independent** IOPC investigation is used for incidents that cause the greatest level of public concern, have the greatest potential to impact on communities, or have serious implications for the reputation of the police service (for deaths in custody). These require a wholly independent investigation conducted only by IOPC staff.

There is no right of appeal against an IOPC-managed or independent investigation except through judicial review, a form of court proceedings which checks that the correct procedures have been used.

5.6.3.3   Notification

The officer in question must be notified for all investigations that are:

- referred to the IOPC;
- into a complaint where special requirements apply; or
- into conduct matters where it seems likely there has been misconduct or gross misconduct, a notifiable offence, a death, or serious injury.

The notice must be served in writing and as soon as practicable. It will be served under reg 15 of the Police (Conduct) Regulations 2012 or reg 16 of the Police (Complaints and Misconduct) Regulations 2012. (The same form is used for both conduct matters and complaints.) The notice may be referred to in police circles as a 'reg 15' (with a hard 'g'). A notice may also be given for less serious investigations.

The notice will include a description of the conduct, the outcome of the severity or threshold test, and a reminder that the officer has the opportunity to seek advice from the Police Federation. The Police Federation advises any officer receiving a reg 15/16 notice not to say anything before seeking advice from a Federation representative. If the officer is to be interviewed, once again the advice is to contact a Federation representative who will arrange to attend the interview or, in some circumstances, help to arrange for legal representation.

5.6.4   Outcomes and sanctions

After the evidence has been collected in an investigation the appropriate authority decides if the officer's behaviour amounted to misconduct or gross misconduct. The various outcomes are shown in the flowchart.

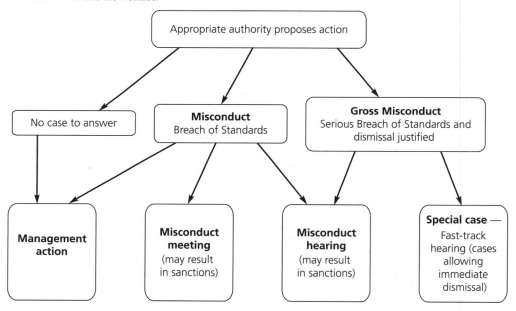

A misconduct meeting may be held for an officer falling slightly short of the standards of professional behaviour, and a misconduct hearing will be held for more serious failures or when the officer already has a final written warning.

Management action would involve pointing out how the behaviour fell short of the standards of professional behaviour, and identifying expectations for future conduct. It could also include establishing an improvement plan and addressing any underlying causes of misconduct. It can therefore be seen as supportive.

After a **misconduct meeting or hearing** the outcome could either be no further action, management action, a written warning, or a final written warning. An officer could also be dismissed (with or without notice) after a misconduct hearing. The 'services' of a trainee officer can be dispensed with at any time under reg 13 of the Police Regulations 2003 (see 5.4.4).

In the recent past there was a public perception that some officers under investigation for gross misconduct were resigning to avoid being held to account for their alleged failings. This loophole was closed by the Police (Conduct, Complaints and Misconduct and Appeal Tribunal) (Amendment) Regulations 2017 which came into force in December 2017. These regulations allow for an investigation into a retired officer to continue in certain circumstances, even if the officer has left the police service.

5.6.5 Unsatisfactory performance or attendance

Unsatisfactory performance or attendance is an 'inability or failure of a police officer to perform the duties of the role or rank [he/she] is currently undertaking to a satisfactory standard or level' (Police (Performance) Regulations 2012). The 2017 Home Office Guidance document *Police Officer Misconduct, Unsatisfactory Performance and Attendance Management Procedures* (Home Office, 2018g) suggests that early interventions by a manager ('management action') should be sufficient to improve and maintain a police officer's performance or attendance (see also 5.6.4). It also states that formal action should not be taken unless the police officer has earlier been offered supportive action but had declined or failed to cooperate, resulting in no improvement.

The Unsatisfactory Performance Procedures (UPP) can also be invoked for officers who are on long-term sick-leave and supported by management action, if a return to work within a reasonable timeframe is unrealistic. Note that the UPP do not apply to officers during their probationary period; reg 13 of the Police Regulations 2003 would be used instead (see 5.4.4).

There are three stages in the UPP with 3–12 months between each. During this time there must be improvement, and the satisfactory performance must be maintained for a year in order to avoid moving on to the next stage (for a full explanation of how this process works, see Home Office, 2017c).

5.7 Police Representative Organizations

Until April 2015, the Police Federation had a unique status as a police representative organization in that all trainees automatically joined. However, in 2014 the Home Secretary announced the law would be changed so police officers would not simply become members by default (Home Office, 2014d). To that effect, in 2015 the Police Federation (Amendment) Regulations 2015 (a Statutory Instrument, see 4.2) was introduced, with a clause added to the 1969 Regulations. These changes mean that when a trainee joins the police service he/she can now decide whether to opt in to join the Police Federation (and currently, most choose to join). Note that in 2016 the Home Office decided that Special Constables should not be represented by the Police Federation. Other staff organizations are described in 5.7.2.

5.7.1 The Police Federation of England and Wales

England and Wales have a single Police Federation (s 64(1) of the Police Act 1996, Membership of Trade Unions), as do Northern Ireland and Scotland. Here we describe the Police Federation of England and Wales (the PFEW), but many of the observations also apply to Scotland and Northern Ireland. (Note that some of the details given here may be subject to change.)

The PFEW has eight regions, with each region electing representatives to form the national Joint Central Committee. For example, Region No 2 of the Federation (North East) consists of the police forces of Cleveland, Durham, Humberside, Northumbria, North Yorkshire, South Yorkshire, and West Yorkshire. The Joint Central Committee is responsible for the national policy of the Federation.

The Federation is not a trade union in the usual sense of the term, and indeed, police officers are forbidden from joining a trade union:

> Subject to the following provisions of this section, a member of a police force shall not be a member of any trade union, or of any association having for its objects, or one of its objects, to control or influence the pay, pensions or conditions of service of any police force. (s 64(1) of the Police Act 1996, Membership of Trade Unions)

The Federation therefore does not have the right to call for any kind of industrial action such as a strike and cannot affiliate itself to the Labour Party or any other political organization. However, in many other respects the Federation was established to represent the views of its members (police officers below the rank of superintendent) on local, regional, and national levels in much the same way as any other staff association.

Each of the police forces in England and Wales has a Joint Branch Board (JBB). Within the JBB there are separate boards, representing the interests of constables, sergeants, and inspectors, as shown in the diagram. These boards each have separate agendas and meetings but also combine to form the force JBB. The JBB represents the views of police officers to the chief constable or commissioner, and to others in positions of responsibility.

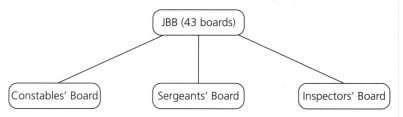

5.7.1.1   The role of the PFEW

On behalf of its members, the PFEW negotiates aspects of pay, pensions, and allowances through the Police Remuneration Review Body (PRRB). This body consists of representatives from the Police Federations (England and Wales, and Northern Ireland), the Superintendents' Association, and the National Police Chiefs' Council (NPCC) and was established through the Anti-social Behaviour, Crime and Policing Act 2014. The members of the body meet with representatives of the government ministers responsible for the police (the Home Secretary, the Northern Ireland Secretary) and representatives of the local authorities and magistrates. The PRRB has an independent chair and deputy chair (appointed by the Prime Minister). Scotland was not included in the remit of the PRRB, and continues to use its own Police Negotiating Board.

The Federation is also represented at Police Advisory Board meetings (chaired by the Home Secretary), which consider professional subjects such as training, promotion, and discipline. After taking these discussions into account, the Home Secretary may then make proposals to amend the Police Regulations.

One of the primary functions of the Federation is to give advice and assistance to its members who are the subject of a formal complaint or internal investigation. In such circumstances the Federation's advice to an officer is to remain calm and contact his/her local Federation representative if unsure of what to do next. The IOPC have produced a leaflet concerning complaints, available from the IOPC website (IOPC, 2017a). The Federation also offers advice and assistance to police officers (including trainee officers) who sustain injuries while on duty and who wish to claim compensation from the Criminal Injuries Compensation Authority (CICA). It also offers advice and assistance to police officers (including trainees) on matters arising from the conditions of service set out in the various Acts and regulations governing the police service.

5.7.2   Other police representative organizations

There are other organizations that represent particular groups and interests, and some have links with the Police Federation. For example, the British Association for Women in Policing (BAWP) is represented on the Equality Subcommittee of the Police Federation. The BAWP seeks to address women's issues in policing and not simply to represent women; membership is open to both men and women. Further information is available on their website.

The National Black Police Association UK (NBPA) is an independent charitable organization which seeks to further the position of all police officers of 'African, African-Caribbean, Middle-Eastern, Asian or Asian sub-continent origin'. A trainee officer may join the NBPA through membership of his or her local Black Police Association (BPA), of which there are about 40 in the UK, covering nine regions. Further information is available on their website.

The National LGBT Police Network UK promotes inclusiveness and equality for LGBT people who work in the police service and other crime agencies.

The Disabled Police Association (DPA) was founded in 2012 to help provide a coordinated response to national police matters that could affect disabled police officers and staff in the UK (see their website for further information).

The Police Superintendents' Association of England and Wales (PSAEW) represents the ranks of Superintendents and Chief Superintendents (there are similar organizations for Scotland and Northern Ireland). As with the Police Federation (see 5.7.1), the PSAEW represents its members at the national Police Negotiating Board.

The National Police Chiefs' Council (NPCC) represents the interests of chief officers in England, Wales, and Northern Ireland, and replaces ACPO. Chief officers are defined as police officers of the rank of ACC or above (commander in the MPS), and senior police staff equivalents. The NPCC states that its remit is to enable independent chief constables and their forces to work together to improve policing for the public, and that every police force is represented in the work of the NPCC through attendance at Chief Constables' Council. While all chief officers have the opportunity to be involved in and shape the work of the NPCC, it is not a membership body in the traditional sense (NPCC, 2015b).

The College of Policing (CoP) is the professional body for policing, with the remit to find the best ways of delivering policing, and to ensure that all officers and staff working for the police have the right knowledge and skills to do their jobs. The College of Policing sets the standards of professional practice within the police, accredits training providers to deliver qualifications, and sets appropriate learning and development outcomes (CoP, 2018m). They also:

- identify, develop, and promote good practice in policing based on evidence;
- support police forces and other organizations and encourage cooperation to protect the public and prevent crime; and
- identify, develop, and promote ethics, values, and standards of integrity within the police service as a whole.

Further information on the College of Policing is provided in 2.2.3.1.

> **TASK 11** If you are a trainee police officer, does your local force have a BPA? If it doesn't, try and find out why there is no BPA or equivalent.

5.8   **Managing Police Information**

Here we examine the need for police officers to protect the confidentiality of information and data under the Data Protection Act 2018 (DPA). We also consider the procedures around the sharing of some information under the requirements of the Freedom of Information Act 2000.

Sections 35–40 of the Data Protection Act 2018 require that personal data must be:

- processed lawfully and fairly;
- collected for specified, explicit, and legitimate purposes;
- adequate and relevant and not excessive;
- accurate and kept up to date;
- kept no longer than is necessary;
- processed in a secure manner.

Police data gathering must be accurate, adequate, relevant, and timely. Once information is collected it is important the police adhere to legal requirements. In addition, the recording of information and the confidentiality policies of the police service concerned should be explained to victims, survivors, and witnesses.

5.8.1   **Confidentiality**

Police officers (including trainee officers and special constables) will frequently encounter information of a sensitive and confidential nature. It is probably obvious, but confidentiality must be maintained, particularly in relation to witnesses, victims, and intelligence. The DPA 2018, the General Data Protection Regulation 2018 (GDPR), and the Human Rights Act 1998 (HRA) were enacted partly as a response to European legislation for protecting individual

Qualifications and Training

rights. Individual force policies may also make reference to these (particularly those sections relevant to the right to privacy).

Police forces will collect and request information from a range of sources. The collection, storage, and disclosure of this information is subject to controls under the DPA and the Management of Police Information (MoPI). Each force has a 'data controller' who receives and considers applications for information, and decides whether the information requested can be disclosed. The DPA also provides certain rights to individuals (including witnesses and victims) for information. It is an offence under the DPA to disclose personal information without the consent of the data controller, except for the purposes of crime prevention or detection.

Confidentiality is one of the standards of professional behaviour (see 5.3.1). Police officers are expected to 'treat information with respect and access or disclose it only in the proper course of police duties'. The evidence for demonstrating this ability could take the form of artefacts such as records, or direct observation by an assessor (normally a tutor constable), or witness statements. It is very unlikely that simulations in a classroom environment would meet the requirements for this criterion.

5.8.2 Management of Police Information (MoPI)

The means by which the police collect, record, share, and retain information has been the subject of some controversy in recent years, most notably as a result of the inquiry into the circumstances preceding the Soham murders (where a school caretaker killed two pupils) and the subsequent police investigations (see Bichard, 2004). The College of Policing document, *Management of Police Information* (available online) sets out the basic principles that police organizations should adopt for the collection, recording, sharing, and retaining of information relevant to their usual work. At the level of the individual police officer, the information may take the form of intelligence and evidence gathering, details concerning domestic crime, search form completion, and pocket notebook entries. We cover the use of the PNB and other police record-keeping documents in 10.2.

The Human Rights Act (HRA, see 4.4) requires all UK legislation to correspond with the European Convention on Human Rights (ECHR). This means that any act by a public authority (such as the police) that contravenes the ECHR will be unlawful. An individual's rights to privacy and family life (Article 8) can be 'interfered' with by the collection of personal information, and this interference is only permitted under certain circumstances.

The DPA places additional constraints on those holding 'personal data' (defined in the Act as any information which can identify a living person). However, exemptions are permitted when such data is used for the prevention or detection of crime, or the apprehension or prosecution of offenders (see the College of Policing *Management of Police Information* for further guidance.)

The Code of Ethics, the HRA, the GDPR, and College of Policing information all set out obligations to manage police information in ways that are both effective and meet certain ethical and professional standards. Many of these obligations are made manifest through standing orders, policies, strategies (the force 'Information Management Strategy'), and similar instruments. However, the same principles also apply for all levels of police staff, regardless of rank or role, and are likely to feature as part of police in-service training.

5.8.3 Freedom of information

The Freedom of Information Act 2000 (FoI) gives a general right of access to all types of recorded information held by public authorities, such as police forces. Each force will publish (normally online) details concerning the public's right under the FoI to access information kept by the force, and the procedures for accessing it, and will also have a publication scheme listing what information is available as a matter of routine, thereby reducing the number of requests for the same information. Not all requests for information will be successful—some of these are obvious, for example, requests relating to the identity of a Covert Human Intelligence Source (see 23.3 on the use of a CHIS), but the right to information is the norm rather than the exception. Requests can be made, and are made, on all kinds of topics.

There are two main ways that the FoI might directly affect a trainee police officer. First, he/she may personally receive a request for information under the FoI, perhaps in the form of a letter or by email. (Many people will know, for example, that a police work email is likely to be of the form x.y@force.pnn.police.uk where x is the first name, y is the surname, and 'force' is a shortened version of the name of a police force, for example BTP.) The officer should not normally respond in person but should promptly pass the request to the person responsible for handling FoI requests. Secondly, all trainees and officers should always be aware when recording information as a police officer, that someone, someday, may apply to view that record, and as this will normally be permitted it is very important to choose your words accurately and carefully.

5.9 Operating IT and Communication Systems

Trainee police officers will use IT systems on both a general level (such as basic word-processing tasks and sending emails), and will also learn how to use specific police related systems such as the Police National Computer (PNC) and the Airwave radio communication system. Particular police forces may also have their own information systems which officers will need to be able to use. The ability to use 'force information management systems' is one of the requirements under the PAC 'Information Management' heading.

5.9.1 Police information systems and databases

There are two large national databases of information for police use in the UK: the Police National Computer (PNC) and the more recently established Police National Database (PND). The PNC tends to be used by officers for 'street level' checks on a suspect, while the PND is more often employed within the context of an investigation, and is likely to contain much more detailed intelligence on individuals (both convicted and suspected). The police in the UK also have access to the Schengen Information System II (SIS II) which operates across Europe and provides alerts concerning people and property. However, at the time of writing it is not clear whether this access will continue after the UK leaves the European Union.

Apart from these national and international systems, each local police force is likely to have its own databases, and you will learn about these when you enter training.

5.9.1.1 The PNC

The PNC is a large database containing information on, amongst other things, people (eg those with criminal records), vehicles (including registered keepers), driving licences, and property. It is also used by other agencies such as the Crown Court (for checking potential jurors), the Environment Agency, the Gangmasters and Labour Abuse Authority, and United Kingdom Border Agency. A police officer could use the PNC to establish, for example, whether a driver is disqualified, or to assess the potential for a particular suspect to respond with violence. However, the PNC can do more than perform these relatively simple checks. For example, the Driver and Vehicle Standards Agency (DVSA) database is linked to the PNC, so a police officer is able to check the expiry date of an MoT and other details (such as 'advisory notices'). The linked DVLA database will reveal information relating to tests, endorsements, and so on (see 19.3.1). The PNC can also be used to search for more 'fuzzy' information such as nicknames used by offenders, tattoos, scars, hair colour, and similar distinguishing features.

The PNC is normally accessed by radio and speaking to an operator based at the Force Control Room. There is a routine to be mastered; a particular sequence of requests is made to the operator, first specifying the nature of the request (eg a vehicle check). The officer then provides his/her name and force number before stating the reason for the check. The phonetic alphabet is used to spell out words to ensure there is no mistake in transmitting the information (see 5.9.4). Officers must make a PNB record (see 10.2) of the details of the checks carried out so that their work is auditable. Trainee officers (on the PCDA or DHEP) are likely to be instructed on using the PNC, and demonstrating the ability to use the PNC effectively is likely to be required before Independent Patrol Status is achieved.

> **TASK 12** What are VODS and QUEST? You may need to use the internet or (if you are a trainee officer) ask more experienced colleagues.

It will certainly be emphasized during police training that there is a requirement to access the PNC in a responsible and professional manner. Inappropriate use of the PNC is viewed by police forces as a serious matter, and could lead to dismissal of a trainee police officer. (Not only is it a contravention of the PNC Code of Practice, but it is also against the law.) Alleged misuse of the PNC can lead to an IOPC inquiry (see 5.6.3) and a subsequent prosecution.

Unfortunately, examples of inappropriate use of the PNC are only too easy to find. For example, in 2016 an Avon and Somerset officer was involved in an incident on a road whilst off duty. The incident was appropriately reported to the police, but the officer subsequently used the PNC to check details of the driver involved in the incident (Avon and Somerset Constabulary, 2017). In another instance, following a court case in 2018, a Staffordshire Police officer was dismissed and given a six-month community order for conducting checks for personal reasons on her neighbours, an ex-husband, and on the family of her new partner (Ross, 2018).

Police forces and other non-police organizations such as the Environment Agency are subject to HMICFRS inspections for PNC-compliance (see the HMICFRS website for further details).

5.9.1.2 The PND

The PND enables information and intelligence to be shared between police forces. It was set up in 2011, partly as a consequence of the inadequacies uncovered during the Bichard inquiry into the Soham murders in 2002, and replaced the IMPACT Nominal Index. The PND contains 'POLE' data, which is information about:

- *People* (eg offenders and suspects) or organizations (companies);
- *Objects* (eg stolen vehicles);
- *Locations* (eg addresses of offenders); and
- *Events* (eg crime reports).

The data is located within five discrete but interconnected sets of records: custody, intelligence, crime, domestic abuse, and child abuse. A police force is able to check what information or intelligence is held on an individual (a 'nominal') by any other police force. Much of the information to be found on the PNC will also be present in the PND and vice versa.

5.9.1.3 Schengen Information System II (SIS II)

The Schengen Information System acts as a 'central hub' within Europe for member countries to distribute alerts across member states. UK police and border agency staff can set up and respond to alerts with international significance through the PNC. For example, alerts can be raised for persons wanted for arrest for extradition, missing persons who need police protection (including minors and adults not at risk), witnesses, absconders, people or vehicles requiring checks, and lost/stolen objects that need to be seized. Once an alert is raised it is distributed to all member states.

At the time of writing it is not clear whether these arrangements will continue after the UK leaves the EU. It is hoped that a post-Brexit UK will be able to negotiate a similar agreement to that which already exists with non-EU member states such as the USA and Australia.

5.9.2 TETRA and Airwave communication

The communication protocol used by police forces in England and Wales (as with most of the other countries in Europe) is known as 'TETRA'—Terrestrial Trunked Radio. 'Airwave' (the product of a commercial company, Airwave Solutions Ltd) employs the TETRA protocols, and is the radio communications network used by the police for voice communication (eg between a police patrol and the force control room) and for communication of data. The system has replaced what many people still think of as police 'radio'. Airwave can also be used to communicate with other rescue and emergency services, and the terminals have an emergency button for use in the case of imminent personal danger. The system can be used for conventional point-to-point communication between two individuals, or it can be used by a number of people to communicate as a group (see 5.9.2.1). It is currently considered secure as it employs relatively sophisticated forms of encryption.

Trainee officers will be provided with full details about how to communicate over Airwave, including codes and protocols which are restricted to the police service (and hence not reproduced here). The phonetic alphabet is used where appropriate (see 5.9.4). Trainee officers will also be required to learn 'AirwaveSpeak', which reduces the amount of time needed to communicate information, and reduces the incidence of error or ambiguity. The table describes some of the basic rules (but be aware that there are many more).

Process	Description	Example
Starting the call ('calling up')	A police officer repeats the call-sign of the person (or control room) that he/she is calling and then adds his/her own call-sign	'Charlie romeo, charlie romeo...this is tango two three...'
Exchange	A police officer finishes his/her part of the exchange with 'over'	'Charlie romeo, charlie romeo...this is tango two three...over'
Conveying information, asking questions, etc		'Charlie romeo, charlie romeo this is tango two three, disturbance in Tontine Street, over'
Confirming	A confirmation is often given that the message has been received and understood	'Tango two three, received, over'
Finishing the call	The police officer (or the control room) finishes the sequence of communication with 'out'	'Charlie romeo, tango two three, suspects under arrest, out'

Airwave has limited capacity so careful management of operational use is important for police effectiveness. (There is, however, a 'surge' facility that provides additional capacity in times of emergency.) Capacity is particularly limited in rural areas and in underground train stations (where strict protocols are therefore particularly important). Coverage is good throughout the road systems of England, Wales, and Scotland, but there are limitations in remote areas, with no coverage at all in some places. It appears to function effectively in most circumstances, although claims were made after the riots in England during the summer of 2011 that Airwave had become 'overloaded' and police officers were forced to use their own personal mobile phones to communicate (Police Federation, 2011, p 6). This was subsequently denied by the company concerned.

The government are currently planning to replace the Airwave system with the new Emergency Services Network (ESN) which according to the Home Office (in *Emergency Services Network: overview* (November 2018)) will provide the next generation integrated critical voice and broadband data services for the three emergency services (police, fire and rescue, and ambulance), and other agencies such as the NCA. The ESN will be a 4G mobile communications network with extensive coverage, high resilience, appropriate security, and public safety functionality which will allow users to communicate even under the most challenging circumstances. It is claimed it will 'transform how our blue-light services respond to incidents, offering better coverage leading to faster response times' and 'enable emergency service professionals to work together better and more efficiently when incidents and accidents occur by sharing data across the new digital network' (Home Office, 2018d). At the time of writing, the intention is that ESN will be incrementally introduced and will be fully functional by 2022.

5.9.2.1   ICCS

Radio communication in policing operates within the Integrated Command and Control System (ICCS). This links telephony, radio, and other digital technologies, and allows police services to communicate internally, with one another and with other emergency services. In 'trunked mode operation' (TMO) a number of airwave users can communicate as a 'talk group'. (A talk group could comprise, for example, all the police officers involved with a particular enquiry, or staff from a variety of agencies when responding to a major incident.) Direct Mode Operation (DMO) provides voice communication between two or more handheld or mobile terminals without using Airwave. It can be used in areas with little or no coverage, but is usually limited to line of sight so has a more limited range than TETRA, and uses more battery power than TMO.

Capacity, congestion, and coverage are important factors for ICCS; for example 'telephony' and 'point-to-point' occupy a lot of capacity and their use should therefore be limited. The most efficient use of Airwave is through an open talk group (this uses the same capacity as a single point-to-point airwave communication). Mobile terminals should be set to the correct talk groups and unnecessary monitoring or usage avoided.

All users must also consider data security when using ICCS. Information that may be sensitive or operationally significant can be sanitized (see 23.5.1), or an alternative means of communication could be used. In the event of an Airwave system failure, emergency services control staff will revert to using mobile phones or the Airwave mobile phone facility, while others could use status and text message with certain limitations.

For further information on ICCS and the various functions and capabilities the following sources are available online: *Standard Operating Procedure Guide on Multi-Agency Airwave interoperability* and *Standard Operating Procedure Guide on Police to Police and Inter-Agency Airwave interoperability* (both published by the NPIA in 2010), and *Airwave TeTRa (Terrestrial Trunked Radio) Technology Procedure* from Surrey Police.

5.9.3 Mobile data devices

A number of police forces allocate mobile data devices such as smartphones, tablets, and laptops to their officers, with the intention of reducing the amount of 'paperwork'. A mobile data device provides an electronic means of:

1. entering and sharing data (eg a witness statement collected in electronic format at the scene of an incident);
2. recording and sharing location data (eg using GPS); and
3. printing some types of completed forms on a 'mini-printer' connected by Bluetooth or similar methods.

In recent years there has been considerable investment in mobile data devices for the police service, typically in the form of customized smartphones and vehicle-mounted mobile data devices. The intention is to free up police officer time and to improve efficiency. For example, both Surrey and Sussex constabularies are now using mobile technology for issuing speeding tickets and completing drink- and drug-driving forms, using digital versions of the forms available via officers' mobile devices (Digital by default news, 2017). In broad terms, the devices allow a police officer to access the PNC, local force tasking and briefing bulletins, missing person reports, police intelligence systems, other information systems (eg the PNLD), and information relating to an individual's name and address (eg the electoral roll, the Quick Address System), and to send emails. In addition, mobile data devices normally incorporate a digital camera, which (in some forces) a police officer can use to record potential evidence. The exact functions and applications used on the mobile data devices are specific to each force and normally kept confidential, but it is assumed that all data is securely encrypted.

Trainee police officers issued with a mobile data device will be informed of the relevant protocols and rules. For example, when a force-issued mobile data device is switched on it is likely to become 'visible' to the control room, therefore many police forces forbid their use whilst off duty.

Despite this progress, deployment of these devices still appears patchy; HMICFRS stated in 2019 that 'there are still forces where this is not the norm and, at a national level, systems are not integrated well enough (HMICFRS, 2019, p 36). Concerns have also been expressed over both the cost of the devices and of ongoing data usage, but it seems inevitable that the police use of mobile data devices will increase.

5.9.4 Conveying information

If you have ever attempted to spell out a word on the phone to another person you have probably experienced the difficulty of clarifying the difference between 'm' and 'n', 's' and 'f', and so on. Mistakes made in the context of ordinary phone calls are seldom life-threatening, but if these same mistakes were made during a police communication it could prove costly, both in time and in terms of safety. This is the reason the 'phonetic alphabet' (sometimes referred to as the 'radio alphabet') and conventions for communicating numbers, time of day, and dates were developed and subsequently adopted by police forces throughout the UK.

5.9.4.1 The phonetic alphabet

With the phonetic alphabet each letter is given a phonetic equivalent. This is to avoid confusion over letters which sound the same, such as 'p', 'b', and 'd'; Instead of saying 'd' the police officer will say 'delta'. The following is a list of the phonetic alphabet as normally employed by police forces in the UK (and beyond).

The Phonetic Alphabet					
a	Alpha	j	Juliet	s	Sierra
b	Bravo	k	Kilo	t	Tango
c	Charlie	l	Lima	u	Uniform
d	Delta	m	Mike	v	Victor
e	Echo	n	November	w	Whisky
f	Foxtrot	o	Oscar	x	X-ray
g	Golf	p	Papa	y	Yankee
h	Hotel	q	Quebec	z	Zulu
i	India	r	Romeo		

You may well be asked to memorize and use it after you join the police. A number of tests are available online for self-testing.

5.9.4.2 Numbers

When communicating a number (eg the age of a person), each digit of the number is said individually. There is a further convention that zero is referred to as 'zero' and not 'naught' (nor as the letter 'O'). Hence the number 2,306 (two thousand, three hundred, and six) is communicated as 'two-three-zero-six'. A less common rule is to give large numbers in pairs, for example 245,671 being conveyed as 'two-four, five-six, seven-one'. However, practice does vary in this respect (particularly with phone numbers).

5.9.4.3 Time and date

As you might guess, police forces tend to use the 24-hour clock for conveying the time of day. So 7.26 pm is written as 19.26 hrs and hence said as 'one-nine, two-six hours'. Dates are given as the day-month-year, in the UK style.

5.9.4.4 IC and SDE codes

There are a number of different situations in which a police officer might need to communicate or record a person's ethnicity, based upon an individual's appearance. The system used by some police forces to communicate the perceived ethnicity of a person is known variously as 'IC codes', 'IC 1 to 6 codes', 'PNC Codes', and 'ID codes'. An officer could use this to describe a suspect's ethnicity when searching for a record on the Police National Computer (or the Police National Database) as shown in the table. (Note that ethnicity and nationality are not the same, and that the examples shown here are for illustration only.)

'IC' Code	Ethnicity	Example of a nationality
IC 0 (sometimes IC 7)	Unknown	N/A
IC 1	White North European	Swedish
IC 2	White South European (sometimes 'Dark European' or 'Mediterranean')	Greek
IC 3	Black (sometimes 'African-Caribbean')	Nigerian
IC 4	Asian (sometimes 'South Asian')	Pakistani
IC 5	Chinese/Japanese/SE Asian (sometimes 'Oriental' or 'East Asian')	Chinese
IC 6	Middle Eastern (sometimes 'Arab')	Egyptian

Note that IC 0/IC 7 is not always used, and some forces may use a different system.

A person can also be asked to define his/her own ethnicity, for example when a police officer is completing a form. The Self-defined Ethnicity (SDE) codes have 18 different options plus the option of 'not-stated' (also known as '18 + 1'), as shown in the following table.

General ethnic group	Self-defined ethnicity	SDE Code
White	British	W1
	Irish	W2
	Gypsy or Irish Traveller	W3
	Any other white background	W9
Mixed	White and black Caribbean	M1
	White and black African	M2
	White and Asian	M3
	Any other mixed background	M9
Asian or Asian British	Indian	A1
	Pakistani	A2
	Bangladeshi	A3
	Chinese	A4
	Any other Asian background	A9
Black or black British	Caribbean	B1
	African	B2
	Any other black background	B9
Other ethnic group	Arab	O2
	Other ethnic group	O9
Not stated	Not stated	NS

TASK 13 Previously, some forces used unofficial IC codes. What are the inherent problems when using police officer-defined codes for radio communication?

5.10 Police Equipment and Technology

Police officers and special constables carry a range of equipment and technology when on patrol. The various items are used for personal protection (see 5.12.5), for controlling violent or potentially violent people, and for communication with other police staff. Training will be given in both the function and appropriate use of the issued equipment and technology. (Note that officers are usually prohibited from carrying unauthorized equipment or technology, but policy details vary between forces.) Here we provide a brief overview of police equipment and other items.

Police uniforms vary from force to force, and according to the role a police officer may be performing at a particular time. The photograph shows the typical clothing and equipment worn and carried by an operational police officer. A trainee officer will become familiar with the 'Standard' (or 'Default'), 'Ceremonial', 'Public Order', and 'Specialist' (eg Dog section) uniforms for his/her force.

The standard uniform is worn for operational activities. It includes the custodian helmet for male officers and the bowler for female officers if on foot patrol, the cap if in a patrol car, and a black wicking shirt. The public order uniform includes a helmet, overalls, a face cover, and protective gloves. Every officer is also required to display a badge showing his/her name and/ or number.

For operational duties police officers wear protective equipment such as body armour and/or a stab vest, and carry equipment such as a first aid kit, handcuffs, PAVA ('pepper') incapacitant spray (or CS spray), a baton (eg an ASP), an Airwave terminal (see 5.9.2), and a torch. In some forces officers might also carry a mobile phone and a 'Taser' (see 18.8.1 for more details on these weapons). Recently, an increasing number of police forces have been issuing officers with body worn video cameras (BWV) which can capture evidence of criminal behaviour and also reduce the time needed to complete statements (MPS, 2014).

Each force makes its own arrangements for purchasing equipment and technology, and some items (such as body armour) must meet Home Office quality assurance guidelines. There are opportunity costs in this approach for as the Home Office noted in 2012 'The police service currently procures equipment and services … in up to 43 different ways at a total cost of £3.3bn across 43 forces' (Home Office, 2012d, p 5). However, the head of the National Audit Office stated that 'Agreement between forces on collaborative ways of buying and common specifications for equipment can deliver better value for money—but implementing this is a challenge where forces are used to doing their own thing' (National Audit Office, 2013). The Police ICT Company, a private company, was founded in 2015 to act as a link between policing organizations and the companies providing technological and commercial equipment. This resulted in savings of more than £28.8 million in the financial year 2018/19 alone (Police ICT, 2020).

5.11 **Effective Interpersonal Communication**

Police officers need to be able to listen carefully, and explain things well, focus on the key points, and talk to people using language they understand. This applies in all circumstances, many of which can seem mundane to a police officer, but can be extremely upsetting for some members of the public. Survivors, victims, or witnesses can understandably be upset and disturbed by their experiences of crime and anti-social behaviour for example.

In all policing incidents it is important that officers are aware of people's reactions and that sufficient time and 'space' are allowed for people to communicate what they have experienced in the course of the incident under investigation. It may be that practical and emotional support in the form of listening and reassurance is sufficient, but careful assessment might be required to determine whether additional support is required (eg medical assistance, counselling, and victim support services). It is important to communicate effectively, building a rapport and gaining trust, being supportive, and keeping those affected up to date.

The ideas presented here should help you become more aware of the way you speak, and the effect it has on other people. In turn, this will help you develop strategies to help you communicate more clearly in the future, and to choose the most appropriate way to speak to another person. In 5.11.3 we will also examine the other side of the communication equation—listening skills. Non-verbal communication (NVC) is also covered (in 5.11.2) as this is an important means of communication that can easily affect exchanges between all individuals, including police officers.

Transactional analysis (TA) is explained in 5.11.1 as just one example of a theory about human communication. Other theories might also be applicable, for example Shannon and Weaver's Information Theory, and we are not asking you to buy into transactional analysis to the exclusion of other theories. We use it here to show how a careful and structured analysis of interactions can provide useful insights, which can then help improve communication.

The topics covered in 5.11 are likely to contribute to the learning required for the National Policing Curriculum subject areas: 'Leadership and Team-working' and 'Communication Skills'.

5.11.1 Transactional analysis

Transactional analysis was originally developed by Eric Berne (for an introduction see Berne, 1968), and is based upon the assumption that at any one time people tend to adopt the characteristics or 'ego states' of a parent (critical or nurturing), adult, or child (adapted or free). The ego state affects their attitudes and the way they speak to each other. The ego states and the type of language used and the associated typical behaviours and attitudes are shown in the table.

Ego state	Typical words/phrases	Typical behaviour	Typical attitudes
Critical parent	'That's disgraceful!' 'You ought to...!' 'Always do it!'	Furrowed brow, pointed finger.	Condescending, judgemental.
Nurturing parent	'Well done, that's clever!'	Benevolent smile, pat on back.	Caring, permissive.
Adult	'How...'? 'When...'? 'Where...'? 'What...'?	Relaxed, logical, attentive.	Open-minded, clear-thinking, interested.
Adapted child	'Please can I?' 'I'll try harder.'	Vigorous, nodding head, downcast eyes, whiny voice.	Compliant, defiant, complaining.
Free child	'I want...' 'I feel great.'	Laughing with someone, uninhibited.	Curious, fun-loving, spontaneous.

Note that no one operates in any of these states on a permanent basis, but switches between states, even within the course of a single conversation.

TASK 14 If this Handbook were a person, which of the ego states would fit best and most often?

According to the theory of TA, the way a person responds will vary, partly due to the way the other person behaves or speaks (influenced by their own ego state). A trainee officer needs to be able to analyse (to some extent) the way he/she speaks and responds, and the ways that others speak and respond, and then to be able to identify the most appropriate way to manage the conversation. Having identified the ego states in play, the next task is to recognize the category of conversation or transaction, ie whether it is complementary, crossed, or ulterior.

Complementary transactions occur when the ego state of each side of the conversation corresponds. Here is an example of a complementary transaction between a trainee police officer 'P' and a member of the public 'M'.

P stops a car to give advice to the driver.

M   I don't know why you've stopped me. Haven't you got anything better to do?
P   Is this your car? I've stopped you because I've got the right, and what's your problem anyway?
M   Get lost.
P   You can't say that; any more lip and I'll have you.

The opening transaction is from M who appears to be in the child ego state. P's response is in the 'critical parent' ego state. The ego states correspond, so it is a complementary transaction sequence:

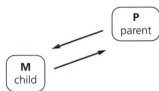

The exchange will continue in this way as long as the transactions are complementary. However, P can change the flow of the conversation by deliberately changing his/her tone and behaviour, and communicating a different ego state to create a 'crossed transaction'.

A **crossed transaction** breaks a complementary transaction. To change the style of the transaction, either P or M could employ a different ego state; let us begin the conversation again with P reacting differently.

M   I don't know why you've stopped me. Haven't you got anything better to do?
P   Hello, just a quick word, I'm PC Williams from Lewes police station. I've stopped you because one of your brake lights isn't working did you know? This could affect your safety as well as the safety of others.
M   Oh right, I didn't realize—thanks for telling me—I'll get it fixed ... soon.
P   Thanks for your cooperation. Good afternoon.

In this case P deliberately ignores M's child ego state and adopts an adult ego state. It is a reply that has reasoning in its content, and this has an effect on M, who may not have expected this type of response. M responds accordingly in the adult ego state, which brings about a satisfactory conclusion. This is referred to as a crossed transaction, as P's response has broken the parent–child–parent pattern, and the transaction has crossed over into a different style.

In an **ulterior transaction** there are actually two different messages, an open message and a hidden message. Frequently with ulterior transactions, the open message is adult–adult, but the hidden message is parent–child or child–parent.

For example, M begins the transaction sarcastically, and emphasizes the word 'such'.

M   It's nice to see the local police making such good use of their time.
P   Yeah, it's all part of the service to you.

This transaction is not just about words: it is also about body language and the tone of voice. The opening transaction has a hidden meaning: M dislikes the police (or at least P) and feels that the police (or P in particular) waste time, rather than catching real criminals; hence the sarcastic emphasis on the word 'such'. P's response also has a hidden meaning: hence the smirky tone and the emphasis on the word 'you'. Each component is complementary. So, unless one of the participants crosses a transaction, the dialogue will continue in this manner. The skill, therefore, is to be aware of what is happening, and to be able to cross an unproductive transaction, and thereby change the ego state of the other person.

Try using these ideas to help you understand your own and other people's styles of communication, and then choose the most appropriate way of saying what it is that you want to say.

> **TASK 15** Over the next two days, listen carefully to conversations around you. What ego states are operating and what type of transactions are taking place? Write down three brief extracts and explain what is happening in terms of transactional analysis.

5.11.2 Non-verbal communication

People may communicate anxiety, confidence, despair, or any other emotion through body language, also known as non-verbal communication (NVC). You may be able to use NVC to help build up trust with other people. It has been observed that adopting similar body postures and mannerisms communicates a positive attitude. A trainee police officer or special constable could use such techniques (in a discreet manner) when communicating with witnesses, suspects, victims, or other members of the public.

However, be wary of popular accounts concerning NVC; particular actions never have definite meanings and hand gestures (for example) are not 'windows on the soul'. (Unfortunately, these kinds of scientifically unjustified 'tips and tricks' have featured in police training in the past.) In particular, the use of 'body language' in an attempt to identify deception or lying is problematic (see Vrij, 2008, for a comprehensive consideration of this). You should also be alert to 'ethnocentrism' in your interpretations of NVC, such as a refusal to make eye contact—for some ethnic groups this is related to cultural attitudes to authority, and does not necessarily indicate guilt or remorse.

5.11.3 Listening skills

Of all the skills that we develop during our lives, the ability to listen is probably the most difficult of all. We hear, but we do not always listen; this ability has to be learned and practised, and a trainee police officer will benefit from developing the ability more fully. Even the little things people say may be of critical importance when dealing with a public order situation or when investigating a crime.

Here we shall simply offer some basic advice on listening. Police training will include more detailed advice on listening skills. It is best to:

- pay full attention to the other person as he/she is speaking and to avoid looking away (think what it feels like for you when you are speaking to a person who keeps glancing away!). Use verbal and non-verbal feedback (eg nodding) to show you are listening
- let the speaker finish before asking another question or make a comment, and don't interrupt. Most of us think we already do this but research shows that this is rarely the case! (However, there may be occasions when a police officer **must** interrupt for operational reasons.) A good way of training yourself to let someone finish is to mentally count a few seconds after he/she has stopped before you respond. You may also notice that he/she then fills this silence, and carries on speaking, almost as an afterthought. Sometimes, this extra information is of critical importance. Family doctors have long known this: often the most important part of the consultation is when the patient stands to leave and remarks, 'Oh yes doctor, there is one more thing …'
- try echoing back to the speaker if you need to clarify something, for example by using a phrase he/she has already used—'You said, "He asked me for a cigarette," …'. The speaker is likely to pick up the thread and continue to explain further.

5.11.4   Communication with colleagues

There are many reasons why good working relationships are important including: maintaining trust, contributing to professional performance, effective cooperation, and encouraging commitment. There is a need to communicate effectively, but also to manage conflict, challenge some attitudes and behaviour, build relationships, and work in teams. It is important to be aware of the needs of work colleagues. Communication style is also important (see also 5.11.1). In this example of reflective practice the officer realizes that within his team some styles of communication work better than others.

Reflective Practice

Several of my officers dealt with an incident which resulted in a suspect attempting suicide. I was aware that the officers were young in service, and experience, ... I carried out reflection with three individual officers and focused on each element of the model. I found myself initially being quite 'corporate' with the way I probed each stage of the cycle when speaking with the officers, but soon realised that there are many ways to ask and word the questions ..., giving it a more personal approach [which] allowed me to gain more information. Upon conclusion of these debriefs I spoke with the team as a whole, I felt better prepared speaking with the team as I knew of the concerns of the individual officers and so could explain things to the whole audience.

(DS G Collins, Metropolitan Police)

The ability to prioritize accordingly can be crucial in providing an effective response. Failure to do this can result in additional pressures placed on the supervisor and the team, put the public and police colleagues at greater risk, and undermine public confidence in the police. Often these situations can be highly pressured and having an appreciation of the available support and advice from colleagues and appropriate organizations (see 11.2) can improve the speed and quality of the service to the public.

Inappropriate behaviour in policing has been a source of criticism and one that the police service continually attempts to address. There are a variety of different ways in which inappropriate behaviour can occur such as unwittingly using potentially offensive language, ignorance, and intended insults and discrimination. All police officers are expected to understand cultural sensitivities, inappropriate sexist or racist behaviour, and language. If police officers disregard these important issues it undermines the police service, supports discrimination within the service, and can put police officers and the public at risk. It could also result in disciplinary action for the officers concerned. For this reason all police officers including trainees have a responsibility to address (and where appropriate challenge) inappropriate behaviour of colleagues. When taking such actions, however, it is important to recognize the limitations of your own abilities—it may sometimes be better to seek advice or guidance from a supervisor.

5.11.4.1   Teamwork

Officers can demonstrate their commitment by taking a full share of the workload and responding promptly to requests for help from other colleagues and external partners. It is also beneficial to communicate clearly about any difficulties encountered; this is far better than just trying to transfer the responsibility to someone else as the problems are unlikely to go away! A positive team spirit is beneficial to everyone, and all team members must take responsibility for maintaining productive working practices. The same principles apply for situations where an officer is working more as an individual rather than as part of a team; face up to responsibilities, take appropriate actions, and ensure all communications are clear.

The need to work effectively as a member of a team is reflected in the new 'Policing Professional Profiles' from the College of Policing, and linked to their 'Competency and Values Framework' (CVF). One of the CVF competencies is about the need to work collaboratively, and therefore includes teamworking. For a description of the CVF, see the College of Policing website.

5.11.4.2   Resolving conflicts

Occasionally, there can be disagreement between team members or with a supervisor. It is important to resolve disagreement diplomatically in order to avoid undermining police responses, as this might otherwise result in poor performance. Unless conflicts are resolved, a sense of distrust is likely to develop between team members and supervisors, and they will no longer be able to work together effectively. Individual interpersonal skills are important in trying to avoid conflict as they can help people to understand the views and opinions of others, and to respond in an appropriate manner. You will need to understand the problem from the opposing perspective, identify the various solutions, and agree on the most appropriate way forward. One model of conflict resolution is 'CUDSA' (Confront, Understand, Define, Search, and Agree). This provides that a step-by-step approach begins with confronting and understanding the problem before moving on to search for and agree to solutions.

TASK 16 List some examples of questions that a trainee police officer might ask people, to help demonstrate he/she can apply the principles of equality, diversity, and anti-discrimination practice.

5.11.5 Communicating personal authority

Communicating authority is a key concept for the police and of particular interest to the trainee police officer and students undertaking pre-join programmes. The exercise of authority is often viewed as a mark of a professional although 'authority' is often expressed or described instead as autonomy or credibility and related concepts. If you are a trainee police officer your authority will certainly be challenged on occasions, and you will no doubt find yourself thinking deeply about your authority, and maybe about how to manage the use of it. There are a number of personal qualities that you need to exhibit before completing your training (see Chapter 6) and some of these are clearly related to personal authority.

In the 1960s and 1970s, the educational philosopher Richard Peters (often referred to as RS Peters, who usually wrote and worked in collaboration with Paul Hirst) argued that there are different forms of personal authority which nonetheless interrelate (Peters, 1973). Although his focus was on authority in education we have adapted his work here to apply to policing.

5.11.5.1 The main forms of personal authority

The main forms of personal authority are considered to be:

- **epistemic**: authority from knowledge (knowing more than the next person);
- **natural** (sometimes called 'charismatic authority'): derived from personality, demeanour (non-verbal communication);
- *de facto* (from fact): authority that exists through convention rather than as a matter of right;
- *de jure* (from right): authority as a matter of right; and
- **moral**: authority that arises from a moral high ground.

Note that these categories are not intended to be mutually exclusive. As we shall see later, *de facto* and moral authorities, for example, are often linked. It is also important to note that authority here can relate to two distinct concepts; the general authority of the police service, which is often thought about in terms of legitimacy (see 2.2.5), and the individual authority of each police officer. It is the latter authority which concerns us here.

5.11.5.2 Personal authority and police officers

We will now examine each of the components of police officer personal authority in turn. The different types of authority are important, particularly as personal authority will inevitably vary between officers, and a good understanding of these topics can help an individual officer improve his/her authority.

A police officer's **epistemic authority** stems from knowledge of the law and procedure. The public expect a police officer to know the rudiments of the law. Although members of the public may know that an offence has occurred (by applying their common sense), they will expect an officer to know which particular law or laws have been broken. In part, this expectation is fed by media portrayals of the police which often feature a police officer using the words 'I arrest you for [specifics of the offence]'. Therefore, if in a particular situation it is seen that a police officer's grasp of the law or proper procedure seems uncertain, then his/her epistemic authority will decrease. The law, policy, and guidelines studied during training provide the basis for establishing epistemic authority.

Some people appear to have more **natural authority** than others through sheer presence (charisma), and are more able to take control when required. This form of authority can be developed, and trainee police officers will receive training on demeanour, use of language, non-verbal communication (body language), and other more subtle ways in which natural authority can be enhanced. Other factors are important too; being smartly dressed (polished shoes, clean and tidy uniform, etc) may seem a strangely old-fashioned topic for a Handbook of this kind but they are important aspects of a trainee officer's personal authority when, for example, giving evidence in court.

Police officers are seen to have *de facto* **authority** in certain circumstances, for example in the aftermath of a road traffic collision, or the expectation that road users will move out of the way of police patrol cars deploying sirens and blue lights. This authority comes not just from the law, but through custom. In terms of the extent to which citizens trust the police and see the police as a legitimate authority, Tom Tyler in the USA and a number of academics in the UK have shown empirically that citizens appear to be more concerned with how police officers conduct themselves and carry out their duties, rather than what they achieve (see Tyler, 2003; Bradford *et al*, 2009; Myhill and Bradford, 2011; and Jackson *et al*, 2013). The focus of this research is on how perceptions of procedural justice inform the legitimacy of police authority. The *de facto* form of authority is easily lost if abused (or perceived as such), and members of the public will no doubt carry on making wry comments about the police using their sirens and lights to get back to the station more quickly for a cup of coffee and a biscuit!

It is a simple fact that police officers have powers that are not granted to other members of society. These powers are the main source of an officer's *de jure* **authority**, and many are covered in this Handbook. The wearing of a uniform symbolizes this form of authority, to separate a police officer from the rest of society, as does the possession of a warrant card.

Police officers are expected to subscribe to a code of ethics and behaviour which is of a higher standard than the rest of society, and this gives them not only moral authority but also moral responsibilities. There are certainly greater moral obligations on the police when compared to many other occupational groups, for example in terms of honesty, integrity, fairness, impartiality, politeness, and general conduct. Gross examples of inappropriate police behaviour (such as the ill-treatment of prisoners) undermine the moral authority of the police service as a whole, but there are other less dramatic examples at the level of the individual. Put simply, members of the public do not expect to witness police officers swearing in public, smoking on duty, or acting other than professionally in the role. These restrictions on the personal behaviour of police officers and the effect on their moral authority also extend to life off-duty. Where is the moral authority of a police officer who arrests an acquaintance for possession of cocaine during a raid on Saturday, having smoked cannabis with him the previous evening? How is a police officer's moral authority affected if she uses her warrant card to gain free entry to a nightclub? Retaining moral authority also requires police officers to maintain a moral perspective when dealing with the public. It is not appropriate, for example, to judge a member of the public by the same high standards that a police officer must follow, and it is partly for this reason that the 'attitude test' (see 5.5.3.5) is an unacceptable means of deciding whether to arrest a person.

If you are a trainee police officer, then it is likely that there will be opportunities for you to develop your personal authority during your initial training. These may include:

- preparing and delivering presentations to others, including groups of students and training staff;
- increasing your knowledge and recall of the law and procedure; or
- observing your own behaviour, including your demeanour and use of language, for example by analysing video of your performance whilst undertaking a particular task.

Feedback from others, including your trainers, assessors, fellow trainees, and representatives of community groups (eg whilst undertaking your community attachment) can help you find out more about how to communicate your authority.

TASK 17 Imagine you are a police officer and you have arrested a woman on suspicion of assault and theft in a shopping centre. The victim has identified the suspect, who cannot explain her possession of the victim's mobile phone. Give examples of how the five forms of personal authority would feature in this particular scenario.

5.12 Health and Safety

By its very nature, policing has always been and will continue to be a potentially hazardous occupation. Whilst risks are present in all work activities, operational staff are more frequently exposed to risks, for example when dealing with environmental incidents or disorderly behaviour. All employers have a duty to ensure (as far as is reasonably practicable) the health, safety, and welfare of their employees. In turn, each employee has a duty to take reasonable care for his/her own health and safety and that of other persons who might be affected by his/her acts or omissions. All decisions must be taken with the National Decision Model in mind (see 5.5.2). It is also important for frontline police officers to be fit and to be provided with (and use) suitable personal safety equipment.

Health and safety may seem at times to be just another bureaucratic burden, but it is an issue police officers must consider and have in mind at all times during their day-to-day work. Health and safety duties are covered by ss 2–7 of the Health and Safety at Work etc Act 1974, and became applicable to police officers, special constabulary officers, and cadets by virtue of the Police (Health and Safety) Act 1997. Home Office publications from 1996 onwards provide guidance for police managers. A police force will also have its own published health and safety policy (eg see the 2017 Essex Police Health and Safety policy, available online).

Health and safety-related assessment criteria are likely to feature learning required for the National Policing Curriculum subject areas: 'Understanding the Police Constable Role', 'Public Protection', 'Managing Conflict', and 'Response Policing'.

5.12.1 The employer's role in health and safety

Section 2(2) of the Health and Safety at Work etc Act (HSWA) 1974 sets out the employer's role for health and safety, stating that employers are responsible for:

- providing and maintaining plant and systems of work that are, so far as is reasonably practicable, safe, and without risks to health;
- making safe arrangements for the use, handling, storage, and transport of articles and substances;
- providing necessary information, instruction, training, and supervision for ensuring, so far as is reasonably practicable, the health and safety at work of employees;
- maintaining places of work under the employer's control in a condition which is safe and free from health risks, with safe means of entry and exit; and
- providing and maintaining a working environment for employees that is, so far as is reasonably practicable, safe, without risks to health, and has adequate facilities for their welfare at work.

(Adapted from the Home Office publication *A Guide for Police Managers*, 1997.)

5.12.2 The employee's role in health and safety

Health and safety legislation places general duties on employees for example to:

- take reasonable care for their own health and safety and that of other persons who might be affected by his or her acts or omissions (s 7(a) HSWA);
- cooperate with the employer to enable the employer to comply with statutory duties for health and safety (s 7(b) HSWA);
- use correctly all work items provided by the employer, in accordance with training and instructions received (reg 14(1) of the Management of Health and Safety etc Work Regulations 1999); and
- inform their employer, or the person responsible for health and safety, of any work situation which might present a serious and imminent danger and any shortcoming in the health and safety arrangements (reg 14(2) of the Management of Health and Safety etc Work Regulations 1999).

(Adapted from the Home Office publication *A Guide for Police Managers*, 1997.)

All decisions must be taken with due regard to the National Decision Model (see 5.5.2).

5.12.3 Hazards, risks, and threat level

Consider the potential threats to the health and safety of a trainee police officer on foot patrol. You have probably thought of several scenarios in which the trainee police officer could be harmed. But how much harm, and how likely is it to happen? This is a matter of judgement for each different situation, but it makes it easier to judge if you think of each type of harm in terms of the hazard, the risk, and the threat level.

A hazard is something with a potential to cause harm, for example, slipping over on a wet surface, being hit by moving traffic, pricking yourself on a used needle, or being hit by a meteorite. The hazard criteria are about how serious the consequences would be if the event occurs. The formal levels of classification for the hazard level are:

- high—death, major injury, or serious illness may result;
- medium—serious injuries or ill health; off work for more than three days; and
- low—less serious illness or injury; off work for less than three days.

The risk is the likelihood of such an event actually happening (see also 5.5.2 on the National Decision Model). The levels of classification for the risk level are:

- high if the event is very likely or near certain to occur;
- medium if the event is likely to occur; and
- low if the event is very unlikely to occur.

The threat level (sometimes referred to as overall risk) is a combination of the hazard and the risk. (Note the possibility of confusing 'risk' and 'overall risk'; you will need to seek clarification if the context does not make the meaning clear.) The grid shows different combinations of hazard and risk, and the resulting threat levels.

THREAT LEVEL ↘		HAZARD		
		High	Medium	Low
RISK	High	INTOLERABLE **high** threat level	SUBSTANTIAL **high** threat level	MODERATE **medium** threat level
	Medium	SUBSTANTIAL **high** threat level	MODERATE **medium** threat level	ACCEPTABLE **low** threat level
	Low	MODERATE **medium** threat level	ACCEPTABLE **low** threat level	TRIVIAL **low** threat level

(Adapted from Home Office, 1997)

Another way of looking at assessing the threat level is to multiply the hazard and risk in an equation: hazard × risk = threat level. This is not the conventional kind of formula—after all there are no numbers to put into it. But it is another way of emphasizing how the threat level is determined by the combination of the hazard and the risk levels.

The following examples illustrate the interaction between hazard, risk, and threat level:

1. Death by meteorite—the hazard is very high as meteorites can be heavy and fall from the sky at high speeds. But the risk is low as this event is very unlikely to occur. So the threat level is low.
2. Bruising from arresting a drunken suspect—the hazard is minor. However, the risk is high as this is quite likely to occur. But the threat level is low as the consequences are unlikely to be serious.
3. Gunshot wounds when pursuing armed suspects—the hazard is serious, and there is quite a high risk of shots being fired. In this situation the threat level is high (and special precautions should be taken).

Consider another example. Imagine you are a trainee police officer on duty at the scene of a road traffic collision. Your colleague is dealing with an injured person in one of the vehicles and you are directing the traffic.

Hazards	You could be struck by a motor vehicle and your colleague could also be hit whilst attending to the injured person, therefore the hazard level is high, as death or major injury is likely to occur if another vehicle collides with you or your colleague.
Risk	Take into account the time of day, volume of traffic, weather conditions, and location: the risk level is medium as it is likely or possible that you might be struck by a vehicle.
Threat level	The threat level is therefore assessed as substantial.

There has been criticism of apparent 'risk aversion' amongst some police officers, but the College of Policing state (2013f) that 'Police decision makers can, therefore, be more accurately described as professional risk takers, with risk taking being at the core of police professionalism'. Further information is available online in *Striking the balance between operational and health and safety duties in the Police Service* produced by the Health and Safety Executive.

5.12.4 Control measures

Control measures are steps that can be taken to lower the risk and therefore reduce the threat level. A five-step approach can be used, as illustrated in the following example; imagine you are a trainee police officer on foot patrol.

- **Step 1: Identify the hazards.** As a pedestrian you are exposed to danger from moving vehicles, and you could also face unpredictable confrontation with members of the public.
- **Step 2: Who may be harmed, and how?** You, a colleague, or a member of the public could be harmed by a moving vehicle, or a weapon used by a member of the public, resulting in death or major injury. Therefore, the hazard level would be high.
- **Step 3: Evaluate the risks.** You are always at risk of walking into an unexpected situation in which harm is possible/likely to occur. Your up-to-the minute location is not always known, and you are sometimes alone, so harm is possible/likely. You may face difficulties with radio communication, reception, and transmission, or other faulty systems, which could lead to harm. Therefore, the risk potential is medium.
- **Step 4: Record your findings.** The threat level grid shows the threat level would be substantial, so you should use control measures to lower it.
- **Step 5: Review your assessment from time to time, and revise it if necessary.**

The following control measures could be used to lower the threat level:

- in relation to the road network, adopting the correct procedures learnt during training, wearing the correct personal protective equipment (fluorescent), and using First Aid if required;
- applying techniques from training sessions for control and restraint, firearms and knife awareness, and using personal protection equipment;
- keeping the Control Room updated with your location;
- using your local knowledge and requesting all available information to assess situations; and
- being aware of the limitations of communications equipment.

> **TASK 18** Imagine you are a trainee police officer carrying out a search of an aggressive young man (under s 1 of the PACE Act 1984: see 9.3). What would be your considerations in relation to your own and your colleagues' safety while searching him? What is your estimation of the threat level and what could be done to lower it?

5.12.5 Personal safety training

Police officers are permitted to use reasonable force if necessary to prevent crime or to arrest a person (see 15.5.1). This right exists under common law and s 3 of the Criminal Law Act 1967. In addition, s 117 of the PACE Act 1984 allows a police officer to use reasonable force to exercise powers granted by other parts of PACE. A police officer may also use reasonable force in self-defence (see *R v McInnes* [1971] 1 WLR 1600 (CA)). In all cases the force used must be proportionate and exercised with due regard to the human rights of the individuals concerned. The definition of reasonable force is covered in 15.5.1.

A PCDA or DHEP trainee police officer will receive practical training in protecting both him/herself and others from attack, and about how to use reasonable force against others. The relevant National Policing Curriculum subject area is 'Managing Conflict'. Pre-join programmes are not likely to include practical training unless the programme is also for special constables.

The precise title of the training may vary, but most forces call it Personal Safety Training (PST) or the Personal Safety Programme. The term PST is preferred to Officer Safety Training (OST), because some or all of the training is also used for some members of the extended police family. Alternatively, a force may have contracted with the College of Policing to deliver the 'Personal Safety—Basic Course'.

The training normally takes place in specialist facilities over a period of five to ten days. The typical components of PST are conflict management, searching people and places, protective equipment, using handcuffs and limb restraints, 'unarmed' self-protection skills, considerations when attending particular types of scenes, edged weapon skills, using incapacitant sprays, and using batons and ASPs. Further information is available in the NPCC *Personal Safety Manual 2016* (available on the College of Policing website), and the NPCC *Guidance on the use of Handcuffs* and *Guidance on the use of Incapacitant Spray*, available online.

Successful completion of PST is a target within the early stages of the PCDA and trainee officers have to achieve it before Independent Patrol. However, many trainee officers will be expected to successfully complete PST much earlier, before their first Supervised Patrol, and in many cases before any community engagement. Police officers may also be expected to undertake and pass 'refresher' PST training courses later in their career.

> **TASK 19** Each force will have police officers trained in the use of equipment used for protection in Chemical, Biological, Radiological, or Nuclear incidents (CBRN incidents, see 11.6.3). What is the standard personal-protective equipment used by the UK police for such incidents?

5.12.6 First aid training

It is the duty of every police officer to 'protect life'. Inevitably police officers find themselves at incidents where there are seriously injured people, and they may also be called upon by members of the public to assist in helping with a whole range of conditions, from a sprained ankle or scalding by hot water through to heart attacks or epileptic seizures. The public will expect a police officer to know what to do, and although specialized medical personnel will also be present (or on their way) on most occasions, a police officer will sometimes be the first person on the scene who has received any training for dealing with such emergencies.

It is for this reason that, pre-join programmes and the induction phase of training include basic First Aid. The training is likely to be based around Module 2 of the College of Policing First Aid Learning Programme (FALP). The assessment might involve the four elements of NOS Unit 4G4 'Administer First Aid' which was developed by the British Red Cross in consultation with the St John Ambulance Service.

Elements of Unit 4G4—Administer First Aid	
4G4.1	Respond to the needs of casualties with minor injuries
4G4.2	Respond to the needs of casualties with major injuries
4G4.3	Respond to the needs of unconscious casualties
4G4.4	Perform cardio-pulmonary resuscitation (CPR)

Successful completion of First Aid training is likely to be a necessary condition for Independent Patrol (see 6.6.1). First Aid training is likely to cover some or all of the following:

- **managing scenes and casualties:** for example, assessing the extent of casualties, communicating with others;
- **Basic Life Support (BLS) for Adults:** a series of actions to administer as immediate life support, including the need first to ensure the safety of yourself and others. BLS involves checking the injured person for a response, checking airways and breathing, and what to

do next (recovery position, chest compression, rescue breaths, depending on the situation), and performing cardio-pulmonary resuscitation (CPR);

- **Basic Life Support (BLS) for Infants and Children**: variations on the system used for adults;
- **specific critical medical conditions**: eg shock, bleeding, spinal injuries, heart attacks, and epilepsy;
- **choking**: techniques employed to counter choking;
- **sprains, strains, and fractures**: dealing with broken bones and similar injuries;
- **scalds and burns**: what to do before more specialist medical treatment can be obtained; and
- **hypothermia, frostbite, heatstroke, and heat exhaustion**: how to treat such potentially complex medical conditions, especially for vulnerable individuals.

Most police forces expect police officers to maintain their level of First Aid training after the initial probationary period. Typically, this involves a 'refresher course' every three years or so. For more specialist roles, officers may be required to undertake specialist First Aid training.

TASK 20 Read and reflect on the contents of Chapter 10 ('First Aid') of the 1999 Macpherson Inquiry into the death of Stephen Lawrence, at <https://www.gov.uk/government/publications/the-stephen-lawrence-inquiry>.

5.12.7   Coping with stressful situations

All professional work has the potential to create stress, but policing presents its own unique challenges in that it involves not only the usual sources of stress when working for a large organization (bureaucracy, differences with colleagues, etc) but also coping with crises, emergencies, and crime. These particular sources of stress can also affect the other people involved, for example suspects, victims, and witnesses, and hence police officers often have to manage the reactions of others who are also experiencing stress. There has been a significant increase in the last few years in the number of sick days taken by police officers on the grounds of 'stress-related illness'.

It is difficult to scientifically define exactly what it means when we say that somebody is suffering from 'stress' (as distinct from the perfectly normal short-term reactions most of us have to a challenging situation). However, most definitions of longer term stress emphasize that it is more continuous than a transient state, and includes a persistent set of 'symptoms' such as anxiety, feelings of insecurity, and physiological effects such as palpitations or diarrhoea.

It is important to recognize the symptoms of long-term stress both within yourself, and others. These are many and varied and include feeling generally 'tensed up', irritable, having a short temper, sleep disturbance (particularly insomnia), problems in relationships, poor appetite, and physical symptoms such as headaches. However, professional medical advice is required to properly identify stress as a cause of these problems. Stressful situations do not necessarily give rise to long-term stress and, likewise, a person may be 'stressed' for no apparent reason.

The sources of stress in policing can be thought of as originating from three interrelated contexts: from within the person, from being a member of a police force, and from the external demands placed on police officers. It could be that some personality types are more susceptible to stress, or that the very types of people who are attracted to policing are also more vulnerable to stress (although there is only limited research to support this idea). In addition, being a member of a large, complex, and demanding organization such as a police force can easily lead to exposure to sources of stress. The demands placed on police officers, in terms of dealing with the results of crime and disorder (including death and injury), interacting with members of the public, offenders, and the legal profession are also obvious sources of stress, particularly as police officers' mistakes may have serious consequences and are sometimes very visible. Responding to a critical incident can be particularly stressful as police officers may witness very disturbing events; this can lead to 'Post-Traumatic Stress Disorder' (PTSD).

There are numerous articles, books, and websites with advice on coping with stress. Police forces also have counselling facilities as well as occupational health support (eg through the

'Occupational Support Unit'). The advice typically centres on dealing with both the symptoms (which may require specialist medical help) and the causes of stress.

5.13 Answers to Tasks

TASK 1 There are many techniques for memorizing information (the author Tony Buzan, for example, has written extensively on the subject). We describe one straightforward technique here for memorizing the declaration:

1. Gather ample supplies of blank paper!
2. Now write out (or word-process) the declaration on a blank piece of paper by copying the original. Check and double-check that you have the words exactly as they should be.
3. Read the first sentence several times (not the whole paragraph) and try to commit this to memory.
4. Now turn the page and try and write the first sentence on another piece of paper from memory.
5. Check your recollected version against the original, word for word.
6. Repeat stages 3–5 until you have the sentence completely correct.
7. Now attempt to memorize the first two sentences together in order.
8. Repeat the process until you have the first two sentences completely correct.
9. Now add the third sentence and so on, until you have committed the complete declaration to memory.

This may take you some hours to achieve. The same technique can be used for memorizing other information—for example, your force might expect you to learn 'definitions'.

TASK 2 Although the police officer concerned was off duty when the alleged incidents took place you have probably noted that the standards for general conduct apply for officers both on and off duty. The standards apparently breached here include Honesty and Integrity, Duties and Responsibilities, and Discreditable Conduct.

TASK 3 In many police forces, such as Kent Police, you would need permission from at least the BCU commander, and the written notice must be given to the chief constable using the form *Notification of Secondary Business Interests*. This should be forwarded through the individual's line manager to the divisional commander or head of department for endorsement.

In many forces, the responsibility for monitoring the 'secondary business interests' of police officers and police staff is delegated to the head of HR.

TASK 4 You will have your own response to the first part of the task. In relation to receiving an unlawful order, this is most unlikely to occur, but you should still be clear about your own position. Knowing whether or not an order is unlawful may not always be immediately obvious, however officers must oppose any improper behaviour or command, and report it where appropriate. The College of Policing Code of Ethics (2014a) goes on to state:

> 5.3 There may be instances when failure to follow an order or instruction does not amount to misconduct. For example, where a police officer reasonably believes that an order is unlawful or has good and sufficient reason not to comply.

> 5.4 Any decision to not obey orders or follow instructions, or that transgresses policing policies and other guidance, must be able to withstand scrutiny.

TASK 5 The assumption is that consent should be achieved in a positive sense, through gaining the support of the public and involving them in policing decisions and strategies. There is also an emphasis on the need for police to be ever more responsive to community needs, see, for example, *Policing Vision 2025* (NPCC, 2016). In 1829, we would argue, the notion of consent was slightly different—it was measured negatively in the sense that people were consenting only to the extent that they were not proactively objecting to or protesting against policing initiatives.

TASK 6 As we suggested, there are no certain answers to this task, but the following two could be examples:

Low pay → Police accept bribes → Politicians bribe the police

And:

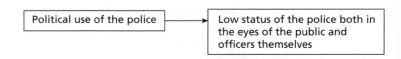

Political use of the police ⟶ Low status of the police both in the eyes of the public and officers themselves

There have been a number of interesting attempts in other countries to tackle, for example, corruption amongst their police officers through using the kind of analysis that you have just undertaken. For example, in Kenya, police wages in 2004 were almost doubled and corruption subsequently fell. (However, proving that this was cause and effect is somewhat more difficult.)

Task 7 You have probably spotted our intentions with this task; the two situations are very similar. The first scenario is the more serious in policing terms as you are told that the woman appears to be slightly drunk, whereas the young man is simply clutching a can of lager. In the first case, the fact that she is a medical student who will soon (presumably) join the medical profession may well have influenced your thinking towards exercising discretion. However, you were not appointed to be a moral guardian of society: the place that a person holds in society should not feature in your decision whether or not to exercise discretion.

In terms of your answer you might well have considered other aspects such as the intentions of each person concerned, the precise nature of the apparent offence, and so on. The problem with presenting these scenarios in a written form (or as simulations in training) is the lack of detailed context; this is so important when making decisions.

When exercising discretion it is important that you would be able to justify your actions to an outsider looking in—that is, to show how discretion is the result of rational decision-making rather than instinct or some other gut reaction. Being clear about your justification will also help you meet the assessment requirements during training and assessment; you must evidence your decision-making because your assessor cannot read your mind!

Taylor (1999) produced a useful checklist for the exercise of discretion. It suggests you consider issues such as fairness, justice, accountability, consistency, and wider community interests and expectations.

TASK 8 Drugs policing, in particular, gives rise to a number of opportunities for corruption, both in type and frequency (Lee and South, 2003). These include theft from arrested drug dealers, planting drugs to imply guilt, illegally protecting drug dealers (eg by classifying them as a CHIS), and participation in dealing.

TASK 9 The five opportunities from the list are:

- first arrival at the scene of a crime where cash or goods are present;
- handling and storing drugs from police investigations;
- the excessive exercise of discretion without challenge;
- managing informants without adequate supervision or scrutiny; and
- lack of effective supervision.

TASK 10 The free cup of coffee theory may seem to you to be an unlikely explanation, but imagine if a police officer uses his warrant card to secure financial advantage—for example to gain free entry to a club. Even if he justifies this to himself on the grounds that his (non-uniformed) presence would somehow be to the benefit of the club concerned, would this not lead to at least a small sense of obligation on his part, and a potential compromise of his position? As they say in the USA, 'nobody ever gave a cop something for nothing'. The situation is even more complex when a police officer has a second job.

This is not to say that accepting gratuities is always wrong. It will depend on the circumstances, and on force policy. For example, you may be offered a cup of tea by well-meaning members of the public if you are engaged in long and tiring public order duties, and it seems there would be little to lose and much to be gained by accepting the offer on those occasions. For a comprehensive discussion of police corruption you might want to read Caless (2008a and 2008b), as well as Newburn (1999) and Miller (2003).

TASK 11 You can find out whether your local force has a branch of the BPA by searching the database on their website.

TASK 12 They are both features of the PNC. VODS is a Vehicle Online Descriptive Search application to help identify vehicles. It can search for combinations of details such as make and model, colour, and VIN (see 19.2.1.1). QUEST is a Query Using Extended Search Techniques facility within PNC, and is the fuzzy capability we referred to earlier. The operator can input partial descriptions of people and produce a list of names that match the characteristics. HMIC have reported the following example of a successful outcome when using QUEST:

> In the West Midlands, counterfeit currency was used in a public house. A search was carried out on the description of a white male, 6' tall, thin build with a skinhead haircut, brown hair, aged 20–22 years. The offender had a tattoo of a swallow on his left hand. Enquiries at the scene suggested he lived in Solihull and may have been called 'Barry'. A QUEST search produced one suspect who was subsequently dealt with for the offence. (HMIC, 2005b, p 36)

You might like to conduct further research on the use of Boolean search techniques that use AND, OR, and NOT. These are also useful for conducting internet searches. Further information is available at <http://www.inbrief.co.uk/police/police-national-computer.htm>.

TASK 13 In 1975 the police in London replaced their 'RC code' ('Race Code') with a new 'IdentiCoding' ('IC') system. This assigned 'white-skinned European types—English, Scottish, Welsh, Scandinavian and Russian' to IC1; 'dark-skinned European types—Sardinian, Spanish, Italian' to IC2; 'Negroid types—Caribbean, West Indian, African, Nigerian' to IC3; 'Indians and Pakistanis' to IC4; 'Chinese, Japanese, Mongolians, Siamese' to IC5; and 'Arabians, Egyptians, Algerians, Moroccans and North Africans' to IC6. Even at the time this caused some controversy (Mackie, 1978). An example of an unofficial IC code is 'IC 9' for people from the gypsy, Roma, or traveller community.

For operational reasons the police obviously require a quick, efficient, and timely means of accurately communicating the ethnic appearance of a missing person, victim, or suspect. Care and thought is always needed to ensure the codes are not used in a way that could appear to others to be racist or discriminatory.

TASK 14 Agreed, this task requires a gross oversimplification of the theory. However, on most occasions the Handbook would appear to be in adult mode—but there are certainly also aspects of the critical and nurturing parent.

TASK 15 We obviously provide a simplified account of transactional analysis (TA). You might want to read further. A good starting point is Berne's very readable and popular 1968 book *Games People Play* (reissued in the late 1990s). The games that Berne refers to are transactions that lead inevitably to predictable outcomes.

Note that TA is not without its critics, and some of its academic standing has been damaged by popularized and oversimplified accounts. Another frequent approach (in police training) to analysing the interactions between individuals (or groups) is the use of the so-called 'Johari' window. The unusual name Johari originates from its two inventors, Joseph Luft and Harry Ingham (Luft, 1970). It proposes that one way of analysing aspects of human interaction is to identify areas of personal awareness and ignorance:

	Known to self	Not known to self
Known to others	Open area	Blind area
Not known to others	Hidden area	Unknown area

For example, the blind area includes aspects which the person does not know about him/herself but which others know. This can range from straightforward information (such as a medical complaint like halitosis) to more developed personality features, such as feelings of inadequacy, which may be barely discerned by the individuals concerned and yet can be easily seen by others.

TASK 16 The questions you might ask could refer to your actions, such as entering a person's home, touching a person when conducting a search, and religious requirements for the treatment of the dead.

TASK 17 The following are examples of how the five forms of authority might feature in the scenario:

Form of authority	Examples
Epistemic	You have a clear understanding of the definition of the possible offences involved in this incident. You have knowledge of the appropriate procedures to be followed and this is conveyed in speech to those present, including the victim and the offender
Natural	You use your demeanour and language to take control of the situation, including indicating when you wish a person to answer a question and in which order
De facto	Your right to question those involved is probably accepted without challenge (but not necessarily with good grace!)
De jure	You have the authority to arrest if the circumstances require this
Moral	You demonstrate, through your behaviour and attitudes, that you do not immediately jump to conclusions concerning the sequence of events, nor attribute guilt or innocence

TASK 18 The hazards include him injuring you with a weapon or an object he is carrying (or picks up, or takes from you, such as your own personal safety equipment). He might also have an infection or infestation (such as hepatitis C, TB, or scabies) and could pass it on to you. He may also have needles concealed in his clothing. Therefore the hazard level is medium, as you could be absent from work for more than three days if he does attack or harm you.

In terms of the risks, you should take into account his level of agitation and aggression, how long the search is likely to take, the extent to which you provide an opportunity for him to use force against you, the locality of the search (in terms of its proximity to any colleagues and members of the public) and the level of illumination. As it is likely or possible that you might be injured, the risk level is medium, so in conjunction with the hazard level, the threat level can be calculated to be moderate.

There are many control measures you could take, for example:

• requesting a cover officer (if you are alone);
• carrying out personal safety techniques such as standing at his side when conducting the search;
• being aware of his movements at all times during the search;
• engaging him in conversation (because he will find it difficult to think of answers to questions and do other things at the same time);
• wearing gloves to reduce the risk of injury, and washing your hands (and other exposed body parts) afterwards; and
• carrying out the search in the sight line of a CCTV camera, if possible.

TASK 19 The 'CR1' is the standard CBRN personal protection equipment issued to trained police officers in the event of an incident (CR stands for Civil Responder; the military are issued with their own version). The CR1 is also used by the fire service in similar circumstances. CBRN incidents are covered in 11.6.3.

TASK 20 Naturally, much media attention at the time of the Macpherson Inquiry report centred on the charge of institutional racism. Unfortunately, this inadvertently diverted national attention from the very serious issue of police officers' First Aid skills, and the need to maintain such skills throughout their careers and at all ranks. Although the Report is clear that Stephen Lawrence's death from his injuries was probably unavoidable, Chapter 10 remains a shocking catalogue of incompetence and ineptitude. It concludes with the observation that:

> [t]his evidence reinforced the Inquiry's views as to the lack of satisfactory and proper training in First Aid for officers of all ranks. Not only should officers be properly trained and be given proper refresher training at regular intervals, but it must be made plain that more senior officers need instruction just as much as junior officers. An officer in the position of [name] must be able to ensure that what is being done by his juniors is proper and satisfactory and in accordance with well-coordinated and directed training. The notion that it may be good enough simply to wait for the ambulance and the paramedics must be exploded. (Macpherson, 1999, s 10.6)

6 Qualifying as a Police Officer

6.1 Introduction

In this chapter we examine the National Policing Curriculum, the new Pre-join Degree in Professional Policing ('Pre-join Degree'), the Police Constable Degree Apprenticeship (PCDA), and the Degree Holder Entry Programme (DHEP). We then look at applying to join the police, the probationary period, Independent Patrol Status, and Full Operational Competence.

6.2 The National Policing Curriculum

The National Policing Curriculum (NPC) was developed by the College of Policing to form the basis of training for a range of policing roles, responsibilities, and levels. It is aligned with the College of Policing Authorised Professional Practice (APP), and the curriculum is structured around seven themes (CoP, 2016d) with the 'Core Learning' theme being central to all parts of the curriculum. A 'curriculum' normally refers to all the learning that is considered necessary for a student to achieve specified learning outcomes. It will therefore usually include or make reference to an accepted body of knowledge, but might also refer to the teaching and learning methods to be employed and the skills to be gained, and will generally articulate with formal qualifications.

The NPC informs the curriculum of the pre-join degree (see 6.4.1), and also informs the 'structure, content and academic progression' (CoP, 2018j) of the new Police Constable Degree Apprenticeships (see 6.4.2), and the new Degree Holder Entry Programmes expected to start in 2020 (see 6.4.3).

6.3 Overview of Qualifications

Until relatively recently the usual qualification route for police officers was through joining a police force and undertaking a two-year full-time probationary period of training. There was little, if any, accreditation of prior learning, and the same model of entry applied to all applicants. The new Policing Education Qualifications Framework (PEQF) has led to major changes, and from 2020 all new police constables will be required to already have a degree level qualification, or be working towards a degree level qualification through the Police Constable Degree Apprenticeship programme. Parallel developments are occurring with PCSO training, with some forces introducing a new 'Police Community Support Officer Apprenticeship' (eg Thames Valley Police, 2019).

The table summarizes the various routes to qualification that have been available in recent years. The final three routes in bold are the current routes available as of 2020.

Course	Qualification	APL arrangements	Comments
Traditional police training (two years)	Diploma in Policing*	N/A	In the past this was the only form of training
Foundation Degree in Policing, Police Studies, or related discipline	FdA or FdSc. Often linked with joining Special Constabulary. HE Level 5*	Towards knowledge requirements, and competence requirements if linked with Special Constabulary	Students complete Diploma in Policing* before or after joining Two-year, full-time programme
Honours Degree in Policing, Police Studies or related discipline	BA (Hons) or BSc (Hons), HE Level 6*	Towards knowledge requirements, and competence requirements if linked with Special Constabulary	Students complete Diploma in Policing* before or after joining Typically three years in duration (full-time)
Pre-join Degree in Professional Policing ('Pre-join Degree')	Title of degree prescribed (and its use sanctioned) by the College of Policing through an approval process, but typically 'BSc (Hons) Professional Policing' HE Level 6	APL for Special Constables towards the NPC	Graduates from this degree apply to join the police *after* completing their degree. Is expected to meet the CoP 'Pre-join Degree in Professional Policing National Programme Specification'. May include membership of the Special Constabulary. Two-year probationary period
Police Constable Degree Apprenticeship (PCDA)	Prescribed by the College of Policing through an approval process, but typically 'BSc (Hons) Professional Policing Practice' HE Level 6	Determined by universities and partner forces, using CoP guidelines	Applicants apply to join the police *before* taking the PCDA. Validated using Apprenticeship Framework, university regulations together with College of Policing accreditation. Successful End Point Assessment leads to confirmation as Police Constable. Three-year probationary period
Degree Holder Entry Programme (DHEP)	Prescribed by the College of Policing but typically a 'Graduate Diploma in Professional Policing Practice'	APL will depend on the degree subject studied but likely to be limited	Graduates apply to join the police *after* completing their degree, prior to starting the DHEP. Two-year probationary period

There are now a number of 'direct entry' schemes in several police forces, such as the 'fast-track' inspector scheme. The recruitment policy has changed to allow direct entry to the rank of superintendent, and the possibility of appointment of chief constables from overseas (Home Office, 2013g). The first few evaluations of the outcomes of these schemes are now available. A more recent initiative has been the recruitment to 'Detective constable' via direct entry schemes (eg Kent Police). In this case entrants are expected to pass the National Investigators' Examination within 12 months of joining and then achieve PIP Level 2 in the second year of training.

The 'Police Now' initiative offers another route into policing. This 'two-year national leadership programme' aims to train 'outstanding graduates' to become police officers (Police Now, 2018b). It is loosely based on the 'Teach Now' scheme, and is currently run in partnership with 17 police forces. The programme consists of an intensive six-week summer training course followed by a two-year period of 'leadership and problem solving skills' (Police Now, 2018a). Note that from late 2019 the 'Police Now' entry route is likely to be through the DHEP (see 6.4.3).

6.4   The New Routes to Qualifying as a Police Constable

It is likely that from 2020 there will be three possible pathways to confirmation as a police constable:

- successful completion of a 'College of Policing-approved' pre-join professional policing degree, for which students fund themselves, followed by applying to join a police force, being accepted, and a two-year probationary period (see 6.4.1);
- a 'Police Constable Degree Apprenticeship' (PCDA, see 6.4.2) where recruits gain an undergraduate degree whilst training as a police constable (and receiving a salary, but at the level of an 'apprentice police officer'), with a three-year probationary period;
- a 'post-join' postgraduate 'conversion' programme into policing (the Degree Holder Entry Programme, DHEP, see 6.4.3) funded by a police force, for graduates from disciplines other than policing, such as the social sciences.

All three routes share a common curriculum, with only minor variations between them. Note that the curricula for all three entry routes are subject to revision and change.

6.4.1 The pre-join degree in professional policing

Pre-join degrees in professional policing are typically three years in duration (when taken full-time) and include most of the 'knowledge' (as distinct from skills and behaviours) required to become a police constable. After completing your degree you will need to apply to join a police force within five years (CoP, 2019c). It is important to note that the successful completion of pre-join degrees will not guarantee entry to the full-time police, or even an interview with a police force; the nationally determined recruitment assessment process will still apply (see 6.5).

Entry requirements for pre-join degrees are determined by the university concerned and will normally be expressed as a number of UCAS tariff points (eg 104 points), the holding of a BTEC Diploma at a particular grade or above, or similar qualifications. As with other undergraduate degrees, students on pre-join degrees are expected to pay tuition fees to the university concerned. If you plan to undertake a pre-join degree you should check at the outset that you have no good reason to think you might be automatically rejected by a police service once you finish your degree. You could be rejected, for example, because you do not meet the requirements for unaided eyesight.

Students on pre-join degrees may be offered the option of joining the special constabulary of the local police force. This will provide the opportunity to gain practical experience of policing while studying for a degree (CoP, 2018k, p 6). Note, however, that being a special constable while on the pre-join degree is no guarantee of being accepted as a full-time police constable. Unfortunately, there are many examples of 'specials' being rejected as full-time police constables despite having years of good service.

After completing the degree and a successful application to join a police force, new recruits will undertake a conversion course and two years' probation. Graduates from College of Policing approved pre-join degree programmes are expected to progress quickly and soon be able to undertake Independent Patrol with 'minimal orientation' (CoP, 2019b, p 5), and unlike the other two routes, it is unlikely that further qualification will be required. The conversion courses are not yet in place but are likely to be shorter than would be the case with a 'non-policing' degree (see 6.4.3 on the DHEP).

The College of Policing expects the content of all 'approved' pre-join degrees to meet its 'Pre-join Degree in Professional Policing National Programme Specification' (CoP, 2018l, p 9) and to include the core professional knowledge required in the National Policing Curriculum (CoP, 2018k, p 7) such as 'evidence based policing' and 'digital policing' (ibid, p 8). The College of Policing operates a licensing scheme for the pre-join degree, and at the time of writing (early 2019) a total of 27 universities were planning on offering approved pre-join degrees in professional policing from September 2019.

6.4.2 The Police Constable Degree Apprenticeship

The Police Constable Degree Apprenticeship (PCDA) is one of the three entry routes into policing and is likely, after 2019, to become the main route (possibly the only route) to qualification as a police constable for applicants without a degree. The apprenticeship combines the knowledge and skills required for full operational competence as a police constable (see 6.4.2 and 6.6) and culminates in both 'confirmation' in position and the award of an undergraduate degree.

6.4.2.1   The PCDA entry requirements

The entry requirements will be determined by police forces in consultation with partner universities/colleges, and will follow the guidance provided by the College of Policing and the Secretary of State. Typically, the requirements are that applicants:

- are aged 18–54 years;
- must hold a Level 3 qualification (or equivalent) prior to entry; and
- meet the police recruitment requirements (see 6.5).

The 'functional skills' qualifications of English and Mathematics at Level 2 (or equivalents) will also be required before completion of the PCDA. In some forces these qualifications are one of the entry requirements, but in others they can be achieved during the three-year PCDA.

Although the entry requirements for the PCDA are normally Level 3 (such as 'A' Level), a number of police forces and Higher Education Institutions (HEIs) are offering an alternative of online tests. It is not clear, however, just how these equivalents have been validated, nor how they will be moderated.

In all cases, entry to the PCDA also requires success at an 'Assessment Centre' (see 6.5.3). Forces select the starting dates for new recruits to their programmes in order to meet their recruitment requirements, and so programmes will not necessarily start in September/October (as is common with many undergraduate degrees).

6.4.2.2   The PCDA programme

The PCDA programme is taken over a three-year period full-time (around 48 weeks per year). It may also be possible in some cases to complete it on a part-time basis over a longer period.

The final PCDA qualification is an HE Level 6 'honours' degree, for example BSc (Hons) Professional Policing Practice. The year-by-year achievements are shown in the table.

PCDA year (full time)	HE level	Features
1	4	Independent Patrol Status
2	5	PIP Level 1 All five specialisms are studied, including work-experience placements
3	6	Full Operational Competence. One specialism is selected (PIP Level 2 may be gained through the Conducting Investigations specialism)

The course content is a mix of practice-based learning, operational policing skills acquisition, and academic (knowledge-based) courses (eg 'police legislation'). In the final year students undertake one of the five specialisms: Response Policing, Policing Communities, Roads Policing, Information and Intelligence, and Conducting Investigations.

Students will learn through workplace studies, scenarios, taught lessons, and mentorship (for practical policing). In common with other degree apprenticeships (such as in engineering), apprentices divide their time between working, training, and learning. A minimum of 20 per cent of the learning takes place 'off the job', for example at a force training centre or university. Independent study and learning will also be required (eg through the NCALT and a university's virtual learning environment).

From the outset, apprentices are in full-time employment with a police force; they are attested 'probationary police constables' (or 'student police constables'), and will receive a salary, although it will be lower than for confirmed police constables. In 2019 the Dorset Police starting salary was £18,000 rising to £23,586 once Independent Patrol Status (see 6.6.1) has been achieved (Dorset Police, 2019). Apprentices do not pay tuition fees to partner universities. However, you are advised to check with the HE institution and police force concerned whether you would be expected to pay back the tuition fees (that the force would have passed to the university), if you chose to leave before the end of the three-year apprenticeship.

PCDA programmes (in common with all degree apprenticeships) blend together employer-defined knowledge, skills, and behaviour ('KSB') into an undergraduate degree in Professional

Policing Practice. The KSB requirement for the PCDA is evidenced by portfolio-building throughout the programme (see 6.6.1 and 6.6.2). Each KSB element is described separately, but in practice they interlink, and a single PCDA student assignment might well include the ability to generate evidence for all three. Independent Patrol Status (IPS) (see 6.6.1) is normally achieved at around the 30- to 35-week point in Year 1 (the exact timing varies from force to force), and Full Operational Competence towards the end of the apprenticeship. The PCDA culminates in the End Point Assessment (see 6.6.3). After successful completion of this final stage the student will be 'confirmed' as a police constable.

PCDAs offered by universities and partner police forces are required to fully align with the College of Policing PCDA National Curriculum, the PCDA Standard, and the PCDA End-Point Assessment Plan (see 6.6.3). Courses and modules on approved programmes are mapped against the learning outcomes of the College of Policing PCDA National Curriculum.

6.4.2.3   PCDA knowledge requirement

The PCDA knowledge requirement is derived from the National Policing Curriculum (see 6.2). Much of the learning for PCDA knowledge acquisition will take place through a blend of classroom-based learning (at a police force training centre and/or university) and online materials and delivery. Knowledge acquisition tends to feature more extensively in the first two years of the PCDA.

Once an apprentice police constable is ready for 'confirmation' he/she will be expected to know and understand all the information summarized in the table.

Knowledge area	Components
The ethics and values of professional policing	Including: duty of care, service delivery, employment practice, efficiency, effectiveness and value for money, Code of Ethics, professional standards, and equality, diversity and human rights
Key cross-cutting and inter-dependent areas of policing	Including: roles and responsibilities, criminal justice, counter-terrorism, vulnerability (including public protection and mental health) and risk
Applicable aspects of College of Policing Authorised Professional Practice	The legal and organizational requirements relating to the operational policing context (response, community, intelligence, investigation and roads/transport), including how to: • effectively respond to incidents, preserving scenes and evidence when necessary; • manage and resolve conflict safely and lawfully; • arrest, detain, and report individuals safely and lawfully; • conduct diligent and efficient, priority and high volume investigations; • effectively interview victims, witnesses, and suspects; • systematically gather, submit, and share information and intelligence to further policing-related outcomes; • meticulously and ethically search individuals, vehicles, premises, and outside and virtual spaces; • optimize the use of available technology; • risk manage health and safety for self and for others
How to interpret and apply the letter and essence of all relevant law	As related to any policing situation, incident, or context encountered by trainees
Social behaviour and society	Including their origins, development, organization, networks, and institutions and how this relates to policing across diverse and increasingly complex communities
The causes, mitigation, and prevention of crime	[In particular] how this knowledge and understanding can influence and be applied to accountable decision-making in all operational policing environments
In-depth knowledge, understanding, and expertise relevant to organizational/local needs	Including the following operational policing contexts: response, community, intelligence, investigation, and roads/transport
Different approaches to systematic evidence-based preventative policing	Including how to critically analyse, interpret, implement, share, and evaluate findings to problem solve and further positive outcomes. These may relate to internal organizational practice or external social or criminal factors

Based on Institute for Apprenticeships & Technical Education (2018b) with text reproduced under the terms of the Open Government Licence (http://www.nationalarchives.gov.uk/doc/open-government-licence/version/1/open-government-licence.htm). Crown copyright © 2019.

Qualifications and Training

The knowledge aspects of the PCDA will often be grouped into courses or modules (eg 'Evidence-based Policing'). The courses or modules will outline the required learning outcomes and how the learning will be assessed. A typical PCDA programme structure consists of a number of modules with pre- and co-requisites, credit ratings, and HE levels (see this example from Canterbury Christ Church University—which is part of a Police Degree Apprenticeship Consortium, along with Portsmouth, Cumbria, and Middlesex universities).

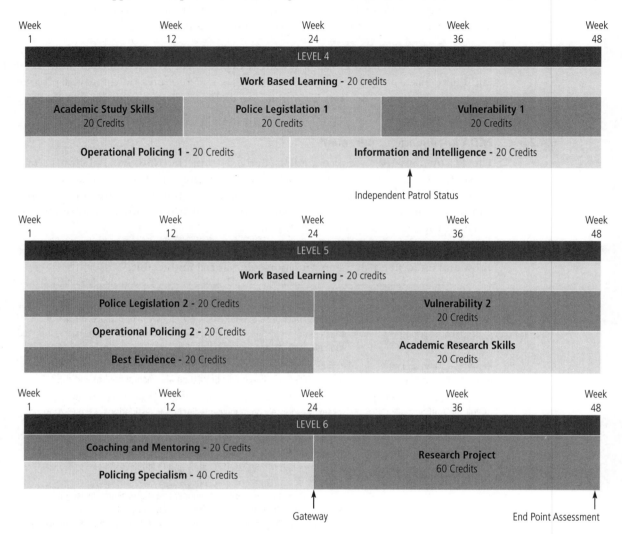

The PCDA knowledge requirement concerning the need to 'Understand key counter terrorism concepts' would probably be broken down for teaching and learning purposes into 'extremism', 'terrorism offences', and so on, and be delivered within a module about Vulnerability. In the first two years there tend to be fewer optional modules. In the third year the options consist of the five policing specialisms.

6.4.2.4   PCDA skills requirement

The Institute for Apprenticeships and Technical Education defines skills as the 'practical application of knowledge needed to successfully undertake the duties that make up the occupation'—in this case initial policing as a police constable.

Skills development is introduced during the first year of the PCDA, but greater emphasis is placed on it during the second year of training. The skills that an apprentice police constable is expected to demonstrate before confirmation are listed here.

Skills—the police constable will safely and lawfully be able to:

• Apply Authorised Professional Practice and any local policy applicable to the operational policing context.

- Communicate effectively, in accordance with the varied needs of differing situations, individuals, groups, and communities. Use own communication skills to manage planned and uncertain situations, and to persuade/lead others as needed.
- Gather, handle, and accurately analyse information and intelligence from a variety of sources to support law enforcement and to maximize policing effectiveness.
- Manage dynamic conflict situations in policing through leadership, and by dealing with a wide range of behaviours and incidents, taking personal accountability for the use of proportionate and justifiable responses and actions.
- Manage effective and ethical searches for evidence and information in differing environments. Take responsibility for courses of action required to follow up on findings (within remit of own role) to maintain the peace and uphold the law.
- Provide an initial, autonomous, and ongoing response to incidents, which can be complex, confrontational, and life-threatening, to bring about the best possible outcomes. Provide an initial, autonomous response to crime scenes, where encountered, that require the management and preservation of evidence and exhibits.
- Provide leadership to protect the public, and empathetic and appropriate support to victims, witnesses, and vulnerable people.
- Manage and conduct effective and efficient priority and high volume investigations. Use initiative to diligently progress investigations, identifying, evaluating, and following lines of enquiry to inform the possible initiation of criminal proceedings. Apply an investigative mind-set when decision-making. Present permissible evidence to authorities where required.
- Interview victims, witnesses, and suspects (including those who may be non-compliant, or have been intimidated or coerced) effectively, in relation to a range of investigations, some of which may be multi-dimensional.
- Assess risk and threats across increasingly complex policing contexts, to take decisions and evaluate initiatives and their outcomes, including the impact of differing actions and methods, in accordance with the policing national decision-making model and evidence-based principles. Take account of the best available evidence from a wide array of sources, including research and analysis, when making decisions. Apply justified discretion when it is appropriate and in the public interest to do so.
- Use police legal powers to deal with suspects, victims, and witnesses across various challenging situations, conducting all actions in a balanced, proportionate, and justifiable manner.
- Proactively introduce new ways of working and innovation to police work where appropriate and possible, and apply critical thinking across policing activities within own area of responsibility.

The list is based on Institute for Apprenticeships & Technical Education (2018b) with text reproduced under the terms of the Open Government Licence (http://www.nationalarchives.gov.uk/doc/open-government-licence/version/1/open-government-licence.htm). Crown copyright © 2017.

All trainees undertaking the PCDA will be expected to evidence the development and attainment of these skills, possibly through creating an electronic portfolio or journal. This will involve reflecting on his/her practice (see 6.6) throughout the whole programme, and he/she will need to select examples to match each skill description. This provides evidence of skills, which will then be 'signed off' (ie approved) one by one, by a work-based mentor or tutor.

The skills are assessed during the End Point Assessment (see 6.6.3), mainly through the 'Professional Discussion' between the apprentice and an independent assessor. It is also likely that the evidence for some skills will be derived from the 'Evidence Based Project' and the 'Presentation and Panel Discussion'. Note also that a subset of the required skills relates to PIP Level 1. For PCDA trainees choosing to specialize in investigation during their final year, PIP Level 2 will also be relevant.

6.4.2.5   PCDA behaviours requirement

According to the Institute for Apprenticeships and Technical Education, behaviours are 'mind-sets, attitudes or approaches required for competence'. The table below lists the behaviours required of the apprentice police constable.

Behaviour	Requirement
Taking accountability	Being accountable and taking ownership for own role and responsibilities, whilst being effective and willing to take appropriate, justifiable risks
Professional integrity	Maintain the highest standards of professionalism and trustworthiness, making sure that values, moral codes, and ethical standards are always upheld, including challenging others where appropriate.
Emotionally astute	Understand and effectively manage own emotions in stressful situations, understanding motivations and underlying reasons for own behaviour and that of others, including colleagues. Value diversity and difference in approaches to work, thinking and background, and treat people with sensitivity, compassion, and warmth
Curious and innovative	Have an inquisitive and outward-looking nature, searching for new information to understand alternative sources of best practice and implement creative working methods. Be committed to reflecting on how own role is undertaken, learning from success and mistakes, to continuously review and adapt approach
Collaborative	Work effectively with colleagues and external partners, sharing skills, knowledge, and insights as appropriate to lead to the best possible results
Supportive and inspirational leading	Role model the police service's values in day-to-day activities, providing inspiration and clarity to colleagues and stakeholders. Consider how the wider organization and others are impacted, and help others to deliver their objectives effectively

Based on Institute for Apprenticeships & Technical Education (2018b) with text reproduced under the terms of the Open Government Licence (http://www.nationalarchives.gov.uk/doc/open-government-licence/version/1/open-government-licence.htm). Crown copyright © 2017.

These behaviours are assessed during the programme through tripartite review meetings between the apprentice, line manager/mentor, and university tutor. They are summatively assessed through the Professional Discussion about the apprentice's Operational Competence Portfolio (see 6.6.3), but the assessment of some behaviours (such as professional integrity) will also involve input from a partner university. For example, behaviours such as plagiarism and other forms of academic cheating will be taken seriously by the university, and are also likely to be viewed adversely by the partner police force.

6.4.3 The Degree Holder Entry Programme

A third route into training as a police constable is the Degree Holder Entry Programme (DHEP). As the title of the programme implies, applicants to such a conversion programme will already have a degree, and then apply to join a police force that offers a DHEP through the usual application process involving attending an Assessment Centre (see 6.5.3). The DHEP applicant's degree can be in any subject but cannot be an approved pre-join degree in professional policing (see 6.4.1). As with the PCDA, the programmes will be offered by partnerships between police forces and universities.

Taken full-time, the DHEP is two years in duration and culminates in qualification as a police constable and the award of a university-issued 120 credit HE Level 6 Graduate Diploma in Professional Policing Practice. The knowledge content of the DHEP shares much in common with the PCDA.

6.5 Applying to Join the Police

Some readers of the Handbook might already be full-time trainee officers (eg undertaking the PCDA), in which case the information in this section (6.5) might only have limited value to you. However, if you are a student on a pre-join degree in professional policing at a college or university, or wishing to undertake the DHEP or are currently a special constable or a PCSO seeking to become a full-time police officer, then the following will provide a useful overview of gaining entry to the full-time police service.

In 2019 the government announced plans to increase police officer numbers, thus requiring police services in England and Wales to plan for a significant recruitment drive following a temporary freeze in recent years. Remember that as well as the territorial police forces (such as the MPS) you could also consider other police forces such as BTP. There are three main sources of information on becoming a police officer:

- the recruitment departments of the police forces in England and Wales, accessible via the force websites;

- the College of Policing website (at <http://recruit.college.police.uk/Pages/home.aspx>); and
- websites which claim to list all current vacancies in all UK police forces (eg <http://www.allpolicejobs.co.uk>).

There are a number of requirements that apply for joining the police service as a full-time police constable. Each police service can also set additional entry requirements (eg having certain qualifications or experience and passing an in-force interview), so you will need to check with the organization you wish to join. There may also be a pre-application questionnaire.

Requirements to join the police service as a full-time police constable are subject to change and variation across police services so you need to check the requirements with the police service of your choice.

6.5.1 Eligibility

Eligibility in this context refers to both your general suitability for the police service, and the technical requirements on you in terms of your age, fitness, and so on. There are many books and websites providing advice on the former. Many of the chapters of this Handbook will also provide insight into the knowledge, skills, and behaviours expected as part of the role of police constable.

In terms of the technical requirements, in order to apply to become a full-time police constable you must be 18 years of age or over, and be in good health and reasonably fit. Officially there is no upper age limit, but the normal retirement age for police constables and sergeants is at 60 years of age, so you are not likely to be selected if you are aged 57 or over. The College of Policing website provides more detail on eligibility requirements, including in terms of any previous convictions, tattoos etc.

6.5.2 The application process

After careful consideration and research, your next step after checking eligibility is to apply to a police force with vacancies. None of the stages are straightforward and there is always a possibility of failure, and this applies particularly for completing the application form. It may still need to be completed by hand (in writing), although many forces now provide the opportunity to register and submit forms online, for example Northamptonshire Police. Some forces also allow applicants to take an online test in lieu of the Level 3 qualification normally required (eg Dyfed Powys Police, 2019).

Many applicants fall at this first hurdle, the application form, because they do not assign sufficient importance to this part of the process. The guidance that accompanies the form should be read carefully. Most applications are now made online, so you may wish to consider 'copying and pasting' information from a Word document that you have written and checked.

The application form is likely to involve the following:

Section(s)	Notes
Biographical details—name, DoB, place of birth, nationality, address(es), family details, employment details, etc	Straightforward information is required, but double-check that you have these right
Convictions, financial background, membership of BNP/National Front/Combat 18 or similar organizations	Criminal convictions are likely to mean your application is rejected. Your family will also be subject to checks Financial problems include County Court Judgments (CCJs) Membership of certain organizations will exclude you
Tattoos	Be honest about tattoos, even if they are not on parts of the body normally exposed to the public. Force policy may vary but generally no tattoos on the face, visible above the collar line, or on hands are acceptable. Offensive or racist tattoos are likely to be problematic
Education and qualifications	List of your qualifications (exams passed) with dates, etc. Remember that you might be asked to show your certificates at some stage so check that you have the details correct.

Section(s)	Notes
Personal referees	Choose your referees with care. Ensure that they can respond authoritatively on your employment or educational record
Competency questions	Usually four questions testing your understanding of the skills and qualities required of a police constable. In many respects the most important part of the form (see below)
Motivation questions	Usually five questions exploring the reasons why you wish to become a police officer

Your application form will join hundreds of others as part of an application 'sift'. The police staff responsible for assessing and grading your application will not have view of certain biographical details such as your ethnicity and so on (this is deliberate). They will instead judge how effectively you have answered the competency and motivation questions, and look for evidence in your answers of specific behaviours from the Policing Professional Profiles, and grade them accordingly. At the time of writing the behaviours are decision-making, leadership, professionalism, public service, and working with others. Read and think carefully about these competency behaviours (the details are to be found in the document *Police SEARCH Recruit Assessment Centre: Information for Candidates* on the College of Policing website).

If you pass the paper sift you will be invited to attend an 'Assessment Centre' (this is usually a reference to the assessment process itself rather than its physical location). It will probably take place at a venue within the relevant police force area, and be conducted according to national guidelines. A new approach to Assessment Centres (the 'Day One Assessment Centre') is currently being piloted by the MPS, South Wales Police, Surrey Police, Sussex Police, TVP, West Midlands, and West Yorkshire. Depending on the outcome of the pilots, new arrangements may be introduced from 2020, with a national process for the recruitment of police constables (CoP and NPCC, 2018, p 23).

6.5.3 The Assessment Centre

If you are invited to attend an Assessment Centre to apply to join a police force we advise you to familiarize yourself with the relevant information on the College of Policing website. We offer some guidance here, but there is no substitute for reading and understanding the official documentation in depth.

Prior to attending all applicants are sent a 'welcome pack' containing preparation materials. It is usually available via the College of Policing website, referred to as the 'Westshire Welcome Pack' (Westshire© is a registered trademark owned by the Home Secretary). The Assessment Centre process follows a nationally agreed format, often referred to as SEARCH© (also a registered trademark). The pack will include information about this, although you can also download the information in advance from the College of Policing website. Your preparation could also include learning more about the force you have applied to (eg the name of the chief constable), practising for the interview (discussed later), and attempting sample numerical and reasoning tests.

The pack will also provide information about a fictitious shopping centre that underpins the storyline for the exercises to be completed at the Assessment Centre. During these exercises the applicant will play the role of a customer services officer; this might appear strange for applying for a position in policing, but the intention is probably to ensure that all candidates have a fair chance regardless of background (after all, a policing scenario might give a special constable an advantage). It assumes that the generic competences required by a constable can nonetheless be assessed.

The Assessment Centre takes about five hours and has five main stages: an interview, a numerical test, a verbal ability test, two written exercises, and four role-play exercises. The candidates are allocated to syndicates (groups) so the exercises can be carried out in turn. All candidates will be under observation, even during breaks—and surreptitiously using a mobile phone during a briefing (for example) will be noticed and not be favourably viewed.

6.5.3.1   The interview

The interview (normally lasting around 20 minutes) consists of four questions, and will focus on exploring how the candidate has handled situations in the past. Six different competencies will be assessed during the interview, some more than once. The competencies are decision-making; service delivery; serving the public; professionalism; openness to change; and working with others. Oral communication will also be assessed throughout.

Typically the questions will begin with 'Can you give me an example of …?' and then refer to a generic situation such as overcoming a particular challenge. Examples of 'mock' Assessment Centre interviews can be found on YouTube and these might be useful in terms of appreciating the format of the interview. However, a candidate should avoid being too practiced and therefore too polished during the interview, and must genuinely understand and mean what he/she says.

6.5.3.2   The exercises

The numerical test consists of a 23-minute, multiple-choice examination with 21 questions and four choices for each answer. Each of the number-based simple mental arithmetic problems requires a calculation (without a calculator) involving addition, subtraction, multiplication, division, and simple percentages.

The verbal ability test has 28 multiple-choice questions. Information is provided about a situation, and the questions assess the candidate's ability to make sense of the situation. In Section A there is a choice of three possible answers for each question, and in Section B there are four options. There is only one correct answer to each question. A full briefing will be given before the test. Many people find the verbal ability test more demanding than the numerical test.

The two 20-minute written exercises based on the contents of the welcome pack are regarded by many as being even more demanding. Each exercise is about a problem at the shopping centre, based on (for example) a memo from a colleague or letters from a customer about the problem. The candidate, as the customer services officer, has to write a 'proposal document' using the template provided. The following aspects will be assessed: the ability to comprehend and summarize information accurately; logical structure of the responses; and spelling and grammar. An example of the written exercises is available on the College of Policing website.

The four role-play exercises each consist of a ten-minute exercise; five minutes for preparation (with written information provided about the situation) and five minutes for a role-play between the candidate as the customer services officer and an actor playing a certain role, for example a customer with a complaint. This is an opportunity for using some of the information from the welcome pack such as the policies of the fictitious shopping centre. Making notes in advance is a good idea as these can be used during the role-play.

6.5.3.3   After the Assessment Centre

Each of the Assessment Centre stages is marked by the assessors, and an overall mark is then calculated. The marking schemes are confidential. You should be notified of the result after a couple of weeks.

If you are successful you may be asked to attend an interview with your chosen police force (this does not apply in all forces). However, not all applicants who meet the minimum national standard are guaranteed a post. This could be because the number of candidates meeting the standard exceeds the number of vacancies in the force, and the force may therefore choose to prioritize candidates with higher scores, or add an additional assessment or an interview. If you are going to be interviewed in such circumstances you should find out carefully what is involved, and why an interview is being conducted at this stage.

6.5.4   Background, security, and medical checks

The police force concerned will conduct a background and security check on successful applicants, and their family and associates. The force are likely to take up the references you supplied in the application form, and check the PNC and other intelligence databases for your right to work in the UK, your address and other biographical details, any criminal convictions or cautions, your financial background, and whether you are known to 'associate' with criminals. If you are refused entry to the police on grounds of security there is little you can do.

You will also be asked to complete and submit a detailed medical questionnaire, countersigned by your GP. Home Office circular 59/2004 (available on the www.gov.uk website) outlines the recommended medical standards for recruitment into the police. The police force might request further information from you and/or your GP, and there might also be a 'medical' involving a hearing test, blood pressure measurements, a lung function test, and tests for alcohol, drug or substance abuse. Your BMI (Body Mass Index) might also be calculated (this involves measuring your height and weight to assess if you are overweight). There is a BMI 'limit' of approximately 32 for most forces.

6.5.4.1 Fitness and eyesight test

If you are selected for the next phase of recruitment, you will be invited to attend a fitness assessment. At the same time you will need to have your eyesight examined by an optician and get the form completed and countersigned, or the force will carry out an eye-test. Your unaided eyesight will need to meet certain minimum standards, you should check this with the force you are applying to.

All applicants also undertake a 'multi-stage fitness test' (the MSFT), an endurance test which involves running to and fro on a 15-metre track in time with a series of bleeps, with the time interval becoming shorter every time (the 'bleep test'). Some forces replace this with a 'circuit' of a 15-metre track. Most reasonably fit applicants have no real problem in meeting this requirement. To test your level of fitness mark out a 15-metre distance (or use your local sports centre) and then download the mp3 file with the 'bleeps' from the College of Policing website (search for MSFT), and attempt the running exercise.

6.6 Key Milestones in Training

All trainee officers are on (or in) probation. The probationary period thus covers the entire period of training until 'confirmation'. During this time the trainee should achieve Independent Patrol Status (IPS), and then Full Operational Competence (FOC). During probation a trainee is not a confirmed constable and is subject to the specific regulations that apply to trainee police officers (see 5.4).

The probationary period is currently two years for full-time trainees but is likely to become three years for those apprentices entering policing via the PCDA route (Home Office, 2018a). Part-time training has an extended probationary period calculated according to Annex C of the Police Regulations 2003. In some forces accredited prior learning (APL) shortens the length of training and the probationary period. This may be particularly relevant for PCSOs and special constables who subsequently join up as police officers.

6.6.1 Independent Patrol Status

Attaining the right to undertake Independent Patrol (achieving Independent Patrol Status, or IPS) is a key milestone in the professional development of a trainee police constable. Training is far from over, but he/she can now undertake many police functions associated with fully qualified (confirmed) officers without the need for constant supervision. IPS is normally achieved after about weeks 30–35 in full-time training, although this does vary from force to force.

A trainee's suitability for Independent Patrol is assessed against various criteria, including a subset of the 'knowledge, skills and behaviours' required of a qualified police constable, and the 13 operational competence criteria (see 6.6.2). For example, in terms of the knowledge requirements for IPS there could be a pass-mark in named modules delivered at Level 4 (eg a module on 'Information and Intelligence'). As you would expect, the main aim is to ensure that the trainee is competent and safe to undertake Independent Patrol, including holding the appropriate values, behaviours, skills, and competences. Some forces may also expect trainees to have acquired advanced driving skills before granting IPS.

Evidence towards achieving IPS is gathered over many months, and is collated in a portfolio (for some HEIs and partner police forces an e-portfolio is used). After IPS has been granted the trainee adds further evidence to the portfolio, towards achieving Full Operational Competence (see 6.6.2) and for the End-Point Assessment (see 6.6.3).

6.6.2 Operational competence

There are 13 areas of operational competence, as shown in the table. Throughout training the trainee will keep a record of evidence in his/her 'Operational Competence Portfolio' (OCP) to show how he/she has demonstrated competence. The OCP is a continuation of the IPS portfolio (see 6.6.1).

To achieve Full Operational Competence (FOC) a trainee police constable will need to demonstrate that he/she has met all 13 areas of operational competence, and if studying for the PCDA, that they have also satisfied the academic requirements of the PCDA. This evidence is collected over the first 24 months of the full-time PCDA (when taken in full-time mode).

Area of operational competence	Candidates will be able to provide evidence of the following in order to demonstrate competence
Operating in accordance with the law, Authorised Professional Practice, and the Code of Ethics	In the operational policing workplace, demonstrate knowledge and understanding of the legal and professional practice requirements relating to the professional policing activities set out […] below, having due regard to the Code of Ethics and the National Decision Model
Providing an initial response to policing incidents	Provide an initial response to incidents in line with legal and professional practice requirements, including: • Using the THRIVE approach • Communicating effectively with those at the scene • Controlling incidents, preserving the scene and potential evidence • Recognizing and providing support to vulnerable individuals (including casualties) • Providing support to victims and witnesses of the incident • Engaging in appropriate multi-agency referrals • Recording actions taken
Managing conflict in a professional policing context	Apply conflict management and personal safety techniques with issued equipment, including: • Making threat assessments using all available information • Using approved and appropriate communication techniques • Recognizing danger cues • Applying appropriate and proportionate tactical options and conflict management techniques • Recording and reporting all actions taken and decisions made in line with legal and organizational procedures
Providing support to vulnerable people, victims, and witnesses	• Communicate effectively with vulnerable people, victims, and witnesses • Provide appropriate support to vulnerable people, victims, and witnesses • Demonstrate an understanding of the factors pertaining to vulnerable individuals, victims, and witnesses that may influence their ability and willingness to receive support • Assess the resilience and capability of the individual, and provide further support (including referrals), as appropriate
Using police powers to deal with suspects	Arrest and detain suspects in line with legal and organizational requirements and timescales Report suspects in line with legal and organizational requirements and timescales Apply alternative options with regard to disposal of suspects, in line with legal and organizational requirements
Conducting police searches	Conduct safe, lawful, and effective police searches of premises, vehicles and outside spaces, including: • Communicating appropriately with those at the search scene • Identifying the correct search areas • Protecting search scenes • Preventing loss or contamination of potential evidence • Utilizing approved search techniques • Analysing the significance of items found during the search • Seizing items covered by identified search powers • Maintaining the integrity of seized items • Leaving the search scene in the required condition • Documenting all decisions, actions, options, and rationales

Qualifications and Training

Area of operational competence	Candidates will be able to provide evidence of the following in order to demonstrate competence
Conducting police searches of individuals	Conduct police searches of individuals in line with legal and organizational requirements, including: • Using authorized and appropriate systematic search methods • Communicating appropriately with the individual before and during the search • Controlling individuals in order to prevent loss or contamination of evidence, escape of individual(s) and/or harm to any person • Maintaining personal safety using approved and appropriate techniques • Seizing any identified items covered by the relevant search power • Maintaining the integrity of seized items • Informing individuals being searched of the results of the search and any further actions to be taken • Documenting all decisions, actions, options, and rationales
Conducting priority and volume investigations	Conduct priority and volume investigations, including: • Planning and conducting an initial investigation • Gathering information, intelligence, and evidence to support the investigation • Undertaking investigative and evidential evaluation throughout the investigation • Briefing relevant others regarding the progress of the investigation • Identifying the need for any additional support, including escalation • Identifying and working with victims, potential witnesses, and suspects • Dealing with suspects in line with investigative decision-making • Providing victims, witnesses and their families with information, support, and protection in accordance with their needs • Retain and record the details of an investigation
Interviewing victims, witnesses, and suspects	Plan and prepare interviews with victims, witnesses and suspects Conduct interviews with victims, witnesses, and suspects, including: • Explaining the interview process to those present and confirming understanding • Maintaining the security and welfare of those present • Using approved interview and communication techniques to obtain accurate accounts • Using exhibits in line with approved interview techniques • Addressing any contingencies that may arise during the interview • Completing all necessary documents and records • Closing the interview, informing all present of the next steps And, for suspect interviews: • Delivering pre-interview briefings to legal representatives • Using the required cautions, evidential, or special warnings and checking suspects' understanding • Evaluate interviews with victims, witnesses, and suspects and carry out post-interview procedures
Response policing	Provide an effective initial response to a critical incident
Policing communities	Communicate and engage proactively with communities, including through use of social media Foster productive partnerships in community policing
Information and intelligence	Conduct effective analysis and evaluation of information and intelligence Develop information and intelligence to inform the tasking and co-ordination process
Conducting investigations	Demonstrate appropriate strategies for dealing with more complex police interviews Apply appropriate investigative procedures in respect of internet-facilitated crime Manage cases through the criminal justice process

Based on Institute for Apprenticeships & Technical Education (2018b) with text reproduced under the terms of the Open Government Licence (http://www.nationalarchives.gov.uk/doc/open-government-licence/version/1/open-government-licence.htm). Crown copyright © 2017.

6.6.3 The End-Point Assessment and Confirmation

Once Full Operational Competence has been achieved (and the trainee has also achieved Level 2 Mathematics and English), a 'Gateway' is opened, and the police force arranges the End-Point Assessment (EPA). The End-Point Assessment has three components as shown in the table.

EPA component	Notes	Grades available
OCP-based professional discussion	The 'Independent Assessor' reviews the portfolio against a number of assessment criteria, looking at the evidence for the 13 areas of operational competence. A 60–75 minute one-to-one discussion then takes place with the apprentice.	Fail: (one or more criteria *not* met) Pass: (all criteria met) Distinction: (all criteria met plus going beyond what could reasonably be expected)
Evidence-based research project	Project derived from one of the five policing specialisms (academic level equivalent to a 10,000 word final year degree dissertation).	Fail: (under 50%) Pass: (50–69%) Distinction: (70% or over)
Presentation and panel discussion	Presentation (around 30 minutes) on the 'evidence-based research project', followed by a panel discussion (30–40 minutes). Can also be used to gather further evidence of attainment of knowledge, skills, and behaviour requirements (if needed). The Independent Assessor leads the discussion and 'signs off' the result.	Fail: (under 50%) Pass: (50–69%) Distinction: (70% or over)

Based on Institute for Apprenticeships & Technical Education (2018a) (but authors' interpretation) with text reproduced under the terms of the Open Government Licence (http://www.nationalarchives.gov.uk/doc/open-government-licence/version/1/open-government-licence.htm). Crown copyright © 2017.

Trainees must achieve at least a pass in all three components to pass overall. A candidate who achieves a distinction in all three components achieves a distinction overall (Institute for Apprenticeships & Technical Education, 2018a). The EPA is mapped to the full police constable 'apprenticeship standard' consisting of the knowledge, skills, and behaviours required for confirmation in role (see 6.4.2). The EPA typically carries 60 credits at HE Level 6, and is 'owned' by the university (or other HE institution) involved.

At the time of writing the necessary and sufficient conditions for confirmation as a police constable for those undertaking the PCDA were not clear, but these are likely to include an EPA graded at least a 'pass' and FOC. In effect the degree is likely to be awarded only to those who meet the academic and professional requirements.

6.6.4 Extension of probationary period and dismissal

At the outset it is important to note that, as for qualified police officers, most trainee police officers/apprentices are not employees in the usual sense of the term. Technically they are 'holders of public office' (and for BTP the situation is especially complicated). This means that the conditions of employment for trainee police officers are particularly complex. In terms of dismissal (officially called 'dispensing with your services') and resignation ('retirement'), the main source of definitive information is the Police Regulations 2003, SI 2003 No 527. The Regulations can be found on the www.legislation.gov.uk website, but the important detail is set out in separate annexes.

Here, we cover regulations 12 and 13 of the Police Regulations 2003 (often known colloquially as reg 12 and reg 13, where 'reg' is pronounced with a hard 'g' (rhymes with egg)). Some of the other police regulations are covered in 5.4 and 5.6. As with many aspects of police training, the position regarding probation, the Regulations, and complaints is subject to review; the new Police (Conduct) Regulations 2020, and the Police (Performance) Regulations 2020 came into force on 1 February 2020. It is also the case that the existing regulations have not been 'tested' against the new PCDA route to confirmation. For example, there may be implications for an apprentice who fails to achieve IPS before the end of the first year of training; one university has stated that 'Failure to do so, may result in a Police Force evoking regulation 12/13, (Discharge of a probationer)' (Liverpool John Moores University, 2018, p 4).

Regulation 12 of the Police Regulations 2003 provides for the usual probationary period (two years for full-time student police officers) to be extended. Details are given in Annex C to the Regulations. The usual reasons for extending the probationary period are interrupted training due to illness or personal problems, or when an officer is 'back-coursed' and required to retake a stage of training, perhaps because of failure. Forces are unlikely to allow an indefinite extension to the probationary period and will usually provide a trainee officer with detailed information concerning the implementation of 'reg 12' on the local level.

Regulation 13 of the Police Regulations 2003 allows for dismissal, but it is rarely used and would normally come at the end of a long process during which support and guidance would be offered. We suggest you contact your representative at the JBB (the Police Federation, see 5.7.1) or take other advice if you find yourself in this situation.

Note that the grounds for dismissal ('not fitted, physically or mentally, to perform the duties of [his/her] office, or that [he/she] is not likely to become an efficient or well conducted constable') are quite broad. For example, persistent failure in assessments or examinations could be considered grounds to consider that a trainee is not mentally fit to continue training. However, more common reasons for being dismissed or resigning are inappropriate behaviour, or failing to maintain a certain level of fitness. The 'balance of probability' is used as the standard of proof for deciding whether the grounds for dismissal have been met.

There are obvious reasons for resigning before being dismissed, particularly in terms of future employment prospects. However, this would not mean the trainee would escape prosecution if the grounds for dismissal arose from a criminal act.

7 Learning and Critical Thinking

7.1 Introduction

The role of education in policing is significantly changing with the movement in making policing a graduate profession. In 2016, the professional body for policing, the College of Policing (CoP) introduced the intention to develop a Police Education Qualification Framework (PEQF). The framework stipulated that all new entrants to the profession must be degree educated or be committed to a programme or an apprentice scheme to ensure consistent educational standards are applied in the policing profession. Now, nearly four years later, these intentions are a reality. Universities are working collaboratively with police forces to implement the delivery of a degree via the three entry routes. These new entry routes to the profession have implications for the existing workforce. Many already serving officers may not wish to study for a degree, however, this option may be appealing with new recruits entering the profession with a degree level qualification. Therefore, training and education is aimed at those prior to joining a force (pre-join degree), whilst they join (Police Constable Degree Apprenticeship and Degree Holder Entry Programme), and those who are serving officers with an already established experience base in practice.

In this chapter we look at the various ways in which learning occurs for police officers, apprentices, and students on pre-join programmes. We acknowledge that learning about 'policing' and how to 'police' can sometimes be a confusing and disorientating experience. In some cases we even have to unlearn before we can learn. For example, if you do not know that there are major legal differences between the offences of robbery and burglary, you will have to unlearn what you thought you knew already, which can be disconcerting and discouraging. Taylor (1986) suggests that the discomfort we experience is actually a necessary part of adult learning, and she discerned four distinct phases of the learning experience, as shown in the diagram.

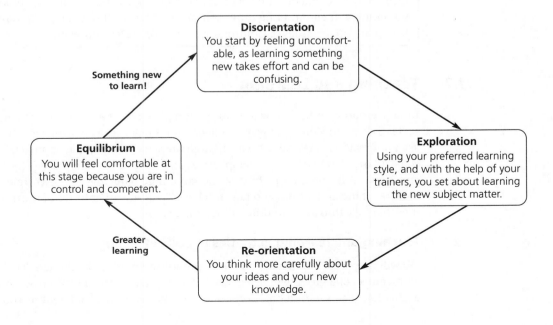

In summary, learning something new is often initially characterized by feelings of discomfort and anxiety. Bear this in mind when studying and it will help you cope; it is quite normal to have some ups and downs as you learn. The following reflection from a serving police sergeant outlines her experiences when she joined policing. She describes her continuous efforts to learn and demonstrates how she consciously reflects on what shapes her experiences. She explains some challenges throughout this piece but neatly illustrates the importance of both formal and informal learning processes.

Case study 1:

I was losing sight of who I was and what my real potential and achievements were or could be. As time has passed, I have come to realise just how much police culture has dictated when, how and who was most deserving, and who was not. I call it the 'likeability factor.' There were pros and cons of 'fitting in', and although a hard work ethic always paid dividends, there was always an extra factor, which I came to realise, I would have no control over. Ultimately, whether my Line Manager liked me or not. Simples. So no matter how hard you could find yourself working, and no matter what the 'policy or processes of application were' it would boil down to a 'likeability factor.'

It was not going to be good enough, to show your monthly figures of arrest, or other statistical relevance, but my professional development was on the knife-edge of whether my team, my sergeants and my inspector liked me. I'd also built up a wide range of work and voluntary experience and training prior to joining the police which I deposited at the door, when I entered training school, as again to dare to relate or identify to this past experience, was quickly identified as 'not befitting' with my new role. This equally equated to identifying as a graduate. I had prior to joining the police, undertaken a distance learning BSc (Hons) degree course at University, whilst working within Youth Offending Service. The amount of life, work and voluntary experiences gained, as well as professional development, which I could have utilised to evidence my justification to apply for various roles, was not recognised. Equally, I soon realised that it was better to remain silent on my true ability or experiences, choosing to eradicate them, realising I was going to have to start over again, but equally, they were to remain firmly hidden, if I was to fit in.

What has become apparent over the years is just how much I failed to be myself. In developing myself, I have had to be creative, innovative and to look for 'other ways', mainly through volunteering or project work to develop myself and upskill. In doing so, I have been able to through reciprocity overcome at times the requirement of 'likeability' and 'service.' The informal networks, skills and knowledge achieved through deviating away from the usual pathways, has enabled me to gain feedback, recognition and permission to challenge the police culture or lack of organisational justice, I've come to find myself within. Furthermore, there have equally been times where I have been lucky, and not solely on ability, I've been able to negotiate the same with some Line Managers, in a system which can feel like playing the lottery at times. On reaching this point, and in using reflective practice, I have been able to recognise how I can self-empower and have self-efficacy in empowering other colleagues and myself to change the way we recognise informal opportunities of Continuous Professional Development.

7.2 Teaching and Learning

In any group of officers engaged in learning, there is every chance that each person will prefer to learn in a different way. Therefore, it is obviously a challenge for the training staff to accommodate each learner with an appropriate activity. A popular approach in police training is 'facilitation', where trainers adopt styles and techniques to bring out (or 'tease out') ideas and views from the group whilst at the same time reducing their own role as conventional didactic 'stand at the front and talk' teachers. There are other forms of learning training activities that take into account different learning styles.

7.2.1 Teaching and learning activities in police training

We will describe a number of activities commonly employed by trainers. The intention is that all members of a group will be engaged at least once during a session. Some trainers will use evaluation sheets to find out more about the effectiveness of different methods.

The **'boardblast'** is a very popular teaching method used by police trainers. The tutor will invite responses which will be written down on a board or flipchart and then discussed. This will be assessed by the tutor and revisited at different stages of the lesson, and is often a very effective method (but is sometimes used to excess). Another occasional disadvantage to the boardblast approach is that most of the class will have very limited knowledge and hence the suggestions might not cover all the required aspects for the topic.

Written case studies are also used. These involve working on a practical example of a police-related problem. Details will be given to an individual or a group, who will then read the material and form conclusions about its content to demonstrate understanding of the subject.

Demonstration can be used for practical topics involving the use of the body in the psychomotor domain. The tutor will demonstrate the movements so the student can repeat the activity afterwards.

Group-work is a very common method in police training. For small-groups, students share ideas among the group and for this to work well, each member should be actively involved in the task. When the group reports back its findings, the trainer or trainers will probably act as a facilitator and will tease out the learning.

Large-group work usually involves allocating responsibility to small groups for researching part of a larger topic. They work away from the training room, and use books, reference material, and computer-based learning. After an agreed time the large group reassembles and the small groups each present their findings to everyone. Alternatively, a large group of students may be presented with information, perhaps from a specialist or a guest speaker, or by watching a video clip.

Individual work provides an opportunity for the student to work alone. This could take a variety of forms, ranging from conducting interviews for research to writing an assignment under exam conditions.

Electronic learning often uses computer-based learning (CBL) packages, which are now available both nationally and locally. CBL activity can be carried out individually or in small groups, both inside and outside the classroom environment. Trainee officers and/or special constables may have access to the resources on the NCALT website (a username and password are needed). There are an increasing number of electronic resources available through NCALT, particularly case studies that link with the NPC learning outcomes.

Facilitated discussions/action-learning sets are particularly useful for exploring attitudes and behaviour. The discussion might be initiated by watching an online video, or by reflecting on the presentation of a guest speaker. Trainers may also encourage students to share their thoughts with others. If this is the case, officers should be prepared to maintain confidentiality as private and sensitive matters may be disclosed (but remember that confidentiality does not protect a trainee from disciplinary action concerning inappropriate language, attitudes, or behaviour).

Presentations are used for some topics and will often use PowerPoint. Throughout the presentation, trainees are given the opportunity to ask questions and make notes. Different trainers will have different approaches to delivering presentations, which may or may not coincide with a student's learning style. For example, some may use the technique of progressively revealing bullet points which, although it will keep the attention of many in the class, can be irritating to some (most trainers welcome feedback on matters such as this). Finally, a Virtual Learning Environment (such as Blackboard) may contain copies of the presentations.

Role-plays involve trainees 'playing' given roles in an imaginary situation, for example in a simulated 'stop and account' scenario, one trainee will act as a police officer and the other a member of the public. Role-plays are normally used when a trainee has gained sufficient knowledge and skills (particularly in terms of police procedure) to make them meaningful. Some police forces use semi-professional actors or volunteers from the local community to play roles, and this can contribute to diversity training. The debrief also provides useful learning opportunities (a trainee could even be videoed to assist with this). Note that role-plays and simulations cannot normally be used as evidence against achievement of the skills and behaviours required of the PCDA. However, a trainee officer can reflect on what has been learnt from a role-play.

Syndicate exercises involve students working in small groups as a syndicate. A syndicate is a group of people where each assumes a certain role. For example, one student might be a member of the public complaining about anti-social behaviour in her street. Other members of the syndicate will play the role of the local PC, the police BCU commander, and so on. The various issues are explored from the different perspectives. Syndicate exercises can be useful learning devices but need to be carefully organized and managed by trainers, with detailed instructions and briefing on the roles played by students. For example, if the syndicate group is quite large (six or more) certain members of the group might not participate, or the issues might only be examined in token and ineffective ways because of time restraints.

Self-facilitated learning—an important part of training for police officers is for them to take an active part within their own learning experience. This involves self-reflection and the confidence to organize and manage their learning independently outside the classroom. The types of activity that may be included in self-facilitated learning might be undertaking additional reading and exercises, to best prepare knowledge for assessment or practice in the field. The tutor may well provide additional resources for reflection. The ownership of self-facilitated learning is beneficial in so many ways. It helps to consolidate the knowledge gained and to consider it in more complex ways, it seeks to ask further questions when clarity is required, and it provides an opportunity to consider the implications of knowledge in practice.

7.2.2 Coaching: expectations and considerations

In police training, coaching is normally carried out one-to-one by a police mentor or coach, particularly when a trainee is based with a Professional Development Unit (PDU). The stage at which coaches are allocated to trainees will vary between forces, but as soon as you have been given details of your coach you should arrange to meet up. At the meeting you may find yourself talking about your background, your motivations to join the police, and your future aspirations. You should also mention the name you would like your coach to use for you. However, bear in mind that your relationship with your coach will develop over time—so do not say too much at first if it makes you feel uncomfortable. You may have written assessments or reports with feedback from your training staff at university or training centre—you can share this so your coach can start to get to know you. Together you can use these to create a development plan for the future. Making a list of subjects that you have already learned in theory can help with planning how to create opportunities for applying the learning in the workplace.

> **TASK 1** Take a moment to write down all of your motivations to join the police. Then consider and write down what you are aiming to achieve over the next three to five years. Next reflect on what you think your main challenges might be.

Your coach will use a variety of techniques to help you learn. For example, he/she may use questioning techniques involving closed questions (requiring a yes or no answer), open questions (requiring you to provide more of an in-depth response), and reflective questions (requiring you to think back on how or what you have learnt); all of these are useful. If your coach uses multiple questions, you need to answer one question at a time to avoid confusion. Be aware of 'leading' questions from your coach as these might lead you to agree with something when you don't! Remember, this could equally well apply to your own use of questions, so you should always be aware of what style of questions you are using and what you want to gain from the answer—affirmation or explanation.

Coaching often takes place before and after attending an incident as part of Supervised Patrol. The incidents may have been carefully selected by the PDU: that is, they wait for a particular type of incident to be reported (such as a suspected shoplifting incident) and then accompany you to that incident. Or you might attend any incident that day, regardless of its nature. Your response (but not necessarily on the first occasion) will be important in terms of your subsequent assessment against the skill and behaviour requirements of the PCDA or DHEP.

Pre-briefs are a good way of preparing. During a pre-brief your coach may ask you questions about the information you have in relation to the incident, and how you intend to deal with the incident. Your coach may also ask you to reflect back on the theory you have covered in the training room to prompt you to apply your learning. After the incident, your coach may ask you to reflect on what happened whilst you responded to the incident. It will be helpful to think about what you felt went well and, conversely, what you felt did not go quite so well. Critical thinking and reflective practice are covered later in this chapter (see 7.4 and 7.5) and it is important to consider the principles covered here, when you are reflecting after an incident, particularly to aid your own development and think about what you may do differently next time.

Your coach will also provide you with feedback. This serves two main purposes: to reassure you that your contribution has been recognized and noted, and to help you develop the skills and abilities required. Feedback is often structured as a kind of sandwich; first an observation on something you did well, then discussing a developmental point (something that you need to focus on improving), and then returning to something else you did well.

7.2.3 Studying and study skills

There are numerous guides, books, and websites which can be used to help develop your study skills. For example, if you are also undertaking a higher education award as part of your education and training, then you may find it useful to work through Dr Stella Cottrell's *Study Skills Handbook* (Cottrell, 2019). Students based at a college, a university on a pre-join degree, or studying as a PCDA apprentice will almost certainly find that support for study skills is available. The following skills are normally required:

- reading skills;
- note taking and writing skills;
- memorizing and revising for assessments;
- using libraries, learning centres, and e-learning resources;
- researching and using internet search engines; and
- time management.

Finally, note that you may have undiagnosed difficulties in learning which could affect your ability to study. Colleges and universities often offer screening for such problems when students first join. They may have a specific department within the university to help support any diagnosed needs, so it is important to liaise with the course lead, should you have any concerns.

> **TASK 2** Find out about the reading technique SQ3R, perhaps by using Google or another internet search engine. This will also prove useful to you if you decide to train as an investigator over the next few years.

7.3 Theories about Learning

Many of our day-to-day actions centre on learning. Finding out more about how you learn will help you to assess your own competencies and evaluate your own educational and training needs. Therefore, understanding some of the theories put forward about learning will help you make these assessments.

7.3.1 Domains of learning

Learning can be seen as part of three separate domains, referred to as the 'learning domains' (eg Bloom *et al*, 1956 and subsequent publications in this series). They are:

- The cognitive domain which is associated with the ability to reason and includes the ability to learn subject matters such as: law, legislation, policy, and procedure, about which we have to think.
- The affective domain which is associated with feelings and emotions. For example, the way people react to situations (such as provocation), and their values and prejudices. A cliché in police training is that 'attitudes can be caught or taught'. Therefore, a great deal of your training will involve you learning to adopt appropriate attitudes and behaviours towards the public and your colleagues. This will involve areas such as respect, race and diversity, team working, community and customer focus, effective communication, problem solving, personal responsibility, and resilience.
- The psychomotor domain is associated with physical dexterity, co-ordination and use of the major and minor motor skills. The psychomotor skills used in policing would include, for example: patrolling, undertaking physical training such as personal safety training, or using hand signals to direct traffic.

Within each domain there are levels of complexity, beginning with the easiest (on the left) and progressively becoming more difficult towards the right, as shown here.

Qualifications and Training

For the cognitive domain ('the head'):

Knowledge→	Comprehension→	Application
The ability to recall facts, words, or phrases, eg a definition of an Act or a section of law	To understand and be able to explain component parts of policy, procedure, or legislation, eg the meanings of words within definitions, the variations and exceptions	To use this knowledge and understanding to apply previous learning to a set task which is either simulated, paper-based, or in the work place

For the affective domain ('the heart'):

Receives→	Responds→	Values
Listens to or sees demonstrated an attitude which is to be learned, eg 'We want you to be a non-discriminator, regardless of the prejudices you may actually have'	Outwardly shows the learned attitude or behaviour, but does not necessarily believe in it, eg 'I have prejudices, but I will not discriminate because I've been told I must not'	Adopts the learned attitude or behaviour and, without request or prompting, owns the feeling personally, eg 'Even though I have prejudices, I believe it is wrong to discriminate and therefore I will not do so'

For the psychomotor domain ('the hands'):

Imitation→	Manipulation→	Precision
Performs the skill as a result of copying or repeating what has been observed, eg resuscitation techniques in First Aid	Executes the skill with some instruction or coaching	Carries out the skill alone without copying, instruction, or the necessity for coaching

For a session involving mainly the cognitive domain, you will probably be asked to assimilate at least some of the knowledge about the subject in advance. This could involve, for example, learning an offence in the form of a definition. Such activities are sometimes referred to as a 'pre-read' but you are of course required to learn material, and not just read it! There may be a check to assess whether you have gained the appropriate level of knowledge. A trainer will then probably move you on to the next level in the cognitive domain (from knowledge to comprehension) and check your understanding and clarify any misunderstandings. Finally, you will be given an opportunity to develop your learning further; the third level of the domain—applying your learning.

Similar activities will be used in the other two domains for attitudinal and skills-based subjects, probably starting at the simplest level and moving incrementally to the more complex. Trainee officers will be coached and mentored in preparation for assessment against the skills and behaviours required of the PCDA or DHEP.

7.3.2 Preferred learning styles

People seem to prefer to learn in different ways (Kolb, 1984), and researchers have discerned the existence of four main learning styles; activist, theorist, pragmatist, and reflective. Most people employ one or two of these styles. The **activist** learning style involves being actively involved with a task, for example taking part in simulations or role-plays; setting tasks or writing questions or case studies; taking part in computer-based learning, for example through the NCALT website; and/or using pre-formed questions before sessions so that learning can be continually checked. The **theorist** learning style involves having a logical outlook and developing underlying theories; reading about a subject and drawing independent conclusions; challenging the underlying assumptions; and/or designing logical diagrams to summarize the subject matter as a sequence of points to be learned. The **pragmatist** learning style involves thinking or dealing with the problem in a practical way, rather than using theory or abstract principles; finding the use of theory and discussion frustrating; and/or looking for the practical applications for learning. The **reflective** learning style involves learning in a slow, deliberate way; taking a step back and looking at a subject from all angles before drawing a conclusion; discussing issues. Participation in simulations or role-plays may not seem that useful.

You can find out more about your own learning style(s) by taking part in an online questionnaire. A popular method in police training is to use Honey and Mumford's Learning Styles Questionnaire.

Through understanding your own learning styles you will be able to think about how you interpret your experiences. It is important to have a conscious understanding and awareness of how we process our thinking and apply criticality to our decision-making.

7.4 Critical Thinking

In recent decades increasing evidence has been found of the existence of two systems of decision-making at work within the human brain (mind):

- 'System 1'—a mental process which helps us make decisions intuitively, quickly, and unconsciously (and often employing mental shortcuts called 'heuristics'); and
- 'System 2'—decision-making which is more deliberate, conscious, and slower.

In this part of the Handbook we are interested in a particular example of System 2 processes: critical thinking skills. This is not to say that System 1 is not without its merits in policing, for intuition can play a valuable part when decision-making is by necessity urgent (see Bryant, 2019, in Roycroft and Roach, 2019, for a discussion), and as Lyons and Ward note 'Reasoning is not *necessarily* any more reliable than intuition' (Lyons and Ward, 2018, p 7, their emphasis). Critical thinking skills complement and occur alongside professional judgement, communication, and other policing skills.

There is no consensus on the precise definition of 'critical thinking skills' but for our purposes we can define 'critical thinking' as a conscious, deliberate, purposeful, and reasoned form of thinking. The meaning of the word 'critical' in this context should not be confused with the meaning in the policing of 'critical incidents' (see 11.5)—although critical thinking skills might well be needed in such circumstances. 'Critical thinking skills' are the methods, techniques, and activities that support critical thinking. These skills include 'clarity, accuracy, precision, consistency, relevance, sound evidence, good reasons, depth, breadth, and fairness' (Scriven and Paul, 2004, p 1).

Critical thinking is an important skill, and is part of being an 'evidence based' police officer. Although some policing is of a routine nature, in many policing situations you will need to be able to respond to novel situations, where the best action to take is less than obvious. Certainly, the importance of critical thinking skills is reflected in their explicit inclusion within the NPC and the PCDA, DHEP, and pre-join curricula. For the apprentice police constable such skills will be of value not only in terms of actual policing, but also in terms of assimilating the required knowledge, skills, and behaviours. You could try the free 'Watson-Glaser' online critical thinking skills test available via the University of Manchester website at <http://www.careers.manchester.ac.uk/applicationsinterviews/psychometric/criticalreasoning/>.

The table summarizes the main skills required of critical thinking in policing, together with an example of their use. Note that the skills are not mutually exclusive, nor is this a complete list. In practice, critical thinking incorporates a range of skills.

Skill	Explanation	Example
Questioning and challenging	Not simply taking claims at face-value, separating facts from opinions, seeking out alternative viewpoints. Identifying and assessing assumptions and presumptions. Informed scepticism.	Questioning the claim that police stop and search data 'proves' that the police are discriminating on the basis of race
Being objective and neutral	Remaining as dispassionate as possible, not allowing emotions to affect judgement. Considering and taking into account your own limitations Being open-minded, avoiding 'motivated reasoning' (finding apparently logical reasons why you should arrive at a conclusion you desire). Avoiding 'group think'.	In a dispute between two individuals, not making rapid snap judgements on the basis of appearance
Observing	Careful and active observation of events, behaviour, data.	Noticing the presence of a child's seat in a suspect's car and how this is at odds with an account

Skill	Explanation	Example
Reasoning and applying sound argument	Using reasoning to draw inferences, construct sound arguments, and identify fallacies (see 7.4.2).	Identifying and testing what would follow, if a suspect's account were true
Analysing and synthesizing	Identifying the key features of a situation and how they interrelate. Interpreting evidence, identifying both strengths and weaknesses in arguments, not rushing to conclusions. Linking ideas together.	Analysing a developing public order situation and deciding on a sequence of actions to take
Problem solving	Approach problems in a systematic way, checking validity of assumptions, assessing options and likelihoods.	Using 'Routine Activity Theory' to help solve a problem of frequent thefts from a car park
Evaluating and reflecting	Systematically reflecting on consequences of actions and outcomes. Generating alternative explanations for events.	Reflecting on whether an arrest required the use of force, what decisions were made, what alternative courses of action might have been open

Critical thinking skills are covered in the PCDA modules called 'Research Methods and Skills' or similar. However, most authorities agree that these skills are also learned as part of the practice of policing itself, using reflection, rather than in the abstract. In any event, critical thinking is not easy, and high levels of motivation and frequent practice are needed to develop such skills. Kolb's (1984) ELC conceptualizes how we learn and develop knowledge from our experiences. This cycle is useful to use to prompt critical thinking.

7.4.1 The Experiential Learning Cycle (ELC)

We all know the sayings that 'if you don't succeed the first time, then try, try again' or 'we all learn by our mistakes'. Much of your learning will take place through your own experiences, and as adults we can actually teach ourselves, at least in part. This process can be represented as a diagram showing the experiential learning cycle (ELC), adapted from the work of David Kolb (Kolb, 1984).

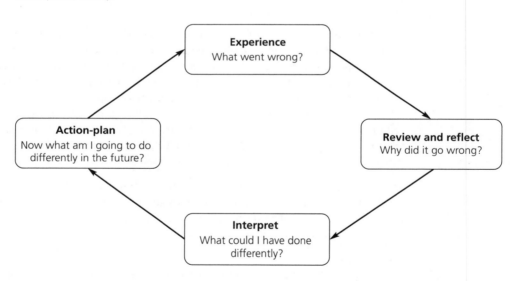

> **TASK 3** Think of a situation you found yourself in recently where afterwards you decided to do something differently next time. Now relate those circumstances to the ELC diagram, starting with 'Experience' and moving clockwise through the diagram. Note there is no correct answer to this task.

The four stages to the cycle can be seen in the context of police training as follows:

- **Experience** (called 'Concrete Experience' in the Kolb original): this is direct experience, often through practical application. A trainee police officer will often want to know what the practical applications of the session will be and get 'hands on' as soon as possible. A police trainer may provide prompts, for example 'think of times in your own life when you have been subject to bullying or harassment'.

- **Review and reflect** ('Reflection'): what does the experience mean to me? This stage is the beginning of understanding. A task such as 'describe your feelings when you were bullied or harassed' may be given.
- **Interpret** ('Abstract Conceptualization'): this involves placing the experiences in some form of theoretical and more abstract framework such as 'How do victims feel about this?'
- **Action-plan** ('Active Experimentation'): the stage of action-planning is how we take this learning forward and test it against reality, such as 'What can a police service do to support victims of harassment?'

TASK 4 An apprentice police officer, as part of Personal Safety Training, starts learning how to handcuff a suspect by taking part in supervised practice using a manikin (dummy). Whilst the trainer observed the apprentice practice their cuffing technique, the trainer then asked: 'Were there any risks to you during the cuffing? How tight did that feel for the suspect? What might you have done differently?'

That night the apprentice reads up on how to handcuff suspects; the reasons for doing it in particular ways, force procedure, and the human rights of the suspect. The next day, presented with a fellow trainee to handcuff, she thinks: 'Now what did I do wrong yesterday and what did it say in those notes I read? I'll try it like this today.'

Identify in the above, each of the four stages of Kolb's ELC.

Reflective practice applies similar principles and is regarded as highly beneficial for police officers and trainees. Christopher (2015) suggests that given the varied and difficult role that police play in society, reflective practice has many benefits and can help promote good practice. He believes that reflective practice enhances police officers' understanding of complex problems, in that it prompts an evaluation of what happened, and can therefore help with understanding what went well, and areas for improvement for next time. Reflective practice is explained in more detail in 7.5.

7.5 Thinking and Learning from Experiences: Reflective Practice and Reasoning

Reflective practice is a complex theory that is debated and considered at length in a considerable number of books and other publications. Its origins can be traced back to the work of John Dewey in the 1930s, often regarded as a founder of the 'cognitivist school' of psychology. He introduced the concept of 'reflective action', based on the idea that people try to develop and improve their performance, but in order to learn, they need to think about (reflect upon) their actions. There are three key questions that can be asked when considering the outcome of any particular course of action:

- What went well?
- What did not go well?
- What would I do differently next time?

This is certainly easier when considering your actions with the benefit of hindsight. Schon (1983) calls this 'reflection-on-action' and likened it to a professional tennis player taking a split second to plan a shot, which if thought about too much would be impossible. The intuitive understanding of the game, the way his/her opponent moves, and recognizing his/her own abilities will all be relevant factors. Thus, the tennis player will almost instantly assess and react to this situation, changing the circumstances to his/her advantage.

This 'reflection-on-action' could equally be termed 'learning by your successes' (or 'learning by your mistakes'). For example, if an apprentice officer hurts his/her back when picking up a heavy load from the back of a police van, his/her reflection-on-action might look something like this:

- What went well? I managed to pick up the heavy load.
- What did not go so well? I hurt my back when lifting it.
- What would I do differently next time? Either bend my knees and keep my back straight or, if it was still too heavy, get some help.

7.5.1 Models of reflective practice

A number of different reflective cycles and models have been put forward to support reflection and encourage people to develop plans based on some sort of analysis of their previous actions. In this way they can then explore new ways to improve future actions. Along with Kolb's (1984) ELC (see 7.4.1), other reflective models include Borton's (1970) Framework for Guiding Reflective Activities. This process asks three key questions: 'What? So what? Now what?', and was further developed by Driscoll (2007). Another popular approach is Gibbs' (1988) Reflective Cycle. Gibbs suggests there are six distinct phases, as shown in the diagram:

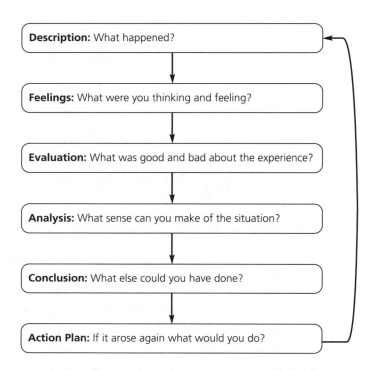

Description: What happened?

Feelings: What were you thinking and feeling?

Evaluation: What was good and bad about the experience?

Analysis: What sense can you make of the situation?

Conclusion: What else could you have done?

Action Plan: If it arose again what would you do?

There are a number of variations of the cycle in use, for example the 'analysis' and 'evaluation' stages are often combined. Detailed descriptions of each of the stages of the cycle are widely available, and these often take the form of directed questions. For example, the 'Description' stage will generally involve the reflective practitioner answering questions about when and where the situation occurred, who else was involved, what actions were taken (or not taken), and so on.

All of the suggested ways of modelling reflective practice are equally valid, as long as there is a conscious attempt to reflect. The process of reflection is supported by using a systematic way of questioning regarding what went well, what did not go well, and how our actions may be different in the future.

7.5.2 Reflective practice in policing

Reflective practice is one of the critical thinking skills required of modern policing. The police are often subject to intense scrutiny after incidents, for example the manner in which the 'Hillsborough' football stadium disaster investigation was conducted or, more generally, how 'Stop and Search' powers are exercised on a day-to-day basis. National enquiries into tragedies such as at Hillsborough will often include questions about the training and experience of the officers involved, how and why they made certain decisions, and whether other officers would have acted in the same way in the same circumstances. These enquiries are generally focused upon 'learning the lessons' to improve future practice. In other words, the police service is asked by the public to reflect upon their actions, the outcomes of their actions, and any problems their actions caused and to consider how they (the police service) will ensure the same problems will not recur.

Reflection on practice also occurs at the level of the individual police officer, and you may be expected to undertake reflective practice as part of the PCDA or DHEP. As Norman and Williams (2017) argue, the complexity of policing and the changing nature of crime (eg the growth in online crime) mean that police officers need to be more reflective in their approach to problem solving in order to meet these new challenges. The reflective model currently encouraged by the College of Policing is Gibbs' (1988) Reflective Cycle (CoP, 2019e). This is perhaps not surprising, given this model has often been used in police training in the past, and is used in other professions such as nursing.

> **TASK 5** Look up reflective practice on the College of Policing website and read the guide at <https://www.college.police.uk/What-we-do/Development/professional-development-programme/Documents/Resources_for_reflective_practice_v1_0.pdf>. You could also watch the Avon and Somerset Constabulary video ('Reflective Practice—reflecting on a tutorial') available on You Tube at <https://www.youtube.com/watch?v=DlaLxXZSHC0>.

In practice, police officers often do not have enough time to formally reflect when in the throes of dealing with incidents, but they do use their knowledge and experience, accumulated through education, training, and practice, to respond to change . This could be a type of automated reflection (as described in 7.5), or making decisions intuitively using system 1 processes (see 7.4).

The ability to reflect on what you have done or what you are doing is an important part of being a professional. The PCDA and DHEP require a foundation of underpinning knowledge, behaviour, and skills (see 6.4.2.2), and the demonstration of operational competence. By applying the basic tools of reflective practice, a police officer can develop him/herself as a professional. For example, one of the areas of operational competence is to 'conduct police searches of individuals in line with legal and organizational requirements' (see 6.6.2). Although this is a simple procedure for an experienced police officer, for some apprentices this can be an embarrassing and traumatic experience, especially if it is the first time he/she has conducted a search. Through the use of reflective practice, apprentices can hone their skills, and learn to consider a range of factors that might affect the way they conduct future searches (such as the location of the search, the age, physical, and emotional state of the person, and the language to use).

7.5.3   Why is it so important to reflect?

In this section of the chapter, we have suggested that reflective practice is a very useful tool for officers, which can be used throughout their career in policing, as well as during qualification and training. We now present some real-life case studies from police officers that demonstrate the use of reflective practice, including their explanation of how the process aids their thinking at work.

> **Case study 2: Extract from a Detective Sergeant who used reflective practice when newly promoted**
>
> I was the manager of a team of detectives who investigated emotionally traumatic events. As a result of this exposure to trauma, the team's stress levels increased. I sought to improve my management of the team and make efforts to account for the trauma incurred when distributing work. My team are dedicated individuals who conduct thorough investigations, however, I did not fully consider their existing work before allocating new investigations. I decided to improve this aspect of my management style.
>
> By reflecting, I identified that work related stressors were causing me to make decisions without fully considering the possible ramifications and that this was affecting the way I allocated work. Failing to consider this was causing increased stress amongst my team. To improve this, I set a personal action plan which consisted of speaking to more experienced managers as to how they managed this, researching management styles and seeking peer reviews. As a result, I understood that I needed to improve my supervision of workload. By not wanting to make my team feel 'micro-managed', I had gone too far in the opposite direction and I realised that I could improve supervision without making staff feel like I was being overbearing. I also identified that by taking more time to listen, I could better understand my staff and what was going on in their lives. I also understood, that I could not expect the same response from each member of my team in relation to their workload.

Having reflected, I have introduced regular conversations with my team, encompassing work and private life. This has enabled me to consider their existing pressure when allocating new work. As a result there have been improvements in staff morale and increased efficiency in processing work. This experience has been positive and I have used it to reflect on other aspects of my work and am seeking ways to introduce this practice to my team. As with all things new, there are some drawbacks. These are mainly getting others to see the benefits of the practice and a small increase in work. To overcome these, I have been an advocate of the benefits I have experienced. Furthermore, I understand that by investing a little time in reflecting you break the cycle of doing things the same way and I have more than recouped the time spent on reflecting in increased productivity and improved ways of working. Using reflective practice has been beneficial to my leadership style

Case study 3: Extract from a Trainee Chief Inspector

I find reflecting on past experiences as a police officer helps me to deal with the incidents which are often of a nasty nature in a more structured and matter of fact way, rather than dwelling on the 'what ifs?' that the situation may have left in my mind. I often reflect back on incidents that happened many months or even years previously, to see whether I would do anything differently, now given my additional years of experience.

For example, the first time I remember consciously reflecting on a work situation I was a uniformed PC, and stopped a motor vehicle that was driving on the wrong side of the street, and went through a red light directly in front of the marked police vehicle I was in.

The driver was a female approx. 30 years of age and she was not driving fast at all, in fact the recording from the personal radio tape in coroners court later reminded me that she was travelling at just 16 mph, however she was not stopping despite the blue lights and sirens on the police vehicle. I assumed she was drunk. When the driver eventually stopped she fell out of the driver's seat, again adding weight to my assumption that the female was drunk, however I noted to my colleague that she did not smell of any form of intoxicating liquor. Had she smelt of such, I imagine she would have been simply arrested under sec.4 RTA, and found herself in a police cell shortly after. I requested a breathalyser and breathalysed her. This female literally took her last ever breath into my breathalyser machine, which incidentally showed she had no alcohol in her breath, and despite extensive emergency life support measures she was pronounced life extinct upon the arrival of a doctor at the scene.

As you can imagine I was quite affected by this mentally, and for quite some time blamed myself for this woman's death. I was the butt of many parade room jokes, as we all know police officers like to joke about situations many others wouldn't, about how I had killed someone. This added to my feeling of guilt, but of course I never let this show to anyone. I simply internalised it. I also hated using the breathalyser for quite some time, I was completely paranoid that this would happen again. The case went to Coroners court with a jury, and I was extremely nervous, especially coming face to face with the woman's family. Following the hearing which declared she died by natural causes, having discharged herself from hospital against doctor's advice, the family approached me and actually thanked me for trying to save their loved one's life. It was at this time that I actually realised that no one except myself held me responsible for this woman's death. I made a decision to consciously reflect on the situation in order to talk it through in my own mind ... what had actually happened? If I had not breathalysed the female would she still be alive? If I had not stopped the vehicle would she have died at the wheel of her vehicle and potentially killed or seriously injured other people in the process? What could I have done differently? What would I do differently if a similar situation would ever happen again?

Reflecting on this situation in a structured way has enabled me to deal with my own feelings relating to it. At the time I wasn't aware of any official models of reflection, however subsequently having learnt more about this subject I reflect on my practices on a regular basis, and actively encourage my staff to do so also.

Case study 4: extract from a Police officer working within a Counter Terrorism department

I am always looking to improve and refine how I and we operate, and reflective practice is a big part of this. When I encounter a barrier to optimal performance I like to run through a process of asking What (is the issue)? So what (are the implications)? Now what (am I going to do about it)? This process led me to a simple but innovative solution to keep officers and staff briefed on fast-moving international developments that affect our day to day work.

What?

Counter Terrorism Border Policing officers work in a complex operating environment, using controversial powers under Schedule 7 to the Terrorism Act 2000 to determine if a person is, or has been involved in the commission, preparation or instigation of acts of terrorism. It can be difficult to keep up to date with fast-moving international developments which might have a bearing on the UK's national security. Historically, much of the information these officers relied upon was held on secret systems and was not readily accessible outside of a secure environment.

So what?

This was problematic as many of the interactions that officers have with the travelling public in ports require a dynamic assessment of the threat and risk posed by individual passengers. The National Decision Model places the Code of Ethics at its heart, meaning officers are accountable for their decisions to use police powers. Decisions should be fair and objective, but transparency in decision-making can be difficult to achieve in a national security context, especially if the information being relied upon is non-disclosable due to its nature or origin. This lack of openness poses a potential threat to police legitimacy, and to the scope or existence of these powers.

Now what?

Reflective practice led me to develop an interactive resource for computers and mobile devices called QuickBrief. This assists Counter Terrorism Border Policing officers around the country in finding reliable open-source information in quick time to aid defensible operational decision-making, and to provide a level of transparency and accountability to our practice. QuickBrief can be accessed from an officer's computer or smart phone and allows them to monitor, in real time, the situation on the ground in a given country of interest via mapping of social media reports. It also provides an overview of relevant news stories, allows officers to access the profile of the country, travel advice, and the profiles, motivation and modus operandi of terrorist organisations active in the country. This innovation means officers can tailor their interactions with persons of potential interest based on up-to-date reliable information, ensuring that questions are pertinent and that answers can be challenged. Whilst developing QuickBrief I had to examine a number of sources of information, narrowing them down to a selection of the most credible and operationally useful. I also had to ensure QuickBrief required minimal maintenance, to protect police time. In the end, this self-updating briefing tool incorporated links to a range of sources including the media, UN, government, an intelligence agency and universities to aid my colleagues and me in reaching defensible operational decisions. I have been able to use QuickBrief to justify the use of police powers to examine passengers under the Terrorism Act, but have also used it to justify not using these powers and identified alternative options instead.

In all three of these case studies you can see that the officers used reflection techniques to identify: the key features of the situation; how they each reacted at the time; and what they changed as a result of a particular issue. The officers each highlighted some of the benefits of utilizing reflective practice, to enhance leadership style, process traumatic events, and identify new means of improving decision-making.

Qualifications and Training

TASK 6 Reflection techniques develop with practice; try it yourself for the following scenario, putting yourself in the role of the constable.

You are patrolling at night when you see a man lying on his back on the pavement. You approach him and establish that he is unconscious and his breathing is very shallow. You immediately call the control room and ask for an ambulance to attend. You then try to speak to the man, whilst checking the pulse in his throat. His pulse is present but weak, so you turn him to the recovery position and note that his breathing has improved. You check him for signs of bleeding but find none, then you cover him with your jacket to keep him warm and wait for the ambulance to arrive. When it arrives the paramedic asks you what happened, and you reply, 'I don't know, I found him here unconscious.' The paramedic then asks, 'Do you know who he is?' and you reply, 'No, I'll check his pockets.' In his jacket pocket you find his name and address and a medic alert card stating that he is diabetic (see 13.7.1.2). The paramedic immediately carries out some checks and administers the appropriate medication; the man regains consciousness within a few minutes and is taken to hospital to be checked.

Now reflect on this scenario, what do you consider went well, what did not go so well, and what would you do differently next time?

On a less positive note, it is also important to reflect on any enquiry into a police action that may have gone wrong. In such a situation investigators delve into all relevant actions 'from the smoking gun, backwards'; in other words, they will look not only at what happened but also why it happened and whether such actions and the accompanying rationales were reasonable. As a holder of public office, a police officer is accountable to the public for actions carried out in their name, so there is a moral imperative, reinforced by the police Code of Ethics (see 5.3), to take the right action, and for the right reasons. The ability to reflect will also be of great assistance if an officer is involved in a disciplinary process. Obviously, there will be a significant difference in the officer explaining why he/she carried out certain actions during the normal course of duties compared with potentially defending him/herself against a serious allegation, but anyone who is accustomed to the process of reflective practice will find it really can help when having to provide an explanation.

One of the first major milestones in a policing career is gaining Independent Patrol Status (IPS) (see 6.6.1). This will require the demonstration of practical skills to a supervisor, to show that the officer is competent and safe to undertake these duties alone, and also can provide a rationale of why certain actions were taken in a particular manner. Note that assessing competence is entirely different to assessing knowledge. For the latter, apprentices must be able to explain important aspects of their role, for example they must show, either verbally or in writing, that they know what legal powers they have as a constable. For the former, they must be able to demonstrate that they can consistently exercise their powers in a legal manner, and in a way that meets the requirements of the PCDA.

7.5.4 Forms of reasoning and arguments

An important critical thinking skill, for apprentice police constables and experienced police officers alike, is a **logical and structured** approach to problem solving. This is not to deny the use of intuition as a problem-solving approach: in some cases, it can be very effective (see Bryant, 2019, in Roycroft and Roach, 2019, for a discussion). However, it is important to develop an awareness of when using intuition is appropriate (and when it is not).

Many people would probably claim to be naturally logical, and hence not require any particular training. However, logical ways of thinking are skills that need to be nurtured and developed, and no one should simply assume they already possess such skills at the appropriate level. Logic underpins the development of sound arguments (explained more fully in 7.5.4.4). We use 'arguments' to express ourselves, sometimes in a formal context (such as in court), or on other occasions, probably less formally, in a piece of reflective practice (see 7.5.2). Perhaps just as important in the policing context, is the ability to identify **fallacious** (incorrect) lines of argument. On occasions these have contributed to miscarriages of justice and to innocent people enduring long prison sentences.

7.5.4.1   Inductive reasoning

Inductive reasoning involves generalizing from a number of previous examples to establish a rule or theory. This form of reasoning is very commonly employed in everyday life and, indeed, was the basis for much scientific discovery in the past. There are some suggestions that this form of reasoning is hardwired into our brains, as most people appear able to apply it without any training. The more this confidence is reinforced by subsequent events, the more we are persuaded by the truth of the generalization. This is known as the **rule of inductive generalization**.

Despite induction being a widespread technique for reasoning, it has an inherent weakness. Sometimes there is no **logical reason** why the generalization should follow from an observation. Additionally, you may have incomplete information and therefore might then draw false conclusions; this can be the case even with accurate observations. However, this is not to say that inductive reasoning has no value, but simply that we should be cautious in its application. The danger for apprentice police constables (and indeed, for all of us) of using inductive methods resides in the problem of generalization from observation, particularly if these observations are limited in number, or unrepresentative. For example, consider the white detective investigating knife crime in east London. In all likelihood, given the social demography of the area, there is greater chance that these crimes involve members of ethnic minorities to an extent that might appear disproportionate to a detective who is new to the area (particularly if he/she does not appreciate that there are significant numbers of ethnic minority people living in that area). A false generalization here would be for our detective to conclude, using induction, that knife crime is somehow endemically black in nature, rather than a product of geography and symptomatic of other social factors (such as poverty) that have independent links with knife crime and being black. East London is one of the poorest areas in Britain (along with parts of Manchester and Birmingham), and there is no evidence to show that ethnicity can cause knife crime. In some senses the detective's incorrect reasoning would be a natural response, hence we need to recognize the nature and limitations of inductive reasoning. The detective mistook association for causality, through the incorrect application of inductive reasoning.

Similarly, unless unchecked, we all have a tendency to look for evidence which supports our generalized inductive theories, and to ignore other evidence. This is particularly problematic in investigations. The proper scientific approach is to look for evidence which might contradict our theories.

> **TASK 7** You are given the numbers 2, 4, 8, and 16. What is the next number in the pattern? Check the answer—it is not 32!

7.5.4.2   Deductive reasoning

Deductive reasoning is the form of reasoning where a conclusion (the 'deduction') must necessarily follow if the assumptions (often called the 'premises') are true. One of the most well-known forms of deduction is that of the 'syllogism'. A famous example is that of 'All men are mortal', 'Socrates is a man', therefore 'Socrates is mortal'. A more everyday example of deduction at work would be 'if a person is in one place then they cannot be in another at the same time'. Hence, if we observe a suspect on CCTV in real time outside London St Pancras railway station then it cannot be the same suspect that we are currently observing at Liverpool Lime Street.

The strength of using deductive reasoning flows from its 'watertight' nature: the conclusion must by necessity follow from the assumptions. However, the 'fatal flaw' with deduction (and particularly in policing contexts) is that we can only be completely certain about the truth of a conclusion if both the assumptions are correct and the deductive reasoning has been correctly applied.

> **TASK 8** Classify the following statements as examples of inductive or deductive reasoning or a combination of the two (use only the statements given to you—make no other assumptions).
>
> (a) Every person's fingerprint is unique to him/her, as no two fingerprints have ever been found to match.

(b) If any liquid that consists mainly of water boils at approximately 100ºC, and blood is mostly water, then blood must boil at roughly 100ºC.

(c) You need to take care when searching the clothes of a suspect as many criminals are drug addicts and they may have syringe needles hidden somewhere.

(d) Defence barristers cannot have a conscience, because they are prepared to defend somebody like Myra Hindley (a notorious child killer).

(e) Anyone who works long and difficult hours in their job should be paid well. Police officers work long and difficult hours, so they should be paid well.

(f) If DNA is entirely inherited and two people are found with identical DNA then they must be identical twins.

7.5.4.3 Abductive reasoning

'Abductive reasoning' is 'reasoning to the best available explanation' or deriving the most likely explanation that fits the observed facts, observations, or assumptions. We often employ abduction when we observe effects and infer causes. For example, if during supervised patrol a trainee police officer observes members of the public running away from a particular location, he or she is likely to infer that they were caused to do so by some event. He or she considers other possible explanations sufficiently unlikely in the circumstances to be discounted.

In practice the three forms of reasoning we have outlined in this section (induction, deduction, and abduction) are often combined. For example, reasoning during a police critical incident might involve employing abduction as an initial 'guess' which is then tested using deduction (what would follow, for example in terms of the consequences?) and induction (what information/evidence supports or refutes this?)

7.5.4.4 Arguments

Technically speaking, an argument is a group of propositions of which one is claimed to follow from the others. Of course, in everyday policing, arguments are not usually expressed in this way, line by line. Instead they are incorporated into sentences, sometimes with information extraneous to the argument, and often with the conclusion presented first. Written arguments also often contain hidden premises (the starting points or assumptions) which are not immediately obvious to the untrained eye. It requires practice and skill to identify the premises, forms of argument, and the conclusions and, most importantly, to decide whether these arguments are logically justified or not.

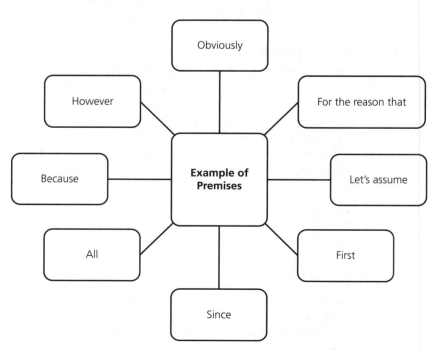

However, there are various key words which can help identify the premises, as shown in the diagram. We can also look for certain words to identify the conclusion within an informal statement about a particular situation. Conclusions are often associated with words and phrases such as:

- it follows that ...
- thus ...
- therefore, ...; and
- so ...

Looking for these informal terms can provide clues about the underlying structure of the argument being presented.

TASK 9 Now that you have read more about critical thinking, and just for fun, try the following Critical Thinkers' Questionnaire to test yourself (some questions are adapted from Facione (1998), most are original). Answer each question 'agree' or 'disagree'. Then calculate your critical thinker index using the answer to task 9.

(a) I dislike those parts of talk shows where people just state their opinions but never give any reasons at all.

(b) I'm entitled to my opinions.

(c) If a person's DNA is found at the scene of a crime then they must have been there.

(d) No matter how complex the problem there is probably a simple solution.

(e) God either exists or doesn't exist. Therefore, the chances that he exists are 50:50.

(f) Rather than relying on someone else's notes, I prefer to read the material myself.

(g) Working out what people really mean by what they say is important to me.

(h) If somebody is really sincere in their arguments then the case they are making is more likely to be correct.

(i) I prefer not to make decisions until I've thought through my options.

(j) I try to see merit in other people's opinions even if I disagree with them.

(k) The reason why the US has such a high murder rate is because of the widespread availability of guns.

(l) The validity of an idea is enhanced by effective communication skills.

(m) A theory is always false if it is incorrectly argued.

(n) I dislike it when tutors discuss problems rather than just giving the answers.

(o) You can't disprove the existence of leprechauns.

7.5.4.5   Forms of argument

As you have seen, an argument is the process of drawing inferences from premises. As well as logic, arguments also tend to take certain assumptions as being inherently true. For example, the 'law of the excluded middle', which states that it is not possible for something to be and not be at the same time. So, either a person committed arson, or they did not. Similarly, we have the 'law of identity': if A is the same as B, and B is the same as A, then A and B are the same. So, if a substance is tested by a forensic laboratory and is found to have the same chemical composition as diamorphine, then the substance is diamorphine.

There are many forms of argument which are logically justifiable and we will examine those that are most relevant to both learning as an apprentice police constable, and more widely in policing itself. Likewise, there are some forms of arguments which are not valid arguments at all and, unfortunately, these **fallacies** are very common (see 7.5.4.7). In order to learn, it is important that we avoid fallacies, and so we need to be able to spot them.

The most famous forms of deductive argument are drawn from a family of arguments referred to as **syllogisms** (eg categorical, disjunctive, and hypothetical syllogisms). For example, the categorical syllogism is an argument consisting of two premises and a conclusion; usually employing the concepts of 'all', 'some', and 'none'. Probably the most famous syllogism is as follows:

- All men are mortal (called the major premise).
- Socrates was a man (called a minor premise).

Therefore (as before, this is the inference)

- Socrates was mortal (conclusion).

In general terms, the categorical syllogism goes something like this:

- All As are Bs.
- C is an A.

Therefore:

- C is a B.

As another example of a syllogism, consider the famous logic of Conan-Doyle's Sherlock Holmes (paraphrased as 'the dog that didn't bark'):

> The Simpson incident had shown me that a dog was kept in the stables, and yet, though someone had been in and had fetched out a horse, he had not barked enough to arouse the two lads in the loft. Obviously the midnight visitor was someone whom the dog knew well (Conan-Doyle, 1894, p 9).

However, there are many other forms of argument beyond the syllogisms (some of which are potentially probably more useful to you). An example is the **modus tollens** form of argument:

- If P then Q (a premise).
- Q is false (a premise).

We conclude:

- P is false (the conclusion).

An everyday example of modus tollens might occur during an investigation into homicide (adapted from an example written by Thomas R O'Connor, Associate Professor of Justice Studies):

- If Mary's boyfriend is to be considered as a suspect, he must have a motive (a premise).
- Mary's boyfriend does not have an apparent motive (a premise).

We then have a conclusion:

- Mary's boyfriend is probably not the offender (the conclusion).

The first premise ('If Mary's boyfriend is to be considered as a suspect, he must have a motive') might well have been established using inductive reasoning (see 7.5.4.1) as most victims of murder are murdered by those they know, and there is normally a motive for the murder.

It is important to note that, if we begin our arguments with correct premises and then argue logically, we can be assured that our conclusions are also correct. However, if we start with false premises then, although we may use a logical and deductive argument, **we cannot say anything** about the truth of our conclusions: they may be true or untrue. This is an important observation in the context of policing.

For example, consider the following argument:

- All humans are self-centred (a premise).
- Criminals are humans (a premise).

Therefore:

- Criminals are self-centred (the conclusion).

This is a perfectly valid argument but the validity of the conclusion depends entirely upon the truth of the premises. The premise that 'All humans are self-centred' might not be correct.

The relationship between premises, arguments, and conclusions is summarized in the table below:

Premises	Argument	Conclusion
Valid	Valid	Valid
Invalid	Valid	Valid or invalid (we do not know)
Valid	Invalid	Valid or invalid (we do not know)
Invalid	Invalid	Valid or invalid (we do not know)

As an example, consider the following written argument from a report in the late 1990s:

> Human rights training in the RUC also lags behind other police organizations we have spoken to. In the new curriculum . . . of 700 sessions of training there are only 2 sessions dedicated to human rights, compared with 40 of drill and 63 of firearms training (Patten Commission, 1999, para 4.5).

We can summarize this argument as follows:

- The proportion of time taken in training a skill or subject reflects its relative importance (a premise).
- A new curriculum provided an opportunity for the Royal Ulster Constabulary (RUC) to reassess the relative importance of these skills and subjects (a premise).
- The RUC spends proportionally more time training drill than human rights compared with other police organizations (a premise).
- The RUC spends proportionally more time training firearms than human rights compared with other police organizations (a premise).

Therefore

- Human rights training in the RUC lags behind other police forces (the conclusion).

How valid is the conclusion based upon the premises?

Well, we can probably take issue with a number of the premises. For example, the first—that the time taken is proportional to the relative importance. But what else could it be proportional to? Drill is an example of a psychomotor skill, and these kinds of skills quite often take longer to perfect than others. For example, a joiner could relatively easily explain to you the theory of how to plane a door to fit its frame, but in practice, fitting the door neatly is an entirely different matter. Taking longer to perfect a skill does not, by itself, prove that we attach more importance to it. So, even though the argument here is valid, if we have serious doubts about the premises then we must also have doubts concerning the validity of the conclusion. In this example we are not saying that Patten's conclusion concerning human rights in the RUC was wrong; we are saying that his conclusion cannot be justified on the grounds given. The Commission could well have been correct on this point, but perhaps should have used a different set of premises.

Understanding the reasoning used (or sometimes the lack of it) is an important tool in learning. As a trainee police officer, you will be presented with many arguments on the streets, in the training room, and by fellow apprentices. Without making yourself too unpopular, you may wish to subject some of these arguments to scrutiny in terms of the validity of their premises and arguments and hence the validity of the conclusions.

TASK 10 Which of the following are arguments?

(a) The registration numbers of all cars can be found on the Police National Computer (PNC). Hence if I stop a car I should be able to check its details on the PNC.

(b) Forensic investigators have a particularly stressful occupation. They are an important part of the criminal justice system. Some work for police forces, whilst others work in the private sector.

(c) I'm tall, so the sight of blood doesn't worry me.

7.5.4.6 Proof

Within logic, **proof** is the means by which we demonstrate that a deductive argument is valid. In mathematics there are many such proofs. In everyday life, and criminal investigation in particular, it is rare to be in possession of such a proof.

Indeed, within criminal investigation and policing in general the word proof may also assume other meanings beyond a strictly formal meaning and is often related to the level of certainty. After all, we speak of proving a person's guilt beyond reasonable doubt. Osterburg and Ward (2004) provided a useful summary of the levels of certainty that may be involved within criminal investigation, as shown in the table (reprinted from Criminal Investigation, 4th edition, with permission. Copyright 2004 Matthew Bender and Company Inc, a member of the Lexis Nexis Group. All rights reserved).

Levels of Certainty and Levels of Proof

Level of Proof	Intuition	Probable cause	Preponderance of evidence	Clear and convincing	Beyond reasonable doubt	Scientific certainty
Evidence	Hunch, guess, or gut feeling	Facts a reasonable person would accept	Corroborated facts, eyewitness testimony, physical evidence, or evidence interpreted by an expert			Precise facts with known accuracy
Quantity	Articulable suspicion about possible facts	Prima facie, presumptive but rebuttable facts	Over 50% of facts are in support	Slightly less facts than beyond reasonable doubt	Sufficient facts to preclude every reasonable alternative hypothesis	Overwhelming facts
Certainty	Apparent	Possible	Basis for hypothesis formulation		Basis for theory construction	Seldom achieved
Law	Suppressed	Basis for binding over to next stage	Civil law standard of proof	International law standard of proof	Criminal law standard of proof	Seldom used
Investigation	Useful during early stages	Basis for arrest or search warrant	Basis for confession and informant law		Basis for conviction	Seldom used

7.5.4.7 Fallacies

Fallacies are incorrect forms of argument (the full technical term is 'informal logical fallacies'). At the risk of stating the obvious, fallacies are a bad thing and should be avoided. There are dozens of fallacies, some of which are so infamous that they have been given Latin names. Indeed, it is quite a long list; here are just a few:

- affirmation of the consequent;
- anecdotal evidence;
- argumentum ad antiquitatem;
- argumentum ad baculum.

There are many websites and books on these, but we will concentrate here on some of the more common fallacies. These are not necessarily mutually exclusive: a single statement may contain more than one logical fallacy. Some common fallacies are:

Anecdotal evidence. One of the most common fallacies is to use personal experience or hearsay as a form of argument. There are a number of problems with this, not least of which is the fact that each of our experiences is unique to us. An example of the anecdotal evidence fallacy is:

> Miscarriages of justice are more common today as evidenced by increased coverage in the media.

Appeal to force ('Argumentum ad baculum'). Appealing to force is the fallacy of using force (or more usually simply the threat of force) in order to try and win an argument. An example of the appeal to force fallacy is:

> If you are innocent you shouldn't be concerned about having your fingerprints taken. However, your consent is really irrelevant as the authorities can force you to give your fingerprints anyway. So, the most sensible policy is cooperation.

Attacking the person ('Argumentum ad hominem'). This is a particularly common form of fallacy. It divides into two distinct forms: **abusive** and **circumstantial**. The abusive form is the fallacious argument that seeks to undermine the position of an opposing view by attacking the person or people that hold that view. An example of the abusive form is:

> It is the policy of the Britain First that we should restore capital punishment for paedophiles, terrorists and murderers (reported by Sky News, 2017) and this demonstrates how wrong the policy is.

The circumstantial form is an attempt to undermine a particular conclusion by drawing attention to the (irrelevant) personal circumstances of the person constructing the argument. An example would be:

> Naturally you are against speed cameras as you drive a fast car.

Argument from ignorance ('Argumentum ad ignorantiam'). This fallacy takes two forms: arguing that since something has not been proven false it must be true, and the converse (the argument that since something has not been proven true, it is therefore false). An example of an argument from ignorance is:

Of course taking an intimate forensic sample from a victim is psychologically damaging. Nobody has proved otherwise.

Appeal to pity ('Argumentum ad misericordiam'). With this fallacy we try to persuade somebody of our argument by appealing to their pity, often the dire consequences that will follow if the argument is not accepted. An example of an appeal to pity is:

The government must accept the recommendations of the undercover policing inquiry. It will not be finished until 2023 and will have taken millions of pounds to produce and this will all be wasted if the recommendations are not accepted.

Appealing to the people ('Argumentum ad populum'). This is the fallacy of claiming that a proposition is true because it is subscribed to by popular opinion. An example would be:

The most appropriate penalty for child murder committed by paedophiles is the death sentence. Opinion poll after opinion poll demonstrates that the British people believe this to be the case.

Appeal to authority ('Argumentum ad verecundiam'). This fallacy needs to be carefully distinguished from the acceptable argument of referring to an authority in a particular field of study as evidence to support an argument **within** that field. The fallacy occurs when an authority is invoked in an irrelevant context. This is sometimes quite subtle. An example of an appeal to authority would be:

Sir Alec Jeffries invented the DNA profile. His support in 2001 for a National DNA database for all UK citizens lends credibility to the idea.

The issue here lies with the fact that while Sir Alec is an undoubted expert on DNA genetic fingerprinting, was he an expert on the possible implications of a national DNA database?

Accident ('Dicto simpliciter'). This fallacy occurs when a generalized rule is applied in circumstances for which it was not intended or designed. An example would be:

The law states that we are not allowed to 'jump' the red lights at a set of traffic lights. It is therefore wrong for the police to be allowed to do so, even in an emergency.

Converse accident. Needless to say, this is the converse of the fallacy of accident. It occurs when a generalization is based upon an exceptional case. An example is:

The government is being asked to consider allowing patients with MS to use cannabis for pain relief. If this happens it is only right that they should legalize cannabis for everyone's use.

False cause and effect ('Non causa pro causa'). This fallacy often occurs when we assume association (often measured as mathematical correlation) is the same as causation. Just because two events occur together does not automatically mean that one caused the other. To assume so is a fallacy. An example of an argument that assumes association and causation are the same would be:

The widespread availability of guns is a major contributory factor to the murder rate of a country. This is demonstrated by the fact that the countries with the highest gun ownership (such as the US) also have the highest rates of homicide.

There is also the fallacy of assuming an event to be the cause of another event simply because it happened before that event. An example would be:

Since the availability of hard-core gay pornography on the internet we have witnessed a significant increase in the incidence of anal rape of men.

Begging the question ('Petitio principii'). This fallacy may take various forms, some of which are quite difficult to spot. In its simplest form, a begging the question fallacy starts with a questionable premise before making a deduction or sometimes repeating the premise in different words. In more subtle cases the premises are actually a consequence of the conclusion, rather than the converse (as it should be). The fallacy often takes the form of circular argument. An example of begging the question would be:

Freedom of speech is an essential right in a police service, because every police employee should have the right to express him or herself with complete freedom.

An even more subtle example would be:

Transgender people should not be encouraged to join the police. The reason is that any police officer who is 'outed' as transgender would find it very difficult to remain in the police after it was revealed that he kept this secret from his fellow officers. Therefore, transgender police officers will do anything to keep their assigned sex secret and will thus be open to blackmail. Therefore, transgender people should not be allowed to join the police.

Irrelevant conclusion ('Ignoratio elenchi'). This is a fallacious argument which sets out to prove a certain conclusion but instead proves a somewhat different conclusion. An example would be:

Hundreds of rare bird's eggs are stolen each year, even though we have the Wildlife and Countryside Act. Clearly, we should repeal the Act.

Non sequitur. This is a particularly infamous fallacy, which probably accounts for why there is no common equivalent English phrase. A non sequitur is an argument where the conclusion is derived from a set of premises which are not logically connected with the conclusion. The non sequitur fallacy happens more often in spoken arguments rather than in a written form. An example would be:

We should return to 'bobbies on the beat' in this country. If the police need additional powers then they should receive them.

In our list we use everyday language as the name for the fallacy but have also included their more traditional Latin names where appropriate. If nothing else, this may impress your family and friends. Please bear in mind that the conclusions in some of our examples may not be true because they are drawn from an incorrect premise, but this does not matter; we are only interested in the validity of the argument, ie that the conclusion can be drawn validly from the premises.

7.6 Learning through Research: Evidence-based Policing

The College of Policing and academic authorities have promoted the idea of 'evidence-based policing' (EBP) as an approach to improving policing strategies and countering crime in the UK. EBP has been inspired by the success of evidence-based practice in other professions, notably medicine. EBP is concerned with research on what works best (when implemented properly under controlled conditions), followed by further research into ongoing outcomes over time. Put simply this means making changes to existing practices, or introducing new initiatives, and measuring the difference the changes make, to see whether they are effective. The aim is to use research to aid decision-making and policy-making by the police and partnership organizations.

EBP was first put forward by Profession Lawrence Sherman in a presentation to the American Police Foundation in 1998 (Sherman, 1998). He based his initial ideas on what was then a recent development in 'evidence based medicine', and further developed his ideas in the 1970s, in the light of academic work from others. The College of Policing explains that, by using an EBP approach 'police officers and staff create, review and use the best available evidence to inform and challenge policies, practices and decisions' (CoP, 2020).

When adopting an EDP approach there is often an emphasis on using quantitative data (eg from randomized control) rather than qualitative data—for example as gained from interviews. However, there is growing acceptance that both quantitative and qualitative approaches to police research can help with decision-making, and add value in their own right. This is reflected in the College of Policing's EBP description cited earlier, about using the 'best available' evidence.

In order to support the use of EBP, the College of Policing organizes 'evidence base camps' (most recently in 2017) where police officers and police staff meet to learn about how to implement EBP, and examine the evidence base for a number of policing and crime issues (eg mental health). The College of Policing also organizes regular 'Research Surgeries' (seven planned for 2020, CoP (2019d)) to support EBP research projects undertaken by police officers and other police staff. There are also a number of College of Policing guides on particular aspects of EBP including a *Policing Evaluation Toolkit* and a *Crime Reduction Toolkit*, both available online.

Further information on EBP is available on the College of Policing website, and from other organizations such as the Center for Evidence-Based Crime Policy (CEBCP) and the Society of Evidence-based Policing (SEBP). The CEBP and SEBP both have public access websites.

The results of applying EBP methods can also be found in academic journals such as the *Cambridge Journal of Evidence Based Policing, Crime and Criminal Justice, Criminal Justice Matters*, and *Policing: A Journal of Policy and Practice and Policing and Society*. In 2018 Thames Valley Police launched their own journal to 'share some of the recent evidence based research and thinking from across the force' (Thames Valley Police, 2018, p 1).

> **TASK 11** In 1978 an award-winning documentary called 'Scared Straight!' was shown on US television. It featured 'juvenile delinquents' (young people convicted in most cases of relatively minor offences) visiting a high security prison and interacting with prisoners serving life imprisonment. Watch the documentary (or at least the first 20 minutes or so) on YouTube at <https://www.youtube.com/watch?v=gXRIR_Svgq4>. Note that offensive language is used throughout so avoid watching the video in a public place.
>
> What do you think the initiative (taking the young offenders into prison) was trying to achieve?'

Undertaking Task 11 will hopefully have demonstrated to you the importance of adopting a more rigorous, systematic, and scientific approach to evaluating initiatives in crime prevention and policing.

EBP is often contrasted with supposedly less effective approaches to policing from the past: the so-called 'three Rs' of random patrol, rapid response, and reactive investigations (Sherman, 2013, p 2). EBP in contrast emphasizes the 'three Ts' of targeting, testing, and tracking (ibid, p 3). However, the suggestion by some that policing before the formal advent of EBP was somehow all 'non-evidence based' is clearly not the case; there are numerous examples of 'experimental' approaches dating back to at least the 1970s.

EBP is included in the curricula of all three entry routes into policing. It is one of the 23 subject areas in the National Policing Curriculum (NPC), and trainees on the PCDA programme will need to conduct their own EBP project. Some aspects of the NPC subject area 'Research methods and skills' are also covered here.

7.6.1 The five steps of EBP research

EBP research is a relatively recent innovation, both in terms of its introduction into initial police training and its day-to-day use in the police service. A number of different models are emerging on how to undertake EBP research, in terms of addressing particular issues, testing interventions, and/or evaluating policing initiatives. The College of Policing advocates the use of a 'logic model' for evaluating policing initiatives, based on a sequence of 'Problem', 'Response', 'Outputs', and 'Outcomes' (see the College of Policing website).

In general terms there are five key stages in any EBP research project:

1. State the question
2. Gather the existing evidence
3. Assess the existing evidence and undertake research
4. Implement the findings
5. Evaluate the implementation

7.6.1.1 Stating the question

This can include increasing our understanding of a policing challenge or crime problem, and how national/international research might apply to our particular local force or community circumstances. The question should be defined as precisely as possible and, importantly, be such that it can actually be answered. Questions which relate to the specifics of the circumstances are often more productive, for example what recent interventions have been found to reliably reduce the theft of mobile phones from people in an urban location? A well-formulated question helps police researchers devise the best ways to gather the evidence.

7.6.1.2 Gathering the existing evidence

What evidence might help answer the question? University-based readers should note this is more than simply drawing up an academic 'literature review'; some of the evidence might be exclusively professional. For some questions (such as a crime prevention technique) the answer might already be available, for example in a database of research, an academic publication, or a policing professional body website. However (particularly if it is related to initiatives that seek to change policing practice), it might even be necessary to conduct empirical research, such as a randomized control trial (see 7.6.2) or analyse existing data (see Task 12).

For non-empirical (or 'desk-based') research, locating the evidence requires good searching and sifting skills, and access to a wide number of databases, some of which may not be available on the open web (such as subscription-only databases). While undertaking desk-based research researchers use inclusion/exclusion criteria, using a range of key words to locate relevant studies and findings, for example, while excluding others. The available databases include the results of one-off studies, case studies, cohort studies, the outcomes of 'randomized trials' and 'randomized control trials', other types of experiment, 'trial and error' approaches, and many other forms of evidence. Essentially EBP researchers are looking for 'what works' (or at least 'what is probably working') in circumstances similar to the context of their own research question.

The 'What Works Centre for Crime Reduction' (part of the College of Policing) can provide useful evidence. The Centre reviews, collates, and shares the best available evidence for crime reduction. The College of Policing also has a repository of its own research publications which are 'peer reviewed to ensure that government standards are met' (CoP, 2018c). These include the categories of 'Community Engagement and Crime Prevention' and 'Crime and Investigation' (ibid).

The Center for Evidence-Based Crime Policy (CEBCP), based at George Mason University in the USA, has an 'Evidence-Based Policing Matrix' which includes all those EBP studies that it deems meet threshold standards to 'qualify' (CEBCP, 2018a). In 2019 there were 165 studies on the Matrix, most US-based and carried out between 1970 and 2016 (CEBCP, 2018b).

Of course, it is just as important to find out about 'what didn't work', although unfortunately, for a number of reasons, not so much of this kind of research gets published. In all cases you will need to critically examine the methodology used, whether the publication was peer-reviewed, and if any conclusions are justified. This is particularly the case where only a few studies have been published. Such critical examination requires considerable skill and knowledge on behalf of the researcher.

Systematic reviews of existing evidence may also be available (similar to the 'Cochrane Reviews' in the context of health care). These are particularly important, but should be carefully scrutinized. In terms of EBP the 'Campbell Collaboration' (<https://www.campbellcollaboration.org/>) is often recommended, but in 2019 the Campbell Library listed only 45 reviews for 'Crime and Justice', not all of which are relevant to EBP in the UK, and those that are can be of variable quality (see Task 13). Fortunately, there is also a growing number of 'Rapid Evidence Assessments' to inform EBP, for example *What Works in Supporting Victims of Crime* (Wedlock and Tapley, 2016).

7.6.1.3 Assessing the existing evidence and undertaking research

You will then need to establish just how 'good' the evidence found (or generated) is, and what relevance it might have to your own EBP research question; this will often be challenging. We can never be certain about any conclusions derived from EBP evidence, even if the evidence is considered to be 'good'. Many types of error (eg 'false positives') are unavoidable.

The criteria for assessing the quality of evidence focuses on the following:

- quality (validity, robustness, and reliability) and
- 'relevance' (how far the evidence pertains to the specific circumstances under study, for example any research about the police use of firearms in the USA (where police carry guns on a routine basis) might not be relevant to the UK.

The 'EMMIE' framework system (Effect, Mechanism, Moderators, Implementation, Economic cost) can be used to help EBP practitioners 'rate and rank' evidence. The origins and justification for using EMMIE are covered in a 2016 academic paper by Nick Tilley (Tilley, 2016, p 307). The system was originally developed by the College of Policing in conjunction with University College London.

Other forms of assessing evidence are also available, for example the 'Maryland Scientific Methods Scale' can be used for evaluating crime prevention evidence (the 'randomised control trials' score at the higher end of the scale).

Statistical testing might be needed for evidence generated through new empirical enquiry, for example, as part of an EBP initiative in a local police force. A hypothesis test, at a specific level of significance, could be used in relation to a particular outcome, for example. Randomized control trials (see 7.6.2) will normally involve measuring the numerical differences between 'intervention' and 'control' groups, to see if the difference is large enough to be a true effect. While techniques such as randomized control trials 'rank' highly as 'robust' methods they are not without their critics, and as with all research you need to critically examine the findings not just accept them as 'fact' (see 7.6.2).

7.6.1.4 Implementing the findings

A 'full-blown' EBP initiative would include deciding whether to implement a change of practice based on the findings of the review. Student police officers are unlikely to be involved in this decision, or in evaluating the results of any implementation.

7.6.1.5 Evaluating the Implementation

Put simply, was the implementation successful? For example, did a particular intervention lead to a desired change in outcomes, such as an increase in arrest rates? These might appear to be relatively straightforward questions, but providing accurate answers can be more of a challenge. For example, we might correctly discern an improvement immediately after an EBP implementation, but subsequent testing might find that the effect 'fades away'. A further complication is that the circumstances in which a change is made might also be changing, which could be confounding any effects.

> **TASK 12** Download the Campbell Collaboration review 'Interview and interrogation methods and their effects on investigative outcomes' from the website <https://www.campbellcollaboration.org/library/interview-interrogation-effects-on-investigations.html> (note that you need to download and unzip all files to locate the review itself, rather than simply the summary). When was the review conducted (note this is not the same as the year it was published)? How many studies (in total) were analysed? What was the search strategy for finding research in this field?

7.6.2 Randomized control trials

A randomized control trial (RCT) is essentially an experiment that is conducted in a rigorous and scientific manner in order to reduce bias. It is considered as the 'gold standard' in many forms of empirical research. If you tried Task 12, you would have seen that RCTs are an important feature of EBP research. Indeed, it may sometimes seem that all EBP research by necessity involves experimental methods such as RCTs, for as Hough *et al* point out, '[t]he EBP movement has given much more priority to ... experimental evaluative research—and has tended to assume that this is the model applied in the archetypal profession of medicine' (Hough *et al*, 2018, p 23). However, EBP research in fact embraces a whole variety of techniques designed to 'get to the truth'.

An RCT is generally used to try and gain knowledge about a 'population'. Here, a population is a scientific term that refers to the complete set of objects that share a common quality or characteristic (often called a 'variable') that we wish to discover more about. These 'objects' could be people. The 'quality or characteristic' is normally something that can be measured and numerically assessed. The diagram shows the key stages of an RCT.

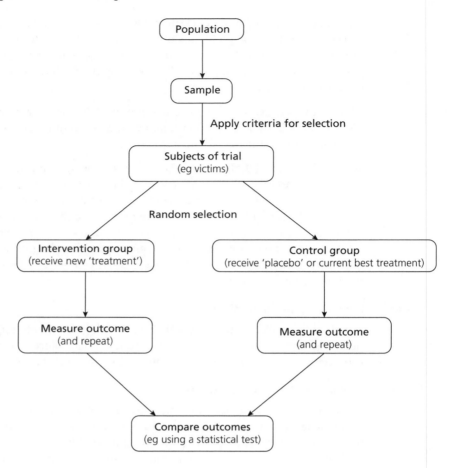

To illustrate how an RCT might be used, consider the following: we are interested in domestic abuse in Greater London and the impact a particular intervention may have on the incidence of repeat victimization. We would need to consider the population of all victims of domestic abuse in the Greater London area in a certain time period, for example the calendar year 2019. In practice we need to be as precise as possible about the population, so for example for this study the exact meanings of 'victim', 'domestic abuse', and 'Greater London area' would need to be carefully defined. All of the subjects (the victims) will probably have suffered repeat victimization, and we might want to find out if a particular police action (eg the attending officers providing a leaflet to the victim) seems to have an effect. To put it simply, does providing a leaflet seem to be mathematically correlated with a decreased, increased, or unchanged likelihood of further victimization? This is often referred to as 'testing the hypothesis'.

7.6.2.1 Selecting the sample

A sample of victims from the population will usually be studied, because the population itself will be too large to be included in the experiment. This is the first scientific compromise in the experiment, because the sample might not be representative; any effects seen for the sample might not hold true for the whole population. One particular problem in sampling (and often a major problem in EBP) is that a sample might be in part 'self-selecting'. For example, people who have had a more positive experience of interactions with the police are more willing to agree to be part of the trial. Therefore, the sample will probably be biased as they are not entirely representative of the population of victims of domestic abuse. For this reason, EBP researchers need to be particularly careful in extending sample-based conclusions to the whole population. Indeed, the methods for selecting a sample, and just how confident we can be in generalizing from the sample to the population, are subjects of separate academic study.

After the sample from the population has been determined, the next stage is to decide who will take part in the RCT. We might start by wanting every member of the sample to be included as a subject of the experiment, but this might not be possible. There may be good reasons why we need to exclude some members of the sample—for example some victims might be 'vulnerable adults' (see Chapter 13 on vulnerability) who are not able to give informed consent. This is likely to be the second significant scientific compromise in the trial, because the application of the inclusion criteria might unwittingly introduce some form of bias to the outcome.

7.6.2.2 Allocation to treatment groups

After the inclusion/exclusion criteria have been applied we now have a new smaller experimental sample. The members of the sample (in our example, victims of domestic abuse) are then allocated to one of two groups: the 'intervention group', and the 'control group'. In some RCTs there could be more than two groups, or example there could be more than one type of leaflet, and we would be comparing three groups; 'no leaflet', 'leaflet A', and 'leaflet B'.

Selection for the groups is by random allocation using a 'double blind' method. It is random in that every member of the sample group (the 'subject') has an equal chance of being selected, and 'double blind' because neither the subject nor the researchers involved (the 'experimenters') know who has been allocated to which group. A double-blind random allocation can even be automated (to avoid human intervention and therefore possible bias). In our example the allocation could occur automatically when the police force concerned responds to the report of domestic violence.

The 'intervention group' then receives the new treatment and the 'control group' does not. In medical trials the control group would receive an inert placebo or current best treatment, so in our example the people in the control group would receive the usual approach. For a proper double-blind trial, the experimenters (which in our case will include the attending police officers) should not know whether the 'treatment' or the placebo is being administered. However, the officers will be handing out the leaflets so obviously they will know whether they are applying the treatment or the placebo, thus the experiment will not be a true double-blind trial. The validity of any conclusions drawn will therefore be undermined; this type of situation presents major difficulties for RCTs in EBP research.

7.6.2.3 Collecting the results of an RCT

The outcome(s) of the trial are measured for both the intervention group and the control group, and will often be a numerical quantity, such as the number of times a particular event has occurred or the average rate at which it has occurred. In our example we would be measuring and comparing the rate of re-victimization for each group. As with other aspects of the RCT, we would need to carefully define from the outset what exactly is meant by 'rate of re-victimization' and how to measure it. Note that in many medical trials the outcomes for each group are measured again after a period of time, maybe several times, to check that any effect of the new treatment does not simply fade away over time. Unfortunately this approach is rarely used in EBP research.

7.6.2.4 Analysing the results of an RCT

The culmination of the RCT is the comparison between the outcomes for the intervention group and the control group. Often this means comparing two numerical values (such as 16 per cent and 22 per cent). The two values are very likely to be different, but we need to know whether the difference is big enough, ie is the difference 'significant'? Is it safe to conclude that the outcomes are significantly different, or could the difference be simply due to chance? For example, 16 per cent and 22 per cent are quite close in value, particularly if there were only a small number of participants in the trial, so has the leaflet really made any difference? However, deciding whether a difference is significant (or not) is not a matter of judgement (even if the researcher is very experienced and qualified). Instead, the decision is made using a predetermined statistical test for significance. There are hundreds of different statistical tests but only a few will be appropriate for a particular RCT. Researchers are trained in choosing the appropriate test (it will be part of the design of the RCT from the outset), and then interpreting the results. The so-called 't-test' and 'chi-squared test' are often used, but the correct choice depends on the nature of the data collected, the design of the RCT, and so on.

The result of such a statistical test is often stated as a level of significance, usually cited as the probability value 'p'. The p value is essentially a statistical judgement on how probable it is that a difference can be put down to chance effects. If $p = 0.01$ (ie 1 per cent), it would mean that, assuming the leaflet had no effect, the observed difference between the groups would be seen 'erroneously' in only 1 per cent of cases if the experiment was rerun a number of times (with the same underlying assumptions and surrounding circumstances). The test would then provide evidence that the observed difference is 'real' and that the difference in the treatments for each group has had an effect. A rule of thumb is that the smaller the value of p the more certain we can be that a genuine effect has been measured. Generally, the value of p needs to be 0.05 or less; the lower the 'better' (in terms of statistical significance). It is important to note, however, that a single RCT that meets the criterion of statistical significance (however small the p value) is rarely sufficient evidence on its own that an intervention has had an effect: repeat trials will be needed, and additional evidence will have to be obtained through different means before we can be sufficiently confident.

An example of a recent randomized control trial in policing concerned the issue and use of conducted energy devices ('tasers') during routine police operations in England and Wales (Ariel *et al*, 2019). The authors of the RCT set out to test the 'effect of mass deployment of TASERs on policing' (ibid, p 280). They concluded that the simple presence of a taser caused an increase in the use of force (ibid). The form of randomization they used was 'cluster randomisation'—this involved groups of police officers, over particular time periods, with one group carrying tasers and the other not. The randomization here involved groups and shifts (early, late, and night shifts). The researchers measured and tested for statistically significant differences between the two groups, and found that in the intervention group (those carrying tasers), 'offenders committed more assaults against officers, and officers more frequently responded with force' (ibid, p 295).

However, their RCT involved only the City of London police force—a very small police force which in many respects is 'atypical' of police forces in England and Wales (they police a very small geographical area (approximately one square mile) forming the financial centre of London). A further problem with the trial was that police officers could (and did) move from control to intervention groups during the course of the study (ibid, p 288). Finally, 'responding with force' included drawing the taser, or aiming it, and red-dotting as well as firing (there were just two cases of the latter during the entire period of experimentation, ibid, p 293). Issues with the design of RCTs, such as these, mean we need to take care when interpreting and acting on any findings.

7.6.3 Undertaking an evidence-based research project

If you are training via the police apprenticeship you will be required to undertake an evidence-based project (equivalent to an honours degree dissertation) as part of the 'End Point Assessment' during the final year of study. Before undertaking your EBP project you may need to agree the project with your sponsoring police force.

As part of the project you may be expected to undertake at least the first three stages of any EBP research, namely: stating the question, gathering the evidence, and assessing the evidence (see 7.5.1 and 7.5.2). The 'question' in this case will be derived from one of the five specialist learning policing areas (response, community, intelligence, investigation, or roads/transport) and will also articulate with the needs of your local communities and police force. For gathering and assessing the evidence (stages (b) and (c), see 7.5.1) you will need to develop the ability to search, evaluate, synthesize, and critically assess (and sometimes add to) the evidence. In particular, the inclusion and exclusion criteria will need to be established early on. Advanced searching skills will also be needed, together with familiarity with how different search engines work.

It is unlikely you will undertake a full-blown RCT as part of your project (due to lack of time, the expense, and the technical assistance that would be needed). However, it is possible that you may undertake a more limited form of empirical research as part of your project—for example a survey. This will complement the desk-based research carried out for the project, but will not replace it. In the case of empirical research as part of an evidence-based project, ethics approval will be required from the university that accredits the degree apprenticeship.

TASK 13 An apparent racial 'disproportionality' in the police use of stop and search powers could form the basis of a relevant evidence-based research question. As well as searching for, and assessing, the relevant evidence, you also decide to look at the currently available data. Go to <https://www.data.police.uk/> and download the MPS police force data for stop and search for the last 36 months. After extracting you should have a number of folders containing Excel CSV files. Note that some of the columns of the spreadsheet may be redundant as the information will have been removed by the police force concerned (eg 'Part of policing operation'). Make sure you are familiar with the meaning of the headings of the files containing data. Explore this data, and in particular critically examine the claim that 'black' people in greater London have an increased chance of being stopped and searched compared with 'white' people. Note that in order to undertake this task you will need to understand and be able to use statistical techniques.

Many quantitative approaches, such as RCTs, help us understand what works in police initiatives. However, other research techniques can be used within EBP to uncover answers to other questions such as, why or how? Qualitative approaches such as conducting interviews or running focus groups with people (eg members of staff, stakeholders, partners) may help you to understand the context of a particular problem. This can be beneficial when you need to explore in-depth why something has happened, to help develop a new or more effective approach.

7.7 Answers to Tasks

TASK 1 How did you get on identifying your own motivations to join the police? Do you have a sense of what you want to achieve in the first instance, what you might be keen to learn, and where you might want to go in the future?

TASK 2 SQ3R stands for:

- Survey/Skim the material you need to read;
- Questions: formulate the questions you expect the material to answer;
- Read the material;
- Recall what you have read; and
- Review.

TASK 3 Not everyone finds that the Kolb process works for them. Indeed, there are a number of more general critiques of the theory underlying ELC. Rogers, for example, has argued that 'learning includes goals, purposes, intentions, choice and decision-making, and it is not at all clear where these elements fit into the learning cycle' (Rogers, 1996, p 108).

TASK 4 The stages are as follows:

- The supervised practice with a dummy is the experience stage.
- The trainer asked, 'Were there any risks to you during the cuffing? How tight might that feel for the suspect? What might you have done differently?'—this is the review and reflect stage.
- The trainee reads up on how to handcuff suspects and reads about the reasons for doing it in particular ways, including force procedure and the human rights of the suspect—this is the interpret stage.
- The next day she has the chance to practise handcuffing again and thinks, 'After what happened yesterday, and because of what I read last night I'll try it a bit looser'—this is the action-planning stage.

TASK 5 The CoP guidance for Reflective Practice is useful. It provides a template for reflective practice based on Gibb's model. It might be worth using these to prompt your own reflections at work or to prepare for your discussions with your mentor.

TASK 6 In terms of what went well, it was good that the victim recovered and appears to have suffered no ill effects, which may have occurred if I had not found him and arranged for him to be treated.

- And for what did not go so well? If I had carried out a full search at the start, I would have found the card sooner and he would not have been endangered for quite so long. I had no intention of searching him, so if I had not been prompted by the paramedic or if the ambulance had been delayed in arriving, the prognosis for the victim may have been poor.
- What would I do differently next time? Once the victim was breathing, I would conduct a more detailed survey, including a check for medic alerts or medicines being carried.

TASK 7 We gave you 2, 4, 8, and 16 to look at and asked you the next number. You would probably have given the answer as 32, if we had not ruled this out. The answer we were thinking of is 31. This is not a trick question!

To explain this, consider the following ways of dividing up a circle:

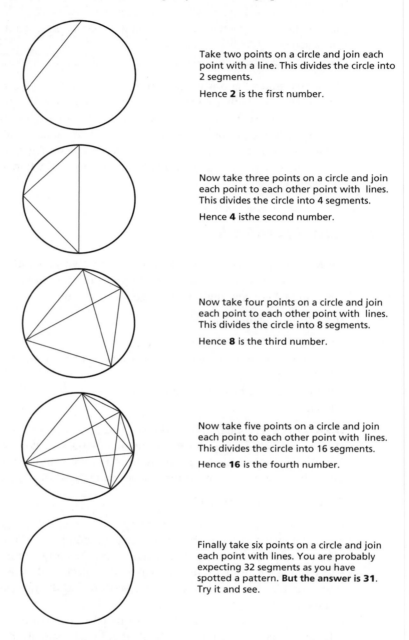

Take two points on a circle and join each point with a line. This divides the circle into 2 segments.

Hence **2** is the first number.

Now take three points on a circle and join each point to each other point with lines. This divides the circle into 4 segments.

Hence **4** is the second number.

Now take four points on a circle and join each point to each other point with lines. This divides the circle into 8 segments.

Hence **8** is the third number.

Now take five points on a circle and join each point to each other point with lines. This divides the circle into 16 segments.

Hence **16** is the fourth number.

Finally take six points on a circle and join each point with lines. You are probably expecting 32 segments as you have spotted a pattern. **But the answer is 31.** Try it and see.

If you want to know the next numbers in the list then look up 'Moser's circle'.

By this stage you might well be thinking, 'What has all this got to do with training as a student police officer?' There are a couple of points here:

• Guessing '32' is a form of inductive reasoning—we are generalizing from past events and making predictions about the future. As explained in this chapter, there are inherent dangers in this that we should be aware of—for example the likelihood of being wrong. This is easy to spot with 2, 4, 8, 16, and 31 but less easy to identify when we encounter our third example in a week of arresting a member of a minority community for theft.

• When establishing a hypothesis it is tempting to look for evidence which supports the hypothesis rather than refutes it. Remember that when investigating and interviewing, your main objective is to establish the truth, not to prove a point.

TASK 8 (a) and (c) are inductive reasoning, the others are all deductive reasoning.

TASK 9 Score 1 point for each of the following answers, otherwise score 0. Total your score.

(a) Agree

(b) Disagree

(c) Disagree

(d) Disagree

(e) Disagree

(f) Agree

(g) Agree

(h) Disagree

(i) Agree

(j) Agree

(k) Disagree

(l) Disagree

(m) Disagree

(n) Disagree

(o) Disagree

Remember, this is just for fun. If you scored:

- 12–15 points You are already a critical thinker.
- 6–11 points You are close to being a critical thinker, but there is room to develop your skills.
- 0–5 points Consider developing your critical thinking skills.

TASK 10

(a) This is an argument.

(b) This is not an argument.

(c) This is the basis of an argument but, as it stands, is not really an argument.

TASK 11 As the title of the documentary suggests, the intention was to scare the young offenders into going 'straight', so they would no longer commit petty crime, and certainly not the kind of crimes that would see them imprisoned alongside the kind of prisoners shown in the documentary. The experiences obviously had an immediate impact on the young people, and it would seem to be 'common sense' that if you want to deter a person from doing something then you should show them the adverse consequences of such behaviour. After the documentary was shown several other states in the USA introduced similar initiatives in the late 1970s and early 1980s, as did a number of other countries. A number of other deterrence programmes employing a similar philosophy have been used since.

However, even at the time of the documentary some people were expressing scepticism about the efficacy of 'Scared Straight!' (Kilby, 2015). Did it really work? And, in retrospect, how should the programme have been evaluated? One reasonably obvious approach was to measure its impact in terms of the subsequent levels of offending of the young people involved, perhaps including some sort of mathematical weighting to adjust for the seriousness of any offences. If the levels of offending had decreased would this be an indication that the programme had been a success? Possibly, but how would we know that this was because of the programme and not some other cause, for example that many of the youngsters had simply 'grown out' of crime? One way of checking would be to introduce a control group for comparison, ie compare the rates of recidivism (the tendency to reoffend) with a similar group of youngsters who had not been part of the 'Scared Straight!' programme. We would also need to choose the group undertaking the programme at random. Otherwise, if we allow self-selection or nomination by probation officers, we may be inadvertently introducing bias. This suggests a form of 'clinical trial' as used, for example, in testing the efficacy of new pharmaceuticals. A number of 'randomised control trials' (see 7.5.2) were conducted on initiatives such as 'Scared Straight!' and, perhaps surprisingly, many trials found that the programmes did not succeed in dissuading young offenders from committing further crimes. Indeed, it was found that some of the programmes seemed to make young people *more likely* to commit further crime. For further details and explanation you might want to look at <http://www.library.college.police.uk/docs/Petrosino-scared-straight-2012.pdf>.

TASK 12 The review consisted of carrying out keyword searches of the following sources:

- 'more than 20 databases' (although only 16 are listed);
- bibliographies of 'relevant' books and 'compendiums' (a total of eight documents including three books);
- abstracts from conferences (no details given); and
- requests made by researchers and practitioners (unlisted).

Although the review was first published in September 2012, the search for evidence was 'executed' (carried out) in July 2010, ie nearly a decade ago. It is claimed that 'the review will be updated every three to five years', but the Campbell Collaboration website does not appear to house any such review.

TASK 13 Before going too far with the data analysis it is worthwhile looking at published research to see how others have tackled this issue. You will need to use your search and sifting skills to do this. Be careful to look at all sides of the 'statistical story', for example in terms of resident and available populations (Waddington *et al*, 2004). When exploring the data you might want to first reflect on the reliability and validity of the data. What variables are involved? What levels of measurement are involved (eg ratio, interval, ordinal, nominal)? How are 'black' and 'white' to be defined? How should we handle 'open-ended' categories such as 'over 34'? What forms of visual representation of the data are possible/should be avoided?

You should then use statistical techniques to explore the stop and search data (and where necessary, other relevant data) in terms of type of search, age, gender, ethnicity, trends over time, legislation used, outcome, 'disproportionality', and other issues. You might wish to consider any of the following: how the data has been presented visually; measures of central tendency, for example mode, median, mean (eg for grouped data); measures of dispersion, for example range, variance, and standard deviation (eg for grouped data); trends and seasonality in overall numbers stopped and searched over time, for example time series, trend line(s), and the ratio of 'black' to 'white' people stopped during the period of study.

8 Policing Local Communities

8.1 Introduction

This chapter is concerned with the nature of policing local communities, with a key focus on community and neighbourhood policing strategies in England and Wales. We will explore a series of issues related and linked to these strategies including: the development of this approach; the function and impact of neighbourhood policing; the value of working in partnership; and effective engagement with the community. We will consider the role of the community in fostering and maintaining social cohesion, and evaluate the challenges and future role of this style of policing in the UK.

The National Police Chiefs' Council have stressed the importance of the relationship between communities and the police, referring to it as 'the bedrock of British Policing' (NPCC, 2016). They have declared that public security and protection will be driven by identified 'local priorities' and 'evidence based demand analysis'. There will also be a need to engage with partners in effective problem solving, thereby setting the future direction for all police forces in England and Wales. Neighbourhood policing has long had a focus on the public priorities of reducing crime and the fear of crime, and has also aimed to improve public confidence in the police by maintaining police legitimacy. A number of studies have outlined the most effective elements of neighbourhood policing: Skogan and Steiner (2004), Tuffin *et al* (2006), and Connell *et al* (2008) have all highlighted the value of targeted foot patrol, community engagement, partnership working, and problem solving approaches to solving community priorities. A systematic review undertaken by Gill *et al* in 2014 also provided evidence of the value of a neighbourhood policing approach in increasing trust and confidence and the perceived legitimacy of the police.

In 2018 the College of Policing produced new evidence-based guidelines on implementing neighbourhood policing (CoP, 2018h) to support and guide chief constables and police and crime commissioners. This chapter explores some of the key points in relation to delivering and supporting neighbourhood policing, and identifying where new solutions may be needed, including conducting further research. You may well have seen a renewed drive for neighbourhood policing in your force, and this chapter will help you understand the context of the approaches used in your local area.

The policing of local communities impacts at the very heart of community safety in England and Wales. Community/neighbourhood policing strategies are particularly important in that no other policing strategy has such potential to engender community cohesion and confidence, and reduce the fear of crime. For neighbourhood policing to develop and progress further, it is crucial that police forces 'buy-in' to the offered guidance. The demands on police resources have changed over the years (due in part to the emergence of new technologies and new threats), so the strategies for neighbourhood policing will need to continually evolve. We strongly recommend that you examine the College of Policing guidelines for yourself as they are firmly linked through case studies and guidance to practical everyday policing initiatives, as well as to an evidence-based approach to practical policing. The guidelines are available on the College of Policing website.

The future of neighbourhood policing has been a 'hot' topic in recent years. The Home Office, the College of Policing, the HMICFRS, and the Police Foundation are all active in reviewing and promoting neighbourhood policing as a strategy and style of local policing in England and Wales. Almost every police force in England and Wales includes a positive reference to this strategy on their websites. HMIC (2017) sparked a debate on the future of policing when they highlighted concerns about reductions in dedicated neighbourhood officers. Andy Higgins of the Police Foundation (2018) draws attention to a service that he argues should be:

> connected not remote, human not just transitional, collaborative not authoritarian, incisive, not blunt, inquisitive not ignorant, proactive not reactive, responsive to need but also fair and just, committed to becoming smarter and better skilled and yet cognisant of gaps in its own knowledge.

The topics covered in this chapter will contribute to the learning required for the National Policing Curriculum subject areas: 'Understanding the Police Constable Role', 'Response Policing', 'Policing Communities', 'Problem Solving', 'Criminology and Crime Prevention', and 'Valuing Difference and Inclusion'.

If you are undertaking the PCDA or DHEP then the content will also be relevant to many of the knowledge and skills requirements but in particular to the need to develop 'in-depth knowledge, understanding and expertise relevant to organisational/local needs, including the ... operational policing contexts of ... community'.

8.2   Neighbourhood Policing in Context

Government policies and media soundbites have regularly focused on the policing of communities and neighbourhoods. Often perceived as the 'softer' side of policing (and by some as having a lower status than other policing roles such as criminal investigation), community-orientated approaches to policing provide a crucial opportunity to engage with the public, proactively combat crime (through crime prevention strategies), and address community safety and quality of life issues. This engagement is important to community problem solving, developing public confidence in the police, and providing a visual presence. There have been many attempts over recent decades (see 8.2.2) to improve police presence and increase community activism to protect local neighbourhoods, and fundamental changes have now been made in the development and application of the relevant legislation.

8.2.1   The definition of neighbourhood policing

Most definitions of neighbourhood policing place great emphasis on the importance of access and communication between local police personnel and local community members (see eg CoP 2018g). This two-way communication should then lead to community engagement, and the development of trust between the local community and their local police service. The specific needs of the local community can then be more easily ascertained, and the community is more likely to have a sense of ownership of the findings. The next stage will be to identify possible community support projects, including solutions to any problems.

In summary, neighbourhood policing involves:

- access (accountable named police officers and police community support officers (PCSOs));
- two-way communication, involving careful listening so trust can develop;
- working together with other agencies and local communities to identify joint priorities; and
- collaboration on developing solutions (which can involve the local community, the police, voluntary groups, and the private sector).

The key aims of a neighbourhood policing approach are to prevent and control crime, and to reduce the fear of crime. Although these aims would predominantly appear to target low-level crime, it should be noted that the fear of crime and nuisance behaviour, the role of intelligence collection, and effective communication with the police have wider implications. As HMIC so succinctly put it (2017, p 27):

> Neighbourhood policing can be a powerful force for protecting the vulnerable and tackling petty crime and anti-social behaviour that blights people's lives. But it can also be the eyes and ears in communities, and can therefore help with gathering intelligence for disrupting serious and organized crime and terrorism.

8.2.2   Neighbourhood policing—a brief history

Looking back at the history of policing, even before the creation of what we now know as the public police, there is clear evidence of participation of the community in policing (Rawlings,

2002). The notion of local policing and community involvement in policing can be traced back to before the 1800s when community representatives became sheriffs or local watchmen. Consider also the 'Hue and Cry', the pursuit of an offender in the King's name as portrayed in fictional historical accounts such as Dickens' *Oliver Twist,* with the baying crowd pursuing Bill Sikes. Contrast this historical (and fictionalized) scenario with the situation in more recent times; in the twenty-first century there is an increasingly distant relationship between the public and the police, particularly in relation to the contribution of communities to policing their own localities.

The community policing model has been widely recognized since the 1960s in the UK, and was strongly supported by John Alderson (former chief constable of Devon and Cornwall Constabulary) in the late 1970s (Mawby, 2008). The serious consequences of failing to work with communities or respond to their needs were demonstrated in the Notting Hill disorders in 1958, the Brixton riots in 1981, and disturbances in Burnley, Bradford, and Oldham in 2001 (Fielding, 2005; Bowling, Parmar, and Philips, 2008). These outbreaks of community discontent resulted in civilian and police casualties and millions of pounds of damage, and sent local community relations with the police into further decline. After such disturbances the inevitable examination of the causes usually results in recommendations to improve dialogue between the community and the police. The lack of partnership approaches in the 1980s was criticized, and various reforms in policing were proposed to support the building of partnerships and community engagement (see eg the 1991 Morgan Report).

In the late 1990s, there was an increasing public demand for a more accessible and visible police service, and the emphasis in policing also began to shift away from a focus on crimefighting to a broader recognition of behaviours that impact on the quality of life and the fear of crime. These underpinning influences provided the impetus for changes in policing, for example the Police Reform Act (2002) which paved the way for the introduction of PCSOs (see 2.2.2.4). PCSOs increased the visible uniformed presence, and the introduction of neighbourhood policing initiatives and the promotion of the 'big society' (Newburn, 2007; Herbert, 2011) provided a further step forward. These changes represented attempts to develop local approaches to policing and improve police engagement with communities, with the aim of increasing the public's contribution to policing objectives. In a review conducted in 2008 (*Engaging Communities in Fighting Crime*), the government put forward 30 proposals aimed at reducing crime, creating safer communities, and increasing public confidence. The focus was on the public as the most important weapon for tackling crime, and one of the central roles for the police was engagement with the community. They called for 'greater consistency in posting police officers to local communities', with more police officers on the streets, deployed from local neighbourhood teams.

In 2010 the Home Office produced the consultation document *Policing in the 21st Century: Reconnecting police and the people* (Home Office, 2010b). This set out the government's vision of 'cutting crime and protecting the public' and a more 'directly accountable' police service, offering 'value for money'. It also made proposals to 'empower communities' and provide 'greater visibility and availability'.

8.2.3   Community and neighbourhood policing today

There is clear evidence of continued support and use of a neighbourhood model of policing in England and Wales, as can be seen in the strategic plans published on all police force websites. However, concerns were raised by HMIC (2017), that the nature of neighbourhood policing was being eroded. In response to these concerns and the intentions outlined by the National Police Chiefs' Council (NPCC, 2016), the College of Policing produced new guidelines to promote a revised neighbourhood policing strategy (CoP, 2018h). The Police Foundation (2015, 2017, 2018) has also focused its research efforts into exploring and examining neighbourhood policing in the UK.

The College of Policing claims that its guidelines were developed through a 'What Works' process, by independent committees working collaboratively. The participants included specialist and generalist practitioners, subject-matter experts from academia and partner agencies, and the third sector. The guidelines are therefore informed by evidence (eg practitioner knowledge and experience and/or social research), and are supported by practical case studies. The three key areas of the guidelines (CoP 2018h) are:

General Procedures

- Delivering neighbourhood policing;
- Supporting neighbourhood policing;
- Identifying evidence gaps.

> **TASK 1** Is neighbourhood policing a strategy in your city or county? How does it work? Who is involved? What are the features of it in your police force?

8.3 Delivering Local Policing

A key feature of the community policing approach is an emphasis on communication and problem-solving activities between the police and the community. The police seek to involve the various communities and partners in their locality in working towards local policing priorities and objectives. The community can also help set priorities and engage in policing activities. Neighbourhood policing teams (NPTs) involve PCSOs and police constables being assigned to patrol particular geographical areas, and to use proactive, intelligence-led, and evidence-based problem-solving approaches to tackle crime and anti-social incidents therein. NPTs engage with the public and hear their concerns, and are also tasked with providing solutions and engaging the community in creating safer neighbourhoods.

A number of different policing models and approaches have been employed to develop, support, and deliver local policing in the UK during the past 40 years. These include zero-tolerance policing, problem-orientated policing, hot-spot policing, and intelligence-led policing. Each approach has a different focus, and can contribute in some way to community policing. Problem-oriented policing, as the label suggests, attempts to model crime or disorder in terms of specific problems, so this is clearly applicable to policing communities. Zero-tolerance policing focuses on dealing robustly with all minor offending in order to make this outcome less likely. For example, the intelligence-led policing model (see 2.2.4.1) could be used to help target high-volume repeat criminals. Community-based and neighbourhood policing are predicated on the view that crime and disorder should be seen in the wider context of the community or communities from which it originates.

8.3.1 Community engagement

Community engagement is vitally important for effective local policing strategies. A two-way dialogue between the public and police is essential for the police to gain a better understanding of communities and their 'needs, risks and threats'. Section 34 of the Police Reform and Social Responsibility Act 2011 provides a legal requirement for chief officers to make arrangements to consult with the public in each neighbourhood, provide local information about crime and policing, and hold regular public meetings. Police and crime commissioners (PCCs) are responsible for engaging with local communities to inform them of any planned reforms and changes to policing, and to seek their views and opinions on local policing, which then informs the local policing plan. The Policing Vision 2025 (NPCC, 2016) stresses that PCCs 'will continue to be at the heart of engaging communities'. All national police forces publish details of local community initiatives, consultations, and meetings on their own webpages.

Community engagement is a core element of effective community and neighbourhood policing approaches. It takes many different guises, ranging from formal structured meetings and consultations to more informal contacts such as meeting officers during their regular patrol duties. It provides opportunities for the public to become involved in decisions that affect them and have an impact on their quality of life. Although formal engagement structures are important, research has indicated that informal rather than formal contacts can be at least as beneficial. It has also been found that the quality of the contact is important: negative encounters can have a 'much greater impact on public and victim satisfaction and confidence than positive ones' (Police Foundation, 2015, p 38). 'Procedural justice' is also important in maintaining good community relations (see 3.6.6 for further details).

Different social media platforms (eg Facebook, Twitter, Instagram) are now key communication channels for the police to gather, use, and share information, and they provide a simple and effective method of engaging with the public in a more direct and immediate way. The use of social media is now firmly embedded in all police force communication strategies throughout England and Wales, backed up with robust guidelines to ensure it is used in a positive way, requiring the same standards of behaviour as would be expected offline.

It is also important to consider here a long-established method of engaging with the community, and one which has formed the basis for a local policing strategy—foot patrol. It continues today as a positive activity which is strongly supported by the general public. 'Today this preventative measure, and high visibility approach to protecting local neighbourhoods is still an entrenched feature of contemporary British Policing' (Police Foundation, 2015). Although there is little evidence to show that foot patrol is an effective means of reducing crime rates, there is certainly public demand to see officers on patrol, and evidence suggests that it can improve community relations and reduce the fear of crime.

The first PCSOs were employed across England and Wales in 2005, their main purpose being to provide a visible presence, to tackle low-level disorder, gather intelligence, and interact with the public. PCSOs have become an effective means of providing community engagement, enabling interaction with the public, acquiring local knowledge, addressing problems, and gathering intelligence. Effective use of the PCSO role, including targeted foot patrols, can facilitate an ongoing two-way dialogue between the police and the public, and enable the police to develop a better understanding of communities and their needs, risks, and threats. However, PCSO numbers have fallen over recent years from a high of 17,198 in 2010 to an all-time low in 2018 of 9,547 (Home Office, 2019i). This reduction in resources has been a challenge to forces wishing to sustain local policing through community engagement.

Key ingredients of successful community engagement can be summarized as a commitment and interest in the community's views and concerns, actively seeking ways to engage with hard to reach groups, ensuring continued informal contacts, as well as structured, relevant, and measurable approaches. Community engagement is most powerful when it is targeted through effective problem solving (see 8.3.2).

> **TASK 2** Some communities are harder to reach, and as we have discussed poor community engagement can have devastating effects on crime in the area. Consider what could be done to ensure effective community engagement.

8.3.2 Collaborative problem solving

Overall, there is strong evidence to support the idea that the police collaborating with the public for the purposes of problem solving can reduce perceived disorder, and increase trust and perceived legitimacy in the police (College of Policing 2018d). Collaborative problem solving also ensures that police resources are used in the most efficient manner and enables the areas of greatest concern to be addressed by using effective interventions and solutions. Attempting to solve problems within communities requires innovative responses, discretion, and imagination. There is no instruction manual for solving community problems, as every situation is different and bespoke solutions are often required to address specific problems in a unique context. Problem solving is based upon personal judgement informed by individual values and the information available to the decision maker at the time. However, there are models of problem solving that can be useful for individuals working in the community, for example the PAT (Problem Analysis Triangle) and the SARA (Scanning, Analysis, Response, and Assessment) process. These provide practitioners with a framework for tackling problems.

8.3.2.1 The Problem Analysis Triangle

The Problem Analysis Triangle (PAT) provides an officer with a basis to begin to analyse a problem. This approach has been associated with routine activities theory (see 3.6.1) and problem-orientated approaches (Tilley, 2008a). The PAT model considers three main points of analysis: victim, location, and offender. Solutions are then found through identifying practical measures to address one or more of these points, for example:

- protection of the victim through crime prevention or target-hardening measures;
- providing surveillance or additional patrols in the location concerned; and
- targeting or persuading offenders to cease their disruptive activities.

While some might consider this to be a simplistic model, it does provide a rationale for responding to problems and collecting the information needed to find solutions. It demands critical and objective thinking, which can in turn inform decision-making. Although this concept is predominantly aimed at uniformed work, there is clearly scope for it to be used more widely, including for non-crime problems.

The SARA process takes the process a step further through to assessment and review. It involves continual re-evaluation of decisions with the intention of improving practice and tackling the root causes of local problems (Weisburd *et al*, 2010). The key stages are:

- **Scanning:** identifying a problem or a crime;
- **Analysis:** assessment of available information surrounding circumstances;
- **Response:** strategy chosen to deal with event;
- **Assessment:** review and evaluation of impact or effectiveness.

Although this model may seem rather mechanical, it does provide a framework in which to confront problems and make decisions (Bullock and Tilley, 2003, p 3). There are other problem-solving models (with acronyms) which focus on different aspects of decision-making or problem-solving processes. Each practitioner needs to identify a method of working that suits the problem and the particular context.

8.3.2.2 Problem-orientated policing

Herman Goldstein developed the concept of problem-orientated policing (POP) as a means of achieving the purposes of policing through tackling problems in communities (Tilley, 2008a). He defined POP as follows:

> In its broadest context, problem-orientated policing is a comprehensive plan for improving policing in which the high priority attached to addressing substantive problems shapes the police agency, influencing all changes in personnel, organisation, and procedures. Thus problem-orientated policing not only pushes policing beyond current improvement efforts, it calls for a major change in the direction of those efforts. (Goldstein, 1990, p 32)

This view was particularly important in the context of the police repeatedly responding to particular crimes or calls for assistance (these could be non-crime anti-social behaviour) in a reactive manner. This responsive approach or 'fire brigade policing' (Rowe, 2008, p 165) would not necessarily address underlying problems in the community, and could stretch the police beyond their capacity without improving public safety. Goldstein suggested the police should analyse the calls from the public, and examine the underlying factors causing the need for police assistance. Particular attention would be given to cases where repeat call-outs and minor cases could escalate to more serious problems (Rowe, 2008). The emphasis of POP in this context encourages a shift from reactive to proactive approaches to policing. Durham Constabulary have been notable employers of the POP approach in the UK, encouraged by the enthusiasm of the current Chief Constable, Mike Barton. In 2016 Durham Constabulary were the only police force in England and Wales to be rated by HMIC as 'outstanding' in their effectiveness in tackling crime.

POP's systematic way of dealing with community problems presented certain challenges in terms of organizational and cultural resistance, including 'crude performance management regimes, staff turnover, lack of trained analysts and interagency hostilities' (Tilley, 2008b, p 226). In addressing underlying community problems, Goldstein argues that the police frequently need to engage with other private, public, and voluntary organizations. Such partnership approaches (often referred to as 'inter-agency' or 'multi-agency' approaches, see 8.4) may create tension, due to different organizational cultures, levels of authority, and objectives (Tong, 2008). So although POP might appear a sound proposal in principle (and has had some notable successes), we also need to consider the barriers to implementing such an approach. Only through the support and willingness of practitioners to engage with new approaches will the intended objectives be met. The website <https://popcenter.asu.edu> provides further useful information about this model, and provides an array of information, guides, and problem solving tools for addressing common crime and disorder problems.

Problem solving approaches are unlikely to be used in response to an isolated incident, and are generally used to address long-term issues, where the same problem recurs. Problems can be identified by the community, by partners, through the National Intelligence Model (see 23.6), or from information provided by local policing teams. Collaborative problem solving is a jointly owned process, through which partners and members of the community provide different views and perspectives, and facilitate wider access to funding and resources. They can work together to implement problem solving approaches.

The College of Policing (2018nh) has found that in order to implement an effective problem solving approach with a neighbourhood policing model, key issues need to be considered:

- *defining the problem*—a detailed specification of the problem needs to be formulated;
- *assessing the impact*—ensuring on-going monitoring and assessment of actions and outcomes;
- *working with partners*—to ensure capacity and lack of duplication of effort;
- *ensuring strong governance and accountability*—commitment to finding solutions, recognizing the good work of staff, and effective leadership.

8.3.3   Targeting policing activity in a community setting

The police have historically focused on making sure that their resources are aligned to targeting the highest-risk neighbourhoods and offenders. Several different policing models and activities have been employed over the years to ensure this happens. This section explores hot-spot policing in local community contexts and zero-tolerance policing. Other models of policing that may be relevant to policing communities include intelligence-led policing and predictive policing (see 2.4). Note that members of the public are able to view local crime patterns at <http://www.police.uk>.

8.3.3.1   Hot-spot policing

A study undertaken by Sherman *et al* in 1989 highlighted that crime is clustered in small areas. Hot-spot policing aims to identify locations where crime and disorder are most common, and then take targeted action in those areas as a deterrent. This involves analysing crime patterns and targeting resources to a local area where there is evidence of high concentrations of crime. It has been shown to be an effective model when it is combined with initiatives designed to reduce opportunities for committing crime. The College of Policing (2013h) notes that hot-spot policing is 'an effective crime reduction strategy, but only modestly' and that it 'works best for drug offences, violent crime and disorder, while it was less effective (but still had some positive effect) for property crimes'.

Some people, premises, or organizations are repeat victims of certain crimes, such as burglary, and the reasons for this are not always clear. There is some evidence (although not conclusive) that the original offender returns to the same places and reoffends. From a thief's perspective it may be that 'it worked once so it will work again'. (For burglary this would include that a burglar deliberately allows enough time for a resident to claim on insurance for a valuable item, before returning to steal the replacement (see eg Bowers *et al*, 2004).) Whatever the explanation, we should emphasize that the data strongly suggests that victims of crime who fail to take elementary precautions after the event should not be surprised if they are targeted again. We also know that those who repeatedly victimize the same target tend to be more established lifestyle or career criminals. This all suggests that intelligence about the nature of a crime and why it is repeated in the same spot with the same victim, should help police forces predict where, when, and by whom the next attempt will be made (see 2.2.4.2 on predictive policing). Local officers engaged in neighbourhood policing where trust has been established may well be in a position to obtain relevant information from members of the local community.

A regular police presence can no doubt help reduce the level of crime in a particular area, but may not be sustainable. However, other crime prevention initiatives (such as installing CCTV or improved street lighting) can demonstrate long-term positive outcomes, and the local knowledge of patrol officers can contribute to devising such initiatives. More information about the hot-spot policing model can be found in 3.5.2.

8.3.3.2   Zero-tolerance policing

Zero-tolerance policing came to prominence in the 1990s. New York City had suffered high levels of crime throughout the 1970s and 1980s, and the police decided to adopt a more aggressive and robust approach to policing. It came to be known as zero-tolerance policing because it responded vigorously to all acts of low-level criminality, and to incivility and

General Procedures

behaviours that detracted from the quality of life for ordinary citizens. The approach was loosely premised upon the 'Broken Windows' thesis presented by Wilson and Kelling (1982). This argued that neglect and the consequent physical problems in a community foster social disorder and eventually crime, and they outlined the need to 'nip bad behaviour in the bud'. The approach was accompanied by a systematic process of managerial accountability known as Compstat, which made the achievement of crime reduction outcomes more open and transparent.

There appeared to be a reduction in crime following the introduction of zero-tolerance policing in New York, but critics later pointed to the fact that similar reductions had also occurred in other parts of the USA that had not adopted such methods. The overzealous and aggressive approach adopted by New York City officers enforcing a zero-tolerance policing strategy also began to attract criticisms from some local citizens, particularly after crime rates had fallen. In England and Wales, zero-tolerance policing was adopted in the late 1990s in Cleveland under the direction of Detective Superintendent Ray Mallon. However, controversy led to his suspension and eventual retirement from the force, and the image of zero-tolerance policing was somewhat tarnished by association.

Nonetheless, the notion of zero-tolerance policing regularly comes to the fore, for example following the outbreak of rioting across London and other English towns and cities in August 2011. Likewise, variations on the zero-tolerance policing approach have been developed and implemented by a number of police forces in England and Wales. A previous commissioner of the Metropolitan Police Service (MPS), Sir Bernard Hogan-Howe, came to prominence during his time as chief constable of Merseyside Police through the successes of his strategy of 'Total Policing', which was seen by some as a form of zero-tolerance policing.

8.3.3.3 The importance of accurate information

Targeting policing resources effectively can lead to positive outcomes, but the quality of problem solving and the intelligence gathered is paramount. Each stage of a problem-solving process requires some analysis to be undertaken, be it statistical analysis, hot-spot mapping, or analysis of relevant research such as social media. To make correct decisions and target resources effectively it is important to avoid making assumptions, and instead to develop and test theories (see 3.7 on evidence-based policing). It is crucial that officers and staff think analytically, access the appropriate data and information, and share the outcome of their findings. The Chicago Alternative Policing Strategy provides an example of employing effective problem solving through a detailed analytical strategy and dedicated commitment from the organization; it was seen by many as a key feature in the successful implementation of the new strategy (Chicago Community Policing Evaluation Consortium, 2004).

For neighbourhood problem solving to be successful, police personnel must consider the best means of securing data and information. All police forces employ skilled analysts and use appropriate software to look for patterns and repeat problems as part of the problem-solving process. Information to help identify the specifics of a problem can be derived from crime data, incident data, environmental visual audits, and information from the community and partners, as well as other national records.

Sharing good practice across police forces is vital, but it is also important to share data and information with other non-police partners. Police forces are engaged in developing systems and protocols to ensure this is done securely, and it is hoped that the sharing of good practice will encourage innovation, prevent duplication, promote best practice across forces, and support the professional development of staff. Local policing delivery should aim to promote community engagement, quality problem-solving techniques, prevention, and early intervention. Intelligence, analysis and problem solving should inform resource deployment decisions, and coordinate responses with partners.

TASK 3 Consider anti-social behaviour. How would intelligence-led policing, problem-orientated policing, and community-based or neighbourhood policing, adopted in their purest form (ie to the exclusion of all other approaches), address this problem?

8.4 The Partnership Approach

Working in partnership and engaging with communities is a defining feature of neighbourhood policing. The police are required and encouraged to collaborate with a number of agencies in investigating crime, and on issues concerning public protection. A 'multi-agency' (sometimes 'inter-agency') approach to reducing crime and disorder and investigating crime is officially endorsed by the Home Office and others. Police force policies and protocols set out how multi- and inter-agency cooperation should operate. Multi-agency collaboration is particularly evident in the following areas:

- Child welfare and protection: this is likely to involve cooperation between the police, health and social services, and education and children's services. For example, if you are a student police officer who has attained Independent Patrol status, you might attend an incident concerning alleged drink-driving, and notice that a child in the care of the suspect appears malnourished, bruised, and psychologically withdrawn. You will report this to your force or divisional public protection desk. Children's services will then become involved and the circumstances further investigated.
- Domestic abuse: similarly, the police response to domestic abuse is likely to include working with specialist domestic abuse services (such as the local Women's Aid), social and health services, housing, education, and voluntary organizations (such as Relate). A multi-agency approach is recommended to provide protection and support to the victim and their dependants (see 13.6.1.7 and 13.7.5). Note, however, that none of this detracts from the presumption that the police will arrest and take action against the alleged offender if possible.
- Reducing crime and disorder: the Crime and Disorder Act 1998 established the statutory obligation for the police and other agencies to work together to counter and reduce anti-social behaviour and other types of crime and disorder in their localities. This takes place formally within the context of a community safety partnership (see 8.4.1).
- Partnerships with local councils or authorities over fixed-penalty notices (see 10.13.2.2): fixed-penalty notices are often issued for parking infringements or driving offences (such as those recorded by speed cameras). The partnership is likely to include close cooperation with local authority CCTV monitoring teams, especially for city centres and popular club or pub venues.

Multi-agency protection arrangements (MAPPA) are covered in 13.7.5.

8.4.1 Community safety partnerships

The Crime and Disorder Act 1998 (as amended by the Police Reform Act 2002) established community safety partnerships (CSPs), and made partnership-working a statutory requirement for organizations such as police authorities, local authorities, fire and rescue authorities, primary care trusts, the Probation Service, and the Drug and Alcohol Action Team. There are around 320 CSPs in England and Wales, and each works with their local Police and Crime Commissioner to identify and respond to crime problems within a specific area. Their key objectives are to:

- establish the level and extent of crime and disorder within the area;
- consult widely with the local population;
- develop a strategy aimed at tackling problems with a clear action plan with organizational responsibilities;
- review the current strategy periodically; and
- work closely with the local Police and Crime Commissioner.

The aim is to reduce crime levels and improve community safety and quality of life. This promotes the sharing of information, and working with other local public, voluntary, and private organizations. Student officers are most likely to encounter CSPs in terms of the local force priorities.

> **TASK 4** In order to develop your local knowledge and understanding further, search the internet for information on your local Community Safety Partnership.

General Procedures

8.4.2 Community safety units

Community safety units (CSUs) coordinate the work of the police locally, in collaboration with the other local agencies such as district and county councils and primary health care trusts. (In some forces this coordinated multi-agency work might have a different name.) Each police force contributes resources to their local CSU.CSUs implement CSP strategic decisions and respond to local need through a full-time community safety team.

Given the local focus of CSUs there will be different priorities in different areas, but there are several common roles and functions. For example, they have an obligation under the Crime and Disorder Act 1998 to audit the crime and disorder problems in their respective areas, and to devise suitable strategies (every three years) to prevent and reduce crime. This includes addressing quality of life issues and the fear of crime. Chief officers must consult with the public in each neighbourhood, provide local information about crime and policing, and hold regular public meetings (s 34 of the Police Reform and Social Responsibility Act 2011). This is achieved through partnership working between CSPs and CSUs.

8.4.3 Youth offending teams

Youth offending teams (YOTs) work with young people who are at risk of offending or reoffending, and offer support through education, employment, work placements, psychological support, and mentoring. They are run by local authorities and bring together and help coordinate the work of several different agencies, including the police. YOTs also provide support for young people who have been arrested or must attend court.

8.5 Diversity and Equality in Local Policing

For a local policing strategy to work effectively it is crucial that the public are treated with respect and impartiality, and treated fairly and equally (see 4.4.2 on the Equality Act 2010 and 'protected characteristics'). Lister *et al* (2015) have highlighted the need for community engagement to involve minority and marginalized groups.

Involving the public in decision-making and working towards understanding local issues and concerns helps provide reassurance and improves public confidence. Building local community trust and confidence will result in greater public involvement and engagement with crime detection and prevention. Respecting diversity and equality and using discretion are vital, so police staff and officers must receive suitable development and training to meet these demands. The complex issue of discretion is covered in 5.5.3.

8.5.1 Diversity and equality

Society is becoming increasingly diverse, for example in terms ethnicity, religious beliefs, and gender and sexual orientation. More importantly, we have become more conscious of such differences and much more determined and willing to afford equal status to individuals from diverse backgrounds. Difference, expressed through the concept of diversity, can be represented as something to be celebrated. Many people believe that the coming together of different values, beliefs, cultures, and perspectives makes life more interesting, more dynamic, and ultimately richer in a variety of ways.

It is important to note that diversity is not just about the differences between people; it is perhaps more about our perceptions of such differences. For example, in most of the UK the divisions within the Christian faith are of little significance for many people in modern times. However, we know that historically this has not always been the case, and more recently the divisions between Catholics and Protestants have been important factors in the conflicts in Northern Ireland. However, the existence of differences does not necessarily lead to tensions or problems (as some may suggest), nor are differences necessarily the source of a dynamic society as others may claim. Either way, if you are (or plan to be) a professional police officer then you will need to think carefully about issues of diversity within society, and about the various ways in which the concept of diversity informs policing. Moreover, it is the responsibility of police forces to end discrimination within their own organizations, so there is a heightened sensitivity concerning the conduct of police officers when dealing with issues around diversity.

People who are clearly identifiable as minorities in society will often find themselves victimized by members of majority groups, for example when individuals from minority ethnic groups are targeted by racists. Sometimes the victimization can be more subtle, and trainee police officers need to think carefully about how their own actions are perceived. Some actions could be deemed offensive by others, even though this was not the intention. As a professional, a police officer has the responsibility to do everything possible to resolve problems, and should certainly not be adding to them. This includes ensuring that police actions are not misunderstood or misinterpreted (see 5.11 on communication).

> **TASK 5** We have already referred to race and ethnicity as part of diversity. Suggest some other differences between people that contribute to diversity.

8.5.2 Diversity and vulnerability

One important way in which diversity informs policing is in relation to the responsibility the police have towards vulnerable people (see Chapters 4 and 13). Vulnerability can arise from belonging to a minority group, but this is not always the case. (For example, women are not a minority group but could be considered to be more vulnerable than men in some circumstances, for example where physical strength or financial independence are significant factors.) However, a police officer needs to ensure that any judgement that a particular person may be vulnerable is based as far as possible on the likely facts about the person and the situation, rather than on the officer's own social conditioning and unconscious bias. After all, some women are physically strong and/or financially independent, and some men are physically and financially dependent on others.

It would also be a mistake to assume that every individual from a minority group or a group that has traditionally been discriminated against in a community will feel vulnerable. Indeed in relation to all aspects of diversity, police officers need to tread a fine line that recognizes diversity without imposing any preconceptions. Cosgrove and Ramshaw (2015) recognize that some vulnerable people may lack trust in the police, and that this can put them off wanting to engage. Officers can often reassure people through effective and just procedural practice and by understanding the different needs of social groups.

The issue of mental health is particularly useful in illustrating the complicated nature of diversity. Mental health issues exist to varying degrees in the general population and can have serious effects in terms of individual and collective well-being. But many people have preconceived ideas of what is healthy and unhealthy, which makes recognizing diversity and difference in relation to mental health particularly difficult. Police actions in relation to people with a mental illness are covered in 13.2.

8.5.3 Diversity and discrimination

Police forces have been under scrutiny for discrimination on the grounds of race for a number of decades. Both the Scarman Report, published in 1981 after the Brixton riots in London, and the Macpherson Report, published in 1999 following the murder of Stephen Lawrence, refer to racial discrimination by the police and a failure to address it. In 2009 the Home Affairs Committee published an evaluation of the impact of the Macpherson Report on tackling 'institutional racism' in the police. It concluded that there were clear positive changes in the way that the police dealt with ethnic minorities, and in the investigation of homicides where the victims were from ethnic minorities. There are, however, still concerns regarding the apparently disproportionate number of stop and searches being conducted on individuals from ethnic minorities as well as a disproportionate number of individuals from African-Caribbean backgrounds featuring on the National DNA Database. These are clearly important issues for policing communities.

The Mental Health Act 2007 and the Disability and Equality Act 2010 reinforce the need to address ways in which people with mental health problems are treated, especially since the majority of such individuals report having experienced discrimination. This is of particular relevance for police officers, given that people with mental health problems often come into contact with the police in the community (see 13.2), and feature disproportionately within

General Procedures

the criminal justice statistics (see Bradley, 2009). We cover the legislation around incidents concerning people with mental ill health in 13.2.

8.6   Answers to Tasks

TASK 1 You will be able to find out if neighbourhood policing strategy applies in your local force by looking on the force website. Some forces include it in their 'Vision' statement, others have a 'Strategy' document. If you can't locate the documents easily then use the 'search' facility.

TASK 2 Effective community engagement can include using more informal ways of communicating, and being more visible in the area—targeted foot patrol, informal conversations, asking questions about local problems, and using social media. Demonstrating to the community that action is being taken is important, and social media can be an effective tool for this. More formal ways of communication are also important, for example holding public meetings and seeking the views of the community through questionnaires and out-reach workers. Telling people about opportunities to get involved and setting up a neighbourhood watch or citizen patrol scheme can be effective ways to engage and reassure the public.

TASK 3 You might start by speaking with those that can really help us: members and representatives of the local community and the patrol officers who work with them. If young people are involved then how can we mobilize their parents and others in the community to address both the anti-social behaviour and its underlying causes? What support can be offered? In summary, do not simply view this as a matter of law enforcement; it is very likely to be part of a wider issue concerning the stability and cohesion of the local community. In terms of anti-social behaviour and the various approaches to policing, you might have suggested the following:

- **Problem-orientated policing**—the fundamental problem needs to be identified. The anti-social behaviour may simply be the visible manifestation of a less obvious problem or change. For example, the removal of fences between the gardens of local-authority-owned houses could have created open areas which encourage anti-social behaviour. If so, other agencies might need to be involved in an agreed and concerted strategy to address the underlying problem.
- **Intelligence-led policing**—target the most active and serious perpetrators. This might require the use of informants and surveillance. When the individuals have been identified, you should examine all appropriate means within the law to prevent or dissuade them from exercising leadership and direction over others. For example, consider what offences they might have committed, whether ABCs (acceptable behaviour contracts) or CBOs (criminal behaviour orders) might be suitable (see 14.2). Alternatively other agencies may be engaged to bring pressure to bear, for example do we have information that they are illegally claiming benefits? If we cannot detect the crime, it could be disrupted instead.

TASK 4 Community safety partnerships all have their own internet sites, for example the Kent CSP can be found at <https://www.kent.gov.uk/about-the-council/partnerships/kent-community-safety-partnership>. Many CSPs have a newsletter which you can subscribe to (eg see <https://www.kent.police.uk/kent-community-safety-newsletter/>), and some use social media (eg see <https://www.facebook.com/CanterburyCSP> and <https://twitter.com/CanterburyCSP>).

See what you can find out about your own Community Safety Partnership.

TASK 5 You would probably have picked up on race and gender, but did you get sexual orientation, age, or belief? And disability?

9 Stop, Search, and Entry: Police Powers and Procedures

9.1 Introduction

This chapter outlines the police procedures around stop, search, and entry, including searching people, premises, and vehicles, and the powers and policies around entering premises.

'Stop and search' can be a very useful tool for police officers, and is certainly one of the most frequently utilized powers. It can be employed in a wide range of situations.

The main purpose of stop and search powers is to 'enable officers to allay or confirm suspicions about individuals without exercising their power of arrest' (PACE Act 1984 Codes of Practice Code A, para 1.4). Carrying out a stop and search is where a police officer detains a person in order to search them and their belongings, including anything they are carrying or being carried in. In order to do this, an officer must have reasonable grounds to believe the person they are stopping and detaining has been involved in a criminal activity, is about to be involved in criminality, or is in possession of a prohibited article. There are some situations where reasonable grounds are not required; however these will be discussed throughout the chapter.

The College of Policing has produced extensive Authorised Professional Practice for the police use of stop and search and, if you are undertaking initial police training then you may be expected to familiarize yourself with the guidance. For example, police officers are expected to adopt a 'procedural justice' approach to stop and search, as this can have a 'positive influence on people's attitudes' (CoP, 2017b), and see also 3.6.6 in this Handbook.

If you are undertaking the PCDA or the DHEP you will be expected to demonstrate that you know how to 'meticulously and ethically search individuals, vehicles, premises and outside and virtual spaces' and are able to safely and lawfully 'manage effective and ethical searches for evidence and information in differing environments' and 'take responsibility for courses of action required to follow-up on findings (within remit of own role) to maintain the peace and uphold the law'.

Despite its usefulness, police use of stop and search has often been criticized, usually on the grounds of alleged discrimination against visible ethnic minorities, but also (some claim) on the basis of lack of effectiveness or incompetent use. For example, in 2013 HMIC published an inspection report that indicated the police had very little understanding of how the powers should be used effectively and fairly (HMIC, 2013b). Others have countered that the apparent discrimination that emerges from the statistics around stop and search should be seen in the light of the difference between 'available populations' (those members of the public the police are most likely to encounter on the streets) and 'resident populations' (the population that lives in an area, whose demographics are often measured through the Census). A full discussion of the 'rights and wrongs' of stop and search is beyond the scope of this Handbook.

After 2009 there was a significant reduction in the number of searches being conducted by police, with the government introducing reforms in 2014 to encourage this reduction. These reforms included the 'Best use of stop and search scheme (BUSSS). However, in the last couple of years, Home Office figures show that police use of stop and search has increased; for the year ending March 2019 there being 383,629 stop and search incidents recorded, an increase of over 36 per cent compared with the previous period (House of Commons Library, 2019). This dramatic increase could be due to officers being more confident in their use of stop and search powers, or to the increase in knife crime across the UK, or other reasons (or a combination of reasons). Furthermore, the number of stop and searches carried out under a s 60 of the Criminal Justice and Public Order Act 1994 authorization has increased significantly, which is reflected in the official figures released by the Home Office (see 9.4.3). This increase may be in part due to the change in rank of the officer who can authorize s 60 powers and the reduction in level of certainty required by the authorizing officer—from belief that violence 'will occur' to 'may occur'.

Stop and search can be used under many different powers, for example s 1 of the Police and Criminal Evidence Act 1984 (PACE) and s 23 of the Misuse of Drugs Act 1971. Every search must conform to the guidelines set out in Code A of the PACE Codes of Practice (see 4.6.1), and be recorded. The data collected from these records shows which areas and ethnicities are involved, and what types of criminal activity are being encountered by officers. It is also used as one of the quantitative measurements of police performance. Any person who has been searched can access a copy of their search. Members of the public could want a copy for various reasons, for example to establish whether the search complied with the Codes of Practice. A failure to comply can result in the search being deemed unlawful, and could lead to a police misconduct investigation.

Police powers in searching properties and entering premises will be covered in this chapter, along with the practicalities regarding searching premises, open spaces, and vehicles. Post arrest searches, under s 32 of the PACE Act 1984 will be covered, as will s 18 of the PACE Act 1984, and the differences between the two. We will also cover searches of properties under a warrant issued by a court (s 8 of the PACE Act 1984).

In 2019 the government set out discussions for the possibility of increasing police powers in stop and search. Some of these measures have already been put in place, with a successful outcome.

As a result of the increase in knife crime and stabbings in some parts of the UK, in March 2019 the Home Secretary enhanced s 60 search powers (see 9.4.3), and allowed the authority to be granted by a police inspector rather than an Assistant Chief Constable.

Further to this, it has been recognized that the law does not currently extend to cover some new problems that have recently arisen, and that stop and search could be an important part of the response. The alarming trend of attacking people with corrosive substances such as strong acids is still very much a problem, and the Offensive Weapons Act 2019 was introduced to tackle this. In February 2019 the government decided to introduce a stop and search power to cover the use of corrosive substances as weapons. However, s 1 of the PACE Act 1984 can still be used for these substances, although it does not cover certain situations (eg when the corrosive substance is in its original packaging).

9.2 Stop and Search

There are currently over 19 different stop and search powers available to police officers. The powers permit officers to search people, vehicles, and/or premises for drugs, weapons, stolen items, fireworks, and even animals. Each stop and search power varies slightly in terms of the grounds necessary to carry out the search, and the location in which it can take place.

The most commonly used stop and search powers are s 1 of the PACE Act 1984 and to a lesser extent s 23 of the Misuse of Drugs Act 1971. Section 1 of the PACE Act 1984 allows officers to search for stolen items and prohibited articles and is covered in more detail in 9.3.

Some powers (such as s 1 PACE) require officers to have reasonable grounds to search individuals, while others do not (such as s 60 of the Criminal Justice Act 1994 (see 9.4.3)). However, for every stop and search there must be some justification for the search. The reasons should be based on objective criteria and an honest appraisal of an on-going situation, and failure in this respect would render the stop and search unlawful. It might even amount to the officer having committed common assault.

Stop and search is governed by the PACE Codes of Practice, and the precise meanings of the wording for stop and search legislation is set out clearly in PACE Code A. The Code governs the use of searching prior to arrest, including the beliefs officers should have, the protocol they should follow, and the time-frame for recording the search.

The Best Use of Stop and Search Scheme (BUSSS) was introduced in 2014. It supports a more intelligence-led approach, and aims to achieve greater transparency and community involvement with regard to the use of stop and search (Home Office, 2014b). The BUSSS involves recording the powers and laws used for each stop and search, the ethnicity of the person stopped, and the outcome of every stop. HMICFRS inspections check for compliance with the scheme's requirements, and any force that fails to comply can be suspended (Home Office, 2017a, p 7).

In 2019 the Home Secretary announced that a number of police forces (including the MPS) would no longer be expected to follow the BUSSS guidance on 'no suspicion' stop and searches, ie s 60 implications, and the seven police forces concerned were issued with amended guidance. This is a nationwide trial where the results will be assessed later this year (Home Office, 2019c). As with many police procedures you are well advised to ensure you remain up to date with current policy.

In summary, any decision to carry out a stop and/or search must be fair, and the reasons must be lawful and be able to withstand legal scrutiny. The conduct of the search must follow the proper procedures, and a record must be made to that effect. In addition, the interactions with the public during the whole encounter must be professional; it is vital that stop and search powers are used in a manner that is transparent and accountable. According to PACE Code A, para 3.1 and the Terrorism Act 2000 Codes of Practice, para 5.1.1, 'all stops and searches should be carried out with courtesy, consideration and respect for the person concerned. This has a significant impact on public confidence in the police'. Procedural justice is also concerned with such matters; see 3.6.6 for further details.

It should be noted that 'stop and account' is different from a stop and search. An officer in uniform or in plain clothes can speak to any person during the course of his/her duty; this could include a 'stop and account'. The interaction could be in order to prevent crime or carry out investigations to locate suspects. There is no requirement for a police officer to make a record of every person he/she speaks to during the course of a shift. Should a person provide information about a crime he/she has witnessed, that person's details should be recorded in line with the required crime report. Or if the individual provides some intelligence, again, this information should be recorded, and his/her details noted. Some forces have systems in place for officers to record stop and accounts, but others do not. It is advisable to record an interaction if the officer was considering carrying out a search but then decided against it, or if the individual was not happy about being approached by the police. In the course of such a conversation the officer may become suspicious and grounds to search may emerge (for instance from the person's manner or behaviour), and the stop and account may become a stop and search. As soon as this happens Code A applies, and the search will need to be recorded. As with searching, or reporting crime, or any interaction with the public, if a person is dissatisfied with his/her treatment, and requests the officer's details, the officer should provide the information.

9.2.1   General procedures for stop and search

Code A, para 1.1 of the Codes of Practice states that police officers must use their powers to stop and search 'fairly, responsibly, with respect for people being searched, and without unlawful discrimination' (see 4.4.2 on 'protected characteristics'). In addition, 'any misuse of the powers is likely to be harmful to policing and lead to mistrust of the police' (Code A, para 1.4). The police also have a responsibility to safeguard and promote the welfare of all persons under the age of 18 (s 11 of the Children Act 2004), and stop and search can sometimes help protect young people from harm.

For each stop and search, it is the officer's responsibility to conduct a risk assessment. If it seems necessary to handcuff the individual before or during the search, the officer must be able to provide justification. This could relate to the individual's behaviour (he/she may be resisting, or being verbally and/or physically aggressive), or to the item the officer is looking for, such as a knife. Many officers now wear a body-worn camera, and this should most certainly be used during a search as it records all actions of the officer and the individual. Such information could prove useful at a later point, for example as evidence of an offence, or to defend against complaints about police officer conduct.

9.2.1.1 Locations for searches

The location in which a person can be legally searched varies with each stop and search power. Various categories of locations that apply to searching are referred to and defined in different pieces of legislation. In order for a search to be legal, it must comply with the location in which a person is stopped; for example a search conducted under s 1 of the PACE Act 1984 must be in a public place, whereas a search conducted under s 23 of the MDA 1971 can be carried out in any place.

A **public place** is anywhere 'the public or any section of the public has access, on payment or otherwise, as of right or by virtue of express or implied permission' (s 1(1)(a) of the PACE Act 1984).

Some locations are only public areas at certain times, for example a park that closes and is locked between 10 pm and 8 am each day; during these hours it would not be a public place. Similarly, the public have express permission to enter cinemas, theatres, or football grounds having paid an entrance fee, and they can remain there until that particular entertainment is over, when permission to be there ends. Again, following this, it could be argued a location is NOT a public place, unless a person has a reasonable excuse for continuing to be within that area. There is an implied permission for persons to enter any privately owned building to carry out business transactions with the owner, and to use a footpath to the front door of a house to pay a lawful call on the householder. That implied permission remains until withdrawn by the householder or the owner of the business premises.

Private places to which the public has ready access are also regarded as public places, for example a private field (if it is regularly used, even by trespassers), or a garden (if it is accessible by jumping over a low wall). Ultimately, it would be a question of fact for the court to consider whether members of the general public can gain ready access to the place, and whether a landowner has given permission for the public to use a privately owned place.

A **private place** is land or premises which are privately owned to which the general public does NOT have ready access, for example a private residence or a private office block. Privately owned land or premises that is used by the general public during opening hours (and is therefore a public place at that time) reverts to being a private place during closing times.

Premises is a very general term and under s 23 of the PACE Act 1984 includes vehicles, vessels, aircraft, hovercraft, offshore installations, renewable energy installations, and tents and other moveable structures.

A **place of residence** is not defined in law so would be a question of fact for the court to decide.

9.2.1.2 Reasonable grounds

For a search to be lawful, an officer must be able to justify why the search is necessary. This justification is referred to as 'reasonable grounds', and is required in most searches. Under Code A of the PACE Act 1984 (para 2) the grounds for reasonable suspicion have two parts:

1. a genuine suspicion in the mind of the officer that he/she will find the object for which the power of search is being used; and
2. the suspicion must be reasonable, formed on an objective basis from facts, information, and/or intelligence which help make it likely that the object will be found, and that a reasonable person would also draw the same conclusions.

The grounds must be a true representation of the situation and can be derived from many different factors such as the individual's general behaviour, the location, and the time of day. The grounds can also stem from intelligence (about the area, that particular person, or the vehicle he/she is driving) or from speaking to members of the public. The grounds make up part of 'GO WISELY' (see 9.2.1.3); the information that must be provided to the individual before the search, and recorded after the search.

Descriptions from witnesses that refer to personal factors about a suspect (eg age, clothing, hair colour, and height) can contribute to reasonable grounds as these would help pinpoint a particular person (Code A, para 2.4). But the reason for stopping and searching a suspect cannot be based upon physical appearance alone, particularly with regard to 'the protected characteristics', such as age, sex, race, religion, or belief (see 4.4.2 for a full list). Generalizing (ie stereotyping) groups of people as being more likely to take part in criminal activity must be avoided (Code A, para 2.2B(a) and (b)). Sufficient grounds for carrying out a stop and/or search require more specific information, for example intelligence giving a specific description of a suspect, or reports from a member of the public that the person was carrying a weapon.

An example of a situation providing grounds for reasonable suspicion

A police constable is informed during a daily briefing that a male who often carries a large knife for protection has been dealing drugs to school children by the 'chicken shop'. He rides a moped which is described as black in colour, and the year reference on the number plate is '67'. The male has been described as white, about 16–20 years old, he carries a small 'man bag' and always wears a puffer jacket.

At about 4.45 pm, officers see a young white male loitering by the chicken shop. He is about 17 years old, has a man bag, and is wearing a cap, grey tracksuit, and a black puffer jacket with a fur hood. As police slow down, he goes to a black moped with the registration MK67JPW and makes to get on it. On questioning he would not give a reasonable explanation about what he is doing, or where he has been, and refuses to give his details.

TASK 1 List the relevant information which could be used to gather grounds for a search. Which search power would you use?

Refusing to answer any questions, on its own, can never be used to provide reasonable grounds for suspicion (Code A, para 2.9), nor can grounds be established retrospectively through questioning (Code A, para 2.11).

The requirements for reasonable grounds are different for certain categories of people (eg 'gangs' and protest groups) and in certain situations. For example, a police officer may have reasonable grounds to stop and search a person who is believed to be a member of a 'gang' if there is reliable and relevant information or intelligence to that effect and the person may be in possession of certain prohibited items (PACE Code A, para 2.6 and Note 9A). The same applies for protest groups, where unlawful objects could have been brought to a demonstration (Code A, para 2.6A). In such circumstances it is not always necessary for the searching officer to have reasonable suspicion that each and every member of the group is in possession of a prohibited article before carrying out a search of an individual from the group (*Howarth v Commissioner of Police of the Metropolis* [2011] EWHC 2818 (QB)).

9.2.1.3 Information to provide before conducting a search

Prior to searching a person, the officer must provide certain information to make the search legal (s 2 of the PACE Act 1984, and PACE Code A). The required information is summarized by the mnemonic 'GO WISELY' as shown here:

G	Grounds of the suspicion for the search
O	Object/purpose of search
W	Warrant card (if the officer is in plain clothes or if requested by the person)
I	Identity of the officer performing the search
S	Station to which the officer is attached
E	Entitlement to a copy of the search record
L	Legal power used
Y	You are detained for the purposes of a search

General Procedures

GO WISELY does not need to be given in a particular order, but should be given prior to the search.

Consider the following example:

> A police constable is informed during a routine briefing that there has been a spate of burglaries in a particular area, occurring between 2 am and 3 am. CCTV has captured images of a white male getting into a large white van near the location of one of the burglaries. Whilst on mobile patrol at 2.30 am, the officer sees a white male, who appears to be carrying something, run out from a side gate. The white male gets into a white van which moves off at speed. The officer stops the van, and speaks with the driver, who is impatient, aggressive, and evasive. He says he is visiting a friend, but does not provide a name or address for the friend when asked. The police officer says the following:
>
> 'I am PC JONES from COLINDALE police station and you are detained for the purposes of a search. I am going to search you under section 1 of PACE. Here is my warrant card. I am searching you for stolen items, as I have seen you run from a gate down the side of a house, in an area which is being targeted for burglaries. You cannot give me a good reason to be in the area at this time of day and you are driving a vehicle which is similar to that seen in recent burglaries. You are entitled to a copy of this search.'

> **TASK 2** Consider what PC Jones says in the example above. Identify where she covers each aspect of GO WISELY.

It is not always possible to provide GO WISELY in full before searching, for example when dealing with an aggressive shoplifter. However the officer should at least state his/her name and station, the power of search, and that the person is being detained in order to conduct the search.

There have been several cases where failing to provide the GO WISELY information prior to the search made the search unlawful. In the case of *O (a juvenile) v DPP* (1999) 163 JP 725, it was decided that a breach of s 2 of the PACE Act 1984 renders a search (and probably any later arrest and detention) unlawful. In another case (*R v Bristol* [2007] EWCA Crim 3214), a search had been carried out under s 23 of the Misuse of Drugs Act 1971. The defendant was convicted of obstructing a police officer, but the conviction was overturned on appeal because s 2 of the PACE Act 1984 had not been followed. A search was also deemed unlawful in another case (*Browne v Commissioner of Police for the Metropolis* [2014] EWHC 3999 (QB)), as the searching officer failed to abide by s 2 of the PACE Act 1984 and used excessive force; damages were also awarded for assault.

9.2.1.4 Conducting the search

The search must be conducted thoroughly, but in a reasonable period of time. The person should be detained for as short a period as possible. The officer should seek cooperation from the person, and should take extra care and be patient if the person could be considered vulnerable (eg due to age, mental or physical illness, or any disabilities, see Chapter 4).

The extent of the search must relate to the object the officer is looking for, for example if you stop someone and tell them you can smell cannabis and describe your search grounds are linked to drugs, you should not then search them under s 1 of PACE. However, should an officer be searching for drugs, and then find a weapon (for example), he/she should still act upon this.

Under s 117 of the PACE Act 1984 reasonable force may be used as a last resort (see 15.4.1.1 on 'reasonable force'), but only after attempts to search have been met with resistance (para 3.2).

When conducting a search on the street or in public view, an officer can do the following;

- place his/her hands inside the pockets of outer clothing;
- feel round the inside of collars, socks, and shoes (para 3.5);
- search a person's hair, if this does not require the removal of headgear (para 3.5);
- require the person to remove his/her outer coat, jacket, and gloves.

The person cannot be required to remove any further clothing in public, but can be asked to remove more clothing voluntarily. If he/she refuses, an officer has no grounds to insist. It should be noted that for this type of search the sex of the officer is irrelevant; for example there is no legal requirement that only female officers can search female members of the public.

Officers should methodically cover all areas thoroughly but in a reasonable time. Items from pockets should be removed and placed in a safe place, such as on a table or in a bag, until the search is concluded. Officers should be aware of a person wearing multiple layers, and be aware of pockets inside tracksuit bottoms worn underneath jeans; such places can be used to conceal smaller items.

A more thorough search (eg requiring the removal of a T-shirt) can be conducted, but this must be out of public view, for example at a nearby police station (see para 3.6). If anything beyond an outer coat, jacket, gloves, headgear, or footwear is removed, the searching officer and any other officers present must be the same sex as the person being searched (unless the person specifically requests otherwise). A search that exposes intimate parts of the body can be carried out if necessary (see 9.2.1.6), but not as a routine extension of a less intrusive search where nothing has been found.

Whilst conducting a search, you must act in accordance with the Codes of Ethics, abide by Code A of PACE, adhere to the nine Policing Principles (see 5.3.1), and comply with the Standard of Professional Behaviour (see 5.3.1). A search which doesn't abide by these outlines would be one that is dishonest, disrespectful, uses excessive use of force, is unfair and not based on the law under which it is being conducted. You must also ensure that all persons present (you as the searching officer, the individual, and your colleagues) are safe.

- The search must be conducted thoroughly, but in a reasonable period of time; the detention time for a search should be as short as possible.
- The search must also be relevant in that the extent of the search must relate to the object the officer is looking for. However, should an officer be searching a person for weapons under s 1 PACE, and find drugs (for example), he/she should still act upon this
- The officer should seek cooperation from the person. Under s 117 of the PACE Act 1984 reasonable force may be used as a last resort (see 15.4.1.1 on 'reasonable force'), but only after attempts to search have been met with resistance (para 3.2)

Extra care and patience should be taken when dealing with people who are considered vulnerable (eg due to age, mental or physical illness, or any disabilities).

9.2.1.5 Recording the search

A record of the search needs to be made as soon as possible, and in any case within 24 hours of the search. It must include the following information:

- the date, time, and location of the search;
- the officer's name and any other officers present;
- the name, age, self-defined ethnicity, and address of the person who has been searched; and
- the grounds or authorization for the search.

Should the individual refuse to provide his/her details, a record of the search containing the available information will still need to be made.

If the search required intimate parts of the body to be exposed, the search record should explain the reasons for this, where it took place, which supervisor was contacted, and what time the authorization was given (see 9.2.1.6). The search is recorded on an electronic database, each created with a unique reference number.

Any objects found also need to be recorded on the search record, and described or photographed. If a vehicle has been searched, its registration, make, and model should be recorded. After searching an unattended vehicle (or anything in or on it) a record of the search must be left, preferably inside the vehicle. If the vehicle is locked the record should be attached to the outside (see Code A, para 4.8, and s 2(7) PACE).

Many police officers in England have body-worn cameras, and these should be used to record all stop and searches. The footage should be attached to any electronic record. This can help to ensure that professional standards are met and prevent or counter unjustified formal complaints from the public. For video-recorded searches, the links or access to video content should be noted in writing.

General Procedures

The individual being searched might request a copy of the search at the time, and this should be provided on the spot. Some forces issue officers with a portable tablet or laptop, so the search can be recorded, and the unique reference number given, immediately. Failing that, a paper record can be given straight away. Alternatively the officer could explain how to obtain a full copy of the search, possibly as an electronic record, or at least provide the reference number. Any request for a copy of the search record must be made within three months of the search (Code A, para 3.8(e)).

9.2.1.6   Intimate searches

An intimate search is a search that requires an individual to remove his/her clothing and expose intimate body parts (genitals and female breasts). The officer must have reasonable grounds to suspect that the person has concealed something inside his/her clothes ('below the clothesline'), for example drugs hidden inside underwear.

Before conducting this level of search it is advisable to contact a supervising officer, to explain your grounds for the search, and why you think it is required. Although a supervisor's permission is not required (the final decision rests with the officer at the scene), the searching officer would need to be able to justify why he/she believed the extent of the search was necessary.

An intimate search should be conducted at a police station or at another location out of the public view (but not in a police vehicle). The search should be conducted by at least two officers of the same sex as the individual being searched, and the individual should also be completely out of sight from anyone of the opposite sex (other than when an appropriate adult of the opposite sex is present).

The search should be conducted as quickly as possible, and at no point should the individual be completely undressed. The person should be asked to remove one half of his/her clothing first (eg from the top part of the body), and the exposed areas will then be searched. Then he/she should replace that clothing and remove his/her other clothing for the rest of the search. Examinations of the genital area must be only visual (no touching).

9.3   Searches under s 1 (of the PACE Act 1984)

In the year ending March 2019, the Home Office reported that there were 370,454 stop and searches conducted under s 1 of PACE, of which 58,251 resulted in an arrest. Other outcomes would include inviting someone in for an interview at a later date, or issuing a street caution (see 10.13.2.3).

Searches under s 1 of PACE can be conducted by any officer, in uniform or in plain clothes, and must be conducted in a public place. Any items located during the search can be seized as evidence and the individual dealt with accordingly.

9.3.1   What items are included in s 1?

A search under s 1 of PACE 1984 must be for a stolen or prohibited article, and this covers a wide range of offences and items. A stolen article is one that an officer suspects or knows to have been stolen, and there must be reasonable grounds to suspect this (such as intelligence, the officer's own personal knowledge of the person/item, the time of day, and the location).

Prohibited articles include bladed or sharply pointed items, fireworks, offensive weapons (including acid or corrosive substances), or items which could be used to commit a criminal offence. The table provides more details on the definition of a prohibited article.

Prohibited article	Description
Offensive weapons (including firearms (see 18.3.1)	Includes any article 'made, intended, or adapted' for causing injury to a person (see 18.2.1), for use by anyone. See also s 1(9) PACE and Code A, Note 23
Bladed or sharply pointed articles	Includes any bladed or sharply pointed article apart from a small folding pocket-knife (see 18.2.3)
Any articles used in the course of or in connection with certain criminal offences	Includes any article made, intended, or adapted for use (by anyone) in the course of or in connection with: burglary (see 16.4), taking a conveyance (see 16.8.2), fraud (see 16.9), or criminal damage (see 20.2)
Fireworks	Only if possessed in contravention of any firework regulations (see 14.9)

General Procedures

9.3.2 The location of a search under s 1 PACE

A search under s 1 of PACE 1984 must occur in a location considered a public place such as on the street, in a park, in a car park, or on the forecourt of a petrol station. Under no circumstances can a s 1 search be conducted within a dwelling. This applies even if the person in the dwelling is an intruder and does not have the resident's permission to be there (in such circumstances the person would probably be immediately arrested on suspicion of burglary and searched under s 32 PACE). A person can be searched under s 1 PACE in the garden attached to a dwelling (eg the front garden of a house) but only if the person:

- does not live in the dwelling, or
- does not have the resident's permission to be on the property.

If the person lives in the attached dwelling or has the resident's permission to be there, the person cannot be searched under s 1 PACE.

9.3.2.1 Vehicles and searches under s 1 PACE

When an officer sees a vehicle in a public place, and believes there are reasonable grounds to search it or anyone in the vehicle for prohibited or stolen items, the vehicle and any person in it can be searched under s 1 PACE. The flowchart provides further details.

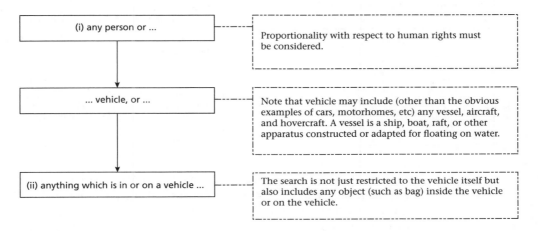

If a vehicle is on land attached to a dwelling (such as a driveway or garden) and the resident of the dwelling owns the vehicle or has given permission for it to be there, the vehicle would be considered as part of the dwelling. It could not therefore be searched under s 1 PACE.

9.4 Other Stop and Search Powers

In addition to s 1 of the PACE Act 1984 there are many other pieces of legislation that include search powers. These include (amongst others):

- The Misuse of Drugs Act 1971;
- The Psychoactive Substances Act 2016;
- The Criminal Justice and Public Order Act 1994;
- The Terrorism Act 2000;
- The Proceeds of Crime Act 2002;
- The Animal Welfare Act 2006; and
- The Firearms Act 1968.

We cover some of the more frequently used and important powers here.

9.4.1 Searches for controlled drugs

Section 23 of the Misuse of Drugs Act 1971 (MDA 1971) provides a police officer (in uniform or plain clothes) with the power to search any person, place, or vehicle for controlled drugs. The officer must have reasonable grounds for suspecting that person is in possession of illegal drugs, or is involved in manufacturing or supplying a controlled substance. The flowchart outlines some key points.

General Procedures

If a person smells of cannabis, has dilated pupils, is evasive to police questions, and appears nervous and agitated, this would be more than enough grounds to consider detaining him/her for the purpose of a search. The reasonable grounds could also be derived from intelligence, personal knowledge, or local knowledge (ie the person displaying these behaviours is in a known drug-dealing hotspot).

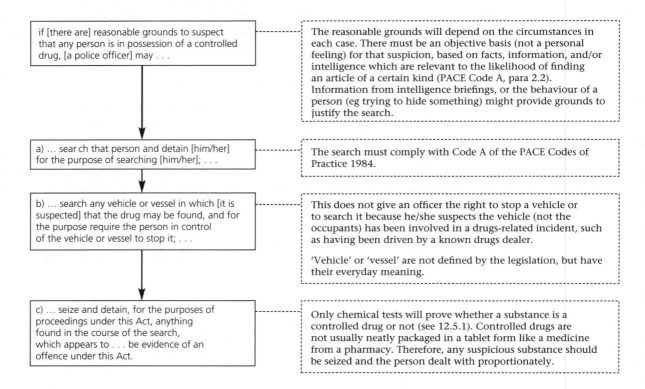

In contrast to searches under s 1 PACE, a s 23 search can be conducted in any place, public or private. However, to search a person under s 23 within a dwelling, the officer must have been invited or allowed on the premises by the resident. Alternatively a search warrant could be used (see 9.5.1.3) under which any person in the property can be searched.

The person's mouth can be searched as this is not considered to be part of an intimate search, but such searches should be exercised with caution (a suspect died after swallowing drugs in similar circumstances in an incident in East London in 2017). Should an intimate search be required, the authority of a senior officer must be obtained.

An individual who attempts to obstruct a drug search commits an offence under s 23(4) of the MDA 1971. The officer must have told the person his/her name, station, and that the detention is for the purposes of a search under the power of s 23. Should the person then continue to obstruct the search, the offence is complete.

9.4.2 Searches for psychoactive substances

In 2016 the Psychoactive Substances Act 2016 (PSA) was introduced to tackle the supply and production of psychoactive substances (see 12.5 and 12.6). The PSA includes its own power (under s 36) to detain and search people for psychoactive substances. The officer must have reasonable grounds to suspect that the person is committing or has committed an offence under the PSA. Such an offence would need to relate to the supply or production of psychoactive substances, as personal possession is not an offence (apart from in a custodial institution).

A s 36 PSA search can be conducted in any place to which the officer has lawful access (see 9.4.1), whether or not it is a public place. Any relevant items found during the search should be seized and then exhibited and submitted for forensic examination (under ss 36–38 and s 43). Small amounts of suspected psychoactive substances can only be seized if they are deemed to be for more than just personal use, because possession of psychoactive substances is generally not an offence.

9.4.3 Searches related to public order incidents

Section 60 of the Criminal Justice and Public Order Act 1994 (CJPOA 1994) provides additional search powers for the police if there is a belief that an incident of serious violence is likely to occur, or has already occurred. Authorization under s 60 of the CJPOA 1994 (often referred to as a 'section 60') is required (see 9.4.3.1). The authorization provides police officers with the power to search any pedestrian or vehicle (or anything being carried in that vehicle or by that person) for dangerous instruments and offensive weapons.

The Home Office reported that 13,175 stop and searches were carried out when a 'section 60' was in place (Home office 2019c). This is five times higher than the previous year's figures, but still low in comparison with the total number of stop and search incidents. The power was used many times during 2019 by officers in London and other cities in response to an upsurge in knife and other violent crime. It should only be used to tackle violent crime, and only when necessary and in a proportionate manner.

9.4.3.1 Authorization

A 'section 60' must be authorized as shown in the flowchart, and the authorizing officer must have a reasonable belief that there has been or is likely to be a serious breakdown in public order. Where possible, a rank of at least Inspector should be consulted. A section 60 will be authorized for a specific geographical area, and the area should be relevant to where the violence has already occurred, is believed to have occurred, or might occur.

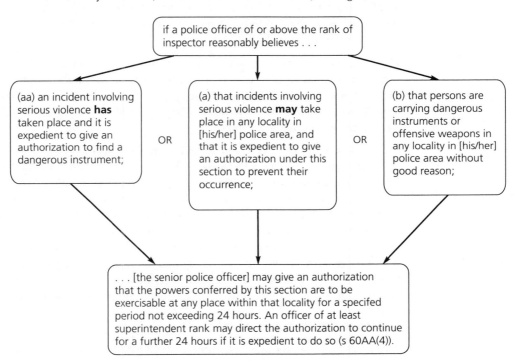

The authorization must be in writing (as soon as this is practicable) and the public should be made aware that it is in place by means of local posters, leaflets, or social media such as Twitter and Facebook. A map of the area it covers is usually included. The initial period is for a maximum of 24 hours, but it can be extended for a further 24 hours if required. Such an authorization must not exceed 24 hours.

9.4.3.2 Powers provided by a s 60 authorization

A section 60 power, once authorized, allows officers in uniform to conduct stop and searches without reasonable grounds (in the relevant locality). The search must be for:

- a dangerous instrument, (see 18.2.2.1); or
- an offensive weapon, (see 18.2.1), which includes 'any article used in the incident to cause or threaten injury to any person, or otherwise to cause intimidation'. This could include a firearm (Code A, Note 23).

The person to be searched must have the item in his/her actual possession, and vehicles can also be searched.

General Procedures

The authorization also provides officers in uniform with a power to require any individual to remove clothing such as masks or scarves, if it seems that a person may be using it to conceal his/her identity. The officer should have reasonable grounds for believing that the item is being worn for that purpose. It is an offence to fail to remove such items when required to do so, and the individual could be arrested for not complying (s 60AA of the CJPOA Act 1994). Note that this is not a power to stop and search a person for items that could be used to conceal his/her identity; it is only a power to stop a person and make the requirement to remove the item.

When making the decision on who to target within the geographical area, officers must take care not to discriminate. There have been concerns about the potential for racial discrimination in such a situation, but in *R (on the application of Roberts) v The Commissioner of the Metropolitan Police* [2012] EWHC 1977 (Admin), it was agreed that although there was potential for discrimination in such situations, searches under s 60 remain compatible with the European Convention on Human Rights.

9.4.4 Searches under the Terrorism Act 2000

The Terrorism Act 2000 provides search powers under ss 43, 43A, and 47A. Section 43 allows police officers to stop, detain, and search any person who they suspect to be a terrorist, or any person who may be in possession of an item which may constitute evidence of being involved in terrorist activity. As with previous search powers, an officer would be required to give GO WISELY prior to conducting the search, and give reasonable grounds for believing that the individual is involved in terrorist activity. These searches can be conducted by police officers in uniform or in plain clothes.

The s 43A power is similar, but relates to vehicles. The search should be for evidence of terrorist activity, and applies to everything in or on the car, for example bags inside the car or in a roof box. The owner of the vehicle does not need to be present for the search. If any relevant items are found, they should be seized as evidence. Any information gleaned should be written up as an intelligence report.

Section 47A of the Terrorism Act 2000 relates to authorizations which are in some ways similar to those made under s 60 CJPOA (see 9.4.3). A s 47A authorization allows any officer within a specified area and time period to search any person or vehicle. The search can only be for evidence of terror activity, but there is no need for the officer to have reasonable suspicion that the particular individual or vehicle is connected to terrorist activity. The search includes searching anything a person is carrying, or has with him/her in or on the vehicle. The officer carrying out such a search must be in uniform. The s 47A power needs to be authorized by a senior officer, who, in most forces, would be at least an assistant chief constable. He/she would have to reasonably suspect that a terrorist act would be forthcoming, and that the authorization would allow police actions that could prevent the act of terrorism.

9.4.5 Searches for proceeds of crime

Section 289 of the Proceeds of Crime Act 2002 (see 16.5) provides officers with the power to search people, vehicles, and properties for cash. The power can only be exercised when the officer is lawfully within the property, for example having been let into the property by the occupier, or if exercising another power (eg searching for drugs under a warrant).

The officer should have reasonable grounds to suspect that at least £1,000 cash is present, and that it is either proceeds of criminal activity, or is intended for use in unlawful conduct. Where possible, a senior or supervising officer should be contacted before the search.

9.4.6 Searches in relation to animal welfare

Under s 54 of the Animal Welfare Act 2006, officers in uniform have the power to stop and detain any vehicle in order to search it for animals that are believed to be suffering, or are likely to be suffering, or are likely to suffer should the circumstances not change (s 19 of the Animal Welfare Act 2006). The officer must have reasonable grounds for such a belief. An animal suspected to be involved in animal fighting can be seized under s 22 of the Act. Officers also have the power to enter a property with a warrant, to search for evidence that may support the commission of an offence (see 9.5.1.3).

Further powers to stop, search, and seize in relation to animal protection are also provided under:

- The Wildlife and Countryside Act 1981 (s 19(1)), to help prevent the taking and killing of wild birds and other animals; and
- The Wild Mammals (Protection) Act 1996 (s 4), which relates to vehicles as well as to persons.

9.4.7 Searches for firearms

Under s 47 of the Firearms Act 1968 any person or vehicle can be searched by an officer, if the officer has reasonable cause to suspect that the person is in possession of a firearm, with or without ammunition, in a public place, and is committing (or is about to commit) a serious firearms offence such as an armed robbery or a shooting. This power can be used instead of searching for an offensive weapon under s 1 PACE, if the search is specifically for a firearm. It should be noted that possession of a firearm is often an offence in itself, with a few exceptions. Chapter 18 (18.3 onwards) provides details on firearms and ammunition.

9.5 Searching Premises, Vehicles, and Open Land

Police officers often need to search premises and places for evidence, for example after searching a person who has been at the location. During a search of a vehicle or premises you may uncover evidence of other illegal activities. For example, in the course of a search in relation to card fraud or drug sales, the officers may also find documents supporting terrorist ideologies (indeed, the proceeds of the fraud could be funding terrorist activities). If such searches uncover evidence that provides grounds for further suspicion, the information should be passed to the appropriate authority.

The flowchart shows which powers can be used to search a property or place. Please note that a 'NO' answer to questions in boxes 2b and 3b requires you to seek further advice as they lead to dead ends in the flowchart. This is shown in the arrows numbered 3d and 4b respectively as SFA—seek further advice.

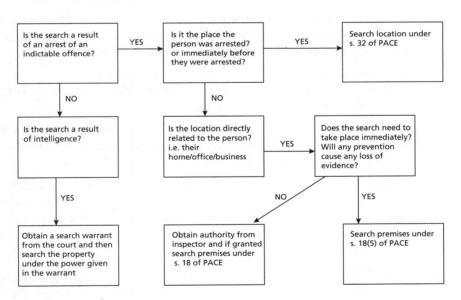

9.5.1 Search powers for premises

It will often be necessary to search premises in relation to a suspected offence. Most of these searches will be under section 32 or 18 of the PACE Act 1984, and will follow an arrest. Search warrants can also be used.

9.5.1.1 Searching the premises where a person has been arrested

A search under s 32 of the PACE Act 1984 is conducted following the arrest of an individual for an indictable offence. It allows an officer to search the location where the person was actually arrested, and his/her location immediately before the arrest (see the flowchart). (The arrested person will also almost certainly be searched on arrest, see 10.8.4.)

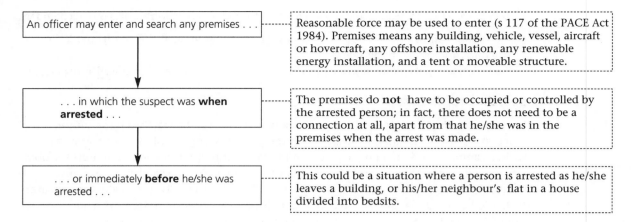

If a man was stopped and arrested outside the block of flats where he lived, his flat could be searched, as could the communal area. Other flats in the block could not be searched, unless there was evidence that he had been in a different flat just before he was arrested. The search must be for evidence of the offence.

It should be noted that if the arrest was found to be unlawful, a search conducted under s 32 would also be considered unlawful, as ruled in *Lord Hanningfield of Chelmsford v Chief Constable of Essex Police* [2013] EWHC 243 (QB).

9.5.1.2 Searching other premises after a person has been arrested

After an arrest for an indictable offence, other locations relating to the arrested person (such as his/her home address or workplace) may need to be searched for evidence. This type of search is conducted under s 18 of the PACE Act 1984. The search must be for evidence of the indictable offence for which a person has been arrested. This power is particularly useful because the s 32 power of search only applies to the location of the arrest (see 9.5.1.1), and the investigation may be concerned with other locations.

Written authority from an inspector is needed for a search under s 18 (except when the presence of the person is necessary), and officers should record the time and date the authority is given. There must be reasonable grounds for suspecting that:

* the person has access to and has used the location; and
* there is evidence on the premises that relates to the offence in question, a similar offence, or to another related indictable offence.

If possible, the authority should be recorded on the Notice of Powers and Rights, and signed. Details of the grounds and the evidence sought should be recorded on the notice, on the custody record, in the search record, and in the officer's PNB.

Anything found during such a search can be seized and retained (s 18(2)) for long as necessary (s 22 of the PACE Act 1984). As for s 32 searches, officers should be aware that evidence relating to other offences could be found whilst conducting the search (see 9.5). The flowchart provides additional information.

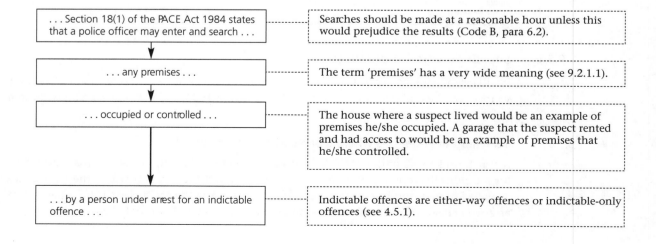

The suspect's home address may need to be searched promptly to prevent evidence being removed. For example, imagine that two burglars are seen to run away from a burglary, and one is stopped and arrested while the other gets away. The suspect who is still at large could go to his accomplice's flat and quickly remove any incriminating evidence. In such relatively urgent circumstances, a search can be carried out under s 18(5) of the PACE Act 1984. This differs from a s 18 search, as it can be carried out without prior authorization, and therefore without delay. An inspector should be made aware of it as soon as possible, but advance authority is not required.

9.5.1.3   Search warrants

Not all premises searches take place after an arrest. Police intelligence could suggest a person is involved in an illegal activity, or officers may even come across such activity by chance. If the activity seems to amount to an indictable offence the police can obtain a search warrant which allows officers to enter and search a particular premises, vehicles, or land for evidence of this criminal activity. The grounds and procedures for applying and carrying out a warrant can be found under s 8 of the PACE Act 1984.

A warrant is issued by a Justice of the Peace, and the application can be made at a court of law, or via an appointment booked with the judge, and conducted over the phone. An on-call judge can be contacted if an 'out of hours' warrant is needed. There must be reasonable grounds for believing that an indictable offence has been committed, and that the object of the search is likely to be of substantial value to the investigation (but is not subject to legal privilege, excluded material, or special procedure material). In addition, at least one of the following conditions must apply:

- it is not practicable to communicate with a person who is entitled to grant entry to the premises or to the evidence;
- entry to the premises will not be granted without a warrant; and/or
- the purpose of a search may be frustrated or seriously prejudiced unless a constable arriving at the premises can secure immediate entry.

The warrant would be granted under the legislation that provides the relevant search power, for example s 23 of the MDA 1971. Other statutes provide particular powers for the police to enter and search premises in certain circumstances, such as the Theft Act 1968 (for stolen property), and in such cases the police will be able to obtain a search warrant under the relevant Act. Any search warrant application (as well as the subsequent search) must comply with ss 15 and 16 of the PACE Act 1984.

There are two main categories of warrant. A 'specific premises warrant' applies for just one premises, and an 'all premises warrant' applies to any premises occupied or controlled by the person specified in the application (and can include specified premises). For an 'all premises' warrant the Justice of the Peace must be satisfied that it is really necessary, for example due to the particulars of the offence, or because it is not reasonably practicable to specify each and every premises which might need to be searched. Premises may be entered and searched on more than one occasion under the same application, but this must be separately authorized by an officer of the rank of inspector or above, and there must be an extremely good reason for returning.

When conducting a warrant, assistance from a specialist unit may be needed, for example a dog unit with dogs that have been trained to detect money or drugs, or a crime scene investigator (CSI) who is able to 'make safe' firearms. The specialist units can be organized prior to conducting the warrant, or for quick time events, contacted to attend immediately. The s 8 PACE power also allows police to seize any relevant evidence found during the search.

9.5.2   General considerations for searching premises, vehicles, and open land

Officers conducting a search should keep an open mind and consider all material at the location as possible evidence for the offence in question, and for other offences. They should also remember that some items or materials might have health and safety implications, such as chemicals for producing drugs. For major and serious crimes, the senior investigating officer may require that a forensic examination is carried out before a search for intelligence materials, to ensure preservation of all the available forensic evidence.

The officer in charge of the search should oversee and closely control the whole process, and keep a record of all decisions made and all items found. All objects that have been moved should be returned to their original positions (as when first found), and any damage recorded in the search log. Failing to do this could lead to complaints and disciplinary procedures.

9.5.2.1 Planning a search

Proper planning is essential for the success of a search. The size of the area and the objects that are sought are key factors. The number of officers required will vary, for example searching a bedsit for evidence during a s 18 search or under a warrant could require just two officers, but in a large or complex search up to ten officers might be needed. Clearly, searching a wheelie bin would require fewer officers than searching a cluttered bedroom.

Officers with special skills such as trained entry officers, or taser-use officers, or a dog handler may also be needed. Search dogs are an invaluable tool for specialist targets such as people, drugs, cash, blood, and firearms (although dogs can damage fragile forensic evidence). A CSI may be useful for photographic recording, and advising on specialist packaging. When searching for a person out of doors, a police helicopter with heat sensors may be required. In searches related to cybercrime (or involving digital materials), a member of the Digital Forensics Unit may be required. PolSA officers (Police Searching Advisors) are specially trained to help searches of vast or particularly difficult areas, or in searches for tiny or very significant pieces of evidence.

When conducting searches in the open air, further considerations apply, such as the weather, terrain, and any surface vegetation. Small items can be easily missed in heavy vegetation, or in wet or snowy conditions. The search officers can obviously be more widely spaced when searching for a larger object on short grass, but may need to work more closely when searching woodland for small items. All these factors must be taken into account during the planning phase.

Personal safety equipment such as helmets, gloves, and knee protectors may be required, as well as tools to access hides, dismantle equipment, or dig in gardens. If it is likely that several items will be seized, it is best practice to allocate an exhibits officer who will record and exhibit all pieces of evidence at the scene. He/she can help ensure that force protocols regarding the handling, exhibiting, and storage of exhibits are closely followed. It is important that sufficient packaging material, transport, and storage facilities are available for the anticipated quantity of evidence. The evidence must be correctly packaged to avoid items being destroyed or damaged in storage (see 26.7 on packaging exhibits), or becoming forensically contaminated.

The IIMARCH mnemonic can be used when planning a search (ACPO, 2006c), as a reminder to consider all of the following:

- Information—why the search is needed, intelligence, local issues.
- Intention—the aim or reason for the search, the target material.
- Method—how the search and management of it will be conducted.
- Administration—maps, plans, transport, equipment.
- Risk assessment (see 5.12).
- Communications—such as which channel to use, mobile and landline numbers, and code words.
- Human rights compliance.

A senior officer, such as a sergeant or inspector, usually conducts a risk assessment of the venue prior to the search. This will take into account the physical risks, such as the safety of buildings and their contents, as well as the likelihood of resistance from occupants. Force intelligence systems and local knowledge could provide information on any contingency plans already in place for particular premises, and any warnings regarding possible occupants. The assessment will inform decisions regarding the number of officers and whether a PolSA and/or a specialist search team are required.

9.5.2.2 After the search

If any items are located during the search, the officer who found the item should complete a statement describing it, and stating where it was found and whether he/she exhibited it or handed it to another person (see 11.2.6).

When the search is complete, officers should ensure they remove all of their equipment. Appropriate paperwork should be completed, including a record of the search. For locations with an identifiable owner or occupier, a copy of the record should be provided, or left in a place where he/she will easily find it. If any damage has been caused, this should be reported to the officer in charge, recorded in notes, and photographed. If the occupier is present, then he/she should be shown the condition of the property. The property must be left secure if force was used to secure entry.

In some searches intelligence-related items might be found. The intelligence might be relevant for the safety of officers who attend later, or it might suggest that some illegal activity could be occurring at the location. In both cases, an intelligence report must be completed.

9.5.3 Procedures for searching buildings

A search of a building should be logical and systematic. For houses and flats, the space is already divided into zones by the walls and floors which can help ensure that all areas are covered, but larger structures can be more complex. It is essential that every effort is made to ensure all areas are searched effectively—there are likely to be voids behind drawers and under cupboards, and any access panels must be removed. Remember that many enterprising criminals attempt to hide evidence, for example beneath floorboards, behind sliding panels, or in a freezer.

Upon arrival at the premises, or if any person arrives during the search, the officer in charge should identify him/herself and state the purpose and grounds of the search. Any other officers involved should also be identified and introduced (Code B, para 6.5). This does not apply if there are reasonable grounds for believing that alerting the occupier would frustrate the object of the search, or put officers in danger (Code B, para 6.4). No consent is required for unoccupied premises, or if the people present or available are not entitled to grant access. In a lodging house, a search should not be made solely on the basis of the landlord's consent; every reasonable effort should be made to obtain the consent of the tenant, lodger, or occupier (Code B, para 5.2). If practicable, the consent must be given in writing on the Notice of Powers and Rights before the search (Code B, para 5.1).

If any items are found during the search, a police officer who is lawfully on any premises has a general power under s 19 of the PACE Act 1984 to seize anything where he/she has reasonable grounds for believing that it:

- has been obtained in consequence of the commission of an offence;
- is evidence that relates to an offence which he/she is investigating, or to any other offence; and
- it is necessary to seize it to prevent it being concealed, lost, damaged, altered or destroyed.

The seized items can be retained for only as long as necessary (s 22, PACE Act 1984; see also 10.9.1).

9.5.4 Procedures for searching open spaces

Searching open spaces can be very difficult, but is often required, for example in missing persons investigations. The weather, drains, and outbuildings can all present additional challenges and make such searches even more difficult. The best way to search will depend on the location, the size of the area, and the officers present; there are a number of different search patterns to choose from such as spiral, zone, grid, or strip search patterns.

Planning is critical, and local knowledge can assist in locating any dangerous points. Copies of plans and maps of the search area and any relevant intelligence should be provided to each officer. Police helicopters and drones can also be used to assist outdoor searches for missing people, suspects who have recently made off from incidents, or vehicles in on-going situations. The offender, any accomplices, the public, and the media may also have access to the search area, especially when cordoning is impractical. This can cause further difficulties, especially when utilizing dog handlers or a police helicopter.

On open and featureless ground, police tape is normally used to divide the area into strips, grids, or zones. If a line search with a return 'sweep' is used, the boundary of the previous sweep is always covered again. The whole line stops when an object such as a ditch or hedge bars the way, and the object is normally searched immediately.

A search of remote areas and woodland can sometimes reveal caches of weapons or explosives, or hides containing stolen materials. In is common to find a wide variety of material that is unrelated to the offence under investigation. Obviously any item such as a timer, knives, or a mobile phone found in a surprising, suspicious, or unexpected place should be treated with caution. These are very rare events, but see 11.6 for more details on the actions that should be taken, in particular at the scenes of suspicious devices.

9.5.5 Procedures for searching vehicles

When searching vehicles, they can be regarded as comprising five main areas: the engine bay, the passenger cabin, the boot, the exterior, and the underside. These should be searched systematically in turn. Vehicles contain a significant number of possible voids that could be used for concealing things, and indeed commercial vehicles intended for illegal drugs importations may have specially constructed voids built into their structure. Officers should be aware of any loose panels, and be sure to check the gear sticks, air vents and CD player/radio.

All officers must keep their own personal safety at the forefront of their minds whilst conducting the search. At a roadside search, safety with regard to traffic should be considered, and it may be necessary to install traffic control systems. Searches should certainly not be carried out on blind bends or adjacent to fast-moving traffic. Officers should also be aware of all the moving and electrical parts within the vehicle. They should ensure the key is always removed from the ignition prior to commencing the search, and ideally held in police possession to prevent suspects from attempting to get back into the vehicle and drive away.

9.6 Answers to Tasks

TASK 1

The grounds for this task are simple. The male is in the area where the drug dealing takes place, and is in possession of a moped which was produced in the year the intelligence has suggested. The male is evasive to police questions, won't account for his movements, and his description—being a young white male, wearing a puffer jacket and a man bag—matches that of the drug dealer.

You could search this male under s 23 of the Misuse of Drugs Act 1971, as intelligence suggests he has been drug dealing, or you could search him under s. 1 of PACE, for weapons. This is because the intelligence has suggested that he is also in possession of a large knife, and often drug dealing and carrying weapons go hand in hand.

TASK 2

I am PC SMITH from HACKNEY police station	I, S
and you are detained for the purposes of a search.	Y
I am going to search you under section 23 of the Misuse of Drugs Act	L
Here is my warrant card (if not in uniform).	W
I am searching you for drugs,	O
as I have seen you driving erratically and at speed, and when speaking to you I can smell cannabis coming from within your vehicle. You appear anxious; your pupils are dilated, and you look dazed. I can also see drug paraphernalia within your vehicle.	G
You are entitled to a copy of this search	E

10 Initial Investigation, Arrest, Detention, and Disposal

10.1 Introduction

In this chapter, we look in detail at the law surrounding detention and arrest, and collecting evidence—both from a crime scene and from people, such as victims, witnesses, or perpetrators of a crime. Some form of initial investigation will be needed to help decide the appropriate course of action. It is of course vital that police officers know the law and how to apply it in relation to detaining a person, carrying out an arrest, and taking a suspect into custody. Moreover, in all situations officers should use the National Decision Model (see 5.5.2) to ensure that all decisions are made lawfully in accordance with the Code of Ethics, national and local policies, and procedures. Further details on investigation, interviewing, and forensic procedures are covered in detail in Chapters 23 to 26.

If you are undertaking the PCDA or DHEP you will be expected to demonstrate that you know how to 'arrest, detain and report individuals safely and lawfully' and 'conduct diligent and efficient, priority and high volume investigations'. You should also be able to safely and lawfully 'use police legal powers to deal with suspects, victims and witnesses across various challenging situations, conducting all actions in a balanced, proportionate and justifiable manner'.

The use of police powers to detain, arrest, and gather evidence must be shown to be justified and proportionate to events in question. The exercise of powers should be consistent with the Human Rights Act 1998 and the provisions of the Police and Criminal Evidence (PACE) Act 1984, and the associated Codes of Practice (see 4.6.1). A professional approach is of prime importance when processing the arrest and detention of a suspect. A fundamental liberty is being taken away from the detained person, and officers must be clear about the police powers to take such an action.

Risk assessments must also be made when a person is detained, especially when there is a risk of self-harm. 'Death in custody' is a devastating occurrence to all concerned (eg the death of Darren Lyons in 2015 following his arrest by Staffordshire Police), and is treated very seriously (IPCC, 2016). In addition, any failure to follow proper procedure could lead to a criticism of police actions, and can help the defence counsel; a case could be lost as a result. A guilty person might walk free and possibly offend again, all because of a procedural or technical lapse.

Many people will not be familiar with the criminal justice process. Over the years, police officers become very familiar with the layout of a police station, the location of the cells, the role of the custody officer, interview procedures, cautions, statements, and legal jargon. They become so used to it in fact that much of it becomes automatic—part of the nature of

General Procedures

professionalism. However, witnesses, suspects, and victims might be anxious or confused, so they will need to have things explained, and their uneasiness or discomfort anticipated. Reassurance can be offered from day one in law enforcement. In addition, people are also much more likely to respond positively if they are treated with respect. A suspect may start to talk, a victim may feel able to describe what happened, a witness may explain what he/she saw, felt, smelt, touched, or tasted. All this could provide vital evidence in a case.

10.2 Police Notes and Records

Police officers need to keep accurate notes and records of their work, particularly if there has been an interaction with a member of the public. The usual place for such records is the pocket notebook (PNB). However, a PNB entry is not normally necessary if other relevant official police documents have been used, such as 'stop and search' forms, 'evidence and action' books (EAB) following an arrest, or a 'collision/accident report book' for road traffic collisions (C/ARB).

Most forces now equip officers with mobile data devices, including body-worn video (BWV), which can be used for some tasks instead of the handwritten PNB. The software is designed to provide secure access to databases such as the PNC and electoral roll. These devices have a facility to complete standard *pro forma* documents that can then be uploaded to a force network, are increasingly used to record other information, for example statements made by suspects and witnesses.

In the longer term, the Emergency Services Network (ESN) should allow for a more standardized approach, and avoid the need for officers to carry two hand-held devices. The programme has been described as 'one of the most technologically advanced systems worldwide', but also as 'inherently high risk' (National Audit Office, 2016). Implementation of the ESN has been delayed a number of times. However, in 2019 the government reiterated that the ESN 'will transform emergency services' mobile working, especially in remote areas and at times of network congestion' (Gov.uk, 2019).

Home Office regulations and all police forces place obligations upon officers to record certain matters (Home Office, 2018b), and the courts can examine any record used by an officer while giving evidence (eg the officer's PNB, see 27.5.3). Therefore, certain rules apply, and if these are not followed then the accuracy or even the authenticity of the entries could be questioned. The National Policing Curriculum (as part of the Policing Education Qualifications Framework, PEQF) refers to the need to keep accurate, legible, and complete records.

10.2.1 The Pocket Notebook

The pocket notebook (the PNB) has been historically used to make a written record of the details of incidents and other pertinent information, particularly whilst on patrol, for example a statement made by a suspect or a description given by a witness. Increasingly though, PNB also refers to the recording of information, such as statements, through the use of electronic devices, which are becoming the norm.

The main functions of the PNB are to:

- note the start and finish time of each period of duty;
- keep a record of significant information collected during an incident in order to comply with the Criminal Procedure and Investigations Act 1996 (see 24.3);
- make a contemporaneous account (as the events unfold) or, if this is impossible, as soon as reasonably practicable afterwards;
- state clearly where another police officer (eg your assessor whilst on Supervised Patrol) has been consulted when writing an entry (see 10.2.3); and
- increase the extent and accuracy of recall in court (see 10.2.3 and 27.5.3).

Officers are usually issued with a PNB soon after joining a police force. The local force policy will be explained on how to complete a PNB, where it should be stored, its surrender, the issuing of new PNBs, and so on (in accordance with the Management of Police Information procedures: see 5.8.2). Note that the rules of disclosure apply to PNB entries (see 24.3.3). The language used in PNB entries must be clear, factually based, and avoid the use of exclusionary terms. Police officers must keep their PNB in a safe place whilst on and off duty and inform their supervisor straight away if it is lost.

It is not normally necessary to complete a PNB entry if other relevant official police documents have been used (such as 'stop and search' forms) but local policy should be followed. In most forces officers use mobile data devices instead of a paper notebook, but in some forces trainee officers will still use the traditional police pocket notebook.

10.2.1.1   How to use the pocket notebook

The importance of the PNB and its proper use cannot be overemphasized. Police officers are obliged to record certain matters within it, and the courts can examine an officer's PNB if he/she refers to it when giving evidence in court (see 27.5.3).

The following depicts some pages from a PNB outlining the general rules that police officers should apply for making PNB entries. These rules must be followed so that the accuracy and authenticity of the entries cannot be put in doubt.

01

<u>Write the day, date, and year at the beginning of entries for each day and underline them</u>

DO NOT LEAVE SPACES

If spaces are left then ———— draw ———— a ———— line, to ————
indicate nothing further can be added. ————

Always make the pocket book entries in, black, ink. ————

Make all entries legible. ————

WRITE THE TIME IN THIS COLUMN USING THE 24 HR CLOCK

Entries should be made in the pocket book as the event happens. If the ————
circumstances make it impossible to do so at the time, then the entry should be made as soon as practicable after the event, and the reason for the delay should also be noted eg: 'Whilst using officer safety techniques, I was unable to make any entries'. ————

Each entry should include the time and name the location where the notes ————
were made. ————

Entries must only be written in single lines of writing on the lines of the pages of the book (except when drawings are made, in which case, draw across the page). ——

Use every line and page of the pocket notebook and do not write anywhere else in the book such as inside the cover. ————

Do NOT overwrite errors. ————

Do NOT erase or obliterate errors. ————

Any mistake should be crossed out with a single line (~~so it can be read~~) and ————
initialled beside the deletion. Any correction should then be written straight after the initials. ————

If two pages are turned over by mistake a diagonal line should be ————
drawn across the blank pages and 'omitted in error' written across the page. ————

Do NOT tear out or remove any of the pages or parts of the pages. Write all ————
SURNAMES in BLOCK CAPITALS. ————

Write down the names and addresses of victims, suspects, and witnesses. ————

Write down all identifying features such as serial numbers of property, including vehicles or documents, e.g. the registration numbers of vehicles. ————

What a person says should be 'written down in direct speech!' and the conversation recorded verbatim or word for word. ————

General Procedures

TASK 1 Why should we avoid the term 'Christian name' when referring to a witness?

10.2.1.2 Example of a PNB entry

The following shows how the rules are applied in a PNB entry.

		01
	Wednesday 16 th January (0000)	
	Duty 0600–1600 ———————— Patrol ZZ 10 ———————	
	Refreshment time 0900 and 1400————————————————	
0545	Briefing at ZZ———————————————————————	
0550	Collected keys for ZZ 10 patrol vehicle index number ZZ 00 ZZZ ———	
0600	Checked vehicle seats and feet areas for property—no trace of any property ———	
0605	Commenced patrol ————————————————————	
0610	At the time stated on the date above, I was alone on mobile patrol in uniform ———	
	travelling in an easterly direction along Sheerbury Road, Ramstone, ———————	
	approximately 50 metres east of the junction with Applebreaux Road, when I saw —	
	a Fordover motor vehicle, index number YY 00 ZZZ being driven in the same ———	
	direction approximately 20 metres in front of me. There was a clear unobstructed —	
	view of this vehicle. I caused the vehicle to stop in Sheerbury Road, 20 metres ———	
	West of the junction with Applebreaux Road and spoke to the driver who was the —	
	sole occupant of the car. The driver identified him/herself to me as First Middle —	
	LASTNAME, born 00/00/00 address 101 Hernegate Road, Ramstone, Kentshire. ———	
Q	'May I see your driving licence and insurance for this vehicle please?' ————	
R	'Haven't got my insurance with me because I have only just bought the car ———	
	yesterday, but here's my driving licence'. Driving licence details ———————	
	LASTN000022FM9ZZ —————————————————————	
Q	'As you are unable to produce your insurance to me right now and as I need to ———	
	ask you some more questions relating to your insurance, I would like to take the —	
	opportunity to inform you of your rights at this point'. I cautioned Mr LASTNAME	
	and told him was not under arrest. ———————————————	
Q	Where is your insurance certificate right now?' —————————————	
R	'I guess it's on its way in the post, I rang them yesterday' ———————————	
Q	'What is the name of your insurance company?' —————————————	
R	'I'm not sure—can't remember.' ————————————————————	
Q	'How much did you pay for the insurance?' ————————————————	
R	'Again, sorry, I can't remember.' ———————————————————	
Q	'How long have you owned this vehicle?' —————————————————	
R	'One day, I bought it yesterday.' ———————————————————	
	PNC check no trace LASTNAME. PNC vehicle check LASTNAME RO at address ———	
	given. Voter's register check confirmed LASTNAME living at address I completed —	
	an HO/RT/1 form. ————————————————————————	

Q	'As you haven't been able to produce your insurance to me now, please produce your certificate of insurance and this form at a police station within 7 days. Have you — got any questions, and do you understand what you have to do?' LASTNAME gave — no reply.
Q	'I have been making a record of our conversation, would you please read these —— notes I have made, and if you agree they are a true record of what we have said, and then sign my notes to that effect?' This is a true record. FM Lastname
Q	'As you have been unable to produce your certificate of insurance to me here, I — am going to report you for the offence of failing to produce or not having a — certificate of insurance for this vehicle.' I cautioned LASTNAME and there was — no reply. These notes were made at the time between 0610 and 0630. CL Underwood PC 118118:
0630	Resumed patrol.
0900	Refs ZZ
0945	Resumed patrol.
C	No insurance—unacceptable because of possible consequences for passengers —— in the vehicle, pedestrians and property owners if vehicle was involved in a collision.
I	PNC check showed vehicle had no insurance.
A	Vehicle was stopped safely , driver spoken to on the footpath beside car.
P	S 136 RTA 1988 to stop vehicle, no insurance covered by s143 RTA 1988.
O	Could have used verbal warning, but due to the serious offence and possible —— outcome, prosecution is in public interest.
A	20 minutes for questioning and reporting the driver was proportionate here.
R	Driver remained calm. Safe environment throughout.

The reasons for making a particular decision need to be clear. The National Decision Model (see 5.5.2) provides an 'official' framework for making decisions, and the mnemonic CIAPOAR can be used to ensure that a PNB entry includes all the aspects that need to be taken into account, that is the Code of Ethics, Information, Assessment, Powers and policy, Options, Action and Review. Further information is available on the College of Policing APP website.

Top Ten Hints for Using a PNB

1. It should be carried at all times on duty.
2. It should be used to record evidence (not opinion, except in cases of drunkenness).
3. It is a supervisor's responsibility to issue a new one when needed.
4. The general rules (see ELBOWS(S)) should always be applied.
5. Make use of the useful information it contains (such as an aide-memoire for the caution).
6. It may be referred to while giving evidence.
7. It remains police property.
8. Diagrams should be included (where appropriate) as part of the written notes.
9. On duty, additional pieces of paper should not be used to supplement the PNB, or as an alternative.
10. Don't lose it!

The rules concerning PNB entries can be summarized by the mnemonic 'no ELBOWS(S)', commonly used in police training.

General Procedures

E	no Erasures
L	no Leaves torn out/Lines missed
B	no Blank spaces
O	no Overwriting
W	no Writing between lines
S	no Spare pages
(S)	but Statements should be recorded in 'direct speech'

10.2.1.3   PNB entries and conferring with others

To comply with the Code of Ethics it is important that an individual officer's account is an honest and accurate account of what he/she actually saw, heard, and did. If an officer did not see or hear see something it should not appear in his/her notes, even if another conferring officer did.

The College of Policing APP is clear that as a general principle, a police officer should not confer with others prior to recording his/her personal account of an incident (CoP, 2013d). However, if other police officers have been involved in the same incident, then there may be occasions when it is necessary for them to consult with each other so that the notes can be as full and comprehensive as possible, but a record to the effect that consultation has taken place (including names, dates, times, locations, and the reasons for consultation) must be made. Police officers who are involved in an incident are legally permitted to confer with each other about their involvement together, before they give their first account in a PNB or statement *(R (on the application of Saunders & Anor) v The Association of Chief Police Officers & Ors* [2008] EWHC 2372 (Admin)).

Firearms officers have come under particular scrutiny in recent years with regard to conferring. In 2005, Jean-Charles de Menezes was shot and killed by MPS firearms officers in the mistaken belief that he was a 'suicide bomber'. In the subsequent inquest the coroner criticized the practice of MPS firearms officers having 'conferred' when writing their notes some 36 hours after the fatal shooting. The same practice was criticized after Mark Saunders was shot dead by MPS firearms officers in 2008 *(R (on the application of Saunders & Anor) v The Association of Chief Police Officers & Ors* [2008] EWHC 2372 (Admin)). MPS firearms officers were also challenged over conferring after they shot Mark Duggan in 2011 *(R (Delezuch) v Chief Constable and R (Duggan) v ACPO* [2014] EWCA Civ 1635). As a result, the following guidance was issued for firearms officers: officers should not as general practice confer with others before writing their accounts, although there may of course be a need to converse in order to resolve an ongoing safety or operational matter. Most importantly, each officer's honestly held recollection of the incident should be recorded individually, as there should be no reason why an officer should need to confer about what was in his/her mind at the time force was used. However, if discussion must take place on other issues, then a record must be made of the time, the date and place of the conferring, the content of the discussion, who was involved and the reasons why it took place.

In 2017 the IPCC recommended that police officers directly involved in fatal incidents should be separated as quickly as possible to prevent conferring, but at the time of writing (early 2020) this has yet to be agreed.

> **TASK 2** Formulate your own system for remembering the general rules concerning PNB entries—for example, a mind-map or mnemonic.

10.3 **Cautions**

From the moment a police officer suspects a person of committing an offence, the suspect has the right to certain information. A 'caution' or 'warning' is given to protect the suspect's rights, and keep him/her informed of the possible consequences of what he/she says (or doesn't say) during an investigation. Code C, para 10 of the PACE Codes of Practice outlines when a warning or caution must be used during the investigative process. Case law states that a caution is required 'when, on an objective test, there are grounds for suspicion, falling short of evidence which would support a *prima facie* case of guilt, not simply that an offence has been committed, but committed by the person who is being questioned' (*R v Nelson and Rose* [1998] 2 Cr App R 399). The type of caution described here should not be confused with the cautions used in out of court disposals (see 10.13.2.3).

There are three different cautions for use during investigations, and each is used at a different stage. The 'when questioned' caution is used at arrest and interview, the 'now' caution is used just before a person is charged with an offence, and the 'restricted' caution is used only for interviews after charge. In all cases the suspect is being warned about how his/her words can be used as evidence, and that whatever he/she says (or doesn't say) can be used in evidence.

There is no need to provide a caution:

- when asking for a person's identity or the identity of the owner of a vehicle;
- when asking for a driver's name and date of birth under the Road Traffic Act 1988 (see Code C, para 10.9, and 19.4.2.2);
- when asking a suspect to read and sign records of interviews and other comments (see Code C, para 11 and Note 11E, and 'unsolicited comments' in 10.4.1); or
- before conducting a search (see Chapter 9).

A police officer using a caution must have a thorough understanding of the 'when questioned', 'now', and 'restricted' variations of the caution, so that the meaning can be passed on to the suspect. Minor deviations in the wording of cautions are acceptable, but any clear breach of the Codes could mean that any evidence obtained will be inadmissible, ie rejected by the court. Police officers must always record when a caution has been given (a PNB entry or on a record of the interview), including the type of caution used (see Code C, para 10.13).

10.3.1 **The importance of the proper use of a caution**

The correct version of the caution must be used or the evidence obtained might be rejected by the court. For example, in *Charles v Crown Prosecution Service* [2009] EWHC 3521 (Admin) the defendant was arrested for being drunk in charge of a motor vehicle (s 5(1)(b) of the Road Traffic Act 1988: see 19.9.3). He provided a positive specimen in a breath test and was informed that he would be charged with a s 5(1)(b) offence. Later he was interviewed about the incident and given the wrong type of caution. During the interview, the suspect admitted to actually driving the vehicle, and the charge was therefore changed to the more serious offence of driving a vehicle on a road above the prescribed limit (see 19.9). The conviction was quashed, however, due to the incorrect procedures.

Some people, particularly those who do not have English as their first language, may not understand the formal wording of a caution. Police officers must ensure that the detained person understands the caution (Code C, para 10.7 and Note 10D). This may not be possible at the time of arrest: a full explanation of the caution might only be possible at interview, once an interpreter is present. When in doubt, an interpreter who is fluent in the suspect's own first language should attend the custody area (and may be needed during the interview process as well, see 25.4). The caution can be given in the Welsh language where appropriate.

10.3.2 **The three parts to a caution**

There are three parts to a caution (Code C, para 10.5), as shown in the diagram:

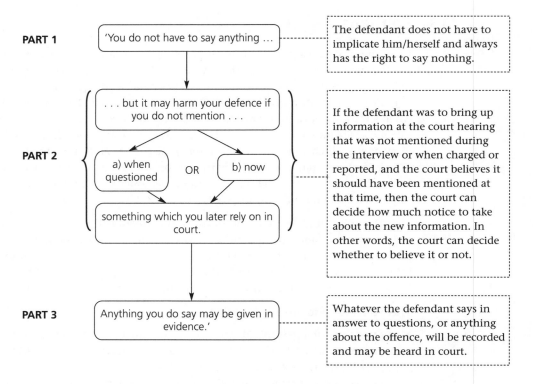

10.3.3 Use of the 'when questioned' caution

The 'when questioned' caution is given to a suspect at the time of arrest, unless:

- it is impossible, for example if the person is very intoxicated, or was violent and needed to be restrained (Code C, para 10.4 and Code G, para 3.4); or
- the caution has been given earlier (eg when a person who is suspected of committing an offence has attended a police station voluntarily to be interviewed (see 10.6 and Code C, para 3.21)).

The 'when questioned' caution is also used at the start of an interview, and when continuing with an interview after a break (see also Chapter 25 on interviewing).

At the same time as being cautioned, certain additional information must be provided, depending on the circumstances. For example, a suspect who has been arrested must also be reminded of the entitlement to free legal advice, and a suspect who has not been arrested must be clearly told that he/she is not under arrest. Further details are provided in 25.5.5.

10.3.4 The use of the 'now' caution

The 'now' caution is the suspect's last chance to have anything recorded about the offence (see Code C, para 16.2). It is used at the end of an investigation, for instance when charging a detained person with an offence, or at the end of reporting a person for an offence (see 10.13.1.1).

Some suspects who are to be prosecuted may not need to be arrested (see 10.6). When informing such a suspect of the impending prosecution there is no requirement under the Codes of Practice to use the 'now' caution, but it can still be used. If it is not used this may help the defendant's case if he/she provides 'new information' at the hearing; he/she could simply claim that there had been no earlier opportunity. This could be seen as a 'fair point' and the court might be more likely to believe the new information (see Code C, Note 10 G, and see 25.5.9.2). Therefore it is advisable to always use the 'now' caution after informing a person that he/she may be prosecuted.

10.3.5 The use of the 'restricted' caution

If a suspect is interviewed after being charged (this is unusual, see Code C, para 16.5) then the 'restricted' caution is used. It is referred to as such because it is shorter than the other cautions. The following words could be used: 'You do not have to say anything unless you wish to do so, but anything you do say may be given in evidence.' The interviewer should also remind the detainee about his/her right to legal advice.

> **TASK 3** Imagine an officer arrests a young woman. First, decide which caution he should use. Secondly, imagine that he uses the standard words but it seems the woman does not understand what he means. Write down a simplified wording he could use to explain the caution to her.

10.4 Unsolicited Comments by Suspects

A suspect who has been arrested must be taken to the nearest designated police station (see 10.8.6) before being interviewed or questioned in any way about the relevant offences (Code C, para 11.1). Asking any sort of questions about his/her involvement in a criminal offence is regarded as 'an interview' and particular rules apply (see Chapter 25 on interviewing).

However, before the interview an arrested suspect may spontaneously say something that is relevant to the offence, and which could be used in evidence. Such utterances are referred to as 'unsolicited' or voluntary comments, and are of two types: relevant comments and significant statements.

A **relevant comment** includes anything which might be relevant to the offence (Code C, para 11.13 and Note 11E), for example 'That other person you've arrested, it was them that did it, you'll see, just ask them you've been talking to, they'll back me up, you'll see!'

A **significant statement** includes anything which could be used in evidence against the suspect (Code C, para 11.4A). The term derives from Part III of the Criminal Justice and Public Order Act 1994 and must have been made in the presence and hearing of a police officer (or other police staff member). It could be a direct admission of guilt, for example 'I wish I never done it now, but I lost it, the knife was on the table and I just kept stabbing, stabbing and stabbing'.

All unsolicited comments made by suspects should be recorded in a PNB entry, noting when the comment was made and signed by the police officer. When practicable, the suspect should be asked to read it, and if he/she agrees that it is a true record he/she should endorse the record with the words 'I agree that this is a correct record of what was said' and then sign (Code C, Note 11E). If the suspect does not agree with the record, the officer should add the details of any disagreement to the PNB recording, for the suspect to read and sign as an accurate account of the disagreement. Any refusal to sign should also be recorded (Code C, Note 11E).

10.5 Identification of Suspects by Witnesses

Some criminal offences are witnessed by members of the public who may feel able to recognize and identify the perpetrator(s). Obviously, this could provide useful evidence. (Here, 'identify' means that the witness can point out the suspect; it is not about providing the suspect's name.) The Codes of Practice must be followed, in order to safeguard the rights of a possible suspect (see 10.5.1). If the witness is successful in pointing out a person, the circumstances under which the identification was made must be recorded (see 10.5.2).

Such an identification process by a witness is only permitted when the police do not have enough information to justify arresting anyone, ie the identity of the suspect is 'not known' (Code D, para 3.2). (The identity of a suspect who has been arrested is regarded as 'known' (Code D, para 3.4) even if the police are not certain of his/her name. When investigating a suspect who has been arrested, different identification procedures are used, such as VIPER video identification parades, see <http://www.viper.police.uk/>.)

10.5.1 The identification process

Before asking a witness to pick out a particular person, the witness should be asked to describe the suspect, and a record should be made of this 'first description' (Code D, para 3.2a). The record is ideally made as a PNB entry, although some report books have a specific section for recording first descriptions. Then the witness can be asked to identify the suspect. The witness's attention must not be directed to any individual (Code D, para 3.2b), as this might compromise the identification (see Note 3F). However, a witness can be asked to look carefully at the people around, or in a particular direction. This might be necessary to ensure he/she does not overlook a possible suspect, or to encourage comparisons between several people. If there is more than one witness, they must be taken separately to attempt an identification (Code D, para 3.2c); additional officers are likely to be required. The police officer accompanying the witness must make a full PNB record of the action taken as soon as possible (Code D, para 3.2e).

The witness will have had two opportunities to see the suspect: first, around the time the offence was committed, and second, when taken to make an identification. The visual evidence from the first sighting may be disputed in court, but this is less likely if the 'Turnbull' guidelines have been followed (see 10.5.2).

10.5.2   ADVOKATE

The guidelines for identifications were set by case law in *R v Turnbull* (1976) 63 Cr App R 132. The mnemonic ADVOKATE is a useful way to remember the main points:

A	Amount of time the suspect was under observation
D	Distance between the witness and the suspect
V	Visibility (eg what was the lighting like, what were the weather conditions?)
O	Obstructions between the witness and the suspect
K	Known or seen before (does he/she know the suspect and, if so, how?)
A	Any reason for remembering the suspect
T	Time lapse between the first and any subsequent identification to the police
E	Errors between the first recorded description and the suspect's actual appearance

In terms of the **Amount** of time the suspect was under observation, for how long was witness looking at the suspect, and from what positions (it is very unlikely that the suspect was in exactly the same position for the whole period) and from what distances? It should also be noted if were there any breaks (however brief) in the observation, and whether it was a frontal, rear, or profile view.

In terms of the **Distance** between the witness and the suspect, how far away was the witness from the suspect when the incident took place? The distance is likely to vary during the course of the observation and will rarely be one measurement, so the longest and the shortest distance, and the timings should all be recorded. In a street, the kerbstones can serve as a guide as they are usually one metre long.

In terms of the **Visibility**, consider the light levels; was it day or night, and if at night were the street lamps on? The weather conditions must be included in detail—it is not sufficient to say 'It was raining'; terms such as heavy rain or drizzle should be used. The effect of sunlight should be considered; where was the sun in relation to the suspect and the witness, and were any shadows cast? If possible, state the distance of available visibility. It is important to record whether the witness was wearing glasses or contact lenses, or if he/she needs corrective lenses.

In terms of **Obstructions** to his/her view of the suspect, any obstruction between the witness and the suspect should be described in detail. It is insufficient to say, for example, that the view was obstructed by a hedge—how tall, how wide, how dense was it? A glass obstruction should be described as clean/dirty, frosted/clear/double-glazed, and whether there was any glare or reflections from the sun or other sources. The extent of the obstruction as perceived by the witness must be ascertained. Record the distance between the witness and any obstructions.

In terms of whether the suspect is **Known** to the witness, is the suspect a friend, relation, or a work colleague? If so, how long has he/she known the suspect, and how well? When did he/she last see the suspect? Has the suspect's description changed in the interim period (eg a change of hair style)?

In terms of the existence of **Any** reason why the witness should remember the suspect, consider any distinguishing feature or peculiarity of the person, or the very nature of the incident itself that made the person memorable. (This can also relate to previous sightings.) What, if anything, first attracted the witness's attention? What has stuck in his/her mind?

In terms of **Time**, how much time elapsed between the witness seeing the suspect at the incident and obtaining a first description? And how much time elapsed between the first description and the subsequent identification?

In terms of **Errors**, how similar is the first description to the appearance of the person identified as the suspect? Any differences must be noted to show integrity of the evidence (eg the identified suspect is wearing a black sweatshirt, and the first description recorded a black jacket).

One of the most important issues to consider when using this process of identification is whether it is actually required. If there is sufficient evidence to justify an arrest, the suspect should be arrested instead.

TASK 4 A police officer attends an incident involving criminal damage to a garden wall. The householder tells her that it all happened about 20 minutes ago and that he would definitely recognize the person who did it, and knows where he is likely to be. What should the officer do, and what should she say?

10.6 Arrest Without Warrant

A police officer may need to arrest a person whom he/she suspects of committing a criminal offence. This would usually be 'arrest without warrant', a general power derived from s 24 of the PACE Act 1984 and governed by Code G of the Codes of Practice. There are other powers of arrest without warrant, for when a person has breached bail conditions for example (see 10.6.5). Warrants for arrest are covered in 10.7.

In the year ending 31 March 2018, 698,737 arrests were made by police in England and Wales, a fall of 8 per cent on the previous year (Home Office, 2017d). The reasons for this decrease are not certain but it could be related to the increased use of voluntary attendance at a police station for interview, and the greater use of other outcomes such as community resolutions (ibid). The right to liberty is an important principle under Article 5 of the European Convention on Human Rights (see 4.4.1) and the power to arrest and detain a person clearly challenges that right (Code G, para 1.2). It is therefore obvious that the power to arrest and detain should only be used for the right reason and at the right time.

Arrest can be used as a means to arrange for a suspect to be interviewed, but it has become more common in recent years to invite the suspect to attend a police station voluntarily for interview. Investigative interviews with suspects are covered in detail in 25.5 and in other parts of Chapter 25. It should be noted that if the rights of such an individual in a police station are not observed (such as being allowed to leave at any time), the investigation will be discredited at best, and at worst discontinued. There could also be claims for damages for an unlawful arrest and false imprisonment (Code G, para 1.3).

Police officers must use the power of arrest fairly, responsibly, with respect for the suspect, and without unlawful discrimination (Code G, para 1.1). Indeed, the Equality Act 2010 makes it unlawful for police officers to discriminate against, harass, or victimize, any person on the grounds of the 'protected characteristics' of age, disability, gender reassignment, race, religion or belief, sex and sexual orientation, marriage and civil partnership, pregnancy and maternity (see 4.4.2).

The information provided here will contribute towards the knowledge evidence to meet assessment criteria requirements of the National Policing Curriculum units on 'Understanding the Police Constable Role' and 'Criminal Justice'.

10.6.1 The two elements for a s 24 PACE arrest to be lawful

Under PACE Code G, para 2.1 two elements must both be satisfied for a s 24 arrest to be lawful:

1. the person has been involved, has attempted to be involved or is suspected of involvement in the commission of a criminal offence; and

2. there are reasonable grounds for believing that the person's arrest is 'necessary' (see *Shields v Merseyside Police* [2010] EWCA Civ 1281).

10.6.2   Reasonable grounds for suspicion

For an arrest to be lawful under s 24 PACE the arresting officer must have a 'reasonable suspicion', relating to both the likelihood that the offence has been committed, and that the suspect is the person who committed that offence (Code G, para 2.3A). Although words such as 'suspicion', 'grounds', and 'belief' are in common usage, they have particular meanings within the context of policing and the law. In a law enforcement context the following meanings apply:

- A **reasonable** conclusion is one that one or more people would agree on as a result of the same personal experience or understanding. It is a practical, level-headed, and logical result.
- **Grounds** for something include a reason or argument for a thought to exist.
- To **suspect** something is to think that it is probably true, although you are not certain.
- To **believe** something is a stronger and more concrete conclusion.

Therefore, in order to decide whether there are reasonable grounds to suspect, the component parts of that offence must be considered, and whether or not a like-minded person who was party to the same facts would draw the same conclusions about the suspect and the offence. The opportunity, motive, presence of mind, means, and incentive for committing the offence should all be considered. Alternatively, certain facts might be known about the suspect, so a person who fits the same profile in terms of employment, description, name, or clothes, or has previous convictions for similar offences and lives near the crime scene, could be considered. Any of these could contribute to grounds for suspecting (see *Chief Constable of West Yorkshire v Armstrong* [2008] EWCA Civ 1582). However, taken individually they may not be enough so, for example, simply having previous convictions would be insufficient grounds for suspicion (see also Code A, para 2.2B(a) PACE).

Information that might dispel suspicion, such as claims of innocence, should also be taken into account (Code G, Note 2). For example, common and statute law provide defences to assault for school staff in relation to the use of 'reasonable force' (see 10.8.3 and 15.5.1) against pupils in their care, so these defences should be taken into account (Code G, Note 2A). An arresting officer as an investigator must pursue all lines of enquiry in order under para 3.5 of the Criminal Procedure and Investigations Act 1996 Code of Practice (PACE Code G, Note 2B, and see also 24.3).

The officer must form his/her own opinion before arresting a person; an arrest can never be justified simply on the basis of obeying the orders of a supervisor or manager. If information that appears to be reliable is given to a police officer, then he/she can use that information as reasonable grounds for making an arrest (*R (Rawlinson & Hunter Trustees) v Central Criminal Court; R (Tchenguiz and R20 Limited) v Director of the Serious Fraud Office* [2012] EWHC 2254 (Admin) ('Tchenguiz')). If the supervisors or managers have information that could justify arrest they must provide it to the arresting officer so he/she can generate his/her own reasonable grounds for suspicion. If the information is too sensitive to be passed to a more junior officer, then the supervisor or manager would have to make the arrest him/herself. Relevant case law on this matter includes *O'Hara (AP) v CC of the RUC* [1997] 1 Cr App R 447; *Commissioner of Police of the Metropolis v Mohamed Raissi* [2008] EWCA Civ 1237; and *(1) Sonia Raissi (2) Mohamed Raissi v Commissioner of Police of the Metropolis* [2007] EWHC 2842 (QB).

10.6.3   Involvement in the commission of a criminal offence

The first element of a lawful arrest under s 24 of the PACE Act is a person's involvement, suspected involvement, or attempted involvement in the commission of a criminal offence (Code G, para 2.1). The guidance in para 2.3 provides more detail on the circumstances in which this might apply. The table provides summaries and illustrative scenarios set in an electrical goods shop, with a police officer who is on duty but not in uniform. (Remember, however, before arresting the person the officer must be certain that it is *necessary* to arrest the suspect (see 10.6.4).)

Level of involvement	Example
A person is about to commit an offence (s 24(1)(a))	The officer sees a woman, who is obviously not a member of the shop staff, walk up to a display of batteries, select a multi-pack, and put it under her coat. She then walks towards the entry/exit of the shop, making no attempt to pay for it. The officer stops her as she is about to leave the shop.
A person is in the act of committing an offence (s 24(1)(b))	The officer sees a man walk up to a display of DAB radios, cut a security link, pick up a radio, and walk towards the door of the shop past the check-outs, without paying for the radio. The store alarm is activated and the man continues to walk out of the shop. The officer concludes that the man is stealing the radio and stops him just outside the shop.
There are reasonable grounds for suspecting a person to be about to commit an offence (s 24(1)(c))	The officer sees a man walk up to a display of mobile phones. He appears to be extremely nervous. The officer sees him take a metal cutter out of his pocket and reach out with the tool towards the security chain of the mobile and appear to be about to cut the chain. But then he is disturbed. He puts the tool back in his pocket and walks away. A few seconds later the same man returns to the display of mobiles, takes out the same tool, places the tool around the security chain, and sets off the alarm. At this moment the officer decides he has reasonable grounds for suspecting that the man is about to commit an offence.
There are reasonable grounds for suspecting a person to be committing an offence (s 24(1)(d))	The officer is just outside the shop and notices a woman standing just inside, near the doorway. She is holding an unpacked, brand-new set of hair straighteners under her arm with the lead hanging down. She has a large handbag and appears nervous. The officer sees her put the straighteners into her bag. She then walks towards the door as if to leave the shop. The officer notes the obvious facts: the straighteners should be in their packaging; the woman should not be so anxious to leave the shop quickly; and she should not have put the straighteners in her bag. This all forms reasonable grounds for the officer to suspect that the woman is in the process of committing an offence of theft.
There are reasonable grounds for suspecting an offence has been committed and that a particular person is guilty of the offence (s 24(2))	The officer is just outside the shop and notices a woman run out of the shop clutching an apparently unpackaged white and chrome-coloured object. The store alarm is activated. He runs after her but loses sight of her in the crowd. A short while later he spots a woman who looks the same as the suspected shoplifter; he believes it is her. He decides he has reasonable grounds for suspecting she had stolen something from the shop.

Section 24 of the PACE Act also caters for situations in which it will be clear that an offence has definitely been committed. For example, a camera shop owner who deals with every sale in his shop sees a woman walk up to a display of cameras, pick one up, and walk towards the door of the shop without paying for it. The store alarm is activated. The shop owner decides that she has stolen the camera and runs out and stops her, and then calls the police. In such circumstances, the officer could arrest any person:

- **who is guilty of the offence** (s 24(3)(a)). For example, the shop owner describes the suspect's actions to the officer in the presence and hearing of the suspect and the suspect does not refute the allegations;
- **concerning whom there are reasonable grounds for suspicion of guilt** (s 24(1)(b)). Imagine that the camera shop owner in the example had run after the suspect, but could not catch up with her. He calls the police and supplies a first description of the woman. The description is passed to an officer who the next day sees a woman fitting the description. He decides therefore that he has reasonable grounds for suspecting her of the theft.

The officer must also believe the arrest is necessary (see 10.6.4).

10.6.4 Reasons that make an arrest 'necessary'

In 10.6.1 we explained that there are two elements for a lawful arrest under s 24 PACE: involvement in the commission of an offence (see 10.6.3); and that the arrest is 'necessary' (Code G, para 2.4). An arrest is deemed to be necessary if one or more of the following reasons (s 24(5)) apply:

1. to ascertain a person's name;
2. to ascertain a person's address;
3. to prevent injury, damage, indecency, or obstruction;
4. to protect a vulnerable person;

5. to ensure prompt investigation; or

6. to prevent a suspect disappearing.

There must be reasonable grounds for believing that the arrest is necessary (*Richardson v The Chief Constable of West Midlands Police* [2011] 2 Cr App R 1, [2011] EWHC 773 (QB)). The officer's belief must be objectively reasonable (*Hayes v Chief Constable of Merseyside Police* [2012] 1 WLR 517), the implication being that any other officer in the same position would be likely to have the same belief. The necessity to arrest an individual using these reasons should be proportionately justified, carefully balanced, and accompanied by substantive grounds. Note that a suspect who attends a police station voluntarily could be arrested on arrival if new information has come to light and it was not practicable to make the arrest any earlier (PACE Code G, note 2G).

These six reasons are set out in full in s 24(5) of the PACE Act 1984 and Code G, para 2.9, available online. The table lists the six reasons and the mnemonic ID COP PLAN.

I	Investigation	To allow the prompt and effective investigation of the offence or the person's conduct.
D	Disappearance	To prevent the person disappearing as this could hinder any prosecution for the offence.
C	Child	To protect a child or other vulnerable person from the person.
O	Obstruction	To prevent the person causing an unlawful obstruction of the highway.
P	Physical injury	To prevent the person causing physical injury (to him/herself or any other person).
P	Public decency	To prevent the person committing an offence against public decency.
L	Loss or damage	To prevent the person causing loss of, or damage to, property.
A	Address	To enable the person's address to be ascertained.
N	Name	To enable the person's name to be ascertained.

10.6.4.1   To ascertain a person's name or address

It should be made clear to the suspect that his/her name and address is required in relation to an offence, so the investigation can proceed. If the suspect refuses, the officer must always explain that it may lead to arrest. The officer should ask the person in an assertive manner, and it may be necessary to ask more than just once. (Remember, this is not a power to arrest any person who simply refuses to give his/her name or address; the officer must suspect that an actual substantive offence has been committed.)

An officer may also arrest a suspect where there are reasonable grounds for doubting the name or address provided is correct (Code G, para 2.9(b)). There must be a logical reason for believing the information is not correct, for example:

- the person cannot provide any identifying documents (eg a driving licence with a photograph);
- there is no record of the name or address in the voters' register or telephone directory;
- the officer suspects the person is using the name or address of a close relative with the same details; or
- the officer suspects the name or address is fictitious because it is the name or address of a famous person or character.

Code D of the Codes of Practice provides guidance on the definition of an unsatisfactory address. It would include an address where the location does not exist. Other examples of unsatisfactory addresses include where the person's name does not appear at the address on the voters' register, or if the person is very soon to leave the UK never to return, or is of 'no fixed abode' and cannot supply a permanent address. However, an address can be regarded as satisfactory if someone else at the address (eg an employer or relative) will accept service of the written charge and requisition on the person's behalf. This procedure could be used for a person whose home address is not in the UK.

10.6.4.2 To prevent injury, damage, indecency, or obstruction

A reason for arresting someone could be to prevent the person:

- **causing physical injury to any other person (Code G, para 2.9 (c)(i))**: for example, if investigating an offence of throwing fireworks in a street or public place (s 80 of the Explosives Act 1875), the officer might conclude that the suspect may harm somebody else;
- **suffering physical injury (Code G, para 2.9 (c)(ii))**: for example, if investigating the offence of being a pedestrian on the carriageway of a motorway (s 17(4) of the Road Traffic Regulation Act 1984), the officer might conclude that the suspect may suffer physical injury from a passing vehicle veering off the main carriageway;
- **causing loss of or damage to property (Code G, para 2.9 (c)(iii))**: for example, if the offence of interference with a motor vehicle or trailer (s 9 of the Criminal Attempts Act 1981), the officer might conclude that the suspect's actions could cause damage to the vehicle;
- **committing an offence against public decency (Code G, para 2.9 (c)(iv))**: for example, if investigating for the offence of using profane or obscene language (Town Police Clauses Act 1847), an officer might conclude that the suspect was committing an offence against public decency; or
- **causing unlawful obstruction of the highway (Code G, para 2.9 (c)(v))**: for example, if investigating for an offence of wilful obstruction of the highway (s 137 of the Highways Act 1980) and the suspect was stopping or slowing vehicles on a road, the officer might conclude that the person needed to be removed.

10.6.4.3 To protect a child or other vulnerable person

It might be necessary to arrest a suspect if he/she is risking the health and safety of a vulnerable person or child (Code G, para 2.9 (d)). For example, a parent is suspected of abusing their children at home and so the arrest is necessary to protect the children.

10.6.4.4 To allow prompt and effective investigation

An investigation might be hindered or delayed if the suspect is not arrested. PACE Code of Practice G, para 2.9 (e) sets out the circumstances for the reason for arrest being 'to allow prompt and effective investigation of the offence or conduct'. For example, it might be necessary to arrest a suspect who is unlikely to attend the police station voluntarily to be questioned (para 2.9 (e)(i), Note 2F). There might also be a need to take fingerprints, footwear impressions, samples, or photographs of the suspect (Code G, Note 2H). All these actions would not be possible unless he/she had either consented or been arrested. Code G, para 2.9 (e) suggests other circumstances where this reason would apply. These include where there are reasonable grounds to believe that the person:

- has made false statements (eg date of birth) or presented false evidence (eg a forged driving licence);
- may steal or destroy evidence (eg disposing of stolen property from a burglary);
- may alert co-suspects or conspirators (who could then arrange to go into hiding); or
- may intimidate or threaten witnesses.

10.6.4.5 To prevent the disappearance of the person in question

Arrest can be necessary if there are reasonable grounds for believing that the suspect will otherwise fail to attend court. Such grounds could include a proven track record of failing to appear at court (or to answer bail at a police station). If an arrest is not necessary then alternatives will be considered (eg the suspect can be reported for summons or later issued with a postal charge requisition (PCR)). Under the ECHR these alternatives should be considered as they would have less impact on an individual's rights and freedoms. Arrest may also be the best solution if a person is homeless and cannot provide a suitable contact address for issuing a written charge and postal requisition. This is explained in more detail in PACE Code G, para 2.9(f).

10.6.4.6 Using the NDM when considering an arrest

The College of Policing NDM (see 5.5.2) should be considered in any situation where arrest is envisaged. Here we provide an example where the police have been called to a local supermarket. The security staff have stopped a man walking out of the store with two large bottles of whisky without making any attempt to pay. The police use the NDM to determine the best course of action.

NDM Stage 1—Gather Information

- Who is the male? Can we confirm his ID?
- Does he have an address? Can we confirm this?
- Are there any health/drug abuse issues?
- What is the value of the property stolen?
- Was the property recovered intact?
- Who witnessed the offence? Will they give formal statements?
- Will the store (victim) support a prosecution? Do they wish to proceed with civil recovery?

NDM Stage 2—Determine the Threat and Risks

- Any officer safety issues with regards to the suspect?
- Any threat to other members of the public?
- Any child or vulnerable person involved?
- Is the suspect a repeat offender?
- Is the store a repeat victim?

NDM Stage 3—What Powers Do the Police Have? What is force Policy?

- Is a search necessary?
- What is the force policy with regards to shoplifting?
- Is there a 'reason to arrest' present (ID COP PLAN)?

NDM Stage 4—Draw Up List of Options

- Confirm suspect details for the store to institute civil recovery?
- Confirm suspect details for the store to ban them from premises?
- No further action necessary?
- Invite suspect for a voluntary interview?
- Arrest suspect for theft?

NDM Stage 5—Take Action and Review what has happened

- Consult the Code of Ethics before making decision to arrest, and only do so if powers allow.

What might you do differently next time?

10.6.5 Arrest without warrant by other persons

Any person may arrest another person, but only in certain limited circumstances, as shown in the diagram.

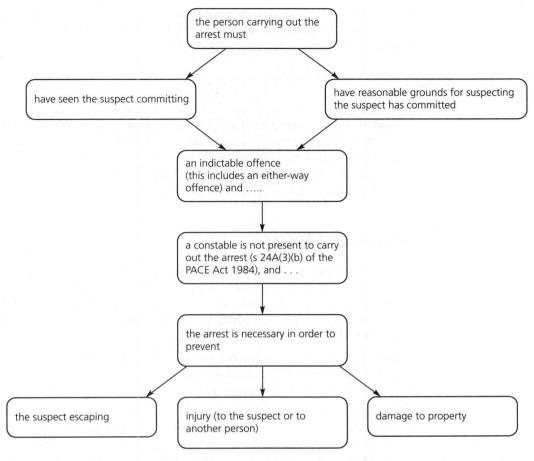

An example of reasonable grounds for suspecting an offence had been committed could be that a man suspects a burglary is being committed because he has seen a young woman he does not recognize climbing into his neighbour's house through a window.

The arrest could also be carried out later (s 24A(2)). For example, a store detective sees a man commit a theft and is unable to apprehend him at the time, but sees him soon afterwards and arrests him.

A person who is not a constable has no right to arrest another person if the offence is a summary-only offence.

10.6.6 Persons wanted for an offence circulated on the PNC

If the identity of a suspect is known and all local lines of enquiry to trace and arrest him/her have failed, or if he/she has not answered bail to a police station or court, a police officer can circulate the person's details on the PNC (see 5.9.1.1). This will need authorization from a supervisor or manager, who will assess the seriousness of the situation. Most volume, priority, and major crime offences (see 24.2.2 for definitions) will be judged as serious enough for a person to be placed as 'wanted' on the PNC. The wanted marker on the PNC should specify the offence, the circumstances (reason), and the necessity criteria for arrest in order to satisfy the legal conditions under PACE for the arresting officer (see 10.6.1). A person who has absconded from prison could also be placed on the wanted list on the PNC.

10.6.7 Arrest in other circumstances

A police officer also has powers to arrest in circumstances that are unrelated to a suspected offence (see PACE Code G, Note 1A). These include arresting a person who:

- fails to answer police bail to attend police station (s 46A PACE, see 10.13.3);
- has been bailed to attend court and who is suspected of breaching, or is believed likely to breach, any condition of bail (s 7(3) of the Bail Act 1976, see 10.13.3);
- is suffering from mental disorder, to remove him/her to place of safety for assessment (s 136 of the Mental Health Act 1983, see 13.2.2);
- is unlawfully at large, to return him/her to prison (s 49 of the Prison Act 1952);

General Procedures

- is a young person who has absconded from the place where he/she is required to reside, and to return him/her there (s 32(1A) of the Children and Young Persons Act 1969);
- might not have the right to remain in the UK, so examination is required (Sch 2, Immigration Act 1971); or
- is causing or may cause a breach of the peace (a common law power, see 14.3).

> **TASK 5** Think of a practical example for each of the following offences: unlawful possession of drugs (see 12.5.2), criminal damage (see 20.2), robbery (see 16.3), and a s 5 Public Order Act offence (see 14.4.3.1). Consider the circumstances under which a member of the public could arrest for these offences. Why might he/she believe the arrest is necessary?

10.7 Warrants of Arrest

A warrant is a formal written document issued by a magistrate or judge that authorizes the arrest of a named individual or a group of people. It is normally addressed to the police and directs them to carry out an action on behalf of the court. A police officer can execute a warrant without having physical possession of the warrant at the time (s 125 of the Magistrates' Courts Act 1980). A warrant of arrest is often used in relation to a failure to:

- pay fines (s 76(1) or (2) of the Magistrates' Courts Act 1980);
- appear at court (s 55(2) of the Magistrates' Courts Act 1980);
- answer bail (s 7(1) of the Bail Act 1976).

A warrant may also be issued for the arrest of a witness required in a court if he/she has not attended despite having been summoned. For non-appearance at court the warrant will be issued under s 97 of the Magistrates' Courts Act 1980 (for a magistrates' court), and under s 4 of the Criminal Procedure (Attendance of Witnesses) Act 1965 for a Crown Court.

There is a power of entry under s 17(1)(a) PACE to search a premises to execute an arrest warrant issued 'in connection with or arising out of criminal proceedings' (subsection (i)). The wording 'is deliberately widely drawn' (Home Office Circular 88/1985, para 8), so for example a constable can enter and search premises to arrest a person for non-appearance in court or failing to pay fines in relation to a criminal offence.

> **TASK 6** Find out how a police officer should execute a warrant to arrest a person.

> **TASK 7** What is the 'European Arrest Warrant'? How does it work?

10.8 Making an Arrest

Here, we deal with the process of making an arrest and a police officer's responsibility to protect the suspect's rights. Making an arrest is an important milestone to achieve within the National Policing Curriculum and is a key activity required to achieve Independent Patrol Status. It also features within the PCDA/DHEP requirements for student officers.

The relevant National Policing Curriculum assessed units are 'Understanding the Role of a Police Constable' and 'Criminal Justice'. The evidence for the achievement will come from successfully conducting arrests whilst under supervision on at least three different occasions.

10.8.1 Preparing to make an arrest

When an arrest is planned or imminent, a police officer must plan in advance where possible. The circumstances might be difficult, for example the precise location and circumstances of the suspect are unlikely to be known. (Note that unless it is unavoidable, a young person should not be arrested at his/her place of education, but if this is necessary the principal (or his/her nominee) must be informed of the arrest (Code G, Note 1B).)

10.8.1.1   Risk assessment and arrest

A police officer should make a risk assessment about a planned arrest, guided by the National Decision Model (see 5.5.2). Inevitably there are risks when force is used to enter and search in unplanned situations: it is impossible to predict who or what the officer(s) might encounter. Consideration should be given to whether it is really necessary to immediately enter the premises. It might be better to stay outside, watch the front and back, and secure the area until colleagues with appropriate equipment and resources arrive (see 5.12 on health and safety).

The risk assessment could be made in advance on the way to an incident or it may need to be done at the incident itself. The assessment will be ongoing, and may need to be modified when approaching a suspect to make the arrest. An officer should consider how his/her demeanour, presence and attitude could influence how the suspect reacts. If he/she becomes agitated or aggressive, the officer could issue a verbal warning outlining the behaviour of the individual and the consequences of his/her actions. (There is no legal obligation to do this.)

10.8.1.2   Power of entry to arrest

There is a power of entry under s 17(1) PACE to enter and search premises in order to arrest a person on warrant (see 10.7), or a person suspected of committing an offence (arrest without warrant, see 10.6). It applies for any indictable offence and for certain summary offences, as listed in the table.

Summary offence with a power of entry in order to arrest	Legislation
Prohibition of uniforms in connection with political objectives	s 1 of the Public Order Act 1936
Causing fear or provocation of violence	s 4 of the Public Order Act (see 14.4.3.3)
Failing to stop when driving a vehicle or cycle when requested	s 163 of the Road Traffic Act 1988 (see 19.4.1)
Driving or being in charge of a vehicle when unfit through drink or drugs	s 4 of the Road Traffic Act 1988 (see 19.9.2)
Being under the influence of drink or drugs when operating railways and trams, etc	s 27 of the Transport and Works Act 1992
Using violence to secure entry	s 6 of the Criminal Law Act 1977 (see 15.7)
Trespassing on premises whilst an interim possession order is in place	s 76 of the Criminal Justice and Public Order Act 1994
Trespassing with a weapon of offence	s 8 of the Criminal Law Act 1977 (see 16.4.3)
'Squatting' on premises	s 7 of the Criminal Law Act 1977
Squatting in a residential building	s 144 of the Legal Aid, Sentencing and Punishment of Offenders Act 2012 (see 14.8.4)
Causing harm or distress to animals	ss 4, 5, 6(1) and (2), 7, 8(1) and (2) of the Animal Welfare Act 2006
Bringing animals into the UK (risk of rabies)	s 61 of the Animal Health Act 1981

Section 17(2) of the PACE Act 1984 explains the factors that must be taken into account before entering, for example whether there are reasonable grounds for believing that the person is on the premises—can the officer see him/her through a window?

This power of search is limited to the extent that is reasonably required to achieve the objective (s 17(4)). For example, if the entry and search was to find and arrest a certain person, there is no justification for looking in a teapot. If a police officer has made an unlawful entry, any evidence of criminality (such as the seizure of controlled drugs) may be excluded by the court under s 78 of the PACE Act 1984 (see *R v Veneroso* [2002] Crim LR 306 (Crown Ct)).

When searching a flat or bedsit, the communal areas such as hallways, stairs, and shared kitchens and bathrooms can also be searched. A neighbouring flat cannot be searched 'just in case', but of course any of the flats could be searched if there was reason to believe that the person was in that particular dwelling.

For arrests that are not related to investigating an offence, other powers of entry are available under s 17(1) PACE. This could include the arrest of a person who has escaped after being arrested, escaped from involuntary custody at a psychiatric unit (but only under circumstances of 'hot pursuit' and not after a period of days or weeks), or escaped from a prison, remand centre, young offenders' institution, or secure training centre. It would also include the arrest of a child or young person who is absent from local authority care, or who has escaped from detention for having committed 'grave crimes' (see also 10.6.7).

10.8.2 Information to be given on arrest

Under s 28(1) of the PACE Act 1984 and Code G para 2.2, when a person is arrested the officer must tell the person at the time of the arrest:

- that he/she is under arrest (even if it seems obvious);
- the reasons for the arrest; and
- the necessity for the arrest (see 10.6.1).

The actual words 'I am arresting you' are recommended (although this is not essential). It is definitely not sufficient for the officer to simply place a hand on the suspect's shoulder; he/she must be clearly informed in words (s 28(2)), and provided with sufficient information to understand what has happened, and why (Code C Note 10B). An arrest is not lawful unless the suspect is fully informed of the arrest and reasons at the time or as soon as practicable (Code C, para 10.3), unless this is not possible because, for example, the suspect is acting in an aggressive manner and needs to be physically restrained. In addition, for an arrest to be lawful, the reason given must be correct.

To fulfil the requirements of both s 28 and Code G, para 2.2 an officer might say to the suspect:

> I have just seen you run out of the shop with a joint of meat under your arm. I heard the store alarm sound at the same time and I therefore suspect that you have stolen the meat. I am arresting you on suspicion of theft of that meat as the arrest is necessary to allow the prompt and effective investigation of the offence by interviewing you at the police station and by searching premises occupied or controlled by you for evidence relating to similar offences.

Here the suspect has been clearly informed that she has been arrested, and the reasons for the suspicion are covered by the words 'I have just seen you run out of the shop with a joint of meat under your arm. I heard the store alarm sound at the same time'. The necessity for the arrest is covered by 'the arrest is necessary to allow the prompt and effective investigation of the offence by interviewing you at the police station and by searching premises occupied or controlled by you for evidence relating to similar offences'.

10.8.3 Using force during an arrest

During an arrest the use of force may be required, but this must be 'reasonable' (eg see s 117 of the PACE Act 1984). The arresting officer must have an honest belief that the force used was reasonable and appropriate in the circumstances. The force would be 'reasonable' if the arresting officer met with force, and had to use equal force to negate it, and then use more force to take control (see also 15.4.1.1). Such procedures are covered in personal safety training.

Section 3 of the Criminal Law Act 1967 (see the flowchart) provides a defence for the use of force for law enforcement activities.

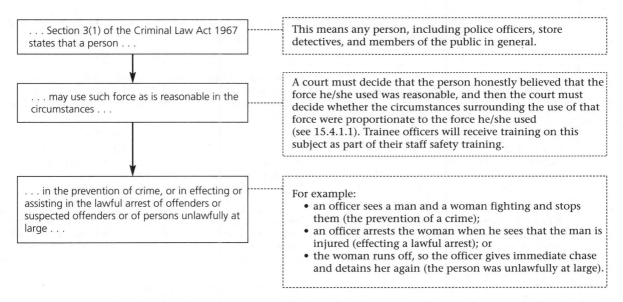

Note that if a police officer restrains a person, but does not at that time intend or seem to intend to arrest him/her, the officer is committing an assault, even if an arrest would have been justified (see *Fraser Wood v DPP* [2008] EWHC 1056 (Admin)).

10.8.4 What to do after an arrest

The suspect must be cautioned (see 10.3), and the officer must make a PNB record (unless it is impracticable to do so) about:

- the nature and circumstances of the offence leading to the arrest;
- the reason or reasons why the arrest was necessary;
- that a 'when questioned' caution was given; and
- anything said by the person at the time of arrest.

If the arrest took place in a location other than in a police station, the suspect can be searched by a police officer (s 32 of the PACE Act 1984) if there are reasonable grounds for believing that he/she may present a danger to any person, or is in possession of anything which could be used to escape from custody or which could be evidence relating to an offence. The search must only be to the extent required to find the particular item—for example, if the search is for a hacksaw, there is no reason for looking in a person's mouth (s 32(3)). In public, a person cannot be required to remove any clothing other than an outer coat, jacket, or gloves, but his/her mouth may be searched (s 32(4)).

A person who has been arrested can be photographed on the street (s 64A(1A) of the PACE Act 1984) and consent is not required. In order to take the photograph, the person can be required to remove anything covering part of the head or face (out of public view if the covering is a religious garment). If a person refuses to remove a covering garment a police officer has the right to remove it (s 64A(2)).

10.8.5 Searching premises after an arrest

After a person has been arrested for an indictable offence, the premises he/she was in immediately prior to the arrest can be searched (s 32(2)(b) of the PACE Act 1984). In addition, any other premises associated with that person can also be searched under s 18 of the PACE Act 1984, with authorization. Further details of these types of searches are given in 9.5.1, and the practical procedures for searching premises are covered in 9.5.3.

10.8.6 Taking the suspect to a police station

A person who has been arrested must be taken without delay to a designated police station (s 30(1) of the PACE Act 1984 and Code C, para 11.1A). (A 'designated police station' is any of the 'police stations in the area that are to be used for the purpose of detaining arrested persons' (s 35 of the PACE Act 1984).)

The only reasons for delaying (s 30(10), and see diagram) are that taking the person to a police station could:

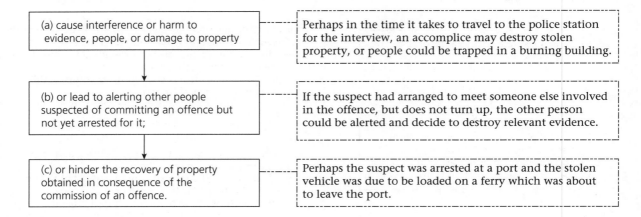

Before placing the detainee in the police vehicle it is advisable to:

- search the suspect (see 10.8.4) for possible weapons;
- use restraints such as handcuffs (whilst considering human rights (see 4.4.1) and the limitations of reasonable force (see 10.8.3));
- search the area in the vehicle where the suspect will sit to locate any unexpected items, and remove police equipment such as items of clothing, stationery, and bags;
- check that rear-door 'child' locks are activated and that electric windows are deactivated;
- position another officer (rather than the suspect) behind the driver, if the vehicle has no barrier between the front and rear seats;
- accompany the suspect in the rear of a van, or in its cage, and be able to communicate with the driver at all times; and
- search the vehicle on arrival at the police station (in the presence of the suspect).

Any discussion of the alleged offence on the way to the police station should be avoided. This is because any questioning of a person regarding his/her involvement or suspected involvement in a criminal offence is considered to be an interview, and interviews must be carried out under caution in a suitable place (Code C, para 11.1A). However, if a suspect freely provides information, then follow the guidelines in relation to significant statements and relevant comments (see 10.4, and 25.5.5 on how this can be used during interviewing).

10.8.7 'De-arresting' a suspect

Any person arrested in a place other than at a police station must be released if there are no longer any grounds for keeping him/her under arrest (s 30(7) of the PACE Act 1984). For example, a suspect might initially refuse to provide his/her name but then provides it on the way to the police station. A PNB record must be made of such a release, explaining the circumstances, and why the reasons for the arrest no longer exist.

10.8.8 The suspect has committed further offences

After the arrest and taking the suspect to the police station it might become apparent that he/she has committed further offences. The police officer has to decide whether to arrest the suspect again, for the further offence(s). The officer will need to reflect as follows: if the suspect had committed only the further offences and was not at a police station, would there be a need to arrest? If the answer is 'yes' then he/she should be arrested for the further offences (s 31 of the PACE Act 1984). All the procedures that apply for any arrest must be carried out in full for this second arrest (such as stating why the arrest is necessary (see 10.6.4) and cautioning the suspect appropriately (see 10.3)).

General Procedures

TASK 8 Consider the following scenario:

An officer is on patrol just outside a tool shop. He sees a man run out of the shop carrying an unpacked, brand-new drill with the label still attached. The shop alarm is activated. During the earlier briefing at the police station the officer had been told that this particular shop had suffered a number of walk-in thefts over the last few days. He therefore decides to arrest the man.

The officer says (on a bad day):

> Hey … you're not going anywhere, you've got to come with me, I'll tell you why later … for now just do as I say … have you got a problem with that? Got anything to say, well it doesn't matter. Come on, give me that drill.

Take a moment to write down what is wrong as far as the PACE Act 1984 and the Codes of Practice are concerned. Next write down what he should have said to the person. This task will help with the National Policing Curriculum assessed unit competences 'Understanding the police constable role' and 'Criminal Justice'.

10.9 Retaining Items in Relation to an Offence

Certain items found on a suspect or at a crime scene may be required as evidence during a subsequent investigation and prosecution. These items are often referred to as 'seized property'. (The use of the word 'property' in a policing context means any article, object, or item which comes into the possession of the police (whether ownership details are known or not), and includes 'found property' (eg lost items handed to the police, see 13.7.1.1).)

Property can be seized directly from the suspect after arrest. The item(s) may either be directly linked to the crime (eg objects suspected to have been stolen), or be other items which need to be sent for forensic examination, such as a suspected illegal substance. Any other items can also be seized at or near the scene of the crime, such as a crowbar found in a front garden, even if they cannot immediately be linked to the suspect. Such items are likely to require forensic examination to establish if there is a link between the suspect and the offence.

10.9.1 Retention and storage of seized property

The main guidance regarding retention of seized property is found in s 22 of the PACE Act 1984, although detailed guidance will also be given during training with a police force. Note that s 22(4) states that 'nothing may be retained if a photograph or copy would be sufficient'.

The legislation describes two main reasons for retaining items:

(a) for the purposes of a criminal investigation, for use as evidence at a trial for an offence, or for forensic examination or for investigation in connection with an offence;

(b) in order to establish its lawful owner … where there are reasonable grounds for believing that it has been obtained in consequence of the commission of an offence.

Contamination must be minimized when seizing and retaining items, and a record of continuity must be kept (see 11.2 and 26.2). Seized items 'may be retained so long as is necessary in all the circumstances' (s 22), but common respect for the property rights of others (as described, for example, in the Human Rights Act 1998) would suggest that any item that is no longer relevant to an investigation should be returned to its owner as soon as possible. Each police force is likely to have a 'Property Management Policy' that sets out the protocols for return (see eg that of Merseyside Police, available online). For mobile phones, each phone has a unique serial number which may be listed on the National Mobile Property Register (NMPR), available online. This can be used to identify the registered owner and establish whether the phone has been stolen. Further details are available online.

TASK 9 If you are a trainee police officer you should familiarize yourself with the forms and procedures relating to seized property. Once seized, where are such items initially stored and, if required, where are they stored for longer periods of time?

General Procedures

10.10 **Presentation of Suspects to Custody Officers**

For most suspects, being arrested is a highly charged emotional event, and police officers must maintain a professional approach throughout. An arrest is the start of a long process, and all staff involved have a responsibility to preserve the suspect's rights throughout their detention.

The information provided here is relevant to the curriculum area of 'Understand and apply the processes for detaining and escorting a suspect to custody' and is an area of occupational competence you will be expected to perform thoroughly.

10.10.1 **Arrival at the police station with an arrested person**

Once at the police station, the person should be taken before a custody officer as soon as practicable (Code C, para 2.1A). The police officer who brings in the suspect should note the arrival time (the 'relevant time' (s 41(2) of the PACE Act 1984)) in his/her PNB. This is to provide continuity of evidence between time of arrest and of arrival at the police station, and any subsequent authorization of detention by the custody officer. A suspect cannot normally be detained for more than 24 hours from the relevant time without being charged.

10.10.2 **The custody officer**

The custody officer is usually a police officer of at least the rank of sergeant, but in some forces a police support employee is designated as a 'staff custody officer'. The custody officer's main duty is to ensure that any person in police detention is treated according to the PACE Act 1984 and the Codes of Practice, and that certain events are recorded on the custody system. The entered information will automatically update the Police National Computer (see 5.9.1.1), and will also be available for officers to use when preparing case files (see 27.4).

When an arrested suspect is taken to the custody suite, the custody officer must be informed of the relevant circumstances of the arrest; ie the suspect's involvement in the commission of a criminal offence, and the reason(s) why the arrest was necessary. This is obligatory under s 24 of the PACE Act 1984 and Code G, para 2.2. The arresting officer would say for example:

> At 11.00 hours today I was on duty outside an electrical shop in the High Street when I saw this person run out of the shop with a brand-new digital radio under his arm. I heard the store alarm sound at the same time and I therefore suspected that he had stolen the radio. I arrested him on suspicion of theft of the radio to allow the prompt and effective investigation of the offence by interviewing him here at the police station, and also to obtain authority from an inspector to search any premises occupied or controlled by him for evidence relating to similar offences of theft.

The officer should stay with the suspect during the initial stages of the custody process.

If there is insufficient evidence to charge a detainee but the investigating officer still has further enquiries to complete, then the person may be 'released under investigation', or bail could be used. But it may become clear that there is neither sufficient evidence, nor further lines of enquiry to pursue. In such circumstances, and if the investigating officer agrees, the custody officer will release the person without charge (Code C, para 1.1). This process is called 'refused charge', and it will usually be the end of the matter unless fresh evidence is found.

The custody officer will also assess whether the detainee will be a risk to him/herself or to others, for example is he/she dependent on drugs or alcohol, does he/she have any welfare concerns, is there a risk of self-harm, or is vulnerability an issue? This will include checking the PNC, and consulting with the arresting officer and appropriate healthcare professionals, for example the custody nurse (Code C, para 3.6).

10.10.3 **Charging and detaining a suspect**

The custody officer must decide if there is already enough evidence to charge the arrested person at this point (s 37(2) of the PACE Act 1984). If there is not, the suspect can be detained if the custody officer has reasonable grounds for believing that the detention is necessary to secure or preserve evidence relating to the offence (eg to carry out searches for evidence), or to obtain such evidence by questioning the suspect.

General Procedures

The precise time that the custody officer authorizes the detention is called the 'authorised time' (s 41(2) of the PACE Act 1984). (This is different from the 'relevant time' referred to in 10.10.1.) The need for continued detention will be reviewed not more than six hours after the 'authorised time', and further reviews will be conducted at nine-hourly intervals after that. The reviews are carried out by an inspector, and the timings are sometimes referred to as the 'custody clock' (see 10.13.3). Section 40A(2) of PACE permits a review of a detention by telephone, but only when it is not reasonably practicable to use video-conferencing (s 45A).

10.10.4 The detainee's rights after arrest

If the custody officer decides to detain the person he/she must inform the detainee of the grounds, and record the grounds for detention in the his/her presence (Code C, para 3.4). If the detainee cannot be informed because he/she is incapable of understanding, is violent, or is in need of medical attention, the grounds must be given as soon as practicable (para 1.8). The custody officer must also make sure the detainee is clearly informed about certain rights that apply throughout the whole period of detention (PACE Act 1984, Code C, para 3.1). The rights are:

1. to have someone informed of his/her arrest;
2. to consult privately with a solicitor and receive free legal advice; and
3. to consult the PACE Act 1984 Codes of Practice.

The detainee must be given two written notices explaining the rights and other arrangements (Code C, para 3.2). Detainees who need an interpreter must be given appropriately translated notices (Code C, para 13.1). The first notice sets out the three rights noted above and also the arrangements for obtaining legal advice, the right to a copy of the custody record, and an explanation of the caution. The second notice sets out the detainee's entitlements while in custody, for example the provision of food and drink, and access to toilets (see Code C, Notes 3A and 3B).

The custody officer (or other custody staff as directed) must ask the detainee whether he/she would like legal advice and for someone to be informed of the arrest. The detainee will be asked to sign the custody record to confirm his/her decision (Code C, para 3.5). The custody officer must also note on the custody record whether the detainee requires:

- medical attention, for example as a result of an injury or lack of medication;
- an appropriate adult, for example the parent or guardian for a juvenile, or a relative or guardian for a mentally vulnerable person (see 25.5.1.1);
- help with checking documentation, for example providing clarification of any of the rights; or
- an interpreter, for example for a detainee with a speech or hearing impairment, or who cannot speak English well enough.

10.10.4.1 The detainee's right to have someone informed of the arrest

The detainee may have one friend, relative, or interested person informed of his/her whereabouts as soon as practicable (s 56 of the PACE Act 1984 and Code C, para 5.1). If the first attempt fails, the detainee can suggest two other people to be contacted. Any number of further attempts can be made (at the discretion of the custody officer or the officer in charge of the investigation) to contact other people until the information has been conveyed to one person. For a young person in detention (under 18 years) the person responsible for his/her welfare must be informed.

The detainee should be allowed to telephone one person in addition to the person informed above, and speak for a reasonable time. Writing materials should be provided if requested.

10.10.4.2 Delaying the detainee's right to contact

The right to contact people and to legal advice can be delayed if the offence is an indictable offence, or if it seems that the communication is likely to lead to:

- interference with or harm to evidence or other people;
- alerting other people who are suspected of committing an indictable offence, but not yet arrested; or
- hindrance to the recovery of property.

General Procedures

Delaying a detainee's right to legal advice (s 58 of the PACE Act 1984 and Code C, Annex B) is very rare, and must be authorized by an officer of the rank of superintendent or above. With regard to trying to inform another person of the detainee's whereabouts (under s 56, see 10.10.4.1), any decision to delay must be authorized by an officer of at least the rank of inspector, and the delay must not exceed 36 hours (s 56 of the PACE Act 1984 and Code C, Annex B).

10.10.4.3 Receiving visits

At the custody officer's discretion, the detainee can receive visits from friends, family, or others who are likely to take an interest in his/her welfare, or from a person in whose welfare the detainee has an interest (Code C, para 5.4). Such visits are subject to the availability of supervising staff, and any possible hindrance to the investigation will also need to be considered (Code C, Note 5B).

10.10.5 Searching the detainee

The custody officer has the power to search the detainee, or can ask another officer to carry out a search. The searching officer must be of the same sex as the detainee (see s 54(9) of the PACE Act 1984 but also refer to your force policy on how to accommodate individuals who wish to be treated according to their preferred gender). The custody officer will decide the extent of the search, but it must not be intimate without further authorization (ss 54(6) and (7), and see also 26.6.1). The forensic examination of suspects is covered in 26.6.

A record of all of the items found during a search must be made. This could be on the custody record, or elsewhere (in which case the location must be noted on the custody record (Code C, para 4.4)). Clothes and effects can only be seized if there are reasonable grounds for believing they may provide evidence relating to an offence, or if the custody officer believes the detainee would use the items to harm him/herself, to damage property, to interfere with evidence, or to try to escape (s 54(3) and (4)). It has been held that taking away clothing under s 54 to avoid its use as a ligature is not a breach of Article 8 of the ECHR (see 4.4.1), as long as the requirements of the Codes of Practice are followed (*Davies (by her mother and litigation friend) v Chief Constable of Merseyside Police* [2015] EWCA Civ 114).

The custody officer is responsible for any of the detainee's possessions that are unrelated to the offence and not to be used as evidence (Code C, para 4.1), and must arrange their safekeeping.

10.10.5.1 Strip searches and intimate searches

A 'strip search' involves removal of clothing, and the detainee can be required to lift his/her arms and stand with his/her legs apart. It requires authorization from the custody officer, who must reasonably consider that the detainee has concealed an article which he/she would not be allowed to keep, and that a strip search is necessary to find the article (Code C, Annex A, para 10). The search must be conducted in accordance with Code C, Annex A, para 11. For example, it must be carried out by an officer of the same sex with at least two people present (other than the detainee), or in line with force policy regarding individuals wishing to be treated according to their preferred gender, but away from other people in general and in a safe place. The search should be conducted with regard to sensitivity, and as quickly as reasonably possible. In relation to establishing the gender of persons for the purposes of searching, see Code A, Annex F.

An intimate search is more detailed than a strip search and involves the examination (including touching) of any part of the body, including orifices (see Code C, Annex A, para 1 and the College of Policing Authorised Professional Practice). Such a search must be authorized by an officer of at least the rank of inspector, who must have reasonable grounds for believing that at the time of the arrest the detainee had concealed on his/her person:

- anything which could be used to cause physical injury to him/herself or others; or
- a Class A drug (see 12.5.1.1) with the appropriate criminal intent (s 55(1)). (The criminal intent must relate to a further criminal offence such as an intent to supply (see 12.6.2), or exportation with intent to evade a prohibition or restriction (s 68(2) Customs and Excise Management Act 1979).)

> **TASK 10** In Task 8 of this chapter a police officer saw a man run out of the shop carrying an unpacked, brand-new drill and heard the shop alarm go off. The officer knew from recent briefings that this shop had suffered a number of walk-in thefts over the last few days. He had therefore arrested the man and taken him to the police station. What should the police officer say to the custody officer?

10.11 Statements from Witnesses and Victims

An important part of any investigation is supporting witnesses (who may also be victims) through the process of making a witness statement. This is recorded on an MG11 form, which will be included in the case file (see 27.4.2). Victim personal statements (see 10.11.2) are also recorded on an MG11 form, either following on from the first part of a witness statement or on a separate form. Detailed and accurate accounts are required and no abbreviations and jargon should be used.

The MG11 form is available as a paper or an electronic version. The paper version has a front sheet and continuation sheets if required (use paper clips rather than staples). On hand-written copies black ink should be used, and any written mistakes crossed out with a single line and initialled in the margin—do not overwrite or use correction fluid. The back of the form (once completed) is for police and prosecution use only, in order to protect witnesses.

Some of the guidance provided here is adapted from the unpublished document 'A Guide to Form MG11, General Completion' by Kent Police, as interpreted by the authors.

10.11.1 Witness statements

Witness statements are generally compiled by the interviewing officer after he/she has interviewed the witness (see 25.6), and they have together agreed the facts that are to be recorded. The officer should outline the consequences of the witness stating anything he/she knows to be false or does not believe to be true, and draw attention to the need for the witness to sign a declaration that he/she believes everything in the statement is true.

The witness's name should be written out in full at the top of the form, using capitals for the family name only. (If capitals are used throughout, then the family name should be underlined.) Any people named in a witness statement should be referred to by the name the witness used. For all descriptions of a person, object, or incident, ADVOKATE must be adhered to in full (see 10.5.2). Descriptions should be recorded in detail, and any uncertainties fully recorded.

General Procedures

General Procedures

MG 11 (T)

RESTRICTED (when complete)

WITNESS STATEMENT

(CJ Act 1967, s.9; MC Act 1980, ss.5A(3) (a) and SB; MC Rules 1981, r.70)

URN ☐ ☐ ☐ / ☐ ☐

Enter your rank and force number.

Statement of: *Charlotte UNDERWOOD*

Age if under 18: *over 18* (if over 18 insert 'over 18')   Occupation: *Police Constable 118118*

This statement (consisting of *one* page(s) each signed by me) is true to the best of my knowledge and belief and I make it knowing that, if it is tendered in evidence, I shall be liable to prosecution if I have wilfully stated anything in it, which I know to be false, or do not believe to be true.

Sign with your rank and number.

Signature: *C. Underwood PC 118118*   Date: *01.03.00*

Tick if witness evidence is visually recorded ☐ *(supply witness details on rear)*

Use the 24 hour clock and use 'at' not 'at approximately'.

Always begin with the time, day, date, location, and other persons present. Do not include your name, title, number, or station in the main body of the text.

At 1600 hours on Wednesday 1st March 0000 I was on uniformed patrol in a marked police vehicle with PC 69900 HODDIM. At this time we attended Kerrie's Corner shop, 98 High Street, Maidbury, Kentshire. As we arrived I saw a man who I now know to be Nathan JONAH born 09.09.1973 sitting on the pavement holding a plastic carrier bag approximately 1 metre from the front door of the shop on the pavement outside. I got out of the car and walked towards JONAH. I would describe JONAH as... The plastic carrier bag JONAH was holding looked as if it contained something lumpy. I heard JONAH shout 'That's it, you're all for it now!' and he tried to stand up, but stumbled and fell. As I approached him I could smell intoxicating liquor on his breath, his speech was slurred, and his eyes were glazed. He tried to stand up again but could not. He was drunk or otherwise intoxicated. He was groaning and looking downwards with his eyes shut sometimes.

This is hearsay evidence (she said that he said), and should be recorded in direct speech; see 24.2.5.1

A woman came up to me and introduced herself as Mrs STONER. She said in the presence and hearing of the suspect 'I heard him say "what's it to you if some of us 'ain't got nothing to eat"' and then I heard a long bang—I think he pushed the shop assistant against the wall behind the door and ran out'. PC HODDIM came over with a shop assistant from the store, a person I now know to be Janis DEE. In the presence and hearing of the suspect I said to Mrs DEE 'Can you please tell me what happened?' Mrs DEE replied 'I was filling the refrigerator with packets of bacon when this bloke here took a pack from out of the box on the floor. He walked around the store for a little while, well staggered really. I tried to stop him and then he just walked out without paying for it.' At 1635 hours the same day I said to the suspect JONAH 'As a result of what this person has told me I am arresting you on suspicion of theft of a pack of meat from the shop. Your arrest is necessary for the prompt and effective investigation of the offence and because you are drunk you may suffer physical injury to yourself'. I then cautioned him to which he replied 'It wasn't me, you've got the wrong person ... why me?' ... As JONAH was drunk I believed that he may present a danger to himself or others if he had possession of a weapon. I also believed he may have other articles from the store which he had not paid for. Therefore I searched him before placing him into the police vehicle. I looked inside the bag he was carrying and it contained a large packet of meat which I seized (exhibit labelled and marked CW/1). JONAH was placed in a police vehicle and conveyed to Maidbury Police Station arriving at 1645 hours the same day where he was introduced to the custody officer PS BENN.

Arrests must be recorded in direct speech, but the caution does not have to be. Any response from the suspect must be accurately recorded.

Sign and date after the last word of the statement, and include your rank and number.

For a duty statement, the signature does not need to be witnessed.

C. Underwood PC 118118, 01.03.00

Sign at the foot of every page, and include your rank and number.

Signature: *C. Underwood PC 118118*   Signature witnessed by: *n/a*

PTO

MG 11 (T)

**RESTRICTED—FOR POLICE AND PROSECUTION ONLY
(when complete)**

Witness contact details

Home address: *31 JENNER ROAD, MAIDBURY, KENT*

.... Postcode: *MA99 1XX*

Home telephone No: *1234567* .... Work telephone No: *123456789* ....

Mobile/Pager No: *1234567* .... E-mail address: *N/A* ....

Preferred means of contact: *HOME PHONE*

~~Male~~/Female (delete as applicable)   Date and place of birth: *12.00.65 BIG CITY*

Former Name: *N/A* .... Height: *163cm* Ethnicity Code: *W1* ....

Dates of witness non-availability: *see MG 10*

....

Use capital letters for all this part.

For example, if previously married.

If no MG 10 form is available, then record the relevant information here.

Witness care

(a) Is the witness willing and likely to attend court? ~~Yes~~/No. If 'No', include reason(s) on form MG6. What can be done to ensure attendance?

....

(b) Does the witness require 'special measures' as a vulnerable or intimidated witness? ~~Yes~~/No. If 'Yes' submit MG2 with file.

(c) Does the witness have any specific care needs? ~~Yes~~/No. If 'Yes' what are they? (Healthcare, childcare, transport, disability, language difficulties, visually impaired, restricted mobility or other concerns?)

....

....

....

Witness Consent (for witness completion)

a) The criminal justice process and Victim Personal Statement scheme (victims only) has been explained to me: Yes/~~No~~

b) I have been given the leaflet 'Giving a witness statement to the police—what happens next?' Yes/~~No~~

c) I consent to police having access to my medical record(s) in relation to this matter: Yes☐ No☐ N/A☑

d) I consent to my medical record in relation to this matter being disclosed to the defence: Yes☐ No☐ N/A☑

e) I consent to the statement being disclosed for the purposes of civil proceedings e.g. child care proceedings (if applicable): Yes☐ No☐ N/A☑

f) The information recorded above will be disclosed to the Witness Service so that they can offer help and support, unless you ask them not to. Tick this box to decline their services: ☑

Remember to get the witness to sign here.

Signature of witness: *AMStoner*

Statement taken by (print name): *PC 118118 UNDERWOOD* Station: *Maidbury Police Station*

Time and place statement taken: *17.50 01.03.00 MAIDBURY POLICE STATION* ....

The time and date the statement was made should be recorded in your PNB.

General Procedures

Witness statements must record only what the witness has experienced directly through his/her own senses. The statement though written (or taken) by a police officer should be in the witness' own words, and avoid police jargon. Opinion should not be included, unless the witness is a relevant expert providing an expert opinion, or a competent witness stating whether another person was drunk (see 12.2.1).

Exhibits (items that could be used as evidence in court) must be given a reference number that includes the initials of the person who handed the item to the police officer. So, for example, the bag of shopping Alice Stoner gave to PC Hoddim will have the reference number AMS/1. The other bag (the orange bag held by the man on the pavement) will have the reference number CU/1 because it was the first item of evidence collected by PC Underwood in this incident (see 11.2.6 for more on numbering of exhibits).

10.11.2 Victim personal statements

The victim will provide a statement as a witness, but can also make a further statement as a victim. Such victim personal statement (VPS) provides extra information on how the crime has affected the victim, and what support may be needed. A VPS can also be made by the relatives or partners of homicide victims, or the parents (or carers) of children or of adults with learning difficulties. It will form part of the case file and is used during the court process, particularly in sentencing and applications for bail.

A VPS is normally made immediately after a witness statement, on the same MG11 form. This is known as a Stage 1 VPS. A caption should be inserted between the evidential part of the statement and the VPS, to emphasize this separation, for example:

> I have been given the Victim Personal Statement leaflet and the VPS scheme has been explained to me. What follows is what I wish to say in connection with this matter. I understand that what I say may be used in various ways and that it may be disclosed to the defence.

A separate or an additional VPS (a Stage 2 VPS) can be made at a later date. The same caption should be used to emphasize it is a VPS and not an evidential witness statement. If a previous VPS has been made, the caption should include the phrase 'This statement adds to what I said in my previous victim personal statement'.

The officer should explain that the victim can express anything he/she chooses, including:

- whether he/she wants to be told about the progress of the case;
- whether he/she would like extra support (particularly if appearing as a witness at a trial);
- whether he/she feels vulnerable or intimidated;
- whether he/she is worried about the suspect being given bail (eg if the suspect and victim know each other);
- if racial hostility is felt to be part of the crime, or if he/she feels victimized because of his/her faith, cultural background, or disability;
- whether he/she is considering trying to claim compensation from the offender for any injury, loss, or damage suffered; and
- whether the crime has caused, or made worse, any medical or social problems (such as marital problems).

Victims can choose whether the VPS will be heard in court (either read out by the victim or the CPS, or from a recording). There may be consequences for a victim's privacy if the statement is heard in open sessions, particularly if reported by the media. If it is not heard and the defendant is found guilty, the contents of the VPS will still be considered as part of the evidence prior to sentencing. All this must be clearly explained to the victim.

The completed statement should be sent to the CPS with information on any arrangements made, and the victim's preferences. Further guidance on victim personal statements is available on the Ministry of Justice website.

10.12 Duty Statements

A duty statement is a witness statement made by a police officer as a witness to events. The general guidance for completing MG11 forms still applies (see 10.11.1) but there are additional considerations. On the back of the MG11, for the 'home' contact details (at the top) a police officer should use his/her work address, email, and telephone number. The Witness Care and Witness Consent sections do not need to be filled in for a duty statement: simply put 'N/A' where appropriate.

MG 11 (T)

RESTRICTED (when complete)

WITNESS STATEMENT

(CJ Act 1967, s.9; MC Act 1980, ss.5A(3) (a) and SB; MC Rules 1981, r.70)

URN ☐ ☐ ☐ ☐

Statement of: *Charlotte UNDERWOOD*

Age if under 18: *over 18* (if over 18 insert 'over 18')   Occupation: *Police Constable 118118*

This statement (consisting of *one* page(s) each signed by me) is true to the best of my knowledge and belief and I make it knowing that, if it is tendered in evidence, I shall be liable to prosecution if I have wilfully stated anything in it, which I know to be false, or do not believe to be true.

Signature: *C. Underwood PC 118118*   Date: *01.03.00*

Tick if witness evidence is visually recorded ☐ *(supply witness details on rear)*

At 1600 hours on Wednesday 1st March 0000 I was on uniformed patrol in a marked police vehicle with PC 69900 HODDIM. At this time we attended Kerrie's Corner shop, 98 High Street, Maidbury, Kentshire. As we arrived I saw a man who I now know to be Nathan JONAH born 09.09.1973 sitting on the pavement holding a plastic carrier bag approximately 1 metre from the front door of the shop on the pavement outside. I got out of the car and walked towards JONAH. I would describe JONAH as... The plastic carrier bag JONAH was holding looked as if it contained something lumpy. I heard JONAH shout 'That's it, you're all for it now!' and he tried to stand up, but stumbled and fell. As I approached him I could smell intoxicating liquor on his breath, his speech was slurred, and his eyes were glazed. He tried to stand up again but could not. He was drunk or otherwise intoxicated. He was groaning and looking downwards with his eyes shut sometimes.

A woman came up to me and introduced herself as Mrs STONER. She said in the presence and hearing of the suspect 'I heard him say "what's it to you if some of us 'ain't got nothing to eat" and then I heard a long bang—I think he pushed the shop assistant against the wall behind the door and ran out'. PC HODDIM came over with a shop assistant from the store, a person I now know to be Janis DEE. In the presence and hearing of the suspect I said to Mrs DEE 'Can you please tell me what happened?' Mrs DEE replied 'I was filling the refrigerator with packets of bacon when this bloke here took a pack from out of the box on the floor. He walked around the store for a little while, well staggered really. I tried to stop him and then he just walked out without paying for it.' At 1635 hours the same day I said to the suspect JONAH 'As a result of what this person has told me I am arresting you on suspicion of theft of a pack of meat from the shop. Your arrest is necessary for the prompt and effective investigation of the offence and because you are drunk you may suffer physical injury to yourself'. I then cautioned him to which he replied 'It wasn't me, you've got the wrong person ... why me?' ... As JONAH was drunk I believed that he may present a danger to himself or others if he had possession of a weapon. I also believed he may have other articles from the store which he had not paid for. Therefore I searched him before placing him into the police vehicle. I looked inside the bag he was carrying and it contained a large packet of meat which I seized (exhibit labelled and marked CU/1). JONAH was placed in a police vehicle and conveyed to Maidbury Police Station arriving at 1645 hours the same day where he was introduced to the custody officer PS BENN.

C. Underwood PC 118118, 01.03.00

Signature: *C. Underwood PC 118118*   Signature witnessed by: *n/a*

PTO

Enter your rank and force number.

Sign with your rank and number.

Use the 24 hour clock and use 'at' not 'at approximately'.

Always begin with the time, day, date, location, and other persons present. Do not include your name, title, number, or station in the main body of the text.

This is hearsay evidence (she said that he said), and should be recorded in direct speech; see 24.2.5.1

Arrests must be recorded in direct speech, but the caution does not have to be. Any response from the suspect must be accurately recorded.

Sign and date after the last word of the statement, and include your rank and number.

For a duty statement, the signature does not need to be witnessed.

Sign at the foot of every page, and include your rank and number.

General Procedures

When referring to other police officers, for the first mention the family name should be in capitals, with the officer's rank and number. If the same officer is mentioned again, only the rank and name is needed. Witnesses should be referred to using either both names, or Mr/Mrs (etc) and the family name in capitals. The first time a suspect is named in a duty statement, the full name should be used with the family name in capitals, but in the rest of the statement only the family name is used.

10.13 Methods of Disposal of Criminal Suspects

Here we describe the various methods of 'disposing' of a criminal suspect. By disposal we mean the result of an investigation and its outcome for the suspect. We have split these into three main categories: directing to court, out-of-court disposals, and bail.

The disposal can be final, leading to a 'positive disposal' such as a charge, caution, or penalty notice, or a 'No Further Action' when no crime can be confirmed or there is not enough evidence to support a prosecution. These disposals usually signify the end of the investigation, although if further evidence comes to light they can be reopened. However, some disposals, such as release under investigation or police bail, can be 'interim' if further investigation is to be undertaken.

10.13.1 Directing to Court

Once an investigation has been concluded and a decision to prosecute has been made by the police or the Crown Prosecution Service (see 27.2), the defendant will be formally accused of committing a criminal offence. In less serious cases, the defendant will receive a formal accusation by way of a written charge and postal requisition by a public prosecutor. In more serious cases the charge will be read out to the suspect in a police station.

10.13.1.1 Written charge and postal requisition by a public prosecutor

Criminal proceedings can be instituted by a written postal charge and requisition (PCR) (s 29(1) and (2) of the Criminal Justice Act 2003), after a police officer reports a suspect at the roadside for a road traffic offence, or a suspect attends a police station voluntarily at an officer's request (reporting for an offence). This has largely replaced the former practice of issuing a summons to attend court.

To report a person for the purposes of issuing a written charge, the officer must:

1. state the offence(s) involved;
2. gather evidence in the usual way, ie using the senses, for example what was seen or heard;
3. point out the offence(s) to the suspect;
4. caution the suspect using the 'when questioned' caution (follow PACE Code C, para 10.2) and also inform the suspect that he/she is not under arrest, but that any failure to cooperate or to answer particular questions may affect his/her immediate treatment;
5. make a PNB record of the questions and answers about the offence(s), including points to prove and negations to available defences;
6. offer the PNB to the suspect to read and sign that the notes are a true record of the interview (see Code C, para 11.11);
7. tell the suspect 'I am reporting you for the offence(s) of ...';
8. caution the suspect (using the 'now' caution: see 10.3).

The evidence is used to form a case file (see 27.4) which is then submitted by the officer-in-the-case for review. If the decision is to prosecute, the public prosecutor will issue a written charge to the suspect. This will describe the relevant offence and state the Act under which the offence was created. The public prosecutor will also issue a requisition which requires the suspect to appear before a magistrates' court. The documents will be served by post, with copies sent to the court named in the requisition.

10.13.1.2 Charging at a police station

For less serious offences the Evidential Review Officer (the ERO, usually a sergeant) will decide whether a suspect should be charged or released without charge. This applies for summary-only offences or either-way offences with an anticipated guilty plea. For either-way offences with anticipated not guilty pleas, and for all indictable-only offences, the ERO will refer the matter to the CPS for a decision (see also 27.3). For a juvenile or a vulnerable adult, any action taken should be taken in the presence of an appropriate adult (Code C, para 16.1 and Note 16C).

The suspect to be charged (or the appropriate adult) is given a written notice (an MG4 form, see 27.4.2) which includes the following details:

- reference number of the case and custody record number;
- time and date the charge is made;
- the suspect's details, including name, address, and date of birth;
- the name of the police officer who charged the suspect, and the name of the custody officer who 'accepted the charge'; and
- any reply from the suspect in response to charge.

The charge will always include the 'now' caution (see 10.3.4) and is likely to be worded as follows (in this example the charge is for an assault):

> You are charged with the offence(s) shown below. You do not have to say anything. But it may harm your defence if you do not mention now something which you later rely on in court. Anything you say may be given in evidence. On (date) at (town) in the county of (name of county) you assaulted (name of victim) contrary to Section 39 of the Criminal Justice Act 1988.

After a suspect has been charged or informed that he/she may be prosecuted for an offence, no further interviews should be conducted unless it is necessary for the following reasons (listed in Code C, para 16.5):

- to prevent or minimize harm or loss to some other person, or the public;
- to clear up an ambiguity in a previous answer or statement; or
- to put new information (relevant to the offence) to the detainee, in the interests of justice.

A 'restricted' caution must be given at the start of such an interview (see 10.3.5).

After being charged, the suspect will usually be released, with or without bail (see 10.13.3.2). The custody officer may, however, decide that the suspect should be kept in custody, if for example he/she has no current abode, his/her name is not known, or if the charge is for a serious offence (see s 38(1) PACE and s 25 of the Criminal Justice and Public Order Act for a full list). A suspect who has been charged and kept in custody will be brought before a magistrates' court at the next sitting.

10.13.2 Out-of-court disposals

Custody officers and other decision-makers have a duty to consider whether an out-of-court disposal (OOCD) would be more appropriate for the offender than prosecution. Prosecution can have serious consequences for the offender and OOCDs are an attempt to avoid disproportionate criminalization of citizens. The seriousness of the offence and the proportionality of the outcome will both be taken into consideration. The National Decision Model (see 5.5.2) can help ensure consistent and effective decision-making when considering an OOCD. The College of Policing APP provides further information on the Out-of-Court Disposals Framework (CoP, 2015g).

10.13.2.1 Restorative justice

Restorative justice (RJ) is a form of OOCD which has been successfully used over a number of years for some offences and some offenders, and can take a variety of forms. At its simplest, police officers can deal with minor crimes and incidents on the spot with a 'community resolution'. These are aimed at adults or youths for lower level crime (see 14.2.1.3 in particular). Community resolutions can also be used after investigations into low-level crime and antisocial behaviour. They have the advantage of not criminalizing suspects, but still deal with the incident to the victim's satisfaction, and also amount to a documented clear-up for the police. The NDM can be used when making decisions on whether to use RJ in a particular situation.

A more formal RJ procedure may also be used if the victim and offender agree, in which they are brought together in a restorative meeting facilitated by an appointed police officer or volunteer. For more serious or persistent matters which cannot be dealt with immediately, a series of meetings with additional participants may be needed to seek longer-term reparative solutions. Research suggests that RJ conferencing can reduce reoffending rates particularly for violent crimes (What Works, 2015).

Using the NDM

An officer is called to the scene of a group of young people who are committing acts of anti-social behaviour outside a local resident's home. They have been repeatedly kicking a football against the resident's wall, and this reverberates inside his living room. The man came out to remonstrate with the them, and they verbally abused him.

NDM Stage 1—Gather information

- Who are the young people involved? Local? Do you have their names/addresses?
- Why have they chosen this location to play football? Are there any alternative locations?
- How does the resident confront the young people? Are they aggressive?
- What form does the verbal abuse take? Language, aggression, swearing? Does any of it amount to a substantive offence?
- Are the young people aware of the impact they are making?

NDM Stage 2—Determine the threat

- Is this a one-off, or ongoing problem?
- Does the officer need to act straight away?
- Have officers dealt with this before? How recently?
- What is the likely outcome/implication if the officer does/does not act straight away?
- Are the police the most appropriate people to deal with the problem? Local authority? School?

NDM Stage 3—What powers do the police have to deal with the problem?

- Arrest? Dispersal? Warnings?

NDM Stage 4—Draw up list of options

- High visibility patrols as deterrence?
- Arrest for Breach of the Peace (if immediate) or Public Order?
- Penalty Notice for Disorder?
- Speak to the young people in question and verbally warn them of their behaviour (and complete a community resolution form)?
- Report the ASB to the local authority?
- Invite young people, parents, and resident to a sit-down Restorative Justice Conference?

NDM Stage 5—Take action

- Based on all the information, options, and referring to the Code of Ethics to ensure proportionality, officers can take one or more of the options. On completion, officers should return to NDM Stage 1 to determine if intervention(s) were successful.

10.13.2.2 Penalty notices

A Penalty Notice for Disorder (PND) allows perpetrators aged 18 or over to pay a fine without going to court. The scheme was introduced in 2001 under ss 1–11 of the Criminal Justice and Police Act 2001, and its key aims and objectives are:

- to reduce the amount of time that law enforcement officers spend completing paperwork and attending court;
- to increase the amount of time law enforcement officers spend on the street;
- to reduce the burden on the courts; and
- to deliver swift, simple, and effective justice that carries a deterrent effect.

The term 'Fixed Penalty Notice' is used in a number of different circumstances, but the common factor is that the recipient has to pay a fixed penalty or charge. The first penalty notices were introduced over 50 years ago for motoring and road traffic offences (see 19.12.4). The Anti-Social Behaviour Act 2003 also provided for local authority personnel and PCSOs to issue penalty notices (also sometimes referred to as fixed penalty notices) for graffiti, and other minor offences such as littering, or dog control offences. The Anti-social Behaviour, Crime and Policing Act 2014 enabled police officers, PCSOs, and council officers to issue fixed penalty notices for failing to comply with a community protection notice, and for public spaces protection offences (see 14.2.2). Civil Enforcement Officers issue penalty charge notices (PCNs) for decriminalized parking/waiting offences in most parts of the UK. PCNs are also used in London for some moving traffic offences related to bus lanes, no-entry signs, restricted turns, red routes, and yellow box junctions.

A police officer who has reason to believe that a person aged 18 or over has committed a relevant offence can issue a penalty notice (s 2(1) of the Criminal Justice and Police Act 2001).

The offences for which a PND can be used are shown in the tables.

PND Offence with a fine of £90	Legislation
Wasting police time/giving false report	Criminal Law Act 1967, s 5(2)
Using public electronic communications network in order to cause annoyance, inconvenience, or needless anxiety	Communications Act 2003, s 127(2)
Knowingly giving a false alarm to a person acting on behalf of a fire and rescue authority	Fire and Rescue Services Act 2004, s 49 (England only) Fire Services Act 1947, s 31 (Wales only)
Causing harassment, alarm, or distress	Public Order Act 1986, s 5
Throwing fireworks	Explosives Act 1875, s 80
Drunk and disorderly	Criminal Justice Act 1967, s 91
Selling alcohol to person under 18 (anywhere)	Licensing Act 2003, s 146(1)
Supply of alcohol by or on behalf of a club to a person aged under 18	Licensing Act 2003, s 146(3)
Selling alcohol to a drunken person	Licensing Act 2003, s 141
Purchasing or attempting to purchase alcohol on behalf of a person under 18 (includes licensed premises and off-licences)	Licensing Act 2003, s 149(3)
Purchase of alcohol for consumption in licensed premises by person under 18	Licensing Act 2003, s 149(4)
Delivery of alcohol to person under 18 or allowing such delivery	Licensing Act 2003, s 151
Destroying or damaging property worth £300 or less	Criminal Damage Act 1971, s 1(1)
Unlawful possession of cannabis and its derivatives	Misuse of Drugs Act 1971, s 5(2)
Theft (retail) of property worth £100 or less (but see* at the end of this table)	Theft Act 1968, s 1
Breach of fireworks curfew (2300–0700hrs)	Firework Regulations 2004, reg 7 (Fireworks Act 2003, s 11)
Possession of a category 4 firework	Firework Regulations 2004, reg 5 (Fireworks Act 2003, s 11)

* For 'theft from a shop' (other than by an employee) only one such PND should ever be issued to an individual, and only for incidents where the value of the goods is £100 or less and the property has been recovered (consuming the stolen property may be an exception).

PND Offence with a fine of £60	Legislation
Dropping or leaving litter or refuse except in a receptacle provided for the purpose in a Royal Park or other open space	Royal Parks and Other Open Spaces Regulations 1997, reg 3(3–5), and the Parks Regulation (Amendment) Act 1926, s 2(1)
Using a pedal cycle, a roller blade, etc except on a Park road or in a designated area	
Failing to remove immediately any faeces deposited by an animal of which that person is in charge	
Depositing and leaving litter	Environmental Protection Act 1990, ss 87(1) and 87(5)
Throwing stones at a train	British Transport Commission Act 1949, s 56
Trespassing on a railway	British Transport Commission Act 1949, s 55
Drunk in the highway	Licensing Act 1872, s 12
Consumption of alcohol by a person under 18 in a bar	Licensing Act 2003, s 150(1)
Allowing consumption of alcohol by a young person (aged under 18) in a bar	Licensing Act 2003, s 150(2)
Unlawful possession of khat and its derivatives	Misuse of Drugs Act 1971, s 5(2)

A PND can be issued on the spot by an officer in uniform ('street issue'), or at a police station by an authorized officer, usually the custody officer. In many forces PNDs can be issued using mini digital printers instead of handwritten PND tickets; officers will need to be familiar with the type of PND forms used locally. The national data-sharing system for recording PNDs (PentiP (Penalty Notice Processing)) can be used to check for unpaid penalties from previous incidents.

A person who accepts a PND is not admitting to a crime; he/she is simply supporting a suspicion by a police officer that an offence has been committed, and recognizing there will be no further proceedings. It would not affect a person's 'good character' (see 24.2.5.2, 27.4.5, and *R v Hamer* [2010] WLR (D) 235). The recipient has 21 days to either pay the penalty or request a court hearing. In some areas an education option is available as an alternative; the recipient must pay for the course and complete it. Failure to take any of these options may result in a fine (one and a half times the penalty amount) or court proceedings.

If after receiving a PND it comes to light that the person may have committed a more serious and non-penalty offence during the same incident, the further offence can be investigated and prosecuted separately (see *R v Gore; R v Maker* [2009] EWCA Crim 1424; WLR (D) 240). The flowchart shows the process model for issuing a PND (adapted from the current Home Office operational guidance (Home Office, 2013b)).

General Procedures

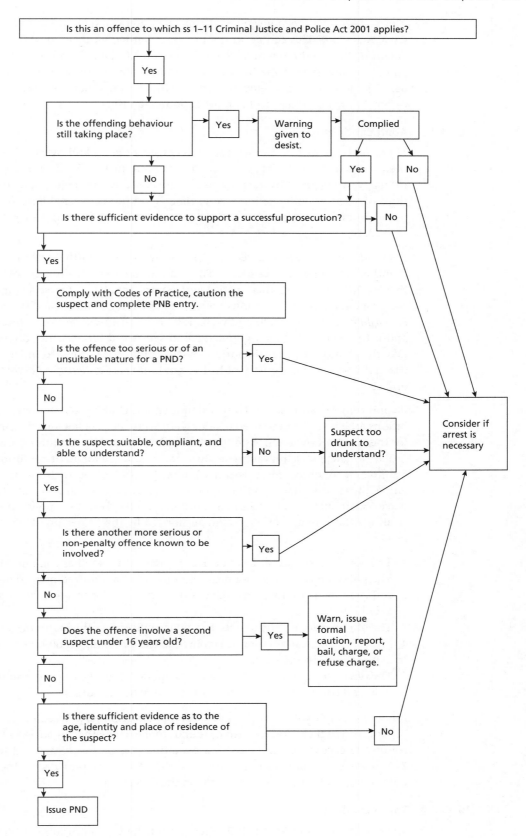

General Procedures

A person who has been given a PND may be photographed on the street (s 64A(1A) of the PACE Act 1984). This can be without consent (either withheld, or if it is not practicable to obtain it). Before the photo is taken the person can be required to remove anything worn on or over any part of the head or face, and an officer can remove it the person refuses (s 64A(2)). However, for a religious garment the person should be taken out of public view before removing the garment and being photographed.

10.13.2.3 Adult cautions

There are two types of caution for adults (aged 18 years and over), the *simple caution* and the *conditional caution* (ss 22–27 of the Criminal Justice Act 2003). They both involve a formal warning given by a senior police officer (or by a more junior officer on the instructions of a senior police officer). Note that the cautions covered here are a method of disposal, and must not be confused with the other forms of cautions used in investigations (see 10.3).

A simple caution can be given to a person who has admitted guilt for certain summary or either-way offences (see 4.5.1). They cannot be used for the offences listed in SI 2015/790 (s 17(3) of the Criminal Justice and Courts Act 2015). To use a simple caution, all of the elements of the offence must be proved (*R (on the application of W) v Chief Constable of Hampshire Constabulary* [2006] EWHC 1904 (Admin)). The caution is recorded on the PNC, and if the recipient is later convicted and sentenced for a further offence, the court can take the caution into consideration. Further details are provided in Home Office Circular 016/2008 and in the Ministry of Justice guide *Simple Cautions for Adult Offenders*, available online.

A conditional caution is similar to a simple caution but has rehabilitative or reparative conditions attached. It can be used to address the offender's behaviour, and to make reparation for the effects of the offence on the victim and others. The conditions must be appropriate, proportionate, and achievable (see the Code of Practice for adult conditional cautions). For example, a condition for a person who has been involved with low-level alcohol-related crime and/or disorder could be 'no possessing an open container of alcohol in a public place for six months'. Conditional cautions can be given by a police constable, an investigating officer, or any other person authorized by the prosecutor. Five requirements must be met:

1. The police officer has sufficient evidence that the person has committed an offence.
2. The police officer or relevant prosecutor (or other authorized person) decides that there is sufficient evidence to charge the person with the offence and that a conditional caution should be given.
3. The offender admits the offence to a police officer (or other authorized person).
4. The effect of a caution and the consequences of failing to observe a condition must be explained to the offender.
5. The offender signs a document that sets out details of the offence, and that he/she admits guilt and consents to the caution and the attached conditions.

Failing to comply with the conditions will result in criminal proceedings, and the caution will be cancelled. If there are reasonable grounds for believing that an offender has failed (without reasonable excuse) to comply with a condition, he/she can be arrested without warrant (s 24A of the Criminal Justice Act 2003). Further details are provided in the CPS Conditional Cautioning Code of Practice, available on the CPS website.

10.13.2.4 Youth cautions

The Crime and Disorder Act 1998 provides for the youth caution (s 66Z(1)) and the youth conditional caution (s 66A) for young people aged between 10 and 17 years. They can be used even if the recipient has previous convictions (for any offence). The suspect must admit the current offence, and must also be referred to the Youth Offending Team (YOT, see 8.4.3) as soon as practicable. Further information can be obtained from the *Youth Out-of-Court Disposals Guide* (Ministry of Justice and the Youth Justice Board, 2015).

For a youth caution the officer must have sufficient evidence to charge for the offence, and must also believe it is not in the public interest to prosecute or give a youth conditional caution. An appropriate adult must be present when the caution is given. For a young person receiving a second youth caution, the YOT will be expected to make an assessment, and if appropriate arrange a voluntary rehabilitation programme.

Youth conditional cautions are the next level up from a youth caution, and involve conditions being placed on the perpetrator. The five requirements listed in 10.13.2.3 must all be met, and both the views of the victim and the behavioural needs of the young person should be taken into consideration.

10.13.2.5 Foreign national offender conditional cautions

Some offenders will be foreign nationals who have entered the country illegally and have no right to remain in the UK. It may be in the public interest if such a person simply receives a caution and leaves the UK, rather than being prosecuted. The primary conditions for these cautions are that the offender must cooperate with the authorities and then leave the UK and not return for five years. Secondary rehabilitative conditions can be imposed, including attending a treatment course (for drug addiction for example) prior to departure. Reparative conditions can also be imposed such as paying compensation, repairing damage, and apologizing to the victim.

10.13.3 Police bail

Bail is a process of attempting to ensure that a person appears at a specified time at a specified place, such as a police station ('police to police bail') or court ('police to court bail'). It is now used less frequently than in recent years. There have been considerable changes to the procedures for granting police to police bail under the Policing and Crime Act 2017. There is now a presumption of release without bail in almost all cases (Release Under Investigation (RUI)), unless the need for bail meets the strict criteria for necessity and proportionality.

Bail is still used during some investigations to allow more time for further enquiries, as there is a time limit on how long a suspect can be held without being charged (see 10.10.3). The 'custody clock' is stopped when a suspect is released on bail, but restarts when he/she returns to the police station on the specified date (carrying on from the time it was stopped). Bail can also be used to bind a defendant who has been charged to appear in court.

Any initial police bail must be authorized by an officer of at least the rank of inspector, and may only be for a maximum period of 28 days. An extension of up to three months can be authorized by an officer of at least superintendent rank. Any longer extensions must be authorized by a magistrates' court (ss 62 and 63 of the Policing and Crime Act 2017).

10.13.3.1 'Street bail'

Street bail allows police officers to release a suspect on bail without going to a police station. The suspect must then attend a specified police station on a specified date (ss 30A–30D of the PACE Act 1984). Street bail is also subject to the new more stringent conditions in relation to authorization and time limits (see 10.13.3), and most officers now proceed by inviting the suspect to a police station for a voluntary attendance interview, unless there are pressing reasons to arrest, for example if the offender is drunk and likely to become violent.

The following questions must be considered when deciding whether to grant street bail.

1. What type of offence has been committed and is it too serious for street bail to be used?
2. What has been the impact of the offence?
3. Would the delay caused by using street bail result in loss of vital forensic evidence?
4. Is the person fit to be released back onto the streets?
5. Does the person understand what is happening? Is he/she vulnerable (see 25.5.1.1)?
6. If released on bail, is the person likely to commit a further offence?
7. Has the person provided a correct name and address? This is needed for street bail.

Note that statements concerning guilt are not relevant to the decision to grant bail—interview and examination of evidence will take place later.

A decision to grant street bail should be explained to the offender, and a notice issued covering points 1–7 above. The person must understand the requirement to attend a police station on a specified date, and that he/she is not being legally discharged and may be subject

General Procedures

to court proceedings or other disposal actions. The notice will list any conditions imposed, and name the police station at which the conditions can be varied. There is a power to arrest without warrant if there are reasonable grounds for suspecting any of the conditions have been broken, or for failing to answer bail at the specified time (s 30D, PACE 1984).

10.13.3.2 Bail from a police station

The overarching power for the police to grant bail and to require individuals to report back to the police station is contained in s 47(3) of PACE. There are five main circumstances for granting bail:

Circumstances for granting bail	PACE subsection	Return location	Conditions can apply?
Further investigation and evidence gathering is planned as there is insufficient evidence to support a charge at present	s 34(5)	police station	No
Insufficient evidence to support a charge and no further investigation planned, but review is required	s 37(2)	police station	Yes
Sufficient evidence to support a charge but consultation with the CPS is required to agree charges	s 37(7)(a)	police station	Yes
Sufficient evidence to support a charge but consultation with the CPS is required to agree on an alternative form of disposal, such as a caution (see 10.13.2.3)	s 37(7)(b)	police station	Yes
After a person has been charged with an offence	s 37(7)(d)	Court	Yes

A person who fails to attend the police station or court at the appointed time, or breaks attached conditions can be arrested without warrant under s 46A(1) of the PACE Act 1984 (see 10.6.5).

> **TASK 11** What offence, if any, is committed by a person who fails to return on bail to a police station, or fails to surrender to custody at a court after having been bailed?

10.14 Handover Procedures

After initial enquiries into a suspected crime (eg taking statements, collecting potential evidence, the arrest of a suspect) the arresting officer may 'hand over' responsibility for the subsequent investigation to another colleague, for example a volume-crime investigator (see Chapter 24). In some forces the case files are handed over to a Criminal Justice Unit or Department where 'case-builders' obtain further statements and evidence, and (if appropriate) prepare files for submission to the CPS (see 27.4.2). Practice varies; in some forces the arresting officer may be expected to see the process through to a more advanced stage.

The key principle for handovers is that the information provided will enable the receiving colleague to become as familiar with the circumstances of the alleged offence as the arresting officer. The 'handover package' will include documents and references to artefacts (eg forensic evidence and special property). It will also include a general checklist (the 'single source document'), which will be likely to list the following:

Checklist entry	Examples/notes
Names of the alleged offender(s)	Provide names, DoB, and custody numbers
The arresting officer's account of the circumstances leading up to arrest	Remember to avoid offering opinion in this section
Investigation checklist	<ul><li>A series of tick-box lists addressing the arrest (including a copy of PNB entries);</li><li>searches;</li><li>exhibits;</li><li>scene and forensic evidence;</li><li>detainee and custody considerations; and</li><li>PNC/force intelligence database checks</li></ul>

Checklist entry	Examples/notes
Witness details and statements	• names, addresses, and contact numbers of witnesses; and • a summary of witness statements
Other officers involved	• details of those who also attended; and • copies of their PNB entries and statements

Note that the single source document could be 'relevant material' (see 24.3.1), so it must be included on the MG6C form.

10.15 Answers to Tasks

TASK 1 The 'first' or 'given' name is the term to use, rather than 'Christian' name. The latter is a reflection of a time when the assumption was made that all UK residents subscribed (at least notionally) to Christianity as a religion.

TASK 2 The use of mind-maps as tools for learning and analysis was pioneered by Tony Buzan and others. The website <http://www.mindtools.com/pages/article/newISS_01.htm> has some useful advice on the application of Buzan's ideas. Of course, we have provided you with the no ELBOWS(S) mnemonic already, but developing your own mnemonic is good practice and will help fix the ideas in your long-term memory.

TASK 3 There are many examples, but you might have considered the following:

The caution means that you have the right to silence and you do not have to say anything or reply to any question you are asked. Anything that you say now or during the rest of the investigation can be given to the court for consideration. However, if you choose not to say anything now or during the investigation, but decide to say something in court, they can ignore it.

TASK 4 She should:

1. obtain and record a first description from the householder;
2. ask the householder if he would accompany her to the locations mentioned to attempt an identification;
3. explain to him that she will not direct his attention to any individual but that he should look carefully at each person present.

TASK 5 Whatever examples you chose, each should have clearly addressed:

• a person's involvement, or suspected involvement, or attempted involvement in the commission of a criminal offence; and
• the reasonable grounds for believing that the person's arrest is necessary.

TASK 6 She should:

• locate the man through the use of intelligence, a stop check, the PNC, or her local force database;
• identify herself, then confirm his identity, and then arrest and caution him;
• endorse the back of the warrant (also known as 'backing up');
• record the event in her PNB;
• send the 'backed-up' warrant to the appropriate court, following local procedures.

If she is not in possession of the warrant at the time of the arrest and the man asks to see it, she must show it to him as soon as is practicable.

TASK 7 The European Arrest Warrant (EAW) is an EU-wide arrest warrant which allows for the extradition of a person suspected of a serious crime from a participating EU country. The application is made by a judge in one country to a judge in the country where the suspect is known to be present. The process is therefore within and part of the criminal justice systems of both countries. Previously, 'extradition' was highly politicized, and people or cases were subject to long delay, political processes, appeals, and so on. The aim of the EAW is to speed things up.

General Procedures

Further details may be found at <http://www.asser.nl/Default.aspx?site_id=8&level1=10783>, but the process may change in the future (after the Brexit transition period).

TASK 8 You probably considered the following:

- An arrested person must be informed by the arresting officer that he/she is under arrest (s 28(2) and Code G, para 2.2).
- The arrest is not lawful unless the arresting officer at the time, or as soon as is practicable, informs the person of the grounds for the suspicion (s 28(3)).
- The arrested person must be informed about his/her involvement (or suspected or attempted involvement) in the commission of a criminal offence, and the reasonable grounds for believing that arrest is 'necessary' (Code G, para 2.2).
- The officer must caution the arrested person (Code G, para 3.4).

For the second half of the task, your answer was probably along the following lines:

> I have just seen you run out of the shop with a brand-new drill under your arm. I heard the store alarm go off at the same time and I suspect that you have stolen the drill. I am therefore arresting you on suspicion of theft of the drill. Your arrest is necessary to allow the prompt and effective investigation of the offence, and also, because you were running away, to prevent any prosecution for the offence being hindered by you leaving the area. You do not have to say anything, but it may harm your defence if you do not mention when questioned something which you later rely on in court. Anything you do say may be given in evidence.

TASK 9 The different categories of seized property might have separate forms for recording the details, but similar information is likely to be required such as:

- sequential number (to be attached to the item(s) for the purposes of recognition);
- name and address of the person from whom it was taken;
- location where it was taken into police possession;
- details of the police officer who took possession;
- exhibit reference (if known);
- description of article(s);
- reasons for taking into police possession;
- proposed disposal method for the property (eg returned to owner or destroyed); and
- current location of the property.

The appropriate form should be completed and a copy attached to the property before it is stored. Each force will have its own procedures but if the main property store cannot be accessed because it is closed (eg at night), the property will have to be kept in a 'transit store' (a secure cupboard). It will later be transferred to the main store by the property officer.

TASK 10 You probably considered the following:

> I have just seen this person run out of a shop with a brand-new drill under his arm. I heard the store alarm sound at the same time, and I suspected he had stolen the drill. I arrested him on suspicion of theft of the drill. This was necessary to allow the prompt and effective investigation of the offence by interviewing him, and also to prevent him leaving the area as this could prevent a prosecution for the offence.

TASK 11 Section 6(1) of the Bail Act 1976 states that it is an offence for a person who has been released on bail in criminal proceedings to fail without reasonable cause to surrender to custody. This is a summary offence and the penalty is three months' imprisonment and/or a fine.

11 | Attending Incidents

11.1 Introduction

This chapter is primarily concerned with the general procedures to be followed when attending incidents, including crime scenes. Throughout we link the subject matter to police officer initial training, undertaken through the PCDA or DHEP, but the content will also be useful to those undertaking a pre-join programme. We also examine attending and dealing with incidents involving loss of life, often untimely deaths, although not necessarily of a suspicious nature.

The police have a responsibility to respond and deal with many types of incident, but the majority of police everyday activities can be described as 'Steady State' policing. There are also major incidents, which are unexpected and cannot be planned for. Examples include large-scale rail, road, air, and sporting disasters or acts of terrorism. They may be classed as emergency, major, or critical incidents (see 11.5). 'Planned Operations' are where the police have had advanced warning of a situation (eg a large demonstration) and will have contingency plans in place (see 11.7).

The police attend volume crime scenes and minor incidents more often than major crime scenes, due to crimes such as burglary, theft, and domestic abuse occurring with greater frequency than serious crimes such as rape and murder. However, in a number of key respects, the principles of attending a volume crime scene are no different to those employed when attending the scene of a serious crime: the differences might simply be those of scale. However, as we note in 11.5, emergencies, major, and critical incidents may give rise to crime scenes of significant geographical size and complexity (such as the bombings in London in July 2005 or the Salisbury Novichok poisonings in 2018) and might require multi-agency emergency responses, adding to the demands of crime-scene management. Much of the information in this chapter relates to crime scenes, but the police also attend non-crime incidents.

The topics covered in this chapter are likely to contribute to the learning required for the National Policing Curriculum subject areas: 'Response Policing', 'Conducting Investigations', 'Public Protection', and 'Counter Terrorism'.

If you are undertaking the PCDA or DHEP then you will need to know and understand how to 'effectively respond to incidents, preserving scenes and evidence when necessary', to 'manage health and safety for self and for others'. For qualification as a police constable you will need to be able to safely and lawfully:

> manage dynamic conflict situations in policing through leadership, and by dealing with a wide range of behaviours and incidents, taking personal accountability for the use of proportionate and justifiable responses and actions.

Further, you will be expected to safely and lawfully 'provide an initial, autonomous and ongoing response to incidents, which can be complex, confrontational and life-threatening, to bring about the best possible outcomes' and to 'provide an initial, autonomous response to crime scenes, where encountered, that require the management and preservation of evidence and exhibits'.

11.2 General Procedures at Crime Scenes

Deployment to any incident has the potential to generate numerous challenges, for example unlawful violence against persons and premises, and public disorder. Victims and witnesses may also need support, including first aid, and in the case of more serious injuries, an ambulance or paramedic may be required. As such, an officer may need to make difficult decisions on how to respond and which actions to take first. The rationale for the decision(s) should be recorded, unless the officer, using his/her professional judgement, regards it as obvious.

The scene of an incident (such as a road traffic collision) normally requires a police officer to make a judgement about the scale and type of response required so that the appropriate help and support is made available through the police and other agencies. We discuss this issue later, but initially concentrate on crime. A crime scene is frequently the most important component of any criminal investigation, because it is very likely to contain physical and electronic evidence which could identify suspects, corroborate or refute statements made by witnesses, and demonstrate guilt or innocence. Early and effective protection of the crime scene ensures that the greatest amount of potential evidence is available for recovery and, therefore, maximizes its value to the investigation.

Crime scenes are not purely geographical locations to which we can apply an address, post-code, or map reference; a victim or suspect in a crime such as a sexual assault is also a crime scene. Treating a person (especially a victim) as a crime scene may be distressing and potentially offensive to the person and to his/her family or friends, but it is vital that we consider people as sources of evidence and intelligence. This is to ensure that we effectively 'protect and preserve' them, and recover the evidence or intelligence we need. Anything that could be a source of evidence or intelligence is also part of a crime scene, including articles related to the offence, such as weapons and vehicles, computer hard drives, digital storage media, as well as the intangible, such as networked environments.

Some of the biggest 'offenders' in relation to poor scene preservation are victims of crime, so any opportunity to encourage good scene management is vital, and will pay dividends. Call centre staff should be trained to explain what the victims or informants could do to help preserve evidence, and the FAO (First Attending Officer) can instruct victims and the public on simple issues such as staying clear of the crime scene and not handling evidence. Victims are often vital sources of physical evidence (especially in offences against the person and sexual assault) and preventing their contamination by others (such as supportive family members) is important. Sexual assault victims should be forensically examined before they smoke, eat, drink, wash, or go to the toilet (unless absolutely necessary) because such activities can destroy evidence. This is sometimes very difficult to explain and may be a source of considerable conflict, yet the problem can often be solved with a diplomatic and respectful approach.

Nearly all officers carry a personal mobile phone with a camera, and it might be tempting to use it to photograph a crime scene. This may occasionally assist an investigation in the early stages (eg when a wet shoe mark is evaporating). However, generally, it is better not to use the camera on a personal mobile phone at a possible crime scene because the phone would then become a source of evidence and would normally be retained for analysis of the image in its original state.

11.2.1 Early priorities at crime scenes—the FAO

The overriding principle at any incident is that all attending officers rigorously ensure the safety of the public, their colleagues, and themselves. Some of the people present at a scene of a criminal offence may be emotional, aggressive, or confused and might represent a danger. In addition, damage to premises, such as by fire, may weaken the structure of a building, resulting in further hazards.

Prior to responding to an incident, officers should ensure that they have the basic information they need to ensure they are prepared and safe. This includes a meaningful address or location, an idea of the incident type and the location of any rendezvous points (RVPs). While travelling to the scene of an incident, a 'dynamic' risk assessment should be made based on the information gathered from the initial report (see the introduction to 24.4.1). The assessment should be based upon:

- what is known (objective fact/information) or believed (subjective fact/information) to have happened;
- the number of people likely to be present;
- any information on the PNC and local intelligence databases about the individuals involved (eg that a suspect has been violent in the past);
- if any weapons are present at the scene;
- any risks associated with the location, and local community sensitivities.

11.2.1.1   Arriving at a crime scene

The first police officer who attends the scene (possibly as the result of an emergency call) is known variously as the FAO, the First Officer at the Scene (FOAS), or sometimes the Initial Responder; different forces use different terms. We use FAO in the remainder of this chapter. The FAO may be of any rank and position within the organization—indeed, it could be a trainee police officer undertaking the PCDA—this will entirely depend on who happens to arrive first. For example, it was a special constable in Community Safety at Thetford (Norfolk) who was first on the scene of a serious assault, and he had to manage the scene and deal with first aid as well as keeping his control room informed.

The first few minutes after arriving at the scene of a major crime may be confusing. The FAO should first control any person in the vicinity, including colleagues, and direct them to carry out urgent tasks where appropriate. Many members of the public who were close to the location at the time of the incident could be valuable witnesses and must be identified swiftly. The FAO may also have to arrest a suspect.

It should be remembered that all physical evidence is expendable when balanced against human life. Hence the FAO should not preserve a crime scene to the extent that it causes delays which aggravate a victim's injuries or increase any risks to life and limb. This is not to say that physical evidence can be disregarded during the life-saving process; the FAO can advise the ambulance crew where not to tread and can carefully move furniture away from the victim to facilitate medical aid when *necessary*. However if items are moved they should be left in their new position and not moved again in an attempt to recreate the original crime scene, because moving furniture, switching on lights, and even opening doors removes items from their original context, and is likely to cause 'contamination' (see 11.2.5.1). All these actions must be reported to the crime scene investigator (CSI) early on in the investigation and should also be recorded as PNB entries (see 10.2). It is good practice in these instances for the officer to also note the decision-making process and the rationale for the action, as both may be useful when writing a statement or appearing in court. For example, imagine that an officer moves a piece of furniture to allow paramedics to access an injured person. The officer would need to note the original location of the furniture, time and date of the move, the reason for deciding to move it, and how she came to this decision. The decision-making process in this instance would refer to the National Decision Model (see 5.5.2) and the Code of Ethics.

As soon as the initial response and emergency treatment of any casualties has been completed all police officers, including the FAO, and other personnel attending crime scenes should withdraw. They should only re-enter if approved, and protective clothing must be worn for their own safety, and to avoid adding more misleading material to the scene. Chapter 26 provides further details on forensics, and Chapter 24 covers investigative actions at crime scenes more generally.

11.2.1.2   The 'golden hour'

The first period of any incident, particularly in major crime and critical incidents, is often described as the 'golden hour'. This is a shorthand reference to the need to identify witnesses and preserve a scene quickly so that evidence can be protected or gathered while it is still fresh and undisturbed. For example, bloodstains should be sampled or protected before they are diluted by rain, shoe impressions (shoe marks) may need to be covered in poor weather, and the body of a deceased person could be initially examined before rigor mortis sets in.

It is also advantageous to identify and interview witnesses whilst their recollections are still clear. Suspects, however, should only be questioned or interviewed once a caution has been given and the suspect's rights have been fully protected (see 25.5). A police officer should always listen carefully to witnesses and evaluate what they say in the light of what is already known. He/she will of course record what is said as a PNB entry, and may also make a note of further questions to ask or other lines of enquiry (see 24.4.1.2 and 24.4.3).

11.2.1.3   Cordons

Cordons are erected as a visible barrier to identify the parameters of crime scenes or other incidents. The flimsy cordon tape that is most often used is clearly not a physical barrier: it is more of a 'statement' to help limit and control access for relevant personnel. In criminal investigations, cordons are generally only used for more serious offences such as major crimes and fatalities.

Cordons should be set up promptly to completely prevent public access, and the cordoned area should be a larger area than might seem immediately necessary. The tape should be securely attached to carefully chosen fixed objects, but any objects that might be a source of evidence should not be used as the evidence might be at risk. For example if the tape was attached to a parked car any movement of the tape due to gusts of wind could erase bloodstains and finger marks.

The size of the cordon should not be determined by the location of convenient fixed objects: if necessary, the tape can be affixed further out until poles are available. Whilst installing the tape the officer must also control witnesses and keep them out of the freshly cordoned area, and this is sometimes difficult. Further information about cordoning bomb scenes is provided in 11.6.2. A single cordon (or the inner or first cordon) must encompass:

* the venue of any incident or suspected offence;
* all possible routes into or out of the venue;
* any location where physical evidence could possibly be found: for example, communal bins, under cars in the street, nearby gardens; and
* any location identified as significant by witnesses.

A secondary cordon (the outer cordon) can also be installed to restrict public access and viewing. As a guide, if the public can see significant evidence then the cordon is almost certainly too small. It also makes sense to position the outer cordon so the movement of traffic is not affected, to minimize local congestion.

Once the inner cordon is in place, nothing may leave or enter it until sanctioned by a CSI, unless it is required to save life—for example, an ambulance or fire appliance. Vehicles moving through a cordoned area may damage vital evidence, for example at a bomb scene components of the device may be picked up by the tyres of emergency vehicles which are then driven out of the scene, and the evidence is likely to be lost. Or, an offender might have leant against a vehicle outside the venue of the offence when they made off, so CSIs may need to examine every vehicle within the cordon or, on occasions, every vehicle in the street.

The powers available to the police to secure crime scenes were considered in the case of *DPP v Morrison* [2003] EWHC 683 (Admin). In a serious incident in a shopping centre involving groups of young people, the police had sought to cordon off four areas in the shopping centre to secure and preserve evidence. Morrison was arrested for obstruction of a police officer in the lawful execution of his duty and for an offence under the Public Order Act 1986. He had walked into one of the cordoned areas, despite being told not to do so by police. He was initially convicted but appealed, and the Crown Court allowed the appeal, stating that there was no lawful authority to erect the cordon, and therefore the police were not acting in the lawful execution of their duty. The prosecution in turn appealed to the High Court. The High Court considered case law and existing legislation and decided that it was unlikely that anyone would have a right to stop police installing a cordon in a public area, and that on private property the police were entitled to assume that the owner would consent to cordoning. The shopping area in the *Morrison* case was privately owned but had a public right of way, so the cordoned areas were in a public place (see 9.2.1.1), and the police were therefore entitled to install a cordon. The appeal was successful. On a practical level, this decision makes it clear that in certain circumstances police officers might need to obtain search warrants (under perhaps s 8 of the PACE Act 1984) in order to remain on private premises for the purposes of a crime-scene search.

11.2.2   The rendezvous point and the common approach path

The rendezvous point (RV point or RVP) is vital to the smooth running of the investigations at the scene, and should be carefully chosen at an early stage. It may have to accommodate a number of vehicles, rest stations, major incident vehicles, and even a command tent. RVPs should always be in a roadway or on land with good access, which is unconnected to the investigation, and should never be placed in a narrow street with restricted access. When attending the scene of a suspicious explosion, care must be taken to search the selected RVP for secondary devices. These are sometimes deliberately placed to cause maximum casualties to the emergency services. In incidents involving firearms officers, the forensic personnel and other emergency services will normally attend the RVP rather than the crime scene as a matter of safety.

The 'common approach path' (CAP) is a designated route from the edge of the cordon into the crime scene proper. It should not be the route likely to have been taken by victim or offender, nor should it necessarily be the route taken by the FAO, as he/she was acting early on without full knowledge of the facts. If the scene is 'empty' (ie there are no living victims) there will be more time to choose the most suitable route. The selected route should minimize damage to potential evidence, particularly material which is small or almost two-dimensional—such as shoe marks and blood. Wherever possible, the CAP should be laid on solid ground as this will help prevent evidence being accidentally concealed (eg if personnel walked on a CAP over soft soil). Ideally the CAP should be marked with tape but, in the early stages, this may not be possible. If tape is used it should not be anchored with rocks and other debris found in the vicinity, since one of these may have been a weapon.

Some of the other problems associated with CAPs include:

- having no choice of route when a building has only one entrance;
- having too much choice when selecting the route for a CAP in a flat, featureless field—how do you decide?;
- establishing a CAP through the rear of the premises—entering the premises via a back door and searching for a key may destroy vital evidence; and
- having no immediate available means to mark the CAP.

One of the early tasks of the CSI is to search the CAP for evidence; he/she may want to re-route it if any evidence is found or at least record and remove potentially valuable material. The CAP should be guarded by a scene control officer.

11.2.3   The crime scene log and attending personnel

Perhaps the most important document at the crime scene is the log, a booklet or a paper form for recording the details of all attending personnel. In essence, it records any event that could have led to contamination of evidence. The log should contain a description of the CAP so that every person attending the scene can familiarize themselves with it prior to entry. It must also record details of:

- every person already at the scene when the FAO arrived;
- every person who subsequently attended the scene and the time of attendance; and
- every person who entered the crime scene or inner cordon, with the time of attendance and the reason.

Whilst the scene control officer should be on hand and easy to find, it is the responsibility of all attending personnel (including trainee police officers on Supervised or Independent Patrol) to seek him/her out. Note that logging or resourcing databases which manage deployments and information at incidents (such as STORM and the older systems like CAD and OIS) do not record officer deployments in sufficient detail and should not be relied upon.

The scene control officer and every individual must ensure the log is completed correctly. It will be copied and probably be disclosed to the defence (see 24.3.3), who will study it and compare it to statements, PNBs, and other scene logs. If it has not been properly maintained then some (or even all) of the evidence from the scene could be deemed inadmissible.

11.2.3.1   Non-police personnel at crime scenes

Ambulance crews should be allowed controlled access in order to save life. They are generally aware of how to behave in a crime scene but may have to be reminded not to touch anything needlessly, and to show caution where they walk. The FAO could accompany the crew and point out apparently significant evidence so they can avoid it, and should also take their names in case they need to be contacted for later elimination (particularly for evidence relating to shoes, clothing, and finger marks). Clearly, ambulance personnel should wear gloves, as should the FAO. Efforts to resuscitate by ambulance staff can generate very considerable quantities of debris, such as wrappers and used medical equipment. This material should be left at the scene for the attending CSI.

If a death has occurred, a doctor is not always required to establish this since ambulance crews can make a 'recognition of life extinct' (ROLE), sometimes referred to as 'Fact of Death' (FOD). In such circumstances the attending officer should take any forms completed by ambulance crew or doctors and ensure they are returned to the police station. If a doctor attends, he/she should wear protective clothing, and disturb the body as little as possible. The use of oral, rectal, or deep-tissue thermometers is not generally permitted because this can interfere with biological evidence in particular, such as DNA. If there is any concern that the death may be suspicious (see 11.3) the doctor or ambulance crew should be requested to not turn the body or search through clothing to view hypostasis or injuries until a CSI is in attendance. The attending personnel could be asked for an opinion as to the cause of death, particularly if the deceased has apparently suffered a sudden death and is known to the doctor. Certification of death is carried out by a doctor afterwards. There is no requirement for a senior officer to enter the scene once a death has been confirmed or to confirm that a death is suspicious. Every additional person in the crime scene can potentially destroy or contaminate evidence.

Other police colleagues (including senior officers) should not enter the inner cordon unless:

- the offender is likely to be within and must be apprehended;
- they are saving life;
- they can assist in urgent and immediate acts to prevent loss of the scene (eg putting out a small and manageable fire); and/or
- a dog is required to pick up a track from within the cordon.

The CSI will attend at the RVP (see 11.2.2) and will liaise with the FAO and other personnel, to decide how to proceed. In general terms, the CSI's initial role is to gather information, start with photography where appropriate, and advise detectives and uniformed police on the arrangements for any arrested persons. Once this has been achieved he/she will examine the CAP, record and recover vulnerable evidence from it, and occasionally move the CAP to another location. It is common for the CSI to enter the scene with the doctor to certify deaths or examine a deceased person.

A **crime scene manager** (CSM) is appointed in a major crime enquiry to manage the scene and deal with scientific resources. Typically, the CSM will be hands-on, but will also be flexible enough to attend strategy meetings and deal with other issues. In a more serious or complex case there may be a number of CSMs, and a **crime scene coordinator** (CSC).

A variety of **emergency personnel** may attend a scene and will be recorded in the log if they enter the crime scene, unless it is a serious incident and is impractical. The following groups will also keep their own records of attendance:

- the Fire and Rescue Service (FRS);
- Explosives Ordnance Disposal (EOD) in the case of explosions or suspected explosive devices;
- HM Coastguard and RNLI;
- mountain rescue and lowland search organizations (with dogs).

Other personnel who may attend as required include forensic scientists, borough or district surveyors and structural engineers (to assess the safety of damaged buildings), National Grid (for gas leaks), and scaffolding contractors (to support damaged structures in order to prevent collapse). However, once cordons are in place, no one should enter the crime scene until sanctioned and briefed by a CSI unless the safety of the public or attending personnel is at risk.

The following powers of entry apply:

- police officers have a power of entry in relation to a person who is under arrest for an indictable offence (s 18 of the PACE Act 1984, see 9.5.1);

- a civilian designated as an 'investigating officer' has a power of entry in relation to a person who is under arrest for an indictable offence (s 38 of the Police Reform Act 2002);
- a civilian designated as a 'designated person' (see PACE Code B, para 2.11) can attend with the police when executing a warrant to search and seize evidence (s 16 of the PACE Act 1984).

In many cases, however, formal permissions are not required because the occupier will invite the police and other investigators to attend and enter the property.

11.2.4 Fast-track actions

In every major crime the senior investigating officer (SIO) will consider fast-track actions which might rapidly resolve the investigation. These decisions are taken after careful thought, and are noted in the decision log or policy file (which records the decision-making process of the senior officer). However, in the very early minutes of an investigation, some actions may be necessary to prevent the loss of evidence or facilitate the apprehension of a suspect. These can include the following:

- using a dog to track the offender, particularly if the scent is not contaminated—the dog may have to enter the inner cordon;
- collecting evidence which is in danger of being lost immediately, such as wadding and cartridge cases being blown away by the wind, photographing the image on a computer screen, or powering off a smartphone (which might otherwise be remotely 'wiped');
- switching off a cooker if it might start a fire;
- covering shoe marks and tyre marks in poor weather (boxes or bin lids taken from an area well away from the crime scene could be used);
- conducting an urgent search of the street (sometimes called a 'flash search') for evidence which has been discarded, especially when the area is busy; and
- controlling large groups of people in confined situations (eg a pub) which might cause the loss (or gain) of fibres which could be used as evidence.

In these circumstances care must be taken to make the right decision. Protective clothing (at the least, clean medical-style gloves) might be needed to prevent contamination of the evidence. Police officers (including supervised trainees) should be prepared to justify their actions (or lack of them) to the senior investigating officer.

11.2.5 Forensic considerations at volume crime scenes

The attending police officer may need to take a crime report, assess the likely *modus operandi* of the offender, record losses, identify potential witnesses, and assess the scene for the potential attendance of a CSI. Overall, fewer actions will be taken by CSIs and police officers at a volume crime scene (compared with a major crime scene). The police will also try to minimize disruption to normal life in the immediate vicinity of the crime. If the CSI is delayed, a police officer may need to:

- close doors to control children and pets (instead of using cordon tape);
- close windows and consider boarding up in inclement weather (if windows are to be boarded-up, ensure the contractor leaves the original window in place);
- cover shoe marks inside premises with a chair (not a piece of paper which is more likely to be moved or trodden on);
- bring broken glass and property inside (as moisture makes fingerprinting difficult), handling it by the edges and wearing gloves;
- cover shoe and tyre marks outside with bin lids, trays, or boxes, even in sunny weather;
- on a bed use the blanket or quilt to funnel any material to a corner; and
- allow the victims to make drinks and food, unless it would damage good evidence or cause a health risk.

In the presence of DNA-rich material a mask should be worn (if available) to prevent contamination from the officer. Protect any articles that have to be moved by wearing gloves, and handle the material carefully: **gloves do not protect finger marks from being destroyed**. Continuity must be considered, as the police officer who moves articles of interest should—technically—exhibit them. Local protocols should be followed on this issue. Details of investigative forensic procedures are covered in Chapter 26.

11.2.5.1 Preventing contamination

Contamination is the transfer of trace evidence by any means other than direct or indirect involvement with the crime, be it accidental or deliberate. The term is also broadly used to describe damage to evidence or altering its state in some way that is not required for its preservation. Contamination could occur, for example, if a police officer is tasked to deal with a suspect and has previously been to the crime scene; the officer could potentially contaminate the suspect with material from the scene. This may reduce the value of evidence that links the suspect with the crime scene.

Certain forms of forensic evidence are, in all practical senses, incontrovertible (eg DNA evidence, see 26.5.3), but are at risk of contamination. Such evidence will be scrutinized by the defence in a criminal case, to try and cast doubt on the integrity of an exhibit (see 11.2.6) and to have it disallowed by the judge. An effective defence team will look for errors in continuity, packaging, and handling, and for any possible source of contamination. The following general advice applies to reduce the risk of contamination:

* wear new surgical-type gloves and a face mask as a minimum, when dealing with exhibits or whilst inside a crime scene (in the absence of a face mask, at the very least, all persons present should avoid coughing or talking over exhibits);
* store exhibits properly to prevent decay and damage. Property stores should be cool and dry. Electronic exhibits should not be stored on plastic shelving or near a magnetic field (from motors or speakers for example);
* never deal with exhibits from two facets of the same offence, such as from the victim and the suspect;
* do not deal with clothing from one person in an offence (eg take it out of packaging) in a room that has previously been used for sampling another person;
* do not place a prisoner in a cell until it has been cleaned.

In relation to vehicles, two people from the same offence (such as victim and suspect) should never be conveyed in the same vehicle, even at separate times, until all parties have been forensically examined. Police vehicles which could contain blood in any form should be cleaned or washed down once any forensic examination has been completed, and all patrol cars should be regularly and fastidiously valeted.

11.2.6 Exhibits and exhibiting

According to common law 'it is within the power of, and is the duty of, constables to retain for use in court things which may be evidence of crime' (*R v Lushington, ex p Otto* [1894] 1 QB 420). The 'things' can include physical objects (eg a knife) and are often referred to as exhibits (as they may be exhibited to a court or 'shown to a witness [at interview] and referred to by him in his evidence' (ibid)). The 1894 ruling in *Lushington* later formed the basis of important sections of the PACE Act 1984 (s 19 on the seizure of material, s 20 in relation to computers and digital evidence, and s 22 on police powers to retain seized material). Under a Code of Practice within the Criminal Procedure and Investigations Act 1996, any police officer investigating alleged crimes 'has a duty to record and retain material which may be relevant to the investigation' (see 24.3.2 on recording and retaining).

A police officer or a member of the public who finds an article which could be used as evidence should 'exhibit' it. This involves formally recording certain details about the object. If the item was originally found by a member of the public a police officer will complete the process, but the finder's initials and name will be recorded on the exhibit label and used as part of the exhibit number. The officer will also be responsible for taking a statement from the person about how and where it was found. The items will be packaged and labelled by the officer who found or received the item from a member of the public. Police officers and CSIs are advised not to accept an unpackaged exhibit from anyone other than a member of the public, as this is a potential cause of contamination.

The item must be properly packaged to preserve the evidence (see 26.7 for details) and labelled. Packaging materials normally have blank labels printed on the outer surface, or a simple label can be attached. The basic information required on the label is:

* the **name** of the person exhibiting (ie the person who first found the item);
* an **exhibit number**: normally the initials of the person exhibiting the item and a sequential number (see 10.11.1 for an example);

- a **description**, which should be brief and to the point—to prevent other people shortening the description for convenience (any index s or serial numbers should be included for clarity); and
- the **date, time, and place** the exhibit was found.

It is the mark of a professional to make detailed notes about the exhibit to assist other investigators. If the records on the contents of a package are not sufficiently detailed then another person might open it to check the contents, which could cause contamination. The notes should record the precise location and orientation of the exhibit at the scene, any identifying marks, the size of clothing, any damage or stains, any logos or identifying features, and serial numbers. The procedures for storing items as they come into police possession are described in 10.9.

11.2.6.1 Signing exhibit labels

The exhibit label records the continuity (or chain of custody) of the exhibit. Ideally, the chain should be unbroken from its seizure until it arrives at court, so unless local protocols dictate otherwise, every person who takes control of the exhibit should sign the label (and later write a statement). The movement of bulk quantities of exhibits is often recorded on a *pro forma* by the driver, and major crime exhibits officers do not normally write a statement for every receipt of every exhibit. If, however, police officer X temporarily passes a packaged exhibit to officer Y for comment but it remains in X's custody, then Y need not sign the label. An example might be where X asks Y for a casual opinion, for example 'Is this a ball-peen hammer?' However, if Y gave a professional opinion or transported the exhibit to another place, then he/she should sign the label and write a statement describing his/her actions.

11.2.6.2 Firearms as exhibits

Safety must always be considered when dealing with firearms as exhibits. That said, firearms are excellent sources of evidence. They provide ballistics evidence, their smooth surfaces are good sources of finger marks, and DNA can be collected from their rough control surfaces such as the grip, slide, and trigger (and from the muzzle if it has been in contact with skin or saliva). We will look at the different types of firearm, their component parts, and the associated law in Chapter 18.

All police forces will have strict protocols in place for accepting weapons from members of the public, and seizing them during searches. For health and safety reasons, all personnel at a crime scene should treat every weapon as if it is loaded and call for a firearms officer to make it safe. For weapons suspected of being involved in crimes it is normal practice for a photographer or CSI to be present during the making-safe process. Whilst making it safe a firearm should not be pointed at the floor or wall if people could be below or on the other side of the wall. None of the controls should be tampered with apart from those necessary to make it safe, nor should it be 'dry-fired'.

In addition no-one should:

- handle or move a firearm unnecessarily or place another article on top of a firearm;
- move a firearm by poking a pen, or any other object, into the barrel or trigger guard;
- stand in front of a firearm or point a firearm at any person, even when it has been 'made safe'.

Every person who handles a firearm, for example when passing it to or receiving it from another person, should clearly demonstrate that it is safe. In terms of labelling, there may be force policies for firearms at scenes or in storage (often a red label means it has not been made safe, and a green label that it has). Loaded firearms should not be conveyed to the police station or laboratory unless this is necessary and suitable safety measures are in place.

Above all: presume every firearm is loaded and ready to fire. In reality, very few guns can fire by being dropped or knocked as most have in-built safety features, but the consequence of a weapon firing by accident can obviously be extremely serious.

11.2.7 Attending major crime scenes

Many of the actions that should be taken by the first attending officer at a major crime scene are common to any crime scene (see 11.2.1 onwards). The FAO should attempt to:

- provide first aid and get assistance from an ambulance crew when necessary;
- cordon off the scene (as wide as practicable) and prevent unauthorized entry, except to preserve life or prevent further damage; and
- create a CAP (see 11.2.2) and begin a 'scene attendance log' (see 11.2.3).

General Procedures

If deaths have occurred the bodies should not be covered, but if they are in public view the public should be removed or screening should be installed until the first attending CSI arrives with a small tent.

Evidence collection can also commence, such as recording witness details and any comments they make, and recording if anything is disturbed or moved. Assistance may be needed to preserve the scene. It is vital to maintain communication with the force control centre and keep them informed. The FAO should also of course remain calm, be positive, and manage the situation until help arrives.

> **TASK 1** In what ways might an investigation into a major crime differ from other investigations?

Most police forces have specialist (often centrally based) departments or units which deal with major crime investigations. Chapter 24 provides more details on the process of criminal investigation.

11.3 Incidents Involving Deaths

Police officers will certainly encounter fatalities that have occurred during criminal offences, but will also deal with incidents where a death seems to be due to natural causes such as illness and old age. For example, the local police station might be called by the neighbour of an elderly person who has not been seen for some time or there are other circumstances which give cause for concern. Of course, these situations are not restricted to the elderly: it is a particularly distressing task to attend a scene of the death of a child or young person.

Any death which occurs outside the hospital environment and is in some way unexpected is referred to in police circles as an 'untimely death'. All such deaths will be subject to some form of investigation, but of course this does not mean that the death is associated with criminal activity. A police officer in early attendance at a scene of a fatality could reflect on the following:

- For an apparent suicide, were the means available to the victim?
- Are any of the injuries puzzling? (For instance there may be unexplained bruises to limbs or the head and neck.)
- Would the victim have been physically capable of the act? (Was he/she strong or tall enough? Could a woman of this stature have pulled the trigger of the rifle and shot herself?)
- Is there any sign of a struggle? (The location may appear particularly disordered, but it could have been like that anyway.)
- Is anything apparently missing? (eg an ornament, jewellery box, firearm, or car—and what is the evidence for this?)
- Is there evidence of a possible forced entry? (Damaged door locks, scratched or dented paintwork around windows, footwear marks on doors, and splintered frames are all suspicious, but there may be an entirely innocent explanation.)
- Does the position or state of the body fit logically with the information received?

In relation to suicides there are some commonly held misconceptions, for example that there will always be a suicide note, and that a person who cuts his/her wrist or throat always makes tentative cuts first (although many do). Other misconceptions are that women never shoot themselves in the face, that farmers always use a shotgun to commit suicide, and that vets always use animal tranquilizers or other drugs (although many do). Suspicion and an enquiring mind can be beneficial at any untimely death but investigators should rely on observation and experience rather than generalization. The chief issues with suicide are that the person must have had access to the object which caused their death and must have been physically capable of committing the act.

If there is any uncertainty, the scene can be treated as 'suspicious' until proven otherwise.

11.3.1 Police actions for incidents with deaths

The general procedure to follow for untimely deaths will vary from force to force, although all subscribe to certain basic principles (and relate to the procedures for attendance at a crime scene: see 11.2). A police officer should:

1. ensure his/her own safety before approaching, as the scene of a death can be dangerous (particularly if there have been multiple deaths);
2. decide whether there is a chance the person is still alive: could First Aid be administered—is an ambulance required?
3. establish and use a CAP (see 11.2.2) to preserve the scene;
4. touch nothing until a visual inspection has been made, and beware of bodies in contact with live electrical systems, as well as toxic fumes, poisons, firearms, needles, and body fluids;
5. consider that any death might be the result of crime if it is in any way suspicious.

The officer should make a PNB entry (see 10.2) which records the location, position, and general description of the body, including any visible injuries. Any potential evidence should also be noted, such as physical evidence in the immediate area, or from witnesses. The officer should also note any disturbance he/she has made to the scene, including the time and nature. Details of any person (such as member of the emergency services or a witness) already within the scene or subsequently allowed into the crime scene should be recorded. If it seems that evidence could have been compromised in any way, the officer should record this and also the decision-making process for taking any actions. Obviously, if the identity of the deceased is known this should be included—any relatives or friends who are present can be asked.

There are also administrative considerations. The attending officer should arrange for the death to be certified by a doctor, nurse, or paramedic, and take any paperwork they produce. For any unexpected death (such as unexplained, apparent suicide, accident, fire, decomposed remains, etc) a supervisory CID officer and a CSI should be contacted as appropriate. If the victim is under the age of 18 then this must be reported clearly to the control room because an investigative policy regarding the death of a child will be activated. If the deceased is a visiting serviceman/woman (on or off duty), the Visiting Forces Act 1952 may be relevant, and the investigation could be taken over by a foreign authority, such as the US Air Force, but the police should meanwhile maintain control of the investigation.

The officer should take control of the scene and anything within it or near it which may be associated with the death (a weapon, drugs, alcohol bottles, suicide note). If the death is not suspicious then force policy may require the officer to search the deceased for signs of injury and to take from him/her any valuables—these should be packaged and stored securely according to local protocols. However, any sudden death could be the result of a crime, so an investigative mindset should be employed throughout, because the scene could have been staged to delay or avoid a murder investigation.

After the examination at the scene the body will be removed. If relatives need to be informed this must be done as soon as possible by a police officer (in person, unless the conditions are exceptional). Police forces across the UK carry out this task for each other when distance makes it difficult. A family liaison officer can be used in cases of murder, road fatalities and other incidents.

Some police officers will suffer psychologically after dealing with a sudden death, ranging from being generally upset to severe changes in behaviour. Many appear to shrug off what they have seen but may still be affected, perhaps by depression or post-traumatic stress disorder (PTSD). A person who is accustomed to taking control in difficult situations may feel powerless and overwhelmed when confronted by the distress of relatives, and the very fact that he/she is unaccustomed to such feelings can cause additional difficulties. Some officers are not apparently affected by a large-scale incident, yet may become upset at a single death when they identify (in some way) with the deceased, or their family and friends. Every police force has structures in place to provide support and assistance: getting help is not a sign of weakness (see also 5.12.7).

General Procedures

11.3.2   Certifying death

If there is the slightest chance a victim is alive, medical assistance should be obtained. A medical professional (a doctor, nurse, or ambulance crew) is required to attend the scene to certify that death has occurred or to make a ROLE ('recognition of life extinct', see 11.2.3.1). There are some exceptions to this rule, based upon the notion that a person is 'obviously dead' but for the trainee officer it is better to err on the side of caution and seek advice.

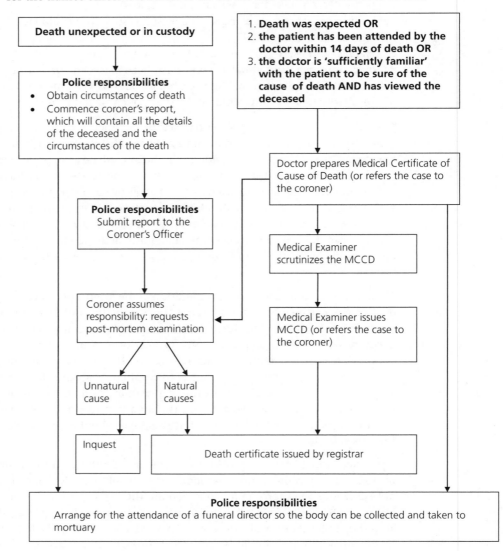

TASK 2 Suggest a type of injury which would definitely cause death (and therefore not require a medical professional to certify death).

The procedure for certifying death depends on whether the death was expected or unexpected, as shown in the diagram.

The role of 'Medical Examiner' was created in 2012 as a second check on the findings in the MCCD, consequent to the offences committed by Dr Harold Shipman .

11.3.3   Changes to the body after death

A body changes quite quickly and predictably after death, so this can assist investigations. The most immediate change is the colour of the skin, which can appear lifeless and wax-like within a few seconds of losing its blood flow.

Hypostasis occurs when the blood settles to the lowest parts due to gravity, and enters parts of the skin creating a port-wine colour (dark red) stain. This is also known as post-mortem lividity or *livor mortis*. Where a body is upright, the blood drains to the lower parts of the limbs, cheeks, and ears. After three to four hours, the blood clots (solidifies) and can no longer flow, so if the body is subsequently moved, the dark areas will no longer be on the lower or underside parts of the body. Pressure can cause distortion to the pattern of hypostasis, for example any areas of skin that have been under pressure will be pale because they are uncoloured by blood. These effects can be produced by the weight of the body on the textured fabrics and clothing seams, and even by floor tiles.

Rigor mortis occurs when chemical changes in the muscles gradually cause them to stiffen. The process normally begins in the head and works down the body. In very general terms it might start after four hours and disappear after 24 hours (when the body begins to break down biologically). However, the process is dependent upon a number of factors, particularly the ambient temperature (the process is quicker at higher temperatures). Crucially, immediately after death the body becomes limp and will flop to rest on adjacent structures, and if left for a number of hours, rigor mortis will stiffen it in that position. If subsequently moved, the body will be rigid and fixed in that initial posture—it will not flop until the rigor mortis fades.

The core temperature of the deceased will gradually equalize with the ambient temperature after death, so it will usually fall in the UK climate. The relationship between the rate of fall in the core temperature and the ambient temperature is well documented, but cannot provide an estimated the time of death to the nearest few minutes (as commonly depicted in fictional accounts!). The ambient conditions (eg air flow), the amount of clothing, and the previous general health of the victim may all affect how fast the temperature falls. Later, decay and insect activity can cause the body temperature to increase.

Other changes to the body will depend on the conditions. If the weather is not too cold it will begin to break down quite rapidly, which may attract a variety of animals which will feed upon it. Blowflies are the most mobile carrion feeders and will appear first, followed by successive waves of insects and other animals. The results include putrefaction and even dispersal of bones over time. In hot or dry environments the body may become mummified. The process of change in a body after death is covered by a specialist field: forensic taphonomy.

11.3.4 Murder investigations

Murder investigations involve a huge investment of police time and resources. Most murders are committed by close family members, or others known to the victim, and although the circumstances leading to such events are often shocking on a domestic scale, it is the abduction and murder by strangers (particularly of children) which attracts most media attention and police resources.

> **TASK 3** What is the CATCHEM database and what does it tell us about a particular category of victims and their murderers?

The level of resources put into a murder investigation depends on the classification of the murder. Murders are classified as Category (Cat) A, B, or C within a more general system of categorizing major crime. Cat A and Cat B murder investigations will be led by an SIO who will probably be centrally based, while a Cat C murder could be investigated by detectives in a local BCU. However, there are variations on these basic categories, and a Cat C murder can often turn out to be more complicated than first thought, requiring more than just a local response.

The 'Murder Investigation Manual' (the 'MIM') and the 'Practice Advice on Core Investigative Doctrine' (ACPO, 2006a and ACPO Centrex, 2005, respectively) provide a five-stage investigative model which is used by most police forces as the template for major violent crime enquiries. The five stages are fast track, theoretical process, planned method of investigation, suspect enquiries, and disposal.

> **TASK 4** Imagine you are a trainee police officer undertaking the PCDA. You are called to a crime scene in a part of town with many multiple-occupancy dwellings. The body of a young woman is slumped on the floor of a blood-splattered bed-sitting room. Curious and worried onlookers are present, and the landlord of the property (who discovered the body) is nervously waiting for you just inside the bedsit door. He says that he heard a disturbance and a lot of screaming. He used his master key to open the door and has not touched anything. What do you do to ensure proper incident management, remembering Stage One of the MIM includes 'crime-scene and evidence preservation'? What are your tasks in priority order?

General Procedures

11.4 Fires and Railway Incidents

Any scene where there is (or has been) a fire, and railway property present particular risks. The policing of most railways and the London Underground is the responsibility of British Transport Police (BTP) but other forces will sometimes be involved, for example pursuing suspects, searching railway property for missing persons or property related to crime, assisting at incidents and accidents, or providing cover when BTP are not immediately available. BTP officers' training is augmented by Personal Track Safety (PTS) courses: most other police forces do not offer this certification.

11.4.1 Attending a fire

Fires are caused by the oxidation of fuel which creates heat. In order for a fire to occur three elements are required: a fuel source (such as furniture, hay, or petrol), oxygen, and an external heat source to cause ignition. Once a fire has started the heat generated can speed up the rate of burning so yet more heat energy is liberated, causing a chain reaction effect. A fire can be extinguished by removing one of the three elements; removing the fuel, starving the fire of oxygen, or reducing the temperature with water. Fires in buildings will often self-extinguish or smoulder once most of the available fuel or oxygen has been consumed. However, in such a situation opening a door or window will introduce fresh air (containing oxygen) to any remaining hot fuel, and the fire can suddenly explode into an inferno within seconds.

The heat from fires spreads by convection (hot air rises), conduction (heat travels through solid objects), and radiation (glowing heat that crosses empty space). Fires can grow very fast, and the chain reaction effect means that small fires, which appear to be insignificant, can spread quite rapidly. During a drought the fuel load in outdoor environments such as grasslands, forests, and gardens, is so dry that the fire spreads far faster than would normally be expected.

Fires are emotional scenes: people whose homes have been damaged or destroyed will be suffering from a combination of fear, relief at surviving, anger, grief, and utter despair at perhaps losing everything they own. There may be irrational or angry outbursts levelled at anyone, and this might include physical assault. A number of agencies are available to assist such victims, for example the local authority can provide temporary accommodation, and practical assistance may be sought from the Salvation Army or Citizens' Advice. If a family member or colleague has died or been injured as a result, then more specialist support can be arranged through Victim Support, the NHS, a Family Liaison Officer (FLO), and charities such as Cruse Bereavement Care.

11.4.1.1 The role of the police at fires

The overriding principle at fire scenes is to prevent the loss of human life. The critical issue of your own safety as a police officer is covered in 5.12, and this principle extends to fighting fires: police officers should not attempt to take action against anything but the smallest of fires. Police officers have powers under s 17 of the PACE Act 1984 to enter a premises to save life or prevent damage, and PCSOs have powers under the Police Reform Act 2002, Sch 4, Part 1, but no unnecessary risks should be taken to save lives, protect property, or rescue animals.

Putting out the fire and saving lives is the role of the FRS, but police officers can assist by controlling the public (s 37 of the Road Traffic Act 1988), assisting with evacuations, and closing roads (ss 35 and 163) as appropriate. If the cause of the fire is unknown or suspicious then force policy will almost certainly require the attendance of a patrol supervisor or inspector, CID, and a CSI. An incident may be deemed to be 'serious' if injury or significant loss occurs, and an appropriate police response and investigation will take place. If the Fire and Rescue Service (FRS) is at the scene the FAO should make contact with the senior fire officer and provide information as required. Police officers are likely to have relevant local knowledge about occupants, business activity on the premises, and/or information about any perceived risks or relevant force contingency plans in place in the area.

If the FRS is not in attendance police officers should employ the JESIP M/ETHANE mnemonic (see 11.5.1). During the early phase of an incident a fire may be small enough to tackle with available fire-fighting equipment, or imaginative use of a hose or towel. The attending police officers will need to make a judgement and keep the control room informed, particularly if it seems the fire could spread. The control room will contact the FRS who will decide whether or not to attend, and will also contact relevant security companies, homeowners, and key holders of houses or businesses so that they can take appropriate action. If there is any conceivable risk to people in nearby properties, the street, or in passing vehicles then decisive action must be taken: evacuate all nearby properties and keep everybody clear. Follow the old adage: GET OUT and STAY OUT.

People in or near a fire may have burning clothes or hair, and these can also 'spontaneously combust' at a distance due to the radiant heat. Such victims may well panic and be unable to follow advice. They should be pushed into a lying position on the ground, and the flames smothered with a coat or blanket. A horizontal position is particularly important to prevent convected heat rising from burning clothes and damaging the eyes and mouth. Victims may need urgent first aid and hospitalization, but such early decisive actions can save lives and reduce further injury.

Any large fire will inevitably attract onlookers, many of whom will merely wish to watch, but some may be intent on stealing rescued property or may even try to enter the property to steal. Scene security, management of the public, and a continuing eye on traffic problems need to be maintained. Some arsonists will return to observe the activity at the scene and a few may even obstruct attempts to extinguish the fire. At one fire in Kent, the offender was at the scene and repeatedly tried to disable the nearest fire hydrant, until police arrived and arrested him. Offences involving the deliberate obstruction of firefighters are covered in 11.4.1.2.

11.4.1.2 Fire and Rescue Service powers and obstruction offences

The Fire and Rescue Services Act 2004 confers a number of powers on the FRS and its members in relation to emergencies, particularly for incidents which are likely to cause death or serious illness or injury, or serious harm to the environment and any plants or animals in it. This applies for emergencies such as fires (or situations where there is a major risk of a fire) and road traffic incidents. It also covers actions required to prevent consequent damage to property (s 44(1)). Authorized FRS staff can enter premises by force, move or break into vehicles, close roads, control the traffic, and restrict access in order to achieve these aims (s 44(2)).

If a person interferes with or obstructs firefighters in the course of their work, he/she could be charged with an offence, for example:

- obstructing or hindering personnel engaged in emergency operations when extinguishing a fire or protecting life and property in relation to a fire (or going anywhere to deal with it or prepare for it) (s 1 of the Emergency Workers (Obstruction) Act 2006);
- obstructing a person who is assisting a firefighter (s 2 of the Emergency Workers (Obstruction) Act 2006);
- obstructing or interfering with an employee of a fire authority who is entering a property or vehicle by force, or carrying out other emergency work (s 44 of the Fire and Rescue Services Act 2004).

The full Acts are available on the www.legislation.gov.uk website.

11.4.2 Incidents and offences on railway property

Railways and their associated infrastructure are exceptionally dangerous places. As well as bumps, trips, and falls, the risks include being struck by a train whilst crossing a track (even at a level crossing or pedestrian gate) or when walking onto a track to retrieve property or rescue a person or a pet, and electrocution by power conductors or signalling equipment.

The electrical conductors which carry the power for trains are either a third rail or overhead, suspended between gantries. It should always be assumed they are 'live' because the power runs continuously—it is not switched off when no train is present. Given that they carry so much power, death is almost certain if a person (or anything he/she is touching) comes into contact with railway power conductors. Overhead power lines can also arc, transmitting electricity through the air to nearby objects. If a person has fallen onto the third rail there is nothing which can realistically be done until the power is turned off, so police officers should be absolutely certain that this has been done before acting in such circumstances; there is no room for ambiguity.

General Procedures

Further dangers are posed by 'rolling stock' (engines and carriages), particularly as modern trains are fast and relatively silent in operation. Railway apparatus (ie railway equipment other than rolling stock) is also dangerous: electrical components, moving parts, and trip hazards are universal. Therefore, police officers engaged on foot pursuits or assisting on railway property, for example at a station, should continuously consider their safety and that of colleagues and the public. **Essentially: there is no reward worth the risk of stepping onto a railway line**. Most force policies will require the abandonment of foot pursuits if the suspect enters railway property, unless there is an immediate risk to life and the officer feels that the situation warrants entry to the track area (after a dynamic risk assessment).

For searches, special measures called 'Safe Systems of Work' (eg stopping trains and cutting the power) should be arranged before carrying out *any* search on operating railway lines or associated property, and it is wise to post a lookout for any carriages or engines that are still moving, however slowly. When searches of railway property are required, close negotiation with Network Rail and train operating companies is essential to reduce the risk of accidents and—where practicable—minimize disturbance to the network. Under the Railway Safety Accreditation Scheme, BTP can accredit organizations and selected personnel with powers to deal with anti-social behaviour by issuing Fixed Penalty Notices and enforcing by-laws. Such staff can act as a visible deterrent and provide reassurance, and free up BTP officers for more frontline duties.

Apart from the common offences which might be committed on railways (thefts, assaults and criminal damage) specific legislation applies for crime and trespass on the railway network. Some of it is quite old, and 'translation' of the Victorian English can be difficult.

11.4.2.1 Trespass and authorized crossing point offences

Under s 16 of the Railway Regulation Act 1840 it is an offence to wilfully trespass on any railway or railway premises, and to refuse to leave when asked to do so by any officer or agent of the railway company. Another piece of Victorian legislation is the Regulation of Railways Act 1868, which prohibits a person from crossing a railway line other than in an authorized place (eg level crossings). Under s 23 a person commits an offence if he/she crosses at an unauthorized place after being warned to desist by a servant or agent of the railway company.

Nearly a century later the British Transport Commission Act 1949 added legislation on trespass to cover trespass along 'railway lines, embankments, tunnels and sidings or any "works" (equipment) and electrical installations' (s 55). The section raises the issue of being in 'dangerous proximity' of lines and electrical installations. It is important to note that the investigating officer must produce evidence of a notice exhibited at the station nearest the place of the offence providing a clear public warning not to trespass on a railway. These signs are most obviously seen at the ends of platforms and at pedestrian and level crossings. Such trespass is a summary offence and can be dealt with by a £60 PND (see 10.13.2.2).

11.4.2.2 Throwing objects and causing damage to railway property

Section 56 of the British Transport Commission Act 1949 makes it an offence to throw, or cause to fall, any object (likely to cause damage) into or upon any rolling stock or static equipment on any railway or siding or any 'works', or which is likely to cause injury. It is immaterial whether the train or equipment is in motion or is static. This is a summary offence and can be dealt with by a £60 PND (see 10.13.2.2).

The Offences Against the Person Act 1861 is a more complex but overarching piece of legislation which discusses 'unlawfully and maliciously' throwing or causing objects to fall. If an intent to injure or endanger any person on a train can be proved, then an offence has been committed (ss 32 and 33). Drunkenness and failing to follow by-laws are covered in s 34, and other acts of misconduct by railway employees are covered in s 17 of the Railway Regulation Act 1842.

The Malicious Damage Act 1861 (s 35) covers placing items (eg a railway sleeper) on a railway, and also covers the removal of rails, turning (or switching) points, and showing or hiding signals. There must be intent to obstruct, overthrow, damage, or destroy an engine, carriage, or truck. This offence is triable on indictment only and the maximum penalty is life imprisonment. Section 36 deals specifically with obstructing engines, or carriages, or railways. The offence is triable either way and it is not necessary to prove intent.

11.5 Attending Emergency, Major, and Critical Incidents

Initial police training is likely to cover the police role in handling emergencies, major incidents, and critical incidents, and emergencies. These categories of incident are all similar in terms of their scale and significance, and it is for this reason that we have grouped them together here. Of all of these types of incident, trainee officers are most likely to attend emergency scenes.

An **emergency** is defined by s 1 of the Civil Contingencies Act 2004 as 'an event or situation which threatens serious damage to human welfare in a place in the United Kingdom', and will include one or more of the following:

- human illness, injury, or loss of life;
- homelessness or damage to property;
- disruption of a supply of money, food, water, energy, or fuel;
- disruption of transport, communication, or health systems and services;
- serious environmental damage (eg radioactive contamination);
- war or terrorism which threatens serious damage to the security of the UK.

(Note that the College of Policing subdivides emergencies into 'rapid onset emergencies' and 'rising tide emergencies' (see CoP, 2017a for further details).)

A **major incident** is an emergency that requires the implementation of special arrangements by one or more of the emergency services, the NHS, or local authority. It is likely to involve serious harm, damage, security risk, disruption, or risk to human life or welfare, such as floods or widespread illness. (Adapted from material provided by Wiltshire Police, no date.)

A **critical incident** can be defined as 'any incident where the effectiveness of the police response is likely to have a significant impact on the confidence of the victim, their family and/or the community' (NPIA, 2011). This definition was subsequently adopted by the College of Policing. Any incident—such as harassment—can escalate to being critical, while other incidents are obviously significant from the very start (such as an apparent murder, train crash, or a large fire).

Police officers in training will practise and rehearse effective ways to intervene to resolve a problem such as a domestic dispute, dealing with a shoplifter, or calming people down who have been involved in a minor road collision. They will learn to defuse, control, restrain, or manage a wide range of such incidents. But for more serious incidents—those with the potential to 'go major' and get really out of hand—there are far fewer opportunities for practice.

> **TASK 5** Try and imagine what your first response would be if you were the first police officer to arrive at:
>
> - a serious road collision;
> - an accident on a railway line;
> - a burning house where people are trapped on upper floors; or
> - a situation where a child is being held hostage.
>
> What would your responsibilities be, as opposed to your instincts? What would you be expected to do? Is there an order in which you should do things? What seem to be the priorities at the scene? What should be your priorities at the scene? What communication is needed and with whom?

Every force and every emergency service will have contingency plans to deal with a whole variety of emergencies and incidents, and for some types of incident this will be a legal requirement under the Civil Contingencies Act 2004. They will have generic plans for certain types of emergency such as an aircraft crash, an influenza pandemic, or a siege incident with a hostage.

The Joint Emergency Services Interoperability Programme (JESIP) was set up for coordinating major incidents requiring a multi-agency response. It developed procedures which allow for joint working between police, fire and rescue, and ambulance services, enabling each organization to work with others, but still maintain autonomy and follow their own procedures. These guidelines facilitate coordinated and coherent decision-making in situations that can

General Procedures

be very fluid and demanding. The JESIP procedures also permit a shared assessment of risk to be made, and take into account that each organization will have its own operational focus during an incident. Trainee officers are unlikely to be involved in the management of a major incident, but should be aware that the JESIP procedures will be used.

Large-scale incidents of any type are not simply 'dealt with' and then closed: after the incident there will be serious issues to consider concerning the impact upon the community at large, such as a fear of further crime and disorder, or where the public's expectations of the police have not been met. Thus the perception of a high level of vulnerability, the scale of the incident, and the feelings held by victims and families must be appropriately addressed through effective and closely managed communication. Liaison with victims, their families, and the community at large is important for a number of reasons, not least of which is to restore public confidence.

11.5.1 JESIP 'M/ETHANE' emergency procedures

The JESIP M/ETHANE mnemonic (JESIP, 2017b) can be used to guide decisions during the early stages of managing a major, or multi-agency, incident (with 'ETHANE' being used for incidents that would not be classified as 'major'). Any police officer may find him/herself as the first responder at an incident, and if the control room has not already decided whether a multi-agency response is required the first responder may need to make that decision.

The mnemonic for the standard JESIP procedure for incidents (full details available from the JESIP website) is M/ETHANE as follows:

- Major incident declared?
- Exact location;
- Type of incident;
- Hazards, present or suspected;
- Access—routes that are safe to use;
- Number, type, severity of casualties; and
- Emergency services—those present and those required.

When a major or multi-agency incident has been declared, it can take time to implement the appropriate strategic and tactical response, so it is vital to ensure that incidents are identified and declared as soon as possible. Accurate information is essential. A number of 'apps' are available for smartphones and tablet devices which claim to help with recording and conveying the information associated with 'M/ETHANE', but you should only use these if instructed to do so by your police force.

Out of all the services that may attend such an incident, only the police will be constantly alert to the possibility that a crime has been committed, and that the emergency, major, or critical incident could also be a crime scene (see 11.2). For example, after a road traffic collision, consideration must be given as to whether the driver was under the influence of drink or drugs; and after a fall from a height, did the woman fall or was she pushed; is this a natural or a suspicious death? Police officers should be suspicious and be alert to any signatures or characteristic signs that there is something wrong. Given the recent prevalence of marauding terrorist incidents, this awareness is increasingly important, as a scene may not be what the FAO initially believes it to be; further lives may be at risk. Additional information and problem-solving skills can help illuminate the incident beyond the initial assessment. For example, a witness may remark 'funny thing—that man hanging round all morning', or an officer may spot an article at the scene (or nearby), such as an empty suitcase. This might suggest that all is not what it seems, and problem-solving skills can help clarify ideas.

> **TASK 6** Describe a problem-solving and decision-making model you have encountered.

The actions of the FAO are crucial to the proper and managed outcome of the incident, and relying on instinct is not sufficient in such situations. For example, a trainee officer may be tempted to act heroically at a house-fire, but without the proper apparatus or an understanding of how fires develop (see 11.4.2) and the risk of structural collapse of the building, he/she may become a victim rather than a rescuer. A police officer needs to follow proper procedures, and to think and act calmly and rationally in order to:

- assess the situation and work out what is going on;
- communicate as quickly as possible; and
- prioritize actions.

> **TASK 7** Imagine you are a police officer attending an incident in which a man with a hostage appears to have barricaded himself into a semi-detached house in a cul-de-sac. About a dozen people are milling about, and the event has been described to you by two very excited and incoherent witnesses. You have one other police officer to assist you. Assuming that police back-up will arrive within ten minutes and other emergency services (fire and rescue service, ambulance) are also on their way (with an estimated time of arrival of 15 minutes), what would be your list of things to do in priority order at such an incident?

11.5.2 Control and responsibility

The FAO is in control of the incident (as 'Silver', the forward Commander: see 11.5.3) until he/she is relieved by someone of superior rank. The incident may include a crime scene, so preservation of evidence and keeping the scene clear and untouched is very important. In an emergency involving firearms or the risk of violence, current practice is that the FAO would not let other emergency services go forward into the 'line of fire' either. Currently most ambulance trusts will also not permit their personnel to enter ongoing firearms-related crime or terror-related scenes as a matter of safety: in 2019 the London Ambulance Service explained to the media that its response to an incident in Streatham (where two people were stabbed by an assailant later shot dead by armed police) involved waiting at a 'rendezvous point until the police confirmed it was safe for them to approach patients' (Evening Standard, 2019). However, policy evolves and, as with all matters concerning attending incidents, ensure that you are familiar with local force policy (see also 11.5.2.2).

In scenes where additional risk is present (such as a firearms incident, terrorist attack, or CBRN attack), areas will be designated as 'hot', 'warm', and 'cold' depending on the risks within those areas. 'Hot' zones contain the most risk for those within and emergency personnel that enter, with the risk reducing through the 'warm' and 'cold' zones. Changes following the Kerslake Report now allow for emergency personnel to be sent into a 'hot' zone (see section 11.5.2.2). Remember to always follow force guidance on attending high risk scenes.

In practice it is unlikely that an FAO would be alone for that long, unless the incident is in a really remote and inaccessible place, or there are corollary problems (such as a natural disaster of some kind) and access roads are blocked. A senior officer may arrive quite quickly but, if not, the golden hour is the responsibility of the officers present. All this sounds complicated and difficult to remember; however, training and experience enable police officers to maintain clear priorities and to follow procedures properly, acting calmly, positively, purposefully, and promptly.

11.5.2.1 Levels of Command

The standard command sequence in use in all police forces across the UK is Gold, Silver, Bronze (GSB). The levels refer to the function of the command level and not necessarily to the rank of the officers concerned (see the College of Policing APP *Operations and Command Structures* for further information). The Home Office guidance document *Critical incident management, Version 11.0* provides the role descriptions shown in the table.

Gold	Strategic command of the incident, usually at police headquarters or at a designated strategic police command centre
Silver	Tactical police command at a forward point closer to the scene of immediate crisis
Bronze	Operational local response at the crisis point itself (eg cordons or firearms), often carried out by a number of people (Operational Response Commanders or ORC), rather than one designated commander

When a more senior officer becomes available, he/she will assume the command level. Therefore a trainee officer on Independent or Supervised Patrol may be 'Silver' for a short period of time, but only until a more senior or more experienced officer arrives on the scene. This tiered structure is considered by many in the police service to work effectively (and has been exhaustively tested) at local or force level and also at national level.

11.5.2.2 Responding to marauding terrorist attacks

There have been an increasing number of such attacks in recent years, such as the Manchester Evening News Arena attack and the London Bridge attacks in 2017 and 2019. The response to the Manchester Evening News Arena attack was evaluated in the Kerslake Report and the system by which areas were designated as 'hot', 'warm', or 'cold' to direct emergency services support was judged as insufficient in the context of responding to a marauding terrorist attack.

The Joint Operating Principles (JOP) for emergency services response to a marauding terrorist attack were changed in 2019, and unarmed police officers can now be required to enter areas of high risk, to preserve life and provide first aid. In addition, emergency services staff may now be directed to 'hot' or 'warm' zones without an armed police escort. This was highlighted as being good practice in the inquests into both the Manchester and the London Bridge terrorist attacks.

11.5.3 Risk assessment and deployment decisions

A risk assessment must be carried out to facilitate a proportionate response in the right sequence. The senior officer carrying out the assessment will ask the person who is 'Silver' at the time for information about the situation.

Resources should not be committed too early unless there is a clear picture of what is happening on the ground. Police officers attending an incident are clearly not available for deployment elsewhere, and swamping a site with armed officers, dog teams, and underwater search personnel may turn out not to be necessary.

> **TASK 8** What problems could arise within GSB command structures? Make a list of what could go wrong and how to try and avoid problems.

In the case of missing persons (especially when there may be other factors, possibly criminal) there are many components to the response: search teams are called out, assessments of transport needs are made, command and control, strategic, and tactical responses are all set up, and the control room will alert other emergency services.

For larger incidents the military might be required and 'military aid to the civil authority' (MACA) will be invoked. Specialists such as explosives ordnance (bomb disposal), helicopters, search and rescue, engineers, nuclear, chemical, and radiological detection and containment units, and a host of others may be called upon. Note that deployment of armed officers is usually a top-level command decision ('Gold'), made by a chief superintendent or chief officer.

General Procedures

11.5.4 Information management at incidents

At some incidents there may be bystanders; they may be a help or a hindrance so will need to be controlled, even at a relatively limited incident. Well-intentioned people may offer to help, and in some circumstances volunteers can be used effectively until more help arrives, for example to instruct and contain people, to direct traffic, and conduct evacuation. However, bystanders may not always be so helpful; police and other emergency service support can be delayed because of passers-by who want to see what is going on. Police officers should always be prepared to move such onlookers away. There is another and very important reason why the area itself must be controlled: it could be a crime scene, and controlling access and the preservation of evidence is vital (see 11.2).

Newspapers, internet sites, social network sites, radio, and television have apparently inexhaustible appetites for crime stories, and this quest has produced an edgy, sometimes fraught, relationship between the media and the police. The media can be rather superficial and sensationalist in an endless quest for headlines (see Leishman and Mason (2003) for more detail), and the unfair presentation of witnesses, victims, or suspects by the media can undermine their credibility before due process has taken place. However, there is no doubt that the media can help with appeals for information to help solve complex crimes, raise awareness of danger, alert the public to emergencies or major disruption, or appeal for help with searches for missing people. The media can very quickly engage with large numbers of people over a large geographical area, and this can help, for example, locate suspects or witnesses who have left the local area.

Communications from the police to the media must be carefully managed. Too much information could put informants at risk, limit the range of questions that could be asked of a potential suspect, or encourage him/her to dispose of items that could provide crucial evidence. An individual police officer should never be tempted to communicate with the media; each force will have a specialist unit for these functions (and some BCUs have their own media relations staff too). An officer's comments might inadvertently be misleading—he/she might not have the full picture and is unlikely to have much experience in communicating through the media. In major incidents the police will hold a press conference to brief the press and provide up-to-date and appropriate information.

11.6 Attending Scenes with Suspect Devices

Suspect devices include bombs, incendiary devices (designed to start or sustain a fire), and CBRN devices (containing chemical, biological, radiological, and/or nuclear material). Obviously, an incident involving a suspect device can become a major or critical incident. CBRN incidents are very rare, but they have been known. In 1995, a small and secretive Japanese sect called Aum Shinrikyo released small quantities of diluted Sarin (a nerve gas) inside a crowded Tokyo subway in the morning rush hour. Twelve people died and around 5,000 people required hospital treatment for their injuries. Had the gas been in concentrated form, the Japanese authorities believe that thousands could have died. CBRN events have also occurred in the UK; in 2006 a former Russian KGB officer Alexander Litvinenko, who had taken asylum in Britain, was poisoned with radioactive polonium whilst at a central London hotel, and died a few weeks later in hospital. And in 2018 Sergei Skripal, a former Russian army officer, and his daughter suffered the effects of a nerve agent whilst in Salisbury city centre. The first Wiltshire police officers on the scene also required hospital treatment.

Terrorist incidents can be regarded as those incidents that involve the use or threat of violence (often extreme violence) to attempt to instil fear in order to further or to publicize a political or extremist belief. The Terrorism Act 2000 provides both an 'official' definition of the meaning of 'terrorism' and the particular powers for situations which might involve terrorism. Similar powers are available under other primary legislation or procedure, but the Terrorism Act 2000 provides wider powers to stop and search and to arrest (see 9.4.4).

The precise nature of any suspect device cannot be determined by visual means alone. The cardinal rule is: do not touch it. At such an incident the FAO should create a very wide space around the device (as wide as is practicable) and get people out of the area. The preservation of evidence is a high priority, but at all times is secondary to public safety.

11.6.1 Cordons and the Terrorism Act 2000

An area can be 'designated' as a cordoned area under s 34 of the Terrorism Act 2000. The designating officer will usually be at least superintendent rank, but could be any rank if he/she considers it urgent (s 34(2)). Police officers have certain additional powers in a designated cordoned area (s 34(1)). Once an area has been cordoned, under s 36(1) a police officer can:

- order a person to immediately leave a cordoned area or any adjacent premises, and to move a vehicle from a cordoned area (if he/she is the driver or in charge of the vehicle);
- arrange for the removal of a vehicle from a cordoned area or for it to be moved within a cordoned area; or
- prohibit or restrict pedestrian or vehicular access to a cordoned area.

(Note that slightly different legislation applies for BTP and MOD police officers.)

Failing to comply with any of these requests (without reasonable excuse) is a summary offence (s 36(2) of the Terrorism Act 2000), and the penalty is three months' imprisonment and/or a fine.

11.6.2 Suspected explosive devices

Alerts for suspected explosive devices present major demands on police and other emergency service resources. However, it must be assumed that every suspect device has the potential to kill and injure. The National Counter Terrorism Security Office (NCTSO) provides extensive advice (updated in 2017) on what to do in the event of a suspected explosive device (available on the gov.uk website). The advice was written for the public and employees such as shop staff, but much of it is also relevant to police officers in training.

The advice in this context can change on a frequent basis, partly in response to emerging terrorist threats and tactics. For example the NCTSO advice states that in some circumstances complete evacuation is not the ideal action (if eg a suspect device has not been found, or the presence of multiple devices is suspected (see *Recognising the Terrorist Threat* available on the gov.uk website)). They suggest instead a partial evacuation or no evacuation at all; officers should seek advice from the emergency coordinator and senior officers and follow local force procedures.

For 'cordoning' at the scene of a suspect device, many police forces adopt the practices shown in the table (but as in all matters involving critical incidents, be guided by local force policy).

Size of object (approximate)	Distance between cordon and device
Brief case	100m
Car or small van	200m
Van or larger vehicle	400m

The initial cordons may be installed by the fire or ambulance services during the rescue phase, using red and white tape. The outer cordon will generally be installed by the police using blue and white tape, and will be managed by scene control officers who permit authorized entry as required, and record activity in their crime scene log (see 11.2).

In an urban area, streets lined with buildings create a potential blast corridor for any explosion so personnel are safer behind 'hard cover' (eg concrete buildings) with no line of sight of the suspected device. No person should be located behind or beneath windows or other glass panels, however far away from the device.

The CAP to the object should be marked out if practicable (see 11.2.2), consistent with the overriding priority of personal and public safety. The force control room should be informed of the precise location of the device, especially if a wider evacuation is taking place outside the immediate cordon, but note that hand-held radios or mobile phones must not be used within 10 metres of the suspect object, and vehicle-based radios must not be used to transmit within 50 metres.

11.6.3 CBRN incidents

A chemical, biological, radiological, or nuclear (CBRN) incident has the potential to cause extreme devastation and very widespread loss of life. Fortunately this type of incident is rare and all forces will have detailed contingency plans—the considerations and procedures are the same as for any other type of suspect device. Some CBRN attacks can be hard to recognize (eg involving nuclear radiation), but any reports of groups of people suddenly collapsing or feeling unwell, or of a strong or noxious smell could indicate the presence of chemicals.

In a suspected CBRN incident the Steps procedure should be followed (Home Office, 2015c). Here, the step number corresponds with the observed number of casualties. For a Step 3 incident, a JESIP M/ETHANE assessment should be made if at all possible, but police safety must not be compromised.

Step	Number of casualties	Procedure
Step 1	One	Approach the site using the usual procedures.
Step 2	Two	Approach with caution and do not discount any possibility. Report arrival and do not touch any object. Report updates continually.
Step 3	Three or more	Do not enter the scene. Create an RV point outside the area, identify safe arrival routes, and await instructions.

11.6.4 Attending the scene of a bomb explosion

After a bomb explosion there is likely to be devastation, wreckage, smoke, flames, badly injured people, dead bodies (and parts of bodies), noise, and confusion. The role of the FAO is the same in principle as for a train crash or major road traffic accident: take charge, clear those who can walk out of the area, close off the area with a cordon, attend to the injured if possible, and treat the area as a crime scene.

As well as complying with the JESIP M/ETHANE guidelines (see 11.5.1), all officers should ensure they continue with their duties at a major incident as defined by their force procedures. Every attempt should be made to preserve the scene for further investigation, but the first priority is always the preservation of life. There may be members of the public who need to be led to safety, or who are injured and require medical services. Onlookers may need to be directed away.

The control room must be kept informed of the situation, so appropriate support can be dispatched to the incident and the commanders have all the information they require. Overall, an officer will usually find that his/her duties will be centred on three main priorities: preserving life, organizing the response to the incident, and maintaining order at the scene.

Nothing can really prepare a trainee police officer (or anyone) for the emotional impact of witnessing such scenes; indeed, many police officers present at the immediate aftermath of a major disaster report experiencing an initial sense of helplessness. However, it has been said (and in our view rightly) that what distinguishes a police officer from the general public is not his/her exercise of powers, or uniform, or knowledge of the law, but knowing what to do in an emergency. That knowledge can only come from training and experience.

> **TASK 9** Note the priority actions now in response to (1) a suspect CBRN device; and (2) a subsequent detonation. What should be done first and thereafter?

11.7 Planned Operations

'Planned Operations' are where the police have had advanced warning of a situation or event and therefore will have developed suitable contingency plans, tactics, and strategies. Examples include disruption at sea and airports due to strikes, pre-planned demonstrations, and large music festivals. As soon as the necessity for such an operation has been identified, it is given an operational name to distinguish it from other incidents. The 'operation' covers the period from instigation, through planning, execution, and debrief. We provide a summary here, but more details are available on the College of Policing website.

General Procedures

11.7.1   Planning an operation

All police organizations have contingency plans for identified risks in their own areas, with a degree of flexibility to cover all eventualities. A range of tactical options can be used for planned operations. Some are also employed in 'steady state' policing (see 11.1) such as using police dogs and batons, and entering buildings, but others are more specialized, for example armed response personnel who can fire attenuating energy projectiles and CS smoke. Other tactical options include shield tactics, air support, barricade/obstacle removal, cordons and intercepts, water cannon, containment, and evidence-gathering teams.

The GSB hierarchy of command (see 11.5.3), is nationally recognized by the police, partner agencies, and other emergency services. At each level of command, tactical advisers from the police and external organizations provide knowledge, understanding, and skills for the planning phase and for responding to changing circumstances throughout the duration of the operation. For example, Gold Command could elect to convene a 'strategic coordinating group', or Silver Command could assemble a 'tactical planning group' to develop a strategy.

Commanders and coordinating groups require specific, accurate, and relevant information at each stage of the operation, so a dedicated intelligence function will be required (see Chapter 23). This could be located at the GSB incident room, or elsewhere, for example at the Force Intelligence Bureau. A Community Impact Assessment (CIA) will be conducted to assess the extent to which businesses, community groups, families, and individuals may be affected by the proposed police response; all vital information for planning a successful operation. Personnel from within the police family (eg neighbourhood teams), and external representatives from the third sector (charitable and non-profit-making organizations, community bodies) can all provide input for the CIA.

Gold Command determines the strategy, and will plan the police response accordingly. All the relevant information is recorded in a single document, the 'operational order'. The personnel participating in the operation are briefed as required, following the categories set out in the JESIP IIMARCH model as shown in the table.

Heading	Key features
Information	Such as evaluated intelligence, results of the community impact assessment, length, duration, and location of the operation
Intention	Objectives of GSB strategies, tactics, policies, powers, and procedures
Method	Process by which the tactics, policies, powers, and procedures will be used
Administration	Logistics pertaining to start times, location, and lengths of duty and periods of refreshment
Risk assessment	Based on gathered information from intelligence sources
Communications	Including media broadcasts and inter-operability between personnel
Human rights and other legalities	Preserving the rights of individuals and groups and adhering to codes of practice in the use of legislation

Derived in part from JESIP (2017a) and Home Office (2014e) but authors' interpretation and description.

The police information (see 5.8.2) generated by an operation must be collected, recorded, shared, and retained in accordance with local force and national guidelines. These specify the use of the Government Security Classifications Policy (GSCP), under which information is classified as either Official, Secret, or Top Secret.

11.7.2   Participating in a planned operation

In the course of a planned operation police officers will of course follow the tactics outlined in the operational order, but within these limits individual officers will probably need to decide what specific actions to take. They should use the College of Policing National Decision Model (see 5.5.2) as a framework for taking a decision. Records of any decisions made and actions carried out should be made in accordance with the PACE Codes of Practice (see 4.6.1) and the rules of disclosure (see 24.3.3). The decisions and actions should be recorded as a PNB entry (see 10.2), although this might not be possible at the time, depending on the circumstances.

The operational order may specify the use of personal protective and operational equipment (see 5.10), particularly if the use of force is likely to be required. The use of force to challenge unacceptable behaviour will be covered under personal safety training (see 5.12.5) and limited by legislation such as the Human Rights Act 1998 (see 4.4.1) and common law. Each individual officer must remember that his/her own health and safety is just as important as maintaining the health and safety of others (see 5.12).

11.7.3 Effective communication for planned operations

Effective communication with partners, communities, and other stakeholders helps to build trust and confidence, and ensure that the appropriate strategy is adopted. Openness and transparency can help identify potential problems, and make it less likely that the situation will escalate and result in the use of unplanned (and less suitable) police response tactics. All officers participating in an operation have an individual responsibility to maintain effective interpersonal communication (see 5.11). Various communication channels are available to GSB during planning and during the operation itself, such as:

- face-to-face, for example public meetings, under-represented groups, independent advisory groups, partnership working, and information sharing;
- digital and social media, for example platforms such as Facebook, Twitter, YouTube, and blog, social media monitoring, and digitally enabled meetings;
- corporate communication (traditional media), for example press releases and statements, television, radio, and newspaper interviews.

After a planned operation there will be a debriefing process to identify examples of good practice and opportunities for improvement. This could help streamline procedures and reduce demands for frontline staff in the future. The information from the debrief should be recorded and retained for revelation and disclosure (see 24.3.3). Further information on debriefing can be found on the College of Policing APP website.

11.8 Answers to Tasks

TASK 1 You may have noted that major-crime investigations are often long term and complex, especially when dealing with 'stranger murders' or 'stranger rapes'.

You could note, too, that crimes of violence attract considerable media interest and widespread publicity which, whilst helpful in publicizing the crime, have the potential to adversely affect an investigation if not handled properly.

TASK 2 When a person is decapitated.

TASK 3 Although it is beyond the scope of this Handbook (and not something that you are likely to encounter unless you become an SIO) you might like to research the CATCHEM (Central Analytical Homicide and Expertise Management) database. Research conducted on child murder with a sexual motive revealed complex mathematical relationships between places of abduction, and aspects of the offender. This is described in Aitken *et al* (1995). One inferential model the authors describe suggests that, in the case of an abduction of a boy aged 0–10 years, there is a 75 per cent chance that the offender lives within five miles of the contact point, and a 77 per cent chance that he/she is more than 21 years old. The pioneering work of Aitken *et al* continues to be developed and extended by, amongst others, the Serious Crime Analysis Section (SCAS, now part of the NCA).

The research has now been applied to the more general crime of homicide (Francis *et al*, 2004). For example, if the victim is aged 18–24, male, ethnically of Asian background, unemployed, and 'stabbed in a rage', then the model predicts that the offender is over 21 (68 per cent likelihood), also Asian (55 per cent), and an acquaintance of the victim (60 per cent).

TASK 4 The priority at the scene of a major violent crime is the preservation of life followed by the preservation of evidence.

You would probably note that the first priority would be not to let anyone else over the threshold of the crime scene, and that might well extend to the area outside the bedsit, to include stairs, stairwell, communal areas, and adjoining corridors or passages. You would clear people away (including the landlord), and close off the scene as swiftly as possible. You would enter the room, principally to ascertain whether the presumed victim is still alive. If she is alive you would follow your National Policing Curriculum training (probably modules 1 and

General Procedures

2), for example applying the 'DRAB' procedures (Danger, Response, Airway, Breathing). Your duty is to support her until the paramedics arrive, and you would also ensure that nothing else was touched.

You would be in urgent communication with your force control centre, describing what you can see, the location, and any other relevant requirements, such as the attendance of paramedics, an ambulance, and a doctor. You would request the attendance of CSIs and probably the duty SIO or duty detective officer, since it is evident that a violent crime has been committed, possibly murder.

Then what? If you had a colleague with you, you could share the note taking, including the names and addresses of witnesses and all other people present. (Bear in mind the need to 'record, retain, reveal, and disclose' that we discuss in 24.3.) You would ask the landlord (whose details you have also recorded) for information about the victim and possible visitors she had had that day, including of course any information about the other person or persons present at the apparent altercation. You would log your actions, begin arranging the CAP, and note anything which you observed (such as a murder weapon, scattered possessions, blood splashes, and so on).

TASK 5 Your answers could well have been 'I do not know', which would have been entirely understandable, even if you are a trainee police officer. (In fact your trainers might be more worried if you claimed already to know the answers to these questions.) We aim to go on to provide you with some general principles and some possible answers.

TASK 6 There are many. The usual model taught during police training (see diagram) adopts a six-stage process, starting with defining the problem:

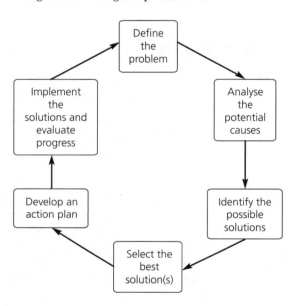

TASK 7 Your list could read something like this:

- Keep in constant communication with your control centre, making sure that they know what is happening and what you are doing.
- Clear the immediate scene and note any injuries to anyone.
- Ensure that the area around the house (the 'stronghold') is evacuated and move people as far from the scene as possible.
- Continue to ask for information on what has happened, but calm any hysterical or over-excited people.
- Create a CAP in and out of the incident (see 11.2.2).
- Clear a wide area to receive the support once it arrives, and identify a suitable RVP (ensure that arriving vehicles are kept away from the scene itself).
- Use your colleagues proactively to control the immediate area, to talk to witnesses, and to communicate with incoming support.
- Find out all you can about the alleged hostage-taker, including name and any relationship with anyone likely to be inside the house with him.

- Make notes: keep a careful log (see 11.2.3) of what has taken place to the best of your knowledge, recording names and addresses of witnesses (see 24.4).
- If it is safe to do so, try to open a dialogue with the hostage-taker, making sure that he understands that you are a police officer and emphasizing that your aim is to end this incident peacefully, without anyone getting hurt.

PCDA trainee officers could compare this list to the one provided during training. No doubt there will be many points in common.

TASK 8 The 'Gold, Silver, Bronze' system has been criticized. One problem could be that as command is transferred from one officer to another, not all the relevant information is passed on.

In his report into the investigation of the Soham murders, Sir Ronnie Flanagan made the following observation:

> Ironically, the overlaying of the Gold, Silver and Bronze command structure on this operation contributed to a lack of clarity of command of the incident, particularly in relation to the role of the SIO and was subject to comment in the internal review. (Flanagan, 2004, p 13)

The report also contained a recommendation that the system should be clarified for homicides. A number of the Flanagan recommendations were subsequently adopted in NPIA guidance, and now feature in the College of Policing Authorised Professional Practice.

TASK 9 The role of the police officer does not include identifying the type of device. His/her role would be to contain the scene, evacuate anyone within the cordon, and manage the site until help arrives. He/she should be communicating to the force control centre to tell them everything he/she can see and otherwise perceive, including the location of the device and its description, following the JESIP M/ETHANE mnemonic. Note that it would be unwise to allow the walking injured to simply leave: even if they appear well they may be contaminated and require decontamination and treatment. Secondary devices would be a major concern. Further information is available from the *Civil Contingencies* section of the College of Policing website.

General Procedures

12 | Alcohol, Drugs, and Substance Abuse

12.1 Introduction

Many of the incidents encountered by police officers will be alcohol or drug-related, particularly on late shifts. The health and safety of all persons present must be considered, as the potential for injury can be very high. Intoxicated people are sometimes subject to rapid mood swings, happy one minute and then violent the next, and others who are normally quite reserved may lose some of their normal social inhibitions and behave unpredictably. Alcohol or drugs was recorded as an 'impact factor' in nearly 90 per cent of the 428,000 recorded incidents where a police officer had to use force in the year ending March 2019 (Home Office, 2019j).

Alcohol and drug consumption is not only confined to adults. According to a 2018 survey involving 13,664 pupils aged 11 to 15, around 44 per cent had consumed alcohol at some time, generally provided in their own homes at weekends by parents or guardians (NHS Digital, 2019b). In the same survey 24 per cent of pupils reported they had taken drugs, compared with 15 per cent in 2014. This increase may be explained at least in part by the use of nitrous oxide and new psychoactive substances.

In terms of illegal use of drugs and other substances, the 2018/19 Crime Survey for England and Wales found that 9.4 per cent of adults (aged 16–59) had taken a drug controlled by the Misuse of Drugs Act 1971 in the previous year. This amounts to around 3.2 million people, about the same as the previous year's figure. The same survey reported that around 0.5 per cent of adults had used a psychoactive substance during 2018/19 (with the 16–24 age group accounting for over half of this figure), and that 2.3 per cent of adults had used nitrous oxide (also known as 'laughing gas').

Although this chapter is mainly concerned with the application of the law surrounding alcohol- and drug-related incidents, the PCDA, DHEP, and pre-join programmes often also provide an introduction to the wider issues surrounding alcohol and other forms of drug and substance abuse. In recent years 'county lines' have become a problem in many forces, and as well as increasing access to drugs this often involves exploitation of vulnerable people. We cover this complex topic in 12.7. Drink- and drug-driving is covered separately in 19.9.

The topics covered in this chapter are likely to contribute to the learning required for the National Policing Curriculum subject areas: 'Understanding the Police Constable Role', 'Policing the Roads', 'Vulnerability and Risk', and 'Managing Conflict', as the legislation and procedures around alcohol and drugs are an important part of police work.

12.2 Alcohol-related Offences and Powers

There is no doubt that alcohol causes problematic behaviour for a minority of users. In the year 2017/18 there were an estimated 1.2 million alcohol-related hospital admissions in the UK, which was 3 per cent higher than the previous year (NHS Digital, 2019c). Alcohol seems to be a key feature in many incidents where violence is involved. In the year ending March 2018, 39 per cent of victims of violent incidents believed their assailants to be under the influence of alcohol (ONS, 2019i), and the police recorded that 14 per cent of violence against the person offences were alcohol-related, with the offence of 'assault without injury on a constable' being the most common at 32 per cent.

Here we explore the legislation and powers available to a police officer to deal with people who have drunk alcohol to excess, and to help to prevent the consumption of alcohol by young people. The word 'alcohol' is used in some legislation; it is defined in s 191(1) of the Licensing Act 2003 as spirits, wine, beer, cider or any other fermented, distilled, or spirituous liquor (in any state).

12.2.1 Drunkenness as an offence

Drunkenness is an offence in certain circumstances (s 12 of the Licensing Act 1872, and see diagram).

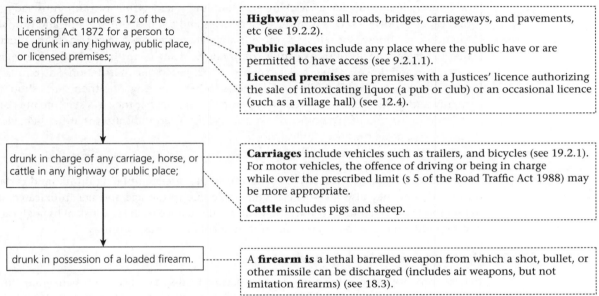

It is an offence under s 12 of the Licensing Act 1872 for a person to be drunk in any highway, public place, or licensed premises;

Highway means all roads, bridges, carriageways, and pavements, etc (see 19.2.2).

Public places include any place where the public have or are permitted to have access (see 9.2.1.1).

Licensed premises are premises with a Justices' licence authorizing the sale of intoxicating liquor (a pub or club) or an occasional licence (such as a village hall) (see 12.4).

drunk in charge of any carriage, horse, or cattle in any highway or public place;

Carriages include vehicles such as trailers, and bicycles (see 19.2.1). For motor vehicles, the offence of driving or being in charge while over the prescribed limit (s 5 of the Road Traffic Act 1988) may be more appropriate.

Cattle includes pigs and sheep.

drunk in possession of a loaded firearm.

A **firearm is** a lethal barrelled weapon from which a shot, bullet, or other missile can be discharged (includes air weapons, but not imitation firearms) (see 18.3).

Note that it is irrelevant whether the person is on the highway or in the public place of his own volition or recently ejected from nearby premises (*Winzar v Chief Constable of Kent*, The Times, 28 March 1983).

The terms 'drunk' and 'drunkenness' are not defined in law, but the case of *R v Tagg* [2002] 1 Cr App R 2 determined that the everyday meaning of 'drunk' should be used as a precedent. The *Oxford English Dictionary* defines drunk as 'having drunk intoxicating liquor to an extent which affects steady self-control' (*Shorter Oxford English Dictionary*, 2002, although the 1933 edition was cited in the case). The Court of Appeal also accepted that the *Collins Dictionary* definition (used by the judge in the original case under appeal) and the *Shorter Oxford English Dictionary* definitions were essentially the same, and were helpful in determining the existence of a state of drunkenness.

The court itself must decide whether or not a suspect was drunk. Generally, the opinion of a witness is inadmissible as evidence, but for drunkenness a 'competent witness' may give evidence that, in his/her opinion, a person was drunk (*R v Davies* [1962] 1 WLR 1111). A competent witness is defined as a person who understands questions, and can respond coherently, and would of course include a police officer. The witness should also provide facts to support the opinion, for example, that the person was unsteady on her feet, had glazed eyes and slurred speech, or that her breath smelt of intoxicating liquor. This offence is triable summarily and the penalty is one month's imprisonment or a fine. A penalty notice can also be used (see 10.13.2.2).

During your studies, you might hear this offence referred to as 'drunk and incapable', which is not strictly correct as the word 'incapable' is not used in the current legislation. The term 'incapable' probably came into use after it appeared in s 1 of the Licensing Act 1902, which provided any person with the power to apprehend any other person found drunk, if he/she appeared 'to be incapable of taking care of himself'. This legislation was repealed by the Serious Organised Crime and Police Act 2005. (The power for a police officer to arrest a person for drunkenness under s 12 of the Licensing Act 1872 is now provided by s 24 of the PACE Act 1984 (see 10.6).)

Whilst the word 'incapable' does not need to be proved for the offence to be committed, you might find it useful to consider how the notion of being incapable might apply in relation to vulnerable people; one such scenario is presented here from the perspective of a police officer on night duty, around midnight.

> Two police officers are deployed to a local hospital at the request of NHS staff who have refused admission to an apparently drunk woman and subsequently called upon their security personnel to eject her from the premises. On arrival at the entrance to A&E, she can be clearly seen standing next to a uniformed member of staff. She appears to be uninjured and capable of walking and standing unaided, but is a little unsteady on her feet. The police officers introduce themselves and ask her for her name and how she intends to get home. She refuses to provide any details and it becomes clear to the officers that her breath smells of intoxicating liquor and that she seems to be drunk. She begins to pace up and down and her facial expression changes to one of irritation. She refuses to communicate and her breathing rate appears to be increasing. She then starts shouting angrily and making erratic movements, pointing her finger at the NHS staff member and demanding treatment. The officers take these signs as an indication that her behaviour may be escalating towards physical violence.

They know she may be suspected of committing the offence of being drunk (and certainly incapable), but they also know she is vulnerable due to her age and her intoxicated state. Rather than taking her into custody, they call an ambulance as she is at risk of hypoglycaemia and hypothermia, due to the large amounts of alcohol she has consumed.

12.2.2 Drunk and disorderly behaviour

It is a summary offence for any drunken person to display 'disorderly behaviour' in any highway, public place, or licensed premises (s 91(1) of the Criminal Justice Act 1967). This is a very common problem, indeed in year ending June 2018, 43 per cent of all PNDs were issued for this offence (Ministry of Justice, 2018a). The precise meaning of 'disorderly behaviour' is not defined by statute but its everyday meaning is 'unruly or offensive behaviour'. The penalty is a fine, a penalty notice, or one month's imprisonment.

It is widely accepted that excess alcohol causes aggression in some people and in some circumstances (Bushman and Cooper, 1990), and the link between alcohol use and certain forms of anti-social behaviour and violence, has been examined (Ostrowsky, 2014). Such violence can inevitably lead to conflict, so you might find it useful to consider how police officers can deal with such situations in practice.

> Two police officers are deployed to a reported incident of anti-social behaviour outside a house on a large estate. The previous shift had attended the location earlier that evening and no offences had been identified. On arrival, the police officers see a number of people in the street outside a house where loud music is being played. The officers inform them that their actions are disturbing neighbours and ask them to go back inside, and they comply. As the officers turn to leave the area, they notice a teenage female slumped against the wall of the house. The officers ask her to stand up. She appears to be aged around 15 years, and is very unsteady on her feet. She is unable to walk or stand unaided and appears to be unaware of her own actions. Her eyes are glazed and her breath smells of intoxicating liquor. She is also shaking, appears dizzy and is sweating profusely even though the air temperature is quite cool. They ask about her welfare and she seems unable to fully understand what is being said, and becomes irritable and nervous. The officers knock on the door of the house several times but get no response; they must now decide what to do.

A potentially violent situation such as this is not always easy to control, particularly as things can happen very quickly without warning; there is little time to make an assessment and prepare a response. Medical professionals often find themselves in similar situations and Harwood (2017) promotes prevention and de-escalation as an initial response. Good communication is key, and a consideration of transactional analysis (see 5.11.1) could be useful in this situation. If the police officer is friendly, polite, and shows respect this might help the situation, so he/she should informally explain his/her role, including aims and objectives, to help resolve the situation in a way that is acceptable to all. General conversation using simple, everyday language may help to build a rapport between the participants, and the officer should communicate in a calm and non-threatening way. The potential aggressor might remain in a heightened state of anxiety, so humiliation, contradiction, and embarrassment should be avoided at all costs.

Should the situation escalate to violence, officers will need to be proactive and employ rapid initial restraint, using, for example, rigid handcuffs, an asp, or incapacitant spray. Some officers may also have been trained in the use of a Taser, or such an officer could be summoned if necessary (see also 15.1 on managing conflict in such situations).

It would clearly be an advantage to know about any known medical conditions, or about warning signs and risk factors for physical violence, but it is unlikely that such information will be available in this type of situation. However, general principles apply in relation to restraint; to reduce the chances of positional asphyxia, a person who is initially restrained lying face down, should as soon as possible be sat up, placed on his/her side, or put in a kneeling or standing position (see 15.4.1.2 for further details). If the person is subsequently taken into custody, the custody officer should be informed of any force used during the arrest or escort.

12.2.3 Drunk in charge of children

Under s 2 of the Licensing Act 1902, it is an offence for a person to be drunk while 'having charge' of a child under the age of 7 years in any highway, public place, or licensed premises. The precise meaning of 'having charge' is not defined by statute, but probably means some sort of care or control over the child(ren); the suspect must be the only person with the child, or alternatively everyone in a group with the child must be drunk. This is a summary offence and the penalty is one month's imprisonment or a fine.

12.2.4 Controlled drinking zones

Under s 235 of the Local Government Act 1972 a local authority can designate an area as a 'controlled drinking zone' (CDZ) to help control anti-social behaviour. It is not an offence to drink alcohol in a CDZ, but it is an offence to fail to comply with a request to surrender alcohol or to cease drinking. However, note that Home Office advice is that 'it is not appropriate to challenge an individual consuming alcohol where that individual is not causing a problem' (Home Office, 2009b).

Local policies will determine how to dispose of any confiscated alcohol. The offence of failing to comply is triable summarily and the penalty is a fine, often imposed through a penalty notice (see 10.13.2.2).

> **TASK 1** Imagine you are a trainee police officer undertaking the PCDA. In your area you often see a habitual drunk who often drinks large quantities of strong lager and then becomes very abusive to passing members of the public. You are requested to deal with this. How would you approach her in terms of her vulnerability and what long-term solution could improve the situation? Look at s 34(1) of the Criminal Justice Act 1972 to help determine a suitable course of action.

12.3 Alcohol and Young People

Alcohol is a problem for a significant minority of young people. In the year 2017/18, there were 7,206 young people under the age of 18 in treatment for alcohol problems in England and Wales (NDTMS, 2018). The same report indicates that early initiation to drinking, drunkenness, and drinking to excess are all associated with increased risk of alcohol disorders and dependency, unplanned and unprotected sex, and injury in young people. Certain legislation is available to help limit their alcohol consumption in public places, while other legislation relates to young people on licensed premises.

On a more general note, if an officer encounters a 'child' carrying unopened cans of alcohol, then he/she should at least consider how he/she acquired the cans (by gift or purchase?), and take action accordingly. This applies even if there are no grounds to reasonably believe that the child has been consuming alcohol, or is about to consume it.

12.3.1 Confiscation of alcohol from young people

A police officer (in or out of uniform) or a suitably designated PCSO may confiscate alcohol (or anything reasonably believed to be alcohol) from a young person in a 'relevant place' (s 1(1) of the Confiscation of Alcohol (Young Persons) Act 1997). A relevant place includes:

- any public place, for example streets, parks, and shopping centres (but not licensed premises such as pubs or clubs); and
- a place to which the person has unlawfully gained access, such as gate-crashing a party at a private house.

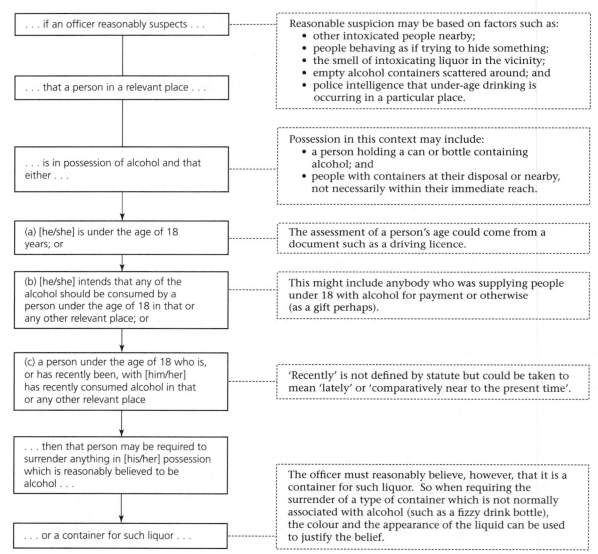

The officer must inform the person of his/her suspicion under s 1(1) (s 1(4) of the Confiscation of Alcohol (Young Persons) Act 1997). The young person can also be required to state his/her name and address (s 1AA), and if suspected to be under 16 can be removed to his/her place of residence or a place of safety (s 1AB) (see 13.3.3 and 14.2.2.1). Failing to comply without reasonable excuse with a requirement under s 1(1) or (1AA) is an offence, and the young person must be informed of this. The offence is triable summarily and the penalty is a fine. The policies on how to dispose of any surrendered alcohol vary between forces.

12.3.2 Persistently possessing alcohol in a public place

It is an offence for a person under 18 to be in possession of alcohol without reasonable excuse in any relevant place on three or more occasions within a year (s 30 of the Police and Crime Act 2009). The offence is triable summarily and the penalty is a fine.

> **TASK 2** Imagine you are a police officer and you see a young male at a bus station drinking alcohol. What requirements can you make? Write down a list of things you would have to say for the requirements to be lawful.

12.4 Premises Licensing Legislation

The Licensing Act 2003 includes legislation to address drunkenness in 'relevant premises'. Relevant premises in this context are premises where alcohol can be sold by retail (eg a pub or a shop), club premises with a certificate (eg a working men's club where alcohol is supplied by or on behalf of a club to members), but also any premises with 'permitted temporary activity' (eg a village hall hired out for a wedding reception).

Staff managing or working in places where alcohol is served have a legal responsibility to try to prevent drunkenness and disorder. People with these responsibilities are listed in s 140(1) of the Licensing Act 2003, and are referred to here as 'responsible staff' (a term of our own invention, not a legal term). They include:

- the holder of a premises licence;
- the designated supervisor of a licensed premises;
- any person who works at the premises in a capacity which authorizes him/her to prevent disorderly conduct;
- any member or officer of a club (with a club premises certificate) who has the capacity to prevent disorderly behaviour; and
- the user of a premises with permitted temporary activity, at the permitted time.

12.4.1 Disorderly conduct on licensed premises

An offence is committed by responsible staff (see 12.4) who knowingly allow disorderly conduct on licensed premises (s 140(1) of the Licensing Act 2003). This offence is triable summarily and the penalty is a fine.

A drunk or disorderly person commits a summary offence under s 143(1) of the Licensing Act 2003 if without reasonable excuse he/she:

- fails to leave relevant premises (when requested to do so by a police officer or a responsible staff member); or
- enters (or attempts to enter) relevant premises having been requested not to enter.

A police officer must respond to requests from responsible staff to help expel or refuse entry to a drunken person (s 143(4) of the Licensing Act 2003). Reasonable force may be used to encourage the person to comply (see *Semple v Luton and South Bedfordshire Magistrates' Court* [2009] EWHC 3241 (Admin) and 15.5.1).

12.4.2 Providing a drunk person with intoxicating liquor

Responsible staff who knowingly sell (or attempt to sell) alcohol to a person who is drunk on relevant premises commit an offence under s 141(1) of the Licensing Act 2003. It is also an offence for anyone to obtain or attempt to obtain alcohol for a drunken person on relevant premises (s 142(1)). These offences are triable summarily and the penalty is a fine; a PND can also be used.

12.4.3 Powers of entry

There is a power of entry to any place if there is reason to believe that an offence under the Licensing Act 2003 is being committed or is about to be committed (s 180(1) of the Licensing Act 2003). Reasonable force can be used (s 180(2)). The term 'any place' is defined in s 193; it includes vehicles, vessels, or moveable structures, licensed or not.

For premises (or any other place) with a club premises certificate, there is a similar power of entry (also under the Licensing Act 2003), if there is reasonable cause to believe that:

- a breach of the peace may occur (s 97(1)(b)); or
- an offence relating to supplying a controlled drug has been committed (see 12.6.2), or is about to be, or is being committed at that moment (s 97(1)(a)).

Reasonable force may be used when exercising this power (s 97(2)).

For premises with permitted temporary activities, a police officer may enter the premises at any reasonable time to assess the effect of the event in relation to prevention of crime and disorder, public safety, the prevention of public nuisance, and the protection of children from harm (s 108(1) of the Licensing Act 2003). There is no specific offence of obstructing a police officer under s 108, but an offence under the Police Act 1996 could be considered (obstruction in the lawful execution of police duties (see 15.4.2)).

12.4.4 Selling alcohol to children and young people

Alcohol cannot legally be sold to a person under the age of 18 years. It is an offence to:

- sell alcohol to a person under 18 in any place (s 146(1) of the Licensing Act 2003)—this is a penalty offence (see 10.13.2.2); or
- knowingly allow the sale of alcohol on relevant premises to an individual aged under 18 (s 147(1) of the Licensing Act 2003).

A further more serious offence is committed if on two or more occasions (within three consecutive months) alcohol is unlawfully sold on the same licensed premises to a young person under 18 (s 147A of the Licensing Act 2003). These offences are triable summarily and the penalty is a fine.

> **TASK 3** In the course of an investigation into offences concerning public indecency and criminal damage it is found that many of these offences are committed by people who have consumed large amounts of intoxicating liquor on relevant premises. This intake of alcohol may have contributed towards these offences being committed. How could the licensing authority of the premises be informed about such activities?

12.5 Controlled Drugs and Psychoactive Substances

Police officers will frequently encounter people who have been using controlled drugs or psychoactive substances. According to police recorded crime in the year ending March 2018, victims of violent incidents believed their assailants to be under the influence of drugs in 21 per cent of cases (ONS, 2019i).

In February 2019, Dame Carol Black was appointed to lead a major independent review of illegal drugs in the UK. The review will summarize the available evidence surrounding the effects of illegal drug use and supply, including current trends and future risks. It will also identify gaps in that evidence and suggest how to address them. When published the results will be available on the gov.uk website.

Risk and hazard levels should be carefully assessed when dealing with people 'under the influence'. Personal safety equipment may be required as the consequences of contamination from bodily fluids or equipment used by a drug addict can be very serious. The merest micro-cut from a virus-contaminated sharp article could cause a life-threatening infection. Understanding of appropriate health and safety measures is included in the PCDA knowledge requirement.

12.5.1 Definitions of controlled drugs and psychoactive substances

A controlled drug is a drug that is subject to legal control. They are classified as such because of their harmful effects on the human body, in particular the brain, and the fact that some people find the psychoactive effects of these substances enjoyable and hard to resist. New substances are added to the Home Office list as they come to the attention of the authorities. However, any alteration, however minor, to the chemical structure of a controlled drug makes it a different substance, and the new substance will therefore not be subject to the existing controlled drugs legislation. Any such altered substance that has a psychoactive effect and is classed as a 'psychoactive substance' would, however, be covered by the Psychoactive Substances Act 2016 (see 12.5.1.2).

12.5.1.1 The definition of a controlled drug

Controlled drugs contain one or more defined chemical compounds with recognized effects, and are classed as Class A, B, or C (Misuse of Drugs Act 1971) according to the potential for harm they are thought to present.

Class A	eg Ecstasy, heroin, cocaine, crack cocaine, 'magic mushrooms' (containing psilocin or psilocybin), 'crystal meth' (methamphetamine), and LSD
Class B	eg cannabis leaves, cannabis resin, 'Spice' (a synthetic cannabinoid), mephedrone, amphetamines (but not methamphetamine), and barbiturates
Class C	eg khat, tranquillizers (such as Temazepam), anabolic steroids, and some painkillers

A full list of controlled drugs can be found on the Home Office website. (Note that medicinal cannabis is now available on prescription.)

The illegal use of controlled drugs often involves particular equipment, to smoke or inject a substance for example. Some examples of this equipment are shown in the photographs.

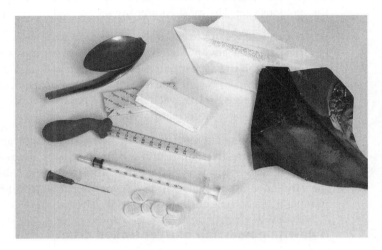

(Photographs from Drugscope 2013, copyright free)

Recognizing controlled drugs is very difficult as there are so many different forms, shapes, colours, and sizes including pills, tablets, liquids, powders, and resins. Therefore, a police officer who finds such a substance without pharmaceutical company packaging should not try to identify it, but should act on the suspicion that it is a controlled drug. The excellent 'encyclopaedia' resource available on the DrugWise websitewill be a helpful resource: <https://www.drugwise.org.uk/drugsearch-encyclopedia/>.

In the financial year ending 2019, there were 153,082 seizures of Class A, B, and C drugs, with around 75 per cent being for Class B drugs, mainly cannabis (16,692 kg). The table shows further information on drug seizures.

Class of drug	A	B	C
Number of seizures in the year ending March 2019	32,753	115,047	5,282
Change in seizures compared with previous year	+13%	+11%	+4%
Most commonly seized drug	cocaine	cannabis	

TASK 4 If you are a trainee police officer undertaking the PCDA or DHEP, find out the common street names, prices, and the appearance for the most common Class A, B, and C drugs in your policing area.

12.5.1.2 The definition of a psychoactive substance

In the legislation a 'psychoactive substance' is any substance (other than controlled drugs, alcohol, or tobacco) which is capable of producing a psychoactive effect in a person who consumes it (s 2(1)(a) of the Psychoactive Substances Act 2016).

In recent years, many new psychoactive substances (sometimes referred to as NPS) have been manufactured, perhaps with a view to circumnavigating the controlled drugs legislation. These substances are often referred to as 'legal highs' and include 'spice' (a synthetic cannabinoid), 'GBL' (gamma butyrolacetone), and 'GHB' (gamma hydroxybutyrate). The Psychoactive Substances Act 2016 (PSA 2016) was drafted to counter production and supply of such substances. In 2018/19 there were 2,973 NPS seizures, an increase of 25 per cent on the previous year. The most commonly seized type of NPS was synthetic cannabinoids.

It is not an offence to possess an NPS (except in a custodial institution (s 9 of the PSA 2016)), but there are dedicated police powers to stop and search for such substances (see 9.4.2 for further details) and there are offences of production and supply (see 12.6). The Crime Surveys for England and Wales now include references to psychoactive substances, and a *New Psychoactive Substances Resource Pack* is available on the gov.uk website. The DrugWise website also provides 'evidence-based information' on NPSs.

Some everyday retail items also contain psychoactive substances. These items include solvent-based glues, correction fluids/thinners, marker pens, aerosols, anti-freeze, nail varnish, nail varnish remover, and whipped cream canisters. Where substances are sold by a retailer for their intended use the sale will not be an offence unless the cashier suspects or believes the product is likely to be consumed for its psychoactive effect.

12.5.2 Unlawful possession of a controlled drug

The most frequently encountered drugs offence is unlawful possession. In order to commit this offence (s 5(2) of the Misuse of Drugs Act), as the diagram shows, a person must:

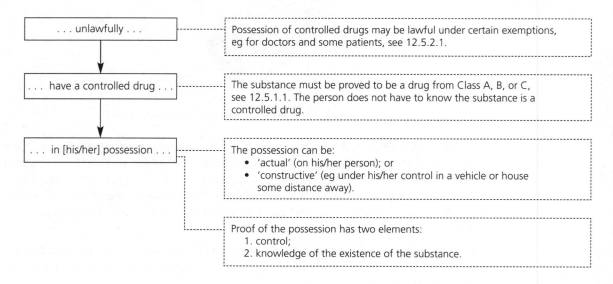

Control of a substance is indicated by the rights the person has over the substance, and generally amounts to ownership. It would include:

- items found on a person (eg in the pocket of a jacket he/she is wearing);
- items found in a person's property; and
- items a person has ordered and paid for but has not yet received.

Having control would also include having custody of an item when a person knows he/she has temporary or partial responsibility for an item, with the owner's consent or knowledge.

Knowledge of the existence of a substance is also required. If a woman has something in her pocket she must know it is there. If the substance was inside a container, it must be proved that she both knew the container was in her pocket and that it contained a substance.

As an example, imagine that a man is searched using the powers under s 23 of the Misuse of Drugs Act 1971 (see 9.4.1). The police officer conducting the search finds some kitchen foil with traces of brown powder on it tucked into the top of the man's sock. After examination, the brown powder is identified as heroin. To prove the offence of possession it must therefore be shown that:

- the foil with the powder was in the man's sock;
- the man knew the foil and powder were there (it does not matter whether or not he knew the substance was a controlled drug);
- the powder was heroin; and
- he was not lawfully entitled to possess heroin.

In relation to stop and search, s 23(2) of the Misuse of Drugs Act 1971 has its own power of search (see 9.4.1).

12.5.2.1 Exemptions permitting lawful possession of a controlled drug

Possession of a controlled drug is lawful for some workers as part of their job, for example as suppliers to the pharmaceutical trade, or as doctors (note that proper prescribing records must be kept). Such exemptions are provided under the Misuse of Drugs Regulations 2001 and made by the Home Secretary under s 7 of the Misuse of Drugs Act 1971. Patients who have been prescribed controlled drugs are also provided for under the exemptions (see 12.5.3.4). Regulation 6 allows police officers, police support employees, customs officers, and postal workers to possess drugs whilst acting in the course of their duties.

12.5.3 Unlawful possession of cannabis and khat

Cannabis is a Class B drug, and khat (a herbal stimulant which is usually chewed) is a Class C drug. The majority of cannabis available illegally in the UK is 'skunk', which generally contains higher concentrations of psychoactive compounds, compared with other forms of cannabis.

12.5.3.1 Intervention model for the unlawful possession of cannabis and khat

The intervention model helps provide a justifiable and proportionate response, and the intention is to send out the message that cannabis and khat are harmful and illegal. There are three levels of intervention (see the diagram) but the guidance emphasizes that arrest remains the first presumption, although discretion can be used at all times. Cannabis and khat warnings are covered in more detail in 12.5.3.2.

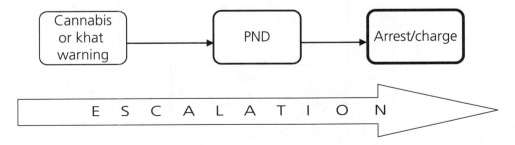

Under the intervention model, PNDs and warnings can only be used if the person:

- is aged 18 years or over and has verifiable personal details (name, date of birth, and address);
- is not vulnerable (see 13.2);
- is competent enough to grasp the meaning of the officer's questions and can reply to questions coherently;

- is not under the influence of alcohol or drugs at the time the warning or PND is issued;
- possesses an amount of cannabis or khat only suitable for personal use (in the officer's judgement);
- is not in possession of any other drug; and
- admits the possession of cannabis or khat (this only applies for warnings, and not for PNDs, see 12.5.3.2).

Aggravating factors must be taken into consideration when deciding which option to take in the intervention model. The location where the person is found to be in possession can be an aggravating factor. This could be a previously identified 'hot spot' for anti-social behaviour due to cannabis/khat use (eg a corner of a park) or any place young people are more likely to be such as a playground or youth club. Other possible aggravating factors include smoking cannabis or chewing khat in a public place or in the view of the public, being a repeat offender (including other criminal offences) or someone who continually engages in anti-social behaviour, and appearing to fail to recognize the seriousness of the situation. If there are one or more aggravating factors, then professional discretion (see 5.5.3) should be used to decide whether to issue a PND or make an arrest. If there are no aggravating factors then a warning is the likely outcome.

The PNC can be used to find out whether the suspect has received a relevant warning or a PND, as these cannot be used more than once. Professional police discretion should be applied, but there is no need to employ each stage of the model in sequence: arrest can be used even if the suspect has never received a relevant warning or a PND. When a suspect does not admit the unlawful possession, a PND can only be used if there is sufficient evidence (see 12.5.2) to prove the offence. For suspects aged under 18, a youth caution can be used as an alternative (see 10.13.2.4).

The large flowchart with the shaded boxes shows the main factors to take into account when dealing with suspects in possession of cannabis or khat. Individual circumstances and the use of discretion mean that the diagram can only provide an indication of the more usual outcomes, and does not cover every eventuality. The shaded boxes relate to the intervention model.

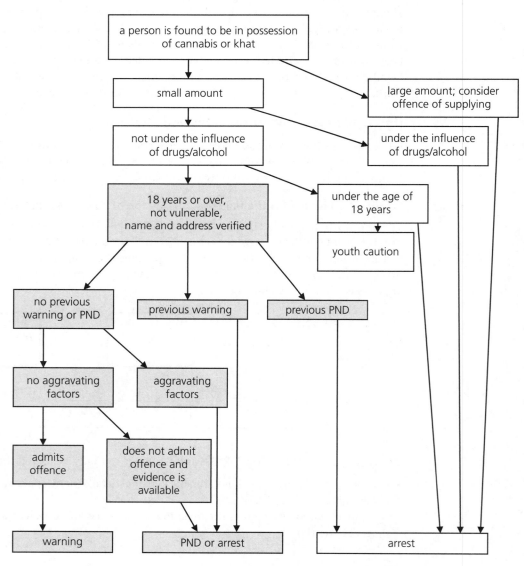

12.5.3.2 Cannabis and khat warnings

These warnings can only be issued when there are no aggravating factors (see 12.5.3.1), and when the person is compliant with the procedure, admits to the offence, and has no previous records of relevant warnings, PNDs, or convictions. The current guidance is that no more than one warning should be issued to an individual. However, under the previous guidance two warnings were allowed, so warnings issued before 26 January 2009 should not be taken into account (except as part of the general previous offending history).

There is no formal group of words for a cannabis or khat warning, but the terms 'cannabis warning' or 'khat warning' should be used (rather than 'street warning'). The officer should tell the suspect that the warning will not amount to a criminal record or conviction but will:

- be recorded and added to local police databases for future reference;
- produce a record of a detected crime for the purposes of statistics as a recordable crime; and
- lead to the issuing of a PND or arrest if he/she is found in unlawful possession of cannabis or khat in the future.

Further guidance on cases involving khat can be found in the document *National Policing Guidelines on KHAT Possession for Personal Use Intervention Framework*, available online.

12.5.3.3 Possession of small amounts of cannabis or khat: practical aspects

For suspects in possession of small amounts of cannabis or khat a police officer should investigate the suspected unlawful possession, remembering to follow the PACE Codes of Practice to protect the rights of the individual (see 10.3 on cautions). The officer should try to establish whether there is any lawful excuse for possession (see 12.5.2.1 and 12.5.4), or if there is any evidence of a more serious offence such as intent to supply (see 12.6.2 and 12.6.3). The drugs should be seized and secured according to local policy (see 10.9 and 11.2.6). The incident should be recorded at the time as a PNB entry. The recording requirements must also be satisfied, and stop and search forms will need to be completed (see 9.2.1.5). Intelligence reports and crime reports can be completed later.

Any arrest must be 'necessary' (see 10.6.4). For details on issuing a PND for possessing cannabis or khat, see para 3.2 of the Home Office operational guidance available at <http://www.justice.gov.uk/downloads/oocd/pnd-guidance-oocd.pdf>.

12.5.3.4 Medical prescription of cannabis-based products

Cannabis-based products can now be prescribed by doctors for medicinal use (SI 2018/1055 The Misuse of Drugs (Amendments) (Cannabis and Licence Fees) (England, Wales and Scotland) Regulations 2018). The drug is often prescribed in the form of a mouth spray, for example Sativex. Note that the 2018 Regulations still prohibit the smoking of cannabis and cannabis-based products for medicinal use.

You might find it useful to consider how the new regulations might apply in practice in relation to valuing difference and inclusion within the community; one such scenario is presented here from the perspective of a police officer.

A police officer has been deployed to managed accommodation for senior citizens on a large housing estate. On arrival, the manager reports that one of the inhabitants, a 70-year-old man, has not been seen for a couple of days and there is cause for concern. The officer receives no answer at the front door and so accesses the rear of the flat via a communal garden, where the officer is able to look through the ground-floor bedroom window. Inside the room, he can see an old man sitting upright in bed—he is startled by the officer. One of the small windows of the bedroom is partially open and a strong smell of cigarette smoke emanates. The officer calls for the front door to be opened and the man gets out of bed and opens the door and invites the officer in. Once inside the flat, the officer can clearly make out an earthy, herbal, woody aroma and asks the man what he is smoking. He replies that he has been prescribed cannabis by his doctor for the relief of chronic pain, and says 'so there is nothing to worry about'. He shows the officer a small Sativex container, a quarter ounce bag of cannabis resin, some rolling tobacco, cigarette papers, and a repeat prescription form in his name.

The senior citizen appears to be in unlawful possession of the cannabis resin and the officer is obliged to take action and clarify the situation with him. The intervention model described in 12.5.3.1 can be used in these circumstances, and taking into account the elderly man's rather unusual circumstances, the officer decides to simply issue a warning (after seizing the cannabis resin, and checking all the criteria for a warning have been met).

12.5.4 Defences and penalties for unlawful possession of a controlled drug

In addition to the possession being lawful (see 12.5.2.1), a number of other circumstances can provide a defence (s 5(4), the Misuse of Drugs Act 1971). The flowchart provides more details about these particular circumstances and the conditions that must be satisfied.

Preventing unlawful possession under s 5 of the Misuse of Drugs Act 1971 is defined as:

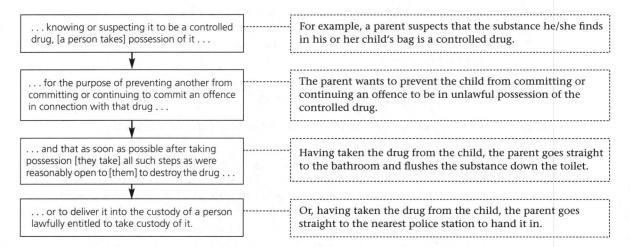

Other defences are available under s 28 of the Misuse of Drugs Act 1971. These relate to two main issues: whether the suspect knew or believed the substance was a controlled drug, and whether he/she was entitled to possess that particular drug (s 28(3)(b)(i) and (ii) respectively). The onus is on the suspect to prove that he/she did not know or suspect some relevant point of fact alleged by the prosecution. Trainee police officers are unlikely to be involved in this process.

Offences involving Class A, B, or C drugs are triable either way and the penalty is imprisonment and/or a fine. The lengths of prison sentences are shown in the table. Unlawful possession of cannabis can also be dealt with by issuing a PND for £90 (see 10.13.2.2 and 12.5.3).

Class	As a summary offence	As an indictable offence
A	Six months	Seven years
B	Three months	Five years
C	Three months	Two years

TASK 5 Establishing whether someone is in unlawful possession of controlled drugs is not always straightforward. Identifying a substance as a controlled drug is relatively straightforward but proving possession is more complicated. Consider the following three scenarios and try and decide whether possession has been established in each case.

1. Before going out to a party one night Ethan puts some cannabis into a wallet. He goes out and gets very drunk and can't remember the night's events. He returns home the next day and puts his coat containing the wallet back into his wardrobe. Some days later he puts the coat on again forgetting it contains the wallet with the cannabis. He is subsequently stopped and searched by the police and the cannabis is found. Is he guilty of unlawful possession?

2. Fred is searched under s 23 of the Misuse of Drugs Act 1971 and the officer finds tablets suspected to be controlled drugs in his trouser pocket. He claimed that they had been prescribed by a doctor some months ago but that he had lost them, so obtained another prescription from his doctor for some more tablets. He says he later found the missing tablets at the back of a

drawer and put them in his pocket, where they are found by the police. Was he in unlawful possession of the tablets at the time?

3. Georgina was entertaining visitors when a search warrant under s 23(3) of the Misuse of Drugs Act 1971 was executed. A small quantity of heroin was found on the sofa in between two guests and she admitted to the police officers present that she was the owner. But when she was formally interviewed she withdrew the admission and named the person she claimed was of the true owner. She also stated that one of her visitors had probably had drugs in his possession in her flat, and that another had been preparing to take heroin before the search took place. Are the circumstances sufficient for Georgina to have been in control of the drugs?

12.6 Production and Supply Offences

Drugs legislation has been carefully worded so that it is not only the illegal end user who is subject to prosecution, but also (and perhaps more importantly) the people involved in the supply chain. The legislation relating to the illegal production and supply of controlled drugs is in ss 4–6 of the Misuse of Drugs Act 1971. Defences to production and supply offences relate to proving possession, and whether the substance in question actually is a controlled drug, but see also 12.5.6 on s 28 and other defences for possession. For psychoactive substances, production and supply offences are covered in ss 4–7 of the PSA 2016. As for controlled drugs, certain activities such as approved scientific research, or work carried out by health care professionals are exempted for the purposes of this Act (s 11).

The supply of drugs to smaller towns often occurs through 'county lines'. Investigating such matters often involves a number of forces working together, which creates additional challenges. We cover county lines in 12.7.

12.6.1 Production of controlled drugs or psychoactive substances

It is an offence to produce a controlled drug or be concerned in the production without a licence from the Secretary of State (s 4(2) of the Misuse of Drugs Act 1971). Growing plants and carrying out chemical processes are included under the umbrella term 'producing', while 'being concerned in the production' would include delivering chemicals, providing premises, or providing finance.

For production of cannabis plants, the Home Office recommends charging under s 4(2) as the charge of 'cultivation of cannabis' (s 6(2)) does not allow for confiscation proceedings (Circular 82/1980). The defences outlined in s 28 of the Misuse of Drugs Act 1971 (see 12.5.4) apply to both these offences.

Offences involving production of controlled drugs are triable either way and the penalty is imprisonment and/or a fine. The maximum lengths of prison sentences are shown in the table.

Class	As a summary offence	As an indictable offence
A	Six months	Life
B	Six months	14 years
C	Three months	Five years

Section 4(2) offences for a Class A drug are 'trigger' offences under s 63B of the PACE Act 1984: this means a sample can be demanded from a person in police custody (see 26.6 on taking samples from people).

The intentional production of a psychoactive substance is an offence under s 4(1) of the PSA 2016. The person must know or suspect that the substance is a psychoactive substance and also:

- intend to consume it for its psychoactive effects; or
- know (or be reckless as to whether) it will be consumed by another person for its psychoactive effects.

Specific Incidents

This offence is triable either way, and the penalty is a fine and/or imprisonment (12 months if tried summarily, and up to seven years' imprisonment on indictment).

12.6.2 Supply offences

These offences (including offering to supply) are covered under s 4 of the Misuse of Drugs Act 1971 for controlled drugs, and under s 4 of the PSA 2016 for psychoactive substances. A court must treat a supply offence more seriously if it was committed in or near to a school, or if the suspect used a courier under the age of 18.

For controlled drugs, supply offences are covered under s 4(3) of the Misuse of Drugs Act 1971 as shown in the diagram.

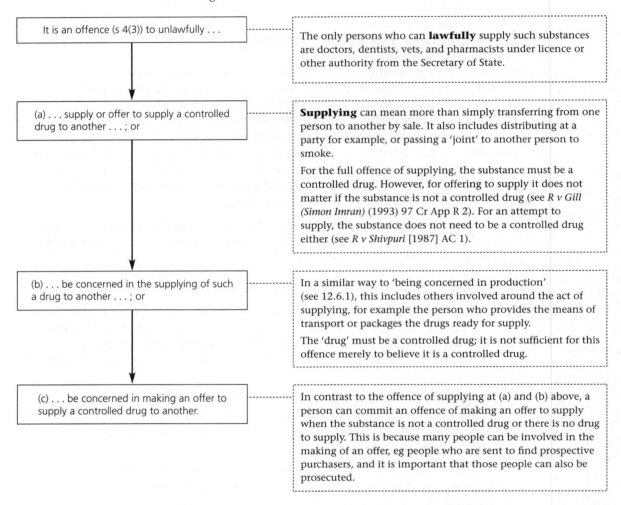

| It is an offence (s 4(3)) to unlawfully . . . | The only persons who can **lawfully** supply such substances are doctors, dentists, vets, and pharmacists under licence or other authority from the Secretary of State. |

(a) . . . supply or offer to supply a controlled drug to another . . . ; or

Supplying can mean more than simply transferring from one person to another by sale. It also includes distributing at a party for example, or passing a 'joint' to another person to smoke.

For the full offence of supplying, the substance must be a controlled drug. However, for offering to supply it does not matter if the substance is not a controlled drug (see *R v Gill (Simon Imran)* (1993) 97 Cr App R 2). For an attempt to supply, the substance does not need to be a controlled drug either (see *R v Shivpuri* [1987] AC 1).

(b) . . . be concerned in the supplying of such a drug to another . . . ; or

In a similar way to 'being concerned in production' (see 12.6.1), this includes others involved around the act of supplying, for example the person who provides the means of transport or packages the drugs ready for supply.

The 'drug' must be a controlled drug; it is not sufficient for this offence merely to believe it is a controlled drug.

(c) . . . be concerned in making an offer to supply a controlled drug to another.

In contrast to the offence of supplying at (a) and (b) above, a person can commit an offence of making an offer to supply when the substance is not a controlled drug or there is no drug to supply. This is because many people can be involved in the making of an offer, eg people who are sent to find prospective purchasers, and it is important that those people can also be prosecuted.

The defences outlined in 12.5.4 also apply here. The penalties are the same as for the production of a controlled drug (see 12.6.1). The offence is a trigger offence: a police officer can demand a sample from a suspect in custody.

For psychoactive substances, it is an offence to intentionally supply such a substance to another person (s 5(1) of the PSA 2016), but this only applies if the suspect:

- knows or suspects (or ought to) that the substance is psychoactive; and
- knows or suspects (or ought to) or is reckless as to whether another person is likely to consume it for its psychoactive effects.

The parallel offences concerning an offer to supply are covered under s 5(2). These offences are all triable either way, and the penalty is a fine and/or imprisonment (12 months if tried summarily, and up to seven years' imprisonment on indictment).

12.6.3 Possession with intent to supply

Possession of a controlled drug with intent to supply is an offence under s 5(3) of the Misuse of Drugs Act 1971. The substance in question must be a controlled drug (unlike the s 4(3) supplying offence), but need not be the drug the suspect believes it to be, so a suspect who believed the drug was heroin can still be guilty even if it is found to be cocaine. It is not relevant whether the possession is lawful, so a chemist or police officer in lawful possession could commit this offence if he/she intended to unlawfully supply the drug. The defences outlined in s 28 of the Misuse of Drugs Act 1971 also apply to s 5(3) (see 12.5.4). The penalties are the same as for the production of a controlled drug, and the s 5(3) offence is a trigger offence: a police officer can demand a sample from a suspect held in custody (see 12.6.1).

For psychoactive substances, possession with intent to supply is covered under s 7(1)(a) of the Psychoactive Substances Act 2016. The suspect must know (or suspect) that the substance is psychoactive (s 7(1)(b)), and intend to supply it to another person for consumption (by any person) for its psychoactive effects. Offences under s 7 are triable either way, and the penalty is a fine and/or imprisonment (12 months if tried summarily, and up to seven years' imprisonment on indictment).

12.6.4 Occupier or manager of premises used for controlled drug offences

This offence (s 8 of the Misuse of Drugs Act 1971) concerns persons who occupy or are concerned in the management of a premises, and who 'knowingly permit or suffer' any of the following activities to take place there:

(a) producing or attempting to produce a controlled drug;
(b) supplying, attempting to supply, or offering to supply a controlled drug to another;
(c) preparing opium for smoking;
(d) smoking cannabis, cannabis resin, or prepared opium.

There must be evidence that one of these activities has actually occurred (see *R v Auguste* [2003] EWCA Crim 3329). For example, in relation to (b) above, there must be evidence of a controlled drug actually being supplied on the premises: the simple existence of sufficient quantities and equipment for supplying controlled drugs is insufficient to prove the offence (see *R v McGee* [2012] EWCA Crim 613). The suspect does not need to know what type of controlled drug is involved.

To be an 'occupier' the person does not have to be a tenant or owner, but needs to have sufficient control over the premises such that he/she could prevent drug-related activities. A student who pays for a room on campus would be regarded as an occupier. A person 'concerned in the management' does not have to have a legal interest in the premises, and would include a trespassing squatter (see *R v Tao* [1976] 3 All ER 65). A cleaner would be neither an occupier nor concerned in the management. To 'knowingly permit or suffer' would include the person having suspicions but choosing to take no action, and also trying to stop the activity but without success. Powers are available to close premises that are being used for controlled drug offences (see 14.2.2.4).

Offences under s 8 are triable either way. If tried summarily the penalty is a fine and/or imprisonment (six months for Classes A and B, and three months for Class C). On indictment the penalty is a fine and/or up to 14 years' imprisonment.

12.6.5 Import and export of controlled drugs or psychoactive substances

The legal import and export of controlled drugs requires a licence, and is covered under s 3(1) of the Misuse of Drugs Act 1971. Without a relevant licence it is an offence under s 170 of the Customs and Excise Management Act 1979 to knowingly acquire possession or be concerned in transporting, storing or concealing such drugs, or be concerned in any fraudulent evasion or attempted evasion of such a restriction. These offences are triable either way. The penalty for a Class A or B drug is imprisonment (life and 14 years, respectively), and for Class C on summary conviction three months' imprisonment and/or a fine, and on indictment, five years' imprisonment.

For psychoactive substances, it is an offence to intentionally import or export such a substance (s 8(1) and (2) PSA 2016, respectively). The person must know or suspect (or ought to know or suspect in the circumstances) that the substance is psychoactive. He/she must also intend to consume it for its effects, or know or be reckless as to whether some other person is likely to consume it for its effects. Offences under s 7 are triable either way, and the penalty is a fine and/or imprisonment (12 months if tried summarily, and up to seven years' imprisonment on indictment).

TASK 6

1. Make a list of factors and circumstances that would provide reasonable grounds for suspecting a man is in unlawful possession of drugs with intent to supply.
2. What would a police officer have to say to him before carrying out a search under s 23 of the Misuse of Drugs Act 1971?
3. Having found an unidentifiable substance, what are some of the reasons that would make it necessary to arrest him?

12.7 County Lines

A 'county line' is where an organized criminal group run a drug dealing operation in a county location outside their usual urban operating area. County lines have become more evident since around 2013. In the words of Coomber and Moyle, county lines are 'a new insidious drug-dealing model, fast permeating provincial drug markets in the United Kingdom' (Coomber and Moyle, 2018, p 1338). In January 2019 the NCA estimated that there were at least a thousand county lines operating in the UK, with approximately 300 originating in the Greater London area (NCA, 2019a, p 2). It is likely therefore that county lines are operating in almost all police force areas in the UK.

Criminal groups (possibly a 'gang') create a network between an urban 'hub' (such as areas within London, Manchester, Liverpool) and county locations (typically towns in counties such as Kent) to supply recreational and other types of illegal drugs to the county locations. In doing so the urban group may force out local illegal drug suppliers. There is some evidence that county lines developed because drug suppliers needed to establish new markets owing to 'market saturation' in city locations (Robinson *et al*, 2019, p 695), and also to avoid police attention (Stone, 2018, p 286).

There are a number of informal terms associated with county lines which student police officers might find useful, as shown in the table.

Term	Explanation
'Trap House'	A building in the county location which is used as a base from which drugs are sold. Occupants include drug users. Examples include homes of those 'cuckooed' but also short-term lets, cheap hotel accommodation.
'Cuckooing'	When a county lines group will take over the home of a vulnerable person (eg those experiencing drug dependency, mental health problems, financial insecurity) using acts of intimidation and violence. (The term is a reference to the nesting behaviour of cuckoos—they take over the nests of other birds). The group will then use the property as their trap house.
'Going Country' (or 'Out There', 'OT')	This has different meanings such as: county lines activity in general, an individual becoming involved in county lines, or the act of travelling to another area, city, or town to deliver drugs or money.
'Trapping'	Either the selling of illegal drugs via a county line, or the moving of drugs from the urban hub to the county location.
'Deal line'	The branded mobile phone number operated by the county line group and used to communicate (primarily to take orders for drugs) with possibly hundreds of drug users.
'Taxing'	Use of violence to exercise control over a county lines member (eg marking or injuring).

A dedicated 'branded' mobile phone line (or multiple lines) is set up to take supply orders from local illegal drug users, usually operated by a 'third party'. The urban hubs are often also the locations for the storage of imported drugs. Drugs are supplied according to the orders taken on the 'branded' phone, and the payments are collected by locally recruited couriers. The NCA reports that vulnerable children, such as those experiencing family breakdown or developmental disorders, are frequently targeted by county line offenders (NCA, 2019a, p 3) to work as couriers and runners. The recruits may also be involved in cutting and bagging illegal drugs. As the NCA notes, the groups involved in running county lines will often employ coercion, intimidation, and violence (NCA, 2019a). Sexual exploitation, modern-day slavery, and human trafficking can also be present as part of the functioning of a county line. The Home Office has published guidance for law enforcement and other professionals, aimed at helping to counter the criminal exploitation of children and vulnerable adults (Home Office, 2018c).

A recent example of a law enforcement initiative against a county line was the Devon and Cornwall Police 'Ligament' operation to take down the 'Billy Line', which had been running a drugs supply network from London to Cornwall. In July 2018 local police had visited a house in Newquay after reports from members of the public concerning apparent drug dealing. A 16-year-old boy was found in possession of a large quantity of drugs and enquiries showed that the boy had been reported as missing. It emerged that the boy had been moved by a county line group to the flat of a 56-year-old heroin addict in Bodmin after failure to meet a debt (*The Guardian*, 2019). The boy had found himself caught up in a county line supplying over 90 drug users in that part of Cornwall. The group had used hire cars to transport drugs from their north London hub to Cornwall; a total of 18 vehicles were hired and 65 return journeys made between January and December 2018 (Cornwall Live, 2019). Five different mobile phones were used to operate the 'Billy Line'. The whole scheme was run by a prisoner from his cell in Wandsworth prison (BBC, 2019).

12.7.1 Offences associated with county lines

The offences associated with county lines include:

- Illegal drugs supply offences—the illegal distribution and dealing in potentially dangerous drugs from town to town, eg s 4(3) of Misuse of Drugs Act 1971 (see 12.6.2).
- Use of firearms, offensive weapons, and bladed objects—the Firearms Act 1968, the Prevention of Crime Act 1953, and the Criminal Justice Act 1988 are relevant here (see Chapter 18).
- Violence—Gangs can use violence to intimidate children and young people in order to recruit them. Offences to be considered include those offences set out in the Offences against the Person Act 1861; and attempted murder (see 14.11 on gangs).
- Abuse and exploitation—Young people and children are exploited to move drugs and money. Both young girls and boys may be subject to grooming and coerced into relationships and made to perform sex acts. Women who have entered into relationships with county line members are often controlled, coerced, and subject to sexual abuse and exploitation; relevant legislation will include the Sexual Offences Act 2003 (see Chapter 17) and the Modern Slavery Act 2015 (see 13.5).

There are sometimes complex issues for police and CPS about whether some of those involved in committing offences whilst involved with a county line (particularly children and young people) were also at the same time victims of trafficking and/or exploitation. In principle, s 45 of the Modern Slavery Act 2015 provides a statutory defence for victims of trafficking. The CPS has published guidance on the approach to be adopted in these circumstances.

12.7.2 Detailed characteristics of county lines

Research is ongoing concerning the structures and MOs typically employed by county lines and, in any event, these are likely to change over time. There are also likely to be significant local and regional variations. What follows is a summary of current thinking but, for obvious reasons, confidential details have been removed. (If you are a trainee police officer your force training is likely to provide greater detail and local contextualization).

A county line group will be based in an urban location, typically a metropolitan area such as Greater London or Merseyside. It is likely to have an informal structure, but may include some sort of hierarchy with 'teenies, runners, youngers, links, baby mamas, baes/wifeys, gangster girls, elders and faces/olders' (Williams and Finlay, 2018, p 730). Many county line operations will operate over 50 to 75 miles, but some may span several hundred miles.

Although almost any county town or district may be attractive to the groups involved, some coastal towns appear to be particularly at risk. Locations experiencing economic problems, with plentiful availability of cheap accommodation and higher concentrations of at-risk individuals seem to have been targets. However, houses in more affluent towns, and locations such as rooms at university halls of residence (with a strong local market in 'recreational' illegal drugs) have also been subject to county lines 'takeovers'.

County lines groups often use public transport or hire cars to move illegal drugs and other commodities from the urban hub to the county locations. Runners from hubs sometimes stop short of the final destination in order to avoid detection by law enforcement, or complete the journey by a different means. Runners are often young people, particularly young women, and the illegal drugs might be 'plugged' within the body of the runner (typically in the rectum and/or vagina).

To promote and organize the selling of illegal drugs the county line will probably use a 'branded' mobile phone number to create a brand that drug users can associate with. The number is then marketed in the area, for example through social media, business cards, and free cigarette lighters (Wigmore, 2018, p 6). Unlike some other criminal activities where mobile numbers are frequently changed, these numbers have value and so are maintained and protected. However, there are some signs that offenders may now be moving to more 'secure' forms of communication that use end-to-end forms of encryption, such as WhatsApp (PNLD, 2018).

At the end of the line are the county line drug distribution centres (the 'trap houses', some of which have been 'cuckooed'). The trap house could be a house or flat near the railway station in a seaside town, but could also be a short-term let (including holiday and AirBnB lets) or a budget hotel room. County line gang members will probably 'assess what such a base could offer (e.g. proximity to the town centre, nearby alleyways, the absence of CCTV etc.)' (Jaensch and South, 2018, p 8). The trap house is local base for the county line and will be the centre for providing illegal drugs for not only the town, but for surrounding estates and other nearby towns as well. Drug orders made through the branded line are collected from the trap house by the purchaser or delivered by locally 'recruited' runners. The runners are often children and young people, and 'clean skins' are preferred (ie those without previous convictions). Forms of 'recruitment' include not only financial inducements (cash, designer clothes), but also coercion, grooming, deception (eg apparent friendship and status), intimidation and threats, and forms of 'debt bondage' (services provided to the county line in lieu of repayment of debts, eg payment for drugs). There is some evidence that county lines groups deliberately target vulnerable children and young people, such as those excluded from school (eg at Pupil Referral Units), young people living in care homes, or those with learning difficulties (The Children's Society, 2020).

12.7.3 Law enforcement response

Given the complex nature of county lines and their geographical spread, a multi-agency approach (see 13.7.5) is usually adopted to detecting or disrupting their activities. This will include the police forces concerned working in collaboration. They will also work in partnership with other agencies (such as local authority social services), and with their Regional Organised Crime Unit (ROCU). (A ROCU covers many forces over a large area—the North-West ROCU, for example, covers Cumbria, Cheshire, Lancashire, Greater Manchester, Merseyside, and North Wales.) The police will need to agree on how to utilize intelligence on county lines operating in their areas, and then select the best disruptive measures in the particular context and make arrangements for joint investigation.

In 2018 the NCA and NPCC launched the National County Lines Coordination Centre (NCLCC). The NCLCC is responsible for 'mapping out the threat from county lines nationally and prioritising action against the most significant perpetrators' (NPCC, 2019), and also provides support for front line police officers. During 2019, the NCLCC coordinated four separate weeks of intensive law enforcement action resulting in over 2,500 arrests. In addition over 3,000 individuals were safeguarded, and the police seized significant quantities of weapons and drugs.

The safeguarding issues for children, young people, and other vulnerable individuals (such as those with mental health problems) will necessitate a multi-agency response. Where the local police service has reason to believe that a child is involved in a county lines network they are expected (without delay) to make a safeguarding referral using a locally agreed 'pathway' process. (If there are reasonable grounds to suspect that a child is suffering or is likely to suffer significant harm, a s 47 Enquiry (Children Act 1989) is initiated, see 13.3.1).

The police or prosecution can also use orders and injunctions in addition to prosecutions for offences, or where such prosecutions might be difficult to mount. The injunctions and orders include:

- Slavery and Trafficking Risk Orders (STRO, see 13.5.3.4);
- Drug Dealing Telecommunications Restriction Orders Regulations 2017 (under the Digital Economy Act 2017), though these are unlikely to cause long-term disruption to county lines communications as the operators are likely to keep separate records of customers' contact details to transfer to a replacement phone (it is easy in the UK for anyone (including drug dealers) to anonymously buy a replacement 'burner' mobile phone and number through 'pay as you go' services);
- injunctions under the Policing and Crime Act 2009 to prevent gang-related violence and gang-related drug dealing activity to be sought against an individual;
- 'closure of premises' powers under the Anti-social Behaviour, Crime and Policing Act 2014 (see 14.2.2.4) can be used to close down 'trap houses'; and
- Criminal Behaviour Orders (see 14.2.1.2) are available for people convicted of offences associated with county lines.

Student police officers should be aware of the local recruitment strategies employed by county line offenders, including through social media. Increasing your knowledge and understanding of the street-level slang language associated with drug dealing and county lines is also useful; you can then listen out for it. You should also pass on any intelligence, using the NIM approach adopted by your force. Relevant intelligence could include:

- changes in drug supply patterns;
- unusual hire car use;
- the names of any local branded lines (a weakness of a county line set up is that their 'business' model depends on promoting the existence of the semi-permanent branded line);
- changes in 'ownership' of the line (it is not unknown for these to be traded or sold between groups);
- signs and symptoms of cuckooing at local properties;
- signs of targeting of vulnerable children and adults, such as control mechanisms employed by county lines.

In particular, where children go missing or absent (see 13.4 on missing persons), even if only for a few hours or overnight, consideration should be given to a possible connection with a county line (see the Safeguarding Hub, 2020).

12.8 Answers to Tasks

TASK 1 Look at s 34(1) of the Criminal Justice Act 1972 to help with the answer.

- The health and safety of the individual is paramount—is she injured in any way, and how drunk is she?
- What offence has she committed? Is she just drunk, or 'drunk and disorderly'?
- Is arrest necessary to prevent her from causing physical injury (to herself or others) or could the matter be dealt with in another way?
- What other agencies could be contacted? If there is an approved treatment centre for alcoholism in the area, the officer could treat her as being in lawful custody for the purposes of the journey (s 34(1) of the Criminal Justice Act 1972).

TASK 2

- Introduce yourself, giving your name and your station.
- Explain that you suspect he is under 18 years of age.
- Tell him that he is in a public place.
- Make clear to him that you wish him to surrender any intoxicating liquor in his possession, and to give his name and address, and that failure without reasonable excuse to comply is an offence.

TASK 3 Some forces have a member of staff who is responsible for representing the police at applications for premises licences or renewals. He/she should be notified of incidents where suspects have been drinking excessively so this can be taken into account when deciding on granting or renewing licences.

TASK 4 Some common unlawfully used controlled drugs (and their prices in 2017, the most recently available *Drugwise* survey) are:

- **amphetamines** (speed, whizz, w, billy, uppers, phet, amph, wizz, white, sulphate, snow, sprint, bomb, base, paste, dexies). The average UK street price is £5 upwards per gram;
- **cocaine** (coke, crack, charlie, sniff, white, ching, powder, snow white, snuff, rock, nose candy, okey cokey, fairy dust, Bolivian marching powder, toot, wrap). The average UK street price is £30–40 per gram, and £10–20 for a 'rock' of crack cocaine weighing 0.25 grams;
- **heroin** (smack, crack, brown, gear, shit, jack, skag, henry, horse, needles). The average UK street price is £10 per 0.1g bag; and
- **cannabis** (weed, skunk, pot, dope, bud, green, blow, hash, ganja, grass, draw, puff, gange, shit, spliff, wacky backy, pukka, rocky, joint, hashish, resin, doobie, gear, bush, smoke, leaf, stash, buddha, rasta pasta, chill, mary jane, to blaze, marijuana, squidgy black, rock, purple haze, sensimilia, hemp, herb, blow, soap, blunt). The average UK street price per quarter ounce is £37 for standard herbal cannabis, £55 for high-strength 'skunk'. The street cost of 'Spice' varies considerably but is approximately £10 per gram.

(Information derived from a number of sources including <http://www.drugwise.org.uk/how-much-do-drugs-cost/>.

There are other online sources of information, see for instance <http://www.dnalegal.com>.

TASK 5

1. Yes. In *R v Martindale* (1986) 84 Cr App R 31 (CA), Lord Lane stated that:

   Possession does not depend upon the alleged possessor's powers of memory. Nor does possession come and go as memory revives or fails. If it were to do so, a man with a poor memory would be acquitted, he with a good memory would be convicted.

2. Yes, his possession was lawful. The original possession of the tablets was lawful and the lawfulness continues with time (see *R v Buswell* [1972] 1 WLR 64).
3. No, she cannot be said to be in control of the drug. There is insufficient actual or physical control of the heroin in this situation (see *Adams v DPP* [2002] All ER (D) 125 (Mar)).

TASK 6

1. Factors and circumstances that would provide reasonable grounds for suspecting he is in unlawful possession of drugs with intent to supply might include:
   - intelligence that drugs are being supplied or used in that particular area;
   - descriptions of people supplying or using drugs in that area;
   - his behaviour (eg he may seem to be trying to hide something, or preparing to secretly throw something away); and
   - other people's behaviour (eg do a series of individuals approach him in turn, and exchange small items and then walk away? Note that these may be very open acts, to try and avoid attracting attention).
2. Before the search, the police officer must explain the purpose of the search, explain the grounds, tell him about his entitlement to a copy of the record of search, show a warrant card (if out of uniform), and explain to him that he is being detained for a search under s 23 of the Misuse of Drugs Act 1971. The officer must also provide his/her name and station. This can be summarized by the mnemonic GO WISELY (see 9.2.1.3 for full details).
3. Here, the reasons for making an arrest (see 10.6.4) could be to prevent injury through the use of the drug(s), or to ensure a prompt investigation by questioning him and arranging for analysis of the drug(s).

13 Protection from Violence, Abuse, and Neglect

13.1 Introduction

In the police environment, the term 'Public protection' has a broad meaning. Although it is often associated with the management of violent and sexual offenders the term is also applied to protecting victims through investigating incidents involving sexual offences, violence, child abuse, vulnerable adult abuse, domestic abuse, hate crime, and missing persons. The police will often be tasked with the initial protection of vulnerable people, young people, and people who may lack the mental capacity to make decisions. In this chapter we explore how the police can respond to these situations, and describe the procedures and available powers. An initial assessment will often be needed to help establish the most appropriate course of action. For example, the police inevitably come into contact with people with mental health difficulties, but they are not obliged to assume responsibility. Other partner agencies are often better equipped to deal with such issues and may have statutory responsibility for providing support and services (although the police will often assist). It is also important that individuals are treated fairly and do not suffer discrimination (s 149 of the Equality Act 2010). This means that, where possible, the police have a duty to make reasonable adjustments to ensure that individuals with protected characteristics are not discriminated against. Note that women and individuals from ethnic minorities are 'over-represented' in the mental health system, and may require specific forms of intervention when displaying unusual forms of behaviour.

If you are a trainee police officer, undertaking the PCDA or DHEP, then responding to a public protection incident as a 'First Responder' may differ from other incidents to which you may be deployed. The introduction to Chapter 15 provides information on how to manage violent and aggressive people. Responding to a domestic abuse incident is covered in detail in 13.6. After ascertaining the initial circumstances on arrival and having taken any immediate actions to prevent any further harm to individuals, you would conduct a risk assessment. When completing such an initial assessment, THRIVE is now often the preferred model adopted by police forces, in conjunction with the National Decision Model (see 5.5.2).

The victim may need support, and this needs to be done in an ethical and appropriate manner. Other people present may also have been affected, and may need just as much support. You need to consider the physical, psychological, and emotional impacts and adapt the support that you can offer accordingly. The type of support that a victim or witnesses may need will vary depending on the type of incident they are involved in. However, normally you would begin by providing reassurance and first aid if necessary (a victim may need specialist medical support depending on the type of incident). Information about procedures involving legislation and courts, and details of available support services such as Victim Support can also be provided (CoP, 2018c). The topics covered in this chapter contribute to the learning required for the National Policing Curriculum subject areas 'Understanding the Police Constable Role', 'Vulnerability and Risk', 'Public Protection', 'Victims and Witnesses'. As part of the PCDA the police constable is expected to know and understand 'Key cross-cutting and inter-dependent areas of policing, including: ... vulnerability (including public protection and mental health) and risk'.

Specific Incidents

13.2 Mentally Vulnerable People

Police officers and others working in law enforcement will often encounter people who behave in unusual ways. This could be due to a mental illness that causes distorted thoughts and feelings that means they may find it hard to take in basic facts and make decisions. They may also be under the influence of drugs (illegal or otherwise). A person suffering from mental ill health may often find it hard to make rational choices. This condition may be transient or more persistent, depending on the person's health. The College of Policing APP provides comprehensive guidance on responding to people with mental health problems or learning disabilities (CoP, 2016c), and the mental health charity MIND and Victim Support published a good practice guide for the police (2013), and a guide for prosecutors and advocates (2010). Note that the Policing and Crime Act 2017 introduced changes to ss 135 and 136 of the Mental Health Act 1983 (MHA); we will discuss these later, but you may also find useful information on how to interpret some of these changes in the guidance published by the Department of Health (2017).

The police may be involved with individuals with mental ill health in two rather different ways: as part of accessing healthcare or in a law enforcement capacity (CoP, 2016c). Here, we will examine the relevant legislation, particularly the Mental Capacity Act 2005 and parts of the MHA Code of Practice (Department of Health, 2015). The MHA is used in relation to people with mental illness; the Mental Capacity Act 2005 (MCA) is used if a person is incapable of making a decision and requires care for any other reason, such as a medical condition. The scenario in 13.2.4 illustrates this further. Police training will include guidance on how to recognize the symptoms of mental illness, and if you are undertaking the PCDA or DHEP further advice is provided through NCALT. Note that, under the MHA, dependence on alcohol or drugs is not considered as a disability or a disorder (s 1(3)).

13.2.1 Interacting with mentally vulnerable people

A common misconception is that people who suffer from mental illness are likely to be violent, but this is often not the case. Mental ill health comprises a variety of disorders, including psychotic disorders (such as schizophrenia), mood disorders (such as depression or bipolar disorder), and personality and anxiety disorders (such as panic attacks and phobias). This should not be confused with learning disabilities, which cover a wide range of conditions with 'significant impairment of intelligence and social functioning' (s 1(4) of the MHA). With such wide definitions, officers need to assess each situation on an individual basis to determine how best to intervene. Trainee police officers will be expected to learn how to deal with these situations effectively and maintain their own and others' safety.

Individuals with learning disabilities can be especially vulnerable, and may have a limited understanding of the police and the justice system. Some may also have difficulty recalling events, understanding questions, and communicating effectively. Others may acquiesce to suggestions of events and actions in order to appease the interviewer. It is therefore very important that individuals with learning disabilities are identified when giving witness statements (see 10.11 and 25.6), and that this information is passed to the CPS. A doctor or a mental health practitioner can help determine whether an individual has a learning disability. Support agencies, such as Victim Support, can provide assistance to people with mental disabilities (eg if they are asked to testify in court).

People experiencing fear, confusion, anger, frustration, and even psychiatric disturbances such as paranoia and hearing voices, may become aggressive when police officers intervene. Officers need to know how to minimize any harmful effects of their intervention. For example, when dealing with individuals displaying signs of mental ill health, you should look out for possible signs of aggression such as sweating, clenched fists, rapidly moving eyes, frowning, increased reaction to sound, raised voices, and threats. You should also avoid any physical contact, unless you are sure that it will not be perceived as threatening. Consider taking a step backwards to show you are giving the person space, move slowly and as little as possible, but keep your hands visible. Make a visual check for weapons and remove anything dangerous, particularly sharp objects, from the individual's reach. You should maintain an adequate distance and may want to remove your headwear as this may be seen as threatening. However, you should be cautious, and keep in a safe position.

Establishing good communication may be difficult but is essential when dealing with a person with mental ill health. You should explain what you are doing and repeat it, to ensure that you are being understood. Use a calm low-pitched tone, short sentences, and simple language and reassure the individual of what you are trying to achieve.

The individual may carry a medical information card, or a Crisis card (eg if he/she finds it difficult to express things clearly), or a Medic Alert bracelet (see 13.2.1). These could provide useful information and the individual should be asked about them. Ask the person why he/she is upset but avoid challenging or reasoning against delusions.

When you call for further assistance ask for lights and sirens to be turned off. Ensure that only one officer talks at a time, do not whisper to your colleagues, and avoid using your radio where possible. Any onlookers should be removed from the scene.

A person experiencing mental ill health may be unpredictable, so you may need to prevent him/her from engaging in harmful behaviour. You may need to use force to do this, but make sure that it is only as a last resort, and that it is absolutely necessary and proportional in the circumstances. You may also need to use force to protect the public and yourself, and again, the degree and type of force must be necessary and reasonable. Before using any force, however, consideration should be given to the various strategies mentioned earlier that can be employed to help minimize aggression.

There will probably be local policies and multi-agency protocols in place between law enforcement agencies and practitioners to ensure a fair and adequate treatment of individuals experiencing mental ill health. You should familiarize yourself with these to ensure that you can provide best service in such situations. You could, for example, refer someone for an assessment with a local authority, under Part 1 of the Care Act 2014, and share or request relevant information from other agencies. This should be done on a 'need to know basis' and may include the name and address of the individual (and his/her carer, if applicable), as well as any other information regarding the person's mental and physical health, and engagement with any services.

Other sources of information that may be of use include the person who reported the incident, the call handler, any medical or support staff available at the scene, and CCTV footage. Parents, carers, and family members can also provide important information which can help establish the best way to engage with a person. However, police officers should not share information with these other people without prior consent from the person in question, unless not sharing would conflict with statutory duties to protect that person or others, hamper the prevention or investigation of a crime, or put a child at risk of significant harm or an adult at risk of serious harm).

13.2.2   Responding to disturbed behaviour

Many people who live in the community suffer from mental ill health and cope well with their everyday lives. The police, however, may become involved if the person's immediate safety is in doubt, or if he/she is causing any other person's safety to be at risk. The police have powers to detain a disturbed person who is a possible danger to him/herself or others, and arrange for him/her to be removed to a place of safety. The procedure and the police powers depend on whether the person is in a public or a private place (see 9.2.1.1 for definitions of public and private places). If the person is also suspected of committing an offence, there may be reasons that could justify an arrest, but this is not necessarily the most appropriate way of dealing with a mentally disordered person.

A police officer can initially talk with the person to try to assess their state of mind. If they seem to need help and the person is receptive, the police can explain the need for treatment, and see if friends or relatives can be contacted. If there is a physical medical emergency, then treatment for this should be addressed first, ie he/she should be taken to an emergency department immediately. Similarly, if it seems clear that a person is becoming aggressive or confused due to an underlying medical condition (such as diabetes or a stroke), this should be treated as a medical emergency.

After talking with the person the police officer might conclude that there are no significant mental health problems, but if a breach of the peace seems likely, the person can be detained to prevent this (see 14.3 on 'breach of the peace' and the use of force). Removing a person to a place of safety should be used only as a final resort. A person can be 'sectioned' for admission to hospital if he/she seems to need urgent psychiatric treatment, but will not seek it voluntarily and presents a danger to him/herself or to others. A police officer may be asked to help remove the person to hospital (but see 13.2.3.2), by force if necessary (s 6 of the MHA). A 'section application form' must be completed and signed prior to any such police involvement.

13.2.2.1 Disturbed behaviour in public places

It is not an offence to be mentally disordered in a public place. However, if a person in a public place (see 9.2.1.1) seems to be in need of immediate care and control, a police officer has the power to remove him/her to a place of safety (s 136 of the MHA).

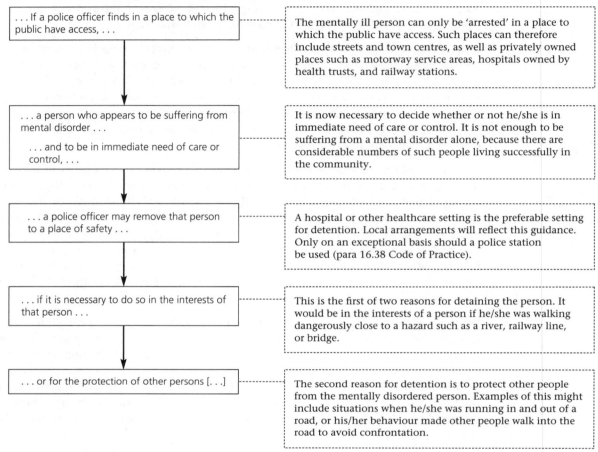

... If a police officer finds in a place to which the public have access, ...

> The mentally ill person can only be 'arrested' in a place to which the public have access. Such places can therefore include streets and town centres, as well as privately owned places such as motorway service areas, hospitals owned by health trusts, and railway stations.

... a person who appears to be suffering from mental disorder ...

... and to be in immediate need of care or control, ...

> It is now necessary to decide whether or not he/she is in immediate need of care or control. It is not enough to be suffering from a mental disorder alone, because there are considerable numbers of such people living successfully in the community.

... a police officer may remove that person to a place of safety ...

> A hospital or other healthcare setting is the preferable setting for detention. Local arrangements will reflect this guidance. Only on an exceptional basis should a police station be used (para 16.38 Code of Practice).

... if it is necessary to do so in the interests of that person ...

> This is the first of two reasons for detaining the person. It would be in the interests of a person if he/she was walking dangerously close to a hazard such as a river, railway line, or bridge.

... or for the protection of other persons [...]

> The second reason for detention is to protect other people from the mentally disordered person. Examples of this might include situations when he/she was running in and out of a road, or his/her behaviour made other people walk into the road to avoid confrontation.

If a person needs to be transported to a place of safety, then hospital or ambulance transport should be used (as set out in agreed local policies). Police transport should only be used in cases of extreme urgency or where there is a risk of violence (Code of Practice, para 16.32).

13.2.2.2 Disturbed behaviour in private places

The police are sometimes called to a house, flat, or other private place to restrain or help a mentally disordered person. They will, of course, first try and communicate with the person to try and reach some agreement on how to help.

The police may need to use powers under s 135 of the MHA which allow them to enter and search a premises to remove persons believed to be suffering from mental disorder (using force if necessary). A warrant issued by a magistrate is required and an Approved Mental Health Professional (AMHP) must be present. The police can also use force to enter premises if there is a breach of the peace, or if the entry is necessary to save life or limb, or to prevent serious damage to property (see 14.3, 13.7.2, and 20.1, respectively).

If the person seems to need help but does not agree to it, an AMHP will be required. The police should remain until he/she arrives to take over responsibility and carry out an assessment for possible detention (Code of Practice, para 14.41). Police officers have no obligation to stay for the assessment, unless it is unsafe to leave (Code of Practice, para 16.34). The AMHP will arrange transport to hospital if required (see 13.2.3.2).

13.2.3   Removal to a place of safety

A place of safety could include social services residential accommodation, a hospital, a police station, an independent hospital or care home for mentally disordered persons, or any other suitable place (if the occupier is willing temporarily to receive the patient). If a detained person is excluded from a hospital as a place of safety and taken to a police station, the name of the person who made the exclusion decision (and the reasons for it) must be recorded (Code of Practice, para 16.62).

13.2.3.1   A police station as a place of safety

Police station cells can only be used as a place of safety for adults, who are suffering from mental ill health in certain circumstances (s 136A of the Policing and Crime Act 2017). Police cells must never be used for a person under the age of 18 years. A person who is kept in a police cell as a place of safety for lack of a suitable alternative should not be detained there for more than 24 hours (Code of Practice, para 16.40).

When a person is taken to a police station as a place of safety under the MHA ('Use of police stations as places of safety'), then PACE Code C (with the exception of s 15) applies even if the person has not been arrested (Code of Practice (para 16.66)). He/she would therefore have the same rights as a person who has been arrested, and a police officer would have the power to search him/her under s 32 of the PACE Act 1984 (see para 16.68).

If an offence seems to have been committed, the person may be interviewed as part of an investigation. An appropriate adult must be present when a 'mentally vulnerable' or 'mentally disordered' person is interviewed (see 25.4.2 and 25.5.1.1). There are exceptions to this requirement, namely if it seems it could lead to: interference with evidence; alerting someone else suspected of committing an offence; or preventing the recovery of illegally obtained property. In line with the general application of the law for non-vulnerable individuals, should the appropriate adult be a solicitor, he/she can be removed from an interview if deemed to be preventing 'proper' questioning (PACE Code C, para 6.9). An interview without an appropriate adult must be approved by an officer of the rank of superintendent or above, and it must not cause further harm to the individual (PACE Code C).

13.2.3.2   Transporting the person to a place of safety

An ambulance or other health service transport should be used to transport a disturbed person from a public or private place to a place of safety. The police should only be involved for more challenging forms of behaviour. The extent of such police involvement will be set out in locally agreed policies (Code of Practice, para 14.48).

13.2.3.3   Procedures at the place of safety

The detention period under ss 135 and 136 must not exceed 36 hours from the time of arrival in the first place of safety. This is comprised of a maximum period of detention for 24 hours, with a possible extension for a further 12 hours, should the assessment of the detained person not have been possible, or is still ongoing, within the initial time period (ss 135(3ZA), 136(2A), and 136B).

A person removed from a public place to a place of safety may be detained there, but only:

- to be examined and assessed by a registered medical practitioner;
- to be interviewed by an approved social worker; or
- while necessary arrangements are made for his/her treatment or care.

13.2.3.4   Disturbed behaviour in a place of safety

A person who is already in a health service place of safety (such as a hospital) may develop signs of apparent mental ill health, and therefore need additional care and control. This should be provided by the doctors and nurses (using their powers under s 5 of the MHA and Code of Practice, para 16.20) and the police should not be called to intervene under s 136 of the MHA.

On occasions there are suspicions that a person in a place of safety has been suffering ill-treatment or neglect, or is not being kept under proper control. In such circumstances, the officer can execute a warrant under s 135 of the Policing and Crime Act 2017 to initiate

Specific Incidents

procedures for alternative provisions to be made in the current location. The officer is not obliged to remove the person to another place of safety (s 135(1A)).

13.2.4 The Mental Capacity Act 2005

Consider the following scenario:

Two police officers have been asked by a paramedic team to attend a bedsit in town. An extremely thin and naked man is lying in bed with several open wounds on his body which look as if they could have been caused by hypodermic needles. He appears to be heavily intoxicated and is suspected of using controlled drugs. Blood-filled syringes are strewn all around the bed and the floor of the room and the man appears to be bleeding from body orifices. The police officers consider the health and safety of the people around them as a priority, so they and the paramedics don protective clothing and remove dangerous and contagious items to a toxic chemical receptacle and a 'sharps box'. The paramedics try to persuade the man to go to hospital but every time they get close to him, he mumbles and moves away violently. The police officers also try to communicate with him, but without success. They must now decide how to help him, and under which legislation.

The Mental Capacity Act 2005 (MCA) provides a broad legal framework which aims to protect vulnerable people aged 16 years or over (s 2(5)) who do not have the capacity (ability) to make their own decisions. (This could be through illness, unconsciousness, alcohol, drugs, or a severe learning disability that has been present since birth.) The Act also empowers and offers protection to carers and others (such as police officers) who are involved in protecting people who may be vulnerable. Of particular interest is s 5, which provides the power to carry out acts related to the care or treatment (including restraint) of a person who lacks capacity. The MCA Code of Practice (Department for Constitutional Affairs, 2007) provides guidance on how the Act should be interpreted. The National Mental Capacity Forum was set up in 2015 to work with a variety of stakeholders (including health services, police, and social care) to improve local implementation of the MCA. The Mental Capacity (Amendment) Act 2019 introduced a Liberty Protections Safeguard (LPS) scheme that replaces the Deprivation of Liberty Safeguards scheme (DoLS) and allows for the deprivation of liberty of individuals who have a mental disorder, cannot make decisions for themselves regarding their care, and may put themselves in situations of harm (eg due to an advanced state of dementia). Previously such a deprivation of liberty was only permitted in a care home or hospital. LPSs are likely to be approved in 2020 and run alongside DoLSs for the first year of their implementation. A code of practice that will guide the implementation of LPSs is also expected to be issued in the future. The Mental Capacity Act 2005 is due to be reviewed in 2020.

In the circumstance described in the scenario, the Mental Health Act 1983 cannot be used, partly because the man is not in a public place (and so s 136 would not apply), but also because he is in need of immediate medical care. Although he might be suffering from a temporary mental disorder, the immediate concern is his apparent inability to make a decision about his medical care. The Mental Capacity Act 2005 can be used in these circumstances, to facilitate making arrangements for transporting him to hospital for medical treatment.

13.2.4.1 General principles underlying the Mental Capacity Act 2005

Section 1(1) of the MCA provides some key principles, for example that a person:

- must be treated as if he/she has capacity (see 13.2.4.2) unless it can be established otherwise (s 1(2));
- must not be treated as incapable of making a decision unless all practicable steps have been taken to help him/her to do so, without success (s 1(3)); and
- must not be treated as if he/she is unable to make a decision just because he/she is known to have made an unwise decision previously (s 1(4)).

The Act also specifies that any decision or action that is taken must be in the person's best interests (s 1(5)) and must avoid (as far as possible) interfering with his/her rights and freedom (s 1(6)).

13.2.4.2 Judging a person's mental capacity

In this context 'capacity' is the ability to take in information and use that information to make decisions. A lack of capacity could be caused by an impairment or disturbance in the functioning of the mind or brain (s 2(1) of the MCA), for example through a learning disability, dementia, brain damage, or toxic confusion caused by drugs or another noxious substance. The lack of capacity could be permanent or temporary (s 2(2)). Any evaluation can only be made on the balance of probabilities.

The process of judging a person's capacity focuses on his/her ability to make decisions, and is regulated by s 3 of the Act. In determining capacity, no reference can be made to the person's age or appearance, nor should any unjustified assumptions be made based solely on the person's condition or behaviour (s 2(3)). A functional test may be used to check, for example, if he/she is able to understand and retain any information relevant to a decision, use information to help make a decision, or inform another person of a decision (CoP, 2016a). The communication used by either party could include talking, writing or typed text, a sign language, or other gestures.

13.2.4.3 Acting on behalf of a person who lacks capacity

Under s 4 of the MCA, the decision made and any subsequent action must be in the person's best interests. He/she must be encouraged to participate as fully as possible in any act or decision, and all reasonably practicable steps should be taken to achieve this. The likelihood of the person having the capacity at some point in the future must be considered, and if there is no immediate need to make a particular decision, and he/she is likely to regain the capacity to make the decision, then it should be delayed until he/she has recovered sufficiently.

If the person cannot make decisions and therefore lacks capacity, a decision might need to be made on his/her behalf. As far as possible, the person's wishes and feelings should be considered, especially his/her usual beliefs and values (if known). The views of the following people should also be taken into account:

- his/her carer;
- anyone else he/she would like to be consulted; and/or
- anyone with power of attorney or a deputy appointed by a court.

Actions carried out in connection with the care or treatment of a person do not incur any liability (s 5) if, prior to those acts, reasonable steps were taken to establish that the person lacked capacity, and it was reasonably believed that the actions were in the person's best interests. If a decision relates to life-sustaining treatment, any consideration that it would be better if the person was allowed to die should be avoided.

If the actions are resisted (despite efforts to communicate and to encourage participation), then restraint may be needed. But there must be a reasonable belief that restraint has to be used to prevent harm to the person, and the restraint must be proportional (s 6). Actions defined as restraint under s 6 include using force (or threatening to use it) in order to apply care or treatment, and restricting a person's liberty of movement, whether or not he/she resists. It does not include depriving a person of his/her liberty (within the meaning of Article 5 of the ECHR), or contravening a decision made by a court or a person with a relevant power of attorney.

13.2.4.4 Applying the Mental Capacity Act 2005

In the illustrative scenario at the start of 13.2.4, all practicable steps to help the man have been unsuccessful. The attending police officers and paramedics believe he needs urgent treatment in hospital. On the balance of probabilities, he is suffering from toxic confusion which has caused an impairment or disturbance of his mind or brain. He is therefore unlikely to have the capacity to make the decision to go to hospital and appears to be incapable of understanding the information relevant to the decision—ie that he is seriously ill and needs treatment. There is no information pertaining to family, friends, or carers, and there is no indication of how he might have wished to be treated when he had capacity.

The police officers and paramedics have taken all reasonable steps required to establish that he lacks capacity, and that he cannot make the relevant decision. Therefore, they need to make a decision on his behalf. The least restrictive action or decision to avoid interfering with his rights and freedom is to ensure he receives hospital treatment. They judge that the least restraint required under the circumstances is to help him onto a stretcher for transportation to hospital.

13.2.4.5 Ill-treatment or neglect of a person who lacks capacity

Some people have particular caring or legal responsibilities for an individual who lacks capacity, and may also have a power of attorney. It is an offence under s 44 of the MCA for any such carer or responsible person to ill-treat or wilfully neglect the person. This includes physical, psychological, financial, domestic, discriminatory, and sexual abuse.

The offence is triable either way and the penalty is a fine or imprisonment (summarily 12 months, and five years on indictment).

TASK 1

1. What is your local force policy on the use of s 136 MHA powers?
2. A police officer is called to the home of the parents of a young man (over 18) who seems to be suffering from a mental disorder. On arrival, the parents inform her that he is in his bedroom, and holding the door handle to stop anyone opening the door. Using the minimum force necessary (and limiting your answers to the Mental Health Act 1983):
   (a) how could she gain entrance for the parents, and
   (b) what options are available should she decide that the young man is in need of medical attention in relation to his apparent mental disorder?

13.3 Safeguarding Children

Child abuse can come in many forms and can occur in all walks of life. It is defined as any action by another person, adult or child, that causes significant harm to a child. It can be physical, sexual, or emotional, but can also be the lack of love, care, and attention. The available evidence suggests that most child abuse occurs within families. Child abuse and neglect differs from other types of abuse due to the long-lasting effects it may have on the victim, and different children will have their own response to the trauma. Offences of child abuse and neglect are found in the Offences Against the Persons Act 1861 and the Sexual Offences Act 2003. Sexual offences involving children are covered in 17.7.

The police have an obligation to safeguard children under s 11 of the Children Act 2004. The police should support other agencies when there are concerns for a child's well-being (ss 17 and 47 of the Children Act 1989), even if no crime has been committed (Home Office, 2015e, p 34). The centrality of protecting children's welfare and the importance of effective multi-agency work in this respect is clearly stated in the government's 2018 *Working Together to Safeguard Children* policy (HM Government, 2018) and the Children and Social Work Act 2017. The latter created 'safeguarding partners', such as local authorities, clinical commissioning groups, and the police.

The Children Act 1989 was an important development in safeguarding the welfare of children in the UK. It covers any person under the age of 18 (s 105) but there are also references to children or young people of a particular age, for example 'under the age of 12'. The Children Act 1989 places great emphasis on encouraging multi-agency working and supporting children and families, and reinforces approaches to child welfare that make children the primary concern.

A number of high-profile cases had demonstrated that more was needed to protect children from harm. The inquiry into the death of Victoria Climbié in 2000, headed by Lord Laming, led to a number of key recommendations which help to ensure the thorough investigation of potential crimes, proper training for investigators, and appropriate and effective inter-agency working. In response, the government produced *Every Child Matters*, and eventually the Children Act 2004. These promote child welfare and inter-agency working, and place statutory obligations on local authorities to cooperate with other agencies. The role of child commissioner was created, and Local Safe-guarding Children Boards (now disbanded) were set up throughout the country to ensure that clear guidance and procedures were in place, and to provide multi-agency training.

The violent death of Peter Connelly (also known as Baby P) in 2007 demonstrated that despite the recommendations, ongoing failures in child protection procedures had not been properly addressed. Lord Laming published a new report in 2009 (Laming, 2009) which highlighted the lack of appropriate action, both individually and collectively, from a number of the services involved. The death of Daniel Pelka in 2012, at the hands of his mother and her partner, further highlighted the need to improve the way vulnerable children are identified and the subsequent procedures for effective communication between institutions (Lock, 2013). Victoria Climbié, Peter Connelly, and Daniel Pelka had each been the subjects of contact with doctors, the police, social services, and schools, and these services had identified areas of potential neglect or abuse. They had, however, failed to take appropriate action to prevent the deaths of the children.

The government's 2018 guide to inter-agency working to safeguard and promote the welfare of children *Working Together to Safeguard Children* is available online.

13.3.1 Investigating child abuse

All police forces have a specialist Child Abuse Investigation Unit. Whilst there may be local and regional differences in the exact nature and scope of their work, these teams will usually be staffed by nationally trained investigators (trained in ICIDP or equivalent) and are likely to have successfully undertaken the College of Policing National Specialist Child Abuse Investigator Development Programme (SCAIDP). In some forces such specialist officers are known as 'Child Abuse Investigators'. Officers involved in interviewing children in relation to abuse should also be trained to a very high standard in witness interviewing.

Once a referral is made to such a team, either from an internal notification or from an external agency (eg social services), the investigators will decide what type of investigation is required. These may often begin as joint agency investigations, but the police will take a lead role if criminal offences are suspected. According to s 47 of the Children Act 1989, the local authority has a duty to investigate where it believes that a child might be suffering significant harm. The police have certain powers under s 46 of the same Act in relation to police protection (see 13.3.3), and the first consideration will be to secure the welfare of a child or children. Once this has been achieved a thorough criminal investigation can take place, and other agencies will work to assure the current and future welfare of the child.

A wide range of incidents may be associated with child abuse, such as:

- domestic abuse;
- missing children, including those truanting from school;
- children engaged in criminality, including bullying and abusing others;
- children abusing animals;
- children involved in sexual exploitation or prostitution;
- parental drug or alcohol abuse.

The Child Abuse Investigation Units can help trainee officers (such as those undertaking the PCDA or DHEP) with decision-making where a child's welfare might be a concern. Further information is available from a number of online sources, including the College of Policing document *Risk and associated investigations*. There is also a College of Policing Professional Role profile for Child Abuse Investigators; this could also help trainee officers understand how such investigations are carried out.

13.3.2 Protecting children from harm

Children are sometimes exposed to significant harm by their parents, relatives, and other people involved in their care and supervision. The Children Act 1989 (s 31(9)) states that harm can include:

- ill-treatment or the impairment of health or development;
- impairment suffered from seeing or hearing the ill-treatment of another;
- sexual abuse; and
- forms of ill-treatment which are not physical.

An alternative definition categorizes child abuse into four distinct types: physical, emotional, sexual, and neglect (ACPO, 2009). Unsurprisingly, risk factors associated with suspicious child deaths include a previous history of violence to children (ACPO, 2014).

Specific Incidents

A more recent concern has been the involvement of children in terrorist acts. Local authorities are now obliged (under s 36 of the Counter-Terrorism and Security Act 2015) to establish 'Channel' panels to try and prevent children being drawn into terrorism. The panels (which include the local chief officer of the police) assess the likelihood of this, and arrange for support to be provided (Home Office, 2015e, p 19).

Some of the legislation in the Children and Young Persons Act 1933 (CYPA) is considered here (see also 13.1.1.2). The Offences Against the Person Act 1861 and the Sexual Offences Act 2003 are also relevant (see Chapters 15 and 17 respectively).

13.3.2.1   The offence of child cruelty

The offence of cruelty to a child (s 1(1) of the CYPA). can be committed by a person aged 16 or over, who is responsible for caring for a child under 16.

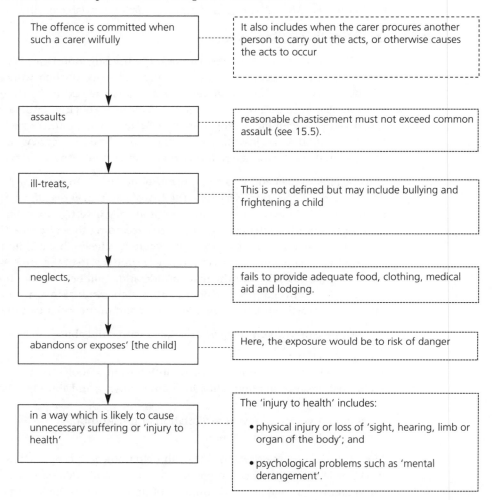

Incidents should be assessed in terms of the history of acts and omissions to determine whether they constitute a criminal offence. The offence is triable either way and the penalty is a fine or imprisonment (summarily six months, and ten years on indictment).

13.3.2.2   Cigarettes and young people

A constable in uniform has a duty to seize any cigarettes, tobacco, or cigarette papers in the possession of a young person who is smoking in a street or public place (s 7(3) of the CYPA). This applies for a young person who either is, or appears to be, younger than 16. Any seized items should be disposed of according to local force policies and procedures.

Selling cigarettes, cigarette papers, or tobacco to young people under the age of 18 years is an offence under s 7 of the CYPA (including sales from automatic machines). The sale of e-cigarettes (commonly known as 'vaping') to under 18s is also an offence under the Nicotine Inhaling Products (Age of Sale and Proxy Purchasing) Regulations 2015. However, under s 7(1A) of the CYPA 1933 it is a defence if it can be proved that a shopkeeper 'took all reasonable precautions and exercised all due diligence to avoid the commission of the offence'.

The offence is triable summarily and the penalty is a fine. If a person is convicted of a s 7 offence on two or more occasions within two years, a magistrates' court can apply a restriction order under s 12. This bans the offender from selling or managing premises for selling tobacco-related products. It is a summary offence for a person to knowingly contravene such an order, and the penalty is a fine.

13.3.2.3 Injuries to children from heating appliances

Carers have a responsibility to ensure that children are kept safe when heating appliances are in use. Under s 11 of the CYPA, a person over 16 commits an offence if a child under 12 is killed or suffers serious injury because the carer allowed 'the child to be in a room containing an open fire grate or any heating appliance'. The appliance must have been 'liable to cause injury to a person by contact with it' and 'not sufficiently protected to guard against the risk of being burnt or scalded without taking reasonable precautions against that risk'. The penalty for this summary offence is a fine.

13.3.3 Police protection

The police have a statutory duty to safeguard the well-being of children (s 11 of the Children Act 2004). Police officers have a power to take children or young people under 18 into police protection, if the child's safety seems to be at immediate risk were no action taken (s 46 of the Children Act 1989). This power is only used in emergency situations and as a last resort and when absolutely necessary; any decision to remove a child/children from a parent or carer is usually made by a court, by means of an Emergency Protection Order (Home Office, 2015e, pp 31, 58). Police protection is not a measure for circumventing the usual legal process; see the Safeguarding Hub document *Police Protection—A practical guide*, available online.

Where possible, officers should speak with the child, and the child's responses should be recorded word for word. Care should be taken to avoid 'contaminating' any future interviews. If a criminal investigation is initiated, the guidance set out in *Achieving Best Evidence in Criminal Proceedings: Guidance on interviewing victims and witnesses, and guidance on using special measures* should be followed. Once officers have secured the safety and well-being of the child, the case should be referred to the Specialist Child Abuse Investigation Unit or its equivalent (see 13.3.1). A child can be kept in police protection for up to 72 hours (s 46(6) of the Children Act 1989).

13.3.3.1 Procedure for police protection

Police protection can involve moving the child to a safe place, or preventing his/her removal from a safe place. Section 46(1) of the Children Act 1989 states that where a police officer 'has reasonable cause to believe that a child would otherwise be likely to suffer significant harm' he/she may:

- remove the child to suitable accommodation and keep him/her there; or
- take all reasonable steps to ensure that his/her removal from a hospital (or other place in which he/she is accommodated) is prevented.

There are two separate and distinct roles for the police in relation to police protection: the initiating officer who takes the key actions in relation to the child, and the designated officer who independently overviews the circumstances in which the child was taken into protection (Home Office Circular 17/2008). The designated officer will be at least the rank of inspector and cannot be the initiating officer for the same case.

Apart from in exceptional circumstances, no child should be taken into police protection until the initiating officer (see 13.3.3.2) has seen the child and assessed the circumstances.

13.3.3.2 The role of the initiating officer

The initiating officer takes the child into police protection, undertakes the initial enquiries, and completes a Police Protection Form as soon as possible. Under s 46(3) of the Children Act 1989, the initiating officer must as soon as is reasonably practicable also:

- inform the local authority where the child was found, of the police protection steps that have been taken (and are proposed) concerning the child, and the reasons;
- tell the authority in which the child usually lives ('the appropriate authority') where he/she is now being accommodated;

- inform the child (if he/she appears capable of understanding) about the steps taken and the reasons, and about any further police protection steps that may be taken;
- try and establish the wishes and feelings of the child;
- ensure that a designated officer has been assigned for the case; and
- arrange for the child to be moved to local authority-provided accommodation ('suitable accommodation' (see 13.3.3.4), if the child is not already in care.

In addition, as soon as is reasonably practicable, the initiating officer must contact the adults who have been caring for the child (s 46(4)). As well as the child's parents, this would include every person who has parental responsibility for the child (see 13.3.3.3) and any other person with whom the child was living immediately before being taken into police protection. The adults who have most recently been caring for the child must be told about the police protection steps taken (or planned) concerning the child, and the reasons.

13.3.3.3 The meaning of 'parental responsibility'

Parental responsibility in terms of the Children Act 1989 means 'all the rights, duties, powers, responsibilities and authority which by law a parent of a child has in relation to that child and [his/her] property'. It can be held by parents, step-parents, and by other people or administrative bodies such as a local authority. The question of who has parental responsibility is covered in ss 2 and 3 of the Children Act 1989. The key points are:

(a) If the father and mother were married to each other when the child was born, they will each have parental responsibility (s 2(1)). (The father is no longer the 'natural guardian' of his legitimate child (s 2(4)).)

(b) If the biological parents were not married to each other when the child was born, the mother will have parental responsibility, and so will the father if the child was jointly registered after 1 December 2003 (s 2(2)).

(c) More than one person can have parental responsibility for the same child at the same time (s 2(5)), and each may act alone to meet that responsibility (s 2(7)).

(d) A person who has parental responsibility for a child does not cease to have the responsibility simply because another person acquires such responsibility for the child (s 2(6)).

The spirit of the legislation is that all the parties including the parents, the child, and the local authority must be kept informed and given reasons for any actions. The child's wishes must be listened to, but not necessarily followed.

13.3.3.4 Suitable accommodation

Suitable accommodation will be local authority accommodation, a registered children's home, or foster care (see Home Office Circular 44/2003). Relatives or other appropriate carers can also be used if the designated officer and social services consider it appropriate. The child may also be taken to hospital if medical attention is required.

The circular also emphasizes that a child under police protection should not be taken to a police station unless there is absolutely no alternative, and under no circumstances should he/she be taken into the custody suite or cell area.

TASK 2 Jo is a single parent struggling to care for 4-year-old Sam. The child has been ill, and Jo does not want to take any more time off work. Her parents often care for Sam while she is at work.

However, on one occasion the parents are unavailable to help. Jo realizes that there is no food in the house and, goes out shopping when Sam is asleep. During the journey, her car breaks down.

Sam wakes up and becomes distraught. Having heard the child screaming hysterically, the neighbours call the police. All the doors and windows are shut and Sam cannot open the door.

1. What power of entry, if any, is available?
2. What offence might Jo have committed?

Protecting children includes situations when they may be exposed to harm due to domestic abuse, female genital mutilation, and forced marriages. These will be covered in more detail in 13.6.

13.4 Missing Persons

It is worth bearing in mind at the outset of this section of Chapter 13 that whilst a 'misper' is a relatively common and often routine matter for the police (the NCA estimate that approximately 180,000 people are reported missing every year in the UK) for the carers, families, and friends of the missing person it can be a highly traumatic and stressful few hours or days. For a very small number of people an incident of a missing loved one may culminate in a tragedy. It is also the case that there are links between children and young people going missing and forms of serious criminality: for example, child sexual exploitation (where going missing can be both a cause and effect) and human trafficking (see 13.5). Further information can be found on the *Missing People* charity's website (<http://www.missingpeople.org.uk>).

Adults, children, and young people can all 'go absent or missing' and for a number of reasons. These include:

- vulnerable adults, such as those with mental health issues, dementia, or other problems, who go missing as a result of confusion, despair;
- adults who deliberately absent themselves, often in an attempt to escape from problems in their home lives, such as a break up with a partner, domestic abuse, or financial problems;
- children or young people who run away from home, or residential care, normally for one or two days (possibly because of neglect, abuse, unhappiness);
- children who are missing through abduction (by a non-custodial parent, a stranger, or through other means such as internet grooming (see 17.7.6));
- adults (predominantly men) who go absent, often in an attempt to escape from problems in their home lives;
- children and young people who are victims of Child Criminal Exploitation (CCE), for example 'County Lines' (see 12.7)
- adults who have been abducted, for example for purposes of sexual assault or people trafficking;
- Children who are missing through abduction (by a non-custodial parent, a stranger, or through other means such as internet grooming (see 17.7.6)).

The vast majority of absent or missing persons are found quickly. For example, 90 per cent of children are found within two days (Missing People, 2019) and have suffered no harm, or the report turns out to be unfounded. A few are found dead after many weeks, and some are never found. Some individuals, particularly children in care, are reported missing repeatedly, and this might include when they leave a place of care without authorization, or fail to return at the expected time. This may occur quite frequently, but it is important to remember that on any occasion a person is reported as missing there may be a risk of harm, particularly if he/she is vulnerable.

A person will be categorized as 'absent' if there seems to be no apparent risk, or he/she is simply not where expected (CoP, 2018g). In these circumstances the police are not likely to launch an investigation. However, 'absent' cases must be carefully monitored, and the actions to locate the individual should be agreed early on, as should a review to reassess level of risk. 'Going absent' must be considered as a possible indicator of something more serious, for example a child might go absent because he/she is being abused at home, and in such circumstances the safe recovery of the child might be just the start of further investigations.

A person is 'missing' if his/her whereabouts cannot be established, and the circumstances are out of character, or the context suggests he/she might be subject of crime, or at risk of harm to him or herself or another. In such circumstances the risk will be assessed as very high (CoP, 2018m). To summarize then, in situations when a person's whereabouts are not known, the level of risk is lowest when he/she is 'absent' and highest if there is a likelihood of serious harm to the individual or the public.

Missing person incidents sometimes become critical incidents (see 11.5), requiring the support of services other than the local force. A search for a missing person can entail a considerable expenditure of resources and time, including rural and urban searches, dragging waterways, and exhaustive enquiries, particularly if the missing person is vulnerable. A police major crime unit (or equivalent) could be involved if there is a criminal aspect to the disappearance such as a suspicious death.

Specific Incidents

The national policy on the police response to missing person incidents was extensively redrafted in the light of the Soham murders in 2002. Huntley had previously come to the attention of Humberside Police for several allegations of sexual offences, which were not taken into account by Cambridgeshire Constabulary when vetting him to work at Soham Village College. The case also highlighted the insufficient sharing of information, and the reliance of smaller police forces on 'mutual aid' for large-scale searches.

The National Crime Agency's Missing Person's Unit is the UK's point of contact for cases of missing persons and unidentified bodies, both at national and international levels. They hold a national database, and provide and facilitate the sharing of information with the aim of maximizing police resources. The database can be a valuable resource when investigating cases of missing persons (NCA, 2018a; UK Missing Persons Unit, 2018).

13.4.1 Missing person enquiries

For all missing person reports the minimum initial response should consist, broadly, of recording the incident, conducting a risk assessment, agreeing the first steps to trace the missing person, and setting a timeline for reviewing decisions taken. Each case varies but there are standard considerations that always apply when the initial report is received by the call-taker, not least of which is to identify the likely level of risk for that person (see 13.4). The majority of missing person enquiries relate to children, so a thorough knowledge of the procedures related to the disappearance of a child is vital (see 13.4.2).

It is also important to keep an open mind about why the person is missing. Officers should avoid making assumptions, and should communicate with those who have more experience in cases of missing persons. The safety of the missing person should be the prime consideration of everyone involved in the investigation. If relevant, forensic evidence should be collected as soon as possible before it is compromised or lost (within 24 hours for high-risk cases and within seven days for medium-risk cases). This will help speed up the investigation by ruling out suspects, and will also avoid the need for later requests to the person's family as this could cause them further distress (CoP, 2016b). Police forces should consider how to provide the best support for the missing person's family, as they are likely to be under considerable stress, but may also be required to provide detailed information on the disappearance. If a person had left intentionally then certain items (eg credit cards and money) are likely to be missing. He/she might be involved with crime or have employment or financial problems—there may be evidence of this. If there seems to have been a violent struggle the person may have been abducted, and the scene must be preserved for evidential and investigative purposes.

The main guidance is available online as follows:

- *Major investigation and public protection: Missing persons* (CoP, 2018g);
- *Missing Children and Adults—A Cross Government Strategy* (Home Office, 2011);
- *Interim Guidance on the Management, Recording and Investigation of Missing Persons 2013* (ACPO, 2013); and
- the *Missing Persons Unit* website (NCA, 2019b).

The first task in a 'misper' enquiry is to conduct a risk assessment. Information is required about the person and his/her circumstances prior to the disappearance, particularly any factors which indicate vulnerability (eg a child is on the Child Protection Register) and their lifestyle. Police forces often utilize a checklist to collect the information required for the risk assessment (see the College of Policing APP on Missing Persons (CoP, 2018m) for further details). The police may ask those reporting someone as missing for a photograph of the missing person, details of their friends or relatives, details of the places the person often visits, whether the missing person has a medical condition (see *Report or find a missing person* on the gov.uk website). They might also ask for a sample of the DNA of the missing person, for example from a toothbrush (ibid).

The levels of risk suggested by the College of Policing (2018m) are 'no apparent risk' (or, if the person is absent), 'low risk', 'medium risk', and 'high risk'. The particular actions needed for each level of risk are covered in police training, but searching for the missing person is an obvious early step to take, assuming that carers, friends, or relatives have already tried to make contact with the missing person by paying a visit, or sending a message by mobile,

WhatsApp, email, or other means. The search would probably begin with the person's home (or last known address), garden, and any adjoining premises (bearing in mind that children can hide in very small spaces). At the same time enquiries could be made concerning admissions to local hospitals.

The search could then be extended to include the surrounding area, concentrating on the person's 'habitual haunts', and then moving on to hazardous places such as pools, streams, caves, and empty buildings. In high risk cases, and particular locations, searching might also be conducted by air.

Preparation should be made to widen the search systematically, including making house-to-house enquiries. It may also be appropriate to request the services of a Police Search Advisor (PolSA) who can provide more specialist advice on planning searches and controlling search teams, including volunteers, who may assist in the search.

Work-place or school absence records can help establish a person's recent movements and activities. Personal papers belonging to the missing person could be viewed (depending on the circumstances), and retained as possible evidence. Local and national police databases should also be interrogated. A list should be made of all relatives, friends, contacts, and work colleagues/fellow trainees in case these are needed, and recent photographs that are a good likeness should be obtained. It may seem an obvious idea to examine any digital devices known to belong to the missing person (smartphones, tablets, etc) and their online activities (such as any social network sites they might use), but there is no automatic legal right for the police to do so (the missing person has the right to privacy)—so be guided by local force policy (see also 21.5 on digital devices as evidence). CCTV footage might also be examined. Depending on the assessed level of risk, the police may decide to enlist the help of the local media.

The reliability of any person giving information should be considered. Ian Huntley, a caretaker at a school in Soham who murdered two young girls, provided false information to the police early in the investigation. Due to an inadequate system of recording and sharing information by Humberside Police and social services, Huntley's previous contacts with law enforcement were not identified. To avoid such omissions in the future all police forces now have to collate information on all absent and missing persons. After a person has been missing for three days the local police force will inform the Missing Persons Bureau and enter the details of the missing person on the PNC to alert other police forces (but see your local force policy).

13.4.2 Special considerations for missing children

All cases of missing children must be properly investigated, and are never considered as low risk. The disappearance of a child (taken here to mean a person under the age of 18) is always medium or high risk, and concern would be even higher for a child on the Child Protection Register. Missing children are particularly at risk of abuse. The Human Rights Act 1998 places a duty on public authorities to protect any person who may be at risk, therefore the police have a duty of positive action on the investigation of missing persons.

Carers and parents are expected to help with finding a child whose whereabouts are not known (eg to make enquiries if a child is unexpectedly and significantly late returning home). They should, however, be provided with support if some level of risk has been identified, or the parents are highly distressed, or unable to make enquiries (CoP, 2018m).

Looked-after children (children 'in care') make up a large proportion of cases of missing children, and they often have other needs that compound their vulnerability. Carers may use the term 'unauthorized absence', but the police should avoid using it when recording a missing child (ACPO, 2010a, p 17) as this might cause confusion. If a looked-after child is not where the carers expect, but his/her whereabouts are known or thought to be known (eg staying with a friend), it is the responsibility of the care staff to search and make enquiries. If the child is then reported to the police as missing, the police might want to consider searching the area.

Child Rescue Alert procedures (CRA) can be used if there is suspicion that a child may be at risk of serious harm. This involves seeking help from the public, for example through television, radio, text messages, and other social and digital media, as well as the charity Missing People (Missing People, 2018). Care should be exercised when using media in the case of

Specific Incidents

children missing from care as their whereabouts may be deliberately being hidden from their birth parents (CoP, 2018m).

13.4.3 The 'Herbert Protocol'

As Age UK explain, the 'Herbert Protocol' is a 'national scheme that encourages carers, family and friends to provide and put together useful information, which can then be used in the event of a vulnerable person going missing' (Age UK, 2018). To date many, but not all police forces in England and Wales have adopted the protocol: the MPS were one of the first to do so.

Many people who go missing are vulnerable elderly adults with dementia, and some will be residents at a care home. The Herbert Protocol includes the use of a form (completed before any likelihood of the person going missing) with a recent photograph and information about the person such as:

- 'background' information (first, last names, nicknames, mobile phone number, etc);
- 'physical description' (DoB, sex, build, ethnicity, hair colour, etc);
- whether he/she has been given a 'GPS tracker'—this potentially provides a very effective way of locating the person;
- 'medical history', including any communication and/or physical disabilities; and
- 'life history' (including hobbies, favourite places, which modes of transport they tend to prefer, favourite destinations when going out, etc).

If the person goes missing an additional form (or section of the initial form) is completed. This will include information such as the time and place he/she was last seen, the clothing he/she was wearing, what items might be in his/her possession.

The form(s) is passed to the police if the vulnerable person goes missing, and will be returned to the carer or care home when the person is located and safely returned.

TASK 3 Consider the following scenario:

A 16-year-old boy has been reported as missing by his mother. Checks with his school showed that he did not arrive at school that morning, despite having left his house (an isolated farm) at the normal time and in school uniform. His whereabouts are unknown and he may have been missing for as long as ten hours. There are indications that he has recently become moody and depressed, and may have been subject to some bullying at school. He is asthmatic and needs regular medication. He is a keen shot and has his own shotgun for using on the farm. He had a quarrel with his father the night before; his father had refused to allow him to go out with friends that evening. The father says the boy acts rebelliously.

1. You might note that there are a number of vulnerabilities, or potential areas for concern, in this case. What further information is required?
2. If the missing person enquiry becomes prolonged, what national guidance is available to help plan the ongoing police investigation?

TASK 4

Why is the 'Herbert Protocol' so called? Has your local force adopted the protocol?

13.5 Modern Slavery and Human Trafficking

Modern slavery is an umbrella term that includes human trafficking and slavery, servitude, and forced or compulsory labour. These crimes all involve exploitation. Slavery is one where one or more persons seem to have ownership over another person(s) and can therefore exploit the victim. Human trafficking occurs when one or more persons make travel arrangements for a person, to a destination where they become a victim of exploitation of one kind or another.

Slavery is prohibited under the European Convention on Human Rights (Article 4 of the ECHR). Slavery, servitude, and forced labour were first criminalized in 2010 under s 71 of the Coroners and Justice Act 2009. The Modern Slavery Act 2015 (MSA) consolidated these offences and explicitly addressed human trafficking. Slavery, servitude, and forced or compulsory labour are all offences under s 1 of the MSA. The Act also introduced an Independent Anti-Slavery Commissioner, with a UK-wide remit to improve the prevention, detection, investigation, and prosecution of modern slavery offences and identification of victims (MSA, Part 4).

The UK's strategy to address modern slavery is organized around four 'Ps' (HM Government, 2014a). These are:

- pursue (by prosecuting and disrupting offenders);
- prevent (individuals from offending);
- protect (vulnerable people from exploitation and raising awareness and resilience for modern slavery); and
- prepare (by improving victim identification and support).

13.5.1 Human trafficking

Human trafficking is often a complex phenomenon of significant national and international concern. It consists of arranging or facilitating the travel of a person, with the view to that person being exploited (by the trafficker or someone else). Note that human smuggling is different from trafficking; smuggling involves bringing a person into a country illegally, but on arrival the relationship between the parties ceases.

The victim can be of any age, and whether he/she consents to travelling is irrelevant, and the travelling can be to or from the UK, or within the UK (s 2 of the MSA). Human trafficking impacts different areas of policing and incorporates a variety of offences, offenders, and forms of victimization. Police officers may come across trafficking victims whilst on patrol or when responding to incidents. Human trafficking does not always entail a sophisticated and complex operation; the exploitation of any one individual by another, for example with the promise of work in another part of the country, may also fall into this category.

13.5.1.1 Exploitation of trafficked persons

In 2018, 6,985 individuals were identified as having been trafficked, an increase of 36 per cent compared to 2017. Of these cases 45 per cent involved children, mainly of UK origin (Home Office, 2019a, pp 44, 46). Labour exploitation is the most common form of exploitation, followed by sexual exploitation (Home Office, 2019a, p 45). The circumstances under which a person is found can be used to help to determine whether he/she is being exploited, as can factors such as vulnerability due to age, familial relationship to the offender, or mental or physical illness (s 1(4) of the MSA).

Sexual exploitation is more likely to affect women and girls. Some victims are forcibly taken from their homes, while others voluntarily travel to another destination unaware of the exploitation that will ensue. Some victims initially agree to travel to work in the sex industry, but are unaware of the working conditions that will be imposed (eg number of clients, type of sexual activity, and pay). Most of the offences relating to sexual exploitation following trafficking can be found in the following legislation:

- Part 1 of the Sexual Offences Act 2003;
- s 1(1)(a) of the Protection of Children Act 1978 (indecent photographs of children); and
- s 33A of the Sexual Offences Act 1956 (related to the offence of keeping a brothel).

Labour exploitation is when the victim is forced to work under unacceptable conditions, often in factory work, agriculture, construction, catering, and hotels. It often involves threats or physical harm, restrictions of movement, debt-bondage, withholding wages, retention of identity documents, and threatening to reveal the illegal status of the worker to the authorities.

Servitude involves providing services through threat or coercion. For example, domestic servitude is when victims are forced to clean or cook in other people's homes. Unlike slavery, servitude does not involve 'ownership', but the victim will often have little chance of improving or changing his/her conditions, and may also be the target of sexual abuse. Offenders may have attracted victims through the promise of employment or patronage (eg promising the parents of a child that they will provide her with an education). Most victims of servitude are from abroad.

Specific Incidents

Commercial organizations operating in the UK with an annual turnover over £36 million are now required to either disclose the steps they have taken to ensure their business does not involve modern slavery (including their supply chain), or to make a statement that they have taken no such action (s 54 of the MSA).

13.5.2 The context of modern slavery and human trafficking

Victims often come from the poorer communities in their country of origin. Poverty places individuals at a greater risk of victimization, especially where there is a pressing need for money (such as a relative being ill). Any country with a relatively low socio-economic status is likely to be targeted for victims by human traffickers, and women are more likely to be victimized for two reasons: they usually have lower wages and greater difficulty in accessing education in their home country, and secondly, they may be more in demand in the country of destination (eg as female sex workers). The victims are recruited in a variety of ways, from advertisements for work, to abduction and kidnapping. Their travel documents may or may not be legitimate, for example a trafficker may arrange a new identity for a child and appoint him/herself as a guardian, thus controlling almost every aspect of the child's life. Corruption in the country of origin (including by government officials) can impede the investigation and prevention of human trafficking. Victims are brought into the country through various points of entry.

Initial indicators that a person may have been trafficked include: human rights breaches; threats or actual harm to family members; deprivation of food, water, and sleep; the withholding of medical care; being forced to perform sexual acts; having wages partly or totally withheld; debt-bondage; working excessive hours; not having access to identity documents such as a passport; or having restricted freedom of movement.

Victims are often reluctant to come forward and report their exploitation, so its true prevalence is difficult to assess. Public authorities (including police authorities) have a statutory duty to notify the Secretary of State, or designated person, when there are reasonable grounds to suspect that a person may be a victim of slavery or human trafficking (s 52 of the MSA), and this should at least help improve the accuracy of the data.

13.5.2.1 Child victims of trafficking

Children are not deemed capable of consent, so any child who is transported to do work is a victim of trafficking; there is no need for there to be any coercion, force, or deception. Some children may not be aware that they are being trafficked and others may deliberately conceal the fact. Child victims are more likely to be exploited for their labour than for sexual purposes.

Child victims may have particular characteristics such as unexpected possession of goods and money, and may exhibit self-confidence and maturity beyond their years. Others may appear to have no money or have debts to pay, but are in possession of goods that would suggest otherwise, such as an expensive mobile phone. A trafficked child may be unable to give details of a contact person or an address. For children trafficked within the UK, there may also be indications of physical abuse, sexual activity, substance abuse, self-harming behaviour, and homelessness. They may also have unexpected contacts or relationships (including online) with adults who are significantly older, or outside their normal circle.

If cared for by adults, the carers may not be the child's parents, or he/she might have a difficult relationship with them, or be one of several unrelated children living at an address. In addition, such children are unlikely to be registered with a GP or be enrolled at a school. Some children who are trafficked have gone missing from local authority care.

13.5.3 Responding to trafficking

In March 2019, the police had recorded 5,059 offences of modern slavery (Home Office, 2019a, p 7). Cooperation from victims is often essential for the successful investigation and prosecution of human trafficking offenders, so every effort must be made to form a supportive and trusting relationship.

Front line police staff have a statutory duty to report cases of modern slavery to the Home Office (s 52 MSA). This is generally done through the National Referral Mechanism (the NRM, see 13.5.3.3). Alternatively an anonymous MS1 form can be used if, for example, the victim is an adult and does not consent to the referral via the NRM.

13.5.3.1 The police response

Police officers should ensure that suspected victims are safe and receive medical assistance as required, and inform a supervisor and a senior detective officer of the situation. An intelligence report should be submitted and the NRM procedures should be followed (see 13.5.3.3).

It is important to be supportive and not to judge or stereotype possible victims, as their circumstances are often unique and difficult to understand for the outsider. The victim may not understand English, might have learning and communication disabilities, or may have physical or mental ill health due to having suffered trauma. Some victims may have experienced long periods of isolation, and may as a consequence feel dependent on their captor, and therefore may not want to cooperate with bringing him/her to justice. Other victims might be fearful of reprisals from traffickers, and fearful of any authority due to an insecure or illegal immigration status. Cultural or religious beliefs and shame and fear of dishonour can present additional difficulties. Forensic medical examination can be traumatic, especially for victims of sexual abuse.

Each of these aspects should be taken into account when interviewing suspected victims. Efforts must be made to communicate with them effectively and to reassure them of the role of the police and to explain any procedures that are required such as searches or medical examinations. Police officers should be mindful of their own conduct, gender, and appearance, and the possible effects on victims. It is essential that adequate physical, psychological, and medical support is provided from the early stages of the investigation, for the well-being of the trafficked person but also to increase the chances of mounting a successful prosecution. Note that detailed information on interviewing is provided in Chapter 25.

Some individuals may be both perpetrators and victims of modern slavery, ie they may have been forced to help exploit others. In these cases, a victim can use the statutory defence under s 45 of the MSA, but not for murder, kidnapping, and false imprisonment (see Schedule 4 to the MSA). If a perpetrator is identified as a victim during the interviewing process, he/she should be referred under the NRM, with his/her consent.

13.5.3.2 Special considerations for child victims of trafficking

Child victims (ie those under 18) have additional vulnerabilities. Any victim suspected of being under 18 should be provided with immediate access to protection and support, as stipulated under s 51 of the MSA.

An officer who suspects that a child may be a trafficking victim has the power to remove the child to a safe place (or prevent the child's removal from a safe place) for a maximum of 72 hours (s 46 of the Children Act 1989 (see 13.3.3)). If there is a risk to life or likelihood of serious harm, the police can apply to a court for an Emergency Protection Order (see 13.3.3). The local authority children's social care service and police Child Abuse Investigation Unit should also be notified.

13.5.3.3 The National Referral Mechanism and investigation

The National Referral Mechanism (NRM) is the system for triggering the formal identification and the provision of support for victims of slavery and human trafficking. Police officers and other first responders (such as ambulance staff) must refer potential victims to the 'Single Competent Authority' (see Home Office, 2019g). Specially trained 'case owners' will then determine whether the individual is a victim of modern slavery, and if this seems likely, the victim is entitled to state-funded support while further evidence is gathered.

Every report of modern slavery must be investigated as soon as possible, and the victim's safety and the types of exploitation must be taken into account. Many offences involve cross-national investigations, which add complexities (see also the College of Policing APP guidance on *Major investigation and public protection* and *Investigation*).

13.5.3.4 Prevention of trafficking

To prevent a person from engaging in modern slavery the police can apply for a Slavery and Trafficking Prevention Order (STPO) or a Slavery and Trafficking Risk Order (STRO). The application is made to a magistrates' court, under s 2 of the MSA. An STPO lasts for at least five years, and can be imposed following a conviction for a modern slavery offence, or as a stand-alone order. An STRO lasts for at least two years and is issued if there is evidence 'beyond reasonable doubt' that an individual poses a risk of harm.

Breaching an STPO or an STRO is a criminal offence, punishable with up to five years' imprisonment. The maximum custodial sentence for slavery (including human trafficking) is 12 months if tried as a summary offence, and life imprisonment if tried under indictment (s 5 of the MSA).

13.6 Domestic and Family Violence and Coercion

Here we cover a variety of offences that can occur when some members of a family or social group seek to maintain control over other members of the group. This includes domestic abuse, 'honour'-based violence, female genital mutilation, and forced marriages; these issues have recently been addressed by governmental policy, particularly in terms of violence against women and girls (Home Office, 2016a), but see also the report from the National Police Chiefs' Council (NPCC, 2015b). Abuse within families can also include abuse of older people, child to parent abuse, and sibling abuse.

Managing incidents of violence in family settings presents particular difficulties, particularly because investigations into domestic or 'honour'-based violence (HBV) may be hampered by the non-cooperation of the extended family or the community. Officers should also be aware that when a victim has an insecure immigration status, the records of any police investigation may become part of his/her application to stay in the UK.

Certain victims will have specific needs or characteristics that make them particularly vulnerable, such as age, gender, sexual orientation, disability, cultural background, immigration status, or profession. In relation to vulnerable adults, consideration should be given to the Local Government Association's *Guidance on adult safeguarding and domestic abuse: a guide to support practitioners and managers*.

13.6.1 Domestic abuse and controlling or coercive behaviour

There is currently no legal definition of domestic abuse. The Home Office (2013a) proposes the following definition:

> any incident or pattern of incidents of controlling, coercive, threatening behaviour, violence or abuse between those aged 16 or over who are, or have been, intimate partners or family members regardless of gender or sexuality. The abuse can encompass, but is not limited to psychological, physical, sexual, financial and emotional [abuse].

A new offence of controlling and coercive behaviour in an intimate or family relationship was introduced by the Serious Crime Act 2015. The offence is designed to address patterns of non-violent abuse, which had proved difficult to prosecute under other legislation. The repetitive nature of the behaviour and its cumulative effect on the victim did not always meet the criteria for common assault or stalking and harassment offences. A new Domestic Abuse Bill has been proposed, which includes a legal definition of domestic abuse and consolidates provisions contained in previous legislation. Although accepted as a positive step by some charities and support services in this field (eg Women's Aid, 2017), there is some concern regarding the suitability of responding to domestic abuse from a purely legal perspective (see Walklate, Fitz-Gibbon, and McCulloch, 2017, p 2).

Violence in the domestic context is prosecuted under the same legislation as any other violent crime (see Chapter 15). In terms of police action, the approach should be pro-arrest, and as much evidence as possible should be gathered. Detailed guidance on the investigation of domestic abuse is available in *Authorised Professional Practice on Domestic Abuse* published by the College of Policing in 2015. It emphasizes a multi-agency approach, and the need for officers to take 'positive action'.

A Domestic Violence Disclosure Scheme ('Clare's Law') was introduced in 2014 (UK Parliament, 2013). It allows an individual to find out whether his/her partner has a history of violence. Members of the public have a 'right to ask' (similar to the Child Sex Offender Disclosure

Scheme) and a 'right to know'. If the police receive relevant information, they can disclose it to the person at risk, after making the appropriate checks (Home Office, 2012b).

13.6.1.1 Civil responses to domestic abuse

The Family Law Act 1996 (FLA) provides opportunities under civil law to counter domestic violence and abuse. The FLA was modified by the Domestic Violence, Crime and Victims Act 2004 and provides the basis for most of the provisions covered here.

A non-molestation order requires a person to refrain from molesting another named person. The applicant could be a spouse, ex-spouse, civil partner, or a current or former cohabitant. Under s 42A of the FLA, it is a criminal offence to breach such an order without reasonable excuse (the person must, however, know of the existence of the order). If the CPS fails to act, the victim may be able to use contempt of court proceedings. The offence is triable either way and the penalty is a fine or a maximum of five years' imprisonment.

An occupation order allows an owner, tenant, spouse, or civil partner to seek the removal of an occupant from his/her home (s 33 of the FLA), and the recipient will be forbidden from entering the property (s 33(3)). A breach of the order is a civil offence, but there is an associated power of arrest under s 47(1). These orders can be difficult to obtain, often because of the recipient's property rights (Herring, 2007, p 270). The lengthy procedures involved are an obvious disadvantage for applicants.

Domestic Violence Protection Orders (DVPOs) and Domestic Violence Protection Notices (DVPNs) were first introduced in the UK in 2014, to give victims more time to decide whether to leave the abuser or to apply for a non-molestation or occupation order. A DVPN is imposed by the police in the immediate aftermath of a domestic violence incident, and prevents the abuser from having contact with the victim or returning to the victim's home for up to 48 hours. During this timeframe, an application needs to be made to a magistrates' court for a DVPO, a civil order under which there will be a further period of no contact for 14–28 days.

Prohibited Steps Orders (PSO) are used to prevent a suspect removing a child from the applicant (s 8 of the Children Act 1989). They can impose restrictions on certain activities unless prior permission is obtained from the court (eg taking the child abroad or out of the local area). Anyone with parental responsibility for the child can apply for a PSO (as described by Part 1 of the Children Act 1989, see 13.3.3.3). A breach of a PSO is a civil contempt of court; there is no associated power of arrest.

The National Centre for Domestic Violence (NCDV) can help victims apply for emergency injunctions, and includes an electronic third-party injunction referral system. It also has a secure online ASSIST programme which allows police officers to access court papers related to non-molestation and occupation orders (NCDV, 2015a; NCDV, 2015b).

The Bright Sky app provides information for victims about nearby services, and also provides a dedicated system for recording particular incidents of abuse by text, images, or video. The victim can then share the recordings with the police and other support services (Vodafone, 2018; Hestia, 2018).

13.6.1.2 Responding to domestic abuse incidents

The Crime Survey for England and Wales estimates that approximately 1.6 million women and 786,000 men (aged between 16 and 59 years of age) experienced domestic abuse in the year ending in March 2019 (ONS, 2019g). However, this data does not record how many times each person is abused, and as such does not provide an accurate picture of the true extent of the problem. For example, 47 per cent of the victims interviewed for the BCS 2009/10 who had experienced domestic abuse had been victimized more than once, and 30 per cent three or more times (Flatley *et al*, 2010). Similarly, a 'rapid evidence review' of repeat violent victimization in Scotland in 2019 suggests that 46 per cent of victims had experienced two or more incidents in the previous year (authors' calculations based on Scottish Government, 2019, pp 15–16), and many will not have contacted the police on each occasion. So if there has been no previous contact with the police, you cannot assume there has been no prior abuse. It is also common for victims of domestic abuse to experience other forms of inter-personal violence, such as sexual assault and stalking (Walby and Allen, 2004). The police should address the incident in its wider context, and take into account, for example, whether the perpetrator has previously committed similar abuse, or if the victim has already been subject to a risk assessment.

Despite the commitments made by many forces, reviews of police responses to domestic violence suggest that positive steps have been taken, but some areas still need to be improved. These include how well police officers understand the nature of coercive and controlling behaviour, identify risk factors, and use positive action (eg arrest powers and charging perpetrators) (HMIC, 2014c; HMICFRS, 2017c).

The call-taker or the front desk staff usually provide the initial response to a report of domestic abuse. This will include gathering and recording information (see 24.4.1.1 on call-handling) and ensuring the safety of victim. The victim's demeanour (and that of others present) and any background noise should also be noted as it may provide clues about the overall situation. The caller should be told when the police are likely to arrive, and that he/she should avoid disturbing any possible evidence. Note that some victims may be calling from unfamiliar locations, or the situation may be changing fast; call-handlers must ask about this and other particular circumstances. Some victims might also have a safety codeword for contacting the police (CoP, 2015a) when seeking assistance (having been through a MARAC, for example (see 13.6.1.7)). Any electronic or paper-based records should be checked for relevant information.

If the suspect is at the scene, the call-taker should keep the caller on the line in order to gather evidence (which could be used in a subsequent prosecution). If the suspect is no longer present, the caller should be advised to keep safe, for example by locking all doors and windows, and carrying a mobile phone, or keeping phone lines open if using a fixed line. A suspect who has left may also return at any time, so a key word should be agreed for the caller to use if he/she comes back. The call-taker should obtain a description of the suspect, and checks on the suspect should be made, including using ViSOR (see 13.7.5.1) and the PND. Note that if the caller says that the suspect has left, this might not be the case as the suspect could be forcing the caller to say as much. If the caller is a child, as much information as possible should be gathered, particularly to ensure the child's safety (CoP, 2015a).

All the information should be recorded and disseminated, including informing the attending officer whether his/her supervisors have been briefed of the incident. An abridged version of the information can be used when a rapid deployment is required. Officer safety must be considered and back-up may be necessary.

An incident or crime report should be completed using the appropriate force system. This will ensure that domestic abuse incidents are not ignored, and that proper support will be provided to victims, and any follow-ups are also fully completed. The computer-aided dispatch (CAD) must remain open for domestic abuse incidents until a risk assessment has been carried out and the victim has been contacted (CoP, 2015a).

The College of Policing provides full guidance on the appropriate response for call takers and front staff in cases of domestic abuse in *Call handler and front counter staff response to a domestic abuse incident* (CoP, 2015a). There is also a College of Policing course on domestic abuse for police officers and CPS professionals.

13.6.1.3   Attending a domestic abuse crime scene

The first priority is the safety of everyone at the scene. The victim could be taken to a place of safety if this cannot be assured in his/her own home. The risk for the victim, children, and officers present (particularly in relation to the use of weapons) must be reassessed as new information is likely to have come to light so the initial risk assessment might no longer apply. A dynamic risk assessment process is needed, and risk management safety planning must be initiated. Chapter 11 provides more details on general procedures to be followed when attending crime scenes. The responding officer should try to build a rapport with the victim to provide reassurance; this will also help with the initial investigation and ensure a successful handover (CoP, 2015e).

Officers should also ensure the preservation of the relevant evidence if any prosecutions seem likely. Everything said by the suspect, victim, or children must be accurately recorded. The information obtained by the call-taker should be double-checked with the caller. Any apparent discrepancies should be investigated, for example the arrival of the police might change the dynamic of the situation, and cause the victim to mistakenly believe that he/she is no longer in danger.

Access to the premises may be denied by the victim and/or the suspect . If the victim refuses to grant entry, the officer will have to judge whether he/she is being controlled or coerced (to prevent entry or to say that the suspect has left). Should the suspect deny entry, officers should ask to speak to other members of the household. There may be grounds to use the power of entry under s 17 of the PACE Act 1984 (to arrest for an indictable offence or to save life and limb, see 13.7.2). If this power is used, a full PNB record must be made, including the reason. Arrest for a breach of the peace (see 14.3.2) may also be considered. If a suspect has left the scene, then his/her description should be confirmed and circulated.

Officers should then speak in more detail with the persons present. First accounts should be obtained from each individual as soon as possible after the events, especially any description of an absent suspect. Each person should be seen separately in a safe environment, and video recording can be used. If the various accounts differ considerably and suggest a different version of events it can be difficult to establish who is the victim and who is the assailant. An injured person could be the victim, but the aggressor can also be harmed when a victim acts in self-defence. The arrest of both parties should be avoided if at all possible. The apparent victim(s) should be offered immediate support (see 13.6.1.6).

If any children are present, a record should be made about each child's welfare, communication ability, demeanour, name, date of birth, sex, address, doctor, primary carer, and school. If no children are seen, officers should still be alert for signs of children, as they may have been kept away from the immediate scene but still be on the premises. If children are deemed to be in danger, s 48 of the Children Act 1989 can be used (see also 13.3.3 on using police protection powers).

Evidence can be vital in a subsequent prosecution, so officers must gather as much as possible. Forensic evidence can be particularly important to avoid over-reliance on the victim's statement in a future prosecution. If a sexual assault seems to have occurred, an early evidence kit (EEK) can be used (see 17.6.1.1). Officers should be proactive in gathering and using photographic evidence, and any non-intimate injuries should be photographed as soon as possible after the event, and again when injuries may become more apparent. The photographs should be used at interview and to help make decisions about bail, and copies should be attached to the evidence file for the CPS and judiciary. Body-worn video might help increase the number of criminal charges in situations of domestic abuse, as it can help officers gather evidence, and provide information about the context of the offences (Owens, Mann, and Mckenna, 2014).

Risk assessments must be carried out for all incidents involving domestic abuse, as soon as possible. Many forces use an aide-memoire (such as the DASH risk assessment checklist, see 13.6.1.8) to ensure officers ask all the required questions when attending an incident. Police officers are responsible for assessing the level of risk, and must complete the process even if the victim refuses to answer questions. Note also that victims should not be asked to sign risk assessments. In some forces the risk assessment is the responsibility of specially trained staff, such as the domestic abuse specialist officer or coordinator, but the FAO may still conduct the risk assessment under supervision.

The degree of risk should be continuously reviewed to ensure the correct level of protection for victims. The primary risk assessment underpins the immediate safety planning, and if several risk factors are identified it may be necessary to inform the victim and notify the relevant support services. In some forces a secondary risk assessment is conducted in some cases, by specially trained staff.

13.6.1.4 Investigating and follow-up for domestic violence incidents

The management of the investigation is dependent on local practices and on general guidance. The 'right first time' principle applies; the investigation should be thorough. It does not need to be conducted by domestic abuse specialist officers, but they can provide useful information and guidance. The investigation should consider the following points:

- any history of domestic abuse;
- any relevant police intelligence (local, national, and international), sources of intelligence include the Police National Database (see 5.9.1.2), the Violent and Sex Offenders Register, house-to-house enquiries, other information from witnesses, CCTV images, and covert surveillance (see 23.4);
- any relevant medical information (with consent);

- information held by housing, social care, and probation services;
- any civil orders and child contact agreements (including disputes);
- evidence from professionals and staff from the emergency services who witnessed the abuse;
- hearsay evidence—this may be acceptable, for example a witness's report of something said by a suspect or a child's account of events (see 24.2.5); and
- technology and social media, this may provide useful information, for example the victim may have received threats.

Other lines of enquiry include house-to-house enquiries, automatic number plate recognition (eg to ascertain the victim and suspects' whereabouts), bank accounts and other financial information (the victim's earnings might be under the suspect's control), covert surveillance (eg in situations of harassment), and prison intelligence. Bad character evidence (see 24.2.5) can also help secure a conviction (CoP, 2015c).

Interviews should explore details of the incident and possible existing evidence, for example details of witnesses; the victim's physical and emotional injuries; details of family members; the history of the relationship and any previous incidents or threats (including with other partners); whether children were present; whether the parties are separated; whether any civil action has been taken; whether any sexual offences have been disclosed; the points to prove; and the victim's perception of the future relationship in terms of the likelihood of further abuse. When interviewing a suspect, the victim's safety must be considered if the interviewer discloses information provided by the victim. The FAO should also be interviewed when relevant, and the interview recorded.

When a victim decides to withdraw from the investigation, the domestic abuse officer should take a comprehensive withdrawal statement to explain the witness's decision. He/she must be asked whether his/her original statement is true, and whether he/she was put under pressure to withdraw, with whom he/she has discussed the matters, whether he/she is considering civil proceedings, and the perceived impact on the witness and any children were the prosecution to continue. This statement and a report from the officer for the case should then be sent to the CPS. The statement may be used as evidence in the prosecution of the current or other incidents. The risk assessment and safety plan for the victim should also be reviewed.

All reports of domestic abuse must be recorded following the National Crime Recording Standards, particularly as domestic abuse may be associated with other crimes such as child abuse and harassment. All relevant information should be passed to police domestic abuse coordinators, who will liaise with the Tasking and Co-ordination Group (see 23.6). The accuracy of the existing data can then be monitored and further statistical information can be produced for sharing with partner agencies and other police personnel.

> **TASK 5** A woman in a long-term domestic relationship complains that she has been punched by her partner. What offence(s) could have been committed?

13.6.1.5 Methods of disposal of suspects

Police officers have a duty of positive action when responding to incidents of domestic abuse (CoP, 2018m). This often means arresting the suspect, but this is not always possible or the best solution. Alternatives to arrest include removing the suspect from the location to prevent breach of the peace and issuing a DVPN, or other civil order (see 13.6.1.1).

The decision to arrest a suspect should not be influenced by the victim's opinion or whether previous complaints have been withdrawn. If the decision is not to arrest, the reasons need to be recorded. However, in some situations both parties have committed acts which could justify arrest, or it may be difficult to differentiate between the perpetrator and the victim. Dual arrests should be avoided, particularly if there are children involved. A thorough assessment of the situation and an understanding of the context of coercive and controlling behaviour are therefore necessary to establish the best course of action.

Cautions are rarely appropriate in situations of domestic abuse (although they are sometimes used for a first incident where there is no intelligence of related incidents), and penalty notices for disorder are never appropriate (CoP, 2018m).When deciding whether to charge a suspect the following CPS documents (available online) all provide guidance: *The Director's*

Guidance On Charging 2013, Domestic Abuse Guidelines for Prosecutors, Domestic Abuse Charging Advice Sheet, and *Code for Crown Prosecutors.* The victim should be informed if the decision is against prosecution.

Bail can be used for a suspect who has been detained, but risk factors should be taken into account and the victim consulted (see 10.13.3 on bail). Any attached conditions should ensure that the victim, children, and witnesses are protected. The conditions must be such that they can be policed effectively, and not conflict with existing court orders. If the suspect is forbidden from contacting the victim this includes indirect contact and contact through social media. It is important to be clear that the conditions of bail apply to the suspect's behaviour (not the victim's), and that breaches of bail will be treated seriously, even if the suspect and the victim become reconciled. Before a suspect is released from a police station, the victim should be informed where possible and the notification recorded. The suspect or the victim may need to remove his/her belongings from a joint residence, and the police should help arrange this, especially if the removal could otherwise lead to a breach of bail conditions. All control rooms and databases should be updated regarding the suspect's bail conditions.

13.6.1.6 Safety and support for the victim

In providing support for victims and ensuring their safety, it is paramount that communication is clear, that the risk assessment is accurate and consistently reviewed, and that appropriate safety planning is devised. Domestic abuse victims are entitled to an enhanced level of service under the *Code of Practice for Victims of Crime* published by the Ministry of Justice (2015).

The following points should be explained to the victim:

- the reasons for the method of disposal;
- how to access support services;
- that the incident will be recorded on police IT systems; and
- that the information and evidence from the current incident could be used to support future prosecutions.

A victim of domestic abuse is often most vulnerable at the point he/she decides to leave an abuser, so information about the risks and risk mitigation will be required as part of a safety plan. He/she might also need help to arrange moving into a refuge, or installing a panic alarm. The location of temporary emergency accommodation (if used) should of course never be revealed to the suspect.

Victims should be informed as soon as possible (within one working day) of any developments regarding the suspect (such as his/her arrest, interview under caution, a decision on prosecution, or information about a first court hearing). Victims must also be informed if the suspect is released, whether on police bail or without charge. If the suspect is released on bail, any conditions imposed (and any change to or cancellation of the conditions) must be communicated to the victim. Reports of a breach of bail should of course be followed up promptly.

The victim must be offered the opportunity to make a Victim Personal Statement (see 10.12) to capture the context of the offending and to convey the impact of the events to the court. A restraining order could be used on the suspect (see 14.5.7.1), and the implications of this should be fully explained. Victims should be told about the possibility of seeking help from Victim Support (VS), and about community support services, and places of safety. They should also be given referral details for an IDVA (Independent Domestic Violence Advisor). Note that a referral to support services should only be made with the victim's explicit consent (CoP, 2015d).

The police should assist the victim and the IDVA in developing and implementing a safety plan. This can include advice on home security (from Crime Prevention Officers), personal alarms, mobile phones (including the possibility that the perpetrator may be tracking the victim), and CCTV. Other safety initiatives include:

- cocoon watch schemes (neighbours, family, and relevant agencies contact the police in case of further incidents);
- police watch schemes (regular patrolling of a certain area);
- sanctuary schemes (extra support so the victim does not have to go out, and the creation of a safe room from where he/she can call the police);

Specific Incidents

- installing a panic alarm (particularly if the victim does not live with the perpetrator);
- TecSOS phone or equivalent (issued to victims and linked to a monitoring service or directly to the police, and enabling victims to be easily located); and
- proximity tagging devices for perpetrators (alerts the victim and the police of the perpetrator's proximity to a certain area).

Neighbourhood policing teams should be kept informed about domestic abuse and associated levels of risk in their geographical area.

A victim of domestic abuse with an unstable immigration status may have his/her access to benefits restricted, thus causing additional financial difficulties. Some perpetrators use a victim's immigration status as a form of control, to dissuade the victim from contacting the police. If the abuse occurred within the first two years of the relationship, the victim can, however, appeal for indefinite stay in the UK.

When a person is killed by a partner or former partner, a domestic homicide review will often take place, with the aim of preventing further deaths (s 9 of the Domestic Violence, Crime and Victims Act 2004). Such a review usually involves chief officers of police, local authorities, probation officers, and health and social services.

13.6.1.7   Multi-agency work and wider initiatives to counter domestic abuse

Multi-agency approaches are very important in preventing and addressing domestic abuse. Provision varies across the country, but good practice often involves a Local Strategic Partnership (LSP), which brings together representatives from local authorities, public and private sectors, community and voluntary organizations. Multi-agency approaches are covered in more detail in 13.7 5, and include:

- MAPPA (Multi-Agency Public Protection Arrangements);
- MARACs (Multi-Agency Risk Assessment Conferences)—high risk victims of domestic abuse should be referred to MARACs;
- SABs (Safeguarding Adult Boards);
- MASHs (Multi-Agency Safeguarding Hubs); and
- ISAs (information-sharing agreements) which can facilitate multi-agency cooperation.

Specialist services for family and domestic violence and abuse include:

- IDVAs (Independent Domestic Violence Advisors), who work with police officers to provide independent support, risk assessment, and safety planning for victims—they are important in helping the police fast-track the investigation of domestic abuse incidents and can testify as an expert witness and should be kept informed of any changes in police practice and updated regularly on cases;
- SDVCs (Specialist Domestic Violence Courts), set up to improve victim protection, increase offender accountability, and to promote multi-agency cooperation;
- DHRs (Domestic Homicide Reviews), a multi-agency review where a person aged 16 or above has died due to possible abuse, neglect, or violence in a domestic context;
- YPVAs (Young People's Violence Advisors), who support domestic abuse victims aged 16 to 18 in a similar way to IDVAs' support for adult victims; and
- ISVAs (Independent Sexual Violence Advisors), who provide targeted support to victims of sexual violence.

Sharing information with the family court system (through the Children and Family Court Advisory and Support Services (CAFCASS)) is also important. Police forces should have protocols in place to this effect.

13.6.1.8   DASH risk assessments

The DASH risk assessment can be used with victims of domestic abuse, stalking and harassment (DASH), and honour-based violence. It involves answering a number of questions; the version used by the police has 27 questions to judge which risk factors may apply in a certain situation. Relevant information often includes the frequency of repeat victimization, the seriousness of the injuries, any escalation of violence, and details of the victim and the suspect. All staff involved with the ongoing investigation, including the custody officer, should be encouraged to contribute information.

13.6.2   'Honour'-based crime

'Honour'-based crime can include domestic or sexual abuse, forced marriage, female genital mutilation, or a combination of all of these. It involves attempts to maintain control in a family or social group to protect certain conceptions of honour and will often involve violence, hence the term 'honour'-based violence (HBV). The perpetrators believe that an individual has brought shame to the family or community through his/her behaviour. We use inverted commas for the word 'honour' in this context, because although the perpetrators may believe they are defending a certain notion of honour, this is not accepted in the UK as an excuse for violence or oppression. It should be noted that an HMIC report criticized the police response to HBV, forced marriage, and female genital mutilation. It found that few forces correctly understood the issues, or had adequate procedures in place to handle such cases (HMIC, 2015c, p 8).

It is very difficult to establish accurate numbers of 'honour'-based crimes, due to high levels of unreported cases and inconsistencies in police recordings of such crimes. There have been some extremely violent and high-profile cases, such as the murder of Banaz Mahmod in 2006 by her relatives. These draw attention to the need to clearly identify cases as HBV so proper support can be provided for the victims. Although most victims of HBV are women (cases tend to occur in very male-dominated cultures), men can also be the targets of HBV, for example if they are homosexual or if they support victims of HBV.

It is important that cases of HBV are identified early on, so they are managed properly. Cases are prosecuted under the specific offence committed (eg assault, kidnap, rape, threats to kill, or murder) but should be flagged up as HBV in the case file. The victim may be at risk from his/her own family and community, so great care is needed when discussing the case with anyone else, for example translators from within the same community. In some cases, a person may be hired to kill a particular family member, or distant relatives living in other areas of the country can pose a threat. Thus, a victim can be at risk even after leaving his/her community. Ensuring the victim's safety is a priority, and the level of risk should not be underestimated. Information should be gathered not only about the victim but also about the alleged offender—he/she may be using younger members of the family to commit the criminal acts or to deflect attention from him/herself.

13.6.3   Forced marriage

Forcing a person to marry is a criminal offence (s 121 of the Anti-social Behaviour, Crime and Policing Act 2014) and the maximum custodial penalty is 12 months if tried summarily, and seven years on indictment. The Forced Marriage Unit (FMU) provided assistance for 1,764 possible cases of forced marriage in 2018, a 47 per cent increase compared with 2017 (Home Office, 2019d, p 7). Of the recorded instances 75 per cent of the victims were recorded as female and 17 per cent male (Home Office, 2019d, p 9). It is very likely that many forced marriages remain unreported.

The victim can be physically, emotionally, or psychologically pressured to marry by means of threats, physical or sexual violence, or other forms of coercion directed at the victim or a third person. If the victim lacks the capacity to consent under the Mental Capacity Act 2005 (see 13.2.4), any type of conduct can amount to the offence. Some victims are not coerced or threatened but are deceived into going abroad, and are unaware that the purpose of the trip is a forced marriage (for a prosecution it is not relevant whether the marriage took place). A forced marriage should be distinguished from an arranged marriage; the latter is a legal practice in which a third party arranges for two consenting people to marry.

Possible cases of forced marriage must be identified and flagged up in the early stages so that appropriate management can be put in place. Most cases involve individuals from South Asian communities, however, forced marriage also occurs in communities from the Middle East, Europe, Africa, and North America (Home Office, 2019d, p 8). While some victims self-refer, around 60 per cent of referrals come from professionals such as specialized support agencies and NGOs (Home Office, 2019d, p 7). Information must be gathered about the alleged offender, the victim, and the community to ensure the case is managed appropriately.

Specific Incidents

13.6.3.1   Investigating forced marriage

In such investigations there may be only one chance to speak to a victim (eg because travelling is imminent)—the 'one chance rule' (HM Government, 2014, p 21). The attending police officer should therefore contact the designated person in their organization with expertise in forced marriages (often the same person leading the response in cases that involve the safeguarding of children, protection of vulnerable adults, or victims of domestic abuse). If access is not immediately possible, then information should be gathered to establish the facts and help with the referral.

The suspected victim must be seen in person, alone, and in a place where the conversation cannot be overheard, to try and avoid retaliation from other family members. He/she should be reassured of the confidentiality of the conversation. All the available options should be fully explained, but his/her decision must be accepted.

A DASH risk assessment exercise should be performed (see 13.6.1.8), and any evidence of abuse or threats of abuse should be explored and documented. Any criminal offence committed in the context of a forced marriage (either before or after the marriage) will also be prosecuted (CPS, 2018c).

The case should be discussed with the Forced Marriage Unit, and the victim referred to appropriate local and national support groups if he/she agrees. The FMU have produced a number of support materials for professionals and those who are in (or at risk of) a forced marriage. These include leaflets, video clips, and a 'survivors' handbook', all available on the FMU section of the gov.uk website.

Police and social service records should be checked for previous referrals of family members, for example in relation to domestic abuse or missing persons. If relevant, a restricted entry in the force intelligence system should be created, and a crime report submitted. Officers should reassure the victim about confidentiality, assess the need for immediate protection, and agree an effective method of contacting the victim discreetly in the future. If the person is under 18, a police protection referral should be made (see 13.3.3). Similarly, for adults with support needs, a referral should be made to the designated person responsible for safeguarding vulnerable adults, and local safeguarding procedures should be activated (see 13.7.3).

Extensive guidance on best practice in responding to situations of forced marriage can be found in *Multi-agency Practice Guidelines: Handling Cases of Forced Marriage*.

13.6.3.2   Forced Marriage Protection Orders

A Forced Marriage Protection Order (FMPO) can be issued by a civil court to a person who seems to be planning to implement a forced marriage. The recipient of the order is obliged to hand over the passport of the person at risk, or to reveal his/her whereabouts if missing. Breaking an FMPO is a criminal offence, with a penalty of up to five years' imprisonment (s 120 of the Anti-social Behaviour, Crime and Policing Act 2014).

13.6.4   Female genital mutilation

Female genital mutilation (FGM) occurs when part or all the external female genitalia are removed or injured for no medical reason (see WHO, 2008, for a typology of different forms of FGM). FGM is referred to in a number of ways at community level (such as female circumcision, cutting, or being 'clean'), and is usually performed before a girl starts puberty. Perpetrators of FGM (sometimes known as cutters) often believe that they are protecting an important part of their cultural identity, and FGM may be presented as an occasion for celebration and a rite of passage. It may also be linked to ideas of family 'honour', in which sense it would be a form of 'honour'-based violence.

FGM is a violation of human rights, particularly the rights to health, security, and physical integrity, and the right to be free from torture and cruel, inhuman, or degrading treatment. It can also cause serious health problems and even death. The NHS recorded 6,415 individual instances of FGM in the year 2018/19 (NHS Digital, 2019a), and although FGM has been a crime under English law since the 1980s, the first prosecution was not made until 2014.

The College of Policing APP guidance on FGM pivots on prevention, protection, and prosecution (CoP, 2015b), and further information is available online in *A Protocol between the Police and the Crown Prosecution Service in the investigation and prosecution of allegations of FGM*. The latter document stresses the importance of early consultation between the police and the CPS. The NHS and the NSPCC websites provide further information and statistical data on FGM.

13.6.4.1 FGM offences

FGM offences are all listed in the Female Genital Mutilation Act 2003 (FGMA). The offences are:

- carrying out FGM (s 1);
- assisting a girl with carrying out FGM on herself (s 2);
- assisting a non-UK person outside the UK to perform FGM on a UK person (s 3); and
- failing to protect a girl from FGM (s 3A);

The offences under ss 1, 3, and 3A also apply for offences that take place outside the UK, if the suspect is a UK citizen (s 4).

For a victim under 16 years of age, the persons responsible for her (such as a parent, or someone assuming similar responsibility even if only temporarily) are committing an offence of failing to protect her, with a maximum penalty of seven years' imprisonment (s 3A).

FGM offences are punishable with a maximum of 14 years' imprisonment (FGMA, and ss 70–75 of the Serious Crime Act 2015).

13.6.4.2 Prevention of FGM

Police officers who suspect that FGM is likely to occur should consider the need to take immediate action to protect anyone at risk, and inform a supervisor or specially trained officer. There may be indicators that suggest that FGM is being planned for a particular girl, for example preparing for a trip, absence from school, and/or a special ceremony. The safety of the girl is paramount, and an assessment of risk of significant harm should be conducted. It could be classed as a critical incident and the 'Golden Hour' principle applied (see 11.2.1). The girl could be taken into police protection for up to 72 hours (see 13.3.3).

A strategy meeting will be arranged (within a day at most) between the local authority children's social care department and health professionals. The parents will be informed of the law and the dangers of FGM, but if it seems that the girl is still at risk, the emergency protection powers and orders under the Children Act 1989 can be used (see 13.6.4.4).

A risk assessment should also be conducted for other female family members. If it is known that a particular woman has already undergone FGM, a multi-agency meeting must be convened and a risk assessment carried out for any girls in her family.

13.6.4.3 Investigating FGM

Indicators that FGM has occurred include absences from school and noticeable changes in behaviour when the girl returns (such as difficulty sitting straight, complaining of pain, and being secretive). FGM is a crime and when carried out on girls it also amounts to child abuse, so a robust investigation must be conducted. Victims may not know that the events they experienced amounted to FGM and/or that it is illegal in the UK. They are often unwilling to report FGM and support a prosecution. Perpetrators may see the act as culturally justifiable and in the best interest of the child, and might not know it is illegal. Other members of the family or the community may share these attitudes and beliefs, or be reluctant to come forward for fear of being ostracized.

Police officers may also be reluctant to address cases of FGM for fear of being branded racist or culturally insensitive, but this should not deter them from exercising their duty of protection. A female police officer should conduct the interview, and no member of the victim's family or community should be present. The language used should be sensitive and non-judgmental. An interpreter may sometimes be required, but if he/she has the same ethnic background as the victim this can inhibit the victim as she may fear a lack of confidentiality.

Officers rely heavily on information and support from other agencies to identify and address FGM. Covert tactics should also be considered and any opportunities for gathering intelligence should be maximized. The risk of FGM occurring to other female members of the same family should also be taken into account.

For suspected cases of FGM, local safeguarding procedures should be followed. For known cases of FGM where the victim is under the age of 18 years, all registered health and social care professionals and teachers have a duty to report it to the police (s 5B of the FGMA). A case would be 'known' if the FGM has been verbally disclosed by the victim or visually identified by the professional involved. Failing to report a known case to the police is not a criminal offence, but is treated as a serious disciplinary matter (CoP, 2015b). Medical evidence will be required for known cases of FGM.

The anonymity of the victim must be preserved for life, so no information that could allow members of the public to identify her should be published. Any breach of this principle is punishable with a fine (s 4A of and Sch 1 to the FGMA).

13.6.4.4 FGM Protection Orders and Emergency Powers

FGM Protection Orders (FGMPO) can be issued to protect girls at risk of FGM (s 5A of and Sch 2 to the FGMA and the Serious Crime Act 2015). They can also be used for girls who have already undergone FGM, as they may be threatened by other witnesses in an investigation into FGM. Note that although the term 'girl' is used, the legislation applies to females of any age.

Applications for an FGMPO can be made to the High Court or a family law court by the victim, local authorities, or a third party authorized by the court (such as the police, a healthcare professional, a teacher, a friend, or a family member). The order provides flexibility for the courts in setting prohibitions and restrictions, and can, for example, require the surrender of passports or travel documents to prevent FGM being arranged or carried out abroad. Breaching an FGMPO is an either-way offence (the penalty is up to 12 months' imprisonment if tried summarily, and 5 years on indictment). A breach can also be treated as a civil matter, as contempt of court (see s 5A of and Sch 2, para 4(3) and (4) to the FGMA).

Emergency powers under the Children Act 1989 are also available when children are known to be at risk of FGM, for example under ss 44 and 46 (see 13.3.3).

13.7 Providing Public Protection

Law enforcement is often seen as the main police priority, but this is not the only role of the police. In terms of police legitimacy (see 2.2.5) there is a clear need to engage with the community, and to act as a 'police service' in addition to being a 'police force'. Here, we will cover some of the ways in which the police are expected to provide a service. This includes dealing with lost property and illness on the street, and the use of force to enter property to save life and limb in emergency situations. Providing protection to children and vulnerable adults is a particular priority, as is providing adequate support for all victims and witnesses so that they can provide good evidence during prosecutions. Vulnerability is covered in more detail in Chapter 4.

13.7.1 Providing support for members of the general public

Some of the services provided by the police are unrelated to law enforcement, such as dealing with lost property, and helping people who become ill in the street. It could be argued that the role of the police in the twenty-first century should not include these 'time-honoured' and traditional activities, but others might suggest that they serve to enhance and secure police legitimacy in an ever more demanding society.

13.7.1.1 Lost property

Traditionally, although not a statutory obligation, the police have provided the repository for property found in public spaces. The police also maintain records of property reported as lost so that any article that has been found can be returned to its owner at the earliest opportunity. Other organizations provide a similar service, such as road and rail transport companies, but only for property lost or found in their own vehicles or premises.

A person finding property is not obliged to hand it over to the police, but should take all reasonable steps to find the owner to avoid being suspected of committing theft (see 16.2). This might include reporting it to the police, and indeed, items such as passports and driving licences are more likely to be quickly and safely returned to the owner if the police take responsibility for making the contact. Generally, police policy is that a police officer (and others such as a PCSO) who finds lost property should record and deposit it at the police station.

Police staff on patrol or at the front counter of police stations will inevitably be handed lost property from members of the public. It is vital that the officer makes an accurate record, and a full entry should be written if a PNB is used (see 10.2). The description of the item(s) should refer to simple facts, such as measurements and unique identifying features (eg serial numbers). Assumptions should be avoided; a shiny gold-coloured watch may not be real gold! The description of such an article should state that it is a watch made of yellow metal, together with the wording on the face.

13.7.1.2   Illness in the street

Police officers on patrol will often encounter individuals who are ill, or seem ill. A police officer in this situation will need to decide whether it is likely the person is ill, and to try and determine the nature of the illness. Note that a person who appears to be drunk or under the influence of drugs might instead be unwell, or have been assaulted or otherwise injured.

It is worth checking to see if the person is carrying documentation or wearing MedicAlert jewellery (see photograph) relating to an illness or medical treatment, a medical information card, or a Crisis card (see 13.2.1).

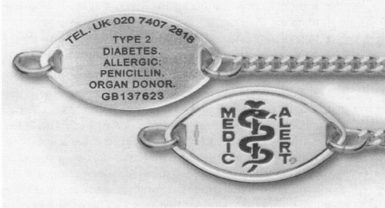

Image reproduced with permission of the MedicAlert foundation.

Police officers should call for an ambulance if it seems necessary, without assuming that a bystander or witness has already done so. A person cannot be forced to go to hospital but the ambulance staff will be able to provide support. Where appropriate, the police officer should provide First Aid as the preservation of life is always paramount.

The identity of the person should be established where possible. If the person cannot provide the information on request and checks on personal documentation (and any medical information jewellery or card) do not help, another person at the scene may know the person and be able to provide useful information. The PNC wanted or missing persons indexes can also be checked for descriptions that match. If necessary, CCTV can be checked to establish the person's prior movements. A supervisor could arrange for the description of the person to be circulated if all else fails.

Officers on patrol may also encounter people who are suffering from memory loss. It is important to try and find out whether this is due to an injury or some pre-existing condition, such as dementia, as this will influence the steps to take next. Determining the cause of memory loss can obviously be difficult, but witnesses might be able to help. We cover dealing with mentally vulnerable people in 13.2.

An officer also has a responsibility to safeguard any property the person might have, for example, a bag or money in a pocket. If possible, this should be kept with the person, for example if he/she is taken to hospital. However, if this is not practical, the property should be taken to a known relative, or as a last resort to the police station for safekeeping. The police officer should, where possible, also ensure that the appropriate relatives are notified. The ill person may not wish a relative to be informed, but this will be a matter of judgement. The police officer must ensure that decisions are justifiable and clearly documented, and a supervisor should be consulted if in any doubt.

Specific Incidents

The officer should accompany the person to hospital if the illness seems to be serious and/or life-threatening as the information he/she can provide could be important for a medical diagnosis.

13.7.2 Entering property to save life or limb

The police have the legal power to enter and search premises to save life or limb (s 17(1)(e) of the PACE Act 1984). The power of search is limited to this purpose (s 17(4)), for example if a property is entered and searched in order to find a person who needs medical treatment, there is no justification for searching a bathroom cabinet. If the conditions do not satisfy s 17 then the entry is unlawful, and any evidence of criminality (such as the presence of controlled drugs) may be excluded by the court in a subsequent prosecution (under s 78 of the PACE Act 1984 (see *R v Veneroso* [2002] Crim LR 306 (Crown Ct)). The officer does not need to have reasonable grounds for believing that anyone is on the premises. For a building with flats, all the flats can be searched.

In the case of *Baker v Crown Prosecution Service* [2009] EWHC 299 (Admin), it was further decided that entry and search under subsection (e) can be carried out:

* without seeking the permission of the occupant (this might be self-defeating);
* without giving the occupant a reason if it is impossible, impracticable, or undesirable to do so;
* to save someone from him/herself as well as from a third party; but
* only to the extent that is reasonably required to satisfy the objective for using the power of entry (s 17(4) PACE Act 1984).

These powers should only be used if 'something serious' seems to have occurred (or is likely to occur) within the property, and not 'simply on the basis of concern for the welfare' of someone in the premises, as shown in *Syed v DPP* [2010] EWHC 81 (Admin). In this incident the officers attended after a neighbour reported a disturbance. On arrival, there was no sign of a disturbance but the officers attempted to enter the premises, stating to the occupant that they were 'concerned about the welfare of person(s) within'. The occupant refused entry, assaulting one officer and spitting at the other, and was subsequently charged with an offence under s 89 of the Police Act 1996 (see 15.4.2.2). On appeal, the conviction was quashed; it was held that the officers had not been acting in the lawful execution of their duty because the criteria for using s 17(1)(e) had not been met.

Reasonable force may be used to secure entry (s 117 of the PACE Act 1984) where any part of the PACE Act 1984 grants a power of entry. If met with force, an officer might have to use equal force to negate it, and then use even more force to take control. This is covered as part of personal safety training. In a prosecution, the court has to determine whether an officer honestly believed that the force he/she used was reasonable and proportionate in the circumstances (see 15.4.1.1). The principles are similar to the use of force during an arrest (s 3 of the Criminal Law Act 1967, see 10.8.3).

13.7.3 Abuse of vulnerable adults

Some adults are deemed to be vulnerable due to a mental, physical, or learning disability, age or illness. Such a person may be unable to take care of him/herself, or protect him/herself against significant harm or exploitation. Vulnerability, including its definition, is discussed in detail in Chapter 4. There are two main types of incidents where adults may suffer abuse: those involving serious abuse, such as GBH or serious sexual assault, and those which involve a serious incident in a care or healthcare environment (ACPO, 2012b).

The abuse can be physical, sexual, psychological, discriminatory, institutional, or financial, and can also include acts of omission and neglect. It can take place in a range of contexts, including day care, residential or nursing situations, as well as hospitals or indeed the person's own home. Offenders can be from any section of society and can include relatives, care workers, professional staff, volunteers, and strangers. Some perpetrate multiple offences against one person a number of times, while others abuse groups of people at the same time. A victim may be reluctant to report the abuse if the suspect is his/her primary carer, as he/she might then be obliged to move into institutional residential care. Some victims may not even realize that the acts amount to abuse, or be able to communicate about it.

The key responsibility of the FAO is to protect the victim from further harm, to preserve evidence, and identify any criminal offences. When communicating with a vulnerable victim, an officer should take into account the victim's level of comprehension, age, and preference (see 13.2.4 and 25.6). Judging the risk of harm is difficult, partly because the adult has the right to make his/her own decisions and choices, and may not see him/herself as vulnerable. For a vulnerable adult in custody, the PACE Codes of Practice provide a number of safeguards to protect his/her rights, including the appointment of a responsible adult.

The Human Rights Act 1998 and the Care Act 2014 provide an important legal framework against which policies for the safeguarding of vulnerable adults have been developed. There is currently no single statutory framework for safeguarding adults equivalent to the Children Act 1989 (which legislates for child protection (see 13.3)).

A multi-agency approach to communication and decision-making may safeguard the victim and prevent further abuse by addressing the immediate protection needs of the victim at the earliest opportunity. Such an approach seems to have been lacking in the case of Fiona Pilkington, who killed herself and her severely disabled daughter in 2007 after years of harassment. The police officers involved in the case were later disciplined for failing to develop adequate support for Fiona and her daughter; she had made over 30 complaints of harassment over a period of ten years. A damning IPCC report drew attention to the fact that Leicestershire Police had failed to properly identify the Pilkingtons as vulnerable and failed to liaise with other agencies in order to provide proper support (IPCC, 2012, pp 179–81). The case highlights the importance of effective communication between agencies in the implementation of effective protection strategies for vulnerable adults.

Further information is available online in the ACPO *Guidance on Safeguarding and Investigating the Abuse of Vulnerable Adults*, the Department of Health *No Secrets: Guidance on Developing and Implementing Multi-Agency Policies and Procedures to Protect Vulnerable Adults from Abuse*, and the *Office of the Public Guardian's Safeguarding Policy*. The Home Office *Code of Practice for Victims of Crime 2015* (available online) can also be helpful in making decisions about how to best meet victims' rights and entitlements.

13.7.4 Providing support for victims and witnesses

Officers at the scene of an incident need to consider the support of victims, witnesses, or suspects (and others affected by the incident) in an ethical and appropriate manner (see 5.3 on ethics). Victims and witnesses may have suffered a physical injury and stress, and may be emotional, confused, aggressive, angry, and/or scared. The type of support required will vary depending on the incident and those involved, and could include providing reassurance, first aid, and information on issues or procedures relating to the incident (legislation, courts, and available services). Specialist medical help might also be required. It is important that the appropriate procedures and legislation are followed and that anxiety or vulnerability is not exacerbated. The support needs of witnesses, survivors, and victims can change over time, so this should be taken into account. It is also important that officers provide updates to minimize anxiety and vulnerabilities. Where vulnerability has been identified (see Chapter 4) the person's wishes should be discussed with them and met where appropriate (this could include further support such as 'Special Measures' (see 27.5.2.5).

13.7.4.1 Information and support for victims

All victims are entitled to support under *The Code of Practice for Victims of Crime 2015*. The Code defines a victim as:

- a person 'who has suffered harm, including physical, mental or emotional harm or economic loss which was directly caused by a criminal offence' or
- is a close relative of a person 'whose death was directly caused by a criminal offence'.

The entitlements for adult and child victims are different (Chapter 2 Part A, and Chapter 3 Part A respectively). The entitlements still apply once a suspect is charged or convicted of the crime, and it is not relevant whether the victim is involved with the investigation.

Working with victims of crime is an important part of police work, but victims and their families often find it hard to understand the complexities of criminal investigations and legal proceedings. Establishing a good relationship with victims increases the chances that they will cooperate effectively with the investigation and prosecution. Victims must be treated with dignity and respect, regardless of the specific circumstances of the crime. They may have experienced very traumatic events and require particular support. Some victims are considered as vulnerable (eg due to their age or the type of crime suffered) and are entitled to additional forms of support. Police officers should consider the well-being of individuals from a broad perspective and be aware of the full range of support services available. Specialist support for victims of domestic abuse is covered in 13.6.1.6, and for sexually motivated offences in 17.6.1. For further guidance in relation to intimidated witnesses, see 14.6 and 25.4.

The Code of Practice also sets up duties for service providers, including the police. All victims making an allegation of criminal conduct should be provided with the *Information for Victims of Crime* leaflet within five days (or be referred to a relevant website with the same information). 'Priority victims' (as identified by the police) are entitled to an 'enhanced service', and must be given this information within one day. This would include victims of the most serious crimes, persistently targeted victims, and vulnerable or intimidated victims. Victims must be told how to access the Code's provisions, including special measures. If it seems that a victim will need any specific measures to help give evidence, then these should also be recorded and shared with Witness Care Units and the CPS.

Victims must be given information and contact details about relevant support services (see 13.7.4.2). The police must explain that victim details are usually passed on to victims' services unless the victim requests otherwise. For victims of sexual offences or domestic abuse, or bereaved close relatives, however, explicit consent must be obtained before forwarding their details to victims' services. (Victims can choose to self-refer to the services at a later date.) The police referral should be done within two working days of an allegation being reported by a victim. Victims of the 'most serious crime' should also be informed of the availability of pre-trial therapy.

A Victim Personal Statement (VPS) can also be made (see 10.11.2), and this must be raised at an early stage for the most serious crimes, for persistently targeted, and vulnerable or intimidated victims, and for parents or guardians of vulnerable or child victims. (Other categories of victim will be informed of this opportunity only when completing a witness statement.) A police officer can, however, use his/her discretion, and offer the opportunity to make a VPS to any victim at any stage.

The police must keep victims informed about the suspect. Victims must be informed within five days (one day for enhanced service) of a suspect being arrested, interviewed under caution, released without charge, released on police bail, or if there are changes in the conditions to their bail or it is cancelled. Any decisions to prosecute or to give the suspect an out-of-court disposal must be communicated to the victim within the relevant time limits (one or five days), including all police cautions and decisions and reasons not to prosecute. The police must also inform victims of the date, time, and location of the first court hearing and bail conditions (including any decisions regarding breaches of these conditions). When considering out-of-court disposals, a victim should also be asked for his/her views when practicable, and these should be taken into account.

Once a trial has started the CPS, Witness Care Units, and other agencies take over responsibility for providing information to victims. The exception is when the police are nominated as the single point of contact with victims.

13.7.4.2 Support services for victims

Victim Support (VS) is a non-governmental agency that offers support primarily to victims and witnesses of crime, and to anyone else who may have been affected, such as the family members of a victim. It also runs the Witness Services in courts across the country, and provides assistance to witnesses. The full range of VS services are listed and described on their website. The service is staffed by specially trained volunteers who offer free and confidential service to victims of crime. (All VS volunteers carry photographic identity cards.) They offer support such as advice on how to improve personal safety or how the criminal justice system works, crisis management, and long-term help. A crisis is often due to a serious form of crime but could also result from non-crime incidents such as a road traffic collision or a sudden death. Specially trained support staff can provide assistance to bereaved family members of victims of violent deaths. Finally, VS also offers information on compensation and insurance schemes.

Other support services include Citizens Advice; social services; mental health, bereavement, and relationship counsellors; and medical practitioners. Particular care needs to be taken with vulnerable people (eg due to age, disability, mental health issues, children, and those who feel intimidated). Note that police officers are in a good position to inform victims of violent crime about the Criminal Injuries Compensation Scheme.

13.7.4.3 Crime prevention advice for victims

The security of a building should be considered after a fire (see 11.4.1) or a burglary (see 3.5.2) as other criminals can exploit perceived weaknesses and commit further crimes. Simple crime prevention and reduction advice, access to good information (perhaps from a Crime Reduction Officer), ideas on alarm installation, and other 'target hardening' techniques can all be useful. Cybercrime prevention advice is covered in 21.3.4. We cover crime reduction in more general terms in Chapter 3

A basic level of support can be offered by patrols occasionally visiting vulnerable victims to check on their welfare and give advice. Neighbourhood Watch schemes should be encouraged (see 2.2.2.9), and victims and their neighbours can be told how to contact Neighbourhood Policing Teams to promote engagement with the local police and build a rapport. Some victims are repeatedly targeted by offenders (see 3.5.2 on 'hot victims') and, in many cases, the scale of the offences can become quite alarming, particularly property repair scams, or in households where domestic violence is an issue.

13.7.5 Multi-agency public protection arrangements

Multi-agency public protection arrangements (MAPPA) are considered by many organizations as key to the successful management of violent and sexual offenders, especially their reintegration into society after a prison sentence. The police, probation, and the prison service in each area form a 'responsible authority' for MAPPA, and work together with other agencies such as social services, electronic monitoring providers, registered social landlords, youth offending teams, children's services, local health services, local housing authorities, and Jobcentre plus. MAPPA guidance identifies a framework with four core functions: identifying MAPPA offenders; ensuring relevant information is shared with appropriate agencies; assessing the risk of serious harm; and managing risk.

The guidance identifies three broad categories of offenders (with some overlap):

- Category 1—registered sexual offenders as defined in Part 2 of the Sexual Offences Act 2003;
- Category 2—violent offenders sentenced to 12 months' or more imprisonment, sexual offenders not included in Category 1, and offenders disqualified from working with children; and
- Category 3—other dangerous offenders who are not included in the first two categories but are nonetheless still regarded by the responsible authority as presenting a serious risk to the public (eg they have a previous conviction or caution that indicates that they have the potential to cause serious harm to others).

There are three identified levels of risk management. Level 1 is for offenders who can be managed by one primary agency without necessarily involving other agencies. Level 2 management involves more than one agency but is not considered to be overly challenging or complex. Level 3 is used where managing the risk requires active conferencing and senior representation from the responsible authority and other agencies with a duty to cooperate.

The number of 'MAPPA-eligible offenders' in the UK has been steadily increasing since 2007, at an annual rate of about 7 per cent. In 2017 the Ministry of Justice reported there were almost 77,000 offenders in the UK (72 per cent Category 1; 27 per cent Category 2; and less than 1 per cent Category 3) and that 98 per cent of cases were managed at Level 1 (Ministry of Justice, 2017b).

In deciding on what course of action to take it is important that 'defensible decisions' are made. This is to ensure that the responsible authority has taken all reasonable steps, and that the assessment methods utilized are reliable. A thorough evaluation of the collected information needs to be demonstrated, and decisions need to have been recorded and acted upon. Throughout it is important to demonstrate that the appropriate policies and procedures have been followed, and that a proactive approach has been adopted by the practitioners and

Specific Incidents

managers. An important function of MAPPA is to ensure that public protection work is communicated to the public and all interested parties in a consistent manner.

MARACs (Multi-Agency Risk Assessment Conferences) are often coordinated by local police forces. They provide a forum for the sharing of information, developing a multi-agency risk management plan for each case. The police have a significant role in the work of a MARAC, particularly in detaining perpetrators and referring cases. High risk victims of domestic abuse should be referred to MARACs.

Other bodies have a particular role within MAPPA, such as:

- SABs (Safeguarding Adult Boards), which make decisions on whether and how to intervene when there is suspicion that an adult in the area has needs for care and support, is experiencing (or is at risk of) abuse or neglect, and is unable to protect him/herself due to that lack of care and support;
- MASHs (Multi-Agency Safeguarding Hubs), where services are co-located to facilitate communication in a given area, mainly in relation to child protection;
- Independent Domestic Violence Advisors (see 13.6.1.7);
- Specialist Domestic Violence Courts (see 13.6.1.7);
- Domestic Homicide Reviews, which are multi-agency reviews where a person aged 16 or above has died due to possible abuse, neglect, or violence in a domestic context;
- Young People's Violence Advisors (see 13.6.1.7);
- Independent Sexual Violence Advisors, who provide targeted support to victims of sexual violence; and
- ISAs (information-sharing agreements), which can facilitate multi-agency cooperation.

13.7.5.1 ViSOR

Information about dangerous offenders is stored in a central database called ViSOR (also known as the Dangerous Persons Database). The data can be accessed by the three responsible authority agencies (see 13.7.5), and the cases are called 'nominals'. When a case ceases to be an active MAPPA case, the information is archived and can be retrieved at a later stage if necessary. The police have a responsibility to create and maintain a ViSOR record for offenders in Categories 1 and 3 when this is not the responsibility of the Probation Trust. Nominal records will normally be removed at the 100th birthday of an individual, after a review is conducted.

13.8 Answers to Tasks

TASK 1

1. There are likely to be policy agreements with local Social Services and the Healthcare Trusts.
2. Advice to the police officer would be as follows:
   (a) A dynamic risk assessment of the situation should be made first. Can she safely enter the room or should she seek the assistance of other officers with appropriate personal safety equipment? Entrance can be gained by seeking the permission of the parents/owners of the property to unscrew the door handle and withdrawing the bar a little, so the handle on the other side no longer works. Then she could turn the handle herself to open the door.
   (b) She should find out if the young man will voluntarily go to hospital. If not, an AMHP should be called to see if he can be taken into hospital under the MHA.

TASK 2

1. Under s 17(1)(e) PACE an officer 'may enter and search any premises for the purposes of saving life or limb or preventing serious damage to property'. The witness evidence of hearing hysterical screaming and the suspicion that the child is alone and cannot open the door together justify the use of s 17 to save the life and limb of the child.
2. It would appear that Jo has committed an offence under s 1 of the Children and Young Persons Act 1933. This is committed by any person who is 16 years old or over who has responsibility for a child under the age of 16 years and who 'wilfully assaults, ill-treats, neglects, abandons or exposes the child in a manner likely to cause unnecessary suffering or injury to health'. In these circumstances Jo has 'abandoned' Sam in a manner likely to

cause unnecessary suffering or injury to health. It appears that, although an offence has been committed, the child is no longer in immediate danger and arrangements could be made (perhaps with relatives) for the child's safety while Jo is absent. If there was any reason to believe the child was in immediate danger the officer could consider taking Sam into police protection and arresting the mother. However, prosecution guidelines must be followed and the guidance of a CPS representative would be required. Whatever action is taken, it must be proportionate.

TASK 3

1. The boy needs regular medication: has he taken it with him? Are there factors which will make his medical condition worse (such as stress-induced asthma)? Can the condition be life-threatening in any way? Is his shotgun (and any other weapons on the farm) accounted for? Has any ammunition gone missing? Has he mentioned any particular individuals in connection with the apparent bullying at school, or about revenge? Was the quarrel with his father more serious than usual? What could have caused his depression and anxiety? Has he ever talked (or hinted) about suicide? Does he have a religious belief or strong ethical principles? Has he taken drugs? Has he ever been in trouble with the police?
2. The College of Policing APP provides guidance in *Major investigation and public protection: Missing persons* (CoP, 2016a).

TASK 4 The 'Herbert Protocol' initiative for helping to locate vulnerable adults who go missing is named after George Herbert, a veteran of the 1944 D-Day landings in Normandy during the Second World War. As an elderly man, Mr Herbert developed dementia and was cared for in a residential home. He went missing in 2011 (apparently looking for his childhood home) but was found dead before he could be helped to return to his residential care. The Protocol was developed in response to this.

Police forces that have adopted the Herbert Protocol include the MPS, Cheshire Constabulary, Cumbria Police, Derbyshire Police, Devon and Cornwall Police, Humberside Police, North Yorkshire Police, Sussex Police, and West Yorkshire Police.

TASK 5 Through questioning, a police officer would be able to determine whether the injury affects the health or comfort of the victim in more than a trivial way. The officer would be able to collect and collate evidence concerning the injury. Remember that the police officer him/herself is a witness too. If there is no evidence of the offence of actual bodily harm, then common assault could be considered as an alternative (see 15.2.1).

Specific Incidents

14 | Policing Anti-social Behaviour, Public Order, and Harassment

14.1   Introduction

In this chapter we look at the policing of anti-social behaviour, public order, and harassment.

Examples of anti-social behaviour include:

> nuisance, rowdy or inconsiderate neighbours; vandalism, graffiti and fly-posting; street drinking; . . . littering, dumping of rubbish and abandonment of cars [and the] inconsiderate or inappropriate use of vehicles (Home Office, 2020a).

Not all anti-social behaviour is necessarily a 'crime' as such, but the term covers a number of disruptive activities, some of which are criminal offences. Consequently, this chapter looks not only at these offences but also considers some of the powers designed for the policing of social disorder generally, in both private and public places.

Note that the responsibility for dealing with many anti-social behaviour activities is shared by the police with local authorities and other partner agencies such as the local Fire and Rescue Service, and social housing landlords.

Dealing with civil disputes (eg trespass or debt) and court orders (concerning, eg, access to children or repossession of property) is not normally the responsibility of the police service in England and Wales, but the police are often first at the scene when such a situation escalates and their role is usually to keep the peace. For some cases of civil dispute, and where no offences have been committed, the police can suggest an alternative remedy to pursue in the civil courts. If, for example, a person is harassed by a neighbour, an injunction can be brought about under s 3(1) of the Protection from Harassment Act 1997 (see 14.5.1.4). In other circumstances, the police can apply for a civil order such as a Domestic Violence Protection Notice (see 13.6.1.1).

The methods for policing demonstrations have drawn attention in recent years, particularly the controversial use of 'kettling' to contain and control crowds. The police have a 'negative duty' to **not** restrict, hinder, or prevent peaceful protest, as well as a positive duty to protect citizens who want to exercise their right to demonstrate—'the right to peaceful assembly' in the European Convention on Human Rights (ECHR). This right is now enshrined in the Human Rights Act 1998, as the freedom of thought, conscience, and religion (Article 9), the freedom of expression (Article 10), and the freedom of assembly (Article 11)—see 4.4.1. There have been a number of HMIC reports on the policing of protest, including a major review in 2009 after the protests at the G20 summit (HMIC, 2009, revised 2011); and a report in 2011 recommended that the police retain an adaptable response to the changing nature of protest (HMIC, 2011). In this chapter we examine the common law employed by the police to contain protesters to reduce the threat of large-scale disorder.

The topics covered in this chapter are likely to contribute to the learning required for the National Policing Curriculum subject areas: 'Public Protection', 'Policing Communities', 'Understanding the Police Constable Role', and 'Response Policing'.

The College of Policing has APP on 'public order' (including the policing of football), and 'stalking and harassment' (under the heading of 'Major investigation and public protection'). If you are undertaking the PCDA or DHEP you will probably be expected to familiarize yourself with the relevant APP.

14.2 Countering Anti-social Behaviour

The definition of anti-social behaviour (ASB) is behaviour which has 'caused or is likely to cause harassment, alarm or distress to any person' (s 2(1)(a) of the Anti-social Behaviour, Crime and Policing Act 2014 (ASBCPA)). There has been increasing interest in the role of the community and victims in working with the police to address ASB.

The Anti-social Behaviour, Crime and Policing Act 2014 provides powers and injunctions to help the police and local authorities address ASB and disorder. In terms of these powers, ASB is broadly categorized as either housing related or non-housing related. The latter occurs in a public place such as a shopping precinct or city centre. Housing related ASB, on the other hand, will include disputes between neighbours over lifestyle clashes, high hedges, litter, noise, boundary disputes, and the behaviour of children. It also includes more serious incidents of ASB, where the behaviour of one household causes serious problems within a whole neighbourhood and may involve harassment, violence, and criminality. The Home Office guidance *Anti-social Behaviour, Crime and Policing Act 2014: Reform of anti-social behaviour powers: Statutory guidance for frontline professionals* (updated December 2017) is available online.

14.2.1 Tackling ASB at the level of the individual

A police officer can require any person who has been acting (or is acting) in an 'anti-social manner' to provide his/her name and address (s 50(1) of the Police Reform Act 2002). An 'anti-social manner' is defined as behaviour that 'caused or is likely to cause harassment, alarm or distress to any person' (s 2(1)(a) of the ASBCPA). It is a summary offence for such a person to fail to give his/her correct name and address when required (s 50(2) of the Police Reform Act 2002)), and the penalty is a fine.

Further measures are available under the ASBCPA to deal with anti-social behaviour, such as civil injunctions and criminal behaviour orders (CBOs). The latter can also be used to deal with individuals who engage in criminality.

14.2.1.1 Civil injunctions

Injunctions to Prevent Nuisance and Annoyance (IPNAs) can be used at an early stage to stop or prevent individuals engaging in ASB. They are intended for use in non-housing related ASB where the behaviour either caused or was likely to cause harassment, alarm, or distress, and for housing related ASB where the conduct is capable of causing nuisance or annoyance.

A wide range of organizations can apply for such an injunction, such as local councils, social landlords, the police, and Transport for London. The injunction is issued by the county court and High Court for over 18-year-olds, and the Youth Court for under 18-year-olds (the relevant Youth Offending Team (YOT) must also be consulted (see 8.4.3)). There is no need to prove an injunction is 'necessary', and they are obtainable on a civil standard of proof (balance of probability). IPNAs can require the perpetrator to address the causes of their ASB, and can also include prohibitions.

Breaching an injunction is not a criminal offence but there are penalties, and the breach must be proved to criminal standard (beyond reasonable doubt). The penalty for a breach for under 18-year-olds is a supervision order or, as a very last resort, a civil detention order of up to three months for 14–17-year-olds. For over 18s the penalty is civil contempt of court with an unlimited fine or up to two years in prison.

14.2.1.2 Criminal Behaviour Orders

Criminal Behaviour Orders (CBOs) can be used to deal with the most persistently anti-social individuals who engage in criminal activity. CBOs (issued under the ASBCPA) are issued by a criminal court on conviction for any criminal offence, but the ASB does not need to be part of the offence. The court must be satisfied beyond reasonable doubt that the offender had already engaged in behaviour that caused or was likely to cause harassment, alarm, or distress to any person, and that making the order would help prevent the offender from engaging in further similar behaviour (s 22 of the ASBCPA). For example, a defendant could be brought before a court and found guilty of criminal damage, and if there was additional evidence that he had engaged in ASB, the court could be asked to make a CBO. The CBO can require the perpetrator to address the causes of his/her ASB (eg attend an anger-management course), and can also include prohibitions. For under 18-year-olds, Youth Offending Teams must be consulted (see 3.3.4).

Breaching a CBO is a criminal offence, so the breach must be proved beyond reasonable doubt. On summary conviction the penalty is up to six months' imprisonment or a fine or both and, on indictment, up to five years' imprisonment or a fine or both.

14.2.1.3 Out-of-court disposals for young people

Out-of-court disposals (OOCDs) are favoured by the government for dealing with young people who engage in ASB in the first instance, in order to prevent the criminalization of such young people and its negative future consequences (Home Office, 2014a). Examples of OOCDs include:

- Acceptable Behaviour Contracts (ABC): a written agreement between a local agency and the perpetrator of ASB to desist from the unacceptable behaviour. To encourage compliance, the terms contained in the contract should be discussed with the perpetrator before they are drafted.
- Community Resolutions: these can be used with both adults and juveniles to help draw up an informal agreement between parties, and are a type of restorative justice (see 10.13.2.1). They are aimed at first-time perpetrators who show genuine remorse for their victim(s).
- Mediation: this is another restorative justice option which consists of a facilitated conversation between the perpetrator and victim (all parties attend voluntarily). Any solution should be agreed by all parties, and the mediator can draw up a document to formalize the decisions.
- Parenting Contracts: this can be considered if it seems that the parent or guardian is a bad influence on the child under 18, or if supervision is lacking. They are similar to an ABC, but are signed by the parent or guardian. They could be considered if the perpetrator is under the age of criminal responsibility and there are no other more appropriate interventions for the child.
- Support and counselling: drug and alcohol dependency can contribute to causing ASB, so early supportive interventions can be instigated.
- Verbal warnings: these are issued by the police, the council, or a housing officer if ASB has occurred (or is likely) and the individual's behaviour is considered as unreasonable.
- Written warnings: as with a verbal warning, these should include details of the behaviour, why it is unacceptable, and its impact on any victims.

14.2.1.4 Community triggers and victim engagement

Community triggers and community remedies provide a means for victims and others to contribute to decisions about managing ASB in their area.

The community trigger system allows victims of ASB or another person acting on their behalf to formally request that ASB incidents be reviewed by the police and local councils (or other relevant bodies). They will then determine whether a certain threshold has been reached, usually three complaints over a six-month period (although this can be locally defined). The persistence and harm (or potential harm) caused by the ASB will also be taken into consideration. Agencies must inform the victim if the threshold has been met, and if it has, a case review will take place with a problem-solving approach. Where an action plan is required, it will be discussed with the victim and a timescale for action agreed.

A community remedy allows victims of ASB to be able to choose the most appropriate out-of-court punitive, reparative, or rehabilitative actions to be taken against perpetrators of low-level crime and the ASB. This will be recorded in a community remedy document which can be used by a police officer, PCSO (if designated), or a relevant prosecutor when a conditional or youth conditional caution is proposed (see 10.13.2.3 and 10.13.2.4). To invoke a Community Remedy there will need to be:

- evidence indicating that the person has committed an offence or ASB that would warrant the use of a caution or court proceedings for a civil injunction;
- an admission from the perpetrator of the behaviour or the offence, and an agreement to participate in the community remedy.

If the perpetrator fails to comply with a conditional or youth conditional caution, court proceedings can be used.

14.2.1.5 Evicting tenants and absolute ground for possession

Absolute Ground for Possession (AGP) can be used by landlords to evict tenants where ASB or criminality has already been proven by another court. The police should not be directly involved in any AGP-related action (it is a civil matter), but they should be aware of its existence in providing advice to landlords etc. It can be used for secure and assured tenancies in both the social and private sector.

The landlord does not need to prove that it is reasonable for him/her to be granted possession if the property has been closed for more than 48 hours under a closure order for ASB, or the tenant, a member of the tenant's household, or a person visiting the property has breached a civil injunction or been convicted of certain offences. These offences include the breaching of a criminal behaviour order or a noise abatement notice, and serious offences such as violent and sexual offences, criminal damage, possession of offensive weapons and drugs. The behaviours amounting to the breach or the convicted offence need to have occurred in the locality of the property, or to have affected a person with a right to live in the locality, or the landlord or his or her staff/contractors.

A landlord seeking AGP first needs to serve a notice of the proceedings on the tenant. This must be within three months where a closure order has been used, or within 12 months of the relevant conviction or finding of the court in relation to a breach. The notice is valid for 12 months.

14.2.1.6 Nuisance or disturbance on hospital premises

It is an offence (s 119(1) of the Criminal Justice and Immigration Act 2008) for a person on NHS premises to cause a nuisance or disturbance (without reasonable excuse) to an NHS staff member who is working there or is otherwise there in connection with work, and to refuse (without reasonable excuse) to leave when asked to do so by a police officer or an NHS staff member. In this context, an NHS staff member includes agency and contract workers, students, and volunteers, and NHS premises include:

- all NHS hospitals in England, and any building or other structure on hospital grounds (land in the vicinity of the hospital and associated with it); and
- vehicles associated with the hospital and situated on hospital grounds (includes air ambulances).

This offence cannot be committed by a person who is there to obtain medical advice, treatment, or care for him/herself, but can be committed by someone who has already received it or has been refused it during the previous eight hours. A police officer who reasonably suspects that a person is committing or has committed a s 119(1) offence can remove him/her from the premises, using reasonable force if necessary (s 120(1)). The offence of causing a nuisance (s 119(1)) is triable summarily, and the penalty is a fine.

14.2.1.7 Smoking in a smoke-free place

Under s 7 of the Health Act 2006, a person commits an offence if he/she smokes in a 'smoke-free' place. Smoking includes the smoking of cigarettes (hand-rolled and manufactured), pipes, cigars, herbal cigarettes, and the use of water-pipes (eg 'hubble-bubble' or hookah shisha pipes).

Smoke-free places include 'enclosed or substantially enclosed premises which are open to the public, and shared workplaces', and are defined in the Smoke-free (Premises and Enforcement) Regulations 2006. Briefly, 'enclosed premises' have a ceiling or roof and are wholly enclosed except for doors, windows, or passageways, while 'substantially enclosed premises' have a ceiling or roof and the permanent openings in the walls are less than half of the total areas of walls, known as the '50% rule'. (Here, 'walls' include structures which 'serve the purpose of walls and constitute the perimeter of premises', and a 'roof' includes any fixed or moveable structure or device which is capable of covering all or part of the premises as a roof, including, for example, a canvas awning.) Therefore premises with a ceiling or roof, but with large permanent openings in the wall (more than half of the total wall area) are not subject to this legislation.

This offence is triable summarily and the penalty is a fine. It can also be dealt with by way of a fixed penalty.

14.2.1.8 Dangerous dogs and anti-social behaviour

Dogs must be kept under control, and prevented from injuring people or other dogs. The owner of a dog or the person in charge of it at the time (A) commits an offence under s 3(1) of the Dangerous Dogs Act 1991 if the dog is dangerously out of control in any place. The offence is aggravated if the dog causes injury to a person (B) or an assistance dog. However, these offences do not apply if the dog is in a dwelling or forces accommodation (in the building, or partly in it, or in part of it) and B was in (or entering) as a trespasser, or if A was present and believed B to be trespassing.

The basic offence is triable summarily and the penalty is six months' imprisonment and/or a fine. The aggravated offence is triable either way. If tried summarily the penalty is six months' imprisonment and/or a fine. On indictment the penalty is 14 years if a person dies as a result of being injured, five years in any other case where a person is injured, and three years if an assistance dog is injured or dies.

Guidance for dealing with owners or breeders of dangerous dogs (defined in s 1 of the Dangerous Dogs Act 1991) can be found in *Dangerous Dogs Law Guidance for Enforcers*.

TASK 1 The case of *Rice v Connolly* [1966] 2 QB 414 clearly decided that a person need not give his/her name and address unless there is power to make an arrest for a crime. In the case of a woman who has not been arrested but is nonetheless acting in an anti-social manner, can a police officer require her to provide her name and address?

14.2.2 Community-based measures for tackling ASB

The police often work with the local council to find long-term sustainable solutions in areas where ASB is a regular problem. However, police officers can often deal with an individual's behaviour straight away and provide immediate short-term respite to a local community.

14.2.2.1 Dispersal Orders

A dispersal order allows a police officer in uniform or a designated PCSO to direct any person committing or likely to commit ASB, crime, or disorder to leave an area for up to 48 hours. The orders can be used for a person over the age of 10 (or who appears to be over 10). The ASB must be contributing (or be likely to contribute) to causing harassment, alarm, or distress to members of the public in the local area or to the occurrence of crime and disorder.

The direction to leave must be necessary to remove or reduce the likelihood of the behaviour. The order must be authorized by an officer of at least the rank of inspector. The direction to disperse must be given in writing unless it is impracticable, and should specify the area to and the time period for which it applies, and can also determine the route and the time recipient(s) should leave by. Breaching a dispersal order is a summary offence for which the penalty is up to three months in prison (for adults only) and/or a fine.

The police officer or PCSO can require the person to hand over any items that could be used to commit ASB, crime, or disorder, but this is not a power of seizure so no force can be used. However, failure to hand over such an item is a summary offence, the penalty for which is a fine.

A young person under 16 receiving such a direction can be taken home (unless there are reasonable grounds for believing that he/she would be likely to suffer significant harm there) or to a place of safety. If he/she is unwilling to go voluntarily, the word 'remove' has been held to mean 'take away using reasonable force if necessary' (*R (W) v Commissioner of Police for the Metropolis and another, Secretary of State for the Home Department, interested party* [2004] EWCA Civ 458).

14.2.2.2 Community Protection Notices

A Community Protection Notice (CPN) is designed to address ASB caused by an individual aged over 16, or by businesses and other organizations. The ASB needs to be having a detrimental effect on the quality of life for people in the locality, and to be unreasonable and persistent/continuing. Council and police officers, PCSOs (if designated), and social landlords can issue CPNs. A written warning must first be given to the perpetrator, stating the problem behaviour, requesting that it should stop, and stating the consequences of continuing. The CPN can include requirements to desist from or stop specified activities, and to take reasonable steps to avoid further ASB.

Breaching a CPN is a criminal offence and the penalties can include a fixed penalty notice (see 10.13.2.2) up to £100, or on summary conviction a fine for contempt of court. In the case of a conviction, the prosecuting authority can ask the court to impose a remedial and/or a forfeiture order. As examples, remedial action could be for the perpetrator to clear up rubbish, and under a forfeiture order, items that were used to commit the ASB could be seized (such as spray painting equipment).

14.2.2.3 Public Spaces Protection Orders

A Public Spaces Protection Order (PSPO) is issued by a council and is designed to manage a specific problem which is caused by individuals or groups in a particular public place, and is injurious to the local community. The ASB must be having (or is likely to have) a detrimental effect on the quality of life for local people, and is (or is likely to be) persistent or continuing in nature and unreasonable. The restrictions imposed by the order must be proportionate and justified, and could include making requirements such as keeping dogs on a lead, and prohibiting the consumption of alcohol in a particular area. A PSPO takes precedence over any by-law which already prohibits an activity in the restricted area, for example a 'controlled drinking zone' (see 12.2.4). Access to public spaces can also be restricted (including certain types of highway) if ASB is occurring there, for example an alleyway could be closed to everyone except the inhabitants of the adjacent houses.

It is an offence for a person, without reasonable excuse, to fail to comply with a PSPO requirement, or to do anything prohibited by a PSPO, apart from in relation to alcohol. A PSPO prohibiting alcohol consumption is only breached when a person is challenged and fails to stop drinking or surrender the alcohol. (This effectively allows peaceful consumption of alcohol in an area with a PSPO relating to alcohol.) Breaching a PSPO is a summary offence and the penalty is a fine. A fixed penalty notice can also be used (see 10.13.2.2).

14.2.2.4 Closure Notices and Orders

These can be used to close premises (licensed, enclosed or open, residential, and business) that are causing nuisance or disorder. A closure notice applies for 24 hours, but can be extended. A closure order is a longer-term solution and can be issued subsequent to a closure notice if necessary. The court must be satisfied that the notice or order is necessary to prevent the nuisance or disorder from occurring, continuing, or recurring. Residents cannot be prohibited from accessing their homes by a closure notice, but will have to leave if a closure order is issued.

A closure notice is initially issued for 24 hours. The council or a police officer (of at least the rank of inspector) must be satisfied on reasonable grounds that the use of the premises has resulted (or is likely to result if the notice is not issued) in nuisance to members of the public, or disorder near the premises. The notice can be extended by up to 24 hours by a council's chief executive officer or a police superintendent. When a closure notice is issued, an application for a closure order must also be made to the magistrates' court. The court can extend the closure notice if necessary for a further 48 hours, so that a closure order can be issued. It is a criminal offence to enter or remain on premises in contravention of a closure notice or extension, and the penalty is an unlimited fine or imprisonment of up to three months, or both. It is also an offence to obstruct a police officer or local council employee who is serving a notice, or entering or securing the premises. The penalty is imprisonment of up to three months, an unlimited fine, or both.

A closure order can be used if it seems necessary. The court must be satisfied that without it there will be serious nuisance to members of the public, or disorderly, offensive, or criminal behaviour on the premises. It is a criminal offence to remain on or enter premises in contravention of a closure order without reasonable excuse, and the penalty is imprisonment of up to six months, an unlimited fine, or both.

> **TASK 2** Imagine you are a trainee police officer on Supervised Patrol in a part of a city which has a significant and persistent problem with anti-social behaviour, and is therefore subject to an authorization under s 34 of the Anti-social Behaviour, Crime and Policing Act 2014. This allows you to disperse people from the locality if you believe this is required. During your patrol, you see a group of children, some seeming as young as six, running in and out of nearby houses and intimidating passers-by. What precise powers would you have to deal with the children involved?

14.3 Breach of the Peace

You have no doubt heard of the phrase 'breach of the peace'. There is some considerable debate concerning both its meaning and whether the police should still have powers in this respect. This is partly because the law surrounding a breach of the peace is somewhat unusual: it is not a criminal offence, nor is it part of statute law, but is instead part of common law (see 4.2). Case law has set a precedent in defining its meaning (see 14.3.1). Some police forces discourage their officers from the use of police powers in relation to a breach of the peace, whereas others continue to view it as an important means of reducing the likelihood of harm taking place. In all cases the police use of breach of the peace should be consistent with Article 5 (the right to liberty and security), Article 10 (the right to freedom of expression), and Article 11 (the right to freedom of assembly and association) of the Human Rights Act 1998 (see 4.4.1). During recent protests the police have used likelihood of an imminent breach of the peace as the reason for the containing ('kettling') of large numbers of protesters at the same location for extended periods of time. The use of 'containment' as a public order measure remains controversial, as does the use of breach of the peace legislation.

Any person committing a breach of the peace can in law be arrested by any other person (although in most cases this will be a police officer, rather than a member of the public). Having been arrested, individuals can be detained until there is no likelihood of a breach of the peace recurring. They may then be released without further action or be 'bound over' (see 14.3.3).

14.3.1 Definition of breach of the peace

The case of *R v Howell* [1981] 3 All ER 383 provides a definition of the meaning of breach of the peace:

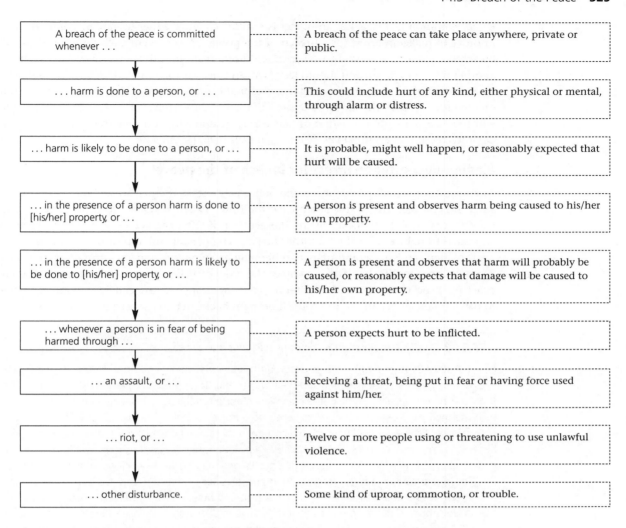

14.3.2 Powers of arrest and entry for breach of the peace

Breach of the peace is unique. It can take place in many different ways, but whatever the situation, it must satisfy the elements set out in the case *R v Howell*.

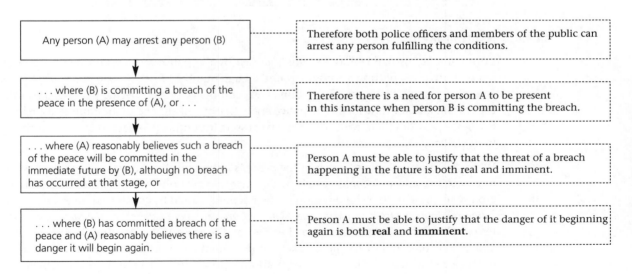

For the arrest to be lawful, the person making the arrest must identify the all-important ingredients of harm and compare the actual circumstances with the definition. The breach must have taken place in his/her presence, or the threat of a breach or its renewal must be both real and imminent.

Under common law (see 4.2) an officer is entitled to enter either private or public premises in order to make an arrest for a breach of the peace, or to prevent such a breach. Once the breach has come to an end the officer should not remain on private premises (unless there is another reason to do so) and should leave within a 'reasonable time'. If he/she is assaulted (eg by a resident of the property) during that reasonable time, this could be regarded as an assault on a police officer in the lawful execution of his/her duty. However, if the officer has not left within a reasonable time, his/her presence may be unlawful and therefore he/she might not be protected under criminal law (*Robson v Hallett* [1967] 2 QB 939).

14.3.3 Binding-over after an arrest for breach of the peace

After arrest for breach of the peace, the police can release the person without further action when it is deemed that a risk of a breach no longer exists. However, in other circumstances the CPS may decide (s 3(2)(c) of the Prosecution of Offences Act 1985) that further action is needed to reduce the risk of another breach. The person will appear before a magistrates' court, which can issue a binding-over order which can refer to general terms of protection, or it can be more specific by naming people. The order can also require the recipient to keep the peace for a specified time, and/or enter into a recognizance for a specified sum (an agreement to pay a financial penalty to the court if brought back after any subsequent breaches).

TASK 3 Compare the use of breach of peace powers in the two situations described below:

- In August 2012 at King's Cross underground station in London a group of around 30 to 40 individuals were stopped from making their way to the Notting Hill Carnival in order to 'prevent a breach of the peace'. Some of the men were reported by the press to be wearing 'body armour'. The men were believed to have travelled from north London in order to 'cause trouble' at the carnival. They were held until the police judged there was no risk of disorder and then released without charge. An MPS Commander was reported as saying 'On the arrests at King's Cross we received intelligence that members of a north London gang were heading towards the carnival. They were spotted on the Underground and they were detained until the carnival was over. There was no doubt they were planning on causing trouble' (*London Evening Standard*, 2012).
- In November 2003, a woman climbed the gates of Buckingham Palace to protest at the visit of US President George W. Bush. She then unfurled the Stars and Stripes flag on top of the gates with the words 'ELIZABETH WINDSOR AND CO ... HE'S NOT WELCOME' written on the flag. After about two hours she voluntarily climbed down from the gates and was reportedly arrested by the police on suspicion of criminal damage and breach of the peace.

14.3.4 Containment

Containment (also known as 'kettling') is used by the police to maintain public order and safety. It involves putting a cordon around a large number of people and confining them to a relatively small, easily managed public area, and police officers decide who remains inside the cordon and for how long. The police argue that the likelihood of an imminent breach of the peace provides them with common law powers to confine people in this way, but this has been challenged in the courts.

When deciding whether a breach of the peace is imminent, the circumstances must be taken into account, and this could cover a wide range of situations. When two or more different groups are present , the combination of their actions should be considered. In *R (on the application of Hannah McClure and Joshua Moos) v Commissioner of Police for the Metropolis* [2012] EWCA Civ 12 the containment was justified by the reasonable apprehension of imminent and serious breaches of the peace likely to be caused by another substantial crowd of protesters arriving at an airbase. The justification was not the violent and unruly behaviour of the main crowd.

Containment is only lawful if the police actions are proportionate, reasonable, and necessary. The police must not use containment until they have taken all other possible steps to prevent the breach or imminent breach of the peace, and protect the rights of third parties (*Austin v Commissioner of Police of the Metropolis* [2009] 1 AC 564). The containment of children is lawful if s 11 of the Children Act 2004 is followed, regarding the welfare of the children (*R (on the application of Castle and others) v Commissioner of Police for the Metropolis* [2011] EWHC 2317

(Admin)). It is accepted that police actions may affect people who are not actively involved in the breach of the peace.

Further case law on containment can be found in *Laporte v Chief Constable of Gloucestershire Constabulary* [2007] 2 AC 105 (see also *Moss v McLachlan* [1985] 1 RLR 76 in relation to the policing of the 1984 miners' strike).

It should be noted that people released from containment have no obligation to provide personal information, nor is it acceptable for them to be photographed (*Susannah Mengesha v Commissioner of Police of the Metropolis* [2013] EWHC 1695 (Admin)).

14.4 The Public Order Act 1986

The Public Order Act 1986 deals with a wide range of behaviours and offences, in descending order of seriousness: riot (s 1), violent disorder (s 2), affray (s 3), fear or provocation of violence (s 4), intentional harassment, alarm, or distress (s 4A), and non-intentional harassment, alarm, or distress (s 5). As you might expect, the least serious offences are the most commonly committed.

14.4.1 Intoxication is not a defence

Some people accused of Public Order Act 1986 offences may claim in their defence that they were intoxicated at the time of the offence. However, s 6(5) of the Public Order Act 1986 specifically states that the court should not accept this as a defence, unless it can be proved that:

- the intoxication was not self-induced (eg it had been caused by a 'spiked' drink); or
- the intoxication was due to prescribed drugs taken as part of a medical treatment.

Note that s 6(5) does not apply to s 4A of the Act, as s 4A was introduced at a later date.

14.4.2 Locations for public order offences

Offences under ss 4, 4A, and 5 of the Public Order Act 1986 are for the most part only committed in a public place, but in certain circumstances they can also be committed within the confines of a private place, for example a communal area such as a shared laundry in a block of flats (see *Le Vine v DPP* (2010) DC (Elias LJ, Keith J) 6/5/2010). These offences can also apply when the conduct occurs in the confines of a private place, but it causes a person who is in a public place to be harassed, alarmed, or distressed. For example, if a householder attaches a poster to the inside of his front-room window, and it offends a person in the street outside (a public street), the offence has been committed. (However, if a poster in a side window was seen by a neighbour from inside his own house (perhaps through his side window), then the offence has not been committed. Other legislation is available for circumstances which are completely private, for example the Protection from Harassment Act 1997 (see 14.5.1).)

The more serious public order offences (riot, violent disorder, and affray) can take place in private, as well as in public places (see 9.2.1.1 for definitions).

14.4.3 Offences under ss 5, 4A, and 4

Sections 5 and 4A of the Public Order Act 1986 are used for relatively minor forms of public disorder such as persistent swearing and shouting. Section 4 is used for more serious public disorder, involving fear or provocation of violence.

The distinctions between offences under ss 5, 4A, and 4 require careful consideration and still cause some debate in legal and police circles. The offences are compared in the table to highlight important differences between them.

	s 4	s 4A	s 5
Intentions of the suspect	Intends to cause fear of violence or to provoke violence	Intends to be threatening, abusive, or insulting	No intention, but is aware that the conduct is threatening or abusive
Recipient of the conduct	Conduct aimed towards a specific person	Conduct does not have to be aimed towards a specific person	Conduct does not have to be aimed towards a specific person (but has to be carried out in the hearing or sight of a person likely to be caused harassment, alarm, or distress)

	s 4	s 4A	s 5
Includes disorderly behaviour?	More than disorderly behaviour		Includes disorderly behaviour
Distribution of material?	Includes distribution of material		No distribution of material
Outcome of the behaviour	No specific outcome is required to prove this offence	An identifiable person must be harassed, alarmed, or distressed	No specific outcome is required to prove this offence

Before looking at the sections in detail, you might find it useful to consider the definitions of key terms used in the legislation:

- Abusive: using insulting or degrading language
- Alarm: a state of surprise, fright, fear, terror, and panic
- Behaviour: a display of conduct involving the treatment of others
- Disorderly behaviour: rowdy, unruly, boisterous, loud, raucous, or unrestrained conduct
- Display: to show or exhibit for all to see, such as placing a sign or poster in a window
- Distress: a feeling of suffering, anguish, and misery
- Distribute: to hand out, share out, give out, or issue to a particular person or people, not just simply leave 'lying about' or displayed
- Harassment: a feeling of annoyance, persecution, irritation, and aggravation
- Sign, leaflet, pamphlet, or poster or other visual representation: containing pictures, text, or images
- Threatening: a physical or verbal act which indicates that harm will be inflicted. It can also include violent conduct
- Words: can be spoken, shouted, or written
- Writing: a notice containing lettering or other visible form of text.

14.4.3.1 Section 5 of the Public Order Act 1986

The offence is also referred to as causing non-intentional harassment, alarm, or distress; or disorderly behaviour/conduct. Section 5 of the Public Order Act 1986 states that a person is guilty of this offence if he/she uses threatening or abusive words or behaviour, or disorderly behaviour, or if he/she displays any writing, sign, or other visible representation which is threatening or abusive, and this is done within the hearing or sight of a person likely to be caused harassment, alarm, or distress thereby. The person who is caused harassment, alarm, or distress can be a police officer, but the level of abuse needs to be at a much higher level as it is assumed that any police officer would be fully accustomed to such language and behaviour (*DPP v Orum* [1989]). The practical implication of this is that in most circumstances police officers, whilst present, will not usually be considered to be a person likely to be caused harassment, alarm, or distress.

The key features of s 5 offences are that:

- the conduct does not have to be aimed towards a specific person;
- the conduct must take place within the presence of a person who can see or hear the conduct, but that person does not need to be identifiable (however, in practical terms the evidence is stronger if his/her identity is known);
- the type of conduct must be likely to cause harassment, alarm, or distress;
- any material used (such as a poster) does not have to be distributed;
- the suspect must intend or be aware that his/her conduct is threatening or abusive in general terms; however,
- there is no need to prove he/she actually intended to cause any person to be harassed, alarmed, or distressed.

You may feel that the last two bullet points appear contradictory, but consider the example shown here where a police officer (PO) is interviewing a suspect (S). This shows that the suspect might intend his/her conduct to be threatening or abusive but has no intention to make any person harassed, alarmed, or distressed, so a s 5 offence has not been committed.

PO	Why did you behave like that, back there in the street?
S	I was trying to be…hard in front of my mates.
PO	Didn't you think about the effect it might have on other people?
S	Not really, no—I was only messing about.
PO	What was the point of it all then?
S	Not a lot—I was only showing off, I'd had a bit, but I wasn't off my head. I knew what I was doing, yeah, and I wanted to be loud and proud, just to show my mates I could do it. They just laughed, made out I was acting stupid.
PO	Yes, and you might have upset a few older people passing by; how do you think they felt hearing that lot?
S	I just didn't think—yeah, I knew they were there…But if I did, I didn't mean to upset them…

There are three defences to this offence (see s 5(3)):

- he/she was in a public place but had no reason to believe that anybody could hear or see the conduct;
- he/she was inside a dwelling (place of residence) and had no reason to believe that the words, behaviour, or conduct could be seen or heard by a person in a public place, for example, a poster was on a wall inside the front room, and could not be clearly seen from outside; or
- that the conduct was reasonable and did not cause anybody to be harassed, alarmed, or distressed, for example he/she shouted at a group of people who were carrying out an unlawful act outside his/her home.

The offence is triable summarily and the penalty is a fine, but can also be dealt with by way of a community resolution (see 14.2.1.3) or a penalty notice for disorder (see 10.13.2.2).

This offence can also be racially or religiously aggravated (see 14.10.4). Note also that 'insulting' or 'offensive' words or behaviour does not form part of this offence, so cannot be dealt with under this legislation.

TASK 4 Take a moment now to consider what evidence a police officer would need before making a decision whether to consider a woman for a s 5 Public Order Act 1986 offence:

1. Who would provide evidence?
2. What evidence would they be able to provide?
3. What evidence would a police officer present at the scene be able to provide?

14.4.3.2   Section 4A of the Public Order Act 1986

A s 4A offence is often referred to as causing intentional harassment, alarm, or distress. A person is guilty of this offence if he/she uses threatening, abusive, or insulting words or behaviour, or commits disorderly behaviour, or displays any writing, sign, or other visible representation which is threatening, abusive, or insulting, with intent to cause a person harassment, alarm, or distress thereby causing that or another person harassment, alarm, or distress.

The key features of s 4A offences are that:

- the suspect intends the conduct to be threatening, abusive, or insulting and to cause a person harassment, alarm, or distress;
- the conduct does not have to be aimed towards a specific person;
- at least one identifiable person must be harassed, alarmed, or distressed; and
- if material is used it need only be displayed (and not distributed).

This piece of legislation is aimed at supporting the most vulnerable members of the community, who may be specifically targeted because of their inability to respond appropriately to intentionally directed acts which cause them harassment, alarm, or distress. These victims may feel particularly uncomfortable as witnesses, so every opportunity should be taken to support them throughout any police or legal process.

As a possible defence, a suspect could demonstrate that:

- he/she had no reason to believe his/her words, behaviour, or conduct inside a dwelling (a place of residence) could be seen or heard by a person anywhere outside, for example a man was reading out loud from a book but the windows were shut (s 4A(3)(a)); or
- his/her conduct was reasonable, for example if a woman opened a window of her house and shouted at two people tampering with her car (s 4A(3)(b)).

This offence is triable summarily and the penalty is six months' imprisonment and/or a fine. This offence can be racially or religiously aggravated (see 14.10.4).

14.4.3.3 Section 4 of the Public Order Act 1986

A s 4 offence is also referred to as fear or provocation of violence. A person is guilty of this offence if he/she uses towards another person threatening, abusive, or insulting words or behaviour, or if he/she distributes or displays to another person any writing, sign, or other visible representation which is threatening, abusive, or insulting. The intent must be to:

- cause that person to believe that immediate unlawful violence will be used (against him/her or another) by any person; or
- provoke the immediate use of unlawful violence (by that person or another); or
- cause that person to believe it is likely either that such violence will be used or be provoked.

For this offence, the intentions of the suspect are the key issue; the actual effect of the behaviour on other people is not relevant. The intention must be to make the recipient (the person (or persons) to whom the conduct is addressed) feel fear, or to provoke other people or another person to be violent. For the suspect's intentions to be held as genuine, his/her conduct must be directed towards a recipient who is present when the words or behaviour are used. The recipient must be able to see or hear the conduct (or the suspect must at least believe that the recipient is able to see or hear the conduct (see *Atkin v DPP* [1989] Crim LR 581)).

If the suspect's intentions are to cause fear of violence, he/she must intend the recipient to fear that violence will be used (or is likely to be used). However, the threatened violent acts do not need to involve the suspect or the recipient directly: the violence could be threatened against another person, or be carried out by a person other than the suspect.

Alternatively, the suspect could be intending to provoke *any* person to use violence. For example, an extremist at a demonstration could be trying to provoke the other demonstrators to be violent by shouting at an animal research worker, 'A dog is for life, not just for you to torture and experiment on, you sadist! You'll get the same, just wait!'.

The key features of s 4 offences are that:

- the conduct must be directed towards a person or persons present at the scene;
- any material used is distributed and not just displayed;
- the suspect must intend or be aware that his/her conduct is potentially threatening, abusive, or insulting (but it does not matter whether the recipient actually feels threatened, abused, or insulted);
- the suspect may intend to cause fear or to provoke violence (but it does not matter whether the conduct actually has either of these effects);
- if the suspect intends to cause fear (that violence will be or is likely to be used), the intention need only be to cause the recipient to feel fear; and
- if the suspect intends to provoke violence, the intention can be to provoke any person present.

A police officer may enter any premises to arrest any person reasonably suspected of committing an offence under s 4 of the Public Order Act 1986 (s 17 of the PACE Act 1984, see 10.8.1.2). The offence is triable summarily and the penalty is six months' imprisonment and/or a fine. This offence can be racially aggravated (see 14.10.4).

TASK 5 Imagine you are a trainee police officer on Independent Patrol. You encounter a man who is shouting in an incoherent and aggressive manner, and it seems to you that the behaviour is likely to be capable of causing harassment, alarm, or distress. Consider how you will deal with this situation if there is no one else in the area at the time at whom this conduct is aimed and hence it appears to be directed solely at you.

While drawing your conclusions, refer to *DPP v Orum* [1988] Crim LR 848 and *Harvey v DPP* [2011] EWCA Crim B1.

TASK 6 Imagine you are a trainee police officer on Independent Patrol. You see a man walk up to the door of a club and adopt an aggressive posture towards the door supervisor. You are about two metres away. The aggressor has clenched fists, bulging eyes, and has taken up a 'boxing' position. The suspect then pushes his shoulder into the door supervisor's chest causing the door supervisor to move back. You hear the suspect say 'You're getting it'. You believe that the door supervisor is about to be attacked and so you arrest the suspect under s 4 of the Public Order Act 1986.

When you return to the club to obtain a statement from the door supervisor, he is not willing to make a statement. Does it seem likely that a successful prosecution could be brought against the suspect under these circumstances?

When drawing a conclusion, consider *Swanston v DPP* (1997) 161 JP 203.

14.4.4 Serious public order offences

These offences under the Public Order Act 1986, in increasing order of seriousness, are affray (s 3), violent disorder (s 2), and riot (s 1). These offences all involve unlawful violence and can be committed in private as well as in public. Violence is essentially aggressive or hostile conduct towards property or persons, and includes acts capable of causing injury even if no injury or damage is caused, for example throwing a full can of beer towards a person, even if it falls short (see s 8 of the Public Order Act).

The legislation describing offences under ss 1–3 also uses the term a 'person of reasonable firmness' (sometimes referred to as the 'hypothetical bystander'). This is not defined under law but can be taken to mean an average person in terms of their reaction to violent incidents around them (ie not someone who is unduly frightened by the most minor of incidents, nor someone who is completely hardened to violent behaviour).

14.4.4.1 Affray

For an affray (s 3 of the Public Order Act 1986) the threat of violence needs to be capable of upsetting others. The primary objective of the law is to protect the general public around the affray and therefore the court will consider how a hypothetical person of reasonable firmness (see 14.4.4) who witnessed the incident would feel (*R v Sanchez*, The Times, 6 March 1996).

Therefore, there are in effect three parties involved in an affray:

- the individual making the threats;
- the person subject to the threats; and
- one or more bystander(s).

In drawing a conclusion about the conduct of the suspects and the person of reasonable firmness, the court can consider evidence from witnesses at the incident (including police officers), the extent of any injuries, and recordings such as from CCTV or the media.

Specific Incidents

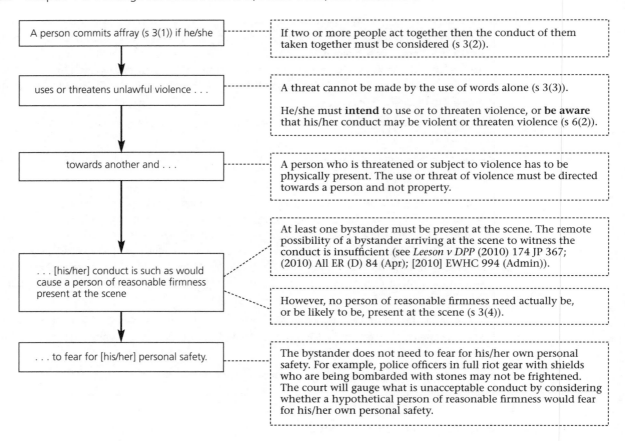

A person commits affray (s 3(1)) if he/she	If two or more people act together then the conduct of them taken together must be considered (s 3(2)).
uses or threatens unlawful violence . . .	A threat cannot be made by the use of words alone (s 3(3)). He/she must **intend** to use or to threaten violence, or **be aware** that his/her conduct may be violent or threaten violence (s 6(2)).
towards another and . . .	A person who is threatened or subject to violence has to be physically present. The use or threat of violence must be directed towards a person and not property.
. . . [his/her] conduct is such as would cause a person of reasonable firmness present at the scene	At least one bystander must be present at the scene. The remote possibility of a bystander arriving at the scene to witness the conduct is insufficient (see *Leeson v DPP* (2010) 174 JP 367; (2010) All ER (D) 84 (Apr); [2010] EWHC 994 (Admin)). However, no person of reasonable firmness need actually be, or be likely to be, present at the scene (s 3(4)).
. . . to fear for [his/her] personal safety.	The bystander does not need to fear for his/her own personal safety. For example, police officers in full riot gear with shields who are being bombarded with stones may not be frightened. The court will gauge what is unacceptable conduct by considering whether a hypothetical person of reasonable firmness would fear for his/her own personal safety.

This offence is triable either way. The penalty if tried summarily is six months' imprisonment, and/or a fine, and on indictment three years' imprisonment.

14.4.4.2   Violent disorder and riot

For the offence of violent disorder (s 2 of the Public Order Act 1986), three or more persons must be present together and use (or threaten to use) unlawful violence. There must be an intention to use or threaten violence, or an awareness that the conduct may be violent or may threaten violence.

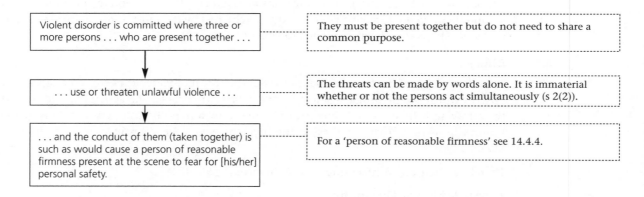

Violent disorder is committed where three or more persons . . . who are present together . . .	They must be present together but do not need to share a common purpose.
. . . use or threaten unlawful violence . . .	The threats can be made by words alone. It is immaterial whether or not the persons act simultaneously (s 2(2)).
. . . and the conduct of them (taken together) is such as would cause a person of reasonable firmness present at the scene to fear for [his/her] personal safety.	For a 'person of reasonable firmness' see 14.4.4.

If it is only possible to arrest and investigate one person out of such a group, then he/she can still be charged with this offence, but it must still be proved that at least two other people using or threatening violence were present, and they must be mentioned in the charge. However, there is no requirement for a common purpose to be held by those using or threatening behaviour (see *R v NW* [2010] EWCA Crim 404). This offence is triable either way. The penalty if tried summarily is six months' imprisonment and/or a fine, on indictment five years' imprisonment.

The offence of riot (s 1(1) of the Public Order Act 1986) is similar to that of violent disorder, but twelve or more people must be present. Charges of riot are very rare. A riot offence is triable on indictment only and the maximum penalty is ten years' imprisonment.

> **TASK 7** Imagine you are a trainee police officer on Independent Patrol. You respond to a call from a customer of a local nightclub alleging that a member of the door staff has pushed a female customer out of the door and that she fell over as a result of the push. There are no other witnesses to the incident and no CCTV footage. Disregarding the investigation of the assault, could an investigation into an affray be sustained? Refer to *R v Plavecz* [2002] Crim LR 837 for your answer.

14.4.5 Hatred on the grounds of race, religion, and sexual orientation

The original Public Order Act 1986 was amended to address 'stirring up' (the phrase used in the legislation) or inciting hatred against a group of people on certain grounds. These offences are a type of hate crime and are sometimes known as 'motivated' hate crimes. The motivations for this type of hate crime are as follows:

- racial hatred, 'hatred against a group of persons defined by reference to colour, race, nationality (including citizenship) or ethnic or national origins' (s 17 of the Public Order Act 1986);
- religious hatred (s 29A of the Public Order Act 1986), hatred against a group of persons defined by reference to religious belief (eg Christianity or Islam) or to a lack of religious belief (eg atheists and humanists);
- hatred on the grounds of sexual orientation (s 29AB of the Public Order Act 1986), 'hatred against a group of persons defined by reference to sexual orientation whether towards persons of the same sex, the opposite sex or both'). Further guidance on this is provided in a Ministry of Justice Circular (2010).

The offences can be committed in a public or a private place, although the effects of the actions must be felt in a public place. The different ways 'stirring up' can be caused are listed in various sections of the Act, as shown in the table. A separate offence (such as criminal damage) can also be aggravated on these grounds, see 14.10 for details. Also note that the offences are committed if the offender 'perceives' that the victim is a member of the group (even if, in actuality, they are not).

Activity	Grounds for hatred	
	Racial	Religious or sexual orientation
Using threatening words or behaviour, or displaying written material	s 18	s 29B
Publishing or distributing written material	s 19	s 29C
Public performance of a play	s 20	s 29D
Distributing, showing, or playing a recording	s 21	s 29E
Broadcasting threatening images or sounds	s 22	s 29F
Possessing racially inflammatory material	s 23	s 29G

In practice, the offences a police officer is most likely to encounter are those involving the use of threatening words or behaviour or the display of written material. Some possible defences are that:

- the acts were part of a programme service (eg on a television programme);
- the acts took place in a private place and were not noticeable to a person in a public place; or
- the suspect was not fully aware of the possible effects of his/her actions.

These offences are triable either way and the penalty is a fine or imprisonment (six months summarily and seven years on indictment).

14.5 Protection from Harassment

Harassment exists in a variety of forms, for example during episodes of stalking, pestering, persecution, and causing annoyance. A number of offences are available to help to deal with the often traumatic experience of being harassed. If complaints are not investigated and

Specific Incidents

addressed in the first instance, relatively minor incidents may develop into much more serious offences such as kidnap, assault, and even murder.

When responding to complaints of harassment, the police priorities are to:

- investigate every report of harassment;
- preserve the safety and protect the lives of all victims;
- approach the harassment proactively;
- use a multi-agency approach when necessary;
- deal with offenders effectively, using any means within the criminal justice system.

Further information can be found in the College of Policing's Authorised Professional Practice statement on *Stalking or Harassment*, available at <https://www.app.college.police.uk/app-content/major-investigation-and-public-protection/stalking-or-harassment/>.

14.5.1 The Protection from Harassment Act 1997

Sections 1–5 of the Protection from Harassment Act 1997 can be applied in a wide range of situations, including disputes between partners in a relationship, disputes between neighbours, stalking, and campaigning. The offences described in the Protection from Harassment Act 1997 are harassment without violence (s 2), stalking (s 2A), breaching an injunction (s 3(6)), putting people in fear of violence (s 4), stalking involving fear of violence or serious alarm or distress (s 4A), and breaching a restraining order (s 5(5)). The stalking offences are covered in 14.5.3.

The behaviour must be oppressive, unreasonable, and unacceptable, such as that displayed during an act of stalking (for which the offence was originally designed), and be of the sort that a reasonable person would find harassing (s 1(2) of the Protection from Harassment Act 1997). Harassing a person includes alarming the person or causing the person distress (s 7(2)). In legal terms, only a person can be harassed, so an employee can be harassed but not a company or a corporate body (s 7(5) of the Protection from Harassment Act 1997).

For these offences (ss 1–5) the perpetrator must know or ought to know that his/her actions are likely to cause the relevant effect on the victim. The judgement on whether a suspect 'ought to know' is made by considering whether a reasonable person in possession of the same information would know that the actions would have these effects. The final decision on the likely effects of a particular behaviour is taken by the court.

Clearly, the Protection from Harassment Act 1997 is a potentially valuable piece of legislation that offers a number of options for providing support to victims of harassment. However, a considerable amount of evidence is required to secure a successful prosecution under this Act, and proving a course of conduct in particular can be difficult. Advice from the CPS should be sought at an early stage.

14.5.1.1 A 'course of conduct'

Under s 1(1) of the Protection from Harassment Act 1997 a person must not pursue a 'course of conduct'. The conduct must be the sort of conduct that the perpetrator knows (or ought to know) amounts to harassment. In addition, it must occur on more than one occasion to be a course of conduct. A course of conduct exists when conduct is directed towards:

- an individual on at least two occasions (s 7(3)(a)); or
- two or more people, and in relation to each person on at least one occasion (s 7(3)(b)).

It is not just the number of incidents, but whether those incidents are connected (*Lau v DPP* [2000] All ER (D) 224). It is, however, less likely that the court will accept that behaviour constitutes a course of conduct if there is a long period of time between the events.

The course of conduct does not have to comprise similar types of conduct: indeed, often it is not obvious that separate incidents are connected, so be aware of this during any investigation. However, a number of irregular and unconnected incidents in a turbulent and unpredictable relationship in which all parties concerned play a part, does not amount to a course of conduct (see *R v Curtis* [2010] EWCA Crim 123 and *R v David Roger Widdows* [2011] EWCA Crim 1500). A court may decide that there was a sequence of separate incidents instead (see *(1) Buckley (2) Smith v DPP* [2008] EWHC 136 (Admin)).

Conduct includes speech, letters, and emails, so evidence will need to be gathered from a wide range of sources such as diary entries, emails, letters, photographs, and interviews with witnesses. A person might make an initial bona fide enquiry for example, but this could become harassing if it is followed up in a manner that is persistent (see *DPP v Hardy* [2008] All ER (D) 315 (Oct)).

The conduct can also involve more than one person. An example of where a group of people could be guilty of harassment would involve three people, X, Y, and Z, who stand along the route which H takes to work in order to give her a threatening letter. They give her the letter, and later Z makes a threatening phone call to her. Provided that H feels alarmed or distressed, and X, Y, and Z knew (or ought to have known) that their actions were likely to be alarming or distressing, then X, Y, and Z would all be committing an offence (s 7(3A) of the Protection from Harassment Act 1997).

That a suspect did not initiate the contact on a particular occasion was held to be irrelevant: in *James v CPS* [2009] EWHC 2925 (Admin), a client who was receiving local authority care made repeated calls to the office but received no reply. The office worker returned the calls on a number of occasions and was verbally abused. Also the offence of harassment does not have to include actually carrying out the conduct; mere planning or otherwise assisting with the course of conduct can amount to the offence.

14.5.1.2   Harassment without violence

It is an offence under s 2(1) of the Protection from Harassment Act 1997 for a person to pursue a course of conduct which involves harassment of one or more persons (s 1(1)(a) and 1(1A) (a)). Once initiated, a person continues to pursue a course of conduct even when he/she does not personally harass the victim but aids, abets, counsels, or procures another who carries it out instead (s 7(3A)). The suspect(s) must know (or ought to know) that the behaviour amounts to harassment (s 1(1A)(b)).

The course of conduct can be to persuade a person to carry out a particular act or to omit to carry out a particular act. The offender might try to persuade a person to do something that he/she is **not** under any obligation to do (s 1(1A)(c)(ii)). For example, an animal rights extremist might pressurize a person working with animals in research to supply information on work practices. This offence can also be committed when there is an intention to persuade a person to omit to do something that he/she is entitled or required to do (s 1(1A)(c)(i)). For example, an animal rights extremist might pressurize a person to stop working for a company that conducts research on animals.

The offence can also be committed when the course of conduct is intended to persuade *any person* to change his/her current routine (s 1(1A)(c)(i) and (ii)). This may form part of a wider campaign about political or social issues. It must be directed towards two or more person(s) in the first instance and occur on at least one occasion in relation to each of those persons.

As a possible defence to a s 2 offence, the suspect could try to show on the balance of probabilities that he/she acted either 'in reasonable circumstances' (this will be for the court to decide, probably using the 'reasonable person' test as in s 1(2)), or in the course of his/her work, for example as a police officer or court official. Full details of the defences are given in s 1(3) of the Protection from Harassment Act 1997.

This offence is triable summarily and the penalty is six months' imprisonment and/or a fine. It can also be racially or religiously aggravated (see 14.10.4).

14.5.1.3   Isolated events causing distress

If distress is caused only on one occasion this does not constitute a course of conduct, and can be dealt with under s 3(1) of the Protection from Harassment Act 1997. The result of a civil claim can be damages (a court order to pay money) and/or an injunction (a court order to impose sanctions on the offender).The injunction can be against a person, or a company. If an injunction is breached, an offence is committed triable either way. The penalty is a fine or imprisonment (six months summarily and five years on indictment). There are no racially or religiously aggravated versions of the civil proceedings under s 3 of the Protection from Harassment Act 1997.

A 'First Incidence Harassment Warning' is another way of dealing with such a situation. This is an official written warning issued by the police, which informs the perpetrator that any further incidents may form part of a 'course of conduct' that could then result in prosecution for harassment offences. The record of the warning provides evidence of the course of conduct, and that the perpetrator 'knows or ought to know' that the conduct amounted to harassment.

14.5.1.4 Putting people in fear of violence

This offence is described in s 4 of the Protection of Harassment Act 1997 and involves more than sending insulting or abusive letters or emails. The conduct must be targeted at an individual and be calculated to cause fear of violence. It must also be oppressive and unreasonable (as identified in *Thomas v News Group Newspapers Ltd* [2001] EWCA Civ 1233, [2002] EMLR 78).

There are several key differences from the harassment (s 2) offence we described earlier. For s 4 offences:

- the victim must believe the violence will happen (as opposed to believing it might happen);
- the victim must fear the violence personally (and not on behalf of somebody else, such as a family member) (*Caurti v DPP* [2002] Crim LR 131); and
- the fear of violence cannot be conveyed through a third party.

In most other ways, the conditions for this offence are similar to those for the offence of harassment (s 2) described in 14.5.1.2; the court decides what is reasonable or unreasonable, it is an offence to pursue or assist the conduct, and there must be a course of conduct amounting to harassment within the meaning of s 1 (see 14.5.1, and *Haque v R* [2011] EWCA Crim 1871). Other relevant case law includes *R v Curtis (James Daniel)* [2010] EWCA Crim 123, [2010] 1 WLR 2770 and *R v Widdows (David Roger)* [2011] EWCA Crim 1500, (2011) 175 JP 345. Stalking is covered in 14.5.3.

The defences to this offence are similar to those for s 2 but with one major addition: that the suspect's course of conduct was pursued reasonably for his/her own protection or for protection of another or of property (belonging to him/her or another). This offence can be racially or religiously aggravated (see 14.10.4) and is triable either way. The penalty is a fine or imprisonment (six months summarily, and a maximum of ten years on indictment).

14.5.1.5 Restraining orders

A court can make a restraining order under s 5 of the Protection from Harassment Act 1997 against a person who has been convicted (s 5(1)) or acquitted (s 5A) of any offence, to protect a person from harassment. A restraining order will place restrictions on a person's future behaviour. It may last indefinitely or for a period stated by the court, and it can be varied or discharged on application. The order will be recorded on the PNC, the police local intelligence database, and the PND. Breaching a restraining order is an offence (s 5(5)) and the penalty is a fine or imprisonment (six months summarily, and five years on indictment).

TASK 8 Imagine you are a police officer. You are requested to attend an address in your area where a complaint of harassment has been made. Write brief answers to the following questions:

1. What evidence would you need to collect to prove an offence under either s 2 or s 4 of the Protection from Harassment Act 1997?
2. What other methods could be used to stop the conduct?
3. How could future evidence be recorded?
4. What reason(s) would make an arrest necessary in these circumstances?

14.5.2 Preventing harassment and the Criminal Justice and Police Act 2001

Harassing or intimidating behaviour by individuals towards a person in his/her home is an offence under the Criminal Justice and Police Act 2001. This legislation should not be seen as a way of stopping people from carrying out their lawful rights to protest peacefully or express strong opinions (even if offensive to some others). Nor is it intended to prevent a fan from standing outside the home of his/her favourite television celebrity, or to stop media commentators from trying to record first-hand comments from people in the news. Rather, this legislation aims to provide a balance between the right to carry out such activities with the rights of residents to be protected from harassment, alarm, or distress in their own homes.

The legislation referred to here provides more than one tool to deal with this type of situation (see 5.5.3 on discretion). The direction to leave is useful, but of course it does not prevent the same protesters from returning and continuing with the same type of behaviour. Charging a person with an offence (causing harassment, distress, or alarm), however, is a more serious matter. Therefore you will need to consider carefully which of the powers to use and this will depend on factors such as the number of people in the vicinity of the person's home, their behaviour and purpose, and the impact of their presence on the resident(s) and people in the surrounding area.

14.5.2.1 Causing harassment of a resident

Behaviour that may cause harassment, alarm, or distress (ss 42 and 42A of the Criminal Justice and Police Act 2001) includes persistent and aggressive hammering on a door; climbing onto the roof of a dwelling, and aggressive use of banners or placards to block or impede access.

As well as causing distress to a resident inside his/her dwelling, other people can also be affected such as friends of the resident inside the dwelling, or people living nearby. Courts will use the 'reasonable person' test to decide if the relevant activities should be regarded as significantly disturbing. A police officer does not have to be present when the behaviour occurs; for example, recordings from a resident's CCTV could be used as evidence of protestors' activities and the distress caused. This offence is triable summarily and the penalty is six months' imprisonment and/or a fine.

14.5.2.2 Giving directions to prevent harassment, alarm, or distress

Under s 42(1) of the Criminal Justice and Police Act 2001 a police officer has the power to give 'directions' to a person (or a group) in order to prevent him/her/them from causing harassment, alarm, or distress to residents (or other people in the vicinity). The wording of a direction (s 42(2)) might be 'You have caused harassment and distress to people living in this area. I therefore require you to leave immediately'.

The direction can be given orally or in writing, and will instruct the person(s) to leave the vicinity and for a specified period (not exceeding three months) and conditions may be attached. An officer of any rank can give the direction (s 42(6)) but it will usually be given by the most senior officer present. An offence is committed under s 7A if a person who has received a direction to leave then fails to leave, or leaves but then returns within the specified time period to try to persuade a resident to follow a particular course of action. This offence is triable summarily and the penalty is six months' imprisonment and/or a fine.

14.5.3 Stalking

The offence of stalking is covered under s 2A of the Protection from Harassment Act 1997. The suspect's acts (or omissions, although no examples are provided) must be associated with stalking. The acts include: following the person, watching or spying on him/her, loitering in any place (whether public or private), contacting (or attempting to contact) him/her by any means, monitoring his/her use of electronic communications (eg social media or email), interfering with his/her property, and publishing any statement or other material relating to or originating from him/her (or purporting to). For stalking that causes fear of violence or serious alarm or distress, see 14.5.3.1.

Research into stalking by Knoll and Resnick (2007) reveals five known stalker types:

- Rejected stalkers—This is the most common type of stalker and can be the most dangerous. The victim is often a former intimate partner, and the perpetrator will often pursue the victim long after the relationship ends. He/she will have a complex and volatile mix of desire for reconciliation and revenge.
- Intimacy seeking stalkers—These want an intimate relationship with someone, and believe that the victim is their 'true love', and project desirable romantic qualities onto the victim. Most perpetrators will have erotomanic (the uncommon delusion and strong belief that someone is in love with him/her despite evidence to the contrary (Ingleston, 2017)). Some will have delusions, and others have morbid infatuations with the victim. Legal sanctions

are seen as a worthwhile price to pay for finding true love, and are unlikely to stop their behaviour.

- Incompetent stalkers—They will probably know that the victim is not interested but will continue hoping that the stalking behaviour will somehow lead to a relationship. They can often be intellectually limited, and have poor social skills which impedes meaningful social interactions. Unlike intimacy-seekers, they do not endow their victim with any unique qualities.
- Resentful stalkers—These types of stalkers intend to frighten their victim. Many have paranoid personalities or delusional disorders. They may pursue a vendetta against a specific victim or may just feel a general grievance and randomly pick a victim. They may also carry out stalking with an attitude of righteous indignation, due to feeling persecuted by someone.
- Predatory stalkers—They will prepare for a sexual attack, and use stalking to discover a victim's vulnerabilities. They do not often give any warning, and the victim is often unaware of the danger. Predatory stalkers often suffer from paraphilias (abnormal sexual behaviours) and are likely to have previous convictions for sexual offences. They may also have a propensity for violence, which can lead to a very violent sexual attack on their victim.

The stalker must pursue a course of conduct (as for s 2(1) offences) that involves harassment (s 2A(2)(a)), and it can be targeted at one or more persons (subsections (1)(a) and (1A)(a), respectively). The behaviour must be such that the suspect(s) must know (or ought to know) that it amounts to harassment (s 2A(2)(c)). A stalker who starts a course of conduct is regarded as continuing it even when the latter acts are carried out by someone else arranged by the suspect (s 7(3A)). This offence is triable summarily and the penalty is six months' imprisonment and/or a fine. It can be racially or religiously aggravated (see 14.10.4).

14.5.3.1 Stalking involving fear of violence or serious alarm or distress

These offences are covered under s 4A(1) of the Protection from Harassment Act 1997. Under s 4A(1)(a) the suspect's course of conduct must amount to stalking (see 14.5.1.3) and also cause the victim:

- to fear on at least two occasions that violence will be used against him/her (s 4A(1)(b)(i)); or
- serious alarm or distress which has a substantial adverse effect on his/her usual day-to-day activities (s 4A(1)(b)(ii)).

For these offences the behaviour must be such that the suspect must know (or ought to know) that his/her acts will have these effects on the victim (ss 4A(2) and 4A(3)). In *R v Qosja (Robert)* [2016] EWCA Crim 1543, it was held that to prove fear of violence, there must be evidence from the victim that he/she feared there would be violence directed at him/her (not just a possibility of violence).

The defences to this offence are given in s 4A(4), and are similar to the defences for s 4 (see 14.5.1.4). The offence is triable either way and the penalty is a fine or imprisonment (12 months summarily, and ten years maximum on indictment). A suspect found not guilty of this offence could instead be found guilty of an offence under s 2 or 2A (s 4A(7)). The s 4A offence can be racially or religiously aggravated (see 14.10.4).

14.5.3.2 The Stalking Protection Act 2019

The Stalking Protection Act 2019 came into force in January 2020. Its purpose is to close a gap in the existing framework for protective orders by creating the Stalking Protection Order (SPO) (Home Office, 2020c). Note that a Stalking Protection Order is not an alternative to prosecution for stalking offences under the Protection from Harassment Act 1997 (see 14.5.3).

An SPO is a civil order granted in a magistrates' court, and will be granted on the balance of probabilities. The criteria for applying for an SPO are set out in s 1(1) of the Stalking Protection Act 2019. The police should consider applying for an SPO if it seems the suspect has carried out acts associated with stalking, poses a risk of stalking to a person, and there is reasonable cause that the proposed order is necessary to protect the other person from that risk (Home Office, 2020c). An SPO application can be made at the beginning of any investigation, and will still apply even if a decision is made not to prosecute.

The person to be protected under the order does not need to have been a victim of the acts described above, but the police must have reasonable cause to believe that he/she may be at risk of such acts. The courts will make an assessment using the criteria set out in the House of Lords judgment in *R (McCann) v Crown Court at Manchester* [2003] 1 AC 787.

Interim SPOs are also available. These short-term temporary orders require a lower threshold of evidence, and can be more quickly obtained. They are useful if immediate protection from harm is required.

Once an SPO is granted it must be recorded on the PNC and include details such as the start and expiry dates, and all the conditions imposed. Breaching an SPO or interim SPO without reasonable excuse is a criminal offence. The person should be arrested as soon as possible, as a delay may result in a loss of victim confidence in the order, and the suspect may cause further harm (Home Office, 2020c). This is an either-way offence and the maximum penalty is 12 months' imprisonment, a fine, or both on summary conviction, and five years' imprisonment, a fine, or both on indictment.

For full guidance on the Stalking Protection Act 2019 and SPOs consult the Home Office guidance (Home Office, 2020c).

14.5.4 Sending nuisance communications

If the harrassment involves communications such as telephone calls or letters, then alternative offences can be considered. This is particularly useful if a course of conduct is not evident.

14.5.4.1 Sending items to cause distress or anxiety

Under s 1 of the Malicious Communications Act 1988 it is an offence for a person to send, for the purpose of causing distress or anxiety, any item (including electronic communications) which contains:

- indecent or grossly offensive content (s 1(1)(a)(i));
- a threat (s 1(1)(a)(ii)) (unless it was made reasonably to reinforce a demand (s 2));
- information which is false and known or believed to be false (s 1(1)(a)(iii)); or
- any article which is entirely or partly, indecent or grossly offensive (s 1(1)(b)).

This offence includes letters and parcels sent by post. It also includes electronic communication such as emails, text messages, and oral or other communication transmitted by means of a telecommunication system, for example landline or mobile telephone (s 2A(a) and (b)). For this offence 'sending' includes delivering by hand, transmitting, and causing to be sent (s 3) by the sender, but does not include the actions of the service provider.

14.5.4.2 Improper use of public electronic communications network

It is an offence under s 127 of the Communications Act 2003 to send (or cause to be sent) a message by means of a public electronic communications network (eg mobile and landline telephones) which is grossly offensive, indecent, obscene, or menacing (s 127(1)), or false, or to persistently use the network for the purpose of causing annoyance, inconvenience, or needless anxiety to another (s 127(2)). These offences are triable summarily and the penalty is six months' imprisonment and/or a fine. A PND can be used for a s 127(2) offence (see 10.13.2.2).

> **TASK 9** Imagine you are a trainee police officer on Supervised Patrol and you have been asked to attend the address of a person who reports being harassed by people in the street outside his house. Suggest some factors you would need to consider in order to decide whether to direct anybody away from the house and whether to investigate for an offence.

14.6 Intimidation of Witnesses, Jurors, and Others

Witnesses often feel vulnerable and concerned about the consequences of their actions, and some become victims of intimidation by the suspect(s) in the case. For example, suspects or their associates might attempt to intimidate witnesses and victims to dissuade them from giving evidence in court. The 'No witness, no justice' project is a joint initiative between the CPS, NPCC, the Home Office, and the Cabinet Office's Office of Public Service

Reform. It highlights the importance of providing support to people who are crucial in the successful prosecution of offenders, and that the police have a duty of care towards them. The Home Office report (1998) 'Speaking Up for Justice' argues that in this context intimidation is not simply a matter of explicit threats of physical harm to a witness or victim, but also includes other less tangible forms: for example, threats made to third parties such as a relative, and financial threats (such as withdrawing support for a dependant). The police must therefore assess the needs of intimidated witnesses and be aware of the various supporting agencies including: Victim Support, the Witness Service, Anti-Social Behaviour Units, Housing Associations, Witness Care Units, Crown Prosecution Service, Prison Service, and other voluntary organizations (eg specific support for victims of sexual violence or domestic violence).

In *Osman v United Kingdom* (2000) 29 EHRR 245, it was decided that national authorities (such as the police) have an obligation to take preventative measures to protect an individual whose life is at risk through the criminal acts of others. In cases involving death threats, there must be a real and immediate risk to the life of the identified individual(s). Reasonable steps must be taken to assess those threats (known as the Osman threshold) and to protect the individuals concerned. However, if the assessment does not suggest that there is a real and immediate risk, the police and other authorities cannot be held negligent if subsequent harm falls upon the victim (*Chief Constable of Hertfordshire v Van Colle (Administrator of the estate of GC, deceased) & Anor; Smith v Chief Constable of Sussex* [2008] UKHL 50).

The offences of intimidation are triable either way and the penalty is a fine or imprisonment (six months summarily, and five years on indictment).

14.6.1 Intimidation relating to civil proceedings

Intimidation relating to civil proceedings is covered under the Criminal Justice and Police Act 2001. For current civil proceedings (s 39(1)) the victim of the intimidation can be a witness in any civil proceedings in the Court of Appeal, the High Court, the Crown Court, a county court, or a magistrates' court. The suspect must have carried out an act which causes intimidation and is intended to either obstruct, pervert, or otherwise interfere with the course of justice.

For civil proceedings in the past (s 40(1)) the person suspected of intimidation must know (or believe) that his/her victim had been a witness in the relevant proceedings, and the intimidation must take place within the period from the start of the proceedings until 12 months after the end of the proceedings.

14.6.2 Intimidation relating to criminal proceedings

This is covered under the Criminal Justice and Police Act 2001. The person suspected of intimidation must have carried out an act (or acts) which either intentionally caused harm to (or threatened to harm) another person. The threatened harm or intimidatory act can be financial or physical, and can be directed against either the person or his/her property (s 40(4)). The person making the threat commits an offence even if a third party is used to convey that threat (s 40(3)). During the relevant periods there is a presumption of an intention to intimidate unless the suspect can prove otherwise (s 40(7) and (8)).

For current criminal proceedings (s 40(1)) the victim of the intimidation must be either assisting in the investigation, a witness or potential witness, or a juror (or potential juror) in proceedings for the offence. The suspect must have carried out an act which causes intimidation and is intended to obstruct, pervert, or otherwise interfere with the course of justice. The act must occur between the start of the investigation and the end of the proceedings, for example at the conclusion of a court hearing.

For criminal proceedings in the past (s 40(2)), the suspected intimidator must know (or believe) whilst carrying out the acts that his/her victim has assisted in an investigation into an offence (eg as a witness), acted as a juror, or concurred in the relevant verdict. In addition, the intimidatory acts must take place within a certain time frame. Note that a person can of course both assist with an investigation and be a witness in court, in which case the longer time frame applies.

Role of the intimidated victim in criminal proceedings	Time period during which the intimidation occurs	
	Starts	Ends
A person who assisted with an investigation	The start of any assistance in the investigation (or the start date as believed by the suspect)	Twelve months after any assistance was given
A witness or juror during the court hearing	The start of the court proceedings	Twelve months after the end of the trial or appeal

14.7 Sports Events Offences

Trainee officers might be involved in policing football matches, particularly in forces covering large towns and cities. Many football clubs will take steps to inform their supporters of the main points of the law and the regulations governing behaviour, for example see Stoke City's 'Customer Charter' online.

The offences described in this section are covered under the Sporting Events (Control of Alcohol etc) Act 1985 and the Football (Offences) Act 1991. Currently, football is the only sport which it is considered necessary to control. Statistics on football-related arrests and banning orders can be found on the gov.uk website. The CPS website provides useful guidance on the policy for prosecutions.

14.7.1 The Sporting Events (Control of Alcohol etc) Act 1985

The Sporting Events (Control of Alcohol etc) Act 1985 only applies to sports grounds, certain sporting events, and designated periods relating to those sporting events. It applies to football matches only if both the particular sports ground and match have been 'designated' by the Secretary of State (see Sch 1, Art 2(1) of SI 2005 No 3204, available online). Note that the list of designations may vary from year to year to reflect changes in the organization of football leagues.

The following events are examples of matches which would be likely to be designated for the purposes of the Sporting Events (Control of Alcohol etc) Act 1985, as they meet both the ground and the match (teams) criteria:

- A football match played between Bristol City and Millwall at Bristol City's ground, Ashton Gate. This is because Ashton Gate is a designated sports ground and both teams are currently members of the English Football League.
- A match played between Dover Athletic and Manchester United at Dover, because Crabble football ground is a designated sports ground and Manchester United is currently a member of the Football Association Premier League.

The legislation does not apply to any sporting event in which players are not paid, nor if spectators are admitted free of charge, such as amateur weekend matches on school sports fields or recreation grounds.

Offences under the Sporting Events (Control of Alcohol etc) Act 1985 can only be considered if they occur during the period commencing two hours before the start of a football match and ending one hour after the end of the match. For example, if a football match is scheduled to start at 7.45 pm and the match ends at approximately 9.30 pm, the period of this match would be from 5.45 pm to 10.30 pm. (We ignore here the added complexity of 'added time' for stoppages, or extra time to decide a match, or the match starting late.)

14.7.1.1 Transport of passengers to sports events

Supporters will often travel to sports events by train, coach, or minibus. Drivers, owners, and passengers of some types of vehicle which are used for the principal purpose of carrying passengers for the whole or part of a journey to or from a designated sporting event are subject to legislation under s 1 of the Sporting Events (Control of Alcohol etc) Act 1985.

Public service vehicles covered by this legislation include buses and coaches, passenger trains, and minibuses. It is an offence under s 1(2) to knowingly cause or permit intoxicating liquor to be carried on such a vehicle. This applies to the operator of the public service vehicle and to the person who has hired it. (It also applies to a 'servant or agent' of the operator or hirer.) It is also an offence for such a person to have intoxicating liquor in his/her possession (s 1(3)) or to be drunk (s 1(4)) while on a vehicle to which this section applies. This offence is triable summarily only and the penalty is a fine for s 1(2) or (4) offences, and three months' imprisonment and/or a fine for an offence under s 1(3).

Minibuses and larger motor vehicles (that are not public service vehicles) are covered by s 1A of the Sporting Events (Control of Alcohol etc) Act 1985. They must be adapted to carry more than eight passengers and be in use for the principal purpose of carrying two or more passengers. It is an offence to knowingly cause or permit intoxicating liquor to be carried (s 1A(2)) on such a vehicle. This offence can be committed by the driver, the vehicle's keeper (or his/her servant or agent), and by anyone who has hired or borrowed the vehicle (or the servant or agent of the person to whom the vehicle is made available).

It is also a summary offence for such a person to have intoxicating liquor in his/her possession (s 1A(3)) or to be drunk (s 1A(4)) on a vehicle to which s 1A applies. The penalty is a fine for a s 1A(2) or (4) offence, and three months' imprisonment and/or a fine for a s 1A(3) offence.

14.7.1.2 Alcohol and drinks containers at a designated sporting event

Section 2(1) of the Sporting Events (Control of Alcohol etc) Act 1985 is often imposed for football matches where there is a potential for disorder. Under this legislation it is a summary offence to possess alcohol or drinks containers likely to contain alcohol. The containers covered by this legislation are defined in s 2(3) as:

> any article or other portable container for holding any drink, which when empty is normally discarded or returned to (or left to be recovered by) the supplier and which is capable of causing injury to a person struck by it.

This obviously includes bottles and cans, including when crushed or broken, and parts of such containers. (Containers for holding any medicinal product (within the meaning of the Medicines Act 1968) are not included.) Section 2(1) applies at any time during the period of a designated sporting event when the person is either in any area of the sports ground from which the event may be directly viewed, or entering (or trying to enter) the sports ground. The penalty for this offence is three months' imprisonment and/or a fine.

It is also a summary offence for a person to be drunk inside the ground, or to be drunk while entering or trying to enter a ground at any time during the period of a designated sporting event at that ground (s 2(2)). The penalty is a fine.

14.7.1.3 Fireworks, flares, and similar articles at a designated sporting event

Section 2A of the Sporting Events (Control of Alcohol etc) Act 1985 covers the possession of fireworks and similar objects at designated sporting events. The prohibited objects (s 2A(3) and (4)) include fireworks, rockets, distress flares, fog signals, pellets and fumigator capsules (for testing pipes), and any other item which is for 'the emission of a flare for purposes of illuminating or signalling, or the emission of smoke or a visible gas'. It does not include matches, cigarette lighters, or heaters.

The times and places to which this legislation applies are the same as for the possession of alcohol at a sports ground, as is the penalty for breaching the prohibition (see 14.7.1.2).

14.7.1.4 Powers of entry and search for sports grounds

Section 7 of the Sporting Events (Control of Alcohol etc) Act 1985 allows a police officer to enter and search any part of the ground if he/she has reasonable grounds to suspect that an offence under the same Act is being committed (or is about to be committed), or to enforce the provisions of the Act. This relates to the possession of alcohol, fireworks, and similar articles and applies during the period of a designated sporting event at any designated sports ground (see 14.7.1). There is a power to search a person (s 7(2)) or a vehicle (s 7(3)) if there are reasonable grounds to suspect that an offence under this Act has been committed (or is about to be committed).

14.7.2   The Football (Offences) Act 1991

The Football (Offences) Act 1991 deals with problem behaviour at football matches. It covers throwing objects, racist chanting, and pitch invasions. The definition of a designated match is very similar to the definition for the Sporting Events (Control of Alcohol etc) Act 1985, as is the time period. The Football (Offences) Act 1991 also applies if the match does not take place, using the advertised starting time as a point of reference.

Throwing objects at a designated football match is an offence under s 2 of the Football (Offences) Act 1991. The objects must be thrown without lawful authority or excuse (for the suspect to prove) at or towards the playing area, or any adjacent area to which spectators are not generally admitted, or any area in which spectators or other persons are or may be present. This offence is triable summarily and the penalty is a fine.

Indecent or racist chanting at a designated football match is an offence under s 3(1) of the Football (Offences) Act 1991 if the chanting is of an 'indecent or racialist nature'. Chanting means the repeated uttering of any words or sounds, by one or more people (s 3(2)) and 'racialist nature' means it is 'threatening, abusive or insulting to a person by reason of [his/ her] colour, race, nationality (including citizenship) or ethnic or national origins'. The offence is triable summarily and the penalty is a fine.

Spectators going onto the playing area (a 'pitch invasion') at a designated football match commit an offence under s 4 of the Football (Offences) Act 1991. This includes 'any area adjacent to the playing area to which spectators are not generally admitted, without lawful authority or lawful excuse (which shall be for [the suspect] to prove)'. This offence is triable summarily and the penalty is a fine.

TASK 10 As a trainee officer on Supervised Patrol, you are deployed to a football match. The club concerned plays within the National League (currently the Vanarama National League), so you can therefore assume that both the ground and the matches played in the ground are designated under both the Sporting Events (Control of Alcohol etc) Act 1985 and the Football (Offences) Act 1991. Consider each of the following offences and match them against the situations given in the table by putting the appropriate letter(s) in the right-hand column. The first answer has been given to you. You may need to consult the original legislation for the detail.

(a) s 2(1) of the Sporting Events (Control of Alcohol etc) Act 1985;

(b) s 2(2) of the Sporting Events (Control of Alcohol etc) Act 1985;

(c) s 2 of the Football (Offences) Act 1991;

(d) s 3 of the Football (Offences) Act 1991;

(e) s 4 of the Football (Offences) Act 1991;

(f) s 1(2) of the Sporting Events (Control of Alcohol etc) Act 1985;

(g) s 1(3) of the Sporting Events (Control of Alcohol etc) Act 1985;

(h) s 1(4) of the Sporting Events (Control of Alcohol etc) Act 1985; and

(i) s 2A of the Sporting Events (Control of Alcohol etc) Act 1985.

1.	You see a fan fumbling for money to pay for a cup of tea from the refreshment stand. When you approach, he is hardly able to stand and his breath smells of intoxicating liquor, his eyes are glazed, and his speech is slurred.	b
2.	You are on duty at the edge of the pitch near the entrance to the players' tunnel as the teams enter after half-time. You see a dark metal object hit the ground near your feet and notice one of the players stop and grab his head in pain. You look up and see a youth in the crowd with his right hand raised as if he has just thrown an object.	
3.	One of the mid-field players is black. Every time he receives the ball you hear opposition supporters make 'monkey' sounds and shout racist abuse.	
4.	You are on duty outside the ground and you see a fan waiting to get a ticket. He has a four-pack of lager cans under his arm.	
5.	Before the start of a match you see a supporter near the front of the ticket queue. He finishes drinking from a can, drops it and crushes it with his foot. He then looks around before picking up the crushed tin, and putting it in his coat pocket.	

6.	One of your responsibilities is to monitor the away supporters as they arrive by coaches and minibuses hired for the occasion. You notice a person drinking from a bottle of cider on one of the minibuses. As the vehicle stops, the driver opens the door and you see one of the other passengers stand up and offer the driver a can of lager. Another passenger then falls down the steps of the minibus, apparently drunk.
7.	At the end of a match when the final whistle is blown the two teams start to leave the pitch. A group of fans go onto the pitch to follow the players and congratulate them.
8.	At the end of a match in early November, you see a youth reach into his pocket as the crowd is leaving the ground. As he rummages in his pocket, a firework falls out.

14.8 Criminal Trespass and Outdoor Gatherings

Travelling people with no fixed abode sometimes find a temporary place to live on privately owned land. This may cause anxiety and distress for the owners of the land or for local residents. However, if the trespassers do not intend to reside, gather, or disrupt lawful activity or if only one trespasser is involved, then the situation might be a civil matter (see 14.8.5). But if it is clear that a trespasser clearly intends to disrupt lawful activity this is likely to amount to a criminal offence (see 14.8.2). Separate legislation is available to deal with problems arising from large outdoor music and dancing events (see 14.8.3).

14.8.1 Criminal trespass or nuisance on land

This offence is described under s 61(1) of the Criminal Justice and Public Order Act 1994. At least two suspects must be planning to live on the land for a period of time, and they must have been asked to leave by the owner or legal occupier. In addition, the suspects must have either:

- caused damage to the land or to property on the land, or used threatening, abusive, or insulting words or behaviour towards the occupier, a member of his/her family, or an employee or agent of his/hers; or
- have six or more vehicles with them on the land (a vehicle includes caravans and unroadworthy vehicles).

A senior police officer present at the scene must reasonably believe that these conditions have been fulfilled. He/she may then direct those persons to leave the land, and to remove any of their vehicles and other property from the land. If the trespassers will not leave, s 62 of the Criminal Justice and Public Order Act 1994 provides a power to seize and remove their vehicles. This also applies if a person fails to remove any vehicle on the land, or leaves and returns within three months (s 62(1)). It is an offence (s 61(4)) for a person to fail to leave as soon as is reasonably practicable, or to leave and then re-enter within three months. These offences are triable summarily and the penalty is three months' imprisonment and/or a fine.

14.8.2 Aggravated trespass on land

Sections 68 and 69 of the Criminal Justice and Public Order Act 1994 cover trespassers who disrupt or obstruct any lawful activity taking place on land or adjoining land (hence the 'aggravated' nature of the trespass). This would include protesters at a military base. Land would include agricultural buildings, footpaths, bridleways, and cycle tracks that cross the land. The summary offence of aggravated trespass is provided under s 68(1), and the penalty is three months' imprisonment and/or a fine.

A senior police officer at the scene of an aggravated trespass has the power to direct a person to leave the land (s 69 of the Criminal Justice and Public Order Act 1994). He/she must reasonably believe that:

- the person is committing (or has committed or intends to commit) aggravated trespass; or
- more than one person is trespassing, and they intend to intimidate other people there who have a right to be there, and deter or obstruct them from lawful activity.

Under s 69(3), it is an offence for a person who has been directed to leave if he/she fails to leave the land as soon as practicable, or having left, re-enters as a trespasser within three months (beginning with the day on which the direction was given). It is a defence if the accused can show that he/she was not trespassing, or had a reasonable excuse for failing to leave as soon as practicable or for re-entering as a trespasser. The offence is triable summarily and the penalty is three months' imprisonment (maximum) and/or a fine.

14.8.3 Open-air gatherings with music at night

Although complaints about excessive noise from gatherings in residential properties are often dealt with by local authority personnel, complaints about larger gatherings in the open air may sometimes require police action. Sections 63, 64, and 65 of the Criminal Justice and Public Order Act 1994 can be used to deal with such situations. The type of gathering (also referred to as an 'open-air rave') is defined in s 63; more than 20 people must be present out of doors at night with amplified music with repetitive beats. The music must be loud or go on for a long time, and be 'likely to cause serious distress to local residents'.

The Act includes the power for police officers to give directions to people present at such gatherings (and to people travelling to the locality). There are some predictable exemptions; the following categories of people cannot be given directions under ss 63–65:

- the occupier of the land ('the person entitled to possession of the land by virtue of an estate or interest held by him [or her]' (s 61(9)) or any member of the occupier's family;
- any employee or agent of the occupier; and
- any person whose home is situated on the land.

14.8.3.1 Dispersal powers for open-air gatherings with music at night

A power is available to disperse people (ten or more) who are at a gathering with music at night, or waiting together at the location for such an event to start (s 63(2)). It also applies for two or more people who are making preparations for such an event.

The direction must be made by an officer of at least superintendent rank, and if not communicated by him/her may be communicated by any constable at the scene (s 63(3)). A person will be regarded as having received the direction if reasonable steps have been taken to bring it to his/her attention (s 63(4)). It is an offence (s 63(6)) if a person (knowing that a relevant direction has been given) then fails to leave the land as soon as reasonably practicable, or leaves and re-enters within seven days. If the suspect can provide a reasonable excuse, this may be a defence (s 63(7)). A person who has been directed to leave a gathering who then moves on to (or prepares for) another similar gathering within 24 hours commits an offence under s 63(7A). The offences are triable summarily and the penalty is three months' imprisonment and/or a fine.

Section 65 of the Criminal Justice and Public Order Act 1994 provides powers to direct persons to desist from proceeding towards a gathering to which s 63 applies. The police officer must be in uniform and within five miles of the gathering. It is a summary offence (s 65(1)) for a person not to comply with such a direction, and the penalty is a fine.

14.8.3.2 Powers of entry and seizure for open-air gatherings with music at night

A power of entry for the police when dealing with night-time open-air musical events is provided under s 64 of the Criminal Justice and Public Order Act 1994; police officers may need to be deployed to determine whether the gathering is covered under s 63 (ie is a 'rave', see the start of 14.8.3). If a police officer of at least the rank of superintendent reasonably believes that the relevant circumstances exist then he/she may authorize any constable to enter the land (s 64(1)). A warrant is not required (s 64(3)). If the s 63 conditions are met, then s 63 directions can be given.

Vehicles and sound equipment belonging to a person (or appearing to) may be seized if he/she has received a s 63 direction and has (without reasonable excuse) failed to remove them, or removed them but then returned within seven days and entered with them as a trespasser.

14.8.4 Squatting in a residential building

It is an offence for a trespasser in a 'residential building' to live or intend to live there for any period of time (s 144(1)(c) of the Legal Aid, Sentencing and Punishment of Offenders Act 2012). The person must have entered as a trespasser, and the means of entry be such that he/she must (or should) know that it was trespass (s 144(1)). The offence does not apply if the person stays on after the end of a lease or licence (s 144(2)). A building includes any temporary or moveable structure or part of a structure, and is 'residential' if it was designed or adapted as a place to live before the time of entry (s 144(3)). A police officer in uniform has the power (s 17 of the PACE Act 1984) to enter and search premises to arrest a person for this offence (see 10.8.1.2). It is triable summarily and the penalty is six months' imprisonment and/or a fine.

14.8.5 Police involvement in civil trespass

Police officers will frequently be called to incidents where a person unlawfully enters land or premises owned by another. This is civil trespass, and is not a criminal offence. The trespasser may become criminally liable if, for example, the acts and/or the intent amount to criminal trespass (see 14.8.1), burglary (see 16.4), or living or intending to live in a residential building for any period of time (see 14.8.4).

Accordingly, in civil trespass incidents the actions of police officers are limited to identifying whether any criminal offences have been committed, remaining to prevent any taking place, and offering advice about civil remedies to both owners and trespassers. The owner should request the trespassers to leave, but if they do not and the owner decides to try and remove the trespassers by force (likely to be difficult), the police should remain in order to prevent a breach of the peace (see 14.3) or to identify any criminal offences, for example unlawful personal violence (see 15.1).

Consequently, at an incident where civil trespass is alleged, a police officer should:

* Locate the owner of the land/premises and speak with him/her to try and establish the circumstances surrounding the complaint, the identity of the trespassers and their location, and if any criminal acts have taken place. If no criminal offences have been committed the limitation of police involvement should be emphasized.
* Locate the alleged trespassers and seek to establish their identity (should they wish) and any claim to lawful entry they might have (in order to help the owner and the trespassers come to a common understanding). The officer should also explain that if they commit a criminal offence or a breach of the peace, they may be liable to arrest and prosecution, and that the owner can obtain an order from a civil court to eject them.
* Attempt to bring about an amicable agreement between the two parties through dialogue, if no criminal offences have been committed.
* Remain at the incident if it seems that criminal offences may be committed.
* Make a full PNB entry (see 10.2) of the events and what was said.

14.9 Fireworks Offences

Under the law, a firework is any device which burns and/or explodes to produce a visual and/or audible effect, and is intended for use as a form of entertainment. Some fireworks offences relate to misuse that could cause danger or annoyance, some relate to the time of year, and some relate to the age of the person buying fireworks. Of particular concern in recent years has been the use of powerful fireworks such as 'aerial shells, aerial maroons, shells-in-mortar and maroons-in-mortar', which can register sound levels above 120 dB—about the noise level of a jet aircraft 100 metres away, and could also be used to damage or even destroy large objects such as cars. The sale of these products to the public in the UK is banned, but people can purchase them abroad and bring them back to the UK.

Relevant legislation includes the Explosives Act 1875, the Fireworks Act 2003, the Fireworks Regulations 2004, and the Fireworks (Safety) Regulations 1997. It is an offence for any person:

* to throw, cast, or fire any firework in or into any highway, street, thoroughfare, or public place (s 80 of the Explosives Act 1875);
* to wantonly (deliberately) throw or set fire to a firework in the street to the obstruction, annoyance, or danger of residents or passengers (s 28 of the Town Police Clauses Act 1847).

It is also an offence for anyone under the age of 18 years to possess fireworks in a public place, except for indoor fireworks (reg 4 of the Fireworks Regulations 2004). Indoor fireworks include caps, sparklers, and 'throwdowns'. (A throwdown is a paper or foil package that contains substances which explode when thrown onto the ground.)

These offences are triable summarily. Alternatively, a PND can be used (see 10.13.2), apart from an offence under s 28 of the Town Police Clauses Act 1847.

14.9.1 Selling fireworks

A special licence is required for a trader to sell fireworks to the public throughout the year. Traders without a special licence can only sell fireworks to members of the public during the following periods:

- first day of Chinese New Year and three days prior to this;
- Diwali and three days prior to this;
- between 15 October and 10 November; and
- between 26 and 31 December.

Under s 12(1) of the Consumer Protection Act 1987 it is an offence to supply fireworks (including sparklers but excluding all other indoor fireworks) to persons under the age of 18 years. This offence is triable summarily, and the penalty is a fine.

14.9.2 Firework curfews

A 'firework curfew' is a period of time where the general use of fireworks is not permitted. Under reg 7(1) of the Fireworks Regulations 2004 it is a summary offence for a person to use an 'adult firework' (essentially all fireworks other than indoor fireworks) between 2300 and 0700 hrs the next day except for during the periods shown in the table. Other exemptions apply for local authority employees using a firework during a local authority display or national commemorative event.

Curfew exemption event or date	Exemption period ends
First day of the Chinese New Year	0100 hrs the following day
5 November	Midnight
Diwali	0100 hrs the following day
31 December	0100 hrs the following day

The penalty for this offence is six months' imprisonment and/or a fine, or a PND can be used (see 10.13.2 on PNDs).

14.9.3 Restrictions on large fireworks for public displays

Public displays frequently use large fireworks, known as category 4 fireworks. They may only be used by an appropriately qualified person (reg 5 of the Fireworks Regulations 2004). Members of the general public are prohibited from possessing such fireworks, except for any person who is employed by a local authority, or who is involved in public or commercial firework displays. A breach of reg 4 or 5 is a criminal offence under s 11 of the Fireworks Act 2003. The offence is triable summarily, and the penalty is a fine.

14.10 Hate Crime

Note that there is no particular offence entitled 'hate crime'. In terms of legislation, hate crimes fall into two main categories, the first being the stirring up offences under the Public Order Act 1986 (see 14.4.5), sometimes referred to as 'motivated' hate crimes. The second group is the 'aggravated' hate crime offences, and these are covered here.

Hate crime is defined on the CPS website as:

> Any criminal offence which is perceived by the victim or any other person, to be motivated by hostility or prejudice based on a person's race or perceived race; religion or perceived religion; sexual orientation or perceived sexual orientation; disability or perceived disability and any crime motivated by hostility or prejudice against a person who is transgender or perceived to be transgender.

The Criminal Justice Act 2003 introduced these changes following the enquiry into the death of the black London teenager, Stephen Lawrence, and a subsequent report into the police investigation chaired by Sir William Macpherson. (The report famously branded the MPS as 'institutionally racist'.)

Specific Incidents

In 2018/19, the police in England and Wales recorded 103,379 hate crimes, an increase of 10 per cent compared with 2017/18 (Home Office, 2019e). This continues an upward trend: the number of recorded hate crimes has doubled since 2012/13. The Home Office (2019e) notes that there were noticeable increases during events such as the EU Referendum and the terrorist attacks of 2017. The various motivations for hate crimes are recorded, but some fall into more than one category (Home Office, 2019e) so the total with regard to motive adds up to more than 100 per cent. The figures for 2018/19 (very similar to the previous year's) are as follows:

- race hate crime (76 per cent);
- sexual orientation hate crime (14 per cent);
- religion-based hate crime (8 per cent);
- disability hate crime (8 per cent);
- transgender hate crime (2 per cent).

A key consideration for the police when identifying a potential hate crime is the victim's perception. In most forces the policy is to record a crime as a 'hate crime' if the victim perceives it as such. Often, victims expect the attacks to continue or are terrified of future victimization. Note that for a hate crime to be classified as such, an identifiable criminal offence (such as assault) must have been committed.

Several Acts refer to hate crime offences, including the Public Order Act 1986 (see 14.4.5), the Football Offences Act 1991 (see 14.7.2), and the Crime and Disorder Act 1998 (see 14.10.1). In all cases of hate crime, the police are expected to identify and record crimes as such, to thoroughly investigate hate crimes, and to offer an appropriate level of support to victims. In addition to the usual considerations (eg forensic awareness), extra sensitivity around the needs of victims from minority communities is often needed. Further guidance can be found in the College of Policing *Hate Crime Operational Guidance*, available online (note that in 2019 the CoP launched a consultation on the Guidance, in response to the HMICFRS 'Understanding the difference: the initial police response to hate crime' report of 2018).

Trainee officers are likely to cover such matters in the initial learning and development phase of their training, and this often involves a contribution from local minority communities or groups. Trainee officers are, however, unlikely to be involved beyond the early stages of an investigation, as such investigations can be complex.

Racially or religiously motivated assaults, criminal damage, public order offences and harassment can be charged under the Crime and Disorder Act 1998 as the 'aggravated' version of the basic offence (see 14.10.1). These carry a heavier sentence on conviction. For a basic offence triable on indictment, a person who is found 'not guilty' of the aggravated version of that offence can still be found guilty of the basic offence. This is known as the 'alternative verdict' (s 6(3) of the Criminal Law Act 1967). For summary-only basic offences, there is no power for the court to return an alternative verdict; therefore the defendant is more likely to be charged with both the basic and the racially or religiously aggravated offence.

Sentence uplifts for disability, homophobic, or transphobic hate crime are available to the courts under s 146 of the Criminal Justice Act 2003. This enables the court to increase a sentence for any offence that is aggravated by hostility on the grounds of disability, sexual orientation, or transgender identity.

For further information on the number of prosecutions for certain types of hate crime, see the CPS report *Hate crime report 2016–2017* (CPS, 2017a). The UK government's programme of actions for tackling hate crime in England and Wales is set out in the Home Office document *Action Against Hate: The UK government's plan for tackling hate crime* (available online).

14.10.1 The definition of racially or religiously aggravated

This is explained in s 28(1) of the Crime and Disorder Act 1998. An offence becomes racially or religiously aggravated for the purposes of ss 29–32 if the offender, on racial or religious grounds:

- demonstrates hostility (s 28(1)(a)): or
- is motivated by hostility (s 28(1)(b)).

Providing evidence for the suspect's behaviour is likely to be easier than providing evidence for his/her motivation. A person is held to have demonstrated hostility even if his/her behaviour might be partly motivated by other factors with no racial or religious basis (s 28(3)), but this is a question of fact for the court to decide. For example, in the case of *Johnson v DPP* [2008] EWHC 509 (Admin), two car park attendants were the victims of hostility, partly based upon their job status and partly upon their membership of a racial group. It was subsequently held that a racially aggravated s 5 Public Order Act 1986 offence had been committed against them. The accused (who was black) had made reference to the skin colour of the attendants, and told them to leave the black community in which they were working and to go to a predominantly 'white' area.

Note that of course people working in law enforcement are themselves fully entitled to protection from any racial or religious aggravation.

14.10.2 Racially or religiously aggravated assaults

Under s 29(1) of the Crime and Disorder Act 1998, the following types of assault as a basic offence can be racially or religiously aggravated:

* common assault (see 15.2.1);
* any offence under s 47 of the Offences Against the Person Act 1861 (see 15.2.2); and
* any offence under s 20 of the Offences Against the Person Act 1861 except for s 18 'with intent' offences (see 15.3).

The motivation for the basic offence must be taken into account—it must be racially or religiously motivated. For example, in the case of *DPP v Roshan Kumar Pal* (unreported, 3 February 2000) the charge of racially aggravated common assault was not proved. Even though the assault on an Asian-heritage caretaker was accompanied by abuse, the assault was held to be motivated by the perceived low status of the victim's job, and not by racism. If the racial or religious aggravation aspect of the offence charged is not proved, the court can substitute the basic offence in most cases.

Aggravated s 20 and s 47 offences from the Offences Against the Person Act 1861 are triable either way and the penalty is a fine or imprisonment (summarily, six months and seven years on indictment). Aggravated common assault offences are triable either way and the penalty is a fine or imprisonment (summarily, six months and two years on indictment).

14.10.3 Racially or religiously aggravated criminal damage

These offences are covered in s 30 of the Crime and Disorder Act 1998. A person is guilty of this offence if he/she destroys or damages property belonging to another (see 20.2), and the acts are racially or religiously motivated. Case law extends the meaning of the term 'belonging' to include having control or custody of property (as used in the Criminal Damage Act 1971 and the Theft Act 1968). There is no need to identify a specific victim and therefore spray-painting racist graffiti on a wall would probably be an example of this offence. The offence is triable either way, regardless of the value of the property damaged. The penalty is a fine or imprisonment (summarily, six months and up to 14 years on indictment).

14.10.4 Racially or religiously aggravated public order offences

Section 31 of the Crime and Disorder Act 1998 covers the aggravated forms of basic public order offences. The table shows the basic public order offences (see 14.4), and the corresponding racially or religiously aggravated offences.

Basic offence (Public Order Act 1986)	Racially or religiously aggravated offence (Crime and Disorder Act 1998)
Fear or provocation of violence (s 4)	s 31(1)(a)
Intentional harassment, alarm, or distress (s 4A)	s 31(1)(b)
Causing harassment, alarm, or distress (s 5)	s 31(1)(c)

In *Norwood v DPP* [2003] EWHC 1564 the regional organizer of the British National Party for Shropshire was found guilty of a racially aggravated s 5 Public Order Act 1986 offence. A few weeks after the 9/11 terrorist attack in New York he displayed a poster which included the words 'Islam out of Britain' and 'Protect the British People' and an image showing one of the 'twin towers' in flames, along with a crescent and star surrounded by a prohibition sign. It was displayed in his flat window and could clearly be seen from the street. However, where the offence is motivated towards the individual victim (and not towards members of his/her racial group) it is not held to be racially aggravated. For example, in the case *DPP v Howard* [2008] EWHC 608 (Admin), an off-duty police officer heard his neighbour shouting 'I'd rather be a paki than a cop.' It was held that the only motivation for the neighbour's shouting was his intense dislike and hostility towards the police (and as a consequence an offence under s 5 of the Public Order Act 1986), and therefore the comments had not been racially aggravated.

The penalty for a s 31(1)(a) or (b) offence (triable either way) is a fine or imprisonment (summarily, six months, and two years on indictment). An offence under s 31(1)(c) is triable only summarily as it relates to a summary-only basic offence (s 5 of the Public Order Act), and therefore has no alternative verdict. The penalty is a fine.

14.10.5 Racially or religiously aggravated harassment

This is covered in s 32 of the Crime and Disorder Act 1998. The offences are racially and religiously aggravated forms of basic offences from the Protection from Harassment Act 1997, s 2 (harassment) and s 4 (putting people in fear of violence).

The offences of aggravated harassment (s 32(1)(a)) and aggravated putting people in fear of violence (s 32(1)(b)) are triable either way and the penalty is a fine or imprisonment (six months for a summary offence, and on indictment two years for a s 32(1)(a) offence and 14 years for a s 32(1)(b) offence. For trials on indictment, a person who is found not guilty can still be found guilty of the relevant basic harassment offence (s 32(5) and (6) of the Crime and Disorder Act 1998).

TASK 11 Consider the following groups of people. In relation to racially or religiously aggravated offences, decide whether they constitute a racial or a religious group, or neither or both:

1. Jews (see *Seide v Gillette Industries* [1980] IRLR 427);
2. Rastafarians (see *Dawkins v Crown Suppliers (Property Services Agency)*, The Times, 4 February 1993, [1993] ICR 517);
3. Muslims (see *J H Walker v Hussain* [1996] ICR 291); and
4. Gypsies (see *Commissioner for Racial Equality v Dutton* [1989] QB 783).

14.11 Syndicate or 'Gang' Incidents

Under s 34(5) of the Policing and Crime Act 2009 a gang is defined (perhaps rather vaguely) as a group that consists of at least three people; uses a name, emblem, or colour or any other identifiable characteristic; and is associated with a particular area. The members of the group may also identify with or lay claim over territory, have some form of 'identifying structural feature', and/or be in conflict with other similar gangs (Home Office, 2012c).

Some researchers (eg Harris *et al*, 2011) suggest that we need to be cautious about labelling offenders as gang members, because such labelling may have the unwanted effect of a 'self-fulfilling' prophecy, and make it more difficult for supposed gang members to break away. As an alternative, the term 'syndicate' is used by some within law enforcement.

Studies commissioned by Westminster Joint Health and Well Being Board have shown there is a higher level of mental health issues within the gang population compared with the general population and the offender population of the same age group (Madden, 2015). Other studies have shown that 86 per cent of gang members were identified as having antisocial personality disorder, over half suffered from alcohol dependence, anxiety disorder, or drug dependence, and 34 per cent had attempted suicide, 25 per cent had suffered psychosis, and 20 per cent had depression. It is becoming more common to see mental health problems in UK gang members (and in the US it has been shown that gang-affiliation is associated with conditions such as anxiety, mood disorder, conduct disorder, post-traumatic stress disorder, and attempted suicide (Hughes *et al*, 2015)). It is clear that more work is required to counter gang cultures, to help reduce the harm caused.

Recently it has become evident that some gang members may be both perpetrators of crime and victims of crime, as they have been coerced, exploited, or groomed into criminal activity (Rigg *et al*, 2018). Some police forces are now utilizing modern slavery legislation (see 13.6) to target certain gang members who are trafficking and exploiting victims (ibid).

14.11.1 Tackling youth violence through legislation

The issue of 'gang'-related violence has received considerable attention in recent years. In 2011, the government claimed in *Ending Gang and Youth Violence: A Cross-Government Report* that 'gang members carry out half of all shootings in the capital and 22% of all serious violence'.

Many measures have been introduced to tackle problems associated with gangs. The Anti-social Behaviour, Crime and Policing Act 2014 created new offences such as threatening with a knife in a public place or school (see 18.2.4) and possessing illegal firearms with intent to supply (s 2(A) of the Firearms Act 1968), the latter carrying a maximum penalty of life imprisonment. The maximum penalty for importation of firearms has also been increased to life imprisonment (ss 50 and 5(A) of the Customs and Excise Management Act 1979).

More recently (2017) the Home Office provided further funding to tackle knife crime, which is often a key feature of gang culture. The Criminal Justice Act 1988 has also been amended to ban the sale, manufacture, rental, or importation of a certain type of long knife often referred to as a 'zombie knife' or similar. These knives can have serrated-edge blades over 60cm long, and are held in high esteem by some gang members as they glamorize violence. In 2017, a number of UK forces made a coordinated response to focus on persistent knife carriers and the people who sell them. The use of amnesty bins has resulted in thousands of weapons being taken off the streets (Newton, 2017).

For investigations into gang-related crime the police can apply for an 'Investigation Anonymity Order' for any person who gives information to the police (see 25.7). This can help persuade witnesses to cooperate as it reduces the risk of reprisals from other gang members.

14.11.2 Gang injunctions

Councils and police chief officers can apply for a 'gang injunction' under s 34(3) of the Policing and Crime Act 2009, to forbid a person from being involved in gang-related violence or gang-related drug dealing activity. The application for over 18s is made to a High Court or county court. It must be shown that the person has engaged in, encouraged or assisted, or needs to be protected from being drawn into more serious activity involving violence or drugs. The 2015 Home Office document *Injunctions to Prevent Gang-Related Violence and Gang-Related Drug Dealing* provides more detailed guidance.

For 14–17-year-olds the application for an injunction is made to a youth court. Local partners can also apply (such as registered social landlords, housing associations, transport agencies, probation, and youth offending teams). Local authority and other key partner agencies may also be involved as they have a responsibility to protect and improve the well-being of a child (s 10 of the Children Act 2004).

A gang injunction can last for up to two years and can prohibit a respondent from:

- associating in public with named gang members;
- visiting or travelling through a particular area or areas;
- being in charge of a particular species of animal (if it has been used to intimidate others);
- posting videos that promote their gang or threaten rival gangs on video-sharing websites; or
- uploading details of gang 'meet-ups' on social networking websites.

If the injunction is imposed for more than a year, the court will hold a review four weeks before the end of the first year to decide whether it should be extended or varied. For a young person, the review must take place at least four weeks before his/her 18th birthday.

Although a breach of a gang injunction is a civil matter, the prohibition is likely to include a power of arrest for any breach. Adults breaching the injunction could be remanded in custody, or on bail with conditions. For 14–17-year-olds, supervision orders (attending regular appointments with a mentor or supervisor), activities orders (attending rehabilitative programmes), or curfews can be used (Home Office, 2015d).

Specific Incidents

14.12 **Answers to Tasks**

TASK 1 A constable in uniform may require a person to give his or her name and address if the constable has reason to believe that a person has been acting (or is acting) in an anti-social manner within the meaning of s 2(1)(a) of the Anti-social Behaviour, Crime and Policing Act 2014. This power is provided by s 50(1) of the Police Reform Act 2002.

Further, s 50(2) states that an offence is committed by any person who:

- fails to give [his or her] name and address when required to do so under subsection (1), or
- gives a false or inaccurate name or address in response to a requirement under that subsection.

TASK 2 Since the young people in the group appear to be local residents, you would not be able to prohibit them from returning to the area within 48 hours, but if you reasonably believe they are between 10 and 15 years old you could take them back to their homes or to a place of safety, having provided them with a written direction first. However, for children who are clearly less than 10 years old such a direction cannot be used, nor is there a legal power to take them home or remove to a place of safety. You could visit the parents and try to offer advice.

TASK 3 In the first example the available intelligence and the use of body armour would appear to provide reasonable grounds for believing that harm was likely to be caused by a person or persons at the carnival.

For the Buckingham Palace example there was no evidence in the description given:

- of harm being done or being likely to be done to a person;
- that, in the presence of a person, harm was done to his/her property;
- of a person fearing being harmed through assault, riot, or other disturbance.

It would therefore be very difficult from the information in the description alone to prove a breach of the peace in this case.

TASK 4 You probably considered the following:

1. The officer would collect evidence from the woman and other people in the area
2. Their statements could provide evidence that the suspect was aware that:
    - while she was in a public place, anyone could hear or see her conduct; and
    - her conduct was unreasonable and was likely to cause harassment, alarm, or distress.
   Evidence could be gathered from people in the public area at the time confirming that they felt alarmed or distressed.
3. The officer could provide evidence about the suspect's conduct (what the officer actually saw and heard), and that there were other people in the public area at the time.

TASK 5 A police officer can also be harassed, alarmed, or distressed, but remember that this is a question of fact to be decided in each case by the magistrates. The magistrates may take into account that police officers often see incidents of disorderly conduct, and may therefore have developed a tolerance of such words and conduct. The evidence of other people in the area is an important factor.

TASK 6 In the case of *Swanston v DPP* (1997) 161 JP 203, the incident had occurred in a very small area and the officer was within about 1.5 m of the suspect. Unless the door supervisor had impaired hearing or sight, he could not have failed to understand what was said or failed to see the actions committed by the suspect. In the *Swanston* case, the prosecution proved that the suspect had the intention of causing the door supervisor to fear that violence was going to be used against him. Those facts were proved by the admissible evidence, including evidence from the police officer who witnessed the incident.

TASK 7 In *R v Plavecz* [2002] Crim LR 837, having been found guilty of affray, the defendant appealed. The court decided that affray is a public order offence and is inappropriate where the incident is essentially 'one on one', and the conviction was therefore quashed. It is doubtful therefore, given the circumstances outside the nightclub, that an investigation for affray could be sustained, but always seek guidance from the CPS in such matters.

TASK 8

1. For either of these two offences to be proven, you would need evidence to prove a course of conduct: for example letters, photographs, or eyewitness accounts. If the harassment involved phone calls, you would seek police force assistance to liaise with the service provider in order to obtain evidence of the calls. You would clarify with the victim whether there had been any previous instances of harassment or being put in fear of violence, and whether the police were informed or any civil remedy taken under s 3 of the Act. You would collect statements from colleagues who had seen the victim on previous occasions, and collect evidence from any other witnesses and paperwork, letters, and photographs from the victim, and exhibit them in a statement (see 10.12). The case could be discussed with a CPS Evidence Review representative or anyone involved in the investigation in an advisory capacity.

2. If the suspect was known and a course of conduct could not be proved but the victim had been harassed or put in fear of violence, you could warn the suspect. The warning would be recorded, preferably in the form of a First Incidence Harassment Warning or as a PNB entry, and you would also make sure it is recorded on the force database for future reference. This could be evidence towards proving a course of conduct in the future.

3. The victim should be advised to:
   - seek legal advice, as pursuing a civil remedy under s 3 of the Act could be appropriate;
   - contact Victim Support;
   - contact his/her phone service provider if the phone was being used to harass or put him/her in fear of violence, to arrange for a block to be placed on 'number withheld' incoming calls; and
   - keep a diary of events, retain physical evidence (such as letters), and take photographs of any visible evidence.

4. If a course of conduct could be proved or suspected, the suspect could be arrested, but only if there was a reason for the arrest being necessary. This could be to protect a child, or to allow the prompt and effective investigation of the conduct of the person in question, or to prevent any prosecution for the offence being hindered by the disappearance of the person in question.

TASK 9 The following are factors for consideration:

- How many times has the victim been harassed by people congregating outside his own home?
- Has he asked the people to leave the area?
- How many people are in the vicinity and what are they doing?
- What is the purpose of their gathering?
- What is the impact on the person in his home?
- Is there sufficient evidence to investigate the offence, or can the situation be better resolved in its early stages by directing the people to leave the area?

TASK 10 The answers are as follows:

1b, 2c, 3d, 4a, 5a, 6fgh, 7e, 8i.

TASK 11 The answers are:

1. Racial group and religious group.
2. Not a racial group but a religious one.
3. Not a racial group but a religious one.
4. Racial group but not a religious one.

Specific Incidents

15 Unlawful Violence Against Persons and Premises

15.1 Introduction

Unlawful personal violence is a common occurrence, and police officers are called to investigate such incidents with alarming frequency, with the number of more serious offences of violence appearing to be rising. The ONS statistics show that, for the year ending June 2019, there had been a 7 per cent rise in offences (totalling 44,076 offences) involving knives or sharp instruments recorded by the police in the previous year (ONS, 2019e). This is the highest number of offences since recording began in March 2011. The 'violence without injury' subcategory (where violence is threatened, or used but no injury is caused) accounted for 41 per cent of all violence recorded by the police and showed an increase of 13 per cent to 691,266 offences. This is a greater increase than the 'violence with injury' subcategory (up 3 per cent to 543,089 offences).

During incidents involving unlawful violence the health and safety of the public and police officer(s) is paramount, so police officers should always consider whether personal protective equipment is required. Incidents involving violence can be difficult to control. Often there is little time to assess a situation and plan a response because the events can be spontaneous.

On receipt of a call requesting police assistance at a violent incident, call-handlers will obtain as much detail as possible and relay it to the attending officers (see 24.4.1.1). If the identity of the suspect is known he/she can be checked on the Police National Computer (PNC). Risk factors for physical violence include a history of violent or disturbed behaviour, substance or alcohol abuse, and previously expressing an intention to harm others. While travelling to the scene, the deployed officers will carry out a risk assessment based on the information from the initial report (see 11.2.1). They should consider the particular risks for each incident, for example in a busy nightclub where many people are drinking alcohol, a glass or a bottle could easily be used as a weapon.

Once at the scene, a reassessment of victim and officer safety should be made, including the immediate risk posed by the availability and possible use of weapons. The need for First Aid or other medical assistance (such as an ambulance) for anyone present will need to be assessed. In a domestic setting, the individuals involved might need to be separated, especially if children are present or nearby (see 13.6). If the suspect(s) are present, the first attending officer (FAO) should watch for warning signs of incipient further violence—as well as verbal threats be aware of other signs of threatening behaviour such as the stance of the person, facial signs (eg snarling, jaw clenching), their use of their arms and hands (eg giving an aggressive 'come on' gesture with the hands or having clenched fists), plus increased breathing rate and pupil dilation (although these are more difficult to identify, particularly at a distance). If you are a trainee police officer or a special constable you will be given further information on this during Officer Safety Training (OST), and particularly the problems of interpreting so-called 'body language'. The National Decision Model (see 5.5.2) should be applied to ensure priorities are met, such as safety of victims and the preservation of evidence (see 11.2).

At any assault, early investigative actions will be crucial for there to be any chance of a successful prosecution; accurate records must be kept of anything said by the suspect (see 10.2), and evidence might need to be recorded, for example by taking photographs. If the alleged offender has left the scene, then his/her identity and description should be obtained from the people still present, and broadcast to other police patrols in the area (see 10.5). If the identity of the offender is known then further searches on any violent history might be obtained through the local force as well as national databases such as the ViSOR (see 13.7.5.1), the PNC for warning markers (see 5.9.1.1), or the PND (see 5.9.1.2), which could hold intelligence on historic out-of-area incidents.

A number of different offences of violence against individuals and premises are covered in this chapter, including:

- common assault under s 39 of the Criminal Justice Act 1988;
- common assault by beating under s 39 of the Criminal Justice Act 1988;
- assault occasioning actual bodily harm under s 47 of the Offences Against the Person Act 1861, often referred to as ABH;
- unlawful and malicious wounding, or inflicting grievous bodily harm (GBH) under s 20 of the Offences Against the Person Act 1861;
- wounding or causing grievous bodily harm with intent to do grievous bodily harm, or to resist or prevent arrest (referred to as 'GBH with Intent') under s 18 of the Offences Against the Person Act 1861;
- assaults on the police and obstructing a police officer under s 89(1) of the Police Act 1996; and
- assault with intent to resist arrest under s 38 of the Offences Against the Person Act 1861.

These general provisions of criminal law of course apply equally to violence and abuse in domestic settings; the only additional offence that relates specifically to domestic violence is coercive or controlling behaviour (s 76 of the Serious Crime Act 2015). This latter offence recognizes the extreme psychological and emotional abuse that some victims may experience (see 13.6).

Before going into the details of the offences of unlawful violence, the various meanings of the word 'assault' must be considered. There is no legal definition of assault. In *R v Brown* [1993] 2 All ER 75, Lord Templeman referred to the definition of assault as that adopted by the Law Commission in their Consultation Paper No 122, *Legislating the Criminal Code: Offences against the Person and General Principles* (1992), para 9.1. This stated:

> in common law an assault is an act by which a person intentionally or recklessly causes another to apprehend immediate and unlawful personal violence and a battery is an act by which a person intentionally or recklessly inflicts personal violence upon another.

Clearly there is a distinction between a victim experiencing the application of force by battery and apprehending the threat of an application of force, although both can amount to an assault (*R v Rolfe* (1952) 36 Cr App R 4). Hence whenever the word assault is used, the intended meaning for that particular context must be considered.

In 2015 the Law Commission submitted a proposal for reforms on offences of violence against a person (Law Commission, 2015). The proposals included recommendations for changes in sentencing for offences, as they argued that the hierarchy of offences should range from the least to the most harm caused. This hierarchy should be better reflected in sentencing, particularly for offences under s 20 (malicious wounding or grievous bodily harm) and s 47 (assault occasioning actual bodily harm). The Law Commission also argued that some of the language in the current legislation is archaic (eg 'grievous' and 'malicious') and therefore required updating. However, the most fundamental changes under consideration for these offences concerned the requirements for intention and recklessness with respect to serious injury. Currently there must be either an intention to cause injury or recklessness as to the risk of injury. The proposed changes would instead create a liability where there is no foresight about the degree of harm that could be caused. As of 2020 the proposed 2015 reforms were still 'pending' (Law Commission, 2020).

Specific Incidents

The topics covered in this chapter are likely to contribute to the learning required for the National Policing Curriculum subject areas: 'Understanding the Police Constable Role' and 'Managing Conflict'. If you are undertaking the PCDA or DHEP you will also be expected to know how to 'interpret and apply the letter and essence of all relevant law, as it relates to any encountered policing situation, incident or context'.

15.2 Common Assault and Occasioning Actual Bodily Harm

Historically, the Offences Against the Person Act 1861 provided magistrates with the opportunity to imprison or fine anyone committing the common law offences of assault or battery (see 15.2.1). The same statute provided the offences of assault occasioning actual bodily harm, GBH, and GBH with intent. Assault and battery remained as common law offences until they became summary offences by virtue of s 39 of the Criminal Justice Act 1988.

The CPS advises prosecutors and the police to consider both the level of injuries and the likely sentence that a court would apply when deciding how to charge a case of assault. They should take into account the *Sentencing Council's Definitive Guideline on Assault* (published in March 2011). In general, if there are no serious injuries, then the offence should be charged as common assault. The police can make the charging decision on common assault, as it is a summary offence (CPS, 2013). If the injury is serious the charge should be ABH, but if it is 'really serious', the charge should be GBH. There may be instances where it is necessary to deviate from this general principle (Sentencing Council, 2012a). If the prosecutors are considering changing the charge from ABH to common assault, the statutory time limit must be taken into account (as common assault is only a summary offence, so must be laid before the court within six months of the offence (*Dougall v Crown Prosecution Service* [2018] EWHC 1367, (Admin)).

15.2.1 Common assault

Under s 39 of the Criminal Justice Act 1988 there are two possible offences:

- common assault as a threat; and
- common assault by battery.

The naming of common assault offences is widely acknowledged to be confusing; various attempts have been made to revise the legislation. The two forms of common assault are mutually exclusive alternatives and should never be charged together (see *DPP v Little* [1992] 1 All ER 299). They are triable summarily only, and the penalty is six months' imprisonment. Note that these offences can be racially or religiously aggravated (see 14.10.2).

15.2.1.1 Common assault (threat)

Common assault as a threat can take a number of forms but does not include any physical contact or physical force on the victim:

- common assault (threat)—any act which makes a victim understand he/she is going to be immediately subjected to some personal violence. An example of this would be: 'I'm going to bitch-slap you bruv!' This could be done by social media, or letter, if there was some immediacy to the threat being carried out and the victim believes violence is going to occur (*R v Constanza* [1997] Crim LR 576). This includes when there is no means to carry out the threat such as holding a replica gun against a person and threatening to shoot him/her, if the victim believes there is a threat of violence (see *Logdon v DPP* [1976] Crim LR 121, DC);
- conditional threat (or conditional assault) conveys a threat on condition of another event, for example 'get out the car or I'll cut you'. It is reasonable for the victim to expect that bodily harm would be likely to follow any refusal. If the victim gets out of the car and the suspect takes no further action, he/she would still be guilty of assault.

Non-conditional threat (or unconditional assault) is not considered an assault, for example John says to Sue, 'Get me some water', Sue refuses and he says, 'If your brothers weren't here I'd thump you.' The wording of the threat shows that John is not going to assault Sue and therefore there is no immediate threat.

In the context of common assault a threat is:

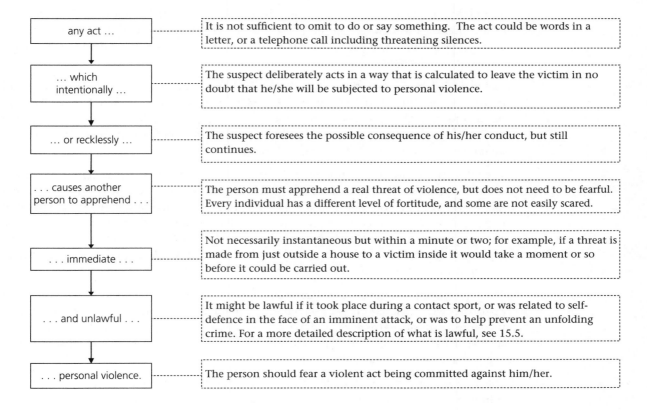

any act …	It is not sufficient to omit to do or say something. The act could be words in a letter, or a telephone call including threatening silences.
… which intentionally …	The suspect deliberately acts in a way that is calculated to leave the victim in no doubt that he/she will be subjected to personal violence.
… or recklessly …	The suspect foresees the possible consequence of his/her conduct, but still continues.
… causes another person to apprehend …	The person must apprehend a real threat of violence, but does not need to be fearful. Every individual has a different level of fortitude, and some are not easily scared.
… immediate …	Not necessarily instantaneous but within a minute or two; for example, if a threat is made from just outside a house to a victim inside it would take a moment or so before it could be carried out.
… and unlawful …	It might be lawful if it took place during a contact sport, or was related to self-defence in the face of an imminent attack, or was to help prevent an unfolding crime. For a more detailed description of what is lawful, see 15.5.
… personal violence.	The person should fear a violent act being committed against him/her.

15.2.1.2   Common assault (battery)

Common assault by battery (beating) involves the actual use of force by an assailant on a victim but only results in very minor or no perceivable injury. It is the intentional or reckless application of force on another, and can range from a push to a punch, and depends on how much harm is done, and the injury received. It can also include spitting in a person's face (although this would not be recognized as assault in terms of witness intimidation legislation (*Normanton* 1997 WL 1103134)).

A 'battery' (as in 'common assault by battery') is any act by which a person:

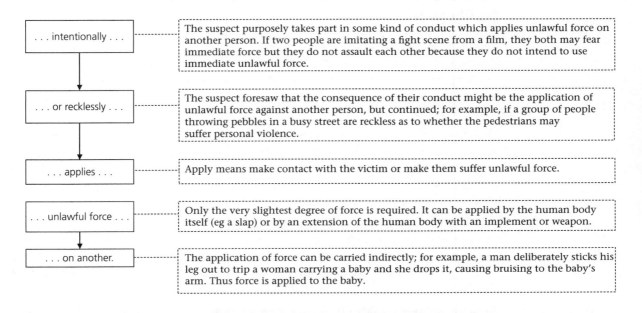

… intentionally …	The suspect purposely takes part in some kind of conduct which applies unlawful force on another person. If two people are imitating a fight scene from a film, they both may fear immediate force but they do not assault each other because they do not intend to use immediate unlawful force.
… or recklessly …	The suspect foresaw that the consequence of their conduct might be the application of unlawful force against another person, but continued; for example, if a group of people throwing pebbles in a busy street are reckless as to whether the pedestrians may suffer personal violence.
… applies …	Apply means make contact with the victim or make them suffer unlawful force.
… unlawful force …	Only the very slightest degree of force is required. It can be applied by the human body itself (eg a slap) or by an extension of the human body with an implement or weapon.
… on another.	The application of force can be carried indirectly; for example, a man deliberately sticks his leg out to trip a woman carrying a baby and she drops it, causing bruising to the baby's arm. Thus force is applied to the baby.

TASK 1 Consider the following incident: two men have been arguing in the street and one man has pushed and shoved the other, but very little force has been used so the victim is therefore uninjured. Is the offence common assault or common assault by beating?

Specific Incidents

15.2.2 Actual Bodily Harm

This offence is covered under s 47 of the Offences Against the Person Act 1861. The full name of the offence is Assault Occasioning Actual Bodily Harm (AOABH) but it is usually referred to as Actual Bodily Harm (ABH). Note that here the word assault is being used to mean some sort of physical attack.

The main factor which distinguishes common assault by beating from ABH is the degree of injury. *R v Donovan* [1934] 2 KB 498 at 509, [1934] All ER Rep 207 suggested that 'bodily harm has its ordinary meaning' and includes 'any hurt or injury calculated to interfere with the health or comfort of the prosecutor. Such hurt or injury need not be permanent, but must, no doubt, be more than merely transient and trifling'.

The injury must therefore be real and it should be capable of being seen or felt by the victim (or by witnesses such as a police officer). It also includes psychiatric injury/illness or psychological damage (*R v Ireland* [1998] AC 147 (HL)), and a hysterical and nervous state of mind brought about by the threat of violence. All of these latter 'injuries to the mind' must be more than emotions such as fear, distress, or panic that might be transient or trivial, and must be supported by medical evidence (see *R v Chan Fook* [1994] 2 All ER 552, [1994] 1 WLR 689, 99 Cr App R 147, [1994] Crim LR 432).

The term 'harm' can have a broad meaning, for example in one case the victim visited her ex-partner who then cut off her ponytail. Although hair grows outside the body and might therefore be considered as dead, and the victim did not feel physical pain in the normal sense, such an act was held to amount to Actual Bodily Harm (see *DPP v Smith (Michael Ross)* [2006] EWHC 94 (Admin), [2006] 2 All ER 16).

The aspects of intention or recklessness are the same for actual bodily harm as they are for common assault by beating; it only needs to be proved that the assault was intended or that it was carried out recklessly. There is no need to prove that the accused intended to cause injuries amounting to actual bodily harm (or was reckless as to whether injuries amounting to actual bodily harm would be caused).

This offence is triable either way, and the penalty if tried summarily is six months' imprisonment and/or a fine, and five years' imprisonment on indictment. The offence can be racially or religiously aggravated (see 14.10.2).

15.3 Unlawful and Malicious Wounding or Inflicting Grievous Bodily Harm

Section 20 of the Offences Against the Person Act 1861 states that it is an offence to 'unlawfully and maliciously ... wound another person' or to 'inflict grievous bodily harm [upon another person]'. The suspect must know that the actions would result in some kind of injury, but does not necessarily have to foresee the degree of injury. The injuries can be caused either with or without a weapon.

To understand this offence, careful consideration needs to be given first to the meaning of certain words. 'Grievous' should be taken to mean 'really serious' (*Director of Public Prosecutions Appellant; and Smith Respondent* [1961] AC 290); see 15.3.1 for details. 'Unlawfully' means 'without lawful justification' (as opposed to cases of lawfully inflicted injury, eg some instances of self-defence, see 15.5). 'Maliciously' means there is:

- an actual intention to do that particular kind of harm; or
- recklessness (unreasonably persisting in taking that risk) as to whether such harmful consequences would occur as a result of the actions taken. For example, in the possible transmission of a sexually transmitted infection by sexual activity, it would be reckless for the suspect to take that risk (*R v Dica* [2004] 3 All ER 593 (CA)).

Note that, although malice (ill-will or a malevolent motive) must be present, it does not have to be towards the victim personally.

15.3.1   The extent of the injury

The injury must amount to either wounding or grievous ('really serious') bodily harm. Wounding is defined as breaking of all the layers of the skin ranging from a minor cut requiring at most just a few stitches, to a deep incision requiring surgery. It does not have to be caused with a weapon (though of course this is often the case, eg using a deliberately smashed glass for an attack). If any of the layers of skin are still intact this would not be considered a wound, even if a bone is broken (*R v Wood and M'Mahon* (1830) 1 Mood CC 278). The CPS Charging Guidelines provide further detail on this.

Grievous bodily harm is not defined in the Act but case law has established that it should be given its ordinary meaning, which is 'really serious bodily harm' (*DPP v Smith* [1960] 3 All ER 161), but the results do not necessarily have to be permanent (ie disability or death). Note that in law there is no distinction between 'serious' and 'really serious'.

The CPS suggests the following as examples of GBH (CPS, 2017b):

- injury resulting in some permanent disability, that is a loss of function;
- visible disfigurement;
- broken or displaced bones;
- injuries with substantial blood loss, usually requiring blood transfusion;
- injuries resulting in lengthy treatment or incapacity;
- psychiatric injury (expert evidence is required).

GBH does not have to include an assault or a battery (see 15.2.1). For example, a person infecting his/her partner knowingly with the HIV virus while concealing the infection from the partner is committing the offence of grievous bodily harm. There have been at least ten convictions for GBH based on the reckless transmission of HIV in England and Wales. Telephone calls that would result in serious psychiatric injury to the victim can also amount to grievous bodily harm.

This offence is triable either way, and the penalty if tried summarily is six months' imprisonment and/or a fine, and up to seven years' imprisonment on indictment. This offence can be racially or religiously aggravated (see 14.10.2).

15.3.2   GBH with intent

The full name for this offence is 'wounding or causing grievous bodily harm with intent to do grievous bodily harm or to resist or prevent arrest'. The main difference between simple GBH and this offence is the element of intent. Inevitably it can be difficult to prove intent, although there will be some obvious examples, for instance if a weapon is used.

Section 18 of the Offences Against the Person Act 1861 states it is an offence to:

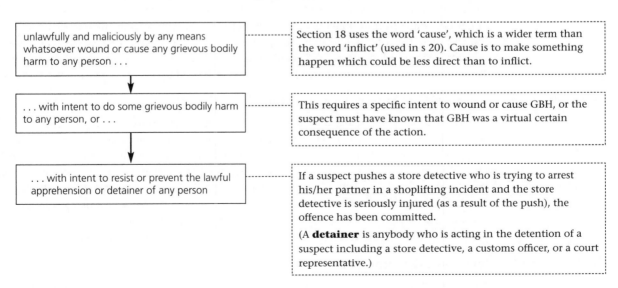

unlawfully and maliciously by any means whatsoever wound or cause any grievous bodily harm to any person . . .

Section 18 uses the word 'cause', which is a wider term than the word 'inflict' (used in s 20). Cause is to make something happen which could be less direct than to inflict.

. . . with intent to do some grievous bodily harm to any person, or . . .

This requires a specific intent to wound or cause GBH, or the suspect must have known that GBH was a virtual certain consequence of the action.

. . . with intent to resist or prevent the lawful apprehension or detainer of any person

If a suspect pushes a store detective who is trying to arrest his/her partner in a shoplifting incident and the store detective is seriously injured (as a result of the push), the offence has been committed.

(A **detainer** is anybody who is acting in the detention of a suspect including a store detective, a customs officer, or a court representative.)

Specific Incidents

This legislation in effect creates two offences under s 18:

- intending to cause GBH and causing GBH; and
- intending to resist apprehension and causing GBH as a result of that resistance.

The offences are triable on indictment only and the penalty is life imprisonment. There was no perceived need to create a racially or religiously aggravated offence for this offence as the maximum sentence is already life imprisonment.

15.4 Police Officers and the Use of Force

In the course of their work, police officers sometimes have to use force to control a situation or to carry out their duties, but they may also have force used against them, for example when a person resists being searched. When a police officer suspects he/she might need to use force a systematic approach is essential, to ensure that using force is absolutely necessary (see 15.4.1).

Members of the public sometimes use force against police officers, and data from the Office for National Statistics (2019) shows there were over 30,000 assaults on police officers in England and Wales (including British Transport Police) in the year 2018/19. New legislation (see 15.4.2.1) has increased the maximum custodial sentence for battery against emergency workers.

15.4.1 The use of force by police officers

Force should only be used by police officers when justified, and must be applied proportionately to protect the officer(s) or others from harm or when detaining a person after arrest or for the purpose of a search. However, it is important that the police officer is always acting in the line of duty, or the officer's actions could be unlawful and even amount to an assault.

If violence seems likely to occur the officer should first ascertain whether his/her mere presence could be sufficient to calm the situation. If this has no impact, then he/she will use communication skills to ask if assistance is required, and use active listening skills to try and calm the situation down. If there is an escalation and the officer perceives the use of force on a person to be required, then primary control skills will be used, ie pushing away with open hands, and using restraining techniques such as arm locks. If the officer struggles to take control and is overpowered, he/she may need to use incapacitant sprays, baton strikes, and 'takedowns'. Increasingly, officers are now being trained and issued with Tasers for use in extreme situations. In a life threatening situation authorized firearms officers (AFOs) can attend.

Officers will assess the risk by profiling a subject's behaviour on a scale ranging from compliant to aggressive (see 15.1), and also consider if there is any prior information on the subject, for example from intelligence. The number of persons present at the scene, the location, and whether any potential weapons are present will also be taken into account. The National Decision Making Model (see 5.5.2) can be used to help ensure that the decisions made and the actions taken are reasoned and justified, and will hold up in any subsequent court case.

15.4.1.1 Reasonable use of force by police officers

The use of force must be reasonable (see 15.5 for a general discussion on the reasonable use of force). For police officers particular considerations apply, for example if a police officer restrains a person without intending or purporting to arrest him/her, this can amount to an assault (as in common assault by beating, ABH, or GBH), and applies even if an arrest could have been justified (see *Fraser Wood v DPP* [2008] EWHC 1056 (Admin)). In another case, it was decided that a police officer who fired a Taser a second time was not using unreasonable force, as the officer genuinely believed that he and others close by were under the threat of immediate attack (*Chief Constable of Merseyside Police v McCarthy* [2016] EWCA Civ 1257).

15.4.1.2 Police restraint techniques

If you are undertaking the PCDA or DHEP you will receive specialist training and undertake practice of police restraint techniques. Both training programmes will require you to be able to 'arrest, detain and report individuals safely and lawfully'. The College of Policing APP on 'control, restraint and searches' (CoP, 2018d) will probably underpin your force training.

What follows is an overview and the details of police restraint techniques will be provided by your force.

Police forces, prisons, and medical organizations generally recommend that restrained persons are held face down (if required) for only the shortest possible period of time. On some occasions the restrainer may need to use his/her knee or body weight to control the person, but the pressure used should be no more than the absolute minimum required to achieve control.

The improper use of restraint by police officers can result in serious injury to the person, or even death. Leaving aside the possibility of a cardiac arrest, one of the more serious risks is positional asphyxia (PA), also referred to as postural asphyxia. This can occur when a person's body position or posture reduces his/her ability to breathe. It may occur through poorly executed or incorrect restraint techniques, or be consequent to some form of accident, such as fainting onto a chair or other raised surface. Asphyxiation can also be caused by keeping a person seated with his/her chest close to his/her knees, particularly if he/she is overweight.

The risk of PA is increased for a person who:

- is under the influence of alcohol or drugs, or unconscious;
- is overweight;
- has a particularly light frame;
- has engaged in a violent struggle or heavy exercise; or
- is under extreme stress.

Prevention is relatively simple: pressure should not be applied to the chest area or the back, and a seated person should not be forced to lean or left leaning forward. A detained person should be made to stand or sit upright as soon as possible, for example after handcuffs have been applied.

Most of the warning signs of impending PA are relatively obvious and include:

- suddenly becoming quiet, limp, or agitated—any change in consciousness should be considered;
- complaining of not being able to breathe—any such complaint should be taken seriously even if the detainee has an aggressive demeanour;
- noisy breathing, gurgling, or choking, foaming saliva, convulsions;
- signs of cyanosis (blue lips, eyelids, or gums—although the latter is often difficult to spot);
- signs of force or stress in the face and neck, such as raised blood vessels or bleeding.

The risk of in-custody deaths from PA is reduced by exercising caution and common sense. Officers should pay close attention if there is a particular risk, and in the event of asphyxiation, any hold or position potentially affecting the subject should be immediately removed and their clothing loosened. If this does not improve the person's condition then CPR should be performed, but it should be noted that resuscitation in such circumstances often fails. More details can be found in Belviso *et al* (2003).

15.4.2 Violence against police officers

Some people deliberately assault officers or emergency workers, and others may resist police actions. There are a number of offences covering such situations. In such circumstances police officers must ensure that their actions, even in the heat of the moment, are lawful, including the use of any degree of force (see 15.4.1).

15.4.2.1 Assaults on Emergency Workers (Offences) Act 2018

This legislation covers the offence of common assault, or battery, when committed against an emergency worker acting in the exercise of functions as such a worker (including when an emergency worker is not at work but is carrying out the same activities as he/she would at work). Section 3 of the Act provides a definition of the term 'emergency worker' (and includes, for example, a police constable (and any person who has the powers of a constable or is otherwise employed for police purposes or is engaged to provide services for police purposes), fire and rescue service staff, and ambulance staff (and some other health workers). It is immaterial whether the employment or engagement is paid or unpaid, and the word 'function' is used (rather than duty) in the Act to encompass a wide range of emergency workers.

Section 1 of the Act creates two new offences:

- common assault of an emergency worker; and
- assault by beating of an emergency worker.

Both these offences are triable either way, and the penalty is a fine or imprisonment for up to a year. Section 2 of the Act also refers to more serious assaults and offences where an emergency worker is a victim; this is now an aggravating factor meriting an increased sentence (the maximum available), and includes the following offences:

- threats to kill (see 15.6);
- wounding with intent to cause GBH (see 15.3.2);
- assault occasioning actual bodily harm (see 15.2.2);
- sexual assault under s 3 of the Sexual Offences Act 2003 (see 17.6.5).

15.4.2.2 Assaulting, resisting, or wilfully obstructing a police officer

This offence (under s 89 of the Police Act 1996) can be committed against police officers acting in the lawful execution of their duties, and against anyone assisting a police officer in the lawful execution of such duties. Note, however, that assault to resist arrest is a separate offence (see 15.4.2.3).

Under s 89 of the Police Act 1996 it is an offence for any person:

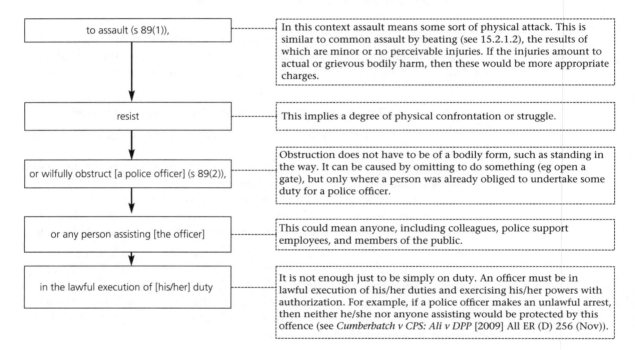

to assault (s 89(1)),	In this context assault means some sort of physical attack. This is similar to common assault by beating (see 15.2.1.2), the results of which are minor or no perceivable injuries. If the injuries amount to actual or grievous bodily harm, then these would be more appropriate charges.
resist	This implies a degree of physical confrontation or struggle.
or wilfully obstruct [a police officer] (s 89(2)),	Obstruction does not have to be of a bodily form, such as standing in the way. It can be caused by omitting to do something (eg open a gate), but only where a person was already obliged to undertake some duty for a police officer.
or any person assisting [the officer]	This could mean anyone, including colleagues, police support employees, and members of the public.
in the lawful execution of [his/her] duty	It is not enough just to be simply on duty. An officer must be in lawful execution of his/her duties and exercising his/her powers with authorization. For example, if a police officer makes an unlawful arrest, then neither he/she nor anyone assisting would be protected by this offence (see *Cumberbatch v CPS: Ali v DPP* [2009] All ER (D) 256 (Nov)).

The police sometimes need to enter and search a premises without the consent of the occupier to save life or limb, including the prevention of self-harm (see 13.7.2 for more detail). If the occupier is present and resists, this offence may be committed. If a police officer receives injuries consistent with common assault, then s 1 of the Assault on Emergency Workers (Offences) Act 2018 would now be the preferred charge (see 15.4.2.1).

The s 89 offences are triable summarily and the penalties are a fine or imprisonment (maximum six months for a s 89(1) offence and one month for a s 89(2) offence).

15.4.2.3 Assault to resist arrest

For the offence of resisting arrest, s 38 of the Offences Against the Person Act 1861 states it is an offence to:

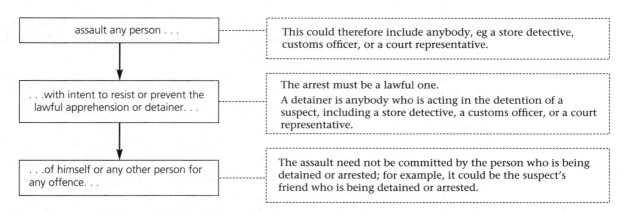

| assault any person . . . | - - - - | This could therefore include anybody, eg a store detective, customs officer, or a court representative. |

| . . .with intent to resist or prevent the lawful apprehension or detainer. . . | - - - - | The arrest must be a lawful one. A detainer is anybody who is acting in the detention of a suspect, including a store detective, a customs officer, or a court representative. |

| . . .of himself or any other person for any offence. . . | - - - - | The assault need not be committed by the person who is being detained or arrested; for example, it could be the suspect's friend who is being detained or arrested. |

The offence of resisting arrest is triable summarily and the penalty is two years' imprisonment.

15.5 General Defences to the Use of Violence

There are a great many defences to the application of force, for example self-defence (also known as 'common law self-defence'). Self-defence is not, however, defined by statute, and therefore it is a question of fact for the courts to decide whether a particular act amounts to self-defence. In *Dewar v DPP* [2010] EWHC 1050 (Admin) it was reaffirmed that there is a two-part test to self-defence:

- that the individual believes that he/she was acting in self-defence; and
- that the force used was reasonable in the circumstances (see 15.5.1).

There is no need to consider which person was the initial aggressor (see *Marsh v DPP* [2015] EWHC 1022 (Admin)). The timing of the use of force can also vary, for example in the case of *R v Bird* ([1985] 1 WLR 816) she believed she was about to be hit and so she hit her partner first. The definition of reasonable force is examined in more detail in 15.5.1.

'Reasonable chastisement' of a child by his/her parent can be a defence, but this does not apply if it involves assault occasioning actual bodily harm, unlawfully inflicting grievous bodily harm, causing grievous bodily harm with intent, or cruelty to a child (s 58 of the Children Act 2004). The Education Act 1996 removed the right of schools to use corporal punishment.

That consent had been given for the use of force can be a defence, for example in some sports (although the level of force used must be appropriate and in keeping with the rules of the game (see *R v Barnes* [2004] EWCA Crim 3246 and *R v Coney* (1882) 8 QBD 534)). Consent can also be used as a defence in a medical context (eg that the act was a necessary part of medical treatment), and for piercings or tattoos. It might also be used where there has been 'horseplay' or rough and undisciplined play where there is no intention to cause injury (*R v Jones (Terence)* [1986] Crim LR 123). The defence of consent cannot, however, be relied on in offences under ss 47 and 20 of the Offences Against the Person Act 1861 where the injuries resulted from sadomasochist activities (*R v Brown* [1993] 2 All ER 75 (HL)).

Intoxication can only be used as a defence for crimes of specific intent, such as offences under s 18 (maliciously inflicting grievous bodily harm with intent). The other more common types of assault (common, causing actual bodily harm, assault of a police officer) require no specific intent and therefore this defence cannot apply. For intoxication to succeed as a defence the court must take into account the degree of intoxication, to determine whether the defendant would have been capable of forming the intent to bring about a specific result. Involuntary intoxication (eg due to spiked drinks) could be considered as a defence for offences of basic intent such as common assault or ABH.

15.5.1 The meaning of 'reasonable force'

The use of reasonable force for self-defence, defence of property, and law enforcement is defined in law, for example its use for certain powers of arrest and entry provided under s

Specific Incidents

117 of the PACE Act 1984 (see 10.8.2 and 13.7.2). The general meaning of 'reasonable force' is expanded upon in s 76 of the Criminal Justice and Immigration Act 2008. Defences that include the notion of 'reasonable force' include:

- self-defence (a common law defence, see s 76(2)(a) of the Criminal Justice and Immigration Act 2008);
- defence of property (a common law defence, see s 76(2)(aa) of the Criminal Justice and Immigration Act 2008); and
- the use of force in the course of prevention of crime, or in making an arrest (s 3(1) of the Criminal Law Act (s 76(2)(b)), see 10.8.2.

For these defences, the person must have had an honest belief that it was necessary to use force and the degree of force used was not disproportionate (see *Palmer v R* [1971] AC 814). Both these conditions must be fulfilled. The person's perceptions of the circumstances at the time will be taken into account, as well as the reality of the situation. For example, the defendant might have had a mistaken belief as to the circumstances but if this misunderstanding is considered to have been reasonable, then a jury could find the defendant not guilty (*R v Williams (Gladstone)* [1987] 3 All ER 411, 78 Cr App R 276). Also, it is not reasonable to expect all defendants in the heat of the moment to be able to judge the precise degree of force required. Therefore, a person who uses the force honestly and instinctively thinking that it was necessary will be provided with some leeway.

15.5.2   Defending against intruders in a dwelling

Where a person is defending him/herself or others from intruders in their home, it might still be reasonable to use a degree of force that might be considered disproportionate in other circumstances. The resident may have been under intense pressure, with little time to think rationally about the minimum level of force required to stop an intruder.

Amendments to s 76(5)(a) of the Criminal Justice and Immigration Act 2008 introduced the idea of disproportionate force, but also the idea that the force used by an individual must always be reasonable in the circumstances as he/she believes them to be. The question as to whether the degree of force used was reasonable in the circumstances is to be decided by reference to the circumstances as they were believed to be. For example, a burglar breaks into a home, and the resident awoken from a deep sleep goes downstairs where a struggle ensues. The resident punches the burglar, knocking him out. This might be considered disproportionate, but is reasonable taking the circumstances into account. However, if the resident then started beating the unconscious burglar, this would be considered grossly disproportionate, and therefore unreasonable and unlawful. A resident who shot indiscriminately at burglars with a gun (*R v Martin* [2002] 2 WLR 1) was held to have used grossly disproportionate force.

The degree of force used will be considered lawful if the resident is acting in self-defence or to protect other people in his/her home, and the force used was disproportionate (but not grossly disproportionate).

Protecting property (rather than people) by using disproportionate force, however, is still unlawful. Further information regarding the defence of property is available in the Parliament briefing paper 'Householders and the criminal law of self-defence' available online.

15.6   Threats to Kill

Section 16 of the Offences Against the Person Act 1861 (as amended by Sch 12 to the Criminal Law Act 1977) is about making threats to kill, and can be committed in two main ways. The simplest form of this offence is when A threatens to kill B and intends that B will believe the threat.

- Annie says to Bob 'You've 'ad it, you're dead, I'll do it ..., you're dead': Annie wants Bob to believe that her threat to kill him is real.

This offence can also be committed in a slightly more complicated way: person A communicates a threat to kill, and intends that B should believe the threat. But the threat is not about killing B, it is about killing another person C. (It is irrelevant whether C knows about the threats.)

- Adam says to Babs 'That Colin—he's finished now, I'll sort it—final like, stone cold, dead': Adam intends that Babs should believe that his threat to kill Colin is real.

To prove this offence, it is not necessary for A to actually intend to kill anyone, but it must be proved that A intends that B should believe and fear that this would be carried out. The threats made by A can be premeditated or spontaneous, and can be communicated by any means including through email or a social networking site. There does not have to be the sense that the killing would be carried out immediately. The offence could be useful where there has been no assault (eg if an assault has been prevented), yet the victim B was in fear that it would be carried out.

Threats to kill are relatively common and it is often difficult to prove an offence has occurred because it is often one person's word against another. The onus is on the prosecution to prove that there was no lawful excuse for making such a threat. (A lawful excuse could be that the defendant honestly believed (with reasonable grounds) that it was necessary in self-defence.) The threat to kill should be plain to see for the jury (*R v Solanke* [1970] 1 WLR 1). If it is not obvious, then perhaps a charge under s 4 of the Public Order Act 1986 or a charge of affray would be more appropriate (see 14.4).

This offence is triable either way, and the penalty if tried summarily is six months' imprisonment and/or a fine, and on indictment ten years' imprisonment.

TASK 2 A police officer attends each of the following incidents. Using the information given here decide what offence or offences may have been committed in relation to the injuries sustained by the victims.

1. Janice is holding a baby and arguing with John. He loses his temper and pushes her shoulder causing her to drop the baby. As a result, the baby sustains a minor fracture to her right arm.
2. Two people are arguing in the street. The dispute reaches a point where one of the couple head-butts the other, who then has a severe nosebleed.
3. An apparently drunken man throws a glass bottle from a moving car in the direction of a woman waiting at a bus stop. The bottle hits the shelter and breaks. A large fragment of flying glass hits the woman on her head, causing a deep wound which bleeds profusely. The woman's skull can easily be seen through the wound. Subsequently, the victim attended accident and emergency at a local hospital and had several stitches inserted.
4. CCTV images show a woman taking goods from a clothes shop and hiding them under her jacket. A store detective follows her out and into the street and stops her. He explains who he is and why he is detaining her. She makes a sudden move, pushing the store detective backwards. He falls over and grazes his hand.
5. After months of alleged harassment by local youths in the street outside her house, the occupant comes out and slaps one of the youths, leaving a large red mark on his cheek.

15.7 The Use of Violence to Enter Premises

It is an offence to use violence to gain entry to premises occupied by any person opposing the entry (s 6 of the Criminal Law Act 1977). Convictions for this offence are usually in the context of domestic disputes, for example a man trying to force his way into his own flat is committing an offence if his live-in partner is inside and does not want him to come in. A police officer suspecting that such an offence may have been committed should run through a mental checklist before acting, to ensure that the circumstances match all the requirements of the relevant legislation.

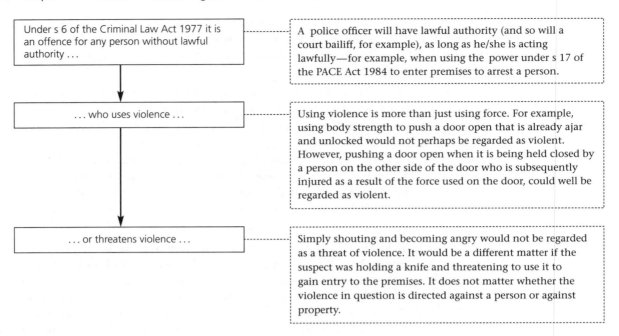

Under s 6 of the Criminal Law Act 1977 it is an offence for any person without lawful authority . . .

A police officer will have lawful authority (and so will a court bailiff, for example), as long as he/she is acting lawfully—for example, when using the power under s 17 of the PACE Act 1984 to enter premises to arrest a person.

. . . who uses violence . . .

Using violence is more than just using force. For example, using body strength to push a door open that is already ajar and unlocked would not perhaps be regarded as violent. However, pushing a door open when it is being held closed by a person on the other side of the door who is subsequently injured as a result of the force used on the door, could well be regarded as violent.

. . . or threatens violence . . .

Simply shouting and becoming angry would not be regarded as a threat of violence. It would be a different matter if the suspect was holding a knife and threatening to use it to gain entry to the premises. It does not matter whether the violence in question is directed against a person or against property.

So for this offence, the suspect must have no lawful authority to enter, and must either use violence or threaten to use violence:

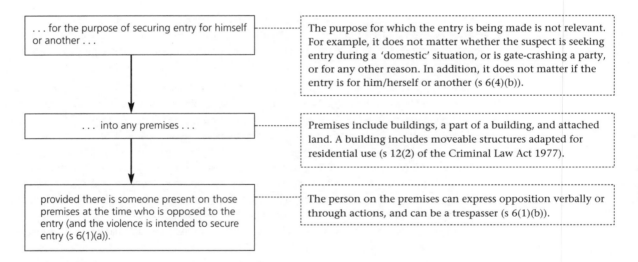

. . . for the purpose of securing entry for himself or another . . .

The purpose for which the entry is being made is not relevant. For example, it does not matter whether the suspect is seeking entry during a 'domestic' situation, or is gate-crashing a party, or for any other reason. In addition, it does not matter if the entry is for him/herself or another (s 6(4)(b)).

. . . into any premises . . .

Premises include buildings, a part of a building, and attached land. A building includes moveable structures adapted for residential use (s 12(2) of the Criminal Law Act 1977).

provided there is someone present on those premises at the time who is opposed to the entry (and the violence is intended to secure entry (s 6(1)(a)).

The person on the premises can express opposition verbally or through actions, and can be a trespasser (s 6(1)(b)).

This offence does not apply for a home-owner, tenant, or legally intended occupier who comes home and finds a person (or several people) in her property; she can legally use or threaten violence to enter the property. The exemption does not include, however, using or threatening violence towards the trespasser; the trespasser can be asked to leave, and it is an offence under s 7 of the Criminal Law Act 1977 if he/she refuses to do so (see also 14.8.4 on squatters and civil trespass).

The offence of using violence to gain entry is triable summarily, and the penalty is six months' imprisonment and/or a fine. There is a power of entry to arrest under s 17 of the PACE Act 1984 for this offence (see 10.6).

> **TASK 3** The police are called to a house at night where a young man is banging on the front door with his fists, shouting 'Open the door!'. The police speak to an older man inside the house. It emerges that the two men live together in the house, and are joint owners. The young man had arrived home in the early hours, very drunk, to find the front door would not open with his key. The neighbours report being woken by the noise and also heard the man inside the house shouting 'Go away!'. In relation to s 6(1) of the Criminal Law Act 1977, has the young man committed an offence by banging on the door?

15.8 **Answers to Tasks**

TASK 1 Common assault by beating (battery): only the very slightest degree of force is required to constitute a battery and little or no visible injury is necessary to prove the offence.

TASK 2 The problem with this type of scenario is that you lack all the other information that would be available in a real incident. However, based entirely on the limited information available to you in the questions, the following are the possible offences that could be considered:

1. An assault can be committed directly or indirectly. So, when John pushes Janice he causes a direct common assault against Janice. As a result of this reckless behaviour, John has also committed a s 20 GBH offence on the baby (see 15.3).
2. Here, in order to have sustained a nosebleed the health and/or comfort of the victim is likely to have been 'interfered with', so ABH (s 47 of the Offences Against the Person Act 1861) would be an appropriate offence.
3. All layers of the victim's skin have been broken and therefore the injury is a wound. More evidence is required to ascertain the suspect's intentions (this will come from witnesses and by interviewing the suspect). The offence could be GBH or GBH with intent.
4. Two options here perhaps; as far as the injury is concerned, a graze may have interfered with the health and comfort of the store detective, therefore ABH could be considered. When the aspect of detention/arrest is also taken into consideration, then assault with intent to resist lawful arrest under s 38 of the Offences Against the Person Act 1861 may also be appropriate.
5. Once again, a large red mark may have interfered with the health and comfort of the young man, therefore ABH could be considered. Alternatively, the red mark could be considered as a minor or hardly perceivable injury, so this might be a common assault by beating (s 39 of the Criminal Justice Act 1988).

Prosecution guidelines or charging standards are available on the CPS website.

TASK 3 Section 6(1) of the Criminal Law Act 1977 states that any person who, without lawful authority, uses or threatens violence for the purpose of securing entry into any premises for [him/her]self or for any other person is guilty of an offence provided that:

- 'a person is present on those premises, and he/she is opposed to the entry which the violence is intended to secure'; and
- 'the person using violence or threatening the violence knows that that is the case'.

In the circumstances it appears that the man is only hammering on the door with his fists and therefore these actions fall short of the 'violence' that is required for this offence. If his actions escalate to the likelihood of damage being caused, or threats or use of violence, then the offence would be committed (provided that he knew his partner was on the premises and opposed the entry).

Specific Incidents

16 | Theft, Fraud, and Related Offences

16.1 Introduction

This chapter examines the law and procedure concerned with a number of criminal offences associated with theft and fraud. We present the basic knowledge of the criminal law required for many approved pre-join degrees and for the PCDA and the DHEP. This Handbook will provide you with the essence of the most relevant law and some interpretations (both academic and from case law or precedent), but there is no substitute for reading and understanding the law itself. Of all the dishonest criminal offences police officers will deal with early in their careers, theft will probably be the most common. Theft includes shoplifting and stealing from an employer, as well as a number of other similar crimes. The primary source of legislation relating to theft is to be found in ss 1–6 of the Theft Act 1968. There are many legal complexities surrounding theft and we will simply examine the basic principles involved. Trainee officers are likely to be involved in most stages of the investigation of theft and 'simple' types of fraud, from reporting to investigation and possibly prosecution. They are less likely to become involved in complex fraud investigations, beyond the initial stages. This is particularly the case for large-scale credit card fraud, where difficult decisions need to be made concerning the 'screening' of reported offences to decide which should be the subject of a secondary investigation (see 24.4.3) and in reference to the National Intelligence Model (NIM) (see 23.6). The investigation is likely to be handled by a specialist unit (which might also deal with cybercrime (see Chapter 21)).

Officers should consider the best way of dealing with certain low-level offences (eg shoplifting items with a value below £100), and exercise their police powers accordingly. The chosen response must fall within the limits of force policy, and you should also check with your workplace tutor and/or supervisors.

The topics covered in this chapter are likely to contribute to the learning required for the National Policing Curriculum subject area: 'Understanding the Police Constable Role'.

16.2 Theft

A person is guilty of theft (s 1 of the Theft Act 1968) if he/she 'dishonestly appropriates property belonging to another with the intention of permanently depriving the other of it'. A thief is a person who commits a theft or, in everyday language, steals something. There are five key concepts relating to the definition of theft: dishonesty, appropriation, property, belonging, and the intention to permanently deprive. We will examine each of these in turn.

16.2.1 Dishonesty

The Theft Act 1968 does not actually define dishonesty, but does state that dishonesty can include where a person would have been willing to pay for property he/she took (s 2(2)). The Theft Act 1968 defines where a person should not be treated as dishonest (s 2(1)). The person is not acting dishonestly if he/she believes that:

- he/she had the lawful right to take the item (eg a man sees a woman leaving with his bag and decides to take it back from her);

- he/she would have had the owner's consent if the owner had known the circumstances (eg your neighbour is on holiday and you are looking after his garden, but your lawnmower breaks down so you take his from his shed to cut your grass); or
- the owner cannot be discovered by taking reasonable steps (eg a person finds cash in the street).

Two tests are applied in court, to establish dishonesty. First, the defendant's genuine and reasonable *knowledge and beliefs* about what actually took place must be established by reviewing the facts of the case. The emphasis is on whether his/her beliefs were *reasonable* in the overall context. The second test (the 'objective test') will consider whether an everyday honest person would consider those acts dishonest. The rather complex case law for these tests is to be found in *Ivey v Genting Casinos (UK) Ltd* [2017] UKSC 67, Lord Nicholls in *Royal Airlines Sdn Bhd v Tan* [1995] 2 AC 378, and Lord Hoffmann in *Barlow Clowes International Ltd (in liquidation) v Eurotrust International Ltd* [2005] UKPC 37.

16.2.2   Appropriation

Appropriation (s 3(1) of the Theft Act 1968) is assuming the rights of an owner of property by keeping it or controlling its movements. This would include a girl who takes a pen from a shop display and puts it in her pocket, and a person who borrows a keyboard from a friend, and chooses to keep it in the hope the friend forgets about it.

A person can agree to the appropriation, but the consent may be in doubt if the person:

- has been deceived about the nature of the circumstances;
- is not of sound mind (including having serious learning difficulties) (see *R v Hinks* [2000] 4 All ER 833); or
- cannot understand the language being spoken (*R v Lawrence* [1972] AC 262).

If a person buys an item in good faith, but later finds out it is stolen property, the purchase can amount to theft, including if the person tries to sell it on, destroy it, get rid of it, or keep it.

16.2.3   Property

Property within the Theft Act 1968 (s 4) has its usual common meaning of a moveable object (such as items for sale in a shop, money, and physical items) or being an individual's personal property (which includes a wide variety of things such as purses, illegal drugs, pets). However, it also includes other things such as ideas, and intangible items, for example air in an oxygen tank, space in a skip, and trademark logos (but not electricity (see 16.7)).

'Things in action' are also taken to be property under the Act. By 'things in action' the law is referring to rights rather than tangible objects, for example the right to sue (to take civil legal action against another). For the trainee police officer, considering property as a 'thing in action' is most likely to occur in connection with alleged crime involving bank or building society accounts, for example when a person entrusted by an organization makes out a cheque to him/herself. (When we deposit funds in a bank account the ownership of the money passes to the bank but in turn we gain under the law the right to 'sue' the bank for this amount back (this right to sue is the 'thing in action'). If somebody else tries to dishonestly debit our bank balance by transferring money to their own account, they are unwittingly attempting to steal our right to sue for the money, not the money itself.)

16.2.3.1   Land and buildings as property

Land itself generally cannot be stolen so if, for example, a homeowner goes on holiday and her neighbour moves the fence over a little to increase the size of his garden (and hence decrease the size of hers), this would not be regarded as theft. (The victim would have to pursue such a matter in a civil court.)

However, if a trustee in charge of an estate or a person with a power of attorney chose to sell another's land for profit, this could amount to theft. Turf, top soil, and cultivated trees and shrubs on land are sometimes removed without permission, as are parts of buildings such as roof tiles, fireplaces, and fixtures and fittings. These items are all regarded as 'real property' so taking such items could therefore amount to theft. Whole buildings, however, cannot be stolen as such.

16.2.3.2   Wild plants and animals on land

The taking of wild plants, fruit, flowers, and fungi only amounts to theft if taken for sale, reward, or a commercial purpose, or taken in such a manner that the plant or fungus cannot grow back (eg the plants have been uprooted).

The taking of wild animals from land can be regarded as theft but only if:

- the animal had been tamed and was being kept in captivity such as in a zoo or a home; or
- the animal had been killed there without the landowner's permission, and taken.

Note, however, that other legislation such as the Wildlife and Countryside Act 1981 might prohibit the taking of certain wild animals and plants in a wider range of circumstances.

16.2.4   Belonging to a person

When something belongs to a person, under s 5 of the Theft Act 1968 this means that the person is either the owner or he/she has:

- a proprietary right or interest, for example the owner of a car takes her car to a garage for repairs. The mechanic spends time and money on parts repairing and servicing the car. He would now have a proprietary right of interest in the car as he has put an investment into it, and now has part ownership until the debt is settled or agreed. If the owner takes the car without settling or agreeing the debt this might be theft (see *R v Turner (No 2)* [1971] 1 WLR 901);
- possession, for example whoever has the vehicle in his/her possession. Whether that possession is lawful depends on the circumstances and the timing. If the owner of the car took it without having paid then his/her possession might not be lawful; or
- control, for example the mechanic who carries out the repairs on the car.

16.2.5   The intention to permanently deprive

This is shown by a person treating another person's property as if it were his or her own, and is described in s 6(1) of the Theft Act 1968. It could include:

- borrowing and lending over an extended time scale (eg borrowing a sewing machine and then lending it to someone else); or
- pawning an item that belongs to another person (eg going to a pawnbroker's shop with your flatmate's laptop and receiving a loan of money in exchange).

It has even been held to include a person stealing a car and then offering it back to the owner in the same condition for money (*R v Raphael* [2008] EWCA Crim 1014).

> **TASK 1** Now that you know what constitutes a theft, think of three incidents of theft that you are aware of, either through the media or other means, and try and identify the five elements of theft within each of those incidents.

16.2.6   Mode of trial and penalties for theft

The offence of theft is triable either way, depending on the value of the goods in question. For retail property worth £100 or less a PND can be used (see 10.13.2). The offence is tried summarily if the value of the property stolen is less than £5,000 (s 22A of the Magistrates' Courts Act 1980), and the penalty is six months' imprisonment and/or a fine. The penalty when tried on indictment is up to seven years' imprisonment.

The police powers for entry and search provided under the PACE Act 1984 for indictable offences (see 10.8.5) apply for all suspected thefts (s 176 of the Anti-social Behaviour, Crime and Policing Act 2014).

16.3   Robbery and Blackmail

Robbery and blackmail are two separate offences under the Theft Act 1968, but there are some similarities. Robbery is theft involving the use of physical force (or the threat of force) to appropriate property belonging to another person. For blackmail, pressure is put on the victim with the aim of causing him/her a loss. However, for blackmail no property needs to have been taken and no physical force needs to be involved for the offence to be proved.

Consideration should be given as to how victims of both robbery and blackmail are supported. Victim support and crime prevention advice should be offered as appropriate (see 13.7.4 and 3.6.3 respectively).

16.3.1 Robbery

Robbery is the act of stealing from a person whilst using (or threatening the use of) force or violence (s 8 of the Theft Act 1968). It is an aggravated form of the primary offence of theft and therefore, for robbery to be proved, theft has to be proved first. Force or a threat of force must be used immediately before, at the time of the theft, and in order to carry out the theft.

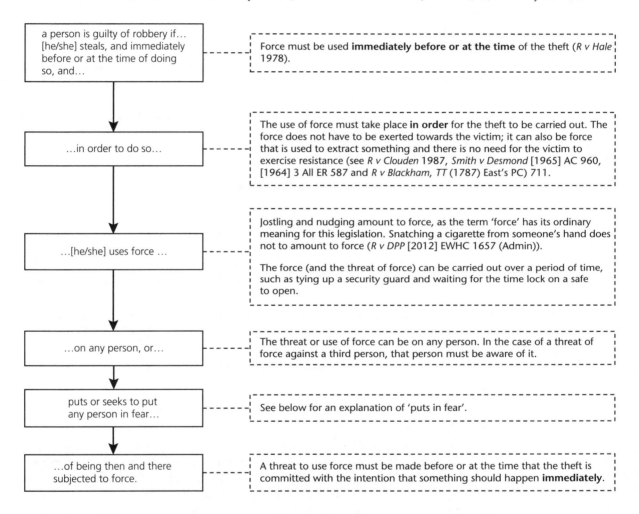

a person is guilty of robbery if… [he/she] steals, and immediately before or at the time of doing so, and…

> Force must be used **immediately before or at the time** of the theft (*R v Hale* 1978).

…in order to do so…

> The use of force must take place **in order** for the theft to be carried out. The force does not have to be exerted towards the victim; it can also be force that is used to extract something and there is no need for the victim to exercise resistance (see *R v Clouden* 1987, *Smith v Desmond* [1965] AC 960, [1964] 3 All ER 587 and *R v Blackham, TT* (1787) East's PC) 711.

…[he/she] uses force …

> Jostling and nudging amount to force, as the term 'force' has its ordinary meaning for this legislation. Snatching a cigarette from someone's hand does not to amount to force (*R v DPP* [2012] EWHC 1657 (Admin)).
>
> The force (and the threat of force) can be carried out over a period of time, such as tying up a security guard and waiting for the time lock on a safe to open.

…on any person, or…

> The threat or use of force can be on any person. In the case of a threat of force against a third person, that person must be aware of it.

puts or seeks to put any person in fear…

> See below for an explanation of 'puts in fear'.

…of being then and there subjected to force.

> A threat to use force must be made before or at the time that the theft is committed with the intention that something should happen **immediately**.

There are two main ways the 'puts in fear' element of the offence could be established:

- the victim's statement could show that he/she was put in fear—the degree of fear is not important, because the fortitude shown by different people will inevitably vary (see *R v DPP; B v DPP* [2007] EWHC 739 (Admin), 171 JP 404); or
- the state of mind of the suspect (intending to make a person fear that force will be used) could be evidenced from the suspect's statement, evidence from other witnesses, or circumstantial evidence, such as the suspect had been holding an offensive weapon.

When force is threatened, but the force is to be used against a third person, he/she must know about it; he/she must 'apprehend' the force. For example, imagine a man goes into the bank and passes a note to the bank teller to hand over cash or he will stab the woman behind him in the queue. The woman does not know the threat has been made, so even if the teller hands over the money this would not be robbery (although it might be blackmail, see 16.3.2).

In terms of the timing of the force or threat of force, if a suspect says 'Give me your mobile now, or I'll stab you', and the mobile is handed over it would be robbery. If, however, a suspect says to a victim, 'If you don't give me your mobile tonight, I'll stab you', it is not robbery as the threat of force is for the future (although it might be blackmail). If force is used after the theft, it would not be robbery but the two separate offences of theft and assault could be considered. An example of this could be a man snatching a woman's mobile phone from her hand without force and then pushing her over. Similarly, if at the end of a fight, as an afterthought, a man sees the opportunity to dishonestly take an item of property from somebody he has injured in the fight, then that is not robbery; it is assault and theft.

Note that all five elements of theft must be proven (see 16.2) to have applied at the time of the robbery. For example, in *R v Zerei* [2012] EWCA Crim 1114, where a car had been taken by violence and abandoned shortly afterwards, a conviction for robbery was held to be unsafe as the intention to permanently deprive was not proved.

The offence of robbery is triable on indictment only and the maximum penalty is life imprisonment.

16.3.2 Blackmail

A person commits the offence of blackmail if he/she makes any unwarranted demand with menaces, with a view to making a gain (for him/herself or any other person), or with intent to cause a loss to any other person (s 21(1) of the Theft Act 1968). The demand must be unwarranted and unreasonable (some demands may be considered reasonable, eg in relation to repaying a debt). The communication can be made by phone, text, or letter, and will be considered made the moment a text is sent or letter posted, not upon receipt (*Treacy v DPP* [1971] 1 All ER 110).

The evidential requirements are shown in the table.

Evidential requirement	Explanation
Demand	The demand can be made orally or in writing
With a view to gain or loss	The loss or gain must be financial in nature
Menaces	This should be given its ordinary dictionary meaning, for example the person's actions or words have a threatening quality, and are not trivial
The demand must be unwarranted	The court must decide whether the demand was unreasonable, and whether the suspect believes it was reasonable and proper

The offence of blackmail is triable on indictment only and the maximum penalty is 14 years' imprisonment.

TASK 2

1. Chris is carrying a bag full of shopping in the town centre when the handle breaks and she drops the bag. Jo grabs it and makes off, but the bag breaks open, spilling the contents onto the ground. Jo picks up one of the items and then runs into Chris, causing her to fall over heavily and break her arm. Has Jo committed the offence of robbery?
2. Mike is a bailiff and he arrives at Stav's home to collect £500 on order of a court. Mike tells Stav if he does not hand over the money he will come in and seize £500 worth of property. Has Mike committed the offence of blackmail?

16.4 Burglary and Trespassing

Burglary is a so-called 'volume' and 'acquisitive' crime. Trainee police officers will undoubtedly encounter crimes of burglary whilst on Supervised and Independent Patrol. It is a serious offence; aggravated burglary (see 16.4.2), for example, carries a maximum sentence of life imprisonment. Not all burglaries are reported, sometimes because the victim is unaware that the burglary has occurred or is reluctant to be involved with the police. Research also suggests that an increasing number of burglaries are committed with the main aim of obtaining vehicle keys to steal vehicles (Allcock *et al*, 2011 and Chapman *et al*, 2012).

There is also the phenomenon of distraction burglary (in some forces called 'artifice' burglary), where entry is gained to the home of a person (very often an elderly person) by an offender pretending to be an official. An important case in establishing this type of offence was *R v Boyle* [1954] 2 QB 292, [1954] 2 All ER 721. Boyle was charged with burglary (or 'house breaking' as it was then known) as he had falsely represented himself as employed by the BBC to locate radio disturbances. He thereby gained admittance to the person's home and stole a handbag. On appeal against conviction it was held that the use of deception to gain entry meant he was a trespasser. Artifice burglars usually commit a series of similar crimes within a short period of time ('spree offences').

The legislation concerning burglary is to be found in ss 9–10 of the Theft Act 1968. We look separately at the basic offence of burglary, then at aggravated burglary, and finally at various aspects of trespass associated with this type of crime.

16.4.1   The basic offence of burglary

The basic offence of burglary is set out in s 9 of the Theft Act 1968. There are two subsections (s 9(1)(a) and s 9(1)(b)) which describe the main ways the offence can be committed, as shown in the diagram (see also 16.4.1.1).

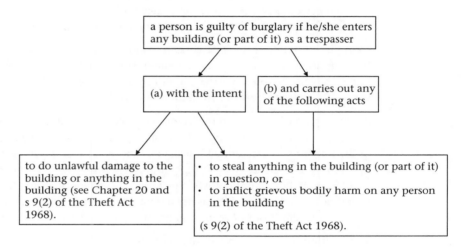

Certain terms, such as 'entry', 'trespasser', and 'building' need to be carefully defined in order to fully appreciate the range of activities that might count as burglary under s 9(1) of the Theft Act 1968.

Entry can be gained in a number of clearly defined ways:

- In person, by walking or climbing into a building, either completely or by inserting a body part (eg an arm or a leg) through a window or letter box. However, there must be more than minimal insertion; sliding a hand between a window and frame from the outside of a building in order to release the catch would be insufficient.
- Using a tool or article as an extension of the human body to carry out one of the relevant offences. In these circumstances no part of the body needs to be inserted, only the article that is being used to gain entry. The article must be used for more than just gaining entry; using a crowbar just to prise open a door would not qualify as the full offence, but a length of garden cane pushed through the letter box of a shop to hook a scarf from a display would qualify as the full offence.
- Using a blameless accomplice in a similar way to using an article as an extension of the suspect's body. Here, for example, a child under 10 years of age (below the age of criminal responsibility) could be lifted through a small window to obtain property from inside. Note that if the child only prepared an entry point the offence has only been attempted.

Trespass involves a person entering a building or part of a building (for the purpose of committing burglary) in one of the following ways:

- entering a building for a purpose other than the intended purpose of that building, for example going into a shop with the intention to steal (rather than an intent to browse or buy);

- entering by some kind of deception, for example pretending to represent a utility company for the purpose of reading a meter and being invited into the building ('distraction burglary', referred to earlier);
- crossing over a demarcation line of some kind, unlawfully and without invitation or permission;
- exceeding a general consent to enter premises, such as entering your father's address at night to take something (see *R v Jones; R v Smith* [1976] 3 All ER 54, [1976] 1 WLR 672).

The person must have guilty knowledge (*mens rea*: see 4.3.2) that what he/she is doing amounts to trespass, or alternatively, not care about whether he/she is trespassing. The trespass must also be voluntary.

Burglary involves entering a building as a trespasser. The word **'building'** is used within the Theft Act 1968, but is not defined there. However, the meaning of 'a building' is reasonably well established through case law:

- 'building is an ordinary word, which is a matter of fact' (*Brutus v Cozens* [1973] AC 854, 861);
- a building is 'a structure of considerable size and intended to be permanent or at least to endure for a considerable time' (*Stevens v Gourley* (1859) 7 CBNS 99); and
- 'a building need not necessarily be a completed structure; it is sufficient that it should be a connected and entire structure' (Judge Lush in *R v Manning & Rogers* (1871) CA). A house under construction becomes a building when it has all its walls and a roof.

Examples of buildings include garages, bandstands, garden sheds, even a walk-in freezer if it has been there for a while and will remain. However, telephone kiosks, bus shelters, and lorry trailers have been ruled not to be buildings in this context. Force policy and procedures may vary with regard to burglary from different types of building.

A dwelling is defined within the Theft Act 1968 as an inhabited building or a vehicle or vessel which is inhabited at the time of the offence (the occupier need not be present at the time of the burglary). An inhabited houseboat moored at a river bank is regarded as a building for the purposes of the Theft Act 1968. Similarly, a motor home or caravan inhabited during a holiday is a building (but not when it is parked and empty during the winter). However, a tent would not be included since it is not a semi-permanent structure. We provide further information on the definitions of premises and locations in 9.2.1.1.

This legislation also covers part of a building, and when a person is lawfully within a building but enters a part of it that he/she is not meant to enter (eg if a customer in a shop goes behind the counter to take money out of the till). It will be a matter for the jury to decide whether the area in question amounts to 'part of a building' from which the general public are excluded (see *R v Walkington* [1979] 2 All ER 716, [1979] 1 WLR 1169).

(Image © Zoe Lawton-Barrett)

Burglary involves entering a building as a trespasser

Burglary involves entering a building as a trespasser

Specific Incidents

16.4.1.1 Sections 9(1)(a) and 9(1)(b)

Section 9(1)(a) relates to intent only, while s 9(1)(b) relates to actually carrying out the acts (as shown in the diagram at the start of 16.4.1).

For an offence under s 9(1)(a) of the Theft Act 1968 the suspect must enter a building (or part of a building) as a trespasser and intend to commit a further act as follows:

- steal something from the building;
- inflict grievous bodily harm on anyone in the building; or
- unlawfully damage the building or anything inside it.

However, the further acts do not have to be committed, only intended. The intent can be proved in a number of ways (or in combination), such as the suspect admitting to having guilty knowledge or criminal intent to commit the offence. Alternatively, other suspects (who admit to involvement in committing the offence) might name the suspect as an accomplice.

Circumstantial evidence can also help to prove intent, such as finding the suspect in the building in possession of property that is known to originate from the premises. Witness statements, and the arresting officer's observations on the suspect's proximity to the crime scene when he/she was arrested could also be used. Fingerprint evidence could also indicate the suspect had been at the location (see 26.6).

If the offence relates to an intent to inflict GBH then the entry must have been made with that in mind. Consequently, in relation to proving the offence, the same degree of evidence of intent will be required as would be needed to prove intent under s 18 of the Offences Against the Person Act 1861 (see 15.3.2).

Under s 9(1)(b) of the Theft Act 1968, burglary involves trespassing and committing acts which amount to:

- theft (or attempted theft); or
- inflicting GBH (or attempting to inflict GBH).

(Note that subsection (b) does not include inflicting unlawful damage.) In relation to inflicting GBH, the meaning of 'inflict' includes situations where force is applied indirectly (*R v Wilson* (1983)). For example, it would include a situation where a woman in her home is frightened by a burglar and as a result falls down the stairs and breaks her leg; harm has been inflicted by the suspect, even though there has been no application of force. For further information on judging whether the acts amount to an attempt, see 22.2.

An offence under either subsection is triable either way, and the penalty if tried summarily is six months' imprisonment and/or a fine. If tried on indictment the maximum penalty is ten years' imprisonment (14 years if the building or part of the building was a dwelling), and at least three years for a third or subsequent domestic burglary.

16.4.2 Aggravated burglary

Aggravated burglary (s 10 of the Theft Act 1968) involves the use of weapons or explosives to commit burglary. The types of weapon or explosive (articles) covered by this legislation are shown in the table, and can be recalled by the mnemonic WIFE.

Article	Details	Theft Act 1968
Weapon of offence	Any article made or adapted for use for causing injury or incapacitation to a person, or intended for such use (see 18.2.1 on offensive weapons)	s 10(1)(b)
Imitation firearm	Anything which has the appearance of being a firearm, whether capable of being discharged or not (see 18.7)	s 10(1)(a)
Firearm	Includes air weapons (see 18.3) and 'component parts' of a firearm (ie parts essential to discharging the weapon), but not 'additions' (see 18.3.1.1)	s 10(1)(b)
Explosive	Any article manufactured for the purpose of producing a practical effect by explosion (excluding fireworks or matches), or intended for that purpose by the person who has it.	s 10(1)(c)

The phrase 'has with him' means 'constructive possession', ie the person is carrying the item, including carrying it in a bag. (The meaning is therefore not the same as under the Firearms

Act 1968 where the item can be at a short distance, eg in the boot of a car 50 metres away.) Anyone else who is present and knows about the constructive possession is also regarded as having constructive possession.

The point in time when the offence is committed depends upon the subsection and the type of burglary:

- for a s 9(1)(a) burglary, the offence is committed the moment a person enters a building with intent (and has in his/her possession one of the WIFE articles);
- for a s 9(1)(b) burglary, the offence is committed when the person commits the theft or grievous bodily harm (and has in his/her possession one of the WIFE articles).

This offence is triable by indictment only and the penalty is life imprisonment.

16.4.3 Trespass offences related to burglary

A trespass or vagrancy offence may be committed if an offender enters a premises but his/her actions do not amount to burglary.

Trespassing with a weapon of offence is committed when a person is on any premises as a trespasser (after having entered as such) and has a weapon of offence in his/her possession without lawful authority or reasonable excuse (s 8 of the Criminal Law Act 1977). It is different from burglary under s 9(1)(a), because there is no intent to commit theft, GBH, or damage. The offence is triable summarily and the penalty is three months' imprisonment and/or a fine.

Trespassing with an intent to commit a sexual offence is covered under s 63 of the Sexual Offences Act 2003. The offender must be on premises or land without the owner's or the occupier's consent and know that he/she is trespassing (or be reckless as to whether he/she is trespassing). There must also be an intent to commit a sexual offence while there, and this could be proved from statements from the offender or intended victim, or items seized from the offender at the scene (such as a knife). The intent can be formed at any time, for example before entering the premises, or only later while on the premises. It is immaterial whether any sexual offence is actually committed. The s 63 offence is triable either way, and the penalty if tried summarily is six months' imprisonment and/or a fine not exceeding the statutory maximum, and ten years' imprisonment on indictment.

16.4.3.1 Trespass and vagrancy

The Vagrancy Act 1824, particularly s 4, could be used when a suspect is found on enclosed premises in the open air or land for an unlawful purpose, such as preparing to commit a burglary or theft.

'Enclosed premises in the open air' would include a house, a shed, or a warehouse, and can mean inside a room or a building. But it does not include the situation where a person is on premises where he/she is entitled to be, but has been found in a particular room. For example, a man could not be found guilty of this offence if he wandered from a communal hallway into a private room which was part of the same premises, because the room itself would not be an enclosed area in the open air (*Talbot v Oxford City Justices*, The Times, 15 February 2000). Enclosed premises can also include an outdoor area such as an enclosed garden or yard with a defined boundary, even if there are gaps in the fence or boundary enclosure. It would not include a university campus truncated by roads and footpaths (see *Akhurst v DPP* [2009] WLR (D) 96). The unlawful purpose for which the person is on the enclosed premises must be a current purpose, so it would not include a person who is hiding from the police following a burglary (*L v CPS* [2007] EWHC 1843, Admin), or a homeless person who sleeps in a shed for just a night or two, or a consenting couple finding somewhere quiet to have intercourse.

The offence under s 4 of the Vagrancy Act 1824 is triable summarily and the penalty is three months' imprisonment and/or a fine.

TASK 3 Georgia enters a house as a trespasser with intent to steal jewellery for which there is a demand at local car boot sales. While she is on the premises, and as a precaution against capture, she takes a screwdriver from a cupboard under the stairs. She continues the search, with the screwdriver in her pocket. Twenty minutes later, the occupier returns and Georgia stabs her, causing serious injury. Has Georgia committed burglary? Give reasons for your answers.

16.5 **Stolen Goods and the Proceeds of Crime**

Stolen goods includes 'money and every other description of property, except land, and includes things severed from the land by stealing' (s 34(2)(b) of the Theft Act 1968). For this offence goods are considered to be 'stolen goods' if they have been obtained through theft, blackmail, or fraud (ss 1 and 21 of the Theft Act 1968, and s 1 of the Fraud Act 2006, respectively).

Stolen goods also include any gain or return from the disposal of the original stolen items such as money or other items which have been received in exchange (s 24(2) of the Theft Act 1968). These are known as 'notionally stolen goods'. After the original theft there is often a whole chain of events, and each of the handlers in this process commits the offence of handling stolen goods, if each has guilty knowledge (*mens rea*) that the goods were originally acquired by a theft. The chain will only be broken when a person receiving the goods is unaware of their origins.

It is not always possible for a criminal to benefit from a crime if stolen items remain in their original state. In the majority of cases, the profits have to be realized, exchanged, or hidden to be of any worth, for example through money laundering. Such activities consequent to a theft are covered by the Proceeds of Crime Act 2002.

16.5.1 **Handling stolen goods**

This offence is described in s 22 of the Theft Act 1968 and is committed when a person handles goods that they know or believe to have been stolen. The person can receive the items, or agree to or assist with their retention, removal, disposal, or realization by another person. This could be for the benefit of another person. It is also an offence to make arrangements for any of these acts.

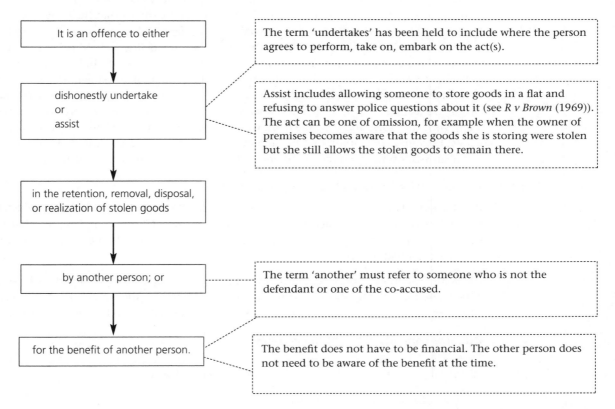

The meaning of receiving has been established through case law as 'gaining possession or control', and would obviously include carrying or holding the goods. But it also includes having control over goods, which is when a person has remote possession; the goods could be kept in storage in a garage or lock-up, for example. The receiver does not need to gain in any way from handling the goods, but he/she must know that the goods are stolen at the time of their receipt, and there must be proof that the goods were actually received. If the receiver is still negotiating the receipt of the goods, then such an act might be construed as 'arranging' so this would also constitute handling. When a person has been charged with receiving stolen goods the onus is always on the prosecution to prove the case. The suspect would have been given an opportunity at interview to explain how he/she had innocently acquired the stolen property. If the jury sees the explanation as reasonable then the defendant might be acquitted. If no explanation is given then the judge might direct the jury to the fact the defendant had been found with stolen property and did not account for this (see *R v Schama; R v Abramovitch* (1914) 11 Cr App R 45, 79 JP 184).

The offence of handling stolen goods can also be committed by a person who is involved in the retention, removal, disposal, or realization of the goods, where:

- retention means continuing to possess something (especially when someone else wants it);
- removal means taking something away from the place where it was;
- disposal means passing on, getting rid of, giving away;
- realization means obtaining money or profit by selling something.

The offence of handling stolen goods is triable either way. The penalty if tried summarily is six months' imprisonment and/or a fine, and on indictment up to 14 years' imprisonment. Note that all five elements of theft must be proven (see 16.2) to have applied at the time of the incident.

16.5.1.1 Knowing or believing that items are 'stolen goods'

The handler must know or believe that items have been stolen for his/her actions to be dishonest; suspicion would not be enough. A suspect would know the goods were stolen if he/she had been told by the thief or someone with first-hand knowledge, or might believe that they were stolen if there was no other likely explanation in the circumstances (see *R v Hall* [1985] 1 QB 496), for example the goods having non-standard packaging.

The court has to decide what is dishonest by everyday standards, and whether the suspect was aware he/she was dishonest by those standards. The suspect may claim to have had a right to the property in law, or would have had the owner's consent, or that the owner cannot be traced, but none of these is relevant. It would also be perfectly correct to direct a jury to use common sense, such as when a person chooses to become deliberately blind to the circumstances of goods being stolen (see *R v Griffiths* (1974) 60 Cr App R 14). In the case of *R v Hall* (1985) 81 Cr App R 260, two men carried out a burglary, and took the stolen property (mainly silver and ornaments) away in three suitcases. The following morning the police observed the two men meeting Hall at his flat, and raided it 10 minutes later. The property was recovered along with the cases, and all three men were arrested. Hall was convicted of receiving stolen goods. He appealed, arguing that he did not know or believe the goods to be stolen, but this was dismissed on the grounds that there could be no other reasonable explanation.

16.5.1.2 The distinction between 'handling' and 'theft'

It is important to distinguish clearly between 'handling' and 'theft'. The court will take a number of key factors into account such as whether the theft was complete, whether there was a break in the proceedings, and whether the suspected handler became involved only after the theft had occurred.

For example, Ellis goes to a large out-of-town electrical store. She takes two smart speakers from a shelf, and hides them in a bin outside the store. Sal then takes them away. The table presents a number of different scenarios to illustrate some differences between handling and theft.

Offences committed by Sal the accomplice

Sal's actions …	Offence committed by Sal
Sal is waiting by pre-arrangement and takes the radios away	Theft
Sal arrives half an hour later by pre-arrangement, and takes the radios away	Theft, particularly if the proceeds are to be shared out between Ellis and Sal. However, handling may be considered if Sal subsequently pays Ellis for the goods
Sal is told where the radios are, but only after they have been stolen. Sal then collects the radios	Handling

A thief can become a handler of the property that he/she originally stole, but only if he/she loses control of the property and later decides to have dealings with the property once again (whilst the goods can still be referred to as stolen goods).

A thief will often attempt to move stolen property on swiftly. Therefore, when an individual is caught with items very recently reported as stolen, he/she owes an explanation as to how he/she came by the property. An item that has recently been stolen is 'hot property' and local criminals are likely to know about it, so it is unreasonable for a person to claim he/she did not know it was stolen property. But months later it would be harder to prove the person knew it was stolen, unless of course it was a particularly unusual item. In the case of *R v Cash* [1985] QB 801, [1985] 2 All ER 128 nine days was considered a reasonable period of time for the possession to be 'recent', and the so-called 'doctrine of recent possession' could apply.

16.5.1.3 Wrongful credits

In this context a credit is 'wrongful' if the funds concerned were derived from theft, blackmail, fraud, or stolen goods. A person is guilty of an offence under s 24A of the Theft Act 1968 if he/she fails to take reasonable steps for a wrongful credit to be cancelled. The wrongful credit must have been made to an account kept by him/her (including a joint account or any account in which the person has any other right or interest). He/she must know or believe the credit is wrongful. The maximum sentence for this offence is ten years' imprisonment.

16.5.2 Proceeds of crime offences

It is an offence under the Proceeds of Crime Act 2002 (POCA) to benefit from any kind of proceeds of crime. Criminals will often try and convert the proceeds of crime into assets in order to make their origin appear legitimate, often referred to as money laundering.

The legislation makes reference to the proceeds of crime as 'criminal property', defining it as any property which the suspect knows or suspects to be, or represent, the benefit from any criminal conduct (s 340(3)) in the UK (s 340(2)). Criminal property is defined in s 340(9) and includes:

- money (including cryptocurrencies);
- property (real, personal, inherited, and moveable);
- things in action such as patents, copyrights, and trademarks; and
- other intangible or incorporeal property such as property rights, leases, or mortgages.

The definition of criminal property under POCA is very similar to the definition of property in s 4 of the Theft Act 1968 (see 16.2.3). Real property is land and things forming part of the land, such as plants and buildings, and moveable property is not attached to the land (eg furniture, art, books, or household goods). Although you cannot generally steal land it can be seized if it has been gained through criminal activity.

There are three main offences under POCA, and these cover most eventualities in benefiting from the proceeds of crime:

- **Concealing, converting, or transferring criminal property** (s 327(1)). A person commits an offence if he/she conceals, disguises, converts, transfers, or removes any criminal property from the UK. For example, a man knows that his wife brings back large quantities of tobacco from cross-Channel ferry trips to sell on to local people. He hides the money behind the panel of the bath in their house. He is guilty of concealing criminal property. Lodging, receiving, retaining, or withdrawing can amount to converting (*R v Fazal* [2009] EWCA Crim 1697).
- **Involvement in arrangements for criminal property** (s 328(1)). A person commits an offence if he/she enters into (or becomes concerned in) an arrangement which he/she knows (or suspects) will help with the acquisition, retention, use, or control of criminal property, by (or on behalf of) another person. The suspect must know or believe it was criminal property when the arrangement was made (see *R v Geary* [2010] WLR (D) 228). For example, a man derives a considerable income from targeting vulnerable householders. He carries out an electrical inspection and deceives the householder about the condition of the wiring, and carries out unnecessary 'repairs' for cash. His girlfriend knows how the money is obtained, and has opened several bank accounts for depositing the profits, and has therefore been concerned in an arrangement that will help in the retention or control of criminal property.
- **Acquisition, use, and possession of criminal property** (s 329(1)). For example, a small-time drug supplier gives some of her profits from selling drugs to her brother. He knows where the money comes from and uses it to buy food; he has 'used' criminal property.

There is a power of search for premises (s 289(1) POCA) if a police officer has reasonable grounds for suspecting the presence of cash obtained through unlawful conduct (s 304(1)), or intended to be used by any person for an unlawful purpose. The officer may also search a suspect and any article he/she possesses at that time (s 289(2) and (3)). The officer's presence must be lawful, and he/she must comply with s 2 of the PACE Act 1984 and the PACE Codes of Practice (see 9.2 and 9.4.5).

16.5.2.1　Defences and penalties

Three defences are available for offences under ss 327(1), 328(1), and 329(1) of the POCA 2002:

- the suspect makes or intends to make (with reasonable excuse) an 'authorized disclosure' to a police, Border Force, or nominated officer, concerning his/her actions;
- the suspect knows (or reasonably believes) that the criminal conduct took place outside the UK and that it was not unlawful in that other country (s 327(2) and (2A)); and
- law enforcement authorities (such as the police) have a defence if they convert or transfer seized criminal property, for example they place seized money in an interest-earning account.

An additional defence is available for s 329(1) where a person acquires, uses, or has possession of the criminal property for 'adequate consideration'. A shopkeeper could claim this defence if she sells goods to a customer and the customer pays with money that comes from crime. Solicitors or accountants who receive money for costs also have this defence.

The ss 327, 328, and 329 offences are all triable either way and the penalty is a fine or imprisonment (six months summarily or up to 14 years on indictment).

TASK 4

1. In the context of 'handling stolen goods', which, if either, of the following statements is true?
   (a) For the purposes of committing an offence of handling, 'stolen goods' includes money but not land.
   (b) Property obtained as a result of a fraud under s 1 of the Fraud Act 2006 is considered to be 'stolen goods' for the purposes of the offence of handling.
2. A police officer carries out a lawful s 1 PACE Act 1984 stop and search on Terri, and complies with the PACE Codes of Practice throughout the process. Terri is an 18-year-old persistent offender and prolific shoplifter. His current favoured MO is to steal items such as meat and clothes from shops, to sell on quickly and cheaply. He is registered unemployed, receives state benefits, and has no close family. Local intelligence has indicated that he has an extremely modest lifestyle (he does not own any vehicles and lives alone in a one-room bedsit) and has recently become a courier for local drug suppliers. During the search, £10,000 in used £50 notes is found concealed in various locations in his clothing. Terri cannot account for this money and there is no evidence of its origin. Assess the likelihood of a successful prosecution for acquiring, retaining, using, or controlling the criminal property under s 328(1) of the POCA 2002. Refer to the cases of *R v NW, SW, RC & CC* [2008] EWCA Crim 2 and the conjoined cases of *R v Allpress; R v Symeou; R v Casal; R v Morris; R v Martin* [2009] EWCA Crim 8 for your answer.

16.6　Going Equipped

This offence is described in s 25 of the Theft Act 1968. A wide range of articles are used to carry out (or help carry out) thefts, such as equipment for removing security tags from clothes, or for gaining entry to vehicles or buildings (including keys). The offence is not committed by simple possession of the articles alone. The suspect must also be on his/her way to carry out a theft (see *R v Ellames* [1974] 3 All ER 130). A direct connection to a specific burglary or theft does not need to be established, but it must be possible to prove that the article is intended to be used to commit crime (by the suspect or another person). The offence cannot be committed when coming away from the crime.

In terms of possession of the article, the phrase used in the legislation is 'has with him' which includes having it ready to hand, such as in a nearby bush a few feet away, or in a car parked outside the address he intends to break into. Note that the meaning of 'has with him' here is not the same as for aggravated burglary (for which constructive possession is required (see 16.4.2)).

Specific Incidents

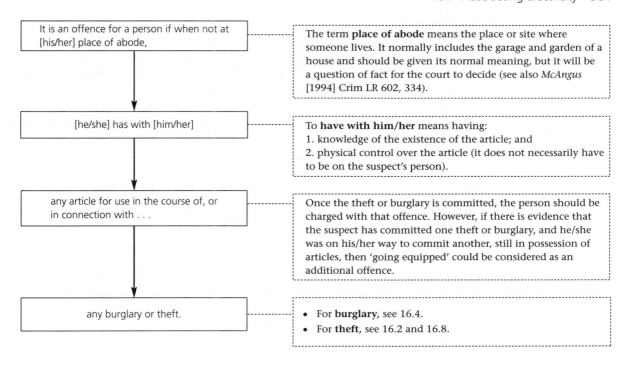

It is an offence for a person if when not at [his/her] place of abode,	The term **place of abode** means the place or site where someone lives. It normally includes the garage and garden of a house and should be given its normal meaning, but it will be a question of fact for the court to decide (see also *McAngus* [1994] Crim LR 602, 334).
[he/she] has with [him/her]	To **have with him/her** means having: 1. knowledge of the existence of the article; and 2. physical control over the article (it does not necessarily have to be on the suspect's person).
any article for use in the course of, or in connection with . . .	Once the theft or burglary is committed, the person should be charged with that offence. However, if there is evidence that the suspect has committed one theft or burglary, and he/she was on his/her way to commit another, still in possession of articles, then 'going equipped' could be considered as an additional offence.
any burglary or theft.	• For **burglary**, see 16.4. • For **theft**, see 16.2 and 16.8.

This offence is triable either way, and the penalty is six months' imprisonment and/or a fine if tried summarily, and up to three years' imprisonment on indictment.

16.7 Abstracting Electricity

Electricity does not fall within the definition of property in the Theft Act 1968, and therefore it cannot be stolen, in legal terms. Here, the term 'abstracting' means illegally taking and using without due authority, such as a householder reconnecting the supply after it has been cut off (see *Boggeln v Williams* [1978] 2 All ER 1061). The abstracted electricity could be from the mains or from a battery, in a caravan for example. As electricity is not property within the Theft Act 1968, entering premises with the sole intention of abstracting electricity does not amount to burglary.

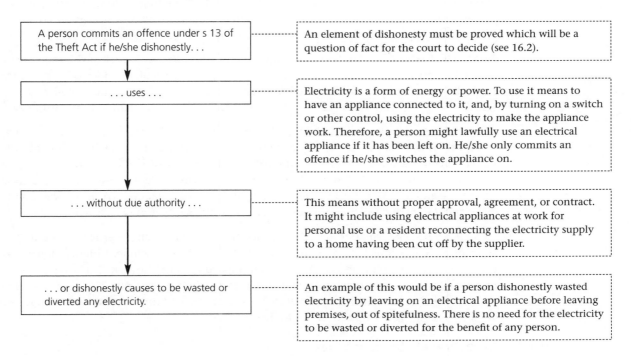

A person commits an offence under s 13 of the Theft Act if he/she dishonestly. . .	An element of dishonesty must be proved which will be a question of fact for the court to decide (see 16.2).
. . . uses . . .	Electricity is a form of energy or power. To use it means to have an appliance connected to it, and, by turning on a switch or other control, using the electricity to make the appliance work. Therefore, a person might lawfully use an electrical appliance if it has been left on. He/she only commits an offence if he/she switches the appliance on.
. . . without due authority . . .	This means without proper approval, agreement, or contract. It might include using electrical appliances at work for personal use or a resident reconnecting the electricity supply to a home having been cut off by the supplier.
. . . or dishonestly causes to be wasted or diverted any electricity.	An example of this would be if a person dishonestly wasted electricity by leaving on an electrical appliance before leaving premises, out of spitefulness. There is no need for the electricity to be wasted or diverted for the benefit of any person.

Specific Incidents

This offence is triable either way and the penalty is six months' imprisonment and/or a fine if tried summarily, and up to five years' imprisonment on indictment.

> **TASK 5**
>
> 1. At each of her BCU briefings throughout the past week, a police constable has been informed about a series of car thefts in her area. One night, she is on patrol in a residential street and a car draws up outside a house. She knows that a prolific car thief lives there. She goes over and speaks to the driver and notices gloves, a large bunch of approximately 40 car keys, and a short length of scaffolding pole in the foot-well of the passenger seat. What could she say to him? Could the offence of 'going equipped' have been committed? What questions should she ask?
> 2. Which of the following offence(s) are neither a 'theft' nor a 'burglary'?:
>   - robbery;
>   - entering a building as a trespasser with the intent to cause damage; and
>   - by-passing a meter to obtain free electricity.

> **TASK 6** On the way home from a nightclub in the early hours of the morning, Daisy walks through an industrial estate where there are a number of storage warehouses. One of them has an open door, and she decides to go in to shelter from the rain. Inside the warehouse she notices a separate office, and forces open the door, damaging the lock. She switches on an electric fire to keep warm and falls asleep. She is woken by a security guard patrolling the industrial estate. Has she committed burglary? Give reasons for your answers.

16.8 Theft of Vehicles and Related Offences

Every year thousands of cars are stolen in England and Wales. Here we examine some of the legal aspects and police procedures surrounding a number of vehicle crimes, particularly stolen vehicles.

The police will receive reports of vehicles being stolen by telephone, through online crime reporting systems, and occasionally personally whilst on patrol. The Police National Computer (PNC) (see 5.9.1.1) will be updated, and if the registration number of the stolen vehicle is spotted by a police officer or an automatic number plate reader system (ANPR), action will be taken. If a stolen vehicle is found by the police, they usually arrange for an approved recovery operator to take it to a secure location (reg 4 of the Removal and Disposal of Vehicles Regulations 1986), and it may be examined by a crime scene investigator, depending on local policy. The owner of the vehicle or their insurance company has to pay the recovery and storage fees (Removal, Storage and Disposal of Vehicles (Prescribed Sums and Charges) Regulations 2008).

Some vehicles are stolen for resale, and their origin will often be disguised when sold on (see 16.8.1.1). Other vehicles may be broken down for parts, particularly older vehicles, as they might be worth more as parts. The cost of vehicle repairs motivates some owners to arrange (or merely claim) that the vehicle has been stolen, so he/she can claim on the insurance.

Other vehicles are taken for 'joyriding'; the vehicle is driven for excitement or as a means of transport, usually for only a brief period of time. This is not theft because there is no intention to permanently deprive the owner of the vehicle. The offence of TWOC (taking a conveyance without consent, see 16.8.2) was created to cover these circumstances. TWOC may also result in damage and injury, so we also describe 'aggravated vehicle taking'. We also cover 'interference' and 'tampering' with motor vehicles, along with the theft of pedal cycles.

As vehicles become 'smarter' (as wi-fi connected hotspots or self-governed vehicles) cyber-security considerations will loom larger. A 2017 government document highlighted the key cyber-security principles for connected and automated vehicles (Gov UK, 2017) to help vehicle industry designers, manufacturers, and suppliers to promote security. This area is likely to require on-going research to inform future investigations, and to provide drivers with suitable advice on reducing the opportunities for hacking.

16.8.1 Detection of stolen vehicles

There are a number of ways of establishing that a particular vehicle is a stolen vehicle, and some everyday clues can trigger an alert police officer to investigate a little further. For example, is it a type of vehicle that is more likely to be stolen? (see Task 8). The registration plates can also provide clues; for example do the plates look as though they have been replaced or have new plates been stuck over the old plates? Do the plates seem different from the rest of the car—for example is the car clean and the plates old and dirty (or the other way round); or are the plates plain, with no reference to a vehicle dealership? To investigate further, a police officer will need to establish the specific identifying features of a vehicle (see 19.2.1.1).

16.8.1.1 Disguising stolen vehicles

When a vehicle is reported as stolen, it is recorded on police and other databases using the VICE identifying features (see 19.2.1.1). So if it is to be sold on or used long term it would need to have a new 'identity' to evade detection.

Criminal gangs will often produce desirable vehicles with new identities to sell on. The perpetrator first obtains an in-demand but damaged vehicle. It must have a V23, the form sent to the DVLA either by an insurance company whenever a total loss payment is made on a vehicle, or by a police officer when reporting a vehicle that has been 'written off' in an accident. (It is legal to repair such a vehicle and use it on the roads.) The criminal then steals a very similar vehicle in good condition—the colour and make must be the same as for the damaged vehicle. The identifying features from the damaged vehicle are then transferred to the stolen vehicle, which will then be sold to an innocent purchaser. Some vehicles are exported as their resale value may be higher in other countries.

Thus police officers must be alert to vehicles with identifying features that do not exactly match the database records, as such a vehicle may have been stolen and provided with a new identity. Also, any vehicle on the roads which has had a V23 should show evidence of extensive repairs; if these are not noticeable then further investigation may be required.

16.8.1.2 Procedure for checking vehicle VICE details

The recommended procedure is outlined in the diagram. If the vehicle needs further examination, a force vehicle examiner can carry this out.

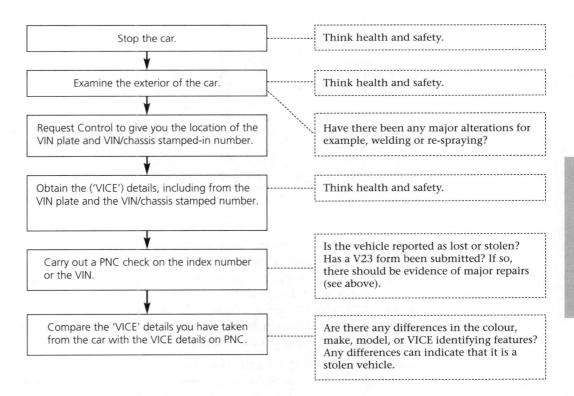

TASK 7 In 16.8.1.2, references are made to stopping the car, examining the car, and locating the VIN and VIN/chassis number. What powers or regulations (1) allow a police officer to stop and examine a car; and (2) require the car to have a VIN or chassis number?

16.8.2 Taking a Conveyance without the Owner's Consent or Authority (TWOC)

This offence (TWOC) is described in s 12 of the Theft Act 1968. 'Taking a conveyance' is a very common offence in England and Wales and, unfortunately, modern technology has failed to deter criminals from this activity.

A conveyance is any equipment constructed or adapted for the carriage of a person or persons whether by land, water, or air. In this context, a conveyance does not include anything constructed or adapted for carrying items other than people, such as the pedestrian-controlled trolleys used by postal workers to transport mail. Pedal cycles are not included under this legislation either; taking a cycle is covered by another subsection (see 16.8.3).

The term 'taking' has its ordinary meaning and can include loading a conveyance onto a trailer (see *R v Pearce* [1973] CrimLR 321).

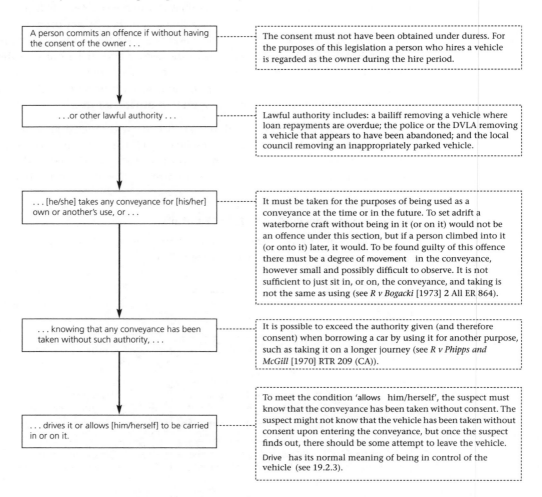

Case law provides a number of clarifications in relation to this offence. For a floating conveyance the movement can be caused by a sail, but cannot 'be natural movement' created by waves or water currents (see *R v Miller* [1976] Crim LR 147). A conveyance must be taken for the purpose of being used as such (including future use), and not just for 'mischief' (see *R v Stokes* [1982] Crim LR 695). A vehicle ceases to be 'taken' once it has been recovered by the victim, police, or insurance company, but this would probably not include simply receiving a report from a member of the public reporting its whereabouts.

A possible defence (s 12(6) of the Theft Act 1968) is that the person believes that he/she has the consent of the owner or had other lawful authority. This offence is triable summarily and the penalty is six months' imprisonment and/or a fine.

In law, the basic offence of taking a conveyance cannot be attempted (see 22.2 on criminal attempts), as the offence is not indictable. If some form of attempt has taken place, the offence of vehicle interference or tampering with a motor vehicle could be used (see 16.8.2.2), or an attempted offence of theft (as theft is an indictable offence).

> **TASK 8** Every day around a thousand vehicles are taken without the owner's consent in the UK. What type of vehicle is most likely to be taken in your area? If you are a trainee police officer, your area should be able to provide you with factual information on this, including where the vehicles are stolen from, and what happens to them.

16.8.2.1 Aggravated vehicle-taking

When a vehicle is taken without consent, an aggravated offence can be committed (s 12A of the Theft Act 1968). The aggravating circumstances for this offence are that after it was taken without consent:

- the vehicle was driven dangerously on a road or other public place (see 19.8.1 on dangerous driving, and for definitions of 'road' see 19.2.2, and for 'public place' see 9.2.1.1);
- an accident occurred (due to the driving of the vehicle) which caused injury to a person, or damage to property other than the vehicle. Here an 'accident' is an unintended occurrence which has an adverse physical result, and the court can also take into account what an 'ordinary' person would consider to be an accident (see *R v Morris* [1972] RTR 201). Injuries include shock, and damage includes any damage caused during the whole incident and does not have to be deliberately inflicted.

The aggravating events must occur after the vehicle has been taken without consent, and before it is recovered by its owner, the police, or the insurance company. The person who is driving at the time of the aggravating events commits the s 12A offence. He/she need not be the same person who first took the vehicle without consent (the s 12 offence).

Possible defences include that the dangerous driving, damage, or accident had occurred before the suspect took the vehicle, or that he/she was not in or on the vehicle, or in its 'immediate vicinity' when the dangerous driving, accident, or damage occurred (s 12A(3)). Immediate vicinity is a question of fact for the court to decide. If the suspect can disprove aggravating factors, he/she can still be found guilty of the basic offence (s 12A(5)).

This offence is triable either way, being tried summarily if the value of the property damaged or destroyed is less than £5,000 (s 22 of the Magistrates' Courts Act 1980). The penalty is a fine (no upper limit) or imprisonment (six months summarily, or two years on indictment). If the accident caused death, the penalty is up to 14 years' imprisonment.

16.8.2.2 Interference and tampering with motor vehicles

When a suspect takes a conveyance without the consent of the owner, in many cases he/she will go through a process of selecting a vehicle, gaining entry either forcibly or by trying door handles, overcoming anti-theft devices such as alarms and steering locks, and then applying a technique such as 'hot wiring' to start the engine. This process inevitably takes time, and sometimes the suspect can be apprehended before the vehicle is taken. However, TWOC is a summary offence, and therefore cannot be attempted under s 1(1) of the Criminal Attempts Act 1981 (see 22.2). So the offences of interfering with and tampering with motor vehicles were created to cover situations where TWOC seems to have been attempted.

Section 9(1) of the Criminal Attempts Act 1981 states that it is an offence for a person to interfere with a motor vehicle or trailer, or with anything carried in or on a motor vehicle or trailer with the intention of committing:

- 'theft of the motor vehicle or part of it';
- 'theft of anything carried in or on the motor vehicle or trailer'; or
- the offence of taking a conveyance.

However, actually proving intent is tricky. In 4.3, we discussed the two main building blocks to a criminal act: *actus reus* (the act itself), and *mens rea* (an intention to commit an act). In this case, the act cannot simply be preparation but needs to go further than this. Unfortunately, case law provides us with little guidance on what interference actually means in practice. Nonetheless, it must be proved that the suspect had at least one of the three intentions, but it is not necessary to prove which particular one. This is a summary offence and the penalty is three months' imprisonment and/or a fine.

Tampering as an activity is more readily understood than interference, and the legislation (s 25(1) of the Road Traffic Act 1988) refers specifically to vehicle brakes. It is an offence for a person without lawful authority or reasonable cause to tamper with the brake or any other part of its mechanism, or to get on or into the vehicle. This applies to motor vehicles on a road or in a local authority parking place. It is a summary offence and the penalty is a fine or imprisonment for up to three months.

TASK 9 Which of the following would constitute an offence of interfering with a motor vehicle?

1. Trying to remove a horse box from the tow bar of a vehicle in order to steal the horse box.
2. Attempting to remove a go-kart from the garden of a house in order to steal it.
3. Opening the unlocked front driver's door of a car to steal a satnav fixed to the dashboard.
4. Putting super glue in a car door lock to prevent the owner from opening the door.

16.8.3 Taking a pedal cycle

Taking a pedal cycle is an offence under s 12(5) of the Theft Act 1968, and is not a TWOC offence (because a pedal cycle is not a conveyance for the purposes of s 12(1) of the Theft Act 1968). The offence would include riding a pedal cycle knowing it to have been taken by another person without consent or lawful authority. The penalty is six months' imprisonment and/or a fine.

16.9 Fraud and Bribery Offences

The continual evolution of technology opens up new ways for fraud to be committed via computer misuse offences or cybercrime (see Chapter 21). The annual UK losses due to fraud are estimated to be around £110 billion (Copper-Ind, 2018), of which around a third is through the public sector. Many frauds relate to procurement, and involve the use of fake invoices (ibid), but others involve tax fraud, housing and benefit fraud, grant and NHS fraud. In terms of individual susceptibility to fraud, people aged 35–44 years are most likely to be victims of fraud (ONS, 2018f). The National Fraud Initiative tackles public sector fraud by cross-matching data from all public sectors to identify fraud and overpayments, and resulted in annual savings of nearly £200 million (Experian, 2018). This might sound impressive but it is in fact only a tiny proportion of the losses; for every £100 of public sector losses a mere 54p was saved. It is believed that many businesses could reduce fraud by simply improving identity checks (ibid).

Much of the law surrounding the crime of fraud is now encapsulated in the Fraud Act 2006. Section 1 states that the offence of fraud can be committed in one or more of three distinctive ways:

1. by false representation, for example presenting a stolen credit card to pay for goods at a till, thereby implying it is yours to use (s 2);
2. by failing to disclose information, for example omitting important information when applying for a job or for health insurance (s 3); and
3. through abuse of position, for example demanding fares from local residents whilst driving a local authority minibus that is intended as a free service (s 4).

For all of these offences there is the same intent; to make a gain for him/herself or another, or to cause a loss to another, or to expose another to a risk of loss. The gain or loss can be temporary or permanent and could involve 'personal' property, 'real' property, things in action, and other intangible property, such as the name of a company or the copyright to a product. This is similar to the definitions of property under the Theft Act 1968.

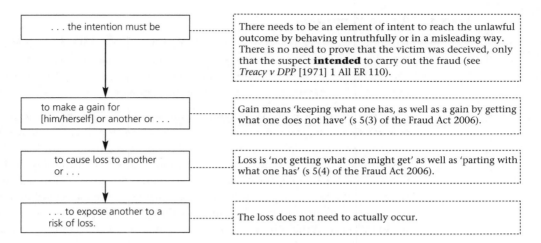

| ... the intention must be | There needs to be an element of intent to reach the unlawful outcome by behaving untruthfully or in a misleading way. There is no need to prove that the victim was deceived, only that the suspect **intended** to carry out the fraud (see *Treacy v DPP* [1971] 1 All ER 110). |

| to make a gain for [him/herself] or another or ... | Gain means 'keeping what one has, as well as a gain by getting what one does not have' (s 5(3) of the Fraud Act 2006). |

| to cause loss to another or ... | Loss is 'not getting what one might get' as well as 'parting with what one has' (s 5(4) of the Fraud Act 2006). |

| ... to expose another to a risk of loss. | The loss does not need to actually occur. |

The fact that a person has created a risk is analogous to a bullet that has been fired from a gun; once it has left the chamber it cannot be taken back .

The offences are all triable either way and the penalty is a fine or imprisonment (12 months summarily or up to ten years on indictment).

16.9.1 False representation

Section 2 of the Fraud Act 2006 states that a person commits an offence if he/she 'dishonestly makes a false representation and intends ... to make a gain for [him/herself] or another, or to cause loss to another or to expose another to a risk of loss'. The suspect must intend that the false representation will cause a gain or loss (*R v Gilbert* [2012] EWCA Crim 2392). The meaning of the term 'dishonesty' is covered in 16.2.1.

This would include a person who advertises an item for sale (including online), purporting it to be a genuine brand when he/she knows it is a fake. Even if nobody sees the ad or responds, the person has still risked causing somebody a loss—the offence is committed the moment the item is offered. False representation means misleading or lying about a fact or law, for example a roofer who knowingly presents a grossly inflated estimate to a customer (see *R v Silverman* [1987] 86 Cr App R 213). The representation can be made verbally or in writing (including online), or through actions. A false representation can also be made to a device or machine which is designed to receive, convey, or respond to communication; for example, using forged coins at a coin-operated snack dispenser (s 2(5)).

16.9.2 Failure to disclose information

Section 3 of the Fraud Act 2006 states that a person commits an offence if he/she 'dishonestly fails to disclose to another person information which [he/she] is under a legal duty to disclose, and intends, by failing to disclose the information to make a gain for [him/herself] or another, or to cause loss to another or to expose another to a risk of loss'.

The failure to disclose can be made by an oral or written omission. The legal duty to disclose (and some examples of a failure to disclose) derives from:

- statute, for example where a company must publish yearly accounts under company law, but fails to do so;
- assumed good faith, such as failing to disclose a serious illness in order to reduce health insurance premiums;
- the express or implied terms of a contract, from the custom of a particular trade or market, such as an estate agent failing to reveal to a client all the bids she received for a property;
- the existence of a fiduciary relationship (where a person is entrusted with another person's financial arrangements), for example where a solicitor does not tell his client there is another beneficiary to a contract.

To provide evidence for this offence, it is often easiest to show that there was a failure to pass on information to the victim. He/she will then have a legitimate claim for seeking damages for non-disclosure, and will also be able to clarify his/her position regarding future consent.

Specific Incidents

16.9.3 Abuse of position

This offence (s 4) can be committed by a person who occupies a position in which he/she is expected to safeguard (or not to act against) the financial interests of another. The offence is committed if he/she dishonestly abuses that position intending to make a gain for him/herself or another, or to cause loss to another or to expose another to a risk of loss.

The offence could apply for anyone who has relied upon or has knowledge of another person's financial affairs, such as between an employer and an employee, between a trustee and a beneficiary or between cohabitees. The meaning of the term 'abuse' in this context is not defined in law but is held to have its normal everyday meaning, and includes a failure to act (s 4(2)). Examples might include a woman who has access to her elderly uncle's bank account and takes money for her own use, or where housemates pool money to pay bills and the person entrusted to pay the bills uses the money to pay his car insurance without any consultation with the others. The abuse must take place at the time the suspect occupies the position of trust, and not later. For example, a woman might leave a company but still have the contact details of clients on her laptop, and she then decides to sell the information to another company. As she was not in post at the time she formed the intent, the s 4 offence is not committed (although she might have committed an offence of possessing an article for committing fraud, see 16.9.4).

16.9.4 Possession, making, or supplying of articles for committing fraud

A person can commit an offence by 'going equipped' (see 16.6) to carry out a fraud, rather than actually having committed the fraud itself. In this context, going equipped means being in possession or control of articles for use in a fraud (s 6 of the Fraud Act 2006) or making or supplying such articles (s 7).

The articles can include clothing to imitate company representatives, mechanisms to slow down electricity meters, false identity cards (see 16.9.7), credit cards, cheque books, shopping bags, till receipts, passports, and driving licences. It also includes a computer program or data held in electronic form (see 21.2).

Section 6 of the Fraud Act 2006 covers possession or having the article under his/her control. For possession, the person must have immediate physical control over the article and know that it is there. Having control would include having physical control at a distance (eg having the key to a cupboard where the item is kept) and also knowing that the article was there. If one person is shown to be in possession of an article, then any other person present who is also aware of the possession is also guilty of possession. Unlike most other statutory preventative measures (legislation designed to prevent criminal offences from taking place, for example 'going equipped' to steal), this offence can be committed anywhere, including when the articles are located in the suspect's home.

Section 7 of the Fraud Act 2006 states that a person commits an offence if he/she makes, adapts, supplies (or offers to supply) any article, knowing that it is designed or adapted for use in the course of or in connection with fraud (or intending it to be used to commit or assist with the commission of fraud). An example of this could be a man offering to make a false ID card for a woman, when he knows she is going to use it to pose as a charity collector and collect donations from the public. Under s 1 of the PACE Act 1984, a police officer has the power to search (see 9.4.2) for articles made or adapted for use in fraud.

The offences are triable either way and the penalty is a fine or imprisonment (12 months summarily, five years on indictment for a s 6 offence, and ten years on indictment for a s 7 offence).

16.9.5 Dishonest obtaining of services

Section 11 of the Fraud Act 2006 covers obtaining a service by dishonest means. The services must be of a type for which payment is generally required and would include bus or train rides, haircuts, a stay in a hotel room, dry-cleaning, admission to a sports event, table attention at a restaurant, and tuition. The service must be obtained through a dishonest act (not an omission), such as using a false credit card, giving false personal details, and making false promises or agreements of payment in full or part with no intention of meeting them (see

16.2.1 on dishonesty). The offence is triable either way and the penalty is a fine or imprisonment (12 months summarily or five years on indictment).

16.9.6 Making off without payment ('bilking')

If a person makes off without paying, but made no dishonest representation and had every intention to pay for goods before the property was obtained, this is an offence under s 3 of the Theft Act 1978 (rather than fraud under s 1 of the Fraud Act 2006). This particular offence is often referred to as 'bilking'. For example, a person might fill up with petrol on the forecourt of a filling station with every intention of paying for the petrol, but on seeing the staff otherwise engaged and no other customers around, decide to drive off without paying. Note that this offence only applies if 'payment on the spot' is the norm in that particular situation, such as collecting goods on which work has been done (eg shoe repairs) or paying for a service which has been provided (eg a haircut). It does not apply if a customer has a credit arrangement or a 'tab' with the service provider. The offence is triable either way and the penalty is a fine or imprisonment (six months summarily or two years on indictment).

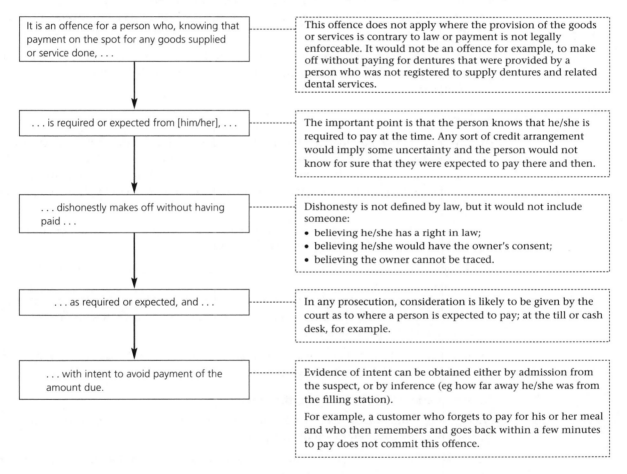

It is an offence for a person who, knowing that payment on the spot for any goods supplied or service done, . . .

> This offence does not apply where the provision of the goods or services is contrary to law or payment is not legally enforceable. It would not be an offence for example, to make off without paying for dentures that were provided by a person who was not registered to supply dentures and related dental services.

. . . is required or expected from [him/her], . . .

> The important point is that the person knows that he/she is required to pay at the time. Any sort of credit arrangement would imply some uncertainty and the person would not know for sure that they were expected to pay there and then.

. . . dishonestly makes off without having paid . . .

> Dishonesty is not defined by law, but it would not include someone:
> • believing he/she has a right in law;
> • believing he/she would have the owner's consent;
> • believing the owner cannot be traced.

. . . as required or expected, and . . .

> In any prosecution, consideration is likely to be given by the court as to where a person is expected to pay; at the till or cash desk, for example.

. . . with intent to avoid payment of the amount due.

> Evidence of intent can be obtained either by admission from the suspect, or by inference (eg how far away he/she was from the filling station).
>
> For example, a customer who forgets to pay for his or her meal and who then remembers and goes back within a few minutes to pay does not commit this offence.

TASK 10 Diners at a restaurant can sometimes fail to pay for a meal, and this could be a criminal offence under s 1 or s 11 of the Fraud Act 2006, or under s 3 of the Theft Act 1978, depending on the sequence of events. Complete the following table; the case of *DPP v Ray* [1974] AC 370 may assist.

Scenario	Possible offence
People order a meal in a restaurant, even though they know they cannot pay for it. They leave before it is served.	
A man orders a meal and it is served to his table. He claims it is inedible and leaves without paying.	
Two women finish their meal. Then they decide not to pay and quickly leave the restaurant.	

16.9.7 False identification documents

A false identity document is:

- a genuine and unadulterated document being used by a different person;
- a genuine document that has been altered; or
- a fake document (a copy of a genuine document, or a form of ID that does not exist).

The Home Office has published *Guidance on Examining Identity Documents*, which gives details of some of the documents that might be used, such as passports, driving licences, and national identity cards.

In licenced premises some customers may present false identity documents during age verification checks (required by the Licensing Act 2003 (Mandatory Licensing Conditions). Such documents can also be used by a fraudster to present false personal information about him/herself, or to induce another to ascertain personal information about the person named on the document (s 4(2) of the Identity Documents Act 2010). Possession of a false identity document which the person intends to use in this way is an offence under s 4(1). The offence is triable on indictment only and the maximum penalty is ten years' imprisonment, a fine, or both.

Possession without reasonable excuse of a false identity document is an offence under s 6(1) of the Identity Documents Act 2010, triable either way. The penalty is a fine or imprisonment (six months summarily or two years on indictment).

16.9.8 Bribery

The Bribery Act 2010 provides an effective legal framework to combat bribery in the public and private sectors. It also includes offences relating to bribery of foreign officials, and to commercial organizations that allow their agents to commit bribery. An organization will have a defence if it provides evidence of having policies and practices in place that prohibit bribery.

The offences relate to bribing another person and to accepting a bribe. Two particular terms used within the legislation have particular meanings:

- 'improper performance' means failing to perform a function or activity with good faith, or impartially (s 4); and
- 'relevant function or activity' includes all functions of a public nature, for example those carried out by public authorities (such as the police), and all activities connected with a business, trade, or profession (s 3).

The offences are triable either way and the penalties are a fine or imprisonment (one year if tried summarily, and 12 years on indictment).

16.9.8.1 Bribing or attempting to bribe another person

Under s 1(1) of the Bribery Act 2010, it is an offence for a person to offer, promise, or give a financial or other advantage to another person in order to:

- bring about an improper performance by any person of a relevant function or activity; or
- reward any person for such improper performance (s 1(2)).

It is sufficient for the perpetrator to intend to induce or reward the misconduct; the actual outcome of his/her actions is irrelevant. It is also sufficient for him/her to know or believe that the acceptance of the advantage in itself constitutes the improper performance of a function or activity (s 1(3)). The advantage can be offered, promised, or given by the perpetrator or through a third party (s 1(5)).

16.9.8.2 Requesting, accepting, or benefiting from a bribe

Under s 2(1) of the Bribery Act 2010, a person commits an offence if he/she requests, agrees to receive, or accepts an advantage if:

- he/she intends improper performance (by anyone) to follow as a consequence (s 2(2));
- his/her request (in itself), agreement, or acceptance amounts to improper performance (s 2(3));
- he/she accepts the reward for anyone's subsequent improper performance (s 2(4)).

It is irrelevant whether the perpetrator actually receives any advantage. The meaning of 'advantage' is a question of fact for the court to decide.

16.10 **Answers to Tasks**

TASK 1 You probably considered the following:

1. Was the person dishonest?
2. Did he/she take the property?
3. To whom did the property belong?
4. Did the person show an intention never to give the property back to its owner?

TASK 2

1. The circumstances do not amount to an offence of robbery because violence was not used in order to steal. This is because Jo picked up the bag and attempted to run off with it; she did not use force to steal it. Jo then picked up an item from the ground and ran into Chris, causing her to fall over and break her arm, and it was only then that force was used. It was used only after the theft had taken place. Force was not used immediately before, at the time, nor in order to steal the bag and the goods, and therefore robbery has not been committed.
2. The circumstances do not amount to blackmail. Although the threat is unpleasant and detrimental to Stav, it is perfectly lawful as Mike is acting on behalf of a court, and the request is reasonable.

TASK 3 The following offences are likely to have been committed:

- burglary with intent to steal (s 9(1)(a) of the Theft Act 1968), since Georgia entered as a trespasser with the necessary intent;
- burglary (s 9(1)(b) of the Theft Act 1968) has been committed since Georgia, having entered as a trespasser, inflicts grievous bodily harm on the occupier; and
- aggravated burglary (s 10 of the Theft Act 1968) has taken place because, whilst committing the s 9(1)(b) burglary, Georgia was armed with a weapon of offence at the time of the search for something to steal.

TASK 4

1. Both statements are true.
2. Without identifying the specific criminal conduct (or at least recognizing the type of criminal conduct which produced the money in the first place), a successful prosecution is unlikely. The case of *R v NW, SW, RC & CC* [2008] EWCA Crim 2 was important with respect to the interpretation of the POCA 2002. The Court of Appeal ruled that the CPS could not just focus on inexplicable affluence, and then make the assumption that there was no lawful reason for its presence, so presuppose that the affluence must result from the proceeds of crime. Unless there is evidence that Terri had the necessary knowledge or suspicion that the property represented a benefit from criminal conduct, a successful prosecution under s 328(1) of the POCA 2002 would not be possible. Even if it could have been proved that the money was from the unlawful supply of controlled drugs, if his only role was as a courier for the money, the money did not amount to property that could be confiscated from him under the POCA 2002 (see *R v Allpress; R v Symeou; R v Casal; R v Morris; R v Martin* [2009] EWCA Crim 8). For a successful prosecution under s 328(1), it would be necessary to prove that he had benefited, for example by receiving payments for passing on the money.

TASK 5

1. In response to this task you may have considered:
   - Has he 'control' over a pair of gloves, a large bunch of approximately 40 car keys, and a short length of scaffold pole? Yes, they are in his car and in his sight.
   - Can the gloves, a large bunch of approximately 40 car keys, and a short length of scaffold pole be considered as 'any article'? Yes.
   - Could the articles be used in the course of or in connection with any 'burglary' or 'theft'? Yes, these are articles which are often used for breaking into cars. (For example, the short length of scaffold pole can be used to break a steering lock.) However, it is not clear at

Specific Incidents

this point whether or not the person has used the articles for any burglary or theft, or whether he was going to use them for such in the future. In order to be found guilty of going equipped the suspect must have some future intention to carry out a burglary or theft and therefore this would need further investigation.

A further consideration is whether the suspect is 'at his place of abode'. There are two issues here. Is the man parked outside his own house? The police officer will need to verify whether it is his house; confirmation could be acquired by making a personal visit to ask inhabitants of the house, checking the voters register, or perhaps asking to see utility bills. And if it is his house, is sitting in a parked car outside a house (with no driveway) equivalent to being 'at his place of abode'? This would be a question of fact for a court to decide.

2. Only abstracting electricity. Interestingly, even though it was mentioned in 16.8 that TWOC is not theft, the Theft Act 1968 (s 25(5)) specifically states that for the purpose of going equipped, TWOC will be treated as theft.

TASK 6 No burglary has been committed. Although Daisy entered the storage warehouse as a trespasser, she had no intention to commit theft, criminal damage, or GBH (the offences specified in s 9(1)(a) of the Theft Act 1968). Once inside the warehouse, she damaged the door (which is property), and also abstracted electricity by using the fire, but neither damage to property nor abstraction of electricity are relevant to s 9(1)(b) of the Theft Act 1968 (see 16.4.1.1).

TASK 7

1. Section 163 of the Road Traffic Act 1988 states that 'a person driving a mechanically propelled vehicle on a road must stop on being required to do so by a constable in uniform' (see 19.4.1). A police officer will be authorized as an examiner by his/her chief officer (see 19.5) and will therefore have the authority to test a vehicle on a road, for the purposes of ascertaining compliance with:
   • the construction and use requirements including lighting; and
   • the requirement that the condition of the vehicle is not such that its use on the road would involve a danger of injury to any person.
2. All wheeled vehicles first used on or after 1 April 1980 should be equipped with a plate which clearly shows the vehicle identification number, the name of manufacturer, and the type approval number (possibly on a separate plate). The plate should be in a conspicuous and readily accessible location on a part not normally subject to replacement (see 19.2.1.1). This is described under reg 67 of the Road Vehicles (Construction and Use) Regulations 1986. The VIN should also be stamped on the chassis or frame and together these identifying features can be matched against details on PNC to enable identification of stolen vehicles.

TASK 8 The Home Office no longer collect data on car thefts, so reliable national statistics about the cars most likely to be stolen are not available. However, many internet sites list the number of different types of cars stolen, but it is not clear whether these take into account the actual numbers of such cars on the road (the 'available population'). However, data from West Midlands Police provides more detailed information at <https://www.westmidlands-pcc.gov.uk/news/news-2018/car-thefts-nearly-triple/>. This shows that Ford cars are very common (17 per cent of all new car registrations), so we might expect 17 per cent of stolen cars to be Fords, but the WMP data revealed the figure to be 31 per cent. This strongly suggests that some Ford brand cars are more targeted by thieves, compared with other makes. The data also revealed that Audis and BMWs are particularly targeted (together they make up only 10 per cent of cars on the road, but 20 per cent of all stolen cars).

The number of vehicle thefts has fluctuated over the years, declining dramatically between 2003 and 2013, but there has been a steady increase in more recent years. Keyless vehicles are particularly vulnerable to hacking techniques.

TASK 9

1. This would be interference (a horse box is a trailer).
2. No, because a go-kart is not a motor vehicle adapted or intended for use on the road.
3. Yes, there is an intention to commit theft of an item which is 'carried in or on the motor vehicle' so this counts as interference.
4. No, there is no intention to steal the vehicle, anything in or on it, or take it without the owner's consent so this would not count as interference.

TASK 10

Scenario	Offence that is likely to have been committed
People order a meal in a restaurant, even though they know they cannot pay for it. They leave before it is served.	This is 'false representation', an offence under s 1 of the Fraud Act 2006. This is because the 'dishonest representation' took place before the property was obtained. By entering a restaurant people imply that they have the means and intention to pay for goods they order (unless there is a special credit agreement where payment can be delayed).
A man orders a meal and it is served to his table. He claims it is inedible and leaves without paying.	The man intended to pay for his meal, but changed his mind when it was served. He has received service, which is part of the charge for the *meal*. He implied that he was an ordinary customer by accepting the service so an offence of 'obtaining services dishonestly' may have been committed (s 11 of the Fraud Act). The dishonesty has occurred after obtaining the property, so this cannot be a s 1 offence.
Two women finish their meal. Then they decide not to pay and quickly leave the restaurant.	The dishonesty takes place after obtaining the property and therefore the offence is more likely to be s 3 of the Theft Act 1978; ie 'bilking'.

The CPS can provide advice on choosing the most appropriate charge (see 27.2).

17 Sexual Offences

17.1 Introduction

The incidence of sexual offences in England and Wales is notoriously difficult to determine, beset as it is by issues of under-reporting and lack of definitional clarity. The most recent data from the Office for National Statistics (ONS, 2019d) reports that the police recorded 162,030 sexual offences during the year ending March 2019. (This combines data from the Crime Survey for England and Wales (CSEW), Home Office police recorded crime, the National Fraud Intelligence Bureau, and the Ministry of Justice Criminal Justice Statistics Quarterly Update.) The figures suggest there has been an overall increase of 7 per cent in sexual offences on the previous year, with a 9 per cent increase in reported rape (58,657 recorded offences during year ending March 2019). The ONS report (2019d) suggests the overall increase may be due to improved police recording practices relating to these kinds of offences, as well as willingness of members of the public to report such crimes.

In the past there were a number of pervasive beliefs surrounding sexual offences that research has now demonstrated to be unfounded. These include 'rape myths', such as assuming that rape only happens to certain types of women, or that women in some way provoke the offence (Croall, 2011, p 267). These spurious arguments have been used, for example, as a defence for rape prosecutions where the victim was a prostitute. Another myth is that a rape is usually committed by a stranger in a dark alley attacking a woman, whereas the reality is that around 90 per cent of female victims of the most serious sexual offences already knew their attacker (Ministry of Justice *et al*, 2013, p 6). However, so pervasive are some of these myths, particularly in relation to the expected behaviour of victims, that in 2015 the Crown Prosecution Service and the Metropolitan Police developed a joint action plan on rape that aimed to address some of these misconceptions (CPS and MPS, 2015a).

Establishing that the victim did not consent to a sexual act is another problematic aspect of this type of offence. The Sexual Offences Act 2003 defines consent and presumptions about consent (ss 74–76). It is also presumed that there is no consent if the victim is under 16. In relation to marriage, it has never been the case that by marrying a man, a woman irrevocably consents to sexual intercourse with her husband (*R v R* [1992] 1 AC 599 (HL)). A man was convicted of raping his wife on a number of occasions from 1970 onwards, and this case credited the *R v R* decision as exploding the myth that it was ever acceptable (*R v C* [2004] EWCA Crim 292). More generally, however, the situation is not always clear in relation to consent, for example when a victim has consumed large amounts of alcohol, or changed his/her mind about engaging in sexual activity. The issue of consent will be discussed in more detail in 17.6.2.

More recently, there has been increasing concern about the sexual abuse of children, and particularly the use of online means to facilitate grooming of victims and to share images of child abuse. The possession and sharing of illicit images of children will be covered in more detail in 17.4.2. Individuals concerned with the safety of children can raise concerns with the police, who in certain circumstances will be able to disclose information in order to protect children, under the Child Sex Offender Disclosure Scheme (see 17.8.3).

The police tend to define policy in terms of 'serious' sexual offences and 'other' sexual offences. There is no collective official definition of 'serious' and in a sense every sexual offence is a serious one. For example, 'flashing' (see 17.2) is not normally included within the category of serious sexual offences, but its impact on victims might well be serious, and it has been suggested by some that this type of sexual crime, alongside voyeurism and image-related offences, may be precursors to more serious offending. However, the police consider that a distinction between 'other' and 'serious' is needed for a number of reasons, including the pragmatic necessity to make decisions on the deployment of resources and the development of policy. Many police forces will make reference to the use of the word 'serious' in the context of the Sexual Offences Acts of 1956 and 2003 and derive definitions in this way. In broad terms the following are normally considered as serious sexual offences when committed against adults (including attempts to commit these offences):

- rape (vaginal, anal, and oral);
- sexual assault by penetration;
- sexual assault where the assault is particularly serious (or is aggravated, for example by the involvement of a person with a mental disorder); and
- causing a person to engage in sexual activity without consent;

Where the offences relate to children, they will always be treated as serious because by their very nature they relate to issues of safeguarding, and other abuse may have occurred.

Reports to the police of sexual offences will arise from a variety of circumstances and in a number of forms. For example, the police may attend the scene of an alleged rape at a club, or a victim might phone the police or attend in person at a local police station. There may also be referrals from a Sexual Assault Referral Centre (SARC). The report might be of a very recent sexual assault, or of a rape that took place some 20 or more years ago. Because the vast majority of laws are not retrospective, when a sexual offence is reported many years after the event, the law that applied at the time of the offence still applies (as illustrated in the convictions of high-profile celebrities such as Rolf Harris, Gary Glitter, and Stuart Hall). Even though the range of sexual offences currently on the statute books appears to cover many eventualities, it may not cover historical reports. For instance, rape law prior to the 1990s would only cover vaginal penetration, and not anal or oral. The latter form of penetration was added to the definition of rape in the Sexual Offences Act 2003. As a result, on a practical level, the date upon which the offence was committed focuses the investigation towards a particular piece of legislation and case law. For example, although oral penetration was not considered rape in the 1990s, it could still have constituted an offence of indecent assault within the 1956 Sexual Offences Act. The difference is that indecent assault carried a maximum sentence of ten years' imprisonment, whilst since 2003 oral rape has carried a potential maximum sentence of life imprisonment.

The investigation of sexual offences has been a problematic area for the police, although the situation has improved markedly since the documentary made by Roger Graef in 1982. This showed the bullying and unsympathetic police interrogation of a woman who had reported rape. Moreover, the woman suffered mental health problems and these seem to have increased the officers' suspicions and concerns over the truthfulness and accuracy of her account. Given the particular controversies surrounding the police investigation of rape in the past, it is perhaps not surprising that detailed information on best practice is now available. The guidance from ACPO (the predecessor of the NPCC) is a key document; access to the full version is restricted but the abridged version can be viewed online (ACPO, 2010a).

The rate of attrition (between a report being made to the police and successful prosecution) is particularly high in sexual offences cases and has been the subject of much official, professional, academic, and media interest. There is undoubtedly an increased emphasis within the police service on improving both the rate of reporting of sexual crimes and the proportion that are brought to a successful prosecution or outcome (Angiolini, 2015). That said, it has been powerfully argued that rape investigations, and the treatment of victims in these cases, is a measure of women's equality in society (Hohl and Stanko, 2015), and consistent failings and poor conviction rates do little to allay concerns in this regard. Domestic abuse cases also suffer from high-profile shortcomings, where women (as for rape) make up the majority of victims; and perhaps these types of cases, together with scandals over gender pay inequalities, and the treatment of women in the film industry, serve to demonstrate that real equality is

Specific Incidents

far from realized. Moreover, recent high-profile cases where charges have been dropped at court due to poor police investigations and a lack of disclosure will not serve to enhance the credibility of the police in this regard. Former Lord Chief Justice, Lord Judge, suggests that juries could even find suspects not guilty at trial for fear they have not been provided with all of the relevant material (Polianskaya, 2018). Recent controversies over the potential early release of serial rapist John Worboys are unlikely to encourage victims to report rape, especially given the large number of allegations against him that were not pursued by the Crown Prosecution Service, and the apparent lack of notification to survivors that he could be released. Worboys was initially granted parole in 2018, but this decision was successfully challenged by survivors. He has since been prosecuted for a number of further attacks. The problem for the police is that high-profile 'exceptional' case failures seem to arise all too regularly, despite reviews, government papers, guidance, and significant developments in practice (Jordan, 2011).

The topics covered in this chapter are likely to contribute to the learning required for the National Policing Curriculum subject areas: 'Understanding the Police Constable Role', 'Public Protection', 'Vulnerability and Risk', and 'Response Policing'.

17.2　Acts of a Sexual Nature in Public Places

Exposure is covered by s 66(1) of the Sexual Offences Act 2003. It is commonly referred to as 'flashing'. A person commits an offence if he/she exposes his/her genitals and intends that someone will see this and be caused alarm or distress. It is not necessary for a person to actually have seen the exposed genitals or to have been distressed as a result; the offence is still committed. It can be committed in a private or public place (see 9.2.1.1 for definitions of places).

The important points to prove would be the double intention specified in the offence—an intent that someone will see, and an intention to cause alarm or distress. Therefore, a 'streaker' planning 'merely' to cause amusement by intending others to see his exposed genitals, does not commit this offence, because he had no intent to cause alarm or distress. Similarly, a nudist at a site specifically set aside for naturism, who does not conceal his or her genitals but has no intention to cause alarm or distress, will not commit the offence.

This offence is triable either way and the penalty is imprisonment (summarily, six months and two years on indictment).

Outraging public decency is covered by common law which states that it is an offence:

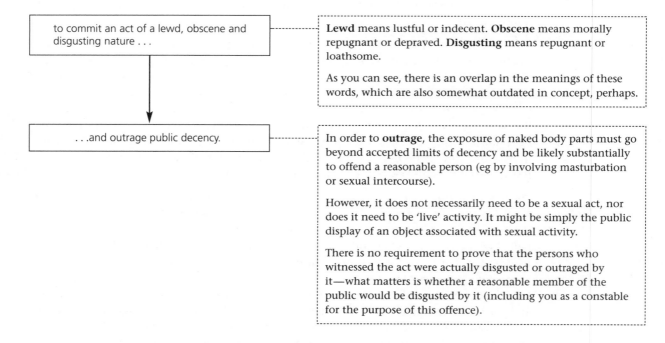

to commit an act of a lewd, obscene and disgusting nature . . .

Lewd means lustful or indecent. **Obscene** means morally repugnant or depraved. **Disgusting** means repugnant or loathsome.

As you can see, there is an overlap in the meanings of these words, which are also somewhat outdated in concept, perhaps.

. . .and outrage public decency.

In order to **outrage**, the exposure of naked body parts must go beyond accepted limits of decency and be likely substantially to offend a reasonable person (eg by involving masturbation or sexual intercourse).

However, it does not necessarily need to be a sexual act, nor does it need to be 'live' activity. It might be simply the public display of an object associated with sexual activity.

There is no requirement to prove that the persons who witnessed the act were actually disgusted or outraged by it—what matters is whether a reasonable member of the public would be disgusted by it (including you as a constable for the purpose of this offence).

The public must have access to (whether they have a right to such access or not), or be able to see the relevant location, such as a private balcony in public view (*R v Walker* [1996] 1 Cr

App R 111; *Smith v Hughes* [1960] All ER 859). It must also have been possible for more than one person to witness the act.

This offence is triable either way and the penalty is imprisonment (summarily, six months and unlimited on indictment).

Sexual activity in a public lavatory is an offence under s 71 of the Sexual Offences Act 2003. There is no need for any person to witness the activity, and if there are witnesses, they do not have to be in any way outraged or distressed. The activity must be such that a reasonable person would regard it as sexual in nature. This offence is triable summarily only and the penalty is six months' imprisonment and/or a fine.

17.3   Voyeurism

Voyeurism is an offence under s 67(1) of the Sexual Offences Act 2003. Usually a suspect (commonly known as a 'Peeping Tom') secretly observes another person undressing or having sexual intercourse (a 'private act') for the purposes of the suspect's own sexual gratification.

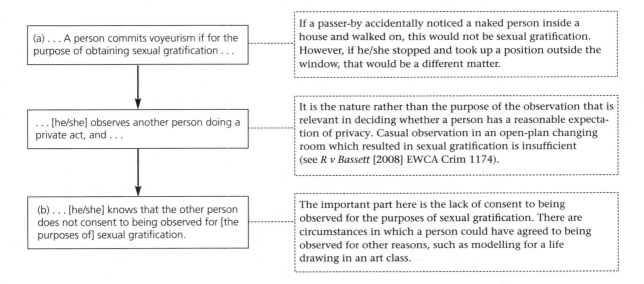

(a) . . . A person commits voyeurism if for the purpose of obtaining sexual gratification . . .

If a passer-by accidentally noticed a naked person inside a house and walked on, this would not be sexual gratification. However, if he/she stopped and took up a position outside the window, that would be a different matter.

. . . [he/she] observes another person doing a private act, and . . .

It is the nature rather than the purpose of the observation that is relevant in deciding whether a person has a reasonable expectation of privacy. Casual observation in an open-plan changing room which resulted in sexual gratification is insufficient (see *R v Bassett* [2008] EWCA Crim 1174).

(b) . . . [he/she] knows that the other person does not consent to being observed for [the purposes of] sexual gratification.

The important part here is the lack of consent to being observed for the purposes of sexual gratification. There are circumstances in which a person could have agreed to being observed for other reasons, such as modelling for a life drawing in an art class.

Section 68(1) of the Sexual Offences Act 2003 explains that, for the purposes of s 67, a person does a private act if he/she is in a place which would reasonably be expected to provide privacy, such as in a home or hotel (but not on a beach or in an open-plan changing room) and at least one of the following conditions is met:

- his/her genitals or buttocks, or her breasts are exposed or covered only with underwear (see *R v Bassett* [2008] EWCA Crim 1174);
- he/she is using a lavatory; or
- he/she is participating in 'a sexual act that is not of a kind ordinarily done in public' such as sexual intercourse, masturbation, or oral sex.

There is a form of voyeurism linked to 'dogging' (outdoor sexual activities); however, if the 'doggers' encourage people to watch, the offence of voyeurism is not committed because consent has been given. Other offences, however, may have been committed, depending on the particular circumstances. Aggravating factors for voyeurism include threatening the victim to dissuade him/her from reporting the offence (CPS, 2017d).

17.3.1   Facilitating voyeurism and the use of equipment

Voyeurism using live link equipment is covered by s 67(2) of the Sexual Offences Act 2003. Person A commits an offence if he/she operates equipment with the intention of enabling another person B to observe, for sexual gratification, a third person C doing a private act. Person A must know that C has not consented to this. For example, a landlord commits an offence if he operates a webcam so that people on the internet can gain sexual gratification from viewing his tenant having sex. The landlord must know that the tenant did not agree to this. There is no need to prove that the landlord personally gained sexual gratification.

The recording of images in relation to voyeurism is covered by s 67(3) of the Sexual Offences Act 2003. It is similar to the legislation under s 67(2), except that the acts are recorded and not just transmitted. Circulating images or recordings are deemed aggravating factors by the Sentencing Guidelines Council, particularly when offenders are motivated by commercial gain (Sentencing Guidelines Council, 2007).

Installing equipment and adapting structures for voyeurism is covered by s 67(4) of the Sexual Offences Act 2003. The offence is committed even if the installation or adaptation is never used. A 'structure' can include a tent, vehicle, vessel, or some other temporary or moveable structure.

These offences are triable either way and the penalty is imprisonment (summarily, six months and two years on indictment).

17.3.2 Upskirting

The term 'upskirting' is used to describe practices where an individual photographs or films from below under another person's clothing (without consent), with the intention of viewing the victim's genitals or buttocks. The victims are usually female, and the offence can be committed even if the area is concealed or partly concealed by a garment such as underwear. There had been a tendency to minimize the intrusive effects of such conduct, but one victim (Gina Martin), finding that the activity was not illegal, initiated a campaign to make it a criminal offence (*Telegraph*, 2019). From 12 April 2019, two specific offences were added to the existing voyeurism legislation under s 67a of the Sexual Offences Act 2003. The new offences relate to operating equipment without consent, and the recording of images without consent. It must be proven that the offences were committed for sexual gratification of the person or anyone else, or for humiliating, alarming, or distressing the victim. The offences carry a maximum sentence of two years' imprisonment on indictment, and six months if tried summarily.

TASK 1 Consider the following scenarios, and what offences might have been committed:

1. On the drive back to their home ground, four members of a rugby club team have taken to celebrating their wins by exposing their naked buttocks ('mooning') at the rear window of the team bus. A police officer is asked to deal with the most recent incident, that had occurred in the busy main high street. What offence might have been committed?
2. John is visiting his friend's house. He is having a meal when he decides to go to the toilet upstairs. When he reaches the landing he realizes that his friend's daughter Jane (aged 17) is using the lavatory with the door ajar. Rather than retreat until she has finished, John is aroused and stays on the landing watching her. He is disturbed by one of his friends. Could John be guilty of voyeurism? Does Jane's age matter?

17.4 Sexual Images Offences

Many aspects of adult pornography are completely legitimate, but if it involves 'extreme images' or indecent images of children, it will be illegal.

17.4.1 Possession of extreme pornographic images

This offence is covered by s 63(1) of the Criminal Justice and Immigration Act 2008. It is an offence to be in possession of an 'extreme pornographic image' (s 63(2)). An image includes moving images and electronic data that can be converted into an image, and/or stored on mobile phones or a computer drive for example (s 63(8)). An image is said to be pornographic if it appears to have been produced solely or principally for the purpose of sexual arousal (s 63(3)), and it must be explicit and realistic. An image is regarded as 'extreme' (see s 63(7)) if it depicts (or appears to depict) activities which:

- threaten a person's life;
- depict rape or non-consensual sexual penetration (this was added by the Criminal Justice and Courts Act 2015, and therefore does not apply to material held prior to 13 April 2015);
- result in (or are likely to result in) serious injury to a person's anus, breasts, or genitals (including surgical reconstructions);

- involve sexual interference with a human corpse (necrophilia); or
- involve a person having intercourse or oral sex with an animal (bestiality), and the act, person, or animal depicted in the image is real, or appears to be real.

The offence of possession of an extreme pornographic image does not apply for 'excluded images' as defined in 17.4.1.1 (s 64(2)). Defences for possessing extreme images (s 65 of the Criminal Justice and Immigration Act 2008) include that the person: had a legitimate reason for possessing it; had not seen it and did not know (nor had any cause to suspect) it was an extreme pornographic image; or had received it without requesting it, and did not keep it for an unreasonable time.

The offence cannot be prosecuted without the consent of the Director of Public Prosecutions. It is triable either way and the penalty is 12 months' imprisonment and/or a fine if tried summarily. For trials on indictment the penalty is imprisonment (three years for images which depict life-threatening acts or involve serious injury, and two years for images which involve necrophilia or bestiality).

The Ministry of Justice has issued guidance for dealing with the offence of possession of extreme pornographic images, available on the CPS website. The Internet Watch Foundation operates an internet hotline for the public and IT professionals to report potentially illegal websites.

17.4.1.1 Excluded images

These images are excluded in the sense that they would not be of concern for the offences under s 63(1) of the Criminal Justice and Immigration Act 2008 (see 17.4.1) or s 62(1) of the Coroners and Justice Act 2009 (for child sex abuse imagery, see 17.4.2). For material to be regarded as an excluded image, it must be part of a full-length mainstream or documentary film classified by the British Board of Film Classification (BBFC), and will not be considered as pornographic if shown as part of the complete film. However, if parts of the classified work have been extracted solely or principally for the purpose of sexual arousal, they will no longer count as 'excluded' (s 63(3)). Such cases will be a question of fact for the court to decide, for example, part of a film could have been unintentionally recorded, or reproduced for a purpose other than pornography.

17.4.2 Images of children and pornography

Sexualized images of children are used by sex offenders as 'stimulus' masturbatory fantasy material, and for some this usage can also produce sexual disinhibition in the offender making the actual abuse of children more likely. To help protect children from harm and exploitation, the general legislation relating to extreme pornography applies (see 17.4.1), but additional legislation applies in relation to images of children. Early legislation only applied to photographs and pseudo-photographs, but new legislation specific to drawings and other fantasy-style images was introduced in 2009. For the purpose of legislation relating to child sexual abuse imagery (colloquially 'child pornography'), any person under the age of 18 is a child, except where defences of marriage apply.

Some photographs of children may appear indecent but are not indecent in terms of the legislation (s 1 of the Protection of Children Act 1978). Exception 1A is that the photograph was of a person aged 16 or over, and that at the time of the alleged offence, the person and the suspect were married or lived together as partners in an enduring family relationship. Exception 1B is that the photograph is for use in criminal investigation or proceedings, in any part of the world.

17.4.2.1 Possession of an indecent photograph of a child

Section 160(1) of the Criminal Justice Act 1988 states that it is an offence for a person to have in his/her possession any indecent photograph or pseudo-photograph of a child. A pseudo-photograph of a child could, for instance, involve a child's naked body with an adult face added to it. The law does not define 'indecent'. According to *R v Stamford* [1972] 2 QB 391, it is up to a jury to decide whether an image is indecent or not based on 'recognized standards of propriety' (not necessarily their personal views—see also *R v Neil* [2011] EWCA Crim 461).

Defences (s 160(2)) include: having a legitimate reason for possessing the image; having not seen the image, nor having cause to suspect what it was; and receiving the image without requesting it and not keeping it for an unreasonable time. The offence is triable either way, and the penalty is a fine or imprisonment (six months if tried summarily, and five years on indictment).

17.4.2.2 Producing and distributing indecent photographs of children

This offence is covered in s 1 of the Protection of Children Act 1978, and is explained in more detail in the flowchart.

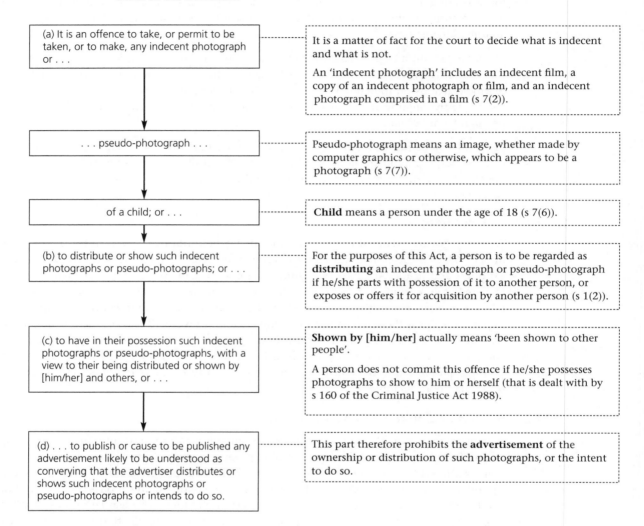

(a) It is an offence to take, or permit to be taken, or to make, any indecent photograph or . . .	It is a matter of fact for the court to decide what is indecent and what is not. An 'indecent photograph' includes an indecent film, a copy of an indecent photograph or film, and an indecent photograph comprised in a film (s 7(2)).
. . . pseudo-photograph . . .	Pseudo-photograph means an image, whether made by computer graphics or otherwise, which appears to be a photograph (s 7(7)).
of a child; or . . .	**Child** means a person under the age of 18 (s 7(6)).
(b) to distribute or show such indecent photographs or pseudo-photographs; or . . .	For the purposes of this Act, a person is to be regarded as **distributing** an indecent photograph or pseudo-photograph if he/she parts with possession of it to another person, or exposes or offers it for acquisition by another person (s 1(2)).
(c) to have in their possession such indecent photographs or pseudo-photographs, with a view to their being distributed or shown by [him/her] and others, or . . .	**Shown by [him/her]** actually means 'been shown to other people'. A person does not commit this offence if he/she possesses photographs to show to him or herself (that is dealt with by s 160 of the Criminal Justice Act 1988).
(d) . . . to publish or cause to be published any advertisement likely to be understood as conveying that the advertiser distributes or shows such indecent photographs or pseudo-photographs or intends to do so.	This part therefore prohibits the **advertisement** of the ownership or distribution of such photographs, or the intent to do so.

Two defences to this offence are listed in s 1(4) of the Protection of Children Act 1978:

- the defendant had a legitimate reason for distributing, showing, or having possession of the photographs or pseudo-photographs; and
- the defendant did not see the photographs or pseudo-photographs, or saw them and did not know they were indecent or have any cause to suspect them to be indecent.

The offence is triable either way. If tried summarily the penalty is six months' imprisonment and/or a fine, and on indictment the penalty is ten years' imprisonment.

17.4.2.3 Possession of a prohibited image of a child

Under s 62(1) of the Coroners and Justice Act 2009 it is an offence to be in possession of a prohibited image of a child (under 18 years of age). The image can be moving, still, or in data form, and is said to be prohibited if it is either:

- pornographic (produced for the purpose of sexual arousal); or
- 'grossly offensive, disgusting or otherwise of an obscene character'.

The image must either focus solely or principally on a child's genitals or anal region, or portray a child as a witness or participant for: sexual intercourse or oral sex with a person or an animal (the animal can be dead, alive, or imaginary); masturbation; or penetration of the anus or vagina.

Defences for possession of a prohibited image of a child (s 64) are similar to those for possessing an indecent photograph of a child (see 17.4.2.1). The offence is triable either way and the penalty is a fine or imprisonment (12 months if tried summarily, and three years on indictment).

17.4.3 Disclosing private sexual images with intent to cause distress

'Revenge pornography' is when private sexual images, usually of a former partner, are made available to the public as a form of revenge against that other person. It is now an offence to disseminate to the public (or a section of the public) films or photographs of a sexual nature, without the consent of the portrayed person, and with the intent of causing him/her distress (s 33(1) of the Criminal Justice and Courts Act 2015). It is not an offence to disclose the images to the portrayed person. Images that have been altered are also included in the remit of this offence (eg using software that enables the manipulation of photographs), but not if the unaltered images were non-sexual, and only became sexual due to the alteration(s).

Defences include that the disclosure: is necessary to prevent, detect or investigate a crime (s 33(3)); or relates to preparation or publication of journalistic material which is in the public interest (s 33(4)). A further defence is that there was reasonable belief that the images had already been released for reward, and there was no reason to doubt the portrayed person had not consented to the release, for example as commercial pornography (s 33(5)).

The offence is triable either way, with a penalty of a fine and/or 12 months' imprisonment if convicted summarily and a fine and/or a maximum of two years' imprisonment if convicted on indictment. One of the first people to be convicted was sentenced to six months' imprisonment (suspended for 18 months), ordered to undertake unpaid work, fined costs, and became subject to a restraining order. This relatively robust approach is intended to act as a deterrent to what is judged by the authorities to be an increasingly common phenomenon.

17.5 Prostitution

A prostitute is defined as 'a person ... who, on at least one occasion and whether or not compelled to do so, offers or provides sexual services to another person in return for payment or a promise of payment to [him/her] or a third person' (s 51(2) of the Sexual Offences Act 2003). Almost all public manifestations of prostitution are illegal. So, for example, it is an offence for a prostitute to be clearly waiting for potential customers in a public place, or for a person to be seen to actively seek the services of a prostitute in a public place.

The strong association between street prostitution and drug dependence, and between off-street prostitution and organized crime was recognized by ACPO in its 2011 *Strategy & Supporting Operational Guidance for Policing Prostitution and Sexual Exploitation* (available online). Although prostitution is illegal in many of its manifestations and not all prostitutes are exploited, many are in a vulnerable situation, a fact that was particularly evident in the case of the Ipswich murders in 2006. Drug dependence, violence, and intimidation may play a large part in explaining prostitution, but low self-esteem and having been abused as a child are also significant factors. Some victims of trafficking are also forced into prostitution. It is therefore important to determine whether an offence was committed, whether the person prostituting him/herself needs any kind of assistance, and which support organizations could help.

17.5.1 Soliciting in a public place

Some of the activities relating to prostitution are described in s 1(1) of the Street Offences Act 1959. This states that it is an offence for a person (male or female) to:

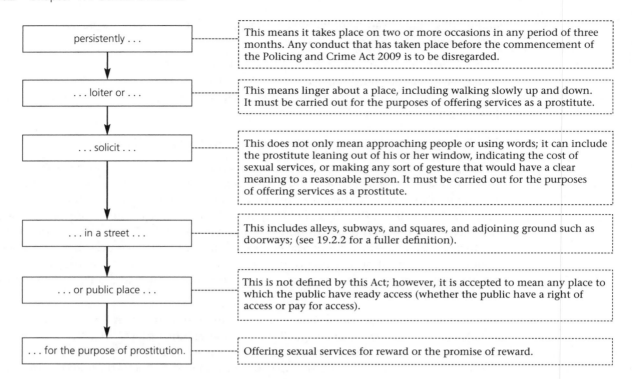

This offence is triable summarily and the penalty is a fine or a court order requiring the offender to attend three meetings with a 'suitable person' (specified in the order).

17.5.2 Procuring the services of a prostitute

It is an offence for a person to solicit the services of a prostitute in a public place (s 51(A) of the Sexual Offences Act 2003). This is known as 'kerb crawling' when carried out from a vehicle. The offence is triable summarily and the penalty is a fine.

The penalties are more severe in relation to paying or offering to pay for the service of an 'exploited prostitute'. This is when a third person motivated by gain (for him/herself or another) has used exploitative conduct to induce or encourage provision of the sexual services anywhere in the world (s 53A of the Sexual Offences Act 2003). The conduct can include the use of force, threats (not necessarily violent), coercion, and deception. It is irrelevant whether the services are actually provided, or whether the 'client' is aware of the exploitative context. ACPO emphasized that anyone exploited through prostitution needs help and support, most often in the form of access to health and welfare services (ACPO, 2011b, p 4). This offence is triable summarily and the penalty is a fine.

17.5.3 Sex for rent

In recent years there has been an increase in the number of reports of sex for rent scandals, where a landlord takes advantage of financially vulnerable individuals to secure agreement to waive or lower rent in exchange for sexual favours. Whilst there is considerable debate about the actual criminality of these arrangements, the CPS (2019) have recently issued amended legal guidance which suggests the practice may amount to an offence under ss 52–54 of the Sexual Offences Act 2003.

Section 52 concerns causing or inciting prostitution for gain and states that a person commits an offence if he/she:

(a) intentionally causes or incites another person to become a prostitute in any part of the world; and

(b) does so for or in the expectation of gain (for him/herself or a third person).

Section 54(1) defines gain as being wider than purely financial advantage and includes the provision of sexual services whether gratuitously or at a discount. The wording of the offence thus appears to cover these kinds of arrangements, although it was probably not written with sex for rent arrangements in mind.

The guidance on these offences observes they may be difficult to prove. It also specifies some circumstances where the s 52 offence might not apply, such as where the tenant proposed the arrangement. In this type of case, the CPS suggests s 53 as a possible alternative offence (controlling prostitution for gain). The offences under ss 52 and 53 both carry a maximum sentence of seven years' imprisonment on indictment.

It is hoped that these penalties will act as a deterrent to would-be perpetrators. That said, it will be interesting to see whether prosecutions for these offences in such situations will succeed. Until a case of this nature reaches the appeal courts, we will not know; it may be that statutory intervention in the form of new law is required.

TASK 2

1. Two police officers are on uniformed patrol near a railway station and notice a woman standing in the car park. As they approach she walks away towards the town centre, but returns a few minutes later. Later, the officers see two cars stop next to her. Each time the occupants of the cars talk to the woman and then drive off. What could the officers do?
2. A person offering a professional body-piercing service passes round a mobile phone amongst a group of strangers. It shows images of genitals and female breasts into which sharp metal objects of various shapes and sizes have been inserted. In relation to the possession of extreme pornographic images, have any offences been committed?
3. Police are told that landlords Rita and Ken have four rental houses, and seem to have suggested to several prospective tenants that the rent would be cheaper if they have sex with them. What potential offences, if any, might have been committed?

17.6 Sexual Assault, Rape, and Other Sexual Offences

This part of Chapter 17 covers the following offences within the Sexual Offences Act 2003:

- rape (s 1);
- assault by penetration (s 2);
- sexual assault (touching) (s 3); and
- causing another person to engage in sexual activity without consent (s 4).

In law, for these offences the offender must be aged 10 or over, and the victim can be of any age. Remember that the question of consent is of paramount importance when considering whether a sexual act relevant to these sections amounts to an offence.

The term 'sexual' now appears in ss 2, 3, and 4, as well as many of the child sex offences. An activity will be sexual if a reasonable person would consider it is obviously sexual (s 78 of the Sexual Offences Act 2003). This would cover, for example, masturbation, which most people would consider to be sexual.

Paragraph (b) of s 78 covers more ambiguous activities which may or may not be sexual, depending on the circumstances or the intentions of the perpetrator (or both). A two-stage test may be applied:

1. Would a reasonable person consider the general nature of the act to be potentially sexual in nature? For example, if another person penetrates a woman's vagina with his/her finger, this is likely to be considered by most reasonable people to be a potentially sexual act.
2. What are the specific circumstances of the person carrying out the potential sexual act? (This might include his/her intentions.) For example, if the penetration was carried out by a GP as part of a necessary medical examination, it would be unlikely to be considered as sexual.

If a person has a hidden sexual motive to an apparently innocent activity, this will not be considered sexual for the purpose of the Act; in effect the activity would fail the first part of the test. The general opinion is that the definition under s 78 excludes obscure sexual fetishes.

Whatever the situation, the term 'sexual' is defined so as to make it clear that not every potentially sexual activity will automatically be considered as sexual under s 78. However, a number of observers have pointed to the possible tautological problems with s 78 definitions of sexual (it defines sexual in terms of itself) and you might consider researching this further.

17.6.1 Initial police response to sexual crime

All reports of serious sexual assault made by complainants should be taken seriously, although there has been considerable debate recently as to whether all complaints should automatically be assumed to be true. Certainly, an investigation should be initiated. As noted earlier, the historical context to rape complaints was the poor response from the police, as Roger Graef demonstrated in the 1982 documentary about the Thames Valley Police. Victims felt that they were being subjected to investigation rather than the perpetrator, and that they were having to convince the police that they were genuine victims. To redress this balance, it then became police practice to treat the victim as if he/she was always telling the truth. Recently this approach has been criticized, because by simply believing the complainant the police effectively reverse the burden of proof against a suspect, and label the suspect as guilty at the outset of an investigation (Henriques, 2016). An independent review of 'Operation Midland' (the MPS investigation into historic sexual offence allegations against prominent people) was critical of this practice. For example, Lord Bramall was subjected to a home visit from the police in circumstances that were stressful for himself and his elderly wife, and she later died without knowing that he had been exonerated. The review suggested that even cursory investigation of the claims against Lord Bramall would have demonstrated that parts of the complaint did not withstand scrutiny, and that no further investigation could be justified.

Interestingly, Henriques (2016) also suggested that even the use of the term 'victim' was value laden. Whilst this observation was disputed by some parts of the police service, Henriques suggests that people who report alleged crimes to the police should be regarded as 'complainants' as they only become 'victims' in the truest sense once a court has decided guilt. However, for the purpose of this part of the Handbook, the words 'victim' and 'complainant' will be used synonymously, with no value judgements attached to either term. Whatever terminology is ultimately used within policing circles, there is little doubt that an objective investigation is the fairest and most appropriate approach, consistent with the values of the Criminal Justice System. There is also little doubt that a person reporting such an incident is entitled to the full services offered by both the police and other supportive agencies, whatever their designation.

The initial investigation into an alleged serious sexual offence will be conducted by the response officers and detectives allocated to investigate the crime. Guidance for first responders attending the report of rape or sexual assault has been produced by the College of Policing (2018b), available on line. Some police forces have specialist units dedicated to investigating rape and serious sexual assault (eg the MPS Sapphire Teams). If the victim is a child (under 16) then other specialist police staff may also be involved. An officer of at least detective sergeant rank will be appointed to lead the investigation, and will review its progress on a regular basis. ACPO's *Guidance for the Investigation and Prosecution of Rape* (ACPO, 2010a) remains applicable to other types of 'serious' sexual offences. It promoted the use of a multi-agency approach to the investigation of rape.

Some forces (eg Kent Police) also provide extra training to uniformed response officers to ensure that appropriate levels of investigation and support are provided at the initial investigation stage. Most forces also have specially 'SOIT' officers (where SOIT stands for Sexual Offences Investigative Trained, Sexual Offences Investigation Trained, or Sexual Offences Investigative Technique). The SOIT training is at PIP Level 2. A SOIT will become the single point of contact (SPOC) between the victim and the investigative team, and also provide early support to the victim. In theory, the same officer will support the victim throughout the investigative process through to court, and sometimes beyond. In practice this role is shared with Independent Sexual Violence Advisors and other volunteer agencies.

17.6.1.1 Information from the complainant

A rape or serious sexual assault is often first reported to the police by the complainant but often some time after the event. It may also initially be reported as domestic violence perhaps due to mistrust in the justice system, fear of not being believed, or fear for his/her personal safety (or that of his/her children). Maintaining the complainant's anonymity is therefore an important part of investigating sexual offences.

A victim of rape or other serious sexual offences may be reluctant to disclose events of a traumatic and intimate nature. He/she could also suffer from 'post traumatic stress disorder', which can take on a variety of expressions: a very emotional or a very withdrawn initial reaction; symptoms of extreme anxiety or depression; denial; rage; hyper-vigilance; flashbacks; and other behavioural disorders. There may also be severe disorientation before he/she can begin to readapt to 'normal' life where the incident no longer takes a central role (Mason and Lodrick, 2013).

A trainee officer is unlikely to be involved much beyond the initial stages of investigation into an alleged serious sexual offence. As for other incidents, the priority of the first attending officer (FAO) will be the protection of the victim and any other individuals at risk (see 11.2.1). An initial report should be taken (eg location, identity, times, description of suspect, etc) and accurate and relevant entries made in the PNB (see 10.2), followed by rapid referral to line managers and the SOITs. A trainee officer would not be expected to take a detailed account from the victim (this would be the SOIT's responsibility if one is deployed), but he/she would need to be mindful that this could be the first stage of a prolonged investigation. The FAO should remain the single point of contact with the victim until a SOIT is appointed. The College of Policing APP (2018b) specifies the minimum response at initial attendance of a report of rape or serious sexual assault.

Report-takers should display active listening (see 5.11.3) and concern for the victim when taking the statement. It is important to establish a relationship of trust with the victim early on as this will encourage him/her to provide as much detailed information as possible at a later stage. The focus should be on assessing the immediate safety of the victim, and be sufficient for briefing of the officers investigating the events.

Certain questions must be addressed during the initial stages. These depend on the urgency of the report and include, amongst other things, asking the identity of the person making the report (and for phone calls, his/her location), the location and time of the incident, whether the person making the report is the victim or a third party (and if the latter, in what capacity), the nature of the incident, the location and identity of the suspect, and details of any known injuries (ACPO, 2010a, pp 24–5). Later, victims should be provided with information on rape crisis centres and local victims support organizations. Any decision to arrest the offender (or involve him/her in any other way in the investigation) should consider the risk that this may present to the victim.

Forensic requirements must be considered (see 11.2), including the use of evidence-recovery methods if appropriate (see 26.6). Sexual assault victims should not smoke, eat, drink, wash, or go to the toilet (unless absolutely necessary) until they have been forensically examined as the preservation of physical evidence is essential. An Early Evidence Kit (EEK) can be used during the initial response to secure relevant forensic evidence. The kit usually includes a plastic container to collect urine samples, sheets of toilet paper, a mouth swab and a mouth rinse.

17.6.1.2   Information from others

Reports may be made by third parties, in which case the report-taker should try to establish in which capacity the third party is acting (eg as a witness or a member of a victim support organization). The third party should be provided with the contact details of an investigating officer (IO) so that any further information can be provided later if necessary. Direct police contact with the victim should usually be avoided without the knowledge of the third party. This does not mean, however, that contact with the victim should be avoided altogether; a risk assessment should be made under the supervision of an IO, who should consider using a SOIT to take matters forward. If the third party identifies an offender, the IO should consider further investigation and arrest if there is reasonable suspicion of the offence having taken place. If the third party making the report is from another agency, the recording and investigation should follow the pre-agreed information-sharing protocols. The information should be auditable (eg recorded in an IT system) and can be used, for example, to analyse trends and patterns of offending. Specialist sexual violence services should be made aware of any anonymous reports. The IO will need to decide whether there is enough evidence to justify reasonable suspicion and a subsequent arrest.

17.6.2 Consent

In many sexual offence prosecutions, particularly those relating to ss 1–4 of the Sexual Offences Act, the court will focus on the issue of consent. A defence is available if the suspect believes that consent was given, but the suspect has to prove that his/her belief was reasonable. The court will decide whether the belief was reasonable after considering the circumstances and the steps that the suspect took to obtain consent (s 1(2) of the Sexual Offences Act 2003). In general terms, the court will seek to establish whether the suspect made a conscious effort to initially establish consent and then monitor the consent—the other person might change his/her mind and withdraw consent, indicated by a change of physical expression or voice tone, for example.

The Sexual Offences Act 2003 introduced two sets of presumptions which courts can make in relation to the guilty knowledge of the defendant about consent: 'conclusive presumptions' (see 17.6.1.1) and 'evidential presumptions' (see 17.6.1.2). These set out certain situations where it is clear that consent cannot truly have been given.

If evidential and conclusive presumptions about consent do not apply then establishing that consent was given is often more difficult, as in many cases the only way to do this is by assessing the statement of the complainant against that of the accused. In order to address this difficulty and to ensure that officers steer away from the myths surrounding rape (see the introduction to this chapter) in 2015 the CPS and the Commissioner of the Metropolitan Police issued a joint action plan. This encourages the police to look more closely at the behaviour of the accused when trying to establish whether consent was granted or not, rather than focusing solely on the complainant (CPS and Police, 2015b). The action plan includes an aide-memoire with information on consent that summarizes relevant legislation and dispels some of the myths associated with rape.

Before considering s 74 of the Sexual Offences Act 2003 further we say more about s 76 and s 75, as understanding the reasoning underpinning each section of the Act in this way is more straightforward and hopefully easier to follow.

17.6.2.1 Conclusive presumptions about consent

Conclusive presumptions about consent are covered in s 76 of the Sexual Offences Act 2003. This sets out specific circumstances where a victim has been deceived and has engaged in sexual activity as a consequence. It must be proved that the defendant intentionally:

- deceived the complainant about the nature or purpose of the relevant act (eg telling the victim it was a necessary medical procedure); or
- impersonated an individual personally known to the victim, with whom the victim would have consented to such activity (eg the defendant pretends to be the victim's current sexual partner during complete darkness, and engages in sexual activity).

The presumption about consent (ie the lack of consent) is conclusive and final: if the victim has been deceived in any of these ways, no amount of evidence can prove that consent had been given or that the defendant believed that consent had been given.

17.6.2.2 Consent and s 75 of the Sexual Offences Act 2003

Section 75 of the Sexual Offences Act 2003 covers evidential presumptions about consent.

Under s 75 the court will presume that the victim did not consent if evidence presented in court proves that the circumstances involved any of the following:

- use of or fear of immediate violence against that or another person;
- any kind of unlawful detention;
- being asleep or unconscious;
- inability to communicate due to physical disability; and/or
- substances that are capable of stupefying or overpowering (such as drugs) that were non-consensually administered.

It also has to be proved that the defendant knew of these circumstances and carried out the act in question, except in the last example, where the section does not require it to be the person who administered to be the person taking advantage of the situation. For example, if A is aware that drugs or alcohol have been administered to B by C without their consent, but A nevertheless engages in sexual activity with B, the presumption in section 75 could still apply to A, even though C administered the substance.

The defence may provide evidence to prevent the presumption being applied. They will need to convince the judge that there is a definite issue about consent, and then produce relevant evidence from the defendant, a witness, or the victim. The defendant's belief (that consent had been granted) and his/her reasoning cannot be merely 'fanciful or speculative' (*R v Ciccarelli* [2011] EWCA Crim 2665).

17.6.2.3   Consent and s 74 of the Sexual Offences Act 2003

Section 74 of the Sexual Offences Act 2003 states that a person consents if he/she agrees by choice, and has the freedom and capacity to make that choice. Whilst sections 75 and 76 appear more clear cut because they list specific circumstances that demonstrate a lack of consent, section 74 plays an important role in providing the general definition of consent capable of encompassing many more circumstances that could amount to non-consent than the specific lists.

A choice has not been made freely if the person has, for instance, taken part under duress, through being blackmailed, or if deceived into thinking negative consequences might follow non-compliance. Capacity to agree means the ability to decide either way, and to be able to communicate the decision. If a person is 'unable to refuse', through intoxication (see *R v Bree* [2007] EWCA Crim 256) or mental disorder, for example, then he/she does not have the capacity to make the choice.

The general definition of consent under s 74 of the Act is wide enough to encompass circumstances where the victim has been deceived in relation to giving consent. For example in *R v Jheeta* [2007] EWCA Crim 1699 the victim felt compelled to have sex after being deceived into believing she would otherwise be fined by the police. Because of the deception, it could not be said that she legally gave consent.

Case law has established a number of other situations where the victim has been deceived and consent is negated under s 74. This includes deceptions concerning the gender of the perpetrator, whether a condom will be used, and blackmail. There have been some successful convictions involving deception and s 74, for example in 2019 Jason Lawrence was convicted of rape where he lied to the victim about having had a vasectomy (Brewis, 2019).

There is, however, considerable debate on the limits of s 74, for example an old case, *R v Linekar* ((1995) 2 Cr App R 49), suggested that a man lying to a prostitute that he would pay for her services did not constitute deceptive conduct sufficient to negate consent. Consideration has also been given to deceptions such as: 'I will marry you'; 'I am a millionaire'; 'I am an airline pilot' and so on, that have been used to secure sexual activity. Such deceptions are undoubtedly morally questionable behaviour, but are unlikely to negate consent under s 74.

The limits to s 74 were further considered in a recent case relating to sexual activity between a male undercover police officer and a female environmental activist. The whole relationship was based on the activist being deceived, and she said that had she known his true identity she would never have consented to sexual activity. The CPS decided that the case could not constitute rape and declined to prosecute. The activist legally challenged this decision in the Divisional Court, which rejected the challenge after reviewing the ambit of consent in older offences (eg of rape and procuring sexual activity by deceptive conduct (now repealed) under the Sexual Offences Act 1956), and the more recent definition of consent provided in s 74 of the Sexual Offences Act 2003. The Court suggested it was inappropriate to introduce a subjective element into the law to considerations of consent, as the victim would need to show that the fraud/deception was regarded by her as fundamental or critical to her decision-making.

It had previously been assumed that a person lying about his/her HIV status could not negate consent under s 74 of the Sexual Offences Act 2003. However, in *R v McNally* [2013] EWCA

Crim 1051 the Court of Appeal clarified that in *R v B* the assailant was silent about his HIV status, and that this is different from deception as to HIV status).

17.6.3 Rape

This is detailed in s 1 of the Sexual Offences Act 2003 and can only be committed by a man, but the victim can be male or female.

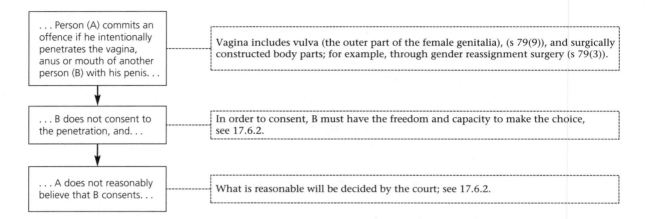

There are some important points to consider about penetration, which also apply for other sexual assaults:

- the very slightest degree of penetration is still penetration (*R v Hughes*, 1841);
- penetration is a continuing act from entry to withdrawal (s 79(2)); person (A) may have penetrated person (B) with B's consent, but B then changes his/her mind (quite legitimately) and makes this clear. If A does not withdraw, this amounts to a continuing penetration (and potentially rape);
- references to a part of the body also include surgically constructed parts (in particular through gender reassignment surgery) (s 79(3)). This leaves open the possibility that the offence can be committed by a person who was not born a man but who has a surgically constructed penis.

The offence of rape is triable on indictment only and the maximum penalty is life imprisonment.

17.6.4 Assault by penetration

This is an offence under s 2 of the Sexual Offences Act 2003; person A commits an offence if he/she intentionally penetrates (with a part of his/her body or anything else) B's vagina or anus without B's consent. Person A must be sexually motivated and not have a reasonable belief that B consents. Penetration is a continuing act from entry to withdrawal, and references to body parts include surgically constructed parts (see 17.6.3). The issue of consent can be considered by looking at the general definition under s 74, or any of the evidential or conclusive presumptions in s 75 or 76 (see 17.6.2). Rather than seeing this offence as a form of rape (because it involves the act of penetration), it is perhaps more appropriate to see it as an aggravated form of sexual assault. It is now (since the Sexual Offences Act 2003) a separate offence with higher penalties than previously. The penalty for penetrative sexual assault offence can be life imprisonment, whereas prior to 2003 the maximum sentence was only ten years. The offence of assault by penetration is triable on indictment only.

17.6.5 Sexual assault

This is covered under s 3 of the Sexual Offences Act 2003, and the details are shown in the flowchart.

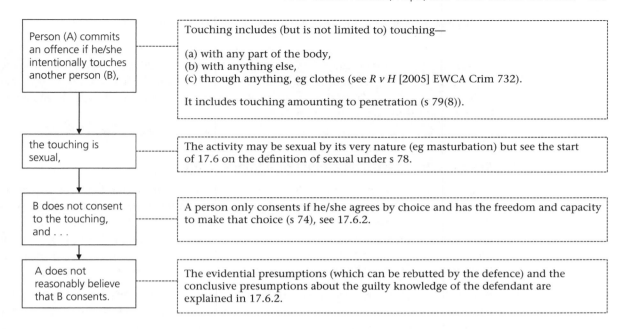

Unlike the old offence of indecent assault, the s 3 offence requires an actual touching of the person (along with the other relevant points to prove) before an offence is complete. Note the very broad definition of 'touching' provided in the flowchart. In circumstances where the suspect has only tried to touch in a sexual manner, but failed to touch the person targeted, this could be an attempted offence (see Chapter 22).

Unlawful sexual touching is triable either way. The penalty is six months' imprisonment and/ or a fine if tried summarily, and ten years' imprisonment on indictment.

17.6.6 Causing another person to engage in sexual activity without consent

It is an offence to intentionally cause another person to engage in sexual activity if he/she does not consent, and the perpetrator does not reasonably believe that consent has been given (s 4(1) of the Sexual Offences Act 2003). An example of this type of offence is where a man threatens to stab a woman with a knife if she does not perform a sexual act in front of him. She performs the sexual act for fear of being assaulted. He has caused her to engage in sexual activity, although there was no contact between the two of them. It would also need to be proven that there was no consent and no reasonable belief in consent. The difficulty for police investigators in these types of cases is that these offences are often committed in private with no witnesses present. A thorough investigation will be needed, as other elements of proof might be uncovered, for example evidence from the suspect's phone. Aggravating factors include a large age difference between offender and victim, general vulnerability of the victim, and the use of weapons to commit the offence. The penalty is six months' imprisonment and/or a fine if tried summarily, and ten years' imprisonment on indictment.

If the sexual activity involves penetration, the offence is more serious. Under s 4(4), the perpetrator (A) can cause penetration involving person B in a number of different ways. It can be:

(a) penetration of B's anus or vagina by anything;
(b) penile penetration of B's mouth (with person A's penis or any other man's penis);
(c) penetration of any person's anus or vagina by B, using part of B's body, or any item; or
(d) penetration of person A's or any other person's mouth with B's penis (if B is a male).

This would cover situations where groups of people cause others to engage in penetrative sexual activity with other people in the group. Some of the group may facilitate the offences by restraining the victim whilst others engage in the penetrative activity. The participants could of course be prosecuted for rape or conspiracy to rape, but this has often proved difficult when groups of people have been involved. However, the s 4(1) offence can be used to cover the conduct of all persons involved, and is classed as a serious sexual offence. Therefore any of the people involved who were found guilty could be placed on the Violent and Sex Offenders Register (ViSOR), not just those who actually penetrated the victim.

It is triable on indictment only and the penalty is life imprisonment.

> **TASK 3** Many victims of rape will be concerned about their identity becoming known during the investigation and any subsequent court case. What legislation is available to provide anonymity in relation to complaints of rape and restrictions on evidence at trials for rape? Is there any anonymity afforded to a defendant in these cases?

17.6.7 Sexual activity with an animal or a human corpse

Sexual intercourse with an animal is covered under s 69 of the Sexual Offences Act 2003. It involves penile penetration of animals by humans, and of humans by animals. The animals and the human participants must be alive and the penetration can be of the vagina or the anus. This activity is also known as bestiality. The offence can also be committed by allowing or causing such an act. (Note that penetration of an animal with an object does not come under this legislation but could be pursued through legislation for prevention of cruelty to animals.)

Penetration of a human corpse is covered under s 70 of the Sexual Offences Act 2003 and can be committed by men or women. Any part of the body or any object can be used to perform the penetration, and any part of the corpse may be penetrated. The offender must have some kind of sexual motivation, and must know or be reckless about whether he/she is penetrating a corpse.

These offences are triable either way. The penalty if tried summarily is six months' imprisonment and/or a fine not exceeding the statutory maximum, and two years' imprisonment on indictment.

17.7 Children, Young People, and Sexual Offences

Sexual activity between an adult and a child under the age of 16 is unlawful. Here we cover some of the sexual offences legislation that applies specifically to offences involving younger victims. (The offences listed in 17.6 can also be considered where the child did not consent.) For a victim under 13 years of age the law considers that he/she cannot give consent in any sense, so the offences are of strict liability.

Sexual contact may take place between an adult (aged 18 or over) and a child under 16, or between children both of whom are aged under 16. Whilst all of these activities might be sexual offences, some of the activities will attract criminal sanction whilst others might not.

First, where a person aged 10 or over engages in sexual activity with another child, and the activities are clearly non-consensual, the prosecutor could employ any of the offences in ss 1–4 of the Sexual Offences Act 2003 (see 17.6).

Secondly, where an adult engages in sexual conduct with a child under the age of 13, there are offences of rape, assault by penetration, sexual assault, and causing or inciting sexual activity that do not rely upon proof of lack of consent (ss 5–8 of the Sexual Offences Act 2003). In essence, these offences are of strict liability due to the age of the child. In many ways the offences covered by ss 5–8 effectively mirror the offences under ss 1–4 of the Sexual Offences Act, apart from the requirement to prove the age of the child, the irrelevance of consent and the addition of the term 'incitement' in s 8 to criminalize conduct aimed at encouraging children under 13 to engage in sexual activity. In all other respects the requirements of proof are the same (eg for rape, intentional penetration of the vagina/anus/mouth with a penis must be proved).

Thirdly, where an adult (aged 18 or over) engages in sexual activity with a child between the ages of 13 and under 16, where lack of consent does not feature, the Sexual Offences Act 2003 creates a series of further offences designed to criminalize such conduct (ss 9–12 of the Sexual Offences Act 2003). Again, there is no need to prove that consent was not given, although consent may be relevant to mitigation and/or sentence if a person is convicted. In these cases, the adult might be able to use a defence of reasonable belief that the child was 16 or over, but this would be dependent upon the circumstances of the case.

Finally, there may be circumstances where both parties engaging in sexual activity are under the age of 16. Section 13 of the Sexual Offences Act 2003 makes it possible for those under the age of 16 to be guilty of sexual offences under ss 9–12. However, provided there is true agreement (and, for instance no coercion by one of the parties), a prosecution is not always considered to be in the public interest. Further details on this are given in the Rape and Sexual Offences Guidance on the CPS website. Under s 13 of the Sexual Offences Act 2003, children charged with any of these offences would be subject to a lower maximum sentence of five years' imprisonment.

Grooming and child sexual exploitation have received particular attention in the political and law enforcement fields in recent years, particularly due to a number of high-profile cases involving individuals, groups of individuals, and gangs that sexually exploited children. As with prostitution, such practices may form part of lucrative and international business empires. We consider some of the measures to tackle these problems in 17.7.6 and 17.8.

17.7.1 Child rape

Rape of a child under the age of 13 is an offence under s 5 of the Sexual Offences Act 2003. It can only be committed by a man, but the victim can be male or female. For this offence, the victim's anus, vagina, or mouth must be penetrated by the offender's penis. The sexual organs can have been constructed through surgery (as with s 1 rape: see 17.6.3) and penetration is a continuous act from entry to withdrawal (s 79(2)).

Whether the victim appears to consent or otherwise agree to the activity is of absolutely no relevance, nor can the defendant contend that he thought the victim was aged 16 or over. Proof that the victim was under the age of 13 must be provided for a prosecution. This offence is triable on indictment only and the maximum penalty is life imprisonment.

For a victim aged 13–15 years there is no specific offence, so the offence will need to fit the general definitions for rape under s 1 (see 17.6.3), and lack of consent would need to be proven. Where lack of consent is difficult to prove, or the circumstances reveal willing participation, then offences from ss 9–12 could be considered (see 17.7.3, for example).

17.7.2 Sexual assault of a child

Sexual assault by penetration of a child under the age of 13 years is an offence under s 6 of the Sexual Offences Act 2003. The penetration can be carried out using any part of the body (such as a finger) or a separate object, and can be committed by a male or a female. The child does not need to be aware of the nature of the penetrating object. As for other offences, penetration is a continuous act from entry to withdrawal (s 79(2)). This offence is triable on indictment only and the maximum penalty is life imprisonment.

Sexual assault on a child under the age of 13 without penetration is covered by s 7(1) of the Sexual Offences Act 2003. It involves intentionally touching a child under the age of 13 in a sexual manner (see 17.6.5 for more detail on the meaning of 'touching' and 'sexual'), and can be committed by a male or a female. This offence is triable either way and the penalty is six months' imprisonment and/or a fine if tried summarily, and 14 years' imprisonment on indictment.

For these offences (s 6 and s 7) the victim must be less than 13 years old, and proof of this must be provided for a prosecution. Whether the victim appears to consent or otherwise agree to the activity is of absolutely no relevance. Nor would it be possible for a defendant to contend that he/she thought the victim was aged 16 or over.

For a victim aged 13–15 years old with non-consensual activity, offences under ss 1–4 can apply. If, however, the activities seem to have been consensual, a prosecution under s 9 or 10 could be considered.

17.7.3 Sexual activity with a child

It is an offence under s 9 of the Sexual Offences Act 2003 for a person (male or female) to intentionally touch a child in a sexual manner. For further explanation of the terms 'touching' and 'sexual', see 17.6.5. Where the child is less than 13 years old it is more likely that the suspect would be prosecuted under s 6 or 7 for such activities, but the prosecutor will decide which is the most appropriate.

For a s 9 offence the child victim has to be under 16, and proof of age is required. The accused will have a defence if he/she reasonably believed the victim was aged 16 or over, so the investigation should seek evidence that could justify the suspect's belief. Prior to 2003, only young men under the age of 23 were able to use this defence, but any person charged with child sex offences can now use it. Where a child is aged under 13 years, the defence is not available.

The s 9(1) offence (assault with no penetration) is triable either way, and the penalty is six months' imprisonment and/or a fine if tried summarily, and 14 years' imprisonment on indictment. If the sexual activity involves penetration, then a more serious form of the offence is committed, under s 9(2). (Such an activity where the victim is under 13 would be prosecuted under s 6.) Section 9(2) describes the acts carried out by the suspect (person A) that can constitute this more serious offence:

(a) he/she penetrates the child's anus or vagina (with a part of A's body or anything else);
(b) person A is a man and uses his penis to penetrate the child's mouth;
(c) he/she causes a part of the child's body (eg a finger) to penetrate A's anus or vagina; or
(d) person A forces a boy to put his penis in A's mouth.

This offence is triable by indictment only, and the penalty is up to 14 years' imprisonment.

17.7.4 Causing or inciting a child to engage in sexual activity

These offences (under ss 8 and 10 of the Sexual Offences Act 2003) can be committed by a man or a woman, and can involve the child acting alone or with another person. The offender might not be physically involved and no sexual activity actually has to occur; incitement alone can amount to the offence.

Causing or inciting a child under 13 years old to engage in sexual activity is covered by s 8 of the Sexual Offences Act 2003. If the sexual activity caused or incited involves no penetration, the offence is committed under s 8(1), and under s 8(2) if penetration is involved. Section 8 therefore creates four separate offences: causing non-penetrative sexual activity; causing penetrative sexual activity; inciting non-penetrative sexual activity; and inciting penetrative sexual activity. Proof of age is once again required, consent is irrelevant, and the defendant will not be able to use a defence that he/she thought the child was older.

Section 8(1) offences (no penetration is caused or incited) are triable either way. The penalty is six months' imprisonment and/or a fine if tried summarily, and 14 years' imprisonment on indictment. Section 8(2) offences (penetration is caused or incited) are triable on indictment only and the maximum penalty is life imprisonment.

For a victim under 16 years of age, these activities are covered by s 10 of the Sexual Offences Act 2003. Non-penetrative sexual activity is covered under s 10(1) and penetrative sexual activity under s 10(2). Reasonable belief that the child was aged 16 or over is available as a defence for this offence. The s 10(1) offence is triable either way. Consent is again irrelevant to the offence, but might be relevant to mitigation and sentence. The penalty is six months' imprisonment and/or a fine if tried summarily, and 14 years' imprisonment on indictment. An offence under s 10(2) is triable on indictment only and the penalty is imprisonment for up to 14 years.

17.7.5 Causing a child to witness sexual acts

There are two offences under the Sexual Offences Act 2003 where the offender causes a child to witness sexual acts: where the offender commits the sexual acts him/herself (s 11) and where other people commit the acts (s 12).

For the s 11 offence the offender must know or believe that the child will be aware of the sexual acts in some way (eg seeing it live, or on a webcam, or hearing it), and gain some sexual gratification from the child's presumed awareness. However, the victim does not actually have to be aware of the activity (eg if the child does not notice). For the s 12 offence the offender must gain sexual gratification from causing a child to watch a third party involved in sexual activity (live or recorded). The child need not be coerced to watch, and may even agree to watch; this is irrelevant to whether the offence has been committed. In the case of *R v Abdullahi (Osmund) Mohammed* [2006] EWCA Crim 2060, the Court of Appeal made it clear that the showing of material and the sexual gratification did not have to occur at the same time. It was possible therefore to show a child sexualized videos with the intention to gain sexual gratification some hours later.

These offences are both triable either way. The penalty is six months' imprisonment and/or a fine if tried summarily, and ten years' imprisonment on indictment.

> **TASK 4** Imagine you are a trainee officer and you are asked to attend the home of a 15-year-old girl. She alleges that a family friend has been visiting the house on a regular basis, and he has sometimes massaged her genitals. If the allegations are substantiated could he have a defence to any possible charge? Would it make a difference if the victim was 12 years old?

17.7.6 Countering grooming and organized child sexual exploitation

Grooming and child sexual exploitation has gained considerable attention in the political and law enforcement fields in recent years, particularly due to a number of high-profile cases involving individuals, groups of individuals, and gangs that have sexually exploited children. Grooming is now addressed under several offences, and measures are being put in place to counter child sexual exploitation.

17.7.6.1 Sexual grooming

There are two main offences associated with sexual grooming under the Sexual Offences Act 2003:

- A meeting, travelling to meet with a child (B) following sexual grooming, or a child (B) travels to meet A following sexual grooming (s 15); and
- communicating with a child for the purpose of sexual gratification for the sender (s 15A)

For both offences the perpetrator must be over 18 years of age, and the victim must be under 16 years of age. However, if the perpetrator reasonably believes the victim was 16 or over this can be a defence. The s 15A offence was introduced in 2017 to fill a perceived gap in the law, where sexualized communication with a child with no intention of meeting up was not previously a criminal offence.

Under s 15 of the Sexual Offences Act 2003, it is an offence to meet with or travel to meet a child following sexual grooming (s 15 of the Sexual Offences Act 2003). The overall aim of this legislation is to criminalize behaviour where an adult contacts a child on one or more occasions and meets (or intends to meet) the child in order to commit any offence under Part 1 of the Sexual Offences Act 2003 against him/her.

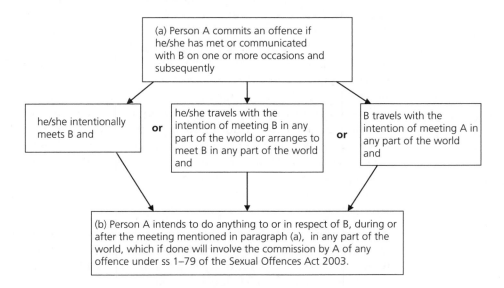

The communication between the two need not be sexualized, for example it could seem to be about attending a sporting event. The contact can be by any means, and includes meeting up, a letter, an email, messages on a social networking site, and SMS texts. Bearing in mind the rapid growth in the use of the internet and social media by young people, it would seem likely that some 16 or 17-year-olds commit such acts, but surprisingly this offence cannot be committed by a person less than 18 years old (see s 13 of the Sexual Offences Act 2003).

A Sexual Risk Order (SRO) can be used to try and prevent online sexual approaches to children under 16, if it is feared that the person intends to meet a child and commit sexual abuse (see 17.8.2).

Section 15A of the Sexual Offences Act 2003 makes it an offence for a person aged 18 years or over to communicate with a person under the age of 16 years if the communication is for the purpose of sexual gratification for the sender. The communication must either be sexual or be made with the intention of encouraging the recipient to make a sexual communication. The maximum penalty on indictment is two years' imprisonment.

17.7.6.2 Child sexual exploitation

Child sexual exploitation (CSE) occurs whenever a child under 18 years of age engages in sexual acts for a reward such as drugs, alcohol, food, accommodation, treats, money, gifts, or even simply some attention from a particular person. The reward can also be to a third person, in which case it is more likely to be money or drugs. For this offence, the sexual act can be carried out by the young person on another person, or by another person on the young person. The exploitation can involve technology (eg asking the child to send sexual images on a mobile phone). People who sexually exploit children generally have power over them, usually as a result of being older, more 'savvy', and having more disposable income. Instances of violence, coercion, and intimidation are not uncommon, and usually occur because the child has no means of escape (Department for Children, Schools and Families, 2009, p 9).

Child sexual exploitation can be difficult to identify. Common indicators of abuse have been covered in 13.3, and include from the most obvious signs of physical violence (such as bruises or cigarette burns), to the child having expensive possessions that cannot be easily explained. Such children may also have health problems, including sexually transmitted diseases, and can also display a range of behavioural problems such as going missing for periods of time, skipping school or being disruptive in class, having mood swings, using drugs and alcohol, and inappropriately sexualized behaviour (NHS, 2013).

Any child can suffer sexual exploitation, including those from stable and loving families, but risk factors include being homeless or in care, having had a recent bereavement, experiencing low self-esteem, or caring for a family member with an illness (NHS, 2013). A history of domestic violence in the family, living in a chaotic environment, a history of abuse, having parents with a history of substance abuse, and experiencing social exclusion are added risk factors. Girls are more likely to be sexually abused than boys (although it is likely that victimization of boys is underestimated), and there is a higher rate of victimization amongst black and ethnic minority children when compared to their proportion in the overall population (Office of the Children's Commissioner, 2012, p 14). Other factors that may place a child at risk of sexual abuse are: unsupervised use of social networking websites, having learning difficulties, suffering from mental ill health, being unsure about his/her sexual orientation, having a history of substance abuse, having friends who are sexually abused, being excluded from mainstream education, being bullied, and belonging to a gang or living in an area with gang associations (CoP, 2014b). Sexual exploitation can have a devastating impact on children, with many suffering from health problems (such as drug and alcohol abuse, self-harming, and mental health problems), going missing or offending as part or as a result of their exploitation (Office of the Children's Commissioner, 2012, pp 49, 50).

'Hotel Notices' can be used to help investigate organized groups involved in child sexual exploitation. Under the Anti-social Behaviour, Crime and Policing Act 2014 the police can require the owner, operator or manager of a hotel or B&B (or similar) to provide information about their guests (including name, address, and age). Failure to comply with the notice without a reasonable excuse, or giving information without taking reasonable steps to verify it, or knowing that it is incorrect, are criminal offences under s 118 of the Anti-social Behaviour, Crime and Policing Act 2014, punishable with a fine of up to £2,500.

17.8 Protecting the Public from Sexual Harm

Records of sexual offenders are kept by the police on what is commonly called the 'sex offenders register' (part of ViSOR, see 13.7.5.1). Part 2 of the Sexual Offences Act 2003 determines that offenders convicted for certain sexual offences, for example rape and certain child sex offences committed by adults, are required to notify the police of personal information such as their name and address (s 80) and this information is stored on the register. The requirements were extended in 2012 to include other offender information such as bank and credit card details, and if he/she is living in a household with a child (s 83(5A)(h)). Notification requirements are imposed for a fixed or indefinite period, depending on the sentence received, and offenders have three days to notify the police of any relevant changes. The offender can appeal against the notification requirements and these can be revised (s 82). Failure to comply with a notification order is an either-way offence under s 91, with punishment ranging from a fine to five years' imprisonment.

17.8.1 Sexual Harm Prevention Orders

A Sexual Harm Prevention Order (SHPO) is applicable to anyone convicted or cautioned for a sexual or violent offence. It can be issued by a court upon conviction, or the police or the National Crime Agency (NCA) can apply to a magistrates' court. The order is issued if it is deemed necessary to protect the public or a specific member of the public (in the UK or overseas) from sexual harm. The offender must have committed any of the acts in Sch 3 or 5 to the Sexual Offences Act 2003, and been convicted as a result, either in the UK or abroad. SHPOs have a fixed term of not less than five years and can prohibit an individual from travelling overseas. Individuals with an SHPO are subject to the same notification requirements as registered sex offenders and must notify the police of their name and address within three days of the order being served. The breach of an SHPO is an offence, triable either way. The punishment is up to six months' imprisonment or a fine if tried summarily, and a maximum of five years' imprisonment if tried on indictment.

17.8.2 Sexual Risk Orders

A Sexual Risk Order (SRO) is a preventative order applicable to an individual who seems likely to present a risk of sexual harm to the public, as a result of having committed an act of a sexual nature. Unlike an SHPO, the individual does not need to have been convicted or cautioned for committing this act (s 122A of the Sexual Offences Act 2003). The order prohibits the individual from committing specified actions, which can include travelling overseas. It also requires the recipient to provide his/her name and address to the police within three days of the order being served. The police or NCA apply to a magistrates' court for an SRO, and must have a reasonable belief that it is necessary to protect the public or specific members of the public in the UK or overseas from sexual harm. SROs have a fixed term of at least two years, except for those with international travel prohibitions, which must last for at least five years. Breaching an SRO is a criminal offence, with a maximum penalty of five years' imprisonment.

17.8.3 The Child Sex Offender Disclosure Scheme

Under this scheme (CSODS) a member of the public can ask the police about a particular person who has access to children, to find out whether he/she has a record for child sexual offences. (This is sometimes referred to as 'Sarah's law' in memory of Sarah Payne who was killed by a convicted sex offender.) The police will confidentially disclose any relevant information to the people who are deemed most capable of protecting the children at risk (usually parents, guardians, and carers), but only if the police believe it is in the child's interests. The information will not necessarily be disclosed to the person who actually made the original request. Information on convicted sexual offenders is not immediately and widely disclosed to the public to avoid any public backlash, and also to ensure that registered sex offenders engage with the system, rather than 'going underground'.

The CSODS request can be made in person, by telephone or email. Individuals making the request in person (eg by walking into a police station) should be allowed to do so privately, and will be informed about how the process will be conducted and the associated timescales. Within 24 hours there should be an initial risk assessment and minimum standard checks using PNC, ViSOR, and other local intelligence systems. Immediate action must be taken if it seems there is an imminent risk to a child; the procedures for safeguarding children are followed (see 13.3.3). There are five further stages for the CSODS (see the Home Office's *Child Sex Offender Disclosure Scheme Guidance*, available online).

17.8.4 Police officers and abuse of trust

Over the last few years attention has been drawn to a form of police corruption which involves police officers and staff abusing their positions to enter into sexual relationships with members of the public. Abuse of position is defined by the NPCC (2017, p 6) as:

> Any behaviour by a police officer or police staff member, whether on or off duty, that takes advantage of their position as a member of the police service to misuse their position, authority or powers in order to pursue a sexual or improper relationship with any member of the public.

Some individuals coming into contact with the police are clearly vulnerable, and there is an imbalance of power between the parties (see for instance IPCC and ACPO, 2012; HMIC, 2017b). In such circumstances a completely professional approach is required, to protect the vulnerable.

The NPCC has issued a national strategy (NPCC, 2017) to address the problem, and emphasized the importance of having mechanisms in place to receive reports of such conduct, investigate appropriately, and ensure that cases are also referred to the Independent Office of Police Conduct (IOPC).

17.9 Answers to Tasks

TASK 1

1. Section 66 of the Sexual Offences Act only applies to exposure of a person's genitals, not the buttocks (although it is possible that 'mooning' may also result in exposure of the genitals, even though this was not intended). However, in any case the suspects might claim their intention was to entertain or amuse, not to alarm or distress. In the common law offence of Outraging Public Decency, there must be a deliberate act that is lewd, obscene, or disgusting. In *R v Rowley* [1991] 4 All ER 649, Lord Simon decided that outraging public decency goes considerably beyond offending the sensibilities of 'reasonable' people. Therefore the local evidence-review representative or CPS representative should be asked whether the common law offence might be committed by members of the rugby team. The public order offences could also be considered, for example s 5 of the Public Order Act—non-intentional harassment, alarm, or distress.

2. Section 67(1) of the Sexual Offences Act 2003 appears to have been committed in these circumstances. The voyeurism offence can be committed within private premises. Jane is engaged in a private act (going to the lavatory) and John is observing her under conditions where it is reasonable for her to expect privacy. It is clear from the circumstances that John did not seek consent and it is unlikely that it would have been given in these circumstances (such evidence could be provided by Jane). Her age is irrelevant in these circumstances. The most tricky element in the case would be to prove that John's observations were for the purpose of sexual gratification, although it is likely that this would be left to a court to determine.

TASK 2

1. The woman could be investigated under s 1(1) of the Street Offences Act 1959 as 'persistently loitering or soliciting in a street or public place for the purposes of prostitution'. To prove 'persistently' there must be evidence of the behaviour on two or more occasions in any period of three months. The police officers should speak to the woman and, having found out her name, address, and date of birth, check whether she has any record of soliciting in the last three months. If she is a persistent offender they may need to consider further action. Otherwise they could warn her about the possible consequences of continuing her behaviour, ensuring of course that the warning is recorded in the appropriate place according to local procedures. This will provide evidence that she has already been acting in this way to any police officer who may need to check in the future. Each police officer should record the incident in his/her PNB.

2. This offence can certainly be committed by the possession of extreme images stored on a mobile telephone. However, body piercing carried out hygienically and with consent is unlikely to result in serious injury to a person's breasts or genitals. If the owner of the mobile was a professional piercer trying to get business he/she could claim the images were for advertising and not for sexual arousal, and is likely to have a defence.

3. Current guidelines suggest there may be a *prima facie* criminal offence committed by both landlords under s 52 of the Sexual Offences Act 2003, so it would be legitimate to investigate the matter to discover whether any offences have in fact been committed. CPS guidance suggests that where the agreement might be suggested by the tenant, the s 52 offence might not apply, so the prospective tenant and landlords will need to be questioned carefully. In this situation the CPS suggests the s 53 offence might be more appropriate.

TASK 3 Section 7 of the Sexual Offences (Amendment) Act 1976 provides anonymity for victims of rape. This includes attempted rape, aiding, abetting, counselling, and procuring rape or attempted rape, incitement to rape, and conspiracy to rape. The anonymity can be waived by a victim at any time, and some victims choose this route to raise awareness for the benefit of other victims (eg the late Jill Saward, who was sexually assaulted in an Ealing vicarage in 1986). Anonymity for defendants in rape cases was removed by s 158 of the Criminal Justice Act 1988. Celebrities such as Sir Cliff Richard and Paul Gambaccini, both publicly accused of sexual offences but later not convicted, have campaigned for a change in the law to provide anonymity for those accused of sexual offences.

TASK 4 For the offence of sexual activity with a child (s 9(1) of the Sexual Offences Act 2003), there is a defence available if the girl is at least 13 years old and the perpetrator reasonably believed that the girl was aged 16 or over. There would be no defence if the girl was younger than 13 years, assuming proof of the behaviour.

Specific Incidents

18.1 Introduction

In this chapter we outline the legislation that covers the use and ownership of weapons (including firearms), and which prohibits possession of weapons in certain circumstances. In the past year (2018/19), the UK has once again seen a significant rise in offences involving knives or other bladed weapons. The police recorded 44,076 offences involving a knife or sharp instrument in the year ending March 2018, a 7 per cent increase compared with the previous year (ONS, 2019b). As in previous years, about half of the offences were assault with injury or assault with intent to cause serious harm, and just over one–third were part of a robbery. The largest increases compared with the previous year were for threats to kill and attempted murder, with figures for homicide showing a fall.

Type of offence involving a bladed or pointed instrument	Number of offences	Percentage change compared with the previous year
Assault with injury and assault with intent to cause serious harm	19,994	+2
Robbery	18,987	+10
Threats to kill	3,764	+20
Rape	503	+10
Attempted murder	412	+22
Homicide	235	−13
Sexual assault	181	+8
Total	44,076	+7

Data source: ONS, 2019b.

Many of the policies aimed at reducing the number of offensive weapons being carried in public are part of the multi–agency approach described in 8.4. For example, in some schools there are walk–through scanners for detecting weapons, and staff can search pupils (both allowed under the Violent Crime Reduction Act 2006). In addition, Part 7 of the Education and Inspections Act 2006 allows for the use of reasonable force by school staff, and describes the circumstances in which confiscation from pupils would be lawful. In most cases school policies on searching and seizing of offensive weapons will have been agreed with the local police.

Health and safety should of course be of primary concern for the police constable when weapons are suspected to be present (see 6.12). The topics covered in this chapter are likely to contribute to the learning required for the National Policing Curriculum subject areas: 'Understanding the Police Constable Role', 'Policing Communities', and 'Response Policing'.

18.2 Weapons Offences

Firearms, knives, clubs, crossbows, batons, and swords are all clearly weapons, but so is a simple length of rope in the wrong hands (see 18.2.1). Firearms are clearly weapons, but are covered under separate firearms legislation (see 18.3–18.8). Note that the law regarding weapons is different in some other countries; some items are easily and legally obtained abroad and then brought into the UK.

In some cases, individuals found in possession of weapons fear attack from others, and their fears may be justified. However, whatever the circumstances, police officers have a duty to attempt to prevent criminal use of these weapons and, if at all possible, locate and remove such items before they can be used.

18.2.1 Offensive, dangerous, and specified weapons

An offensive weapon for the purposes of the Prevention of Crime Act 1953 is any article 'made, adapted, or intended' for causing injury (s 1(4)). A 'made article' is something that has been made or manufactured for the purposes of causing injury to people, for example a flick knife or telescopic baton. The courts need no proof of its intended use.

An 'adapted article' is something which has been modified in some way for the purposes of causing injury, for example a broken bottle with sharp edges, or a potato used as a mount for protruding razor blades. A jury would need to decide whether or not articles have been specifically adapted to be offensive weapons. For example, in the case of *Prosecution right of appeal (No 23 of 2007), sub nom R v R* [2007] EWCA Crim 3312 it was decided that gloves filled with sand should be regarded as offensive weapons, because the prosecution had produced evidence that similar gloves had been advertised for sale on a website as 'self–defence gloves'. The jury would also need to be convinced that the defendant had no reasonable excuse for possessing the item(s).

An 'intended article' is any item in the suspect's possession, with which he/she intends to cause injury. The precise nature of the article is not important: a pillow can be an offensive weapon if it can be proved that the suspect intended to use it to cause injury (eg to a frail relative). Once again, gathering evidence through interview is important because it must first be proved that the suspect intended to cause injury with the article. Only then would any reasonable excuse for the possession be considered (see *R v Sundas* [2011] EWCA Crim 985).

18.2.1.1 Dangerous weapons

Some offensive weapons are classified as 'dangerous weapons' under s 28 of the Violent Crime Reduction Act 2006 (because they are listed as 'specified weapons' under s 141 of the Criminal Justice Act 1988). The table lists some examples with descriptions (quotes are taken from the relevant Acts and Statutory Instruments).

Item	Comments
Disguised knife	'Any knife which has a concealed blade or concealed sharp point and is designed to appear to be an everyday object of a kind commonly carried on the person or in a handbag, briefcase, or other hand luggage (such as a comb, brush, writing instrument, cigarette lighter, key, lipstick or telephone)'
Stealth knife	'A knife or spike, which has a blade, or sharp point, made from a material that is not readily detectable by apparatus used for detecting metal and which is not designed for domestic use or for use in the processing, preparation or consumption of food or as a toy'
Knuckleduster	'Band of metal or other hard material worn on one or more fingers, and designed to cause injury'
Telescopic truncheon	'A truncheon which extends automatically by hand pressure applied to a button, spring or other device in or attached to its handle'
Baton	'A straight, side–handled or friction–lock truncheon'
Shuriken, Shaken or Death Star	'A hard non–flexible plate having three or more sharp radiating points and designed to be thrown'
Push dagger	'A knife the handle of which fits within a clenched fist and the blade of which protrudes from between two fingers'
Belt–buckle knife	'A buckle which incorporates or conceals a knife'
Swordstick	'A hollow walking–stick or cane containing a blade which may be used as a sword'
Handclaw	'A band of metal or other hard material from which a number of sharp spikes protrude, and worn around the hand'
Hollow kubotan	'A cylindrical container containing a number of sharp spikes'

Item	Comments
Footclaw	'A bar of metal or other hard material from which a number of sharp spikes protrude, and worn strapped to the foot'
Balisong or Butterfly knife	'A blade enclosed by its handle, which is designed to split down the middle, without the operation of a spring or other mechanical means, to reveal the blade'
Blowpipe or blow gun	'A hollow tube out of which hard pellets or darts are shot by the use of breath'
Kusari gama	'A length of rope, cord, wire or chain fastened at one end to a sickle'
Kyoketsu shoge	'A length of rope, cord, wire or chain fastened at one end to a hooked knife'
Manrikigusari or kusari	'A length of rope, cord, wire or chain fastened at each end to a hard weight or hand grip'
Samurai sword (or other similar curved blade)	'A sword with a curved blade of 50cm or over in length which is measured in a straight line from the top of the handle to the tip of the blade'

18.2.2 Possessing an offensive weapon in a public place

Section 1(1) of the Prevention of Crime Act 1953 states that it is an offence for:

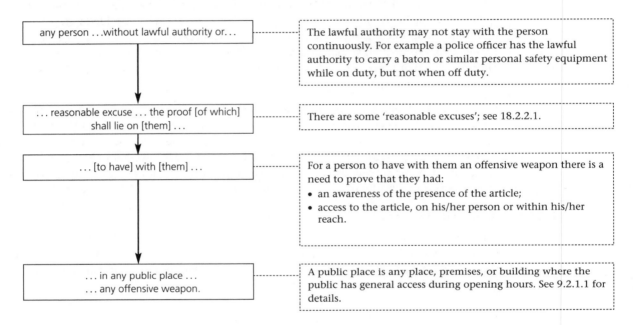

Of course, some items that might be classed as offensive weapons may have innocent uses, and the person would therefore have a reasonable excuse for carrying such an item (see 18.2.2.1).

A police officer has the power to search for offensive weapons under s 1 of the PACE Act 1984 (see 9.4.2). Possessing an offensive weapon in a public place is an either–way offence, and the penalty is a fine or imprisonment (six months if tried summarily and four years if tried on indictment).

18.2.2.1 Reasonable excuses

A person may have a reasonable excuse for possession of an offensive weapon in a public place if he/she fears for his/her safety: for example, a woman who feels she is about to be assaulted (and cannot escape) and picks up a chair to defend herself. Other reasonable excuses include having an innocent reason, such as a chef carrying kitchen knives on his way to work.

Unreasonable excuses include:

- Forgetfulness—for example a man forgetting he has a cosh in the glove compartment of his car (see eg *R v McCalla* (1988) 87 Cr App R 372). However, when the forgetfulness is combined with other circumstances (eg 'relating to the original acquisition of the article') there might be a reasonable excuse, but it will be for the court to decide (see *R v Vasil Tsap* [2008] EWCA Crim 2679). An example might be when a weapon is left by a passenger in a taxi and the driver moves it to the front seat footwell intending to dispose of it later. If the taxi is later stopped by the police the driver may claim to have forgotten that the weapon was there (see *R v Glidewell* LTL 19/5/99, The Times, 14 May 1999).

* Ignorance—not knowing the true identity of the item, for example believing that a truncheon is an umbrella.
* General self–defence—having a weapon just in case, when there is no reason to fear an attack; this would be for a court to decide.

The burden of proving a reasonable excuse for possession of an offensive weapon lies with the defendant. Therefore, officers should gather as much evidence as possible (before, during, and after interview under caution) about any reasonable excuse the defendant might put forward.

18.2.3 Possessing a bladed or sharply pointed article in a public place

The Criminal Justice Act 1988 (CJA 1988) created the offence of having a bladed or sharply pointed article in a public place (s 139(1)) in an attempt to prevent serious crimes involving the use of such items. Historically, under the Prevention of Crime Act 1953, if the defendant had been in possession of a kitchen knife, pair of scissors, or large pocket knife, he/she would not be found guilty if the court could be persuaded on the balance of probabilities that he/she had had a reasonable excuse (see 18.2.2.1). The CJA 1988 makes this less likely. We define some key terms as follows:

* 'Bladed' includes any kind of bladed article, for example a kitchen knife, a retractable blade knife ('Stanley® knife'), scissors, a craft knife, a pocket knife, a dagger, or any article which has been given a cutting edge or blade. Pocket knives with a blade less than 7.62 cm (3 inches) long which cannot be locked in the open position are exempt from this legislation.
* 'Sharply pointed' includes any kind of sharply pointed article, for example a needle, geometry compasses, or any article which has been given a sharp point.

A court must decide whether an article has a blade or is sharply pointed, so the onus is on the prosecution to prove that the article fits the relevant description. For example, in *R v Davis* [1998] Crim LR 564 the suspect was carrying a screwdriver which the court was asked to consider as a 'bladed article capable of causing injury'. The court decided that it was more important to determine whether the screwdriver had a cutting edge or point than to consider whether it was capable of causing injury. Therefore, unless a screwdriver has a pointed end or has been sharpened to make a blade, it is not an article for the purposes of this Act. A power to search for bladed, or sharply pointed articles is provided under s 1 of the PACE Act 1984 (see 9.3).

The table shows some possible defences to this offence. General self–defence, ignorance, or forgetfulness are not accepted as a defence (see 18.2.2.1). It is very important to gather evidence to counter any defences that may be offered later.

Defence	Example
Lawful authority	The lawful authority may not stay with the person continuously. For example, a police officer would have lawful authority to have a bladed or sharply pointed article after seizure and before placing it into a property store. Members of the armed services will also have lawful authority to carry articles such as bayonets whilst on duty, but may be liable for prosecution if such an article was carried off duty
For use at work	A joiner uses wood chisels with very sharp cutting edges and may need to carry them in a bag in the street while moving between jobs. The work can be casual and the bladed article does not have to be used on a regular basis (see *Chahal v DPP* [2010] EWHC 439 (Admin)). He/she, however, would not be able to use this claim if he/she had a chisel in a nightclub whilst socializing
Religious reasons	Followers of the Sikh religion may carry kirpans (a small rigid knife) for religious reasons
Part of any national costume	Whilst wearing national costume, some Scots carry a skean dhu (a small dagger, tucked in the top of the socks). However, this defence could not be used if the person was carrying the knife but not wearing national costume

The offence is triable either way and the penalty is a fine or imprisonment (six months if tried summarily and four years on indictment).

> TASK 1 A police officer on patrol stops a vehicle and notices two bayonets, in their scabbards, in the foot–well of the passenger seat. What should the officer consider and what actions may be needed?

18.2.3.1 Tackling knife crime

Knife crime is widespread and can present an immediate and devastating danger to people in all sectors of society, so police forces are under great pressure to take the lead in initiatives to reduce this threat. The criminal use of knives and other bladed weapons is probably best viewed in the context of wider social issues such as vulnerability (see Chapter 4 in particular). The phenomenon often features in press and media reports, having been commented upon at the highest levels of government, and in May 2019 the Offensive Weapons Act received Royal Assent. This Act makes it illegal to possess dangerous weapons (see 18.2.1.1) in private, including knuckledusters and zombie knives. This will help prevent such knives being bought online and sent to residential addresses; the seller must not send such an item unless he/she has made arrangements with the delivery company to ensure it is not delivered to a person under 18. The Act also creates Knife Crime Prevention Orders to help the police target those most at risk of being drawn into knife crime, and to help set them on a more positive path.

In addition to tough law enforcement, the government announced in 2019 that £220 million (including the £200 million Youth Endowment Fund) will be invested in early intervention projects to divert young people away from serious violence. In addition, the Anti–Knife Crime Community Fund will be allocated a further £1.5 million of new funding (£4 million has already been spent on relevant community projects). The Home Secretary also announced in October 2019 a number of measures to tackle county lines gangs (see 12.7.3), underpinned by £20 million of Home Office investment.

18.2.4 Weapons in schools

Section 139A of the Criminal Justice Act 1988 prohibits certain weapons on school premises (s 139A(1) for bladed or sharply pointed articles, and s 139A(2) for other offensive weapons). Here, a 'school' is an educational institution providing primary and secondary education (s 14(5) of the Further and Higher Education Act 1992), and school premises include land used for the purposes of a 'school' such as playing fields and playgrounds (s 139A(6) of the CJA 1988).

The classification of these offences and powers of search are the same as for possessing an offensive weapon in a public place (see 18.2.2). For searching a person, the officer does not need to have grounds to suspect that the particular person is in possession of a weapon, but the decision should still be based on objective factors connected with the reason for searching the premises (PACE Code A, para 2.29). This is covered in more detail in Chapter 9. The officer does not have to be in uniform to enter school premises if he/she suspects a s 139A offence, and reasonable force can be used to secure entry. If offensive weapons, or bladed, or sharply pointed articles are found, they can be seized (s 139B of the CJA 1988).

Defences for s 139A offences include that the article or weapon was for use at work, educational purposes, religious reasons, or as part of a national costume (see also 18.2.3). The offence is triable either way with a penalty of a fine or imprisonment (six months if tried summarily and four years on indictment).

18.2.5 Threatening with a weapon in a public place or school

It is an offence to threaten a person in a public place or on school premises with:

- an offensive weapon (s 1A of the Prevention of Crime Act 1953); or
- a bladed or sharply pointed article (s 139AA of the CJA 1988).

The threat must be intentional and unlawful (see 18.2.2) and create an immediate risk of 'serious physical harm' (harm that amounts to grievous bodily harm (see 15.3.1)).

Due to the location, these offences are aggravated versions of the basic possession offences. Many terms mean the same as for the basic offences and have been described elsewhere in detail. For example, for the definitions of public place, school premises, offensive weapons, and bladed or sharply pointed article see 9.2.1.1, 18.2.4, 18.2.1, and 18.2.3 respectively.

The offences are triable either way with a penalty of a fine or imprisonment (one year if tried summarily and four years on indictment). If the suspect is found not guilty of the aggravated offence at court, he/she can still be found guilty of one of the relevant basic possession offences (s 10 of the Prevention of Crime Act 1953 and s 12 of the CJA 1988).

18.2.6 Possession of a weapon in a private place

The offences we have discussed so far relate to the possession of weapons in public places or schools. For similar incidents on private property (eg inside a dwelling) s 64 of the Offences Against the Person Act 1861 could be considered. For this, it is an offence to possess, make, or manufacture any item with intent to commit, or enable any other person to commit, any other offence within the Act. The items include explosive substances, machines, and 'any other dangerous or noxious thing'. The penalty is imprisonment for up to two years.

18.2.7 Manufacture, import, sale or hire etc of offensive weapons

For certain types of weapon, it is an offence for a person to manufacture, sell, or hire such an item. This includes offering such an item for sale or hire, or exposing it or possessing it for the purpose of selling, hiring, lending, or giving it to another person.

If the weapon in question is a 'specified weapon' (see 18.2.1), the offence is committed under s 141 of the Criminal Justice Act 1988. For a 'flick knife' or a 'gravity knife' the offence is committed under s 1 of the Restriction of Offensive Weapons Act 1959 (A flick knife opens automatically by hand pressure, and a gravity knife opens by the force of gravity or by centrifugal force.)

These are both summary offences, with a penalty of six months' imprisonment and/or a fine.

18.2.7.1 Selling bladed or pointed items to young people

Selling a knife, a knife blade, a razor blade, or an axe to a young person under 18 is an offence (s 141A(1) of the Criminal Justice Act 1988). This offence also applies for any other bladed or sharply pointed article which is made or adapted for causing injury to a person. The offence is triable summarily with a penalty of six months' imprisonment and/or a fine.

18.2.8 Arranging the minding of a dangerous weapon

It is an offence to make arrangements for another person to look after, hide, or transport a 'dangerous weapon' to help make it available for an unlawful purpose (s 28 of the Violent Crime Reduction Act 2006). These weapons include those in the table in 18.2.1, the sharp and bladed articles referred to in 18.2.7.1, and firearms (excluding air weapons).

The arrangements must help make the weapon available for the offender to use at a particular time and place, and possession of the weapon must either constitute an offence in itself, or be likely to lead to the commission of an offence. The 'minder' would not be committing a s 28 offence, but might be committing a weapons possession offence (see other parts of this chapter). The s 28 offence is triable either way.

> **TASK 2** Ahmed, a 17–year–old at a local FE College carries a knife 'for his own personal protection'. He is under threat from others at the college and has good grounds to fear for his safety. Putting aside any discussion of whether Ahmed has a reasonable excuse: what factors should be taken into account when deciding what action (if any) to take?

18.3 Firearms

Any police officer could find him/herself unexpectedly at the scene of a firearms incident, or may come across a firearm during a premises search. Officers may also be called to investigate incidents where air weapons have been used, or to establish where there is doubt that a firearm is legally owned. For these reasons it is important for all police officers to have a basic knowledge of firearms, particularly with regard to safety.

The injuries caused by firearms are almost always catastrophic and frequently fatal. Therefore, when handling or being in the vicinity of firearms remember that:

- all bullet wounds are serious—the movies do not necessarily reflect reality, so anyone who has suffered such an injury must receive professional medical care as soon as possible;
- the entry wound is usually small and the exit wound is often much larger;
- when a bullet enters flesh it causes a large temporary cavity, which collapses to form a smaller permanent cavity where hot gases will have burned internal structures, and infection will be a major risk;
- body armour struck by a bullet can cause blunt trauma injuries such as broken bones, internal bleeding, and organ damage.

When a firearm is found at an incident there are particular procedures to be followed, as described in 11.2.6.2. The forensic aspects of firearms are covered in 26.5.7. The most important consideration is safety; the safety of the evidence but more importantly the physical safety of anyone who will come into contact with the firearm.

The types of firearms most commonly used by criminals are shown in the table.

Type of firearm	Number encountered by the police in 2018/19 (and where available, percentage change in brackets)
Air weapons	3,203
Handgun	2,733 (–3%)
Imitation	1467 (+2%)
Unidentified	1,060 (+18%)
Shotgun	677 (+7%)
Other	748 (+33%)
Rifle	49 (–50%)

Data derived from ONS, 2019j, apart from air weapons data which is from House of Commons Briefing paper SN03641.

18.3.1 Definition of a firearm

Section 57(1) of the Firearms Act 1968 provides a definition of a firearm as shown in the flowchart.

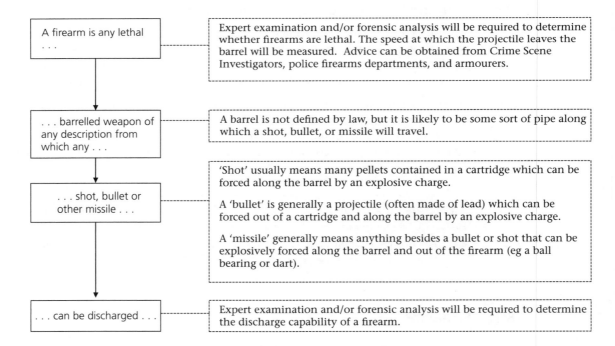

There are many different types of firearm such as revolvers, pistols, and rifles. Firearms are loosely grouped into four categories under the Act: 'Section 1 firearms' (covered under s 1 of the Firearms Act 1968), shotguns, air weapons, and prohibited weapons. The legislation relating to imitation firearms was significantly changed in the Violent Crime Reduction Act 2006, see 18.7 in particular.

Specific Incidents

18.3.1.1 The parts of a firearm

A firearm consists of 'component parts' which are essential for it to work (such as the trigger mechanism and the firing pin), and 'additions' such as magazines, sights, torches, trigger guards, grips, sound moderators, and flash eliminators (also known as accessories). The component parts are all vital to the functioning of a firearm and are therefore legally controlled, so that they cannot be acquired separately and then assembled to make an uncertificated firearm (see 18.3.2).

The photograph shows a self–loading pistol (SLP) with the main parts of a firearm identified. Note that this particular SLP would be classed as a prohibited weapon due to its short barrel (see 18.8).

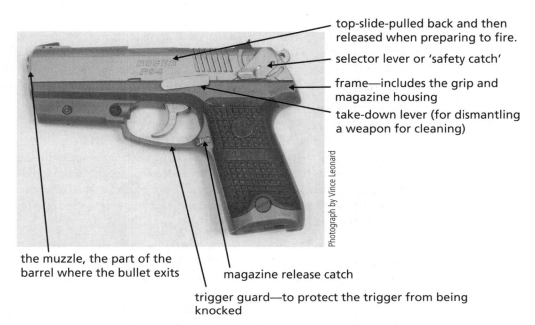

top-slide-pulled back and then released when preparing to fire.

selector lever or 'safety catch'

frame—includes the grip and magazine housing

take-down lever (for dismantling a weapon for cleaning)

Photograph by Vince Leonard

the muzzle, the part of the barrel where the bullet exits

magazine release catch

trigger guard—to protect the trigger from being knocked

The ammunition is stored in a 'magazine', which is located in the frame. Pulling and releasing the top–slide moves a round of ammunition from the magazine into the breech end of the barrel, and also 'cocks' the action. The safety catch prevents the weapon from firing unless it is in the 'fire' position.

The second photograph shows another SLP (also a prohibited weapon, see 18.8), which has been partly disassembled to reveal some of the internal mechanism.

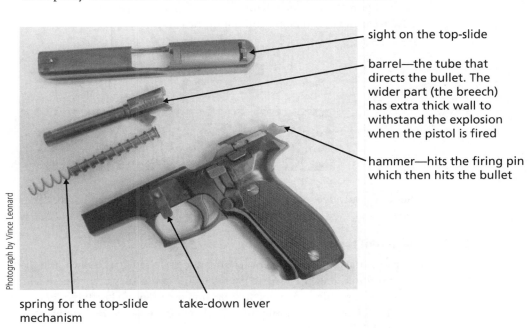

sight on the top-slide

barrel—the tube that directs the bullet. The wider part (the breech) has extra thick wall to withstand the explosion when the pistol is fired

hammer—hits the firing pin which then hits the bullet

Photograph by Vince Leonard

spring for the top-slide mechanism

take-down lever

Pulling the trigger fires the weapon—the propellant powder ignites and produces hot gases that force the bullet down the barrel. It also pushes the top–slide backwards which releases the empty cartridge case. The mechanism is 'self–loading' in that it also feeds the next round of ammunition from the magazine into the breech end of the barrel. The trigger can then be pulled again to fire another round, and the whole process can be repeated until the magazine is empty. (This is different from an 'automatic firearm' for which simply maintaining pressure on the trigger will cause it to fire repeatedly.)

The barrel of a firearm can be smooth or rifled. Smooth–bore weapons enable the easy passage of shot, and although normally associated with lead shot (as used in sport shooting) these weapons can also fire a single or several larger lead 'slugs'. Generally, smooth–bore weapons have a limited range, are less accurate than rifled firearms, and produce a spread of shot. They are often used to commit crimes, partly due to their greater availability to criminals but also because the spread of shot means that accuracy is not required. Rifled–bore weapons are a more recent development, with the inside of the barrel being grooved (rifled) in a helical pattern. There are between two and 16 curved grooves which cause the bullet to spin. This imparts stability to the round, and increases both firing accuracy and range.

Calibre is the measurement of the diameter of the barrel. In rifled weapons the calibre is normally expressed in metric or imperial figures (eg 7.62 mm, 9 mm, .38 inch, .357 inch). For smooth–bore weapons the calibre is not stated as the diameter of the barrel because it was difficult for engineers in the past to make such accurate measurements. Instead, the calibre is stated in terms of the mass of the largest lead sphere that would just fit into the barrel, the mass being stated as a fraction of a pound. For example, the barrel of a 12–bore (UK) or 12–gauge (US) weapon would just accommodate a lead ball that weighs one–twelfth of a pound (approximately 37 g).

Sound moderators (also known as 'silencers') are designed to reduce the noise or flash of a firearm. A flash eliminator reduces the flash from the round exiting the barrel and thereby aids the firer's vision (especially when firing in low light). Detachable sound moderators are generally subject to certificate control, but integral sound moderators, and those for air weapons are not. It will be for a court to decide whether a particular sound moderator or flash eliminator could be used with the firearm in question, and whether the suspect had it for that purpose.

18.3.1.2 Ammunition

A conventional round of modern ammunition for a handgun, rifle, or carbine consists of a cartridge and a bullet.

The base of the cartridge has a 'primer' which will ignite when struck by the firing pin. This sends a flame through a 'flash–hole' to the main body of the cartridge, which ignites the propellant powder. The propellant burns and creates expanding gases which force the bullet out of the cartridge, and along and out of the barrel.

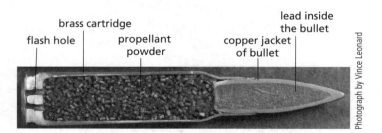

Shotgun cartridges work on the same basic principle, but the outer covering is plastic or cardboard, and they contain a number of shot rather than a single bullet (see 18.5).

18.3.1.3 Different types of firearm

Firearms have many different features such as the barrel length, the loading mechanism for ammunition, and the kinetic energy of the projectiles fired. These features affect how dangerous a particular weapon could be, and are used in classifying firearms under the Firearms Act 1968 (see 18.5 on shotguns, 18.6.1 on air weapons, 18.7 on imitation firearms, and 18.8 on prohibited weapons).

Firearms can also be classed in terms of their design, for example:

- a revolver is a hand–held firearm with a cylinder that revolves as it is fired, to align a new round of ammunition with the breech of the weapon. There are usually spaces for six rounds, hence the 'six gun' of the American cowboy. A revolver with a short barrel would be a prohibited weapon (see 18.8 for a photograph of such a weapon);
- a pistol is a hand–held firearm, often fed by a removable magazine (see 18.3.1.1). A pistol with a short or rifled barrel will be a prohibited weapon, as would any self–loading pistol (often mistakenly referred to as an 'automatic' pistol (see 18.3.1.1));
- a rifle has a long rifled barrel, and is designed to be an intrinsically accurate long–distance weapon (many have a large sight mounted on the top). The ammunition is usually fed from a magazine but each round has to be manually fed into the breech by operating a 'bolt'.

Some types of firearm can fire in automatic mode, ie pulling and holding the trigger will cause a continuous discharge of rounds until the magazine is empty; all such weapons are classified as prohibited under the Firearms Act 1968. Other features that could cause a weapon to be classed as a prohibited firearm are listed in the table in 18.8.

18.3.2 Firearms certificates

A certificate is needed for s 1 firearms, shotguns, some types of ammunition, and any component parts of a firearm (see 18.3.1.1). Other categories of firearm such as air weapons (in England and Wales) and some imitation firearms do not require certificates. It is an offence to have a s 1 firearm or a shotgun without the requisite certificate (see 18.4.2 and 18.5.1, respectively).

A police officer has the power to demand the production of a firearm certificate from any person whom he/she believes to be in possession of any firearm(s) or ammunition requiring a firearms certificate (s 48(1) of the Firearms Act 1968). The interpretation of the term 'demand' varies between forces; for some it means the certificate should be produced on the spot, while in others it could be produced at some specified time in the future. A police officer can also require such a person to give his/her name and address.

If the person does not produce the certificate and permit a police officer to read it (or otherwise show that he/she is entitled to have the items in his/her possession), then the firearm or ammunition may be seized and retained (s 48(2)).

18.3.3 Other offences relating to possession of firearms

Apart from not having the relevant certificate for a firearm (see 18.3.2), there are other offences related to possession of a firearm. For example, under s 19 of the Firearms Act 1968, it is an offence to have certain types of firearm and ammunition in a public place, without lawful authority or reasonable excuse (see 18.2.2.1 on excuses). This applies to loaded shotguns, air weapons (loaded or not), any s 1 firearm (loaded or not), prohibited weapons (loaded or not), imitation firearms, and ammunition suitable for use in a s 1 firearm. So, if a young man was carrying an unloaded air weapon in a sports bag in the street on his way to his sister's house to show it to her, he would have to be able to prove he was old enough to possess the weapon and had a reasonable excuse (ie he was taking it to show her). This offence is triable either way, except for air weapons where the offence is triable summarily. The penalty is six months' imprisonment and/or a fine.

Possessing a firearm with the intention that a person (any person) will cause any other person to fear that violence will be used is also an offence (s 16A of the Firearms Act 1968). This offence can be committed in a public or a private place; for example by a farmer brandishing a shotgun and shouting 'Get off my land!' at a rambler, causing her to fear she will be shot. The offence is triable on indictment only and the penalty is ten years' imprisonment and/or a fine.

It is also an offence to be in possession of a firearm or an imitation firearm at the time of arrest, for example if a man is arrested for shoplifting and is found to have a firearm in his pocket (s 17(2)).

Specific Incidents

18.3.4 Requesting a person to hand over a firearm or ammunition

Health and safety always come first. Health and safety in relation to firearms found at crime scenes is covered in 11.2.6.2.

A police officer can require any person to hand over a firearm (and/or ammunition) for examination (s 47(1) of the Firearms Act 1968). The officer must have reasonable cause to suspect that the person is in possession of a firearm (with or without ammunition) in a public place, or is committing or is about to commit a 'relevant offence'. Here, a relevant offence would include other offences from the Firearms Act 1968, such as carrying a firearm with criminal intent (s 18), trespassing in a building with a firearm (s 20(1)), or trespassing on land with a firearm (s 20(2)). It is a summary offence to fail to hand over a firearm or ammunition when required to do so (s 47(2)), and the penalty is three months' imprisonment and/or a fine.

18.3.5 The power to stop and search for firearms

This is provided by s 47 of the Firearms Act 1968 (s 47(3) for a person, and s 47(4) for a vehicle). It applies if a firearms offence has been committed or is about to be committed. A power of entry (s 47(5)) is available to search for firearms. For such a search, s 2 of the PACE Act 1984 and the associated Codes of Practice must be followed (see 9.4.1), and as ever, health and safety comes first.

18.3.6 Young people and access to firearms

For all types of firearms (including imitations and ammunition) it is a summary offence under the Firearms Act 1968 to sell or hire such an item to a person under 18 (s 24(1)), and for a young person under 18 to purchase such an item (s 22(1)). It is also an offence to give, lend, or otherwise part with a s 1 firearm or ammunition to a person under 14 (s 24(2)). A defence is available for the s 24 offences if it can be shown that there were reasonable grounds to believe the young person was older than the relevant age limit (s 24(5)).

Other legislation applies to specific types of firearms and this is covered where the various categories of firearm are described separately.

18.3.7 Trading in firearms

Any person who trades or carries out any business with firearms (including air weapons) without being registered as a firearms dealer commits an offence (s 3(1) of the Firearms Act 1968). This includes manufacturing, selling, exposing for sale, repairing, and testing firearms. These offences are triable either way, and the penalty is six months' imprisonment and/or a fine if tried summarily, and five years' imprisonment on indictment.

18.4 Section 1 Firearms

Section 1 firearms are defined in s 1 of the Firearms Act 1968. They include any firearm that is not a shotgun, a legal air weapon, a prohibited weapon, or an imitation firearm. (A 'sawn–off' shotgun, however (see 18.5), is classed as a s 1 firearm.)

The photograph shows a rifle that would be classed as a s 1 firearm.

Photograph by Nathan van der Nest

18.4.1   Legislation relating to s 1 Firearms

It is an offence to have a s 1 firearm without the appropriate certificate (s 1), as shown in the flowchart.

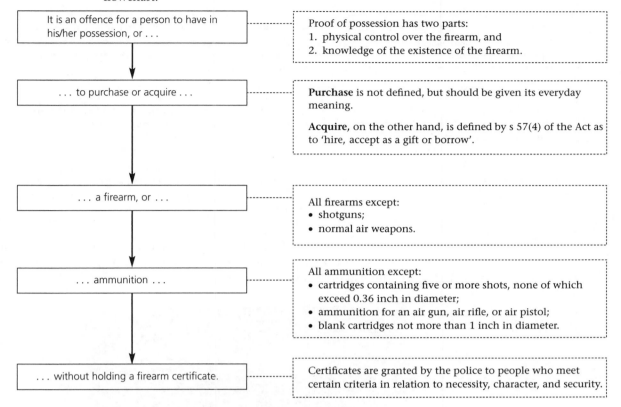

This offence is triable either way and the penalty is a fine or imprisonment (six months if tried summarily, but if on indictment five years, and seven for a 'sawn–off' shotgun).

In some circumstances a s 1 firearm might not require a certificate. This may apply for handguns for killing animals, and for antique firearms (although criminals have been known to take advantage of this possible loophole by legally acquiring antique firearms and ammunition to carry out street shootings and robberies). Members of rifle and pistol clubs and visiting overseas forces are also excluded from the requirement to hold a firearms certificate.

The age restrictions for s 1 firearms are shown in the table. Note that a person of any age can carry a s 1 firearm for a person over 18 during a sporting activity.

The person may	Under 14	Age 14+	Age 15+	Age 17+	Age 18+
Hold a firearm certificate	*	✔	✔	✔	✔
Carry a firearm for a person over 18 during a sporting activity	✔	✔	✔	✔	✔
Receive a s 1 firearm as a gift	–	✔	✔	✔	✔
Purchase or hire a s 1 firearm	–	–	–	–	✔

* A parent can be granted a certificate (or have an existing certificate varied) that includes a child under 14, if for example the child is to participate in competitive target shooting.

18.5   Shotguns

The definition of a shotgun is provided in s 1(3)(a) of the Firearms Act 1968 , as shown in the flowchart.

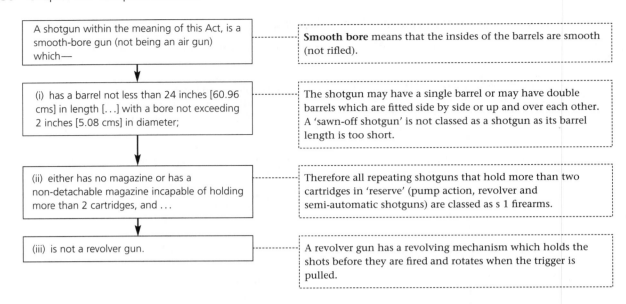

A shotgun within the meaning of this Act, is a smooth-bore gun (not being an air gun) which—	**Smooth bore** means that the insides of the barrels are smooth (not rifled).
(i) has a barrel not less than 24 inches [60.96 cms] in length [...] with a bore not exceeding 2 inches [5.08 cms] in diameter;	The shotgun may have a single barrel or may have double barrels which are fitted side by side or up and over each other. A 'sawn-off shotgun' is not classed as a shotgun as its barrel length is too short.
(ii) either has no magazine or has a non-detachable magazine incapable of holding more than 2 cartridges, and ...	Therefore all repeating shotguns that hold more than two cartridges in 'reserve' (pump action, revolver and semi-automatic shotguns) are classed as s 1 firearms.
(iii) is not a revolver gun.	A revolver gun has a revolving mechanism which holds the shots before they are fired and rotates when the trigger is pulled.

A typical shotgun cartridge consists of a plastic or cardboard tube containing shot and protective wadding, with a brass battery cup at the base containing the primer. The photograph shows a cartridge with part of the casing cut away.

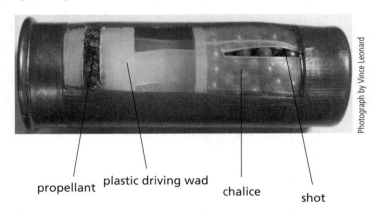

Photograph by Vince Leonard

propellant plastic driving wad chalice shot

The propellant is contained in the cartridge directly adjacent to the primer, and separated from the shot by a 'driving wad', a circular piece of plastic or compressed fibrous material. In modern shotgun ammunition, this wad is usually integral to a 'chalice' which holds the shot. When the shotgun is fired the propellant ignites and forces all the shot and wadding out through the barrel. The wadding prevents the shot from being deformed when the weapon is fired (non–spherical shot would tend to stray from the intended path). Shotgun and cartridge forensics are covered in 26.5.6.

There are different designs of shotguns, with different loading systems. The most commonly owned and used type of shotgun is double barrelled (side–by–side or over–and–under) and has no magazine. The double barrel allows for two shots before reloading is required. The cartridges are individually loaded into each barrel by 'breaking' the weapon to allow access to the rear part of the barrel.

Pump–action shotguns have a single barrel and a magazine for cartridges. After firing, the empty cartridge is extracted by sliding the fore–end backwards, and the next one loaded by sliding it forwards. Such a weapon is classed as 'prohibited', see 18.8.

Photograph by Vince Leonard

magazine

'fore-end' that 'pumps' the cartridges into the breech end of the barrel

A self–loading shotgun (often referred to as a semi–automatic) has a magazine from which the cartridges are loaded into the breech and then discharged (in a similar manner to a self–loading pistol). The loading and ejection mechanism is operated by the gas created when a cartridge is discharged. This allows the weapon to be fired as fast as the trigger can be pulled. Such a weapon is classed as 'prohibited', see 18.8.

18.5.1 Shotgun certificates and age restrictions

A shotgun certificate (also referred to as a 'licence') is granted by the chief police officer of the force area where the applicant lives. Shotguns are frequently used for sporting purposes (eg clay pigeon shooting) and for shooting game, and unless there is a specific reason to refuse an application it will normally be granted, in marked contrast to the issue of certificates for s 1 firearms. Possessing, purchasing, or acquiring a shotgun without holding the relevant certificate is an either–way offence under s 2(1) of the Firearms Act 1968. The penalty is a fine or imprisonment (six months if tried summarily and five years on indictment).

A number of conditions are placed upon the holder of a shotgun certificate, for example that shotgun(s) will be kept secure when not in use (eg in a specially designed steel gun cabinet). It is a summary offence for a person to fail to comply with a condition relating to a shotgun certificate (s 2(2)), and the penalty is six months' imprisonment and/or a fine.

In certain circumstances a person may 'have' a shotgun without a shotgun certificate, such as when borrowing a shotgun from a person who holds a certificate, and then using it on that person's land in his/her presence. Nor is a certificate required for possession of shotgun cartridges with many small pellets (ie five or more shot pellets in a cartridge with pellets not more than 0.36 inches in diameter).

The age restrictions specifically for shotguns are shown in the table. Note that there is no age limit to having a shotgun certificate, and that any person of any age can have an assembled shotgun in his/her possession if supervised by a person aged at least 21 years with a certificate.

The age restrictions that apply for firearms in general are covered in 18.3.6.

The person may	Under 14	Age 14+	Age 15+	Age 17+	Age 18+
Hold a shotgun certificate	✔	✔	✔	✔	✔
Possess an assembled shotgun if supervised by a person aged 21 or over with a certificate	✔	✔	✔	✔	✔
Receive a shotgun as a gift	–	–	✔	✔	✔
Have an uncovered/unsecured shotgun	–	–	✔	✔	✔
Purchase or hire a shotgun	–	–	–	–	✔

It is an offence to gift a shotgun or ammunition to a young person under 15 (s 24(3)). A defence is available if it can be shown that there were reasonable grounds to believe the young person was 15 or over (s 24(5)).

> **TASK 3**
>
> 1. Describe the general characteristics of a firearm.
> 2. What are the powers to demand production of certificates?
> 3. Under what circumstances can a person be required to hand over a firearm or ammunition for examination?
> 4. What types of firearms are covered by s 1, and so require a s 1 certificate?
> 5. What ammunition is covered by s 1 and therefore requires a s 1 certificate?
> 6. Describe the specifications of a shotgun that would be legal in the UK.

18.6 Pellet Firearms

There are various types of firearm that fire small pellets. They are usually less dangerous than other firearms because the pellets are discharged from the barrel relatively slowly and have a relatively small mass. Pellet weapons include air weapons (such as air rifles), BB guns, and airsoft weapons.

Specific Incidents

18.6.1 Air weapons

Air weapons include air pistols, air guns, and air rifles. The velocity of the projectiles is low because the pellets are propelled by a spring or compressed gas or air, rather than by an explosive charge. However, air weapons can still cause serious injury including blindness, and fatalities are not unknown, particularly children—in 2016, a 13–year–old died in Bury St Edmunds after being shot in the neck with an air rifle. Air weapon offences make up more than half of all recorded firearms offences and it is clear they should be taken very seriously.

The photograph shows an air pistol that uses a sliding mechanism to generate the air pressure to 'cock' the spring so it is ready to fire.

Photograph by Vince Leonard

The pressure in an air–weapon can also be generated by folding the barrel into the 'broken' position; this system is used for air rifles, as shown in the photograph.

Photograph by Vince Leonard

There are many different types of design of air weapons, so unless you know how to safely handle firearms you should always ask someone who knows about firearms to assist you in their safe handling and storage.

An air weapon does not require a certificate under s 1 of the Firearms Act 1968 unless it exceeds the authorized kinetic energy. The kinetic energy can be measured by a forensic laboratory.

Any air weapon that uses self–contained gas cartridges (containing compressed gas and a pellet) is automatically classed as a prohibited weapon (see 18.8). For further information see the Firearms (Dangerous Air Weapons) Rules 1969.

18.6.1.1 Age limits for possessing and firing air weapons

The legislation on the specific age limits for air weapons is covered here, and there are a number of associated offences (all triable summarily, with a fine as the penalty). The age restrictions that apply to all firearms (including air weapons) are covered in 18.3.6.

For a person under the age of 18 it is an offence to 'have' with him/her an air weapon or ammunition for an air weapon anywhere and at any time (s 22(4)) unless:

- he/she is a member at an air rifle club and firing at targets; or
- the weapon does not exceed .23 calibre and is being fired at a gallery (s 23(2)).

On private land with the landowner's permission, a young person under 18 years can use (ie fire) an air weapon, but under 14s must be supervised by a person of 21 years or over. It is an offence if the pellets go beyond the premises (eg a house, garden, or other enclosed private place), unless the owner of the adjoining property gave permission (s 23(1) and (1A) and s 21A(1) and (2)).

For other locations, a young person aged 14–17 years can use an air weapon anywhere if supervised by a person aged over 21 (s 23(1)). This includes a public place, provided the young person and supervisor have a lawful authority or reasonable excuse, for example if employed in the authorized and licensed destruction of feral pigeons.

18.6.1.2 Young people and access to air weapons

The legislation described in 18.3.3 helps prevent young people having access to firearms in general, including air weapons, but other legislation applies specifically to air weapons. Subject to the exemptions for supervisors of young people outlined in 18.6.1.1, it is an offence:

- to make a gift or to otherwise part with any air weapon or ammunition to a young person under 18 (s 24(4));
- for a person in possession of an air weapon to fail to take reasonable precautions to prevent a young person under 18 from having an air weapon (s 24(ZA)(1)).

A defence is available if it can be shown that there were reasonable grounds to believe the young person was aged 18 or over (s 24(5)). These offences are triable summarily and the penalty is a fine.

TASK 4

1. A 16–year–old boy has been firing an air rifle from his parents' bedroom window at drinks cans on top of their garden wall and some of the pellets have clearly gone into the neighbour's garden. What offence has the boy committed?
2. A young person is seen carrying an air rifle in a street. Police questioning establishes that she is 17 years old. What offence, if any, has she committed?

18.6.2 BB guns

BB guns fire small round plastic or aluminium balls which resemble ball bearings, hence the term BB guns. They were originally manufactured for recreational target practice and for shooting vermin, so they have some capacity to injure. More recently some BB guns are manufactured to look like real firearms, so may also be 'realistic imitations' (see 18.7.1). Many 'firearms incidents' involve BB guns; a national overview can be found at <http://www.infertrust.org/issues_bb_guns.asp>.

The force to fire the projectiles from a BB gun is derived from a spring, batteries, or from gas in an external aerosol canister. However, if the gun appears to be more powerful than a typical BB gun or has large projectiles, it may need to be assessed by a forensic laboratory because it might be sufficiently powerful to be classified as an air weapon or a 'Section 1 firearm'. Any air weapon with a self–contained cartridge (resembling a bullet and casing, and using gas to propel the projectiles) will be classed as a prohibited weapon (see 18.8).

18.6.3 Airsoft guns

Airsoft guns fire plastic pellets or marking projectiles not exceeding 8 mm diameter, and are generally less powerful than BB guns or standard air weapons (see s 57A(2) of the Firearms Act 1968 (as amended by the Policing and Crime Act 2017) for a fuller definition). They are generally used in leisure activities, for example 'skirmishing' competitions between individuals or teams, and historical re–enactments. The UK Airsoft Retailers Association (UKARA) holds a database of registered skirmishers.

Some airsoft weapons appear identical to real firearms, as shown in the photograph, and are therefore classed as 'realistic imitation firearms' (see 18.7.1 for further details).

Photograph by Vince Leonard

Other airsoft weapons are brightly coloured so they do not resemble real firearms (see 18.7.2 on imitation firearms). The restrictions on the sale of airsoft weapons depend on whether the weapon is classed as an imitation or a realistic imitation, see 18.7 for further details.

18.7 Imitation Firearms and Blank–firers

Police officers are likely to encounter objects which resemble firearms (such as some 'airsoft' guns, see 18.6.3), and these imitations can cause considerable fear and alarm. If they can fire lethal projectiles (ie over a certain power limit), such firearms will not be regarded as imitations and will be subject to the Firearms Act 1968 (see 18.3), and all the relevant legislation will apply, for example any requirements for certificates or licences.

The terms 'replica firearm', 'imitation firearm', and 'realistic imitation firearm' can appear to mean the same thing, but there are important differences. We cover the key points here, but the full details are provided in the Violent Crime Reduction Act 2006 (VCRA). Note that imitating possession of a firearm by putting a hand with extended fingers inside clothing to look like a gun does not amount to possession of an imitation (*R v Bentham* [2005] UKHL 18).

The sale of all imitation firearms is restricted to adults (aged 18 or over), and additional restrictions apply for realistic imitations (see 18.7.1.1).

18.7.1 Realistic imitation firearms

Any item that looks like a modern real firearm (same size and colour) but does not meet the definition of a firearm under the Firearms Act 1968 (see 18.3.1) is now classed as a realistic imitation firearm (s 36 of the VCRA). Realistic imitation firearms (RIFs) do not have to be capable of firing projectiles, although many are (eg see 18.6.3 on 'airsoft guns').

Realistic imitations of the types of firearms made before 1870 are not subject to this legislation, so can still be sold by anyone over the age of 18 years. Prior to 2006, RIFs were known as replica firearms, and could be owned, bought, sold, and imported with very few restrictions. The photograph shows a RIF which is also a cigarette lighter.

Photograph by Vince Leonard

RIFs are easy to mistake for conventional firearms and can cause alarm and distress to others if seen in public places; this can cause significant problems for the police.

18.7.1.1 Restrictions on realistic imitation firearms

The sale of RIFs is restricted to adults (aged 18 or over), and under s 37 of the VCRA the seller must be certain that the purchaser will use the weapon for:

- the purposes of a museum or gallery;
- the purposes of theatrical productions, films, and television programmes;
- historical re–enactments (under regulations set by the Secretary of State);
- duties concerned with service as a Crown servant; or
- skirmishing at a registered site (see 18.6.3 on airsoft weapons);

The carrying of RIFs in a public place is also restricted to the above purposes. In any other circumstances, carrying any imitation firearm in a public place is a summary offence under s 19 of the Firearms Act 1968, and the penalty is a fine or six months' imprisonment.

18.7.2 Imitation firearms (non–realistic)

These imitations do not look like real firearms due to their colour and/or size. The principal colour must be mainly bright red, orange, pink, yellow, green, blue, or purple, or they must be formed from transparent materials (s 38(3) of the VCRA). In terms of size, for an imitation of normal colour (ie dark or metallic) to be classed as a non–realistic, it must be small, ie no more than 38 mm in height or 70 mm in length.

Their use is subject to fewer restrictions than for realistic imitations as they are more clearly identifiable as imitations. However, it is important to note that some 'customized' and fully functional firearms are also manufactured in bright colours and designs, so police officers should carefully examine such an item to determine its true nature. If there is any uncertainty the officer should seize it for examination at a specialist laboratory

18.7.3 Readily convertible imitation firearms

Some imitation firearms (including realistic imitations) can be converted into a functional firearm, of a type requiring a certificate under s 1 of the Firearms Act 1968 (see 18.4.1), or even fall into the category of a prohibited weapon (see 18.8). If the conversion process is simple and does not require special skills or special tools (s 1(6)), the firearm is regarded as being 'readily convertible'. Here, a 'special tool' is a tool which would not generally be used in the home for construction and maintenance, so, for example, if the conversion can be carried out with a normal screwdriver, the weapon would be regarded as readily convertible.

Any object will be regarded as a firearm under s 1(1) and (2) of the Firearms Act 1968 if it:

- has the appearance of a firearm;
- can be readily converted into a weapon from which a shot, bullet, or other missile can be discharged; and
- when converted, would fall under s 1 of the Firearms Act 1968.

Possession of a readily convertible imitation firearm without a certificate is an offence, as it would be regarded as a functioning firearm. Ultimately only a court can decide whether a particular article requires a certificate, and testing at a forensic laboratory would usually be required before commencing any prosecution. There might be a defence if it can be shown that the owner did not know (and had no reason to suspect) that the item was readily convertible (s 1(5) of the Firearms Act 1982). Possession of a tool or article with the intention of using it to convert an imitation firearm into a working firearm is an offence (s 127 of the Policing and Crime Act 2017). It is also an offence to unlawfully supply, or offer to supply, a defectively deactivated weapon to another person in the UK or in a member state of the EU (s 128 of the Policing and Crime Act 2017). This would cover a firearm that could relatively easily be re–activated (eg by re–drilling a blocked barrel).

18.7.4 Blank–firing firearms

A blank–firing firearm is one that cannot discharge a projectile. Blank cartridges contain powder or propellant, but no bullet (the casing is simply 'crimped' where the bullet would be). For a blank–firer to comply with the Violent Crime Reduction Act 2006 and the Firearms

Act 1968, it must discharge gas from the top of the weapon and have a solid, blocked barrel. Blank–firers sold in Europe and the USA are often manufactured to fire out of the muzzle, and are therefore not legal in the UK. In terms of their appearance, blank–firing firearms can be imitation or realistic imitation firearms.

It is legal for an adult (at least 18 years old) to buy, sell, and own a blank–firing imitation or realistic imitation firearm without a certificate. However, these items may not be carried in public and may only be used on private land or property with the landowner's permission. Further details on the buying, selling, and importing of blank–firers are provided in the Violent Crime Reduction Act 2006.

TASK 5

1. Imagine you are a police officer on foot patrol. A store detective stops you in the street and points out a woman who has a firearm in her handbag. What questions could you ask to try and determine the type of firearm, and what could you do next?
2. A motorist stops you to say he has just seen a man down a side lane with a long gun. What questions could you ask to try and find out more about the type of firearm, and what would you do next?

18.8 Prohibited Weapons

Parliament decided that the general public have no reasonable need to possess certain types of potentially highly dangerous weapon such as many types of handgun, machine guns, PAVA (an incapacitating pepper spray), or CS spray.

Images courtesy of Kent Police

The two canisters on the left are examples of CS Spray and those on the right, pepper spray. All are examples of s 5 prohibited weapons.

Under s 5 of the Firearms Act 1968, it is an offence to possess or make such items without special authority. The table shows some features which cause a weapon to fall into the prohibited category, along with some examples. There are some exceptions to these prohibitions (ie such firearms would not be prohibited), as shown in the final column of the table (information derived from the CPS website).

Prohibited feature	Example of a prohibited firearm	Permitted exceptions
Short barrel (less than 30 cm) or short overall (less than 60 cm)	short handguns and short revolvers or designed as signalling apparatus	any air weapon, muzzle–loading gun
Can discharge a noxious substance (liquid, gas, or other thing)	stun guns (including a 'Taser') and aerosol incapacitant sprays	
Two or more missiles can be successively discharged without repeated pressure on the trigger	any machine gun	
Self–loading or pump–action with a rifled barrel	short–barrelled rifles	if chambered for .22 inch rim–fire cartridges

Specific Incidents

Prohibited feature	Example of a prohibited firearm	Permitted exceptions
Self–loading or pump–action with a short smooth–bore barrel (barrel less than 24 inches, or overall length less than 40 inches)	short self–loading shotguns	if it is an air weapon, or is chambered for .22 inch rim–fire cartridges
Smooth–bore revolver gun	'Dragon'	if it is either a muzzle–loading gun, or is designed for 9 mm rim–fire cartridges
Can project a stabilized missile	rocket launcher	if designed for line–throwing, pyrotechnics, or as signalling apparatus
Has a self–contained gas cartridge system	Brococks	
Ammunition designed to explode on or just before impact, or containing a noxious substance		
Any firearm disguised as another object	pen guns, key fob guns, and phone guns	

This revolver is a prohibited weapon as its barrel is less than 30 cm in length.

The rifle shown in the second photograph is a prohibited weapon because it can be converted (using the 'change lever') to automatic mode, so it can discharge two or more rounds successively (see 18.3.3).

The third photograph shows a carbine, a type of rifle with a short barrel. It is a prohibited weapon due to the barrel (the barrel is rifled, shorter than 30 cm, and the calibre is more than .22 inch).

Specific Incidents

It is an offence to possess, purchase, acquire, manufacture, sell, or transfer a prohibited weapon or ammunition (s 5(1) of the Firearms Act 1968) without written authority from the Defence Council (the Secretary of State for Defence, other MoD ministers, the Chiefs of Staff, and senior civil servants). This offence is triable either way and the penalty is a fine or imprisonment (six months if tried summarily and ten years on indictment).

18.8.1 Police use of prohibited weapons

Tasers are in widespread use by police forces across the UK, and most taser–trained officers are not firearms officers (see 5.10). Tasers are a conducted energy device (CED) and classed as a prohibited weapon. The cartridge is fired from the main part of the weapon but remains attached by fine wires that conduct electricity, so delivering a series of electrical shocks to the target. This interferes with the body's neuromuscular system and causes acute pain. The only Home Office approved devices at the time of writing are the Taser X2 (at the top, with its cartridge on the right) and the Taser X26e (marked X26, with its cartridge on the left) below.

Photograph by Vince Leonard

These 'less–lethal' weapons bridge the gap between a baton and a firearm, and are designed to temporarily incapacitate a person rather than be lethal. However, the use of such weapons can have fatal consequences, for example if the subject was soaked in flammable liquids or was fitted with a pace–maker. Most injuries caused will be due to the way in which the person falls, especially if the head impacts with a solid surface. A full explanation of the rules and procedures governing the issue and use of these devices can be found on the College of Policing website.

TASK 6 Sixteen pupils and one teacher were killed in a firearms incident at Dunblane in Scotland in 1996. Consider the report by the Hon Lord Cullen *The Public Inquiry into the Shootings at Dunblane Primary School on 13 March 1996*, and the subsequent Firearms (Amendment) Act 1997 and the Firearms (Amendment) (No 2) Act 1997. What changes were introduced by this legislation, and why was this thought to be necessary?

18.9 Answers to Tasks

TASK 1 You probably considered the following:

1. Does the driver have a reasonable excuse for the presence of the items? (eg the items could be antiques and part of a collection, or they could be props for use in theatrical productions or historical reenactments.
2. Who do the items belong to?

3. Has an offence been committed?
4. If an offence has been committed, can the person be arrested?
5. You could explain the law, including how a display of such weapons could be misinterpreted and cause fear and alarm.

TASK 2 You probably considered the following:

1. Is Ahmed above the age of criminal responsibility?
2. What type of knife is it?
3. Has it been made, adapted, or intended to cause injury?
4. For how long has Ahmed been carrying the knife?
5. Will he hand it over?

TASK 3

1. Any lethal barrelled weapon of any description from which any shot, bullet, or other missile can be discharged. This includes a prohibited weapon (lethal or not), any component part of a lethal or prohibited weapon, and any accessory designed or adapted to diminish the noise or flash caused by firing any such weapon.
2. A police officer may demand the production of the relevant certificate from any person whom he/she believes to be in possession of a s 1 firearm (or ammunition) or a shotgun.
3. When a police officer has reasonable cause to suspect a person of having a firearm in a public place (with or without ammunition), or to be committing (or be about to commit) an offence relevant to the Firearms Act 1968, anywhere other than in a public place.
4. All firearms except shotguns, prohibited weapons, air weapons (unless 'especially dangerous'), or imitation firearms (unless converted).
5. Any ammunition for a firearm except:
   - cartridges containing five or more shot, none of which exceeds .36 inch in diameter;
   - ammunition for an air gun, air rifle, or air pistol; and
   - blank cartridges with 1 inch maximum diameter.
6. The shotgun must have a smooth bore and the barrel must be at least 60.96 cm long and no more than 5.08 cm in diameter. It must not be a revolver gun, and must have either no magazine, or a non–detachable magazine that can hold only one or two cartridges.

TASK 4

1. It is generally an offence for a person under the age of 18 to have an air weapon (or ammunition for an air weapon), but there are exceptions. For example, it is not an offence for a person aged 14 years or over to possess the air weapon on private premises with the consent of the occupier, and he/she does not have to be supervised. However, it is an offence to use an air weapon to fire a missile beyond those premises (s 21A of the Firearms Act 1968).
2. A person commits an offence if, without lawful authority or reasonable excuse, he/she has with him/her in a public place any loaded or unloaded air weapon (s 19 of the Firearms Act 1968).

TASK 5

1. The questions could include colour, size, shape, and if there were any distinguishing features such as sights, magazine, and whether the grips were wood or plastic. The actions could include consideration of powers, consideration of offences once the firearm is identified, safe handling and firearms safety rules, safety of the public and self. It would seem safe to approach the woman, as the 'alleged' firearm is in her handbag and not in her hand. It is, however, readily accessible so the approach should not be rash. If, based on the available information, the officer fears for his/her own safety or that of the public, then armed support should be summoned.
2. Questions could include whether there was more than one barrel, whether the weapon was 'broken', whether the weapon had a telescopic sight, whether the weapon had a bolt, whether the witness saw a magazine, and whether the man he saw appeared to be alone. Actions could include consideration of whether there had been other such reports, whether the man might be part of a shooting syndicate or a farmer shooting on his own land, or whether the man might be poaching. Considerations could include whether the road was a public place, whether the man had the appropriate documentation, what powers exist to seize the weapon, and consideration of any offences as well as safe handling, firearms safety rules, and requesting armed support.

TASK 6 The private ownership of handguns was completely banned. Handgun ownership had been increasing in the 1990s with, generally, the fast–growing sport of 'combat' shooting the only legitimate reason for owning a handgun. Cullen recommended a cautious approach, for example storing firearms at clubs and/or police stations, and although this was considered to be unworkable by shooters, the restrictions had public backing. The 'Snowdrop' campaign (so called because snowdrops bloom in March) called for a complete ban on the private ownership of handguns, and gathered around 750,000 signatures. This put the government under significant political pressure, and the new restrictions were introduced. The first new Act banned the 'higher' calibre handguns, classing them as prohibited weapons, and the second new Act added .22 calibre firearms to the prohibited list.

These changes introduced some of the world's toughest gun control laws, and halted the spread of legal activities with handguns. There were, however, some unintended consequences; a new market for realistic imitation firearms (see 18.7.1) developed, along with new criminal supply routes and an upsurge in the re–activation of de–activated firearms.

The 2015 HMIC report *Targeting the Risk* recommended tough new licensing conditions for the owners of shotguns and other firearms, including improving the process of checking applicants' medical fitness to own such weapons. These recommendations were enacted in the Policing and Crime Act 2017.

19.1	Introduction	441	19.8	Offences Relating to	
19.2	Definitions for Vehicles,			Standards of Driving	484
	Roads, and Driving	442	19.9	Drink- and Drug-driving	489
19.3	Vehicle and Driver Documents	448	19.10	Using Vehicles to Cause Alarm,	
19.4	Stopping a Vehicle and			Distress, and Annoyance	500
	Examining Documents	459	19.11	Other Offences Relating to	
19.5	Construction and Use			Vehicles and Highways	500
	of Vehicles	462	19.12	Methods of Disposal for	
19.6	Pedestrian Crossings and			Motoring Offences	503
	Road Signs	475	19.13	*Answers to Tasks*	509
19.7	Road Traffic Collisions	478			

19.1 Introduction

Trainee police officers will be expected to demonstrate competence in many areas of road traffic policing during Supervised and Independent Patrol. This chapter covers the terms commonly used in the legislation, the offences related to circumstance and manner of driving, collisions (the preferred term for accidents), and drink- and drug-driving. It also covers non-driving highways offences such as wilful obstruction and the use of fireworks near highways.

Much of the legislation and regulation surrounds safety and the protection of road users, with pedestrians, motorcyclists, and cyclists being particularly vulnerable (Department for Transport, 2019c). There were 1,782 road traffic deaths and 25,484 serious injuries on the roads of Great Britain in 2018 (Department for Transport, 2019c). Road transport collisions are a common cause of death in the 5–19 years and the 20–34 years age groups in England and Wales, ranking second and third for males in these age groups respectively, and third and fifth for females in both age groups (ONS, 2019f). We consider the reasons why collisions occur and the trends over recent years in 19.7.

Road death and injury are of course tragedies for the individuals concerned, as there are often long-term physical and psychological consequences, but they also have a significant financial cost to society as a whole, with estimates for 2018 amounting to around £1.96 million for each fatality (£3.5 billion in total) and £220,000 for each serious injury (£5.6 billion in total) (Department for Transport, 2019a). For some reason there is little public outrage at such high levels of death and injury on the roads compared to homicides and physical assaults (there were 785 homicides over the same period (ONS, 2019h; Scottish Government, 2018)).

Research suggests there is a link between offending on the roads and other forms of criminality. Rose (2000) demonstrated that 79 per cent of disqualified drivers had a criminal record (four times higher than the average for the general population), approximately 50 per cent of dangerous drivers had a previous conviction, and approximately 25 per cent were convicted of an offence within a year (three times the average). Interestingly, drink-drivers were less likely to have a criminal record (40 per cent) than other groups of serious traffic offenders, and 'only' 12 per cent were convicted again within a year. However, these figures are still about twice the average for the general population. Nunn (2018) found that 82 per cent of drug-drivers had previous convictions, of which 82 per cent related to drugs and 53 per cent were for serious motoring offences. Junger *et al* (2001) also identified links between 'risky' traffic behaviour and more general violent crime, and similarly Chenery *et al* (1999) demonstrated in a famous study the links between the relatively minor offence of illegal parking in disabled bays, active criminals, and illegal vehicles. All of this leads us to the notion of 'self-selecting' road and traffic behaviour that police officers could usefully consider as indicators of perhaps more serious criminal predisposition (Roach, 2017).

Specific Incidents

It has been identified that the following crime types are facilitated by the use of the road network: drug smuggling, human trafficking, child exploitation, counterfeit goods, and organized crime groups, as well as many volume crimes such as shoplifting, burglary, and motor vehicle crime (Roach, 2017). The enforcement of road traffic offences and the imposition of penalties will of course deny criminals the use of the roads and hence disrupt their other criminal activities, but the information also provides an invaluable source of up-to-date intelligence on individual criminals. Traffic cameras and automatic number-plate readers allow individuals in vehicles to be tracked across the road network, and this provides additional information that can be used in crime prevention and detection.

The National Police Chiefs' Council roads policing strategy *Policing our Roads Together: A 3 year strategy 2018–2021* aims to reduce the number of collisions leading to road death and serious injury, and to combat organized crime and terrorism through flexible enforcement based upon intelligence, professional judgement, and discretion. Through working with partners, the aim is to provide a visible and technological presence on our roads, and to penalize and educate errant drivers, thereby influencing the behaviour of all road users. Further information is available in the *Roads Policing* section of the College of Policing APP, available online.

'Working in the carriageway' accounts for a significant number of police fatalities and is one of the most dangerous working environments for police officers. The police are governed by the Health and Safety at Work etc Act 1974, and each police service will therefore have risk assessments (see 5.12.3) for this type of work. Trainee constables should be familiar with these assessments and the associated risk mitigation strategies. Working in the carriageway is also governed by the New Roads and Street Works Act 1991 and the Highways Act 1980. These require all individuals (including police officers) to wear suitable high visibility clothing whilst working in the carriageway (and failing to do so may constitute a criminal offence). For roads with a speed limit over 50 mph the jacket must comply with the European Standard EN 471 to class 3 (service-issue high visibility jackets will comply with this).

Trainee police officers will be instructed, shown, and assessed on the police procedures for stopping a vehicle, the actions to be taken when attending the scene of a recent collision, and so on. Where appropriate, we provide some of these details (in 19.4.1, eg on stopping vehicles). Officers should also be guided by local policies and the College of Policing *Road Policing* Authorised Professional Practice, available online.

The topics covered in this chapter contribute to the learning required for the National Policing Curriculum subject areas: 'Roads Policing', 'Understanding the Police Constable Role', and 'Response Policing'.

19.2 Definitions for Vehicles, Roads, and Driving

Road traffic legislation has inevitably developed as times have changed, and new terminology has been introduced to deal with advances in technology. Terms that were valid for the Highways Act 1835 may seem archaic but should be seen in context. It is, however, essential that an officer understands what the terms mean, as they often determine the relevant powers and responsibilities.

19.2.1 Definitions of vehicles

Within road traffic legislation various terms are used to describe the different types of vehicle and other wheeled objects, such as carriages, conveyances, and cycles. The following table explains some of these terms, but is by no means comprehensive.

Vehicle type	Definition	Examples
'Vehicle'	According to the Vehicle Excise and Registration Act 1994, a vehicle is: 'a mechanically propelled vehicle, or anything (whether or not it is a vehicle) that has been, but has ceased to be, a mechanically propelled vehicle' The ordinary dictionary meaning can also be used	Milk float, ride-on grass cutter

Vehicle type	Definition	Examples
'Mechanically propelled vehicle'	'Mechanically propelled' means that the vehicle is powered by a motor (driven by electricity, petrol, diesel, or other fuels). The meaning is not defined by any Act of Parliament, so whether a particular vehicle is a mechanically propelled vehicle is therefore a question of fact for a court to decide	Car, van, lorry, go-ped, quad bike, speedway motorcycles, Formula One racing cars, self-balancing personal transporters (Segways, hoverboards, etc), invalid carriages such as powered wheelchairs and scooters
'Motor vehicle'	This is a mechanically propelled vehicle that is intended or adapted for use on roads (s 185 of the Road Traffic Act 1988)	Car, van, lorry, bus, coach, self-balancing personal transporters (Segways, hoverboards, etc)
'Motor bicycle'*	This means a motor vehicle which has two wheels and a maximum design speed exceeding 45 kph. If powered by an internal combustion engine, the cylinder capacity must exceed 50 cc. It includes a combination, such as a motor vehicle and a side-car (s 108 of the Road Traffic Act 1988)	Motorcycle with two wheels, includes those fitted with a sidecar.
'Bicycle'	This includes a 'motor bicycle' (ie a motorcycle) for the purposes of vehicle excise duty	
'Moped'*	A moped is a motor vehicle with three or fewer wheels and maximum design speed of 50 kph (note this covers electric-powered two-wheelers). If propelled by an engine, the cylinder capacity must not exceed 50 cc (s 108 of the Road Traffic Act 1988). Older models with an engine (first used before 1 August 1977) can also have pedals for propulsion.	
'Pedal cycle'	This must be designed so it can be propelled by pedals, and includes electrically assisted pedal cycles (reg 3 of the Pedal Cycles (Construction and Use) Regulations 1983)	Mountain bike, racing bike, BMX bike
'Carriage'	This means a motor vehicle or trailer (s 191 of the Road Traffic Act 1988). The ordinary dictionary meaning also applies	Any motor vehicle described above, and caravans
'Conveyance'	This is a vehicle constructed or adapted for transporting person(s) by land, water, or air, but not one constructed or adapted for use 'only under the control of a person not carried in or on it' (s 12(7) of the Theft Act 1968)	Motorcycle, bus, boat, and plane

* De-restriction kits are available for mopeds (to allow speeds over 50 kph and/or increase the cylinder capacity), and for 125 cc learner motorcycles, to increase power. If such alterations are made the vehicle becomes a motor bicycle and the rider must conform to the relevant licence requirements (see 19.3.1.3).

Some vehicles do not fit within obvious categories. These include mini-motos (small motorcycles designed for use on private land), scooters with a petrol or electric engine but no seat (eg Go-peds), and self-balancing personal transporters such as Segways and hoverboards. All of these have been held to be motor vehicles (carriages) for the purposes of s 185 of the Road Traffic Act 1988. The Crown Prosecution Service provides advice on their website in the *Definitions of a motor vehicle* section, including references by case stated (ie the relevant case law) regarding mini-motos, Go-peds, and self-balancing personal transporters. Full details of the legal requirements are also given on the CPS website; see also *Coates v CPS* [2011] EWHC 2032 (Admin). In some circumstances, the use of such vehicles may be an offence against the Highways Act 1835 (see 19.11.3).

Commercial vehicles are either passenger-carrying vehicles (PCVs) or goods vehicles. Some are very large, for example 'large goods vehicles' (LGVs, previously known as heavy goods vehicles) and can therefore cause immense damage in a collision. The general construction and use regulations for all vehicles (eg see 19.5.4 on loads) also apply to large commercial vehicles, depending on the number of passenger seats or the vehicle weight. However, additional rules apply for commercial vehicles such as:

- driver licensing and operator licencing (see 19.3.1.4); and
- restrictions on driver hours (see 19.5.5).

Note that a commercial vehicle may on occasions be driven for other purposes (eg a vintage lorry at a motor show, or a minibus transporting people for a charity on a voluntary basis).

Specific Incidents

In such circumstances the regulations for commercial purposes may not apply, but the individual circumstances will need to be ascertained in each case.

19.2.1.1 Vehicle identification features

Vehicles normally have a number of identifying features unique to each vehicle, and these can be easily recalled by using the police mnemonic VICE, as shown in the table.

V	Vehicle identification number (VIN)	VINs on EU-market vehicles have 17 characters in a unique combination of numbers and letters. A few vehicles have non-standard VINs, usually on imported vehicles that were originally sold outside the EU (often right-hand drive vehicles from Japan). The VIN is displayed on the dashboard (visible through the windscreen) on most vehicles.
I	Index number or registration plate	All mechanically propelled vehicles used on public roads require a registration mark (number).
C	Chassis number (same as VIN)	All vehicles used on or after 1 April 1980 will have their 17-character VIN stamped into the chassis or frame of the car. The location is often described in the vehicle handbook.
E	Engine number	Engine numbers are often tucked away in locations most easily seen when (or if) the engine is taken out of the vehicle. Engines are also sometimes replaced, so the fact that an engine number cannot be found should not in itself be a cause for suspicion.

All vehicles in use on or after 1 April 1980 have the VIN on a metal plate attached to a part of the vehicle not normally subject to replacement, and in a conspicuous and accessible position. The VIN will also be stamped on the chassis or frame. The VIN plate will also show the manufacturer, and may also show the type approval number (indicating that the vehicle meets EU standards), and the vehicle weight and axle loadings. The VIN plate shown here displays the vehicle weight information (see 19.5.4), but on many vehicles this will be on a separate plate. For UK registered goods vehicles over 3.5t a separate plating certificate will be issued, see 19.5.4.

(Image © Kevin Lawton-Barrett)

Example of a VIN on the chassis of a VW camper van.

The four weights in this case (from top to bottom) refer to:

- the total weight of the vehicle, including any people or loads;
- the gross train weight (the vehicle and any trailer attached) including any people or loads;
- the weight limit for the front axle (axle 1) (includes the vehicle and anything (including people) being carried); and
- the weight limit for the second axle (axle 2) (includes the vehicle and anything (including people) being carried).

Vehicles with more than two axles will continue the number sequence.

All the identifying features articulated in the VICE mnemonic are recorded on DVLA databases along with the colour, make, and model of the vehicle. Police control-room personnel have access to databases listing the positions of the stamped-in VIN, the VIN plate, and the engine number for all vehicle makes and models.

19.2.2 Roads, highways, and related terms

Legislation relating to road and traffic policing often includes the words 'road', 'highway', and 'public place'. Each term is used in different pieces of legislation, though the term 'road' is used far more frequently, particularly since the introduction of the Road Traffic Act 1988.

- A 'road' is any (length of) highway to which the public has access, and includes bridges over which a road passes (s 192 of the Road Traffic Act 1988). The limits of a road are the hedgerows, walls, fences, or building lines on each side, so a public footpath alongside a road is part of the road.
- A 'highway' (s 5 of the Highways Act 1835) is a road, bridge, carriageway, cart-way, horseway, bridleway, footway, causeway, church way, or pavement.
- A 'public road' is a road maintained at the public's expense (for the purposes of vehicle excise duty legislation), as defined in s 62 of the Vehicle Excise and Registration Act 1994. Note that just because a road is not gated or blocked, it is not necessarily a public road; if in doubt consult the Highways Authority for the area.

Note the potentially confusing overlap between a road and a highway: in practice this does not matter as each relates to individual pieces of legislation.

A number of other terms are also used:

- 'other public place' is a place that any member of the general public has access to, without needing specific permission (see also 9.2.1.1), but it will be for a court to decide. It is likely to include car parks, turning areas, and parks. The term is used in the Road Traffic Act 1988, for example in relation to insurance (s 143(1)(a)), collision reporting (s 170), driving standards (ss 2 and 3), offences surrounding driving-related death (ss 1, 2B, 3ZB, and 3A) and drink or drug drive offences (ss 4, 5, and 5A);
- a carriageway is a 'way' that is marked or arranged in a highway, over which the public have a right of way for the passage of vehicles, but does not include cycle tracks (s 329 of the Highways Act 1980);
- a bridleway is a highway on which the public have a right of way on foot, on horseback, or leading a horse (s 329 of the Highways Act 1980);
- a footpath is a highway that is not adjacent to a road, over which the public have a right of way, but only on foot (s 329 of the Highways Act 1980);
- a footway (such as a pavement) is a highway adjacent to a road, and to which the public have a right of way on foot only (s 329(1) of the Highways Act 1980);
- a street includes roads, lanes, alleys, subways, squares, and any other similar places open to the public. It also includes doorways, entrances to premises, and any ground adjoining a street (*Smith v Hughes* [1960] 2 All ER 859).

The maintenance of a private road is usually the responsibility of the landowner; the road in the photograph is in a good state of repair. Private roads may or may not be subject to public rights of way.

(Photo by Kevin Lawton-Barrett)

19.2.2.1 Road and road network classifications

As well as the legal definition of a road set out in 19.2.2 there are also a number of other terms, such as 'A road' and 'minor road', which are used to describe individual roads and combinations of roads. Many of these will not be used when dealing with offences but are used by police and partner organizations when communicating, and when determining responsibility for, and reporting, collisions. Some of the terms are officially recognized and others used anecdotally; an understanding of them is important when dealing with drivers, witnesses, and other agencies. We provide a summary here but for a full explanation see *Guidance on Road Classification and the Primary Route Network* from the Department for Transport.

The Strategic Road Network (SRN) and the Primary Road Network (PRN) form the network of main roads across the country. The Department for Transport is responsible for defining the SRN and the PRN. The SRN includes all the larger roads (eg motorways) that are used for the national distribution of goods and services, and for public travel across the whole country. The roads that form the SRN are also known as trunk roads. The PRN is used for transport on a regional or county level, and also feeds into the SRN for longer journeys. The PRN also includes all the SRN in a particular area.

Motorways are subject to particular rules regarding the movement of vehicles, such as direction of travel (see also the table). The Motorway Traffic (England and Wales) Regulations 1982 describe the designation of each part of the motorway (such as 'central reservation' and 'hard shoulder'), and the particular rules that apply. Pedestrians and mopeds are prohibited on motorways, as is stopping (apart from on the hard shoulder in emergencies).

The Department for Transport is responsible for classifying roads according to their size and usage as shown in the table. Most UK roads (60 per cent) are unclassified D roads.

DfT road type	Example	Road sign	Key features	Identification in police communications
Motorway	M6	Blue with white text	Each has a unique identifying number Motorways form part of the SRN	By number
A Road	A21	Non-PRN: White with black text Part of PRN: Green with white and yellow text Road number will be shown	Each has a unique identifying number Some are subject to the motorway regulations and are referred to as A(M), for example the A1(M). May also have a name (often used by local people)	By number
B Road	B1231	White with black text Road number will be shown	Each has a unique identifying number May also have a name (often used by local people)	By number
Classified Unnumbered Road ('C roads')	'Mill Lane'	White with black text (No number will be shown)	Each usually has a name (but may also have a locally designated number)	By name
Unclassified Road ('D roads')	'Church Road'	White with black text	Each has a name	By name

For identifying roads when reporting collisions, the Department for Transport guidance (2011) states that the relevant road(s) should be identified as a motorway, A(M), A, B, C, or unclassified (even though C is an unofficial term), including the number of a motorway, A(M), A, or B road.

The Highways Act 1980 includes particular terms for different types of road, although these are not widely used in other contexts, for example:

- a 'special road' is a road where certain types of traffic are prohibited, and includes all motorways and some high-grade dual carriageways;
- a principal road is any A road or motorway, so includes 'special roads';
- a secondary road is any road that is not a principal road.

Other unofficial terms are also used, for example a 'major road' is generally any A road or motorway, and a 'minor road' is generally any classified unnumbered or unclassified road (the unofficial C and D categories in the table).

19.2.2.2   Responsibilities for roads

The highways authorities are responsible for the SRN. English and Welsh traffic officers have some powers related to the control and direction of traffic, but they are obliged to follow the direction of a police constable. The authority in England is 'Highways England', staffed by Highways England Traffic Officers Service (TOS), but often still referred to as HATOs (the previous term, derived from the now defunct Highways Agency). In Wales there are two agencies; the North and Mid Wales Trunk Road Agent and the South Wales Trunk Road Agent, staffed by Welsh Government Traffic Officers.

All roads that are not part of the SRN are the responsibility of the relevant local county council, unitary authority, or town council. In London, the City of London is responsible for all roads in its local authority area except those on designated red routes. Red routes (the major road network in London with special stopping, loading, and unloading restrictions indicated by red lines) are administered by Transport for London. If an incident occurs at a boundary between different highway authorities, the relevant authorities will need to work together.

19.2.3   Driving

Legislation relating to road and traffic policing often refers to 'driving' and 'attempting to drive'. The term 'driving' is not defined in any legislative Act, but there are precedents which provide guidelines, and the final decision rests with the court. The court will consider:

* the degree to which the person had control over the direction and movement of the vehicle;
* the length of time the person had control;
* the point at which the person stopped the driving; and
* the use of the vehicle's controls by the person in order to direct its movement.

Attempting to drive is not defined by statute, but the general principles for attempted offences should be applied; an attempt is the last action before the full offence is committed, and is more than merely preparatory to the act (see 22.2.1). For example, trying to start a vehicle which will not start because it has a fault could be considered as attempting to drive. The definition of being 'in charge of a vehicle' is covered in 19.9.1 as it only relates to drink- and drug-driving.

19.2.4   Using, causing, permitting use of, and keeping a vehicle

Many road traffic offences are committed by the people who use the vehicle, but some offences relate to causing or permitting a vehicle's use. This would apply to vehicle owners and people who hold supervisory responsibilities, for example. You need to have a clear understanding about the meanings of 'using', 'causing', and 'permitting'. The level of knowledge of the circumstances is the key to determining each individual's liability. We will illustrate the principles in the context of an employer, an employee, and a defective vehicle, but 'using', 'causing', and 'permitting' also occur in other circumstances, for example within families or between friends. It is also important to note that it will be for the courts to decide as a question of fact whether any of these offences have been committed in particular circumstances; the descriptions we provide here are only general guidelines.

We can briefly summarize the differences between using, causing, and permitting as follows: imagine an employer runs a company van which has a defective tyre, and his female employee drives it. Even if he is not aware of the defect then the offence of 'using' would still be committed. If, knowing about the defect, he sent her out in the vehicle this would be 'causing', and if he allowed her to borrow the van and use it at the weekend for her own purpose, this would be 'permitting'. We provide more details in the following paragraphs.

Using a vehicle is not the same under road traffic law as driving a vehicle; for example, a vehicle can be 'in use' while parked, or while being towed. The user of a vehicle can be:

* the driver of a vehicle, including an employee driving a company vehicle for business purposes;
* the employer, if the vehicle is a company vehicle used on company business. The employer can be held responsible for committing an offence (as a user) relating to a vehicle defect even if he/she is unaware of the defect: in some circumstances, both the employer and the driver (an employee) can be held responsible;
* the owner of a vehicle, if it is being driven by another person with the owner present and for the benefit of the owner; or
* a person steering a vehicle, for example when being towed.

For causing the use of a vehicle, the 'causer' must have the authority to make a subordinate carry out a particular action, and must know about the unroadworthy state of the vehicle. In some cases, a company rather than a person can be held responsible for causing the use of an unroadworthy vehicle if the company director knows the vehicle is defective. However, many companies allow employees to use company vehicles for private purposes, and in such circumstances it is unlikely that the employer could be held responsible for causing the vehicle to be used. Also, note that if a person tows a vehicle, then he/she is causing it to be used on a road.

'Permitting use of a vehicle' is a further legal concept. The 'permitter' must be in a position to either allow or forbid its use and the permission can be given verbally, in writing, or merely implied. The 'permitter' (an employer, eg) would commit an offence if he/she has knowledge of (or 'turns a blind eye' to) the unroadworthy state of the vehicle or its lack of documentation and allows an employee to drive it for business purposes (for relevant case law see the House of Lords judgment in *Vehicle Inspectorate v Nuttall* [1999] 1 WLR 629, available online). If either of these elements cannot be proved, then offences relating to the 'use' of the vehicle could be considered.

Keeping a vehicle is when a person ('the keeper') has day-to-day responsibility for a vehicle. It is a question of fact for a court to decide who is a 'keeper', as no legislative definition exists. The 'registered keeper', however, is the person to whom a vehicle is registered, ie whose details appear on a national register of vehicles (see 19.3.3). Consequently the registered keeper is not necessarily the keeper (see *Mohindra v DPP* [2004] EWHC 490 (Admin)).

The legal owner of a vehicle could be the 'keeper' or the 'registered keeper', although this should not be assumed. It could alternatively be a financial institution which provided a loan for the purchase, or an insurance company that has paid out on a claim in relation to the vehicle.

TASK 1 Imagine you are a police officer. You see a car being towed by a van, driven by an older man, in a car park with unrestricted access used as a cut through between two roads. The car has all four wheels on the ground and is being towed with a tow rope. There is a person who looks quite young in the driving seat of the car, turning the steering wheel. You stop the vehicles and speak to both individuals. The van driver is the owner of both vehicles, and the person in the car is his 15-year-old son. You also note that one of the car tyres is defective. The car engine will not start and they say they are taking it to a local garage for repair.

What is the status of each vehicle, each individual, and the location? Who may be liable for any offences discovered?

19.3 Vehicle and Driver Documents

The act of driving and the use of vehicles are subject to licensing, statutory requirements, and testing. These regimes create various documents which a police officer needs to understand in order to deal with incidents, and we will explain the key points here. We will also cover some of the offences which may be committed if all is not in order, and some of the police powers which may be available in such circumstances.

19.3.1 UK driving licences

In the UK, a driver must have the appropriate licence entitlement for the classes of vehicle that he/she drives. The licence shows the categories of vehicle that a person is entitled to drive. UK driving licence regulation and design has changed a number of times over recent years, mainly to bring the UK into line with EU regulation, the latest amendments being in July 2015. This section will primarily deal with UK driving licences but also provides some information on licences from other countries. UK driving licences are administered by the Driver and Vehicle Licensing Agency (DVLA).

The DVLA database contains a 'driver record' for each driver, which shows his/her licence and driving history, and any Driver and Vehicle Standards Agency (DVSA) test passed. Updates are indicated by a 'marker' on the record, for example 'test passed' or 'licence revoked'. The PNC contains up-to-date copies of all the DVLA driver records as 'driver files', and such a file will have a 'DD' tab if the driver is disqualified.

Offences relating to driving licences under the Road Traffic Act 1988 include:

- driving a motor vehicle on a road otherwise than in accordance with a licence authorizing him/her to drive a motor vehicle of that class (s 87(1)); this includes drivers on provisional entitlements who fail to comply with licence requirements;
- causing or permitting another person to drive on a road if that person does not have a licence authorizing driving that class of vehicle (s 87(2)); and
- failure to update a change of address on a driving licence (s 99(5)).

When a driver commits a road traffic offence, penalty points can be 'endorsed' on his/her driving licence, or a marker can be added to his/her licence record. Endorsements are not made on the physical licence itself; the points are recorded electronically on the driver record. For endorsable offences, the number of penalty points depends on the offence.

19.3.1.1 Vehicle categories and codes on driving licences

There have been several changes to the licence vehicle category designations over time, and some older licences will still display some of the discontinued categories. The first table shows the categories that currently apply (early 2019) for vehicles with four or more wheels. For a full explanation of the pre-2013, pre-1996, pre-1990, and pre-1986 arrangements, see the gov.uk website.

Licence vehicle category	Type of vehicle	Minimum driver age
B1	Light vehicles and quad bikes, 4 wheels up to 400 kg (550 kg if designed to carry goods)	17
B	Cars and light vans	17
B auto	Cars and light vans with an automatic gearbox	
BE**	Cars and light vans with a trailer up to 3,500 kg	
C1	Goods vehicles between 3,500 kg and 7,500 kg (with or without a trailer; 750 kg maximum trailer weight)	18*
C1E**	As for C1 but with a trailer over 750 kg, but combined weight not exceeding 12,000 kg	
C	Any goods vehicles over 3,500 kg, with or without a trailer (750 kg maximum trailer weight)	21*
CE**	As for C, but with a trailer over 750 kg	
D1	Passenger-carrying vehicles max length 8 m, with 9–16 passenger seats (minibuses), and trailer up to 750 kg	21*
D1E**	As for D1 but with a trailer over 750 kg (combined weight not exceeding 12,000 kg)	
D	Bus with more than 8 passenger seats, and trailer up to 750 kg	24*
DE**	As for D but with a trailer over 750 kg	
F	Agricultural tractors	17
G	Road rollers	21
H	Tracked vehicles	
K	Mowing machines or pedestrian-controlled vehicles	16

* These categories can be driven at a younger age in some circumstances, for example if the driver: is a member of the armed forces; a learner driver (only some categories); or received a licence for certain categories prior to 1997.
** A full licence for the towing vehicle category must be obtained before the test can be taken for towing a trailer.
Details can be found on the *Information on Driving Licences* leaflet available from the gov.uk website.

The categories that apply to motorcycles are covered in 19.3.1.3. Powered wheelchairs and powered scooters designed for people with disabilities do not require a driver licence.

19.3.1.2 The driver and issue number

Every UK driving licence holder has a driver number. This is the unique reference by which DVLA identifies an individual, and is assigned to a single driver record. A foreign licence holder (with no UK licence) can have a UK driver number if he/she has been dealt with for an offence in the UK and issued with penalty points. It is essential to check the details of a foreign licence holder against the 'driver file' on the PNC, because the driver may have UK penalty points or even be disqualified. It should be noted that a person may have more than one driver number if he/she has been dealt with by the DVLA using slightly different data on different occasions (eg omitting a middle name, giving names in different order, an error in the date of birth). There is a means by which a number of such driver records can be brought together (police service DVLA liaison officers can provide details).

The driver number contains three clusters of information about the driver: family name (five letters); gender and date of birth (six numbers); and a final cluster (five characters). The table shows how to interpret the driver number WILLI 611205 RS9KY for the driver Robert Stuart Williamson.

Cluster	Description	Example
1	The first five letters of the family name. If the name has less than five characters, the remaining spaces are made up using the figure 9 (ie TODD9))	WILLI
2	The first and last digits are derived from the year of birth	611205 shows the year of birth is 1965
	The second and third digits represent the month of birth and the gender. For a female, 5 is added to the second digit, so for a female born in November the cluster would be x61xxx, and for a female born in July, it would be x57xxx	611205 shows he was born in November and is male.
	The fourth and fifth digits show the day of birth:	611205 shows he was born on the 20th of the month
3	The first two characters represent the person's initials	RS9KY (if there is only one initial, 9 is used in place of a second initial, eg R9)
	The third number and the final two letters are computer-generated, and are used to avoid duplicate records. If the first 13 digits of the driver number are unique then the third digit will be a 9, otherwise it will be an 8 (or a 7 in the case of a triplicate, and so on).	RS9KY

The issue number on the driving licence is shown adjacent to the driver number on the front of the licence. A driver's first issue number is randomly generated, and is increased by one on his/her subsequent licences (ie if on first issue the number is 35, the next licence will be 36 and then 37, and so on). Only the current licence is valid as drivers are not allowed to hold more than one licence. The driver file on the PNC shows the issue number of the current valid licence, so this should be checked against any licence provided.

19.3.1.3   Motorcycle licensing and training requirements

To legally ride a motorbike on a road, the driver must first obtain a licence with a provisional entitlement for the relevant category, and also complete Compulsory Basic Training (CBT). This training takes place at approved centres and includes basic handling and bike control, a practical on-street assessment, and a knowledge test of the Highway Code. A CBT certificate is valid for two years and is shown as a marker on the DVLA driver record. It can be retaken if it expires. Once a full motorcycle entitlement has been obtained a valid CBT is no longer required. A full explanation of the process for obtaining motorcycle licences can be found on the gov.uk website.

The motorcycle categories in the table came into force on 19 January 2013. Note that electrically assisted pedal cycles are classified as pedal cycles (see 19.2.1) so a driving licence is not required.

Licence vehicle category	Type of vehicle	Minimum driver age
Moped AM	2- or 3-wheeled vehicles, top speed 15.5–28 mph (25–45 km/h)	16
	Small 3-wheelers (up to 50 cc and below 4 kW), light quadricycles (under 350 kg, top speed 25–45 km/h)	
Moped p (no longer issued)	2-wheeled, top speed 28–31 mph (45–50 km/h), maximum engine capacity 50cc if powered by internal combustion.	

Licence vehicle category	Type of vehicle	Minimum driver age
Moped q	2- or 3-wheels, top speed 15.5 mph (25 km/h), engine size less than 50 cc if internal combustion, granted with an AM licence entitlement	
A1	Small motorbikes up to 11 kW and 125 cc (power-to-weight ratio not more than 0.1 kW per kg)	17
	Motor tricycles with a power output 15 kW or less	
A2	Medium motorbikes up to 35 kW (power-to-weight ratio not more than 0.2 kW per kg). If the engine is restricted its power must be at least half its original (or it will be category A)	19
A	Motorbikes, unlimited size/power, with or without a side-car.	17 (armed services only)
	Motor tricycles with power output over 15 kW	21 (progressive access*)
		24 (direct access**)

* Must hold A2 licence for at least 2 years before taking the practical test.
** No need to hold the A2 licence for 2 years before taking the practical test.

For further details and older licence categories, see the gov.uk website.

19.3.1.4 Additional licensing requirements for commercial vehicles

Drivers of larger vehicles are subject to extra licencing requirements when the vehicles are driven for commercial purposes. This applies for large goods vehicles (classes C1, C1E, C, and CE) and for larger passenger vehicles (classes D1, D1E, D, and DE); see 19.3.1.1 on licence categories. The regulations are numerous and complex, for further details see the gov.uk website. Some key features of the regulations for commercial driving are that the driver must:

- be aged at least 18 years (under certain conditions the minimum age is 21 or 24 years, see 19.3.1.1);
- hold a full car licence; and
- complete a medical form when first applying (includes a section for his/her GP and optician to complete) and on each renewal.

As for any driver, the E categories can only be obtained after obtaining a full category for the towing vehicle. For commercial drivers up to the age of 65 the driving licence categories are only valid for five years, and need to be renewed (renewal is required every year for drivers older than 65 years).

Drivers of commercial vehicles of classes C, CE, D, and DE must also hold a Driver Certificate of Professional Competence (CPC), obtained by attending a certified training course and passing four tests. They must also complete 35 hours of ongoing training every five years to remain qualified.

19.3.1.5 UK photocard driving licences

A UK driving licence photocard is about the size of a credit card and is valid for ten years. The licence can be a full or provisional licence, and shows the driver's current driving entitlements and personal information. Additional licence information can be accessed online using the driver number and the holder's NI number and postcode. The issue number should be checked on the PNC driver file to confirm it is the driver's most recently issued licence. Penalty points should also be checked on the PNC as these are no longer endorsed on the actual licence. Note that a driver may produce an old-style paper licence which is still valid, usually because he/she has not recently changed his/her name or address.

Provisional licences have a green background with a clear pictogram of an L plate on the front. It will show only provisional entitlements, as they are not issued to drivers with a full entitlement in any category. Full licence photocards have a pink background with an EU flag on the front, and show all the holder's full entitlements. Full licence photocards do not show any provisional entitlements so these would need to be checked against the driver file on PNC.

The latest version of the full driving licence photocard (from 6 July 2015) is shown here. The card has improved security features such as tactile (raised) surfaces, engraved text, changing colours, and complex background designs.

Specific Incidents

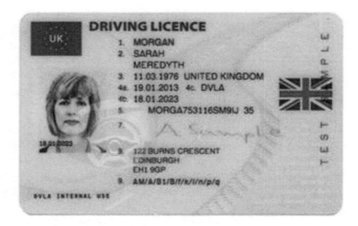

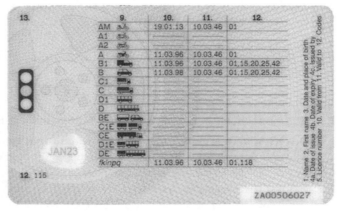

On the front of the card, the issue and expiry dates are shown ((4a) and (4b) respectively). The driver and issue number are shown at (5). The categories of valid vehicle entitlement are shown at (9), with EU directive categories in capitals and UK local categories in lower case.

On the back of the card column 9 shows all the possible entitlements (see 19.3.1.1 and 19.3.1.3) and columns 10 and 11 show the valid entitlements for the licence holder, with start and expiry dates. Column 12 lists the DVLA restriction codes that apply for each entitlement. There are many restriction codes, for example code 01 is 'eyesight correction' for the driver, code 40 is for 'modified steering' on a vehicle (this may apply to a disabled driver), and code 101 is 'not for hire and reward' and may be applied to the minibus entitlement. A breach of the restrictions would amount to driving not in accordance with a licence.

The DVLA leaflet ref INS57P provides a good explanation of most of the features shown on photocard licences. It is available on the gov.uk website, and can be printed off and kept as a reference.

19.3.1.6 Provisional entitlements and learner drivers

All provisional entitlements impose certain requirements on the driver, and these vary according to the category of vehicle. A breach of any of the requirements will amount to the offence of driving otherwise than in accordance with a driving licence (s 87(1) of the Road Traffic Act 1988). The conditions under which a provisional licence holder can drive a vehicle are set out in reg 16 of the Motor Vehicles (Driving Licences) Regulations 1999. The main requirements relate to 'L' plates and supervision.

L plates must be displayed on front and back of the vehicle while it is being driven by a provisional licence holder in England. The plates must be clearly visible to other road users within a reasonable distance (reg 16(2)(b)). The correct dimensions for an L plate are shown in the diagram, and it can have rounded corners. D plates can be displayed in Wales, but they must be replaced with L plates if driving in England.

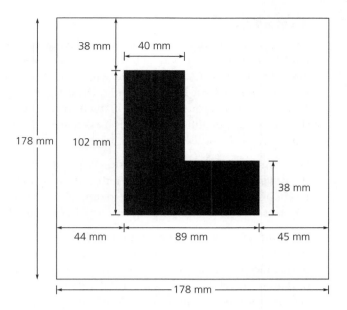

L plates are often 'cut down' for mounting on motorcycles, but this is not permitted. Any vehicle with a cut down L plate (see the photograph) is not displaying a proper L plate, so is not complying with a provisional entitlement requirement, and is therefore driving 'not in accordance with a licence'.

Supervision is required for drivers with a provisional entitlement when driving vehicles with four or more wheels (such as those in category B, C, D, and derivatives of these). The supervision must be provided by a 'qualified driver' (reg 16(2)(a)) who must be at least 21 years old, have the relevant driving experience, and have had a full British (including Northern Ireland) or an EU Community licence with the relevant entitlements for at least three years (reg 17(1) and (2)).

There are some situations where a driver with a provisional entitlement can drive without supervision, such as:

- driving certain categories of motor vehicle, for example a three-wheeled vehicle;
- riding a moped, or a motorcycle (with or without a side-car);
- driving on an exempted island (except for large goods vehicles and passenger-carrying vehicles); or
- driving a motor vehicle having just passed the relevant driving test (but the driver must have a relevant certificate authorizing the driving).

Provisional licence holders should not drive a vehicle with a trailer (reg 16(2)(c)), unless learning and being supervised for a vehicle in the E category. In such circumstances the towing vehicle should have an L plate on the front and the trailer should have a L plate on the back (reg 16(5)).

19.3.1.7   Disqualification

A driver who has been disqualified cannot legally drive any motor vehicle on a road. This is a punishment for the individual but also serves to protect the public. When a driver has been disqualified the DVLA driver record will be marked as such, and a Disqualified Driver (DD) tab will appear on the PNC names file. The driver's licence will also be revoked (see 19.3.1.8). A person can be disqualified even if absent from court, so a driver might not know that he/she has been disqualified, but this is no defence. Such individuals should be dealt with in the same way as any other disqualified driver.

Disqualification can be imposed once 12 penalty points have been recorded ('endorsed') on the driver's DVLA driver record in a three-year period. This can be after a series of relatively minor offences. It is not obligatory to disqualify a driver with 12 points, and a driver can present reasons to the court and explain why he/she should not be disqualified.

Disqualification is also one of the penalty options for certain offences, and can be discretionary, for example for 'failing to stop after an accident' (see 19.7.2). For more serious offences disqualification is obligatory, such as for driving over the prescribed limit for alcohol or drugs, or dangerous driving. The court will decide the duration of the disqualification, taking into account the offence and the driver's offending history. Permanent disqualification is very rare (*R v Tunde-Olarinde* [1967] 2 All ER 491).

A further option is a DTTP disqualification ('Disqualified Til Test Passed'). This requires the driver to pass a DVSA test to regain his/her licence, and is often imposed in addition to a conventional disqualification, for example 'disqualified for two years and DTTP'. Once the disqualification has reverted to DTTP-only, the driver will be allowed a provisional licence so he/she can practise for retaking the test. All the requirements of the provisional entitlement apply (see 19.3.1.6), and if they are not fulfilled the driver is dealt with in the same way as any other disqualified driver, ie under s 103(1)(b).

While disqualified from holding or obtaining a licence, it is an offence to obtain a licence or drive a motor vehicle on a road (s 103(1)(a) and (b) of the Road Traffic Act 1988 respectively). The court will require evidence of the original disqualification (see *Mills v DPP* [2008] EWHC 3304 (Admin)) such as a certificate of conviction under s 73 of the PACE Act 1984, the defendant's admission (at interview or in court), or a statement from a person who was in court when the disqualification was imposed.

These offences are triable summarily and the penalty for obtaining a licence while disqualified is a fine. The penalty for driving a motor vehicle on a road while disqualified is imprisonment for up to six months and/or a fine, discretionary extension of the disqualification, and obligatory endorsement (six penalty points).

19.3.1.8   Revocation

When a licence is revoked the individual's licence is effectively suspended, pending resolution of the circumstances, and the person is no longer authorized to drive under any of the entitlements on the licence. Licences can be revoked by the DVLA for a number of reasons, such as:

- failing to surrender a licence when required, for example when an endorsement is imposed. The DVLA will write to the licence holder requesting surrender of the licence within 28 days, and stating that if it is not surrendered it will be revoked. If it is not surrendered the DVLA will inform the individual by post that the licence has been revoked. The record will be updated to show the licence as expired;
- disqualification—when a driver is disqualified (see 19.3.1.7), the DVLA will mark the licence as revoked on the driver record and add the disqualification. At the end of a fixed period disqualification the individual must re-apply for a licence, and until it is issued the DVLA driver record will still show it as revoked;
- medical grounds—the licence holder (or a third party with an obligation to inform) tells the DVLA that the person has a notifiable medical condition (see the gov.uk website for a list). The revocation will only be cancelled after suitable medical reports have been received or a specified symptom-free period has passed;
- the licence has been issued in error by the DVLA.

The circumstances under which a licence can be revoked will often need to be explained to individuals, as many people do not understand the process. Depending on the reasons for the revocation, the DVLA driver record will show the licence as revoked or expired. Sometimes the DVLA will alter the expiry date of the licence rather than revoke it in the normal way. Note that a person with a revoked licence is not disqualified from driving; this would need to be imposed by a court. Driving with a revoked licence is 'driving not in accordance with a licence' which is a different offence from driving while disqualified.

New drivers can also have their full entitlement revoked to a provisional entitlement (on one occasion only). This was introduced in the Road Traffic (New Drivers) Act 1995 after research revealed that new drivers (during the first two years of driving, and generally young people) were more likely than other road users to be involved in collisions due to poor driving. The full entitlement licence is automatically revoked if the driver receives any obligatory endorsement(s) (s 2(1)(b)) which accumulate to six or more penalty points (s 2(1)(d)).

TASK 2

1. Could a disqualified driver or 'new driver' with a revoked licence conceal the fact that he/she is disqualified?
2. How could a police officer on patrol check whether a driver is disqualified?

19.3.1.9 Foreign licences

There are significant numbers of non-UK drivers now residing in the UK, and their status with regard to driving and licensing depends on the person's country of origin.

If he/she holds a licence from an EU country (a 'Community licence') or a country in the European Economic Area then the holder is treated as if a UK licence is held, and can continue to drive on it (until the age of 70). Such a licence can be exchanged for a UK licence at any time, but this is not compulsory.

For a driver with a non-EU licence, the licence will remain valid for 12 months after either entering the UK as a visitor or becoming a resident. An individual's status as either a visitor or resident and any change in status will be a matter of fact for a court to decide, but a permanent address, employment, or enrolment of children at a local school may all be indicators of residence. Once the 12-month period has expired an appropriate UK licence must be obtained.

A person holding a non-EU licence must comply with the above requirement; however, a person from certain designated non-EU countries or territories can exchange his/her licence for a UK licence within five years of arrival, although this is not compulsory. This applies for Australia, Barbados, British Virgin Islands, Canada, Falkland Islands, Faroe Islands, Hong Kong, Japan, Monaco, New Zealand, Republic of Korea, Singapore, South Africa, Switzerland, and Zimbabwe.

A driver with a non-UK licence can still be dealt with for driving matters. If endorsements are imposed, a UK driver number will be allocated and a 'non-licence holder' driver record will be created at the DVLA. A full explanation of the particular circumstances of drivers with a non-UK licence is provided at: <https://www.gov.uk/driving-nongb-licence>, but officers should also follow local policies.

19.3.2 Insurance

All motor vehicles used on the road or other public place in the UK must have a valid third party liabilities insurance policy, or a 'security' (a financial deposit by a large organization). Third party insurance means the policy will pay out if another person's property is damaged, or if someone other than the policy holder is killed or injured (s 145(3)(a)). Insurance cover is usually described as fully comprehensive, third party only, or third party fire and theft (TPF&T). The cost is based on the risk as assessed from the information provided by the policy holder, and any failure to disclose correct or full information may amount to fraud under s 2 or 3 of the Fraud Act 2006. Some vehicles have a black box fitted in the vehicle to record aspects of the driving, which could permit a discount.

The policy will specify the cover in terms of the use of the vehicle and the individuals concerned, and if any of the conditions listed on the policy are breached the vehicle will not be insured. The cover will only apply to specific uses such as Social, Domestic and Pleasure (SDP), commuting to a fixed place of work, or business use. The policy can apply to the policy holder only or to the policy holder and named drivers. 'Any driver' policies are sometimes issued (often for company vehicles) and these usually have conditions, for example that all drivers must be over 25 years old or employed by the policy holder.

'Any vehicle' clauses often cause confusion. These allow the policy holder to drive any vehicle with the owner's permission, and were previously standard on all comprehensive policies. However, this is no longer the case, and some drivers do not realize this. An 'any vehicle' clause cannot be used by an individual who owns more than one vehicle as a way of avoiding insurance payments for all of the cars that he/she owns. So it does not allow the policy holder to drive another vehicle that he/she owns, without insuring each vehicle separately or as part of a multi-car policy. The same restriction applies for any named drivers on a policy. Some any-vehicle clauses require that the vehicle is also insured separately by its owner, and may also include a further clause stating that this cover does not extend to recovering vehicles seized by the police for a 'no insurance offence'. It should also be noted that 'any vehicle' clauses only ever provide basic third party cover.

The policy must be issued by an insurer registered with the Motor Insurers' Bureau (MIB) to be valid in the UK. The policy holder will receive a certificate of insurance (hard copy or electronic) from the company, and this will include at least the following features:

Insurance Company Name and Address:
AAA Insurance Ltd.
The High Street
Maidbury MB1 1AB
Registration Number: AA 00 AAA

Certificate number: 000/999/123
Policy holder's name: Orlando SMITH Expiry date: Noon 16th December 2019
Permitted Drivers: Verity SMITH, Noah KAY
Limitations as to use: Use for social, domestic, and pleasure purposes, including travel between the driver's home and place of work.

Note that the existence of an insurance certificate does not prove that a vehicle is insured—the policy might have been cancelled after the certificate was issued. The MIB maintains a database of all insured vehicles, available via the vehicle file on the PNC, so officers should always refer to this. Short duration policies are often not shown on the MIB database, so further enquiries would be required to establish an accurate picture of the insurance status. The MIB run a help line for police officers who have stopped a vehicle on the street and have enquiries regarding its insurance, although this is not available 24/7 at the time of writing. The force control room can provide current telephone numbers for officers to call direct.

19.3.2.1 Driving a vehicle without adequate insurance cover

If a vehicle is not properly insured, any individual who uses, causes, or permits (see 19.2.4) its use on a road or other public place commits an offence contrary to s 143(1) and (2) of the Road Traffic Act 1988. The registered keeper (see 19.3.3) is guilty of an offence (s 144A of the Road Traffic Act 1988) if it is kept (see 19.2.4) without insurance (unless the vehicle has a Statutory Off Road Notification (SORN, see 19.3.5). A vehicle without adequate insurance can be seized under s 165A of the Road Traffic Act 1988 (see 19.4.3 for details of the procedure).

There are a number of exceptions to the offence of driving without adequate insurance, which must be substantiated. These include vehicles:

- kept by the registered keeper at a location which is not on a road or other public place;
- not kept by the registered keeper at the relevant time, for example whilst lent to another person;
- that have been stolen and not recovered before the relevant time;
- driven by an owner who has deposited £500,000 with the Accountant General; or
- owned by authorities (such as councils, police authorities, the NHS, Army, or Air Force).

If it can be proved that the user did not own the vehicle (or had not hired it), and he/she was acting in the course of her/his employment and had no reason to believe that the vehicle was not properly insured, this can be a defence (s 143(3) of the Road Traffic Act 1988).

19.3.2.2 Foreign insurance

A driver visiting the UK with a foreign-registered vehicle will probably have valid insurance from his/her home country, but it may be time-limited by the policy terms and conditions. Once a visitor becomes a UK resident (see 19.3.1.9) a policy with a UK MIB registered insurance company is required (see also 19.3.3 on UK-registering a foreign vehicle).

19.3.3 Vehicle registration and licensing

A new vehicle is generally first registered in the UK by the motor trade. The DVLA issues a registration document to the keeper and assigns the vehicle a registration mark (also known as a registration number or an index number). The Vehicle Excise and Registration Act 1994 (VERA) provides much of the relevant legislation.

Some older vehicles will need to undergo registration in the UK, for example when the vehicle has only been used on a private estate or has been imported. Vehicles brought into the UK by a visitor must be registered in the UK after six months or when he/she becomes a resident, whichever is sooner. Once a vehicle is registered (or becomes subject to registration) it is also subject to the UK insurance and testing criteria.

The registration mark of a particular vehicle can be changed for a number of reasons. These include a 'cherished transfer' (also referred to as a 'private plate', although the DVLA term is 'personalized vehicle registration numbers'). Another reason for a change is that a vehicle was exported and then imported back into the UK. Records are cross-referenced on the PNC vehicle file so any previous registration numbers for a particular vehicle will be shown, as will all vehicles that have had a particular registration number.

19.3.3.1 The vehicle registration document and number plates

The vehicle registration document is proof that the vehicle is registered, and shows the details recorded on the register. The current version (the V5C with a red front cover) was introduced in 2010, and revised in 2012. The older version (the V5) has a blue front cover and is still valid if the keeper of the vehicle has not changed since 2010. The document contains a wealth of information regarding the vehicle which can be useful in the investigation of a variety of offences.

A vehicle is not properly registered if any of the particulars recorded in the register are incorrect or incomplete. It is an offence to use a vehicle that is not properly registered on a road or in a public place (s 43C(1) of VERA 1994). Other registration documents offences include failure to notify the DVLA about the disposal of a vehicle, or a change of vehicle details. Most of these offences are covered under the Road Vehicles (Display of Registration Marks) Regulations 2001 and VERA 1994. Defences for using a vehicle that is not properly registered include that no reasonable opportunity was given to supply the name and address of the registered keeper (eg if the person had only just bought the vehicle), or if there were reasonable grounds for believing that the recorded particulars were correct.

The registration mark or index number is shown on the 'number plate' of a vehicle. The plate should use a standard font, and it should not be customized in any way. These and further details on number plates may be found on the DVLA website.

Local **memory tag** denoting where a vehicle is first registered. AB refers to Peterborough.

Age identifier which changes twice yearly in March and September. The number 51 refers to September 2001.

Random letters which will never include I or Q and which uniquely define the vehicle.

(Image reproduced with the permission of the DVLA)

Specific Incidents

Offences relating to number plates (mostly under the Road Vehicles (Display of Registration Marks) Regulations 2001) include: no number plate or an obscured number plate; forgery of a number plate; incorrect fitting, number, or position of plates; and incorrect style, size, and spacing of characters. These are all summary offences.

19.3.4 Annual testing and 'MOT' test certificates

The majority of vehicles used on roads will be subject to testing. Any motor vehicle registered under the Vehicle Excise and Registration Act 1994 must be tested every year (after a certain period from registration) if it is to be used on a road (s 47 of the Road Traffic Act 1988). This also applies to any vehicle that is subject to registration, even if it has not actually been registered (eg a newly imported vehicle). The MOT test system is administered by the Driver and Vehicle Standards Agency (DVSA). The test is know as an 'MOT' because the 'Ministry of Transport', a predecessor of the Department for Transport, administered the system. Vehicles are grouped into different categories for the purpose of testing and test fees (see the gov.uk website for details and the DVSA MOT testing manuals for each vehicle category).

For most vehicles, the first test is required three years from the date of first registration of the vehicle (s 47(2)). For large goods vehicles, coaches, buses, ambulances, and private hire vehicles the first MOT is required one year from registration (s 47(3)). For vehicles up to 40 years old that are newly registered in the UK (see 19.3.3) the schedule for MOT testing starts from the date of manufacture (taken to be the last day of the year during which its final assembly was completed). Vehicles built and registered more than 40 years ago and without substantial modifications in the last 30 years are now classed as 'historic' and no longer require an MOT (but may be submitted on a voluntary basis for a test).

It is an offence under s 47 for a person at any time to use (or cause or permit to be used) a motor vehicle on a road without a test certificate apart from:

- driving to a pre-arranged MOT test;
- driving from a failed MOT test to a garage for repairs by previous arrangement (reg 6(2)(a)(i) of the Motor Vehicle (Test) Regulations 1981); or
- being towed from a failed MOT for scrapping (reg 6(2)(a)(iii)(B)).

The results of tests are uploaded immediately and the 'MOT expiry tab' on the PNC vehicle file will be updated. Police officers should cross reference the information with the MOT data held on the vehicle file of the PNC. The MOT history of any vehicle is available to anyone on the gov.uk website.

19.3.5 Vehicle excise duty

Vehicle excise duty (VED) is payable on any vehicle used or kept on a public road, and is covered under s 1 of VERA 1994. The system is also referred to as 'vehicle licensing' and 'road tax'. The registered keeper is responsible for paying VED, and for arranging a Statutory Off Road Notification (SORN). A vehicle with a SORN can be kept off road without paying VED. The PNC vehicle files include an excise licence field, and any vehicle's excise duty status can be accessed on the gov.uk website. It has been held that a vehicle is 'kept' on a public road even if it is only there for a very short period (s 62).

The taxation classes include private/light goods vehicles (PLG, such as family cars and light vans), buses, and heavy goods vehicles. (Note that the category 'bicycle' refers to two-wheeled motorcycles rather than pedal-powered bicycles.) Some types of vehicle are exempt from duty such as vehicles for disabled people, fire engines, ambulances, and most vehicles manufactured before 1 January 1978 (except for LGVs and buses (see s 5(2) of and Sch 2 to VERA 1994)). Exempted vehicles are subject to a 'nil licence' and will appear as such on the vehicle licensing register.

It is an offence for the registered keeper to keep an untaxed vehicle off-road without making a SORN (s 31A(1)) or for any person to use or keep a non-exempted vehicle on a public road if no VED has been paid (s 29(1) of VERA 1994).

19.4   **Stopping a Vehicle and Examining Documents**

Police officers on foot or mobile patrol will sometimes need to stop vehicles in relation to driving standards, or because the vehicle is being used for some other criminal activity. Stopping vehicles and inspecting documentation are covered by particular police powers, and further powers may be available if any offences are disclosed.

19.4.1   **Police powers to stop a vehicle**

All police officers have the legal power to stop any mechanically propelled vehicle on a road (s 163 of the Road Traffic Act 1988) and do not need to have any form of suspicion or authorization. The police officer must be on duty and in full uniform, and give a clear direction to the driver to stop. Health and safety considerations are key in relation to where the officer makes the request, and to where the vehicle can actually stop (see 19.1). Failing to comply is a summary offence and the penalty is a fine. If the driver flees, the police have a power of entry into premises in order to arrest for this offence (s 17 of the PACE Act 1984 (see 10.8.1)).

19.4.2   **Driver and vehicle information checks**

Police officers can now check all driver and vehicle documentation electronically by the side of the road, and there is now a clear expectation that officers will verify the status of the documentation before allowing a driver to proceed.

Here, a 'driver' is:

- any person driving a motor vehicle on a road;
- any person the officer has reasonable cause to believe had been driving a motor vehicle on a road at the time it was involved in an accident; or
- any person who the officer has reasonable cause to believe has committed an offence in relation to the use of a motor vehicle on a road, for example 'quitting' (see 19.5.2.3).

Driving licence checks are carried out on the PNC (including by the person's home post code if there seem to be discrepancies). MOT status can be checked through the PNC vehicle file or over the internet, and insurance details can be accessed on the MIB database (through the vehicle file on the PNC). The MIB help line can also provide useful information.

19.4.2.1   **Requiring documents for examination**

If it is not possible to make electronic checks at the scene of an incident, a police officer can request production of the following documents:

- the driver's driving licence (s 164(1));
- an appropriate insurance certificate (s 165(1)) (on paper or in electronic format on a suitable device (s 165(2A)));
- the vehicle's MOT test certificate (s 165(1)); and/or
- CBT certificate (only motorcyclists without a full entitlement) (s 164(4A)).

These requirements also apply for supervisors of learner drivers (s 164(1)(d)) in some circumstances (ie when a learner driver on a provisional entitlement is driving a motor vehicle on a road or is believed to have been involved in an accident or to have committed a road traffic offence (see 19.4.2 for details)). A police officer can also request any person driving or otherwise 'using' a registered vehicle (see 19.2.4) to produce the vehicle's registration document (s 28A(1) of VERA 1994).

Under the Road Traffic Act 1988, if the driver cannot produce the insurance or MOT certificate when required, a police officer can require the person to state his/her name and address and the vehicle owner's name and address (s 165(1)), and in some forces there may still be the option of issuing an HO/RT/1 form for production of documents within seven days (see 19.4.2.3).

19.4.2.2   **Requesting information from a driver**

A police officer may require a 'driver' (see 19.4.2) to state his/her date of birth (s 164(2)) if he/she fails to produce his/her licence, or produces a licence that is unsatisfactory (eg it seems to have been altered or it contains information that seems incorrect). This also applies for a person who is supervising a learner driver at the time of an accident or an offence, and there is reason to suspect that he/she (the supervisor) is under 21 years of age.

19.4.2.3 Failing to produce documents or provide information

Under the Road Traffic Act 1988 it is a summary offence for a person when required to fail to:

- produce his/her licence or state his/her date of birth (s 164(6));
- produce his/her CBT certificate (motorcyclists only) (s 164(6));
- state his/her name and address and the name and address of the owner of the vehicle (s 165(3));
- produce a certificate of insurance or an MOT certificate (s 165(3)).

Failing to produce the registration document is an offence under s 28A(3) of VERA 1994 (except when the vehicle is subject to a lease or hire agreement). However, a person will not be prosecuted for failing to produce any of these documents if the officer then issues an HO/RT/1 form (not used in all forces) and the driver then produces the documents within a specified time:

- within seven days in person at a police station (specified by the driver at the time of the request);
- as soon as reasonably practicable (a question of fact for a court to decide); or
- at a later time if the driver can prove it was not reasonably practicable to do so before the day on which written charge proceedings were commenced.

For pedal cyclists and drivers of any mechanically propelled vehicle who are suspected of dangerous, careless, or inconsiderate driving or cycling (ss 2, 3, 28, and 29; see 19.8 onwards) there is a separate offence of failing to provide his/her name and address to any person having reasonable grounds for requiring the information (s 168 of the Road Traffic Act 1988). Note that 'a mechanically propelled vehicle' is a very broad category (see 19.2.1).

TASK 3

1. What checks should be undertaken to verify the identity of a driver and the validity of any documents produced?
2. What problems might there be in establishing a person's true identity?
3. What extra checks could a police officer carry out to make sure he/she has been given the person's real name and address?

19.4.3 Seizing a vehicle

Under s 165A of the Road Traffic Act 1988, a police officer has the power to seize a vehicle if he/she has reasonable grounds for believing that the driver does not have a suitable licence or that the vehicle is not adequately insured. To seize a vehicle a police officer must be in uniform and have requested to see the relevant documents. He/she must also warn the driver that the vehicle will be seized unless the documents are produced immediately. However, if it is impractical to warn the driver then a warning is not required (s 165A(6)). More than 1.8 million uninsured vehicles have been seized since the power became available in 2005, with some 133,000 seized in 2018 alone (Motor Insurers' Bureau, 2018; 2019).

If the driver has failed to stop or has driven off, the vehicle may be seized at any time in the 24-hour period following the incident. A police officer has the legal power to enter premises to seize a vehicle, including from the driveway or garage associated with a private dwelling-house. The officer must have reasonable grounds for believing the vehicle to be present, and reasonable force may be used if necessary.

TASK 4 Imagine you are a police officer. You stop a high-performance car using your powers under the Road Traffic Act 1988. The driver is young but has an appropriate licence and the PNC check shows that the vehicle is insured. A driving licence enquiry shows he has nine current points on his licence for three speeding offences.

- What questions would you put to him about his insurance policy?
- How would you check that the insurance company knows about the endorsements on the driver's licence and that the policy has been issued in full knowledge of the risk?

TASK 5 Imagine you are a police officer. Whilst on Independent Patrol you have stopped a vehicle using your powers under the Road Traffic Act 1988 and a vehicle check on the PNC shows the MOT has expired.

- What are the defences to not having a valid test certificate?
- What questions will you put to the driver to negate any defences?

19.4.4 Police pursuits

Pursuits should be avoided if at all possible. Pre-emptive action such as requesting a vehicle to stop is preferable if suitably trained officers are available, but some drivers and motorcyclists refuse to stop when requested to do so. If a driver's actions or manner of driving suggest that he/she does not intend to stop and the police driver believes that the driver is aware of the requirement to stop, the police need to decide on the best course of action. Any pursuit must be justified, proportionate, cause the minimum level of risk, and be suitably authorized. Some pursuits will be part of a pre-planned operation, if, for example, suspects in a moving vehicle are under surveillance, and the police decide that the best tactics are to try and stop the vehicle. It would be obvious that the suspects might not comply, and that this could lead to a pursuit. In this situation a pursuit would be considered as part of a pre-planned operation.

Pursuits are split into two phases; an initial phase and a tactical phase. The initial phase is the period of a spontaneous pursuit before tactical resolution can be considered and actioned. For any phase of a pursuit, the vehicle must be fitted with audio and visual warning equipment. Certain types of vehicle must not be used for pursuits under any circumstances, for example personnel carriers, vans, hired vehicles, and personal vehicles. Any four-wheel drive vehicle is inherently less stable than other vehicles and only specific vehicles with suitable handling characteristics should be used for pursuits. Drivers involved in pursuits must be suitably qualified and have attended suitable refresher training every two to three years.

For the initial phase of a pursuit, unmarked cars can be used if driven by an advanced driver. Otherwise, suitable marked cars and police response motorcycles can be used, as can any vehicle deemed suitable for the tactical phase. Tyre deflation systems may also be employed at the initial stage. Pursuit trained standard/response drivers and motorcyclists (with suitable vehicles) may be authorized by an appropriate member of staff from the control/communications room to continue with a pursuit as it moves into the tactical phase. However, their role would be to support the pursuing vehicle, and they must not play an active part in tactical resolution.

An appropriate resolution tactic must be selected (such as tyre deflation devices or implementing tactical pursuit and containment (TPAC) tactics). The pursuit then moves into the tactical phase. The driver must be an advanced driver trained for the tactical phase of pursuits. One of the officers in a pursuing vehicle will be identified as the 'pursuit commander', and will direct the pursuit and the tactics used. Marked or unmarked cars can be used but the vehicle must be deemed fit for use in tactical phase pursuit, and any unmarked vehicles should be replaced with marked vehicles at the earliest opportunity (as such vehicles are more visible and therefore safer).

The use of pursuit as a tactic by police is controversial, and the reputation of the force can be tarnished if a pursuit related injury or death occurs. The risk must be assessed against the objective(s), applying the national guidance (see the College of Police APP) and any local policy.

19.4.5 Road checks (s 4 of the PACE Act 1984)

Road checks can be used to determine whether a vehicle is carrying people connected with an indictable offence (a witness or suspect), or who are unlawfully at large (s 4 of the PACE Act 1984). There must be reasonable grounds for suspecting that the person is, or is about to be, in the locality. When directing vehicles to stop s 163 of the Road Traffic Act 1988 must be followed (see 19.4.1), and the road check must comply with PACE Code of Practice A. Road checks cannot be used for road traffic or vehicle excise offences.

The road check must be authorized by a senior officer in writing because the rights of all the individuals stopped must be considered—every vehicle will be stopped in a certain area. The authorizing officer must be a superintendent or above but if unavailable, an officer of a lower rank can authorize a road check (see s 4(5) of the PACE Act 1984). The authorization must specify the time, place, and reason for the check.

19.5   Construction and Use of Vehicles

Construction and use legislation relates to the maintenance of a vehicle to a roadworthy standard, and the circumstances in which it may create a danger to other road users. The legislation is written in the form of regulations, notably the Road Vehicles (Construction and Use) Regulations 1986 and the Road Vehicles Lighting Regulations 1989. There are also offences under the Road Traffic Act 1988 where no specific regulations apply. Some construction and use offences can be evidenced with a superficial examination of the vehicle, while other more complex matters will require expert training. Conducting a roadside vehicle examination can be dangerous, and should not be undertaken if the officer has any doubts concerning safety.

A police authorized vehicle examiner can test a vehicle (and drawn trailer) on a road to check compliance with construction and use requirements, and also assess the risk of making such checks in particular circumstances. This requires specialist training (s 67 of the Road Traffic Act 1988). If a vehicle examiner is not available the assistance of a DVSA advanced or forensic vehicle examiner can be sought; in some forces there are specific arrangements between the DVSA and local police control rooms.

19.5.1   Tyres

When dealing with tyre offences it is important to record sufficient information so the specific tyre on a vehicle can be identified when presenting evidence. This will include a description of the tyre including its size and rating, the dimension and description of any defects, and its location on the vehicle. For the location the usual system is to state front (F) or rear (R), and nearside (N/S) or offside (O/S). Nearside is the side closest to the kerb when driving on the left, and offside is the side further from the kerb (and the driver's side on a right-hand drive car). So the tyre at the front of the car on the driver's side would be the F/O/S.

The terms used to describe the various parts of a tyre are shown in the diagram. It may also be necessary to specify whether a side wall was the inner (the side you cannot see from beside the vehicle) or the outer (the side to the outside of the vehicle).

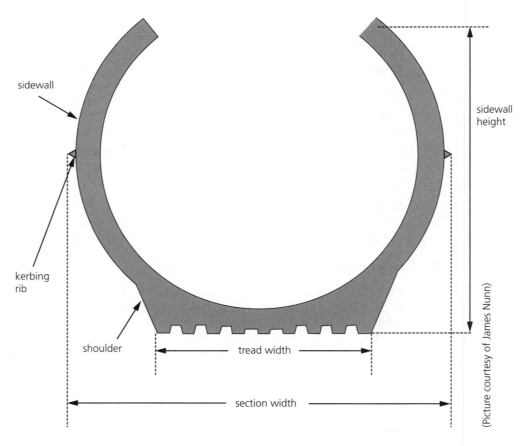

(Picture courtesy of James Nunn)

For use as evidence, all the identifying details, codes, and features on the wall of a tyre should be noted, including serial numbers and characters relating to the type of tyre. This will include the make and model of the tyre, ie Pirelli P6000.

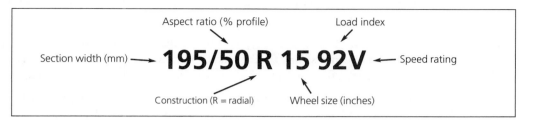

On initial examination the side wall information can appear confusing as the format has been developed over time, and uses various international standards and units of measurement.

The side wall information shown in the box can be interpreted as follows:

- the section width is 195 mm, this is the distance between the outer edge of each sidewall (under normal inflation), and is always greater than the tread width as tyres bulge out;
- the aspect ratio compares the height of the side wall with the section width, and is stated as a percentage (a 'low ratio' is also known as a 'low profile' in common parlance). In this case the figure is 50 per cent, so as the section width is 195 mm the side wall height must be 97.5 mm. Some older tyres may not have a stated aspect ratio; it is generally 80 per cent in such cases;
- the letter 'R' denotes that the tyre has a radial construction, and indicates the way the steel or fabric belts are arranged within the structure of the tyre. Almost all tyres on cars now are radial; other belt arrangements include bias-belted ('B') and cross-ply ('-') which are now used primarily for motorcycle tyres. There may also be another letter (H, V, or Z); this is a duplication of the speed rating information;
- the wheel rim diameter (the metal part) in inches;
- the load index (or rating); and
- the speed rating (H, V, or Z; in increasing order of maximum speed).

Other information may be present on the side wall, such as whether the tyre is 'tubeless' or 'tube type' (ie it requires an inner tube). If there is an arrow (often with the word 'direction') the tyres must be fitted so that the wheel rotates in that direction when the vehicle moves forwards. There may also be an 'inside' or 'outside' marker; again tyres should be fitted as indicated. The week and year of manufacture is indicated by a set of numbers preceded by 'DOT', and the final numbers will be the week and the year. For example, 2317 would indicate the 23rd week of 2017; this information can help identify a tyre.

19.5.1.1 Offences relating to tyre condition and maintenance

Tyres on vehicles and trailers must be in good condition and suitable for the purpose for which they are being used. They must also be inflated to the correct pressure. The photograph shows an under-inflated tyre.

(Photograph courtesy of James Nunn)

Regulation 27 of the Road Vehicle (Construction and Use) Regulations 1986 applies for vehicles and trailers used on roads with pneumatic (inflatable) tyres, and covers a range of problems relating to tyre condition and use. (This regulation does not apply to agricultural motor vehicles with a maximum speed of 20 mph; for vehicles that have broken down or are en route for breaking up; or vehicles being towed at not more than 20 mph.) In all cases, however, tyres should not be in such a condition that they could cause damage to the road surface or persons (reg 27(1)(h)).

Tyres must be the correct type for the vehicle (taking into account the types of tyres fitted to the other wheels), and for the road conditions or purpose. Some wear is permitted, depending on the type of vehicle, but the following types of damage are not allowed:

- cuts anywhere on the surface of the tyre, longer than 25 mm or 10 per cent of the section width of the tyre (whichever is the greater), and also deep enough to reach the ply or cord;
- lumps, bulges, or tears;
- exposed ply or cord.

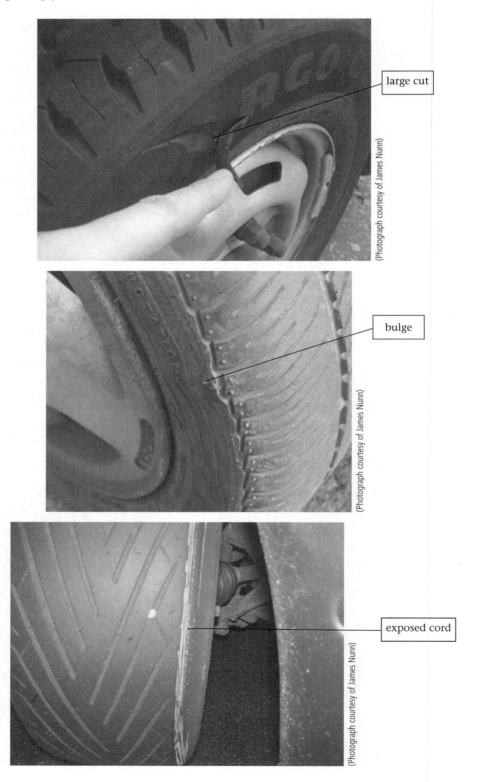

For private cars and vans (driving licence category B and Private Light Goods vehicles (see 19.3.5)) and their trailers, the tread grooves should be at least 1.6 mm deep over the whole central three-quarters of the tread-width. A depth gauge should be used to measure accurately. Areas where there is no visible tread pattern remaining are described as 'devoid of tread'.

The width of the central three-quarters of the tread-width can be calculated as follows:

1. Measure the width of the tread, ie the surface of the tyre in contact with the road (total width = 160 mm).
2. Obtain the width of the central three-quarters of the tread-width by dividing the total tread-width by 4, then multiplying by 3 (160 mm/4 = 40 mm, and then 40 mm × 3 = 120 mm). Or alternatively use a calculator to multiply the tread-width by 0.75 (160 mm × 0.75 = 120 mm).
3. Obtain the width of each of the two outer eighths of the tread-width by dividing the total tread width by 8 (160 mm/8 = 20 mm).
4. Check that your calculations are correct by adding the value for the central three-quarters to twice the value for the outer eighth (120 mm + 20 mm + 20 mm = 160 mm, hence correct).

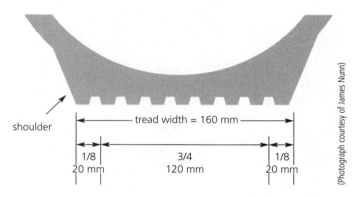

(Photograph courtesy of James Nunn)

One-eighth at the edge of the tread-width is a relatively small amount so if an area with insufficient tread is clearly visible at first glance, it is likely to be more than just the outer eighth (but it will still need measuring!).

The outer eighths (on each side of the tread-width) can have patches with less than 1.6 mm of tread (as long as there are no cuts or exposed cord or ply).

The four photographs show worn areas on different parts of the tread-width, all worn beyond the legal limit (the first shows a tyre with insufficient tread in at least part of the central area, the second shows wear to both outer edges, the third shows wear to just the inner edge, and the fourth to just the outer edge).

(Photographs courtesy of James Nunn)

For other types of vehicle (such as motorcycles, larger passenger vehicles, and larger goods vehicles) the groove depth over at least three-quarters of the tread-face must be at least 1.0 mm. The area with at least 1 mm tread depth must be continuous but can be towards one side (it does not have to occupy the central three-quarters of the tread-face). Therefore a legal tyre can have no tread over the whole of the inner or the outer quarter of the tread-face, or the inner and the outer eighth, or other combinations of areas. (Note, however, that certain types of tyre (usually for high performance motorcycles) are manufactured with no grooves on the outer eighths of the tread-width.)

This motorcycle tyre has some tread across the whole tread-face, but it is worn below the legal limit.

(Photograph courtesy of James Nunn)

For mopeds (see 19.3.1.3), all the original tread pattern grooves must be visible. Here, no tread is visible in the central area, so this is illegal.

(Photograph courtesy of James Nunn)

19.5.2 Lights on vehicles

The position, style, maintenance, and colour of vehicle lights are important for road safety. Police responsibilities include identifying vehicles with faulty lights, testing and inspecting lights, and bringing the faults to the attention of the owner and/or driver. Drivers should use their vehicle lights with consideration towards other road users. Police officers can offer advice to drivers on this; for example, lights should not cause undue dazzle or discomfort to other people using the road.

The following information relates in part to the Road Vehicles Lighting Regulations 1989. There are two main categories of lights: obligatory lights (must be fitted and maintained), and optional lights.

> **TASK 6** A range of lights is now available for temporary attachment to the roof of a vehicle. Find out whether blue lights are permitted for use in this way.

19.5.2.1 Obligatory lights

Here we will examine the obligatory lights required for a car as this is the most common type of vehicle on the road. Other classes of vehicle have different requirements, as described in the regulations.

The obligatory lights on the front of a car are: position lights ('side lights'), dipped, and main beam headlights, and direction indicators. On the back of the car the obligatory lights are: position lights, direction indicators, stop lights (brake lights), fog lights, a registration-plate lamp, and a reflector (albeit not strictly a light). A 'hazard warning-signal device' to operate the direction indicator lights on the front and back of the car is also obligatory. These obligatory lights are often clustered together.

Position lights must be present on all four corners of a vehicle, to indicate the vehicle's presence and width to other road users. The front position lights ('side lights') are white and not particularly bright, and are often switched on by the first click of the switch near the steering wheel. The rear position lights ('tail lights') are red, and are operated by the same switch as the front position lights. They are less bright than brake lights. Position lights must be lit when the vehicle is moving at night (between sunset and sunrise) and during the day if visibility is reduced. They may also be required when a vehicle is parked on a road at night, see 19.5.2.4 for details.

Dipped-beam headlamps are powerful white lights at the front of the car. They illuminate the road ahead, but should shine downward and to the left to avoid dazzling drivers of oncoming vehicles. The dipped-beam headlights are often switched on at the second position of the light switch. They must be lit when the car is being driven during hours of darkness, but are not required by law on roads with street lighting with a 30-mph limit or less (position lights are still required) or if the vehicle's fog lights are illuminated. They should also be used during the day in seriously reduced visibility. The dipped-beam headlights do not need to be illuminated if the car is being towed. The illumination of dipped-beam headlights is usually indicated on the vehicle display by the illumination of a green lamp or pictogram.

Main-beam headlights ('full-beam') are very bright white lights at the front of the car which shine straight ahead to illuminate the road over a long distance. They are usually operated with a pull or push of a switch near the steering wheel when dipped-beam headlamps are already on. If the front fog lamps are in use (in seriously reduced visibility), the use of mainbeam headlights can be counterproductive as the light will reflect back from the fog causing the driver to be dazzled, reducing the distance the driver can see.

The main-beam headlight switch must be wired so that the lights can be 'dipped' to avoid dazzling oncoming traffic. This involves no movement inside the headlamp unit; the power supply is simply switched to the dipped-beam bulbs. The illumination of main-beam headlights is indicated on the vehicle display as a blue lamp or illuminated pictogram.

Direction indicators are found at each corner of the car (and sometimes at the sides) and are used to indicate to other road users that the driver is intending to move the car to the right or left. They must be amber and flash between 60 and 120 times a minute. They are usually operated by pushing a switch near the steering column upwards or downwards. There must be some sort of indicator near the driver to show that the direction indicators are activated. If an indicator flashes very fast this usually indicates that one of the other bulbs in the circuit has failed.

The rear registration-plate lamp is white, and illuminates the rear plate when the position indicator lights are switched on. It should not shine directly backwards (to avoid dazzling the driver of any following vehicle).

Rear stop lamps ('brake lights') are red and very bright. They are positioned at the rear corners of the car and must operate when the main (primary) braking system (eg foot brake) of the car is applied. They warn other road users that the vehicle brakes have been activated and therefore the vehicle may be slowing down or stopping.

Rear fog lamps are red and very bright, similar to stop lamps. They are operated by an independent switch (which may be part of the main lighting switchgear), and will only work when the headlights are illuminated. They should be used only if visibility is reduced, as they might prevent following drivers from noticing any illumination of the stop lamps, and this can obviously be dangerous. They do not need to be used when the car is towing a trailer.

Hazard warning signalling uses the same lamps as the direction indicators. It is controlled by a switching device that makes all the direction indicators flash at the same time. It operates automatically in some vehicles when the driver brakes hard. It should only be used:

- when the vehicle is stationary, to alert other road users of an obstruction;
- when moving on a motorway or dual carriageway, to warn drivers behind of an obstruction ahead; or
- by the driver of a bus when children under 16 are getting on or off, or to summon help.

The switch to activate this device must be in reach of the driver. The switch button often has a small triangle which lights up when the hazard warning lights are illuminated.

19.5.2.2 Optional lamps

Some optional lamps perform the same function as obligatory lights: for example extra front-position lights (side lights), extra stop lamps, extra direction indicators, and extra dim/dipping (the dipped beam headlamps operate at less than their normal brightness to replace the need for front position lights (front side-lights)) and hazard warning devices. As these all have the same functions as obligatory lights, they must be maintained and in full working order, just like the obligatory lights (which must still be fitted as described earlier).

Other optional lamps include lamps such as reversing lights and front fog lights. They are not obligatory so do not have to be maintained. They must not, however, be in such a condition as to cause danger or be used in such a way that they cause undue dazzle or discomfort to other road users.

19.5.2.3 Vehicle lights when driving at night

The position lights must be used as soon as the sun sets and until the sun rises. Dipped headlights should be used during the 'hours of darkness' which starts half an hour after sunset and ends half an hour before sunrise. The times for sunset and sunrise are available on police databases (via the control room), but these times can also be found in newspapers and on the internet.

> Remember:
> - hours of <u>d</u>arkness for <u>d</u>ipped headlights; and
> - <u>s</u>unset and <u>s</u>unrise for <u>s</u>idelights.

19.5.2.4 Parking without lights at night

On a road with a speed limit of 30 mph or less some types of vehicle can be parked without illuminated position lamps between sunset and sunrise. This applies to cars, mini-buses, light goods vehicles, motorcycles, and invalid carriages, but not to a vehicle with a trailer or a projecting load. The vehicle must be parked:

- at least 10 m from a junction, facing the right way (on a one-way street this can be either side) and close to the kerb; or
- in a designated parking area or lay-by.

19.5.2.5 Legitimate use of a vehicle with defective lights

A vehicle with defective lights may be driven in some circumstances without an offence being committed. This is only permitted during the day (between sunrise and sunset), and the lights must have become defective during that journey, or arrangements must have already been made to repair the fault (reg 23(3) of the Road Vehicles Lighting Regulations 1989).

There are numerous other exemptions to the lighting regulations in regs 4–9, so unusual circumstances will need to be considered on a case-by-case basis.

> **TASK 7** Consider each of the following statements in turn, and decide if each statement is true or false:
>
> 1. The term 'hours of darkness' refers to a period from half an hour after sunset to half an hour before sunrise.
> 2. The legislation that covers the use of lights on vehicles is the Road Vehicles (Construction and Use) Regulations 1986.
> 3. The permitted flash rate of an indicator lamp fitted to a vehicle is between 80 and 100 pulses per minute.
> 4. Hazard-warning signals on a vehicle may be used lawfully when the vehicle is being towed by another vehicle.
> 5. A defect occurring during a journey during daylight hours is a defence to a defective light fitted to a vehicle.
> 6. A reversing light is an optional lamp.
> 7. The term 'obligatory light' means a light that is required by the legislation to be fitted to a vehicle.

19.5.3   **Danger of injury from the use or poor maintenance of vehicles or trailers**

There are numerous circumstances where the use of a vehicle or trailer may pose a danger or nuisance to other road users. Some of these are specifically addressed in the legislation (see 19.5.3.1 and 19.5.3.2), but many are not. Section 40 of the Road Traffic Act 1988 and reg 100 of the Road Vehicle (Construction and Use) Regulations 1986 are worded so they can be used to cover a wide range of situations related to maintenance and incorrect use of a vehicle. The offences relate to using a vehicle, including causing or permitting its use (see 19.2.4). The vehicle must be on a road.

If the use involves a danger of injury to any person, this is an offence under s 40A of the Road Traffic Act 1988, if the danger is due to:

- the condition of the motor vehicle or trailer (or of its accessories or equipment);
- the purpose for which it is used;
- the number of passengers carried by it or the manner in which they are carried; or
- the weight, position, or distribution of its load or the manner in which it is secured.

If the use of the vehicle causes nuisance but not danger, then reg 100 of the Road Vehicle (Construction and Use) Regulations 1986 can be used.

Offences under these sections can be used for defects which do not fall within specific regulations. This could include suspension or bodywork defects, or extra wide wheels which stick out far beyond the bodywork (these can make contact with pedestrians or their clothing as the vehicle passes by). Jagged edges on bodywork (see the photograph of the wheel arch of a van) can cause injury to other road users.

(Photograph courtesy of James Nunn)

Bodywork and parts must be secure or they could cause injury or collisions (see the photograph of the loose bodywork on a motorcycle).

(Photograph courtesy of James Nunn)

Specific Incidents

19.5.3.1 Poor maintenance and some associated offences

When considering the condition of a vehicle, a general rule is to take account of how it was first constructed, as this provides a guide to how it should be maintained. If a component part is missing or not working, an offence is likely to have been committed. Specialist equipment and training may be required to deal with some of these matters. Here we list just some of the offences under the Road Vehicles (Construction and Use) Regulations 1986 that relate to poor maintenance of a vehicle:

- The wipers and washers (those that are required to be fitted) must be maintained in efficient working order and be properly adjusted (reg 34). Split blades as shown in the first photograph are not allowed.
- An audible warning instrument (horn) must be fitted to any motor vehicle with a maximum speed of more than 20 mph (reg 37).
- The braking systems (including the handbrake) must be maintained in good working order and be properly adjusted (reg 18(1)). Brake fluid should be clear and amber coloured; in the second photograph you can see it is opaque which shows it is contaminated with water and has formed an emulsion. There should be no evidence of fluid leaking from the brake system (see the next photograph which shows where fluid has leaked over the inside of a wheel).
- Exhaust systems and silencers must be maintained in good working order, and must not be altered to increase the noise made by escaping exhaust gases (reg 54).
- Motorcycle exhausts must be the correct type (for a moped or motorbike first used after 1 January 1985, reg 579A(1) or (4)). The silencer should be either the original fitted by the manufacturer or an approved British Standard replacement, and must comply with noise requirements. (A motorcycle should not be used on a road if its exhaust is marked 'not for road use' or similar.)
- Vehicle emissions must not contain any smoke, visible vapour, grit, sparks, ashes, cinders, or oily substance that causes (or is likely to cause) damage to property, or injury or danger to other road users (reg 61). Some police services have instruments to test vehicle emissions, but this is usually undertaken by local authority environmental services or the DVSA.

(Photograph courtesy of James Nunn)

(Photograph courtesy of James Nunn)

(Photograph courtesy of James Nunn)

19.5.3.2   Incorrect use of a vehicle and some associated offences

There are many ways in which a vehicle can be used incorrectly under the Road Vehicles (Construction and Use) Regulations 1986. The regulations stipulate, for example, that:

- Passenger numbers must not exceed the number that seats allow (reg 100(1) and (3)) so, for example, passengers must not be carried in the rear of a small van with no fixed seating.
- The horn (reg 99) must not be used when the vehicle is stationary (other than in an emergency involving another vehicle, or when using a reversing or boarding-aid alarm). In addition, the horn must not be used by moving vehicles on restricted roads between 2330 and 0700 hrs.
- Excessive engine noise from motor vehicles on roads must be avoided by the driver taking reasonable care (reg 97).

19.5.3.3   Stationary vehicle offences

The regulations on stationary vehicles are covered under the Road Vehicles (Construction and Use) Regulations 1986. The engine must be turned off when the vehicle is stationary for any length of time to prevent noise or exhaust emissions (reg 98), and it is an offence to leave the engine running whilst stationary in a confined space with other vehicles. The engine must also be turned off and parking brake applied when the driver stops and leaves the vehicle ('quitting'), unless there is another person in the vehicle who is licensed to drive it (reg 107, and s 42 of the Road Traffic Act 1988). This would apply, for example, to a driver who parks outside a shop and runs inside to buy something. Certain exemptions apply to emergency service vehicles and to vehicles with machinery that requires the engine to be running.

19.5.3.4   Head and eye protection for motorcyclists

Helmets or other suitable protective headgear must be worn by anyone driving or riding on a motor bicycle (defined in 19.2.1). It is an offence under s 16 of the Road Traffic Act 1988 to drive or ride on a road without such protection. The design of the headgear is regulated by

Specific Incidents

the Motor Cycles (Protective Helmets) Regulations 1998. The helmet must bear a mark indicating compliance with the British Standard (BS 6658:1985) or the equivalent EU standard, or it must be of a type which seems likely to afford similar protection. A helmet must be securely fastened by straps or other fastenings, and an additional strap under the jaw must be used to secure a chin cup (reg 4). Under the regulation, a helmet that is not secured is 'not being worn'. Helmets are not required for some people in some circumstances, such as:

- a person using a ride-on motor mower;
- Sikhs who wear a turban, whilst on a two-wheeled motorcycle;
- passengers in a side-car; and
- a person pushing a two-wheeled motorcycle on foot.

Riders or drivers of three-wheeled vehicles do not need to wear a helmet if the distance between any two wheels on the same axle (front or back) is at least 460 mm. The distance between the wheels is measured between the centre of the area of contact with the road for each wheel. Under reg 4, if the two wheels are less than 460 mm apart they are regarded as a single wheel, so the vehicle would be classed as a motor bicycle.

Eye protection is not required by law, but if used, it must meet the British Standards EN 1938:1999, or an offence is committed under s 18(3) of the Road Traffic Act 1988.

19.5.3.5 Seatbelts

The requirements for the use of seatbelts depend on the age of the person and where he/she is sitting. The requirements are provided in ss 14, 15, 15A, and 15B of the Road Traffic Act 1988, the Motor Vehicles (Wearing of Seat Belts) Regulations 1993, the Motor Vehicles (Wearing of Seat Belts by Children in Front Seats) Regulations 1993, and the Motor Vehicles (Wearing of Seat Belts) (Amendment) Regulations 2006.

A summary of the requirements is shown in the table (based on rules 99–102 of the Highway Code, available online). In addition, some older or classic cars may not have seatbelts fitted.

Seatbelt requirements

	Front seat	Rear seat	Who is responsible?
Driver	Must be worn if fitted	Not applicable	Driver
Child under 3 years of age	Correct child restraint must be used	Correct child restraint must be used. If unavailable in a taxi, the child may travel unrestrained	Driver
Child from 3rd birthday up to 1.35 m in height or 12th birthday (whichever is reached first)	Correct child restraint must be used	Correct child restraint must be used where seat belts are fitted. Adult belt must be used if correct child restraint is not available in a licensed taxi or private hire vehicle, or for reasons of unexpected necessity over a short distance, or if two occupied restraints prevent fitment of a third	Driver
Child aged 12 or 13 years, OR Child over 1.35m tall (any age under 14 years)	Seat belt must be worn if available	Seat belt must be worn if available	Driver
Passengers aged 14 and over	Seat belt must be worn if available	Seat belt must be worn if available	Passenger

If a child seat or restraint is used it should be suitable for the weight of the child concerned, and fitted in accordance with the manufacturer's specifications.

In some situations a seatbelt does not have to be worn, such as:

- a driver engaged in deliveries (eg delivering post or newspapers) or collections if the distance between the stops is less than 50m;
- a driver reversing a vehicle, or supervising a learner driver who is reversing a vehicle (or conducting a manoeuvre which includes reversing);
- an examiner conducting a driving test, if wearing the belt would be dangerous;

- people in vehicles being used for police purposes (see local policy; as a general rule the exemption is not used and may vary in relation to people under arrest) and vehicles being used for fire brigade purposes;
- taxi drivers while 'plying for hire', answering calls for hire, or carrying passengers, and private-hire drivers while carrying passengers;
- people taking part in processions organized by, or on behalf of, the Crown;
- people holding a medical certificate providing exemption from wearing a seatbelt (provided the certificate is produced at the time or within seven days, or includes a relevant letter issued within the EU (in relation to a Community licence holder));
- a disabled person wearing a disabled person's belt;
- the vehicle is driven under a trade excise licence (which allows untaxed vehicles to be driven by the motor trade) for the purposes of investigating or remedying mechanical fault; or
- where the seatbelt is an inertia type which is locked as a result of being, or having been, on a steep incline.

> **TASK 8** Imagine you are a police officer. You suspect a particular vehicle has a number of serious defects so you signal to the driver to stop (using powers under the Road Traffic Act 1988).
>
> - In terms of health and safety, what factors must you consider?
> - What will you to say to the driver, and if you find a defect what will you do next?

19.5.4 Loads

Loads carried by a vehicle must not be a danger or nuisance to any person or property. The weight, packing, distribution, and adjustment of a load must be taken into account (reg 100(1)). An abnormal load is a load which exceeds certain weights or dimensions, and special arrangements are required. The load carried by a motor vehicle or trailer must be secured if necessary, by physical restraint: for example the luggage on the roof bars of a car must be tied down (reg 100(2)).

The weight of the load must not cause the total permitted weight of the vehicle to be exceeded. The gross vehicle, gross train (vehicle and trailer), or gross individual axle weight limits are indicated on the vehicle (see the figure in 19.2.1.1 for an example of a VIN plate with weight limits).

A UK registered goods vehicle over 3.5t will have a plating certificate issued by the Vehicle and Operator Services Agency (VOSA), in addition to the VIN plate. A separate plating certificate is also issued for trailers. The plating certificate will be displayed in the cab of the goods vehicle or fixed to the trailer. The certificate designates the maximum vehicle and axle weights for use on UK roads (often referred to as the plated weight) and these may be different from the manufacturers' weights as different rules apply in different jurisdictions. It is an offence for the vehicle to be used without displaying the plating certificate.

If a vehicle is suspected to be overweight, authorized officers can instruct a driver to have it weighed at a calibrated weighbridge. These are generally located at local authority depots or private companies, and may be some distance from where the vehicle is stopped. Specially trained officers or VOSA vehicle examiners operate the weighbridge, and they can prohibit the use of the vehicle until its weight is sufficiently reduced.

A load is abnormal if any of the following apply:

- the total weight of the vehicle exceeds 44,000 kg;
- the axle load for a single driving axle exceeds 11,500 kg;
- the axle load for a single non-driving axle exceeds 10,000 kg;
- the width of the vehicle and its load exceeds 2.9 m; or
- the length of the vehicle and its load exceeds 18.65 m.

Abnormal loads may cause significant damage to road surfaces and other infrastructure unless carefully managed. Before any such load is moved, the police, highways authority, and the owners of any bridge or other relevant structure (such as Network Rail) must all be informed. The highways authority for the SRN (see 19.2.2.2) is Highways England, and they use ESDAL (electronic service delivery for abnormal loads) for making such arrangements. There may be restrictions on the route and the timing of the transit, and the lead time for notification can be up to ten weeks. Further details can be obtained from the gov.uk website.

Some loads (commercial or private), may contain dangerous materials such as explosives or corrosive substances. The carriage of hazardous goods on the roads is regulated by a European agreement, the International Carriage of Dangerous Goods by Road (ADR), which places responsibilities on both operators and drivers. Drivers must hold the correct ADR certificate for the specific category of dangerous goods being carried. Vehicles carrying dangerous goods are subject to an additional annual test, and must carry appropriate paperwork, markings, and equipment for the relevant load. A hazchem information sign must be displayed, which shows the nature of the goods, the primary hazard, information for fire fighters, and a contact telephone number. There are also regulations on how substances must be stored, packaged, and labelled, and the quantities that can be carried. Some exemptions apply for private vehicles, particularly relating to the quantities of particular materials that can be carried. Further details can be obtained from the gov.uk website.

19.5.5 Commercial vehicle driver and operator regulations

One of the key controls imposed on the drivers of commercial vehicles concerns driving hours, rest periods, and breaks. There are two sets of rules; the 'GB rules' which generally apply for smaller vehicles and shorter journeys, and the 'EU rules' most of which relate to larger vehicles and longer journeys. DVSA or specialist roads policing officers are most likely to be in a position to enforce the rules, but all police officers should be at least familiar with the basics.

All commercial vehicle operators (companies that run fleets of vehicles, including haulage firms and bus and coach companies) are obliged to record driver hours and the number of drivers on each vehicle, and retain this information for two years. Tachographs must be fitted in some types of vehicles to monitor driver hours, although under GB rules a time card can be used instead. There are numerous rules regarding tachographs, including testing regimes (see the gov.uk website for further details).

19.5.5.1 The 'GB rules' for commercial drivers

The GB rules apply for goods vehicles under 3.5 tonnes, for passenger vehicles with eight or fewer passenger seats, and for any regular passenger services of less than 50km (regardless of the number of passenger seats). The daily driving time for each driver must not exceed ten hours (including driving that is not on the public road, ie in a yard or off road). The rules also refer to 'duty time', which must not exceed 11 hours if it includes any driving. The duty time for employed individuals is the whole time at work, and for self-employed individuals is the period driving or otherwise working with the vehicle.

19.5.5.2 The EU rules for commercial drivers

The EU rules apply for goods vehicles over 3.5 tonnes and passenger-carrying vehicles with nine or more passenger seats on any type of journey in the EU (including the UK), except for regular passenger service journeys of less than 50km. These rules may also apply to vehicles being driven on 'permit operations' (such as school minibuses), and those used by voluntary groups, but the specific circumstances will need to be considered (see the gov.uk website for further details).

A driver must not generally drive more than nine hours in total in a day. This can, however, be extended to ten hours on two occasions each week, but the total must not exceed 56 hours a week, or 90 hours in two consecutive weeks. In terms of breaks, the driver must have a break (or breaks) totalling at least 45 minutes for every four and half hours of driving, and the following rest periods:

- a daily rest of at least 11 hours (but this can be reduced to nine hours on three occasions between any two weekly rest periods); and
- a weekly rest of at least 45 continuous hours after six consecutive 24-hour periods of working (12 consecutive 24-hour periods for coach drivers on international trips). The weekly rest can be reduced to 24 hours every other week, but the missing hours must be added to other weekly rests.

Note that this is a summary of the key points of these complex regulations, see the gov.uk website for full details.

19.5.5.3 Commercial vehicle operator's licences

Individuals or companies that run commercial vehicles must obtain an operator's licence.

There are three types of licence depending on the nature of the goods and journeys, and possession of a licence is indicated by an identity disc displayed in the window of the cab. The design and colour of the disc indicates the type of licence held; blue for standard national, green for standard international, and orange for restricted (ie only for carriage of the company's own goods). For interim licences the word interim is overprinted on the disc. Vehicle operator's licences are issued by the Traffic Commissioners for Great Britain, under the Goods Vehicles (Licensing of Operators) Act 1995 or the Public Service Vehicles (Operators' Licences) Regulations 1995.

An operator's licence can be revoked or suspended for breaches of rules and regulations. It is an offence to operate a commercial vehicle without an operator's licence, and there are severe penalties for operating without a licence.

19.6 Pedestrian Crossings and Road Signs

Over the years, the number of road signs and regulations in England and Wales has increased in an attempt to keep the road environment as safe as possible for all road users. These signs and regulations, however, are only of value if road users comply with them. Police officers can of course detect non-compliance offences, but can also help the public develop road-safety awareness. Note that some moving traffic offences have been decriminalized in some boroughs. A comprehensive explanation of road signs is provided in the Department for Transport publication *Know your Traffic Signs* available on the gov.uk website.

19.6.1 Pedestrian crossings

The following table shows the key characteristics of the three main types of pedestrian crossing described in the Zebra, Pelican, and Puffin Pedestrian Crossings Regulations 1997.

Pelican	Pedestrians can push a button to operate traffic lights to bring vehicles to a stop. The traffic light sequence is the same as for normal lights except that, after the red light, the amber light flashes to indicate that vehicles may proceed if the crossing is clear
Puffin	Sensors detect anyone waiting to cross and change the traffic lights accordingly for vehicles to stop. The sequence is the same as for regular traffic lights
Zebra	These are not supported by traffic lights, but are indicated by black and white striped poles with yellow flashing beacons on top. Pedestrians walk across a section of road with wide alternate white and black stripes.

19.6.1.1 Layout of crossings

The limits of crossings are marked out by two parallel lines of studs across the carriageway, as shown here.

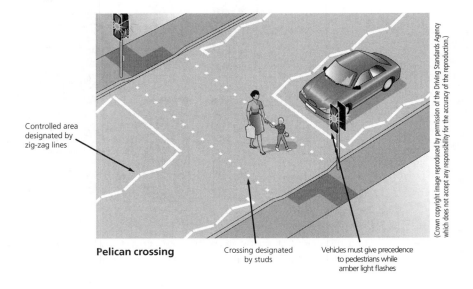

Controlled area designated by zig-zag lines

(Crown copyright image reproduced by permission of the Driving Standards Agency which does not accept any responsibility for the accuracy of the reproduction.)

Pelican crossing

Crossing designated by studs

Vehicles must give precedence to pedestrians while amber light flashes

The stop line for a Pelican or Puffin crossing is a solid white line across the road, just before the first line of studs. The line at the start of a Zebra crossing is a broken white line as the driver has to give way to pedestrians. Drivers and riders must not cross the stop or give-way line if pedestrians are on the crossing (or of course if the traffic lights are red for a Pelican or Puffin crossing).

The controlled area of a crossing is a certain length of road before (entry) and after (exit) a crossing. It is indicated by white zigzag lines painted along the edge and the middle of the road (between two and 18 zigzags, depending on the road layout in the immediate vicinity).

Where there is a refuge for pedestrians or a central reservation on a zebra crossing, each part of the crossing is treated as a separate crossing.

19.6.1.2 The correct use of crossings

The regulations for the use of crossings are given in the Zebra, Pelican, and Puffin Pedestrian Crossings Regulations 1997, and give rise to several offences which can be committed by drivers or pedestrians. Pedestrians have precedence over vehicles at (or approaching) zebra crossings (reg 25), and at pelican crossings when the amber light is flashing (reg 26). They must not delay on a crossing longer than is necessary to use the crossing in a reasonable time (reg 19).

For vehicles, the following rules apply:

- No overtaking within the controlled area when approaching any crossing (reg 24).
- All vehicles must stop at red/steady amber lights at Pelican or Puffin crossings (reg 23).
- No stopping in the controlled area of any crossings (reg 20) unless it is to allow pedestrians to cross, to prevent injury or damage, to make a right or left turn, to carry out building work or maintenance of the road or crossing, or to remove obstructions from the road (regs 21 and 22). (This does not apply to pedal cycles or public service vehicles, nor if the vehicle is beyond the driver's control.)
- No stopping on the actual crossing, unless the way is blocked or it is necessary to avoid injury to persons or damage to property (reg 18).

Contraventions of these regulations amount to an offence under s 25(5) of the Road Traffic Regulation Act 1984, and Sch 2 to the Road Traffic Offenders Act 1988.

19.6.2 White lines along the centre of the road

Solid white line systems are used to prohibit overtaking where visibility and vision is limited, or to separate lanes of traffic on roads going up a hill. The lines may be continuous on both sides, or continuous on one side and broken on the other. The lines may also be separated by a wider hatched area. The various layouts are set out in reg 26 of the Traffic Signs Regulations and General Directions 2002 and are covered on p 64 of *Know Your Traffic Signs*.

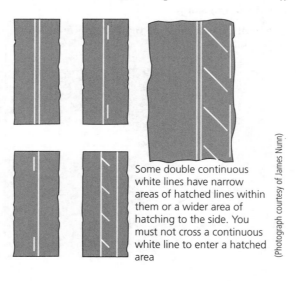

Some double continuous white lines have narrow areas of hatched lines within them or a wider area of hatching to the side. You must not cross a continuous white line to enter a hatched area

(Photograph courtesy of James Nunn)

The presence of at least one continuous central white line means that no vehicle is permitted to stop on either side of the road. Note that this also applies if there is a broken line on one side (reg 26(2)(a)). This regulation does not apply on dual carriageways, nor to vehicles used for fire brigade, ambulance, or police purposes. Exceptions also apply for vehicles that have stopped in order to:

- allow passengers to board/alight from a vehicle;
- allow goods to be loaded or unloaded from the vehicle;
- facilitate building or demolition work;
- enable the removal of any obstruction to traffic, road works, or public utility work; or
- avoid an accident.

Exceptions also apply for vehicles that cannot proceed due to circumstances beyond the driver's control (such as stationary traffic), or are required to stop by law or with the permission or direction of a constable in uniform or a traffic warden.

Crossing or straddling a solid white line is also covered by the regulations (reg 26(2)(b)). The solid line must be closest to the driver in the direction of travel, and it doesn't matter whether the other line in the system is broken or continuous. This does not apply when a vehicle is turning right or when the action is unavoidable when passing a stationary vehicle, a pedal cycle, a horse, a road-maintenance vehicle moving at 10 mph or less, or an accident. Nor does it apply when complying with directions from a police officer or a traffic warden in uniform. The offences relating to crossing white lines are committed under s 36(1) of the Road Traffic Act 1988, reg 10 of the Traffic Signs Regulations 2002, and Sch 2 to the Road Traffic Offenders Act 1988.

19.6.3   Disobeying a traffic sign

This is an offence only in relation to signs of the prescribed type (listed under reg 10 of the Traffic Signs Regulations and General Directions 2002) that have been lawfully placed on or near a road (s 36 of the Road Traffic Act 1988). Drivers are therefore under no obligation to heed informal signs erected by members of the public.

Regulation 10 of the Traffic Signs Regulations and General Directions 2002 creates two lists of relevance to s 36 of the Road Traffic Act 1988:

List 1: contravention of a sign on List 1 is an offence under s 36 of the Road Traffic Act 1988.

List 2: these are selected signs from List 1. Contravention of these signs creates a significant danger, and may lead to disqualification or endorsement of the driver's licence.

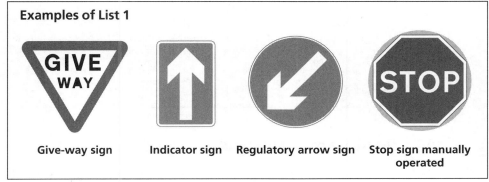

Examples of List 1

Give-way sign   Indicator sign   Regulatory arrow sign   Stop sign manually operated

(Crown copyright images reproduced by permission of the Department for Transport)

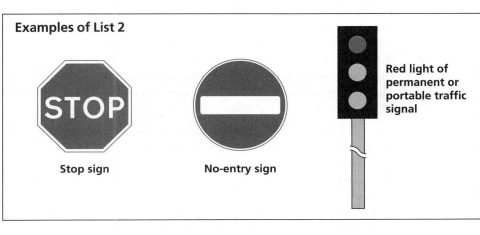

Examples of List 2

Stop sign   No-entry sign   **Red light of permanent or portable traffic signal**

(Crown copyright images reproduced by permission of the Department for Transport)

Specific Incidents

19.6.4   School crossing patrols

Local councils can designate locations where children cross roads on their way to and from schools (or from one part of a school to another) as a 'patrolling place'. Here, a school crossing patrol (in uniform) can hold up a prescribed sign to stop traffic to allow people to cross (s 28 of the Road Traffic Regulation Act 1984). Vehicles must stop before reaching the crossing place (so people crossing are not impeded) and remain stationary for as long as the sign continues to be exhibited (s 28(2)). Police officers may be required to undertake this function on occasions.

It is a summary offence to fail to comply with the requirements of a school crossing patrol, or cause a vehicle to move when the sign is exhibited (s 28(3)). The penalty is a fine, and the driver may also be disqualified.

TASK 9 For each of the following road traffic signs, find an image to show either the symbol for the sign or the sign as marked on the road surface itself.

1. Vehicular traffic entering the junction must give priority to vehicles from the right: for example, a mini-roundabout.
2. Priority is to be given to vehicles from the opposite direction.
3. Warning of a weak bridge.
4. Prohibition of vehicles exceeding a stated height.
5. Drivers of large or slow vehicles to stop and phone for permission to cross a level crossing.
6. Route for use by buses and pedal cycles only.
7. Route for tramcars only.
8. Stop sign, manually operated.
9. Convoy vehicle, no overtaking.
10. Stop for road works.
11. Vehicles to stay to the right of a vehicle involved with mobile road works.
12. Zigzag lines for an equestrian (horse) crossing (also called 'Pegasus') or Toucan crossing (crossing for pedestrian and cyclists to use together).
13. Line markings across a junction at which a vehicle must give way.
14. Variations of double white-line markings, including the use of hatched areas.
15. Variations of yellow bus-stop markings.
16. White lines and hatched areas dividing lanes or a main carriageway from a slip road (on motorways or dual carriageways).
17. Yellow grid markings within a box junction preventing entry without a clear exit.
18. Red-light signal of permanent/portable traffic signals and green filter arrows.
19. Tramcar not to proceed further.
20. Intermittent red-light signals at railway level crossings, swing bridges, etc.
21. Matrix prohibition.

19.7   Road Traffic Collisions

It is common to refer to collisions between vehicles as 'accidents' and the older police term of RTA (for Road Traffic Accident) has even entered popular language. However, it is more common now in police circles to refer to a Road Traffic Collision (RTC) or a 'crash' rather than an accident. This change of terminology reflects the thinking that incidents of this nature are not random acts of chance, but have causes. Most collisions are caused by a combination of factors such as driver error, driver distraction, poor appreciation of a hazard, and so on. However, the term 'accident' is still used frequently during police training and features in much of the relevant legislation.

Road traffic collisions are very common and result in a large number of injuries; 160,378 casualties in 2018 (Department for Transport, 2019b). It is as if the whole population of a town the size of Harrogate in North Yorkshire or the entire district of Wealdon in East Sussex (ONS, 2019k) were to be injured every year, year after year. There has in fact been a general downward trend in total casualties since 2003, but this is mainly due to the decrease in the number recorded in the 'slight injury' category. The number of fatalities has remained around the same since 2010, and serious injuries have been rising since 2013.

Collisions are generally categorized as follows:

- Damage Only (where there is only vehicle damage and no injury);
- Non-Reportable Damage Only (NRDO) where there are no grounds for a police report;
- Personal Injury (often referred to as a PI); and
- Killed or Seriously Injured (the term KSI is widely used).

Officers attending collisions are legally obliged to report certain types of collisions, known as 'reportable accidents' (see 19.7.2.1) to their police service; these reports will also contain statistical data relating to the circumstances. All police services are then obliged to submit the statistical data regarding collisions to the Department for Transport (referred to as STATS19, see 19.7.2.3).

19.7.1   Management of collision scenes

The police have a number of key responsibilities when responding to collisions, and some of these would apply to any potential crime scene (see 11.2). At the scene of a collision the police must:

- preserve life,
- coordinate the emergency services involved (eg the Fire and Rescue Service),
- secure, protect, and preserve the scene (including any electronic evidence from dashcams or telematics, eg),
- lead and manage the subsequent investigation into the incident, and
- liaise with relatives of the injured or killed.

Incidents with a serious injury or fatality should be treated as a crime scene. Specialist officers will undertake forensic reconstruction and related activities, but all officers need to have a basic understanding of legislation and procedures. In the initial response to a collision on the SRN (see 19.2.2.1), the police work very closely with the highways authorities (see 19.2.2.2).

Here we provide a summary of the key police responsibilities, but for further information see also *CLEAR Keeping Traffic Moving*, available online. CLEAR is a mnemonic for Clear, Lead, Evaluate, Act, and Re-open, and is part of a government initiative for improving incident management and traffic congestion on the strategic road network. It aims to clarify the priorities of the various organizations involved in traffic incident management, and promote partnership working. It is hoped that this will improve incident management and reduce the duration of incidents. Further detail on the management of emergency incidents on highways is available on the gov.uk website, and police service training will reflect this best practice.

19.7.1.1   Dynamic risk assessments

When attending incidents on roads, police officers should conduct a dynamic risk assessment. This involves continually evaluating the changing circumstances (the location, the vehicles, and the people involved) and adjusting the assessment accordingly.

In relation to the location, the physical layout or position on a road can increase the risk, for example any bends in the road can prevent approaching drivers from seeing the incident. The weather conditions or a low winter sun can also reduce the visibility. The speed, volume, and movements of passing traffic should also be considered, as should other problems such as fallen trees or electricity cables. Some locations may suffer poor radio and/or mobile phone coverage, hindering communication between officers at the scene and their control rooms.

All the vehicles involved should be identified; as you might expect multi-vehicle incidents can compound risk factors or create new ones. The contents and the post-impact condition of some vehicles may present additional hazards; spillage of fluids, high voltages in modern electric vehicles, chemical hazards from vehicles that have caught fire, and body fluids from casualties should all be taken into account. If you are unsure, take advice from fire and rescue units as they are specialists in such hazards. Some of the vehicles might have been involved in criminal activity (always carry out PNC checks), creating additional complications. Specialist equipment such as lighting or screening is also important and should be available via force control rooms, particularly if there has been a fatality or there are special recovery requirements, for example for abnormally heavy loads or vehicles that have left the carriageway.

All the people at the scene should be accounted for; it is not uncommon for individuals to be thrown some distance from the vehicles. Their demeanour and any need for medical attention should be taken into account, and support provided as appropriate. The PNC could be used to help establish whether any of them have been involved in criminal activity that could present additional risks at the scene.

Specific Incidents

19.7.1.2 ACE-CARD actions for road traffic incidents

The 'ACE-CARD' mnemonic can be used to help remember the sequence of considerations and actions required when responding to a road or traffic incident. This approach is summarized in the table. A fuller explanation can be found in the *Roads Policing* section of the College of Policing APP, available online.

Letter:	Abbreviation for:	Meaning:
A	**A**pproach	Before approaching gather as much information as possible. Approach incidents from the rear, where possible.
C	**C**aution (signs)	Place warning signs and cones correctly (see 19.7.1.4). If on a motorway and the matrix speed restrictions need activating, contact 'Control' (or the local highways control room). Establish an appropriate 'exclusion zone' around the incident.
E	**E**xamine (the scene)	Decide whether further assistance is needed. Employ the critical incident procedures if required (see 11.5).
C	**C**asualties	After protecting the scene check that all casualties have been found and administer first aid if required. Take details of casualties before they are taken from the scene.
A	**A**mbulance (and Fire and Rescue Service and other support agencies)	Control and manage the scene. Provide a safe working area for the support agencies.
R	**R**emove (the obstructions)	Recovery services should be contacted promptly (via the control room) but no vehicle should be removed until potential evidence is secured. Breakdown vehicles should be controlled by police or designated highways agency personnel (see 19.2.2.2 and 19.7.1).
D	**D**etailed (investigation)	Reporting and subsequent investigation according to local and national policy.

19.7.1.3 Special considerations for police use of the motorway hard shoulder

Motorists are only permitted to use and drive on the hard shoulder in emergencies. The police may, however, drive on the hard shoulder ('hard shoulder running'), as specified in reg 16 of the Motorways Traffic (England and Wales) Regulations 1982. The College of Policing suggests that driving on the hard shoulder should be kept to a minimum (APP *Roadcraft: The Police Driver's Handbook*) and that officers should remember that it:

- may be in use by traffic as a live running lane;
- could be obstructed by stationary vehicles or moving vehicles straying into the hard shoulder;
- may be unsafe because of dirt and debris.

Officers driving on the hard shoulder should also keep to an appropriate speed, and remember that if attending a stationary vehicle (especially in darkness), the driver or passengers may be present on the hard shoulder.

19.7.1.4 Cone tapers and warning signs

A cone taper is used to guide motorists into the appropriate lanes if one or more lanes are closed. Warning signs must be used if part of the carriageway is to be coned off, and several signs will be needed for roads with higher speed traffic. On single carriageways, the signs should be placed on both directions of approach. The minimum requirements for cone taper warning signs are shown in the table:

Speed limit	Number of signs	Clear view to the first sign	Distance for the signs (before the start of the cone taper)
70 mph (motorways)	3	100 m	300, 600, and 900 m
50–60 mph	2 or 3 (depends on safety considerations)	100 m	300 and 600 m (and 900 m if a third sign is used)
40–50 mph	2	100 m	200 and 400 m
30 mph or less	1	100 m	50 m

Adapted from College of Policing APP for the management of incidents.

When reopening any road or removing a lane closure, primary consideration must be given to safety.

On fast roads, motorways, or other roads on the SRN there may be multiple closures and diversions which can cause additional complications. A plan should be drawn up in consultation with the other agencies involved, such as Highways England, traffic officers, and contractors. The re-opening will often be phased to reduce any 'conflict' between traffic flows in adjacent lanes.

19.7.2 Driver obligations after a collision

The Road Traffic Act 1988 takes a common-sense approach to collisions (referred to as accidents in the Act) and dictates that the drivers involved must stop and be prepared to provide details to anyone who reasonably requires information, or report the incident to the police (s 170). The information might be needed for compensation claims for repairs, injuries, or deaths. Police officers need to know what information must be exchanged after a collision, and which offences are committed when a person fails to meet his/her obligations in this regard.

19.7.2.1 Reportable accidents

If an accident meets certain criteria, then the driver has to provide particular information to other people, or failing that, report the incident to the police (s 170(1) of the Road Traffic Act 1988); this is known as a 'reportable accident'. The criteria for a reportable accident concern the location of the accident, the vehicle type, and whether there is any damage or injury apart from to the driver and his/her vehicle. The definition of an 'accident' is not provided by statute and remains a question of fact for the courts to decide. However, in *R v Morris* [1972] RTR 201 'accident' was held to be 'an unintended occurrence which has an adverse physical result'.

For an accident to be reportable, the location of the vehicle at the moment of the collision is important. It must have been on a road or other public place (which could include hospital grounds, household garage blocks, private roads, or motorway service areas; see 9.2.1.1 and 19.2.2 for further discussion on the definition of a public place). If the vehicle leaves the road or other public place during or after the accident and comes to rest in a private dwelling, or grounds adjacent to the road or public place, this is still a reportable accident. If a collision takes place at any location other than a road maintained at public expense, evidence will be required to prove that it is a public place (eg concerning the frequency of use, by whom, and under what circumstances).

The vehicle must be mechanically propelled (see 19.2.1) and the collision must be due to its presence on a road or other public place. This includes vehicles intended or adapted for use off-road (eg dumper trucks and off-road motorcycles) and covers a wider range of vehicles than 'motor vehicles' (see 19.2.1). The phrase 'due to the presence' implies that the incident would not have occurred had the vehicle not been there, and does not necessarily mean that the vehicle was directly involved. It may be that the presence of the vehicle purely created the circumstance where other vehicles were involved in an incident. The classic example of this is a legally parked car that creates a slight narrowing of the available space which leads to a collision; had the car not been present the collision would not have occurred.

The damage must be to another vehicle such as a bicycle, or to property such as a road sign, garden wall, or certain animals. Note that lamp posts are the property of the local highways authority or the local council.

(Photograph courtesy of James Nunn)

The damage can be to private property, but the vehicle must have been on a road or other public place immediately before the incident. The damage does not have to be permanent or beyond repair, but the physical appearance must have been altered in some way. Certain types of animals (horses, cattle, asses, mules, pigs, sheep, goats, and dogs) are classed as property in this context. For injuries, the injury must be to a person other than the driver of the vehicle, for example passengers, pedestrians, or people in other vehicles. The injury can be shock as well as actual bodily harm.

When attending a reportable accident, the police officer must record all the details even if no offence has been committed (see 19.7.2.3). A full record of the events should be made (see 10.2) because the officer might be called as a witness in a civil court case, for example if a pedestrian had been seriously injured in a collision and is claiming compensation. The format of the record will be subject to local instruction, see 19.7.2.3.

TASK 10 In many police forces the policy is to conduct a preliminary breath test on every driver involved in a road traffic collision. What legislation provides this power? What computer checks could be carried out on the drivers involved?

19.7.2.2   Information required after a reportable accident

All the driver(s) at a reportable accident must stop and remain at the scene for as long as necessary to provide information to others (s 170(2) of the Road Traffic Act 1988). Failing to stop at any accident is a serious offence and is committed even if the person later reports the accident to the police.

At the scene, a driver must provide particulars to anyone who has reasonable grounds for needing the information; this could include the driver or rider of any other vehicle involved, the passengers in any of the vehicles, property owners, pedestrians, or their representatives. The driver must provide: his/her name and address; the name and address of the vehicle's owner; and the identification marks of the vehicle (eg the vehicle registration number). Failing to stop or report an accident is a summary offence under s 170(4) of the Road Traffic Act 1988. The penalty is six months' imprisonment and/or a fine, and the offender may also be disqualified.

If the driver cannot or does not provide the relevant information at the time of the accident, then he/she must 'report' the accident and provide the relevant information to the police as soon as reasonably practicable, and certainly within 24 hours (s 170(3) and (6) of the Road Traffic Act 1988). He/she must report in person to a constable or police station; it is not sufficient to telephone or email. It is a matter for a court to decide what is 'reasonably practicable' for the particular circumstances.

A relevant insurance certificate must be produced by the driver where personal injury is caused to another person (an 'injury accident'). The certificate should be shown to a police officer and any person having reasonable grounds for seeing it, for example the injured person (s 170(5)). If this is not possible at the time, the driver must report the accident to the police and produce the insurance as soon as is reasonably practicable and, in any case, within 24 hours (s 170(6)). Failing to produce proof of insurance after an injury accident is a summary offence under s 170(7) of the Road Traffic Act 1988 and the penalty is a fine. When the police attend, many of these arrangements no longer apply as officers are generally able to ascertain insurance status at the scene of the incident using the MIB database through the PNC.

19.7.2.3   STATS19 data

STATS19 data is a statistical record of all reportable accidents (see 19.7.2.1). STATS19 data is submitted to the Department for Transport by individual police forces. The Department for Transport collates and analyses the data to produce the annual collision statistics, published each September (see Task 11). Some forces still record collisions on paper records which are then converted to an electronic format, whilst others record collisions electronically. The Metropolitan Police records collisions on its Case Overview Preparation Application (COPA). The Department for Transport is currently reviewing the STATS19 system.

CRaSH is a Department for Transport electronic system devised for recording collisions and submitting the statistical information, and making it available to authorized users such as local authorities. The system has been adopted by about half the police services in England and Wales at the time of writing (the remainder submit paper reports), though more services are scheduled to start using it soon (Department for Transport, 2019c). The use of different reporting systems can affect the way the statistical data is recorded, and this is acknowledged in the annual collision statistics report (ibid).

The STATS19 data reports concern the circumstances of the collision, including the police officer's judgement regarding the contributory factors; the most frequent cause in 2018 was 'failing to look properly'. Other information such as the names and full addresses of parties involved and witness details are not included. It is important that the information contained in the STATS19 data is accurate because it provides the evidence base for road safety and casualty reduction strategies. The Department for Transport document *STATS20* provides guidance on completing the STATS19 reports (Department for Transport, 2011).

The analysis of STATS19 data provides insights into the key factors causing collisions, and can help identify strategies to reduce the number of casualties. Previous interventions include national advertising and enforcement campaigns (such as the Christmas drink-driving initiatives), new locations for speed cameras, setting up community speed-watch initiatives, and the re-engineering of junctions. Casualty reduction policy and activity revolves around the 4Es (enforcement, education, engineering, and evidence); the STATS19 data is fundamental to the success of these processes.

(Photo by Kevin Lawton-Barrett)

TASK 11

1. The following is a list of some of the main contributory factors to reported road accidents from *Contributory factors in reported accidents by severity, Great Britain, 2017, for fatal collisions*, available on the gov.uk website). Before you look at the report, which ones do you think are the most common causes? Put them in order, with the most frequently occurring first.
   - Pedestrian failed to look properly
   - Driver impaired by alcohol
   - Driver illness
   - Driver failed to look properly
   - Loss of control
   - Careless, reckless, or in a hurry
   - Failed to judge other person's path or speed
   - Exceeding the speed limit
   - Vehicle travelling too fast for conditions
   - Poor turn or manoeuvre

2. List three national road policing priorities.

19.8   Offences Relating to Standards of Driving

Standards of driving are assessed as sufficient when a driver passes his/her driving test, but this minimum standard should be maintained. This is defined, for the purposes of the Road Traffic Act 1988, as the standard of a 'competent and careful' driver, and it will be for a court to decide, based on the facts presented. Offences relating to the standard of driving are listed at the start of the Act. Here we cover the following offences (from the Road Traffic Act 1988 unless otherwise stated):

- causing death by dangerous driving (s 1);
- causing serious injury by dangerous driving (s 1A);
- dangerous driving (s 2);
- causing death by careless or inconsiderate driving (s 2B);
- careless and inconsiderate driving (s 3);
- causing death by driving whilst unlicensed or uninsured (s 3ZB);
- causing death by driving whilst disqualified (s 3ZC);
- causing serious injury by driving whilst disqualified (s 3ZD);
- causing the death of another person whilst under the influence of drink or drugs (s 3A);
- careless and inconsiderate cycling (s 29);
- driving elsewhere than on a road (s 34); and
- wanton and furious driving (s 35 of the Offences Against the Person Act 1861).

For ease of explanation the offences will not be dealt with in the order in which they are presented in the Act. We will examine what we mean by dangerous driving and careless and inconsiderate driving, and then consider the offences that relate to the consequences of such activity.

19.8.1   Dangerous driving

The legislation considers there are two main causes of dangerous driving: the driver's manner and actions during driving and the condition of the vehicle. These are fully defined in s 2 of the Road Traffic Act 1988.

Section 2A(1) states that a person is regarded as driving dangerously because (a) the way he/she drives falls far below what would be expected of a competent and careful driver; and (b) it would be obvious to a competent and careful driver that the driving would be dangerous (a question of fact for the court to decide). The minimum standard of driving applies during the driving test, with knowledge and application of the Highway Code also setting the standard at which a competent and careful person should drive. The Highway Code therefore provides a useful guide when interviewing and gathering evidence for this type of offence. The following are examples of driving activities which may support an allegation of an offence under s 2A(1):

- racing or competitive driving style;
- driving at a speed which is highly inappropriate for the prevailing road or traffic conditions;
- aggressive driving, such as sudden lane changes, cutting into a line of vehicles, or driving much too close to the vehicle in front;
- disregard for traffic lights and other road signs which, on careful analysis, would appear to be deliberate, or disregard for warnings from fellow passengers;
- overtaking in circumstances where it could not have been carried out safely;
- impaired driver ability, such as having an arm or leg in plaster, or impaired eyesight, or too tired to stay awake;
- using a mobile phone (*R v Browning* [2001] EWCA Crim 1831; [2002] 1 Cr App R (S) 88).

The dangerous condition of a vehicle (s 2A(2)) is judged from the perspective of a 'competent and careful driver if it would be obvious ... that driving the vehicle in its current state would be dangerous'. The weight or height of the vehicle, as well as any load carried, should be considered in the context of the location and road conditions. Examples of s 2A(2) circumstances include driving with a load which presents a danger to other road users, and driving with knowledge of a dangerous vehicle defect.

When gathering evidence for dangerous driving, the Construction and Use Regulations 1986 and the Highway Code provide useful benchmarks. A wide range of defences are available (see 19.8.3), so where appropriate, evidence should be collected to negate these. It is for a court to decide whether it would be 'obvious' that the driving was dangerous. The penalty is a fine or imprisonment (six months if tried summarily and two years on indictment).

19.8.2 Careless or inconsiderate driving

Legislation concerning careless or inconsiderate driving is provided within s 3 of the Road Traffic Act 1988. An offence is committed by a person who drives a mechanically propelled vehicle on a road or other public place without due care or attention or without reasonable consideration for other persons using the road or public place. Whether the driving was careless or inconsiderate is a question of fact for the court to decide.

Careless driving (driving without due care and attention) is defined in law as when the standard of driving falls below what would be expected of a competent and careful driver (s 3ZA(2)). (Note the difference between this offence and dangerous driving (see 19.8.1), where the standard falls *far* below the expected standard.) Examples of careless driving would include a driver who fails to look behind whilst reversing, or crosses the white line when overtaking without checking for oncoming vehicles, or using the right-turn direction indicator and then turning left. The driver's knowledge of the circumstances can be taken into account, and any factors that he/she should have been aware of.

For inconsiderate driving, another person must be inconvenienced by the suspect's driving. This would include:

- cutting across the path of another vehicle, for example when turning, or changing lanes without prior warning;
- cutting in at the front, after passing a long line of waiting traffic;
- causing traffic problems by failing to conform to directional arrows;
- forcing other drivers to take evasive action by failing to drive correctly;
- deliberately performing skids at high speed or making 'handbrake turns';
- driving on footpaths; or
- driving off-road across grassland, with disregard for other users of the space.

A driver can only be charged with careless or inconsiderate driving, not both. They are both summary offences, and the penalty is a fine, an endorsement, and discretionary disqualification, or a £100 FPN and three penalty points.

19.8.3 Defences to dangerous, careless, or inconsiderate driving

There are various defences for dangerous or careless or inconsiderate driving. These are summarized in the following table.

Defence	Explanation
Automatism	Automatism is 'the involuntary movement of a person's body or limbs' (*Watmore v Jenkins* [1961] 2 All ER 868), and it must occur very suddenly with little or no warning. This could be due to an epileptic fit (with no prior symptoms) or a wasp sting. Case law has established that falling asleep at the wheel or a hypoglycaemic diabetic coma are not automatism
Unconsciousness or sudden illness	This would include situations where a person suddenly becomes unconscious as a result of circumstances beyond his/her control, such as being hit on the head by a stone that has smashed through the windscreen. Case law has established that falling asleep at the wheel or a hypoglycaemic diabetic coma are not beyond the driver's control
Assisting in the arrest of offenders	Here, the driver might have a defence if he/she intentionally shunted a suspect's car off the road in order to help the police arrest the suspect (*R v Renouf* [1986] 2 All ER 449)
Duress by threats	The suspect must be able to show that he/she drove dangerously due to a threat (that he/she could not otherwise avoid or escape)
Duress of necessity (of circumstances)	The suspect must be able to show that he/she had to drive dangerously to avoid death or serious injury (to any person), and that it was not reasonable to act otherwise in the circumstances
Sudden mechanical defect	This does not apply if the driver is already aware of the defect or it could have been easily discovered by superficial examination, for example of tyres (*R v Spurge* [1961] 2 All ER 688)
Authorized motoring event	A person will not be guilty under s 1, 2, or 3 of the Road Traffic Act if he/she drove in accordance with an authorization for a motoring event given by the Secretary of State (s 13(A) of the Road Traffic Act 1988)

Specific Incidents

19.8.4 Other offences involving dangerous driving

Section 35 of the Offences Against the Person Act 1861 states that it is an offence for anyone 'having the charge of any carriage or vehicle ... [to cause] or cause to be done bodily harm to any person' by wanton or furious driving, racing, other wilful misconduct, or wilful neglect. This could be used when there has been dangerous driving but the Road Traffic Act 1988 does not cover the circumstances, for example when the driving was not on a road or other public place, the vehicle was not a mechanically propelled vehicle (eg it was a bicycle or horse-drawn vehicle), or the statutory Notice of Intended Prosecution was not given (see 19.12.5). The offence can only be committed if the driver has a degree of subjective recklessness: he/she must appreciate that harm was possible or probable as a result of the driving (*R v Okosi* [1996] CLR 666). It is triable by indictment only and the penalty is two years' imprisonment. Disqualification is discretionary, although endorsement (three to nine points) is obligatory if the offence was committed in a mechanically propelled vehicle.

Riding a cycle carelessly, inconsiderately, or dangerously on a road is an offence under the Road Traffic Act 1988. This can be riding 'without due care and attention, reasonable consideration for other persons using the road' (s 29), or riding dangerously (s 28(1)). These offences are triable summarily and the penalty is a fine.

19.8.5 Causing death by driving

Road deaths have a devastating effect on families and the community, and the police have a responsibility to investigate and provide support for those affected. A family liaison officer (usually referred to as a FLO) can be appointed to provide information, build confidence, and gather any information from the family which would be helpful to the investigation. Friends and relatives of the deceased may want to visit the scene and leave memorials or tributes (local authority policies might apply).

The offences are all under the Road Traffic Act 1988 and are categorized by the type of driving that caused the death. It is not relevant whether the person who died was in the suspect's vehicle at the time of the incident. The offences are as follows:

- causing death by dangerous driving (s 1);
- causing death by careless or inconsiderate driving (s 2B);
- causing death by careless or inconsiderate driving whilst under the influence of drink or drugs (s 3A);
- causing death by driving whilst unlicensed or uninsured (s 3ZB); and
- causing death by driving whilst disqualified (s 3ZC).

For a s 3A offence there must be evidence of careless or inconsiderate driving whilst under the influence of drink or drugs. The driver can be unfit through drink or drugs (s 4), over the prescribed limit (s 5 or 5A), or have refused to provide a specimen (s 7) within 18 hours of the driving, or refused permission for it to be laboratory tested (s 7A(6)). These are explained in more detail in 19.9.

Note that for a s 3ZB or 3ZC offence, the manner of the driving must have contributed to causing the death but it does not have to be the sole reason. It is not necessary to prove careless or inconsiderate driving, but the mere presence of a vehicle on a road is insufficient (see *R v Hughes* [2013] UKSC 56). Driver licensing, vehicle insurance and disqualification are covered earlier in this chapter.

The table compares some key aspect of the various causing death by driving offences, and also shows the mode of trial and the penalties.

Section of the Road Traffic Act 1988	s 1	s 2B	s 3A	s 3ZB	s 3ZC
Type of vehicle	any mechanically propelled vehicle		mechanically propelled vehicle if unfit to drive (otherwise motor vehicle)	motor vehicle	
The location	on a road or other public place			on a road	
Mode of trial	indictment only	either way	indictment only	either way	indictment only

Minimum mandatory disqualification	two years	one year	two years	one year	two years
Endorsement	obligatory	obligatory 3–11 points	obligatory	obligatory 3–11 points	obligatory
Retaking driving test	compulsory and extended	discretionary	depends on alcohol/drug level	discretionary	compulsory and extended
Maximum custodial penalty	14 years	six months summarily, five years on indictment	14 years	six months summarily, two years on indictment	ten years

19.8.6 Causing serious injury by driving

Causing serious physical injury to another person by driving can be an offence in certain circumstances. Here, serious injury means physical harm, which amounts to grievous bodily harm as set out in the Offences Against the Person Act 1861 (see 15.3.1). There are two specific circumstances, each with its own offence:

- when a mechanically propelled vehicle is driven dangerously on a road or other public place (s 1A of the Road Traffic Act 1988). The penalty is a fine or imprisonment (12 months if tried summarily and five years on indictment); and
- when a motor vehicle is driven on a road by a disqualified driver and the driving has contributed in some way to the collision (s 3ZD of the Road Traffic Act 1988). The penalty is a fine or imprisonment (six months if tried summarily and four years on indictment).

Both offences carry an obligatory disqualification and 3–11 penalty point endorsement on conviction. A defendant found not guilty of these offences could still be convicted of dangerous driving (see 19.8.1), or careless or inconsiderate driving (see 19.8.2).

TASK 12

1. Who would be held to be 'driving' in each of the following scenarios? Use the case suggested as guidance.
    (a) Jerry sits in the driver's seat of a car and lets it freewheel down a sloping road with the steering lock on. See *Burgoyne v Phillips* [1982] RTR 49.
    (b) Maz, a passenger in a car 'driven' by Mel, sees a friend walking along the roadside towards the moving car. To frighten the friend, Maz snatches the steering wheel from Mel's grasp to make the car veer in that direction. Would Maz be held to be 'driving'? See *DPP v Hastings* (1993) 158 JP 118.
    (c) Hari is in the driving seat of the car and 'driving' along the road. Pat leans over from the front passenger seat and steers the car, while Hari manipulates the other controls. Hari's view forward is partially obscured by Pat. After some distance, the car runs into a ditch, while Pat is steering. Pat had been able to reach both the handbrake and the ignition key and knew the consequences of using the various controls, but did not have access to the foot pedals. See *Tyler v Whatmore* [1975] RTR 83. Who was driving?
2. Answer questions (a) and (b) by selecting the correct option(s) from the following list.
    (a) Where can dangerous driving and causing death by dangerous driving be committed?
    (b) In what location(s) does s 35 of the Offences Against the Person Act 1861 apply?
        (i) Anywhere?
        (ii) On a road?
        (iii) In a public place other than a road?
        (iv) In a public place only?

19.8.7 Other offences involving standards of driving

Some acts that amount to poor driving may not fall within the scope of the offences of dangerous, careless, or inconsiderate driving, but they may still amount to an offence, albeit of a less serious nature. Combined with other factors, the poor driving could contribute towards one of the more serious offences but would not, in most circumstances, constitute one of the more serious offences *per se*. Exceeding the speed limit is an important example of poor standards of driving, and is covered by s 89(1) of the Road Traffic Regulation Act 1984.

Members of the police service and other emergency services are granted some exemptions from road traffic regulations. However, police officers are expected to drive at least as well as other motorists and should aim to provide a positive role model for other drivers—consider this in relation to personal authority (see 5.11.5). It is very important that a police officer's driving meets the relevant standards and that he/she is fully aware of local police service policies before taking on any emergency response.

The following driving standards offences are derived from the Road Vehicles (Construction and Use) Regulations 1986:

- driving (or causing or permitting any other person to drive) a motor vehicle on a road if the driver is in such a position in the vehicle that he/she cannot have proper control of the vehicle or have a full view of the road and traffic ahead (reg 104). The penalty is an obligatory endorsement (three points) and a discretionary disqualification or a fixed penalty;
- opening a vehicle door on a road (or causing or permitting it to be opened) and injuring or endangering any person (reg 105). Anyone in the vehicle can commit this offence, but if a child opens the door it is likely the driver would be deemed to have permitted the offence. The maximum penalty is £1,000 fine or a fixed penalty;
- driving a motor vehicle on a road if the driver is able to see directly, or by reflection, a TV or similar apparatus (reg 109). This does not apply to satnav apparatus or other apparatus used to display information about the state of the vehicle, nor to devices that help the driver see the road adjacent to the vehicle;
- driving a motor vehicle on a road while using a hand-held phone or a similar device (reg 110). The meaning of 'using' in this context is explained in 19.8.7.1

19.8.7.1 Mobile phones and driving

The meaning of 'using' a mobile phone while driving has recently been clarified in the case *DPP v Barreto* [2019] EWHC 2044 (Admin). It must include some form of electronic communication from or to the handset (such as data transmission); however, this does not have to continue throughout the use. The communication is to be considered the whole process so, for example, reading or writing texts or emails constitutes using the device for interactive communication even though the data transmission element of the process may only be milliseconds and take place later. (Communication by two-way radio, such as 'CB', is excluded from this offence, although obviously the general need for safe driving still applies.) This offence can also be committed by a person supervising a learner driver. Where an employee commits an offence using a hand-held phone provided by his/her employer, the company can also be held liable if they have failed to prohibit the employee from using it while driving on company business. At the time of writing the government is considering reviewing this legislation.

The penalty is an obligatory endorsement (three points), a discretionary disqualification, and a fine. Alternatively an FPN can be issued (see 19.12.4).

TASK 13

1. What other offences might be considered for a person using a hand-held mobile telephone while driving, apart from the offence derived from reg 110 in the Road Vehicles (Construction and Use) Regulations 1986?
2. Driving while using a phone is clearly a significant distraction; what other circumstances or activities might adversely affect standards of driving?

19.8.8 Driving in places other than a road

The law surrounding 'off-road' driving is covered in s 34 of the Road Traffic Act 1988. This states that an offence is committed by a person who:

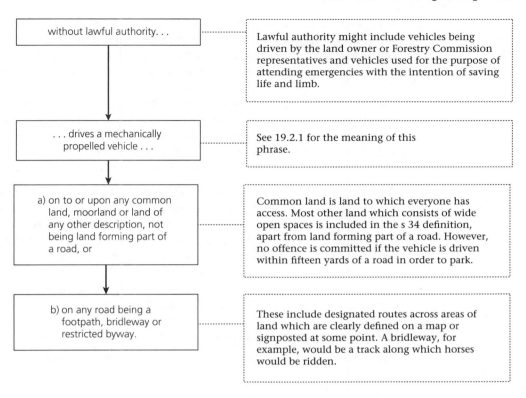

without lawful authority. . .	Lawful authority might include vehicles being driven by the land owner or Forestry Commission representatives and vehicles used for the purpose of attending emergencies with the intention of saving life and limb.
. . . drives a mechanically propelled vehicle . . .	See 19.2.1 for the meaning of this phrase.
a) on to or upon any common land, moorland or land of any other description, not being land forming part of a road, or	Common land is land to which everyone has access. Most other land which consists of wide open spaces is included in the s 34 definition, apart from land forming part of a road. However, no offence is committed if the vehicle is driven within fifteen yards of a road in order to park.
b) on any road being a footpath, bridleway or restricted byway.	These include designated routes across areas of land which are clearly defined on a map or signposted at some point. A bridleway, for example, would be a track along which horses would be ridden.

This is a summary offence, and the penalty is a fine.

19.9 Drink- and Drug-driving

It is an unfortunate fact that a proportion of the driving population choose to drive whilst under the influence of an intoxicant, be it alcohol or some other substance. Police officers inevitably come into contact with such individuals, and must know how to deal with them accordingly.

There are three driving offences relating to driving while under the influence of alcohol or other drugs, and these are all contained within the Road Traffic Act 1988:

- driving, or attempting to drive, or being in charge of a mechanically propelled vehicle whilst unfit to drive through drink or drugs (s 4);
- driving, or attempting to drive, or being in charge of a motor vehicle with alcohol (s 5) in excess of the prescribed limit; and
- driving, or attempting to drive, or being in charge of a motor vehicle with a specified drug (s 5A) in excess of the prescribed limit.

The s 4 offence is very different from s 5 and s 5A offences. For a s 4 offence, the prosecution has to prove that the suspect's ability to drive was actually impaired, whereas for a s 5 or 5A offence the only evidence required is a certain alcohol or drug concentration in the blood, breath, or urine (depending on the offence). They also involve different categories of vehicle.

Due to the complex nature of these offences and the numerous historical challenges to the procedures, the Department for Transport now issues standard forms (MGDD/A to MGDD/F, available online) to be used for investigating these offences. You should check that any hard copies at custody units are in fact the most up-to-date versions.

We will first consider some key terms and concepts in the legislation relating to alcohol, drugs, and driving, and then go on to look at preliminary and evidential tests in more detail.

19.9.1 Key terms from the legislation

The notion of a person being 'in charge of a vehicle' only occurs within ss 4, 5, and 5A of the Road Traffic Act 1988 and there is no legal definition for this, but case law focuses on control of the vehicle and how likely it was for the person to drive. Therefore each set of circumstances is a matter of fact for a court to decide. The court would take into account whether a person had some control of the vehicle, had the keys, or was in or close to the vehicle. Being 'in charge' can also include supervising a provisional licence holder (see *Leach v Evans* [1952] 2 All ER 264 and *Haines v Roberts* [1953] 1 All ER 344).

Specific Incidents

Some defendants claim a defence in relation to being 'in charge', and it may be necessary to negate this. For example, a man might attempt to prove that there was no likelihood of him driving the vehicle in the near future, but it has been held that simply stating there was no intention to drive is insufficient (see *CPS v Thompson* [2007] EWHC 1841 (Admin), [2008] RTR 70). A suitable defence could be that he had booked a hotel room for the night, or that the vehicle had been wheel-clamped (see *Sheldrake v DPP* [2003] 2 All ER 497 and *Drake v DPP* [1994] RTR 411 respectively). If there is no witness evidence that a driver had been driving prior to a collision, the defence might also claim that he/she was too badly injured to drive or that the vehicle was too damaged, but the court can disregard such matters (see s 4(4) of the Road Traffic Act 1988 and *CPS v Thompson* [2008] RTR 70). This is a complex area, and trainee officers should seek advice.

The term 'drug' has a different meaning depending on whether the offence is under s 4 or s 5A. For s 4 offences a drug is any substance which can cause an intoxicating (psychoactive) effect. This includes all 'controlled drugs' and other psychoactive substances (see 12.5.1). For an offence under s 5A, the drug must be one of the 17 drugs listed in s 5A, and no other drugs or substances can be taken into account. A particular individual can be simultaneously investigated for a s 4 and s 5A offence, so the difference in the meaning of the word 'drug' is important. The Department for Transport advises that if there is sufficient evidence, then officers should proceed with both a s 4 and s 5A process.

19.9.2 Unfit through drink or drugs

These offences are covered under s 4 of the Road Traffic Act 1988. The diagram shows this in detail (s 4(1)).

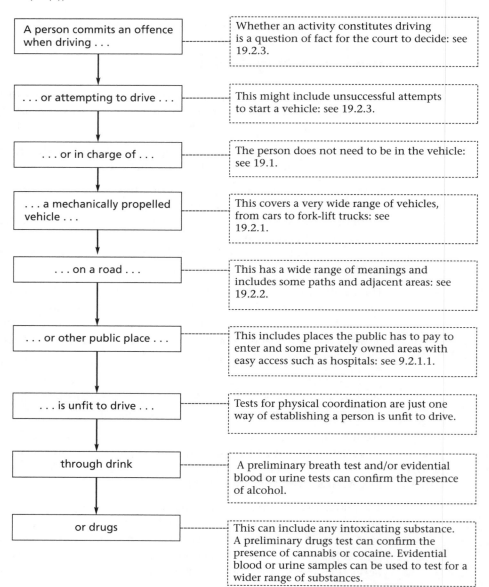

There is no need to administer a preliminary test for alcohol or drug levels before arresting a driver for this offence, but an officer can choose to do so. A positive preliminary test result means there is no need to arrange for medical confirmation that the person's condition is due to the presence of alcohol or a drug, and the officers can immediately arrange for an evidential test (see 19.9.5). Remember that the result of a preliminary test for drugs will be negative if the intoxicant is not one of those covered by the test.

The suspect's level of impairment and ability to drive properly is assessed by the police officer, through observations made during a preliminary impairment test (see 19.9.4.1). However, this would clearly not be required for a man who is so intoxicated that he falls out of the vehicle and is unable to stand.

If a preliminary test for alcohol or drugs had not been carried out or was negative, the doctor or health care professional (custody nurse) at the police station will examine the person and judge if his/her condition is due to intoxication (with any substance). If the examination shows that the person's condition is due to intoxication, then an evidential test will be used (blood or urine) to prove the presence of alcohol or a drug in the body, see 19.9.5.

A suspect arrested for a s 4 offence can also be investigated for a s 5 or a s 5A offence. If there is sufficient evidence, a suspect should be charged with more than one offence, and they will be dealt with independently. Section 4 can also be used if the driver is over the limit for alcohol or specified drugs, but the vehicle involved is not a motor vehicle (assuming there is sufficient evidence of impairment).

The evidence presented to a court for a s 4 offence is likely to include:

- the style of driving before the accused was stopped;
- his/her demeanour at time of stop (speech, unsteadiness);
- the results of any preliminary tests;
- the report by a medical examiner whilst in custody (particularly if screening specimens are not obtained to prove the presence of alcohol or drugs in the body); and
- the results of evidential drug tests (using blood or urine samples).

Remember that it might be necessary to present evidence to counter an 'in charge' defence that the driver was not likely to drive (see 19.9.1).

An arrest for a s 4 offence would be under s 24 of the PACE Act 1984. (There is no power of arrest for a s 4 offence under the Road Traffic Act 1988.) A power of entry to arrest for a s 4 offence is available under s 17(1)(c)(iiia) of the PACE Act 1984, if there are reasonable grounds for believing that the suspect is on the premises (see 10.8.1.2).

Offences under s 4 of the Road Traffic Act 1988 are triable summarily and the penalties are:

- for driving and attempting to drive whilst unfit due to drink or drugs (s 4(1)): six months' imprisonment and/or a fine, and obligatory disqualification; and
- for being in charge of a vehicle whilst unfit due to drink or drugs (s 4(2)): three months' imprisonment and/or a fine, and discretionary disqualification.

19.9.3 Driving, attempting to drive or being in charge of a motor vehicle when over the prescribed limit

There are two prescribed limit offences, s 5 relates to alcohol and s 5A relates to 17 specified drugs. The offences under s 5 and 5A only require evidence that the level of the substance in the suspect was over the prescribed limit, and evidence that the person was driving, attempting to drive, or was in charge of a motor vehicle.

19.9.3.1 Alcohol in excess of the prescribed limit

This offence relates to having alcohol over the prescribed limit in blood, breath, or urine. The flowchart shows the wording for a s 5 offence; bold-edged boxes emphasize the features that distinguish a s 5 offence from a s 4 offence.

Section 5 states that it is an offence for a person to:

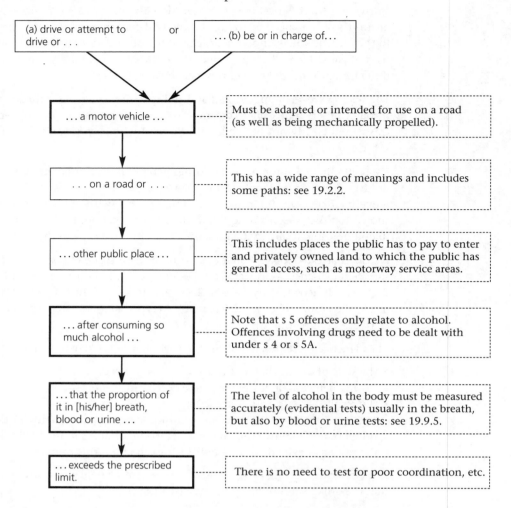

The prescribed limits are shown in the table. Note the units: microgrammes (μg), milligrammes (mg), and millilitres (ml). A good way to help memorize these figures is to remember that the digits in each measurement add up to eight.

Type of sample	Amount of alcohol per 100 ml
Breath	35 μg
Blood	80 mg
Urine	107 mg

These offences are triable summarily and the penalties are:

- for driving or attempting to drive above the prescribed limit (s 5(1)(a)): six months' imprisonment and/or a fine, and obligatory disqualification; and
- for being in charge of a vehicle above the prescribed limit (s 5(1)(b)): three months' imprisonment and/or a fine, and discretionary disqualification.

19.9.3.2 Specified controlled drug in excess of the prescribed limit

Section 5A of the Road Traffic Act 1988 relates to driving with certain specified drugs over the legal limit in the blood. The drugs covered by s 5A and their legal limits are shown in the table.

Specific Incidents

Controlled drug	Limit (microgrammes (µg) per litre of blood)
Amphetamine	250
Benzoylecgonine	50
Clonazepam	50
Cocaine	10
Delta-9-Tetrahydrocannabinol (THC*)	2
Diazepam	550
Flunitrazepam	300
Ketamine	20
Lorazepam	100
Lysergic Acid Diethylamide (LSD)	1
Methadone	500
Methylamphetamine	10
Methylenedioxymethamphetamine	10
6-Monoacetylmorphine	5
Morphine	80
Oxazepam	300
Temazepam	1,000

* The active ingredient in cannabis.

Some of the drugs on the list are regularly prescribed by doctors to help patients with conditions such as anxiety. However, some people obtain these drugs by other means and use them for recreational purposes, often at higher dosage levels than recommended by the manufacturer. For these drugs, the legal limits have been set very high, much higher than the levels for a person taking the drug at the medicinal dosage. This is to avoid penalizing drivers who are taking these drugs for medical reasons.

The wording and layout of s 5A is very similar to that of s 5; this was deliberate as the criminal justice system is very familiar with s 5 and how it is used. The flowchart for the s 5 offence (in 19.9.3.1) can be applied for s 5A, replacing 'alcohol' with 'drugs', and 'breath, blood, or urine' with 'blood only'. The penalties for s 5A offences are the same as the penalties for the equivalent s 5 offences.

Defences are available if the suspect can show that the drug had been prescribed or supplied for medical or dental purposes (s 5A(3)(a)), and had been taken in accordance with the instructions (s 5A(3)(b)), and that immediately before taking the drug, its possession was not unlawful (see 12.5.2). These defences cannot be used if the suspect did not follow professional advice about the amount of time that should elapse between taking the drug and driving (s 5A(4)(a) and (b)). The advice could be from the person prescribing, supplying, manufacturing, or distributing the drug.

19.9.4   Preliminary tests

Preliminary tests are frequently referred to as roadside screening tests. There are two types of preliminary tests; preliminary impairment tests, and tests for the presence of alcohol or certain drugs. Preliminary tests are covered in s 6A (breath), s 6B (impairment), and s 6C (drugs) of the Road Traffic Act 1988. A police officer does not need to be in uniform to require a person to take part in a preliminary test. However, the police officer actually administering a preliminary test must be in uniform (except after an accident). A Home Office statistical return form must be completed after administering a preliminary test. More recent equipment will do this automatically. Preliminary tests can also be used in police stations and hospitals.

The flowchart summarizes the circumstances for administering preliminary tests.

Specific Incidents

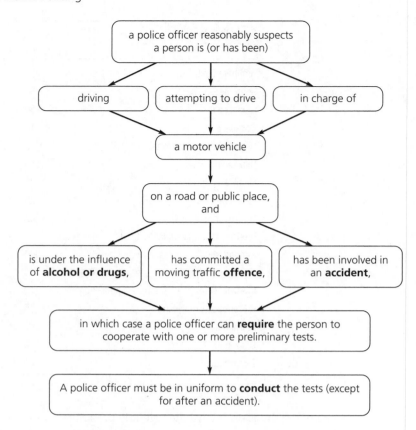

In some situations there may be many individuals at a scene, so it might not be clear who was driving. It should first be clarified who was in each vehicle at the time of the accident; witnesses may be able to help on this matter. However, remember that a police officer only has to 'reasonably believe' that a person was driving a vehicle at the time of the accident, so if no one admits to being the driver then more than one person from the vehicle can be tested. If a number of individuals were 'in charge' of the same vehicle, then all will be subject to testing.

The meaning of the term 'accident' has not been defined by statute and remains a question of fact for the courts to decide (see 19.7.2.1). When any such incident seems to be due at least in part to the presence of a motor vehicle on a road it 'is a fair basis on which a police officer may request the provision of a specimen of breath' (Lord Widgery CJ in *R v Morris* [1972] RTR 201).

A power of entry is available in order to administer preliminary tests (s 6E of the Road Traffic Act 1988), but only after an accident which the police officer reasonably suspects has caused an injury. The power can be used for any place, using reasonable force if necessary.

Any refusal to cooperate with a preliminary test is an offence and the person can be arrested (see 19.9.4.5).

19.9.4.1 Preliminary impairment tests

The Field Impairment Test (FIT) is used as the preliminary impairment test for s 4 offences, and the officer carrying out the test must be suitably trained. The subject is asked to carry out a number of specific actions with his/her eyes closed, such as walking in a straight line or judging time. The tasks and subsequent recording of the observations are set out in the MGDD/F form. Failing the test provides the officer with grounds for arrest.

19.9.4.2 Preliminary breath tests for alcohol

Screening tests for alcohol are primarily used for s 5 offences, but can also be used for s 4 offences. For s 5 offences the preliminary test is used to find out if it is *likely* that there is sufficient alcohol in the subject's system to provide grounds for suspicion that an offence has been committed. If positive, it also allows the officer to consider arrest. For s 4 offences the tests can confirm the presence of alcohol, which avoids the need to arrange for a doctor or other health care professional's opinion (see 19.9.2).

The preliminary breath-test devices sample air that has come from deep within the lungs, and must be approved by the Secretary of State. Electronic devices include models such as the Lion

Alcolmeter 500, the Alcosensor IV, the Draeger Alert, and the Draeger Alcotest 7410 or 6820. Non-electronic devices (such as Alcotest 80 and R80A and the Alcolyser) involve the inflation of a bag, and are used less often. Officers should be familiar with the devices deployed within their area, and ensure that the manufacturer's instructions and local police service policies are followed.

For conducting the test, the police officer must make the requirement of the suspect in a form of words that complies with the legislation, including the implications of failing to comply. There is no prescribed format, but officers will be advised on any locally agreed form of words during training, and it may be specified in local police service policy.

The officer must also ask the person when he/she last drank alcohol or smoked as this can disrupt the test results if the test is taken within a certain time period. However, failing to ask these questions will not invalidate the test (*DPP v Kay* [1998] EWHC 258 (Admin)), nor will an innocent failure to follow the instructions render the arrest and subsequent evidential test unlawful (although the results may be considered as less reliable).

To carry out the test the driver should be asked to take a deep breath and to blow into the machine in one continuous breath until requested to stop. The person should be told the result of the test. A positive result justifies arrest because it provides the officer with the grounds to suspect that the proportion of alcohol in the person's breath or blood exceeds the prescribed limit. The reason for the arrest is the suspicion, not the positive result. The suspect must be told that he/she is under arrest and the reasons for the arrest (s 6D(1) of the Road Traffic Act 1988), and must be cautioned. An evidential test for alcohol should then be carried out (see 19.9.5.1 and 19.9.5.2).

A patient in a hospital must never be arrested (s 6D(3)). However, should such a wrongful arrest take place, a subsequent and lawfully obtained evidential specimen will not become unlawful (*DPP v Wilson* [2009] EWHC 1988 (Admin)).

19.9.4.3 Preliminary drug tests

Screening tests for drugs are used mainly for s 5A offences but can also be used for suspected s 4 offences. For s 5A offences the preliminary test is used to provide grounds for suspecting that an offence has been committed, and therefore arrest. For s 4 offences the tests can confirm the presence of certain drugs. Once confirmed there will then be no need to arrange for a doctor or other healthcare professional to determine 'a condition due to ...' at the police station.

The test is carried out on a sample of saliva and currently identifies the presence of cocaine and cannabis (or more precisely its active ingredient THC). These feature on the s 5A list of drugs, and are two of the most commonly abused drugs. According to recent research, it seems they are likely to account for the vast majority of drivers under the influence of a drug (Department for Transport, 2013). The next drug proposed for inclusion in the saliva test is amphetamine.

There are currently two devices approved by the Home Office for roadside drugs screening; the Draeger DrugTest 5000 and the Suretec DrugWipe 3S. Both use the same technology to detect the drugs but display the results in different ways. Police services may use either or both of the devices, although their use may be restricted to specific departments or units. Any officer who is required to carry out testing will receive device-specific training.

A person may be under the influence of a drug that cannot be detected by the device. If an officers suspects this is the case and can justify an arrest due to the person's demeanour, the fact that it is not possible to screen for a particular drug is not relevant, and is no bar to arrest.

19.9.4.4 What to do after a preliminary test

If the result of a preliminary alcohol or drugs test is positive the person should be arrested so that evidential tests can be carried out. For a suspected s 5 or 5A offence (driving over the prescribed limit) the arrest power is provided under s 6D(1) of the Road Traffic Act 1988. For a suspected s 4 offence (driving while unfit) the arrest power is provided under s 24 of the PACE Act 1984. There is a power of entry in order to arrest a person who has been involved in an injury accident and provided a positive preliminary test (s 6 of the Road Traffic Act 1988).

If the result of a preliminary test is negative but it still seems that the driver is intoxicated then the officer could:

- conduct a preliminary drugs or alcohol test (whichever has not already been done);
- conduct a preliminary impairment test (if he/she is qualified and has the apparatus available) and proceed as for a s 4 offence;
- arrest under s 5A if it seems likely the intoxication is caused by one of the other 15 specified drugs on the s 5A list; or
- arrest the driver under s 24 of the PACE Act 1984 on suspicion of driving whilst unfit (under s 4).

If the result of a preliminary test is negative and there is no evidence of impairment and no other offences have been committed, then the driver is free to leave.

19.9.4.5   Failing to cooperate with a preliminary test

If the driver does not take the test correctly, refuses to participate, or is unable to complete a preliminary test (eg due to a medical condition), this amounts to 'failure to provide'. The number of opportunities that should be provided for completing a preliminary test varies between forces and will be determined locally.

If there is reasonable suspicion that the person is under the influence of alcohol or a drug, then he/she should be arrested and the relevant evidential tests carried out. If alcohol or drugs are not suspected, the person should instead be reported for the offence of failing to cooperate with the provision of a specimen for a preliminary test (s 6(6) of the Road Traffic Act 1988). The person's true identity will need to be ascertained through computer checks with Control and identity documents from the person. The address he/she gives must be checked as genuine. The suspect should be interviewed under caution (all recorded in the officer's pocket notebook), and then reported for the offence of failing to cooperate with a preliminary test and cautioned again. This offence is triable summarily and the penalty is obligatory endorsement (four points) and discretionary disqualification.

19.9.5   Evidential tests

The results of evidential tests for drugs and alcohol can be used as evidence in a court for an offence under s 3A, 4, 5, or 5A of the Road Traffic Act 1988. The specimens are usually provided at a police station (or hospital if the suspect is a hospital patient) but some types of tests can be conducted at the roadside. The requirement for any evidential test is usually made at a police station or hospital, but the requirement for an evidential breath test can also be made at the roadside. It is usual to arrest a suspect before requiring an evidential test, although this is not compulsory by law. Note that a suspect who is also a hospital patient cannot be arrested (s 6D(3) of the Road Traffic Act 1988).

If there is reasonable cause to believe that the suspect has a drug in his/her body (eg from a preliminary drug-test result or the medical examiner's opinion), a blood or urine specimen should be taken for a suspected s 4 offence, and a blood specimen for a suspected s 5A offence. A single blood specimen can be used to investigate a s 4 and 5A offence as long as there is sufficient quantity (the laboratory will need to be informed of this intention). For alcohol, an evidential breath test will always be used in preference to blood or urine tests (s 7(3) of the Road Traffic Act 1988) unless:

- there is reasonable cause to believe that a medical reason prevents the use of a breath test;
- the approved device is not available; and/or
- there is cause to believe the device gave an unreliable result.

A suspect at a police station cannot delay providing a specimen for an evidential test in order to obtain legal advice. There can only be a delay in exceptional circumstances and where a legal representative is available for immediate consultation (*Chalupa v CPS* [2009] EWHC 3082 (Admin)).

19.9.5.1   Evidential breath tests for alcohol

The test can be required and conducted at (or near) a place where a relevant preliminary breath test has been administered, at a police station, or in a hospital (s 7(2) of the Road Traffic Act 1988). For suspected offences of causing death by careless driving when under the influence of drink or drugs, or for being unfit to drive (ss 3A and 4 of the Road Traffic Act 1988 respectively) there is no need for a prior preliminary breath test.

Two samples of breath are required for the test, and the process and period of time in which the two samples are collected is called a 'cycle'. The two samples must be obtained from the same cycle in order for the test to be valid. Only the sample containing the lower proportion of alcohol will be used as evidence, and the other will be disregarded (s 8(1) of the Road Traffic Act 1988). The samples will be analysed by a device approved by the Secretary of State (currently the Camic Datamaster, the Lion Intoxilyzer 6000, or the Intoximeter EC/IR). The person operating the machine (often the custody officer) will have been trained to use it and will check that it is working properly. MGDD forms must be used to record the breath-test procedure and the completed forms will constitute the 'notes made at the time'.

As part of the requirement to provide specimens, the officer must say to the suspect 'I warn you that failure to provide either of these specimens will render you liable to prosecution.' (para A12 in the MGDD/A and s 7(7) of the Road Traffic Act 1988).

Each organization will have its own policy on how many attempts can be allowed for the suspect to provide a sufficient volume of air in a proper manner (s 11(3) of the Road Traffic Act 1988). Note that regurgitation of stomach contents does not affect the accuracy of the measurements (see *McNeil v DPP* [2008] EWHC 1254 (Admin)).

The prescribed limit for alcohol in the breath is 35 μg of alcohol per 100 ml of breath (see 19.9.3), but the police do not proceed unless the level is above 40 μg (see MGDD/A, section A20). After the test, the MGDD forms are completed and if the result is above the prescribed limit the driver can be charged and bailed to court.

If the driver fails to provide two samples of breath, the offence of 'failing to provide a specimen of breath for an evidential breath test' (s 7(6)) has been committed. Refusing to provide suitable samples is equivalent to failure (s 11(2) of the Road Traffic Act 1988), including when not enough breath is provided (see *Rweikiza v DPP* [2008] EWHC 386 (Admin)). The suspect must be allowed sufficient time to provide the samples in each subsequent cycle; otherwise a subsequent prosecution may fail (see *Plackett v DPP* [2008] EWHC 1335 (Admin)). The suspect is not obliged to mention any medical condition which could account for failing to provide enough breath, but the court does not have to accept the excuse if he/she later claims that this is the case (see *Piggott v DPP* [2008] WLR (D) 44). If the testing machine registers an error on the second sample in each of two cycles, then further breath samples can be required (eg at another police station or using another machine), and failing to comply is an offence (s 7(6)), even though previous samples were supplied (see *Hussain v DPP* [2008] EWHC 901 (Admin)). If the suspect does not speak English and a request for a specimen of breath is translated (by an accredited interpreter), a court can draw an inference (ie draw their own conclusions) on whether the suspect would have understood (see *Bielecki v DPP* [2011] EWHC 2245 (Admin)).

19.9.5.2 Blood and urine specimens

These may be required under s 7(3) of the Road Traffic Act 1988 (see the start of 19.9.5). For a suspected s 4 or s 5 offence, either type of specimen can be used, but for a s 5A offence it must be a blood sample. The requirement to provide a specimen of blood or urine can only be made at a police station or hospital. If the driver refuses (or is unable) to provide blood or urine samples, then he/she will have committed the offence of failing to provide samples for an evidential test (s 7(6) of the Road Traffic Act 1988).

Before a blood or urine sample is taken the driver must be told:

- for a suspected s 5 offence, the reason(s) why breath specimens cannot be taken (from the list under s 7(3) (see 19.9.5)); and
- that he/she is therefore required to give a sample of blood or urine; and
- that failing to provide the specimen could result in his/her prosecution.

Where there is an option, blood is the preferred medium. Apart from medical considerations, the driver cannot choose whether the sample will be blood or urine. Before proceeding with a blood test the driver should be asked if there are any medical reasons for not taking a blood sample. The sample must of course be taken by a medical examiner or health care professional. After the sample has been obtained the driver can be bailed to return to the police station when the results arrive back from the laboratory. Blood and urine samples are usually sent to the laboratory by post, although blood samples for a s 5A analysis must remain refrigerated and arrangements vary between police services.

19.9.5.3 Allowing for the delay between the offence and taking samples

As the human body continually breaks down alcohol it is assumed that the level of alcohol in a suspect's breath, blood, or urine at the time of an alleged offence will gradually decrease over time (if no more alcohol is consumed). It is a fact in law that a court will assume the level of intoxicants in the body at the time of the alleged offence were not less than the levels measured in the evidential test (s 15(2) of the Road Traffic Offenders Act 1988).

However, the accused may claim the 'hip-flask defence', insisting that he/she consumed alcohol or drugs after the offence but before the evidential sample was taken (eg that he/she ran off after a collision and went for a drink before the police arrived), or that he/she consumed intoxicants from a container (the proverbial (and sometimes actual) hip flask) in the vehicle after the preliminary test. This is formally referred to as 'post-incident drinking'. If he/she can prove this, the assumption under s 15(2) (see previous paragraph) cannot be made.

If a driver provides an evidential specimen and alleges he/she has consumed further intoxicants since the time of the alleged offence, 'back calculations' can be used to establish that the driver was in excess of the legal limit when the incident occurred. These calculations are based on the time elapsed since the offence, the subsequent consumption of alcohol, and the estimated rate of elimination of alcohol from the human body. Evidence for back calculations should be recorded on Form MGDD/D at the police station. However, if this defence is not raised until later, the relevant laboratory should be provided with as much information as can be obtained from the case papers and the officer in charge of the case.

The following information is relevant, where available:

- the type and quantity of alcohol consumed before the incident and, if possible, the times at which individual units of alcohol were consumed;
- the type and quantity of alcohol allegedly consumed after the incident but before the test;
- the driver's characteristics: weight, height, build, age, sex, and any medical conditions;
- details of any food consumed from six hours before the offence until the provision of a breath or laboratory specimen; and
- details of any medication taken regularly or within four hours prior to drinking.

TASK 14

1. If you are a trainee police officer, find out what preliminary test equipment is available for you to use and how to use it. This information should be available at your police station or from local policy documents.
   - Are you only authorized to use equipment to test for breath alcohol, or could you test for drugs as well?
   - Would you be allowed to carry out a preliminary impairment test?
2. The suspected commission of a moving traffic offence is one reason for requiring a driver to be tested for the presence of alcohol in his/her body. Give some examples of moving traffic offences under the Public Passenger Vehicles Act 1981, the Road Traffic Regulation Act 1984, and the Road Traffic Offenders Act 1988.

19.9.6   Drink- and drug-driving, and admission to hospital

Some drivers need to be admitted to hospital after an accident. Investigations in these circumstances are covered under s 9 of the Road Traffic Act 1988, and an MGDD/C form is used. A hospital is defined by the Act as an institution which provides medical or surgical treatment for in-patients or out-patients. The term 'patient' is not defined and will be a question of fact for the court to decide, but generally speaking a patient is a person who is currently on hospital grounds receiving medical treatment (or waiting to receive medical treatment).

19.9.6.1   Obtaining samples from a hospital patient

The medical practitioner (usually a doctor) in immediate charge of the patient must be notified before a requirement is made, or any test is carried out on the person (s 9(1) of the Road Traffic Act 1988). The procedures (see 19.9.4 and 19.9.5) must be explained as the welfare of a patient is paramount. If the doctor does not object, the patient can be asked to cooperate with a preliminary test.

If the result is negative, the patient must be told that no further action will be taken regarding a drink- or drug-driving offence. If he/she does not cooperate and refuses to have the test, the patient should be reported for an offence under s 6(6) of the Road Traffic Act 1988. Note that a hospital patient cannot be arrested for failing to cooperate with a preliminary test (s 6D(3)).

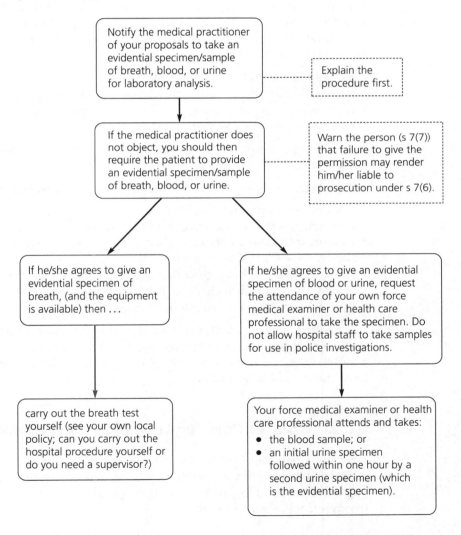

Evidential tests will be carried out if the result of the preliminary test is positive (or the patient fails to complete the test). The outline procedure is shown in the diagram.

If a blood sample is required it must be taken by a police medical practitioner or health care professional. Very rarely no such person is available, and another medical practitioner who is not responsible for the clinical care of the patient should take it.

Specific Incidents

An unconscious patient (described as 'incapable of giving valid consent' on the MGDD/C) cannot take part in a breath test and so a blood sample will be required, and once again the relevant medical practitioner must be notified (see s 9(1A) of the Road Traffic Act 1988). However, the blood sample must not be analysed until the patient regains consciousness and can give permission (s 7A(4)). It is an offence to refuse such permission (s 7A(6)).

TASK 15 A trainee police officer is required to attend the accident and emergency department at the local hospital. There she makes a lawful requirement for a sample of breath, blood, or urine from a patient who was driving a vehicle at the time of a collision. Unfortunately, whilst waiting for the police medical practitioner to arrive, the patient is discharged from hospital and leaves the building.

Does the obligation for the patient to provide that sample still stand? Refer to *Webber v DPP* [1998] RTR 111 for your answer.

19.10 Using Vehicles to Cause Alarm, Distress, and Annoyance

The police have a number of powers under s 59 of the Police Reform Act 2002 for situations where the anti-social use of motor vehicles is causing concern to other people in the area. The driving must amount to careless or inconsiderate driving, unlawful off-road driving (see 19.8.2 and 19.8.8 respectively) or unlicensed on-street racing. It must also cause (or be likely to cause) alarm, distress, or annoyance to other people. In such circumstances a police officer, using reasonable force when required, has the power to:

* require a moving vehicle to stop (s 59(3)(a));
* seize and remove the vehicle, after warning the driver (s 59(3)(b)); and
* enter certain types of premises (but not a dwelling-house or attached garage or garden) in order to stop or seize a vehicle (s 59(3)(c)).

Failing to stop is a summary offence under s 59(6) of the Police Reform Act 2002 and the penalty is a fine.

If the vehicle is to be seized under s 59(3)(b) there is no need for a warning if:

* it would be impracticable to do so;
* a warning has already been given on that occasion;
* there are reasonable grounds for believing that such a warning has been given on that occasion by someone else; or
* the officer has reasonable grounds for believing that the person has been given a warning (by any police officer, in respect of any vehicle being used in the same or a similar way) on a previous occasion in the previous 12 months.

The warning applies to both the driver and that particular vehicle, so it applies to future stops when anyone is driving that vehicle, and to that driver in any vehicle. The wording for a warning notice is not specified in the legislation, so the wording can vary; pre-formatted forms may be available locally.

19.11 Other Offences Relating to Vehicles and Highways

There are a number of offences that relate to vehicles and highways that are not directly related to driving. Here we cover the legislation that restricts the clamping of vehicles parked on private land, and some other non-driving highways offences that might cause distress or inconvenience to other road users.

19.11.1 Immobilizing vehicles parked on private land

Private individuals and organizations have been known to immobilize or move vehicles parked on private land, and then asked the owner/driver to pay a release fee. It is, however, a summary offence under s 54(1) of the Protection of Freedoms Act 2012 for a person without lawful authority to:

- immobilize a motor vehicle by attaching an immobilizing device, for example a wheel clamp (s 54(1)(a)); or
- move or restrict the movement of a vehicle, for example by towing it away or blocking its movement with another vehicle (s 54(1)(b)).

The notion of 'lawful authority' is the significant issue here. The 'law of contract' does not provide the landowner or operator of a commercially run car park with the lawful authority to immobilize or move a vehicle, even when the terms and conditions of the parking are clearly displayed and the vehicle is parked for a longer period than permitted (s 54(2)). So a car park operator who clamps a vehicle in such circumstances is likely to have committed this offence. However, for a car park where the movement of vehicles in and out is restricted by the use of a rising-arm barrier the situation is different. If a car driver does not pay the parking fee and therefore cannot leave because the barrier remains down, no offence is committed by the car park owner or operator because the car has not been immobilized or removed (s 54(3)).

Note that this offence cannot be committed by anyone who is entitled to remove a vehicle, as he/she would have lawful authority for this. An example might be when a representative of a hire company retrieves a vehicle after the hire agreement has expired (s 54(4)). Note also that the offence requires an intention to prevent or inhibit the removal of the vehicle, so a householder who merely moves a vehicle a few metres along the road to remove an obstruction from the entrance to his driveway (for example), does not commit the offence, because he did not intend to prevent the driver from accessing and using the vehicle.

19.11.2 Road-related anti-social behaviour

Some of the more common offences are described here.

Wilful obstruction is an offence under s 137 of the Highways Act 1980. It is an offence for a person:

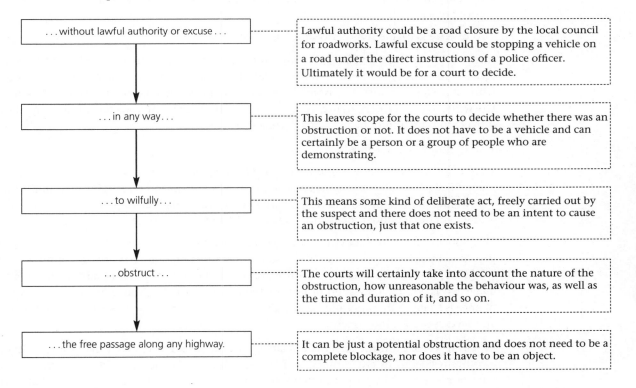

. . . without lawful authority or excuse . . .	Lawful authority could be a road closure by the local council for roadworks. Lawful excuse could be stopping a vehicle on a road under the direct instructions of a police officer. Ultimately it would be for a court to decide.
. . . in any way . . .	This leaves scope for the courts to decide whether there was an obstruction or not. It does not have to be a vehicle and can certainly be a person or a group of people who are demonstrating.
. . . to wilfully . . .	This means some kind of deliberate act, freely carried out by the suspect and there does not need to be an intent to cause an obstruction, just that one exists.
. . . obstruct . . .	The courts will certainly take into account the nature of the obstruction, how unreasonable the behaviour was, as well as the time and duration of it, and so on.
. . . the free passage along any highway.	It can be just a potential obstruction and does not need to be a complete blockage, nor does it have to be an object.

This offence is triable summarily and the penalty is a fine.

Specific Incidents

'Unauthorized campers' can be directed away from 'any land forming part of a highway, any other unoccupied property, or any occupied land without the consent of the owner' under s 77 of the Criminal Justice and Public Order Act 1994. This allows local authorities to direct people who are residing in vehicles in such locations to leave with the vehicles and any other property they have there.

Vehicles or trailers must not be left in a dangerous position on a road (s 22 of the Road Traffic Act 1988). It is an offence for a person in charge of a vehicle to cause or permit:

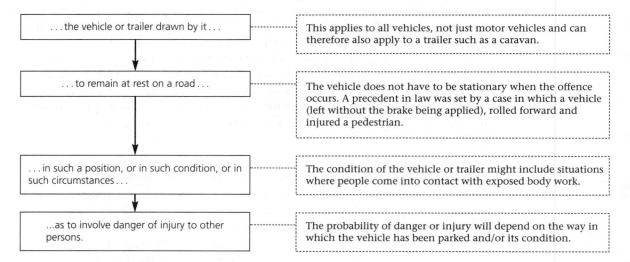

. . . the vehicle or trailer drawn by it . . .	This applies to all vehicles, not just motor vehicles and can therefore also apply to a trailer such as a caravan.
. . . to remain at rest on a road . . .	The vehicle does not have to be stationary when the offence occurs. A precedent in law was set by a case in which a vehicle (left without the brake being applied), rolled forward and injured a pedestrian.
. . . in such a position, or in such condition, or in such circumstances . . .	The condition of the vehicle or trailer might include situations where people come into contact with exposed body work.
. . . as to involve danger of injury to other persons.	The probability of danger or injury will depend on the way in which the vehicle has been parked and/or its condition.

This offence is triable summarily and the penalty is a fine.

Lighting fires or letting off firearms near a highway is an offence under s 161 of the Highways Act 1980. This prohibits any person (without lawful authority or excuse) from:

- depositing anything on a highway which leads to someone getting injured;
- lighting a fire on or over a carriageway; or
- discharging a firearm (or firework) within 50 feet of the centre of a highway if it could injure a user of the highway.

This offence is triable summarily and the penalty is a fine.

Interfering with road signs, other traffic equipment, or vehicles may put other road users at risk. Section 22A of the Road Traffic Act 1988 states that it is an offence to (intentionally and without lawful authority or reasonable cause) cause anything to be on or over a road, or interfere with a motor vehicle, trailer, cycle, or with traffic equipment (directly or indirectly) if this is likely to cause injury to a person or damage to property.

Traffic equipment is defined as:

- anything lawfully placed on or near a road by a highway authority;
- a traffic sign lawfully placed on or near a road by a person other than a highway authority; and
- any fence, barrier, or light lawfully placed on or near a road (eg to protect street works), or any item placed under the instructions of a chief officer of police.

This applies only if the activities would be regarded as obviously dangerous to a reasonable person or bystander. The reasonable person or bystander does not have to be a motorist (*DPP v D* [2006] EWHC 314 (Admin)). It is irrelevant that the suspect was unaware of the potential danger; this will be a question of fact for the court to decide given the circumstances. The offence is triable either way and the penalty is a fine or imprisonment (six months summarily and seven years on indictment).

Repairing vehicles in the street is a relatively common practice, but it may cause nuisance to other residents, or environmental damage. Under s 4 of the Clean Neighbourhoods and Environment Act 2005, it is an offence in some circumstances to 'carry out restricted works on a motor vehicle on a road'. This includes the repair, maintenance, servicing, improvement, dismantling, installation, replacement, or renewal of a motor vehicle (or of any part of or accessory to a motor vehicle). However, a householder who repairs his/her own vehicle in the street and gives no reasonable cause for annoyance to persons in the vicinity does not commit this offence as the work is not for gain or reward or as part of a business. Nor is any offence committed if the work is required after an accident or breakdown and the repairs were necessary on the spot or carried out within 72 hours.

Skips placed on or near highways can present hazards. Permission must be given by a highways authority for placing a skip on a highway (s 139(1) of the Highways Act 1980), and conditions must be met in relation to its size, the way it is lit and its position on the road (s 139(2)). An offence is committed if the skip is placed without permission (s 139(3)), or the conditions are not met (s 139(4)). These are summary offences and the penalty is a fine.

Holding or getting onto a motor vehicle (or an attached trailer) that is moving and on a road, in order to be towed or carried is an offence (s 26(1) of the Road Traffic Act 1988). This is a summary offence and the penalty is a fine.

> **TASK 16** Several complaints have been made by residents in the neighbourhood of a club. They say that at closing time they have seen people throwing rubbish bins and other items about the streets, tampering with traffic lights, and deflating vehicle tyres.
>
> What offences might have been committed?

19.11.3 Riding small vehicles on a pavement

The use of mini-motos (miniature motorbikes), go-peds (petrol-driven scooters), and self-balancing personal transporters (eg Segways and hoverboards) may pose potential risks to the health and safety of other road and pavement users. There have been a number of fatalities and serious injuries, and many members of the public consider their use as an example of anti-social behaviour. All of these types of vehicle have been held to be motor vehicles (see 19.2.1) and must therefore comply with the usual road traffic laws. It is an offence to 'wilfully ride a carriage' on a pavement (s 72 of the Highways Act 1835) and the meaning of carriage includes motor vehicles.

19.12 Methods of Disposal for Motoring Offences

There are several ways of dealing with a suspect who has committed a road traffic offence, and the decision will be based upon a number of factors including local policy and the police officer's discretion (see 5.5.3 on discretion). The methods of disposal for such offences include:

- a verbal warning;
- reporting a suspect for the purposes of issuing a written charge;
- the VDRS (Vehicle Defect Rectification Scheme);
- a TOR (Traffic Offence Report);
- an FPN (fixed penalty notice);
- arrest and charge.

The first flowchart summarizes the early stages of the investigative process for dealing with motoring offences. Note there may be some local variation about the use of police note books (PNB in the flowchart), as well as matters relating to the issue of the HO/RT/1 form, FPNs, and the use of the VDRS. Officers should therefore follow local arrangements.

Specific Incidents

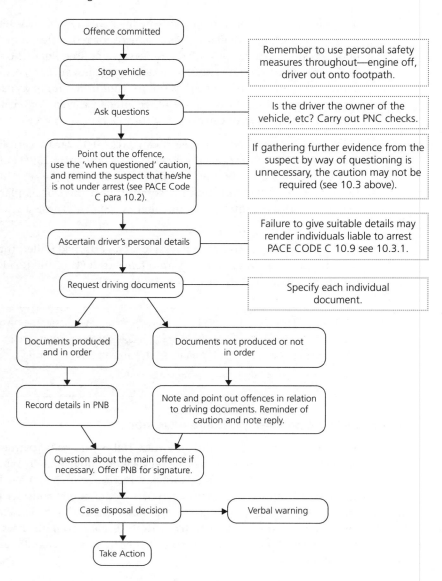

If a verbal warning is not appropriate the VDRS, a TOR, or an FPN can be used (depending on local policy).

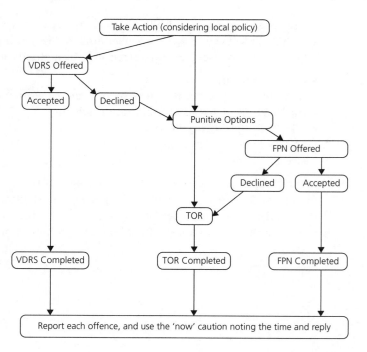

Note that criminals sought in connection with serious crimes often come to the attention of the police through committing minor road traffic offences. If a suspect has been arrested for the other offences, he/she can of course also be charged with the road traffic offences.

19.12.1 Reporting for the purposes of issuing a written charge

The suspect must be reported for the purposes of issuing a written charge (see 10.13.1.1) for all methods of disposal, apart from a verbal warning with no further action. The officer must ascertain the personal details of the suspect, including a suitable address for the issuing of a written charge (often referred to as suitable for 'the service of a summons'), should that be necessary. The processes may vary, for example it is slightly different for completing a Traffic Offence Report (see 19.12.3) compared with issuing an FPN (see 19.12.4). If a person refuses to provide this information he/she may be liable to arrest and could then be charged with the traffic offences once in custody, as for any other offence (see 10.13.1). Sometimes the arrested person provides the required details just prior to being charged; local policies vary on how to proceed.

19.12.2 Vehicle Defect Rectification Scheme

Drivers of vehicles that are found to be in an unsuitable condition due to minor defects can be given the opportunity to use the Vehicle Defect Rectification Scheme (VDRS). This avoids the need to prosecute or issue an FPN. The use of the VDRS will be subject to local police service instructions and officers should be clear about when it can be used. Deciding whether to use the VDRS will also depend on the circumstances of the offence and the officer's discretion.

The advantages of the VDRS include:

- the defects are rectified, which contributes to road safety;
- the offender does not have to go to court; and
- improved police and public relations: many people will only come into contact with the police during the investigation of road traffic matters, and the VDRS is partly supportive, rather than wholly punitive.

When considering using the VDRS the police officer must point out the offence to the person responsible for the vehicle and inform him/her that participation in the VDRS is voluntary and that no further action will be taken if he/she agrees to participate in the scheme. If the driver declines the VDRS, he/she will normally be issued with a TOR or an FPN, but officers should follow local policy.

After receiving a VDRS notice, the driver must have the vehicle repaired within 14 days and submit it for examination at a Department for Transport approved testing station (an MOT testing station) where the VDRS form should be endorsed to confirm the fault is rectified. The driver must then send the completed form to the Central Ticket Office (or as guided by local policy). If the driver fails to return the form within the specified time, he/she could be prosecuted by way of written charge (as if the VDRS had not been used), although local policies may vary.

19.12.3 Traffic Offence Report (TOR)

In the majority of police services most officers either offer advice for minor offences (where there has been no collision) or issue a Traffic Offence Report (TOR). Many police services are moving away from using FPNs in favour of TORs as they provide a range of disposal options, such as driver improvement courses (only available for some offences), conditional offers with the same penalty as an FPN, or a written charge summoning the offender to court.

The procedures for issuing TORs vary between police services so local policy should be followed. A TOR usually has at least two self-carbonating copies to record details of the driver, the offence, and the vehicle. Generally the first copy is kept by the issuing officer (the reverse side is in effect an MG11 duty statement (see 10.12) and should be completed according to local policy). The second copy is given to the driver. As the driver could eventually be prosecuted, the reporting procedures for issuing a written charge (see 10.13.1.1) should be followed and recorded on the notice, and the driver asked to sign the entry. The officer sends his/her copy of the completed TOR to the force central processing department for a decision on disposal. The disposal options include issuing a Notice of Intended Prosecution (see 19.12.6), making a conditional offer (see 19.12.4.3), and referral to the National Driver Offender Retraining Scheme (see 19.12.6).

19.12.4 The fixed penalty system

The fixed penalty system for motoring offences (Part III of the Road Traffic Offenders Act 1988) provides offenders with the opportunity to pay a fixed fine instead of going to court (s 54 of the Road Traffic Offenders Act 1988). The FPN system is similar to the Penalty Notice for Disorder (PND) system for anti-social behaviour offences (see 10.13.2.2). Note that the use of FPNs is subject to local policy, and that most parking offences have now been decriminalized (eg in London officers can only issue FPNs for unnecessary obstruction). There are two types of FPN:

- non-endorsable fixed penalty notices (NEFPN), for offences which do not add penalty points to an offender's driving licence (parking, seatbelts, and vehicle lighting offences);
- endorsable fixed penalty notices (EFPN), for offences which add penalty points to an offender's driving licence (eg contravening a red traffic light, failing to stop at a stop sign, and driving a vehicle with defective tyres).

An FPN can only be issued to the person actually committing the offence or driving the vehicle involved; they cannot be used for people who cause or permit an offence (see 19.2.4 for 'cause' or 'permit'). In some circumstances an FPN can be issued by leaving the documents on the vehicle without the need for the driver to be present, such as a parking ticket affixed to a car's windscreen. An FPN can be issued to non-UK offenders and UK offenders, as well as those with no fixed abode, irrespective of whether the offence is endorsable. A financial penalty deposit can be requested from any offender who does not have a satisfactory address in the UK (see 19.12.4.4). If the FPN is not accepted, the driver will have to be reported. A fine for an FPN must be paid within 28 days (to the Central Ticket Office in the area) or it will be increased by 50 per cent, and can also be recovered by the courts.

For offences involving commercial vehicles (eg breaches of drivers' hours rules, overloading of vehicles) the fixed penalty value can be increased, depending on the circumstances and the severity of the offence (see the VOSA *Guide to graduated fixed penalties and financial deposits*, available online).

19.12.4.1 Issuing a non-endorsable fixed penalty notice

When a police officer in uniform has reasonable grounds to believe that a person is committing or has committed a fixed penalty offence (and local policy indicates this is the suitable disposal option), an FPN can be issued. If the driver is present the police officer should:

1. point out the offence;
2. caution the driver using 'when questioned' and inform him/her that he/she is not under arrest (PACE Code C, para 10.2);
3. question the driver and allow him/her to ask questions (in relation to the offence(s));
4. if the driver fails to cooperate or answer any particular questions after being cautioned, he/she should be informed that failing to provide his/her name and address for example, may make him/her liable to detention or arrest (PACE Code C, para 10.9, see also 10.3.1);
5. check that the driver wishes to proceed with an FPN;
6. complete and issue the NEFPN;
7. report the driver or owner for the offence;
8. use the 'now' caution (see 10.3.4).

Certain parking related NEFPNs can be attached to a stationary vehicle (s 62(1)) if the driver is absent, and it is an offence for any person other than the driver/owner to remove or interfere with the notice.

The flowchart summarizes the process.

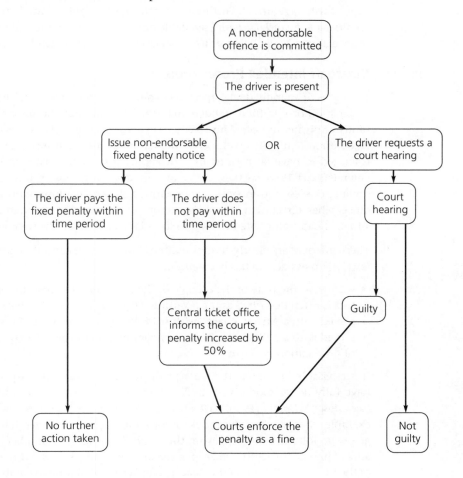

19.12.4.2 Endorsable fixed penalty notices

For some offences the penalty includes obligatory endorsement. An EFPN can be used if:

- the driver's file on the PNC can be checked to view the endorsement history;
- the total number of points including the new proposed points does not exceed 11; and
- the driver accepts an EFPN.

The procedure for issuing an EFPN is the same as that for a standard FPN, except for checking the driving licence status as set out earlier, and recording the driver number. If the proposed new points would take the total to 12 or more the driver will have to be reported for prosecution.

19.12.4.3 Conditional offer of fixed penalty

A conditional offer for a fixed penalty can be sent to the alleged offender if the FPN cannot be handed to a driver or attached to a vehicle (s 75 of the Road Traffic Offenders Act 1988). This could apply for speeding offences detected by automatic camera devices, or when a police officer sees a driver disobeying a road sign but it is impossible or too dangerous to follow, or when a TOR has been issued and no suitable education course is available. The conditional offer will state the circumstances of the alleged offence, and the relevant fixed penalty, and explain that no further proceedings will take place in relation to the offence for 28 days from the date of issue. If payment is made within that period there will be no court proceedings. Police officers and staff at Central Ticket Offices can arrange for conditional offers to be sent.

19.12.4.4 Roadside deposit scheme

If a driver has been issued with an FPN or conditional offer but is unable to provide a satisfactory UK address at the time of an offence, the police officer can request a financial penalty deposit. The officer can prohibit the use of the vehicle and physically prevent its use (eg with a wheel clamp or a wire rope lock through the steering wheel) until the deposit is paid. Once paid, the driver can then choose whether to ultimately pay the FPN and allow the deposit to be used as part-payment, or request a court hearing. If he/she is found not guilty in court the deposit will be returned. Further information is available in the *VOSA Guide to graduated fixed penalties and financial deposits*, available online. This procedure will probably only be available to specialist roads policing units; officers should check which local arrangements apply.

19.12.5 Notice of Intended Prosecution

The rights of an individual suspected of committing certain road traffic offences are safeguarded under the Road Traffic Offenders Act 1988. He/she must be informed at the earliest opportunity of his/her suspected involvement in an offence, usually by means of a Notice of Intended Prosecution (NIP). This will specify the nature of the offence and the time and place where it is alleged to have been committed. It applies for offences listed in s 1(1) of the Road Traffic Offenders Act 1988, such as: dangerous driving; dangerous cycling; careless and inconsiderate driving; careless and inconsiderate cycling; failing to conform with the indication of a police officer when directing traffic; failing to comply with a traffic sign; and speeding offences (see Sch 1 to the Road Traffic Offenders Act 1988 and for a full list on the www.legislation.gov.uk website).

These offences are clearly serious matters, but a person cannot be prosecuted for any of them (s 1(1)), unless he/she has been either:

- warned at the time of the offence of the possibility of prosecution (a verbal NIP, s 1(1)(a)), this is often described as the 'Warning Formula' and is reproduced in report books; or
- served with a written charge within 14 days of commission of the offence (s 1(1)(b)); or
- served with a NIP within 14 days of commission of the offence, setting out the possibility of prosecution (s 1(1)(c)).

It is advisable to provide the NIP as a document, because the suspect may later claim not to have fully understood a verbal NIP, and the prosecution would have to prove the contrary (see *Gibson v Dalton* [1980] RTR 410). The NIP can also be served by post when necessary, for example when a police officer observes a vehicle go through a red traffic light and it is too dangerous to follow. A PNC check on the vehicle's registration number should provide the name and address of the registered keeper. He/she must state who was driving the vehicle at the time of the incident (s 172(2) of the Road Traffic Act 1988); failing to comply is an offence (s 172(3)).

In *Whiteside v DPP* [2011] EWHC 3471 (Admin) it was decided that:

- a NIP has been lawfully served if it has been posted (even if the recipient does not receive it);
- the recipient does not have a defence simply because he/she has no knowledge of the NIP being sent, unless it can be proved that under the circumstances it was not reasonably practicable to have been made aware of it;
- the offence is committed even if a recipient of the NIP does not know that he/she is obliged to state who was driving.

A NIP is not required when the vehicle concerned has been involved in an accident (s 2(1)) unless the driver failed to stop (see 19.7.2), nor is it required if an FPN was issued at the time the offence was committed (s 2(2)). The final methods of disposal after a NIP has been served include a written charge or a conditional offer of a fixed penalty (see 19.12.4.3).

19.12.6 National Driver Offender Retraining Scheme

Another out-of-court disposal option for road traffic offences is the National Driver Offender Retraining Scheme (NDORS). Courses available include the National Driver Alertness Course and the National Speed Awareness Course (s 89(1) of the Road Traffic Regulation Act 1984). The driver must hold a current driving licence, and his/her actions and the circumstances must be such that there would be a realistic prospect of convicting him/her for the offence. If he/she has previously attended an NDORS for the same offence, it must have been more than three years ago. For more information, see the *National Driver Offender Retraining Scheme (NDORS): Guidance on Eligibility Criteria for NDORS Courses*, available online.

TASK 17 Imagine you are a police officer dealing with a driver. Write down the sequence of what you would need to say and do in each of the following three situations:

1. driver unable to produce driving documents;
2. driver has committed an offence for which you can use an FPN; and
3. driver has committed an offence for which you can use the Vehicle Defect Rectification Scheme.

19.13 **Answers to Tasks**

TASK 1 Both of the vehicles are still 'motor vehicles' for the purposes of the legislation regardless of the fact that the car engine does not work and it cannot self-propel. Both of the individuals are 'drivers' as both have control of the movement of their particular vehicle, it is irrelevant that the youth driving the car cannot drive legally due to his age; he is still driving. The location of the incident would be a 'public place' and not a road or highway, therefore, only the offences applicable to public places can be considered. The older man would be 'using' both vehicles; he is driving the van and the car is being used for his purpose, namely being taken to a garage for repair. He will also be permitting the offences committed by his son in the car, knowing they were going to occur but continuing to allow them. The son would be using the car for the purpose of any offences relating to his use of that vehicle, so he would be driving not in accordance with a licence, driving without insurance, and driving with a defective tyre. The MOT status of the towed car would also need to be ascertained.

TASK 2

1. Knowing that he/she was likely to be disqualified from driving, a person might contact the DVLA to obtain a duplicate licence before the court hearing and then submit one and keep the other. Alternatively, the person could obtain a stolen old-style paper licence (without a photograph) and produce it to assume the identity of another person.
2. The officer should carry out PNC checks and local database checks (such as the voters' register), and also ask for the person's name and date of birth to check against the details on the databases. The licence issue number can be checked to find out if the licence is valid. Local knowledge would be very important here as the officer would be able to ask about the description of localities and names of places to help verify the identity of the driver.

TASK 3

1. The PNC will be the primary source of information. The driver file should be checked to verify the driver's identity, driving licence status, and address; this can be cross-referenced with the person's file for marks, scars, and so on. The vehicle file will provide details regarding the vehicle's MOT and excise licence status. It will also link to the MIB insurance database which will show the details of any policy in force. Further enquiries can be made via the MIB help line if further details regarding insurance are required.
2. It is not uncommon for individuals to give slightly different details to an officer on the street to those given to other authorities such as the DVLA; this may or may not be intentional. For example, a different name order, the omission or inclusion of middle names, or a slightly incorrect date of birth can all cause problems.
3. The details should be checked; a police officer should:
- always check the driver and vehicle details with the PNC to establish if they match;
- use the PNC to check whether the driver has a criminal record;
- request further proof of identity, for example passports and credit cards;
- request a voters' register check through the control room; and
- request telephone numbers and ask the control room to call the numbers to verify the existence of the person.

By the cross-referencing of all the information currently available to officers on the street it should be possible to identify an individual and verify his/her driving status. There may be no need to use an HO/RT/1.

TASK 4 Many insurance companies are reluctant to insure high risk drivers in high performance vehicles. If they do, the premiums are likely to be very high. You might ask the driver about his insurance; the cost of the policy, how he pays for it (this could be cross-referenced with employment information, does it seem likely that can he afford it), how was the policy arranged (in person, over the internet, direct with the company, or through a broker), does he have any other driving qualifications, or is a black box fitted in the vehicle that could permit a discount?

The police officer should then contact the insurance company directly (using the information held on the MIB database via the PNC vehicle file) and speak to a police liaison representative, or contact the MIB help line to find out if there was full disclosure when the policy was taken out. If not, the insurance company may cancel the policy on the spot or make a note to contact him for further payment, and there may be evidence of a fraud offence (see 16.9) which can be investigated further. However, such a driver would still have been insured at the time when he was stopped, so could not be prosecuted for driving with no insurance.

TASK 5 Defences to using a motor vehicle on a road without a test certificate are that the vehicle is:

- being driven to a pre-arranged MOT test;
- being driven from a failed MOT test to a garage for repairs by previous arrangement (reg 6(2)(a)(i) of the Motor Vehicle (Test) Regulations 1981); or
- being towed to a place to be broken up for scrap, after failing an MOT (reg 6(2)(a)(iii)(B)).

Possible defences to not having a valid test certificate could be countered by asking the driver for the starting point, destination, and reason of his/her journey.

TASK 6

Blue flashing lights are only allowed for certain types (and uses) of vehicle, such as police vehicles, and those owned by HM Revenue and Customs for use in pursuit of serious crime. The number of types of vehicles on the list continues to grow.

TASK 7

1. True. The term 'hours of darkness' refers to a period from half an hour after sunset to half an hour before sunrise.
2. False. It is the Road Vehicles Lighting Regulations 1989 as amended by the Road Vehicles Lighting (Amendment) Regulations 1994.
3. False. The correct rate is 60 to 120 pulses per minute.
4. False. The lawful circumstances are:
   (a) while stationary, to warn other road users of a temporary obstruction;
   (b) to summon assistance to the driver, conductor, or inspector of a bus (PSV);
   (c) on a motorway or unrestricted dual carriageway to warn following drivers of the need to slow down due to a temporary obstruction ahead; and
   (d) in the case of a school bus, while loading or unloading (or about to do so) passengers (under 16 years of age), provided the bus displays the statutory yellow reflective signs indicating the presence of schoolchildren.
5. True.
6. True.
7. True.

TASK 8 As you approach the vehicle, you would need to consider health and safety implications and consider the potential problems associated with:

- the vehicle moving through deliberate or accidental action by the driver;
- the engine still running (the driver could move off quickly);
- the handbrake not being applied (again for a quick pull away, or the vehicle may roll);
- the location of the ignition keys; and
- traffic passing by the location.

You could follow the following sequence:

1. Speak to the driver, introduce yourself, and outline the reason for stopping the vehicle.
2. Ask the driver for his/her name, address, and date of birth, and for his/her connection with the vehicle (is he/she the owner too?).
3. Ask the driver for details of his/her intended destination and the place where he/she began the journey.
4. Examine the vehicle whilst considering the potential health and safety implications associated with:
   - moving parts inside the engine compartment such as thermostatically controlled cooling fans;
   - high temperatures associated with parts such as brakes, exhaust systems, radiators, and engines;
   - harmful liquids such as hydraulic fluids, battery acid, anti-freeze, and hot engine coolant;
   - sharp objects such as exposed tyre cords or faulty bodywork;
   - movement of the vehicle and anything in, on, or under the vehicle;
   - movement of other vehicles and persons around you; and

- the surface upon which you and the vehicle are positioned and the existence of harmful objects or substances.

5. Note any possible offence(s), detected in the usual way by gathering evidence using your senses (ie what you saw, felt, smelt, and so on).

6. Point out the possible offence(s) to the driver.

7. Caution him/her using the 'when questioned' caution, and follow PACE Code C, para 10.2 by informing the person that he/she is not under arrest.

8. If the person fails to cooperate or answer any particular questions after being cautioned, he/she should be informed that a failure to provide a name and address, for example, may make him/her liable to detention or arrest (PACE Code C, para 10.9 (see 10.3.1)).

9. Note the questions and answers about the offences as PNB entries, for example when did he/she last inspect the vehicle, was he/she already aware of the defect, and how long ago did the journey begin? The PNB entry should be offered to the driver to read and sign that the notes are a true record of the interview.

10. The driver could then be reported for the offences and cautioned.

TASK 9 See the Highway Code (available online) for answers. You can also practise your understanding using the 'Practise your driving theory test' page on the gov.uk website.

TASK 10 The legislation that provides the power to implement such a policy is s 6A of the Road Traffic Act 1988; whilst in uniform or not, if a police officer reasonably believes that a person is driving, has been driving, is attempting to drive, or is in charge of a motor vehicle on a road or public place at the time of an accident, he/she may require the person to cooperate with one or more preliminary tests including a breath test. The officer must be in uniform to administer the test.

The computer checks that could be carried out on such driver include:

1. a PNC check to:
   - discover if the driver is wanted, or disqualified from driving;
   - check the driver's driving licence and insurance status;
   - check the status of any insurance to cover the driving in the circumstances. This may be a policy in the driver's name (on the current vehicle or another), or a policy applicable to the current vehicle permitting the driver's use;
   - check the MOT status of the vehicle;
   - ascertain if there are any reports regarding the vehicles being stolen; or
   - establish details of the keepers of the vehicles;
2. local checks to determine whether the driver's name and address are valid.

TASK 11 The order is as follows, with percentages for 2017. The total is over 100 per cent as some collisions/accidents have more than one contributory factor.

1.

Factor	Percentage of main contributory factors
Loss of control	27%
Driver failed to look properly	26%
Driver careless, reckless, or in a hurry	17%
Poor turn or manoeuvre	15%
Exceed speed limit	14%
Driver failed to judge other person's path or speed	13%
Pedestrian failed to look properly	10%
Travelling too fast for conditions	9%
Driver impaired by alcohol	9%
Driver illness	7%

2. The NPCC document *Policing the Roads in Partnership—5 Year Strategy 2015–2020* (available online) lists four priority areas: 'SAFE', safe roads, free from harm by reducing road casualties; 'SECURE', secure roads, free from criminality and terrorism; 'EFFECTIVE', effective data-led patrolling and partnership working; 'EFFICIENT', efficient roads promotion policies, and improve public confidence.

Specific Incidents

TASK 12

1. (a) Jerry is driving.
    (b) Maz is not driving.
    (c) Both Hari and Pat are driving.
2. (a) (ii) and (iii) it applies on a road or in a public place.
    (b) (i) it applies anywhere.

TASK 13

1. Using a hand-held phone while driving could easily amount to failing to have proper control of the vehicle, or even dangerous driving (see 19.8.1).
2. Other 'careless driving' activities may include lighting a cigarette, turning round and looking at children, searching for a station on the radio, changing CDs, looking for sunglasses, looking in the mirror and applying make-up, or any other similar action that diverts attention from driving.

TASK 14

1. Trainee police officers are likely to receive instruction quite early on in the use of an Electronic Breath Screening Device (ESD), and to use one during Supervised Patrol. It is usually a hand-held device, with a disposable mouthpiece that is changed for each test.
    In relation to preliminary drug test devices, each force has different policies relating to which staff can carry out this procedure, so trainee officers might not be trained in the use of such a device straight away. A preliminary impairment test can only be conducted by an officer who has been approved for it by his/her chief officer.
2. Moving traffic offences include contravention of traffic regulations (eg speed limits), and failing to comply with traffic signs and directions (eg traffic lights).

TASK 15 Yes, in such circumstances the required sample may then be taken at a police station, regardless of whether an appropriate breath-analysis machine is available. See *Webber v DPP* [1998] RTR 111.

TASK 16 Section 22A of the Road Traffic Act 1988 states that a person is guilty of an offence if he/she intentionally and without lawful authority or reasonable cause:

(a) causes anything to be on or over a road;
(b) interferes with a motor vehicle, trailer, or cycle; or
(c) interferes (directly or indirectly) with traffic equipment.

TASK 17 For all of these situations the officer should first point out offence(s), caution and inform the driver that he/she is not under arrest, explain that a failure to cooperate or to answer particular questions may make him/her liable for detention or arrest. Then the officer should question the suspect and note the answers given. The next stage will vary:

1. Driver is unable to produce driving documents when required: the next stage is to check the PNC for all the vehicle and driver-related information. Most police services no longer allow officers to use HO/RT/1 forms requesting production of documents at a police station—check your local arrangements. Then report the suspect, and administer the caution (the 'now' version).
2. Fixed penalty offence: for a non-endorsable offence with driver present the officer should complete and issue NEFPN, and report and caution the suspect (the 'now' caution). The driver can refuse the offer of an FPN and elect to go to court instead. If the driver is not present the completed NEFPN should be fixed to the vehicle.
    For an endorsable offence when the driver is present, the next stage is to offer an EFPN in lieu of court, report the suspect, and give the caution (the 'now' version). The number of endorsement points should be checked through the PNC, so the driver's driver record must be traced. If the proposed points would take the total to 12 or more an EFPN cannot be used. If the points would reach 12 or more, or the driver refuses the offer of an EFPN, then he/she should be reported for the offence, usually via a TOR. If the licence is not available but all the other conditions are met, a provisional EFPN can be issued.
3. VDRS offence: offer VDRS and issue form if accepted, then report and caution the suspect (the 'now' version). If the driver refuses the VDRS he/she should be reported for the offence, usually via a TOR.

20 | Damage to Buildings and Other Property

20.1 Introduction

In this chapter we examine the law surrounding damage to property, much of which stems from the Criminal Damage Act 1971. We also look at legislation to help protect ancient monuments and heritage sites in the UK. An understanding of these aspects of the law will help a student officer undertaking the PCDA or DHEP with achieving the requirement to 'conduct diligent and efficient ... high volume investigations'. It is also relevant to the National Policing Curriculum requirements regarding knowledge of legislation and procedures (part of 'Understanding the Police Constable Role').

Criminal damage is both one of the most common crimes in England Wales and often one of the most visible (it is an example of one of the so-called 'signal crimes' described in 3.4.2). It often comes to the notice of the police through reports from the public, property owners, and others. However, intelligence might also feature, particularly in terms of identifying and taking action for 'taggers' (individuals who spray graffiti on buildings or trains or other objects as a form of stylized self- or group-identification). Likewise, the tags themselves might also provide useful information for building intelligence about the activities of a local criminal 'gang' (see 15.8 and 23.6).

The investigation of criminal damage, arson, and 'heritage crime' (eg the illegal removal of objects from archaeological sites) provides good examples of the multi- and inter-agency approach to crime reduction described in 3.6. For example, detection of criminal damage might well involve (or be led by) PCSOs and local authorities, and investigations into suspected arson are often carried out by specialist fire and emergency service investigation teams (subject to local agreements). Cultural crime detection might well involve the police working in partnership with Historic England, the English Heritage Trust, and others.

Police officers have a power of entry to search premises in order to prevent serious damage to property (s 17(1)(e) of the PACE Act 1984).

20.2 Criminal Damage

In terms of criminal damage, a trainee officer is most likely to encounter graffiti and minor damage to fences, cars, and bus shelters. Occasionally, the damage can be much more serious, when, for example, the damage has been caused by fire or involves culturally important buildings. Graffiti is among the most common forms of criminal damage, and to help reduce its prevalence the sale of containers of aerosol paint to a young person under the age of 16 is a summary offence (s 54(1)) of the Anti-Social Behaviour Act 2003.

Specific Incidents

Section 1(1) of the Criminal Damage Act 1971 describes the offence of criminal damage. It states that an offence is committed by a person who without lawful excuse:

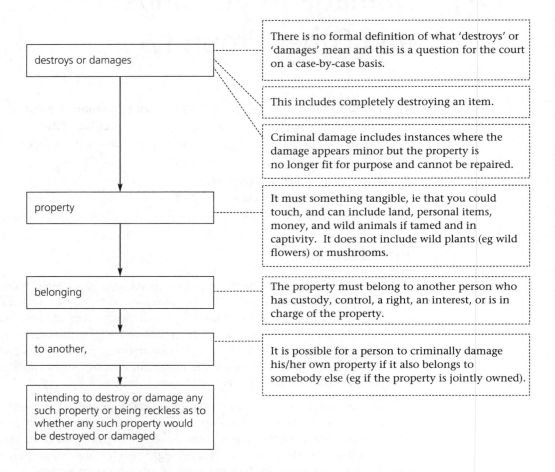

There are some circumstances where a person could have a lawful excuse for causing the damage. He/she would need to have an honestly held belief that:

- he/she had permission from the owner of the property (or an appropriate person) to carry out the relevant acts, for example a recovery operator is authorized by a car owner to load the car onto a recovery vehicle, and damages it in the process; or
- his/her own or another's property was in immediate need of protection by reasonable means (eg a car had slipped down a steep embankment and was likely to slip still further, and a recovery operator damages it when pulling it back up onto the road).

There may even be occasions where an incorrect belief could still constitute an honestly held belief and would therefore negate liability for a criminal act. For example, if a vehicle owner is unconscious in hospital after a car accident, the recovery operator might honestly believe that the owner would give permission for the car to be moved.

The person carrying out the offence must either intend to cause the damage, or be reckless as to whether the property would be damaged. The appropriate test of recklessness for criminal damage is:

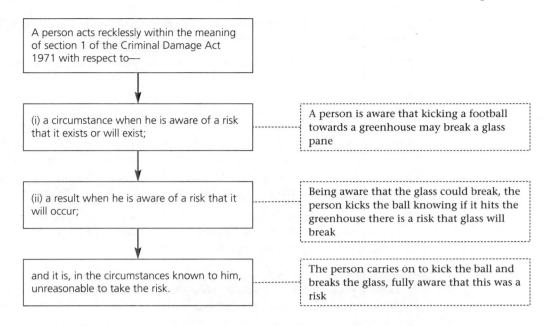

The person who takes the risk must be fully aware of it. The risk may be obvious to others but, as we can see in the case of *R v G* [2003], it might not always be obvious to the defendant(s). In this case two children, aged 11 and 12, set a fire under a wheelie bin in the back yard of a shop, and then left, assuming that the fire would soon go out on the concrete floor. However, it continued to burn and resulted in damage of around £1 million. They were convicted (of arson), but this was overturned by the House of Lords because although the risk seemed an obvious one to most adults, it was not to the children. Therefore the extent of the person's awareness needs to be considered, with regard to whether his/her action was reasonable; and this will be decided by the court on a case-by-case basis.

The offence of criminal damage is triable either way, and will be tried summarily if the value of the property damaged or destroyed is less than £5,000 (s 22 of the Magistrates' Courts Act 1980). The penalty is six months' imprisonment and/or a fine if tried summarily, and ten years' imprisonment on indictment. If the damage is aggravated by religious or racial hatred then the maximum penalty on indictment is increased to 14 years (s 30(1) of the Crime and Disorder Act 1998).

> **TASK 1** Robyn, after her arrest for being drunk and disorderly, smears her own excrement on the walls of the police station cell. Discuss whether this constitutes criminal damage.

20.2.1 Aggravated criminal damage (endangering life)

The offence of 'criminal damage, life endangered' (s 1(2) of the Criminal Damage Act 1971) is committed by a person who destroys or damages property intending (or being reckless as) to endanger life. To prove the offence, there is no requirement for the offender to try to kill someone or for any actual injury or harm to occur. There is only a necessity to prove that the damage was caused intentionally or recklessly and that there was potential for another to be harmed as a result of that damage being caused. In the case of *R v Sangha* [1988] 2 All ER 385 (CA) the defendant lit a fire on a mattress in an empty flat. The flat was in a block which had been constructed to prevent the spread of fire from one flat to another. The court held that it was irrelevant that no lives were actually endangered by the defendant's actions; the fact that the circumstances could be considered to endanger life was sufficient.

For this offence the property can belong to another person or to the offender (in contrast with the basic offence of criminal damage, where the property must belong (at least in part) to another). For example, an angry man deliberately damages the brakes of his own car knowing that his partner will be driving it later that day, and intending her life to be endangered. The damage caused must also be the cause of the danger: for example, shooting at someone in a room through a window both endangers life and damages the window, but it is the bullet that endangers the life rather than the damage from the broken window, so this would not be criminal damage life endangered.

This offence is triable by indictment only and the penalty is life imprisonment.

20.3 Arson

Arson is destroying or damaging property by fire. It is covered under s 1(3) of the Criminal Damage Act 1971. For a person to be found guilty of this offence at least some of the damage must have been caused by fire (excluding smoke damage). For the offence to be proved there must be an intent or an element of recklessness in relation to the use of fire.

If no life is endangered then arson is triable either way, with a penalty of six months' imprisonment and/or a fine if tried summarily, and up to life imprisonment on indictment. If life is endangered this offence must be tried on indictment.

> **TASK 2** For what reasons might the crime of arson be committed? Can the behavioural profiling of arsonists be of potential value to the police and others?

20.4 Threats to Damage

This offence is covered in s 2 of the Criminal Damage Act 1971 and there are two points to prove in relation to such a threat:

- the conduct that is threatened must refer to damage; and
- the extent of the threatened damage must constitute an offence under s 1 of the Criminal Damage Act 1971. This can include acts of simple damage under s 1(1), as well as criminal damage where life is endangered (s 1(2)).

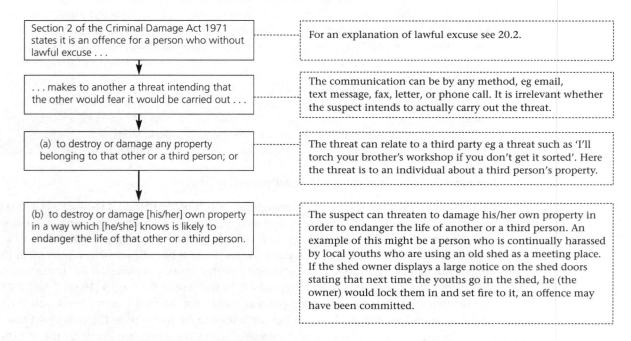

Section 2 of the Criminal Damage Act 1971 states it is an offence for a person who without lawful excuse . . .

For an explanation of lawful excuse see 20.2.

. . . makes to another a threat intending that the other would fear it would be carried out . . .

The communication can be by any method, eg email, text message, fax, letter, or phone call. It is irrelevant whether the suspect intends to actually carry out the threat.

(a) to destroy or damage any property belonging to that other or a third person; or

The threat can relate to a third party eg a threat such as 'I'll torch your brother's workshop if you don't get it sorted'. Here the threat is to an individual about a third person's property.

(b) to destroy or damage [his/her] own property in a way which [he/she] knows is likely to endanger the life of that other or a third person.

The suspect can threaten to damage his/her own property in order to endanger the life of another or a third person. An example of this might be a person who is continually harassed by local youths who are using an old shed as a meeting place. If the shed owner displays a large notice on the shed doors stating that next time the youths go in the shed, he (the owner) would lock them in and set fire to it, an offence may have been committed.

The person who makes the threat must intend that the recipient will believe the threat will be carried out. In any prosecution it will be for the court to decide whether what was communicated had enough substance and immediacy to constitute a threat. In some circumstances it might be more appropriate to consider an offence under s 4 of the Public Order Act 1986 (see 14.4.3.3).

The offence of making threats to damage cannot be committed if the threat involves an element of recklessness as to whether the property would actually be destroyed or damaged (see 20.2 on the meaning of 'reckless'). For example, imagine an angry woman shouts to a neighbour 'If your kid keeps throwing stones over my wall, I'll start chucking them back, and no, I don't care what it does'. She is reckless as to whether damage is caused or not so she would not have committed the offence of 'threats to damage'. Note that the feelings of the person receiving the threat are not relevant for this offence; he/she does not need to be put in fear, or believe the threat will be carried out.

This offence is triable either way and the penalty is six months' imprisonment and/or a fine if tried summarily, and ten years' imprisonment on indictment.

20.5 Possessing an Article with Intent to Cause Criminal Damage

This offence is covered in s 3 of the Criminal Damage Act 1971.

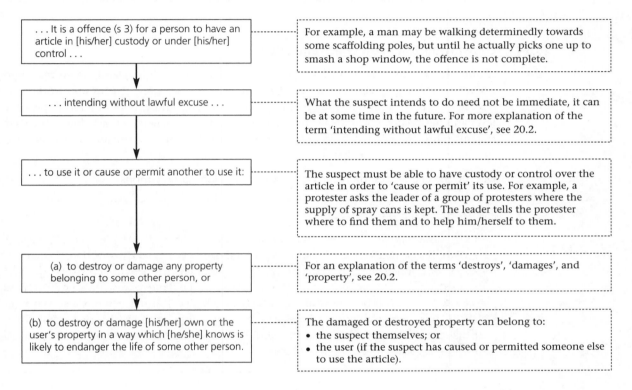

The type of article involved here can be anything tangible. The Law Commission, who advised on the Act, explained that:

> [t]he essential feature of the proposed offence is to be found, not so much in the nature of the thing, as in the intention with which it is held. (Law Commission No 29, para 59)

This offence is triable either way. The penalty is six months' imprisonment and/or a fine not exceeding the statutory maximum if tried summarily, and ten years' imprisonment on indictment.

A power to search for articles made or adapted for use in the course of or in connection with an offence under s 1 of the Criminal Damage Act 1971 is provided under s 1(2)(a) of the PACE Act 1984. Any person or vehicle (and anything in or on a vehicle) can be searched and detained for the purpose of such a search. Section 2 of the PACE Act 1984 and its Codes of Practice must be followed, including providing the person with the GO WISELY information listed in para 3.8 of Code A (see 9.2 and 9.3 on stop and search procedures).

20.6 Causing Damage to Heritage Sites

Buildings and sites of historic interest have had some form of legal protection in the UK since 1882. Initially only the most important ancient sites were protected, such as Stonehenge and some large castles. Over the years, however, further specific legislation has been introduced and this provides protection to many types of historic site such as:

Specific Incidents

- scheduled monuments (an archaeological site or building that is of national importance, eg Stonehenge or Dover Castle);
- listed buildings (includes small houses, street furniture, and lighthouses; over 500,000 in England alone);
- protected marine wreck sites (53 in English coastal waters);
- protected military remains of aircraft and vessels of historic interest (includes losses during peacetime);
- conservation areas (local authority designated areas of special architectural or historic interest; around 9,000 in the UK);
- registered parks and gardens (gardens of stately homes, public parks, and cemeteries on a national register; over 1,600 in the UK);
- registered battlefields (46 in the UK, eg at Hastings); and
- World Heritage Sites (25 in the UK, eg Canterbury Cathedral, Stonehenge, and Hadrian's Wall).

20.6.1 Legislation to protect heritage sites

A number of bodies (local authorities, the police, and Historic England) share the responsibility to enforce legislation designed to protect heritage sites. Partnership-working (see 8.3 and 8.4) plays a fundamental role in tackling heritage crime, both at a local operational level and nationally at a strategic level. However, this is a challenging task due to the shared responsibility, the relative rarity of incidents, and the lack of expertise and understanding of the nature of the possible 'harm'.

Despite the challenges, there have been some successful prosecutions.

Historic England Case (2020)

In 2019 the Mac family were fined a total of £160,000 for causing irreversible damage to Withybrook mediaeval village in Warwickshire over a three-year period. The site is located on land owned by the Mac family, who bulldozed a road across the site and installed pipes, fencing and water troughs. Historic England were consistently refused access to the site (a scheduled monument, see start of 20.6), and issued repeated warnings that the work was not permitted. However they were ignored, and Historic England then instigated court proceedings, but the work had already caused significant damage and a medieval trackway was completely lost.

20.6.1.1 The Ancient Monuments and Archaeological Areas Act 1979

It is an offence under s 28 of the Act to damage or destroy (without lawful excuse) a 'protected monument' (defined in s 28, and includes a scheduled monument). The suspect must know that it is a protected monument and intend to destroy or damage it, or be reckless as to whether it would be destroyed or damaged. The offence is triable either way and the penalty is a fine and/or imprisonment (six months if tried summarily and two years on indictment).

Other sections of this Act may also be relevant to the trainee police officer, for example:

- s 42, under which it is a summary offence to use a metal detector in a 'protected place' without the written consent of English Heritage, and an either-way offence to remove an object in such circumstances;
- s 9, under which it is an either-way offence to damage, demolish, or alter a listed building.

20.6.1.2 The protection of wrecks and military remains

The Protection of Wrecks Act 1973 can be used to designate an area containing a 'protected wreck'. All retrieved wreck material (eg fixtures and fittings, coins, cannon, and wreck timbers) must be reported to the 'Receiver' at the Maritime and Coastguard Agency.

The Protection of Military Remains Act 1986 makes it an offence to interfere (without a licence) with the wreckage of any crashed, sunken, or stranded military aircraft or designated vessel. The Act provides two levels of protection, depending on whether the site is designated as a 'protected place' or a 'controlled site'. Greater restrictions are placed upon activities at the latter. Investigations under this Act usually relate to diving and are undertaken by the

Ministry of Defence supported by the police and Historic England. Most of the offences in relation to this Act are triable either way.

20.6.2 Offences relating to cultural objects and treasure

We have already referred to the legislation around the use of metal detectors (see 20.6.1.1). Further legislation is available to help regulate the trade in 'cultural objects' and 'treasure' found at archaeological or other heritage sites.

A 'cultural object' is defined as an object of historical, architectural, or archaeological interest. It is 'tainted' if a person illegally excavates an object from its original position in the ground, or removes it from a building, structure, or monument of historical, architectural, or archaeological interest in the UK or elsewhere. Dishonest dealing of a tainted cultural object while knowing or believing it is tainted is an either-way offence (s 1 of the Dealing in Cultural Objects (Offences) Act 2003).

'Treasure' includes old gold, silver, or bronze coins, collections of prehistoric metalwork, and objects found with such coins or metalwork (s 1 of the Treasure Act 1996). Such finds must be reported through the Portable Antiquities Scheme. It is a summary offence to fail to notify the district coroner within 14 days of finding 'treasure' (s 8(3) of the Treasure Act 1996).

20.7 Answers to Tasks

TASK 1 The excrement will not have destroyed the walls of the police cell, but the walls will need to be cleaned and have therefore been damaged. The cost of the damage will be equal to the cost of the cleaning operation. The suspect will need to be interviewed to prove or disprove whether she intended to damage the walls or was reckless as to whether or not the damage was caused. One of these must be proved for the offence to have been committed. If the drunken state was self-induced, this will not be an acceptable defence (*DPP v Majewski* [1977]).

TASK 2 Arson is a frequent cause of fires. In 2007 a Home Office analysis of incidents identified particular motives for arson in the UK, as shown in the table.

Form of arson	Motive	Proportion of all arson (year 2000 data)	
		Property	Vehicles
Youth disorder and nuisance	Vandalism and boredom	36%	39%
Malicious	Revenge, racism, clashes of beliefs/rivalries, or personal animosities	25%	3%
Psychological	Mental illness or suicide	26%	13%
Criminal	Financial gain and fraud, or the concealment of other crimes (theft, murder, etc)	13%	45%

Based on Home Office, 2007.

However, there are alternative but complementary ways of understanding the causes of arson. For example, Canter and Fritzon (1998) identified two main categories; person-orientated (towards self or others) arson and object-orientated arson. A further distinction is possible, namely in terms of the motive being either expressive (eg to express some form of emotion or psychological need) or instrumental (eg to serve as a means of achieving another goal). This gives rise to fourfold typology, as summarized in the table:

	Person-orientated	Object-orientated
Expressive	Directed inwards (towards the offender) possibly as the result of anxiety, depression, or suicidal tendencies	Directed at an object (eg building) but for symbolic or emotional needs of the offender
Instrumental	Directed outwards (to others), possibly as revenge for perceived wrongdoing	Directed at an object (eg building), but where arson is a consequence of another motive, for example to hide evidence of a burglary

Based on Canter and Fritzon, 1998 and Fineman, 1995.

Specific Incidents

Canter and Fritzon (1998) found that there were statistically significant associations between each of the four motive categories and the offender's social and psychological background. For example, repeat arsonists tended to fall into the expressive/object-orientated category, whereas an expressive/person-orientated arson was more likely to be committed by a person with a history of psychiatric problems. This approach thus provides a potential to 'profile' unknown offenders on the basis of the types of arson incidents observed. The Home Office and others see some virtue in this approach in terms of aiding arson investigation (Home Office, 2007, p 15).

21 | Cybercrime

21.1 Introduction

The term 'cybercrime' encompasses a wide range of criminal activity that involves some form of electronic or digital technology. Many other terms have been used over the past 20 or more years to describe such crimes, and this has led to confusion among victims, investigators, others in the criminal justice system, and the media. The term cybercrime has been more widely used since the creation of the Council of Europe Cybercrime Convention (commonly known as the Budapest Convention on Cybercrime), and is now the common term for a whole range of criminal activities. Although the terminology may seem confusing, there are, in effect, five main ways that digital technology can impact on crime, as follows:

- Technology as the target of crime—this is often referred to in the UK as 'cyber-dependent' or 'pure' cybercrime. It includes such crimes as 'hacking', where a computer is accessed illegally. The hacker may simply wish to show that they have the knowledge and skills to 'hack' into a security-protected computer or computer system, but there are other more sinister reasons for hacking, such as stealing data stored on the computer, or restricting access by legitimate users to damage a business. This type of crime is usually investigated by highly trained staff from specialized cybercrime or computer crime units at national or local level.
- Technology as an aid to crime—this is where a traditional crime is committed and digital technology is used to support the commission of the acts. In the UK, this is now sometimes called 'cyber-enabled' crime. An example would be a blackmail demand (a traditional crime) made by email or other form of electronic communication. The blackmail offence could be committed without the use of digital technology, but it is easier for the criminal to use digital resources to issue demands and instructions for payment of ransom (and this means of communication is also, unfortunately, often more difficult for an investigator to trace). The internet can also be used to commit crimes such as stalking, harassment, fraud, identity theft, racial abuse, and other hate crimes, as well as the sharing of images of child sexual abuse and exploitation (sometimes colloquially referred to as 'child pornography'). A vast range of crimes can be aided by the use of digital technology. It is now difficult to identify any crime which could not involve digital technology in one form or another.
- Technology as a communications tool to plan or enact crime—this could be, for example, where a group of criminals use digital technology to communicate with each other about their plans, or share other information about a proposed crime. The criminals presume or hope that their communications are not being monitored but, in any case, will often use anonymous services and encryption (this is often built in to popular instant messaging smartphone applications such as WhatsApp, so no extra effort will be needed by the criminal). Law enforcement agencies may find it difficult to even establish that any communication took place.
- Technology as a witness to crime—this is an increasingly important tool in combating criminal activities and other types of behaviour investigated by the police, for example anti-social behaviour. While passive data generators such as CCTV and ANPR are extremely valuable tools for law enforcement, the police are likely to make other enquiries to support or counter the evidence available in digital form. However, the ubiquitous nature of CCTV (see 23.4.1) appears to have led to an over-reliance on such material, to the detriment of traditional investigative techniques. Unfortunately on some occasions a person who has witnessed a crime will post such information online, rather than directly reporting the matter to the police.

- Technology as a storage medium—this includes the deliberate or inadvertent storage of data on any device, which could then be used as evidence in an investigation. It is extremely important that the data and the devices are handled correctly from the very first contact with the police, and throughout the whole of any investigation or legal process. If a 'first officer at the scene' does not preserve it correctly, the evidential value of the data may be lost. In some situations specialist support will be required, although for more straightforward cases all police personnel should have the requisite skills and knowledge to deal with such devices (see 21.4).

If you are undertaking a pre-join degree, the PCDA, or the DHEP then you will cover cybercrime (sometimes called 'digital crime') and the police response ('digital policing') as part of your programme. This might well include an overview of the internet (including some basic knowledge on IP addresses but also more advanced topics such as the 'Dark Web'), social media, the rapidity of technological development, and similar topics.

A police officer must be able to recognize new forms of crime in new environments, and take appropriate and timely actions. Technological change is likely to continue at an ever-increasing pace, and this will inevitably place additional demands on the police who will have to keep abreast of the impacts of technology on criminal behaviour. New ways of abusing technology for criminal purposes will likely always be developed, and this will inevitably present new challenges for policing.

Police officers are also expected to know what to do in cases involving digital technology, including what not to do. They will need to know what actions to take and not take (and why), and these may differ depending on the type of technology that is encountered. Some officers will be very familiar with day-to-day use of digital technology (and others less so), but all officers will be required to deal with the technology in an appropriate way, to ensure the integrity of any evidence from digital devices. The temptation (particularly for the more tech-savvy) to 'take a quick look' at a computer or mobile phone must be resisted. In fact, unless there is a specific power to seize and search through a mobile phone, such a 'quick look' could constitute an offence under s 48(1) of the Wireless Telegraphy Act 2006.

The fact that technology may be involved in the commission of a crime should not in itself make the investigation into an offence more difficult. The vast majority of technology-related crimes can be treated as offences under traditional legislation; specific legislation such as the Computer Misuse Act 1990 is only needed for particular types of crime. Many offences committed online are able to be prosecuted under legislation that exists to counter and prosecute more 'traditional' crime. For example internet facilitated grooming (see 17.7.6) is covered under the Protection of Children Act 1978. (This same Act is now also a key piece of legislation in combating the presence and distribution of sexual images of children on the internet, but was initially used to tackle traditional (non-digital) photographs and methods of distribution.)

The main complication when dealing with cybercrime is often the international nature of evidence gathering. With traditional offences, for example if someone breaks into your house and steals your valuable possessions, the victim, offender, and forensic evidence are usually all co-located at the scene. But for many cybercrimes (eg if someone 'breaks into' (ie hacks into) a UK resident's Instagram account and deletes valuable photos) the victim will be local but the offence may well have been committed by someone in a different country, and the digital forensic evidence (eg data held on cloud storage) is likely to be in yet another country. Jurisdictional issues and access to international cooperation may prove difficult, costly, and time consuming, if not impossible. The Council of Europe is one of the organizations attempting to address this (the UK's membership of the Council is unaffected by Brexit). They propose creating an additional protocol to the Budapest Convention; in 2018, their Secretary General, Thorbjørn Jagland, stated:

> Access to evidence stored on virtual servers in the cloud is vital to protect society and individuals against cybercrime. Without data, there is no proof and therefore no justice. The adoption of a new protocol to secure evidence in the cloud while respecting the safeguards imposed by the rule of law will be another key milestone in this treaty's history (Council of Europe, 2018).

21.1.1   The extent of cybercrime

The extent of cyber-enabled and cyber-dependent crimes is the subject of some debate, and estimates regarding the economic consequences of these crimes for the UK vary widely. Cybercrime and fraud involving the internet are becoming more prominent, and matching other crime types in terms of their prevalence. For example, in the year ending September 2019 there were an estimated 3.8 million frauds (eg fraud conducted using stolen debit or credit card details), up 9 per cent on the previous year's figure, and one million computer misuse offences (unchanged from the previous year) (ONS, 2020). Compare this with 6.06 million 'traditional' types of crime in the same period. The estimated annual cost to the UK of cybercrime runs into billions of pounds. Indeed, UK residents are now more likely to be victims of fraud than any other type of crime (see 16.9 for offences related to fraud). Malware and phishing emails are used to obtain customers' details, and are key drivers of fraud. Such data can be used to commit fraud directly, or to add authenticity to any other fraudulent approach (NCA Cyber Crime Assessment, 2017, p 21).

The volume, range, and variety of cyber-enabled crimes is increasing. In particular, many organized crime groups have moved their activities online, as the potential rewards are greater and detection less likely. These types of crime can be very hard to investigate as they can be carried out from any location in the world. In addition, an attack on a computer system can appear to be an in-house malfunction and the initial response of information security professionals (understandably) is to try to restore normal services as soon as possible. Therefore, some attacks may not even be recognized and reported as such. The extent of the crime can also be difficult to determine, such as whether an attempted fraud or an attack is a stand-alone incident or part of a wider series. However, if an attack involves personally identifiable information being exposed and obtained, the breach must be reported (Data Protection Act 2018).

Online criminals often use automated means to target a huge number of victims at the same time, each for fairly small amounts of money. Victims will sometimes not even notice, but in any case reporting it to the police is unlikely to achieve much, because an individual loss of less than £10, where the evidence is probably abroad, is not likely to be investigated. Criminals adopting this method can make millions of pounds, with very little chance of capture. At the very minimum, such victims should be advised to report low-value online fraud to Action Fraud (see 21.3.3) as the activity might form part of a broader picture.

21.2   Examples of Cybercrime

The Home Office has been working with a number of police forces on collecting information concerning the scale and nature of cyber-enabled crime. This involves 'flagging' crimes where the reporting officer determines (on the balance of probabilities) that the offence was committed in full, or in part, using a digital device such as computer, a computing network, or a device such as a smartphone or tablet. Examples include where a crime involved the use of a social media site (such as Facebook), or other sites such as eBay to commit fraud. However, crimes where a mobile phone has been used to make phone calls or send text messages would not be flagged, nor would crimes where a PC and printer have been used to produce a counterfeit ticket for an event. Inevitably, as we have already noted, there are likely to be numerous cases where the decision on whether to flag falls in a grey area.

Here we outline some of the main types of cybercrime and provide some examples.

21.2.1   Abuse of network activities

Abuse of network activities are cyber-dependent crimes. Computers are often linked by networks within and between organizations and individuals, and this can be exploited by criminals or people who want to cause disruption and commit 'cyber-ASB'. For example, a Distributed Denial of Services (DDoS) attack involves sending multiple requests or messages to the target network. The intention is to overload the processing systems, and impede or even prevent normal functions. The table shows some examples of abuse of network activities.

Activity	Example
DDoS attacks	ICMP flood, peer-to-peer forms of attack
PBX hacking ('phreaking')	Hacking into a business phone network to generate a profit from international calls, at the expense of the business
Spamming	Emotet trojan, contained in a malicious attachment to a phishing email, intended to steal financial information stored on the network.
Botnets	MyKings botnet controlling your computer to mine cryptocurrency

The term 'spam' is frequently used for unwanted and unsolicited emails. Huge numbers of such communications can be sent out to sell a product or to distribute malware—this is known as 'spamming'. The malware could have a variety of functions, such as sending out another wave of electronic communications to cause disruption, for example as part of a DDoS. Spamming can also be used to help set up botnets, where many computers are taken over without the users' knowledge, rather like a parasite can take over and harm a living organism. The affected computers can be linked to form a network and remotely assigned to a variety of tasks. Each user will not know this is happening but might, however, notice that his/her machine seems to be working rather slowly.

21.2.2 Digital trespass, illegal access, or interception

Hacking is when a person intentionally accesses a computer, or other digital device, without the knowledge or permission of the legitimate user. It has inevitably been put to criminal use, for example stealing personal and business data for selling on to organized crime groups. It also includes the interception of VoIP calls (eg Skype services). Simple hacking is a criminal act in its own right, but it is often used to facilitate other criminal activity and then becomes an even more serious matter.

Such unauthorized access to digital devices is required to manually install 'stalkerware' apps. These track and monitor the victim's movements and communications, and are increasing used as part of coercive and controlling behaviours and domestic abuse offending. Globally, the reported number of victims with such apps covertly installed on their devices increased by 35 per cent in the year 2018/2019, and the UK was the eighth worst affected country (Kaspersky, 2019).

21.2.3 Malware

Malware is software that has been created to be used with a malicious intent, to cause harm through disrupting digital devices and networks. It can operate in many different ways, and there are a number of different types, some of which are listed and explained in the table.

Name/type of malware	How it operates	Examples
Virus	Part of the coding helps it spread and replicate by inserting a copy of itself in another program.	'Drive-by' websites, ransomware (eg Citadel malware) and HummingWhale virus (Android operating system).
Trojan	A form of malware which is 'smuggled' into a computer or network and which then performs unauthorized actions such as deleting data or secretly providing a 'backdoor' to enable another person to take over an infected computer.	'Man-in-the-Browser' (and 'Boy-in-the-Browser') Trojans secretly re-route web traffic from a victim's browser through an offender's own system, allowing the offender to capture passwords and other sensitive information (eg banking details).
Spyware	Logs a person's activities on the internet, collecting and collating information that is used to target them.	Spyware that is used for (often unwanted) 'pop up' advertising in web browsers. Also includes 'key loggers' to secretly and remotely record a user's logon and password details.
WORM	A stand-alone program that replicates itself over a computer network (without the need for a host program). 'WORM' is an acronym for 'Write Once Read Many'.	They sometimes are delivered by an email that then looks at a person's address book and sends a copy of itself, often along with a message that purports to come from the sender.

Ransomware (see 21.2.6) is a continuing and major problem, and such viruses now over-shadow the more traditional malware threats such as Trojans (see Europol's *Internet Organised Crime Threat Assessment* (IOCTA, 2019)).

21.2.4 Offensive material and illegal services

The anonymity afforded to internet users is exploited by people who wish to share and obtain offensive images and material, whether for personal satisfaction or commercial gain. Such material includes images of sexual abuse and exploitation of children (see 17.4.2) and internet hate crime (see 14.10 on hate crime). A current phenomenon is the use of sexually explicit images by individuals wishing to humiliate or harm ex-partners (see 17.4.3). The table shows some of the different ways the internet is used as a means of committing hate crime and providing illegal services.

Activity	Description	Example
Internet hate crime	Distributing material electronically intending to stir up hatred	Extremist political webpages glorifying violence against ethnic minority groups
'Cybersex'	Sharing sexual images without the permission of the person portrayed	Sexting via smartphones
Pharmaceuticals, controlled substances, and alcohol	Selling prescription-only and other restricted drugs through the internet	Illegal online pharmacies
Weapons and firearms	Selling weapons and firearms over the internet to people with no legal right to ownership	Alleged market in weapons through the 'Dark Net'
'Revenge porn'	The publication of explicit material portraying someone who has not consented for the image or video to be shared	An ex-partner publishing intimate photographs of a former partner on social media without his/her permission, with the intention of causing him/her distress

The Dark Net (or Dark Web) is increasingly used to commit crimes. This part of the World Wide Web is not visible to the normal user and can only be accessed with dedicated software. One such tool is 'The Onion Router' ('TOR'), which is advertised as 'free software that helps you defend against traffic analysis, a form of network surveillance that threatens personal freedom and privacy, confidential business activities and relationships, and state security' (Tor, 2016). As with many ideas and developments that are created for lawful purposes, criminals exploit these new technologies for their own unlawful purposes. Criminal activity in this arena is typically more difficult to investigate due to the anonymity it provides.

21.2.5 Cyber aggression

This can be on an interpersonal level such as cyber-harassment and cyber-bullying through social media sites (see the table for examples), but would also include conflict and espionage conducted through the internet. Despite anxiety in the media, there have as yet been no clear documented cases of cyber-terrorism. The IOCTA, however, has established that human-trafficking and terrorism are becoming cyber-enabled to an increasing extent.

Activity	Description	Example
Cyber-harassment	Using digital means to harass, threaten, or unreasonably embarrass a person	Repeated sending of bullying SMS texts
Cyber-stalking	Constant monitoring, contacting, and spying by digital means	Stalking an ex-partner using GPS tracking systems on a smartphone
Libel	Libelling of a person online	Allegations made through a Twitter account

21.2.6 Theft, fraud, and extortion

The cyber-enabled crimes of theft and fraud are particularly common, and ransomware is a clear example of extortion. There are numerous ways of conducting theft, fraud, and extortion through the internet, as shown in the table.

Specific Incidents

Activity	Description	Example
Re-chipping, unblocking telecommunication devices	Changing a SIM card; reprogramming a mobile telephone	Unblocking services (via software or hardware)
Advanced fee fraud	Requesting by digital means an upfront payment for non-existent goods or services	Scams such as the West African '419' fraud
Identity theft/identity fraud	Obtaining another person's personal and/or official information online, normally to commit an offence	Creating a false profile on a social networking site using someone else's name and details
Online auction fraud	Offering items which are then not delivered, or are misrepresented in some way	Using digital images to portray a non-existent item for auction
User account theft	Using various means to collect information about a person's computer or network account	User-accounts (eg on websites and forums, and Xbox live accounts) are hacked
Phishing	Trying to steal login, password, and personal identification numbers using electronic means	Emails that seem to be from a tax office, requesting details to be completed online
Spear phishing	Phishing which is personalized and individualized, which can make it seem more credible	An email with authentic details harvested from a social network site, seeming to be from a person's employer, but which contains malware
Phone-based scams	Trying to persuade a person to provide information, which can then be used to conduct theft	Phone call (vishing) purporting to be from recipient's bank, or a message (smishing) stating the person has won a prize; 'SIM-jacking' where fraudsters obtain the code from a person's service provider and take control of the victim's number
Cyber-squatting, domain name piracy	Registering domain names that are similar to well-known brands, intending to gain or profit	A confusingly similar company domain name is chosen to make a profit from unwary consumers
Ransomware	A form of malware that allows a criminal to lock a computer from a remote location, and then display a pop-up window informing the owner that the computer will not be unlocked until a sum of money, a ransom, is paid	Examples in 2017 include Wannacry and Not Petya. Some ransomware demands are accompanied by an accusation of illegal activity, or a pornographic image appears on the locked screen. This makes it more difficult to seek help so the recipient is more likely to simply pay the ransom
Sextortion, webcam blackmail	Blackmail in which sexual information or images are used to extort sexual favours and/or money from the victim	An online relationship develops into performing sexual acts via a webcam, but the blackmailer then threatens to publicly release the recordings if payment is not made
Business Email Compromise (BEC) (also referred to as CEO fraud)	The attacker gains access to a corporate email account and spoofs the owner's identity to defraud the company or its employees, customers, or partners	A bogus invoice is sent from a compromised email account requesting a change in payee information, to transfer payments to the perpetrator's account

Virtual currencies such as Bitcoin are frequently the currency of choice for criminals committing crimes of extortion, for example using ransomware. Although Bitcoin transactions are in the public domain, tracing the individuals involved is more difficult than tracing traditional bank transactions because the participants use anonymous services. As law enforcement has had some success investigating cases involving Bitcoin, criminals are now turning to other types of crypto-currency, such as Ethereum, Monero, and Litecoin.

21.2.7 IPR crime

Intellectual Property Rights crime is frequently cyber-enabled. This includes intellectual property theft where images and designs are taken and used without consent, for example downloading music or text without authority from the owner or composer.

Activity	Description	Example
Intellectual property theft	Stealing intellectual property, such as images and designs	Hacking a company's computer systems to steal software for computer chip design
Copyright infringement	Making unauthorized copies of digital content	Music and video shared with torrents, 'warez' software, commercial DVD copying, android boxes for accessing streamed films and sport without payment
Trademark infringement	Unauthorized use of a registered trademark	Selling goods online, using the logo from another company
Counterfeiting	Producing an imitation version	Using digital means to make forged banknotes
Circumventing conditional access systems	Bypassing the access systems to paid products or services	Satellite TV card-sharing using customized Linux firmware

21.3 Responding to Cybercrime

Cybercrime is considered to be a recent phenomenon, however, it has impacted on UK policing since the 1980s. The first national response was created in 2001 as the National High Tech Crime Unit. Although somewhat of a cliché, 'prevention is better than cure' remains a sensible piece of advice, and this certainly applies to cyber-enabled and cyber-dependent crime. As a policing student you will no doubt receive advice on safeguarding your digital information and remaining safe online, so you should be familiar with such information. Police officers are increasingly likely to be asked by members of the public for advice on computer security (see 21.3.2).

21.3.1 Local level police responses to cybercrime

Police forces in the UK each have their own locally based resources to investigate cyber-dependent crime. The units have often evolved from former fraud squads and tend to be relatively small, but their capabilities are increasing with the development of digital forensic technology. They also provide additional support to other investigations, for example into child sexual exploitation and abuse.

Cases involving complex cybercrime and fraud are investigated by the specialist police investigators at the MPS 'FALCON' unit (Fraud and Linked Crime On-Line). A number of forces (eg Sussex and Surrey, and Kent and Essex) have combined their resources and formed joint units for investigating cyber-dependent crime.

Many cyber-enabled and some cyber-dependent crimes are effectively 'screened' to decide whether further investigation is appropriate. Level 1 or 2 plastic-card crimes, if investigated, are likely to be tackled by a force-based unit, although forces do not have the resources to investigate all reported incidents (particularly credit and debit card offences such as 'card not present' fraud where payments are made over the internet or by phone). Level 3 plastic-card-related crimes are usually passed to the NCA for investigation.

Although the investigation of cyber-dependent crime will invariably involve collecting 'traditional' forms of evidence (eg in written form) there might also be digitally based evidence, such as a deleted file recovered from a PC hard drive, or the address book from a mobile phone SIM card. Police officers at crime scenes must ensure the correct actions are taken to ensure that digital evidence is not destroyed or contaminated (see 21.4). The ACPO good practice guidelines recommend that digital evidence strategies should form part of the wider investigative process (ACPO, 2007a and ACPO, 2012a).

The forensic techniques required from initial data recovery to analysis (often known as digital forensics) are a specialist field within investigation (see 21.4). Once a device is seized and submitted to your Digital Forensics Unit, they will follow the ISO 17025 standards to ensure the integrity and admissibility of the forensic evidence. Police forces may choose to 'outsource' some digital forensic analysis to non-police contractors, who are also expected to meet the ISO 17025 standards and follow the good practice guidelines.

Specific Incidents

21.3.1.1 Cybercrime prevention advice

If you are a police officer, you might well be expected to offer some form of 'cybercrime prevention' advice, especially for people who have been victims of small-scale online fraud. Members of the public should be advised as follows:

- do not open attachments or links that appear in emails, unless such a message from a known source is expected;
- keep anti-virus software up to date;
- download the latest security patches for the operating systems used; and
- choose secure passwords.

Most emails sent out by financial and other organizations now include specific information such as part of a postcode, and also address the recipient personally. Many such organizations also provide guidance for customers to prevent internet-related crime, and it is good practice to remind members of the public to use such information.

In advance of any transaction banks will often send a One Time Password (OTP) to the customer's mobile phone. Any customer receiving such a message unexpectedly should contact the bank immediately. Before travelling abroad, customers should also consider informing their bank which countries will be visited, and about any foreseen transactions in those countries. Two-factor (dual) authentication may also be used by banks and other businesses, especially those in the finance sector. Online purchasing systems will generally employ 'user authentication' methods to help counter potential fraud.

Some people may be more vulnerable to certain crime types, such as widowed or single people. Middle-aged people may become victims of 'romance fraud', and young people may receive sextortion threats (see 17.4.3). However, criminals often target a wide and non-specific audience to try and locate potential victims. They only expect a tiny proportion to respond, but this could still amount to thousands of victims.

There are many online resources with further information and guidance such as:

- the National Cyber Security Centre (NCSC) which provides security advice and information to everyone in the UK, including the public, and members of all kinds of organizations. They have published the '10 steps to cybersecurity', which outline basic measures for protection against cyber-attacks (see <https://www.ncsc.gov.uk>);
- the 'ThinkUKnow' campaign (run by CEOP, the National Crime Agency's Child Exploitation and Online Protection command) which aims to increase young people's understanding of online safety (CEOP, 2013);
- GetSafeOnline.org which provides advice for individuals and businesses, including cybercrime prevention guidance;
- the 'Take Five' campaign, which offers straightforward and impartial advice to help everyone in the UK protect themselves against financial fraud (see <https://takefive-stopfraud.org.uk/>).

Police officers can use these sources to obtain further accurate and appropriate cybercrime prevention guidance, and will then be able to provide bespoke cyber-security advice to individuals within local communities as required.

21.3.2 National measures to counter cybercrime

The National Cyber Crime Unit (NCCU) is responsible for investigations into 'high end' cyber-dependent crime, for example investigating large-scale DDoS and other hacking attacks, and significant cyber-enabled frauds. It is part of the National Crime Agency, it also works closely with the Child Exploitation and Online Protection (CEOP) Centre, and is actively engaged in countering the development of malware. The NCCU works with business and industry to counter cyber-dependent crime, and has close links with the European Cybercrime Centre (EC3) based within Europol in The Hague.

Action Fraud is the national fraud and cybercrime reporting centre for the UK. Complainants for these crime types should be advised to report the crime online at <https://www.actionfraud.police.uk/report_fraud> or by telephone on 0300 123 2040. Action Fraud is responsible for collating all reports of cyber-dependent crime and fraud (including cyber-enabled fraud), and can use the information to identify patterns of criminal activity, and thus facilitate investigations.

The banking industry supplements the police resources available to investigate plastic-card crime: for example, the industry body APACS sponsors the work of the Dedicated Cheque and Plastic Crime Unit (DCPCU).

21.3.3 International measures to counter cybercrime

In 2011, the UK acceded to the Budapest Convention on Cybercrime, a major international treaty designed to harmonize legislation and facilitate the effective investigation of cybercrime. It improves international cooperation between nations, including the rapid transfer of electronic evidence across international borders where required.

From the perspective of the police officer, the importance of the Convention lies in its procedural provisions. It sets out procedures for processes such as:

- the preservation of stored data;
- the preservation and partial disclosure of event data;
- the legal means available to produce evidence;
- the search and seizure of computer data;
- the real-time collection of event data; and
- the interception of content data.

The Convention also facilitates some types of transborder access to stored computer data and helped set up a 24/7 network to help ensure speedy assistance among the signatory parties (see 21.3.4.1). While police officers are unlikely to make use of such procedures on a daily basis, it is nonetheless important to know they exist—there may be vital digital evidence in any investigation, and this by its very nature is often transient.

The number of law enforcement requests for data has reached such a level that companies such as Facebook, Apple, Microsoft, and Google now have their own dedicated procedures for handling such requests. They can choose to provide some types of communications data (see 23.4.3) if the request is lawful, without the need to invoke complex formal legal assistance provisions. Any requests for communications data will have to be made through the 'Single Point of Contacts' within your local Communications Intelligence Unit. The most commonly sought information in investigations is the identity of the subscriber of a communications service ('entity information').

21.3.3.1 The 24/7 system

The 24/7 network makes it easier and faster for signatory countries to seek assistance from one another in cybercrime and electronic evidence cases. The UK point of contact is housed by the National Crime Agency, and, as a party to the Convention, the UK can use the Convention provisions during an investigation. For example, vital data could be preserved in another signatory country, pending an application for legal assistance (which may take many months, during which the requested data may otherwise be deleted by normal business processes).

If information is required from a country that is not a party to the Budapest Convention, there are other options to preserve and obtain data, although these requests are sometimes refused by the host country.

21.4 Seizure and Packaging of Digital Devices

At many police incidents there will be digital evidence. When such evidence is encountered and dealt with by the police, certain procedures must be followed. The importance of this cannot be overstated! The way in which the evidence is handled at this initial stage will impact on its admissibility in any subsequent criminal justice proceedings. Your actions may mean the difference between evidence being accepted or rejected at trial. This type of evidence is volatile (ie the data held on digital devices can be transient and easily altered), so special considerations apply for seizure and packaging of digital devices at crime scenes.

If a computer needs to be seized, the Digital Forensics Unit (or Computer Crime Unit) should be contacted in advance for advice, and may also attend the scene if they think it is necessary. DFU personnel are specially trained to recover data and present it in a form acceptable to the criminal justice system. In doing so, they will be mindful of ss 19 and 20 of the PACE

Act 1984 (which provide the legal basis for the seizure of data) and the *ACPO Good Practice Guide for Digital Evidence* (ACPO, 2012a). This is included within the Investigations Authorised Professional Practice (APP) under the Forensics section. The Good Practice Guide outlines (p 6) the four principles of digital evidence which must be adhered to. The first principle is relevant for all police officers and the remaining three are more relevant to specialists but are included here for completeness:

- Principle 1: *No action taken by law enforcement agencies, persons employed within those agencies or their agents should change data, which may subsequently be relied upon in court.* For the trainee police officer this means, for example, that they should not turn on a PC that is turned off (see 21.4.3) or have a quick look at the contents of a smartphone or other device.
- Principle 2: *In circumstances where a person finds it necessary to access original data, that person must be competent to do so and be able to give evidence explaining the relevance and the implications of their actions.*
- Principle 3: *An audit trail or other record of all processes applied to digital evidence should be created and preserved. An independent third party should be able to examine those processes and achieve the same result.*
- Principle 4: *The person in charge of the investigation has overall responsibility for ensuring that the law and these principles are adhered to.*

Apart from data and programs that may be stored, the plastic, metal, and glass surfaces of a digital device may also provide useful evidence. The outer skin of most computers is usually slightly textured and will therefore not yield latent finger marks. However, the smooth screen can provide latent finger marks, as can areas which are not normally seen such as inside the case, under the support foot, and at the rear.

Local policy must be followed for all seizures and storage of computers and associated equipment, particularly relating to packaging. In serious or major crimes, great care must be taken as DNA and finger mark analysis may be required for whole devices. There may be a conflict of priorities between the physical and digital evidence retrieval—this must be resolved prior to any activity.

A key point is that a computer which is to be seized as part of an investigation that is currently powered on should never be turned off by following a standard shut-down procedure, but should instead have its power supply removed, see 21.4.1 and 21.4.3. And just as important— a digital device that is 'off' when found must not be turned on.

Computers that are attached to networks present particular problems. If you encounter a network during an unplanned seizure and you need to seize one or more of the computers you should contact your DFU or equivalent for advice. Further information may be found in Bryant and Bryant (2014).

The *Electronic evidence guide—a basic guide for police officers, prosecutors and judges* produced by the Council of Europe (COE) provides additional guidance. This is available via law enforcement agencies, but can also be obtained by visiting <https://www.coe.int/en/web/octopus/home> and joining the community, which is in itself an excellent resource for cybercrime-related matters. The guide provides advice on how to handle traditional computer-based evidence, and also deals with Live Data Forensics (see 21.4.2). It also covers the procedures for obtaining evidential materials during online investigations; it is not as simple as just going online and downloading the data. The guide also has easy-to-use flowcharts for using in search and seizure exercises, and these could be printed off and used (in conjunction with local policy) when attending crime scenes with electronic evidence.

Digital forensics scientists are subject to the same codes of practice as forensic science providers, such as the *Codes of Practice and Conduct for forensic science providers and practitioners in the Criminal Justice System*. The codes deal with laboratory-based activity, but the level of scrutiny for those collecting digital evidence will no doubt increase—the correct procedures must be followed. The Forensic Science Regulator (appointed by the Home Office) developed the codes, and also ensures that all forensic science providers meet certain standards.

21.4.1 Unplanned seizures of digital equipment

Where a seizure is unplanned, the Digital Forensics Unit (DFU) or equivalent should be contacted for advice. The scene should be secured and people moved away from the equipment

Specific Incidents

and any power supplies. If a printer is still printing then it should be allowed to complete its run. The display of any active screen should be photographed or captured on Body Worn Video.

In the meantime:

- do not power-on any device;
- do not touch any key or the mouse;
- do not interfere with any other device on a network;
- do not use the telephone system; and
- treat any 'advice' from the owner or user with caution.

The layout of the devices and associated cabling should be photographed or sketched where practicable. Separate photographs should be taken of the computer from the front, sides, and back, and of any cables and devices such as portable drives that may be connected to the computer. For small portable devices, local policy should be followed, but in no circumstances should call lists, pictures, or any other files be viewed as this will be a breach of Principle 1 of the ACPO guidance.

If the devices are unconnected to other devices, then the DFU may suggest a simple seizure. If a device is powered on, unless advised to the contrary, the best course of action would be to turn off the device to prevent the loss of evidence (see 21.4.3.1).

However, care is needed as some devices may be part of a network, and be able to communicate with other systems and devices through Wi-Fi, Bluetooth, NFC, and infrared. The contents of some networked connected devices (eg smartphones, tablets, and similar) can be deleted remotely, and a suspect may want to do this to try and destroy potential evidence. These 'kill commands' can only be effective if the device is switched on and connected to a network. If a device needs to remain powered-on because live data forensics is required (see 21.4.2), then a 'Faraday bag' can be used to prevent such wireless communications being received by the device; a good temporary solution is to completely wrap the device in kitchen foil.

Seized hard drives should be placed in anti-static bags, tough paper bags, tamper-evident cardboard packaging, or wrapped in paper and placed in aerated plastic bags.

Given the growth in internet-connected devices and the increased use of the 'Internet of Things', the number of devices that could hold vital evidence in an investigation has increased dramatically. Virtual assistants, such as the Amazon Alexa, smart TVs, smart watches, games consoles, routers, and even some doorbells and fridges could all be significant. Car infotainment systems and vehicle telematics could equally be valuable sources of evidence. Hence police officers now need to look beyond smartphones, tablets, and computers, but this inevitably creates additional considerations. So, always seek advice from your DFU before seizing any non-standard digital devices; they are not going to be impressed with you speculatively submitting an American-style multi-door internet connected fridge freezer for digital examination without having spoken to them first!

21.4.2 Live data forensics

Live data forensics (LDF) procedures allow data to be recovered from a device that is found powered-on.

It employs relatively novel techniques, but is becoming increasingly important and necessary, as a significant amount of data on devices is held in temporary memory. Such data would be lost if someone turns off the device when seizing it as evidence. Specially trained and equipped staff have the requisite knowledge and skills to recover the data, while at the same time minimizing any 'contamination' (ie changes to the data).

The increasing need for LDF in daily police work reinforces the advantages of contacting your DFU in advance of any search and seizure activity where digital evidence is likely to be encountered.

21.4.3 Procedures for computers and mobile devices that are powered-on

For all powered-on devices, and once any LDF has been completed, the following actions should be taken in this order, to preserve as much evidence and data as possible:

1. photograph the device (particularly the screen);

2. make a PNB record of any on-screen text and imagery that might be visible, and the current activity of the device (eg it may be loading a web page);
3. put the device into 'flight mode' or 'airplane mode' if possible; and then
4. turn it off by doing a 'hard shut-down' or remove the power supply (unless local policy determines that under the specific circumstances it should be left powered-on).

Removing the power supply to a computer prevents automated routines from being activated or drives being formatted—these might otherwise destroy vital evidence on the hard drive.

Every effort should be made to obtain the PIN, password, or other decryption code that is used to unlock the device. Without this, it may not be possible for DFU to recover the stored data and evidence on the device.

21.4.3.1 How to turn off computers and other devices

To turn off a computer the power lead should be removed from the back of the PC base unit. (Unplugging it from the mains would not necessarily cut the power supply as the computer might have an uninterruptible power supply (UPS).) Care must be taken when removing the power lead as there is a low of risk of electrocution to the person doing this. This risk will be very much reduced by not holding the very end of the power lead where it connects to the computer.

Laptops generally have a battery so removing the power lead will not turn them off: this can be a particular problem in unplanned seizures. It would therefore seem necessary to remove both the battery and the power cable, but as in all matters concerning the seizure of digital equipment, local force policy must be followed. If the battery is removed it must also be seized. For laptops with a sealed-in non-removable battery and for tablets, the only option would be to perform a 'hard shut-down'. This is done by holding down the on/off button for several seconds until the device turns off completely. For mobile phones and smartphones that are powered-on, similar general advice applies (but check local policy).

21.4.4 Packaging digital equipment

Force policy must be followed for 'bagging and tagging' digital equipment. Most force policies state that see-through plastic bags should be used. If PC base units or other items of larger digital equipment are seized, then each item should be placed in its own bag. The bag must then be properly sealed and labelled—a cardboard exhibit label should be attached if the bag does not have a pre-printed label. However, note finger marks on smooth surfaces will be obliterated if they come into contact with a polythene bag, so care must be taken. In serious or major crimes, great care and detailed planning will be required as the entire device may be subject to DNA and finger mark analysis.

For small, portable digital devices the following procedures are likely to apply:

- package each device separately in its own individual bag, unless instructed to the contrary;
- where applicable, keep the various media (eg CDs) in their cases;
- check inside all cases at the scene;
- do not place labels directly on any device;
- seize cradles/power packs for tablets, smartphones, and similar equipment; and
- keep packaged devices away from sources of magnetism, including during transport (eg keep devices away from vehicle radios).

Each force is likely to have its own policies for seizure and packaging of smartphones and mobile phones. This may include storage in Faraday bags and boxes to prevent the device communicating with the network.

21.5 Legislation and Cybercrime Offences

For most cyber-enabled crime, existing 'non-cybercrime' legislation, such as the Fraud Act 2006, can often be used to address the particular crime concerned. This also applies for some cyber-dependent crimes, for example hacking will be often prosecuted as extortion (even though hacking is explicitly covered by the Computer Misuse Act 1990 (CMA)). One reason for this is that the penalty for the 'traditional' offence (in this case extortion) will carry the heavier penalty on conviction. Another example of using non-cybercrime legislation to tackle some online offences relates to online harassment. When victims are trolled online, or sent grossly offensive messages, this could constitute an offence under s 1 of the Malicious Communications Act 1988 (see 14.5.3.1). However, the trolling will probably take place more than once, and it would therefore be more appropriate to prosecute under the Protection from Harassment Act 1997 (see 14.5.1).

Other legislation can be used to deal with the 'grey' area between cyber-enabled and cyber-dependent crime. For example, a stolen phone with a blocked IMEI will not work on a UK network. (A mobile phone is uniquely identified by its International Mobile Equipment Identity (IMEI) number, and network service providers can use this to blacklist stolen phones.) Therefore, criminals in possession of a stolen phone will often seek to change the IMEI so it can be used again, possibly in a crime. The phone can be unblocked or otherwise reprogrammed using unofficial hardware and software acquired through the internet. It is a criminal offence to unblock a phone by altering an IMEI (s 1 of the Mobile Telephones (Reprogramming) Act 2002 (MTRA)).

It has, however, been necessary to bring in new legislation to tackle the growing use of digital technology, given that such capabilities were not even imaginable when the older laws were written. This will help close and clarify the grey areas and loopholes that could otherwise be exploited. For example, several elements of the Regulation of Investigatory Powers Act 2000 have been phased out and replaced by the Investigatory Powers Act 2016. In addition s 33 of the Criminal Justice and Courts Act 2015 introduced a new offence of disclosing private sexual photographs and films with intent to cause distress, colloquially known as 'revenge porn', and the Voyeurism Act 2019 created the offence of 'upskirting' (see 17.3.2).

21.5.1 The Computer Misuse Act 1990

For cyber-dependent crime the main legislation in England and Wales is the Computer Misuse Act 1990 (CMA), together with its various amendments (principally within the Police and Justice Act 2006). The four main offences under the amended CMA are shown in the table. Offences under ss 1 and 2 relate to unauthorized access whereas the more serious s 3 offence involves unauthorized acts.

Section	The offence	Explanation and examples
1	Unauthorized access to computer material	Prohibits activities such as accessing a person's iPad using his/her name and pin number. It is simply enough to prove that the suspect knows that the access was unauthorized—there is no need to prove the suspect had any intent to do something (such as steal a password to a website) after gaining access.
2	Unauthorized access with intent to commit or facilitate commission of further offences	An example of this offence would be hacking a person's PC to locate his/her bank details with the intent to access the account online and make payments from it (here, the further offence could be theft).
3	Unauthorized acts with intent to impair	This would include spreading viruses, accessing a victim's social media account and changing the password, and DDoS attacks. The scope of s 3 was broadened to include 'impair' as the original legislation required that changes be made to the files or programs on the computer, which did not cover DDoS attacks.
3A	Making, supplying, or obtaining articles for use in an offence under s 1 or 3	This would include, eg, supplying 'kits' to enable DDoS attacks that would enable the sowing of 'Trojans' within a company's network.

For the purposes of the CMA 1990, the word 'computer' is defined under case law (*DPP v Jones* [1997] 2 Cr App R 155 (HL)) as 'device for storing, processing and retrieving information'. This is a wide-ranging definition that would certainly include tablet devices, smartphones, and even the aforementioned internet connected fridge freezer (see 21.4.1). In terms of the location, the CMA 1990 applies where the perpetrator was in the UK at the time he/she committed the relevant acts, and/or the relevant 'computer' was physically located in the UK.

All CMA offences are triable either way, and the penalty for each when tried summarily is a fine or a maximum of 12 months' imprisonment. For convictions on indictment the penalty is either a fine or imprisonment, a maximum of two years for a s 1 or 3A offence, five years for a s 2 offence, and ten years for a s 3 offence.

22 | Attempts, Conspiracy, and Encouraging or Assisting Crime

22.1 Introduction

In this chapter we discuss legislation designed to deal with suspects or offenders who stop just short of committing indictable offences but can nevertheless be prosecuted for attempting to commit the full offence, or for conspiracy. In addition, those accomplices who are not the actual perpetrators of an offence who encourage or assist in the commission of a crime from a distance are also considered. This relatively new legislation has a slighter wider scope than the common law offence of incitement that it replaces. These kinds of offences are referred to as inchoate— meaning anticipatory or preparatory. People who are accused of the offences described in this chapter are also sometimes loosely or informally described as 'accessories' to a crime.

The rationale for creating the inchoate offences of conspiracy, attempts, and incitement is based on the notion that the perpetrator is no less dangerous or culpable than a person who might commit the full or substantive offence. That is why the maximum sentence for inchoate offences is usually the same as for the actual offence. It is fair to say, though, that charges for inchoate offences are much rarer than those for the full offence.

22.2 Criminal Attempts

A person who is planning or preparing a criminal offence might not actually commit the full offence. This could be because the suspect lost his/her nerve, or was disturbed, or simply found that the intentions or plans were impracticable. Occasionally the police learn of such criminal intentions and will covertly observe the suspect's activities—such evidence can sometimes be used to support a charge for an inchoate offence. This often applies in very serious cases like terrorism, where it is clearly in the public interest that the harmful intent of terrorists is thwarted before the full offence can be committed.

The offence of a criminal attempt can be used to penalize a criminal for carrying out an act just short of committing a full offence. This offence (a criminal attempt) is described under s 1(1) of the Criminal Attempts Act 1981:

> If with intent to commit the offence to which this section applies, a person does an act which is more than merely *preparatory* to the commission of the offence, [he/she] is guilty of attempting to commit the offence.

The attempted offence must be an indictable offence (ie it can be tried on indictment in a Crown Court or either way at a magistrates' court or a Crown Court—see 4.5.1), however, see 22.2.3 for certain indictable offences which cannot be attempted. Summary offences cannot be attempted in terms of the Criminal Attempts Act 1981.

The mode of trial is the same as for the main offence. For either-way offences the penalty is the same maximum penalty as the substantive offence when tried summarily. For an indictable-only offence the maximum penalty is the same as for the substantive offence.

22.2.1 Attempts and criminal intent

The suspect must have formed criminal intent (*mens rea*) in all three of the areas shown in the table:

The suspect must have the intent to	Example
Commit the full offence	The suspect intended to steal a car or to rob a person
Take part in a series of acts which will lead to a final outcome of committing the full offence	The suspect made a point of collecting the tools together, going to a house, and forcing a window in order to break in
Carry out all the elements of the offence	In order to attempt a theft, for example, the suspect must have acted dishonestly with the intention of appropriating the property belonging to another and of permanently depriving the other of it

For a person to be found guilty of an attempt to commit an offence, the suspect must have more than an intention to do it (*R v Campbell* [1991] Crim LR 268). The suspect must demonstrate a guilty intent by carrying out the type of acts which amount to more than merely preparing to commit the full offence. For example, it would not be enough for a suspect to have some rags and a container of petrol in a bag, and to take them to his rival's house; these actions might still be considered as preparatory. If, on the other hand, he went to his rival's front door and pushed petrol-soaked rags through the letter box, and then used a match to try to set the rags alight, this would show a clear intent to carry out arson. These acts would probably be considered as 'more than merely preparatory' and could therefore constitute an attempt under the Criminal Attempts Act 1981.

The final act carried out by the accused must be in combination with all the other preparatory acts, and have no purpose other than to complete the full offence. For example, imagine a group of people arrive in a van at a yard containing copper scrap one night. They cut a large hole in the fence, big enough for a person to pass through, but then spot a security guard and quickly leave. When they are stopped, one of the group has some wire cutters in his pocket and another is seen to quietly drop some bolt croppers on the ground next to the van. Their actions amount to more than preparations to steal; they have committed an attempt under s 1(1) of the Criminal Attempts Act 1981 (see *Davey v Lee* (1967) 51 Cr App R 303).

It is sometimes difficult to identify the fine line between preparatory acts and attempts to commit crime. However, this decision is primarily the jury's to make, based on 'common sense'.

To help make the decision, the following question could be asked: does the available evidence demonstrate that the defendant has performed an action which shows that he/she has actually tried to commit the offence in question, or has he/she merely become ready to put him/herself in a position or equipped him/herself to do so (*R v Geddes* (1996) 160 JP 697)?

It is not sufficient that the defendant made preparations, obtained suitable materials or equipment, got ready, and put him/herself in a position to commit the main offence.

With regard to theft, the law introduced the specific offence of going equipped to steal (s 25 of the Theft Act 1968, see 16.6). It states that a person is guilty of this offence if, 'when not at his place of abode, he has with him any article for use in the course of or in connection with any burglary or theft'. One can see here how the law seeks to cover all eventualities of criminal endeavour—walking down the street with implements to steal a car would not amount to an attempt, but would amount to the offence of going equipped to steal.

For an attempt, if the person **believes** that he/she is committing an offence but does not actually commit it, he/she will still be regarded as having attempted it, even if it is proved later that it would not have been possible to commit the full offence (s 1(3)(b)). For example, a woman is paid money to travel from another country to the UK with a suitcase that she believes contains heroin. On arrival in the UK her suitcase is searched and she admits to importing heroin into the UK. However, tests on the substance in the suitcase reveal it to be harmless vegetable matter, and not drugs. The offence of importing controlled drugs has not been committed, but she has still attempted to commit the crime (*R v Shivpuri* [1987] AC 1).

The more recent case of *L v CPS* [2013] EWHC 4127 (Admin) demonstrates that the prosecution need to prove more than the person's mere presence at the scene of a robbery to convict him/her of involvement in attempted robbery. In this case, a group of youths were accused of acting together to attempt to rob young children of their phones. All were convicted, but an appeal was allowed in the case of individual L, as there was insufficient evidence to demonstrate that he encouraged the attempted robbery at any stage. His mere presence amongst the group of offenders was found to be insufficient to convict him of attempted robbery.

22.2.2 Thorough planning and practical preparation

Section 1(2) of the Criminal Attempts Act 1981 states that there must be evidence that the person actually planned to personally carry out the act, rather than just planning it (in which case someone else could have carried it out): 'the person does an act which is more than merely preparatory to the commission of the offence'. If there is something else to be done before the completion of the offence, it does not amount to an attempt.

As has been alluded to, it does not matter (for the offence of criminal attempt) whether the attempted offence would actually have been impossible to carry out (s 1(2)). Two examples demonstrate this:

- A woman who fires a bullet at the body of a man lying on a bed intending to kill him, but she did not know he was already dead. Even though the full offence of murder is impossible, she has still in fact attempted to kill someone.
- A man tries to steal property from a woman's pocket. He inserts his hand but finds nothing because the pocket is empty. Even though the full offence of theft is impossible he has still attempted to commit the offence of theft.

22.2.3 Offences that cannot be criminally attempted

Section 1(4) of the Criminal Attempts Act 1981 lists several categories of offence that cannot be 'attempted', such as summary offences. There are also a number of indictable offences that cannot be attempted. These include:

- conspiracy to commit an indictable offence: that is, an agreement between people to commit an offence;
- aiding, abetting, counselling, procuring, or suborning the commission of an indictable offence: for example, a person knew all the circumstances concerning a particular murder and did everything apart from deliver the fatal kick to the head; and
- assisting offenders: for example, knowingly helping offenders avoid arrest or concealing information, perhaps by paying money to a witness to stop him/her giving testimony in any trial.

The reason these particular offences cannot be attempted is because they are, of themselves, preparatory (criminal) conduct. In other words, one cannot 'attempt an attempt'.

(Note, however, that some summary offences amount to attempts in themselves, for example 'attempting to drive whilst unfit through drink or drugs' (see 19.9.2), and 'interfering with vehicles' (see 16.8.2.2). The latter was created to cover situations where a person's actions effectively amount to an attempted 'taking a conveyance without the owner's consent' offence (see 16.8.2), but could not be charged as such because TWOC is a summary offence.)

TASK 1 The following case relating to an attempt subsequently went to appeal. Predict the result of the appeal and explain your reasoning.

A man was seen by a teacher in the lavatory block at a school. A cider can with the man's finger marks was found in one of the cubicles. His rucksack, containing a large kitchen knife, some rope, and a roll of masking tape, was found in some nearby bushes. He was charged and convicted of attempted child abduction, the prosecution putting forward the argument that he had been hiding in the lavatories to abduct a child. He appealed on the grounds that he had not attempted to commit the offence (*R v Geddes* [1996] Crim LR 894).

22.3 Conspiracy

The word 'conspiracy' is usually employed to describe a plan made in secret by a group of people to do something unlawful or harmful—bear this in mind when seeking to understand this offence. We have now moved one step further back from attempts. If the full offence is not apparent and neither is an attempt, then what other legal provisions exist to deal with criminals who are apparently engaged in planning to commit offences? The answer lies in the law's provisions for the offence of conspiracy. This brief overview will concentrate on conspiracy to commit an offence, as described in the Criminal Law Act 1977, but it is worth mentioning that under common law there are non-statutory conspiracies, such as conspiracy to defraud and conspiracy to corrupt public morals or outrage public decency. Further information on these is available on the CPS website.

Conspiracy (s 1 of the Criminal Law Act 1977) is seen as an 'incomplete offence' (as are attempts to commit crime). This is because it is committed as soon as the parties agree to carry out a course of conduct that will involve committing the main offence (known as the substantive offence). The conspirator does not have to commit the substantive offence to commit conspiracy. Note that a person can still be found guilty of conspiracy even if the commission of the substantive offence is impossible due to the existence of particular circumstances (subsection (b)). Thus, if two men agree a course of conduct to kill a particular woman, it does not matter if (unknown to the men) she is already dead.

For there to be a conspiracy, at least two people must make the agreement. There can be no criminal conspiracy where a person acts alone, and mere negotiation does not constitute an agreement (*DPP v Nock* [1978] AC 979). Conspiracy, then, is a group activity. However, if a person enters into an agreement and then withdraws, this still amounts to a conspiracy, and the withdrawal would be regarded only as mitigation (*R v Gortat and Pirog* [1973] Crim LR 648). In addition, there are certain classes of people who by definition cannot be guilty of a conspiracy. First, the intended victim of a crime cannot be guilty, and unsurprisingly a conspiracy cannot be said to exist when a child under 10 is the only other person in an agreement to commit crime (s 2 of the Criminal Law Act 1977). Finally, a husband and wife cannot be guilty of conspiracy to commit crime if they are the only people in the agreement. This particular exclusion of liability appears to relate to the traditional notion that when two people are married they become 'one', in the eyes of the law. If, however, they both entered into a conspiracy with a third party (so that there were then three people in the conspiracy) they could all be guilty of the offence.

Evidence for conspiracy can be difficult to obtain because such agreements are usually made in secret, with no other parties present. However, it can be proved by demonstrating the parties' pursuit of a common purpose, for example through clandestine meetings, text messages, emails, and paper-based documents showing plans to commit a crime. The police will often use surveillance to obtain evidence of a conspiracy (see 23.4.2 on covert surveillance). Charges for conspiracy are quite rare and are usually reserved for very serious crimes such as terrorism or organized crime gangs.

The sentence for conspiracy is the same as for the substantive offence planned. Conspiracies are indictable-only offences, and because of this they can only be tried at a Crown Court, and as a Crown Court trial is a costly process, the CPS only support charges for conspiracy when it is in the public interest. If substantive offences have been committed, the CPS are more likely to charge for these rather than a conspiracy, unless many people have been involved only at the conspiracy stage or the crime that was planned was very serious. Where parties conspire to commit other offences abroad, in some circumstances the convictions can be pursued in England and Wales (s 1A of the Criminal Law Act 1977).

22.4 Encouraging or Assisting Crime

The commission of a crime often involves two or more accomplices but they may not all actually perpetrate (carry out) the offence. Some accomplices are at the crime scene but 'merely' offer encouragement, while others might assist in the commission of a crime from a distance, providing information, transport, or financial support.

A person who encourages or assists in a crime (but does not perpetrate the main offence) may believe or claim that he/she was not a true accomplice. However, under the Serious Crime Act 2007 there are three criminal offences which involve encouraging or assisting another person to commit an offence. Together they replace the common law offence of incitement (now abolished), and also provide additional scope for prosecution in cases where the crime has not yet taken place; previously there was no criminal liability for assisting the commission of an offence unless the offence had been committed or attempted. The legislation providing for these offences came into force on 1 October 2008, and does not apply retrospectively, so would only apply for conduct since that time.

Note that a person cannot be convicted of encouraging or assisting a crime for which he/she is the intended victim. For instance, a 16-year-old schoolchild cannot be convicted of encouraging or assisting his/her teacher to engage in sexual activity with them. The teacher would commit the sexual offence of breach of a position of trust, but the young person could not be convicted of encouraging or assisting as he/she is the person protected by that particular piece of legislation (s 51 of the Serious Crime Act 2007).

As for conspiracy offences, prosecutions for encouraging and assisting offences are rare. This is partly due to the difficulties in obtaining the required evidence, but also because the police and the Crown Prosecution Service will generally search for substantive offences wherever possible. The maximum penalties for an offence under s 44, 45, or 46 of the Serious Crime Act 2007, will be the same as the maximum for the relevant main offence.

22.4.1 Intentionally encouraging or assisting an offence

This is covered by s 44 of the Serious Crime Act 2007, which states that an offence is committed by a person who:

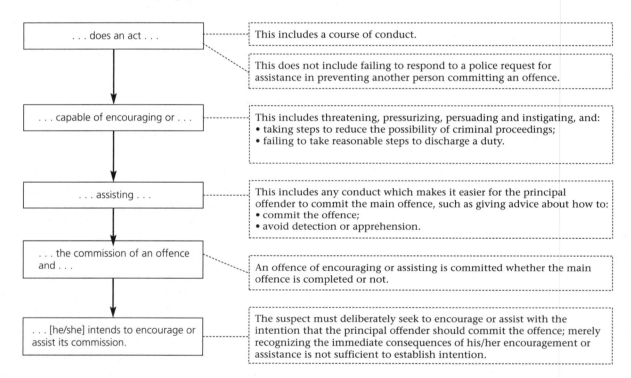

We provide a few examples to illustrate some key points:

- At a noisy and angry street protest, a police officer speaks to Dodie (a protestor) to try and help him calm down, but Dodie becomes increasingly irate and aggressive. Due to the loud noise, the officer is unable to summon assistance from a colleague. Instead the officer requests Neil, another protestor, to help restrain Dodie, but Neil refuses. Neil's refusal would probably not be regarded as encouraging or assisting a person to commit a criminal act.
- Frankie lends a baseball bat to a neighbour who is scared that someone might possibly break into his house to steal antiques. Frankie knows that a baseball bat is sometimes used as a weapon to injure people, but gives it to her neighbour with the sole purpose of helping him feel more confident. Subsequently, an intruder is seriously injured by the neighbour using the baseball bat. For Frankie, this would probably not amount to assistance or encouragement to cause grievous bodily harm.

- Kristoff is married to Shazia but is having an affair with Bella, one of Shazia's workmates. Kristoff intends to murder Shazia and dispose of the body and make it seem that she has moved away. Bella knows all about Kristoff's plan and agrees to provide him with up-to-date information on Shazia's whereabouts during the day to give Kristoff a better opportunity to act without being caught. Another work colleague overhears Bella talking about the plan, and contacts the police. Bella has intentionally assisted in the commission of murder.
- Brown works for a double-glazing firm. In return for payment he provides Mal with a spare key from a recently installed door, knowing that Mal is likely to use the key to burgle the house. Three days later Mal enters the house, and steals cash and jewellery. Brown has intentionally assisted in the commission of burglary (for burglary, see 16.4).

22.4.2 Believing one or more offences will be committed

Offences under ss 45 and 46 of the Serious Crime Act 2007 relate to belief rather than intent. The person providing the encouragement or assistance must believe that the main offence(s) will actually be committed and that his/her act(s) will provide encouragement or assistance. It is immaterial whether the main offence is completed or not.

An offence is committed under s 45 of the Serious Crime Act 2007, when a person 'does an act capable of encouraging or assisting the commission of an offence' (the main offence). He/she must believe that the main offence will be committed and that his/her act will encourage or assist its commission. The following is likely to constitute a s 45 offence.

Black is a car sales person who makes a copy of a key of the most expensive car on the forecourt at the dealership at which he is employed. During an evening out, he gives the spare key to his friend, Stav, knowing that Stav will probably steal the car in the near future. The next day Stav is arrested during a burglary and is found in possession of the spare key. At interview, Stav outlines his reasons for possessing the spare key, including Black's involvement. In this example, Black has committed the s 45 offence because, although he did not intend that Stav should commit theft, Black still believed that Stav would commit the offence. It is irrelevant that Stav did not steal the car.

The s 46 offence is very similar to the s 45 offence, but applies in circumstances where there are a number of possible main offences planned by person B (rather than just one), and person A (providing the encouragement or assistance) does not know which of the offence(s) B is going to commit. No main offence needs to actually be completed. Examples of offences under s 46 include:

- a gun shop owner providing guns to a criminal gang knowing they will use them in criminal enterprises such as robbery, but not knowing where or when;
- providing cutting agents to drug dealers, being unaware of what class of drugs the dealers may be supplying and to whom (*R v Omar Saddique* [2013] EWCA Crim 1150); and
- where a man supplies a crime gang with various number plates for vehicles upon request. He knows they commit robbery, burglary, and murder, and often do so using stolen cars on false number plates. He is unaware which crime will be committed, but he knows the false number plates will be used.

22.4.3 Possible defences to encouraging or assisting offences

If the defendant can prove that it was reasonable for him/her to act the way he/she did (in the circumstances he/she was aware of or believed existed) this may be a defence (s 50) to an offence under s 44, 45, or 46. When determining what was reasonable, the seriousness of the anticipated main offence, the purpose of the act of encouragement or assistance, and the authority under which the person was acting will all be considered:

- With regard to the seriousness of the anticipated main offence, it might be reasonable to encourage or assist in the commission of a minor offence in order to prevent a more serious offence being committed. For example, Peta infiltrates a gang who are conspiring to commit an armed robbery. He tells one of the other members of the gang to steal a car for the gang to use as a getaway from the robbery. Peta's intention is to look credible in front of the other gang members so he can achieve his main objective of preventing the robbery from taking place. Therefore, he may have a 'reasonable' defence.

- When considering the purpose of the act of encouragement or assistance, it might be reasonable to encourage or assist in the commission of a minor offence in order to prevent more serious harm from being inflicted. For example, imagine Manny and Sam are members of a teenage gang who plan to attack a rival gang and stab the leader, Taz. However, Manny does not want to attack Taz and succeeds in persuading Sam to smash the windows of Taz's car instead. Manny is charged with encouraging Sam to commit criminal damage, but may have a 'reasonable' defence that his actions were to prevent a more serious offence.
- The authority under which he/she was acting should also be taken into account, as it might be reasonable to encourage or assist in the commission of an offence if it was done for the benefit of collecting evidence during an investigation by law enforcement agencies. For example, Boris, a 15-year-old, is tasked by a local authority trading standards department with going into a local shop and purchasing a lottery ticket.

The defendant may be able to plead impossibility as a defence. This is because a person can only be convicted if his/her acts are genuinely capable of encouraging or assisting a crime, which cannot apply if it is impossible for the main offence to be committed. However, a person could still be convicted of a criminal attempt as an alternative (see 22.2.2). Remember also a person cannot be convicted of encouraging or assisting a crime for which he/she is the intended victim (see the introduction to 22.3).

22.5 Answer to Task

TASK 1 The suspect had never had any communication nor made any other contact with any of the pupils. As a result, the Court of Appeal concluded that the acts of the suspect were merely preparatory and that the suspect had not attempted to abduct a child or children.

23 | Intelligence

23.1   Introduction

This chapter examines how criminal intelligence is used to support policing objectives. We will also consider some of the components of intelligence gathering: sources, source handling, surveillance, research and development, the intelligence 'target package', and some of the laws and rules about what can, and cannot be done with intelligence. Some of the material may not appear immediately relevant to the work of a student police officer, but you will discover its importance as you move through your training. Many of the serious and organized-crime investigations which result in a successful prosecution have their origins in good intelligence, and the UK's strategy for counter terrorism heavily depends on the UK intelligence community. Very few investigations into level 2 crime (and few of those at level 1) would be effective without intelligence, and certainly much police time would be ill directed and fruitless.

Significant cases, such as the murder of 11-year-old Rhys Jones in 2007, have highlighted the importance of converting intelligence into evidence. In this case the police had information and intelligence from numerous sources, but it proved highly problematic to convert the intelligence into admissible evidence. In the Rhys Jones case, the police obtained recordings of conversations using hidden audio devices, and a key witness gave evidence as a 'protected' witness (see 24.2.4.2). Through these means, and DNA evidence, the identity of the offenders was confirmed.

Criminals will usually go to some lengths to prevent knowledge about their activities leaking out. They often seek to protect key questions about a crime or a criminal; the when, where, how, and why. Covert surveillance can be used to help establish such information. For example, after the 2015 Hatton Garden burglary, police were able to video-record some of the people responsible for the crime while they were in a café discussing their involvement. Without such covert evidence, it would sometimes be difficult to prosecute all the individuals involved in similar cases. Such covert work often infringes upon the private lives of particular members of the public, so this type of activity is carefully controlled under the Regulation of Investigatory Powers Act 2000 (RIPA), and officers would need to seek authority for surveillance.

As a student police officer you will come into contact with the public for much of your working time. You may therefore be in one of the better positions to gather intelligence that could impact upon crime and criminality in your locality and the wider community. You need to be alert to the possibilities of gathering intelligence, understand how you should record it, how you can input it into the intelligence system, how it is assessed, and how it is ultimately utilized. Some of the methods for obtaining intelligence, information, and evidence (and how they are managed) are explained in the remainder of this chapter.

An understanding of the National Intelligence Model (NIM) is an important requirement for student police officers. Your geographical policing area is likely to have an intelligence collection plan, formulated by the force strategic 'Tasking and Coordinating Group' (T&CG) process. This will consider local crime trends and particular crime patterns and then identify what particular information needs to be collected at a particular time (see 23.6.1 for more detail). However, this does not prevent any officer putting other information into the system, as any information may be vital to ongoing investigations. The intelligence can be assessed later by other more experienced colleagues (see 23.5.2 on submission procedures).

As with many aspects of operational policing, extensive APP guidance on this subject is available from the College of Policing (under the Intelligence Management heading). Note that for obvious reasons neither the College of Policing guidance nor this Handbook will provide confidential details of police intelligence gathering, collation, analysis, and dissemination methods.

The topics covered in this chapter are likely to contribute to the learning required for the National Policing Curriculum subject areas: 'Information and Intelligence' and 'Conducting Investigations'.

If you are undertaking the PCDA or DHEP, you will be expected to demonstrate that you can 'systematically gather, submit and share information and intelligence to further policing-related outcomes'. You will also need to develop an 'in-depth knowledge, understanding and expertise relevant to organisational/local needs, including the ... operational policing context [of] intelligence'.

23.2 Information and Intelligence

The police receive information and intelligence in several different ways. Information can be obtained, for example, from a call from the public advising the police of an incident. Intelligence is more difficult to define but is generally considered to be information derived from many sources (some confidential) that has been recorded, graded, and evaluated. If information is received concerning an increase in the number of thefts of radios from cars in a particular area, and this information is linked to a change in payment policy by a local drug dealer (who is now accepting goods in lieu of money in payment for drugs) intelligence can begin to be derived from this information.

23.2.1 Obtaining intelligence

There are many sources of intelligence, ranging from information picked up during conversations with a member of the public (open sources, see 23.2.2) to specialist covert surveillance operations (see 23.3 and 23.4 for details). A police officer can let colleagues know that he/she is interested in an individual, and would welcome any useful information gleaned during interviews. The same applies of course to police patrols, who often spend some part of their duty deployment on open observation and interaction with the public. Information can also be obtained from prisons, via the force Prison Intelligence Officer (PIO). Formal intelligence gathering in prisons is subject to strict protocols and risk assessments, but plenty of miscellaneous and open information about criminal targets is available from prison visits, interviews, preparations for release, and so on (see CoP, 2013b for further details).

Some types of information, particularly financial, can be obtained under the provisions of the Proceeds of Crime Act 2002. This places obligations on certain occupational groups, such as bank managers and solicitors, who must report the handling of sums of money for which there is little or no apparent justification, as this may indicate criminal activity (see 16.5.2). Useful information could be obtained through Action Fraud, the national centre for reporting fraud and cybercrime (see 21.3.2). Certain offences such as cybercrime and fraud are often linked to serious and organized crime or terrorism, so all fraud and online crime should be reported through Action Fraud so intelligence can be gathered. This enables crimes to be linked, and new trends and crimes to be identified that might be part of a wider picture of organized crime or funding terrorism.

Many different intelligence-gathering techniques are used in counter-terrorism. Terrorist activities can generally be divided into two areas of activity: the facilitation and the act itself. The facilitation could include communication, radicalization, funding, money-laundering, and open research. The actual terrorist act may of course lead to major disruption and death or damage. At its simplest, information about the facilitation of an actual terrorist attack could be volunteered by members of the public coming forward, or from the police on routine calls, or when conducting stop and searches. The intelligence gathered will be shared between UK police forces working closely with security and intelligence agencies, as part of counter-terrorism policing to prevent, deter, and investigate terrorist activity. The police regard cooperation with the public as a powerful defence against terrorist threats.

Police forces routinely share information with other forces, particularly through the Police National Database (see 5.9.1.2). Even if it seems trivial or incomplete, police forces should always communicate information as it might have a bearing on the activities of someone in another police force area (Bichard, 2004).

23.2.2 Open sources of information and intelligence

The first and most obvious source of 'open' intelligence about crime and criminality is likely to come from the general public. People notice all kinds of things and should be encouraged to report to the police anything that is odd, suspicious, or out of character. There is much to be gleaned about the lifestyles of criminals from simple observation or from general conversations with members of the public. Criminals live within communities, they have to go shopping, wear clothes, and socialize, and of course they are very likely to have families, hobbies, or interests which have nothing to do with crime. A profile can be built up of a criminal's daily habits: where he/she shops or goes for a drink, what cars he/she drives, and so on. Neighbours, garage mechanics, newsagents, dog walkers, joggers, parking attendants, crossing attendants, fitness instructors, and the like may all have information that could be useful in an investigation.

> **TASK 1** Can you suggest some other sources of intelligence that would be available to any member of the public?

There may be specific practices and policies regarding open source searches in the area where you work, so as a trainee officer make sure you find out about these before you do anything on your own initiative. Some sources can be more straightforward, for example gleaning information from a local newspaper. Most provincial newspapers are served by a small army of volunteers who send in reports every week, and it is sometimes possible to pick up open references to criminal targets (see NPCC, 2015).

23.2.2.1 Online sources of information

The internet is a valuable source of open intelligence—for example through social networking sites and online forums. If you decide to use open online sources within your work, however, it is not as simple as it sounds. First, because the open web is so huge and effectively free from significant control, much of the information lacks provenance and could be inaccurate, unreliable, or even false. It might also be impossible to use such information as evidence in a court of law because the authors may be untraceable.

There are, however, several ways in which open source material might assist a police investigator, for instance by identifying a suspect's associates, or corroborating information that is already suspected.

Remember though that any search leaves a 'footprint'—Locard's principle, that 'every contact leaves a trace' (see 26.2.1)—so without careful planning you may inadvertently leave a digital (police) footprint. You may for instance have searched from a computer with a police IP address. Many criminals, particularly those committing offences online, might well be knowledgeable about such matters, and will be able to find the IP address of anyone who has searched for them. (The IP address allocated to a police force is permanent and can be identified by a simple search on the internet.) Once a suspect realizes he/she has been the subject of an online police search he/she will be alerted and may change tack. As a result, many hours of work could have been wasted by a well-intentioned but inexperienced officer. In summary, open source searches can be of value in gathering further intelligence but must be done properly. The NPCC (2015) have issued guidance to Police officers regarding open source investigation, and it provides minimum standards for officers and staff to obey before engaging in such activities. This includes some training via e-learning plus a good understanding of the legal implications of such activities. Before engaging in any such activities you are urged to seek advice from your immediate supervisor and line manager.

Investigation and Prosecution

23.3 Covert Human Intelligence Sources

The police term for an informant or source is 'CHIS', which stands for Covert Human Intelligence Source. Criminals use other terms (all unflattering), such as 'grass', 'snout', and 'nark'. Many intelligence sources are criminals themselves, as non-criminals are unlikely to have real access to criminals, their plans, and their activities.

It is interesting to note that many government agencies are permitted to use sources to gain intelligence (provided for in the Home Office Codes of Practice under the Regulation of Investigatory Powers Act 2000 (RIPA)). Such agencies and departments include HM Revenue and Customs, the Ministry of Defence, the Department of Health, the Department for Work and Pensions, the Environment Agency, the Armed Forces, and the Food Standards Agency. Any agency using a CHIS must have a responsible authorizing officer and observe the other RIPA requirements. Local authorities must obtain judicial approval for using a CHIS and for other surveillance activities (ss 37 and 38 of the Protection of Freedoms Act 2012).

23.3.1 The definition of a CHIS

A member of the public who simply volunteers information about criminals or crimes is not generally defined as a 'source'. A person is regarded as a source (s 26(8) of RIPA) if he/she establishes or maintains a personal or other relationship with a person for the covert purpose of:

- obtaining information or providing access to information to another person; or
- disclosing information obtained by the use of such a relationship, or as the consequence of the existence of such a relationship.

In essence, a CHIS is therefore someone who cultivates another person to obtain information, or who provides access to information, or who discloses information. Notice that the words criminal or unlawful are not used here. This is because the information need not necessarily be crime-related, at least to start with. It is the 'covert' part which is important. (Thus, solicitors or bank officials who pass details of suspicious activity to the police are not sources because they are working in an open relationship with the police and not acting covertly.)

In general terms the term 'covert' usually means hidden, but RIPA provides a precise legal definition (s 26(9)(b)–(c)):

> a purpose is covert in ... a relationship if it is conducted in a manner which is calculated to ensure that only one of the parties to the relationship is unaware of the purpose [and] ... [a] relationship is used covertly, and information obtained is used or disclosed in a manner that is calculated to ensure that one of the parties to the relationship is unaware of the use or disclosure in question.

What this means in straightforward terms is that the person being cultivated by the CHIS (or from whom information is obtained because of that relationship) does not know that the CHIS is informing the police. As an alternative, consider this as a working (but strictly speaking, 'non-legal') definition: a CHIS is tasked by the police with cultivating or sustaining a relationship with a third person, and that third person does not know about the police involvement.

Under RIPA, any use of a CHIS by the police will always require authorization granted by the force authorizing officer (a senior police officer, usually a detective superintendent or higher) who is answerable to a surveillance commissioner with a national remit. The authorization (or 'authority') will normally last 12 months.

The use and management of a CHIS under the age of 17 presents additional challenges, and the Regulation of Investigatory Powers (Juveniles) Order 2000 and Regulation of Investigatory Powers (Juveniles) (Amendment) Order 2018 apply. In 2019, a UK charity *Just for Kids Law*, challenged the legal basis of the current scheme for using a juvenile CHIS. The court (the High Court (Queens Bench Division)) denied the application, and held that under the scheme there was no unacceptable risk of a juvenile's rights under Article 8 of the ECHR being breached. The response of the court also suggested that the safeguards regarding the welfare of children were adequate. The charity has, however, appealed (*R (on the application of Just for Kids Law) v Secretary of State for the Home Department* [2019] EWHC 1772 (Admin)).

23.3.2   Handling sources

Handlers are usually detectives who have undergone an intensive training programme during which they learn (through scenarios and role-play) how to keep control when tasking informants, arranging secure meetings, and handling sources who may be devious, dishonest, and manipulative. A source-management unit is staffed by a CHIS controller, CHIS handlers, and support staff. The CHIS controller is responsible for the supervision, management, and control of all the staff in the unit. The CHIS handlers are responsible for the day-to-day management and recruitment of CHISs.

> **TASK 2** What qualities do you think are needed for a person to make a good source handler? Make a list of the attributes, skills, and competencies necessary to handle a covert source who has access to criminal information.

Most forces use a qualified and experienced detective constable as a source handler, probably paired with another (perhaps less experienced) handler. It is good practice to have two handlers so that a CHIS (who could be manipulative and might have his/her own agenda) has less chance of exerting control over the handlers. A further advantage is that two can share the responsibility of handling, welfare issues, and recording of meetings with a CHIS. Sometimes, especially when meetings or intelligence taskings are urgent, there have to be 'singleton' meets between one handler and a source, but most forces recommend that this should never be routine.

A handler submits a report with details of the intelligence he/she has obtained from the CHIS, and writes a separate note to his/her controller detailing the meeting itself. The intelligence is passed in its raw state to the Research and Development unit or Force Intelligence Bureau, where it is assessed against what is already known, considered in the wider context, and then sanitized (see 23.5.1).

23.3.3   Restrictions on the use of sources

We have already noted that RIPA provides the definitions of a source and what is meant by covert, but the Act also determines the legal and practical parameters for handling a CHIS. We do not go into all the detail of the Act here, but there are special safeguards for vulnerable or young people, and a regular audit of authorizations by a surveillance commissioner (appointed nationally under a chief surveillance commissioner).

Attention is also drawn throughout RIPA to proportionality and to Articles in the Human Rights Act 1998 legislation, particularly with respect to the right to a private life. In terms of proportionality, a CHIS with excellent access to the upper echelons of criminality would not be used to establish the identity of a local graffitist. RIPA provides the necessary framework for the ethical and legal use of a CHIS by properly trained source handlers who are aware of the full extent of their powers (but will not abuse them), as well as ensuring that the risks are proportionate to the expected gain.

> **TASK 3** We noted earlier that a CHIS is often also a criminal him/herself. What problems might arise for a police force when recruiting and using an active criminal as a CHIS? Aside from the ethical and moral considerations, what practical difficulties might there be? How might they be met and overcome?

23.3.4   The consequences for the CHIS

A CHIS may provide the police with information about a planned crime in which the CHIS will participate. In such circumstances the CHIS can be designated as a participating informant (PI). If he/she is then charged and prosecuted, the sentencing judge would be made aware of the assistance the CHIS had provided.

A CHIS who is not a participating informant may also be able to take advantage of the 'assisting prosecutions' legislation in the Serious Organised Crime and Police Act 2005, under which a formal agreement can be made with an offender in order to secure evidence for the prosecution of other offenders. In most cases, the police and the Crown Prosecution Service will try to keep the identity of a CHIS confidential, and will adopt what they see as a pragmatic approach: if there is a risk to the CHIS, the prosecution is very likely to be withdrawn and charges dropped. An added advantage is that the CHIS can be used again. No one can pretend that these are easy judgements; you may like to read further on this matter: see Harfield and Harfield (2005 and 2008).

As a trainee police officer, you need to be aware of the risks a source may face by talking to you. It is essential that you are cautious and try to minimize any risk by acting professionally. You should keep the information to yourself at all times, even after you are able to input it into the intelligence system. There is no need for you to spread the information to a wider number of people or assume that other people are already aware of it. For instance, just because a person has given you information about a local crime, this does not automatically mean that all his/her family and friends know about it too. Assuming that they all know could have serious consequences for the source, especially if the friends and family find out from you in casual conversation and have different views about assisting the police. It might be useful to see yourself as a sponge, sucking up information and keeping it in, rather than giving information away! You could after all be told anything—from the criminal activities of members of the public to the criminal activities of colleagues or even celebrities. It is important to faithfully record the information as given, and avoid prejudging whether it is true or not; that will be considered later, when the information is investigated.

23.3.4.1 Motivation of informants

The handler should identify a potential source's primary motive or motives because this will affect whether the CHIS should be recruited, and how he/she should be handled. The source's primary motivation must be sufficient to sustain him/her throughout the long period of gathering intelligence. This is a very under-researched area and hence what follows should be treated with some caution.

> **TASK 4** Consider for a moment why someone might decide to become a source for the police. Why would you betray your criminal colleagues? How would you keep it up, week after week, month after month? How do you keep the secret of your relationship over a period of time that may extend to many years?

Many sources will suggest that money is a key motivator, but a potential CHIS might well be able to make more money from the criminal enterprise he/she is reporting on, so we must look a little deeper; motivation is psychologically complex. For example, an experienced and 'lifestyle' criminal might inform on other criminals who are threatening his/her dominance. Other sources may be motivated by distaste for the crimes committed by the target criminal. In one case a young woman with two young children informed on her brother, a prominent local criminal, because she had seen him downloading child sex abuse images on his computer and suspected that he was an active paedophile.

It is easy to overlook the human needs of sources: like most people, they want affection, praise, contact, reward, encouragement, and a sense of being valued. Handlers can provide all these things for a source, but a CHIS who becomes too emotionally dependent upon a handler might become unable to function adequately in other aspects of his/her life without the handler's help. Obviously this can lead to problems. Other ethical dilemmas may also arise: for example, imagine a CHIS drug-user overdoses on drugs purchased with the money he received from the police. To what extent would the police be ethically, morally, or legally responsible?

Police handlers are acutely aware of safety issues surrounding any human sources, and will make complex arrangements to protect a source's identity, particularly from other criminals. The consequences of any mistakes could be catastrophic for the source, hence the need for caution. Police officers have a legal duty of care and confidentiality towards sources, so they must take every step to protect their identities (*Swinney v Chief Constable of Northumbria* [1996] EWCA Civ 1322).

23.3.5   Undercover officers and 'test purchase' operations

A highly trained police officer can work to penetrate a group of criminals, for example posing as a drugs importer or as a document supplier (eg for passports). However, the risk must be proportionate to the outcome, so an undercover officer would only be used in relation to very serious crimes, such as high-profile robberies, conspiracy to murder, organized crime, child grooming, or terrorism. All operations using an undercover officer require authorization, and the risk assessment must be very thorough.

Officers cannot sustain undercover roles for long and need to be reintegrated into the police force before they are compromised or exhausted by the continuous strain ('turned or burned'). This requires fastidious timing by the handler and supervisors, in order to maximize the benefits. Recent problems with undercover police activities have led to calls for more stringent supervision of such police practices. For example, an HMIC report criticized an undercover police officer for defying management instructions when working undercover with a group of environmental campaigners (HMIC, 2012a); the trial against the activists subsequently collapsed. Other revelations relating to the misuse of undercover operatives have turned the spotlight on police decision-making, particularly the decisions to deploy such tactics, for example see the *Stephen Lawrence Independent Review: Possible corruption and the role of undercover policing in the Stephen Lawrence case*, available online. A public inquiry into undercover policing was convened in 2015. In 2017 Sir John Mitting was appointed to lead the inquiry when illness prevented the previous chair from continuing. The inquiry has begun is ongoing and proceedings are updated at <https://www.ucpi.org.uk/about-the-inquiry/>.

Test purchase operations are used relatively frequently, for example a police officer can pose as a potential buyer for an illegally acquired firearm. The whole transaction is monitored carefully (with surveillance teams deployed and uniformed officers on hand), and when the moment is right, the dealer or seller is arrested and charged. The advantage for the police of such 'sting' operations is that an officer only needs to appear once in one location, thereby reducing the risk. The advantage in terms of criminal justice is that the criminal is caught in the act, and is therefore more likely to plead guilty. This saves time and expense, both for the police and the criminal justice system.

Officers planning and undertaking such operations must be sure that the proposed operation is proportionate and does not entrap individuals into committing offences they would not normally commit. If there is a lack of proportionality, or obvious entrapment, the defence could apply under s 78 of the PACE Act 1984 to have the evidence obtained rendered inadmissible (see 25.5.1.2), or will put forward an abuse of process argument for illegality (ie a court will not allow a prosecution to continue as it is 'unfair').

> **TASK 5** What qualities and competences are required for a good undercover officer? What logistical and operational problems might arise? What needs to be considered when planning a test purchase operation?

23.4   Surveillance

For the general public, surveillance generally means watching over something, but in a police and legal sense it generally means covert surveillance, where the subject of the surveillance is unaware that he/she is being monitored, and the monitoring is planned in advance. The use of covert surveillance is tightly controlled by the Regulation of Investigatory Powers Act 2000 (RIPA, see 23.4.2). However, other types of monitoring, such as the use of CCTV by local authorities, generally do not involve the planned observation of a particular person and so are not regulated so closely (but see 23.4.1).

Principles of liberty and freedom must be respected; the surveillance might risk infringing the 'right to privacy and family life' (see 4.4.1). For obvious reasons we only provide a general description of what is involved here. Details are provided during initial training, as and when appropriate.

23.4.1 CCTV

The simplest and most obvious form of open surveillance is the ubiquitous CCTV camera overlooking public and private premises, walkways, town centres, banks, railway stations, airports, and even police stations. The benefit of CCTV is that it can provide 24-hour coverage of a location and its images are retrievable within a certain period; the disadvantage is that the location of the cameras is fixed—cameras cannot follow a target round a corner. In addition, CCTV cameras are usually easy to spot, so an astute criminal will note the locations of cameras and avoid them, or attempt to disguise some of his/her features.

CCTV cameras are usually operated by local authorities or shop security officers. If an operator spots a person behaving suspiciously and decides to observe him/her using the CCTV for a while, this is not covert surveillance as it is not part of a planned operation; the observation is spontaneous as it is in response to immediate circumstances. The police can arrange to have access to recordings from a particular CCTV camera (as in the investigation into the murder of the toddler James Bulger in 1993, when two older children abducted and killed him). Furthermore, some forces have live access to CCTV coverage and can therefore respond immediately to any incidents unfolding on the screens. The procedures for arranging to view CCTV footage are covered in 24.4.1.3.

Some local authorities and other organizations (see Sch 1 to RIPA for a full list) carry out directed surveillance using CCTV for their own enforcement activities, for example to monitor criminal behaviour such as fly-tipping.

Sections 29–35 of The Protection of Freedoms Act 2012 introduced powers for the Secretary of State to issue codes of practice for surveillance camera systems, as well as a system for regulating such activities, spearheaded by a Surveillance Camera Commissioner (Home Office, 2013c). The Information Commissioner's Office has revised in recent years the Codes that regulate the use of surveillance cameras and personal information by businesses and organizations other than public authorities (ICO, 2017). Surveillance is covered in more detail in 23.4.2.

The use of automatic number plate recognition systems (ANPR) by a range of organizations has increased in recent years. The surveillance commissioners have concluded that ANPR cameras are sometimes utilized for covert purposes without proper authorization (see 23.4.2.2). The ANPR Independent Advisory Group is responsible for ensuring that use of ANPR is underpinned by respect for privacy. The Group comprises industry specialists, academics, and lawyers, and is overseen by the Surveillance Camera Commissioner.

Recently, a member of the public challenged a South Wales Police pilot scheme that involved Automated Facial Recognition. He suggested that it was unlawful and was likely to infringe his right to privacy under Article 8 of the ECHR (see 4.4). The Divisional Court refused the application, finding that the current regime provided sufficient legal safeguards with regard to data protection, human rights, and equality. The claimant has now appealed to the Court of Appeal (*R (on the application of Bridges) v Chief Constable of South Wales* [2020] 1 Cr App R 3).

23.4.2 Covert surveillance

Covert surveillance is surveillance that is planned in advance and is covert:

> if, and only if, it is carried out in a manner that is calculated to ensure that the persons who are subject to surveillance are unaware that it is or may be taking place. (s 26(9), RIPA)

The Act divides covert surveillance into two types; directed and intrusive. The type depends on the location of the target and hence the level of intrusion. Directed surveillance is when the person is anywhere apart from residential premises or a vehicle, and intrusive surveillance is when the person is in residential premises or in a vehicle.

Directed surveillance is defined in s 26(2) of the RIPA, as shown in the diagram.

Surveillance is directed [...] if it is covert but not intrusive and is undertaken:
(a) for the purposes of a specific investigation or operation;

This means a pre-planned event and not an immediate response to an incident.

(b) in such a manner as is likely to result in the obtaining of private information about a person (whether or not one specifically identified for the purposes of the investigation or operation); and

Carrying out surveillance of people while they carry out a criminal activity is unlikely to bring about the gathering of private information. However, surveillance of a person who is not engaging in criminal activity is far more likely to result in obtaining private information about him/her.

(c) otherwise than by way of an immediate response to events or circumstances, the nature of which is such that it would not be reasonably practicable for an authorization under this Part to be sought for the carrying out of the surveillance.

Observing unexpected events that are unfolding before your eyes would not be classed as direct surveillance.

For example, while on Independent Patrol, you observe a person on a building site loading material into a vehicle and decide to observe them, using cover until other patrols arrive to support you.

The provisions in RIPA are intended to ensure that police actions are proportionate and justified; the police often use the mnemonic PLAN—Proportionate, Lawful, Auditable, Necessary (and some have added the letter E for Ethical). The JAPAN mnemonic is also used: Justification, Authorization, Proportionality, Auditable, and Necessary.

An example of directed surveillance might be the installation of a concealed camera in a tree opposite a suspect's residence so a surveillance team could see when the suspect was about to leave. The camera would have to be positioned so that only the suspect's premises were under surveillance. If the camera captured a neighbour's house and the neighbours' activities, this would amount to 'collateral intrusion', and authority could be withheld until the risk of intrusion is minimized or avoided. If CCTV is to be used for a covert pre-planned investigation, then authority should be sought.

Intrusive surveillance (s 26(3) of RIPA) is described in the second flow-diagram.

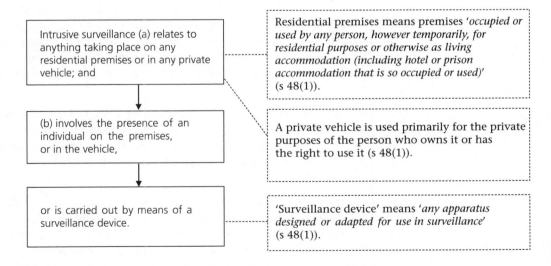

Intrusive surveillance (a) relates to anything taking place on any residential premises or in any private vehicle; and

Residential premises means premises 'occupied or used by any person, however temporarily, for residential purposes or otherwise as living accommodation (including hotel or prison accommodation that is so occupied or used)' (s 48(1)).

(b) involves the presence of an individual on the premises, or in the vehicle,

A private vehicle is used primarily for the private purposes of the person who owns it or has the right to use it (s 48(1)).

or is carried out by means of a surveillance device.

'Surveillance device' means 'any apparatus designed or adapted for use in surveillance' (s 48(1)).

An example of intrusive surveillance would be using a hidden listening device in a hotel room (or outside the room, if it consistently provided information of the same quality and detail as if it was inside the room (s 28(5)). Surveillance is not intrusive if it only provides information about the location of a vehicle, or if it is a one-sided consensual interception (eg of a telecommunication system) with no intercept warrant (s 28(4)(a) and (b) respectively).

In a landmark case, the House of Lords (now the Supreme Court) concluded that covert surveillance of communications between lawyers and their clients is allowed under RIPA Part II. This was somewhat surprising as those communications might well be covered by legal professional privilege, and a person in custody has enshrined rights to consult privately with his/her legal representative (*In re McE (Appellant) (Northern Ireland) & In re M (Appellant) (Northern Ireland) & In re C (AP) and another (AP) (Appellants) (Northern Ireland)* [2009] UKHL 15).

More recently, the Court of Appeal was asked to deliberate on police use of covert surveillance. During the course of an investigation for violent robbery and burglary, the police had 'bugged' the prison van used for transporting the suspects, and overheard incriminating remarks. The trial had allowed the evidence to be heard and the men were convicted. They then appealed against their convictions, arguing that the prison van should have been regarded as akin to a prison cell, which in their view made it a private residential premises within the context of intrusive surveillance. (If this was the case, then the authority for the surveillance should have been provided by a chief officer of police, not the superintendent.) They also argued that the surveillance in itself was not necessary or proportionate, and that their convictions should be quashed because the surveillance evidence should have been rendered inadmissible at trial under s 78 of the PACE Act 1984 (see 25.5.1.2). In a clear judgment, the Court of Appeal did not agree that the prison van was private or residential, and accepted that the police action had been both necessary and proportionate as another suspect had yet to be found. The appeal was dismissed (*R v Plunkett and Plunkett* [2013] EWCA Crim 261). The case is a good illustration of the importance of clear decision-making by the investigators, to demonstrate both reasonableness and good faith.

23.4.2.1   Covert surveillance methods

Surveillance work involves a variety of approaches, depending on the information required.

Static observations can be carried out from a fixed vantage point (an Observation Point or OP), for example from a park bench or an unmarked parked police vehicle. If the OP is on private property the identity and safety of the owner or user must not be compromised. The surveillance could be either directed or intrusive, depending on the location of the subject under observation.

Mobile conventional surveillance involves officers following the subject on foot or in a vehicle. If the location of the subject is the only information recorded, then this is directed surveillance. The teams who undertake this type of work are highly trained and such operations are carefully planned. Two key factors to consider are the location and the awareness of the subject. A tightly knit rural community would be a difficult location as strangers and unknown cars will 'stand out' in a small village or a quiet residential street. Different but equally complex problems occur in busy high streets, where it is difficult to keep the target in sight. Some criminals use sophisticated counter-surveillance techniques to shake off such surveillance, though by doing so they of course demonstrate that they probably have something to hide.

Mobile technical surveillance involves attaching tracking devices to vehicles, packages, or other items. If the device is used to simply identify the position of an object, then this is directed surveillance. Tracking by GPS is commonly used by the police and private sector organizations; you may have seen security vans for transporting money with a sign indicating that the vehicle is being tracked.

Audio and visual surveillance employs devices such as binoculars, cameras, or recording equipment. These can be used when following a subject, or observing and recording him/her from an OP. Microphones and sound-recording equipment can be used to record a subject's speech when an undercover officer engages him/her in conversation in order to obtain evidence or intelligence; 'wearing a wire'. The use of audio-visual equipment for surveillance is tightly regulated and the authorization must relate to the specific methods to be used.

23.4.2.2   Authorization for covert surveillance

Authorization for covert surveillance must be given in writing and is valid for three months. It will be scrutinized (usually monthly in the case of intrusive surveillance) by a surveillance commissioner. The authorization can be withdrawn and the operation cancelled if he/she is not satisfied that the grounds were reasonable and the justification proportionate and any intelligence already obtained would probably be destroyed.

For directed surveillance, the authorization should be given in writing by a police officer not below the rank of superintendent. In urgent cases, a superintendent can provide a verbal authorization for 72 hours, but written authority should be provided within the 72-hour period.

Intrusive surveillance is a highly specialized area of police work and will only be authorized if it involves serious crime. All such operations must be authorized by a person holding the rank of chief officer (ie assistant chief constable rank and above) and the authorization must be approved by a surveillance commissioner.

Some operations involve the use of a CHIS, OPs, and mobile surveillance, so multiple applications for authority will be required. These complex procedures ensure that the police (and other agencies) operate in a system which is open to both scrutiny and monitoring, and in compliance with the Human Rights Act 1998.

23.4.3 Communications data

Communications data (CD) is the 'who', 'when', 'where', and 'how' of a communication, but not its content (the 'what'). It can provide valuable intelligence to the police and other agencies, particularly when investigating organized crime and terrorism, and has two main components:

- 'entity data' (about a person or organization making the communication); and
- 'events data' about the existence and timing of the communication.

The Investigatory Powers Act 2016 (IPA) governs the use of CD and how it is obtained. Trainee police officers are unlikely to be involved in the collection of intelligence from CD but need to be broadly aware of the controls surrounding its request and collection.

23.4.3.1 Entity data and events data

Communications data consists of entity data (about a person or organization) and events data (the timing of telecommunications events) (s 261(5) of the IPA).

Entity data identifies the person or organization making the communication, or the location of the communication equipment being used and/or the network through which the data are transmitted. Examples include:

- the 'header' of an email which identifies the IP address of a sender;
- the postal address on a letter;
- the location of a mobile phone (eg using cell site analysis);
- 'reverse look ups' (eg whose mobile phone is this?);
- a password used by a subscriber.

Events data is concerned with data about how a communication service has been used, such as a list of numbers called by a particular mobile phone, or a list showing when letters have been delivered to a particular address.

23.4.3.2 Communications data and investigation

Communications data can be obtained by the authorities from telecommunications providers for specific investigations or operations (listed in s 61 of the IPA), but the necessity and proportionality criteria defined under the IPA must be met. The public authority must consider (s 2(2) of the IPA):

- whether there are other less intrusive means to obtain the information;
- the sensitivity of the material;
- the public interest in the integrity and security of the telecommunications systems; and
- protecting privacy.

Many police officers use the PLANE mnemonic to assess their approach; it must be Proportionate, Lawful, Auditable, Necessary, and Ethical (see 23.4.2). The data gathering must be authorized by a designated senior officer who is independent of the specific investigation or operation (unless there are exceptional circumstances (s 63(2) of the IPA)). An authorization to obtain under s 61 usually lasts for one month, although extensions are available. The material sought can also be material that does not yet exist (eg on-going communications by a potential suspect). CSPs must comply with requests under this section unless it is not practicable for them to do so (s 66 of the IPA).

23.4.3.3 The Investigatory Powers Act 2016

The Investigatory Powers Act 2016 (IPA) received Royal Assent in November 2016 and aimed to:

- consolidate and clarify existing police and intelligence services powers in relation to obtaining CD (as discussed in 23.4.3);
- create independent oversight of certain warrants (judicial sanction will be required);
- create an office of Investigatory Powers Commissioner; and
- make provision for the retention of internet records.

It is envisaged that the new legislation will help combat serious crime and terrorism more effectively. Whilst extensions are available for some of the powers, the government suggests that built-in safeguards will ensure they are only used in appropriate circumstances. Many of the investigative powers in the Act were already in place (eg under statute law, case law, and EU Directives) and were merely consolidated. The IPA consists of:

- Part 1: this describes responsibilities in relation to privacy, and provides offences relating to unlawful interception of communications and the unlawful obtaining of CD;
- Part 2: this describes the circumstances in which communications interception is lawful, and how any obtained material should be managed;
- Part 3: this sets out the procedures for obtaining CD, including authorization and management of the material;
- Part 4: this concerns the authorizations for retention notices served upon telecommunications operators, and the resulting obligations;
- Parts 5 and 6: these describe the powers and warrants in relation to equipment interference.

Other parts of the Act deal with bulk personal dataset warrants, and other miscellaneous provisions. Note that some Parts of the Act are still not yet in force (see the legislation.gov.uk website for updates and more details).

The IPA 2016 will probably soon be amended following a case in the European courts (Judgment in Joined Cases C-203/15 *Tele2 Sverige AB v Post-och telestyrelsen* and C-698/15 *Secretary of State for the Home Department v Tom Watson and Others*) and the subsequent government consultations. The amendments to the IPA (Smith, 2018) include:

- restricting access to events data so it will only be permitted for serious crime; and
- creating the Office of Communications Data Authorisations (OCDA), a new and independent body to authorize relevant CD requests, to be overseen by the Investigatory Powers Commissioner and Investigatory Powers Commissioner's Office.

23.5 Managing, Processing, and Using Intelligence

Intelligence should be managed, processed, and analysed so that it can be effectively and legally used by the police and other agencies. For Level 3 crimes, the national intelligence agencies link closely with the police and other agencies. For example, the NCA works with police forces, the Serious Fraud Office, HM Revenue and Customs, and other law enforcement agencies to curtail serious and organized criminality. The Security Service (MI5) also uses intelligence from police sources to counter threats to national (internal) security. The commitment to working partnerships with relevant agencies ensures the free flow of intelligence between partners, and much of the system relies upon NIM principles (NCA, 2015).

23.5.1 Data protection and intelligence

The police collect information every day, some of which is personal. Personal data is held on systems such as the police national computer, computer aided dispatch, Police National Database, automatic number plate recognition, and intelligence and crime reporting systems.

Such data must only be accessed for a legitimate purpose. Everyone who uses personal data (including the police) has to follow strict rules called 'data protection principles'. They must make sure the information is:

- used fairly, lawfully, and transparently;
- used for specified, explicit purposes;
- used in a way that is adequate, relevant, and limited to only what is necessary;
- accurate and, where necessary, kept up to date;
- kept for no longer than is necessary; and
- handled in a way that ensures appropriate security, including protection against unlawful or unauthorized processing, access, loss, destruction, or damage.

When the stored information is about a vulnerable person (eg a missing person suffering from dementia, or a child), it may in some circumstances be shared with other agencies, but police officers should check local force policies.

As a trainee police officer you should ensure you do not leave your pocket notebook (PNB) insecure, or leave any electronic devices 'unlocked'. You should also have a legitimate policing purpose for any search for information on police databases or other systems, and the purpose must be recorded in your PNB. In 2017 the Police Federation claimed they were contacted on average twice a week to represent police officers at misconduct hearings for breaches in data protection.

There are several pieces of legislation associated with the management and holding of information, such as:

- Article 8 of the HRA 1998, which gives individuals a right to respect for private and family life, that may not be interfered with;
- the Data Protection Act 2018;
- the General Data Protection Regulation 2016 (implemented in 2018) which includes how the police manage information; and
- the Freedom of Information Act 2000 that allows an individual to request what information is being kept about him/her.

The key point is that information should only be collected if it is deemed relevant for a policing purpose, such as the preservation of life, maintaining order, and investigating and detecting crimes. This provides the legal basis for the police to deal with that information, for instance by recording it, sharing it with other agencies, or simply retaining it for future use. Information is collected (sometimes because of strategic direction, see 23.6) and then collated, evaluated, and disseminated. This is the 'intelligence cycle'.

23.5.2 Intelligence reports

Intelligence is usually reported by police officers on a 3 × 5 × 2 form ('three by five by two'). The numbers refer to 'qualities' of the intelligence, measured in three categories. For example, for a CHIS the scales refer to his/her reliability, the reliability of the intelligence, and the level of security to be implemented.

A summary of the 3 × 5 × 2 approach is given in the table (note that headings might vary from force to force).

Reliability of source (Do we trust him, her, or it?)	Reliability of intelligence (Do we believe the specific intelligence?)	Distribution (Who can see it?)
1. Reliable	A. Known directly (eg direct observation by CCTV)	P. Lawful sharing is permitted
2. Untested		C. Lawful sharing permitted, but with conditions
3. Not reliable (ie intelligence has normally turned out to be incorrect in the past)	B. Known indirectly but corroborated	
	C. Known indirectly	
	D. Not known	
	E. Suspected to be false	

A piece of intelligence may be graded for example as '2 by B by P' (all combinations of scales are possible). A police officer will complete the main body of the form with the intelligence, and the force Intelligence Unit provides the grades concerned with its distribution (sometimes referred to as the 'Handling Code'). The College of Policing has developed further codes to identify the best means for implementing this 'exploitation of the intelligence' (CoP, 2018f), for example:

- Code A1 requires covert development of the intelligence, rather than direct action at the time;
- Code A2 allows for covert action to be taken based upon the intelligence (ie a surveillance operation);
- Code A3 signifies that overt action can be taken on the intelligence, but any action must be specified by the source intelligence owner (usually the area intelligence controller).

Reports dealing with a common theme may be collated from several sources and be circulated as a single composite intelligence item (further protecting each source). The information may be 'sanitized'—this is the removal of any features of the intelligence that could identify the source or the circumstances in which the intelligence was obtained. For example, no R&D staff would allow a report to go into circulation which began:

> At 5.30 pm, on Tuesday 15 August, 'Jimmy the shark' saw Sam 'Toucan' Belmont in the Three Feathers pub in Harpenden, and gave Jimmy . . .

Aside from the inappropriate use of nicknames instead of real names, obvious indicators in the text such as 'Jimmy the shark' could quickly identify the source, which would be likely to compromise his/her access as well as putting him/her at personal risk. The 'need to know' principle applies to protecting sources, because the police want the source to continue his/her covert relationship with the target. R&D staff may return to the handler(s) with requests for directions to pursue and more targets; a productive source will be heavily tasked.

These 3 × 5 × 2 forms are a major part of the intelligence in-flow into a police force 'Research & Development' unit (or 'Force Intelligence Bureau'—the name varies from force to force). They ensure that reports are circulated to those who need to know, for example the Tasking & Coordination Group (see 23.6). The importance of accuracy and objectivity in reporting cannot be overstated. You may be convinced of the accuracy of the information you have gained from a source, however, this raw information still has to go through a process of collation, evaluation, and analysis in order to assess its reliability and validity (see 23.5.3 onwards). It is also essential that information is recorded and input into the system promptly, ie on the day it is received. This professional approach will stand you in good stead in the future.

23.5.3 Analysing intelligence

At some point in the distribution chain (this varies from force to force), analysts will analyse the intelligence, for example to establish and identify the MO (the *modus operandi*). The MO is how the criminal has carried out the offence—how did the burglar gain access to the property, what type of items were taken, where did he/she look? The next stage will be to try and match a particular event with what is already known about other similar crimes. In some forces, this happens with the raw intelligence, in others with the sanitized version. Either way, the assessed intelligence helps analysts to fill out the picture.

The NIM (see 23.6) suggests that intelligence analysis should be undertaken within four main areas.

- Problem profiling—for example the identification of crime hot spots (see 3.5.2).
- Subject profiling—analysing the actions of suspected criminals and their associates, and of victims. This will involve building up an understanding of the criminal networks involved, through link and association analysis.
- Tactical assessment—essentially a management-support function undertaken by the analyst which involves recommendation of the deployment of resources based on the intelligence available.
- Strategic assessment—involves likely future developments in criminal activity (eg the impact of an international event or the introduction of new technologies). Strategic assessment is normally undertaken by a senior or principal analyst.

Many different techniques can be employed by analysts such as 'crime pattern analysis', 'network analysis', 'case analysis', and 'crime trend analysis'. There are up to ten different analytical techniques (ACPO, 2008), although research shows that in practice often significantly fewer than ten are used (eg Cope *et al*, 2005).

Crime analysis can be used in many ways, for example crime trend analysis can help to identify patterns in crimes or incidents in a locality (as described in the College of Policing APP). It could also help to find out whether the number of particular crimes is increasing, decreasing, or remaining steady. This could be important for deciding how to allocate (limited) resources, for example if the problem is in decline then resources could perhaps be deployed more effectively elsewhere. Crime trend analysis would also be able to identify whether particular crimes or incidents are happening within specific time frames. Some crimes, for instance, are frequent in particular seasons, such as robberies at holiday resorts or burglaries at Christmas. Such analysis might also be able to identify where crime has been displaced, for instance a successful drive to remove street crime from a particular location may only serve to move it (or more usually, a proportion of it) to another nearby location. Crime trend analysis might be able to identify this pattern early so that further responses can be managed.

The theoretical and empirical methods that underpin the ten techniques include formulating and testing hypotheses and drawing of inferences. Analysts also use various software packages, for example the 'Analyst's Notebook' from the i2 company. The R&D unit in turn will try to gather enough intelligence to construct a 'targeting package' for the Tasking and Coordination Groups to consider (see 23.6.2).

23.5.4   Intelligence 'packages'

An intelligence package is a number of items of intelligence with related content. They are fundamental to police operational planning at the T&CG level and above. Intelligence packages are not just put together as a response to crime, but may also be used to support other objectives, such as planning appropriate levels of policing for a demonstration.

An ideal package would provide a highly accurate picture of how particular crimes are carried out in a given locality, by whom, with what success, how the acquisitions from the crime are fenced, how money is laundered and by whom, what the likelihood is of repeat victimization, and how the crime series is likely to develop. However, many lack such detail and are much more likely to combine hard intelligence and reasoned hypothesis-testing.

23.5.5   Dissemination

As discussed, intelligence may be disseminated to others within the extended policing 'family', such as other officers and staff in your force, or police forces or agencies elsewhere. Disseminated intelligence is likely to be sanitized to protect sources. However, police forces also have sharing agreements or arrangements with other agencies (eg social services), and various other considerations apply, for example the sharing agreement might be a legal requirement made by a judge in court (for instance in family proceedings). Secondly, and more usually, the police will enter into information sharing agreements with partner agencies to ensure a professional and 'joined up' approach, as, for example, it would obviously be difficult if social services and police could not share relevant information in a child neglect investigation. Despite any agreements, police must give due consideration to issues of proportionality, risk, data protection, and freedom of information, as well as the human rights of those affected by any sharing of information. In some restricted circumstances, dissemination could involve the provision of information under statute or common law, so that a parent could protect his/her child from a potential abuser (the Child Sex Offender Disclosure Scheme, see 17.8.3). Even in these cases, however, particular care needs to be demonstrated to ensure lawful disclosure. For further information, see the Information Management section of the College of Policing APP, under the heading 'sharing'.

23.6   **The National Intelligence Model**

The NIM is concerned with using intelligence to determine key priorities for policing. The Home Office described the NIM as 'a validated model of policing ... representing best practice in the use of intelligence to fight crime' (Home Office, 2001, p 45). All police forces in England and Wales are required to implement the NIM, and it is also used by the National Crime Agency and local Community Safety Partnerships (see 8.4.1).

The NIM is not the same as Intelligence-led Policing (ILP); the NIM is more concerned with using intelligence to determine priorities for policing, while ILP is essentially concerned with using intelligence to counter crime. Further information on the NIM and its associated Codes of Practice (2005), can be found in the College of Policing APP *Intelligence management*.

23.6.1 Key features of the NIM

The key part of the NIM process is shown in the centre of the diagram: the Tasking and Coordinating Process, overseen by Tasking and Coordination Groups (T&CG). This determines the operational responses to crime and disorder, and prioritizes intelligence requirements (eg identifying car-crime hot spots, or obtaining information about a series of burglaries). The arrows on the diagram show how intelligence and other factors influence decision-making.

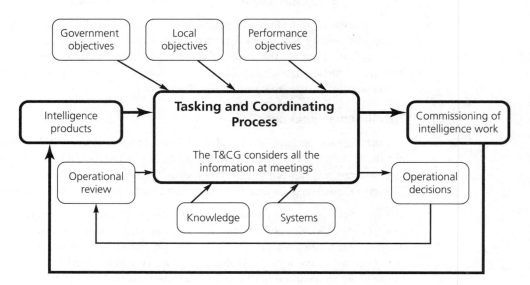

The bold lines indicate the key aspects of the process and emphasize the use of intelligence products to determine what further intelligence work needs to be commissioned. It is a continual cycle of policy development, implementation, and review (and thus bears some resemblance to Kolb's learning cycle, referred to in 7.3.3).

The Tasking and Coordinating Process is conducted at three levels to correspond with the specified levels of crime:

- Level 1 (local BCU level) in relation to local crime capable of being managed by local resources (which may include the most serious crime) and anti-social behaviour;
- Level 2 (force and regional) in relation to force, inter-force, and regional criminal activity, usually requiring additional resources; and
- Level 3 (national) in relation to the most serious and organized crime.

The classification of the crime is significant for resourcing. A single BCU does not have the resources to cope with, say, a group of criminal associates carrying out thefts from ATMs (cash machines) across the force area. A force-level response (level 2) would be needed, and this would usually be centrally coordinated and directed. Level 3 crime is dealt with by linking with national agencies such as the NCA, and its international counterparts if required.

Whether on a national, regional, or local scale, assessed intelligence informs operational decision-making following the same principles as set out in the NIM. Care must be taken to avoid isolating the work at one level from the work at other levels. Related issues at different levels must be taken into account to ensure that opportunities are not missed, and that appropriate resources are allocated.

23.6.2 The tasking and coordinating process

At the heart of the business process are the **Strategic Tasking and Coordination Group** (Strategic T&CG) meetings. Most forces will have a Strategic-level T&CG dealing with serious Level 2 crime. The purpose of the meetings is to initiate a Control Strategy which will establish the intelligence requirement and set the agenda for prevention, intelligence, and enforcement priorities. The Strategic T&CG do not routinely determine the operational tactics to be deployed, but instead maintain an overview of priorities. So, for example, if the Strategic T&CG required that countering ATM raids was to be made a priority, then specialist operations such as surveillance and CHIS recruitment would be 'tasked' to challenge that criminal network. Strategic issues are considered every six months at force-level Strategic T&CG meetings. Members of a Strategic T&CG include the force-wide senior management team, intelligence specialists, crime analysts, and other senior staff as required.

A second category of T&CG meetings also takes place: the **Tactical** Tasking and Coordination Group meetings. At a BCU level (Level 1) the Tactical T&CG meets at least every two weeks. The group comprises the senior supervisory officers and support staff from the local area, and they apply the planned response to the Control Strategy, review progress, and make changes to plans if judged appropriate. They can call on other agencies to assist in tactical decisions, but compared with Strategic T&CG meetings there is generally not such a wide range of senior staff present at Tactical T&CG meetings.

23.6.2.1 Inputs to the tasking and coordinating process

The T&CGs are informed by intelligence products which have been researched and written by analysts working with police officers (see 23.5.3). Both the strategic planning at force level and the local-tasking operational planning at BCU level are guided by these intelligence products and other forms of analysis.

Strategic Assessments are long-term strategy documents, usually produced every six months. Tactical Assessments review the progress of current operations and approaches. The T&CGs also commission, and are subsequently informed by intelligence products. These include target/subject profiles about named offenders, victims, or networks, and problem profiles about issues of concern such as a hot spot or the increased availability of a particular street drug.

The decisions taken by the T&CG will be influenced by a number of other factors such as:

- Government objectives: for example to raise the priority level of thefts from cars, or deal with public order issues.
- Local objectives: including force objectives, such as dealing with so-called 'problem families', 'problem estates', and local disorder. These objectives will have arisen through canvassing both the police (eg through community liaison officers), and local government councillors, local authority officials, and other parts of local government. Their views will be conveyed to the area or BCU commander (usually a superintendent) through routine meetings and consultations, and will be converted into local objectives.
- Performance objectives: the long-term (yearly) objectives for the BCU will also be taken into account. These may be to develop strategies to reduce all crime locally (and might include reducing burglaries by a specific percentage, for example), or dealing with anti-social behaviour, or improving arrest rates, or 'brought to justice' data. These determine the BCU Commander's strategic approach.
- Knowledge: the professional knowledge required by staff in order to contribute fully to the NIM and other aspects of police work. It includes knowledge of legislation, codes of practice, and force policies.
- Systems: the IT systems and associated procedures for the storage, retrieval, analysis, and dissemination of intelligence information.

23.6.2.2 Outputs from the tasking and coordinating process

The Control Strategy will be implemented, for example commissioning of new intelligence work (the intelligence requirement, see 23.6.2) and making operational decisions to improve the management of crime and the local community. Teams may be assembled to tackle particular issues, and budgets will be set; the overtime budget is frequently of particular significance.

As well as the weekly or fortnightly Tactical T&CG meetings at BCU level there are likely to be daily meetings to monitor and direct the daily aspects of police work. The daily meetings (sometimes known as 'Intelligence Daily Briefing' meetings, or more colloquially in some forces as 'Morning Prayers') are part of the process of ensuring that the T&CG strategy is implemented and kept on track.

23.6.3 Links with the wider policing role

The NIM is intended to be the engine room that drives the policing machine. Police officers undertake much of their non-reactive work at the direction of the T&CG, to help policing in their area to be coordinated, specific, and focused. For example, it would not be appropriate for the T&CG to recommend an operation targeting thefts from cars when local priorities were largely focused on reducing alcohol-related violence. (However, the BCU Commander may still judge that disrupting car thefts is a temporary but urgent priority.)

23.6.4 The NIM in practice

To illustrate the way in which the NIM is used in policing we will track through a crime from start to finish.

Suppose we receive several reports of an 'artifice burglary' (see the start of 16.4). The reports will enter the process as information, and a key early requirement will be for analysts to assess the criminal's MO, such as the type and location of targeted property (see 23.5.2). The findings may be incorporated into a subject profile (if the offender is known) or a problem profile (if his/her identity has not yet been established).

The T&CG may then task the police staff who are responsible for gathering intelligence to find out whether there is access to information about criminals known to undertake this type of crime (perhaps through a regular 'fence'), and whether there is local knowledge of such individuals. The T&CG will assign a priority to the investigation and will commission further work, such as checking the force databases, and trying to match other spree offences in the force area, or in neighbouring force areas. (Artifice burglars tend not to 'work their own patch', perhaps because they run the risk of being recognized.) Analysts might note, for example, that the offences have all taken place within half a mile of a railway station, in which case the force may approach British Transport Police for help, and look at relevant CCTV footage.

Suppose the frequency of artifice burglaries increases, and one of the victims becomes seriously ill as an indirect consequence of the theft. At the next T&CG meeting, the priority level for artifice burglary will be raised, and the operational plans will be revised and developed. The BCU Commander will take into account government objectives, local feelings about the nature of the crime, media pressures, and the chances of apprehending the offender(s). Now suppose that a CHIS (see 23.3) provides useful information to her handler and a report is submitted. It is assessed by the R&D unit and compared with other intelligence, and provides a name, a likely location for offences in the near future, and a clear idea of the MO. An operation is mounted, two people are arrested, and a case is prepared. The final outcome for the offender(s) could be a prison sentence, a caution (see 10.13.2), a fine, seizure of assets, or community service. Other outcomes might include displacing the activity of artifice burglars and the development and implementation of a crime reduction (prevention or disruption) strategy (see 3.6), and probably some useful media coverage.

The NIM process has led to an assessment of the nature of the crime, to tasking the intelligence-gathering parts of the force, and giving the crime a higher priority level in the midst of competing claims for attention. The newly acquired intelligence was assessed and used to develop a package of operational measures through the T&CG, and the subsequent police action disrupted that type of crime and probably helped reassure the local community. This is a simple example of the business-process model of policing, and the same principles will operate whether the issue is the vandalizing of cars or a more serious crime enquiry, such as systematic violent assaults on young people near a sports centre.

Investigation and Prosecution

TASK 6 Now it is your turn: using the NIM, describe what would happen if the BCU Commander wanted to deal with:

1. a crime hot spot involving alcohol-fuelled violence;
2. a spate of break-ins into vehicles;
3. a series of attacks on students to steal credit cards.

What factors do you think would influence the prioritizing of the crimes? What would you expect the crime analysts to provide? How would you task the collection of intelligence? What operational considerations would there be?

23.7 Answers to Tasks

TASK 1 Open sources of intelligence have grown rapidly in recent years, largely as a result of developments such as social networks. Whereas in the past we might have needed to search manually through used-car adverts in paper copies of newspapers and magazines for evidence of possible 'ringing' (see 16.8.1.1), we can now use the search facilities available on most websites (which have the added advantage of automating the process of identifying common links and patterns). Indeed, the widespread availability of information is causing some concern with regard to crimes such as identity theft and 'spear phishing'. As an experiment, try to find out as much about yourself as you can by using freely available internet resources. For example, start with <http://www.192.com> and enter your own name. You may be surprised at what you (and anyone else) can find out.

TASK 2 You may have come up with the following:

Integrity and honesty; patience and attention to detail; strong-minded and not easily diverted; adaptable (can think on his/her feet) and flexible; firm sense of duty but objective; understands the 'bigger picture' of force needs and intelligence requirements; reticent or discreet; knowledgeable about crime and criminals; professional in the relationship (courteous but not close); good listener, empathetic ('emotional intelligence'); ordinary/normal in appearance, so can blend into a crowd; resilient and stable as a personality and willing to work long or unsocial hours.

In practice, a combination of these qualities, skills, or attributes appears to be uncommon. A good source handler can be trained to a high level, but there must be strong pre-existing character traits, upon which the training can build. You can see that it takes someone with considerable investigative experience and 'life skills' to succeed in this role.

TASK 3 The first consideration for the police is whether the identity of the informant will be revealed, and if so, whether he/she would be at risk of serious harm, or even being killed. In such circumstances his/her identity would never be revealed. If the informant was the main source of evidence the prosecution of the case in open court would probably be abandoned.

You might also have referred to the difficulty of using an active criminal as a source. If a CHIS takes part in an organized crime, or is involved in criminal planning, he/she could be charged and brought before a court. A further difficulty is deciding whether, in order to obtain the intelligence, the crime should be allowed to go ahead with the source taking part.

TASK 4 Motivation is notoriously difficult to understand and identify, particularly for informants. As Canter and Alison (2000) noted, the motivation a person may provide is not necessarily the most useful for understanding his/her actions, and will be only one of a number of possible explanations. Perhaps an obvious motivation would be money, but this seems unlikely as the amounts paid out to informants are normally quite small, usually less than £100. (The total amount paid out yearly by police forces in England and Wales to all their informants is currently approximately £80,000—figure derived from BBC, 2017.)

TASK 5 For a good undercover officer the following would all be relevant: resilience, self-sufficiency, strong professionalism, the ability to work alone, the ability to deceive, the focus and concentration to know what intelligence is needed, a very good relationship and trust with your handler, and a personal inclination towards the clandestine.

Investigation and Prosecution

There are a host of problems associated with going undercover long term and a team of people are used to support the lone officer. Problems include payment, avoiding anything (in clothing, residence, possessions) that could identify him/her as a police officer, career planning, reassuring family members, diverting curious colleagues, and so on. A good cover story will be needed for the criminal target, but also for the officer's colleagues back in the force (to explain his/her absence).

In planning a Test Purchase (TP) operation, you would have to consider the original intelligence and its reliability, the target criminal's patterns of movement and MO, when to insert the TP officer, how to monitor what is happening, how to intervene and disrupt or arrest, and whether you have the authorization to proceed.

TASK 6

1. You should consider the location of the hot spot, for example is it in a town centre, or close to a series of pubs or clubs? When does crime happen? Would a police presence act as a deterrent? Who is likely to have brought the incidents to police attention? What would be the feelings and fears of the local community?

2. Are the vehicle owners reporting the crime? What items are taken? Is there a pattern? What is the location? Are particular kinds of car targeted? What preventative action would help? (This could include providing CCTV coverage, or using leafleting, media announcements, and social networks to warn car owners not to leave valuables on view.)

3. Are the credit card thefts seasonal (eg do they occur in the summer, at the start of a new term, or in the run-up to Christmas)? What is the MO? What do students do about it? Is violence involved? How is the crime reported? Are women students more at risk than men? Do the local police databases contain entries on criminals who specialize in this sort of crime? What preventative action might you recommend? (Hint: think about crime prevention, raising awareness, liaison with college and university authorities to put ATMs (cash point machines) on campuses, credit card theft-prevention schemes, social networking, talking to the banks, posters near ATMs, security awareness, CCTV, and so on.)

24.1 Introduction

A criminal investigation is defined in s 22 of the Criminal Procedure and Investigations Act 1996 (CPIA) as 'an investigation conducted by police officers with a view to ascertaining whether a person should be charged with an offence, or whether a person charged with an offence is guilty of it'. (This includes investigations set up in the belief that a crime is about to be committed.) Central to the investigative process is the collection, collation, and evaluation of many differing categories of information. However, this is a complex process; as O'Neill (2018, p xix) explains, 'criminal investigation is like trying to complete a jigsaw puzzle without a picture, without all the pieces and without any parameters'.

There are a number of guidance documents on the process and management of investigations, for example:

- the Practice Advice on the Management of Priority and Volume Crime (The Volume Crime Management Model) (2009) (often referred to as VCMM);
- APP available on the College of Policing website under Investigation; and
- the *Murder Investigation Manual* (2006).

The VCMM sets out the minimum standards for volume crime investigations (see 24.2.2), while the *Murder Investigation Manual* (MIM) and APP both identify key stages within investigations, and list the main considerations for making decisions in individual cases. Once a case is allocated to an investigator, the College of Policing APP guidance must be followed on how to progress the investigation.

The CPIA is clearly central to the correct procedures being followed for an investigation, and is covered in detail in 24.3. It is vital that investigators know when any particular investigation has formally started, so they can ensure compliance with the CPIA and the associated Codes of Practice. The CPIA defines the roles of investigator (both police officer and civilian), disclosure officer, and 'officer in the case' (OIC).

As well as the CPIA, the following legislation is also relevant to undertaking investigations and therefore underpins what we describe here:

- the Criminal Justice and Public Order Act 1994 (CJPOA);
- the Police and Criminal Evidence Act 1984 (PACE) and its Codes of Practice 2004;
- the Human Rights Act 1998 (HRA);
- the Regulation of Investigatory Powers Act 2000 (RIPA);
- the Serious Organised Crime and Police Act 2005 (SOCPA); and
- the Investigatory Powers Act 2016.

All investigators, at whatever level of accreditation, are expected to understand the legislation that impacts upon their investigative role, and keep abreast of changes. The College of Policing releases a monthly digest to help officers to maintain and update their knowledge.

Trainee police officers may be directly involved in criminal investigations, and this will provide many opportunities for collecting evidence to demonstrate operational competence (see 6.6). The evidence could include pocket notebook (PNB) entries and witness statements. Trainee officers will be expected to attain PIP Level 1 status which will allow them to 'own' investigations into priority and volume crime offences. They would not take charge of investigations into more serious crimes, but could be present as a first attending officer (FAO). It follows that all trainees need to understand all the principles discussed here, so they can deal competently with any crime incident until other support arrives, or even take ownership of less serious volume crime investigations. If you are undertaking the PCDA or the DHEP you will also be expected to demonstrate that you can 'manage and conduct effective and efficient priority and high volume investigations' and 'use initiative to diligently progress investigations, identifying, evaluating and following lines of enquiry to inform the possible initiation of criminal proceeding' and are able to 'apply an investigative mind-set when decision-making' (Institute for Apprentices, 2017).

24.2 Key Principles for Investigations

Before we look at the detailed process of investigation, there are some key points to consider, for example how investigators should approach their work, and how resources are allocated for investigations where there are many competing priorities. The College of Policing APP makes it clear that all investigators should adhere to some core principles when conducting investigations. These include honesty, integrity, confidentiality, and conducting effective investigations proportionately, within the law, and in a transparent fashion. These core principles echo the Code of Ethics for police officers (see 5.3). Conducting investigations in this manner makes for a more ethical approach, thereby improving public confidence in the effectiveness of investigations, and also the general objective and fair approach.

Investigators also need to be mindful of the Code of Practice for Victims of Crime which provides important standards for updating victims regarding the progress of investigations, the treatment they should expect from the police in given circumstances, and referral to victim support (see 13.7.4.2).

24.2.1 The 'investigative mindset'

There is plenty of guidance from the College of Policing, the National Police Chiefs' Council, and others about the law surrounding investigation, procedural matters, and the application of forensic investigation. However, comparatively little guidance is available on the mental processes involved in investigation: that is, the forms of cognition and decision-making required to see an investigation through to a successful conclusion. The term 'investigative mindset' is often used in the professional literature (eg see ACPO Centrex, 2005, p 60), but it is far from clear what this actually means in practice. It seems to be concerned with the best ways for investigators to make sense of information (eg an eyewitness statement) and potential evidence (eg a DNA sample) gathered over the course of an investigation and how to use it to make decisions. Five principles underpin the investigative mindset (ACPO Centrex, 2005, p 63). These are summarized in the table, and follow the mnemonic UPERE.

Principle	Explanation
Understanding the source of material	Understanding how a deleted SMS has been recovered from a mobile phone
Planning and preparation	This is in terms of the gathering of material, eg planning a witness interview
Examination	This comprises • the account (eg given by a victim); • clarification (eg investigate any apparent contradictions); and • challenge (both the meaning and reliability of material)
Recording and collation	Making adequate records, storing material correctly, establishing access arrangements
Evaluation	Identify further action that may be needed (eg fast-track actions to find other materials). 'Gap analysis' (see 24.4.4)

(Based on ACPO Centrex, 2005, pp 60–3 but authors' own interpretation.)

An investigative mindset helps maximize the amount of information gathered, and also ensures that its reliability is effectively tested, appropriate actions are initiated, proper records are kept, and that material is appropriately stored. The same principles should be applied for every piece of information uncovered in the course of an investigation. As an example, take a piece of evidence discovered such as a CCTV image. Investigators should:

- understand (ie know) the source of the CCTV recording;
- plan and prepare how best to examine the material (eg what is the most appropriate format for the examination);
- examine the material for what it can add to the investigation;
- record the outcome of the examination (eg in note form) and ensure it is properly stored; and
- evaluate it in terms of what is already known within the investigation, for example how it interacts with other evidence and what it means in terms of the future focus of enquiries.

This approach encourages officers to be thorough and thoughtful about the material they have obtained. Rather than accepting material at face value, or making assumptions relating to its importance, investigators must examine it with a critical eye, assuming nothing, believing nobody, and checking everything. Inevitably, the more serious and complex a case, the more onerous this task becomes.

Investigators need to keep an open mind in relation to alternative explanations of the material they uncover. The College of Policing APP suggests it is sometimes useful to generate a number of hypotheses based upon all available facts once all the material evidence has been gathered. They caution against trying to find material that fits the hypotheses; the hypotheses should be made to fit the material. Whether this advice is sufficient is open to debate, but in any case, investigators must try to prove or disprove any given hypotheses, which fits well with the notion of an open-minded and transparent investigation.

Investigators are also encouraged to use the National Decision Model (NDM) when making decisions within a criminal investigation (see 5.5.2). However, most examples of using the NDM relate to circumstances where a one-off decision is required rather than the multiple decisions required in the course of even the most straightforward criminal investigations (CoP, 2014a). A key concern is that neither the VCMM nor the NDM have been subjected to extensive academic research, particularly about whether the NDM is appropriate for all decisions in a policing context, particularly crime investigations (O'Neill, 2018).

24.2.2 Resources for investigations

The investigation of a crime will often depend on whether the crime is a volume, priority, or major crime. Volume crime is 'any type of crime which, through its sheer volume, has a significant impact on the community and the workload of the local police' (NPIA/ACPO, 2009, p 8). It usually includes street robbery, burglary of dwelling-houses and other premises, theft (including shoplifting), theft of vehicles and from vehicles, criminal damage, common assault, and illegal possession of controlled drugs. Priority crimes for many basic/borough command units (BCUs) in recent years have included street robbery, burglary, and car crime. Hence a priority crime might also be a volume crime, and vice versa, but the terms are not synonymous. It is important to ensure that volume crime is accorded sufficient attention, and the VCMM sets out the minimum standards of response to volume crimes identified by the TCG planning process at BCU level (see 23.6.2).

24.2.2.1 Resources for the investigation of more serious crimes

Some crimes are more complex and require significant local resources, for example the deployment of a team of specially trained detectives. The following might also be required:

- the intelligence department could task a covert human intelligence source (CHIS) to find information on a particular crime;
- an analyst could be asked to build a picture of the suspect's associates,
- the financial department could look into the sources of a suspect's income;
- an investigator in communications data and open source intelligence could be asked to fill in gaps about a suspect's communications and private life.

The investigation of major crimes also requires significant resources. A 'major crime' would be any crime that includes serious violence (eg murder, manslaughter, and stranger rape) or the potential for serious violence, and a crime that requires resources beyond those of a single BCU. Any crime of grave public concern (eg the abduction of a child), terrorism, or the threat of terrorism is also likely to come under the umbrella of major crime. Major crimes are classified as shown in the table (ACPO 2006a).

Category	Definition
A+	Public concern and the associated response to media intervention are such that 'normal' staffing levels are not adequate to keep pace with the investigation
A	An incident of grave concern or where vulnerable members of the public are at risk; where the identity of the offender/s is not apparent, or the investigation and the securing of evidence requires significant resource allocation
B	The identity of the offender/s is not apparent, the continued risk to the public is low, and the investigation or securing of evidence can be achieved within normal resourcing arrangements
C	The identity of the offender/s is apparent from the outset and the investigation and/or securing of evidence can easily be achieved

In each force there will be a Major Crime Unit headed by a senior detective officer (eg a superintendent). He/she can designate any crime as a major crime, in order that the appropriate resources can be made available for its subsequent investigation.

The Serious Crime Analysis Section (SCAS), part of the National Crime Agency, can help identify evidence that could indicate that the same offender has committed a number of similar serious offences (for instance murders and rapes). Serious 'live' offences are added to the SCAS database where they can be compared to old cases that remain unsolved. Physical and behavioural aspects of the offender can be used in 'domain searches' to try and find links to other crimes. If potential offenders are identified the relevant forces would then be notified. It is of course very important that such offenders are apprehended at the earliest possible stage.

24.2.3 Managing and recording investigations

Effective communication is a key component in case management, as the investigating officer (IO) will interact with other officers, members of the police family and members of the public. It provides clarity between all of the 'players' within a particular investigation. How else would it be possible to gain information and evidence from others, and to brief other professionals on the status of the investigation and of the needs of the case?

Risk-management is also important, and must be borne in mind throughout an investigation in relation to colleagues, victims, witnesses, and members of the public. There are several examples where police failed to appreciate the real risks posed to victims of crime (for instance, the investigation into the death of Alice Ruggles, 2016). The police have been criticized for their failure to recognize risk, particularly in relation to their poor response to domestic abuse cases (HMIC, 2014) and more recently stalking (HMCPSI, 2017). This is important, especially where the police become aware of a threat to life, as they have a legal duty to protect life where there is a real and immediate risk. This derives from Article 2 of the European Convention on Human Rights and is outlined in an ECHR ruling (*Osman v UK* (2000) 29 EHRR 245).

Consideration should also be given to colleagues who are exposed to distressing situations when investigating crimes. For example a family liaison officer (FLO) will provide support to families and become an investigative asset to cascade information, but he/she is also likely to absorb some of the distress felt by the family. Some people are more at risk than others of developing long-term mental health issues as a result of exposure to these potentially traumatic events at work. Welfare and TRiM (Trauma Risk Management) can be used to identify colleagues within an investigation team who may be particularly vulnerable.

Records of the investigation must be kept so that investigations are auditable and transparent. As such, depending upon the level of investigation, the decisions, actions, and strategies will be recorded in a variety of media by investigating officers. For example, in a volume crime investigation and for routine priority crimes, the investigation is likely to be recorded within the electronic crime report. However, the investigation of a serious or major crime will be recorded on a decision log or policy file, which will set out the key strategic decisions (for further information see ACPO Crime Committee (1999) *Revised Guidelines For the use of Policy Files*). The policy file could be vital if an investigation is transferred to another officer—not uncommon in the uncertain world of policing—so it is crucial to have an accurate record of what has been done. Poor policy file completion was mentioned in the

Macpherson Report (1999), which considered the failings of the Stephen Lawrence murder investigation in 1993.

The early decisions made when initially attending a crime scene become very important at a handover (eg crime scene management, witnesses, victim, forensic opportunities, CCTV, and house-to-house enquiries). The new investigating officer needs to understand what has been done already and what still needs to be done. It also allows the new IO to form his/her own opinion on the sufficiency of those decisions.

24.2.4 Witnesses in investigations

The evidence of a witness (including victim(s)) may be vital in obtaining a conviction. Many, if not all, witnesses will cooperate if officers provide reassurance and information about what to expect.

24.2.4.1 Types of witness

There are various categories of witness, and the dialogue between the witness and the police officer, and the means by which evidence is obtained, will vary accordingly.

A defence witness is a person who the accused is going to call to give evidence at the trial in relation to an alibi or to other matters. The name, address, and date of birth of any such witness must be disclosed in advance to the prosecution (s 6 of the CPIA) as the police may wish to interview him/her. A defence witness may be intimidated or reluctant to assist, fearing, for example, police coercion to change his/her account. In these circumstances consultation with the CPS is advised. Any interview with a defence witness has to comply with the relevant Code of Practice (under s 21A of the CPIA).

A significant or key witness is someone who can provide evidence that is particularly important to a case. They are designated as such by the SIO, usually in a serious or major crime enquiry involving an indictable offence such as murder, manslaughter, rape, or kidnap. The witness may have witnessed the offence (or part of it) or may stand in a particular relationship to the victim, or have other evidence or intelligence to offer. An interview with a significant witness may be visually recorded if it seems that this will contribute significantly to the investigation (see 25.6.1).

A vulnerable witness (s 16, Part II of the Youth Justice and Criminal Evidence Act 1999) is any person:

- under the age of 17;
- with a 'mental disorder' (this is the phrase used in the Act);
- with significant impairment of intelligence and social functioning (eg a learning disability); or
- with a physical disability or a physical disorder.

An intimidated witness (s 17, Part II of the Youth Justice and Criminal Evidence Act 1999) is:

- any elderly and frail person;
- a witness experiencing fear or distress about testifying in the case;
- any witness who self-neglects or self-harms;
- any complainant in a sexual assault case;
- a victim of a domestic violence, a racially motivated crime, or repeat victimization; or
- a relative of the victim in a homicide case.

A 'reluctant witness' is a witness who declines to cooperate, or who makes a statement but then refuses to attend court. He/she may fear repercussions or reprisal, or might simply not want to assist the police. If the police can establish that he/she has important evidence to offer, a witness summons can be issued to compel attendance in court (see Home Office Circular 35/2005).

24.2.4.2 Support for witnesses during investigations

Witnesses are likely to be unfamiliar with the procedures employed during investigations, and some may also be a victim in the case. Victim Support and the Victim Communication and Liaison (VCL) scheme can provide support for victims and witnesses (see also 13.7.4). The VCL reflects the CPS approach to directing services towards victims in greatest need, and takes account of the revised Code of Practice for Victims of Crime (the Victims' Code). The witness service will also offer support at court for witnesses and victims.

Some witnesses and victims will be entitled to 'special measures'. Witnesses under 17 years of age and complainants in sexual cases always require special measures. Other vulnerable or intimidated witnesses may require special measures, but further assessment will be required through the use of an MG2 form. More information on special measures can be found on the CPS website.

A witness may be granted anonymity in the interests of justice. Certain conditions must be met for a 'witness anonymity order' to be issued by a court. For example, the order (issued under the Coroners and Justice Act 2009) must be necessary to protect the safety of the witness or another person, or to prevent any serious damage to property, or to prevent real harm to the public interest—and the court must take the witness's feelings into account on these matters. The order must also be seen as necessary for the defendant to receive a fair trial (and without the order either the witness would not testify or the public interest would be harmed if the witness were to testify without anonymity). The police must obtain as much corroborative evidence as possible in any case where witness anonymity might be involved. An important case involving witness anonymity is *R v Mayers (Jordan)* [2008] EWCA Crim 2989. It dealt with several separate investigations into murder and drug-dealing, and anonymous witnesses were allowed to provide evidence at the trials of several defendants. Appeals were made on the grounds that the witness anonymity orders should not have been allowed, but the Court of Appeal upheld the decision.

24.2.4.3 Offenders as witnesses for the prosecution

Under the Serious Organised Crime and Police Act 2005 (SOCPA), agreements can be made with offenders who offer to assist with the investigation or prosecution of offences committed by others. The agreement must be in writing and could state, for example, that the person will not be prosecuted (an immunity notice under s 71), or that certain pieces of evidence will not be used (a 'restricted use undertaking' under s 72).

In order to benefit from the agreement the person must fully admit his/her own criminality, agree to cooperate in full, provide all the information he/she has regarding the matters under investigation, and give evidence in court if required. A witness against the accused may also be a co-accused, as in the Rhys Jones murder investigation in 2007. In that case the CPS originally planned to charge a co-accused with firearms offences, but instead offered him immunity from prosecution provided he met certain conditions, including attending court and giving a truthful account. He accepted these terms and the CPS was able to use the new evidence to charge a suspect with murder.

24.2.5 Evidence in investigations

Evidence usually falls into one of six categories: oral, real, documentary, secondary, opinion, or hearsay. Evidence can be derived through identification, confessions, and expert evidence. The nature and types of evidence are covered during initial police training, for example modules within the 'Conducting Investigations' subject area of the National Policing Curriculum.

Real evidence exists as an object, for example as microscopic bloodstains or particles of explosive, or a hammer. An item of real evidence is known as 'an exhibit'. The reporting or the arresting police officer is responsible for ensuring the secure retention of exhibits. There must be an auditable trail for real evidence, from the moment it was discovered or recovered until it is produced in court. This is referred to as 'continuity of evidence' or the 'chain of evidence'. In complex cases, an exhibits officer will be appointed, and in some police forces a designated specialist is responsible for safeguarding certain materials, such as forensic items or CCTV footage. Further details on the procedures for ensuring the continuity of evidence are provided in 11.2.6 and Chapter 26.

A document is of course also 'real evidence', but is classed separately because of its referential nature, and because authorship can often be proven. The medium through which it is written can vary from a 'Last Will and Testament' on parchment with spidery copperplate writing, to an electronic file recording the use of a credit card over the internet. A handwriting expert may be needed to testify to offer opinion that, within limitations, the author of one particular document is likely to be the author of another particular document. This becomes even more complex when it comes to electronic text, and specialists differ over degrees of certainty about the authorship of, for example, web documents, particularly if they are not signed or copyrighted. The requirements for 'continuity of evidence' also apply to documents (see also 26.5.5 on forensics). Secondary evidence can be admissible (eg copies of an original document) at the judge's discretion, but ideally the original should be sought and produced.

24.2.5.1 Hearsay evidence

Hearsay evidence is when one person reports in court what another person has said or written outside court. For example, the witness might give evidence that she heard a man say that he stabbed someone after an argument. This would be hearsay, because she did not see the stabbing, she is only reporting that she heard the man talking about it. This kind of evidence has generally been treated with an element of suspicion, and was usually rendered inadmissible in court because of the potential for ambiguity or malice. Part of the reasoning for caution with hearsay evidence is that the defendant cannot cross examine the person who made the supposed statement (ie the man who spoke of the stabbing in the example above). It was considered that hearsay evidence should only be allowed as evidence in court in specific circumstances. The Criminal Justice Act 2003 changed the law relating to the admissibility of hearsay evidence in criminal proceedings, and can be seen as a major shift in attitude towards this type of evidence (see 27.5.2.3 for more details). The 2003 law was predicated upon the assertion that juries in particular could be trusted with more evidence than before, even hearsay or bad character evidence. Properly directed, it was reasoned, they could make decisions without assuming guilt. Whether this is true or not is open to debate, but the net effect of the 2003 changes was to increase the amount of evidence potentially admissible at trial. The old law was criticized (Spencer, 2016) for being too complicated, difficult to find (because it was in different Acts of Parliament or case law, some of which extended back into previous centuries), and too inflexible. In an infamous trial for indecent assault (*R v Sparks* (1964)) the court would not allow a defendant to use certain hearsay evidence and he was convicted, even though that evidence might have exonerated him if the jury had heard it. (He subsequently appealed and was successful, but only on other grounds.) In the 2003 Act there is a specific clause allowing for flexibility and admissibility of evidence, if it would be in the interests of justice for a court to hear it. If a case similar to *Sparks* were to be heard today, it is likely that such hearsay evidence would be allowed.

A trainee officer does not have to learn all the details of all the provisions for hearsay, but a basic understanding serves to underline why it is vital for all officers to make a PNB record of exactly what was said.

24.2.5.2 Bad character evidence

Bad character evidence (BCE) can sometimes be used in criminal cases, and officers should always consider whether relevant BCE exists. Bad character is defined by s 98 of the Criminal Justice Act 2003 as evidence of:

- misconduct (including previous convictions, cautions, and offences for which a person has been charged, but the charge has not been heard or the person was acquitted (s 112)); or
- a disposition towards misconduct, for example 'other reprehensible behaviour' (s 112), which, for example, could include anti-social behaviour, persistent lying, and racist behaviour.

Thus the law makes it clear that reprehensible behaviour falling short of a conviction counts as bad character, as well as obvious instances, such as previous convictions. For instance, a person may have a propensity to be violent if he/she gets drunk, and this may become relevant in a case of assault against a family member, irrespective of whether the accused has been previously convicted in relation to similar behaviour. The evidence for BCE cannot come from the offence currently under investigation, nor can it be related to the process of the current proceeding (eg the defendant not attending court when required). Therefore police officers should record matters that might relate to bad character evidence contemporaneously, and provide such intelligence to the relevant department. This information could be crucial to a subsequent criminal investigation.

Here we have provided a simple overview of BCE to the extent which is relevant to the trainee officer. The CPS website provides information on bad character evidence and the College of Policing APP website also contains further information (under the heading *Prosecution and case management*).

24.3 The Criminal Procedure and Investigations Act 1996

Many see the Criminal Procedure and Investigations Act 1996 (CPIA) as relating only to disclosure, but it also relates to the conduct of investigation overall. The Act makes an important distinction between revelation and disclosure; the former relates to material revealed to the prosecutor by the police on the relevant forms (MG6 series), whilst disclosure relates to material disclosed to the defence by the prosecutor (see 24.3.3). Much of the recent legislation relating to investigation was enacted to combat fears that the police had historically withheld important information, ignored exonerating facts, and constructed cases against individuals who were sometimes innocent. High-profile miscarriages of justice often demonstrated these failings in abundance (such as the 'Guildford Four' and the 'Maguire Seven', the 'Birmingham Six', the case of the Taylor sisters, and Stefan Kiszko). For more information on these and other miscarriage of justice cases, see Eddlestone (2012).

The codes also set out the key roles in an investigation as follows:

- the investigator(s), defined as any police officer or employee who plays an active part in an investigation;
- the officer in charge (OIC) who directs an investigation;
- a disclosure officer (more serious investigations may have more than one, eg there may be a separate disclosure officer for sensitive intelligence-based material); and
- the prosecutor who takes responsibility for the conduct of the criminal proceedings.

The definition of a criminal investigation in s 22 of the CPIA (and honed by the Code of Practice), makes it clear that investigators have certain responsibilities and duties, and that these apply right from the very start of a criminal investigation. Relevant material (any evidence that might be pertinent, see 24.3.1) must be recorded and retained, and lines of enquiry that might exonerate a suspect must also be pursued. Subtly, the Act and Codes promoted a shift towards truth-seeking in investigations, rather than trying to prove the guilt of a suspect. The CPIA should be seen as a set of legal responsibilities that run through an investigation from the moment it begins. In an investigation into a major crime a disclosure officer and other staff will often be appointed at the earliest stage to ensure that all relevant material is dealt with in the correct fashion.

The CPIA requires investigators to provide a list of unused material to the prosecutor, who will then consider what material might need to be disclosed to the defence out of fairness. Seen from this perspective, it might seem that the disclosure procedures do not need to be considered until the very end of an investigation. But in fact, the CPIA and its associated codes require exactly the opposite, and this is by no means fully appreciated, even today.

Material that is not used as evidence for the prosecution case will be revealed to the CPS who then decide which parts of it should be disclosed to the defence (see 24.3.3). (You should note that 'revealing to the CPS' and 'disclosing to the defence' are both often referred to as 'disclosure' and this can cause confusion.) The information presented here is drawn from the CPIA and its associated Code of Practice, and the Disclosure Manual (CPS, 2018b).

To illustrate the importance of this issue, imagine a case in a local magistrates' court. The prosecution counsel opens the case by outlining the circumstances of a major public disturbance in a town centre, witnessed by a number of people. Officers from the nearby police station and surrounding areas had attended and a woman was arrested. Statements from the arresting officer and witnesses provided strong evidence of an assault by the defendant. In court, one of the witnesses gives evidence for the prosecution, and is then cross-examined by the defence counsel. Next, the arresting officer (AO) takes the witness stand and the prosecution asks him to outline the evidence of the arrest. After this has been done, the defence counsel rises, and says:

Defence: Officer, I have only two questions for you ... we will hear shortly from my client that there were several other police officers at the scene of the alleged assault. Who were these other officers and why are they not giving evidence today?

AO: There were approximately ten officers at the scene; I do not know their names as they came from a neighbouring police area.

Defence: Officer, the last witness has told this court that, when you arrived at the location, you had a conversation with him about what actually happened. Where are your notes of that conversation?

AO: I have no record of the conversation; I remembered the name and address and then a statement was taken later.

The defendant now takes the stand and tells the court the reason for the assault was self-defence and that the arresting officer was completely wrong about how drunk she was. The defence counsel asks his client if there is anyone who can corroborate this, and she replies that, if the other police officers and witnesses had been at court, they would be able to confirm her account. The focus of the defence lawyer has now switched from what his client actually did at the scene (which may seem the most important issue), to examining whether the police officer had kept proper records of the events, including whether the identity of the other police officers present had been noted. The defence applies to stay the proceedings on the basis that his client is being deprived of the right to a fair trial under Sch 1, Art 6 to the Human Rights Act 1998 (see 4.4.1), stating that the prosecution has effectively prevented the defence from accessing a number of witnesses who are crucial to their client's defence. Alternatively, they might apply for a stay of proceedings on the grounds of an abuse of process. The magistrates retire to deliberate.

Whether the application would have been successful or not in this imaginary case is irrelevant here: the point we wish to make is that a lot of time and effort can be wasted if certain information is not recorded, and that cases can be lost as a consequence.

> **TASK 1** What sort of information could the arresting officer have recorded in relation to this case?

Some officers regard disclosure to the defence as a process that both confuses the courts and facilitates the work of the defence. However, investigations need to be conducted as a search for the truth, and police investigators are obliged to search for evidence that will not only point to guilt, but also to innocence. It could be said that disclosure helps create a 'level playing field' because the prosecution has access to significant professional services and capabilities for producing evidence for the prosecution, while the defence case is sometimes constructed by only one person, the defence solicitor.

24.3.1   Relevant material

Material is said to be relevant when it has a bearing on any offence under investigation or any person being investigated, or on the surrounding circumstances of the case. 'Material' is any information and objects obtained in the course of a criminal investigation, and includes written materials, moving or still images, mobile data, software, and information given orally.

In general terms, all relevant material obtained or generated during the course of an investigation must be recorded and retained, even if it is not subsequently used by the prosecution. If it is not recorded (or is recorded incorrectly), or is not retained then it is 'lost' to the defence, and hence has not been properly shared with them through the CPS. This could be a serious loophole that can be exploited by the defence, as illustrated at the start of 24.3. The responsibility to record and retain relevant material does not relate just to prosecution material, but also to material that might assist the defence. As an example, imagine that CCTV recordings of an incident involving assault at a nightclub in the centre of a town have been collected. If the recording showed the suspect talking to a security guard (a 'bouncer') outside the club, this could be an alibi for the suspect and the material would be relevant. However, it can be difficult to decide whether materials are or will be relevant, because the defence strategy cannot be predicted in advance.

It is sometimes necessary to liaise with other organizations or individuals when building a case file. This should take into account the circumstances under which the information is shared. There are instances where there is a statutory obligation to share information (eg under a freedom of information request). In other situations, there may be a statutory power to share information, but not an obligation. Any statutory purpose for sharing the information must be identified, and if there is none, the risk of sharing it must be assessed. This will take into account the source of the information and the possibility of its further dissemination, the common law duty of confidentiality, and possible breaches of the Human Rights Act 1998 and the GDPR 2018. Police forces often have Information Sharing Agreements (ISAs) that help to streamline the exchange of information. Any sharing of personal information (eg medical information, or religious or political beliefs) must be necessary for the particular purpose; it must not be shared out of mere curiosity or interest. The information must be accurate, judged on its own merits, and decided on a case-by-case basis, and its relevance should be clearly explained. The College of Policing document *Information management: Sharing police information* (available online) provides further details and explanations.

24.3.2 Record, retain, and reveal

The officer in charge of the investigation is responsible for ensuring that relevant material is recorded in a durable or retrievable form, for example in writing, on tape, or on a computer drive. The record should be made when the material is received or as soon as possible afterwards. The contents of any material (eg a recording) deemed not relevant should be summarized before discarding the material.

The following materials are routinely recorded and retained (para 5.4 of the CPIA Code of Practice):

- crime reports (including crime report forms, relevant parts of incident report books, and officers' PNBs);
- custody records;
- records derived from recordings of telephone messages (eg 999 and 112 calls) containing descriptions of an alleged offence or offender;
- final versions of witness statements (and draft versions, where their content differs from the final version);
- any exhibits mentioned in witness statements (unless they have been returned to their owner, on the understanding that they will be produced in court if required);
- interview records (written, audio, or video records, of interviews with actual or potential witnesses or suspects);
- communications between the police and experts such as forensic scientists (but not the prosecutor), reports of work carried out by experts, and schedules of scientific material prepared by the expert for the investigator for the purposes of criminal proceedings;
- records of the first description of a suspect by each potential witness who purports to identify or describe the suspect, whether or not the description differs from subsequent descriptions by that or other witnesses; and
- any material casting doubt on the reliability of a witness.

There is a particularly important point concerning potential witnesses who the police know about but have not interviewed. In the case of *R v Heggart and Heggart* (November 2000 (CA)), it was determined that the courts should automatically assume that any evidence from uninterviewed witnesses would either undermine the prosecution case, or assist the defence case. Therefore, a record should be made of any witness details, and what they observed in relation to the incident at the scene. There is, however, a notion of proportionality here: there would be no expectation to record the details of all 25,000 spectators at a football match.

Material relevant to an investigation must be retained for a certain period of time. The length of time varies, depending, for example, on whether the case continues to court, the outcome, and the length of sentence following a conviction (see para 5.8 of the CPIA Code for more detail). If the case goes to court, some of the relevant material will be exhibited as part of the prosecution case, but some will not. This 'unused material' will be 'revealed' to the CPS who will then decide whether it should be disclosed to the defence (see 24.3.3).

24.3.3 Disclosure

Disclosure is providing the defence with copies of, or access to, any material which has not previously been disclosed, and which could possibly be used to undermine the prosecution case against the accused, or otherwise assist his/her case. The CPS decides which material should be disclosed, and the police are usually responsible for implementing any subsequent disclosure. In routine and minor cases, the arresting officer or the case officer will also be the disclosure officer. In more serious cases the disclosure officer is a specific and dedicated specialist, and not necessarily a police officer.

The forms used for disclosure are MG6 B, C, D, and E (see 27.4.2 on MG forms). The Streamline Disclosure Certificate (SDC) can be used for a summary case at a magistrates' court where a not guilty plea is anticipated; the SDC will then replace the MG6C. The disclosure officer ensures that copies of these forms are provided to the CPS. The CPS reviews the forms and decides what else should be disclosed and when. Some of the more sensitive information revealed to the CPS will not be disclosed, such as personal details of a CHIS (see 23.3). The police will then disclose the selected items to the defence.

> **TASK 2**
>
> 1. Reference is made earlier to material that is relevant but will not be used as evidence. In relation to the disclosure process, what is the term for this material?
> 2. Who is responsible for examining the records created during the investigation with a view to revealing the material to the prosecutor?
> 3. Who makes the decision regarding what unused material is actually disclosed to the defence?

The failure to disclose certain information led to 20 convictions being quashed in the high-profile case of *R v Barkshire and others* ([2011] EWCA Crim 1885). The appellants had been convicted of conspiracy to commit aggravated trespass in preparation for climate change protests at a power station at Ratcliffe-on-Soar in 2009. The prosecution had failed to disclose the actions of an undercover police officer who had infiltrated the group and could have been seen to be inciting the events. The convictions of a further 29 appellants involving the same police officer were also quashed (see *R v Bard (Theo)* ([2014] EWCA Crim 463)). A number of other high-profile cases have also highlighted the prosecution's failure to provide the defence with potentially exonerating material. The majority of cases coming to light were rape cases where defendants had been remanded for a significant amount of time, and material was only discovered after trials had commenced (Dodd, 2017; Bowcottt, 2018). In one case involving a student, the MPS apologized, explaining that their investigator had missed the material amongst 57,000 pieces of data. The MPS undertook urgent reviews of 600 similar cases to establish the extent of the problem.

24.3.3.1   The Disclosure Management Document

The Disclosure Management Document (DMD) sets out how all seized electronic media and data are managed. The prosecution must explain to the defence and the court what has been done (or will be done) and why. The DMD should be provided to ('served on') the defence and the court before the plea and case management hearing (see 27.5.1). The defence are invited to identify any additional lines of enquiry that they consider to be reasonable. The judge can then manage the case robustly from the outset.

The use of the DMD was extended in November 2019 and it is now used in the following instances:

- all cases where social media/phone evidence is crucial;
- GBH and wounding, and GBH with intent (see 15.3);
- murder and attempted murder;
- drug trafficking and supply offences (see 12.6.3); and
- rape and other serious sexual offences cases (see Chapter 17).

The DMD was introduced in response to problems around the sheer quantity of digital evidence. By 2014, rapid advances in technology and the popularity of social media had led to mobile phones becoming the preferred choice for accessing the internet (Zimmerman, 2017). This has created problems around the management and disclosure of digital media. In the case of *R v R and others* ([2015] EWCA Crim 1941) the police seized 85 computers and other devices between 2007 and 2011, and the subsequent review of the material took several years. This was felt to be far too long and The Hon Sir Vivian Ramsey gave specific advice on how police should manage digital material henceforth. The first recommendation was to put the prosecution 'in the driving seat' at the initial disclosure stage. It was also felt that there should be a more considered approach when deciding between seizing electronic devices or downloading data in situ. Other considerations included selecting the appropriate equipment and software for reviewing data, how to choose the words or phrases to find relevant material (see 24.3.1), and material that might be considered legal privilege.

In 2017, HMICFRS criticized the Crown on how they recorded decisions about what should and should not be disclosed (the endorsing schedules). It was clear there was a problem as 52 per cent of all cases that year (72,000 out of 137,000) were either delayed or had collapsed (Justice Select Committee, 2018). A number of judges also expressed a lack of confidence in the prosecution's ability to manage the disclosure process (HMICFRS, 2017a), and the collapse of the Liam Allen case (see CPS 2018d) drew yet more attention to the problems around reviewing and disclosing digital media. It is hoped that the broader introduction and use of the DMD in 2018 will help avoid such problems in the future.

24.4 The Investigation Stage by Stage

The response to priority and volume crimes involves many different police staff, from call-handlers to trained investigators. Most incidents are dealt with by the first attending officer (FAO), who will often be the only investigator for the case.

The quality of an investigation and the chances of a successful prosecution are enhanced by actions taken early on in the investigation. These actions include locating, gathering, and retaining material, and making an initial report. Call-handlers, frontline support staff, and police officers are all obliged to record, retain, and reveal information to the investigating officer or disclosure officer, and must follow the specified procedures described for the 'Management of Police Information' (see 5.8.2), as set out in the CPIA and its associated Code of Practice (see 24.3). If other investigators are subsequently involved, they may benefit from questioning and gathering evidence from the person who originally reported the crime, and from the person who received and wrote the initial report.

Some of what follows is an interpretation of the VCMM (*Practice Advice on the Management of Priority and Volume Crime (The Volume Crime Management Model)*, 2nd edn (NPIA/ACPO, 2009)). This document and the College of Policing APP provide further detail relating to investigations. Here we have attempted to outline the procedures adopted in a 'typical' police force, with the investigation of priority and volume crime presented as a series of separate activities for clarity. In practice, however, they are more likely to overlap and merge into a single process, and may not all necessarily feature in any particular investigation, nor in the precise order implied.

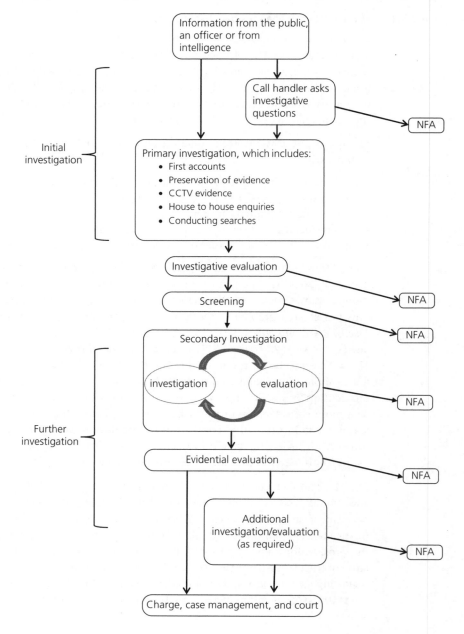

At any stage of the investigation it might become clear that no further action is required (NFA), or that certain actions are necessary, for example to arrest the suspect (see 24.4.3.1). When the decision is NFA, intelligence systems may be updated and the case will be filed as undetected. If further evidence or information comes to light the case can be reopened.

Trainee police officers will be involved in both the primary and secondary investigations into priority and volume crimes during their second year of initial training (or earlier in some forces). The actions outlined here could provide evidence of competence at PIP Level 1 (see 7.5), perhaps as part of the PCDA or DHEP.

24.4.1 Initial investigation

Initial investigation covers a wide range of activities involving police officers and other policing staff. It begins at the very moment a police officer arrives at an incident, or a call-handler answers a call from a member of the public. Some investigations are instigated proactively, for example as a consequence of research and development of intelligence gathering, others reactively, when new information becomes available from sources such as:

- the general public;
- partnership agency reports;
- intelligence derived from other crimes or new information received about an old crime leading to a subsequent re-investigation;
- police actions, for example discovering a cannabis 'factory' through the use of a thermal imaging camera.

24.4.1.1 Call handling as initial investigation

Many investigations start when a member of the public calls the police or emergency services. Call-handlers play a key role in the initial investigation and screening, for example their guidance to a caller may help preserve forensic material at a scene. Their questions are part of an initial investigation and they will then help determine what needs to be done next. Call-handlers collect a large amount of information and may use scripts or computer dropdown menus to help ensure all relevant information is gathered. He/she will use some of the information to conduct a risk assessment, probably using the 'THRIVE' risk management tool, an acronym that stands for 'Threat, Harm, Risk, Investigation, Vulnerability, Engagement' (but to which we can also add 'Prevention and Intervention'). These are the key considerations when evaluating any given situation. The THRIVE tool articulates with both the Code of Ethics and NDM and helps a police force to react with the appropriate level of response. In summary a call-handler will make an assessment regarding:

- Whether A **Threat** exists, or is implied, to harm a person or property.
- Where the **Harm** could be either physical or psychological.
- How likely the **Risk** of action leading to harm is of being carried out.
- What **Investigative** actions are required regarding the scene, people, and evidence and whether attendance is required to find out more about the problem or crime.
- The **Vulnerability** of a person, in the circumstances described (which may impact on them not being able to protect either him/herself or other people, or his/her own property or the property of another).

In addition, the call handler is likely to end the call with:

- **Engagement**—eg consideration of further engagement (particularly if the caller is one of a 'hard to reach' group); signposting to other sources of force information, other agencies etc.

As more and more police forces adopt the THRIVE (or a variant, 'THRIVE +') model of call-handling, its benefits will need to be evaluated. Hopefully it will improve resourcing and prioritizing, and provide new insights into particular problems. Forces might also be able to develop prevention and intervention strategies to reduce problems in the future. The incident that has given rise to the call will be graded according to the level of police response required (typically as 'immediate', 'priority', 'scheduled' (eg a later phone call)). Depending on the BCU deployment policy, officers may be dispatched to a location (there may be a dedicated team of officers for attending volume crime scenes). If immediate attendance is not required the caller will probably be transferred to a 'crime bureau' where details of the incident will be considered and recorded (see also 3.4.1). This may be the end of the investigation for that incident, unless any further relevant information comes to light.

24.4.1.2 Primary investigation

Police officers may be deployed to a location based upon the decisions of the call-handlers, or may encounter an incident whilst on patrol. An officer's initial appraisal of the situation and a few preliminary questions will often be sufficient to determine whether any persons present could reasonably be suspected to have been involved in a criminal offence. The answers to these questions comprise the 'first account', sometimes referred to as an initial account, and would aim to establish:

- the type of alleged offence;
- the approximate time of the alleged offence;
- the scene of the alleged offence—only sufficient detail to understand what might be said in an interview; and
- how the alleged offence came to the notice of the police.

A police officer who is trying to discover whether, or by whom, an offence has been committed can question any person from whom useful information might be obtained (PACE Code A, Note 1). If there are reasonable grounds for suspecting that the person has been involved in a criminal offence then a caution must be given before asking any further questions (see 10.3 and 25.5.5). Any conversation that takes place with a suspect before a caution is given should be summarized in a PNB entry, as it could be used in court. Remember that once a suspect has been arrested he/she cannot be interviewed about the offence except at a police station (Code C, para 11.1) unless the delay would irretrievably hinder the investigation (see 10.8.6).

In the majority of cases you may well have both suspect and victim or witness at the scene of the crime. If so, the most beneficial way of using witness evidence is to ask the witness in the presence and hearing of the suspect(s) to explain what he/she saw or heard. Care must be taken in cases of domestic abuse or sexual offences where the victim might be reluctant to speak in front of the suspected abuser (see 13.6 and 17.1). This will be a judgement call by the officer, based upon the circumstances of the case; a risk assessment regarding his/her own safety; and consideration of the safety of the witness and victim. The answers given by a witness should be recorded word for word in a PNB entry or equivalent. The record could later be used as evidence in court as part of an officer's duty statement (see 10.12 on duty statements, and 27.5.3.2 on using a PNB in court).

First accounts from witnesses can also provide the information required for planning an interview with the suspect, or for constructing a 'handover package' for other officers to conduct the interviews (see Chapter 25 on interviews and 10.14 on handover procedures). A first account can also be compared with an account given under oath verbally at court, and any inconsistencies between the two accounts would require an explanation from the witness.

Information about all the witnesses, and any actions, statements, comments, or other relevant material (see 24.3) must be recorded, ensuring compliance with the CPIA. A case could be undermined in court if the defence asked a police officer about something a witness had said and the officer had no record of it (see 27.5.3). If for some reason a PNB record cannot be made, the record should be made separately. The use of the PNB and making PNB entries is covered in 10.2.

Written police records of early accounts from victims and witnesses may be admissible as hearsay evidence (see 27.5.2.3) if a witness or a victim cannot appear in court in person, for example if he/she is seriously ill or is unwilling to give evidence. The police records of such witness accounts must be recorded verbatim. The names and addresses of any other people the victim has told about the incident should also be noted so these can be followed up.

In addition to obtaining first accounts, other actions are required as shown in the table.

Taking a report of a crime	All actions taken to trace witnesses and suspects should be recorded. A list should be made of any other enquiries that have been made, or could be made
The crime scene	The scene should be preserved for the CSI, to avoid contamination. This might require a cordon (see 11.2.1.3 and 11.6.2) for a large or serious crime scene
CCTV evidence	The location of cameras that could have recorded the incident should be recorded (for CPIA purposes and evidence recovery). The CCTV hard copy should be preserved, recovered, and exhibited where possible (see 24.4.1.3)

Managing witnesses	First accounts must be recorded, including full names and addresses. These accounts might suggest further potential witnesses, and these should be recorded in full
House-to-house enquiries	These are likely to concern witnesses or potential witnesses. A record should be made of all persons spoken to, and of any absent potential witnesses (for a future visit). The content of the discussions should be carefully noted, including any refusal to reply
Other evidence	Photographs, plans, and maps might suggest opportunities for obtaining forensic evidence. All documents, captured texts, images, or sequences from electronic devices should be retained
Taking statements	Statements should be obtained as a matter of urgency where violence has occurred (or been threatened), where a suspect has been detained, or if witness contamination must be avoided (eg where a description of a person is relevant)
Recording actions taken	Before going off duty, full details of all actions taken must be recorded, as handwritten PNB entries or electronic entries (depending on the circumstances)

(Adapted from Practice Advice on the Management of Priority and Volume Crime (The Volume Crime Management Model), 2nd edn (NPIA/ACPO, 2009).)

These would generally be taken during the 'golden hour' or as 'fast-track actions' (see 11.2.4), and a trainee police officer could well be involved. The official recommendation is that the NDM should be used to take any decisions, but this may be of limited use in this context, see 24.2.1. It is usually necessary to prioritize certain early actions, and take into account which can be realistically pursued at the time. All decisions made by officers when gathering evidence should be both legal and ethical to ensure the process, procedure, and source cannot be criticized later in court. A particular decision may be well-motivated but if it steps outside of the law the evidence gathered could be rendered inadmissible, for example the interviews and confessions in the Christopher Halliwell case (see 25.5.1.2).

With regard to possible witnesses, any people in the vicinity who were not involved or who did not see what happened should be eliminated from the enquiry. Careful judgement is needed to establish who was a material witness to the event (who actually saw it) and who was not. This is not as easy as it sounds because some people become over-excited when they think they have witnessed a crime, and will be keen to provide their (possibly derivative) account. Note, however, that an effective response to supporting survivors, victims, and witnesses will improve the quality of investigation by maximizing the availability of evidence (and it will also help increase public confidence in the police).

All the actions listed in the table should be completed so the information can be pieced together. It is important to realize that a primary investigation is not simply a collection of information concerning an alleged crime; it is an integral part of the whole investigation (eg as a precursor to an evidential evaluation and possible secondary investigation) which may lead to prosecution.

The primary investigator produces a crime report which is sent to the principal screener or, in some forces, links directly with the crime bureau to provide information for the crime report. The FAO must be thorough regarding these initial actions so he/she can produce a professional product. The report will be handed to an investigator who may take the investigation further, or it may be filed with no further investigation necessary.

24.4.1.3 Obtaining CCTV evidence

CCTV evidence can also form part of a primary investigation. It can be used to establish the sequence of events and to provide evidence, including supporting the defence case. Relevant material would include footage that showed the suspects were near to the relevant vicinity around the time the crime was committed. The ACPO document *Practice Advice on the use of CCTV in Criminal Investigations* is still available online; we have summarized the key points here. The regulations concerning the use of CCTV are covered in 23.4.1.

In an investigation, CCTV footage should ideally be obtained during the 'golden hour' (see 11.2) to avoid it being lost, but this may be difficult if specialist services are required. In theory, any officer could seize and exhibit CCTV evidence but when and who depends on the circumstances. A trainee officer undertaking the PCDA or DHEP could at least ensure that the recording system is safe and secure before referring the matter to a supervisor.

The storage format and technical requirements for recovering recordings should be established before accessing the equipment. Often the images are stored on a disc, and taking away the machine or its hard drive is not always possible. If the footage is likely to be relevant, it can be dealt with in one of two ways. Either it can be viewed in situ and a decision made about its relevance, or it can be seized without viewing, following the rules on the preservation of evidence (see 11.2.6 on exhibits and 24.3.1 on relevant material). Working copies must be made for any further viewings, following ACPO's four principles (see 21.4). In either case, a record would be made of what was viewed, in accordance with PACE Code D (this covers the procedures for the identification of suspects, see 4.6.1 and 26.6.1.1). The record will also contain any initial reactions to any viewings, so it can be scrutinized at a later date to assess the reliability of any assertion. Seized hard drives should be placed in anti-static bags, tough paper bags, tamper evident cardboard packaging, or wrapped in paper and placed in aerated plastic bags (see 21.5.4 on packaging digital devices).

24.4.2 Investigative evaluation and screening

As part of a first formal investigative evaluation the crime will be screened to decide if it should be classed as mandatory, priority, or non-priority. This process will also assess the quality of the initial and primary investigation, and ensure that all evidence-gathering opportunities have been exploited (for the current incident and for other related incidents). A principal screener will normally be an experienced police officer with investigative skills at PIP Level 2 or above. (The exact role title can vary from force to force, and Crime Management Unit staff may also undertake this role.)

Non-volume serious crimes such as homicide and rape will be classed as mandatory, and will certainly be assigned for secondary investigation. The likelihood of solving priority and/or non-priority crimes will also be assessed. A secondary investigation will be allocated for any crimes which are part of a series, involve a named suspect, or for which there is good evidence or credible intelligence linked to a named offender. To determine the future direction of the investigation, the College of Policing APP suggests four key questions for an investigative evaluation (CoP, 2018a).

- What is known?
- What is not known?
- What are the consistencies between the findings so far?
- What are the contradictions?

The results of the evaluation will lead to a range of outcomes, for example that the investigation is filed with no further action (NFA) because no leads exist and little else can be done, or that it should be handed on for further investigation because there are further lines of enquiry and/or suspects might be known.

In a complicated or lengthy investigation several staged investigative evaluations will be needed to maintain focus. These will form part of an on-going secondary investigation, and will be conducted by the officer leading the investigation. You can see the cyclical nature of the process of investigative evaluation in the flowchart at the start of 24.4. Repeated cycles of further investigation and investigative evaluation will continue until the case is ready for evidential evaluation (assuming a suspect has been arrested at this stage). If a suspect has not been found, despite lengthy enquiries, the investigation may be filed as NFA. Each evaluation should be recorded so that decisions can be reviewed throughout the investigation. The VCMM makes it clear that as a minimum, an investigation plan (sometimes part of a 'handover package' (see 10.14)), should be prepared for any secondary investigation.

If the decision is not to investigate any further then the crime report is filed ('finalized') as NFA and the reasons for the decision are recorded. This process has been criticized, as there are indications that many cases are screened out at an early stage, and therefore receive little investigative attention. In 2018 *The Independent* newspaper's Home Affairs Correspondent, Lizzie Dearden, claimed that police were not responding to crimes as they had in the past due to government cuts (Dearden, 2018), and reported that the head of the Police Federation claimed that the 'financial cake' could only be cut so many ways, so prioritizing was inevitable (*The Independent*, 12 August 2018).

The principal screener can allocate secondary investigations to several investigators, each with a different role. The investigators could be patrol officers, neighbourhood officers, volume crime investigators working as part of a volume crime investigation team, or officers on specialist squads (eg a burglary squad). Depending on force protocols, a trainee officer might be allocated certain volume crimes to investigate as lead investigator; these might include domestic abuse, hate crime, and public order offences.

24.4.3 Further investigation

The investigation plan from the principal screener will help direct any secondary investigation, and identify relevant lines of enquiry. These may be, for instance, to trace witnesses, identify a victim, or protect scenes. The plan will set out the minimum enquiries expected, but for other investigative strategies the investigator will use his/her discretion.

In serious cases the police might, for example, decide to employ a media strategy to ask the public for assistance with a challenging investigation. For some less serious cases where a person is 'caught on camera' committing minor crime but has not yet been caught by police, the police might publish the images to try to find out who the suspect is. Other strategies include house-to-house enquiries, searching, forensic retrieval, e-fit circulation, statements from witnesses with full descriptions, capturing text or other electronically generated data, and interviewing. Each strategy employed must be carefully planned and executed (see the College of Policing APP on investigation for more details).

Any person to be interviewed by the police (witness, victim, or a potential witness or victim) is entitled to be treated fairly and with dignity, so each interviewee's individual needs must be recognized and taken into account (see 25.4). For instance, the person could be a vulnerable witness (see 24.2.4) who would require some assistance when providing evidence to the police, or a vulnerable suspect who would need an appropriate adult, family member, and/or solicitor present when interviewed at a police station. The person may have other requirements, for example be unable to speak English so an interpreter would be needed, or have physical disabilities that would require assistance from a specialist adviser. Professional officers must treat people in an appropriate and respectful manner, but this approach also helps ensure that any evidence obtained cannot be discredited by poor practice. Investigative interviewing is covered in detail in Chapter 25.

The guidance in the College of Policing APP distinguishes between investigative activities that have a specific aim in mind (eg to trace a suspect), and activities that are part of a general trawl for information (eg house-to-house enquiries). Each investigator will apply discretion to decide which strategies to use in a particular context, and record the reasons for each decision.

As more evidence is gathered the investigator will need to conduct further investigative evaluations (see 24.4.2). This might lead to further lines of enquiry, the employment of other investigative strategies, a decision to arrest, or a decision to proceed no further with the investigation. Once a potential suspect is identified, the investigation will move into the suspect management phase (see 24.4.3.1).

24.4.3.1 Suspect management

Once a suspect has been identified, a range of options will need to be explored. If he/she has not already been arrested, consideration would need to be given to arrest, search, and seizure of evidence, and the appropriate timings for each action (see 10.8 on making arrests). Both the VCMM and the College of Policing APP contain detailed information on strategies for making arrests, searching, and interviewing. Trainee officers should also seek advice from peers and supervisors if in any doubt about to how to progress the suspect management phase.

Any arrest must be lawful and necessary (see 10.6). In terms of making the arrest, this must be carefully planned. First, consideration needs to be given to what is known about the suspect and his/her criminal history, for example has he/she been violent to police officers in the past? If so, meticulous planning would be needed on how to safely carry out the arrest. Another issue is if the officers attend, but the suspect is not at home. The suspect might now be alerted to the fact that the police have called, and might decide to go into hiding, or to dispose of possible evidence. An alternative approach would be to obtain a search warrant (from a magistrates' court), providing a power to enter for the police, even if the suspect is absent (see 9.5.1.3); any potential evidence could be secured in his/her absence. Whether this is necessary, proportionate, and legal is a significant issue for the investigator, and requires careful thought and planning. The investigator will also need to plan which police station(s) the suspect(s) will be taken to following arrest, particularly if a number of suspects are to be arrested at the same time.

Once a suspect is in custody, key considerations include the suspect's medical condition, whether there is any 'bad character' evidence, whether any identification procedures are applicable, further searches of premises, when to interview, who is to conduct the interviews, and the exact nature of the interview strategy (see 10.8 on detainees and Chapter 25 on interviewing). The outcome of an investigation could be NFA but there are many other methods of disposal, for example charging with an offence, giving a formal caution, and fixed penalty notices (see 10.13). Once a suspect is charged (see 27.3), the investigation then moves into the case management phase (see 27.4).

24.4.3.2 Evidential evaluation

If the investigation has progressed through secondary investigation, then a further evaluation is necessary—an 'evidential evaluation'. Again, this is likely to be undertaken by the officer in charge of the investigation. The evaluation considers whether there is sufficient evidence to allow for a criminal justice disposal, or whether no further action can be taken because all 'leads' have yielded no further evidence. The strengths and weaknesses of the case will be taken into account, and whether there is sufficient evidence to charge. The evidential evaluation stage never takes place in a vacuum—investigators will liaise with peers, supervisors, case review officers, and evidence review officers (EROs). If it seems there is sufficient relevant evidential material, the investigators will send an advice file (an MG3 form, all key statements, and an outline of the available evidence) to the CPS for a charging decision. The CPS will sometimes provide advice about evidential gaps (see also 24.4.4) that would need to be addressed before deciding whether to charge a suspect (see 27.3 for more on CPS advice and charging).

24.4.4 Gap analysis

Allied to the concept of the investigative mindset, and particularly to the principle of investigative and 'evidential evaluation', is the notion of a 'gap analysis'. This is the periodic examination of material gathered during an investigation in order to identify and then fill any gaps in investigative and evidential knowledge. It often employs the '5WH' approach; the 'Who? What? When? Where? Why? and How?'.

Gap in Knowledge	Explanation
Who?	The identities of witnesses, suspects, victims, etc
What?	The sequence of events leading up to, during, and after an alleged offence
When?	The time(s) of events linked with the alleged offence
Where?	The locations linked with the alleged offences
Why?	Motivation—why this place, this time, this alleged victim?
How?	The means of conducting the alleged offence

Investigators are frequently advised to use such an approach when considering the progress of enquiries, as it is believed it helps ensure a more methodical and thorough investigation.

24.5 Answers to Tasks

TASK 1 A police officer attending an incident is a potential witness (for both the prosecution and the defence). If he/she talks to witnesses or potential witnesses, their details and what they observed in relation to the incident should be recorded. If there are groups of people milling around, the officer might decide to stay in the area in case of any further trouble; such observations and any decision taken should be recorded. In the case of an arrest, any assistance provided to an arresting officer should be recorded (by both officers).

TASK 2

1. Unused material.
2. A disclosure officer is responsible for examining the records created during the investigation (and any criminal proceedings arising from the investigation). He/she will also complete the appropriate forms (MG6 series) to reveal relevant material to the prosecutor.
3. The prosecutor.

25 | Investigative Interviewing

25.1 Introduction

Interviewing witnesses, victims, and suspects is a key part of the police investigation process, and a 'frontline' police officer will carry out an interview nearly every day. The modern approach to police interviewing in the UK is to see the interview as a means of seeking to establish the truth. This sounds obvious but it does in fact represent a marked change in emphasis from the past: it is no longer simply a case of working through a list of 'points to prove'. Instead, interviewing is now much more of an information gathering 'inquisitorial approach'. The term *investigative* is key here as the interview is a central part of any investigation and can significantly affect the outcomes. In the past (particularly in the 1970s and 1980s) the police were sometimes accused of using oppressive techniques for obtaining a confession, and there were a number of notorious miscarriages of justice where innocent people were wrongly convicted, or the guilty were acquitted.

The advent of the PACE Act 1984 represented a major step forward, as for the first time the police were obliged to routinely audio-record interviews. There were many benefits to this (both legally and ethically), but the interviews also provided a rich source of data to be examined by researchers, particularly psychologists and criminologists. They found there were a number of areas of poor practice in interviewing. An influential report (Baldwin, 1992, p 34) notes that when interviewing suspects, the main weaknesses were 'a lack of preparation, a general ineptitude, poor technique, an assumption of guilt, unduly repetitive, persistent or laboured questioning, a failure to establish the relevant facts and the exertion of too much pressure'. This and other reports led to the development of a common approach to interviewing and increased standardization of interview training across the whole of England and Wales. The PEACE model (see 25.3 onwards) was an important step forward in reaction to the perceived shortcomings in police interviewing.

In this chapter we will examine investigative interviewing processes and procedures in depth, and the recommended methods for conducting interviews. Trainee officers will also practice interviewing procedures and techniques, including how to follow the relevant codes and legislation. If you are on a pre-join course at a university, or undertaking the PCDA or the DHEP you might have the opportunity to explore some more of the underpinning theory and research involved in police interviewing—for example, in relation to memory enhancement, lying and deception, and false confessions. The College of Policing has published APP covering investigative interviewing, and further information can be found on their website. The topics covered in this chapter are likely to contribute to the learning required for the National Policing Curriculum subject area 'Conducting Investigations'.

25.2 Key Principles for Interviewing

In order to establish an ethical framework for police interviewing some general principles have been adopted by the police service. These principles apply to all interviews and assist with effective planning and implementation. Home Office Circular 2/1992 on investigative interviewing initially outlined seven principles. These were updated in 2007 and formed part of the National Investigative Interviewing Strategy (NPIA, 2009). The NPIA Strategy was further developed as part of the College of Policing's APP website in 2013 and most recently updated in March 2019 <https://www.app.college.police.uk/app-content/investigations/investigative-interviewing/#:~:text=during%20the%20investigation.-,Principle%201,without%20any%20omissions%20or%20distortion>. The seven principles are as follows:

1. 'The aim of investigative interviewing is to obtain accurate and reliable accounts from victims, witnesses or suspects about matters under police investigation.'
2. 'Investigators must act fairly when questioning victims, witnesses or suspects.' 'People with clear or perceived vulnerabilities should be treated with particular care, and extra safeguards should be put in place.'
3. 'Investigative interviewing should be approached with an investigative mindset. Accounts obtained from the person who is being interviewed should always be tested against what the interviewer already knows or what can reasonably be established.'
4. 'When conducting an interview, investigators are free to ask a wide range of questions in order to obtain material which may assist an investigation.'
5. 'Investigators should recognise the positive impact of an early admission in the context of the criminal justice system.'
6. 'Investigators are not bound to accept the first answer given. Questioning is not unfair merely because it is persistent.'
7. 'Even when the right of silence is exercised by a suspect, investigators have a responsibility to put questions to them.'

An investigative interview should be lawful, in that the information should be obtained in accordance with statute so that it may be usefully admitted in evidence if required. The information should be obtained in an ethical manner, and should respect the individual's rights, such as freedom and dignity. The investigative interview should maximize the opportunity to establish detailed information, which can be used to establish the reliability and truthfulness of the interviewee's account. It should also meet and extend the aims and objectives of the overall investigation. The outcomes of the interview must stand up to judicial review and challenge by the criminal justice system.

The legislation around police interviewing is complex, and here we cover the basics, sufficient for the trainee officer. The following legislation (all available on the www.legislation.gov.uk website) is also important for interviewing:

- ss 76 and 78 of the PACE Act 1984, including provisions under Codes C, E, and F;
- Part III and ss 34, 36, and 37 of the Criminal Justice and Public Order Act 1994 (CJPOA), including 'special warnings' (see 25.5.9);
- the criminal law relating to the offence(s) for which suspects are charged;
- the Human Rights Act 1998 (see 4.4.1);
- the Criminal Procedure and Investigations Act 1996 (CPIA); and
- the Youth Justice and Criminal Evidence Act 1999 (especially on 'vulnerable', 'intimidated', and child witnesses).

Other legislation covers specific provisions which we will refer to later, but those noted here set out the key principles governing what an interviewer can say and do during an interview. Legislation such as the PACE Act 1984 and its Codes of Practice have certainly helped to reassure the public, lawyers, academics, and the police themselves, that interviewing is now more tightly controlled, more ethical, and often more effective. Of course, simply knowing the law is not enough, the law must also be followed and applied, and that is the key role for a police officer. If mistakes are made through incompetence, poor practice, or acting in 'bad faith' during the interview process, parts of the evidence may be rendered void or inadmissible. This could mean that a guilty person might avoid prosecution and be free to offend again, or an innocent person might be wrongly charged and convicted.

25.2.1   Strategic oversight

Investigative interviewing is now seen as a crucial part of the criminal investigation process, and in line with a professionalization agenda, the development of both witness and suspect interviewing is overseen by the National Strategic Steering Group on Investigative Interviewing (NSSGII). It aims to develop policies, practices, and procedures that are appropriate for modern investigative activity. Working in conjunction with the NSSGII, each police force now has a force lead on investigative interviewing, and coordinators at both regional and national levels provide advice and guidance to practitioners on current best professional practice. In addition, at the tactical level, trained and qualified interview advisers are available to support colleagues in formulating both suspect and witness strategies. All of this is a far cry from the pre-1990s, when officers conducted interviews with little or no guidance or support, mainly to obtain a confession. This was sometimes to the detriment of major investigations, as poor and illegal tactics were sometimes exposed at court (see for instance the IRA cases in the 1970s and 1980s, the Maxwell Confait case in the early 1970s, and the George Heron case in the early 1990s).

25.2.2 The investigative interview as a professional conversation

An investigative interview is a 'professional conversation' (ie a 'conversation with a purpose'). A police interviewer cannot approach it in quite the same manner as a social conversation, but can utilize some aspects of everyday experience to help. Investigators manage the 'conversation' in accordance with predefined investigative objectives and overall aims; these are the 'purpose' of the conversation.

Everyday conversation often takes the form of a verbal exchange between two people, with each person taking turns to meet the desired social outcome, for example:

P1: Good morning, how are you?
P2: Very well thank you, and you?
P1: Couldn't be better ... (next topic of conversation)

We have all assimilated the norms of conversation through our everyday lives and have generally learned to follow these 'rules'. Consider a recent conversation you have had, face to face with a friend. It is highly likely to have started with saying 'Hello' in some manner that is appropriate to your relationship and status (eg a handshake, fist bump, kiss, or hug). After that you will have generally chatted, taking conversational turns, exchanging anecdotes, news, and possibly even gossip. When the conversation started to come to an end you will have used language to indicate this to the other person by saying something like 'Oh, it's been really nice talking ...' to see if you are both ready to disengage and depart. If so, you will go through a process of saying 'Goodbye', and again, this will be in a manner appropriate to your relationship and status. Without giving it any conscious thought, you will have started with a form of 'greeting' followed by some kind of verbal 'mutual activity' and ended with 'closure'. Milne and Bull (1999) and Shepherd (2007, p 21) have described a form of professional conversation management that echoes this as the 'GEMAC' model: that is, 'Greeting, Explanation, Mutual Activity and Closure'. GEMAC is used by some investigative interviewers as a framework for 'decoding' the underlying conversational process.

25.2.3 Questioning in interviews

Questioning is a skill that needs to be practiced. With experience, each interviewer will develop a questioning style that suits his/her persona and working context, but there are a few basic pointers that will help all interviewers, for example to:

- listen intently;
- indicate interest in what the interviewee is saying using verbal and non-verbal encouragement;
- pause for a moment after each response, to process what has been said;
- frame the next question as far as possible on the previous answer, as this will help to develop detail and progress beyond the superficial; and
- make a link to your next objective, once the current questioning 'thread' has been exhausted.

When developing an account from an interviewee, the 'narrative' and 'context' are both important. As a rule, if you initially focus on the narrative, ie what happened, and develop this in detail, the contextual elements will gradually emerge. The narrative can be thought of as the outline of a drawing, and context being the shading and colours. To develop the narrative, it is often quite productive to limit the questioning in the early stages to questions that start with:

- 'Tell me ...'
- 'Explain ...'

- 'Describe ...'
- 'What happened next ...'

Remember to focus on your objectives. Once you have developed the full narrative using productive questioning sequences, the contextual detail (the shading and colours) can be developed by a similar process, starting with more open-ended questions. You will then be able to progress to more specific detail by using 5 'Wh' questions, the 'Who? What? When? Where? Why?' and 1 'H' question, How?' (see 24.4.4). This will be followed by closed confirmatory questions. The type of question therefore changes as the interviewer progresses down the basic questioning hierarchy shown in the diagram.

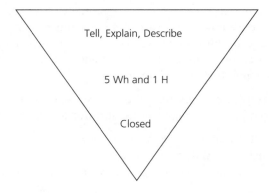

By using questions in a structured sequence, you will develop a systematic and detailed approach to information gathering.

There is no uniform definition of question types and classes, but a few simple concepts should be borne in mind, for example whether a particular question is 'open' or 'closed' and whether it is 'productive' or 'counter-productive' (Shepherd, 2007). Open questions (those which normally cannot be answered with a simple yes or no) are preferable, and generally more productive, as they invite a fuller, richer response. The interviewer should ensure that the interviewee provides as much detail as possible in his/her own words, as this makes any potential evidence more powerful. Leading questions can cause a person to overstate or understate a point, so should be avoided.

In a suspect interview, to prove the *mens rea* (see 4.3.2) the interviewer might ask an open question, for instance starting with 'Explain how you were feeling when you ...?' or 'Tell me what you were thinking when you were ...?'. Open questions such as 'Explain in detail what happened to you last night?' can be very productive as they can initiate a lengthy free narrative. Closed questions can be equally productive too, for example 'Did you assault Donald?' could lead the suspect to replying 'Yes, I did, he was asking for it ...', and providing a detailed explanation of why.

25.3   **What is an Investigative Interview?**

There are a number of definitions of an interview; the one most often used by trainee officers is provided in PACE Code C, para 11.1A. This states that an interview is 'The questioning of a person regarding their involvement or suspected involvement in a criminal offence or offences which, under Code C paragraph 10.1, must be carried out under caution'. However, this definition does not include interviews with witnesses, nor does it provide us with any real focus to the process. To maximize the information gathered, we also need to recognize the importance of the key component of an interview, namely the two-way conversational process (see 25.5.2).

The common element in all investigative interviews, with a witness, victim, or suspect, is face-to-face communication between two persons. The interviewer must therefore be aware that the conversational process is central to the success of the encounter, and that social skill and appropriate conversational behaviour will affect the outcomes of the interview (see 25.2.2). The SE3R approach (Shepherd, 2008) is also widely used ('Survey, Extract, Read, Review,

Respond') This can help the interviewer to gain a fuller and more detailed understanding of the relevant events.

Police forces in England and Wales use the 'PEACE' approach to interviewing: Planning and Preparation; Engage and Explain; Account, Clarification, and Challenge; Closure and Evaluation (CoP, 2013q). Each of these elements will be considered in turn, but the detail will depend on whether the interview is with a suspect or a witness. The key points to consider are as follows:

- **the objectives** (what is to be achieved and how: remember, the emphasis is on establishing the truth (see Chapter 24 on investigation));
- **the relevant** law (eg recent stated cases, and intention, effect of drink/drugs on intention, recklessness, etc);
- possible **defences** (eg statutory defences, reasonableness, mistake, coercion, duress, self-defence);
- possible mitigating and aggravating factors; and
- the **pre-interview briefing** (to solicitors or legal representatives: see 25.5.4).

We devote considerable time to looking at the preliminaries, because establishing an appropriate tone, mood, and format for an interview from the very start is beneficial to the overall process. Most interviewees will not know what is happening and may need reassurance; some may have never even been in a police station before.

Evaluations of the use of PEACE by police forces in England and Wales have been provided by Clarke and Milne (2001) and Walsh and Milne (2008). In the latter case, the two researchers found particular concerns with rapport building and the lack of summarizing during the interview. Clarke, Milne, and Bull looked at PEACE interviewing again in 2011 and found that further improvement in training was required, particularly in terms of the communication skills of interviewers (Clarke *et al*, 2011). It might be worth thinking about this as you read through the rest of this chapter.

Further information on the history of PEACE together with a detailed explanation is provided in *Investigative Interviewing: The conversation management approach* (Shepherd and Griffiths, 2013).

25.3.1 PEACE—planning and preparation

Many aspects of an interview appear to be merely practical issues, but on closer inspection several of these factors could also influence its overall outcome, so careful planning is essential. For example, the number of interviewers present is likely to affect the approach. There is no substitute for careful and detailed planning; every interview is different and every witness, victim, or suspect will behave differently, so interviewers must be prepared for these differences and plan accordingly. The plan should be in writing.

Practical aspects to be covered in the plan include:

- the order of interview, if more than one person is to be interviewed;
- who will be present, and the seating plan (how will this affect communication?);
- the time and location;
- the timing of breaks; and
- how it will be recorded and how the recording will be later used.

For interviews with suspects (see 25.5) there are also statutory considerations, such as recording the interview and the PACE requirements for rest and review times (see the PACE Codes of Practice C, E, and F).

As well as covering the practical aspects, the plan should take into account all the topics that need to be covered; these will be the interview objectives, one of which will be selected as the key objective (see 25.3.1.1). The College of Policing APP suggests that a properly conducted 'wants analysis' will help an investigator in formulating objectives. There is a saying in interviewing, the meaning of which is often overlooked: 'If I know what I want to know, I will know when I have been told it.' At face value this appears obvious, but it can be challenging to actually define what you need to 'know' in order to be able to accept or reject an investigative hypothesis. This always requires careful thought and must be completed prior to the interview.

Investigation and Prosecution

An interview plan helps an interviewer keep track of what has been covered and what remains to be explored. SE3R can be used as an aide-memoire during the interview and will also help you see if the accounts from different interviewees contradict each other or vary significantly from what seem to be the facts. The plan may contain a series of prompts, thereby enhancing topic selection and thoroughness, but these should be used with care to ensure the interviewer appears professional and in control of the interview. Remember also that whatever sort of plan is used, the plan will be 'relevant material' (as set out in the CPIA) and must therefore be retained as a document to be revealed (see 24.3).

Certain information is required about the interviewee in advance as part of the preparation process, for example:

- Has the interviewee's identity been confirmed? A Livescan and IDENT1 check could be used (see 26.5.4).
- How old is he/she? (Establishing the age of a person is not necessarily a simple process. Some adults will claim to be younger in an attempt to avoid prosecution.)
- Is the interviewee on the force's intelligence database? Is he/she suspected of other crimes elsewhere, or flagged as active or of interest to other police forces or agencies (for instance on the PNC or PND)?
- Is he/she already on bail? Is he/she in breach of bail or a court order, or wanted for a crime elsewhere?
- Does the interviewee have any medical or mental health conditions to take into consideration?

Normally the same interview team would conduct all the interviews relating to one incident. However, once the arrest and detention procedures are complete, the responsibility for an interview is sometimes handed over to another investigator (perhaps from a dedicated unit for prisoner handling). In such circumstances, the new investigator will need to be fully briefed so he/she can prepare properly for the interview (see 10.14 on handover procedures). In these situations, SE3R can be used as a tool to assess, analyse, assimilate, and become fully conversant with every detail of a case.

In terms of the general approach, each interviewee is different and will require a different approach. The qualities of an interviewee can be considered in terms of two variables:

- the 'ability' to 'tell', ie what does he/she know that is important and relevant to the investigation;
- the 'willingness' to 'tell', ie the motivation to cooperate.

This can be illustrated as follows:

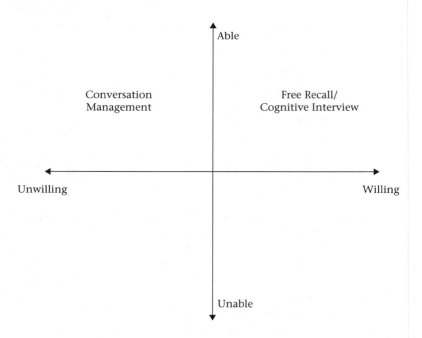

These two variables (willingness and ability) can each vary across their ranges and may change during an interview. If the interviewee has information and is willing to cooperate (ie is 'willing and able'), then a free recall or cognitive style of interview would be most appropriate (see witness interviewing in 25.6). If the person is less willing to cooperate then a more directed, conversation-managed approach should be considered. Both approaches will follow the GEMAC principles (see 25.2.2).

25.3.1.1   Establishing the aims and objectives of the interview

The aim of the investigative interview is to establish a detailed explanation (an account), and to compare it to the material facts that have been established from witness(es) or other evidential sources such as CCTV or forensics. For this we will need interview objectives (see 25.3.1.2 for some examples), and one of these should be identified as the key objective. The key objective will provide a useful focus for the interviewer.

When we formulate objectives, we are defining the parameters of the account to be obtained from an interviewee, and we are seeking to obtain detailed information that can be used to test the reliability and truthfulness of the account given and of other accounts and evidence. For example, we may have physical evidence from the scene of a road traffic collision in the form of a skid mark left by a motorcycle; this indicates the motorcycle is likely to have been moving at a high speed and that the wheel locked. If we obtain witness testimony from the driver of a vehicle overtaken by the motorcycle (indicating a similarly high speed and reckless behaviour), this would put the physical evidence into context and would also help corroborate it. All this information in turn could be used to deconstruct the motorcyclist's account; he stated that he was adhering to the rules of the Highway Code. This illustrates how one interview (in this case with a witness), can inform an interview with another person (in this case with the suspect).

25.3.1.2   Planning the questions

Questions are arguably the principal tool of the interviewer (see 25.2.3). The interviewer's questions will shape the response of the interviewee and the conversational turn-taking (see 25.2.2). The opening questions of the interview are very important as these tend to set the 'agenda' and tone for the rest of the interview and, to a certain extent, dictate interviewing tactics. The first questions should reflect the key objective(s) for the interview. For example, imagine that the interview concerns a case where a man is accused of stealing a chocolate bar from a shop. He was observed to enter the shop, walk to the confectionery display, look furtively over each shoulder, select a chocolate bar, and place it into his pocket. He then walked calmly from the store and was challenged and detained by a member of staff outside, where a chocolate bar was recovered from his pocket.

From this we can identify many key material facts:

- he was inside the shop;
- he carried out various actions inside the shop;
- he walked from the shop;
- he had a chocolate bar in his possession when stopped.

The aim of the interview will be to establish his account in detail, so our interview objectives here could be:

- Explain (in detail) his reason for going to the shop.
- Explain (in detail) his actions inside the shop prior to approaching the confectionery display.
- Explain (in detail) his actions at the confectionery display.
- Explain (in detail) his route after leaving the confectionary display.
- Explain (in detail) his possession of the chocolate bar.
- Explain (in detail) what he was thinking at each of the above points in the chronology.

Note that these are not specific questions but are instead 'questioning areas' that can be developed conversationally by the interviewer who now '... *knows what he/she wants to know* ...'.

The key objective here would probably be 'Explain (in detail) the man's possession of the chocolate bar'. This provides a starting point for the conversation and can be used to formulate an opening question such as 'Tell me in detail how the chocolate bar came to be in your pocket?' or 'Explain in detail how the chocolate came to be in your pocket when you were stopped outside the shop?' Both of these questions are open-ended and both address the key objective. By starting with the correctly selected key objective, the interviewee is drawn towards focusing on the most important issues, which in turn can be used to develop the other objectives. Once all the objectives have been met (in detail), the interviewer has established an account that can be tested against other evidence to determine the reliability and truthfulness of the interviewee's account, which was the overall aim of the interview.

25.3.1.3 Using bad character evidence

Interviewers must carefully assess at the planning stage whether any relevant bad character evidence (BCE, see 24.2.5.2) will be raised. The previous behaviour would have to be relevant to issues in the current investigation. For example, having many theft convictions would add very little to an assault case where the key issue was whether the suspect intended to commit GBH. BCE can be used by interviewers to rebut an innocent explanation, to suggest untruthfulness, or even to demonstrate that the suspect committed the crime on the basis of 'unlikelihood of coincidence'. (For example, a person's offending history might make it seem more likely that he/she is the offender for the current offence (*R v McAllister* [2009] 1 Cr App R 129).) This type of bad character evidence was used in the conviction of Levi Bellfield for the murder of Amanda ('Milly') Dowler (*R v Bellfield*, 2011).

There are no hard-and-fast rules as to when to raise such issues in interview, but it does make sense to include them in the plan as a separate objective to explore, once other objectives have been fully covered. Then each previous conviction or incidence of behaviour can be explored in fine grain detail until all relevant areas have been discussed. Any similarities or other reasons for raising the material should be discussed within the interview.

25.3.2 PEACE—engage and explain

The aim of this phase of the interview is to create an environment that encourages the interviewee to cooperate with the interview process. It builds upon the 'greeting' phase (see 25.2.2) and seeks to establish a productive social and conversational dynamic for the encounter. This is known as 'set induction' and has two important aspects.

1. Orientation of the interviewee regarding the context of the encounter, and orientation towards the task in hand and the expected outcomes.
2. Behaviours required by both parties to undertake the agreed mutual activity.

The interviewer should explain what is going to happen and how things will proceed, as this will help to reassure and relax the interviewee and provide the correct conversational dynamic for the encounter. If the interviewee understands exactly what the interviewer is trying to achieve, and what is expected from him/her in terms of content and detail (and why), then it is more likely that this will be achieved. It will also help to reduce anxiety in the interviewee, and he/she will probably perform better and be more likely to provide the information the interviewer requires. Adopting a consultative and non-threatening manner will improve the chances of the interviewee cooperating; this is vital as encouraging the person to talk is a primary aim of the interview process. The interviewer should definitely not read from a plan as this does not help build a rapport and is likely to convey a general lack of competence and professionalism (see 5.11 on communication).

In this stage of a PEACE interview, the interviewer should:

- establish a rapport by including introductions, concerns, considerations, and by using appropriate humour. This will help establish common ground and hopefully create a cooperative atmosphere;
- **explain the reasons for the interview** (for a suspect, this should include an explanation of the alleged offence, the grounds for arrest, and that the interview provides an opportunity for the suspect to put his/her account of what happened, and for the police to seek the truth);
- **set out the route map**—what happens during and after the interview process, and the general (not the specific) line of questioning;
- **describe the routines**—depending on the nature of the interview this might include explaining why certain persons are present, the recording procedures, the need for interviewers to refer to their notes and make further notes, the production of exhibits, etc;

- **state the expectations**—ground rules such as no over-talking or interruptions, politeness, time to think, and the need to seek clarification of questions and answers; and
- **explain the interviewee's legal rights** and the role of the solicitor and legal advisers.

For suspect interviews, any significant statements or silences must be put to him/her at the start of the interview in compliance with the PACE Codes of Practice (Code C 11.4). Suspect interviews are covered in more detail in 25.5.

Setting the right tone is very important: not all interviewees and suspects are guilty. The rule of thumb would be to treat people as you would wish to be treated yourself. For each interviewee any cultural or behavioural factors should be noted and taken into account. For example, asking directly how he/she wishes to be addressed might provide an easy ice-breaker at the beginning of the interview. An interviewer could also offer the interviewee a cup of tea or other refreshment (if available—there is a certain loss of face otherwise!).

25.3.3 PEACE—account, clarifications, and challenge

This is the main part of the interview. The interviewer should first seek a 'free' account, without any interruption if possible, focusing on the key objective(s). The account should then be developed by conversational probing of what has been said, moving systematically from one objective to another, clarifying or seeking greater detail (see 25.2.3 and 25.3.1.2 on questioning skills and planning questions). Turnbull and the ADVOKATE checklist could be used here, if appropriate (see 10.5.3). Each objective should be explored in 'fine grain detail', thus exhausting relevant questions on that objective before moving on to another.

A good strategy to develop is using the interview objective as a conversational 'opener', and to let a free narrative develop. The ongoing narrative can then be used to formulate the next question. This will create a continuous sequence where each question will seem to flow from what the person has already said. The interview will feel more like a natural conversation, where the interviewer is really listening to what the interviewee says (see 25.2.2 on interviews as a type of conversation). This is almost always more productive than a disjointed series of questions and answers. It requires great concentration on the part of the interviewer and needs practice, and, as you might expect, appropriate training from a skilled practitioner.

The account should then be summarized before selecting the topics that are relevant, in dispute, and checkable. These will then be examined in greater detail. To clarify the account the interviewer may need to seek new/additional information, before summarizing again, with commitment and agreement if possible. The account should make chronological sense. The account and 'topic phase' of the interview should establish the interviewee's full and detailed account.

25.3.3.1 Challenging

Once the complete account is established it can be compared with the evidence, and any inconsistencies can be challenged. Challenging should be restricted to inconsistencies and facts (that can be checked and proved, and are also admissible). The interviewer should take care not to criticize or accuse—but should instead ask for explanation where discrepancies emerge. The challenge phase should not be a confrontation; even hard-to-answer questions can be asked in a socially skilled and conversational manner. The interviewer must also consider whether a special warning is needed, see 25.5.9.

One effective conversational method of challenging is to:

1. Confirm the detail given by the interviewee in the account.
2. Reveal the detail that contradicts or is inconsistent with any aspect of other details.
3. Ask an open-ended question.

This approach can be illustrated in a suspect interview as follows (where I is the interviewer, S is the suspect, and detail X is contradicted by information Y):

   I: In your earlier account you said X (detail), do you agree? [Point 1 above]
   S: Yes
   I: The evidence shows Y. How do you explain that? [Points 2 and 3 above]

The suspect then needs to account for the inconsistency, and this can then be further probed. The interviewer should listen carefully, because the suspect may now start changing his/her account (which should have been fully developed, summarized, and agreed in the topic phase of the interview). An interviewer can be robust and persistent in line with the seven principles (see 25.2) without being confrontational and oppressive.

> **TASK 1** The 'cognitive interview' (CI) technique can be used to help the interviewee's recall, particularly for witness interviews. Find out about the key features of this interview method.

25.3.3.2 The importance of breaks

Breaks are useful for making arrangements and gathering thoughts, particularly if the interview has taken an unexpected turn; the plan may need to be revised. It may be useful to plan breaks as follows:

- Account Phase—use the key objective and develop a detailed account.
- Break—analyse information, review plan, undertake relevant fast-track actions.
- Topic Phase—develop topics that are relevant, checkable, and in dispute.
- Break—analyse information, review plan, undertake relevant fast-track actions, plan challenges.
- Challenge Phase.

After a break it is good practice to summarize what has been said and to invite the interviewee to comment on the accuracy of the summary. This demonstrates that the interviewer has been listening carefully and has realized the significance of what has been said, and that the interviewee is being taken seriously.

25.3.4 PEACE—closure

The interviewer should aim to maintain the good rapport built up during an interview as it might be necessary to interview the same person again. Closure is one of the stages in the GEMAC conversation model (see 25.2.2). Before finishing the interview, the interviewer should:

- review the interviewee's account in full;
- allow the interviewee the chance to correct, confirm, deny, alter, or add to his/her account;
- ensure that all the planned objectives and topics have been covered;
- check whether the interviewee (or the solicitor, if present) wants to ask any questions; and
- explain what will happen in the future.

The interview can then be formally closed. This is likely to include recording the time when the interview finishes. For interviews with suspects, there are additional requirements relating to recording the interview (see 25.5.7).

25.3.5 PEACE—evaluation

The evaluation stage includes what has been achieved, and how well the interviewer's aims and objectives were met. The interviewer should refer to his/her plan and reflect on what went well, what might have gone better, and (for next time) which areas he/she would try to develop or improve. The following questions might be relevant.

- Have other reasonable lines of enquiry (such as an alibi) been discovered?
- Are other forensic opportunities now apparent?
- Have all the points to prove from the offence under investigation been covered?
- Have the statutory defences, mitigation, or explanation, perhaps pointing to innocence been considered?
- Have the objectives been achieved?
- Does the interview add to the investigation as a whole?
- Have the requirements of the CPIA been satisfied?
- How have I performed, and what can I learn from this interview to develop my skills?

Trainee police officers should assess their personal level of skills and knowledge about interviewing and use this in their assessment portfolios. All interviewers should regularly evaluate their performance to ensure continuing professional development.

25.4 The Needs of the Interviewee

Many suspects will be anxious and want to know what is going to happen next and in the longer term. The common questions are 'Will I be released?', 'Will I get bail?', and 'How long will I be here?' Remember that there is a presumption in law that a suspect will be bailed or 'released under investigation' (RUI), and that any bail periods will be generally limited to 28 days (Policing and Crime Act 2017). These arrangements may be changed in the near future, as the matter is currently under discussion.

If the suspect asks such questions the interviewer should explain that he/she cannot determine the decisions of the custody officer or the CPS reviewing lawyer. Obviously, there should be no attempt to gain a confession through promise of favours such as early release or bail, as this could render any subsequent confession inadmissible at court. (Further information on admissibility is provided in 25.5.1.2.)

25.4.1 Meeting the needs of all interviewees

The interviewer and the custody officer should be alert to the special circumstances involved in interviewing a person with a physical impairment, a mental health condition, a mental disorder, or other possible vulnerability (see Chapter 13 on vulnerability). They should always try to ascertain the nature and extent of the vulnerability, although the individual may or may not be willing to divulge it.

There were major changes to PACE Code C in 2018, partly as a result of police failures in identifying suspects as vulnerable. It is now insufficient to rely on the suspect's opinion regarding his/her own vulnerability when determining whether an 'appropriate adult' is required (see 25.5.1.1). Code C, para 1.4 makes it clear that reasonable enquiries should be made to ascertain what information is available. Furthermore, if at any time an officer has any reason to suspect that a person may be vulnerable, in the absence of clear evidence to dispel that suspicion, that person shall be treated as such. In the case of *R v Aspinall (Paul James)* [1999] MHLR 12, the failure to follow the requirements to have an appropriate adult in the interview of a mentally disordered suspect meant that, despite his apparent lucidity in interview, it was unfair to admit material from the interview as evidence.

For a profoundly deaf individual a 'signer' may be required. A partially deaf person will find it easier if he/she can see the interviewer's face in order to lip-read, and people should speak one at a time. A deaf person's attention could be attracted by lightly touching his/her sleeve. The force Diversity and Inclusion Team may be able to provide Braille texts that explain, for example, a suspect's rights, the caution, and the management of the disks after interview (note, however, that not all visually-impaired people can read Braille).

Other impairments, such as speech impediments, may be more difficult to deal with, but interviewers should always be sensitive to the individual's needs and requirements and should try to satisfy these needs. The simple question is: 'Have I done all I can to ensure that this person is not disadvantaged in any way because of a vulnerability or impairment?' If this is the case, then all reasonable steps have been taken. No one should be placed at a disadvantage in a police interview because of physical or mental vulnerability; the criminal justice system is not well served unless this principle is upheld.

25.5 Interviews with Suspects

A suspect interview is defined as 'the questioning of a person regarding his/her involvement or suspected involvement in a criminal offence or offences which must be carried out under caution' (PACE Code C, para 11.1A). This applies to *any* conversation once a caution has been given, and it is irrelevant whether or not the suspect has been arrested. Not all suspects are arrested, for example a suspect on the street being reported for a road traffic offence (see 10.13.1.1), or a suspect who volunteers to be interviewed to assist with the investigation of an offence.

Suspects who have been arrested must always be interviewed at a police station (PACE Code C, para 11.1), unless the requirements for an 'urgent interview' are met (see 25.5.10). Suspects who have not been arrested and who volunteer to be interviewed to assist with an investigation are normally interviewed at a police station, but could be interviewed at another suitable location. Suspects being reported for a minor road traffic offence are usually interviewed at the roadside (under caution, with the suspect's full rights and entitlements fully set out).

25.5.1 General rights of the suspect

The suspect has the normal rights of being treated with dignity, fairness, and objectivity, and the right to free independent legal advice (FILA) during interview, and for a vulnerable person, an 'appropriate adult' should also be present (see 25.5.1.1). A number of laws and associated codes regulate the process of police interviews, in order to protect the interviewee. The suspect should be assessed as 'fit for interview'. If a suspect appears to be ill, hurt, or suffering from a psychological condition a doctor or custody nurse will make this decision, but it can be decided on the person's own say so, supported by the custody officer's independent observations.

Unquestionably, there have been many instances in the past of the police abusing their powers to question suspects (some of which may have been motivated in part by the so-called 'noble cause corruption' discussed in 5.5.4). This could range from using oppressive behaviour to obtain confessions under duress (see 25.5.1.2), to a lack of safety provisions when interviewing a vulnerable person. The custody officer and the suspect's legal adviser both have a responsibility to monitor the suspect's rights and the process of interviewing, and there are now far fewer opportunities for foul play. The rights should be fully explained to the suspect, and reinforced with a written explanation.

The EU Directive 2012/13/EU enhances the rights of suspects at police stations and covers the right to information in criminal proceedings. It enshrines the right of a suspect to:

- information concerning procedural rights (eg rights to free legal advice and to remain silent);
- information relating to the reason for arrest and the suspected offence; and
- access to case file material that relates to the legality of the arrest (Cape, 2015).

So, as soon as the custody officer becomes aware of the existence of material relevant to the legality or otherwise of the arrest, he/she must communicate this information to the suspect. This will allow the defence to make submissions to the custody officer (and beyond) regarding the suspect's continued detention.

Cape (2015) suggests that decisions about how much information is provided to a suspect and/or his solicitor prior to interview (see 25.5.4) can be problematic. The amended PACE Code C 11.1A states:

> they and, if they are represented, their solicitor must be given sufficient information to enable them to understand the nature of [the suspected] offence and why they are suspected of committing it, in order to allow for the effective exercise of the rights of the defence.

R v Roble [1997] Crim LR 449 states that a legal adviser must be in a position to 'usefully advise his client'. Interviewers have discretion when deciding which material will be disclosed to the legal adviser prior to interview, and will need to consider the matter carefully at the planning stage. This area has produced some interesting case law (see *R v Howell* [2003] EWCA Crim 01 and *R v Knight* [2003] EWCA Crim 1977).

25.5.1.1 The presence of an 'appropriate adult'

The PACE Act 1984, Code C, para 3.15 states that an 'appropriate adult' must be provided for any suspect who is a juvenile (under 18) or who is vulnerable. The definition of vulnerable has been significantly widened to also include any suspect who, because of a mental health condition or mental disorder, may, among other things, have difficulty in understanding the full implications for him/her in relation to his/her arrest, detention, or questioning, or be prone to becoming confused or unclear about the situation. PACE Code C, para 1.13d provides a full definition of vulnerable, but see also Chapter 13 on vulnerability.

The role of the appropriate adult is to safeguard the rights, entitlements, and welfare of a suspect (PACE Code C, para 1.7A). He/she will support, advise, and assist the suspect when:

- the suspect is given or is asked to provide information or participate in any procedure;
- observe whether the police are acting properly and fairly;

- assist the suspect to communicate with the police whilst respecting the suspect's right to choose to say nothing; and
- help the suspect to understand his/her rights and ensure that those rights are protected and respected.

PACE Code C, para 1.7 sets out the categories of person who can be an appropriate adult. In the case of a juvenile, it would generally be the parent or guardian. If the juvenile is in the care of a local authority or voluntary organization, it would be a person representing that authority or organization. A social worker may stand *in loco parentis* (in the place of a parent). As a last resort, any responsible person aged 18 or over who is not a police officer or employed by the police may act as the appropriate adult.

For a person who is vulnerable, an appropriate adult should be a relative, guardian, or other person responsible for his/her care and custody. Alternatively, it could be someone experienced in dealing with vulnerable persons, such as an approved mental health professional (AMHP) or a specialist social worker. Any appropriate adult needs to be truly appropriate in order to perform the role. Therefore, for a vulnerable adult, it cannot be any responsible person aged 18 or over who is not a police officer or police employee, but one that is appropriate to deal with that vulnerability.

Some categories of people cannot be the appropriate adult. PACE Code of Practice C, Note 1B states:

> A person, including a parent or guardian, should not be an appropriate adult if they are: suspected of involvement in the offence; the victim; a witness; involved in the investigation, or have received admissions prior to attending to act as the appropriate adult.

The appropriate adult will be invited to sign the custody record to show that he/she understands the responsibilities involved. (The interviewer should check that this has been done before the interview begins.) An interview involving an appropriate adult may take longer, especially if it also involves interpretation, for example by a signer. Translation from one language to another generally doubles the time taken for an interview, so allowances should be made for this. An extended time-frame can have advantages, however, in that the interviewee has more time to consider his/her replies. The interviewer will also have more time to observe and consider the suspect's non-verbal communication (NVC) and demeanour (although of course any interpretations must always allow for cultural and linguistic diversity, see 5.11.2).

25.5.1.2 Confessions, oppression, and unfairness

Any statement that is in any way adverse to a person (eg admitting to a crime or even to being present at the scene of a crime) can amount to a confession under s 82 of the PACE Act 1984. The statement can be made to any person, not just a police officer, and can include written or spoken words, actions, or even silence. However, even if a person confesses in one of these recognized ways, the evidence might not be admissible in court. The defence can argue that a confession should be rendered inadmissible because:

- it was, or may have been obtained by oppression (s 76 PACE);
- something was said or done that is likely to render the confession unreliable (s 76 PACE) (eg inducements were offered, threats were made, or the caution was not properly given);
- the manner in which the evidence was obtained means it is unfair to admit it (s 78 PACE); or
- it is too prejudicial to admit it (eg if the offender has previously confessed to a similar but more serious offence, the bench or the jury might not fully consider the evidence in the current case) (s 82 PACE).

Many of the unfair practices that were adopted in the past by the police to secure a 'confession' from a suspect in custody have been identified and made less likely, if not impossible, by legislation and practice guidelines.

Oppression usually means behaviour akin to breaching a person's human rights under Article 3 of the ECHR (this refers to torture, inhumane or degrading treatment, or the use or threat of violence). Case law has widened the definition of oppression to include 'exercise of authority in a burdensome, harsh or wrongful manner' (*R v Fulling* [1987] 2 All ER 65), as well as:

> questioning which by its very nature, duration or other circumstances (including the fact of custody) excites hope (such as the hope of release) or fears, or so affects the mind of the subject that his will

crumbles and he speaks when otherwise he would have stayed silent (*R v Prager* [1972] 1 WLR 260, 266, adopted by the House of Lords in *R v Mushtaq* [2005] UKHL 25).

This latter definition can encompass many situations, and is often used by defence solicitors. If the court or the defence raise the issue of oppression, the prosecution must prove beyond reasonable doubt that it was not used to obtain the confession.

Inducements to confess could include offers to grant bail, or for the police to refrain from arresting family members. Threats could be suggesting that bail would not be granted or that family members might be arrested.

Section 78 of the PACE Act 1984 underpins many strategies used by defence solicitors. It allows for any potential prosecution evidence to be rendered inadmissible (not just confessions, see *R v Mason* [1987] 3 All ER 481). To use s 78, the defence has to show that the manner in which the evidence was obtained means it should not be admitted as it would be unfair to the proceedings. The defence might argue, for instance, that DNA evidence should not be admissible because the prosecution has not proven continuity of the evidence from the moment it was found to the moment it was examined at the laboratory (implying that it might have been contaminated). Note, therefore, that if a s 76 argument does not succeed the defence could argue that a confession should be rendered inadmissible under s 78 instead.

The Halliwell case is a recent example of where the suspect's rights were denied (Cox, 2012). A superintendent was judged to have breached PACE by interviewing the suspect in circumstances that were oppressive, and that deliberately denied him his rights (both ss 76 and 78 PACE arguments were employed by the defence). Halliwell was arrested for the abduction of Sian O'Callaghan, but some of the interviews were conducted prior to arrival at a police station under the guise of an urgent interview (see 25.5.10). However no caution was given, and he was questioned without a solicitor (without Halliwell's agreement). He confessed to the murder of O'Callaghan and another woman, Becky Godden, and was subsequently charged with both murders. After lengthy legal arguments at the start of the trial, however, all of Halliwell's confessions were ruled inadmissible and the second murder case failed. The O'Callaghan case continued based upon other evidence, and Halliwell was convicted. There was extensive media coverage and an IPCC investigation ensued. The superintendent was found guilty of gross misconduct for the breaches, and was given a final written warning.

25.5.2 Planning suspect interviews

As well as the general PEACE considerations for planning interviews covered in 25.3.1, other factors apply for suspect interviews, such as:

- the legal framework for interviews with suspects;
- the suspect's right to a free independent legal adviser, and for the adviser to be present throughout the interview; and
- the arrangements for recording the interview.

These requirements need to be covered in the interview plan. The interviewer also needs to consider what defences the suspect might employ and how these might be countered.

One of the first things to consider for a suspect interview is what potential offence or offences are being investigated. Remember that, if an offence has actually occurred, the following must be proved.

1. **Criminal intent** (*mens rea*): What was in the suspect's mind at the time? Why did he/she commit the offence?
2. **Criminal action** (*actus reus*): What did he/she actually do? How did he/she do it?

For each offence the following will be required: the points to prove, the evidence that the suspect committed the offence, case law, and the specific parts of the criminal law under which the suspect may be charged. The relevant legislation should be consulted and the key points established. Information such as witness accounts or statements should be considered as they will help clarify what is required from the interview.

25.5.3 Defence solicitors

The defence solicitor is the defendant's legal adviser. He/she is obliged to prevent the defendant from further assisting the police by way of self-incrimination, if that is not in the defendant's interest (PACE Code C, Note 6D). The solicitor's only role in the police station is to protect and advance the legal rights of his/her client (PACE Code C, Note 6D).

A 'duty solicitor' is drawn from a retained panel of solicitors who are available to advise an arrested person who does not have a solicitor of his/her own available for the interview. They provide 'free and independent legal advice' (FILA) and are there to advise their clients at any time. They are of course independent of the police and the CPS. The custody officer will make the initial contact with the solicitor, following a request from the detained suspect (see 10.10), and the interviewer will then become the point of contact for the defence solicitor. (Note that confidential handover documents or witness statements should not be attached to the custody record.)

25.5.3.1 Active defence

A solicitor might adopt an 'active defence' role (Ede and Shepherd, 2000). If the evidence looks weak or merely circumstantial, the solicitor will probably advise the suspect to remain silent or to submit a jointly prepared statement. It is sometimes difficult for a trainee officer to accept that a solicitor can advise a suspect against providing details about a crime or admitting guilt, and more experienced interviewers may also argue that there is no 'level playing field'. It is important to recognize that these are emotional reactions, and should be set aside. It is essential to remain objective and focused on the real evidence. There may be sound reasons for a legal adviser to advise the suspect to remain silent or reply 'no comment', for example there may have been very little disclosed during the pre-interview briefing (see 25.5.4). The decision to make 'no comment' and the possible reasons could be examined by the court (see eg *R v Howell* [2003] EWCA Crim 01), and the jury may be suspicious about a suspect's silence at interview (see 25.5.9.2 on adverse inference).

Sometimes an admission of guilt is better for the client, especially if there is strong or irrefutable evidence, or strong mitigation (an excuse or reason for what has been done). The solicitor might try to dominate an interview (an accepted tactic), particularly if the interviewer seems to lack experience or is unprofessional. If a solicitor is disruptive there is a risk of 'losing the interview', and the interviewer may therefore need to speak out and take control (a good command of the relevant areas of PACE Code C, Notes 6D and 6E will be needed). However, it is very rare for a police interviewer to have to stop the interview and seek to have the solicitor excluded under PACE Code C, para 6.9. In any case, the whole interview is recorded; the court will undoubtedly take a negative view of a disruptive solicitor, and this might even prejudice the suspect's defence.

25.5.4 Briefing a solicitor before an interview

Before the interview begins the solicitor must be briefed (provided with the relevant information) so that his/her client may be usefully advised (see *R v Roble* [1997] Crim LR 449). The interviewer must plan what to disclose, considering:

- what is the evidence?
- what evidence should be disclosed immediately or withheld (at least for the time being)?
- at what stage of the interview will particular evidence be disclosed?
- can the withholding of all/some/any evidence be justified (see *R v Imran & Hussain* (1997))?

Any evidence derived solely from intelligence should not be included in the pre-interview briefing, as the protection of sources is an important consideration. Forensic evidence, or details of a particular MO, can be disclosed at the discretion of the interviewer, being mindful of the amount of detail revealed and how this could be used by the suspect to construct a false alibi or defence. The interviewer can seek advice and guidance about what to disclose from a supervisory officer or qualified interview adviser. In some situations, a fuller disclosure might facilitate a frank and productive interaction between the suspect and the police—the skill is to recognize the situations where fuller disclosure would be beneficial. Where the disclosure is limited, the solicitor is more likely to ask difficult questions and to advise the suspect to remain silent at interview. If further material is disclosed during an interview, the solicitor is likely to immediately ask for a private consultation with his/her client. These consequences should be considered and planned for.

There are two major warnings that must be heeded when briefing the solicitor: never overstate or understate the evidence, and never express a view on the likely outcome for the client.

Investigation and
Prosecution

The case of *R v Mason* [1987] 3 All ER 481 is a good example of where a solicitor was misled (as well as the suspect). Police told both of them that the suspect's finger marks had been found on a broken bottle from the scene of an arson attack, but this was not true. The court took a dim view of investigators having deliberately lied to an officer of the court (the solicitor), and rendered Mason's subsequent admissions as inadmissible under s 78 of the PACE Act 1984.

Ideally, the interviewer and the defence solicitor will meet in a quiet room, and there will be no interruptions. However, they will sometimes end up discussing the matters in a busy corridor, or by phone, which makes it more difficult. At the start of the briefing the interviewer should explain that he/she will invite the solicitor to ask any questions once the disclosure of evidence is complete. Sufficient time should be allowed for the solicitor to take notes, although a video-recording will be made in serious cases. The case against the suspect should be outlined, including the evidence upon which the interview will be based, and up-to-date information about the welfare of the client should also be provided.

Then the solicitor can be invited to ask questions; this needs careful handling, as being over-defensive and disclosing only in response to the solicitor's questions may increase the likelihood of a 'no comment' interview. The interviewer must, however, also guard against saying too much. A solicitor may try different tactics, such as switching abruptly from questions about evidence to questions about other aspects of the case. The interviewer needs to remain calm and self-possessed, and will of course be able to deal more confidently with such situations if he/she knows all the details of the case, and has a thorough understanding of the relevant law.

A written record must be kept of the details that have been disclosed, including the additional questions asked by the solicitor and any responses provided, so that the CPS can be informed of the contents of the briefing on the MG06A form (see 27.4.2 on MG forms). The disclosure process can also be video-recorded, and a copy given to the solicitor. This is common in serious offences and is also advocated by the Law Society to ensure transparency and ethical practice by all parties. Such a recording may be crucial evidence in arguing there has been recent fabrication, particularly when a solicitor has advised 'no comment' on the basis of there having been little or no disclosure of information.

25.5.5 The start of a suspect interview

The time spent on engaging and building rapport with the suspect, explaining what is going to happen, and following the procedures properly may all prove productive later on. In addition, no irregularities will have been provided for the solicitor to use in the defence of his/her client.

There is a legal requirement for certain information to be mentioned at the start of the interview (see PACE Code E paras 3.4–3.7), for example the time, date, and location of the interview. Before asking any questions about the offence (or after any break), the interviewer must caution the suspect (see PACE Code C, paras 10.8 and 11.4) and check his/her understanding of the caution. A detailed account of the various cautions and their use is given in 10.3. It is important that the interviewer is satisfied that the suspect understands the implications of the caution before asking him/her any questions. To that end, the interviewer might say to the suspect, for example:

> You have an absolute right to remain silent if you wish, you do not have to speak to me or answer any of my questions. However, if this matter goes to court and at court you rely on a fact in your defence that the court think you could have reasonably given me here today, then the court are entitled to ask themselves 'why did you not reveal this fact at the time of the interview?' They might think that the facts you give in defence in court are untrue or have been made up since the interview, and they may be less likely to believe you. And remember, everything being said here today is being recorded and could be played in court.

The solicitor should not be asked to explain the caution, or to acknowledge that his/her client understands it—this is the responsibility of the interviewer. The suspect's understanding of the caution should be checked by asking him/her three simple questions, such as:

1. Do you have to answer any of my questions?

2. What might the court think, though, if you tell them something in your defence that you have not told me during interview and the court reasonably believes that you could have done so?

3. Where can this recording be played as proof of what has been said in this interview?

Further information must be provided to the suspect, depending on the circumstances and location of the interview. For example, a suspect who has been arrested and who is being interviewed at a police station must also be reminded that he/she is entitled to free legal advice in person or on the phone, and that the interview can be delayed until it is obtained. Such reminders and the suspect's response should be recorded in the interview record (Code C, para 11.2).

Other information that must be provided to a suspect who has not been arrested is shown in the table.

Circumstances and location of interview with a suspect who has not been arrested	Additional information to be provided to the suspect
Suspect is on the street being reported for an offence	That a failure to cooperate (eg by not providing a name and address when being reported for an offence) could amount to committing a further offence or lead to arrest (Code C, para 10.9)
Suspect has volunteered to assist with the investigation of an offence and is being interviewed	That he/she can leave at any time, and can also obtain free and independent legal advice if he/she agrees to remain (Code C, para 3.21)

Any significant statement (see 10.4) should also be discussed. The suspect must be given the opportunity to clarify, confirm, deny, or add to an earlier statement. Sometimes it may be difficult to distinguish between a significant statement and a 'relevant comment' (again see 10.4), but if there is any doubt, the statement or comment should be put to the suspect at the beginning of the interview, after caution and before questioning.

25.5.6 Tactics during interviews

The interviewer should be polite, rational, and professional, and proceed with the interview as planned. However, interviewees may be hostile and refuse to cooperate. A common temptation for an interviewer in such circumstances is to confront the solicitor or to start rushing the questions, but this must be avoided. The interviewer must not be drawn into asking closed questions (requiring a yes or no reply), or into speeding up, allowing little time for answers (as if a 'no' answer is expected). Nor should the suspect be asked why he/she is not answering the questions. The simple advice in this situation is to adhere to the PEACE model of interviewing, and not to be thrown. Skilful and persistent questioning may slip under a hostile suspect's defences. For example, he/she could be unnerved by a new line of questioning and forget to continue to 'brazen it out' with a repeated 'no comment', and suddenly provide vital evidence or information.

Most defence solicitors, particularly duty solicitors, will have a good understanding and plenty of experience of the PEACE interview model and the approaches that an interviewer is likely to adopt. For example, the solicitor will know that the interviewer will try to build a rapport with the interviewee, but it is very unlikely that he/she will assist with the process. If the interviewer starts with a few informal words about a non-contentious topic (such as whether the suspect would like a drink) to encourage the suspect to open up, the solicitor is likely to challenge its relevance unless it relates directly to the suspect's welfare. Therefore, all opportunities to build a rapport before the interview should be recognized and utilized to the full.

The PACE Codes of Practice provide some guidance on what is acceptable behaviour by the solicitor in an interview. A legal adviser is permitted to seek clarification, offer the client their advice (including to refrain from answering a question), and can also challenge an improper question or the manner in which it is put. A legal adviser may not, however, answer questions on the client's behalf or provide him/her with written responses to quote (see PACE Code C, Notes 6D and 6E.)

The solicitor will also closely monitor the interview process itself. This is because, however overwhelming the evidence, any flaw in police procedure can lead to charges against the suspect being dismissed, or evidence being ruled inadmissible. A solicitor has no obligation to immediately point out any police failing or non-adherence to the appropriate Codes, and may only mention it later when it is of particular advantage to the client, for instance in court. This is one of the reasons why the interviewer needs to know the law and the associated police procedures very well indeed. Asking leading questions, adopting a threatening or bullying manner, or seeking to offer the suspect a lighter sentence in exchange for giving more evidence will all prompt the solicitor to intervene (and rightly so). If, however, the interviewer is acting fairly, proportionately, and properly, then the solicitor's grounds for intervention are much reduced.

25.5.6.1 Prepared statements

The solicitor may present the interviewer with a written 'prepared statement'. This is often written by the solicitor and the suspect, and signed by the suspect. The suspect might then not want to say anything more about the matter and may make this clear at the start of the interview (after the caution). The most appropriate response in such a situation is to temporarily suspend the interview and consider the contents of the statement. It can then be included in a revised interview plan, and the interview restarted. The receipt of a prepared statement does not mean the interview process is over. As an interviewer, you still have the right to ask relevant questions relating to the investigation.

The case of *R v Knight* [2003] EWCA Crim 1977 should be studied by all interviewers as it provides useful guidance on what to do when presented with a prepared statement. If the factual defence is stated in the prepared statement in writing, and the suspect gives oral evidence at court which is wholly in line with the statement, then no adverse inference can be drawn. The case makes it clear that the purpose of s 34 of the Criminal Justice and Public Order Act 1994 is to encourage the early disclosure of a suspect's account (rather than the scrutiny and testing of it by police in interview). Had the latter been intended, Parliament would have used significantly different language, as questioning the contents of a statement would be a significantly greater intrusion into a suspect's general right to silence than the requirement to disclose his factual defence. However, *R v Knight* recognizes that a prepared statement does not give automatic immunity to adverse inference, as the prepared statement might be lacking in detail or deficient in another manner.

All prepared statements should be carefully analysed (eg using SE3R), and any omissions noted. The case of *R v Lewis* [2003] EWCA Crim 223 is particularly relevant in this context. If the prepared statement lacks detail, including explanatory detail, this gives the interviewer the opportunity to ask questions about what is not contained in the statement. In *R v Lewis* it was observed that 'a fact supporting a fact, is also a fact that can reasonably be expected to be mentioned'. The careful analysis of the content then gives rise to new interview objectives, based on information that is not included in the prepared statement. These objectives can then be developed during a further interview, being mindful that it is highly likely this will be a 'no comment' interview.

25.5.7 Recording suspect interviews

The principle of PACE Code E (para 2.1) is that an audio-recording should be made of any interviews under caution with suspects for any offence, but there are some exemptions to this as detailed in 25.5.7.2. Most interviews are now supplemented with a simultaneous visual recording, so Code F will also apply.

25.5.7.1 Recording interviews with suspects who have not been arrested

The information provided to a suspect in order to arrange a voluntary interview is on a par with that provided to an arrested suspect (see PACE Code C, paras 3.21(b) to 3.22). This information and the subsequent consent to the interview must be thoroughly recorded. On arrival for the voluntary interview, a sergeant must conduct a risk assessment on the suspect (similar to the way a custody officer would for an arrested person).

At the start of the interview, the suspect's consent to be interviewed must be confirmed. However, he/she can withdraw consent, and is free to leave at any time (subject to any necessity to then arrest the suspect if that were to be the case under PACE Code G).

PACE Code E, para 2.3 details the circumstances under which a suspect interview would not be audio-recorded as a minimum standard. These include:

- an authorized recording device in working order is not available; or
- such a device is available but a location suitable for using that device to make the audio-recording of the matter in question is not available; and

- the 'relevant officer' (described in para 2.4) considers, on reasonable grounds, that the proposed interview should not be delayed until an authorized recording device in working order and a suitable interview room or other location become available and decides that a written record shall be made.

It is also possible for the interview to be recorded solely in written form if the suspect (or the appropriate adult on his/her behalf) objects to the interview being audibly recorded. The decision to continue recording the interview against the wishes of the suspect may be commented upon in court, as this could be seen as being oppressive (Code E, Note 3D). The evidence could then be rendered inadmissible under s 76 or 78 (see 25.5.1.2).

If the interview takes place other than at a police station, for example at the roadside in relation to a motoring offence, the PNB is the most appropriate place to record such an interview in writing, complying with Code C, para 11.7.

25.5.7.2 Procedures for recording interviews

Audio-recordings of interviews are made using DVDs or secure digital networks, depending on the facilities available. PACE Code E makes various provisions for the use of these different types of media.

For DVD recordings, the sealed disks must be shown to the suspect at the start of the interview to show they are new, sealed, and have not been tampered with. The following information must be recorded as a PNB entry, or on the paper seals to be wrapped around the disks at the end of the interview (see Code C, para 11.7):

- the time, day, date, location of the interview;
- the name, rank, role of the interviewer;
- the name, address, date of birth of the interviewee; and
- the persons present.

When a DVD recorder is first switched on there will be a continuous sound while it is formatting the disks, and this must be explained to the suspect. Two recordings are made simultaneously (sometimes three are made, depending on the equipment). At the end of the interview one of them will be sealed as the 'master recording'. The other(s) will remain with the case file; these are known as the 'working' copy/copies. A further copy will also be provided for the solicitor on request. The master recording is filed by the designated responsible person and will not be opened unless it is needed in exceptional circumstances or is to be examined on the direction of a judge or a senior member of the CPS.

> **TASK 2** Find out what happens to the working copy of the recording

At the end of the interview and before switching off the machine, the interviewer must record the time when the interview finishes. For DVDs, the labels must be signed by everyone present, and the master recording must be sealed in the presence of the suspect. If a suspect or the solicitor refuses to sign the labels, this has to be recorded. (Note that no signing is required for a recording made on a secure digital network.) The suspect should be told what will happen to the recordings, and this is reinforced by handing him/her a pre-written explanation.

Where the interview is recorded onto a secure digital network, Code E makes separate provisions for the start of the interview. In brief, the recording device would need to be switched on as soon as the interviewer enters the room with the suspect; the interviewer must log directly into the secure digital network and commence the recording. The interviewee must be told that the interview is being recorded onto a secure network, that the recording has begun, and of his/her rights of access to it, should a prosecution ensue. At the end of the interview (as with all interviews), he/she will be provided with a notice about the rights of access to the recording. The interviewer should also make a PNB note of the date and time, together with the identification number of the recording.

Interviews are normally visually as well as audio-recorded. PACE Code F states that there is no statutory requirement to do this but suggests circumstances where it should be considered, for example where the suspect is deaf and uses sign language to communicate, where there is a need for an appropriate adult, and where the interviewer wants to invite the suspect to demonstrate his/her actions (Code F, para 2.2).

At the start of a video-recording, the interviewer must explain that a visual recording is going to be made, and then unwrap the DVDs in the presence of the interviewee, load the equipment, and start recording. Similar legal necessities apply to video interviews as for audio interviews (ie cautions and significant statements or silences, etc). The suspect has the right to object to the visual recording at this point; if accepted, the interviewer will explain that the visual recording cannot be completed and then stop the disks (see Code F). The interview will then be recorded using audio-only equipment. Once a video-interview is complete, the DVDs must be sealed in the presence of the interviewee, and the audio-only recording procedures followed.

PACE Code E, para 1.6 extends the range of audio and audio-visual devices that may be used to record suspect interviews. It established the term 'authorised' recording device, which means any device authorized by the chief officer of a force, as long as the interviewer has been trained to use it. This would include the use of body-worn-video (BWV) to record a suspect interview, as long as it meets the above criteria. Even if BWV cannot be used as an authorized device, it is an ideal back-up to a written-only interview record. The contemporaneous written record would be the evidential product, but the video would add transparency to the interview process.

Further details concerning recorded interviews may be found in the 'investigation' area of APP on the College of Policing website. Note that under the PACE Act 1984 there is no requirement to record the suspect's NVC, apart from the interviewer making references to actions.

25.5.8 Taking offences into consideration

Admissions of other offences can sometimes be treated as TICs ('taken into consideration'). These assist police to solve crimes and enable the police to gather essential intelligence relating to criminal activity. For victims they promote 'closure' and allow them to claim compensation. A suspect may wish to tell the police about other offending behaviour in order to 'get it all over and done with', fearing for instance that further evidence of his/her offending behaviour could emerge over time, leading to repeated arrests.

TICs should be discussed with suspects, of that there is no doubt. However, no admissions to crimes should be obtained by inducements or favour (see 25.5.1.2). Safeguards have been put in place to prevent abuse of the TIC system; in the past, some criminals undoubtedly 'assisted' the police by admitting to offences they had not committed, hoping for more lenient treatment. However, the opposite applies—the Sentencing Council (2012b) makes it clear that where a defendant has admitted TICs, the sentence should reflect the totality of the offending. It is legitimate for an interviewer to ask a suspect if he/she wishes any further offences to be taken into consideration, as long as the interviewer adheres to these considerations.

Where a suspect discusses another crime that he/she has committed, the interviewer should obtain sufficient detail of the crime to be able to satisfy the points to prove, as if the case was going to court as a charge. This includes seeking out any evidential material that may already exist, for example forensic evidence. Each subsequent admission should be dealt with in the same manner, providing a thorough and professional response to the investigation of the relevant crime. Interviewers will also need to check whether the admitted crimes have already been reported and recorded, or whether they are new crimes that should be recorded as such. The MG18 form must be completed so that the prosecutor and the court are made aware of any relevant factors, as well as the MG19 form which relates to possible compensation for victims. If the suspect refuses to accept the TICs in court at a later stage, he/she will already have been warned that the offences concerned could be investigated separately.

Sentencing guidelines (issued in 2012) made it clear that TICs are unlikely to be accepted for sexual or violent offences, or for offences more serious than the main charge. If there is any doubt about the appropriateness of certain charges or TICs, advice is available from the CPS (see 27.3), custody officers, and PIP Level 2 investigators. Further information is provided on the CPS website.

25.5.9 Special warnings and adverse inference

Special warnings are used when the suspect fails to, or refuses to, answer questions satisfactorily after due warning. If he/she presents a 'no comment' interview when asked questions, or fails to respond to questions based on special warnings, then at trial a judge may advise the jury that they are entitled to draw an 'adverse inference'.

25.5.9.1 Special warnings

The use of a special warning (ss 36 and 37 of the CJPOA 1994) is, in a sense, a further caution to the suspect and his/her legal adviser. A special warning may be needed for a suspect who has been caught directly in the commission of a crime (*in flagrante* or 'red-handed').

Section 36 warnings relate to a suspect's refusal to account for objects, marks, or substances, or marks on such objects. Further details are shown in the flowchart.

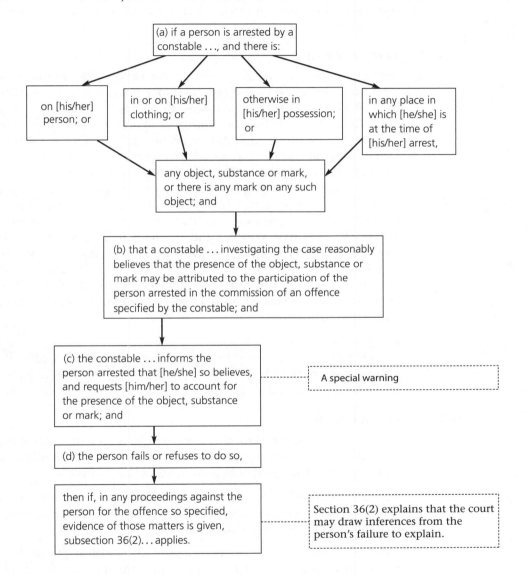

Section 37 warnings relate to the failure of a person to account for his/her presence at a place at or about the time of an alleged offence. If an interviewer believes that the suspect's presence is linked to his/her participation in the offence, then the suspect must be warned that 'adverse inference' could be drawn if no explanation is provided. If a suspect has given a reasonable account of the fact in question, a special warning should not be used as it could be interpreted as oppressive behaviour and the suspect's legal adviser would almost certainly intervene.

The special warning should include the following five points, put in ordinary language which the suspect will understand:

1. the nature of the offence being investigated;
2. the particular fact the suspect needs to account for;

3. that the interviewer believes that the fact arose because the suspect was involved in the offence;
4. that inference may be properly drawn if the suspect fails to account for that specific fact; and
5. that a record of the interview is being made.

Suggested wording and more guidance on special warnings may be found in the 'investigation' area of APP on the College of Policing website. It may be necessary to give several special warnings, if a number of separate material facts have been identified under s 36 or 37.

Once any particular special warning topic has been probed in fine grain detail, it is important that interviewees are made aware of when the special warning no longer applies. Special warnings indicate that he/she needs to explain something, so if he/she does not, an adverse inference can later be drawn at court. When a special warning no longer applies, the interviewee should no longer feel compelled to answer: the normal right to silence would apply.

25.5.9.2 Adverse inference

'Adverse inferences' under ss 34–37 of the CJPOA 1994 can be drawn in court if the defendant presents new significant information. It must be information concerning a fact in his/her defence, that the court would reasonably expect to have been divulged earlier. The information could have been provided at interview following a caution (s 34) or after a special warning (ss 36 and 37), or before the person is charged or reported. The jury would be entitled to ask themselves 'why didn't he/she mention this earlier?' and may conclude that the defendant has recently fabricated the fact, or that the new information is untrue. Therefore, during a police interview the suspect **must** be asked all the relevant questions to cover possible defences. After all, if the crucial grounds for defence were not covered during the interview, then the defence might be able to argue in court that the defendant would have provided the information at interview 'if only he/she had been given the opportunity'. Where an investigator feels that adverse inferences could be drawn as a result of silence or failure to answer questions, the College of Policing APP suggests that an adverse inference package is compiled for the CPS, to highlight where this might be the case. Always seek advice from peers, supervisors, and consult APP guidance before undertaking this work.

> **TASK 3** When should the special warning be used—before caution, during the main questioning phase, or at the end of the interview, as things are being brought to a close?

25.5.10 Urgent interviews

So far in 25.5 we have covered the standard rights and entitlements afforded to people being questioned about involvement or suspected involvement in criminal offences. However, in some very limited circumstances these rights can be withheld.

Normally, this type of interview will involve asking no more than a couple of questions, but is only permitted for indictable only offences and where there are reasonable grounds for believing that the consequent delay might lead to:

- interference with, or harm to, evidence connected with an offence;
- interference with, or physical harm to, other people;
- serious loss of, or damage to, property;
- alerting other people suspected of having committed an offence but not yet arrested for it; or
- hindering the recovery of property obtained in consequence of the commission of an offence.

The interview must cease once the relevant risk has been averted, or the necessary questions have been asked (in order to attempt to avert that risk).

Column one of the table lists the circumstances of the interview, where some normal rights are withheld.

Circumstances of the interview	PACE Code C	Authorization
Prior to arrival at the police station, after arrest	para 11.1	None required, but must be recorded on the custody record
Before suspect has received legal advice, having requested it	para 6.6	Authorization required by an officer of at least the rank of superintendent
No appropriate adult or interpreter (when one is required)	para 11.18	Only authorized in exceptional cases, and if satisfied the interview would not significantly harm the person's physical or mental state.

25.6 Interviews with Witnesses

The PEACE process applies to all interviews (see 25.3) but interviews with witnesses are not governed by the PACE Codes of Practice, so there is more flexibility. Different approaches and techniques for gathering witness testimony can be adopted (eg video- or audio-recording), depending on the category of the witness and the nature of the interview in prospect.

Ideally, interviewers should only know a little about the alleged offence(s) before the interview. This is because too much knowledge might result in the interviewer contaminating the interview by inadvertently introducing information not already mentioned by the witness. Another pitfall can be the interviewer failing to ask all the questions which would be needed to fill any 'gaps' in a witness's account. This can happen when the interviewer subconsciously supplements the account with his/her own knowledge of the offence.

APP suggests that a witness interview strategy should be developed in the early stages of an investigation. Any strategy should consider such issues as:

- appropriate level of interviewer required;
- how the evidence is to be captured (ie audio, video, statement);
- location of interview (ie police station, home address, sexual assault referral centre); and
- any vulnerabilities or particular needs of the witness or victim (see 25.6.2).

The correct strategy is particularly important in complex investigations where there may be a number of victims and witnesses, but can still apply in volume crime cases.

25.6.1 Recording witness interviews

The account from a witness is usually written up on an MG11 as a witness statement (see 10.11). Some categories of witnesses and victims (eg vulnerable or intimidated witnesses, see 24.2.4) are interviewed away from a police station at designated facilities with suitable recording facilities (see 25.6.2).

In a serious crime the interview with a significant witness is often video-recorded to capture his/her initial oral account of events. This has numerous advantages for the investigator; for example, it is less obtrusive and more fluent than the stop/start approach required for a written statement, so the witness may be more forthcoming. In addition, the witness's own words and intonation are recorded, thus reducing the risk of the statement-taker unintentionally influencing the content. A video-recording can also help assess the witness's ability to provide convincing oral evidence from the witness box ('come up to proof')—some witnesses may not be able to perform reliably in court due to nervousness, forgetfulness, or confusion. After the interview a ROVI (record of a video-interview) document may be prepared by the police to help inform decisions on criminal charges, or a full witness statement (MG11) can be prepared. The existence of the video-recording must be revealed (see 24.3) to the CPS. The subsequent use in court of evidence derived from video-recordings is covered in 27.5.2.5. Vulnerable witnesses can be supported by an intermediary which may alleviate communication problems and allow better evidence to be obtained.

25.6.2 Achieving best evidence

Interviews conducted in compliance with Achieving Best Evidence (ABE) guidelines are used for a witness who has been assessed as having a particular vulnerability, or characteristics that will require a particular approach or special measures. The definitions of vulnerable and intimidated witnesses are provided in 24.2.4.1, and vulnerability is covered in Chapter 13. Each witness must be assessed prior to formal interview in order to identify whether ABE procedures are required. Interviewers should use the special measures available so they can offer reassurance in the face of questions from a witness such as 'Will I have to face him in court?' or 'Will everyone be able to hear all this?'

Interviews that are likely to be more difficult or protracted will be conducted by specialist interviewers qualified to at least PIP Level 2, and will follow ABE guidelines. The College of Policing APP makes clear the similarities between the PEACE model of interviewing and ABE. The phases for each have different titles but essentially cover the same ideas. The phases identified in an ABE interview are: establishing rapport, initiating and supporting a free narrative account, questioning, closure (Ministry of Justice, 2011). Guidance is also available regarding the structure of visually recorded interviews with witnesses (NPCC, 2015a), and this should be read in conjunction with the ABE guidance.

Trainee officers may engage with such witnesses in obtaining vital first accounts, or might attend a full interview to brief and assist the interviewers. Where a first account is being obtained, it cannot be stressed enough that it is imperative to ask open, non-leading questions, and to record what the person says verbatim in contemporaneous notes (usually in your PNB).

25.7 Interviews and Criminal Intelligence

An often overlooked by-product of a formal police interview is the 'intelligence interview'. These are used to gather criminal intelligence on the activities and lifestyle of the interviewee and others. It is a separate process from an investigative interview and must be undertaken by specialist intelligence officers. A trainee officer is unlikely to be involved in the detail of any of this, but it helps to know that it happens.

All interviewers should carefully consider whether an interviewee would have access to information about criminals whose criminality comes within the force's strategic intelligence requirement. Such access should be noted and reported to the BCU Intelligence Unit who will arrange for an intelligence interview. This is often carried out by a fully trained intelligence analyst or researcher who does not work 'in the field' (so that other criminals who may be in the vicinity will not recognize him/her). Any interview conducted whilst the subject is in custody (and this is often the only opportunity for a secure approach) must be recorded on the custody record, but there must be no specific reference to the purpose of the interview. The record will simply show the transfer of custody from one investigator to another. In order to enhance confidentiality, intelligence interviews should not be recorded on disk or the secure digital network, and no other people should be present. Any information obtained will be recorded on a 3 × 5 × 2 (see 23.5.2).

An Investigation Anonymity Order (IAO) can be used when a person (other than a witness) can assist the police with relevant information or intelligence, but he/she wants to remain anonymous. It applies for cases involving murder or manslaughter with a firearm or knife, and the suspect must be between 11 and 30 years of age and belong to a group of people of a similar age (Coroners and Justice Act 2009). The group ('gang') should also be identifiable by the types of criminal activity undertaken by its members, and also be likely to use intimidation against a member who provides the police with relevant information about the offence. The legislation is primarily intended to tackle 'gang culture' crime but may in time be extended to cover a wider range of criminal acts. An IAO prohibits the disclosure of information that identifies the person or might lead to his/her identification.

25.8 Answers to Tasks

TASK 1 The 'cognitive interview' uses memory-enhancing techniques such as context reinstatement, which involves recreating the other events that were also encoded at the same time (or before or after) the event of interest. You are probably familiar already with this idea—for example what techniques do you use to locate misplaced keys? If you want to know more about the cognitive interview and other interview techniques then *Investigative*

Interviewing—Psychology and Practice by Rebecca Milne and Ray Bull is a good start (Milne and Bull, 1999). Although CI may be part of PEACE training, it is not often used by investigators in volume crime cases.

TASK 2 A shortened version of the interview will be prepared as a transcript for the reviewing lawyer on an MG15 form (a Short Descriptive Note (SDN)). It is not usual practice for a full transcript (Record of Taped Interview or ROTI) to be made, as this is very time-consuming and therefore costly.

TASK 3 Many police practitioners argue that the best place to use a special warning is after the suspect has had a full opportunity to account for what happened, but has not done so. This would probably be during the 'challenge' phase of the PEACE interview (see 25.3.3.1).

26.1 Introduction

This chapter is concerned with the use of forensic investigation and the role it plays in policing. We will concentrate on the aspects of forensic investigation that are most relevant to initial training, exploring not only the subject of forensic investigation itself (and its relationship with forensic science), but also the role of police officers in assisting the Crime Scene Investigator (CSI), such as 'bagging and tagging' evidence, and collecting evidence from suspects. An understanding of forensic investigation and how a police officer supports that process is vitally important in terms of both convicting the guilty and exonerating the innocent.

The apparent obsession with detail in packaging and exhibiting can seem odd to the uninitiated but making errors or failing to follow accepted procedure can have serious consequences. For example, Weir (2007) quoted from *R v Hoey* [2007] NICC 49 (20 December 2007) as follows:

> It is not my function to criticise the seemingly thoughtless and slapdash approach of police and SOCO officers [CSIs] to the collection, storage and transmission of what must obviously have been potential exhibits in a possible future criminal trial but it is difficult to avoid some expression of surprise that in an era in which the potential for fibre, if not DNA, contamination was well known to the police such items were so widely and routinely handled with cavalier disregard for their integrity.

The topics covered in this chapter are likely to contribute to the learning required for the National Policing Curriculum subject areas: 'Conducting Investigations', 'Understanding the Police Constable Role', and 'Response Policing'.

26.2 Principles of Forensic Investigation

Some key principles underpin the application of forensic science to criminal investigation, for example that:

- all things are unique;
- when two objects come into contact they exchange material; and
- forensic science is context-sensitive, which means that forensic evidence is given meaning when its place or role within the investigation is understood.

Forensic investigation is a tripartite arrangement that involves forensic science, the investigator, and the CJS. It can be used to support both criminal and civil investigations.

26.2.1 Locard's Principle

When we handle an object, a small amount of material is inevitably transferred from our hands to the object and may remain there, for a little time at least. Material may also transfer onto our hands—for example, particles of dust or even tiny fragments which make up the article in question. Edmond Locard (1877–1966) is credited with the development of this 'Principle of Exchange'. His assertion was that material from the crime scene would be found on the suspect and vice versa, and is commonly expressed as 'every contact leaves a trace'. For example, an offender could leave finger marks, blood, and shoe marks at the crime scene and might take away fibres from fabrics such as curtains and carpets, or glass fragments on his/her clothing; the contacts have left a trace.

Locard's Principle has been a mainstay of forensic investigation principally because all matter is divisible if enough force is applied (Inman and Rudin, 2002), that is; objects break down during contact and, potentially, most things ultimately erode to become smaller and smaller. Some of these contacts cannot actually be proven because the quantities of the physical material transferred are too small to be located by current technology. Kirk (1953) wrote that failures by investigators to find or understand physical evidence were the only real problems with forensic evidence, rather than the veracity of the evidence itself. Fortunately, the principle can also be extended to include the impressions left at crime scenes by tools, weapons, and other materials. Locard's Principle is really inductive reasoning by another name and hence cannot be considered a scientific law in the usual sense, but until relatively recently this did not much concern the courts. (Inductive reasoning involves generalizing from a number of previous examples to establish a rule or theory. The fingerprint, for example, is still assumed to be unique and this is based on the assertion by fingerprint experts that no two fingerprints have yet been found to be the same. Perhaps the most famous example of inductive reasoning is that 'all swans are white', which is based upon repeated observations of white swans. It would be entirely natural, therefore, to have every confidence in the statement until the day that a black swan is observed.) In practice, Locard's Principle manifests itself in reverse in forensic investigation—evidence of transfer is used as a demonstration of previous contact; if we find a finger mark then we conclude that the finger touched an object.

Trust in the principle requires a leap of faith but, even after assuming we can find the transferred material or an impression, we then need to show that it came from the particular source in question. This brings us to the concepts of individualization and uniqueness.

26.2.2 Individualization

According to Kirk (1963, p 236) 'all objects in the universe are unique' so no two things can actually be identical, apart from at an atomic or molecular level. Thus, everything we are concerned with in forensic investigation should be considered as unique, or a one-off. This represents another leap of faith on the part of the investigator and forensic scientist because, again, this concept is not strictly a scientific law. (It cannot be considered to be a scientific law because there is no way it could ever be *falsified*.) However, as with Locard's Principle, the criminal justice system (CJS) does not consider this a particular problem and to date there have been few challenges in the courts.

Many objects which appear to be identical are markedly different, and those that are very similar (perhaps too similar to measure any differences) become visibly or measurably unique during use. This unique quality is brought about by the development of individual characteristics. The majority of industrial processes impart very similar characteristics to the same products, so they appear identical to the naked eye. A standard 'slot' screwdriver, for example, will be made on a production line, and every screwdriver will appear identical even though, theoretically, they are all unique. The tip will be hammered flat and the blade ground to pre-set dimensions, creating an edge which is generally very similar in every screwdriver of that type. During subsequent use (and misuse) each screwdriver will, however, develop clearer unique characteristics (as shown in the photograph), which provide the means for the forensic scientist to tell them apart.

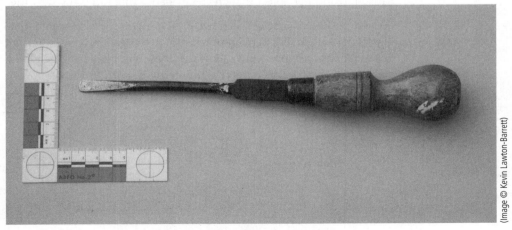

(Image © Kevin Lawton-Barrett)

A used screwdriver has inevitably acquired unique characteristics

Anything which can be associated with its source is said to have individual characteristics: for instance, a finger mark to a finger, a tool-mark to a tool, and so on. There are different types of characteristic in the classification of evidence to help us understand this. Consider, for example, a number of unused, apparently identical screwdrivers of the same brand. These will have:

- class characteristics which are qualities produced by a controlled process, typically a manufacturing process: for instance, a type of screwdriver, where each one is similar to the naked eye. An example could be a 10 mm slot screwdriver;
- sub-class characteristics which are the features on a batch of screwdrivers, particularly those which distinguish them from other batches—these features may be imparted by poor quality control or minute changes in settings, grinders, and so on. A batch of screwdrivers may be almost imperceptibly different to other batches;
- individual characteristics that are unique to that particular screwdriver. It will share the class and subclass characteristics, but Kirk's statement tells us that it is unique—as are all other screwdrivers.

Individualization follows from the premise that two items (such as a screwdriver and a scratch it made) are derived from a common source, so any marks the screwdriver makes can potentially be matched with it. This process is easier if the screwdriver has been damaged or modified by use, because the unique qualities of that screwdriver will be more noticeable.

26.2.3 Applications to criminal investigation

An investigator will use evidence of transfer in an attempt to prove that contact has occurred. Although any police officer may be involved in searching a crime scene—whether a place, person, or thing—the majority of scenes are examined by specially trained CSIs. Transfer can be demonstrated by the so-called traces that comprise debris—glass, paint flakes, hairs, DNA, and fibres, for example (see 26.5.1 for more detail). Second, there are 'impressions' (see 26.5.2) which include 'prints' made by fingers ('finger marks'), shoes, tools, tyres, and printers. Note also that Locard's Principle is not restricted to these traditional and tangible examples: it can also be extended to intangible digital data held by electronic media, such as computers, discs, and mobile phones.

Locard's Principle is primarily used to create physical links between the differing parts of an investigation. This is set out in its simplest form in the following diagram for an offence against a person.

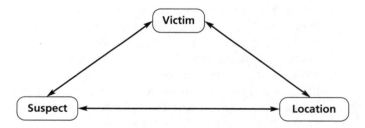

The links are normally created by forensic scientists comparing a 'questioned sample' with a 'control'. It is the examination of articles for individualizing features and subsequent comparison to another object that creates evidence that can be used by the CJS.

Clearly, the link may be between two or more people, a suspect and the scene only, or any permutation of these. A chief aim of forensic investigation is to locate and recover the physical material or impressions which allow the links to be made. The best links are two-way between every facet, because this reinforces the strength of the evidence.

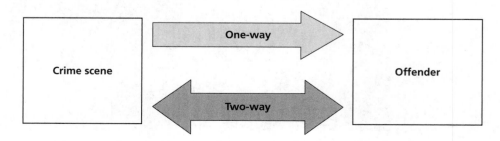

A mechanical fit (sometimes called a physical fit or jigsaw fit) between two or more fragments is an extended application of the theory that all things are unique and can be individualized. In its simplest form, imagine that an object breaks into several parts, and that those parts are later found separately. If the parts can be reconstructed as 'a fit', then it is a reasonable assumption that they must all originate from the same source. This would provide exceptionally powerful evidence in a police investigation. For example, small fragments of a blade were found in the chin of a deceased male and a suspect was found in possession of a damaged craft knife. The blade of the craft knife and the metal fragments were reconstructed successfully to rebuild the blade in its original form. However, whilst this is acceptable to the court as proof that the craft knife was involved in the murder, it does not prove who committed the offence.

In a more common scenario, imagine that a window has been forced using a screwdriver. The CSI will recover control samples from the crime scene (see 26.6.2.1), perhaps a sample of paint and a cast of a tool-mark, and will aim to have these compared with the 'questioned samples'—a sweater and a screwdriver taken from a suspect. This may provide strong evidence of association. However, if a corner of the screwdriver blade had broken off and become lodged in the window frame, it should fit exactly with the damaged screwdriver blade, and this would provide even stronger evidence of association. The actual fit would depend on a number of factors, including whether the screwdriver had been used after the break occurred and how effectively it was preserved by the officer who took control of it. However, the question now arises: Who was holding the screwdriver when it forced the window? The investigator needs to be able to 'put the suspect at the scene', so evidence of transfer between the suspect and the window (or other parts of the crime scene) would be important here. Any paint flakes on the suspect's sweater or other clothing could be compared to the control of paint removed from the crime scene. Thus: two forms of evidence would have been employed—the mechanical fit *proves* the involvement of the screwdriver and the paint flakes are *strongly supportive* of the notion that the suspect was present during the commission of the offence. A variety of other forms of evidence (eg eye witnesses, CCTV, stolen property) can support the contention that the suspect committed the offence in question.

If Locard's Principle is accepted as really meaning all things erode or break down, then it continues to apply after the commission of the offence, so evidence will inevitably continue to change: fibres on the guilty party are lost, shoes continue to wear out, screwdrivers are modified, damaged windows are repaired, and DNA decays. One key objective for the police therefore, is to intervene as quickly after the crime as possible to recover the potential evidence from scene and suspect, to prevent any further changes.

26.3   Forensic Science and Investigations

Forensic science is commonly described as the application of scientific disciplines to the legal system. The fields of science so employed are many and varied: from archaeology through every conceivable speciality to zoology, and any of these may potentially have a role in the investigation of an offence. Experts in these fields may work independently or be employed by a Forensic Science Provider (FSP, but normally just called the 'lab'). They will produce evidence for the investigator by analysing and interpreting the material provided, to determine facts or form opinions about the case. The scientist can later make statements of fact (what he/she did during the examination) and provide expert opinion (what he/she believes the analysis means) even though the offering of opinion is effectively disallowed by the courts. The first expert opinion was offered by John Smeaton in 1782 in a case regarding the silting up of Wells harbour. Lord Mansfield allowed Smeaton's opinion because his opinion was 'deduced from facts which are not disputed' in *Folkes v Chadd* (1782) 3 Doug KB 157.

The evidence may point to the guilt or innocence of a suspect, neither of which should be a consideration for the scientist. There are a number of important ethical principles which the scientist is bound by, the key ones being to discover the truth and to be unbiased. This is also the essence of a police investigation and the primary focus of the criminal court.

Forensic investigation is often concerned with two main forms of (largely physical) evidence: corroborative evidence (material that will confirm or refute a hypothesis about the crime, for instance that a powder is, or is not, heroin) and inceptive evidence (which identifies an unknown, for example a person).

The investigator may employ forensic investigation and forensic science in a variety of ways when considering these two main forms of evidence. These include:

- Describing the *modus operandi* (MO): the attending CSI or scientist can help form a hypothesis about the method used by the offender to commit the crime. This would be at an early stage in a forensic investigation. The data can be analysed for patterns to link offences. For example, a CSI may link a number of burglaries based upon MO, finger marks, or a shoe mark left at several crime scenes, or a scientist may be able to interpret the patterns of blood splashes at the scene of a violent crime to establish the mechanics of an assault.
- Answering questions posed by an investigator in order to progress an enquiry: for instance, whose DNA is on this knife? Is there a connection between the weapon used in this crime and this suspect?
- Establishing that an offence has occurred: by examining exhibits it may be shown that an offence has been committed, for instance: following the analysis of a white powder; the classification of a firearm; the calculation of alcohol in urine or blood.
- Corroborating or refuting witness statements: this is particularly useful when applied to very specific issues raised during interview.
- Establishing physical links between different people, crime scenes, and exhibits, such as drugs or stolen property and weapons.
- Identifying an individual: fingerprints and DNA (and some other techniques) can be employed to identify people, including suspects, arrested persons, or the body of a deceased person.
- Further informing an enquiry: often by clarifying issues or providing some form of descriptive information or intelligence. An example would be a specialist helping to identify the make and model of a vehicle involved in a 'hit-and-run' road traffic incident by examining debris and paint at the scene.

26.3.1 Working with forensic scientists

Efficient communication with forensic scientists is vital to the investigative process. In volume crime this is normally carried out by the CSI, but in major crime it will be a senior CSI, and sometimes one or more investigators assist at a case conference held by a Forensic Management Team (FMT). In order to provide an efficient and effective service to the police, the forensic scientist expects:

- unbroken continuity (or 'chain of custody') of evidence (see 11.2.6);
- correct packaging with intact integrity seals;
- utmost care in preventing contamination (see 11.2.5.1);
- a clear communication which explains the investigative need, and describes the perceived relevance and place of the evidence (ie its context);
- guidance regarding 'points to prove';
- up-to-date information whenever the investigation changes tack; and
- clear guidance on any deadlines, such as bail dates or court appearances.

It is important to remember that forensic evidence is context-sensitive. This can be difficult to understand, the misunderstanding being based upon the notion that a particular type of evidence is 'good' or 'poor'. Finger marks and DNA evidence are often regarded as 'good' because each can easily provide clear differentiations, but their significance depends on their location or 'context'. For example, a finger mark found near the point of entry in the female toilets of a burgled pub was found to belong to the barman. The context of this apparently innocent mark changed when, during interview, he categorically denied ever having been in the toilet. In another case, blood found on an assault suspect's clothing was initially explained by the fact that he had helped an injured stranger in the street. However, on closer analysis it was apparent that the blood must have spattered onto his clothing, which indicated he may have been involved in an offence.

In order to provide the correct information and to explain its importance to the case, an MG21 form is used to guide the investigator through the submissions process (see 27.4.2 on MG forms). Police officers must follow force procedures regarding the submission of exhibits to laboratories, to avoid problems in any subsequent prosecution. Laboratory submission forms, fingerprint documentation (even for negative results), and CSI worksheets are disclosable under the Criminal Procedure and Investigations Act 1996 (CPIA) (see 24.3 on the CPIA and disclosure), and all the physical or digital materials recovered as evidence can be examined by defence experts upon request.

26.3.2 The role of the crime scene investigator

The CSI is typically the first port of call for all enquiries regarding forensic science, such as taking samples from suspects and victims and the examination of crime scenes. Chief amongst the CSI's crime-based activities are:

- photographing crime scenes, articles, or people associated with crime, such as weapons, injuries, victims, and suspects (but not so-called 'mug shots');
- the location, assessment, and recovery of exhibits and physical or biological evidence (including finger marks) from crime scenes;
- the packaging, storage, and documentation of recovered material;
- attending post-mortem examinations for sudden and suspicious deaths;
- providing advice to police officers and investigators on matters related to physical evidence, photography, and laboratory submissions; and
- gathering intelligence (from utterances, personal observations, or physical material) to support the National Intelligence Model (NIM) (see 23.6), and for use in databases.

CSIs are also involved with non-crime incidents such as sudden deaths, suicides, and fatal industrial accidents (on behalf of HM Coroners and in support of Health and Safety Executive investigations). They may also be involved in the recording of loss through fire prior to arson being ruled out, especially at high-value scenes and those of significant public interest.

The majority of CSIs in the UK police are police support staff attached to a force's scientific support department (sometimes shared with other forces). This includes other complementary services such as a photography unit and a fingerprint bureau with experts who identify suspects from crime-scene finger marks and manage IDENT1 (the national fingerprint database), and a laboratory for enhancing finger mark evidence. Computer forensic investigators and technical services (responsible for covert intelligence and evidence-gathering technology) may work in the same department.

26.3.3 Quality standards

It is important to understand that quality is critically important in the crime scene examination arena, and this extends to laboratory analyses. The chief objectives of quality mechanisms are to ensure rigorous standards and integrity are maintained in the 'crime scene to court' process, and—of no lesser importance—that the public can have confidence in the processes involved. The collection and recording of crime scene evidence is covered by ISO 17020, and laboratory processes are covered by ISO 17025 with adherence to other standards, such as ILAC G19. Both sets of ISO standards are administered by UKAS in the UK and are required by the Forensic Regulator as described in her Codes of Practice and Conduct (Forensic Science Regulator, 2017).

26.4 Establishing the Time and Date of an Event

This is about establishing the precise time that an event occurred (eg when an image on a computer hard drive was accessed) and is sometimes known as 'time-and-date-stamping'. Some evidence may occur in a physical form which shows it was created during the commission of the offence, and this is potentially of great value. For example:

- in the investigation of an assault, the distribution of blood on the suspect could indicate that she had been present during the assault, and even establish her distance and position in relation to the victim. DNA analysis of the blood on the suspect's clothing could establish it was from the victim, so proving the suspect's clothing (and probably the suspect) was present when that person was assaulted;
- when investigating a case of criminal damage to a church window the presence of unusual stained glass from the window on the suspect's head hair and upper clothing may indicate that he was in close proximity when that window was smashed;

- for an offence where a firearm had been used, finding firearm discharge residue (FDR) on a suspect may show that he was present when a firearm was discharged. (However, it does not necessarily prove that it was that particular gun that was fired, or that he was the person who fired the weapon since it could have been fired by another person who was present.)

Challenging suspects in interviews, however, can be used to reinforce many forms of evidence. CSIs and forensic managers prefer absolute statements from suspects because this can make the context of the evidence stronger. If a suspect or other person makes an early statement, this information should be carefully considered: it may be of value to the scientist and must, at least, describe any admissions made. In addition, when a laboratory result is received officers might consider their interview strategy; that is, how best to employ the information received to drive the investigation forward.

For example, where a man is suspected of a shooting, the forensic manager and scientist will consider the value of any potential FDR evidence after interview thus:

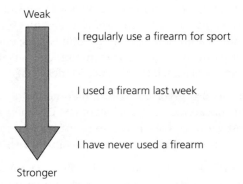

Weak

I regularly use a firearm for sport

I used a firearm last week

I have never used a firearm

Stronger

Clearly, if the man denies the use of firearms on any occasion then any FDR located on his body or his clothes would provide the basis for challenging the veracity of any statement he makes in his defence. The evidence against him would be strong. If this were the case, consideration must be given to his activity in recent days.

- Has he been in the vicinity of a firearm which has been used?
- Was he arrested by an officer who recently used a firearm, say, for sport?
- Was he conveyed in a vehicle which had contained people who were contaminated with firearms residues?
- Was he arrested by an officer who was environmentally contaminated through using firearms at work?

The forensic scientist would need to know this sort of information so that an informed assessment of the significance of any contamination could be made. To explore this further you may wish to look at how FDR evidence was used in the wrongful conviction of Barry George in 2001; the defence raised the possibility that his coat had been contaminated by armed police officers when they searched his home address. He was subsequently acquitted in 2008.

TASK 1

1. What does FSP stand for?
2. Who is credited with the development of the Principle of Exchange?
3. List three things for which an investigator might employ forensic science.

26.5 Types of Forensic Evidence

Forensic evidence can be classified in a number of different ways, but here we have chosen a relatively simple method:

- trace evidence; very small quantities of material (DNA is considered separately);
- impressions or marks (finger marks are considered separately);
- DNA evidence (a type of trace evidence, but with special features);

- finger marks (impressions, which also leave a trace of sweat, and can be printed in blood or other materials); and
- documents, firearms, digital devices, and CCTV.

A great deal of intelligence can be recovered from crime scenes and this can be stored in a variety of databases, such as IDENT1, the National DNA Database, and footwear collections, which will be discussed later. The information taken even from a crime scene with limited evidence can be valuable when it is compared to other crime scenes, including the MO, the size of tool marks, and even the behaviour of the suspect. This information can be stored in crime systems (such as Genesis) or forensic management databases and may be capable of linking offences through their analysis.

It is also worth considering that many types of physical evidence can be derived from digital devices too, for example finger marks, DNA, and fibres (from people and their clothes, and from the environment in which the items have been stored or used). There may be a conflict of priorities when considering the seizure of both physical and digital evidence from a digital device, so advice should be sought from a CSI and computer forensic investigator (see also 21.5).

26.5.1 Trace materials as forensic evidence

Trace material can be any material transferred from the suspect to the crime scene (or a victim) and vice versa. It ranges from common materials such as fibres, glass fragments, and paint flakes transferred during property crimes to the more exotic, such as pollens, soils, and even insects or their fragments. Imagination is important here and consideration should not be limited to any specific groups: creativity is a vital element in forensic investigation. DNA trace evidence is covered separately in 26.5.3.

26.5.1.1 Glass

The manufacturing processes vary depending on the type of glass required and this provides varying degrees of discriminatory power (ie the ability to distinguish one object made of glass from another). The addition of colourants and physical processes can make this outwardly common material very useful in the right criminal circumstances.

Glass is a mix of silica, sodium carbonate, and calcium compounds which are smelted to form the base material to which physical processes or chemical additives are applied, imparting a number of properties. All glass can be chemically analysed and its refractive index measured (how much it slows down light that passes through it). The following types of glass are often encountered in an investigation:

- plain window glass (or float glass): the most common window glass manufactured today. It breaks relatively easily;
- Georgian wired glass: reinforced with wire mesh of varying sizes, used for security (because it is difficult to penetrate), and fire resistance (it remains in situ longer than float glass);
- toughened glass: inherently strong and normally difficult to break—used in telephone kiosks and the side windows of vehicles. It breaks relatively easily if struck with force near the edge by a sharp object, or by throwing a 'ninja rock' (a ceramic fragment from a broken spark plug), and forms thousands of cube-shaped granules;
- laminated glass: two sheets of glass which sandwich a plastic layer which prevents the pane shattering and retains it in the frame. It is used for windscreens and many low-level windows;
- container glass: eg bottles, drinking vessels, and older TV and computer screens;
- optical glass: found in lenses; and
- mirrors.

Shards of glass may be exceptionally sharp and small, and can be very dangerous. Personnel should always wear goggles and gloves when dealing with broken glass and avoid large, unsupported broken windows as these may collapse without warning.

Glass found on the suspect or other articles can be compared to samples recovered from a broken window frame (see 26.6.2.1) by a variety of analytical techniques. Where the glass is unusual (perhaps very old or specially coloured) the scientist may be able to provide a forensically important statement. Glass can be broken in a variety of ways and different authors have different views on classification but, in a criminal context, glass is typically broken by moving objects (varying speeds), by some form of stress, by heat, or by an explosion. Frequently, the cause is deduced at the scene, but windows and glass objects can be reconstructed in order to demonstrate the cause, point of impact, and (using some fractures) even the direction of the breakage. One of the most valuable attributes of breaking glass is a process called backward fragmentation, where breaking glass throws out fine particles which may land on the offender in a characteristic way, and which can demonstrate that he/she was in the vicinity of the window when the glass broke.

26.5.1.2 Fibres, paint, and security marker substances

Fibres can be natural, man-made, or mixed. They are frequently transferred from clothing, seats, and carpets on to receptive surfaces, especially when the contact has been violent or has occurred over a long period. Manufacturers use different fibre mixes and dyes so many fabrics may have an unusual or characteristic mix which can be very useful forensically. Man-made fibres such as polyester and nylon can survive conditions which cause decay in natural materials such as wool or cotton. A process called 'fibre mapping' can be carried out in significant crime scenes, where every fibre is lifted onto adhesive tape (hundreds of pieces of tape are required). In this way, the position of a certain person (eg the suspect) can be established at a crime scene. Poor crime-scene management can of course compromise the success of such procedures.

Paint is found as a protective or cosmetic coating on window and door frames, vehicles, and other manufactured objects. Manufacturers add a wide range of chemicals to paints to give them specific properties, colours, and surface finishes. So, at a crime scene any surface which has been chipped or scraped may be usefully examined and compared with paint fragments found on a suspect's clothing, tools, vehicle, or other objects in his/her possession. The more layers of paint, the more likely the profile can be demonstrated as being unique. Some paints are particularly unusual (eg military coatings (infrared absorbing) and paint used on colour-coded scaffold poles), so their presence should alert suspicion.

Security marking systems increasingly employ pigments and other chemicals. These frequently contain a fluorescent dye which glows under ultra violet (UV) light and may contain a range of unique markers, or 'taggants', such as microdots and chemical traces (including synthetic DNA) that form a unique code. Some types of microdots are virtually indestructible and can even withstand the very high temperatures required to smelt (stolen) metals. Such high-tech security markers can be applied to individual at-risk assets (eg engine components and jewellery), and to larger surfaces such as sheets of lead on church roofs. They can also be incorporated into metals, or into pastes, greases, and sprays which can then be applied to suitable surfaces.

Infrared detectors in alarm systems can deploy these markers in a spray, so when such a system has been activated, or stolen property is recovered, it is good practice to scan the objects (and any suspects) with a UV light: any fluorescence should be seen as suspicious and reported to a CSI, who will take samples from suspects and scenes as necessary and arrange for further analysis.

26.5.1.3 Soil, plants, and insects

Soils are found nearly everywhere, but they can vary significantly within short distances due to geological and geomorphological factors, such as the source rock contributing to the soil. This is a complex topic so we provide only a brief summary here, but in essence the minerals, organic material, and grain size of the sample will each be examined. In some situations soil is modified by the inclusion of chemicals and waste material from industrial and other processes, and this can also be useful in identifying locations. Soil is almost always sampled during exhumations, because if any toxins are found in the body of the deceased, the possibility of the toxins having leached into it from the environment may need to be explored. It can be difficult to demonstrate that soil evidence has come from a *very specific* location (perhaps a few square metres of a field) but this can sometimes be achieved.

Vegetative material can often be used by forensic botanists to identify the species of a plant from small fragments of leaf, stem, seed, flower, or wood. Palynologists can identify the species of plant from the pollen transferred onto clothing, vehicles, and illegal substances such as cannabis resin. The precise mix of plant types at, say, the crime scene, can often provide particularly powerful forensic evidence when compared to the clothing or vehicle of a suspect.

Insects are generally sensitive to their food source and climate (apart from the common pest species) and, as a result, many species are found in limited ranges. When insects are identified during a forensic investigation, they may be helpful in determining the geographical origin of materials. Forensic entomologists can also use known data on insect life cycles—especially those of blowflies—to identify when a body became available for them to feed upon. This may be of value when attempting to determine the time or date of death.

By using all these naturally occurring types of evidence, the source of materials such as cannabis resin, or the previous locations of vehicles and people can often be established.

26.5.1.4   Toxicology

This is a specialist field engaged in the analysis of poisons and drugs and may be crucial to an investigation, for example:

- to calculate whether a person is over the drink-drive limit;
- to establish that alcohol or drugs may explain behaviour such as violence or drowsiness (particularly relevant to 'date-rape' offences); or
- to establish the causes of illness and death.

Roadside breath tests are the most common forms of toxicological measurement carried out by the police, but these are normally used as screening tests (see 19.9.4) prior to more stringent evidential tests (see 19.9.5). A variety of field-test kits and covert-sampling devices can be employed to screen for drugs, but the opinion of an expert toxicologist should be sought to provide evidence suitable for a prosecution, unless force policy allows the suspect to make a guilty plea prior to caution, or if there is an intervention model in place at the time (see 12.5.3.1). Elaborate and expensive analysis would therefore not normally be required (or at best, not even embarked upon), since the case will not go to court in these circumstances.

In driving cases, where the driver claims to have drunk alcohol only after an incident, specialist laboratory submission forms (MGDD/D) should be used to request a 'back calculation' (see 19.9.5.3). Police officers should consider seeking the advice of a CSI (or a Scientific Support Unit adviser), since the forms required for such a calculation can be quite complex and require other factors to be considered, such as medication, food consumed, and any ill health. Regardless of this, original bottles and glasses should be seized where possible, and marked up to show what the suspect claims to have drunk—remembering that a 'gulp' or 'swig' is not a scientifically accepted measurement of alcohol consumption!

Commonly, blood or urine is sent for analysis for toxins, but other samples from the body tissue of deceased victims (including from the eyes) may also be used, depending upon the circumstances. Toxicology samples must always be treated as a potential health hazard.

26.5.2   Impressions as forensic evidence

These are the marks left by fingers, shoes, tools, tyres, stamping machines, printers, and typewriters, etc. Whilst these can be a direct 'stamped' effect, many are made up of irregular scrapes and smudges and even cutting or drilling marks. Finger marks are covered separately in 26.5.4. All forms of impression can be easily destroyed: be cautious about what is touched and where people walk. All forms of impression evidence are capable of providing intelligence, and can be readily compared to the object which is suspected to have left the mark.

26.5.2.1   Footwear marks

Shoe or other footwear marks are a useful but potentially short-lived form of evidence. Footwear is readily modified by use when people walk over surfaces that scratch and tear the soles or add particles such as glass and stones. The resultant damage occurs at random and is therefore unique to every sole. When a shoe leaves an impression at a crime scene the mark can be compared with the shoe in question. However, the shoe must be located and recovered before the relevant damage to the sole is further eroded, as this could reduce the value of any comparison.

The marks can be on a flat, apparently two-dimensional surface, or they can be impressed into a soft substrate to form a three-dimensional pattern. Importantly, the surface must be fine enough to receive the mark: soft clay is clearly better than coarse sand.

Trainers in particular are readily identifiable (either from databases or by an expert) and this data can be used for intelligence purposes in order tentatively to link crime scenes. Forensic Management Systems used in local force databases, or external databases such as the National Footwear Database (NFD) provide a valuable intelligence tool (see also 26.6.1.5). The addition of MO, time of offence, and target properties can make such databases invaluable. Under the PACE Act 1984, police forces can make good use of shoe marks and their intelligence databases by taking shoes from detainees in police custody and scanning the sole patterns for future use (see 26.6.1). The database can also provide information on offences where a very similar sole pattern has occurred and, therefore, assist in linking crimes.

In theory, marks should be present at almost every crime scene, since almost all offenders will walk within the venue. Therefore all attending personnel should use the Common Approach Path (CAP) to a crime scene (see 11.2.2). A variety of techniques can be used to recover the marks: photography, casting, lifting, or removal of the surface upon which the mark rests.

26.5.2.2 Tyre marks

Like footwear, vehicle tyres leave impressions which are commonly found in soft soils, on roads, smooth concrete floors, glass, and paper—particularly at 'ram raids'. They are also modified by the surfaces over which they pass, and may pick up 'inclusions' such as glass and gravel. On a suitable surface these individual details will be impressed as a two or three dimensional pattern. The impression may be of a rotating tyre or a skidding tyre. The full circumference of a car tyre is approximately 3.14 times the diameter, so a full rotation print of a 50 cm diameter car tyre is over 150 cm long. (Finally, that school geometry has proved useful!) You should retain as much as possible of the tread pattern for the CSI.

The laboratory can assist in identifying the make and type of tyre from a recovered mark, which may then include or exclude particular vehicles from the enquiry. If a suspect vehicle exists it is better to seize the entire vehicle rather than to remove the wheels for analysis.

26.5.2.3 Other types of marks

Tool or instrument marks are marks imparted to receptive surfaces by the application of force. These marks can also be left by objects such as rocks, baseball bats, and any suitably hard object which meets a softer surface, but typical examples are those made by forcing a window or cashbox. The marks can be made by:

- levering, to force open a window, door, or cashbox—one edge of the target surface acts as a fulcrum or pivot and both this and the opening part will be marked;
- striking an object, or person, with a weapon or similar;
- cutting—the action caused by scissors, wire cutters, and bolt croppers; and
- drilling—the waste material and hole from drilling can bear the impression of the cutting edge of the drill bit.

These actions impress the shape of the tip or edge of the device into the surface. The shape of the object will have been individualized through its manufacture and previous use (see 26.2.2).

Stamps, dyes, and manufacturing marks also create impressions. The objects making the impressions will all undergo individualization and acquire unique minor changes. Vehicle identification numbers (VINs, see 19.2.1.1) are often faked or amended, so a particular stamp can be compared to VINs on suspect vehicles. Where metal factory waste has been stolen, any remaining material should be taken to scrap dealers to compare its cut edges with that of any scrap they have recently accepted and, hopefully, quarantined on site. Scrap dealers are now expected to be able to identify sellers (Scrap Metal Dealers Act 2013), and it is reasonable to presume all industrial waste has identifying features and unique cut edges, so this can help identify the thieves. If there is a match, the factory cutting machines may also need to be examined.

Any material which is set in a mould or extruded also takes on an impression of the mould or extrusion head, particularly where debris has built up. Examples include apparently identical lead sheets, copper pipes, plastic bags, and plastic components. These can be usefully compared because many objects from a single batch will have similar characteristics. If for instance half a batch of copper pipes has been stolen and is recovered by the police then extrusion marks can show they come from the original batch. Extrusion marks were especially useful in the 1970s and 1980s in investigations of terrorist bombings: the offenders often used several bin bags from the same roll, and the bags were found at different locations so the police could link several offences by examining extrusion marks on the bags.

Printers, copiers, and typewriters can also provide useful evidence. Modern copiers (and all printers) are digital, which means that the pages which have been printed are digitally stored within the device's limited memory for some time after printing. Paper feeders and rollers may also impart marks. Photocopiers superimpose an image of the glass screen (the platen) on the copies they produce, so the more damage (or dried correction fluid) on the platen, the better the scientist's chances of demonstrating an association between a particular copier and paper evidence. Most colour printers also print Machine Identification Code (MIC) onto each printed page. MIC is a series of tiny dots that record the serial number of the machine and the printing date (known as printer steganography); this can be used for tracking forged documents and money. At the other end of the technological scale, even in the twenty-first century, some offenders still use typewriters to produce documents. The fonts are easily identifiable, and plastic ribbons, correction ribbons (which physically lift letters from paper), and other components can be valuable when an offender has used such a machine.

Bite marks are another form of impression, and are valuable sources of evidence. The position, number, layout, orientation, and cutting surfaces of teeth make our dentition highly individual. It is the role of the *forensic odontologist* to compare marks found on victims and in foodstuffs with the teeth of the suspect. This is carried out by taking a three-dimensional dental impression of the suspect's teeth and comparing it with photographs or impressions of the injury or damage. Older bite marks on skin may not be immediately apparent but can still be visible under ultraviolet (UV) lighting and can be photographed some time after the incident. Whenever bite marks are found, DNA may be present and consideration must be given to preserving this evidence.

26.5.3   DNA evidence

Every cell in the human body—with a few exceptions—has a nucleus which contains 23 pairs of chromosomes (one of each pair from each parent), and these are made up of genes which govern the biological and physical processes in the body. The genes are made of DNA, and the nucleus of every cell contains a complete copy of the DNA for the entire organism, so a cell from a person's cheek contains exactly the same genetic material as a white cell from his/her blood. A large proportion of DNA is the same for all humans, but small differences occur between individuals and these account for variations such as hair and eye colour, other physical characteristics, and genetically related illness. However, the chromosomes also contain sections of DNA called Short Tandem Repeats (STRs) which have no clear function. The number of repeats and the number of specific STRs vary significantly between individuals, so they are very useful for forensic analysis.

DNA is typically found on articles or at scenes yielding blood, semen, saliva, hair with roots, some bodily secretions, and pieces of body tissue. Biological material is a potential health hazard, but also needs protecting from investigators if it is to be used as evidence, because our own DNA can easily contaminate it. The DNA is extracted from the sample and copied many times using a process called Polymerase Chain Reaction (PCR) to ensure enough is available for analysis. The different STRs are then measured and compared to the suspect's sample or data stored in the National DNA Database.

26.5.3.1   DNA variability and forensics

Clearly, there would be limited mileage in comparing common genetic material (such as eye colour) to identify suspects. The analysis of DNA samples highlights the differences between the DNA of different individuals. One limitation with DNA is that identical twins and triplets share the same DNA profiles, because they came from the same fertilized egg which divided to produce more than one foetus. There is a very small possibility that their DNA has mutated, but this is not likely to be discovered in routine forensic tests. Twins or triplets from different eggs are called fraternal (or non-identical) twins or triplets and their DNA differs considerably. A DNA 'hit' is a calculation concerning a selection of a person's STRs and is supplied by the scientist as a 'match probability'. If the match probability is one in a billion, it means that there is one chance in a billion that another person selected at random has the same profile. It does not mean that there is a one in a billion chance that the suspect is innocent (the prosecutor's fallacy). If the DNA recovered for analysis is degraded through age or lack of proper handling, the match probability applied to the comparison may be reduced, which can cause some concern, but remember that other evidence should be used to support the prosecution case.

The current system for DNA analysis in the UK is DNA 17. This analyses many STRs including those used in other countries, so a DNA sample from a crime scene in the UK can easily be compared with records on a database in another country (and vice versa).

Mitochondrial DNA (Mt DNA) is a different form of DNA which can be extracted from bone, hair, faeces, and teeth. It is found in the cytoplasm of all cells inside tiny structures called 'mitochondria' (rather than in the cell's nucleus), and forms a loop; this makes it more resilient to external influences so it may last for many years. It does, however, have limitations in that it cannot uniquely identify a person: it can only identify the maternal line. This means, for example, that a person has the same Mt DNA as his/her siblings and mother (and her siblings), all the way up the female line. Fathers do not share their Mt DNA with their children because at fertilization only the sperm head enters the egg (the 'midpiece' containing the mitochondria, as well as the tail, is left outside the egg). Mt DNA analysis can be beneficial when applied to the study of old and degraded samples where normal (nuclear) DNA is unavailable. It was famously used by the Forensic Science Service (FSS) to identify the bodies of Tsar Nicholas II, Tsarina Alexandra, and their three children, whose bodies were found in 1991 near Yekaterinburg in Russia, following their murders by the Bolsheviks in 1919.

Y STRs are a variable genetic feature found on the Y chromosome, so they can only be used for the identification of men (as women do not have a Y chromosome). The Y chromosome can be used to determine paternal ancestry. In Western culture (though not in Iceland, where surnames are passed on in a different way), this is traditionally paralleled by the transfer of the surname; hence Y chromosome analysis has gained commercial popularity as a genealogical tool and may assist in some investigations. The value of Y STRs is, of course, significantly diminished in males with uncertain paternity.

26.5.3.2 The National DNA Database

Whilst an FSP can directly compare a sample of a suspect's DNA to DNA found at a crime scene or on a weapon or other person, the majority of DNA-rich evidence is analysed by the FSPs and the data from it is uploaded to a national resource. The National DNA Database (NDNAD) is a database containing records of the DNA of subjects who are arrested, cautioned, convicted, and charged for recordable offences, with approximately 531,000 new subject samples being added annually. Separate sections of the database also contain records of the DNA from many missing and vulnerable people. The database also stores records on DNA recovered from crime scenes, which may have been found as blood, saliva on cigarette ends, bite marks, and so on. The Biometric Commissioner reports (for the year ending December 2018) that the database contains approximately 6.34 million subject profiles and 616,000 crime-scene samples. Most of the retained samples (approximately 80 per cent) are from males (Wiles, 2019). The elegance of the system is that although many offenders who commit minor crimes will move away from criminal activities, others will continue as volume-crime offenders or will step up their activity to more serious offences. By taking a DNA sample from suspects, the police effectively 'bank' this intelligence for future investigations, as they do with fingerprints. This may also have a deterrent effect. The NDNAD can demonstrate links between crimes, identify the deceased, and, of course, identify the person whose DNA has been found at crime scenes and on exhibits. Currently, it matches over 30,000 crime scenes to subjects annually.

Potentially, its greatest strength lies in making 'cold hits', which is when a sample from a crime scene or victim identifies a suspect, often in older cases where the crime has never been solved. For instance, in 1988 a man sexually assaulted two young girls in Canterbury, Kent, and was not apprehended or identified at the time. In 2001 he was arrested in Derbyshire for shoplifting (only £10 worth of groceries), and the arresting PC took his DNA sample. It was matched to DNA found at the Kent crime scene, and he later admitted the offences and was sentenced to 15 years in prison. Your local force will have similar success stories where the NDNAD has solved old (and new) crimes.

26.5.4 Finger marks

The ridged skin on our fingers leaves marks on many finely textured surfaces we touch. These are called finger marks, and they can be imaged, compared, and used as forensic evidence. The term 'fingerprints' refers to the images made (usually by law enforcement agencies) to record the skin ridge patterns on our fingers. The fingerprint images can be compared with the finger marks found at crime scenes.

Ridge details are found on the skin on the fingers, palms, soles, and toes—about 5 per cent of the total area of skin. Every finger, toe, palm, and sole pattern on every person is considered by the criminal justice system to be unique, including those of so-called identical twins. The tiny ridges consist of small features such as forks and spurs which are normally referred to as 'minutiae'. It is the combinations and positions of these features that make the patterns on the fingers unique (often referred to as 'fingerprints'). The ridges develop in the womb and remain identical (apart from size and scarring) until death—and beyond if the body is sufficiently preserved.

Finger marks can be a three-dimensional impression or a two-dimensional mark consisting of sweat and contaminants. The receiving surface must be sufficiently smooth to accept the mark. (There is an analogy here with the pattern of a shoe impressed into soft clay compared to one impressed into shingle.) For a non-porous surface, the easiest way to determine whether it might yield finger marks is to scratch it gently with a fingernail, although this should be carried out with caution, and never at a serious or major crime scene. If the scratching action makes virtually no noise then the surface could be a good source of finger marks. If it makes a noise (due to it being rough) then the surface might be unsuitable. Porous surfaces such as paper and wood can bear finger marks if the surface is fine enough.

26.5.4.1 Locating finger marks

Finger marks can be positive (visible or 'patent'), latent (invisible), or plastic (impressed into a surface). Positive marks are often printed in dirt or blood, and can be photographed. CSIs usually look for latent marks by using a fine brush to gently dust a surface with powders, and then examining the area with a torch. This is the most common procedure; the fabric of the building can be examined and bulky items left in place, rather than being recovered as evidence. The mark may then be photographed and, where appropriate, lifted with an adhesive material and placed onto an acetate sheet. Plastic marks are three-dimensional patterns impressed into putty, clay, or chocolate, for example. They can also be photographed and even cast using a silica gel if the surface is firm enough.

On some items, such as paper or carrier bags, there may be no visible marks, but it is *presumed* that marks are very likely to be present. These items can be seized and packaged for later chemical or physical enhancement by employing specialist light sources, physical treatments, and chemical dyes to enhance the non-aqueous components of sweat (salts, fats, oils, and amino acids make up about 1.5 per cent of the content of sweat). It is worth bearing in mind that paper exhibits can still produce meaningful finger mark evidence years after being laid. Consider finger marks on documents from the DVLA to show ownership of vehicles in the distant past, and old passport applications, cheques, letters, and diaries.

Occasionally, laboratory personnel visit complex scenes and search the fabric of the building using chemicals and light sources. Whilst CSIs routinely 'dust' smooth non-porous surfaces, marks may also be found on many other surfaces such as textured plastics, polythene bags, paper, smooth wood, and even wall coatings. The majority of marks at scenes or on exhibits are otherwise invisible, which means they are easily damaged by thoughtless actions, and wearing gloves does not prevent people destroying finger marks which are present.

Note that it is always better to preserve a whole crime scene rather than just the point of entry because as an initially nervous and sweaty-palmed offender moves through a building, his/her hands may dry out sufficiently to leave marks of good quality further inside the scene.

26.5.4.2 IDENT1

A suspect's fingerprints can be compared directly to marks left at scenes (print to mark comparisons) but there is, of course, a digital alternative. The IDENT1 database is a national system that contains records of the fingerprints (so-called 'tenprints') and palm prints of arrested persons, and crime-scene marks recovered by CSIs and other personnel. It also contains records from vulnerable people at risk from exploitation. The Biometric Commissioner (Wiles, 2019) reports that IDENT1 contained more than 8.2 million tenprints taken under the PACE Act 1984. The database compares:

- crime-scene marks with other crime-scene marks to search for links between offences;
- tenprints and palm prints against crime-scene marks (and vice versa); and
- new tenprints to those already on file to confirm identity, or establish that an arrested person is not using a pseudonym.

Once the system identifies a suspect print, a chain of at least three experts then verify the result before providing a statement of evidence in a process called ACE-V (Analysis, Comparison, Evaluation, Verification). If a suspect's tenprints are already on the IDENT1 system then his/ her identity can be verified in about ten minutes, a so-called live identification.

IDENT1 is linked to the Livescan tenprint scanners in police stations, which have improved the quality of tenprints (compared with the old ink and paper systems), and portable units can be linked to mobile telecoms for use on patrol. These scanners are linked to IDENT1 through a 'Biometric Services Gateway' and are proving very useful in the rapid identification of living (and even deceased) persons.

26.5.5 Evidence from documents

Under the term 'documents', forensic investigators normally include all letters, paperwork, invoices, cheques, transfers, application forms, handwriting, and any other written material, whether handwritten or printed by typewriter, computer printer, photocopier, or other device.

The writing on a document (eg a hate-mail letter) can be compared with material obtained during the investigation, including samples provided by a suspect. Handwriting samples are used most effectively when a variety of material is submitted for comparison, and not just samples produced in front of a police officer. For example, 'course of business' handwriting samples (such as diaries, letters, general paperwork) can be sourced from his/her home address, work, or other places. (Some samples may be *known* to have been written by the suspect, but for others this might not be so certain.) A document can also be analysed for 'impressed' handwriting. Typically this is found when a pad of paper is used and an impression of writing on one page is transferred to the pages below. It can be enhanced using Electrostatic Detection Apparatus (referred to as ESDA).

Printers and typewriters can also be analysed and compared with a specimen document. The presence of printer-head faults, 'banding', or damage to paper caused by rollers may be reproduced under laboratory conditions and compared with the suspect document (see also 26.5.2.3).

The physical features of paper can also be compared, such as tear marks, staple holes and batch faults in envelopes (such as poor cuts and folds). Other features such as watermarks, obliterations, paper type, security inks, concealed marks, and 'reactive fibres' can be analysed in a number of ways, for example by microscopy and by using a Video Spectral Comparator (VSC). A VSC employs different wavelengths of light and is particularly useful in identifying handwritten additions to cheques and payment forms, and for revealing obliterated text. When a suspect is identified, the investigator should also exploit any finger marks on the paper, and consider the potential for DNA on envelope flaps and stamps.

26.5.6 Evidence from CCTV footage

At some crime scenes, CCTV footage might provide vital information. Most CCTV cameras are automatic and many are actually unmonitored. Even digital storage systems are likely to be overwritten at some stage, so any delay in obtaining recordings should be kept to a minimum. Copies of CCTV recordings can be obtained with appropriate authorization, and a forensic analyst can then enhance the images and conduct a more thorough analysis (see 24.3.1.3). CCTV footage should not be ignored or simply deleted if the activity that concerns the investigator is not seen on the recording. Such actions may be challenged at appeal: in *R (Ebrahim) v Feltham Magistrates Court* (2001) the investigating officer did not seize a CCTV tape because he saw nothing of significance on it, but this was challenged on the ground that a fair trial would not be received as a result. CCTV recordings are disclosable material under the CPIA (see 24.3).

26.5.7 Firearms and forensics

In a typical offence a firearm is used to threaten, injure, or kill a victim, and the offender leaves with the weapon, leaving only a bullet (or lead shot), a spent cartridge, and perhaps some damage to a building showing the impact of a projectile. Later, a suspect might be arrested and his home searched, revealing a suspicious firearm which could be forensically linked to the shooting in question (or indeed any shooting), and to the person who fired the weapon. The categories of firearms, their component parts, and the associated legislation are covered more fully in Chapter 18.

Firearms and spent bullets or cartridges are a rich source of evidence. When a weapon is fired, the barrel and the firing mechanisms leave marks on the bullets and cartridge cases. The National Ballistics Intelligence Service (NABIS) can examine spent (used) bullets and cartridge cases for intelligence purposes at their hub laboratories. The examiners will look for these marks, and use their database to establish links between crime scenes where bullets and cartridges have previously been found. Recovered firearms are also test fired at the hub laboratory to generate spent bullets and cartridges for comparison with evidence already in the database.

The functionality of the NABIS database is similar to that of IDENT1 and the NDNAD, as links can be generated, so crime series can potentially be identified and detected. Clearly, one firearm can be used at a number of crime scenes so the intelligence provided by NABIS can be very useful.

Bulleted cartridge component	Available evidence
Cartridge case	The actions of loading, firing, and ejecting the cartridge will scratch the polished brass casing and leave comparable marks upon it. These marks are caused by the magazine (if used), the ejector, extractor, breech face, and firing pin. Since bullets, cartridge design, and extractors vary, it may be possible to identify the type of weapon from which the cartridge was ejected. Manufacturer's details, calibre, and type of round are normally engraved on the head stamp (the base) of cartridges. Despite the high temperature generated during firing, it is sometimes possible to recover finger marks from the brass case
Bullet	This will normally identify the calibre of the weapon used, and since there is huge variation in bullet design, any specialist rounds and sometimes the type of weapon can be identified. Most important, though, is the scratched impression on the bullet of the rifling grooves inside the gun barrel. Variations in the twist (left or right) and the number of grooves may assist in the identification of the make and model of the gun used, and can be compared to a suspect weapon. Even badly deformed bullets are useful to the scientist as a means of eliminating weapons
Powder	During firing, the powder gives off smoke and particulates which are emitted from the muzzle and frequently around the mechanism of the firearm itself. Minute particles of the bullet, unburnt powder, and other debris are ejected in several directions. This may include small granules of lead, barium, and antimony. These 'firearm discharge residues' (FDRs) can be found on the clothing, face, and hands of the offender and other people and items in the vicinity. Swabbing kits are available to retrieve this material. Suspects should be swabbed as soon as possible because the residues fall off easily. It should be noted that the presence of FDRs does not necessarily prove involvement in the offence

Shotgun cartridges vary both in their overall design and the number and size of lead shot they contain (see 18.5). CSIs and forensic scientists can use these features to derive evidence.

Shot cartridge component	Available evidence
Cartridge case (sometimes called the 'hull' in the USA)	This is normally retained in the weapon until reloading; however, it may be ejected by automatic or self-loading weapons. It can be used to establish the bore of the weapon and the manufacturer and type of cartridge. Scratches on the brass base and the impression of the firing pin and breech face can be compared to suspect weapons. In automatic weapons, marks from the extractor, ejector, and magazine may be found
The shot	The size of the shot may eliminate some types of cartridge from an enquiry. The spread of the shot can be useful in establishing the range of the weapon

Shot cartridge component	Available evidence
Powder	FDRs are available, but note that in most sporting shotguns the FDRs are ejected through the muzzle since the breech is sealed until reloading or ejection
Wadding	The presence of wadding indicates that a shotgun has been discharged. It can frequently give an early indication as to the bore of weapon used, and a hint as to the cartridge manufacturer. Wadding is normally badly deformed during discharge, so irregular lumps of plastic, felt, or cork at the scene should be collected and preserved. Plastic wadding fired from a sawn-off weapon can sometimes be compared to the finish at the sawn-off muzzle: if the finish is poor, the wadding may bear scratches which can be reproduced during controlled tests

Firearms may also require classification for offences relating to their category (such as section 1, 2, or 5, see Chapter 18). Test firing may also be required to check that they function, and to support or refute statements about trigger sensitivity or any issues with the mechanism (for instance when they fire 'accidentally'). The most frequently asked questions at laboratories are:

- Is this weapon a firearm as defined by the legislation (see 18.3.1)?
- Is this an imitation firearm (see 18.7)?
- What type of weapon fired this bullet (or recovered cartridge case)?
- Did this weapon fire this bullet (or recovered cartridge case)?
- How far was the weapon from the victim?
- Can this weapon fire accidentally?
- Do these swabs/items of clothing bear FDR?
- Which is the entry wound/exit wound on this victim?

(Adapted from a number of unpublished Forensic Science Service publications.)

TASK 2

1. List three types of trace evidence or material which might be found at a burglary.
2. List three types of impression.
3. List three sources of DNA.
4. Which does mitochondrial DNA establish: male or female lines?
5. Which parent provides a boy's Y-STR?

26.6 Taking Samples in Investigations

The objective of taking samples from suspects, victims, and crime scenes is to demonstrate a link between them, preferably during the offence in question (see 26.2.3). Forensic evidence has the potential to produce powerful forms of evidence which might 'include' or 'exclude' people and other things from an enquiry, and can also produce investigative leads. Procedures must be strictly followed (such as ISO 17020, see 26.3.3) in order that samples have a clear provenance and do not become contaminated with other material. Typically, if a sample is taken from one person or place then a corresponding sample should be recovered from elsewhere for comparison, but by a different person. A sample taken from a known source, such as DNA from a person or a scraping of paint from a window frame is known as a 'control' (see 26.6.2.1).

Whilst the crime scene is normally examined by CSIs, any people who are suspected of having been involved in the offence will also need to have samples taken. This can be carried out by custody staff, a medical practitioner or police officer in the custody area, a hospital, or at a person's home or place of work (depending on the person and the circumstances).

26.6.1 Taking samples from people

We have already discussed the requirement to link suspects, victims, and venues as part of an investigation but samples are also occasionally used to establish identity.

The samples taken from people can include a variety of trace evidence and DNA-rich material in or on any part of the body, including foreign blood, saliva, and semen (all sources of DNA);

firearm and explosive residues; trace material such as glass, paint flakes, fibres, grease, plant debris, or soil; bite marks, weapon marks, and bruises; chemicals, such as alcohol, toxins, and drugs within the blood and urine, or chemical traces upon the skin; fingerprints; and handwriting.

It is important to distinguish between people in custody and others who are voluntarily providing evidence or material which can eliminate them from the offence. When taking forensic samples from suspects (whether arrested or not) the procedures set out in PACE Code D must be followed (see 26.6.1.1). However, for other people who provide samples to assist police investigations, such as victims and witnesses, there are no equivalent PACE requirements. This means it might not *always* be necessary for a police surgeon or other medical practitioner to take certain types of sample. Police officers must, however, treat victims, witnesses, and volunteers in accordance with the Human Rights Act 1998 (see 4.4.1). This is an important consideration when arriving at a scene or dealing with a victim who attends the police station where no CSI or medical assistance is immediately available.

As noted earlier, people are crime scenes and are sources both of evidence (potentially to be used in court) and intelligence (eg to provide leads in an investigation). Hence, samples from a person can be used to:

- prove or disprove his/her involvement in the offence;
- corroborate or refute statements;
- show a link between him/her and another person, the scene, or an exhibit;
- establish drug, toxin, or alcohol levels in the body; and
- provide a reference sample (DNA, fingerprints, or footwear impressions) for direct comparison, for elimination, or for a database.

Normally DNA and fingerprint samples provided by suspects are retained in databases for 'speculative' (untargeted) searches, but most other samples are destroyed after the case is complete. Ensure you follow local protocols on retention and disposal.

26.6.1.1   PACE Code D

When taking forensic samples from suspects, parts 4–6 of PACE Code D must be followed (see the table).

Part in Code D	Procedure covered
Part 4	Identification by fingerprints and footwear impressions
Part 5	Examinations to establish identity and the taking of photographs
Part 6	Identification by body samples and impressions

This includes suspects who have not been detained but are instead attending a police station 'voluntarily' (see Code D, para 5.19). Note that when PACE refers to a suspect attending a police station 'voluntarily' this is not referring to a member of the public who 'volunteers' to submit to some form of sampling.

Some of the key points from this part of Code D are that:

- samples should be relevant and should be proportional to the offence (unless they are for speculative searching and are covered by blanket policies, such as taking fingerprints, DNA samples, and photographs);
- appropriate adults are required in many circumstances, including taking samples from juveniles, the mentally disordered, or the visually impaired; and
- a full record must be kept about consent, authority, and warnings to the detained person.

The PACE Act 1984 defines two types of sample: non-intimate and intimate. An easy way of remembering the distinction is that: a sample is non-intimate if it is outside the underwear and not an orifice, but if the area to be sampled is an orifice or within the underwear (including a bra), then it is intimate.

A non-intimate sample includes:

- a sample of hair (other than pubic hair) and includes hair plucked with the root;
- a sample taken from a nail or from under a nail;

- a swab taken from a non-intimate part of a person's body (not from inside a nostril or ear);
- an impression of the skin from a non-intimate part of the body (such as the ears, feet, or elbows); or
- saliva.

A non-intimate sample may be taken by a police officer, detention officer, or CSI, and reasonable force may be used but an intimate sample must be taken by a registered medical practitioner (a doctor, dentist, nurse, or paramedic) and force may not be used.

An intimate sample is:

- a dental impression (which must be taken by a registered dentist: Code D, para 6.4);
- a sample of blood, semen, or any other tissue fluid;
- urine (which need not be taken by a registered medical professional: Code D, para 6.4);
- pubic hair; or
- a swab taken from any part of the genitals or from any orifice other than the mouth.

Intimate samples are essential when attempting to establish the existence, or otherwise, of a 'two-way transfer' between the parties (see 26.2.3) to prove a sexual assault, rape, or other serious offences against the person. Note that in cases of sexual assault and murder the intimate *and* non-intimate sampling of prisoners and victims will ideally be conducted by a specially trained Forensic Medical Examiner (FME) or other registered medical practitioner. Police officers and CSIs might assist, however, especially with note taking and packaging.

26.6.1.2 What samples should be taken?

The types of sample taken from victims and suspects will depend on the nature of the offence. The following table describes the *minimum* samples for consideration (represented by a tick in the table). Note that PACE Code D requires that the suspect must be informed about the reason for sampling (including speculative searches) and that an inspector has given authority. The Human Rights Act 1998 must be complied with, and the reasons for taking a particular sample must be noted in each case.

	Cheque or other fraud. Hate mail	Burglary or other property crime	Sexual assault or rape	Theft from motor vehicle with damage caused	ABH and other assaults	Homicide victims and suspects
Blood and/or urine for toxicology			✔		✔	✔
Clothing (inner)			✔		✔	✔
Clothing (outer)		✔	✔	✔	✔	✔
DNA	✔	✔	✔	✔	✔	✔
Fingerprints	✔	✔	✔	✔	✔	✔
Hair (combing)		✔	✔	✔	✔	✔
Hair (pulled/cut)		✔	✔	✔	✔	✔
Handwriting sample	✔					
Photographs of injuries		When relevant	When relevant	When relevant	When relevant	Effectively mandatory
Sexual offence kit			Mandatory			Normally used
Shoes	✔	✔	✔	✔	✔	✔

26.6.1.3 The sampling procedure for taking evidence from people

Upon delivery to a custody area all arrested persons are subject to mandatory sampling where their fingerprints, DNA, and a photograph are taken. Force policies may also require the scanning of shoe patterns. DNA will not be required if a successful profile has been created previously. Sampling of suspects for evidence to link them to recent crimes should be carried out as soon after arrest as possible to recover the maximum available material. Do remember that, in major crimes and sexual offences, you should contact a CSI for advice if you wish to carry out Livescan fingerprinting or DNA swabbing prior to the arrival of the medical practitioner, because evidence can be lost during these processes. If there is a long delay between offence and arrest (even years), the CSI should be consulted because non-intimate samples and material recovered from the crime scene may still be useful.

Brand-new, unused packaging equipment must be used, since old equipment is a source of contamination. Specific kits are available, for example for the sampling of hair or urine, and these should be used where accessible. Personnel should wear gloves as a minimum form of protection and, for serious offences, or where health warnings exist, officers should wear protective clothing to protect themselves and the evidence from contamination. The CSI or forensic support personnel should be informed when samples have been taken, so that correct transport, storage, and subsequent preservation can be arranged. Materials containing potential DNA should normally be frozen immediately. For target materials similar to a paint or oil, it is best practice to air-dry the samples securely, or to freeze them if this is not possible. It is best to seek advice from a CSI.

Samples from the exposed skin, hands, head, and mouth should be taken first (before clothing samples) in order to prevent material from those areas contaminating the clothing or vice versa.

26.6.1.4   Head hair samples

Head hair (including beard hair) may contain glass, plant material, foreign hairs, and other particulates and should be dealt with before clothing is removed. This will limit contamination by or from other samples (especially important in offences where windows have been smashed). Head hair samples can be used for the following purposes:

- recovery of fibres, hair, and particulate material and traces, wet or dry blood;
- comparison (as a control) with the subject's hair (structure, length, colour, and treatments) when found at scenes or on other people;
- chemical analysis to demonstrate long-term drug use or metals poisoning; and
- DNA analysis from the cells forming part of a hair root.

Any hat should be removed and exhibited first. Where religious head coverings are worn, such as turbans, it is good practice to ask permission from the person first and, time permitting, make arrangements for alternative head coverings prior to removal.

The samples must be taken over a sheet of pre-folded paper (at least A4 size) which catches debris. The hair should be combed from front to back all over the head so that debris falls onto the paper, continuing until no more debris is found. Clearly, this is not easy when the person is not compliant. The paper and comb should both be exhibited. For a person with matted hair or dreadlocks, a glove can be worn and the hair gently 'brushed' with the hands, or a new small hairbrush can be used with care. The paper containing the debris, the glove, and the comb or brush should be exhibited. Any blood or other matted material in the hair should be cut out over a sheet of pre-folded paper, and the scissors should be exhibited along with the cut section and the paper.

A 'control' of head hair is also required and ideally this is pulled out (so it contains the root material and can be identified as belonging to that person through DNA), but follow local advice because some forces may prefer the hair to be cut. At least 25 control hairs should be taken, including all colours and length variations.

26.6.1.5   Clothing and footwear samples

Given that footwear can leave marks, and that clothing can leave impressions or fibres at crime scenes, these forms of evidence can be very powerful. In the laboratory the scientist may wish to take test impressions or use control samples of fibres to establish whether the footwear or clothing was worn by a person involved in an offence. Fibres, hair, blood, etc can transfer between different parties during offences against the person and during property crimes, so they are potentially very useful as evidence. Damage to clothing can provide information about weapons used on a victim, and damage to fibres can indicate proximity to fire or an explosion.

When taking clothing from suspects and victims, the person must stand on a clean paper sheet to catch any falling debris, because material recovered from the floor has no known provenance. The clothing should be removed in a logical manner, normally starting with jackets and sweaters, followed by shoes, trousers and socks. Each piece should be separately exhibited and packaged in front of the subject. Notes should be made about its size, the presence of blood, colour, logos, and any damage. This avoids the need to open the packaging later, to screen or describe the contents. A final search of pockets may be carried out within the bag to prevent the unnecessary loss of material.

When all the clothing has been taken the subject's bare feet should be brushed off onto the paper sheet before he/she steps off, because material on the sheet will otherwise adhere to sweaty feet. The paper sheet on the floor is also an exhibit, and must be treated with care before being folded and dispatched for storage or analysis.

Footwear impressions can provide important intelligence information since they can be compared against patterns stored in the National Footwear Database. This can be searched for footwear matches, which is particularly relevant for premises-related crimes such as burglary. Shoes which may be needed for the analysis of trace materials and DNA should not be scanned or photocopied as this can contaminate the shoes or cause the loss of material. It is best to seek advice from a CSI.

26.6.1.6 Skin swabs and nail scrapings

Swabs of blood or other DNA-rich material on the skin should ideally be taken by a CSI or trained custody personnel, but do not permit unnecessary delays to occur. The skin may bear other residues such as explosives traces, security paints and markers, or metals such as lead. Note that bite marks on people may contain another person's DNA that will need to be preserved; a CSI should be contacted immediately. Typically, swabs are taken either wetted with sterile water, or dry if the residue is wet or tacky. An unused 'control' swab from the same batch should be included in the bag.

Nails may have skin or other debris beneath them. They are cut or scraped by using a 'nail module' which typically contains cocktail sticks, A4 paper, bags, and clippers. Hold the hand firmly and carefully clip or scrape the debris from all the nails of one hand onto the pre-folded paper. Place the cocktail stick (or clippers) inside the paper before folding it, then put everything in the bag and seal it in the presence of the suspect. The samples from each hand form separate exhibits.

26.6.1.7 Buccal swabs and other samples for DNA analysis

DNA can be extracted from buccal (mouth) swabs and pulled hair for inclusion in the NDNAD, and for direct comparison to crime scenes and victims. The subject should not eat, drink, or smoke for at least 20 minutes before the test because this allows the lining of the mouth to generate new cells to replace dead or damaged cells. The DNA sampling pack contains a buccal swab kit and a hair sampling kit. The gloves must be worn and every effort must be made to avoid contamination—biological material can be very easily contaminated by people talking, coughing, or sneezing over it, or otherwise mishandling it. The sampling process should be carried out *before* completing the associated paperwork, because if the swab is accidentally dropped, the entire kit must be disposed of and a new form would have to be completed for the replacement swab kit. Force protocols must be followed regarding subsequent record keeping, handling, and storage. Note that although Code D, para 6.7 refers to the use of 'reasonable' force to take non-intimate samples, buccal swabs should not be taken by force because of the risk of causing choking.

A suspect may refuse to provide a buccal swab, in which case he/she may elect to provide a hair sample (pulled, to include the root). The hair sampling site can be chosen by the suspect on condition that it is not in an intimate area. In the unlikely event that the suspect has no hair at all and has refused a buccal swab, then a blood sample will suffice but this would be an intimate sample.

26.6.1.8 Prints and impressions from people

Fingerprints are a useful and non-invasive form of evidence. The regulations governing their use by the police are provided in Code D, paras 4.1–4.15. Police officers receive training on how to fingerprint suspects using Livescan (in all main police stations), portable devices for use on patrol, and sometimes on ink systems. Livescan and portable scanners have the advantage of being digitally linked to IDENT1, so they are quick and accurate. Ink systems include using traditional copper plate and printers' ink, and peel-apart pre-inked strips. The latter have the advantage of being portable, and they are mainly used to take elimination fingerprints from, for example, victims of crime.

Fingerprints can be used to identify a person as part of immigration enquiries, such as for a person detained under the Immigration Act 1971 or the Immigration and Asylum Act 1999. Typically, this is required when a person:

(a) fails to produce evidence of identity and nationality upon arrival to the UK;
(b) is refused entry but temporarily admitted;
(c) is to be removed as an illegal entrant or deported;
(d) is arrested under the Immigration Act 1971;
(e) has made a claim for asylum;
(f) is a dependant of any person listed in (b) to (e).

People requesting visas or asylum in the UK have their fingerprint, facial, and digital documentation data stored in the Immigration and Asylum Biometrics System (IABS).

Whilst many police officers are able to take fingerprints, other impressions can be problematic. For instance Code D, para 6.1(v) covers the more unusual body impressions (eg ears and feet), which can be difficult to do properly, so the advice of a CSI should be sought.

26.6.1.9   Handwriting samples

A person providing a handwriting sample should sit at a table without being able to view any of the existing handwriting evidence. A ballpoint pen is used—not a pencil or a felt tip because they do not always show the construction of each letter, which is important. The officer then dictates what is to be written. Under no circumstances should the subject simply be asked to write 'the quick brown fox jumps over the lazy dog'. This sentence would be of little use since a person's writing style is partly determined by the letters before and after every other letter, so it might not provide the combinations required for the investigation. The sample material must be written in the same format as the document for comparison: if the original is in capitals, then the sample piece must be in capitals, and so on. If the writing was on a specific form, the supplier should be asked to supply blank samples; dummy cheques are available from CSI or Fraud Units if necessary. Typically, the person should be asked to write out the contents of the document a minimum of five times (unless this would be unreasonable), and for cheques, at least 15 samples are needed. He/she should sign and date every page, and each completed sample should be removed so the writing style used previously cannot be seen and copied. The subject may, obviously, attempt to conceal his/her true handwriting style but is likely to revert to type after several samples. (This is why 'course of business' handwriting, perhaps taken from the home or workplace, is useful.) Even though the final results may be 'obvious', the samples should still be submitted to a suitable facility for expert opinion. Note that your forensic supplier may accept scanned copies by email for an initial assessment.

26.6.1.10   Photographs

Taking photographs and searching for identifying marks is covered in Code D (paras 5.1–5.18 for a detained person and paras 5.19–5.24 for a person who is at a police station but not detained). Paragraph 5.1 permits photography of injuries because an image of a suspect's recent injury may indicate his/her involvement in an offence, for example burns from arson attacks, and bruises or lacerations caused by one or more parties defending themselves in an assault case, especially when a victim of strangulation has fought back. Valuable identification evidence can also be provided by taking photographs of certain features such as tattoos and scars.

Code D, para 5.4 states that 'identifying marks' include those that could identify the person as a 'person involved in the commission of an offence'. This means that suspects can be examined with a UV light source to look for fluorescent dyes from marker traps deployed to deter theft of high-value goods and, especially, metal theft (see 26.5.1.2).

TASK 3 Imagine you are a police officer. Consider what you might do if:

1. A woman attends the police station and claims to have been 'date-raped'. GHB and Rohypnol (examples of so-called 'date-rape' drugs) are rapidly excreted from the human body. Would you find a 'urine module' and request an immediate urine sample? How might this affect potential DNA evidence?

2. You attend a robbery and a man says he bit the offender. He can still taste blood in his mouth. Would you ask him to spit into a sterile bottle?
3. A victim claims a man sexually assaulted her and ejaculated over her hand. Would you glove or bag her hand, or even take a swab from it (if trained)?

26.6.2 Sampling from crime scenes

This is a complex area so CSI trainers provide training for new officers and those on refresher or detective training courses. This Handbook can be used as a guide, but local CSIs are best able to provide the most up-to-date information on local force protocols.

A force is likely to employ specialist CSI staff whose chief role is the recovery of physical material from crime scenes. However, a police officer may seize exhibits in the course of duty at crime scenes, for example when part of a search team (see 9.5), or if it seems there are only one or two items to seize and they can be safely recovered without a CSI, such as documents, cheques, or a single moveable shoe mark, but note that local policies on CSI deployment and evidence seizure must be followed. There may also be situations where the CSI is unable to attend, or where evidence could be lost if not recovered immediately (eg a shotgun cartridge on a windy day).

Evidence at crime scenes can include a wide range of potentially valuable material, but it will be mixed up with lots of other 'everyday' items. The best way to identify sources of potential evidence at volume crime scenes is to speak to the victim. The CSI will question the victim at a common domestic burglary regarding probable entry and exit routes, what has been disturbed, and what was stolen. This informs the search for evidence which, typically, follows a common pattern. The CSI then assesses the risks and hazards and examines external areas for evidence first, particularly the point of entry and especially if the weather might destroy it. This is followed by a search of the internal areas and focal points such as searched drawers and other disturbed articles. The victim assists but does not control the process. Contemporaneous notes are taken, and packaging is completed at the scene.

Usually (though not always at volume crimes), photographs are taken first, because the process is non-destructive. Then DNA and other trace evidence are taken, with finger-printing carried out last, because the powders are contaminants. Each piece of evidence is packaged, marked, and labelled according to force protocols, and its position and description recorded on a worksheet. In a standard volume crime scene, common forms of evidence include:

- tool-marks and shoe marks outside the premises, particularly near to the point of entry (these are photographed and then cast using a silicone gel or plaster of Paris);
- broken glass (broken during entry) for use as a control to match to any glass found in the suspect's hair and clothing;
- shoe marks on windowsills (these can be photographed and lifted onto gel or tape). Shoes can also leave prints some distance into a crime scene, especially on recently waxed floors and gloss doors (see 26.5.2.1 for details);
- finger marks left by a suspect climbing into the premises, pulling out a pane of glass, leaving ornaments outside, or while searching (see 26.5.4.1 for details);
- DNA, if the suspect has sustained injuries, left strands of pulled hair, consumed food or drinks, or discarded a cigarette;
- glove and fabric patterns, marks left by the ears, nose, elbows, and even lips, all of which have been found at crime scenes; and
- control samples of fabrics and paint to compare with fibres or debris on the suspect's clothing or tools.

26.6.2.1 Recovering 'controls'

A control is for comparing with other samples, for instance comparing a fibre from a sofa in a crime scene with fibres found on a suspect. A control (in crime-scene investigation terms) comes from a known source, so in this example it would be material cut from the sofa. This would then be compared to fibres found on the suspect's clothing (and vice versa, with his clothing acting as a control). Where only a simple control of material—such as fibres, paint, or broken glass—is needed without a full scene examination then a suitably trained police officer may gather the samples, but for anything more complex the CSI should be tasked.

26.7 **Seizure and Packaging Techniques**

Using the correct seizure procedures and methods for packaging prevents damage and contamination and is, effectively, a demonstration of the care and skill that accompanied the seizure of the exhibits. Local force protocols will be based on those laid down by forensic science laboratories and these must be followed. Guidance can be found in the FSS publication *The Scenes of Crime Handbook* (probably available to police officers through their local force, and available as a PDF online, or from SceneSafe). For the seizure and packaging of objects related to cyber-enabled or cyber-dependent crime, see 21.5.

26.7.1 **Types of packaging and how to use them**

Paper bags should have the top folded over twice (approximately 25 mm (one inch) per fold). The joint should be sealed over with two signature seals (an adhesive label with the officer's signature, name, and number). The entire join between folds and bag should then be completely sealed, preferably with clear one-inch tape. An exhibit label can also be attached if required but most bags have these pre-printed upon them. Note that some forces require the factory-sealed base of the bag to be folded and sealed in the same way as the folded top.

For **polythene bags** a tamper-evident bag should be used if available. The methods for sealing plain (unmarked) polythene bags are more complex: speak to your CSI.

Nylon bags should be sealed by twisting into a 'swan neck' as shown in the photograph, and then secured with tape or a cable tie (without 'teeth' as these could puncture the bag). The sealed nylon bag is then placed in a polythene bag, swan necked, and sealed.

(Image © Kevin Lawton-Barrett)

A Nylon bag 'swan necked' prior to securing with a cable tie

The entire package should then be placed in a rigid container, signature sealed, and labelled. Nylon bags containing hydrocarbons should not be stored close to other samples (see 26.7.2).

Boxes can also be used for large items, but they must be immobilized inside the box with string or cable ties. All the open edges of the box must be sealed with tape and signature-sealed as shown in the photograph. Smaller boxes for mobile phones, etc can be sealed into pre-printed tamper-evident polythene bags.

(Image © Kevin Lawton-Barrett)

Police evidence box

Paper folds are required for the safe collection and storage of dry materials such as powders, paint fragments, and hair combings (but not glass: use a small box). The diagram shows a common technique for constructing a 'paper-fold' container. Pre-fold the paper before adding the loose material, and then tap the paper gently to work the material down into the greyed section before refolding and sealing into a suitable polythene bag.

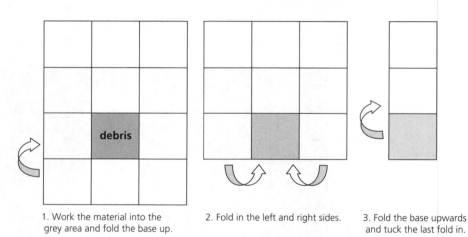

1. Work the material into the grey area and fold the base up.

2. Fold in the left and right sides.

3. Fold the base upwards and tuck the last fold in.

26.7.2 Packaging procedures for some common items

In these examples it is assumed that the officer has access to packaging materials with pre-printed exhibit labels attached. If labels are not printed on the package then separate paper labels should be used, but you should also write onto the package in case the label becomes detached.

Bedding, fabrics, clothes, and shoes must be sealed into paper bags which allow them to breathe. Sealing articles which are even slightly damp into plastic encourages the growth of mould and bacteria. A health hazard warning label should be used if any biological material might be present or where it is known or believed that articles have come from a potentially contaminated source (eg a known drug addict).

Articles that are **slightly wet or soaked** with non-flammable liquids (including blood) need to be dried. A CSI should be contacted *urgently* for advice and assistance with drying. Fabric items bearing wet blood must not be folded as this causes the blood to transfer to other parts of the article. In an emergency the wet items could be placed in a polythene sack for transport but urgent CSI advice is required, and it should all be sealed into a robust paper sack for protection.

Articles which may bear **flammable substances** should not be stored in paper bags because flammable chemicals (ignitable liquids or accelerants) will evaporate through paper sacks and be lost and also contaminate other material in storage and transit. Typically these samples are packaged in nylon bags sealed *within* a polythene bag, and, rather than tape, the necks are 'swan necked' and sealed with cable ties. Where biological material such as blood or semen is also believed present, the CSI should be consulted, since DNA may be destroyed by flammable substances. It is likely that the CSI will recommend immediate transport to a laboratory.

Sharps, bladed weapons, screwdrivers, and other pointed objects represent a very serious health hazard. If specialist syringe and needle storage boxes are not available, consider disposing of hypodermic needles in a sharps bin prior to packaging the syringe (this does not apply in major-crime cases: advice will be required). For knives and blades, a knife tube should be used where possible, but a clean, unused, sturdy box could suffice. Care should be taken with screw-thread knife tubes as the screwing action can easily force the point of a knife blade through the lid and into the hand. The two halves of knife tubes and sharps packs are often sealed together with tape and signature-sealed prior to packaging in a polythene bag. Blood soaked or wet weapons will need air-drying to prevent rusting or DNA decay.

Firearms represent a serious and immediate high-risk hazard. It is best practice to call for the assistance of a Firearms Officer and/or a firearms trained CSI to properly record the making-safe process. Any firearms of forensic interest can then be sealed in boxes with a safety certificate but those surrendered to the police (perhaps after the death of the owner) may simply require a label after they have been made safe. Above all else—avoid transporting or handling firearms which are not known to be safe.

Bottles and glasses must be immobilized in a sturdy box to protect finger marks or DNA, and prevent damage from any sharp edges. Bottles and glasses for back-calculation alcohol analysis (see 19.9.5.3) must be marked to show the levels the suspect claims to have drunk.

Urine samples may be required in a crime investigation or be taken from drivers under the Road Traffic Act 1988 (see 19.9.5.2). Custody officers have access to 'RTA-type' urine kits which contain a special preservative, but the urine can also be collected in a plastic pot, which is then decanted into a suitable bottle containing a preservative. The bottle must be properly secured and placed in a rigid outer container.

Documents should be packed in stout card folders or boxes to prevent people leaning on the documents or writing over them.

TASK 4 If you are a trainee police officer discuss the following questions with a CSI or your trainers. If you are a student you could raise them in a seminar:

1. At a major crime scene, what are the usual problems with the CAP and cordons?
2. What is the better form of evidence: a finger mark or DNA? (People are very likely to have different views, based almost entirely upon the perceived context of the evidence.)
3. What is worse, known contamination of an exhibit, or the suspicion of contamination?

TASK 5

1. A police officer is taking a DNA sample from an arrested person. He accidentally drops the swab on the floor. What should he do now?
2. Which PACE Act 1984 Code applies to fingerprinting suspects?
3. Imagine you have a quantity of fine debris you wish to store. Taking a sheet of A4 paper, make a paper fold to retain it.
4. For forensic purposes, what sort of bag should be used to pack clothing thought to be contaminated with petrol?
5. In an emergency, where a woman claims to have been drugged and raped, can a police officer lawfully ask her to provide a urine sample?
6. A police officer attends a crime scene and takes a control sample of glass. How many pieces should she take? From where? Should the glass be marked at all?

26.8 **Answers to Tasks**

TASK 1

1. Forensic Science Provider. Most forensic services were previously carried out by the Forensic Science Service (FSS) but this was closed by the government for financial reasons and the work has been taken over by a range of private sector companies. The FSS archive still exists for research and cold case investigations.
2. Edmond Locard.
3. A possible list:
   - describing the *modus operandi* (MO);
   - answering investigative questions;
   - to establish that an offence has occurred;
   - to identify an offender or suspect;
   - to corroborate or refute witness statements;
   - to establish a physical link between suspect, crime scene, and victim;
   - to identify an individual; and
   - to further inform an enquiry.

TASK 2

1. Fibres, glass, paint, soil, pollen, etc. You could also include DNA-rich material.
2. Tool marks, shoe marks, impressions from stamps and dyes, extrusion marks, finger marks, clothing, gloves, bite marks, etc.
3. Blood, semen, ear wax, mucus, saliva, etc.
4. Mitochondrial DNA comes from the female line, that is, from the mother, and is found in all her children.
5. The Y-STR comes from the father and is passed only to his sons.

TASK 3 In all these instances you could lawfully have taken the evidence. If you decided not to, the evidence could quite possibly be lost.

It is acceptable, in an emergency and when a CSI or medical assistance is not available, for anyone to take a sample from a victim in cases such as these. Clearly, the dignity and psychological well-being of the victim must be uppermost in your mind, but there are occasions when decisive action will benefit the investigation. Crucially, you would need to have access to the appropriate sterile equipment, and you would preferably have received previous training.

Many police forces have evidence kits at the front counter for just this sort of unlikely situation. Out on Supervised or Independent Patrol these kits might not be available, so personnel may have to 'make do'.

TASK 4

1. Common Approach Paths sound simple but raise many problems, not least of which is selecting a good route and location. Essentially, they should be on a hard surface and should not be the offender's or victim's likely route to or from the crime scene. The next issue is how to mark a CAP on a windy day without anything to secure the tape. This cannot really be done until assistance arrives. CSIs will probably be able to explain that, with hindsight, the FAO could have employed better tactics.
2. Fingerprints are assumed to be unique, but there is disagreement over this issue since it is difficult to actually prove this point in a scientific sense (we cannot compare every finger that has ever existed or that will ever exist). Our DNA is unique too, and many people prefer this type of evidence more readily, possibly because it has been the subject of much recent research. The best evidence, ultimately, only occurs where the context for it is right: thus on one occasion DNA can initially appear to be of little use, whilst in another context it could be very powerful.

   In terms of speed, the turnaround for a fingerprint in an emergency can be a few hours from any point in the UK by using Livescan or digital photography and secure email, or by actually taking non-digital images of fingerprints direct to a fingerprint bureau. For DNA, forensic scientists are now deploying fully automated 'Rapid DNA' technology in some areas, which can reduce the analysis time to about 2 hours, but if this is not available, the best that DNA evidence can manage is around 12 hours.

3. If the CSI knows contamination has occurred he/she can warn the scientist, and occasionally there may be a way to overcome the problem. If there is a suspicion or accusation that it has occurred then there may be no resolution, particularly if the Crown is 'ambushed' in court. By ensuring rigorous standards at the scene (or elsewhere) and by admitting mistakes, the prosecution might be able to offer a rebuttal. The most important point is: never allow contamination to occur. But if it does, then honesty is the best policy.

TASK 5

1. Destroy the entire kit and start again with a new kit.
2. Code D.
3. Compare the result to the diagram in 26.7.1.
4. Nylon. Nylon bags are crinkly and rustle like a crisp packet: remember 'Nylon is Noisy'.
5. Yes. There is nothing to prevent an officer asking for a sample in an emergency (and assisting, to an extent, in its collection). However, the human rights of the individual must be respected and officers should act with common decency.
6. Six pieces from the frame (around the hole), and mark the inside or outside of each piece.

27 Prosecution and Court Procedures

27.1 Introduction

Prosecution, as all experienced police officers know, is often a lengthy and complex affair, and many aspects are not solely in the control of the police. There are two forms of prosecution: written and criminal charge. Written charge is a relatively straightforward process (see 10.13.1.1). Here we cover the more complex process of criminal charge.

The police decide on charging for most 'volume crimes' that are summary only offences. They can also decide for either-way offences as long as a guilty plea is anticipated, and the magistrates have sufficient sentencing powers to deal with the case to conclusion. There are exceptions to this, for example in any cases involving a death, sexual offences where the complainant is under the age of 18, and cases involving hate crime or domestic abuse (see the CPS document *Charging (The Director's Guidance) 2013*—5th edition, available online).

The Crown Prosecution Service (CPS) make the charging decisions for all indictable offences, and for more complex or sensitive cases. Once a decision to charge has been made, the CPS will run the case to conclusion, working closely with the police officer in the case (OIC).

In this chapter we look at the role of the CPS and examine the aspects of the charging, prosecution, and court procedures which are most relevant to trainee officers and students on pre-join programmes. Most of the subject matter relates to the National Policing Curriculum subject areas: 'Conducting Investigations' (one of the specialist areas) and 'Criminal Justice'.

27.2 The Role of the Crown Prosecution Service

The CPS was set up in 1986 under the Prosecution of Offences Act 1985 as an independent prosecuting authority for England and Wales. It is independent of the police, and is therefore an important mechanism for maintaining fairness in the criminal justice system. CPS lawyers (Crown prosecutors) are solicitors and barristers who are responsible for prosecuting criminal cases on behalf of the Crown.

Where a case is serious or complex, Crown prosecutors advise the police in the early stages of the investigation, sometimes about possible lines of investigation, and always in terms of decisions about charging. These types of cases should not be charged by the police without the authority of a Crown prosecutor. Crown prosecutors prepare and then present cases in court. The CPS also provides information and guidance to victims and witnesses, and will help support them through the prosecution process.

The CPS is divided into 13 areas across England and Wales. Each area is headed up by a Chief Crown Prosecutor, who in turn is answerable to the Director of Public Prosecutions. The Director of Public Prosecutions is the head of the CPS and works under the superintendence of the Attorney General. The Attorney General oversees the work of the CPS and is accountable to the government in terms of its performance and conduct.

Crown prosecutors are governed by the Code for Crown Prosecutors. This is a public document and is available on the CPS website (CPS, 2018a). In short, it sets out that before pursuing a case, the Crown prosecutor should be sure that there is sufficient evidence to provide a realistic prospect of conviction, and that it is also in the public interest to pursue a prosecution.

Only when both of these elements are met should a case be charged. The same standard applies in cases where the charging decision has been made by the police. There is one exception to this, and that is where a case is charged on the threshold test (see 27.3.2).

27.3 The Charging Process

As mentioned in the introduction to this chapter, the police are responsible for charging decisions in most cases involving straightforward summary offences, and in lower level either-way offences that are likely to be dealt with in a magistrates' court. The charging decision should be referred to the CPS for indictable-only cases, and for more serious or sensitive either-way offences likely to be heard at the Crown Court. Charging advice is normally provided to the police in one of three ways: CPS Direct; the direct submission of a case file; or through a face-to-face meeting.

CPS Direct provides most of the charging advice given to the police. It consists of teams of Crown prosecutors across England and Wales who are available 24 hours a day, seven days a week, 365 days of the year. The police contact CPS Direct by telephone and electronically transmit the evidence, so the advice may be provided straight away. At this point a suspect could still be in custody and the police may be requesting charging advice on the threshold test (see 27.3.2), or the suspect may have been bailed pending a charging decision—in which case the charging advice is likely to be given in line with the full code test (see 27.3.1). Charging advice is requested on police MG3 forms (see 27.4.2), and the Crown prosecutor sends the advice to the officer electronically, on a CPS MG3 form.

For cases that are more complex and/or sensitive, a file can be submitted directly to the CPS. A Crown prosecutor will then review the file and provide charging advice to the police. Again, charging advice will be sought and given on MG3 forms.

Face-to-face meetings, or sometimes video-conference style meetings, are held for large-scale, complex, sensitive, and serious cases. By their very nature these cases will require more time and may involve the examination of large quantities of evidence.

27.3.1 The full code test

The majority of cases will be charged using the 'full code test'. This is set out in the *Code for Crown Prosecutors*, but it also applies for cases where the charging decision is made by the police. There are two stages to the full code test. First, the prosecutor must be sure that there is sufficient evidence to provide a realistic prospect of conviction. This is different to the test set down for a jury deciding on guilt. A prosecutor does not need to be convinced of guilt beyond any reasonable doubt, but must be sure that a properly directed and impartial jury, acting in accordance with the law, is more likely than not to find the defendant guilty. When the prosecutor is trying to decide whether the evidence is sufficient, he/she needs to be sure that the available evidence is reliable, credible, and can be used in court. If there is insufficient evidence to provide a realistic prospect of conviction then the case fails at this stage and the suspect should not be charged, no matter how serious the offence is. If the prosecutor decides there is sufficient evidence to provide a realistic prospect of conviction the second stage of the test is applied.

The second stage of the full code test considers the public interest. If there is sufficient evidence then a case will normally proceed unless there are significant public interest factors which suggest that the case should not go ahead. Public interest factors can include:

- the age of the suspect;
- the circumstances of, and the level of harm caused to, the victim;
- the impact on the community;
- whether there may be a source of information that requires protection; and
- whether a prosecution is a proportionate response or whether the suspect could be better dealt with by a method which diverts them from the court process, such as a caution.

There is no exhaustive list of public interest factors, and there may well be factors unique to individual cases. If a case meets the full code test then the appropriate charge(s) should be selected and the suspect charged as soon as practicable (CPS, 2018a).

27.3.2 The threshold test

The threshold test is used when there is a time limit and a decision has to be made on whether to charge, grant bail, or release under investigation. It applies in cases where further evidence still needs to be gathered but the suspect would pose a significant risk if released. There are two questions that must be considered when applying the threshold test:

- Is there a reasonable suspicion, using the available evidence, that the suspect committed the offence?
- Is there further identifiable evidence to be gathered that could ultimately provide the prosecution with a realistic prospect of conviction (in line with the full code test)?

If both factors are met, the Crown prosecutor is likely to authorize a charge under the threshold test (CPS, 2018a). Once charged, the suspect must be placed in front of the next available court for the magistrates to decide whether to remand the defendant in custody or grant bail. The CPS, working together with the police, may apply for remand in custody, but the court makes the actual decision.

When a case has been charged under the threshold test and the defendant has been detained on remand, the case must be kept under constant review to ensure that it is progressing as anticipated, to make sure that the decision to keep the defendant on remand is still appropriate. As soon as practicable the full code test must be applied and met in order for the case to continue.

27.3.3 Investigative advice

In the case of very large-scale, complex, or sensitive cases the police may decide to seek advice from the CPS at a very early stage in the investigation to ensure that the correct evidence is identified and gathered from the outset. This may involve a number of consultations, and the CPS may also provide written advice setting out further actions for the police to complete ('action plans') before charges are actually authorized (see 24.4.4). However, this additional effort ultimately saves the police from pursuing unnecessary lines of enquiry and ensures that the appropriate and required evidence is gathered as soon as practicable.

27.3.4 Selecting the correct charge

A CPS 'charging standard' can be used to determine the precise charge (or charges) made against an individual. For example, a suspected shoplifter might be charged with 'Theft contrary to sections 1(1) and 7 of the Theft Act 1968', in which case the charging standard would involve a consideration of the five elements of the offence (dishonesty, appropriation, property, belonging to another, permanent intention to deprive (see 16.2)).

When selecting the charge, the Crown prosecutor or police officer should make sure the charge fairly reflects the seriousness and the full extent of the offending. The charge selected should also give the court adequate sentencing power. Once charged, the 'suspect' becomes a 'defendant'.

27.4 Preparing and Submitting Case Files

It is important that case files are completed accurately, logically, and with integrity for a prosecution to succeed. The case file will include a summary of the interview (see 25.5.7), the MG6 forms (see 27.4.2), charge sheets, and lists of exhibits (often forensic evidence).

27.4.1 The National File Standard

The National File Standard (NFS) is described by the CPS and the College of Policing as providing a 'staged and proportionate approach to the preparation of case files' (CPS, 2013; COP, 2014d). The purpose is to provide the prosecutor, the defence, and the court with proportionate and relevant information throughout the case. The files submitted to the prosecution from the first hearing must contain the core information which the prosecutor will need to complete a Case Management Form. The required content for a case file depends on whether a guilty or not guilty plea is expected.

27.4.2 MG forms

The forms for case files are often referred to as 'MG forms' (see the Home Office document *Manual of guidance and MG forms Version 10.0*). Each MG form will show the suspect's details and the case file reference number (these will have been uploaded when the suspect was first presented to the custody officer upon arrest (see 10.10.2)). The forms are numbered in the official lists, for example MG02, though the zero is often omitted in other written documents (as in this book), and in conversation. Here we cover only the MG forms that a trainee police officer is likely to require for three different categories of case, as follows:

- straightforward cases where a guilty plea is entered (and there are no complications such as certain sensitive disclosure issues);
- contested cases ('not guilty' pleas); and
- Crown Court cases.

The forms required for straightforward and contested cases depend on whether the suspect has been charged. Charging decisions are usually based on the information received by the CPS in a pre-charge expedited case file. This will include forms MG3 and MG3A and any key evidence. Once the charge has been made, a post-charge expedited file is required so that an advanced disclosure pack can be built for the defence and the court. This pack should include a summary of the case and the interview (in the MG5), any available statements and exhibits, and a copy of the defendant's previous convictions.

If a 'not guilty' plea is entered, or if the case is to be heard in Crown Court, upgrading to a Full File is required. If the case is disposed of at the first court appearance, then of course no upgrading is needed.

The forms required for each eventuality are shown in the table. A tick indicates that a particular form will almost certainly be needed, and a question mark indicates that it might be needed.

Form	description	straightforward		contested		full file
		pre-	post-	pre-	post-	
MG2	Special Measures Assessment				?	
MG3	Report to Crown Prosecutor	✓	✓	✓	✓	✓
MG3A	Further report to Crown Prosecutor	?	?	?	?	
MG4	Charge sheet		✓		✓	
MG4A	Conditional bail form		?		?	
MG4B	Request to vary police conditional bail		?		?	
MG4C	Surety/Security		?		?	
MG5	Police Report		✓		✓	✓
MG6	Case file evidence and information	?	?	?	?	
MG6B	Police officer/staff's disciplinary record					?
MG6C	Schedule of non-sensitive unused material					✓
MG6D	Schedule of sensitive material					✓
MG6E	Disclosure officer's report					✓
MG7	Remand in custody application		?		?	?
MG8	Breach of bail conditions		?		?	
MG9	Witness list		✓		✓	✓
MG10	Witness non-availability		✓		✓	✓
MG11	Witness statements	?	?	?	?	?
MG12	Exhibits list					✓
MG15	Interview record: this could be an SDN, a ROTI, or a ROVI*		?		?	✓

Form	description	straightforward		contested		full file
		pre-	post-	pre-	post-	
MG16	Bad character/dangerous offenders				?	?
MG18	Offences taken into consideration		?		?	?
MG19	Compensation form (plus supporting documents)					✓
MG21/21A	Forensic submissions				?	✓
MGDD A/B	Driving under the influence of alcohol/drugs forms	?	?	?	?	?
SDN	Short Descriptive Note; may be written on MG15, MG5, or officer's MG11		✓			✓
Phoenix print	Computer print-out of the suspect's previous convictions, cautions, etc	✓	✓	✓	✓	✓
PNC	Print-out of suspect and key prosecution witnesses' pre-convictions, including cautions, reprimands, final warnings, PNDs etc	✓	✓	✓	✓	✓
Copy of documentary exhibits/photos			✓	✓	✓	✓
Police racist incident form/crime report			?		?	?
Crime report and incident log				✓	✓	✓
Any unused material which might undermine the case		✓	✓	✓	✓	✓
Custody record						✓

* ROTI: Record of a Taped Interview; ROVI: Record of a Video-recorded Interview; both are written documents summarizing the content of the recordings.

27.5 In Court

The role of magistrates' courts and the Crown Court is explained in 4.5. Here, we will concentrate on what happens at court, with particular emphasis on the likely role of a trainee officer.

The course of events in both the magistrates' courts and the Crown Courts follow certain routines and patterns depending on the type of hearing. In the table you will find a description of the people who are most likely to be present in the magistrates' and the Crown Court.

Participants in the court room	Description of the role
The Magistrate(s)	Unpaid, specially trained volunteers who hear cases in the magistrates' court. They are not legal professionals. Also known as 'lay magistrates'
District Judge	A legal professional drawn from the rank of solicitor or barrister—hears cases in the magistrates' courts only
Court legal adviser	A legally trained professional who advises the lay magistrates on matters relating to the law
The defendant	The person who is charged with the offence with which the court is concerned
Representative for the prosecution	In the magistrates' court this may be a solicitor, a barrister, or an associate prosecutor. (Associate prosecutors can review and present straightforward cases, and with further training may present trials involving summary only offences without the penalty of a custodial sentence.) In the Crown Court the representative must be a barrister, or a solicitor who has undertaken further training and obtained 'higher rights of audience'. He/she may be employed by the CPS, or be a barrister from the independent bar who has been instructed by the CPS
Defence	A legal professional acting on behalf of the defendant. Again, this can be a solicitor or a barrister in the magistrates' court. In the Crown Court it must be a barrister or a solicitor who has undertaken further training and obtained 'higher rights of audience'
The Public	Courtrooms are open to the public and anyone may attend a hearing. There are certain exceptions to this, for example where the defendant is under 18
The Judge	Crown Court judges are legally qualified professionals, normally drawn from the rank of solicitor and barrister, who have held their qualification for a period of at least five years

Participants in the court room	Description of the role
The Jury	The jury in the Crown Court consists of 12 members of the public who have been selected from a panel of people who have been 'summonsed' for jury service
Witnesses	People who have witnessed elements of the offence that need to be proved in court. The defence may wish to test a witness's evidence by cross-examination. Professional witnesses may also be called to give evidence in relation to particular evidence, for example a doctor may be asked to give evidence in relation to injuries he/she has examined
The Media	Usually present at major trials, court reporters are sometimes also present at the magistrates' courts and are likely to report on cases of local interest
Probation Service	May be present during some types of hearing so that they are aware of the circumstances of a case, should a probation report be required in order to assist with sentencing. (The report would cover the offender's background, reasons for offending, levels of remorse, and appropriate sentences.)
Young Offender Service	Similar to the probation service, but for young people under 18.

Some courtrooms are still the more traditional, grand, imposing wood-panelled rooms, but many courtrooms are located in modern buildings and are far removed from the scenes you may see in television dramas. Wigs and gowns are not worn in the magistrates' courts, where proceedings are generally a little less formal. To learn about the processes, there is no substitute for visiting courts and observing the procedures live.

For a trainee police officer, giving evidence features as one of the PAC headings, a key aspect of qualifying to undertake Independent Patrol. However, after qualifying, a police officer might not attend court again for some time; indeed, to some extent the opportunities to experience court during training are specially arranged. A police officer is more likely to give evidence in court if he/she is a detective working on volume crime or is involved in a major police operation. Court appearances for police officers are less common now partly due to the increased proportion of early 'guilty' pleas. This increase is likely to be in some part attributable to advances in DNA evidence, the increased availability of discounted sentences in return for a guilty plea at an early stage, and also the increased use of statutory fines and penalties (see 10.13.2). However, as court appearances by police officers now tend to relate to more serious offences and involve a substantial criminal trial, it is all the more important to get it right.

27.5.1 The adversarial justice system in court

In court, contested hearings are undertaken by two 'adversaries' or opponents, these being the representatives for the defence and the prosecution. Occasionally a defendant elects to conduct his/her own defence, but he/she will not always be permitted to cross-examine all witnesses (see 27.6.2.3 for details).

The defence and the prosecution must comply with certain rules concerning the evidence. The prosecution has a duty to ensure that all relevant evidence and unused material is disclosed under the CPIA (see 24.3). The Criminal Procedure Rules govern the process, and these are regularly updated. Part 1 sets out the overriding objective that the court should be able to deal with cases justly:

> 1.1.—(1) The overriding objective of this procedural code is that criminal cases be dealt with justly.
> (2) Dealing with a criminal case justly includes—
> (a) acquitting the innocent and convicting the guilty;
> (b) dealing with the prosecution and the defence fairly;
> (c) recognising the rights of a defendant, particularly those under Article 6 of the European Convention on Human Rights;
> (d) respecting the interests of witnesses, victims and jurors and keeping them informed of the progress of the case;
> (e) dealing with the case efficiently and expeditiously;

> (f) ensuring that appropriate information is available to the court when bail and sentence are considered; and
> (g) dealing with the case in ways that take into account—
>   (i) the gravity of the offence alleged,
>   (ii) the complexity of what is in issue,
>   (iii) the severity of the consequences for the defendant and others affected, and
>   (iv) the needs of other cases.

In accordance with the overriding objective of fairness, the defence is unlikely to succeed if it seeks to ambush the prosecution with a piece of evidence or a point of law at a late stage in the proceedings (eg see *Gleeson* [2003] EWCA Crim 3357).

The defence occasionally challenges the prosecution's case and asks for the prosecution to cease. For example, the judge can be asked to dismiss the case at a Plea and Case Management Hearing (PCMH) before the trial begins. The admissibility of critical evidence might be challenged, and if successful the case for the prosecution inevitably fails. Alternatively, in certain circumstances, the challenge might come later on in the trial by way of a 'half time submission' by the defence, once the prosecution has closed its case. A challenge is very likely to occur if a key witness fails to confirm (orally) the evidence in his/her written statements. The judge can also halt a trial for similar reasons and direct a jury to acquit, but this is rare.

By way of example, the defence could challenge the following issues (this is not an exhaustive list):

- whether the alleged offence actually took place (eg in a rape case, when a point to prove has not been established in the evidence);
- whether the defendant carried out the relevant acts (perhaps he/she has an alibi);
- whether the defendant had the requisite intention (the act was unintentional or there were justifiable reasons for the act, such as self-defence); and/or
- whether the process which brought the defendant to court was at fault.

This last point can be used even if it seems very likely the defendant clearly did commit the crime (eg if there is very strong DNA prosecution evidence) and there is little to be said in mitigation. The defence could claim, for example, that the relevant PACE Act 1984 and CPIA Codes of Practice had not been followed, and suggest that the trial is flawed and unfair, and the judge will be asked to dismiss the evidence and any related charges. Indeed, it is the role of the defence counsel to expose flaws in the prosecution case if that helps the defendant. Some people feel uncomfortable with these aspects of the defence counsel's role, believing such approaches to be morally ambiguous. This misses the point: the role of the defence is to do anything (within legal and ethical bounds) to act in the defendant's best interest, including exploiting 'loopholes' in the law.

So, in this sense, the police have to get it absolutely right, every time. That is why we place so much emphasis here on getting the procedure correct.

27.5.1.1 A court as a public arena

Both the Crown Court and magistrates' courts have a public gallery and, with the exception of youth courts, anyone can watch any trial or hearing in progress. For some cases, however, special measures will apply (see 27.5.2.5) and the public will be excluded so the trial can be held in private.

When friends or relatives of the defendant and the victim are present, public order problems may occasionally occur. If this seems likely the ushers and security staff should be alerted to this possibility. The judge or chairman of the bench may warn the public gallery about the possible consequences of disruptive behaviour, such as removal or arrest for contempt of court. Whilst efforts have been made to alter courtroom layouts to avoid such a possibility, a member of a jury may still be intimidated by glares and gestures from the defendant's circle of associates. In such circumstances the public gallery may be cleared, leaving the press bench to represent the public's interest. It is not just in the courtroom that these problems can arise, as communal corridors, cafes, and smoking areas all provide opportunities for the defendant's associates and the witnesses for the prosecution to meet. Separate rooms are available in most courts for witnesses to sit away from other people, and it may be possible for witnesses to enter the court building via a separate entrance. Intimidation of juries and witnesses is covered in 14.6.

Police officers are not immune from threats or intimidation, and should identify and bring to the court's attention any person who challenges, or seeks to threaten or intimidate, an officer. Common times for attempted intimidation are when a police officer is leaving court at the close of the day, or is away from the court during a lunch break.

27.5.2 Court procedures

Evidence is usually presented in court in the form of the testimony of a witness. Witnesses give evidence of what they heard, saw, smelled, tasted, or felt. Sometimes, an expert witness may be asked to give an opinion, such as a pathologist giving an opinion on the cause of death in a murder case, but ordinary witnesses (including police officers) will seldom be asked for an opinion. Witnesses who attend courts frequently (eg police officers) are known as professional witnesses, as distinct from expert witnesses.

On the basis of the given evidence, the bench or district judge (in a magistrates' court) or the jury (in the Crown Court) will decide whether the accused is guilty or not. In the case of the Crown Court, if the accused pleads guilty, there will be no need for a jury, and the hearing will be much shorter.

27.5.2.1 The notification to attend court

At the outset witnesses are 'warned for court'. For a magistrates' court the notification to attend will be a simple letter or notice stating the date and time. For the Crown Court, there are two forms of witness warning—a 'conditional' and a 'full' warning. A conditional warning is used when the witness's evidence is not likely to be contested and so the witness may not be required to attend court. If nothing more is announced or communicated then he/she can 'stand by' and is unlikely to give evidence (unless either side move to have the witness called—perhaps if the trial takes an unexpected turn). Note, however, that he/she still should not discuss the evidence with any third party. A witness receiving a full warning will certainly be called to attend, but still might not be called to give evidence.

Waiting for a case to get to court can be a frustratingly long and drawn-out process. Delays can be caused by the sheer volume of cases the court has to deal with, or difficulty finding a date when all witnesses and legal representatives can attend. Once in court, a case may still not be heard quickly: it may be put back, postponed, rescheduled, or otherwise not heard on that day for any number of technical or procedural reasons.

27.5.2.2 The oath

Evidence must be given on oath by any witness or defendant at a statutory legal process, including a magistrates' court or the Crown Court. The Perjury Act 1911 and the Oaths Act 1978 require that a person must be sworn in the particular form or manner that is binding on his/her conscience. Those adhering to a religious belief touch or hold (covered or uncovered) their respective holy books when giving the oath, and there may be other observances involved such as a ritual washing. Those who do not hold a particular religious belief may choose to affirm. The affirmation is a promise to tell the truth, and was brought in under the Oaths Act 1978 (s 4(2)) to avoid the possibility of non-religious witnesses claiming their evidence to be invalid.

Perjury is when a person lies under oath. This is a serious criminal offence under the Perjury Act 1911. A person commits perjury when he/she wilfully makes a material statement which he/she knows to be false or does not believe to be true. This could be in a court or tribunal after the person has been sworn as a witness or as an interpreter (s 1(1) and (2)), or before any person legally empowered to hear and assess evidence. A court determines whether the statement was 'material' or not for the proceedings (s 1(6)). The false statement must have been made deliberately and not merely by mistake, and more than one witness must testify that the statement was false for a perjury conviction to succeed (s 13).

Perjury is an offence in criminal and civil proceedings, punishable on indictment with a maximum of seven years' imprisonment or a fine (CPS, 2017c), and the punishment must reflect the seriousness of the original offence (*R v Dunlop* [2001] 2 Cr App R (S) 27). Perjury in most cases will amount to perverting the course of justice, but perjury specifically involves lying in court. Perverting the course of justice can occur in many different ways such as arranging a false alibi, but lying about it in court would be perjury. A prosecution for perjury is appropriate when making a false statement in court is the principal act, but not if the false statement is part of a series of acts aimed at perverting the course of justice. Aiding, abetting, counselling, procuring, or suborning another person to commit perjury carries the same penalty as perjury itself (s 7(1)). Chapter 22 covers conspiracy and encouraging or assisting another to commit an offence.

27.5.2.3 Giving evidence

Oral evidence is the most common form of evidence presented to a court. It is verbal, spoken evidence. A witness will say 'I saw him push the block over the parapet of the bridge', or 'I heard her scream and then felt a hand on my bottom', or 'The drink tasted really bitter after I came back from the toilet'. It is what has been directly experienced by someone on the spot at the time that the alleged offence was committed. A witness to an act must have perceived (seen, heard, felt, tasted, or smelled) that act directly, through his/her senses. Under s 9 of the Criminal Justice Act 1967, if both sides agree, a witness statement can be read out in court in the place of oral evidence from the witness (commonly referred to as a 'section 9 statement').

Real evidence is any article or thing which can be produced for the court, supported by testimony to link to the accused, such as 'This is the iron bar I saw him holding'.

TASK 1 Can you think of potential problems associated with the use, and production in court, of 'real evidence'?

The evidential link to the accused generally has to made through supporting testimony, such as: 'These bloodstains were recovered from the clothing worn by the accused at the time of his arrest, and match the blood type of the man found lying in the stairwell.' The significance of a piece of real evidence often has to be explained in court, especially if the relevant item is not within everyone's common experience, such as an explosive detonator for triggering a bomb. Large items, for example a lorry, a crash site, or piece of machinery, may be visited by a court if the evidence is vital for a case.

There must be an auditable trail for the article produced as real evidence, from the moment it was discovered or recovered until it is produced in court. This is referred to as 'continuity of evidence' or the 'chain of evidence' and is covered in more detail in 11.2.6.

Documentary evidence is a separate class of real evidence. The rules about the legal status of documents are complex but the general point is that the document should be produced in court by the person who created it and who can testify to its contents. This is not always possible (eg for a will) but a court can ask for a handwriting expert to testify that, within limitations, the author of one particular document is likely to be the author of another particular document.

Hearsay evidence is 'any statement not made in oral evidence in the proceedings' (s 114 of the Criminal Justice Act 2003 (CJA 2003)); it is a person's account of what another person said. There have been concerns that hearsay evidence might breach Article 6 of the ECHR (which establishes the right to a fair and public hearing) by not allowing the defence the opportunity, for example, to cross-examine an absent witness. The European Court of Human Rights found that this was unfounded, and stated that the circumstances of each trial need to be taken into account (*Al-Khawaja & Tahery v UK* [2012] 2 Costs LO 139).

TASK 2 There are a number of exceptions which allow for hearsay evidence to be used. Can you think of any possible exceptions that might apply?

The four 'gateways' to admissibility of hearsay evidence are:

1. The CJA 2003 or any other Act indicates it may be used. (This will include, for instance, when a witness cannot attend court due to illness, and statements from a person (eg a victim's friend) about what the victim had said about the incident (s 120 of the CJA 2003).)

2. Any of the common law exceptions preserved by the CJA 2003 (including confession evidence).
3. All parties to the proceedings agree to the evidence being given.
4. The court concludes that in the interests of justice the hearsay evidence should be admitted.

Gateway 4 is particularly useful for hearsay evidence that does not fit any of the recognized exceptions (it is sometimes referred to as the 'safety valve'). It was used when the Court of Appeal (Criminal Division) accepted hearsay evidence consisting of a police officer's record of a conversation with a 14-year-old witness. This contained details of the witness's relationship with the offender, and was accepted on the grounds that it was useful to confirm evidence given by the witness earlier, despite it having been later denied (*Burton v R* [2011] EWCA Crim 1990).

Bad character evidence (BCE, see 24.2.5) can be used in court but the defence or the prosecution must first apply to the judge under s 100 of the CJA 2003. The main principle is to protect a witness or victim from having irrelevant aspects of his/her previous history brought up (see s 101(1) of the CJA 2003 for the full list). Where the defendant wishes to raise the previous sexual history of a complainant, this is likely to be excluded by virtue of s 41 of the Youth Justice and Criminal Evidence Act 1999 (YJCEA), unless it is relevant and admissible. Case law shows that judges are unlikely to allow BCE evidence to be introduced unless it is really significant and relevant (see *R v Bovell* [2005] 2 Cr App R 401).

TASK 3 Find out which MG form is used to record BCE in a defendant's case file.

Witness evidence is given from the witness box (often surprisingly small and modest in reality, unlike those you may have seen on TV or film). The witness should face towards the judge or the bench when giving evidence. Evidence can take a number of forms such as oral, real, documentary, or hearsay, and these are covered in detail in 24.2.5. 'Evidence-in-chief' is the evidence given by the witness in response to the party that called him/her as a witness.

In most straightforward cases oral evidence is given 'directly', which means providing a detailed and accurate chronology of events without any prompting. If there are logistical problems with a witness being able to attend court, evidence can be given via a live television link.

Under s 9 of the CJA 1967, a witness statement can be read out in court in the place of oral evidence from the witness (a 'section 9 statement'). In more complex cases, and always at the Crown Court, evidence is given in response to questions that seek to draw out detail from the witness, usually following the chronology of the events.

A police visual recording of an interview with a significant witness (see 25.6.1) may be shown to the court, particularly if there are inconsistencies between the oral evidence and the recorded evidence. A recording is not usually permitted as the sole source of evidence-in-chief, apart from when 'special measures' apply (see 27.5.2.5); this commonly happens in cases involving rape or sexual abuse, and especially where the witness is a child. The court can exclude a recording if there is insufficient information about where it was made, or if the recording contains serious violations of the rules of evidence.

27.5.2.4   Cross-examination

Cross-examination takes place once the evidence has been given (either directly or in response to the counsel's questions). The opposing counsel is likely to ask questions. This may be quite stressful for the witness, but there are a variety of 'special measures' available for vulnerable and intimidated witnesses (see 27.5.2.5), and aggressive questioning is not normally tolerated by magistrates or judges. If the defendant is conducting his/her own defence it will sometimes be inappropriate for him/her to cross-examine a particular witness, particularly in cases involving domestic violence, for example. In such circumstances an application can be made by the prosecution for a legal representative to be appointed to act on the defendant's behalf, for cross-examination purposes only (s 36 of the YJCEA).

After the cross-examination, the counsel that called the witness has the right to ask further questions (re-examination), but this questioning is restricted solely to matters that arose in the cross-examination, and is usually seeking clarification and removing ambiguity. And finally, the magistrates or judge may need to ask questions of a witness, though they will be very careful not to take over the role of either counsel.

After a witness has finished giving evidence the magistrate or judge gives permission for him/her to leave the witness box. There are two forms of 'permission to leave' and these are:

- to be stood down, which usually requires a witness to be available for recall; and
- to be discharged, which means the court does not expect him/her to be recalled, so he/she may leave the court.

The witness can sit in the public gallery once he/she has been discharged.

27.5.2.5 Special measures in court

Special measures are available to assist some vulnerable and/or intimidated witnesses (see 24.2.4). Special measures are important in terms of witness well-being, which in turn impacts on the quality of the evidence he/she is able to give. All children and young people under the age of 18 are eligible for special measures. Vulnerable witnesses are eligible if the quality of their evidence is likely to be adversely affected due to their personal difficulties, as are intimidated witnesses whose quality of evidence is likely to be diminished by reason of fear or distress. An application is made to the court explaining what type(s) of special measure is being applied for, and how and why this will assist the witness and improve the quality of their evidence. The application is made by the CPS, based on information provided by the police.

The various types of special measure are set out in ss 23–30 of the YJCEA:

- screens are positioned around the witness (s 23). This is helpful in that the witness will not be able to see the defendant and vice versa. However, it does mean the witness will be in the same room as the defendant which may be too difficult for some witnesses;
- a TV live link is used so the witness gives evidence from another room within the court building or, sometimes, a different building altogether (s 24). Evidence is relayed live to the courtroom on large TV screens. This means that the witness does not have to go in to the same room as the defendant. It does mean that the defendant will be able to see the witness on the TV screens, although it is possible to apply for the TV screens to be positioned in court such that the witness cannot be seen by the defendant;
- evidence is given in private—members of the public are excluded from the courtroom and only one nominated member of the press is permitted to stay for the proceedings (s 25). This is not used very often but can be employed in very sensitive cases, or where intimidation is an issue;
- wigs and gowns (judges' and lawyers') are removed to create a less intimidating environment (s 26). This is particularly relevant to cases involving children;
- video-recorded interviews can be used as 'evidence-in-chief' (s 27)—this allows the witness to give his/her account in a more relaxed environment, closer to the time of reporting the offence, hopefully resulting in a fuller more detailed account. The witness will, however, still be cross-examined by the defence;
- a pre-recorded cross-examination is used (s 28). At the time of writing this is not yet fully operational in England and Wales, but recent pilots have provided encouraging results;
- intermediaries (eg a speech and language therapist) are used to help with communication and understanding (s 29); and
- communication aids (eg a computer) are used by the witness when giving evidence (s 30).

Each special measure may be used individually or in combination with others, in order to ensure that the witness has the best possible opportunity to provide high-quality evidence. It should be noted that special measures are not guaranteed until the court has ruled on the application. Therefore, while it is a good idea to explain the available options to eligible witnesses at an early stage, premature promises should not be made.

27.5.2.6 Hostile witnesses

A barrister can ask for a witness to be deemed 'hostile' by the judge. This is when a witness has made a statement previously but declines to confirm certain details in court, and is assumed to be deliberately not telling the truth. (He/she may have been asked to say something different or be silent, to avoid incriminating the defendant.) The judge will announce his/her decision to the court, often giving reasons. The witness can then be cross-examined and challenged about the change of evidence, and the inconsistencies with previous statements and accounts will be explored.

27.5.3   Giving evidence as a police officer

Early on in his/her career a police officer is most likely to give evidence in court as the 'officer in the case', the 'OIC'. The officer's availability will be taken into consideration when the trial date is set.

This is the final phase of the investigation in a sense, because it is the calling to account of the case against the accused and a consideration of the evidence. A police officer's role is to explain what he/she has done, heard, seen, or recorded, as clearly and as concisely as possible. Any witness, including a police officer or an officer in training, should avoid discussing the case in detail with colleagues or associates before, and certainly during, the trial, because recollections can be contaminated by verbally revisiting the circumstances.

27.5.3.1   Preparing for giving evidence as a police officer

After the case file has been prepared, further planning and preparation is needed for the actual process of giving evidence. As the officer in the case you would have to:

- review the case, reread the case papers, and reread your pocket notebook (PNB);
- ensure you have a copy of your duty statement to use as a reminder, if required, while giving evidence (permitted under s 139 of the CJA 2003);
- familiarize yourself with the rules of evidence (particularly on hearsay evidence and opinion);
- speak to the CPS lawyer who will be prosecuting;
- prepare for dealing with predictable but difficult questions from the defence, for example on certain points of evidence;
- check that everything in the case is administratively in order, including labelling the exhibits; and
- check the arrangements for witnesses, for example about any payment due to them, and the holding areas where they will wait to be called, particularly if they feel vulnerable to intimidation—a separate room is often provided.

You could also visit the court premises and sit through part of another case, before checking the exact location of the courtroom for 'your' case.

27.5.3.2   In the witness box as a police officer

It is becoming increasingly common, particularly in magistrates' court cases, for police officers to give their evidence via video link from their police station in order to save time and resources. However, there will be times when you will have to attend court in person, and in any event this guidance applies equally (where practicable) to both scenarios. You will first take the oath or affirm, and then introduce yourself by rank, police number, name, and the police station where you are based. When you are responding to questions try to address your answers to the judge and jury, or the magistrates. Speak clearly, do not rush your words, and try to keep to a steady pace as people will be taking notes of what you say.

If you want to refer to your PNB in court, you should ask for permission. The defence is entitled to object, and may ask you to explain the manner and time of making your notes, and whether your notes represent a 'contemporaneous account' (written at the time), or whether you wrote up your PNB afterwards. Any notes made reasonably soon after the event should be acceptable, however, if there is a significant time lag (two days or longer) the defence is likely to question this very closely. The court, prosecution, or defence may want to examine the entry itself, so make sure that your grammar and spelling are always up to scratch and that your handwriting is at least legible! They might also examine it to look for any evidence of collusion with other officers (see 10.2.3). Heavy reliance on your PNB is not advised and it should not be thought of as a substitute for good preparation. If you ask to refer to it to answer simple questions, it will look as though you have not bothered to prepare, and have no proper recollection of the case, which will reflect badly on your credibility as a witness. Referring to it for specific details, such as times, dates, or car registration plate numbers, is usually acceptable, but do not expect to be allowed to use it as a script.

When giving evidence you could be tempted to try to learn your evidence by heart and then recite from memory, but this is most inadvisable. First, it will sound rehearsed and artificial. Second, the defence may try to put you off with questions so that you lose your thread and flounder, and finally it suggests that maybe you do not have the confidence to rely on your recall of events. There is nothing wrong with referring to your PNB entries—after all, the lawyers and the judge constantly refer to their notes. However, you should not rely on your PNB exclusively as that will not create a good impression. It is much better to speak clearly and confidently, referring only now and then to your PNB to refresh your memory, or to quote a particular detail. Always avoid hearsay or bad character evidence unless it has been confirmed to you that it has been admitted. We discuss how to create a good impression in more detail in 27.5.3.4.

27.5.3.3 Cross-examination

As a witness you can ask the defence or anyone else to repeat a question which you did not hear, did not understand, or which you want clarified. (This also gives you an extra moment to think.) You should remain polite and courteous at all times, and be prepared for the unexpected, for example:

> PC Winn, what formal training have you had in interview techniques and did that training, if indeed you had it, cover the use of oppressive interrogation?
>
> Here the defence is using a common tactic of double questioning, as well as launching straight into querying the officer's qualifications. She might choose to reply as follows:
>
> [To the judge] I was accredited Tier 2 Investigative Interviewing, which means I am qualified by the police in investigative interviewing, which incorporates questioning styles. I did the training at the Police training centre in August last year. I routinely undertake interviews at this level and believe I have an understanding of the term 'oppressive' as it applies in the Police and Criminal Evidence Act 1984, section 76. [Turning back to the defence] Would you repeat the second part of your question, sir?

Note her politeness and refusal to be flustered or stampeded by the defence's approach. In fact, the completeness of her first reply establishes her as a professional and credible witness, and the defence may seem merely querulous (questioning for its own sake). If the defence persisted in making an innuendo in such a deliberately challenging tone the judge might intervene to ask where it is leading and how it is relevant, and whether the defence is raising an issue for consideration for exclusion of the evidence. You might also have noticed how PC Winn 'collects' the question from the lawyer and delivers her answer directly to the judge, before politely asking the defence lawyer for the second part of his question. This emphasizes that she has been attentive and is not to be hurried into giving confused (or confusing) answers to compound or complex questions.

The use of body language can certainly help control pace and speed. It would be best to turn back to a person asking a question only when you think you have given a complete answer and you are ready for the next question. Some eye contact with the jury is always helpful as they are the people you would need to convince on issues of fact. You should avoid a one-to-one 'conversation' with either the defence or the prosecution counsel as this is likely to be irritating to the jury (they may feel distanced from the proceedings).

The defence may use a variety of approaches such as trailer questions, multiple questions, hypothetical questions, 'topic-hopping', or out-of-sequence chronology. These should be dealt with one at a time. It is important to portray yourself to the jury as a competent professional.

The defence counsel will sometimes attempt to persuade juries that collusion has occurred between officers, and that adjustments have been made to match their accounts. It is important that you limit yourself to recollections about matters that you have personal knowledge of, and can convey directly to the court, and do not adjust your evidence. Imagine if you truthfully recalled in your evidence to the jury that your memory is that the car you saw was green, and your colleague following you into the witness box had said it was red? Both of you are telling the truth, one possibly mistaken, but this would be far better than you 'changing your recall' to having seen a red car—when the car was in fact later proved to be green! (See 10.2.1.3 on 'conferring with others' and PNB records.)

There will be occasions when your evidence as a police officer is favourable to the defendant, and naturally enough the defence will want to make use of this. You should expect to be questioned about how you conducted the investigation, and the evidence you have already given, and asked for any additional facts which you have not already given. It is often not what you say that is fertile territory for the cross-examination—but rather what you did not say.

27.5.3.4 Creating the right impression

The impression a police officer creates in court, as noted earlier, will influence his/her credibility, particularly as some members of the jury might be subjective and 'go by feel', rather than by objective fact.

When giving evidence as a police officer you should always watch your general attitude and remain calm, polite, and courteous at all times, even in the face of inflammatory questioning or an apparent attack on your integrity. Rising to the bait will only serve to assist the defence. If in court you appear intolerant or impatient, or reply in kind, then your credibility as a police officer on oath or affirmation in court would be at risk. Police officers are subject to personal scrutiny (as any other witness can be); your record, your training, your job performance, and even your personal life may be closely investigated by the defence. Anything which can undermine your credibility or make the jury dubious about the reliability of your testimony may be exploited by a defence lawyer, who will not hesitate to confront you with it during cross-examination. In the same way, any obvious bias demonstrated by a police officer against a defendant will be deeply unhelpful to the prosecution case and may in fact help the defence.

When giving evidence you should speak clearly, keep your voice at an audible volume, and try not to talk too quickly. Clear concise language should be used. No one would advise you to talk like a legal textbook but you should avoid using colloquial speech or slang terms unless you are repeating something you have heard as part of your evidence, in which case you should say exactly what you heard, no matter how obscene or objectionable the language. Another temptation is to say too much and to keep on talking, but you should keep your answers short and to the point.

For example:

> **Prosecutor**: Constable Winn, did you see the injuries?
>
> **PC Winn**: Yes, I did. This was at first during the initial interview, when Ms Bent showed me an extensive bruise to her left eye and cheekbone. She was then examined by the custody nurse for other injuries.
>
> **Prosecutor**: What did you do next?
>
> **PC Winn**: I arranged for the custody nurse to examine Ms Bent and prepare a body map of injuries, and arranged for them to be photographed.
>
> **Prosecutor**: With what result?
>
> **PC Winn**: We had the injuries photographed and listed. She was advised to attend A&E immediately after the interview, and I have obtained a doctor's report and statement.
>
> **Prosecutor**: Your Honour, I refer to the statement taken from Dr Salim Khan, A&E House Officer at Albright Hospital, in bundle 6, document 44A.

Notice that PC Winn gives clear answers, but does not elaborate (she knows that the prosecution—or the defence—will follow up with another question if more information is required). Note too that she does not try to give a medical opinion, nor to paraphrase Dr Khan's evidence or statement. This would be inappropriate because PC Winn has no medical qualifications and knows that she cannot speak with any authority. However, the court may allow PC Winn to comment on whether the apparent injuries were consistent with assault, based on her knowledge and experience as a police officer. The temptation to use someone else's evidence in your answers can be strong, especially if you know the case well and have carefully read all the statements and written evidence, but you must resist.

The use of acronyms (eg BCU, TIC, ETA, SIO) and overly technical words (eg 'haematoma' (a bruise) or 'lacerations' (cuts)) should also be avoided as they may confuse and irritate the jury. You might appear to be trying too hard to impress if you say something like this (especially if your grasp of the meaning of words is a little shaky).

> I proceeded in a southerly direction towards the connurbative encompassment of commercial premises which is characterized by the soubriquet of 'shopping mall'. The chronological observation which was then essayed by myself was recorded contemporaneously as 13.45 hours, British Summer Time. It was at that juncture that I espied the trio of adult males engaging in what I deemed to be behaviour which warranted a sufficiency of explanation as to make my legitimated suspicions subside . . .

Perhaps all you needed to say was:

> I was on patrol in the shopping centre at 13.45 when I saw three men behaving suspiciously, so I challenged them.

Even this is fairly formal, but it has the great merit of being brief. Remember the impression you are creating as a concise, well-prepared professional.

You certainly need to be organized and to appear to be organized: 'Um . . . I will just check . . .' or 'Um, I seem to have mislaid it . . .' are not likely to impress the jury and you risk losing their attention. The statement 'May I please refer to document 24 in the bundle, your honour?' is far more professional and courteous. Using the correct terminology to address the court will certainly help create a good impression:

- 'Ma'am' or 'Sir' for the lawyers on either side;
- 'Your Honour', 'My Lady', or 'My Lord' for the Judge in the Crown Court (depending on the status of the Crown Court);
- 'Your Worships' for the magistrates' court and 'Ma'am' or 'Sir' if addressing them individually; and
- 'Ma'am' or 'Sir' for a district judge in the magistrates' court.

It would be easy for us to ignore your appearance through some sense of 'politeness' and respect for individual personal style, but non-verbal communication (see 5.11.2) is a powerful influence—you need to look as smart as you sound. A smart uniform, polished shoes, and neat hair can seem petty restrictions, but they help you assert your authority (see 5.11.5) and will boost your confidence in the witness box. Actions also convey attitudes; hands in pockets, fiddling with buttons or your glasses, and constantly shifting through documents create a poor impression.

27.5.3.5 After giving evidence

You should wait in the witness box until the magistrate or judge gives you permission to leave. If you are in doubt about whether you are being 'stood down' or 'discharged' (see 27.5.2.4) you must speak to the CPS lawyer prosecuting the case at a convenient moment, and remain available within the court building.

If you wish to remain in court you are entitled to do so, and can sit in the public gallery. However, witnesses and family for the accused could be there, so you might not feel particularly comfortable. You should also avoid making eye contact or nodding in agreement; this sort of action on your part might encourage the defence to question any influence you may be having on the jury or the magistrates, and could easily lead to criticism of your conduct in open court.

You would also need to take care in relation to other witnesses who have not yet given evidence. Imagine you travelled to court with a colleague and that you have given evidence and been discharged, but she is going to give evidence the following morning. You travelled together by car and intend to return home the same way; however, you would need to take care not to talk about the case. The following morning she may be asked about how she travelled, who with, and whether the case was discussed. The defence may look for forms of collusion, or inconsistency between her written statement and the evidence she gives orally, and suggest that any differences are an indication that she changed her account to suit others. You will need to ensure this type of situation does not arise.

27.6 **Answers to Tasks**

TASK 1 You might have referred to the 'continuity of evidence'. You will remember from many examples in this Handbook that this is a mundane but vital part of case preparation.

TASK 2 The exceptions usually agreed to be taken as evidence are declarations on the point of death, and statements about confessions if the witness heard the confession him/herself.

TASK 3 Form MG16 is used.

Bibliography and References

ACPO (2006a), *Murder Investigation Manual*, 3rd edn (Wyboston: National Centre for Policing Excellence).

—— (2006b), *Practice Advice on Search Management and Procedures 2006* available at <http://library.college.police.uk/docs/npia/search-management-practice-advice-2006.pdf> (accessed 1 May 2018).

—— (2006c), *Practice Advice on Stop and Search 2006* available at <http://content.met.police.uk/cs/Satellite?blobcol=urldata&blobheadername1=Content-Type&blobheadername2=Content-Disposition&blobheavalue1=application%2Fpdf&blobheadervalue2=inline%3B+filename%3D% 22436%2F865%2FPractice_Advice_on_Stop_and_Search.pdf%22&blobkey=id&blobtable=MungoBlobs&blobwhere=1283565271771&ssbinary=true> (accessed 19 March 2014).

—— (2008), *Practice Advice on Analysis* available at <http://library.college.police.uk/docs/npia/practice_advice_on_analysis_interactive.pdf> (accessed 1 May 2018).

—— (2009), *ACPO Guidance on Investigating Child Abuse and Safeguarding Children*, 2nd edn available at <http://library.college.police.uk/docs/acpo/Child-Abuse-ACPO-guidelines-2005.pdf> (accessed 1 May 2018).

—— (2010a), *Guidance on Investigating and Prosecuting Rape* (abridged edn) available at <http://library.college.police.uk/docs/acpo/Guidance-Investigating-Prosecuting-Rape-(Abridged-Edition)-2010.pdf> (accessed 1 May 2018).

—— (2010b), *Guidance on the Investigation, Cautioning and Charging of Knife Crime Offences 2009* available at <http://library.college.police.uk/docs/acpo/knife-crime-offences-2012.pdf> (accessed 1 May 2018).

—— (2011a), *ACPO Uniformed Operations Policing the Roads—5 Year Strategy 2011–2015* available at <http://library.college.police.uk/docs/ACPO/ACPO-policing-the-roads-2011.pdf> (accessed 3 March 2013).

—— (2011b), *Strategy & Supporting Operational Guidance for Policing Prostitution and Sexual Exploitation* available at <http://www.npcc.police.uk/documents/crime/2011/20111102%20CBA%20Policing%20Prostitution%20and%20%20Sexual%20Exploitation%20Strategy_Website_October%202011.pdf> (accessed 1 May 2018).

—— (2012a), *ACPO Good Practice Guide for Digital Evidence March 2012* available at <http://library.college.police.uk/docs/acpo/digital-evidence-2012.pdf> (accessed 1 May 2018).

—— (2012b), *Guidance on Safeguarding and Investigating the Abuse of Vulnerable Adults* available at <http://library.college.police.uk/docs/acpo/vulnerable-adults-2012.pdf> (accessed 31 January 2015).

—— (2013), *Interim Guidance on the Management, Recording and Investigation of Missing Persons 2013* available at <http://library.college.police.uk/docs/college-of-policing/Interim-Missing-Persons-Guidance-2013.pdf> (accessed 1 May 2018).

—— (2014), *A Guide to Investigating Child Deaths* available at <http://www.app.college.police.uk/app-content/major-investigation-and-public-protection/child-abuse/police-response/risk-and-associated-investigations/> (accessed 31 January 2015).

ACPO and NPIA (2009), *National Investigative Interviewing Strategy, Briefing Paper* available at <http://library.college.police.uk/docs/npia/BP-Nat-Investigative-Interviewing-Strategy-2009.pdf> (accessed 16 March 2020).

ACPO Centrex (2005), *Practice Advice on Core Investigative Doctrine* (Camborne: National Centre for Policing Excellence).

Age UK (2018), *The Herbert Protocol* available at <https://www.ageuk.org.uk/calderdaleandkirklees/about-us/latest-news/articles/2018/the-herbert-protocol/> (accessed 16 March 2020).

Aitken, C, Connolly, T, Gammerman, A, Zhang, G, and Oldfield, R (1995), *Predicting an Offender's Characteristics: An evaluation of statistical modelling*, Police Research Group Special Interest Series 4 (London: Home Office).

Alderson, J (1998), *Principled Policing: Protecting the public with integrity* (Winchester: Waterside Press).

Allcock, E, Bond, JW, and Smith, LL (2011), 'An investigation into the crime scene characteristics that differentiate a car key burglary from a regular domestic burglary', International Journal of Police Science and Management 13(4), 1–11.

Angiolini, E (2015), *Report of the independent review into the investigation and prosecution of rape in London* available at <https://www.cps.gov.uk/sites/default/files/documents/publications/dame_elish_angiolini_rape_review_2015.pdf> (accessed 1 May 2018).

APCCS (2013), *Police and Crime Commissioners* available at <http://www.apccs.police.uk/page/ pcc-candidates> (accessed 13 February 2013).

Ariel, B, Lawes, D, Weinborn, C, Henry, R, Chen, K, and Dabo, H (2019), 'The "Less-Than-Lethal Weapons Effect"—Introducing TASERs to Routine Police Operations in England and Wales: A Randomized Controlled Trial', Criminal Justice and Behavior 46(2), 280–300.

Audit Commission (1993), *Helping with Enquiries: Tackling crime effectively* (London: Audit Commission).

Avon and Somerset Constabulary (2017), *Police Employees Misusing Access to the Police National Computer (PNC)* available at <https://www.avonandsomerset.police.uk/about-us/freedom-of-information/previous-foi-requests/data-protection-computer-misuse/police-employees-misusing-access-to-the-police-national-computer-(pnc)/> (accessed 8 March 2018).

Baldwin, J (1992), *Video Taping of Police Interviews with Suspects—An Evaluation.* Police Research Series Paper 1 (London: Home Office).

Banton, M (1964), *The Policeman in the Community* (London: Tavistock).

BBC (2016), *Hundreds of police accused of sexual exploitation* available at <http://www.bbc.co.uk/news/uk-38240524> (accessed 1 March 2017).

—— (2017), *Police pay out at least £22m to informants in five years* available at <http://www.bbc.co.uk/news/uk-38902480> (accessed 1 March 2017).

—— (2018a), *Home Office doubles youth crime prevention scheme funds to £22m* available at <https://www.bbc.co.uk/news/uk-44999299> (accessed 1 January 2019).

—— (2018b), *Kent Police stop using crime predicting software* available at <https://www.bbc.co.uk/news/uk-england-kent-46345717> (accessed 16 March 2020).

—— (2019), *London to Cornwall county lines drugs conspiracy 'run from prison'* available at <https://www.bbc.co.uk/news/uk-england-cornwall-49335302> (accessed 16 March 2020).

Bedfordshire Police (2017), *Probationary officer dismissed for discreditable conduct* available at <https://www.bedfordshire.police.uk/news-and-appeals/probationary-officer-dismissed-discreditable-conduct> (accessed 8 March 2018).

Belviso, M, De Donno, A, Vitale, L, and Introna, F (2003), 'Positional asphyxia: reflection on 2 cases', American Journal of Forensic Medicine and Pathology 24(3), 292–7.

Berne, E (1968), *Games People Play: The psychology of human relationships* (Harmondsworth: Penguin).

Bichard, Sir M (2004), *Return to an Address of the Honourable the House of Commons dated 22nd June 2004 for the Bichard Inquiry, Report HC 653* (London: The Stationery Office).

Blackburn, R (1995), *The Psychology of Criminal Conduct: Theory, research and practice* (Chichester: Wiley & Sons).

Bloom, B, Engelhart, M, Furst, E, Hill, W, and Krathwohl, D (1956), *Taxonomy of Educational Objectives: The classification of educational goals; Handbook I: Cognitive Domain* (New York: Longmans).

Blumstein, A, Cohen, J, Roth, JA, and Visher, CA (eds) (1986), *Criminal Careers and 'Career Criminals'* (Washington, DC: National Academy Press).

Bottoms, A and Tankebe, J (2012), 'Beyond procedural justice: A dialogic approach to legitimacy in criminal justice', Journal of Criminal Law and Criminology 102(1), 119–70.

Bowcott, O (2018), 'Solicitor for student in rape case criticises police and CPS' *The Guardian*, available at <https://www.theguardian.com/uk-news/2018/jan/30/met-police-and-cps-apologise-to-man-after-collapse-of-case> (accessed 8 March 2018).

Bowers, KJ, Hirschfield, A, and Johnson, S (1998), 'Victimisation revisited: A case study of non-residential repeat burglary in Merseyside', British Journal of Criminology 38(3), 429–52.

——, Johnson, SD, and Pease, K (2004), 'Prospective hot-spotting: The future of crime mapping?', British Journal of Criminology 44(5), 641–58.

Bowling, B, Parmar, P, and Philips, C (2008), 'Policing ethnic minority communities' in T Newburn (ed), *Handbook of Policing*, 2nd edn (Cullompton: Willan), pp 611–41.

Bradford, B, Jackson, J, and Stanko, E (2009), 'Public encounters with the police: On the use of public opinion surveys to improve contact and confidence', Policing and Society 19(1), 20–46.

Bradley, The Rt Hon Lord (2009), *Lord Bradley's Review of People with Mental Health Problems and Learning Disabilities in the Criminal Justice System* (London: Department of Health).

Brewis, H (2019), 'Match.com serial rapist Jason Lawrance jailed for two-and-half more years after five more victims come forward', *Evening Standard* (3 October 2019) available at <https://www.standard.co.uk/news/crime/matchcom-serial-rapist-gets-extra-jail-time-after-five-more-victims-come-forward-a4253691.html> (accessed 16 March 2020).

Bryant, R (2008), *Investigating Digital Crime* (Chichester: John Wiley & Sons).

—— (2009), 'Theories of Criminal Investigation' in S Tong, R Bryant, and M Horvath (eds) *Understanding Criminal Investigation* (Chichester: Wiley-Blackwell).

—— (2019), 'Innate Reasoning and Critical Incident Decision-Making' in M Roycroft and J Roach, *Decision Making in Police Enquiries and Critical Incidents* (London: Palgrave Macmillan).

—— and Bryant, S (2014), *Policing Digital Crime* (Farnham: Ashgate Publishing).

Bullock, K and Tilley, N (2003), *Crime Reduction and Problem-oriented Policing* (Cullompton: Willan).

Burke, RH (2019), *An Introduction to Criminological Theory*, 5th edn (Abingdon: Routledge).

Bushman, B and Cooper, HM (1990), 'Effects of Alcohol on Human Aggression: An Integrative Research Review', Psychological Bulletin 107(3), 341–54.

Button, N (2009), *National Fraud Authority Fraud Typologies and Victims of Fraud: Literature Review* available at <https://www.gov.uk/government/uploads/system/uploads/attachment_data/file/118469/ fraud-typologies.pdf> (accessed 23 January 2015).

Caless, B (2008a), 'Corruption in the police: The reality of the "dark side" ', The Police Journal 80(1), 3–84.

—— (2008b), 'Persistent dark matter: Police corruption in the last ten years', Ethics in Policing 1(2), 16–28.

—— and Owens, J (2016), *Police and Crime Commissioners: The Transformation of Police Accountability* (Bristol: Policy Press).

Campbell, A and Muncer, S (1989), 'Them and Us: A comparison of the cultural context of American gangs and British subcultures', Deviant Behaviour 10, 271–88.

Canter, D and Alison, L (2000), *Precursors to Investigative Psychology: Criminal detection and the psychology of crime* (Aldershot: Ashgate).

——, ——, and Fritzon, K (1998), 'Differentiating arsonists: A model of firesetting actions and characteristics', Legal and Criminological Psychology 3, 73–96.

Canterbury Christ Church University (2019), *Faculty of Social and Applied Sciences School of Law, Criminal Justice and Computing Submission for validation of BSc(Hons) Professional Policing Practice in Collaboration with Police Degree Apprenticeship Consortium*.

Cape, E (2015), 'Transposing the EU Directive on the right to information: a firecracker or a damp squib?', Criminal Law Review 1, 48–67.

CEBCP (2018a), *Evidence-Based Policing Matrix* available at <https://cebcp.org/evidence-based-policing/the-matrix/> (accessed 12 March 2019).

—— (2018b), *MatrixAllStudiesNov2017.xlsx* available at <https://cebcp.org/wp-content/evidence-based-policing/the-matrix/MatrixAllStudiesNov2017.xlsx> (accessed 12 March 2019).

Centrex (2005), Level 1 Investigator Professional Development Portfolio.

CEOP (2013), *Welcome to CEOP's thinkuknow website* available at <http://www.thinkuknow.co.uk/> (accessed 23 March 2015).

Chainey, S (2012), *Repeat Victimisation*, JDI Briefs (London: UCL Jill Dando Institute of Security and Crime Science).

—— Curtis-Ham, S, Evans, R, and Burns, G (2018), 'Examining the extent to which repeat and near repeat patterns can prevent crime', Policing 41(5), 608–22.

Chan, JBL (2003), *Fair Cop: Learning the art of policing* (Toronto: University of Toronto Press).

Chapman, D, Whitfield, C, Felitti, V, Dube, S, Edwards, V, and Anda, R (2003), 'Adverse childhood experiences and the risk of depressive disorders in adulthood' Journal of Affective Disorders 82, 217–25).

Chapman, R, Smith, LL, and Bond, JW (2012), 'An investigation into the differentiating characteristics between car key burglars and regular burglars', Journal of Forensic Science 57(4), 939–45.

Chartered Institute of Arbitrators (2016), *Mediation* available at <http://www.ciarb.org/dispute-appointment-service/mediation-new> (accessed 1 May 2018).

Chicago Community Policing Evaluation Consortium (2004), *Community Policing in Chicago, year 10.* (Chicago: The Illinois Criminal Justice Information Authority).

Chenery, S, Henshaw C, and Pease, K (1999), *Illegal Parking in Disabled Bays: A means of offender targeting*, Police and Reducing Crime Briefing Note 1/99 (London: Home Office).

Children's Society (2020), *What is county lines?* available at<https://www.childrenssociety.org.uk/what-is-county-lines> (accessed 16 March 2020).

Chowdhury, H. (2018), 'Kent Police stop using crime predicting software', *The Telegraph* available at <https://www.telegraph.co.uk/technology/2018/11/27/kent-police-stop-using-crime-predicting-software/> (accessed 16 March 2020).

Clarke, C and Milne, R (2001), *A National Evaluation of the PEACE Investigative Interviewing Course*, Home Office Report PRAS/149 (London: Home Office).

——, ——, and Bull, R (2011), 'Interviewing suspects of crime: The impact of PEACE training, supervision and the presence of a legal advisor', Journal of Investigative Psychology and Offender Profiling 8(2), 149–62.

Clarke, RV (1999), *Hot Products: Understanding, anticipating and reducing demand for stolen goods*, Police Research Series Paper 112 (London: Home Office).

Clough, J (2015), *Principles of Cybercrime*, 2nd edn (Cambridge: Cambridge University Press).

College of Policing (2013a), *FAQs* available at <http://www.college.police.uk/Contact/Pages/college-website-FAQ.aspx> (accessed 1 May 2018).

—— (2013b), *Intelligence collection, development and dissemination* available at <https://www.app.college.police.uk/app-content/intelligence-management/intelligence-cycle/#prison-intelligence> (accessed 1 March 2017).

—— (2013c), *Investigation Investigative Interviewing* available at <https://www.app.college.police.uk/app-content/investigations/investigative-interviewing/> (accessed 1 March 2017).

—— (2013d), *Operational Review* available at <http://www.app.college.police.uk/app-content/operations/operational-review/#officers-conferring> (accessed 1 March 2017).

—— (2013e), *Pre-Join to Policing Programmes* available at <http://www.college.police.uk/What-we-do/Learning/pre-join-to-policing/Pages/Pre-join-in-policing.aspx> (accessed 11 March 2016).

—— (2013f), *Professional Entry to Policing: Pre-Join Strategy & Guidance* available at <http://www.college.police.uk/What-we-do/Learning/pre-join-to-policing/Documents/Professional_Entry_to_Policing_Strategy.pdf> (accessed 28 December 2015).

—— (2013g), *The effects of hot spot policing on crime* available at <http://library.college.police.uk/docs/what-works/What-works-briefing-hotspot-policing-2013.pdf> (accessed 12 March 2019).

—— (2014a), *Code of Ethics: A Code of Practice for the Principles and Standards of Professional Behaviour for the Policing Profession of England and Wales* available at <http://www.college.police.uk/What-we-do/Ethics/Documents/Code_of_Ethics.pdf> (accessed 13 January 2017).

—— (2014b), *Major investigation and public protection responding to child sexual exploitation, Risk Factors* available at <http://www.app.college.police.uk/app-content/major-investigation-and-public-protection/child-sexual-exploitation/#warning-signs> (accessed 20 January 2015).

—— (2014c), *National Decision Model: Policing Principles* available at <https://www.app.college.police.uk/app-content/national-decision-model/the-national-decision-model/#policing-principles> (accessed 16 February 2018).

—— (2014d), *Prosecution and Case Management* available at <http://www.app.college.police.uk/app-content/prosecution-and-case-management/charging-and-case-preparation/#summonsing> (accessed 9 January 2015).

—— (2015a), *Call handler and front counter staff response to a domestic abuse incident* available at <https://www.app.college.police.uk/app-content/major-investigation-and-public-protection/domestic-abuse/call-handler-and-front-counter-staff-response/> (accessed 26 December 2015).

—— (2015b), *Female genital mutilation* available at <https://www.app.college.police.uk/app-content/major-investigation-and-public-protection/female-genital-mutilation/> (accessed 28 December 2015).

—— (2015c), *Figures on Disapproved Register published* available at <http://www.college.police.uk/News/College-news/Pages/disapproved-register.aspx> (accessed 1 March 2017).

—— (2015d), *First response* available at <https://www.app.college.police.uk/app-content/major-investigation-and-public-protection/domestic-abuse/first-response/> (accessed 26 December 2015).

—— (2015e), *Investigative development* available at <https://www.app.college.police.uk/app-content/major-investigation-and-public-protection/domestic-abuse/investigative-development/> (accessed 26 December 2015).

—— (2015f), *National Policing Police Community Support Officer: Operational Handbook* available at <http://recruit.college.police.uk/pcso/Documents/National_Policing_PCSO_Operational_Handbook.pdf> (accessed 1 March 2017).

—— (2015g), *Possible justice outcomes following investigation* available at <http://www.app.college.police.uk/app-content/prosecution-and-case-management/justice-outcomes/> (accessed 27 January 2016).

—— (2016a), *Assessing capacity* available at <https://www.app.college.police.uk/app-content/mental-health/mental-capacity/> (accessed 23 November 2019).

—— (2016b), *Major investigation and public protection Missing persons* available at <http://www.app.college.police.uk/app-content/major-investigation-and-public-protection/missing-persons/?s=missing+persons> (accessed 25 November 2016).

—— (2016c), *Mental Health* available at <http://www.app.college.police.uk/app-content/mental-health/?s> (accessed 25 November 2016).

—— (2016d), *National Policing Curriculum* available at <http://www.college.police.uk/What-we-do/Learning/Curriculum/Pages/default.aspx> (accessed 1 March 2017).

—— (2017a), *Civil emergencies* available at <https://www.app.college.police.uk/app-content/ civil-emergencies/civil-contingencies/#critical-incident> (accessed 7 March 2018).

—— (2017b), *Stop and Search* available at <https://www.app.college.police.uk/app-content/stop-and-search/> (accessed 16 March 2020).

—— (2018a), *Authorised Professional Practice: Investigative evaluation: Core 4 Investigations—Process of Investigation—Investigative and Evidential Evaluation* available at <http://library.college.police.uk/docs/APPref/core-investigative-doctrine.pdf> (accessed 7 March 2018).

—— (2018b), *Briefing note: For police first responders to a report of rape or sexual assault* available at <http://library.college.police.uk/docs/appref/C909E0418-First-Responders-Brief.pdf> (accessed 18 February 2019).

—— (2018c), *College of Policing published research* available at <https://whatworks.college.police.uk/Research/Pages/Published.aspx> (accessed 12 March 2019).

—— (2018d), *Detention and custody control, restraint and searches* available at <https://www.app.college.police.uk/app-content/detention-and-custody-2/control-restraint-and-searches/> (accessed 16 March 2020).

—— (2018e), *Impact evidence for engaging communities* available at <https://www.college.police.uk/What-we-do/Support/Guidelines/Neighbourhood-Policing/Pages/engaging-communities.aspx> (accessed 16 March 2020).

—— (2018f), *Intelligence Management: Intelligence report* available at <https://www.app.college.police.uk/app-content/intelligence-management/intelligence-report/> (accessed 14 February 2018).

—— (2018g), *Major investigation and public protection, Missing persons, Risk assessment and response* available at <https://www.app.college.police.uk/app-content/major-investigation-and-public-protection/missing-persons/> (accessed 8 December 2018).

—— (2018h), *Neighbourhood Policing Guidelines* available at <https://www.app.college.police.uk/changes-to-app/neighbourhood-policing-guidelines/> (accessed 7 March 2018).

—— (2018i), *Neighbourhood Policing impact and implementation. Summary findings from a rapid evidence assessment* available at <http://www.college.police.uk> (accessed 16 March 2020).

—— (2018j), *PEQF Supporting Resources* available at <http://www.college.police.uk/What-we-do/Learning/Policing-Education-Qualifications-Framework/Pages/PEQF-Supporting-Resources.aspx> (accessed 7 March 2018).

—— (2018k), *Policing Education Qualifications Framework: National Pre-join Degree in Professional Policing: An Introduction Version 1.0* available at <https://www.college.police.uk/What-we-do/Learning/Policing-Education-Qualifications-Framework/Documents/Pre-Join_Degree_in_Professional_Policing_An_Introduction.pdf> (accessed 12 March 2019).

—— (2018l), *Pre-join Degree in Professional Policing Provider Guidance Version 1.0* (April 2018) available at <https://www.college.police.uk/What-we-do/Learning/Policing-Education-Qualifications-Framework/Documents/Pre-join_Degree_in_Professional_Policing_Provider_Guidance.pdf> (accessed 12 March 2019).

—— (2018m), *Risk* available at <https://www.app.college.police.uk/app-content/risk-2/risk/> (accessed 23 March 2015).

—— (2019a), *College of Policing Vulnerability Conference* available at <https://www.college.police.uk/About/Documents/Conference/The_THRIVE_approach_workshop.pdf> (accessed 16 March 2020).

—— (2019b), *Equality Impact Analysis Regulations for Police Constable: Qualifications for Appointment and Probationary Periods Version 8* (April 2019) available at <https://www.college.police.uk/What-we-do/Learning/

Policing-Education-Qualifications-Framework/Documents/PEQF_Equality_Impact_Analysis_V8.pdf> (accessed 12 March 2019).

—— (2019c), *Pre-join degree in Professional Policing: Information for prospective students* available at <https://www.college.police.uk/What-we-do/Learning/Policing-Education-Qualifications-Framework/Entry-routes-for-police-constables/Pre-join-degree/Pages/Information-for-students.aspx> (accessed 12 March 2019).

—— (2019d), *Research Surgeries* available at <https://whatworks.college.police.uk/Support/Pages/Research-Surgeries.aspx> (accessed 12 March 2019).

—— (2019e), *Resources for reflective practice Version 1.0* available at <https://www.college.police.uk/What-we-do/Development/professional-development-programme/Documents/Resources_for_reflective_practice_v1_0.pdf> (accessed 12 March 2019).

—— (2020), *What is evidence-based policing?* available at <https://whatworks.college.police.uk/About/Pages/What-is-EBP.aspx> (accessed 16 March 2020).

CoP/NPCC (2018), *Workforce Transformation in the Police Service* available at <https://www.npcc.police.uk/Publication/Workforce%20Transformation%20Baseline.pdf> (accessed 12 March 2019).

Connell, NM, Miggans, K, and McGloin, JM (2008), 'Can a community policing initiative reduce serious crime? A local evaluation', Police Quarterly 11(2), 127–50.

Coomber, R and Moyle, I (2018), 'The Changing Shape of Street-level heroin and crack supply in England: Commuting, Holidaying and Cuckooing Drug Dealers across "County Lines" ', British Journal of Criminology 58, 1323–42.

Cope, N, Fielding, N, and Innes, M (2005), 'The appliance of science? The theory and practice of crime intelligence analysis', British Journal of Criminology 45(1), 39–55.

Copper-Ind, C (2018), *Fraud epidemic costs the UK £110bn annually* available at <https://www.internationalinvestment.net/internationalinvestment/news/3500818/fraud-epidemic-costs-uk-gbp110bn-annually-report> (accessed 3 January 2020).

Cornish, DB and Clarke, RV (1986), *The reasoning criminal: Rational choice perspectives on offending* (New York: Springer-Verlag).

Cornwall Live (2019), *The full story of how a gang flooded Cornwall with heroin and crack from London* available at <https://www.cornwalllive.com/news/cornwall-news/full-story-how-gang-flooded-3275472> (accessed 16 March 2020).

Cosgrove, F and Ramshaw, P (2015), 'It is what you do as well as the way that you do it: the value and deployment of PCSOs in achieving public engagement', Policing and Society 25(1), 77–96.

Cottrell, S (2019), *The Study Skills Handbook* (Macmillan Study Skills) (Red Globe Press: London).

Council of Europe (2018), *Conference on cybercrime: evidence in cyberspace, WHOIS data, cyberviolence, global state of legislation* available at <https://www.coe.int/et/web/portal/-/conference-on-cybercrime-evidence-in-cyberspace-whois-data-cyberviolence-global-state-of-legislation> (accessed 27 December 2018).

Cox, LJ (2012), *Preliminary ruling R v Halliwell* (9 May 2012, Bristol Crown Court) available at <https://www.judiciary.gov.uk/wp-content/uploads/JCO/Documents/Judgments/halliwell-ruling.pdf> (accessed 27 April 2018).

CPS (2013), *The Director's Guidance On Charging 2013*, 5th edn, May 2013 (revised arrangements) available at <http://www.cps.gov.uk/publications/directors_guidance/dpp_guidance_5.html#a16> (accessed 26 December 2015).

—— (2014), *Honour Based Violence and Forced Marriage: Guidance on Identifying and Flagging cases* available at <http://www.cps.gov.uk/legal/h_to_k/forced_marriage_and_honour_based_violence_cases_guidance_on_flagging_and_identifying_cases/index.html> (accessed 29 January 2015).

—— (2016), *Former police officer sentenced for preying on domestic abuse victims for sexual gratification* available at <http://blog.cps.gov.uk/2016/04/former-police-officer-sentenced-for-preying-on-domestic-abuse-victims-for-sexual-gratification.html> (accessed 1 May 2018).

—— (2017a), *Hate crime report 2016–2017* available at <https://www.cps.gov.uk/publication/hate-crime-report-2016-2017> (accessed 1 March 2018).

—— (2017b), *Offences Against the Person, Incorporating Charging Standard* available at <https://www.cps.gov.uk/legal-guidance/offences-against-person-incorporating-charging-standard> (accessed 1 May 2018).

—— (2017c), *Perjury* available at <https://www.cps.gov.uk/legal-guidance/public-justice-offences-incorporating-charging-standard> (accessed 1 May 2018).

—— (2017d), *Voyeurism* available at <https://www.sentencingcouncil.org.uk/wp-content/uploads/Final_Sexual_Offences_Definitive_Guideline_content_web1.pdf> (accessed 1 May 2018).

—— (2018a), *The Code for Crown Prosecutors* available at <http://www.cps.gov.uk/publication/code-crown-prosecutors> (accessed 16 March 2020).

—— (2018b), *Disclosure Manual* available at <https://www.cps.gov.uk/sites/default/files/documents/legal_guidance/Disclosure%20Manual_0.pdf> (accessed 29 April 2018).

—— (2018c), *Honour-Based Violence and Forced Marriage* available at <https://www.cps.gov.uk/legal-guidance/honour-based-violence-and-forced-marriage> (accessed 12 December 2018).

—— (2018d), *Joint Review Disclosure Plan* available at <https://www.cps.gov.uk/publication/joint-review-disclosure-process-case-r-v-allan> (accessed 16 March 2020).

—— (2019), *CPS legal guidance on Prostitution and Exploitation of Prostitution* available at <https://www.cps.gov.uk/legal-guidance/prostitution-and-exploitation-prostitution> (accessed 22 December 2018).

CPS and MPS (2015a), *Joint CPS and Police Action Plan on Rape* available at <https://www.cps.gov.uk/sites/default/files/documents/publications/rape_action_plan_april_2015.pdf> (accessed 1 May 2018).

—— (2015b), *What is Consent?* available at <https://www.cps.gov.uk/sites/default/files/documents/publications/what_is_consent_v2.pdf> (accessed 1 May 2018).

Crawshaw, R, Devlin, B, and Williamson, T (1998), *Human Rights and Policing: Standards for good behaviour and a strategy for change* (The Hague: Kluwer Law International).

Croall, H (2011), *Crime and Society in Britain*, 2nd edn (Harlow: Pearson Education).

CSEW (2018), *Crime in England and Wales: year ending March 2018* available at <https://cy.ons.gov.uk/peoplepopulationandcommunity/crimeandjustice/bulletins/crimeinenglandandwales/yearendingmarch2018> (accessed 12 March 2019).

Daly, M (2003), *My life as a secret policeman* available at <http://news.bbc.co.uk/1/hi/magazine/3210614.stm> (accessed 23 July 2009).

Davis, M (1996), 'Police, discretion, and the professions' in J Kleinig, *Handled with Discretion: Ethical issues in police decision making* (Lanham, MD: Rowman & Littlefield).

Dearden, L (2018), 'Police forces are "failing the public" due to cuts, Police Federation chief warns', *The Independent*, 12 August 2018, available at <https://www.independent.co.uk/news/uk/crime/police-uk-stop-responding-crime-budget-cuts-demand-federation-violence-demand-officers-a8485316.htmlon 23/12/2019> (accessed 16 March 2020).

Delattre, EJ (2002), *Character and Cops: Ethics in Policing*, 4th edn (Washington, DC: AEI Press).

Department for Children, Schools and Families (2009), *Safeguarding Children and Young People from Sexual Exploitation* available at <http://www.uknswp.org/wp-content/uploads/SAFEG.PDF> (accessed 1 May 2018).

Department for Transport (2011), *Instructions for the Completion of Road Accident Reports from non-CRASH Sources: STATS20* available at <https://assets.publishing.service.gov.uk/government/uploads/system/uploads/attachment_data/file/230596/stats20-2011.pdf> (accessed 31 October 2018).

—— (2013), *Driving under the influence of drugs: Report from the Expert Panel on Drug Driving* available at <https://www.gov.uk/government/uploads/system/uploads/attachment_data/file/167971/drug-driving-expert-panel-report.pdf> (accessed 11 February 2016).

—— (2018) *Reported road casualties in Great Britain: 2017 annual report* available at <https://assets.publishing.service.gov.uk/government/uploads/system/uploads/attachment_data/file/744077/reported-road-casualties-annual-report-2017.pdf> (accessed 16 November 2018).

—— (2019a), *Accident and casualty costs (RAS60)* available at <https://www.gov.uk/government/statistical-data-sets/ras60-average-value-of-preventing-road-accidents> (accessed 6 December 2018).

—— (2019b), *Contributory factors for reported road accidents (RAS50)* available at <https://www.gov.uk/government/statistical-data-sets/ras50-contributory-factors> (accessed 27 March 2019).

—— (2019c), *Reported road casualties in Great Britain: main results 2018* available at <https://assets.publishing.service.gov.uk/government/uploads/system/uploads/attachment_data/file/820562/Reported_road_casualties_-_Main_Results_2018.pdf> (accessed 16 March 2020).

Department of Health (2000), *No Secrets: Guidance on Developing and Implementing Multi-Agency Policies and Procedures to Protect Vulnerable Adults from Abuse* available at <https://www.gov.uk/government/uploads/system/uploads/attachment_data/file/194272/No_secrets__guidance_on_developing_and_implementing_multi-agency_policies_and_procedures_to_protect_vulnerable_adults_from_abuse.pdf> (accessed 31 January 2015).

—— (2015), *Mental Health Act 1983 Code of Practice* available at <http://www.crisiscareconcordat.org.uk/wp-content/uploads/2015/01/Code_of_Practice.pdf> (accessed 28 December 2015).

—— (2017), *Guidance for the implementation of changes to police powers and places of safety provisions in the Mental Health Act 1983* available at <https://www.gov.uk/government/uploads/system/uploads/attachment_data/file/656025/Guidance_on_Police_Powers.PDF> (accessed 7 February 2018).

Devon and Cornwall Police (2014), *Substance Misuse Referral Schemes* available at <https://webcache.googleusercontent.com/search?q=cache:LaKnP69J9-kJ:https://www.devon-cornwall.police.uk/FOI/Doc/fa8da6bd-cbf3-43b6-bdbd-91da5ba67cbb/p%3FD280.pdf+&cd=2&hl=en&ct=clnk&gl=uk> (accessed 1 May 2018).

Digital by Default News (2017), *Police forces harness mobile technology* available at <http://www.digitalbydefaultnews.co.uk/2017/03/29/police-forces-harness-mobile-technology/> (accessed 16 February 2018).

Directgov (2011), *Uninsured Driving* available at <http://www.direct.gov.uk/en/Motoring/OwningAVehicle/Motorinsurance/DG_067639> (accessed 31 March 2011).

Dodd, V (2017), *Met police deny systemic failure in rape case disclosures. Wednesday 20th December 2017* available at <https://www.theguardian.com/uk-news/2017/dec/20/met-police-deny-systemic-failure-in-case-disclosures> (accessed 16 February 2018).

DoJ (2018), *2018 UK Annual Report 2015 Report on Modern Slavery* available at <https://assets.publishing.service.gov.uk/government/uploads/system/uploads/attachment_data/file/749346/2018_UK_Annual_Report_on_Modern_Slavery.pdf> (accessed 11 December 2018).

Dorset Police (2019), *The Apprenticeship* available at <https://www.dorset.police.uk/recruitment/police-officers/becoming-a-police-officer/the-apprenticeship/> (accessed 12 March 2019).

Dunnighan, C and Norris, C (1996), 'A risky business: Exchange, bargaining and risk in the recruitment and running of informers by English police officers', Journal of Police Studies 19(2), 1–25.

—— and —— (1999), 'The detective, the snout, and the Audit Commission: The real costs in using informants', The Howard Journal 38(1), 67–86.

Dyfed Powys Police (2019), *Frequently Asked Questions* available at <https://www.dyfed-powys.police.uk/en/join-us/police-officer/frequently-asked-questions/> (accessed 12 March 2019).

Eck, JE, Lee, YJ, O, SH, and Martinez, N (2017), 'Compared to what? Estimating the relative concentration of crime at places using systematic and other reviews', Crime Science: An Interdisciplinary Journal 6(8) available at <https://crimesciencejournal.springeropen.com/articles/10.1186/s40163-017-0070-4> (accessed 9 December 2017).

Eddlestone, J (2012), *Blind Justice: Miscarriages of Justice in 20th Century Britain*, e-book, Bibliofile publishers.

Ede, R and Shepherd, E (2000), *Active Defence: Lawyer's guide to police and defence investigation and prosecution and defence disclosure in criminal cases* (London: Law Society Publishing).

EHRC (2015), *Newsletter* available at <http://www.equalityhumanrights.com/college-policing-and-commission-announce-new-police-training-stop-and-search> (accessed 25 January 2016).

Ekblom, P (2001), *The Conjunction of Criminal Opportunity: A framework for crime reduction toolkits* available at <http://webarchive.nationalarchives.gov.uk/20100413151441/crimereduction.homeoffice.gov.uk/learningzone/cco.htm> (accessed 11 March 2014).

Elliott, J, Kusher, S, Alexandrou, A, Dwyfor Davies, J, Wilkinson, S, and Zamorski, B (2003), *Review of the Learning Requirement for Police Probationer Training in England & Wales* (University of East Anglia and University of the West of England).

Ellison, M (2014), *The Stephen Lawrence Independent Review: Possible corruption and the role of undercover policing in the Stephen Lawrence case* available at <https://www.gov.uk/government/uploads/system/uploads/attachment_data/file/287030/stephen_lawrence_review_summary.pdf> (accessed 4 March 2015).

Environmental Audit Committee (2012), *Wildlife Crime* available at <http://www.publications.parliament.uk/pa/cm201213/cmselect/cmenvaud/140/140.pdf> (accessed 30 January 2013).

Everson, S and Pease, K (2001), 'Crime against the same person and place: Detection opportunity and offender targeting' in G Farrell and K Pease (eds), *Crime Prevention Studies*, vol 12 (Monsey, NY: CRC Press).

Experian (2016), *Fraud costing the UK economy £193bn a year* available at <https://www.experianplc.com/media/news/2016/fraud-costing-the-uk-economy-193bn-a-year/> (accessed 1 March 2017).

—— (2017), *Fraud still costing the UK more than £190bn—new analysis released in the Annual Fraud Indicator* available at <https://www.experian.co.uk/blogs/latest-thinking/identity-and-fraud/fraud-costing-uk-more-than-190bn-released-annual-fraud-indicator/> (accessed 11 March 2019).

—— (2018), *New Experian research shows online fraud continues to be a top concern across the globe* available at <https://www.experianplc.com/media/news/2018/84-of-businesses-could-reduce-fraud-risk-if-certain-about-customers-identity/> (accessed 12 March 2019).

Farrall, S and Gadd, D (2004), 'Evaluating crime fears: A research note on a pilot study to improve the measurement of the "Fear of Crime" as a performance indicator', Evaluation 10(4), 493–502.

Felson, M (2002), *Crime and everyday life*, 3rd edn (Thousand Oaks, CA: Sage Publications).

Fielding, NG (2005), *The Police & Social Conflict: Rhetoric and reality*, 2nd edn (London: Routledge-Cavendish).

Fineman, K (1995), 'A model for the qualitative analysis of child and adult fire deviant behaviour', American Journal of Forensic Psychology 13, 31–60.

Flanagan, Sir R (2004), *A Report on the Investigation by Cambridgeshire Constabulary into the Murders of Jessica Chapman and Holly Wells at Soham on 4 August 2002* (London: HMIC).

Flatley, J, Kershaw, C, Smith, K, Chaplin, R, and Moon, D (2010), *Crime in England and Wales 2009/10* Home Office Statistical Bulletin 12/10 (London: Home Office).

Flynn, C (2011), 'Examining the Links between Animal Abuse and Human Violence', Crime, Law and Social Change 55(5), 453–68.

Forced Marriage Unit (2014), *Statistics January to December 2013* available at <https://www.gov.uk/government/uploads/system/uploads/attachment_data/file/291855/FMU_2013_statistics.pdf> (accessed 9 January 2015).

Ford, K, Newbury, A, Meredith, Z, Evans, J, Hughes, K, Roderick, J, Davies, A, and Bellis, M (2019), 'Understanding the outcome of police safeguarding notifications to social services in South Wales', The Police Journal, 1–22.

Francis, B, Barry, J, Bowater, R, Miller, N, Soothill, K, and Ackerley, E (2004), 'Using homicide data to assist murder investigation', Home Office Online Report 26/04 (London: Home Office).

Fuller, E (ed) (2008), *Drug Use, Smoking and Drinking among Young People in England in 2007* (National Centre for Social Research, National Foundation for Educational Research).

Gill, C, Weisburd, D, Telep, CW, Vitter, Z, and Bennett, T (2014), 'Community-oriented policing to reduce crime, disorder and fear and increase satisfaction and legitimacy among citizens: A systematic review', Journal of Experimental Criminology 10(4), 399–428.

GLA (2018), *Police get extra £15m to tackle knife crime* available at <https://www.london.gov.uk/city-hall-blog/police-get-extra-ps15m-tackle-knife-crime> (accessed 7 March 2018).

GMC (2008), *Licensing and Revalidation* available at <http://www.gmc-uk.org/7a_Licensing_and_Revalidation.pdf_25399016.pdf> (accessed 11 March 2014).

Goldstein, H (1990), *Problem-orientated Policing* (New York: McGraw Hill).

Gov UK (2017), *The key principles of vehicle cyber security for connected and automated vehicles* available at <https://www.gov.uk/government/publications/principles-of-cyber-security-for-connected-and-automated-vehicles> (accessed 16 March 2020).

—— (2019e), *About the Emergency Services Network* available at <https://www.gov.uk/government/publications/the-emergency-services-mobile-communications-programme/emergency-services-network> (accessed 16 March 2020).

Greenburg, D (2019), 'Criminal Careers' in E McLaughlin and J Muncie (eds), *The Sage Dictionary of Criminology*, 4th edn (London: Sage Publications).

Guardian (2019), ' "I agreed because I was scared": boy, 16, on county lines ordeal' available at <https://www.theguardian.com/uk-news/2019/sep/03/boy-x-county-lines-ordeal-cornwall> (accessed 16 March 2020).

Gudjonsson, G, Sigurdsson, J, and Einarsson, E (2004), 'The role of personality in relation to confessions and denials', Psychology, Crime & Law 10(2), 125–35.

Halliday, J (2018), *Cheshire PC is jailed for 25 years for sexual assault and grooming* (The Guardian, 13 December) available at <https://www.google.com/url?sa=t&rct=j&q=&esrc=s&source=web&cd=1&cad=rja&uact=8&ved=2ahUKEwje4pqs-MnfAhUEqXEKHQ8JBRIQFjAAegQICRAB&url=https%3A%2F%2Fwww.theguardian.com%2Fuk-news%2F2018%2Fdec%2F13%2Fcheshire-police-officer-is-jailed-for-25-years-for-sexual-assault-and-grooming&usg=AOvVaw3WHA29qswT5Tx_2_Nq7jep> (accessed 31 December 2018).

Harfield, C and Harfield, K (2005), *Covert Investigation* (Oxford: Oxford University Press).

—— and —— (2008), *Intelligence: Investigation, Community, and Partnership* (Oxford: Oxford University Press).

Harris, D, Turner, R, Garrett, I, and Atkinson, S (2011), *Understanding the Psychology of Gang Violence: Implications for designing effective violence interventions*, Ministry of Justice Research Series 2/11, March.

Harwood, RH (2017), 'How to deal with violent and aggressive patients in acute medical settings', Journal of the Royal College of Physicians Edinburgh 47, 94–101.

Heap, D (ed) (2017), *Crime outcomes in England and Wales: year ending March 2017*, 2nd edn (London: Home Office).

Heaton, R (2000), 'The prospects for intelligence-led policing: Some historical and quantitative considerations', Policing & Society 9, 337–55.

—— (2008), 'Measuring crime reduction: Geographical effects', The Police Journal 81(2), 95.

Henriques, R, Sir (2016), *An Independent review of the Metropolitan Police Service's handling of non-recent sexual offence investigations alleged against persons of public prominence* available at <http://news.met.police.uk/documents/report-independent-review-of-metropolitan-police-services-handling-of-non-recent-sexual-offence-investigations-61510> (accessed 1 March 2017).

Henry, S (2013), 'Crime' in E McLaughlin and J Muncie (eds), *The Sage Dictionary of Criminology*, 3rd edn (London: Sage Publications).

Herbert, N The Rt Hon (2011), 'Restorative justice, policing and the Big Society', Restorative Justice Council, Manchester, 22 February.

Herring, J (2007), *Family Law*, 3rd edn (Cambridge: Pearson).

Hestia (2018), 'Bright Sky' available at <https://www.hestia.org/brightsky> (accessed 12 December 2018).

Higgins, A (2018), *Modernising neighbourhood policing guidelines: big cogs turning* available at <http://www.police-foundation.org.uk/2018/07/modernising-neighbourhood-policing-guidelines-big-cogs-turning/> (accessed 16 March 2020).

Highway Code (2004), available at <http://www.direct.gov.uk/en/TravelAndTransport/Highwaycode/DG_070190> (accessed 11 March 2014).

Historic England (2020), *Costly Convictions for Family Guilty of Seriously Damaging Historic Site in Warwickshire* available at <https://historicengland.org.uk/whats-new/news/costly-convictions-for-damaging-historic-site-in-warwickshire/> (accessed 16 March 2020).

HMCPSI (2017), *CPS Response to HMCPSI Thematic Inspection of CMS Case Finalisations* available at <https://www.cps.gov.uk/publication/cps-response-hmcpsi-thematic-inspection-cms-case-finalisations> (accessed 16 March 2020).

HM Government (2014a), *Modern Slavery Strategy* available at <https://www.gov.uk/government/uploads/system/uploads/attachment_data/file/383764/Modern_Slavery_Strategy_FINAL_DEC2015.pdf> (accessed 23 January 2016).

—— (2014b), *Multi-agency practice guidelines: Handling cases of Forced Marriage* available at <https://www.gov.uk/government/uploads/system/uploads/attachment_data/file/322307/HMG_MULTI_AGENCY_PRACTICE_GUIDELINES_v1_180614_FINAL.pdf> (accessed 9 January 2015).

—— (2018), *Working Together to Safeguard Children 2018* available at <https://assets.publishing.service.gov.uk/government/uploads/system/uploads/attachment_data/file/729914/Working_Together_to_Safeguard_Children-2018.pdf> (accessed 28 January 2019).

HM Government and College of Policing (2014), *Out of Court Disposals Consultation Response* available at <https://www.gov.uk/government/uploads/system/uploads/attachment_data/file/370053/out-of-court-disposals-response-to-consultation.pdf> (accessed 23 January 2016).

HMIC (2002), *Training Matters* (London: HMSO).

—— (2003), *Diversity Matters* (London: HMSO).

—— (2005a), *Inspection of Kingston upon Hull BCU Humberside Police July 2005* available at <https://www.justiceinspectorates.gov.uk/hmicfrs/media/humberside-hull-basic-command-unit-inspection-20050629.pdf> (accessed 1 May 2018).

—— (2005b), *Police National Computer Data Quality and Timeliness Second Report on the Inspection by HM Inspectorate of Constabulary* (London: HMSO).

—— (2006), *PNC Compliance Report: City of London* (August 2005) (London: HMSO).

—— (2009), *Adapting to Protest* available at <https://www.justiceinspectorates.gov.uk/hmic/media/adapting-to-protest-20090705.pdf> (accessed 4 March 2017).

—— (2010), *Anti-social Behaviour: Stop the rot* available at <http://www.hmic.gov.uk/media/stop-the-rot-20100923.pdf> (accessed 2 March 2011).

—— (2011), *Policing Public Order* available at <https://www.justiceinspectorates.gov.uk/hmic/media/a-review-of-the-august-2011-disorders-20111220.pdf> (accessed 4 March 2017).

—— (2012a), *A Review of National Police Units which Provide Intelligence on Criminality Associated with Protest* available at <http://www.hmic.gov.uk/publication/review-of-national-police-units-which-provide-intelligence-on-criminality-associated-with-protest-20120202/> (accessed 6 March 2012).

—— (2012b), *A Step in the Right Direction: Policing anti-social behaviour* available at <http://www.justiceinspectorates.gov.uk/hmic/media/a-step-in-the-right-direction-the-policing-of-anti-social-behaviour.pdf> (accessed 2 January 2015).

—— (2013a), *Crime Recording in Kent: A report commissioned by the Police and Crime Commissioner for Kent* available at <http://www.hmic.gov.uk/media/crime-recording-in-kent-130617.pdf> (accessed 11 March 2014).

—— (2013b), *Stop and Search Powers: Are the police using them effectively and fairly?* available at <https://www.justiceinspectorates.gov.uk/hmic/media/stop-and-search-powers-20130709.pdf> (accessed 11 March 2016).

—— (2014a) *Crime Recording: A matter of fact. An interim report of the inspection of crime date integrity in police forces in England and Wales* available at <https://www.justiceinspectorates.gov.uk/hmicfrs/wp-content/uploads/2014/05/crime-data-integrity-interim-report.pdf> (accessed 27 December 2019).

—— (2014b), *Crime-recording: Making the victim count. The final report of an inspection of crime data integrity in police forces in England and Wales* available at <https://www.justiceinspectorates.gov.uk/hmicfrs/wp-content/uploads/crime-recording-making-the-victim-count.pdf> (accessed 2 December 2017).

—— (2014c), *Everyone's business: Improving the police response to domestic abuse* available at <http://www.justiceinspectorates.gov.uk/hmic/wp-content/uploads/2014/04/improving-the-police-response-to-domestic-abuse.pdf> (accessed 6 January 2015).

—— (2015a), *Integrity matters: An inspection of arrangements to ensure integrity and to provide the capability to tackle corruption in policing* available at <https://www.justiceinspectorates.gov.uk/hmic/wp-content/uploads/police-integrity-and-corruption-2015.pdf> (accessed 1 March 2017).

—— (2015b), *Stop and search powers 2* available at <https://www.justiceinspectorates.gov.uk/hmic/wp-content/uploads/stop-and-search-powers-2.pdf> (accessed 11 March 2016).

—— (2015c), *The depths of dishonour: Hidden voices and shameful crimes, An inspection of the police response to honour-based violence, forced marriage and female genital mutilation* available at <https://www.justiceinspectorates.gov.uk/hmic/wp-content/uploads/the-depths-of-dishonour.pdf> (accessed 4 December 2016).

—— (2016), *Best Use of Stop and Search revisits* available at <https://www.justiceinspectorates.gov.uk/hmic/publications/best-use-of-stop-and-search-revisits/> (accessed 1 March 2017).

—— (2017a), *PEEL: Police legitimacy 2016* available at <https://www.justiceinspectorates.gov.uk/hmicfrs/wp-content/uploads/peel-police-legitimacy-2016.pdf> (accessed 12 March 2019).

—— (2017b), *The State of Policing: The Annual Assessment of Policing in England and Wales 2016* available at <https://www.justiceinspectorates.gov.uk/hmicfrs/wp-content/uploads/state-of-policing-2016.pdf> (accessed 5 March 2018).

HMIC and HMCPSI (2013), *Getting cases ready for court a joint review of the quality of prosecution case files*, July 2013 (London: HMIC and HMCPSI).

HMICFRS (2017a), *Making it Fair: The Disclosure of Unused Material in Volume Crown Court Cases* available at <https://www.justiceinspectorates.gov.uk/cjji/wp-content/uploads/sites/2/2017/07/CJJI_DSC_thm_July17_rpt.pdf> (accessed 16 March 2020).

—— (2017b), *Peel: Police efficiency 2017* available at <https://www.justiceinspectorates.gov.uk/hmicfrs/wp-content/uploads/peel-police-efficiency-2017.pdf> (accessed 19 February 2018).

—— (2017c), *A progress report on the police response to domestic abuse* available at <https://www.justiceinspectorates.gov.uk/hmicfrs/wp-content/uploads/progress-report-on-the-police-response-to-domestic-abuse.pdf> (accessed 12 December 2018).

—— (2019), *State of Policing: The Annual Assessment of Policing in England and Wales 2018, Part 1: Overview* available at <https://www.justiceinspectorates.gov.uk/hmicfrs/wp-content/uploads/state-of-policing-2018-part-1.pdf> (accessed 21 February 2020).

Hohl, K and Stanko, EA (2015), 'Complaints of rape and the criminal justice system: Fresh evidence on the attrition problem in England and Wales', European Journal of Criminology 12(3), 324–41.

Home Affairs Select Committee (2015), *The College of Policing in the first two years* available at <http://www.publications.parliament.uk/pa/cm201415/cmselect/cmhaff/800/80005.htm> (accessed 31 March 2015).

Home Office (1989), *Criminal and Custodial Careers of those Born in 1953, 1958 and 1963*, Home Office Statistical Bulletin 32/89 (London: Home Office).

—— (1997), *Police Health and Safety, Volume 2: A guide for police managers, Police Policy Directorate* (London: Home Office).

—— (2001), *Policing a New Century: A blueprint for reform*, Cm 5326 (London: Home Office).

—— (2005a), *Code of Practice for Victims of Crime* available at <http://webarchive.nationalarchives.gov.uk/20100418065544/http://homeoffice.gov.uk/documents/victims-code-of-practice2835.pdf?view=Binary> (accessed 3 April 2012).

—— (2005b), Initial Police Learning and Development Programme (IPLDP), Letter to Chief Police Officers 7 November 2005 (London: Home Office).

—— (2005c), *IPLDP Central Author Practitioner Guidance*, Community Engagement & Professional Development Units (London: Home Office).

—— (2007), *Safer Communities: Towards Effective Arson Control* available at <http://www.stoparsonuk.org/documents/resources/Arson%20Scoping%20Study%201999%20UK%20Home%20Office.pdf> (accessed 1 May 2018).

—— (2009a), *Explanatory Memorandum to the Criminal Justice and Immigration Act 2008 (Violent Offender Orders) (Notification Requirements) Regulations 2009 No. 2019* available at <http://www.legislation.gov.uk/uksi/2009/2019/pdfs/uksiem_20092019_en.pdf> (accessed 20 December 2013).

—— (2009b), *Designated Public Place Orders Guidance* available at <https://www.gov.uk/government/publications/designated-public-place-orders-guidance> (accessed 1 May 2018).

—— (2009c), *National Domestic Violence Delivery Plan Annual Progress Report 2008/2009* available at <http://webarchive.nationalarchives.gov.uk/20100418065544/http://www.homeoffice.gov.uk/documents/dom-violence-delivery-plan-08-09.html> (accessed 10 July 2010).

—— (2009d), *Together We Can End Violence against Women and Girls: A strategy* available at <http://webarchive.nationalarchives.gov.uk/20100413151441/http://homeoffice.gov.uk/documents/vawg-strategy-2009/end-violence-against-women2835.pdf?view=Binary> (accessed 10 July 2010).

—— (2010a), *Call to end violence against women and girls: strategic vision* available at <https://www.gov.uk/government/publications/call-to-end-violence-against-women-and-girls-strategic-vision> (accessed 9 February 2014).

—— (2010b), *Policing in the 21st Century: Reconnecting police and the people* (London: Home Office), available at <http://www.homeoffice.gov.uk/publications/consultations/policing-21st-century/> (accessed 19 May 2011).

—— (2011), *Missing Children and Adults* available at <https://www.gov.uk/government/uploads/system/uploads/attachment_data/file/117793/missing-persons-strategy.pdf> (accessed 11 March 2014).

—— (2012a), *Crime in England and Wales: Quarterly Update to September 2011–19* available at <http://www.homeoffice.gov.uk/publications/science-research-statistics/research-statistics/crime-research/hosb0112/hosb0112?view=Binary> (accessed 10 January 2013).

—— (2012b), *Domestic violence disclosure scheme pilot: guidance* available at <http://www.homeoffice.gov.uk/publications/crime/dvds-interim-guidance?view=Binary> (accessed 21 December 2012).

—— (2012c), *Ending Gang and Youth Violence: one year on* available at <http://www.official-documents.gov.uk/document/cm84/8493/8493.pdf> (accessed 10 January 2013).

—— (2012d), *The Police Act 1996 (Equipment) Regulations 2011 and the Police Act 1996 (Services) Regulations 2011 Impact Assessment* available at <http://www.homeoffice.gov.uk/publications/consultations/cons-2010-police-procurement/police-act-ia?view=Binary> (accessed 7 March 2012).

—— (2013a), *Domestic violence and abuse: new definition* available at <https://www.gov.uk/domestic-violence-and-abuse> (accessed 20 December 2013).

—— (2013b), *Penalty Notices for Disorder (PNDs)* available at <http://www.justice.gov.uk/downloads/oocd/pnd-guidance-oocd.pdf> (accessed 11 March 2014).

—— (2013c), *Surveillance Camera Code of Practice* available at <https://www.gov.uk/government/uploads/system/uploads/attachment_data/file/204775/Surveillance_Camera_Code_of_Practice_WEB.pdf> (accessed 11 March 2014).

—— (2014a), *Anti-social Behaviour, Crime and Policing Act 2014: Reform of anti-social behaviour powers: Statutory guidance for frontline professionals: July 2014* available at <https://www.gov.uk/government/publications/anti-social-behaviour-crime-and-policing-bill-anti-social-behaviour> (accessed 1 March 2017).

—— (2014b), *Best Use of Stop and Search Scheme* available at <https://www.gov.uk/government/uploads/system/uploads/attachment_data/file/346922/Best_Use_of_Stop_and_Search_Scheme_v3.0_v2.pdf> (accessed 26 March 2015).

—— (2014c), *Home Office Counting Rules for Recorded Crime* (London: Home Office).

—— (2014d), *Home Secretary outlines reforms to the Police Federation* available at <https://www.gov.uk/government/news/home-secretary-outlines-reforms-to-the-police-federation> (accessed 26 March 2015).

—— (2014e), *Operational briefings and planning* available at <https://www.gov.uk/government/uploads/system/uploads/attachment_data/file/488513/Operational_briefings_and_planning_v3.0EXT_clean.pdf> (accessed 8 March 2018).

—— (2014f), *Vision and Purpose Statements for Crime Recording (NCRS & HOCR)* available at <https://assets.publishing.service.gov.uk/government/uploads/system/uploads/attachment_data/file/387762/count-vision-december-2014.pdf> (accessed 27 December 2019).

—— (2015a), *Crime Recording General Rules* available at <https://www.gov.uk/government/uploads/system/uploads/attachment_data/file/489732/count-general-january-2016.pdf> (accessed 22 February 2016).

—— (2015b), *Hate Crime, England and Wales, 2014/15* available at <https://www.gov.uk/government/uploads/system/uploads/attachment_data/file/467366/hosb0515.pdf> (accessed 22 February 2016).

—— (2015c), *Initial Operational Response to a CBRN incident* available at <http://www.jesip.org.uk/uploads/media/pdf/CBRN%20JOPs/IOR_Guidance_V2_July_2015.pdf> (accessed 8 March 2018).

—— (2015d), *Statutory Guidance Injunctions to Prevent Gang-Related Violence and Gang-Related Drug Dealing* available at <https://www.gov.uk/government/uploads/system/uploads/attachment_data/file/432805/Injunctions_to_Prevent_Gang-Related_Violence_web.pdf> (accessed 11 March 2016).

—— (2015e), *Working together to safeguard children. A guide to inter-agency working to safeguard and promote the welfare of children* available at <https://www.gov.uk/government/uploads/system/uploads/attachment_data/file/419595/Working_Together_to_Safeguard_Children.pdf> (accessed 23 December 2015).

—— (2016a), *Ending Violence Against Women and Girls Strategy 2016–2020* available at <https://www.gov.uk/government/uploads/system/uploads/attachment_data/file/522166/VAWG_Strategy_FINAL_PUBLICATION_MASTER_vRB.PDF> (accessed 23 October 2016).

—— (2016b), *Home Office counting rules for recording crime; Section A: Whether and when to record*, available at <https://www.gov.uk/government/uploads/system/uploads/attachment_data/file/566188/count-general-nov-2016.pdf> (on 26 November 2016).

—— (2017a), *Best Use of Stop & Search Scheme* available at <https://www.gov.uk/government/uploads/system/uploads/attachment_data/file/346922/Best_Use_of_Stop_and_Search_Scheme_v3.0_v2.pdf> (accessed 1 March 2017).

—— (2017b), *First director general appointed to lead new Independent Office for Police Conduct (IOPC)* available at <https://www.gov.uk/government/news/first-director-general-appointed-to-lead-new-independent-office-for-police-conduct-iopc> (accessed 10 December 2017).

—— (2017c), *Home Office Guidance: Police Officer Misconduct, Unsatisfactory Performance and Attendance Management Procedures* available at <https://www.gov.uk/government/uploads/system/uploads/attachment_data/file/664940/Final_Home_Office_Guidance.pdf> (accessed 7 February 2018).

—— (2017d), *Police powers and procedures, England and Wales, year ending 31 March 2018* available at <https://assets.publishing.service.gov.uk/government/uploads/system/uploads/attachment_data/file/751215/police-powers-procedures-mar18-hosb2418.pdf> (accessed 12 March 2019).

—— (2018a), *Circular 001/2018: amendment to probation periods for constables and pre-entry qualifications* available at <https://www.gov.uk/government/publications/circular-0012018-amendment-to-probation-periods-for-constables> (accessed 27 February 2019).

—— (2018b), *Counting rules for recorded crime* available at <https://www.gov.uk/government/publications/counting-rules-for-recorded-crime> (accessed 11 February 2019).

—— (2018c), *Criminal Exploitation of children and vulnerable adults: County Lines guidance* available at <https://assets.publishing.service.gov.uk/government/uploads/system/uploads/attachment_data/file/741194/HOCountyLinesGuidanceSept2018.pdf> (accessed 16 March 2020).

—— (2018d), *Emergency Services Network* available at <https://www.gov.uk/government/publications/the-emergency-services-mobile-communications-programme> (accessed 3 February 2018).

—— (2018e), *Forced Marriage Unit Statistics 2017* available at <https://assets.publishing.service.gov.uk/government/uploads/system/uploads/attachment_data/file/730155/2017_FMU_statistics_FINAL.pdf> (accessed 12 December 2018).

—— (2018f), *Hate Crime, England and Wales* available at <https://www.gov.uk/government/statistics/hate-crime-england-and-wales-2017-to-2018> (accessed 5 March 2019).

—— (2018g), *Home Office Guidance: Police Officer Misconduct, Unsatisfactory Performance and Attendance Management Procedures* available at <https://assets.publishing.service.gov.uk/government/uploads/system/uploads/attachment_data/file/732466/Home_Office_Guidance_on_Police_Misconduct.pdf> (accessed 31 December 2018).

—— (2018h), *Police powers and procedures, England and Wales, year ending 31 March 2018* available at <https://assets.publishing.service.gov.uk/government/uploads/system/uploads/attachment_data/file/751215/police-powers-procedures-mar18-hosb2418.pdf> (accessed 21 February 2019).

—— (2018i), *Seizures of drugs in England and Wales, financial year ending 2018* available at <https://assets.publishing.service.gov.uk/government/uploads/system/uploads/attachment_data/file/754677/seizures-drugs-mar2018-hosb2618.pdf> (accessed 10 January 2019).

—— (2018j), *Stop and Search: Extending police powers to cover offences relating to unmanned aircraft (drones), laser pointers and corrosive substances. Government consultation* available at <https://assets.publishing.service.gov.uk/government/uploads/system/uploads/attachment_data/file/739629/ 06_09_18_Stop_and_Search_Consultation_Document_pdf> (accessed 4 March 2019).

—— (2019a), *2019 UK Annual Report on Modern Slavery* available at <https://assets.publishing.service.gov.uk/government/uploads/system/uploads/attachment_data/file/840059/Modern_Slavery_Report_2019.pdf> (accessed 23 November 2019).

—— (2019b), *Crime Outcomes in England and Wales: year ending March 2019* available at <https://assets.publishing.service.gov.uk/government/uploads/system/uploads/attachment_data/file/817769/crime-outcomes-hosb1219.pdf> (accessed 16 March 2020).

—— (2019c), *Crime Recording General Rules* available at <https://assets.publishing.service.gov.uk/government/uploads/system/uploads/attachment_data/file/854733/count-general-dec-2019.pdf> (accessed 27 December 2019).

—— (2019d), *Forced Marriage Unit Statistics 2019* available at <https://assets.publishing.service.gov.uk/government/uploads/system/uploads/attachment_data/file/804044/Forced_Marriage_Unit_Statistics_2018_FINAL.pdf> (accessed 26 November 2019).

—— (2019e), *Hate Crime, England and Wales, 2018/19* available at <https://assets.publishing.service.gov.uk/government/uploads/system/uploads/attachment_data/file/839172/hate-crime-1819-hosb2419.pdf> (accessed 19 February 2020).

—— (2019f), *Home Office Counting Rules for Recorded Crime: with effect from April 2019* available at <https://assets.publishing.service.gov.uk/government/uploads/system/uploads/attachment_data/file/845360/count-general-nov-2019.pdf> (accessed 26 November 2019).

—— (2019g), *Independent Review of the Modern Slavery Act 2015: Final Report* available at <https://assets.publishing.service.gov.uk/government/uploads/system/uploads/attachment_data/file/803406/Independent_review_of_the_Modern_Slavery_Act_-_final_report.pdf> (accessed 24 November 2019).

—— (2019h), *Police Powers and Procedures. England and Wales, year ending 31 March 2019. National Statistics* available at <https://assets.publishing.service.gov.uk/government/uploads/system/uploads/attachment_data/file/841408/police-powers-procedures-mar19-hosb2519.pdf> (accessed 16 March 2020).

—— (2019i), *Police Workforce, England and Wales, 31 March 2019.* 2nd edn, Statistical Bulletin 11/19 available at <https://assets.publishing.service.gov.uk/government/uploads/system/uploads/attachment_data/file/831726/police-workforce-mar19-hosb1119.pdf> (accessed 16 March 2020).

—— (2019j), *Police use of force statistics, England and Wales April 2018 to March 2019* available at <https://assets.publishing.service.gov.uk/government/uploads/system/uploads/attachment_data/file/853204/police-use-of-force-apr2018-mar2019-hosb3319.pdf> (accessed 14 February 2020).

—— (2020a), *Anti-social behaviour* available at <https://www.police.uk/crime-prevention-advice/anti-social-behaviour/> (accessed 16 March 2020).

—— (2020b), *Home Office Guidance: Conduct, Efficiency and Effectiveness: Statutory Guidance on Professional Standards, Performance and Integrity in Policing* available at <https://assets.publishing.service.gov.uk/government/uploads/system/uploads/attachment_data/file/863820/Home_Office_Statutory_Guidance_0502.pdf> (accessed 17 February 2020).

—— (2020c), *Stalking Protection Orders: Statutory guidance for the police* (London: Home Office).

Home Office Select Committee (2015), *Evaluating the new architecture of policing: the College of Policing and the National Crime Agency—Home Affairs, Certificate in Knowledge in Policing* available at <http://www.publications.parliament.uk/pa/cm201415/cmselect/cmhaff/800/80008.htm#a13> (accessed 31 March 2015).

Home Secretary (2012), *Conference Speech to the Police Superintendents' Association 11 Sep 2012. Home Office* available at <https://www.gov.uk/government/speeches/police-superintendents-association-conference-home-secretarys-speech> (accessed 26 February 2016).

Hough, M and Stanko, B (eds) (2018), *Developing an evidence based police degree-holder entry programme Final Report, Mayor of London, Office for Policing and Crime* available at <https://www.london.gov.uk/sites/default/files/debpdhp_report_final.pdf> (accessed 12 March 2019).

House of Commons Library (2019), *Police Powers: stop and search* available at <http://researchbriefings.files.parliament.uk/documents/SN03878/SN03878.pdf> (accessed 16 March 2020).

Hughes, K, Hardcastle, K, and Perkins, C (2015), *The Mental Health Needs of Gang-Affiliated Young People* available at <https://www.gov.uk/government/uploads/system/uploads/attachment_data/file/398674/The_mental_health_needs_of_gang-affiliated_young_people_v3_23_01_1.pdf> (accessed 12 January 2016).

Humberside Police (2015), *Wanted Persons* available at <http://www.humberside.police.uk/sites/default/files/Wanted_Persons.pdf> (accessed 27 January 2016).

ICO (2017), *In the picture: A data protection code of practice for surveillance cameras and personal information* available at <https://ico.org.uk/media/for-organisations/documents/1542/cctv-code-of-practice.pdf> (accessed 25 April 2018).

Ingleton, R (2002), *Policing Kent 1800–2000* (Chichester: Phillimore).

Inman, K and Rudin, R (2002), 'The origin of evidence', Forensic Science International 126, 11–16.

Innes, M (2005), 'What's your problem? Signal crimes and citizen-focused problem solving', Criminology & Public Policy 4(2), 187–200.

—— (2014), *Signal Crimes: Social Reactions to Crime, Disorder and Control* (Oxford: Oxford University Press).

Institute for Apprenticeships & Technical Education (2018a), *End Point Assessment Plan for Police Constable Integrated Degree Apprenticeship at Level 6* available at <https://www.instituteforapprenticeships.org/apprenticeship-standards/police-constable-degree/> (accessed 12 March 2019).

—— (2018b), *Police Constable (Degree)* available at <https://www.instituteforapprenticeships.org/apprenticeship-standards/police-constable-degree/> (accessed 15 February 2018).

Institute of Alcohol Studies (2015), *Alcohol's impact on emergency services full report* available at <http://www.ias.org.uk/uploads/Alcohols_impact_on_emergency_services_full_report.pdf> (accessed 1 March 2017).

—— (2016), *Youthful Abandon* available at <http://www.ias.org.uk/uploads/pdf/IAS%20reports/rp22072016.pdf> (accessed 1 March 2017).

IOCTA (2019), *Internet Organised Crime Threat Assessment* available at <https://www.europol.europa.eu/sites/default/files/documents/iocta_2019.pdf> (accessed 3 January 2020).

IOPC (2017a), *Information for police officers and staff* available at <https://policeconduct.gov.uk/complaints-and-appeals/information-police-officers-and-staff> (accessed 5 March 2018).

—— (2017b), *Statutory guidance* available at <https://policeconduct.gov.uk/complaints-and-appeals/statutory-guidance> (accessed 3 February 2018).

—— (2020) *Statutory guidance on the police complaints system* available at <https://policeconduct.gov.uk/sites/default/files/Documents/statutoryguidance/2020_statutory_guidance_english.pdf> (accessed 17 February 2020).

IPCC (2012), *IPCC report into the contact between Fiona Pilkington and Leicestershire Constabulary 2004–2007* IPCC Reference: 2009/016872.

—— (2014), *Police Officers Subject of a Complaint* available at <http://www.ipcc.gov.uk/page/police-officers-being-subject-complaint> (accessed 24 March 2014).

—— (2015), *Statutory Guidance to the police service on the handling of complaints* available at <https://www.ipcc.gov.uk/sites/default/files/Documents/statutoryguidance/2015_statutory_guidance_english.pdf> (accessed 28 December 2015).

—— (2016), *IPCC investigation after death of Staffordshire Police detainee* available at <http://ipcc.gov.uk/news/ipcc-investigation-after-death-staffordshire-police-detainee> (accessed 1 March 2017).

IPCC and ACPO (2012), *The abuse of police powers to perpetrate sexual violence* available at <https://www.policeconduct.gov.uk/sites/default/files/Documents/research-learning/abuse_of_police_powers_to_perpetrate_sexual_violence.pdf> (accessed 12 March 2019).

Iranian and Kurdish Women's Rights Organisation (2014), *Postcode lottery: police recording of reported 'honour' based violence* available at <http://ikwro.org.uk/wp-content/uploads/2014/02/HBV-FOI-report-Post-code-lottery-04.02.2014-Final.pdf> (accessed 10 January 2015).

Jackson, J, Bradford, B, Stanko, B, and Hohl, K (2013), *Just Authority? Trust in the police in England and Wales* (London: Routledge).

Jaensch, J and South, N (2018), 'Drug Gang Activity and Policing Responses in an English Seaside Town: "County Lines", "Cuckooing" and Community Impacts', Revija za kriminalistiko in kriminologijo/Ljubljana 69/2018/4, 269–78 available at <https://www.policija.si/images/stories/Publikacije/RKK/PDF/2018/04/RKK2018-04_JessicaJaensch_DrugGangActivityAndPolicingResponses.pdf> (accessed 16 March 2020).

JESIP (2017a), *IIMARCH template* available at <http://www.jesip.org.uk/IIMARCH-template> (accessed 8 March 2018).

—— (2017b), *M/ETHANE* available at <http://www.jesip.org.uk/methane> (accessed 8 March 2018).

Johnson, SD, Guerette, RT, and Bowers, K (2014), 'Crime displacement: what we know, what we don't know, and what it means for crime reduction', Journal of Experimental Criminology 10(4), 549–71.

Johnston, D and Hutton, G (2005), *Blackstone's Police Manual, Volume 2: Evidence and Procedure* (Oxford: Oxford University Press).

Jones, T and Newburn, T (1998), *Private Security and Public Policing* (Oxford: Clarendon Press).

Jordan, J (2011), 'Here we go round the review-go-round: Rape investigation and prosecution—are things getting worse not better?', Journal of Sexual Aggression 17(3), 234–49.

Junger, M, West, R, and Timman, R (2001), 'Crime and risk behaviour in traffic', Journal of Research in Crime & Delinquency 38(4), 439–59.

Justice (2011), *Mediation and alternatives to court* available at <http://www.justice.gov.uk/courts/mediation> (accessed 21 December 2012).

Justice Select Committee (2018), *Disclosure of evidence in criminal cases inquiry*, p 42, available at <https://publications.parliament.uk/pa/cm201719/cmselect/cmjust/859/85902.htm> (accessed 16 March 2020).

Kaspersky (2019), *The State of Stalkerware 2019, Coalition Against Stalkerware* available at <https://media.kasperskydaily.com/wp-content/uploads/sites/92/2019/11/18053214/Kaspersky_Coalition_The-state-of-stalkerware-in-2019_ENG_fin.pdf> updated online in 2020 at <https://securelist.com/the-state-of-stalkerware-in-2019/93634/> (accessed 10 January 2020).

Kent Online (2013), *Kent Police officer Eileen Arthurs tells misconduct trial of friendship with convicted criminal and ex-Page 3 model* available at <http://www.kentonline.co.uk/gravesend/news/kent-police-officer-eileen-arthu-a54538/> (accessed 1 March 2017).

Kent Police (2017), *Force Control Room* available at <https://democracy.gravesham.gov.uk/documents/s38698/THRIVE%20-%2012102017.pdf> (accessed 16 March 2020).

Kilby, B (2015), *Why Scaring Kids Out of Committing Crimes Doesn't Work* available at <https://www.vice.com/en_us/article/kwxxba/why-scaring-kids-out-of-committing-crimes-doesnt-work-1105> (accessed 12 March 2019).

Kirk, P (1953), *Crime Investigation: Physical Evidence and the Police Laboratory* (New York: Interscience Publishers Inc).

—— (1963), 'The Ontogeny of Criminalistics', Journal of Criminal Law, Criminology and Police Science 54(2), 235–8.

Kolb, D (1984), *Experiential Learning: Experience as the source of learning and development* (Upper Saddle River, NJ: Prentice Hall).

Laming (2009), *The Protection of Children in England: A Progress Report* available at <https://www.gov.uk/government/uploads/system/uploads/attachment_data/file/328117/The_Protection_of_Children_in_England.pdf> (accessed 7 December 2017).

Law Commission (2014), *Reform of Offences against the Person: A Scoping Consultation Paper, Consultation Paper No 217* available at <http://www.lawcom.gov.uk/app/uploads/2015/06/cp217_offences_against_the_person.pdf> (accessed 6 January 2015).

—— (2020), *Implementation Table* available at <https://www.lawcom.gov.uk/our-work/implementation/table/> (accessed 16 March 2020).

Lee, M and South, N (2003), 'Drugs policing' in T Newburn (ed), *Handbook of Policing* (Cullompton: Willan).

Leishman, F and Mason, P (2003), *Policing and the Media: Facts, fictions and factions* (Cullompton: Willan).

Leukfeldt, E and Var, M (2016), 'Applying Routine Activity Theory to Cybercrime: A Theoretical and Empirical Analysis', Deviant Behaviour 37(3), 263–80.

Lister, S, Adams, B, and Phillips, S (2015), *Evaluation of police-community engagement practices* (Swindon: Economic and Social Research Council).

Liverpool John Moores University (2018), *Programme Specification Bachelor of Science with Honours in Professional Police Practice* available at <https://prodcat.ljmu.ac.uk/Specifications/LCP/36029/3580008032/01_08_2018/version_02_01/36029-3580008032.pdf> (accessed 16 March 2020).

Lock, R (2012), *Final Overview Report of Serious Case Review re Daniel Pelka—September 2013* available at <https://cscb-new.co.uk/downloads/Serious%20Case%20Reviews%20-%20exec.%20summaries/SCR_Archive/Coventry%20SCR%20-%20Daniel%20Pelka%20(2013).pdf> (accessed 7 December 2017).

London Evening Standard (2012), 'Notting Hill Carnival: "Body armour" gang held on way to festival' available at <http://www.standard.co.uk/news/crime/notting-hill-carnival-body-armour-gang-held-on-to-festival-one-man-remains-critical-8083875.html> (accessed 20 February 2013).

Luft, J (1970), *Group Processes: An introduction to group dynamics* (Palo Alto, CA: National Press Books).

Lyons, J and Ward, B (2018), *The New Critical Thinking: An Empirically Informed Introduction* (Abingdon: Routledge).

Mackie, L (1978), 'Race causes an initial confusion', *The Guardian*, 14 June 1978.

Macpherson, Sir W (1999), *The Stephen Lawrence Inquiry* available at <https://www.gov.uk/government/publications/the-stephen-lawrence-inquiry> (accessed 4 April 2014).

Madden, V (2015), *Understanding the Mental Health Needs of Young People involved in Gangs* available at <http://www.mac-uk.org/wped/wp-content/uploads/2013/03/Mental-Health-and-Gangs-Report-2013.pdf> (accessed 19 January 2016).

Marinez, NN, Lee, YJ, Eck, JE, and O, SH (2017), *Ravenous wolves revisited: A systematic review of offending concentration* available at <https://crimesciencejournal.springeropen.com/articles/10.1186/s40163-017-0072-2> (accessed 9 December 2017).

Marshall, B, Webb, B, and Tilley, N (2005), *Rationalisation of current research on guns, gangs and other weapons: Phase 1* (London: University College London/Jill Dando Institute of Crime Science).

Mason, F and Lodrick, Z (2013), 'Psychological consequences of sexual assault', Best Practice and Research Clinical Obstetrics and Gynaecology 27, 27–37.

Mawby, RC (2008), 'Community policing' in T Newburn and P Neyroud (eds), *Dictionary of Policing* (Cullompton: Willan), pp 40–1.

McKee, C (2014), *Home Office Statistical Bulletin Crime Outcomes in England and Wales 2013/14* (London: Home Office).

Motor Insurers Bureau (2018), *2018 Annual Report and Accounts* available at <https://www.mib.org.uk> (accessed 23 December 2019).

—— (2019), *One injured every 20 minutes—Police launch national campaign to protect the public from uninsured drivers* available at <https://www.mib.org.uk/media-centre/news/2019/october/one-injured-every-20-minutes-police-launch-national-campaign-to-protect-the-public-from-uninsured-drivers/> (accessed 23 December 2019).

Miller, J (2003), *Police Corruption in England and Wales: An assessment of current evidence*, Home Office Online Report 11/03 available at <http://webarchive.nationalarchives.gov.uk/20110218135832/http://rds.homeoffice.gov.uk/rds/pdfs2/rdsolr1103.pdf> (accessed 23 July 2009).

Milne, R and Bull, R (1999), *Investigative Interviewing: Psychology and practice* (Chichester: John Wiley & Sons).

MIND (2010), *Achieving Justice for Victims and Witnesses with Mental Distress* available at <https://www.barcouncil.org.uk/media/175024/mind_toolkit_for_prosecutors_and_advocates__2_pdf> (accessed 1 May 2018).

—— (2013), *Police and Mental Health: How to get it right locally* available at <http://www.mind.org.uk/media/618027/2013-12-03-Mind_police_final_web.pdf> (accessed 27 February 2014).

MIND and Victim Support (2013), *Police and mental health, How to get it right locally* available at <https://www.mind.org.uk/media-a/2116/2013-12-03-mind_police_final_web.pdf> (accessed 22 November 2019).

Ministry of Justice (2010), *Offences of stirring up hatred on the grounds of sexual orientation* available at <http://www.banksr.co.uk/images/Other%20Documents/Judicial%20material/circular-2010-05-sexual-orientation-hatred.pdf> (accessed 11 March 2014).

—— (2011), *Achieving Best Evidence in Criminal Proceedings* available at <http://webarchive.nationalarchives.gov.uk/20130128112038/http://www.justice.gov.uk/downloads/victims-and-witnesses/vulnerable-witnesses/achieving-best-evidence-criminal-proceedings.pdf> (accessed 23 December 2015).

—— (2013), *Out of Court Disposals* available at <http://www.justice.gov.uk/out-of-court-disposals> (accessed 17 January 2015).

—— (2015), *Code of Practice for Victims of Crime* available at <https://www.gov.uk/government/uploads/system/uploads/attachment_data/file/470212/code-of-practice-for-victims-of-crime.PDF> (accessed 27 December 2016).

—— (2017a), *Criminal justice system statistics quarterly: June 2017* available at <https://www.gov.uk/government/statistics/criminal-justice-statistics-quarterly-june-2017> (accessed 1 February 2018).

—— (2017b), *Multi-Agency Public Protection Arrangements Annual Report 2016/17* available at <https://www.gov.uk/government/uploads/system/uploads/attachment_data/file/655022/MAPPA-annual-report-2016-17.pdf> (accessed 7 February 2018).

—— (2018a), *Criminal justice system statistics quarterly: June 2018* available at <https://www.gov.uk/government/statistics/criminal-justice-system-statistics-quarterly-june-2018> (accessed 10 January 2019).

—— (2018b), *Transforming the response to domestic abuse* available at <https://consult.justice.gov.uk/homeoffice-moj/domestic-abuse-consultation/> (accessed 12 December 2018).

——, Home Office, and Office for National Statistics (2013), *An Overview of Sexual Offending in England and Wales* available at <https://www.gov.uk/government/uploads/system/uploads/attachment_data/file/214970/sexual-offending-overview-jan-2013.pdf> (accessed 20 December 2013).

—— and the Youth Justice Board (2015), *Youth Out-of-Court Disposals Guide for Police and Youth Offending Service* available at <https://www.gov.uk/government/uploads/system/uploads/attachment_data/file/438139/out-court-disposal-guide.pdf> (accessed 27 January 2016).

Missing People (2018), *How Can We Help You?* available at <https://www.missingpeople.org.uk/how-we-can-help/families-and-friends/reporting-a-missing-person/879-what-will-the-police-do.html> (accessed 11 December 2018).

—— (2019), *Key information* available at <https://www.missingpeople.org.uk/about-us/about-the-issue/research/76-keyinformation2.html?start=1> (accessed 17 February 2020).

Morris, W, Burden, A, and Weekes, A (2004), *The Case for Change: People in the Metropolitan Police Service* (Morris Inquiry) available at <http://www.policeauthority.org/Metropolitan/downloads/scrutinites/morris/morris-report.pdf> (accessed 19 July 2010).

MPS (2014), *Met Briefing Note; Body Worn Video (BWV)* available at <https://www.thinglink.com/scene/520889205841199104> (accessed 1 May 2018).

—— (2018), *How to become a police constable* available at <http://www.metpolicecareers.co.uk/newconstable/becoming-a-pc.php> (accessed 7 March 2018).

Myhill, A and Bradford, B (2011), 'Can police enhance public confidence by improving quality of service? Results from two surveys in England and Wales', Policing and Society First 1–29.

National Audit Office (2011), *The Crown Prosecution Service, The introduction of the Streamlined Process* available at <http://www.nao.org.uk/wp-content/uploads/2011/11/10121584.pdf> (accessed 17 January 2015).

—— (2012), *Home Office and National Policing Improvement Agency Mobile Technology in Policing Report by the Comptroller and Auditor General, HC 1765, Session 2010–2012, 27 January* (London: The Stationery Office).

—— (2013), *Police procurement* available at <https://www.nao.org.uk/wp-content/uploads/2013/03/10092-001-Police-procurement.pdf> (accessed 8 March 2018).

—— (2016), *Upgrading emergency service communications: the Emergency Services Network* available at <https://www.nao.org.uk/report/upgrading-emergency-service-communications-the-emergency-services-network/> (accessed 1 March 2017).

National Sexual Assault Hotline (2012), *How Long Does it Take to Recover?* available at <https://ohl.rainn.org/online/resources/how-long-to-recover.cfm> (accessed 8 January 2015).

NCA (2016), *NCA Strategic Cyber Industry Group Cyber Crime Assessment 2016 ver. 1.2* available at <http://www.nationalcrimeagency.gov.uk/publications/709-cyber-crime-assessment-2016/file> (accessed 1 March 2017).

—— (2018a), *Missing Persons Unit* available at <http://www.nationalcrimeagency.gov.uk/about-us/what-we-do/specialist-capabilities/missing-persons-bureau> (accessed 8 December 2018).

—— (2018b), *National Referral Mechanism Statistics—End of Year Summary 2017* available at <http://www.nationalcrimeagency.gov.uk/publications/national-referral-mechanism-statistics/2017-nrm-statistics/884-nrm-annual-report-2017/file> (accessed 11 December 2018).

—— (2019a), *Intelligence Assessment County Lines Drug Supply, Vulnerability and Harm 2018* available at <https://www.nationalcrimeagency.gov.uk/who-we-are/publications/257-county-lines-drug-supply-vulnerability-and-harm-2018/file> (accessed 16 March 2020).

—— (2019b), *UK Missing Persons Unit* available at <https://missingpersons.police.uk/en-gb/home> (accessed 23 November 2019).

NCDV (2015a), *ASSIST* available at <https://www.assist.uk.net> (accessed 26 December 2015).

—— (2015b), *Third Party Injunction Referral* available at <http://www.ncdv.org.uk/information-for-police-agencies/third-party-injunction-referral/> (accessed 26 December 2015).

NCPE/ACPO (2006), *Practice advice on professionalising the business of Neighbourhood Policing* available at <http://library.college.police.uk/docs/acpo/Professionalising-NeighbourhoodPolicing.pdf> (accessed 28 October 2018).

NDTMS (2018), *Alcohol and drug misuse and treatment statistics* available at <https://www.gov.uk/government/collections/alcohol-and-drug-misuse-and-treatment-statistics> (accessed 10 January 2019).

Neighbourhood Watch (2014), *Our mission* available at <http://www.ourwatch.org.uk/about_us/our_mission/> (accessed 11 March 2014).

Newburn, T (1999), *Understanding and Preventing Police Corruption: Lessons from the literature*, Police Research Series Paper 110 (London: Home Office).

—— (2007), *Criminology* (Cullompton: Willan).

—— (ed) (2011), *Handbook of Policing*, 2nd edn (Abingdon: Routledge).

—— (2015), *Literature review—Police integrity and corruption* available at <https://www.justiceinspectorates.gov.uk/hmic/wp-content/uploads/pic-literature-review.pdf> (accessed 27 December 2016).

—— and Neyroud, P (2008), *Dictionary of Policing* (Cullompton: Willan).

Newton, S (2017), *Knife, gun and gang crime* and *Crime prevention* available at <https://www.gov.uk/government/news/government-announces-further-funding-to-tackle-gang-related-violence> (accessed 8 March 2018).

Neyroud, P (2011), *Review of Police Leadership and Training: Volume One* (London: Home Office), available at <http://www.homeoffice.gov.uk/publications/consultations/rev-police-leadership-training/report?view=Binary> (accessed 11 April 2011).

—— and Beckley, A (2001), *Policing, Ethics and Human Rights* (Cullompton: Willan).

NHS (2013), *How to Spot Child Sexual Exploitation* available at <http://www.nhs.uk/livewell/abuse/pages/child-sexual-exploitation-signs.aspx> (accessed 8 January 2015).

NHS Digital (2017), *Smoking, drinking and drug use among young people* available at <https://files.digital.nhs.uk/47/829A59/sdd-2016-rep-cor-new.pdf> (accessed 10 January 2019).

—— (2019a), *Female Genital Mutilation (FGM) Enhanced Dataset—April 2018 to March 2019, England, experimental statistics, Annual Report* available at <https://files.digital.nhs.uk/42/2AB299/FGM%202019%20AR%20-%20Report.pdf> (accessed 16 March 2020).

—— (2019b), *Smoking, Drinking and Drug Use among Young People in England 2018* available at <https://digital.nhs.uk/data-and-information/publications/statistical/smoking-drinking-and-drug-use-among-young-people-in-england/2018/part-6-young-people-who-drink-alcohol> (accessed 16 March 2020).

—— (2019c), *Statistics on Alcohol, England 2019* available at <https://digital.nhs.uk/data-and-information/publications/statistical/statistics-on-alcohol/2019/part-1> (accessed 16 March 2020).

North Yorkshire Police (2020), *How we handle incidents* available at <https://northyorkshire.police.uk/what-we-do/dealing-with-crime/deal-crime-report/> (accessed 16 March 2020).

Nozick, R (1974), *Anarchy, State and Utopia* (Oxford: Blackwell (2003 print)).

NPCC (2015a), *Advice on the structure of visually recorded witness interviews*, 3rd edn, available at <http://library.college.police.uk/docs/appref/NPCC-(2015)-Guidance-Visually-Recorded-Interviews%203rd%20Edition.pdf> (accessed 10 March 2016).

—— (2015b), *Honour based Abuse, Forced Marriage and Female Genital Mutilation* available at <http://library.college.police.uk/docs/appref/Final%20NPCC%20HBA%20strategy%202015%202018December%202015.pdf> (accessed 8 December 2017).

—— (2016), *Policing Vision 2025* available at <http://www.npcc.police.uk/documents/policing%20vision.pdf> (accessed 19 February 2018).

—— (2017), *National Strategy to address the issue of police officers and staff who abuse their position for a sexual purpose* available at <https://www.npcc.police.uk/documents/Abuse%20of%20position%20for%20sexual%20purpose%20National%20Strategy.pdf> (accessed 12 March 2019).

—— (2018), *National Vulnerability Action Plan 2018–2021* available at <https://www.npcc.police.uk/documents/crime/2018/National%20Vulnerability%20Action%20Plan_18_21.pdf> (accessed 16 March 2020).

—— (2019), *Record numbers arrested and hundreds of children protected as County Lines drug networks targeted* available at <https://news.npcc.police.uk/releases/record-numbers-arrested-and-hundreds-of-children-protected-as-county-lines-drug-networks-targeted> (accessed 16 March 2020).

NPIA (2007), *Practice Advice on Critical Incident Management* available at <http://library.college.police.uk/docs/NPIA/Practice-Advice-on-CIM-Jul2011.pdf> (accessed 1 May 2018).

—— (2009), *National Investigative Interviewing Strategy, Briefing Paper* available at <http://library.college.police.uk/docs/npia/BP-Nat-Investigative-Interviewing-Strategy-2009.pdf> (accessed 10 July 2020).

—— (2011), *Practice Advice on Critical Incident Management*, 2nd edn, available at <http://library.college.police.uk/docs/NPIA/Practice-Advice-on-CIM-Jul2011.pdf> (accessed 8 March 2018).

——/ACPO (2009), *Practice Advice on the Management of Priority and Volume Crime (The Volume Crime Management Model)*, 2nd edn, available at <http://library.college.police.uk/docs/acpo/VCMM-191109.pdf> (accessed 1 May 2018).

NPT (1995), *Police Probationer Training Foundation Course Notes* (Police Central Planning & Training Unit, a division of National Police Training), p 4.

NSPCC (2005), *Understanding the links, child abuse, animal abuse and domestic violence* available at <https://www.nspcc.org.uk/globalassets/documents/research-reports/understanding-links-child-abuse-animal-abuse-domestic-violence.pdf> (accessed 4 December 2016).

Nunn, J (2018), 'The Criminal Histories of Drug-Drive Offenders', Policing: A Journal of Policy and Practice, available at <https://academic.oup.com/policing/advance-article/doi/10.1093/police/pay026/4967630> (accessed 21 January 2019).

Office of the Children's Commissioner (2012), *I thought I was the only one. The only one in the world* available at <http://www.childrenscommissioner.gov.uk/content/publications/content_636> (accessed 9 March 2018).

Ofqual (2016), *The Register* available at <http://register.ofqual.gov.uk/> (accessed 16 March 2016).

O'Neill, M (2018), *Key Challenges in Criminal Investigation* (Policy Press: Bristol).

ONS (2014), *Crime in England and Wales, Year Ending June 2014* available at <http://www.ons.gov.uk/ons/dcp171778_380538.pdf> (accessed 6 January 2015).

—— (2015), *Public Perceptions of Crime* available at <http://webarchive.nationalarchives.gov.uk/20160105160709/http://www.ons.gov.uk/ons/rel/crime-stats/crime-statistics/focus-on-public-perceptions-of-crime-and-the-police-and-the-personal-well-being-of-victims-2013-to-2014/chapter-2-focus-on-public-perceptions-of-crime.html> (accessed 28 February 2016).

—— (2016), *Population Estimates for UK, England and Wales, Scotland and Northern Ireland* available at <https://www.ons.gov.uk/peoplepopulationandcommunity/populationandmigration/populationestimates/datasets/populationestimatesforukenglandandwalesscotlandandnorthernireland> (accessed 1 March 2017).

—— (2017a), *Crime in England and Wales: year ending Sept 2016* available at <https://www.ons.gov.uk/peoplepopulationandcommunity/crimeandjustice/bulletins/crimeinenglandandwales/yearendingjune2016> (accessed 1 March 2017).

—— (2017b), *Public perceptions of crime in England and Wales: year ending March 2016* available at <https://www.ons.gov.uk/peoplepopulationandcommunity/crimeandjustice/articles/publicperceptionsofcrimeinenglandandwales/yearendingmarch2016#worry-about-crime> (accessed 3 December 2017).

—— (2018a), *Crime in England and Wales: year ending September 2018* available at <https://www.ons.gov.uk/peoplepopulationandcommunity/crimeandjustice/bulletins/crimeinenglandandwales/yearendingseptember2018> (accessed 24 January 2019).

—— (2018b), *Deaths Registered in England and Wales (Series DR), 2017 (Statistical Bulletin)* available at <http://www.ons.gov.uk/ons/rel/vsob1/mortality-statistics-deaths-registered-in-england-and-wales-series-dr-/2014/stb-mortality-stats-2014.html> (accessed 16 March 2020).

—— (2018c), *Domestic abuse in England and Wales: year ending March 2018* available at <https://www.ons.gov.uk/peoplepopulationandcommunity/crimeandjustice/bulletins/domesticabuseinenglandandwales/yearendingmarch2018> (accessed 12 December 2018).

—— (2018d), *Homicide in England and Wales: year ending March 2017* available at <https://www.ons.gov.uk/peoplepopulationandcommunity/crimeandjustice/articles/homicideinenglandandwales/yearendingmarch2017> (accessed 21 January 2019).

—— (2018e), *Offences involving the use of weapons: data tables* available at <https://www.ons.gov.uk/peoplepopulationandcommunity/crimeandjustice/datasets/offencesinvolvingtheuseofweaponsdatatables> (accessed 21 April 2018).

—— (2018f), *Overview of fraud and computer misuse statistics for England and Wales* available at <https://www.ons.gov.uk/peoplepopulationandcommunity/crimeandjustice/articles/overviewoffraudandcomputermisusestatisticsforenglandandwales/2018-01-25> (accessed 12 March 2019).

—— (2018g), *Population estimates for the UK, England and Wales, Scotland and Northern Ireland: mid-2017* available at <https://www.ons.gov.uk/peoplepopulationandcommunity/populationandmigration/populationestimates/bulletins/annualmidyearpopulationestimates/mid2017> (accessed 21 January 2019).

—— (2019a), *Crime in England and Wales: Annual supplementary tables (Tables S29/S30)* available at <https://www.ons.gov.uk/peoplepopulationandcommunity/crimeandjustice/datasets/crimeinenglandandwalesannualsupplementarytables> (accessed 27 December 2019).

—— (2019b), *Crime in England and Wales: Other related tables* <https://www.ons.gov.uk/peoplepopulationandcommunity/crimeandjustice/datasets/crimeinenglandandwalesotherrelatedtables> (accessed 16 March 2020).

—— (2019c), *Crime in England and Wales: year ending June 2018. Statistical bulletin* available at <https://www.ons.gov.uk/peoplepopulationandcommunity/crimeandjustice/bulletins/crimeinenglandandwales/yearendingjune2018#main-points> (accessed 12 March 2019).

—— (2019d), *Crime in England and Wales: year ending March 2019* available at <https://www.ons.gov.uk/releases/crimeinenglandandwalesyearendingmarch2019>(accessed 16 March 2020).

—— (2019e), *Crime in England and Wales: year ending September 2019, Statistical bulletin* available at <https://www.ons.gov.uk/peoplepopulationandcommunity/crimeandjustice/bulletins/crimeinenglandandwales/yearendingseptember2019#violent-crime> (accessed 10 December 2019).

—— (2109f), *Deaths Registered in England and Wales (Series DR), 2018 (Statistical Bulletin, table 9)* available at <https://www.ons.gov.uk/file?uri=%2Fpeoplepopulationandcommunity%2Fbirthsdeathsandmarriages%2Fdeaths%2Fdatasets%2Fdeathsregisteredinenglandandwalesseriesdrreferencetables%2F2018/referencetablesfinalv22.xlsx> (accessed 16 March 2020).

—— (2019g), *Domestic abuse in England and Wales overview: November 2019* available at <https://www.ons.gov.uk/peoplepopulationandcommunity/crimeandjustice/bulletins/domesticabuseinenglandandwalesoverview/november2019> (accessed 25 November 2019).

—— (2019h), *Homicide in England and Wales: year ending March 2018* available at <https://www.ons.gov.uk/peoplepopulationandcommunity/crimeandjustice/articles/homicideinenglandandwales/yearendingmarch2018> (accessed 5 December 2019).

—— (2019i), *The Nature of Violent Crime in England and Wales: year ending March 2018* available at <https://www.ons.gov.uk/peoplepopulationandcommunity/crimeandjustice/articles/thenatureofviolentcrimeinenglandandwales/yearendingmarch2018> (accessed 16 March 2020).

—— (2019j), *Offences involving the use of weapons: data tables* available at <https://www.ons.gov.uk/peoplepopulationandcommunity/crimeandjustice/datasets/offencesinvolvingtheuseofweaponsdatatables> (accessed 18 February 2020).

—— (2019k), *Population estimates for the UK, England and Wales, Scotland and Northern Ireland: mid-2018* available at <https://www.ons.gov.uk/file?uri=%2Fpeoplepopulationandcommunity%2Fpopulationandmigration%2Fpopulationestimates%2Fdatasets%2Fpopulationestimatesforukenglandandwalesscotlandandnorthernireland%2Fmid20182019laboundaries/ukmidyearestimates20182019ladcodes.xls> (accessed 16 March 2020).

—— (2020), *Crime in England and Wales: year ending September 2019* available at <https://www.ons.gov.uk/peoplepopulationandcommunity/crimeandjustice/bulletins/crimeinenglandandwales/yearendingseptember2019> (accessed 31 January 2020).

Ostrowsky, MK (2014), 'The Social Psychology of Alcohol Use and Violent Behavior Among Sports Spectators', *Aggression and Violent Behavior* 19(4), 303–10.

Owens, C, Mann, D, and Mckenna, R (2014), *The Essex Body Worn Video Trial* available at <http://whatworks.college.police.uk/Research/Documents/BWV_Report.pdf> (accessed 1 May 2018).

PCC Thames Valley (2017), *Police & Crime Plan for the Thames Valley 2017–2021* available at <https://thamesvalley.s3.amazonaws.com/Documents/Police%20and%20Crime%20Plan/Police%20and%20Crime%20Plan%20Final%202017%20-%202021.PDF> (accessed 8 March 2018).

PCeU (2014), *What we do* available at <http://content.met.police.uk/Article/What-we-do/ 1400015320495/1400015320495> (accessed 11 March 2014).

Pease, K (1997), 'Crime prevention' in M Maguire, R Morgan, and R Reiner (eds), *The Oxford Handbook of Criminology*, 2nd edn (Oxford: Oxford University Press).

—— (1998), *Repeat Victimisation: Taking Stock* (London: Police Research Group, Home Office).

—— (2002), 'Crime reduction' in M Maguire, R Morgan, and R Reiner (eds), *The Oxford Handbook of Criminology*, 3rd edn (Oxford: Oxford University Press), pp 947–79.

—— (2018), *Repeat Victimisation* available at <http://www.excellenceinpolicing.org.uk/wp-content/uploads/2018/09/4-1_Repeat_Victimisation.pdf> (accessed 16 March 2020).

Perry, WL, McInnis, B, Price, CC, Smith, SC, and Hollywood, JS (2013), *Predictive Policing: The Role of Crime Forecasting in Law Enforcement Operations* (Washington, DC: Rand Corporation).

Peters, R (1973), *Authority, Responsibility and Education* (London: Allen & Unwin).

PNLD (2018), *PNLD Conference 2018 Helen Hanley, PNLD Legal Adviser, provides an overview of 'County Lines' as presented by DCI Carl Galvin at our Criminal Law Conference on Thursday 4th October 2018* available at <https://www.pnld.co.uk/media/92367/county-lines-overview-by-helen-hanley.pdf> (accessed 16 March 2020).

Polianskaya, A (2018), 'Former Lord Chief Justice warns rapists may now go free after string of prosecutions collapse', *The Independent*, 20 January 2018, available at <http://www.independent.co.uk/news/uk/rape-trial-lord-chief-justice-oliver-mears-samson-makele-snaresbrook-crown-court-disclosure-a8169661.html> (accessed 8 March 2018).

Police Federation (2011), *Policing the Riots* available at <http://www.nypolfed.org.uk/assets/uploads/PDFs/christmas_2011.pdf> (accessed 1 May 2018).

—— (2017), *Police Officers Warned Over Data Protection Breaches* available at <http://www.polfed.org/newsroom/4166.aspx> (accessed 12 March 2019).

—— (2018), *Quick Reference Guide: A basic summary of your main terms and conditions* available at <https://polfed.org/Norfolk/media/1385/quick-reference-guide-v10-october-2018.pdf> (accessed 17 February 2019).

Police Foundation (2015), *Neighbourhood Policing, Past, Present and Future* available at <https://www.researchgate.net/profile/John_Chapman6/publication/277018498_Neighbourhood_policing_Past_present_and_future_-_A_review_of_the_literature/links/555f3bd208ae9963a117f164.pdf> (accessed 14 February 2019).

—— (2017), *Neighbourhood Policing: a police force topography* available at <http://www.police-foundation.org.uk/publication/neighbourhood-policing-a-police-force-typology/> (accessed 14 February 2019).

—— (2018), *The future of Neighbourhood Policing* available at <http://www.police-foundation.org.uk/publication/future-neighbourhood-policing/> (accessed 14 February 2019).

Police ICT (2020), *Commercial Successes* available at <https://ict.police.uk/about/commercial-successes/> (accessed 1 February 2020).

Police Now (2018a), *About the programme* available at <https://www.policenow.org.uk/the-programme/about-the-programme/#1502792978359-486e26a6-6756> (accessed 8 March 2018).

—— (2018b), *Police: Now* available at <https://www.policenow.org.uk/> (accessed 8 March 2018).

Prime Minister's Office (2017), *The Queen's Speech and Associated Background Briefing, on the Occasion of the Opening of Parliament on Wednesday 21 June 2017* available at <https://www.gov.uk/government/uploads/system/uploads/attachment_data/file/620838/Queens_speech_2017_background_notes.pdf> (accessed 8 December 2017).

Public Health England (2017), *Local Alcohol Profiles for England* available at <https://fingertips.phe.org.uk/profile/local-alcohol-profiles/supporting-information/additional-data-and-reports> (accessed 19 January 2018).

Quinton, P, Tiratello, M, and Bradford, B (2017), *Does more stop and search mean less crime?* available at <http://www.college.police.uk/News/College-news/Documents/Stop%20and%20search%20-%20Less%20crime%20-%20Report.pdf> (accessed 18 January 2018).

Rawlings, PJ (2002), *Policing: A short history* (Cullompton: Willan).

Reiner, R (2000), *The Politics of the Police*, 3rd edn (Oxford: Oxford University Press).

—— (2010), *The Politics of the Police*, 4th edn (Oxford: Oxford University Press).

Re-Solv (2013), *Working to prevent VSA* available at <http://www.re-solv.org/> (accessed 11 March 2014).

Reynolds, M (2018), 'Biased policing is made worse by errors in pre-crime algorithms' *New Scientist* available at <https://www.newscientist.com/article/mg23631464-300-biased-policing-is-made-worse-by-errors-in-pre-crime-algorithms/> (accessed 16 March 2020).

Rigg, G, Hill, M, Drew, J, and Gulvin, A (2018), *Our Approach to Ending the Criminal Exploitation of Vulnerable Children and Adults by Gangs, Kent and Medway Gangs Strategy* available at <https://www.kscb.org.uk/__data/assets/pdf_file/0005/81455/Final-Version-Kent-and-Medway-Gangs-Strategy.pdf> (accessed 12 March 2019).

Roach, J (2017), 'Self-selection Policing and the Disqualified Driver', Policing: A Journal of Policy and Practice, available at <https://academic.oup.com/policing/article-lookup/doi/10.1093/police/paw056> (accessed 21 January 2019).

Robinson, G, McLean, R, and Densley, J (2019), 'Working County Lines: Child Criminal Exploitation and Illicit Drug Dealing in Glasgow and Merseyside', International Journal of Offender Therapy and Comparative Criminology 63(5), 694–711.

Rogers, A (1996), *Teaching Adults*, 2nd edn (Buckingham: Open University Press).

Rose, G (2000), 'The criminal histories of serious traffic offenders', HORS 206 (London: Home Office).

Ross, A (2018), 'Police officer sacked after looking up partners on force database' *Express & Star* available at <https://www.expressandstar.com/news/crime/2018/05/22/police-officer-sacked-over-misuse-of-database/> (accessed 31 December 2018).

Rowe, M (2002), 'Policing diversity: Themes and concerns from the recent British experience', Police Quarterly 5(4), 424–46.

—— (2008), *Introduction to Policing*, 2nd edn (London: Sage Publications).

—— (2017), *Introduction to Policing*, 3rd edn (London: Sage Publications).

Safeguarding Hub (2020), *County Lines—Get a step ahead by improving your knowledge* available at <https://safeguardinghub.co.uk/county-lines-get-a-step-ahead-by-improving-your-knowledge/> (accessed 16 March 2020).

Scarman, Lord (1981), *Report into the Brixton Disorders*, Cmnd 8427 (London: HMSO).

Scottish Government (2018), *Homicide in Scotland 2017–2018: statistics* available at <https://www.gov.scot/publications/homicide-scotland-2017-18/pages/4/> (accessed 5 December 2019).

—— (2019), *Repeat Violent Victimisation: A Rapid Evidence Review* available at <http://actiononviolence.org/sites/default/files/repeat-violent-victimisation-rapid-evidence-review.pdf> (accessed 16 March 2020).

Scriven, M and Paul, R (2004), *Defining critical thinking* available at <http://www.criticalthinking.org/aboutCT/define_critical_thinking.cfm> (accessed 12 March 2019).

Sentencing Council (2012a), *Assault: Definitive Guideline* available at <http://sentencingcouncil.judiciary.gov.uk/docs/Assault_definitive_guideline_-_Crown_Court.pdf> (accessed 6 February 2012).

—— (2012b), *Offences taken into consideration and totality—definitive guideline* available at <http://sentencingcouncil.judiciary.gov.uk/docs/Definitive_guideline_TICs__totality_Final_web.pdf> (accessed 1 May 2018).

Sentencing Guidelines Council (2007), *Sexual Offences Act 2003, Definitive Guidance* available at <http://webarchive.nationalarchives.gov.uk/+/http://www.sentencingcouncil.org.uk/docs/web_0000_SexualOffencesAct1.pdf> (accessed 23 December 2012).

Shepherd, E (2007), *Investigative Interviewing: A Conversation Management Approach* (Oxford: Oxford University Press).

—— (2008), *SE3R: A resource book*, 4th edn (East Hendred: Forensic Solutions).

—— and Griffiths, A (2013), *Investigative Interviewing: The conversation management approach*, 2nd edn (Oxford: Oxford University Press).

—— and Kite, F (1988), 'Training to Interview', Policing 4, 264–280.

Sherman, L (1998), *Ideas in American Policing: Evidence Based Policing* available at <https://www.cebma.org/wp-content/uploads/Sherman-Evidence-Based-Policing.pdf> (accessed 16 March 2020).

—— (2013), 'The Rise of Evidence Based Policing: Targeting, Testing and Tracking', Crime and Justice 42(1), 377–451.

Sherman, LW, Gartin, PR, and Buerger, ME (1989), 'Hot Spots of Predatory Crime: Routine Activities and the Criminology of Place', Criminology 27, 27–56.

Shorter Oxford English Dictionary (2002), 5th edn (Oxford: Oxford University Press).

Simmons, AJ (2001), *Justification and Legitimacy: Essays on rights and obligations* (Cambridge: Cambridge University Press).

Skills for Justice (2011), *Policing Professional Framework* available at <http://www.skillsforjustice-ppf.com/?r_id=1> (accessed 3 April 2012).

Skogan, WG and Steiner, L (2004), *Community policing in Chicago, year ten* (Chicago: Illinois Criminal Justice Information Authority).

Sky News (2017), *The far-right: What is Britain First?* available at <https://news.sky.com/story/the-far-right-what-is-britain-first-11149915> (accessed 12 March 2019).

Smith, G (2018), 'The proposed changes to the UK Investigatory Powers Act', Privacy and Data Protection 18(3), January 2018, 16–17.

Smith, J (2016), *Crime-prediction tool may be reinforcing discriminatory policing* available at <http://uk.businessinsider.com/predictive-policing-discriminatory-police-crime-2016-10> (accessed 8 March 2018).

Smith, MJ and Tilley, N (2005), *Crime Science: New approaches to preventing and detecting crime* (Cullompton: Willan).

Smith, W and Swann, J (2016), *College of Policing Vulnerability Conference Presentation by Westley Smith and Joanna Swann* available at <https://www.college.police.uk/About/Documents/Conference/The_THRIVE_approach_workshop.pdf> (accessed 16 March 2020).

Snowdon, C (2016), *Alcohol and the public purse. Do drinkers pay their way?* available at <https://iea.org.uk/wp-content/uploads/2016/07/DP_Alcohol%20and%20the%20public%20purse_63_amended2_web.pdf> (accessed 8 March 2018).

South Wales Police (2015), *YES—I do have the Certificate of Knowledge in Policing* available at <http://www.south-wales.police.uk/apply-for-a-job/police-officer/questions-answered/> (accessed 31 March 2015).

Spencer, J (2016), *Evidence of Bad Character*, 3rd edn (Oxford: Hart Publishing).

The Stationery Office (2016), *Explanatory Notes: Investigatory Powers Act 2016* available at <http://www.legislation.gov.uk/ukpga/2016/25/pdfs/ukpgaen_20160025_en.pdf> (accessed 8 March 2018).

Stelfox, P (1998), 'Policing lower levels of organised crime in England and Wales', The Howard Journal 37(4), 393–406.

Stewart, JK (1985), 'Interviewing Witnesses and Victims of Crime' US Department of Justice, National Institute of Justice, Research in Brief, December1 in R Milne and R Bull (1999), *Investigative Interviewing: Psychology And Practice* (Chichester: Wiley).

Stone, N (2018), 'Child Criminal Exploitation: "County Lines", Trafficking and Cuckooing', Youth Justice 18(3), 285–93.

Stone, V and Pettigrew, N (2000), *The Views of the Public on Stops and Searches* (London: Home Office).

Suffolk Police (2018), *Over 20,000 knives deposited in Suffolk Bin a Blade amnesty* available at <https://www.suffolk.police.uk/news/latest-news/over-15000-knives-deposited-suffolk-bin-blade-amnesty> (accessed 4 January 2019).

Taylor, C (2001), 'Advance disclosure: reflections on the Criminal Procedure and Investigations Act 1996', The Howard Journal 40(2), 114–25.

Taylor, CW (2006), *Criminal investigation and pre-trial disclosure in the United Kingdom. How detectives put together a case* (Lampeter: Edwin Mellen Press Ltd).

Taylor, M (1986), 'Learning for self-direction in the classroom: The pattern of a transition process', Studies in Higher Education 11(1), 55–72.

Taylor, P and Bond, S (eds) (2012), *Crime Detection in England & Wales* (London: ONS).

Telegraph (2019), *Gina Martin: how I got the law changed and made upskirting illegal* available at <https://www.telegraph.co.uk/women/life/gina-martin-got-law-changed-made-upskirting-illegal/> (accessed 6 February 2019).

Thames Valley Police (2018), *Thames Valley Police Sharing Thames Valley Police research and practice* available at <https://www.thamesvalley.police.uk/SysSiteAssets/foi-media/thames-valley-police/other_information/tvp-journal---volume-1---first-edition---april-2018.pdf> (accessed 12 March 2019).

—— (2019), *Thames Valley launches PCSO Apprenticeships* available at <https://www.matthewbarber.co.uk/news/thames-valley-launches-pcso-apprenticeships> (accessed 12 March 2019).

Thornton, S (2007), 'Introduction' in ACPO, *Practice Advice: Introduction to Intelligence-led policing*, ACPO Centrex.

Tierney, J (2009), *Key Perspectives in Criminology* (Maidenhead: Open University Press).

Tilley, N (2008a), 'Modern Approaches to Policing: Community, problem-orientated and intelligence-led' in T Newburn (ed), *Handbook of Policing* (Cullompton: Willan), pp 373–403.

—— (2008b), 'Problem-orientated Policing' in T Newburn and P Neyroud (eds), *Dictionary of Policing* (Cullompton: Willan), pp 225–7.

—— (2016), 'EMMIE and engineering: What works as evidence to improve decisions?' Evaluation 22(3), 304–22.

Tong, S (2008), 'Interagency Approaches to Policing' in T Newburn and P Neyroud (eds), *Dictionary of Policing* (Cullompton: Willan), pp 148–9.

Tor (2016), *Tor* available at <https://www.torproject.org/> (accessed 15 March 2016).

Tuffin, R, Morris, J, and Poole, A (2006), *An Evaluation of the Impact of the National Reassurance Policing Programme* (London: Home Office).

Tyler, TR (2003), 'Procedural justice, legitimacy, and the effective rule of law' in M Tonry (ed), *Crime and Justice: A Review of Research*, vol 30 (Chicago, IL: Chicago University Press), 431–505.

UK Missing Persons Unit (2018), *Who we are* available at <http://missingpersons.police.uk/en-gb/about-mpu/who-we-are> (accessed 8 December 2018).

UK Parliament (2013), *Clare's law: The Domestic Violence Disclosure Scheme—Commons Library Standard Note* available at <http://www.parliament.uk/business/publications/research/briefing-papers/SN06250/clares-law-the-domestic-violence-disclosure-scheme> (accessed 20 December 2013).

Vodafone (2018), *Vodafone Foundation and Hestia launch the UK's first app to provide nationwide domestic abuse support* available at <https://mediacentre.vodafone.co.uk/news/bright-sky-launches/> (accessed 12 December 2018).

Vrij, A (2008), *Detecting Lies and Deceit: Pitfalls and opportunities*, 2nd edn (Chichester: Wiley-Blackwell).

Waddington, PAJ (1999), *Policing Citizens* (London: UCL Press).

——, Stenson, K, and David, D (2004), 'In proportion: Race, and police stop and search', British Journal of Criminology 44, 889–914.

Waddington, PAJ, Wright, M, Williams, K, and Newburn, T (2017), *How People Judge Policing* (Oxford: Oxford University Press).

Wadham, J (2004), 'Conference on data protection and information sharing', 15 July (London).

Walby, S and Allen, J (2004), *Domestic violence, sexual assault and stalking: Findings from the British Crime Survey*, Home Office Research Study 276.

Walby, S, Towers, J and Francis, F (2014), 'Mainstreaming domestic and gender-based violence into sociology and the criminology of violence', The Sociological Review 62:S2, 187–214.

Walklate, S, Fitz-Gibbon, K, and McCulloch, J (2017), 'Is more law the answer? Seeking justice for victims of intimate partner violence through the reform of legal categories', Criminology and Criminal Justice 23(11), 1–17.

Walsh, D and Milne, R (2008), 'Keeping the PEACE? A study of investigative interviewing practices in the public sector', Legal and Criminological Psychology 13(1) February 2008, 395–7.

Wedlock, E and Tapley, J (2016), *What Works in Supporting Victims of Crime, Victims' Commissioner* available at <https://victimscommissioner.org.uk/published-reviews/what-works-in-supporting-victims-of-crime-a-rapid-evidence-assessment/> (accessed 12 March 2019).

Weisburd, D, Telep, CW, Hinkle, JC, and Eck, JE (2010), 'Is problem-oriented policing effective in reducing crime and disorder?', Criminology and Public Policy 9(1), 139–72.

What Works (2015), *Restorative Justice (RJ) Conferencing* available at <http://whatworks.college.police.uk/toolkit/Pages/Intervention.aspx?InterventionID=24> (accessed 12 January 2018).

Wheller, L (2019), *Evidence-based policing: Mapping police practice and building the evidence base* available at <https://www.birmingham.ac.uk/Documents/college-social-sciences/business/research/crime-justice-policing/conference-presentations-2019/cjp-conference-evidence-based-policing.pdf> (accessed 30 November 2019).

WHO (2008), *Classification of Female Genital Mutilation* available at <http://www.who.int/reproductivehealth/topics/fgm/overview/en/> (accessed 1 May 2018).

Wigmore, J (2018), *Recognising & acting on signs of 'county lines' child exploitation: A case study* available at <https://www.england.nhs.uk/wp-content/uploads/2018/11/recognising-acting-on-signs-of-county-lines.pdf> (accessed 16 March 2020).

Williams, A and Finlay, F (2018), 'County lines: how gang crime is affecting our young people', Archives of Disease in Childhood 104, 730–2.

Williams, S and Coupe, T (2017), 'Frequency Vs. Length of Hot Spots Patrols: a Randomised Controlled Trial', Cambridge Journal of Evidence-Based Policing 1(1), 5–21.

Wilson, JQ (1996), 'On deterrence' in J Muncie, E McLaughlin, and M Langan (eds), *Criminological Perspectives: A reader* (London: Sage Publications).

—— and Kelling, G (1982), 'Broken windows', Atlantic Monthly, March, 29–38.

Wiltshire Police (no date), *Major Incident Team* available at <https://www.wiltshire.police.uk/article/1070/Major-Incident-Team> (accessed 1 May 2018).

—— (2018), *Vulnerability Strategy* available at <https://www.wiltshire.police.uk/media/485/Vulnerability-Strategy/pdf/Vulnerability_Strategy.pdf> (accessed 16 March 2020).

Wolfenden Report (1957), *Report of the Committee on Homosexual Offences and Prostitution*, Cmnd 247 (London: HMSO).

Women's Aid (2017), *Women's Aid responds to the Queen's Speech* available at <https://www.womensaid.org.uk/womens-aid-respond-queens-speech/> (accessed 8 December 2017).

Woodhouse, J (2013), *Extreme Pornography Commons Library Standard Note SN/HA/5078* available at <http://www.parliament.uk/business/publications/research/briefing-papers/SN05078/extreme-pornography> (accessed 27 February 2014).

Wright, A (2002), *Policing: An introduction to concepts and practice* (Cullompton: Willan).

Zimmerman, KA (2017), *History of Computers: A Brief Timeline* available at <https://www.livescience.com/20718-computer-history.html 28/05/2019> (accessed 16 March 2020).

Index